Introduction to BUSINESS MANAGEMENT

Second Custom Edition for
the Telfer School of Management at the University of Ottawa

École de gestion
TELFER
School of Management

Taken from:

Business, Seventh Canadian Edition
by Ricky W. Griffin, Ronald J. Ebert, Frederick A. Starke, and
Melanie D. Lang

Management, Canadian Edition
by Michael A. Hitt, J. Stewart Black, Lyman W. Porter, and
Andrew J. Gaudes

Learning Solutions

New York   Boston   San Francisco
London   Toronto   Sydney   Tokyo   Singapore   Madrid
Mexico City   Munich   Paris   Cape Town   Hong Kong   Montreal

Cover Art: Courtesy of DigitalVision/Getty Images

Taken from:

Business, Seventh Canadian Edition
by Ricky W. Griffin, Ronald J. Ebert, Frederick A. Starke, and Melanie D. Lang
Copyright © 2011, 2008, 2005, 2002, 1999, 1996, 1993 by Pearson Education Canada, Inc.
Published by Prentice Hall
Toronto, Ontario

Management, Canadian Edition
by Michael A. Hitt, J. Stewart Black, Lyman W. Porter, and Andrew J. Gaudes
Copyright © 2009 by Pearson Education Canada, Inc.
Published by Prentice Hall

This special edition published in cooperation with Pearson Learning Solutions.

All trademarks, service marks, registered trademarks, and registered service marks are the property of their respective owners and are used herein for identification purposes only.

Pearson Learning Solutions, 501 Boylston Street, Suite 900, Boston, MA 02116
A Pearson Education Company
www.pearsoned.com

Printed in Canada

1 2 3 4 5 6 7 8 9 10 XXXX 15 14 13 12 11 10

000200010270568837

MHB

ISBN 10: 0-558-87458-4
ISBN 13: 978-0-558-87458-2

Overview

Contents

Part Four
Managing the Organizational Environment
117

Part Five
Managing Ethics, Social Responsibility, and Diversity
153

Part Nine
Organizational Culture and Change   323

Part Ten
Accounting and Financial Statements   355

Part Eleven
Motivation   389

Part Twelve
Communication   431

Part Thirteen
Organizational Control   463

Part One

Case Analysis

Case Study Format

"I hear and I forget. I see and I believe. I do and I understand."
—Confucius (551–479 BC)

FOCUS

- Formatting
- Content
- Important points

The Case Solution Format

Since your case is, in fact, a form of business report, it should be carefully prepared using a series of headings and sub-headings. Furthermore, it should be concise and to the point. Be careful, though, that you do not fall into the trap of analyzing the problem on a superficial basis.

In addition, carefully check your completed work for proper grammar, sentence structure, punctuation, and spelling. Your case must also be presented in a professional and visually appealing manner. Poor work in this area is inexcusable and will result in the loss of 10 marks.

Requirements

The following are the required deliverables for every case study that you submit for grading:

1. Title Page

A title page is an opportunity to create a visually appealing first impression on your reader. It is also a medium by which important information is communicated to the reader of the case. The following points of information are required on the title page of the case:

- Name or Title of the case
- Names and student numbers of all who produced the case
- Date
- Course Code and Section
- Professor's name
- Teaching Assistant's name

The following statement must also be present on the cover page for any case submitted for ADM 1300:

In partial fulfillment of the requirements of ADM 1300

When producing a title page, make sure to include all the required information, but do not limit yourself to only that information. As long as the title page is professional and visually appealing, feel free to get creative with it in order to establish a quality first impression on those that read it. You cannot always judge a case by its cover, but you can create a positive outlook for those about to read the case.

Forgetting this sentence is one of the most common mistakes made when writing a case and it will cost you a quick 2 marks.

2. Executive Summary

The executive summary is a tool used by writers to give a synopsis of the entire paper. There are many reasons for incorporating an executive summary, the most important of which is time. Managers and executives do not have the time to read through entire documents, and must rely on those that prepare the documents to summarize the information in a useful fashion on to one page (MAXIMUM!). The format for an executive summary is included on the following page.

3. Assumptions

Students may find it difficult to cope with real life business situations when faced with incomplete information. The lack of information can provide

Important Note:
- Executive Summary must be one page maximum.
- Sentences in point form are necessary.
- Always write the Executive Summary after you have completed your whole case.

- Worth 5 marks
- All based on formatting
- All or nothing: 5/5 or 0/5

Executive Summary

To: Manager/Executive/Professor

From: Name(s)

Subject: Title of the Case

Problem: Primary/Central Problem
- 1–3 sentences explaining the primary problem
- Short and sweet!!!
- No mention of satellite problems

Alternatives:
1. Status Quo/No Change Scenario
2. Mention all other alternatives

Facts Considered:
1.
2.
3. …
- These are facts directly from the case
- These are not assumptions

Recommendation:
- A brief paragraph stating immediate, short-term and long-term goals to solve the primary problem

Do Not Assume the Case Away

Important Note:

Do not build your entire argument on assumptions because rarely are these arguments based on factual information.

Assumptions:
- Worth 0 marks but are not optional.
- Flow from the information in provided in the case.
- State the facts that led you to making the assumption.

Formatting Tips:
- Use bullets.
- All assumptions must be in full sentence format.

Satellite Problems:
- Worth 0 marks but are not optional.
- Lead you to the Primary Problem.
- Stated directly in the case.

Formatting Tips:
- Use bullets.
- All points must be in full sentence format.

....based on the facts of the case....
....satellite problems will be explicitly stated in the case....

opportunities for students, but it can also provide pitfalls in which they can easily get caught. In order to handle the incomplete information, case preparers need to identify assumptions that they make to fill in the blanks that they believe are present.

One challenge that students have is coming up with logical assumptions that will add credibility and depth to the case. Because students all come from different backgrounds and have different life experiences, their perspectives of the cases presented will vary widely.

4. Statement of the problem

One of the most important aspects in producing a quality case is problem formulation. The entire goal of the case format is to identify the primary problem(s) and to recommend methods by which these problems can be solved; if you do not properly identify the primary problem, then you are going to have alternatives that may not be relevant or helpful in solving the case.

Every case that is presented to you will have problems present, and there will be room for improvement each and every time. What you need to do is use the facts presented in the case and your assumptions based on these facts to identify all the problems that exist.

Satellite problems. are the secondary problems that exist. They are either a cause or a result of the primary problem, and they are *based on the facts of the case*. Most often, *satellite problems will be explicitly stated in the case*. Be sure to identify these satellite problems in sentence format (if the satellite problem is taken directly from the case, remember to use footnotes or end notes), and be sure to elaborate on why they are problems (do not assume that the reader will understand why it is a problem). By analyzing the satellite problems, you will be able to arrive at the primary problem.

The primary problem(s). is the key part of the case. You must be concise and to the point to show your understanding of what is plaguing the organization and/or the people involved in the case. When looking at satellite problems, ask yourself "Why?" to determine if it is a cause or a result of the primary problem(s). What is important here is to *pinpoint the basis for which the goal of your case will be built on.*

Implications. are split into two sections, each of which is worth 5 (five) marks; *Implications on the Organization* and *Implications on the Personnel*. By identifying the implications of the problems, you show an understanding of what is happening and what can happen if these problems are not solved. Implications are a look to the future at potential problems that can occur, and we ask you to separate your analysis in to the Organization and the Personnel involved.

The implications on the organization look at the entity/entities involved in the case, and you need to identify what is going to happen to the organization if the problems persist. The implications on the personnel look at the impact of the problems on all the people that are involved in the case.

Whereas the primary and satellite problems identified above are based on the facts of the case, the implications will be your interpretation of the facts. This is your opportunity to show a thorough understanding of the problems and what will happen if they continue. Similar to the writing of the assumptions discussed above, *you should identify the implication and then identify the facts from the case that led you to the implication.*

Primary Problem:

- Worth 5 marks but are not optional.
- Based on clarity and understanding of the situation.
- Always ask yourself "Why?"

Formatting Tips:

- In paragraph format.
- Primary problem should be 2–5 sentences long.
- Do not write a page in length!!!

…pinpoint the basis for which the goal of your case will be built on…

Formatting Tips:

- Bullet form.
- In full sentence format.
- Each set of implications should have five points.

…should identify the implication and then identify the facts from the case that led you to the implication

Example

Do not write

Implications on the Personnel

- Low morale

Write *elaborate and detailed sentences* that justify your claim, such as the example that follows

Implications on the Personnel

- The recent firings of several middle level managers will lead to a low morale amongst the remaining middle level managers, who may now fear for their jobs.

By seeing what is wrong as a result of the problems, you are now ready to look in to how to make things right.

5. Alternative Solutions

Identifying problems within a real life situation creates an opportunity to solve those problems. Be intelligent and innovative in developing methods that could alleviate the problems at hand. This section involves practically applying theories and concepts to real life situations.

The case analysis is a developmental paper that follows the logical thought process incorporated in solving problems. The reason that the **status quo** is

Alternatives:

- Worth 50 marks.
- Each alternative is worth 50 marks/# of alternatives presented.
- If Status Quo is missing, then you lose the marks that should be allocated to that alternative. If you include four alternatives but neglect to analyze a status quo/no change scenario, the fifty marks will be divided by five, and each alternative will be graded out of 10 marks; you will receive zero on ten for failing to analyze the status quo.
- 3–5 alternatives are expected.

....is to ensure that you understand the severity of the situation at hand and be able to outline what will occur if no changes are made...

...must still be presented...

analyzed *is to ensure that you understand the severity of the situation at hand and be able to outline what will occur if no changes are made*. You have been told that all alternatives presented must be capable of solving the problems, but, even though the No Change Scenario will not solve the problems in the best manner, it *must still be presented* and analyzed thoroughly. When formatting your paper, ensure that the No Change Scenario is the first alternative presented; this is to highlight your logical thought process in understanding the current situation before suggesting possible changes.

Alternatives must be presented in a logical and comprehensive manner. In order to leave no room for misinterpretation for the readers, we recommend that you present your alternatives as follows:

Description: Your description should start with a *few sentences which contain the theory or concept* supporting the chosen alternative. The following sentences should *describe how the theory or concept could be practically applied* to the particular problems at hand. This will allow you to apply the material from the course to real life business situations.

Pros & Cons: This section is a basic comparison of the advantages and disadvantages of the alternative put forth as a prospective solution to the problems identified.

Analysis: In this section, it is important to weigh the pros against the cons, and evaluate the applicable consequences, and you must tie the alternative back to the primary problem(s) and the situation presented in the case as a whole. You must conclude each alternative presented with a judgment as to whether or not it will solve the problems presented. Is it the most effective way to solve the problem? Will it solve the problems without creating new ones? Are there options available that are more viable or feasible?

An example of how you could structure and present your alternatives, but that you are not limited to, follows:

Description

Very Important:

...description should start with a few sentences which contain the theory or concept supporting the chosen alternative...

...the following sentences should describe how the theory or concept could be practically applied to the particular problems at hand...

No Change Scenario (or Status Quo)

Your first paragraph should be a paragraph thoroughly outlining what the alternative involves. To not include a description of the alternative and jump right in to the pros and cons of the alternative is to leave too much room for interpretation for the reader, and leaving room for interpretation can often lead to misinterpretations. In order to ensure that you and the reader are both clear on what the alternative involves, describe it here. An insufficient description would be "Allow all things to remain as they are". You need to describe what will continue to happen if nothing changes and elaborate on key points that lead you to believe what your pros and what your cons are. Approximately 15% to 25% of the marks associated with an alternative will be allocated to the description portion.

Pros

Pros and cons can be listed as presented here, or they can be in a table side by side with the cons

- Pros can be listed using bullets as they appear here, but they must be presented here in full sentences – the reader must understand what you are trying to communicate, and saying something to the effect of "It saves money" is insufficient

Be sure to cover all possible pros and cons; a thorough presentation of the alternative will touch on all aspects of the case

Approximately 15% to 25% of the marks associated with an alternative will be allocated to the pros and cons portion.

Cons

There is no magic number for pros and cons that should be listed for each alternative. The status quo will obviously have very few pros and many cons if problems truly do exist, while viable alternatives that can solve the problems can have many pros and few cons.

You must use the listing of pros and cons to differentiate alternatives that are somewhat similar in nature.

Analysis/Summary/Evaluation

Any of the above sub-headings are sufficient for identifying this portion of the alternative. At least 50% of the marks associated with an alternative are allocated to the analysis of the alternative, and this is where you evaluate an alternatives viability in solving the problem. If it's not a viable solution for the problem, then it probably should not be presented.

Your analysis is a paragraph or two in sentence format that gives you the opportunity to weigh the pros against the cons. It is insufficient to simply rehash all the points that you brought up above in the listing of the pros and cons; the first half of the alternative was focused on presenting information, and now is your opportunity to interpret and evaluate that information. Be thorough in your analysis, and come to a conclusion on whether or not the alternative solution presented here is a viable option that could possibly be pursued.

- Avoid "*Hiring Consultants*" as an alternative. You are the consultants, and you've got a problem to solve. Don't pass it off on to somebody else.
- Make sure that your alternatives are reasonable. When seeing that a manager may not be effective, don't immediately propose to fire them. The majority of the cases that you will be presented with have problems where the underlying factors are more than just the individuals involved. Be certain before toying with peoples' lives.
- Be sure to apply any theories that you present to the real life situation of the case study, and do not simply present generic concepts.

Important Tips:
Now that you know how to properly format, present, and prepare an alternative solution, you are ready to learn how to structure your recommended solution.

6. Recommended Solution

Now is your opportunity to select the alternative or combination of alternatives that best solves the primary and satellite problems. In the paragraphs that make up your recommended solution, you must outline:

- which problems the alternative(s) solves, and any problems that it may not solve

- why it solves them better than other viable alternatives,

- how the combination of alternatives, if recommended, is better than any individual alternatives (or vice versa)

- a forecasting look at how the recommendation will benefit the personnel and the organization

The recommended solution should be selected based on all the alternatives that were presented in the case. While each alternative is evaluated independently in the alternative section of the case, each alternative should be evaluated compared with or contrasted against other alternatives presented as

Recommentation:
- Worth 5 marks.
- Always tieback to the primary problem.
- Take the marker step by step through how this alternative solves the primary problem.
- What separates this alternative from the others.

Implementation:
- Bullet form.
- Each section is worth 5 marks.
- Bullets in full sentence format.

viable solutions. Explaining how your solution best solves the problem and setting it apart from the viable alternatives that you are rejecting indicates that you are a practical and reliable problem solver.

Please be thorough and elaborate in these paragraphs so that the readers understand exactly why and how this solution solves the problems. The last step is making your solution come to life!

7. Implementation

The implementation section is the place where a great case can distance itself from a good one. The purpose of outlining methods of implementing your solution is to allow you to outline how your theories and concepts and ideas that you have recommended can become a reality. By defining the problems, you show you understand what needs to be corrected; by recommending a solution, you show you understand the concepts of what needs to be done; by logically and properly implementing a solution, you show that you can comprehend real life situations through a logical dissection.

Implementation is broken down in to three separate sections, with each section being allocated five marks. It can be presented in sentence format in bulleted lists as long as the reader understands what is required.

....must be logical and sequential....→ *Immediate action.* The immediate action required is all that needs to be done between today and six months from now. The business world is a fast paced environment, and if a problem exists, it needs to be dealt with right away. This *must be a logical and sequential* format, and you must reasonably establish a chronological method by which your solution can become a reality. For example, if your solution is to change the management style of the organization, it will be insufficient and illogical for your first step of immediate action to involve telling the manager that he must change his style. Be reasonable and rational, and show an understanding of a real life situation.

....will be following up or adding to things that were completed in the immediate time frame....→ *Short term action.* The action required in the short term needs to be accomplished between six months and one year from the present. Many aspects of the short term action *will be following up or adding to things that were completed in the immediate time frame*; there will also be many aspects of short term action that can only be introduced to the solution in a time frame of at least six months from the present.

...reflect back on the solution and evaluate its success after a year...→ *Long term action.* The long term action is any action required one year from the present and beyond. It is also a combination of items that are following up on items introduced in the previous year, and the introduction of new items. This is also a good time to *reflect back on the solution and evaluate its success after a year*.

8. Spelling, Grammar, and Presentation

Cases that are submitted that include spelling, grammar, punctuation or presentation errors are unprofessional, and for this reason, errors in this category are inexcusable. If your case has one error present, you will receive 7 out of 10; if you have two errors, you will receive 6 out of 10; if you have three errors, you will receive 5 out of 10; if you have more than three errors present from this category, you will receive 0 out of 10 for this section.

Everyone starts off with 10 out of 10, and everyone should be able to keep those 10 marks—the key is to have your case PROOF READ several times. You must resist the temptation to say your case is done when you've finished writing it, and that there is still plenty of work to be done. It is highly recommended that someone other than the preparer(s) proof read the case because they'll be able to catch things that you would not notice having written the paper yourself.

Hopefully the above guidelines and suggestions have cleared up any misconceptions that you may have had regarding preparing a case. You should use this information as a guide, but not limit yourself to the information presented here, presented in ADM 1300 or presented in the seminar. Please feel free to get creative and innovative while working within the boundaries and parameters that have been established.

Part
Two

Managers and Managing

Chapter 1

Managing the Business Enterprise

After reading this chapter, you should be able to:

1. Describe the four basic functions that constitute the *management process*.

2. Identify *types of managers* by level and area.

3. Describe the five basic *management skills*.

4. Explain the importance of *setting goals* and *formulating strategies*.

5. Discuss *contingency planning* and *crisis management*.

6. Explain the idea of *corporate culture* and why it is important.

Taken from *Business*, Seventh Canadian Edition, by Ricky W. Griffin, Ronald J. Ebert, Frederick A. Starke, and Melanie D. Lang.

Corporate Culture

The term *corporate culture* refers to the shared experiences, values, norms, and ethical stance that characterize an organization. It is important for managers to understand the concept of corporate culture because culture influences the behaviour of employees. Managers can use that knowledge to be more effective in leading and motivating employees. Consider these examples of corporate culture:

■ At WestJet, employees have a big stake in the company's success because of profit-sharing, and they contribute ideas about how best to run the airline. For example, a group has formed that calls itself the WestJesters. They do things like developing the cornball jokes that WestJet flight attendants tell during flights.

■ Paul Godfrey, the CEO of the Toronto Blue Jays Baseball Club, says the culture of the club is to make employees feel like they are part of a family. To facilitate the culture, Godfrey invites small groups of employees to have "snacks with the president" so they can talk about how the organization is operating. Godfrey encourages questions from employees on virtually any topic.

■ Rick George, the CEO of Suncor, says the company's culture is open and non-bureaucratic, and that it has a clear strategy that employees can relate to. The company hires many new people, so it must take steps to ensure that the new employees understand the "soul" of Suncor because they have different experiences and different expectations.

■ At Wellington West Holdings Inc., the culture is simple, personal, and fun.

Companies that focus largely on one type of product (for example, Starbucks Coffee Company) may have a fairly homogeneous culture throughout the organization. But large companies with many different divisions and many different types of customers (for example, the Royal Bank of Canada) are likely to have several different subcultures because the various divisions pursue different goals and because different types of people are found in the different divisions. Even in smaller firms, there may be noticeable differences in the culture of the marketing and finance departments.

Culture Surveys

Each year, Waterstone Human Capital conducts in-depth interviews with senior managers at many different Canadian companies and asks them which corporate cultures they admire most. The top three companies named in the 2008 survey were Boston Pizza, Four Seasons Hotels and Resorts, and Intuit Canada. The majority of managers who are interviewed typically say that the culture of their company is not what they want it to be, that their corporate culture is "weak," and that they don't monitor their organization's culture through surveys.

Starbucks is one company that systematically assesses its corporate culture. Once every 18 months employees fill out a Partner View Survey, which contains questions that are designed to help the company determine whether it is making progress toward one of its key values—providing a work environment where people treat one another with respect and dignity. The survey is voluntary, but about 90 percent of employees fill it out (on company time). One reason the participation rate is so high is that the company actually pays attention to what employees say in the survey. For example, when one survey showed that employees were not clear about career progression possibilities in the company, Starbucks held career fairs in several Canadian cities, where company managers spoke with employees about management opportunities at Starbucks.

Cultural Change

Companies sometimes decide that they need to change their culture. A realization of the need for change usually comes after top management sees that changes in the company's external environment are going to require some sort of response from the company. But just because someone recognizes the need does not mean that it will actually be implemented because changing an organization's culture can be very difficult.

In 2007, several RCMP officers alleged that senior management was covering up mismanagement of the RCMP's pension and insurance plans. As a result of these charges, lawyer David Brown was appointed by the government to look into the matter. His report concluded that Commissioner Giuliano Zaccardelli had exercised absolute power, that no one questioned his management style, and that there was a "tone" at the top of the organization that resulted in little respect for employees and put pressure on the employees not to challenge authority. The report also said that whistle-blowers within the RCMP were punished when they pointed out that there were problems. The report concluded that the culture and management structure at the RCMP were "horribly broken." These developments are discouraging because a few years earlier the RCMP had completed a "visioning" process that resulted in a new mission statement, a new set of core values, and a commitment to the communities where it worked. At that time, it was reported that the culture of the RCMP were quite different than it was in the days when military tradition dominated the organization, but subsequent events suggested that the culture had not actually changed.

A similar story can be told about the Canadian Imperial Bank of Commerce. It supposedly had a conservative culture, but as the commercial paper crisis unfolded in 2007 it became clear that CIBC was going to incur billions of dollars of losses because of its exposure to subprime mortgages in the United States. This happened in spite of CIBC's supposed shift to a low-risk culture. ◆

How will this help me?

After reading this chapter, you will have a clearer understanding of how to effectively carry out various management responsibilities. From the perspective of a consumer or investor, you'll be better able to assess and appreciate the quality of management in various companies.

In this chapter, we begin by introducing the idea of the management process and the functions that are necessary in this process. We then identify the different types of managers that are likely to be found in an organization (by level and by area). Next, we describe the basic management skills, paying particular attention to decision-making skills. We then explore the importance of strategic management and effective goal setting in organizational success. We conclude the chapter by examining the concept of corporate culture.

Who Are Managers?

All organizations depend on effective management. Regardless of the type of business they work in, managers perform the same basic functions, are responsible for many of the same tasks, and have many of the same responsibilities. All managers plan, organize, direct, and control day-to-day operations.

Although our focus is on managers in business settings, remember that the principles of management apply to all kinds of organizations. Managers work in charities, churches, social organizations, educational institutions, and government agencies. The prime minister of Canada, the president of the University of Toronto, the executive director of the United Way, the dean of your business school, and the chief administrator of your local hospital are all managers. Remember, too, that managers bring to small organizations many of the same kinds of skills—the ability to make decisions and to respond to a variety of challenges—that they bring to large ones. Regardless of the nature and size of an organization, managers are among its most important resources.

1 Describe the four basic functions that constitute the *management process.*

management The process of planning, organizing, leading, and controlling an enterprise's financial, physical, human, and information resources to achieve the organization's goals of supplying various products and services.

The Management Process

Management is the process of planning, organizing, leading, and controlling an enterprise's financial, physical, human, and information resources to achieve the organization's goals of supplying various products and services. Thus, the CEO of Walt Disney Productions is a manager because he regularly carries out these four functions as films are being made. Actors such as Julia Roberts or Tom Cruise, while they may be the stars of the movies, are not managers because they don't carry out the functions of management.

There are two important overall points to keep in mind when thinking about the management process. First, the planning, organizing, leading, and controlling aspects of a manager's job are interrelated. These activities generally follow one another in a logical sequence, but sometimes they are performed simultaneously or in a different sequence altogether. In fact, a manager is likely to be engaged in all these activities during the course of a business day. Second, it is important to make the distinction between management effectiveness and management efficiency. **Efficiency** means achieving the greatest level of output with a given amount of input. **Effectiveness**, on the other hand, means achieving the organizational goals that have been set. Put another way, efficiency means doing things right, while effectiveness means doing the right things. A manager who focuses on being effective will likely also be efficient, but a manager who focuses on being efficient may or may not be effective.

efficiency Achieving the greatest level of output with a given amount of input.

effectiveness Achieving the organizational goals that have been set.

Planning

Planning is the process of determining the firm's goals and developing a strategy for achieving them. It has five basic steps. In *step 1*, goals are established for the organization. WestJet, for example, may set a goal to fill 90 percent of the seats on every flight. In *step 2*, managers identify whether a gap exists between the company's desire and actual position. Examination of the load factor data may show that the load factor is only 86 percent. In *step 3*, managers develop plans to achieve the desired goal. For example, the fare from Calgary to Winnipeg may be reduced by 10 percent in an attempt to increase the load factor to 90 percent. Note that goals indicate *what* results are desired, while plans indicate *how* these goals are to be achieved. In *step 4*, the plans that have been decided upon are implemented. This involves actually charging the new reduced fare. This is the point in the planning process where thinking is converted into action. In *step 5*, the effectiveness of the plan is assessed. Actual results are compared with planned performance, that is, the load factor data are analyzed to determine whether the 90 percent goal has been achieved. Plans may then have to be modified and a different goal may have to be set.

planning The process of determining the firm's goals and developing a strategy for achieving them.

This is how the planning process worked when Yahoo was created. The company's top managers set a strategic goal of becoming a top firm in the then-emerging market for internet search engines. They started by assessing the ways in which people actually use the web and concluded that people wanted an easy-to-understand web interface. Yahoo also wanted to be able to satisfy a wide array of needs, preferences, and priorities by having people go to as few sites as possible to find what they were looking for. One key component of Yahoo's strategy was to foster partnerships and relationships with other companies so that potential web surfers could draw upon several sources through a single portal. Yahoo managers then began fashioning alliances with such diverse partners as Reuters, Standard & Poor's, the Associated Press (for news coverage), RE/MAX (for real estate information), and a wide array of information providers specializing in sports, weather, entertainment, shopping, and travel.

It may be difficult to predict which plans will be successful. One tool that helps managers assess future possibilities is called **prediction markets**. It involves creating a market where people can buy "shares" in various answers to important questions that need to be answered. At Cisco Systems, for example, 20 employees in a chip-design unit bought shares based on how many defects they thought they would find in a new product (each stock represented a range of possible numbers of defects). The winner of the game received an iPod. The actual number of defects found in the new chip was in the range that was predicted by the group. Other companies that use prediction markets include Microsoft, Best Buy, and Hewlett-Packard.[1]

prediction markets Creating a market where people can buy "shares" in various answers to important questions that need to be answered.

A Hierarchy of Plans

Plans can be made on three general levels, with each level reflecting plans for which managers at that level are responsible. These levels constitute a hierarchy because implementing plans is practical only when there is a logical flow from one level to the next. **Strategic plans**, which are set by top management, reflect decisions about resource allocations, company priorities, and the steps needed to meet strategic goals (we look at strategic planning later in this chapter). General Electric's plan to be number one or number two in all the markets in which it competes is an example of a strategic plan. **Tactical plans** are shorter-range plans concerned with implementing specific aspects of the company's strategic plans. They typically involve upper and middle management. Coca-Cola's plan to increase sales in Europe by building European bottling facilities is an example of a tactical plan. **Operational plans**, which are developed by middle and lower-level managers, set short-term targets for daily, weekly, or monthly performance. McDonald's, for example, establishes operational plans when it stipulates precisely how Big Macs are to be cooked, warmed, and served.

strategic plans Set by top management; reflect decisions about resource allocations, company priorities, and the steps needed to meet strategic goals.

tactical plans Shorter-range plans concerned with implementing specific aspects of the company's strategic plans. They typically involve upper and middle management.

operational plans Plans developed by middle and lower-level managers that set short-term targets for daily, weekly, or monthly performance.

Organizing

organizing Mobilizing the resources that are required to complete a particular task.

Organizing involves mobilizing the resources that are required to complete a particular task (we examine this topic in detail in Chapter 9). The importance of organizing can be seen by considering what happened at Hewlett-Packard, which lost some of its competitive edge a few years ago. One of the major reasons for its slide could be traced back to what had once been a major strength. Specifically, HP had long prided itself on being a corporate confederation of individual businesses. Sometimes these businesses even ended up competing against each other. This approach had been beneficial for much of the firm's history. It was easier for each business to make its own decisions quickly and efficiently, and the competition kept each unit on its toes. By 1998, however, problems had become apparent, and no one could quite figure out what was going on.

Enter Ann Livermore, then head of the firm's software and services business. Livermore realized that the structure that had served so well in the past was now holding the firm back. To regain its competitive edge, HP needed an integrated, organization-wide internet strategy. Unfortunately, the company's highly decentralized organization made that impossible. Livermore led the charge to create one organization to drive a single internet plan. A reorganized HP has bounced back and it has regained its competitive strength.[2]

Leading

leading (or directing) Involves the interactions between managers and their subordinates as they both work to meet the firm's objectives.

Leading (or directing) involves the interactions between managers and their subordinates as they both work to meet the firm's objectives. By definition, managers have the power to give orders and demand results. Leading, however, goes beyond merely giving orders. Leaders attempt to guide and motivate employees to work in the best interests of the organization. Managers at WestJet, for example, have been very successful in motivating employees to go above and beyond normal work practices to ensure the company's (and their own) financial success. We discuss leadership in more detail in Chapter 12; topics include the various approaches to leadership (trait, behavioural, and situational), leadership styles (autocratic, democratic, and free-rein), and recent trends in leadership (e.g., charismatic leadership, ethical leadership, and strategic leadership).

Controlling

controlling The process of monitoring a firm's performance to make sure that it is meeting its goals.

Controlling is the process of monitoring a firm's performance to make sure that it is meeting its goals. Managers at WestJet and Air Canada, for example,

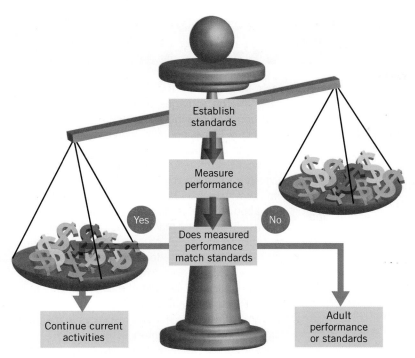

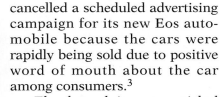

Figure 1.1 The control process.

focus relentlessly on indicators of performance like on-time arrivals, baggage-handling errors, the number of empty seats on an airplane, and results of surveys of employees and customers. If, say, on-time arrivals start to slip, managers focus on the problem and get it fixed. No single element of the firm's performance can slip too far before it's noticed and fixed.

Figure 1.1 illustrates the control process that begins when management establishes standards, often for financial performance. If, for example, a company wants to increase sales by 20 percent over the next 10 years, then an appropriate standard might be an increase of about 2 percent a year. Managers then measure actual performance against standards. If the two amounts agree, the organization continues along its present course. If they vary significantly, however, one or the other needs adjustment.

Control can also show where performance is better than expected and thus can serve as a basis for providing rewards or reducing costs. Volkswagen Canada cancelled a scheduled advertising campaign for its new Eos automobile because the cars were rapidly being sold due to positive word of mouth about the car among consumers.[3]

The boxed insert entitled "What Do Managers Actually Do?" explains in practical terms what it means to be a manager.

Japanese organizations don't usually like radical restructuring, but when Senichi Hoshino took over the hapless Hanshin Tigers, he axed 24 of the team's 70 players and replaced them with free agents. He required everyone on the roster to compete for a position, tracked performance daily, and made individual coaches directly responsible for seeing that players executed certain skills. Soon after that, the Tigers won the pennant—a particularly important achievement because superstition says that when the Tigers win, Japan will soon enjoy a period of prolonged prosperity.

Business Accountability

What Do Managers Actually Do?

Henry Mintzberg of McGill University conducted a detailed study of the work of five chief executive officers and found the following:

1. Managers work at an unrelenting pace.
2. Managerial activities are characterized by brevity, variety, and fragmentation.
3. Managers have a preference for "live" action and emphasize work activities that are current, specific, and well defined.
4. Managers are attracted to the verbal media.

Mintzberg believes that a manager's job can be described as 10 roles (in three categories) that must be performed. The manager's formal authority and status give rise to three interpersonal roles: (1) figurehead (duties of a ceremonial nature, such as attending a subordinate's wedding); (2) leader (being responsible for the work of the unit); and (3) liaison (making contact outside the vertical chain of command). These interpersonal roles give rise to three informational roles: (1) monitor (scanning the environment for relevant information); (2) disseminator (passing information to subordinates); and (3) spokesperson (sending information to people outside the unit).

The interpersonal and informational roles allow the manager to carry out four decision-making roles: (1) entrepreneur (improving the performance of the unit); (2) disturbance handler (responding to high-pressure disturbances, such as a strike at a supplier); (3) resource allocator (deciding who will get what in the unit); and (4) negotiator (working out agreements on a wide variety of issues, such as the amount of authority an individual will be given).

Consistent with Mintzberg's findings, managers in a study conducted by Toronto's Pace Productivity said that their work lives were very hectic and that their focus shifted rapidly from activity to activity. For example, for the average manager, 43 different activities lasted an average of just 16 minutes each. Managers felt that they should have spent about half their time on activities such as managing staff, providing direction, and coaching, but that they actually were able to spend only 18 percent of their time on "people management." Managers also thought that they should have spent about 6 percent of their time on administrative tasks, but they actually spent 25 percent of their time on those activities. The time that managers thought they should spend on planning was about the same as what they actually spent.

Insight into what managers actually do can also be gained by looking at the so-called functions of management (planning, organizing, leading, and controlling). Consider the work of Marina Pyo, who is publisher, School Division, at Pearson Education Canada, the company that publishes the textbook you are reading. Her job is to manage the activities that are necessary to develop resources in math and science for the Canadian elementary school market. Her work is at times intense, fragmented, rewarding, frustrating, and fast paced. In short, she is a typical manager.

Pyo carries out the planning function when she drafts a plan for a new book. She is organizing when she develops a new organization chart to facilitate goal achievement. She is leading when she meets with a subordinate to discuss that person's career plans. And she is controlling when she checks sales prospects for a book before ordering a reprint.

Some of Pyo's activities do not easily fit into this "functions of management" model. For example, it is not clear which function she is performing when she negotiates the size of a reprint run with the manager of the sales division. But this activity is captured in Mintzberg's role approach to management (Pyo is carrying out the negotiator role).

Critical Thinking Questions

1. What exactly is it that managers are accountable for?
2. Why do you think managers spend less time on "people management" than they think they should and more time on administrative tasks? How does this affect managerial accountability?

Types of Managers

2 | Identify *types of managers* by level and area.

Although all managers plan, organize, lead, and control, not all managers have the same degree of responsibility for each activity. Moreover, managers differ in the specific application of these activities. We can divide managers by their *level* of responsibility or by their *area* of responsibility.

Levels of Management

The three basic levels of management are top, middle, and first-line management. As shown in Figure 1.2, in most firms there are more middle managers than

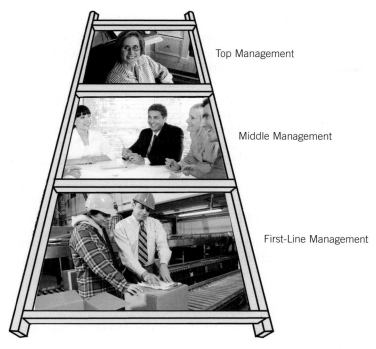

Top Management

Middle Management

First-Line Management

Figure 1.2 Most organizations have three basic levels of management.

top managers and more first-line managers than middle managers. Moreover, as the categories imply, the power of managers and the complexity of their duties increase as we move up the pyramid.

Top Managers

The small number of executives who guide the fortunes of companies are **top managers**. Common titles for top managers include president, vice-president, chief operating officer (COO), chief executive officer (CEO), and chief financial officer (CFO). Top managers are responsible to the board of directors and shareholders of the firm for its overall performance and effectiveness. They set general policies, formulate strategies, oversee significant decisions, and represent the company in its dealings with other businesses and government.[4] In 2006, *Canadian Business* magazine named Denis Turcotte, CEO of Algoma Steel, as the top Canadian CEO for his work in making Algoma the most efficient steel producer in the world.[5]

In some companies, top managers temporarily do the jobs of front-line workers in order to get insights into what employees are actually doing each day and to think of ways to help employees do their jobs better. For example, 150 managers of Loews Hotels in Canada and the United States spend one day every year in an entry-level job at the company. At Amazon.com, top managers deal with customers' phone or email questions one day every two years.[6]

Middle Managers

Middle managers occupy positions between top and first-line managers. Titles such as plant manager, operations manager, and division manager are typical of middle-management jobs. Middle managers are responsible for implementing the strategies, policies, and decisions of the top managers. For example, if top management decides to bring out a new product in 12 months or to cut costs by 5 percent in the next year, middle management will have to decide whether to increase the pace of new product development or to reduce the plant's workforce. With companies increasingly seeking ways to cut costs, the job of middle manager has lately become precarious in many large companies.

top managers Those managers responsible for a firm's overall performance and effectiveness and for developing long-range plans for the company.

middle managers Those managers responsible for implementing the decisions made by top managers.

First-Line Managers

first-line managers Those managers responsible for supervising the work of employees

First-line managers spend most of their time working with and supervising the employees who report to them. For example, a transit supervisor monitors bus schedules, passenger safety, and the behaviour of bus drivers. A first-line supervisor at a building project ensures that workers are carrying out construction as specified by the architect, but the supervisor also interacts extensively with materials suppliers, community officials, and middle and top managers at the home office. Those who hold titles such as supervisor, office manager, and group leader are first-line managers. The manager of a Canadian Tire store and the flight-services manager for a specific Air Canada flight are first-line managers.

Areas of Management

Within any large company, the top, middle, and first-line managers work in a variety of areas, including human resources, operations, information, marketing, and finance.

Human Resource Managers

Human resource managers provide assistance to other managers when they are hiring employees, training them, evaluating their performance, and determining their compensation level. In unionized companies, human resource managers are also involved in negotiations with the union. Imperial Oil has separate departments to deal with recruiting and hiring, wage and salary levels, and labour relations. Smaller firms may have a single department, while very small organizations may have only a single person responsible for all human resource activities. Chapter 12 addresses issues involved in human resource management.

Operations Managers

Operations managers are responsible for the production systems that create goods and services. These include production control, inventory control, and quality control, among others. Manufacturing companies like Steelcase, Bristol Aerospace, and Sony need operations managers at many levels. Such firms typically have a vice-president for operations (top manager), plant managers (middle managers), and foremen or supervisors (first-line managers). In recent years, operations management practices have been receiving increasing attention in service organizations, hospitals, universities, and the government.

Information Managers

Information managers are responsible for designing and implementing systems that gather, process, and disseminate information. Dramatic increases in both the amount of information available to managers and the ability to manage it have led to the emergence of this important function. Many firms, including Federal Express, have a chief information officer (CIO). Middle managers engaged in information management help design information systems for divisions or plants. Computer systems managers within smaller businesses or operations are first-line managers.

Marketing Managers

Marketing managers are responsible for getting products and services to buyers. Consumer product firms like Procter & Gamble and Coca-Cola often have large numbers of marketing managers at various levels. A large firm will have a vice-president of marketing (top manager), regional marketing managers (middle managers), and several district sales managers (first-line managers). Firms that produce industrial products such as machinery and janitorial supplies tend to put less emphasis on marketing and to have fewer marketing managers. We look at marketing in detail in Chapters 16 to 18.

Financial Managers

Management of a firm's finances, including its investments and accounting functions, is extremely important to its survival. Nearly every company has *financial managers* to plan and oversee its financial resources. Levels of financial management may include a vice-president for finance (top manager), division controllers (middle managers), and accounting supervisors (first-line managers).

Basic Management Skills

The degree of success that managers enjoy is determined by the skills and abilities they possess. Effective managers must have five key skills: *technical, human relations, conceptual, time management*, and *decision-making skills*.

Describe the five basic *management skills*.

3

Technical Skills

Skills associated with performing specialized tasks within a company are called **technical skills**. An administrative assistant's ability to type, an animator's ability to draw a cartoon, and an accountant's ability to audit a company's records are all technical skills. People develop their technical skills through education and experience. The administrative assistant, for example, probably took a keyboarding course and has had many hours of practice both on and off the job. The animator may have received training in an art school and probably learned a great deal from experienced animators on the job. The accountant earned a university degree and a professional certification.

    As Figure 1.3 shows, technical skills are especially important for first-line managers. Most first-line managers spend considerable time helping employees solve work-related problems, monitoring their performance, and training them

technical skills Skills associated with performing specialized tasks within a company.

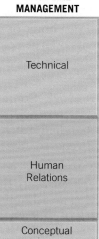

Figure 1.3 Different levels in an organization require different combinations of managerial skills.

in more efficient work procedures. Such managers need a basic understanding of the jobs they supervise. As a manager moves up the corporate ladder, however, technical skills become less and less important. Top managers, for example, often have only a cursory familiarity with the mechanics of basic tasks performed by their subordinates. Michael Eisner, the former CEO of Disney, freely admits that he can't draw Mickey Mouse or build a ride for Disney World.

Human Relations Skills

human relations skills Skills that enable managers to understand and get along with other people.

Human relations skills enable managers to understand and get along with other people. A manager with poor human relations skills will have trouble getting along with subordinates, which will, in turn, cause valuable employees to quit or transfer, and contribute to poor morale. When Development Dimensions International (DDI) asked 944 human resource professionals to state the reasons why newly promoted managers fail, 53 percent said it was because of poor people skills.[7]

Human relations skills are important at all levels, but they are probably most important for middle managers, who must often act as bridges between top managers, first-line managers, and managers from other areas of the organization. Effective managers possess communication skills that help them to understand others (and to get others to understand) and that can go a long way in maintaining good relations in an organization.

Conceptual Skills

conceptual skills A person's ability to think in the abstract, to diagnose and analyze different situations, and to see beyond the present situation.

Conceptual skills refer to a person's ability to think in the abstract, to diagnose and analyze different situations, and to see beyond the present situation. Conceptual skills help managers recognize new market opportunities (and threats). They can also help managers analyze the probable outcomes of their decisions. Top managers depend most on conceptual skills and first-line managers least, although some level of conceptual skill is needed in almost any job-related activity.

Time Management Skills

time management skills The productive use that managers make of their time.

Time management skills refer to the productive use that managers make of their time. In 2008, for example, Onex Corp. CEO Gerald Schwartz was paid a total of $61.7 million (including bonuses and options).[8] Assuming that he worked 50 hours a week and took two weeks vacation, Schwartz earned about $24,680 per hour, or about $411 per minute. Any time that Schwartz wastes represents a large cost to Onex and its stockholders.

To manage time effectively, managers must address the four leading causes of wasted time:

- *Paperwork.* Some managers spend too much time deciding what to do with letters and reports. Most documents of this sort are routine and can be handled quickly. Managers must learn to recognize those documents that require more attention.

- *The telephone.* Experts estimate that managers are interrupted by the telephone every five minutes. To manage time more effectively, they suggest having an administrative assistant screen all calls and setting aside a certain block of time each day to return the important ones.

- *Meetings.* Many managers spend as much as four hours per day in meetings. To help keep this time productive, the person handling the meeting should specify a clear agenda, start on time, keep everyone focussed on the agenda, and end on time.

■ *Email.* More and more managers are also relying heavily on email and other forms of electronic communication. Like memos and telephone calls, many email messages are not particularly important, and some are trivial. As a result, time is wasted when managers have to sort through a variety of electronic folders, in-baskets, and archives. As the average number of electronic messages grows, the potential time wasted also increases.

Decision-Making Skills

Decision making means choosing one alternative from among several options. **Decision-making skills** are critical for managers because decision making affects all the functions of management and all managers at all levels in all organizations. Managers can improve their decision-making effectiveness by following a rational decision-making process.

decision making Choosing one alternative from among several options.

decision-making skills Skills in defining problems and selecting the best courses of action.

The Rational Decision-Making Process

Figure 1.4 shows the steps in the rational decision-making process. The key elements of each step are described below.

Recognizing and Defining the Decision Situation.   The first step in rational decision making is recognizing that a decision is necessary. There must be some stimulus or spark to initiate this process. For example, when equipment malfunctions, managers must decide whether to repair it or to replace it. The stimulus for a decision may be either a problem or an opportunity. A manager

Step	Detail	Example
1. Recognizing and defining the decision situation	Some stimulus indicates that a decision must be made. The stimulus may be positive or negative.	The plant manager sees that employee turnover has increased by 5 percent.
2. Identifying alternatives	Both obvious and creative alternatives are desired. In general, the more important the decision, the more alternaticves should be generated.	The plant manager can increase wages, increase benefits, or change hiring standards.
3. Evaluating alternatives	Each alternatives is evaluated to determine its feasibility, its satisfactoriness, and its consequences.	Increasing benefits may not be feasible. Increasing wages and changing hiring standards may satify all conditions.
4. Selecting the best alternative	Consider all situational factors and choose the alternative that best fits the manager's situation.	Changing hiring standards will take an extended period of time to cut turnover, so increase wages.
5. Implementing the chosen alternative	The chosen alternative is implemented into the organizational system.	The plant manager may need permission from corporate headquarters. The human resource department establishes a new wage structure.
6. Following up and evaluating the results	At some time in the future, the manager should ascertain the extent to which the alternative chosen in step 4 and implemented in step 5 has worked.	The plant manager notes that six months later, turnover dropped to its previous level.

Figure 1.4 Steps in the rational decision-making process.

facing cost overruns on a project is faced with a **problem decision**, while a manager who is trying to decide how to invest surplus funds is faced with an **opportunity decision**. Managers also need to understand precisely what the problem or opportunity is. This understanding comes from careful analysis and thoughtful consideration of the situation.

Consider the situation in the international air travel industry. Because of the growth of international travel related to business, education, and tourism, global carriers such as Singapore Airlines, KLM, Japan Air Lines, British Airways, and American Airlines need to increase their capacity for international travel. Because most major international airports are already operating at or near capacity, adding new flights to existing schedules is not feasible. Rather, the most logical alternative is to increase capacity on existing flights. Thus, Boeing and Airbus recognized an important opportunity and defined their decision situation as how best to respond to the need for increased global travel capacity.[9]

Identifying Alternatives. Once the need for a decision is recognized, the second step is to identify possible alternative courses of action. In general, the more important the decision, the more attention is directed to developing alternatives. If the decision involves a multimillion-dollar relocation, a great deal of time and expertise should be devoted to identifying alternatives, but if the decision involves choosing a name for the company softball team, much fewer resources should be devoted to the task (although it may be difficult to keep the players from arguing about what the name should be!).

Factors such as legal restrictions, moral and ethical norms, and available technology can limit alternatives. After assessing the question of how to increase international airline capacity, Boeing and Airbus identified three different alternatives. They could independently develop new large planes, they could collaborate in a joint venture to create a single new large plane, or they could modify their largest existing planes to increase their capacity.

Evaluating Alternatives. Once alternatives have been identified, they must be carefully evaluated. During its analysis of alternatives, Airbus concluded that it would be at a disadvantage if it tried to simply enlarge its existing planes because the competitive Boeing 747 is already the largest aircraft being made and could readily be expanded. Boeing, meanwhile, was seriously concerned about the risk inherent in building a new and even larger plane, even if it shared the risk with Airbus as a joint venture.

Selecting the Best Alternative. Choosing the best available alternative is the real crux of decision making. Many situations do not lend themselves to objective mathematical analysis, but managers and leaders can often develop subjective estimates for choosing an alternative. Decision makers should also remember that finding multiple acceptable alternatives may be possible, so selecting just one alternative and rejecting all the others might not be a good decision. Airbus proposed a joint venture with Boeing, but Boeing decided that its best course of action was to modify its existing 747 to increase its capacity. Airbus then decided to proceed on its own to develop and manufacture a new jumbo jet called the A380. Meanwhile, Boeing decided that in addition to modifying its 747, it would also develop a new plane (the 787).

Implementing the Chosen Alternative. After an alternative has been selected, managers must implement it. In some situations implementation is fairly easy, but in others it is very difficult. In the case of an acquisition, for example, managers must decide how to integrate all the activities of the new business into the firm's existing organizational framework. When Hewlett-Packard first announced its acquisition of Compaq, managers acknowledged that it would take at least a year to integrate the two firms into a single one.

After a long decision-making process, Airbus decided to design its own jumbo jet. The Airbus A380's design allows seating for up to 850 people, and major airports around the world have been building new runways and terminal areas to accommodate the behemoth. Boeing, meanwhile, went through a similar decision-making process but concluded that the risks were too great to gamble on such an enormous project. Instead, the firm decided to modify its existing 747 design and develop a new fuel-efficient aircraft, the 787.

One of the key things that managers must deal with during implementation is employee resistance to change. The reasons for such resistance include insecurity, inconvenience, and fear of the unknown. Managers must also recognize that even when all alternatives have been evaluated as precisely as possible and the consequences of each alternative have been weighed, unanticipated consequences are still likely.

Following Up and Evaluating the Results. The final step in the decision-making process requires managers to evaluate the effectiveness of their decision—that is, they should make sure that the chosen alternative has served its original purpose. If an implemented alternative appears not to be working, managers can respond in several ways. One possibility is to adopt an alternative that had previously been discarded. Or they might recognize that the situation was not correctly defined to begin with and start the process all over again. In the Boeing/Airbus case, both companies are getting feedback that they made a good decision because they have large order backlogs. But both companies are experiencing delays in meeting their new product development schedules.

Behavioural Aspects of Decision Making

Many managers make decisions with too little consideration for logic and rationality. Peter Tingling, a professor at the Segal School of Business at Simon Fraser University, says that managers too often decide what they want to have happen and then later conduct analyses to support their decision. In his words, instead of using "evidence-based decision making," managers often use "decision-based evidence making."[10] Even when managers try to be logical, they sometimes fail. When Starbucks opened its first coffee shops in New York, it relied on scientific marketing research, taste tests, and rational deliberation in making a decision to emphasize drip over espresso coffee. However, that decision proved wrong when it became clear that New Yorkers strongly preferred the same espresso-style coffees that were Starbucks' mainstays on the west coast. Hence, the firm had to reconfigure its stores hastily to meet customer preferences.

Non-logical and emotional factors often influence managerial decision making. These factors include *organizational politics, intuition, escalation of commitment*, and *risk propensity*.

organizational politics The actions that people take as they try to get what they want.

Organizational Politics.   The term **organizational politics** refers to the actions that people take as they try to get what they want. These actions may or may not be beneficial to the organization, but they do influence decision making, particularly if the person taking the action is powerful and can get his or her way.

intuition An "inner sense" or "hunch" usually based on years of experience and practice in making decisions in similar situations.

Intuition.   Managers sometimes decide to do something because it "feels right" or because they have a "hunch." **Intuition** is usually based on years of experience and practice in making decisions in similar situations. Such an inner sense may actually help managers make an occasional decision without going through a rational sequence of steps. For example, the New York Yankees once contacted three major sneaker manufacturers—Nike, Reebok, and Adidas—and informed them that they were looking to make a sponsorship deal. While Nike and Reebok were carefully and rationally assessing the possibilities, managers at Adidas quickly responded to the idea and ended up hammering out a contract while the competitors were still analyzing details.[11] These occasional successes can be very dramatic, but they should not cause managers to rely too heavily on intuition.

escalation of commitment When a manager makes a decision and then remains committed to its implementation in spite of clear evidence that it was a bad decision.

Escalation of Commitment.   When a manager makes a decision and then remains committed to its implementation in spite of clear evidence that it was a bad decision, **escalation of commitment** has occurred. A good example of this is Expo 86, the world's fair that was held in Vancouver. When the project was first conceived, the deficit was projected at about $56 million. Over the next few years, the projected deficit kept rising until it was over $300 million. In spite of that, the project went forward. Managers can avoid over-commitment by setting specific goals ahead of time that deal with how much time and money they are willing to spend on a given project. These goals make it harder for managers to interpret unfavourable news in a positive light.[12]

risk propensity How much a manager is willing to gamble when making decisions.

Risk Propensity.   **Risk propensity** refers to how much a manager is willing to gamble when making decisions. Managers who are very cautious when making decisions are more likely to avoid mistakes, and they are unlikely to make decisions that lead to big losses (or big gains). Other managers are extremely aggressive in making decisions and are willing to take big risks.[13] They rely heavily on intuition, reach decisions quickly, and often risk big money on their decisions. These managers are more likely than their conservative counterparts to achieve big successes with their decisions, but they are also more likely to incur greater losses.[14] The organization's culture is a prime ingredient in fostering different levels of risk propensity.

Strategic Management: Setting Goals and Formulating Strategy

strategic management The process of aligning the organization with its external environment.

strategic goals The overall objectives that a business wants to achieve.

Strategic management is the process of aligning the organization with its external environment. The starting point in effective strategic management is setting **strategic goals**—the overall objectives that a business wants to achieve. Remember, however, that deciding what it intends to do is only the first step for an organization. Managers must also make decisions about what actions will and will not achieve company goals. Decisions cannot be made on a problem-by-problem basis or merely to meet needs as they arise. In most companies, a broad program underlies those decisions. That program is called a **strategy**—the broad set of organizational plans for implementing the decisions made for achieving organizational goals.

strategy The broad set of organizational plans for implementing the decisions made for achieving organizational goals.

Setting Goals

Goals are performance targets, the means by which organizations and their managers measure success or failure at every level. In this section, we identify the main purposes for which organizations establish goals, classify the basic levels of business goals, and describe the process that is commonly used to set goals.

Explain the importance of *setting goals* and *formulating strategies.*   **4**

The Purposes of Goal Setting

There are four main purposes in organizational goal setting:

goals Performance targets, the means by which organizations and their managers measure success or failure at every level.

1. *Goal setting provides direction, guidance, and motivation for all managers.* If managers know precisely where the company is headed, there is less potential for error in the different units of the company.

2. *Goal setting helps firms allocate resources.* Areas that are expected to grow will get first priority. The company allocates more resources to new projects with large sales potential than it allocates to mature products with established but stagnant sales potential.

3. *Goal setting helps to define corporate culture.* General Electric's goal, for instance, is to push each of its divisions to #1 or #2 in its industry. The result is a competitive, often stressful, environment and a culture that rewards success and has little tolerance for failure.

4. *Goal setting helps managers assess performance.* If a company sets a goal to increase sales by 10 percent in a given year, managers in units that attain or exceed the goal can be rewarded. Units failing to reach the goal will also be compensated accordingly.

Kinds of Goals

Goals differ from company to company, depending on the firm's purpose and mission. Every enterprise, of course, has a *purpose*—a reason for being. Businesses seek profit, universities work to discover and transmit new knowledge, and government agencies exist to provide service to the public. Most enterprises also have a **mission statement**—a statement of how an organization will achieve its purpose. Bell Canada's mission, for example, is to be a world leader in helping communicate and manage information. Chrysler's mission statement emphasizes "delighted customers." Atco Ltd.'s mission is to provide products and services to the energy and resource industries and to invest principally in energy-related assets in North America. The mission of Investors Group is to satisfy clients who need general and comprehensive financial planning.

mission statement An organization's statement of how it will achieve its purpose in the environment in which it conducts its business.

Two business firms may have the same purpose—for example, to sell watches at a profit—but very different missions. Timex sells low-cost, reliable watches in outlets ranging from department stores to corner drugstores. Rolex, on the other hand, sells high-quality, high-priced fashion watches through selected jewellery stores. Regardless of a company's purpose and mission, every firm needs to set long-term, intermediate, and short-term goals:

- **Long-term goals** relate to extended periods of time—typically five years or more into the future. MasterCard, for example, might set a long-term goal of doubling the number of participating merchants during the next 10 years. Similarly, Sony might adopt a long-term goal to increase its share of the digital SLR market by 10 percent during the next five years.

long-term goals Goals set for extended periods of time, typically five years or more into the future.

intermediate goals Goals set for a period of one to five years.

- **Intermediate goals** are set for a period of one to five years into the future. For example, the marketing department's goal might be to increase sales by 3 percent in two years. The production department might want to decrease expenses by 6 percent in four years. Human resources might want to cut turnover by 10 percent in two years. Finance might aim for a 10 percent increase in return on investment in three years.

short-term goals Goals set for the very near future, typically less than one year.

- **Short-term goals** are set for one year or less. For example, Four Seasons Hotels may set a goal to increase the revenue generated by each hotel room by 10 percent over the next six months. Or WestJet may set a goal to increase the proportion of occupied seats on the average flight by 8 percent over the next three months.

SMART goals Goals that are specific, measurable, achievable, relevant, and time-framed.

Whatever the time frame of the goals that are set, research shows that managers who set **SMART goals** (Specific, Measurable, Achievable, Relevant, and Time-framed) have higher performance than managers who don't. The boxed insert entitled "Setting Green Goals" describes the importance of setting goals that take the environment into account.

Formulating Strategy

After a firm has set its goals, it must develop a strategy for achieving them. In contrast to planning, strategy is wider in scope and is a broad program that describes how a business intends to meet its goals, how it will respond to new challenges, and how it will meet new needs. **Strategy formulation** involves three basic steps: (1) setting strategic goals, (2) analyzing the organization and its environment, and (3) matching the organization and its environment (see Figure 1.5).

strategy formulation Creation of a broad program for defining and meeting an organization's goals.

Setting Strategic Goals

Strategic goals are long-term goals derived directly from the firm's mission statement. General Electric Co., for example, is pursuing four strategic goals to ensure continued success for the company: an emphasis on quality control, an emphasis on selling services and not just products, a concentration on niche acquisitions, and global expansion.

Analyzing the Organization and Its Environment

SWOT analysis Identification and analysis of organizational strengths and weaknesses and environmental opportunities and threats as part of strategy formulation.

After strategic goals have been set, managers assess both their organization and its environment using a **SWOT analysis**. This involves identifying organizational **S**trengths and **W**eaknesses, and identifying environmental **O**pportunities and **T**hreats. Strengths and weaknesses are factors *internal* to

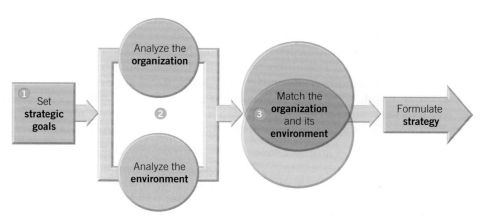

Figure 1.5 Strategy formulation.

The Greening of Business

Setting Green Goals

The logic of goal setting is being extended to making businesses greener. Consider the following:

- Wal-Mart set a goal to reduce the amount of packaging used by 5 percent throughout its huge supply chain; it wants to achieve that goal by 2013.
- The province of Ontario has set a goal to reduce plastic bag usage by 50 percent by 2012.
- Loblaws set a goal of reducing by one billion the number of plastic bags given to customers by 2009.
- Scotiabank has set a goal to be in the top 10 percent of the companies listed on the Dow-Jones World Sustainability Index.

For some organizations, their entire mission is being green. For example, the mission of B.C.–based Greener Footprints (a non-profit organization) is to reduce the use of plastic bags in Canada. For other organizations, the setting of green goals is closely tied to the success of their business. For example, the CEO of Honda, Takeo Fukui, recognized that Toyota's popular Prius hybrid automobile outsold Honda's hybrid car by a wide margin during the last decade, so he set a goal to make Honda the greenest company in the automobile industry. Honda has set a goal to sell 500 000 hybrid automobiles each year (Toyota's goal is one million). In 2008, Honda introduced its Clarity FCX, which is the most advanced green vehicle ever made. It is powered by a hydrogen fuel cell that generates no pollution at all. Honda also launched a new gas-electric hybrid in 2009 and plans to launch several other hybrids by 2015.

Rona Inc., the home renovation chain, has set a goal of doing business only with suppliers who address environmental sustainability and who do not contribute to deforestation. The goal for 2009 was to have all the plywood panels Rona sells made only from lumber that comes from forests that have been certified as sustainable. By 2010, the same goal will apply to spruce, pine, and fir. By 2012,

Rona's goal is to have 25 percent of its total wood sales come from forests that are certified by the Forest Stewardship Council.

Sometimes companies get involved in green activities that are quite different than their main business. For example, Google is involved in a strategic initiative called RE<C, whose goal is to develop electricity from renewable energy resources (solar, wind, and geothermal) that will actually be cheaper than electricity that is produced by burning coal. Larry Page, the co-founder of Google, says the company gained expertise as it developed efficient data centres, and it wants to apply that expertise to the development of generating renewable electricity. The first goal is to produce one gigawatt of renewable energy that is cheaper than that produced by coal. He thinks that can be done within a few years. Once that goal is achieved, the next goal will be to produce renewable electricity on a much larger scale.

Green goals may be developed by managers, or they may be imposed on companies by external groups. In 2007, for example, the federal government notified Canada's biggest industrial polluters that they had six months to provide emissions data that the government would use in setting new emission reduction targets. Discussions also continue at the international level about what the goal for emissions should be, but to date there has been no agreement. A spokesperson for 77 developing nations says that unless there is a goal, there can be no progress.

Critical Thinking Questions

1. What are the advantages associated with setting green goals? Are there disadvantages? Explain.

2. What difficulties might Rona encounter as it tries to reach the goal of having 25 percent of its total wood sales come from forests that are certified by the Forest Stewardship Council?

3. What are the advantages of the government setting emission reduction targets? What are the disadvantages?

---

the firm and are assessed using **organizational analysis**. Strengths might include surplus cash, a dedicated workforce, an ample supply of managerial talent, technical expertise, or weak competitors. For example, Pepsi's strength in beverage distribution through its network of soft drink distributors was successfully extended to distribution of its Aquafina brand of bottled water. Weaknesses might include a cash shortage, aging factories, and a poor public image. Garden.com's total reliance on the emerging internet-based retailing model became its downfall when the dot-com bubble burst.

Opportunities and threats are factors *external* to the firm and are assessed using **environmental analysis**. Opportunities include things like market demand for new products, favourable government legislation, or shortages of

organizational analysis The process of analyzing a firm's strengths and weaknesses.

environmental analysis The process of scanning the environment for threats and opportunities.

raw materials that the company is good at producing. For example, when Pepsi managers recognized a market opportunity for bottled water, they moved quickly to launch their Aquafina brand and to position it for rapid growth. Threats include new products and processes developed by competitors, changes in government regulations, and shifting consumer tastes. For example, Eastman Kodak Co. realized that that it needed to convert from its long-standing silver-halide film business to digital photography, and manufacturers of CDs and CD players now recognize the threat that online music services like iTunes pose.[15]

Matching the Organization and Its Environment

The final step in strategy formulation is matching environmental threats and opportunities with corporate strengths and weaknesses. This matching process is the heart of strategy formulation. More than any other facet of strategy, matching companies with their environments lays the foundation for successfully planning and conducting business. Over the long term, this process may also determine whether a firm typically takes risks or behaves more conservatively. Just because two companies are in the same industry does not mean that they will use the same strategies. The Toronto-Dominion Bank, for example, has been aggressively expanding into the U.S. retail banking industry by acquiring U.S. banks, but the Royal Bank of Canada has been much less aggressive in this area.[16]

Levels of Strategies

There are three levels of strategy in a business firm (see Figure 1.6). A **corporate-level strategy** identifies the various businesses that a company will be in and how these businesses will relate to each other. A **business-level (competitive) strategy** identifies the ways a business will compete in its chosen line of products or services. **Functional strategies** identify the basic courses of action that each department in the firm will pursue so that it contributes to the attainment of the business's overall goals.

Corporate-Level Strategies

There are several different corporate-level strategies that a company might pursue, including concentration, growth, integration, diversification, and investment reduction.

Concentration. A **concentration strategy** involves focussing the company on one product or product line. Organizations that have successfully pursued a concentration strategy include McDonald's and Canadian National Railway. The main advantage of a concentration strategy is that the company can focus its strengths on the one business it knows well. The main disadvantage is the risk inherent in putting all of one's eggs in one basket. These risks can be overcome to some extent by adhering to the following principle: "If you put all your eggs in one basket, watch the basket!"

Growth. Several growth strategies are available, all of which focus on *internal* activities that will result in growth. These strategies include **market penetration** (boosting sales of present products by more aggressive selling in the firm's current markets), **product development** (developing improved products for current markets), and **geographic expansion** (expanding

corporate-level strategy Identifies the various businesses that a company will be in and how these businesses will relate to each other.

business-level (competitive) strategy Identifies the ways a business will compete in its chosen line of products or services.

functional strategies Identify the basic courses of action that each department in the firm will pursue so that it contributes to the attainment of the business's overall goals.

concentration strategy Focussing the company on one product or product line.

market penetration Boosting sales of present products by more aggressive selling in the firm's current markets.

product development Developing improved products for current markets.

geographic expansion Expanding operations in new geographic areas or countries.

Figure 1.6 Hierarchy of strategy.

In the wake of an industry-wide slump a few years ago, Cisco Systems, a giant maker of communications equipment, radically revised its strategic plans. Where engineers once pursued their own pet projects, engineering is now centralized under a group of top managers. Where individual units once chose their own suppliers, a committee now oversees all partnerships. Where the product line once consisted solely of networking apparatus, the company has branched out into a variety of new high-tech markets.

operations in new geographic areas or countries). WestJet, for example, has used a geographic expansion strategy, since it started by offering service in Western Canada but has now added flights to various other cities.

Integration. Integration strategies focus on *external* activities that will result in growth. **Horizontal integration** means acquiring control of competitors in the same or similar markets with the same or similar products. For example, Hudson's Bay Company purchased Kmart and Zellers. **Vertical integration** means owning or controlling the inputs to the firm's processes and/or the channels through which the products or services are distributed. Thus, major oil companies like Shell not only drill and produce their own oil, but refine the oil into different products and then sell those products through company-controlled outlets across Canada. Another example of vertical integration is Irving Forest Products' purchase of Royale Tissue from Procter & Gamble.

horizontal integration
Acquiring control of competitors in the same or similar markets with the same or similar products.

vertical integration Owning or controlling the inputs to the firm's processes and/or the channels through which the products or services are distributed.

Diversification. **Diversification** means expanding into related or unrelated products or market segments. Diversification helps the firm avoid the problem of having all of its eggs in one basket by spreading risk among several products or markets. *Related diversification* means adding new, but related, products or services to an existing business. For example, CN diversified into trucking, an activity that is clearly related to railway operations. Maple Leaf Gardens Ltd., which already owned the Toronto Maple Leafs, also acquired the Toronto Raptors basketball team. *Conglomerate diversification* means diversifying into products or markets that are not related to the firm's present businesses. For example, Brookfield Asset Management (formerly known as Brascan Ltd.) used to own companies in the mining, real estate, electric power generation, and financial services businesses but has now moved away from a diversification strategy.

diversification Expanding into related or unrelated products or market segments.

Investment Reduction. **Investment reduction** means reducing the company's investment in one or more of its lines of business. One investment-reduction strategy is *retrenchment*, which means the reduction of activity or operations. For example, Federal Industries formerly was a conglomerate with interests in trucking, railways, metals, and other product lines, but it retrenched and now focusses on a more limited set of customers and products. *Divestment* is another investment-reduction strategy; it involves selling or liquidating one or more of a firm's businesses. For example, BCE sold its *Yellow Pages* and *White Pages* for $4 billion.

investment reduction
Reducing the company's investment in one or more of its lines of business.

Business-Level (Competitive) Strategies

cost leadership Becoming the low-cost leader in an industry.

differentiation strategy A firm seeks to be unique in its industry along some dimension that is valued by buyers.

focus strategy Selecting a market segment and serving the customers in that market niche better than competitors.

Whatever corporate-level strategy a firm decides on, it must also have a competitive strategy. A *competitive strategy* is a plan to establish a profitable and sustainable competitive position.[17] Michael Porter identifies three competitive strategies. **Cost leadership** means becoming *the* low-cost leader in an industry. Wal-Mart is the best-known industry cost leader. Montreal-based Gildan Activewear is dedicated to achieving the lowest possible costs in producing its T-shirts. The company has captured 29 percent of the U.S. imprinted T-shirt market with this strategy.[18] A firm using a **differentiation strategy** tries to be unique in its industry along some dimension that is valued by buyers. For example, Caterpillar Tractor emphasizes durability, Volvo stresses safety, Apple Computer stresses user-friendly products, and Mercedes-Benz emphasizes quality. A **focus strategy** means selecting a market segment and serving the customers in that market niche better than competitors. Before it was acquired by Nexfor, Fraser Inc. focussed on producing high-quality, durable, lightweight paper that is used in bibles. While it still has a good reputation in the production of bible paper, Nexfor Fraser Papers is now more diversified and produces papers for a variety of uses, including dog food bags and doughnut boxes.

Functional Strategies

Each business's choice of a competitive strategy (cost leadership, differentiation, or focus) is translated into supporting functional strategies for each of its departments to pursue. A functional strategy is the basic course of action that each department follows so that the business accomplishes its overall goals. To implement its cost-leadership strategy, for example, Wal-Mart's distribution department pursued a functional strategy of satellite-based warehousing that ultimately drove down distribution costs.

The strategy of one small company is described in the boxed insert entitled "From a Missouri Garage to Hollywood."

Entrepreneurship and New Ventures

From a Missouri Garage to Hollywood

The feature films *The Red Canvas* and *Way of the Guardian* were not developed by your typical Hollywood production team. For starters, one of the films' co-creators lives and works in Missouri. Adam Boster and his partner, Ken Chamitoff, started Photo-Kicks—a marketing company specializing in action photography—in their garages in 2002. From their beginnings photographing students at local martial arts schools, Boster and Chamitoff built Photo-Kicks into a multimillion-dollar business employing photographers, graphic designers, and marketers throughout the United States and Canada. In 2007, Photo-Kicks came in at number 592 on *Inc.* magazine's list of the 5000 fastest-growing private companies in America.

Just a quick glance at the many photographs on display on the Photo-Kicks website (www.photo-kicks.com) provides an eye-opening introduction to action photography. Athletes young and old punch, kick, and leap their way across the frames. But it's the countless other services that Photo-Kicks provides to its customers that have allowed it to grow so rapidly. Photo-Kicks bills itself as "a fully equipped graphic design and marketing organization," creating such products as customized logos, brochures, websites, posters, and trading cards.

Then, of course, there are the movies. *Way of the Guardian* began as a card game and animated series also developed by Boster and Chamitoff. *The Red Canvas* is more personal. It tells the story of a struggling immigrant who finds success and redemption in the sport of mixed martial arts. Chamitoff acknowledges that the film could not have happened without the years he and Boster spent travelling the country photographing martial arts students. "I learned the stories of every person I encountered," said Chamitoff. "Those stories shaped not only *The Red Canvas*, but Photo-Kicks as well."

Critical Thinking Question

1. What are the key differences between the various types of corporate and business-level strategies? Which strategies do you believe Photo-Kicks is pursuing?

Contingency Planning and Crisis Management

Business environments are often difficult to predict because unexpected events may occur. Managers know that such things can happen, so they often develop alternative plans in case things go awry. Two common methods of dealing with the unknown and unforeseen are *contingency planning* and *crisis management*.

Discuss *contingency planning* and *crisis management*.

5

Contingency Planning

Contingency planning attempts to (1) identify in advance important aspects of a business or its market that might change, and (2) identify the ways in which a company will respond to changes. Suppose, for example, that a company develops a plan to create a new business. It expects sales to increase at an annual rate of 10 percent for the next five years and develops a marketing strategy for maintaining that level. But suppose that an unexpected financial crisis and recession occurs (as happened in 2008) and sales do not reach planned levels. Does the company abandon the business, invest more in advertising, or wait to see what happens in the second year? Any of these alternatives is possible. However, things will go more smoothly if managers have decided in advance what to do in the event of problems like a financial crisis. Contingency planning helps managers do that.

In the summer of 2008, a strike at the PotashCorp. of Saskatchewan created a shortage of potassium acetate, which is the key ingredient in runway de-icer that airports use to prevent airplanes from sliding off runways in sub-freezing weather. The strike ended in November 2008, but by then airports were having trouble obtaining potassium acetate. The U.S. Federal Aviation Administration informed all airports that they should develop contingency plans to get their potassium acetate from alternate sources. Cryotech Technologies, the biggest supplier of potassium acetate to airports, responded by getting supplies of a corn-based de-icer instead. [19]

contingency planning
Identifying aspects of a business or its environment that might entail changes in strategy.

Commercial airlines have contingency plans to deal with problems like major snowstorms. These contingency plans involve making sure that planes are not stranded at airports that are experiencing snow delays.

Crisis Management

crisis management An organization's plan for dealing with emergencies that require an immediate response.

Crisis management involves an organization's plan for dealing with emergencies that require an immediate response. The listeria problem at Maple Leaf Foods in 2008 is an example of a crisis that needed to be effectively managed. CEO Michael McCain acted quickly to handle the crisis and did not hide behind lawyers or let financial implications get in the way of his decisions. The company recalled 686 000 kilograms of tainted meat (which cost the company $19 million). McCain publicly apologized at news conferences and in television commercials and assured consumers that the company would solve the problem.[20] By January 1, 2009, a survey revealed that 78 percent of respondents had recently purchased a Maple Leaf product. That was up from only 20 percent in September 2008.[21]

Italian food giant Parmalat Finanziaria SpA also faced a crisis when it couldn't account for $11.7 billion in funds. Its Canadian division, headed by CEO Marc Caira, responded by auditing the Canadian operation's accounting practices to make sure his division wasn't part of the problem. After he had determined it wasn't, he then took a variety of actions to reassure customers, employees, and investors that everything was fine in the Canadian division. He did this by continuously communicating with the company's key constituents. Caira's actions worked. The year after the Parmalat scandal broke in Italy, the Canadian division recorded its highest sales and profits ever.[22]

Disruption management (DM) stresses internal self-reliance in planning for and preparing responses to disruptions in an organization's external environment. Consider a shutdown caused by a snowstorm at Toronto's Pearson International Airport. An airline's least costly solution would be to simply cancel all incoming flights immediately. This approach cuts the airline's operating costs, but it is a terrible option for passengers who can't get where they're going. A DM approach would consider alternatives such as rescheduling flights into neighbouring airports and providing ground transportation into Toronto. A DM model would quickly simulate the costs and benefits of these and other options to help managers make an effective decision.

Management and the Corporate Culture

6   Explain the idea of *corporate culture* and why it is important.

corporate culture The shared experiences, stories, beliefs, norms, and ethical stance that characterize an organization.

Every organization—big or small, more successful or less successful—has an unmistakable "feel" to it. Just as every individual has a unique personality, every company has a unique identity, called its **corporate culture**—the shared experiences, stories, beliefs, norms, and ethical stance that characterize an organization. This culture helps define the work and business climate that exists in an organization.

The opening case provides several examples of corporate cultures. Here are some more:

■ Magna International, a large Canadian producer of auto parts, is a firm with a strong culture. Its founder, Frank Stronach, is well known for his views about employees, working conditions, daycare centres, unions, the free enterprise system, and profit distribution.[23]

■ Four Seasons Hotels and Resorts has a different, but equally strong, culture. Managers are judged by deeds, not words, and act as role models; employees take their cues from the managers.[24]

■ At Toyota's Cambridge, Ontario, plant the corporate culture stresses values, principles, and trust. The culture is one of continuous improvement.[25]

■ At WestJet Airlines, the corporate culture emphasizes profit maximization. Most of the employees own shares in the company, and all of them get to keep some of the profits. This is a powerful incentive for them to work productively.[26]

In 2008, executives at 340 Canadian companies participated in the Waterstone Human Capital corporate culture survey and expressed the following views:[27]

- Eighty-two percent said that culture has a strong or very strong impact on corporate performance.

- Three-year average revenue growth for the top 10 firms on the list was 63 percent higher than that of the 60 largest public companies in Canada that are listed on the S&P/TSX.

- Fifty-three percent felt that a strong culture reduced turnover, and 57 percent felt that a strong culture gave employees a sense of belonging. This finding is important, since an online survey conducted by Ipsos Reid found that many workers feel that they don't fit in well at work.[28]

A strong corporate culture guides everyone to work toward the same goals and helps newcomers learn accepted behaviours. Cameron Herold is a Vancouver entrepreneur who has had a string of successes in franchising, including College Pro Painters, Boyd Autobody, and 1-800-GOT-JUNK. He says that a cult-like culture is crucial for attracting great employees. He says what's needed is a culture that is "more than a business and slightly less than a religion."[29]

In a strong culture where financial success is the key issue, newcomers quickly learn that they are expected to work long, hard hours and that the "winner" is the one who brings in the most revenue. But if quality of life is more fundamental to the culture, newcomers learn that it's more acceptable to spend less time at work and that balancing work and non-work is encouraged. The survey mentioned above found that only 36 percent of executives felt that the culture of their company was strong.

Forces Shaping Corporate Culture

A number of forces shape corporate cultures. First, the values held by top management help set the tone of the organization and influence its business goals and strategies. Frank Stronach (Magna International), Timothy Eaton (Eaton's), Max Ward (Wardair), Larry Clark (Spar Aerospace), and Jean de Grandpré (BCE) are just a few of the leaders who have had a profound impact on the culture of their respective organizations. Even a large, long-time firm like Ford still bears the traces of founder Henry Ford.

The firm's history also helps shape its culture. The championship banners that line the arena where the Montreal Canadiens play signify that they are winners. Maintaining a corporate culture draws on many dimensions of business life. Shared experiences resulting from norms sustain culture. Thus, working long hours on a special project becomes a shared experience for many employees. They remember it, talk about it among themselves, and wear it as a badge of their contribution to the company.

Stories and legends are also important. Walt Disney has been dead for many years now, but his spirit lives on in the businesses he left behind. Quotations from Disney are affixed to portraits of him throughout the company's studios. And Disney's emphasis on family is still visible in corporate benefits such as paying for spouses to accompany employees on extended business trips. In fact, employees are often called "the Disney family."

Finally, strong behavioural norms help define and sustain corporate cultures. For example, a strong part of the culture at Hewlett-Packard Canada is that everyone wears a name tag and that everyone is called by his or her first name. And at Sony Corporation every employee wears a corporate smock.

These banners hanging in Centre Bell, the home of the Montreal Canadiens, are a dramatic illustration of the history of the team and its winning culture.

Communicating the Culture and Managing Change

Managers must carefully consider the kind of culture they want for their organization, then work to nourish that culture by communicating with everyone who works there. Wal-Mart, for example, assigns veteran managers to lead employees in new territories. As we saw in the opening case, Starbucks surveys employees every 18 months regarding several aspects of its culture. Royal Bank of Canada and Four Seasons Hotels and Resorts also survey their employees to determine how well they are progressing toward their corporate culture goals.[30]

Communicating the Culture

To use its culture to the firm's advantage, managers must accomplish several tasks, all of which hinge on effective communication. First, managers themselves must have a clear understanding of the culture. Second, they must transmit the culture to others in the organization. Communication is thus one aim in training and orienting newcomers. A clear and meaningful statement of the organization's mission is also a valuable communication tool. Finally, managers can maintain the culture by rewarding and promoting those who understand it and work toward maintaining it.

Managing Change

Organizations must sometimes change their cultures. Ontario Hydro, for example, had an "engineering" culture for many years. That meant that everything was planned and analyzed down to the last detail before any action was taken. But Ontario Hydro's culture has changed to a more consumer-oriented, risk-taking culture as it tries to cope with large debt and changes in its markets. When cultural change is required, the process usually goes through three stages:

1. At the highest level, analysis of the company's environment highlights extensive change as the most effective response to its problems. Conflict and resistance typically characterize this period.

2. Top management begins to formulate a new vision and culture for the company. Whatever that vision is, it must include a renewed focus on the activities of competitors and the needs of customers.

3. The firm sets up new systems for appraising and compensating employees, systems that enforce its new values. The purpose is to give the new culture solid shape from within the firm.

Robert Nardelli, the CEO of troubled Chrysler, is trying to change the "old Detroit mind-set" culture of the company, which was characterized by managers focussing on priorities that were important to the company—like running at full capacity—rather than what was important to the customer. As part of the process, Nardelli himself led a management development seminar on what the culture of a customer-driven company should look like.[31] Given the major problems that Chrysler was facing in 2009, it is imperative that the company develop a customer-driven culture if it hopes to survive.

Sometimes the three-stage change process is not completed. Consider what happened at Nortel Networks, which hired a new president and a new chief technology officer in an attempt to resolve some of the company's problems. Both of these individuals had worked at Cisco Systems Inc., and it was thought that they would be a great addition to a troubled company like Nortel. But Cisco has a hard-driving sales culture, while Nortel's culture is much less intense. Within three months, both new managers resigned from Nortel. Nortel's CEO said that their departure was due to different management styles and a different vision for the future of the company. In short, there was a culture clash that caused the new hires to leave the company, and the culture they envisioned will not be implemented at Nortel.[32] In 2009, Nortel declared bankruptcy.

Test yourself on the material for this chapter at **www.pearsoned.ca/mybusinesslab**.

Summary of
Learning Objectives

1. **Describe the four basic functions that constitute the** *management process.* *Management* is the process of planning, organizing, leading, and controlling an organization's financial, physical, human, and information resources to achieve the organization's goals. *Planning* means determining what the company needs to do and how best to get it done. *Organizing* means determining how best to arrange a business's resources and the necessary jobs into an overall structure. *Leading* means guiding and motivating employees to meet the firm's objectives. *Controlling* means monitoring the firm's performance to ensure that it is meeting its goals.

2. **Identify** *types of managers* **by level and area.** Managers can be differentiated in two ways: by level and by area. By *level*, *top managers* set policies, formulate strategies, and approve decisions; *middle managers* implement policies, strategies, and decisions; and *first-line managers* work with and supervise employees. By *area*, managers work in areas like marketing, finance, operations, human resources, and information. Managers at all levels may be found in every area of a company.

3. **Describe the five basic** *management skills.* Most managers agree that five basic management skills are necessary for success. *Technical skills* are associated with performing specialized tasks ranging from typing to auditing. *Human relations skills* are associated with understanding and getting along with other people. *Conceptual skills* refer to the ability to think in the abstract, to diagnose and analyze different situations, and to see beyond present circumstances. *Time management skills* refer to managers' ability to make productive use of the time available to them. *Decision-making skills* allow managers to define problems and to select the best course of action.

4. Explain the importance of *setting goals* and *formulating strategies*. *Goals*—the performance targets of an organization—can be long term, intermediate, and short term. They provide direction for managers, they help managers decide how to allocate limited resources, they define the *corporate culture*, and they help managers assess performance. *Strategies*—the methods that a company uses to meet its stated goals—involve three major activities: setting *strategic goals*, analyzing the organization and its environment, and matching the organization and its environment. These strategies are translated into *strategic, tactical*, and *operational plans*.

5. Discuss *contingency planning* and *crisis management*. To deal with crises or major environmental changes, companies develop contingency plans and plans for crisis management. *Contingency planning* means identifying in advance certain key aspects of a business or its market that might change and thereby affect the operation of the business. This type of planning also identifies the ways the business will respond if the changes actually occur. *Crisis management* means developing methods and actions for dealing with an emergency that requires an immediate response. To prepare for such emergencies, organizations develop crisis plans.

6. Explain the idea of *corporate culture* and why it is important. *Corporate culture* is the shared experiences, stories, beliefs, norms, and ethical stance that characterize an organization. A strong, well-defined culture can help a business reach its goals and can influence management styles. Culture is determined by several factors, including top management; the organization's history, stories and legends; and behavioural norms. If carefully communicated and flexible enough to accommodate change, corporate culture can be managed for the betterment of the organization.

PEARSON
mybusinesslab   To improve your grade, visit the MyBusinessLab website at www.pearsoned.ca/mybusinesslab. This online homework and tutorial system allows you to test your understanding and generates a personalized study plan just for you. It provides you with study and practice tools directly related to this chapter's content. MyBusinessLab puts you in control of your own learning!

Key Terms

business-level (competitive) strategy   (p. 32)
concentration strategy   (p. 32)
conceptual skills   (p. 24)
contingency planning   (p. 35)
controlling   (p. 18)
corporate culture   (p. 36)
corporate-level strategy   (p. 32)
cost leadership   (p. 34)
crisis management   (p. 36)
decision making   (p. 25)
decision-making skills   (p. 25)
differentiation strategy   (p. 34)
diversification   (p. 33)
effectiveness   (p. 17)
efficiency   (p. 17)
escalation of commitment   (p. 28)
environmental analysis   (p. 31)
first-line managers   (p. 22)

focus strategy   (p. 34)
functional strategies   (p. 32)
geographic expansion   (p. 32)
goals   (p. 29)
horizontal integration   (p. 33)
human relations skills   (p. 24)
intermediate goals   (p. 30)
intuition   (p. 28)
investment reduction   (p. 33)
leading (or directing)   (p. 18)
long-term goals   (p. 29)
management   (p. 16)
market penetration   (p. 32)
middle managers   (p. 21)
mission statement   (p. 29)
operational plans   (p. 18)
opportunity decision   (p. 26)
organizational analysis   (p. 31)
organizational politics   (p. 28)

organizing   (p. 18)
planning   (p. 17)
prediction markets   (p. 17)
problem decision   (p. 26)
product development   (p. 32)
risk propensity   (p. 28)
short-term goals   (p. 30)
SMART goals   (p. 30)
strategic goals   (p. 28)
strategic management   (p. 28)
strategic plans   (p. 18)
strategy   (p. 29)
strategy formulation   (p. 30)
SWOT analysis   (p. 30)
tactical plans   (p. 18)
technical skills   (p. 23)
time management skills   (p. 24)
top managers   (p. 21)
vertical integration   (p. 33)

Questions for Analysis

1. How are the four functions of management related to the five basic management skills? Use examples to clarify your answer.

2. What is the relationship between Mintzberg's roles of management and the more traditional functions of management? Use examples to clarify your answer.

3. Select any group of which you are a member (your company, your family, or a club or organization, for example). Explain how planning, organizing, directing, and controlling are practised in that group.

4. Identify managers by level and area at your school, college, or university.

5. In what kind of company would the technical skills of top managers be more important than human relations or conceptual skills? Are there organizations in which conceptual skills are not important?

6. How can managers determine if they are being efficient and effective?

7. Perform a SWOT analysis for the school you are currently attending.

8. Consider the various corporate-level strategies discussed in the text (concentration, growth, integration, diversification, investment reduction). What is the relationship between these various strategies? Are they mutually exclusive? Are they complementary? Explain.

Application Exercises

1. Interview a manager at any level of a local company. Identify that manager's job according to level and area. Show how planning, organizing, directing, and controlling are part of this person's job. Inquire about the manager's education and work experience. Which management skills are most important for this manager's job?

2. Interview managers at several different companies and determine their views on government bailouts of companies that are in financial trouble. Include in your list of interview questions the following one: "Do you think managers should accept bailout money from government during difficult economic times like those that companies experienced in 2008 and 2009?"

Building Your Business Skills

Speaking with Power

The Purpose of This Assignment

To encourage students to appreciate effective speaking as a critical human relations skill.

Background

A manager's ability to understand and get along with supervisors, peers, and subordinates is a critical human relations skill. At the heart of this skill, says Harvard University professor of education Sarah McGinty, is the ability to speak with power and control. McGinty defines "powerful speech" in terms of the following characteristics:

- the ability to speak at length and in complete sentences
- the ability to set a conversational agenda
- the ability to deter interruption
- the ability to argue openly and to express strong opinions about ideas, not people
- the ability to make statements that offer solutions rather than pose questions
- the ability to express humour

Taken together, says McGinty, "all this creates a sense of confidence in listeners."

Assignment

Step 1

Working alone, compare your own personal speaking style with McGinty's description of powerful speech by taping yourself as you speak during a meeting with classmates or during a phone conversation. (Tape both sides of the conversation only if the person to whom you are speaking gives permission.) Listen for the following problems:

- unfinished sentences
- an absence of solutions
- too many disclaimers ("I'm not sure I have enough information to say this, but...")
- the habit of seeking support from others instead of making definitive statements of personal conviction (saying, "As Emily has stated in her report, I also recommend consolidating the medical and fitness functions," instead of "I recommend consolidating the medical and fitness functions")
- language fillers (saying, "you know," "like," and "um" when you are unsure of your facts or uneasy about expressing your opinion)

Step 2

Join with three or four other classmates to evaluate each other's speaking styles.

- Have a 10-minute group discussion on the importance of human relations skills in business.

- Listen to other group members, and take notes on the "power" content of what you hear.

- Offer constructive criticism by focussing on what speakers say rather than on personal characteristics (Say, "Bob, you sympathized with Paul's position, but I still don't know what you think," instead of "Bob, you sounded like a weakling").

Questions for Discussion

1. How do you think the power content of speech affects a manager's ability to communicate? Evaluate some of the ways in which effects may differ among supervisors, peers, and subordinates.

2. How do you evaluate yourself and group members in terms of powerful and powerless speech? List the strengths and weaknesses of the group.

3. Do you agree or disagree with McGinty that business success depends on gaining insight into your own language habits? Explain your answer.

4. In our age of computers and email, why do you think personal presentation continues to be important in management?

5. McGinty believes that power language differs from company to company and that it is linked to the corporate culture. Do you agree, or do you believe that people express themselves in similar ways no matter where they are?

Exercising Your Ethics: Team Exercise

Clean Up Now, or Clean Up Later?

The Situation

The top management team of a medium-sized manufacturing company is on a strategic planning "retreat," and the members are formulating ideas and plans for spurring new growth in the company. As one part of this activity, the team, working with the assistance of a consultant, has conducted a SWOT analysis. During this activity, an interesting and complex situation has been identified. Next year, the federal government will be issuing new—and much more stringent—pollution standards for the company's industry. The management team sees this as a potential "threat" in that the company will have to buy new equipment and change some of its manufacturing methods in order to comply with the new standards.

The Dilemma

One member of the team, James Smith, has posed an interesting option—not complying. His logic can be summarized as follows:

1. The firm has already developed its capital budgets for the next two years. Any additional capital expenditures will cause major problems with the company's cash flow and budget allocations.

2. The company has a large uncommitted capital budget entry available in three years; those funds could be used to upgrade pollution control systems at that time.

3. Because the company has a spotless environmental record so far, Smith argues that if the company does not buy the equipment for three years, the most likely

outcomes will be (a) a warning in year 1, (b) a small fine in year 2, and (c) a substantial fine in year 3. However, the total amounts of the fines in years 2 and 3 will be much lower than the cost of redoing the company budgets and complying with the new law next year.

Team Activity

Assemble a group of four students and assign each group member to one of the following roles:

- management team member
- lower-level employee at the company
- company customer
- company investor

Action Steps

1. Before discussing the situation with your group, and from the perspective of your assigned role, do you think that James Smith's suggestion regarding ignoring pollution standards is a good one? Write down the reasons for your position.

2. Before discussing the situation with your group, and from the perspective of your assigned role, what are the underlying ethical issues in this situation? Write down the issues.

3. Gather your group together and reveal, in turn, each member's comments on James Smith's suggestion. Next, reveal the ethical issues listed by each member.

4. Appoint someone to record the main points of agreement and disagreement within the group. How do you explain the results? What accounts for any disagreement?

5. From an ethical standpoint, what does your group conclude is the most appropriate action that should be taken by the company in this situation?

6. Develop a group response to the following questions: (a) What are the respective roles of profits, obligations to customers, and obligations to the community for a firm in this situation? and (b) Is it possible to simultaneously make an ethical decision and maximize company revenue?

For additional cases and exercise material, go to www.pearsoned.ca/mybusinesslab.

Concluding Case 1-1

The Business of Bagging Customers

Coach Inc. started out in 1941 making virtually indestructible, high-quality handbags. In the 1970s it was bought by Sara Lee Corp., a big company that was pursuing a strategy of diversification. Because Coach was just one of literally dozens of businesses owned by Sara Lee, it suffered from the lack of focussed management attention. Coach's CEO, Lew Frankfort, knew that his company's success depended on finding the right industry niche. In 2000, he convinced Sara Lee to spin off Coach as an independent company.

By 2007, Coach had sales of $2.6 billion, and the company's net income growth had averaged 51 percent per year for the previous five years. In spite of the recession that started in 2008, the company planned to open many new stores in North America and in China. And it had big plans to compete with the best-known brand names in the industry. For example, just a few years ago in China, Louis Vuitton had the largest market share (33 percent), followed by Gucci and Prada (more than 10 percent each). Coach had only 2 percent. By 2007, Coach's share market share had increased to 12 percent, Louis Vuitton's share had dropped to 27 percent, and Gucci and Prada had less than 10 percent each.

These successes have come in the high-fashion business, where fickle customers and rapid changes make planning difficult. Most fashion designers—Ralph Lauren, Donna Karan, Prada, Gucci, Fendi—have adopted a design-driven business model, in which the designer dictates style to the customers. Coach, however, has taken a different approach. The company asks the customers what they want and then provides it. Coach's customer focus has created a competitive advantage for the firm, which annually sells $865 of merchandise for every square foot of store space, compared to an industry average of $200–$300.

Frankfort introduced many new analytical tools for tracking market trends, evaluating effectiveness, and managing risk. The firm's leaders look at sales data for each store and each product type on a daily basis (several times a day during busy seasons). But extensive and intensive customer research remains the cornerstone of his planning. Indeed, the company spends $2 million per year on surveys. The surveys are supplemented with one-on-one interviews with customers from locations around the world,

to quiz them on everything from appearance and quality to the correct length for a shoulder strap.

"The tremendous amount of testing they do differentiates them from a lot of other fashion companies," says industry analyst Robert Ohmes. Analyst Bob Drbul says, "Their execution and business planning is in the league of a Wal-Mart or a Target" (two much larger firms known for their effective business planning). New Coach products are first shown to selected buyers in 12 worldwide markets to gauge initial customer reaction. An initial demand forecast is then made, and six months before introduction, they are tested in another 12 markets. At launch time, sales are monitored closely and adjustments made quickly.

For example, an unexpected spike in sales was investigated, and managers found that buying by Hispanic customers was on the increase. Within a week, the firm had moved up the opening date of a South Miami store and began advertising in Spanish for the first time. Frankfort understands that, to be effective, plans must be translated into appropriate actions. "Not only do you need to know your business and your customers... you also need to be nimble to adapt," he says.

A host of other changes have also aided Coach in its rapid rise. Lew Frankfort hired a former Tommy Hilfiger designer, Reed Krakoff, to update the firm's classic but clunky styles. "Something was missing," says Krakoff. "I had to take these ideas and make them fun—young in spirit." Instead of introducing new products twice a year, a common practice in the fashion industry, Coach releases new styles monthly. Customers now have a reason to visit the stores more often. Outsourcing the production function allowed the company to increase gross profit margins by 24 percent over five years. The firm has diversified into many other related lines of business, including shoes, jewellery, and furniture. There is even a Coach car, a co-branded Lexus, with a Coach leather interior.

Women's Wear Daily, the bible of the fashion industry, named Coach as the "most splurgeworthy luxury brand." Customers agree. Investors, too, like Coach. The firm's share price rose an astonishing 900 percent during its first four years as an independent firm. Krakoff gives the credit for the firm's achievements to Frankfort's planning skills, saying, "The key to Lew's success... is his ability to orchestrate a decision-making process that is both inclusive and incisive."

Questions for Discussion

1. Describe examples of each of the management functions illustrated in this case.

2. Which management skills seem to be most exemplified in Lew Frankfort?

3. Explain the role of goals and strategy in the success of Coach.

4. What corporate culture issues might exist when a former division of a big company is spun off?

Concluding Case 1-2

If at First You Don't Succeed . . .

Warner Music Group Corp. is one of four companies that control about 80 percent of the global recording business. The others are Vivendi Universal Music Group, Sony BMG Music Entertainment, and EMI Group PLC. Warner is trying to profit from increased sales of downloaded music from the web and from cellphone networks. In 2006, downloaded music accounted for just 10 percent of the market, but the International Federation of the Phonographic Industry (IFPI) predicts that figure will rise to 25 percent by 2010.

In the spring of 2007, EMI Group became the first of the Big Four labels to remove so-called Digital Rights Management (DRM) software that restricts how consumers can play and copy music files. The CEO of Warner thought that was a bad idea, but when Universal Music Group followed EMI's lead, Warner finally agreed in December 2007 to remove the software and sell its music on Amazon.com Inc.'s digital music store. Up to that time, Warner had refused to offer songs by its artists in the MP3 format because they can be copied and burned onto CDs and played on Apple's iPod. In July 2008, cellphone maker Nokia announced that it had signed three of the Big Four labels for its "Comes with Music" phone service. It is rumoured that Nokia paid the record companies millions of dollars for the right to offer songs free for downloading.

Industry observers are very interested in whether Warner's strategy will work, partly because Warner's CEO—Edgar Bronfman Jr.—is the person who made a series of disastrous decisions when he was CEO of Seagram, the iconic Canadian company. Seagram was started by his grandfather Sam Bronfman in the 1920s. In 1957, Sam's son Edgar Sr. became CEO of Seagram, and for the next 40 years the company focussed on the production of wine and distilled spirits with well-known brand names like Chivas Regal, Absolut Vodka, and Crown Royal. In the process, Seagram became a household name in Canada and the Bronfman family became very wealthy.

In 1994, Edgar Jr. took over leadership of the company from his father and before long was making some dramatic strategic moves that steered the company away from its traditional products and toward the high-risk entertainment business. For example, the company bought MCA Inc. (now Universal) and Polygram NV. These high-risk moves caused some people to recall founder Sam Bronfman's observation that third-generation family members often dissipate the family fortune. Edgar Jr. was well aware of this criticism, and he was determined not to fulfill his grandfather's prophecy.

Under Edgar Jr.'s leadership, things went reasonably well for a time. Then he met Jean-Marie Messier, the CEO of Vivendi SA, who was trying to convert a French water and utility company into a media conglomerate. In 2000, Edgar sold Seagram to Vivendi for $33 billion of Vivendi stock. But when Vivendi got into financial trouble shortly thereafter, its stock price dropped sharply and the Seagram family fortune declined—from about US$7 billion to less than US$1 billion. Critics charged that Edgar Jr. had exchanged the Bronfman family fortune for a relatively worthless piece of the New Economy dream. Some people started thinking Sam Bronfman was right after all.

After the Vivendi debacle, Edgar moved on to other things in an attempt to repair his reputation as a manager. Determined to get back on the winning path, he first tried to buy Vivendi's film and TV assets, but he was unsuccessful. Later, he and several partners were able to purchase Warner Music Group, which includes record labels such as Warner Bros., Atlantic, Electra, and the Christian music producer Word Records. As CEO of Warner, Edgar Jr. adopted a corporate strategy premised on the belief that consumers would increasingly bypass traditional music stores and instead buy online digital music.

It is not yet clear what the latest developments in digital music mean for Edgar Bronfman Jr. and for Warner Music Group. If Warner's strategy works, Edgar Jr. will be seen as a manager who had the vision and insight to position Warner so that it could capitalize on a major trend. Also, if Vivendi somehow overcomes its financial problems, Edgar Jr. will benefit from its increased stock price because he still holds a lot of its shares. If neither of these possibilities works out, critics will say that old Sam Bronfman was right.

▶

Questions for Discussion

1. What are the various corporate-level strategies that a company might use? Which of these corporate-level strategies did Seagram use under Edgar Bronfman Sr.? Under Edgar Bronfman Jr.? Which strategy is Warner Music Group using now?

2. What is involved in each of the four functions of management? Which of these four functions caused Edgar Bronfman Jr. the most difficulty when he was CEO of Seagram?

3. How do you tell if a person is a good manager? Is Edgar Bronfman Jr. a good manager?

4. What skills do managers need to be effective? In what skill did critics say Edgar Bronfman Jr. was weak? Explain.

Chapter 2

Putting It All Together

After reading this chapter, you should be able to:

1 Answer the question: What is management?

2 Explain why management must be understood within the context of organizations and how organizations affect the practice of management.

3 Describe the role of working with and through people in effective management.

4 Explain managerial paradoxes and how dealing with them lies at the core of management.

5 Specify the nature and extent of commitment required for managerial excellence.

6 Define the term "entrepreneurial mindset" and explain its importance for managers.

7 Describe and compare the different elements of managerial work and the different managerial roles.

8 Discuss the skills necessary to be an effective manager.

Taken from *Management*, Canadian Edition, by Michael A. Hitt, J. Stewart Black, Lyman W. Porter, and Andrew J. Gaudes.

Managing: Putting It All Together

As president of The Home Depot Canada and The Home Depot China, Annette Verschuren confronts change, uncertainty, constraints, and the need to make sound decisions on a daily basis. Throughout her career Annette has succeeded in meeting these managerial challenges decisively using skills and insights that she continues to hone.

Verschuren has a background similar to that of many Canadians. She is the middle of five children of parents that immigrated to Canada from the Netherlands in the post–World War II era. Her parents settled on a dairy farm on Cape Breton Island where Annette was born and raised. She studied business administration at St. Francis Xavier University, and then embarked on a career with the Cape Breton Development Corporation, becoming the director of planning and helping employ displaced coal miners. Verschuren moved to Toronto in 1986 to begin working for the Canada Development Investment Corporation (CDIC), where she was responsible for divesting Crown corporations.

Her first experience with the private sector and retail came in 1989 when she left the CDIC to work for the conglomerate Imasco Ltd. While there, she assumed responsibility for managing Den for Men's 63 Canadian stores. Verschuren later created Verschuren Ventures and convinced Texas-based craft retailer Michaels to expand into Canada. She brought 17 Michaels stores to Canada and employed 1000 people in just over two years, becoming president of Michaels Canada in 1993.

In 1996, Annette received an offer from The Home Depot to take on the role of president of The Home Depot Canada. She would become the first woman and person without home improvement experience to become a president within The Home Depot. When

The Home Depot's Annette Verschuren is credited with the success of the company's Canadian retail operations, but she is quick to deflect credit to the hard work of more than 27 000 employees across Canada. She is described as a chameleon, adapting effortlessly from a meeting with corporate executives to a meeting with tradespeople, and is respected by both colleagues and competitors. Verschuren has subsequently been given the lead role in the expansion of The Home Depot into China while still presiding over the Canadian division.

Verschuren entered The Home Depot there were only 19 stores in Canada, and the outlook from corporate head office in Atlanta was that there was only room for 50 Canadian stores. Arthur Blank, co-founder and then CEO of The Home Depot, thought Verschuren was crazy when she forecast that Canada could accommodate 100 stores. Incidentally, there are now 154 stores in Canada, and plans for more.

Annette Verschuren has not completely relied upon the US model in developing The Home Depot Canada. She has instilled new ways of looking at retail home improvement and has, on a number of occasions, demonstrated that the US model can be improved upon. One particular example is Annette's response to a study that showed the large influence women have in home renovation and large purchase decisions. She introduced a more family-friendly store with wider aisles and a cleaner environment, and created in-store departments

that handled decorative elements, such as window treatments and wall art.

In order for stores to provide a more local appeal, she also decentralized decision making so that store managers could be more responsive to the demands of local customers, encouraging entrepreneurship at the store level. She also reduced the number of products in stores and scaled down the size of stores slightly to improve upon efficiencies and reduce inventory costs. The net result of Verschuren's adjustments has been a chain of Canadian retail stores that collectively generate sales in excess of $5 billion annually.

While riding the wave of success in Canada, in fall 2006 head office asked Verschuren if she would be interested in leading the expansion of The Home Depot into China. Always in pursuit of new challenges, Verschuren said yes. Meanwhile, she continues to oversee the Canadian operations and fend off competitive advances by Rona and Canadian Tire, as well as entry of the United States number two home improvement retailer, Lowe's. Verschuren has stressed the importance of retaining excellent staff, as it is their contributions that have allowed her to take on the role of fronting the corporation's Chinese expansion.

It is often said that little is certain but change, so Annette Verschuren will undoubtedly continue to face tough challenges ahead. Reflecting on her career to date, Verschuren has explained that she has had to reincarnate herself, changing in order to meet business demands. Given the management expertise she has developed over her career and the skills she has demonstrated in applying it to numerous difficult situations, it appears that the confidence The Home Depot has placed in her is well founded. ◆

Sources: The Home Depot Canada, www.homedepot.ca (accessed July 9, 2007); C. Nuttall-Smith and G. York, "Orange China," *Report on Business*, March 2007, pp. 25–38; C. Green and R. Koci, "An Interview with Annette Verschuren," *Hardware Merchandising*, March/April 2006, pp. 43–48; A. Verschuren, "Business Success: How to Prosper in the New Global Economy," address at the Atlantic Economic Summit, September 28, 2004.

Why feature Annette Verschuren in this opening chapter? The answer is simple: Her career to date—especially how she has approached managerial challenges during her career—will illustrate three key themes that are emphasized in this chapter and throughout the book: The importance of change, technology, and globalization.

Managing Effectively in Today's World: Three Critical Challenges

Change, technology, and globalization: These are undeniably three of the most important challenges that will have an enormous impact on managers in the near future. Consequently, we will be highlighting them in this and every other chapter in this book. We view them as three themes that weave continuously through the different topics that make up this subject called "management."

Change

Change is the most persistent, pervasive, and powerful area of challenge that any manager will have to deal with in any type of organization and in any geographical area. No matter how new or experienced you are as a manager, you will be confronted with both the need and the opportunity to change. Not making any changes at all is unlikely to be an option. As a Greek philosopher once wrote many centuries ago, "Change alone is unchanging,"[1] and that is still as appropriate a statement today as it was then.

Certainly, in her managerial experience so far, Annette Verschuren has had to cope with and master the need to change. She has jumped from staid, well-established organizations to the helm of something new and different. Indeed, her success (so far at least) seems to have come as the direct result of her willingness to risk and embrace change. In her current role with The Home Depot China, she faces daily changes that will occur while entering a completely new market. Doing things the same way day after day would be highly unlikely to lead to progress for her or the organization.

Technology

The other two themes that we emphasize throughout this book, technology and globalization, are nearly as important to any manager as is change. No managers in today's world can ignore the impact of technology and the way it affects their jobs and firms. Technology developments, of course, often force managers to make changes—whether they want to or not. One only needs to point to the internet as a case in point. The internet has had far-reaching effects on how managers do their jobs. Another example is the presence of online retail, which has presented Annette Verschuren with new challenges in addressing the needs of customers through the internet—both its numerous opportunities and its potential threats. The playing field for customers, competitors, and one's own organization has changed.

Globalization

The third theme, or overarching type of challenge, that managers face is globalization, the increasing international and cross-national nature of everything from politics to business. No longer can managers say that "what happens in the rest of the world does not affect me or my organization." It doesn't matter whether you will ever manage a firm outside of your country of origin or not, although it's becoming increasingly likely that you will. Rather, the point is that global events will almost certainly come from outside *into* your organization. They will affect how you set goals, make decisions, and coordinate and lead the work of other people.

Exhibit 2.1 Critical Management Challenges for the 21st Century.

Throughout her career, Annette Verschuren has had to engage in managerial activities that went beyond the borders of Canada. Verschuren first brought the Texas-based craft retailer Michaels to Canada, opening 17 stores. She then expanded US retailer The Home Depot from 19 stores in Canada to 154 in just 11 years. Verschuren is now faced with the challenge of expanding the North American home improvement phenomenon to Asia.

While we have discussed the three themes—change, technology, and globalization—separately, these three managerial challenges are often highly interrelated. Both technological and global developments frequently change the direction of organizations and the way they operate. Thus, the three managerial challenges of change, technology, and globalization form an integrated "iron triangle" of exceptionally strong influences on managers and management (as illustrated in Exhibit 2.1).

Managing Strategically to Meet the Challenges

The three major challenges described above combine to create an incredibly complex, dynamic, and competitive landscape in which most managers must operate. To survive and perform well in such an environment, managers throughout the organization are required to manage strategically.[2] Clearly, managers at the top of the organization—like Annette Verschuren—establish goals and formulate a strategy for the firm to achieve those goals. For the goals to be accomplished, the strategy must also be effectively implemented, which requires managers at all levels of the organization to set and accomplish goals that contribute to the organization's ultimate performance.

Increasing globalization and the enhanced use of technology have contributed to greater changes, emphasizing the importance of knowledge to organizational success.[3] The importance placed on the intellectual capital of the organization requires managers to use their portfolio of resources effectively. Of primary importance are intangible resources like the employees and the firm's reputation. Managers are responsible for building an organization's capabilities and then leveraging them through a strategy designed to give it an advantage over its competitors. They usually do this by creating more value for their customers than their competitors do.[4]

Managers are responsible for forming the strategies of the major units within the organization as well. Because the strategy has to be implemented by people in the organization, managers must focus heavily on the human factor. As they implement their strategies they will encounter conflicting conditions. Often this means managing multiple situations simultaneously and remaining flexible to adapt to changing conditions. Additionally, achieving an organization's goals requires that managers commit themselves to always being alert to how strategies can be improved and strengthened in advancing the vision that has been established for the organization. Finally, the dynamic competitive landscape entails substantial change. To adapt to this change, managers are required to be innovative, entrepreneurial, and to continuously search for new opportunities.

Now we turn to a set of basic questions that will be the focus for the remainder of this chapter: (1) What is management? (2) What do managers do? (3) What skills do managers need?

What Is Management?

Before we go any further, it is essential to take time to briefly discuss definitions and terms that will be used throughout this book. So here is how we will be using the following terms as they relate to the overall focus of this book:

Management: This term has several different uses. The primary meaning for the purposes of this book is as an activity or process. More specifically, we define **management** as the process of assembling and using sets of resources in a goal-directed manner to accomplish tasks in an organizational setting. This definition can, in turn, be subdivided into its key parts:

management The process of assembling and using sets of resources in a goal-directed manner to accomplish tasks in an organizational setting.

1. Management is a process: It involves a series of activities and operations, such as planning, deciding, and evaluating.

2. Management involves assembling and using sets of resources: It is a process that brings together and puts into use a variety of types of resources: human, financial, material, and information.

3. Management involves acting in a goal-directed manner to accomplish tasks: It does not represent random activity, but rather activity with a purpose and direction. The purpose or direction may be that of the individual, the organization, or usually a combination of the two. It includes efforts to complete activities successfully and to achieve particular levels of desired results.

4. Management involves activities carried out in an organizational setting: It is a process undertaken in **organizations** by people with different functions intentionally structured and coordinated to achieve common purposes.

organizations Interconnected sets of individuals and groups who attempt to accomplish common goals through differentiated functions and intended coordination.

Management can also have several other meanings in addition to a process or set of activities. The term is sometimes used to designate a particular part of the organization: the set of individuals who carry out management activities. Thus, you may hear the phrase "the management of IBM decided . . . " or "the management of University Hospital developed a new personnel policy. . . . " Often when the term is used this way, it does not necessarily refer to all members of management, but rather to those who occupy the most powerful positions within this set (top management).

Another similar use of the term is to distinguish a category of people (that is, "management") from those who are members of collective bargaining units ("union members" or, more informally, "labour") or those who are not involved in specific managerial activities, whether or not they are union members ("nonmanagement employees" or "rank-and-file employees"). We frequently use the term member to refer to any person (any employee) in an organization without regard to that individual's place in the organization. In this book, we use the term "manager" to refer to anyone who has designated responsibilities for carrying out managerial activities, and "managing" to refer to the process of completing those activities.

Let's now consider the question "What is management?" in a different way: by examining four fundamental *perspectives* of management—the organizational context, the human factor, managing paradoxes, and the entrepreneurial mindset. These perspectives cut across the entire managerial process. When you begin a journey, it's helpful to have a broad overview of the terrain you are about to travel *before* learning the details of the different parts of the trip. This overview helps integrate the different perspectives and facilitates your understanding of them to provide a meaningful and powerful adventure. And learning about the complexities of management is, we strongly believe, a journey that adds up to a definite adventure!

The broad perspectives presented here and throughout the book are based on information and ideas from a wide variety of sources: our personal experiences and observations as educators, managers, and consultants; research findings from the scholarly literature; extensive study of the subject; and, particularly, hundreds of conversations and interviews with practising managers over the years. These perspectives represent complementary points of view about management, but they are not mutually exclusive. Rather, each perspective provides a different lens to help you look at the topic and understand its complexities and challenges. These perspectives are presented to provide you with more understanding about what is meant by "management" than you can gain from a single definition. "Management" is too complex a concept to be captured by a definition alone.

In the next few pages, we first state each perspective, followed by typical questions that might be asked about it and our responses to those questions. Thus, the next part of this chapter uses a Q&A approach. The intent of this approach is to encourage you to become more interested in and involved with the material. We hope that it will increase your curiosity about management and stimulate your interest in learning about it.

PERSPECTIVE 1: *The Organizational Context*

management occurs in organizations

As you begin the formal study of management, it is important for you to understand that organizations serve as the context for management. And managers, much like the stage, are the constant background for actors in a play. For our purposes in this book, this context can be *any type of organization that employs people*: companies, universities, law firms, hospitals, government agencies, and the like.

Management Occurs in Organizations; It Does Not Happen in Isolation

Just as water is the necessary environment for fish, or air is for a plane, organizations are the necessary environment for managers to manage. In fact, stated strongly, "management does not exist without organizations."

Q: **Can't there be management in nonorganizational settings such as families, political groups, or ad hoc groups?**

A: Good question. Managerial activities, such as decision making or communication, can happen in nonorganizational settings such as a family. You can even engage in managerial activities such as planning and goal setting independently, without others being involved. However, these activities in isolation do not constitute management. Management requires integration of all these activities *and* the involvement of other people. This integration only occurs in an organizational context. It is similar to a dialogue taking place only when another person participates in the conversation—otherwise, it's a monologue.

Q: **OK, but does the type of organization matter? Does it make a difference whether the organization is small or large, or whether it's for profit or not-for-profit?**

A: Certainly the nuances of effective management change depending on the situation and type of organization. Managing in a small company where you know every employee—such as 96 percent of the 3040 businesses in Fredericton, New Brunswick, that have fewer than 50 employees—is not the same as managing in a large organization like RBC Financial Group with over 60 858 employees located in offices in Canada and around the world.[5] Although in this book we consider organizations of all sizes, the premium placed on good managers tends to increase as size and complexity increase. However, the cost of failing to manage effectively is high in all types and sizes of organizations.

Regardless of the fact that some dimensions of effective management are affected by the size and type of organization, the fundamental substance of management does not change. If the basic essence and nature of management changed dramatically from one organizational type to another, we would need a separate textbook for small organization management, large organization management, private company management, public agency management, and so on. In our view, the essentials of management are critical and universal activities in all organizations.

Nova Scotia–born Sidney Crosby is a well-known NHL hockey player and is team captain for the Pittsburgh Penguins. Crosby's coach is responsible for managing the team as a whole. Crosby, on the other hand, does not manage the team, but he does provide leadership on and off the ice. Many young hockey players look up to him as a role model. In your opinion, does this make Crosby a manager?

Each Organization Has Its Own Set of Characteristics That Affect Both Managers and Those with Whom They Interact

While it is critical to understand that management occurs in the context of organizations, all organizations are not the same, even those of similar size or complexity. Each organization has its own "personality" (often referred to as the organization's culture), and its own strengths, weaknesses, problems, and opportunities. These various characteristics affect the organization and all who work within it.

Q: What is it about organizations that creates their particular characteristics, and do they influence effective management?

A: Organizations often bring together a variety of people from different backgrounds—different ethnicities and cultures (Asian, African, Arabic, Anglo, Irish, Vietnamese, and so on), different educational levels (high school dropouts, college graduates, and MBAs), different technical backgrounds (engineering, digital arts, and accounting), and different socioeconomic levels (from very poor to very privileged)—who must then work together to achieve common objectives. Thus, developing a degree of shared cooperation becomes essential. This can only be accomplished by gaining acceptance of existing ways of working together, using existing structures and processes, or by developing new structures and processes. These behaviours, structures, and processes over time constitute the personality, or culture, of the organization. Whatever one may think or assume about the personality or culture of, say, a typical unit of Imperial Oil Limited, it is likely to be different from that of Radical Entertainment, a video game developer headquartered in Vancouver where shiatsu massage therapy is provided on site and free passes are given out to local ski and

Good managers can make or break all kinds of organizations—large and small, profit and nonprofit. Although the United Nations Children's Fund (UNICEF) is a nonprofit organization, its many members worldwide—both volunteer and paid—make it a complex organization to manage. Large, far-flung organizations make a manager's job harder to accomplish. As a result, organizations such as these place a premium on top managers, and they are generally paid competitively as a result.

snowboarding hills.[6] The basic principles of effective management are relevant in all organizations, but the specific characteristics of an organization affect how those principles are applied.

Q: Does this mean that if I am an effective manager in "Organization A," I will automatically be an effective manager in "Organization B"? Or does this mean that because organizations have different personalities, effective management practices can't be transferred from one organization to another?

A: Sound approaches to management do transfer from one organization to another. This does not mean, however, that your behaviour can be identical and still be equally effective in all organizations. For example, if you learn how to read music, you can apply that knowledge from one piece of music to another, but it does not mean that you can play each piece of music the same way. Furthermore, even if the musical score were the same, it does not mean that you would play the piece exactly the same way for different conductors or with different musical groups. But making these adjustments does not change your fundamental understanding of how to read music and your ability to adapt that knowledge to different circumstances. In the same manner, for example, becoming an experienced and competent decision maker is important in all organizations. However, some organizations may encourage participatory decision making, while others are more directive. No matter what the style, it remains important to develop the skills needed to make good decisions.

Effective management is similar in all organizations, but the challenges differ by organization. For example, an effective manager in a large government bureaucracy like Health Canada, with its rigid rules, can be quite different from one in a start-up, cutting-edge, high-technology business like a new-venture firm, where each experience is new and the rules are developed along the way. Thus, you will need to change how you put management ideas into practice based on the nature of the organization in which you are working. But this fine tuning does not lessen the importance of acquiring a basic understanding of management. In fact, having that understanding allows you to move more easily from one organization to another and still be effective. This does not mean, however—and we want to emphasize this—that you can ignore the differences from one organization to another; you must adapt the way you manage in each new organization. In fact, one of the quickest ways to become an ineffective manager is to remain rigid in how you carry out your managerial functions!

Managers Must Understand Organizations

Because organizations are the context of management, managers must understand how to operate within them. As we stated earlier, organizations are to management what air is to a plane. Yet for a plane to fly effectively, a pilot must possess essential knowledge about the characteristics and composition of air, like how atmospheric density relates to temperature in order to calculate how much lift it can provide. In the hottest days of summer, planes taking off sometimes have to bump passengers when seats are still available on the plane, because as the temperature rises, the air becomes less dense, lift is more difficult to achieve, and the weight with which a plane can safely take off declines.

Q: But what does it really mean to "understand organizations"? I can't possibly know everything about them, so how do I figure out what is more and less important to understand?

A: Just as a pilot does not have to be an astrophysicist or an aeronautical engineer to skilfully fly a plane, you do not need a Ph.D. in organizational science to be an effective manager. However, you do need a solid understanding of some basic features of organizations. Much of what follows in this textbook is designed to provide you with the fundamental knowledge you need in relation to the challenge of managing with skill. Of course, one textbook and one course in management will not provide you with sufficient knowledge. This book, however, will give you the foundation you need to be an effective manager. Without that foundation, you will either learn the hard way from your errors or be an ineffective manager.

Thus, while it is not practical to fully understand all organizations, you need to know how they can affect management practice. The key point is that just as a pilot cannot simply focus on the plane and ignore the conditions of the air, effective managers cannot only focus on management and ignore the organizational context within which it is practised. Clearly, for example, Annette Verschuren knows the difference between what managerial actions are required on the retail sales floor of a Home Depot outlet and what is required in an executive boardroom.

management requires getting things done through people

The act of managing involves an attempt to achieve an objective through the efforts of two, three, ten, a hundred, or even thousands of other people. Somebody acting entirely alone, whether he or she is writing a poem or making a critical investment decision, may be trying to achieve a particular goal, but that person is not managing. Management is, by its very nature, a people-based activity. Managers, no matter how talented, cannot do everything themselves. They need to use their own skills and energies as well as those of other people if they are to be effective. As one high-level executive within a software firm explained:

> *Hard skills, like sales, come easily to me, yet they produce transitory results. Delegating to others, co-creating performance expectations, and trusting people to carry through is not easy. But over the years, I have found that connecting with people one-on-one, and strengthening soft skills, produce meaningful and lasting results.*[7]

The message is clear: If you don't want to work with and through other people, then don't become a manager. You won't like the activity, and you are unlikely to be successful.

Managers Must Be Adept at Assessing Other People's Capabilities

A critical managerial skill, and one that can be developed, is that of assessing other people's capabilities. Knowing the capability of an individual or a group of people to complete one or more tasks, as well as judging what level of performance they might be able to reach with additional instruction, training, and motivation, is essential for building an effective unit.

 It sounds difficult to be able to evaluate the capabilities of people and to do it accurately. How do you do it?

A: It's not easy and it takes time, effort, and often experience to develop this kind of managerial skill. However, the important point is that being a manager requires that you do this task well. It's critical to being an effective manager.

Effective Managers Must Be Adept at Matching People's Capabilities with Appropriate Responsibilities

Knowing what a particular individual or particular group is capable of doing is only part of the requirement for successfully getting things done through people. Another equally important requirement is being able to match people with tasks they are best able to perform. In addition to finding the right job for the right person, managers must also ensure that their people have the resources necessary to do the job. Therefore, the manager must be a resource provider (a resource finder and enhancer) as well as a resource coordinator.

Q: That sounds good, but aren't resources always scarce in
organizations?

A: Certainly, resources are finite in all organizations. A manager almost
always has limited time, equipment, money, and especially people. That is why
it is vital to use human resources as skilfully as possible—to be able to connect people and tasks effectively. Often, that process involves forming teams,
where the whole is greater than the sum of the parts. Knowing the people in
your organization and their capabilities is vital, but it also is essential to fully
understand the tasks and the jobs that need to be done. Matching resources
and tasks also demands considerable effort to explore whether additional
resources are needed. Management is an activity that requires initiative—not
passive acceptance of the status quo.

Effective Managers Must Be Adept at Motivating People

The third requirement for successfully getting tasks done through people is
motivating them to accomplish the goals. In the current competitive landscape (described earlier in this chapter), formal authority is declining as a

All jobs require specific skills
and capabilities. The job of
managers is to match people
with the jobs they are best suited
to perform. This requires a
considerable amount of
evaluation of the job and the
person applying for it. For
example, a cashier's position
usually requires that the
employee learn how to operate
the cash register, ensure items
are properly priced, and be
knowledgeable of the different
payment methods available.
More importantly, cashiers are
frequently the customer's sole
contact with the firm. What the
customer thinks of him or her is
likely to be what the customer
thinks of the firm.

useful means for influencing people. Thus, managers must have a good understanding of what people value (what they care about) if they are to be superior
motivators.

Q: I don't want to be a psychologist, so how can I understand
what each person values
and wants out of work?

A: You are not expected to become a psychologist, but it is important that you
know some basic approaches to motivate people. In addition, you need to
understand how to apply those approaches when it comes to managing specific individuals. That includes not only those who work for you but also your
peers and superiors.

Q: But isn't management more than motivating people or getting things done through people?

A: Absolutely. Management is a complex process that requires integration of many different tasks, including planning and organizing what is to be done, developing budgets, and evaluating outcomes. Motivating and leading people are only two components of this overall process. Nevertheless, unless managers can get things done through people, not much will be accomplished. Managers must multiply the effects of their own efforts by influencing and directing the efforts of other people.

management requires simultaneously mastering multiple and potentially conflicting situations

Like most things, if management were easy there wouldn't be such a high premium placed on it. One of the important factors that separates great managers from mediocre managers is the recognition, acceptance, and mastery of managing paradoxes—the ability to cope with forces that pull managers in opposite directions. Great managers do not avoid these tensions but embrace them, harness them, and use them.

 Are these opposing forces really trade-offs? If so, managers sometimes have to trade off one opposing force for another. Is this correct?

A: Yes, managers at times have to make decisions about trade-offs. Sometimes they do, in fact, have to go with one set of actions to achieve the desired results—for example, expand the investment in R&D (research and development)—and in the process, forgo another investment and its potential results. That might mean postponing television advertising during *Hockey Night in Canada* for a season. However, great managers do not automatically view competing forces in terms of direct trade-offs; they often recognize that the challenge is to respond to both forces simultaneously in a creative fashion that enables the firm to accomplish both sets of objectives or some portion of them.

Management Is a Complex Process Requiring Integration, Yet Managerial Activities Are Often Fragmented and Do Not Occur in a Logical, Sequential Fashion

Management requires the integration of a variety of activities, such as planning, decision making, communicating, motivating, appraising, and organizing, yet a manager's day is typically fragmented with interruptions, breaks in sequence, and other distractions. In a sense, a manager is like a juggler. The manager may need to keep several balls in the air, simultaneously throwing the balls up and catching them. Rarely does the manager take the time to evaluate the competing "ball" and decide to keep one up while somehow suspending the others in mid-air. All of the balls must be continuously juggled or they will be lost.

Likewise, while managers are constantly confronted with rapidly changing activities and discrete bits or chunks of information, it is the responsibility and challenge of the manager to integrate all of them in a meaningful way. As such, the manager must be capable of seeing patterns of important activities and changes in them, both within the organization and external to it. He or she must then coordinate the resources, people, and activities to achieve the organization's goals.

Q: Although this seems logical, management seems much more simple than you're describing. Isn't the key to simplify management and not make it more complex?

A: Management, as often described by "bestselling" books, may seem simple, and certainly the authors of many of these books would like you to believe that if you just did "X" you would be highly successful. But the reality is that management is complex and requires integration of fragmented actions, information, and resources. Easy solutions may be appealing, but they rarely work. If management were simple, there wouldn't be a new bestseller about it each month—no one would need the new tip of the month.

There may be some value in bestselling management books, but the simple solutions that they offer may work only in a very specific situation; they are unlikely to work in most situations. Solutions that work across a variety of conditions are likely to be more complicated. Effective managers understand that paradoxes—seeming contradictions—lie at the centre of their roles and responsibilities and that one of their key challenges is to deal with those paradoxes effectively.

Management Requires Consistency and Flexibility

Perhaps one of the most important paradoxes is that of simultaneously maintaining consistency and flexibility. Without question, people need some consistency in their organizational lives. Workers could not be expected to perform their jobs well if tasks, or how they were expected to accomplish them, changed each day. Without some consistency, the workplace would be chaotic, and no purposeful organizational objectives could be accomplished. Yet, in the current competitive landscape—with rapidly changing technology, government policies, customer preferences, and competitor capabilities—flexibility, change, and adaptation are essential for survival.

Q: As a manager, how can I be consistent and yet remain flexible at the same time?

A: It is important to understand that as a manager you do not need to make an either/or choice to be consistent all of the time or completely flexible all of the time. For example, your fundamental values and ethical standards need to be fairly stable. People may not agree with your values or ethical standards, but they need to know what they are and that you consistently maintain them. Otherwise, you will appear to be unpredictable and untrustworthy. You also need to exhibit a fair degree of consistency without being overly rigid in your basic approach to dealing with people and problems. People need to perceive that you are open to alternative ideas, but they will have difficulty if you change so often that you seem to be a chameleon.

Managers Must Reflect and Act

Talk to any manager today, and he or she will tell you that one must rapidly deal with often unexpected situations, decisions, problems, and opportunities. One executive put it this way:

> *The fascinating thing about this job is the incredible variability of it . . . It's a never-ending kaleidoscope. I sometimes compare it to playing tennis with an out-of-control tennis-ball serving machine that just keeps shooting balls at you. You've got to keep moving faster and faster to keep up.*[8]

Quick action is often the difference between first and second place or even last place in the competitive marketplace, as Research In Motion has demonstrated with its popular BlackBerry. To some extent, then, capabilities like being able to think and make decisions quickly are admirable managerial qualities.

But there is an inherent problem with focusing on the onslaught of daily activities. This problem is similar to running and focusing on the ground only a metre in front of you. You may notice the stone in the path in time to avoid it, or you may notice a declining or inclining slope in the path and change your pace appropriately. Each individual step you take may be successful, but by focusing on only a metre in front of you, you may not notice that you are running straight toward a wall or cliff. Take, for example, the case of Richard Currie, former president of Loblaw Companies and presently chairman of the board for Bell Canada. Currie is recognized as having turned Loblaw around with innovative products like the "No Name" brand. Under Currie's 25 years of management, Loblaw shares increased 350-fold, becoming the largest private-sector employer in Canada. Two simple dictums that Currie employed through his career have been "don't move too fast" and "no one is as smart as all of us."[9] As this example suggests, taking time to make appropriate decisions and seeking the advice and input from others allows managers to look up and take notice of events beyond their own daily activities.

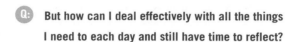

Q: But how can I deal effectively with all the things I need to each day and still have time to reflect?

A: Management is about activity; it is not about philosophy. But managers cannot know if they are headed in the right direction, if their pace is appropriate, or if their current approach is effective, unless they *take* the time to reflect on these things. Because management is about activity, you are unlikely to *find* time to reflect—you are going to have to *make* time. In fact, many of the insights presented in this chapter have come from managers, as we asked them in our interviews to take time to reflect on management. So, while managers must act and often do so quickly, they must also take time to analyze what they are doing, how they are doing it, and perhaps most importantly, why they are doing it.

Increasingly, Managers Need Global Perspective and Local Understanding of Specific Customers, Governments, Competitors, and Suppliers

International management consultants are fond of saying that in the future there will be two types of CEOs: those who have a global perspective and those who are out of a job. The evidence for the increasing globalization of business is nearly overwhelming, and that is why we make it one of our key themes in this book. It is virtually impossible to read a major magazine or newspaper without finding several stories related to global business in some form—companies entering international markets, competing with foreign competitors, responding to a foreign government's policy change, and so on. This requires a global perspective. However, the paradox is that all business occurs at a local level. The business transactions and the management activities all take place in specific countries with specific employees, government officials, competitors, and suppliers. Roots Canada, for example, has made inroads into the United States and has also been successful in expanding internationally. Roots even got the prestigious role of official outfitter for not only Canada, but the United States, Great Britain, and Barbados for the 2004 Olympics in Athens. The knife cuts both ways however; in early 2004 Roots was faced with closing a Canadian manufacturing facility, locating it offshore because of economic pressures to compete with lower-priced products coming into Canada from American and European firms.[10]

A: The key is to be able to recognize the drivers behind these competing forces. For many products, it is much cheaper to build one version for the entire world than to have variations for every country. Yet, for many of these products, customers in different countries have different preferences. One compromise is to design the product so it has the widest appeal, recognizing that, as a consequence, it will not appeal to some potential customers. Nevertheless, more sophisticated managers do not trade off global standardization for local appeal or vice versa. Instead, they recognize the inherent challenge in this paradox and seek to standardize aspects of the product that have common appeal and simultaneously customize those features that need to be adapted to local preferences.

For example, McDonald's has a worldwide identity built around the standardization of both its products and its service. The Quarter Pounder and Egg McMuffin are the same product whether you buy them in Charlottetown, Singapore, or Moscow. The company also attempts to standardize managerial styles by requiring managers to learn the company's specific approaches to human resource practices, marketing, inventory management, and quality control. However, McDonald's corporate managers must also learn to adjust their financial and marketing approaches to local conditions. Similarly, McDonald's store managers around the world must learn when to add specialized menu items to suit local tastes—McLobster in New Brunswick, McPoutine in Quebec, the Teriyaki McBurger in Japan, McFalafel in Egypt, and 100 percent kosher beef in Israel.[11]

You might think of this global/local paradox by comparing it to a view of the landscape from a helicopter. Managers often have to "helicopter up" to a level to get a broad perspective of the "forest," or in other words, to obtain a global view. But then they need to come down closer to earth to see the "trees," or the local conditions and marketplace. Managers who can only see what is immediately and directly in front of them risk being ineffective because they can't see "the forest for the trees." At the same time, though, managers who only fly at 20,000 feet risk being ineffective because they miss the small details and nuances that can influence the success or failure of specific decisions or tasks. Thus, effective management is not a matter of having only a broad global perspective or only a knowledge of the specific local situation; it is a matter of being able to develop *both*.

Agreements like the North American Free Trade Agreement (NAFTA) have thrown open doors to customers and firms worldwide. Managers in Toronto cannot assume their products will be as appealing in Miami or Beijing as they are on their home turf. But they also know that their competitors' products won't be either. In recent years, this has made for a broader playing field with make-or-break competitive consequences.

PERSPECTIVE 4: *Entrepreneurial Mindset*

managers must continuously search for and exploit new opportunities

We previously noted that managers must be committed to continuous learning and to creating value for others. However, to survive in the hyper-competitive landscape that exists in the twenty-first century they are required to regularly search for and be open to new opportunities in their current marketplace or to ideas that could create new markets. Entrepreneurship involves identifying new opportunities and exploiting them; thus, managers must be entrepreneurial.

 I thought that entrepreneurs developed new businesses and then managers operated them. Are you saying that managers are entrepreneurs?

A: You are correct about what entrepreneurs do, but entrepreneurship is not exclusive of management, especially in the current environment. Entrepreneurial activity is not limited to new, small firms. Managers in large firms need to be entrepreneurial and create new businesses as well. Developing new businesses requires that the lead person and perhaps others take entrepreneurial actions. Given the amount of change and innovation encountered in most industries and countries, businesses cannot survive without being entrepreneurial.[12]

 What is required for a manager to be entrepreneurial and be responsible for all of the other activities explained?

A: Managers must develop an entrepreneurial mindset. An entrepreneurial mindset is a way of thinking about businesses that emphasizes actions to take advantage of uncertainty.[13] With an entrepreneurial mindset, managers can sense opportunities and take actions to exploit them. Uncertainty in the environment tends to level the playing field for both large and small organizations and for resource-rich and resource-poor ones. Opportunities can be identified by anyone and exploited to achieve a competitive advantage.

To develop an entrepreneurial mindset, managers must first be alert and open to investing in opportunities today that may provide benefits in the future. They must be amenable to new ideas and to using them to create value for customers.[14]

 So, both large and small firms can be entrepreneurial?

A: Yes. In fact, large and small firms *and* new and established firms can be entrepreneurial. For reasons described earlier, they not only can be, they

must be to survive. Eaton's, once an entrepreneurial company that grew to become one of North America's most influential department stores, no longer exists in part because it lost its entrepreneurial nature when it no longer understood the needs of its customers and was unable to respond to the competitive advances of other retailers in the late 1990s. As a whole, small and new firms tend to be more entrepreneurial, but often lack the ability to sustain this advantage. On the other hand, large, established firms are good at using their size to gain an advantage and in sustaining their strong position as long as new, rival products don't enter the market. However, larger firms have a harder time being entrepreneurial.[15]

An Entrepreneurial Mindset Requires a Commitment to Constantly Learning New Skills and Acquiring New Knowledge

Management is a complex process. It is not just about strategy, or organizing, or decision making, or leadership. It is about all of these activities and more, but it is especially about *integrating them*. To integrate activities, managers require multiple skills (as we discuss later in this chapter): technical, interpersonal, and conceptual. These skills can be learned, or at least greatly improved by learning, if there is a commitment by a manager to such learning. Experience alone does not necessarily provide learning, but the desire for and effort to acquire new knowledge from those experiences often produces learning and the development of new capabilities.

Q: **But do I really have to keep on learning about how to manage throughout my career?**

A: It is dangerous to assume at any point in time that you know all that needs to be known about management. Managers must continuously acquire new knowledge and skills to remain competitive because they constantly confront new situations and challenges. Therefore, a commitment to continuous learning and improvement is vital. Managerial hubris—meaning

Even the best managers with the most experience must stay abreast of the marketplace because conditions can change rapidly. This means not becoming complacent but committing themselves and their staff to continued learning and improvement to meet new challenges and situations.

overbearing pride or self-confidence—has been publicly demonstrated in recent years by the colossal failures of companies such as Enron and WorldCom, which will be better known for the circumstances of their demise than for their products or services. This danger should motivate you to pursue the frontiers of learning and acquire better managerial skills no matter what your level in the organization is.

An Entrepreneurial Mindset Also Requires a Commitment to Adding Value to Other People's Efforts and to Society

At its best, management is not a selfish activity. It should serve others, both in one's own organization and in society at large. This kind of commitment represents a challenge—a challenge to contribute something that benefits people, whether it be employees, customers, shareholders, or others. Meeting this challenge requires not only a sense of obligation and responsibility, but also vision and a burning passion. Otherwise, why be a manager?

What Do Managers Do?

A few years from now when you are getting started on your career, whether in management or some other endeavour, your parents or friends might ask: "What do you actually *do* in your job?" A manager is a manager, right? Well, as we'll see, it's not quite that simple. Just as we tried to provide some different ways of thinking about "what is management?" we will also do the same with respect to the question, "What do managers do?"

Later in this section (see the next two boxes), two managers describe— in their own words—what they do, what they like most about their jobs, and recent changes they've had to cope with in their jobs. These interviews provide a glimpse at some of the flavour and intensity of actual managerial jobs.

There are also other, analytical ways to look at managerial jobs aside from simply asking managers what they do. Over the years, several systems have been developed to classify (a) managerial functions, (b) the roles in which managers operate, and (c) the characteristics and dimensions of managerial jobs. These typologies can provide you with useful ways to examine the extremely varied nature of managerial jobs and responsibilities. In effect, they provide a road map for thinking about what management is.

Managerial Functions

One way to think about the question "What do managers do?" is to analyze the work of managers according to the different functions or processes they carry out. The first such classification system dates back at least 80 years and has sometimes been criticized for not sufficiently characterizing what managers "really do." However, this system is still, after more than eight decades, widely used by management scholars and writers.[16] In fact, as we explain at the end of this chapter, a variation of this traditional typology forms the basis for the general sequencing of the chapters in this book (as well as most other textbooks on the subject of management). The four principal managerial functions that seem most applicable to modern organizations are planning, organizing, directing, and controlling.

planning Estimating future conditions and circumstances and making decisions about appropriate courses of action.

Planning. **Planning** involves estimating future conditions and circumstances and, based on these estimations, making decisions about what work is to be done by the manager and all of those for whom she or he is responsible. This function can be thought of as involving three distinct levels or types: strategic planning, which addresses strategic actions designed to achieve the organization's long-range goals; tactical planning, which translates strategic plans into actions designed to achieve specific and shorter-term goals and objectives; and operational planning, which identifies the actions needed to accomplish the goals of particular units within the organization.

organizing Systematically putting resources together.

Organizing. To carry out managerial work, resources must be put together systematically, and this function is labelled **organizing**. It involves paying attention to the structure of relationships among positions and the people occupying them, and linking that structure to the overall strategic direction of the organization. Since the world today is basically full of uncertainties and ambiguities, the function of organizing is a critical challenge facing managers. At its most basic level, the purpose of this managerial function can be thought of as the attempt to bring order to the organization. Without organizing, it would be a very chaotic environment.

Directing. This function has typically had a number of different labels over the years, including *leading*. The latter term obviously does not have the autocratic connotations associated with the word *directing*. Nevertheless, the core of **directing**, or leading, is the process of attempting to influence other people to attain organizational objectives. It heavily involves motivating those for whom you are responsible, interacting with them effectively in group and team situations, and communicating in ways that are highly supportive of their efforts to accomplish their tasks and achieve organizational goals.

directing The process of attempting to influence other people to attain organizational objectives.

Controlling. In contemporary organizations, the word **controlling** is not entirely satisfactory because it implies, as does the word *directing*, that the activity must be carried out in a dictatorial, autocratic fashion. This, of course, is not the case, although in a particular circumstance a manager might act in this manner. The essence of this function is to regulate the work of those for whom a manager is responsible. Regulation can be done in several different ways, including setting standards of performance in advance, monitoring ongoing (real-time) performance, and, especially, assessing a completed performance. The results of such evaluation are fed back into the planning process. Therefore, it is important to consider these four managerial functions as parts of a reciprocal and recurring process, as illustrated in Exhibit 2.2.

controlling Regulating the work of those for whom a manager is responsible.

Managerial Roles

An alternative approach to describing managerial work was proposed some years ago by Canadian scholar Henry Mintzberg.[17] He based his classification system on research studies about how managers spend their time at work, and focused on "roles," or what he called "organized sets of behaviours." Although this way of viewing managers' work activities has not replaced the functional approach, it has received a great deal of attention because it provides additional understanding and insights not readily apparent in that more traditional set of categories.

Mintzberg organized his typology of managerial roles into three major categories—interpersonal, informational, and decisional—each of which contains specific roles. Altogether, there are 10 such roles in this system, as shown in Exhibit 2.3 and described in the following sections.

Exhibit 2.2 Managerial Functions.

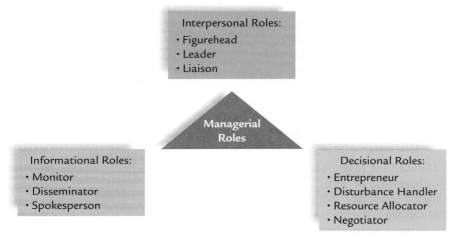

Exhibit 2.3 Types of Managerial Roles.

A Week in the Managerial Life of Deb M.

Deb M. is the director of organizational effectiveness for a Canadian oil and gas company.

QUESTION: Describe the type and range of activities you were involved in, as a manager, this past week.

Last week 70 percent of my time was spent in meetings with others. That's a bit high but not totally unusual.

One of the meetings I organized and led. Actually it was a two-day work meeting with HR peers in other parts of the company. We were working on coordinating our HR activities such as recruiting and performance management across the company. We have four separate operating units and each has its own HR department to some extent.

One of the other meetings involved making a presentation to our corporate senior management team regarding our compensation strategy. I was explaining how changes we proposed to make would help us better attract and retain employees with key skills.

I also had a meeting with my boss to review resource needs for my team in order to manage increasing workloads.

I spent several hours interviewing job candidates for a new hire to join my team.

I also conducted an orientation session with a number of our managers to explain our new job evaluation system.

The rest of the time was spent working on several efforts to better integrate and harmonize certain HR practices, such as pay, across the company. This involved both working with my subordinates as well as working on my own.

QUESTION: What do you like best about your job as a manager?

One of the things I like best about my job is that I have the opportunity to influence the decisions and actions that will have a significant impact on the success of the company. Much of our success depends on the people we attract and select into the company and the performance current employees contribute. My job in HR and the work of my subordinates contribute directly to the quality of people we have and how well they perform.

QUESTION: In the past year or so, what is the biggest change you have had to respond to?

We are going through a lot of changes right now. We have changed our strategy and our structure—but most of these changes were planned. The unexpected changes have involved individuals who have either deviated from the agreed-to plan and/or have not shared key pieces of information that would have caused us to plan differently. In the first case, I've had to rely on my interpersonal skills to try and get the person back on track. In the second case, I've had to incorporate the new information and adjust our plans.

Interpersonal Roles. Interpersonal roles are composed of three types of behaviour and, according to Mintzberg, are derived directly from the manager's formal authority granted by the organization. They are as follows:

1. *The Figurehead Role:* This set of behaviours involves an emphasis on ceremonial activities, such as attending a social function, welcoming a visiting dignitary, or presiding at a farewell reception for a departing employee. A familiar term for this role of representing the organization, borrowed from the military, is "showing the flag." Although one particular occasion where this behaviour occurs may not be important in and of itself, the activity across a period of time is a necessary component of a manager's job. If you doubt this, just ask any manager you know! For example, the next time you meet the dean of a business school, ask how often she finds it necessary to participate in figurehead activities—think of commencement ceremonies, for instance—and how important this is for the long-term benefit of the school.

2. *The Leader Role:* This role, in Mintzberg's system, is essentially one of influencing or directing others. It is the set of responsibilities people typically associate with a manager's job, since the organization gives the manager formal authority over the work of other people. To the extent that managers are able to translate this authority into actual influence, they are exercising what would be called leadership behaviour. The leader

type of behaviour would be demonstrated when, for example, a newly appointed project team leader gathers his hand-picked team members together and discusses his vision and goals for the team and his ideas as to how to accomplish them.

3. *The Liaison Role:* This role emphasizes the contacts that a manager has with those outside the formal authority chain of command. These contacts include not only other managers within the organization, but also many individuals outside it—for example, customers, suppliers, government officials, and managers from other organizations. It also emphasizes lateral interactions, as contrasted with vertical, interpersonal interactions of a manager, and it highlights the fact that an important part of a manager's job is to serve as a go-between for his or her own unit and other units or groups. The liaison role would apply to the situation where a marketing manager interacts with key customers to learn about their reactions to new product ideas.

Informational Roles.   This set of roles builds on the interpersonal relationships that a manager establishes, and it underlines the importance of the network of contacts built up and maintained by a manager. The three specific informational roles identified by Mintzberg are as follows:

1. *The Monitor Role:* This type of behaviour involves extensive information-seeking that managers engage in to keep aware of crucial developments that may affect their unit and their own work. Such monitoring, as previously noted, typically deals with spoken and written information and "soft" as well as "hard" facts. A manager attending an industry conference who spends considerable time in informal lobby and lounge conversations to gather data on current developments in the industry would be engaging in this role.

2. *The Disseminator Role:* A manager not only receives information but also sends it. This often includes information that the receiver wants but otherwise has no easy access to without the help of the manager. A supervisor who finds out about reorganization plans affecting his part of the organization and conveys that information to his subordinates would be acting in a disseminator role.

3. *The Spokesperson Role:* A manager is frequently called upon to represent the views of the unit for which he or she is responsible. At lower management levels, this typically involves representing the unit to other individuals or groups within the organization; at higher management levels, this internal spokesperson role could also be supplemented by an external component in which the organization and its activities and concerns often must be represented to the outside world. When the manager of the western region meets with other regional managers and presents the views of his region's sales personnel about how well a proposed new sales incentive plan is likely to work, he is functioning in a spokesperson role.

Decisional Roles   The final category of roles in this classification system relates to the decision-making requirements of a managerial position. Four such decisional roles are designated by Mintzberg:

1. *The Entrepreneurial Role:* Managers not only make routine decisions in their jobs, but also frequently engage in activities that explore new opportunities or start new projects. Such entrepreneurial behaviour within an organization often involves a series of small decisions that permit ongoing assessment about whether to continue or abandon new ventures. This type of role behaviour involves some degree of risk, but that risk is often limited or minimized by the sequence of decisions. Suppose,

for example, that a lower-level production manager comes up with an idea for a new organizational sales unit that she discusses with her colleagues and then, based on their reactions, modifies it and presents it to upper-level management. Such a manager would be exhibiting entrepreneurial role behaviour that goes beyond her routine responsibilities.

2. *The Disturbance Handler Role:* Managers initiate actions of their own, but they must also be able to respond to problems or "disturbances." In this role, a manager often acts as a judge, problem solver, or conflict settler. The goal of such actions, of course, is to keep small problems or issues from developing into larger ones. If you, as a manager, were to face a situation where your employees could not agree about who would do a particularly unpleasant but necessary group task, and you then stepped in to settle the matter, you would be functioning as a disturbance handler.

3. *The Resource Allocator Role:* Since resources of all types are always limited in organizations, one of the chief responsibilities of managers is to decide how the resources under their authority will be distributed. Such allocation decisions have a direct effect on the performance of a unit and an indirect effect of communicating certain types of information to members of the unit. The manager of front desk services for a large resort hotel who decides how many and which clerks will be assigned to each shift is operating in a resource allocator role.

4. *The Negotiator Role:* This type of managerial behaviour refers to the fact that a manager is often called upon to make accommodations with other units or other organizations (depending on the level of the management position). The manager, in this decisional situation, is responsible for knowing what resources can or cannot be committed to particular negotiated solutions. Someone who serves on a negotiating team to set up a new joint venture with an outside company would be functioning in the negotiator role.

If nothing else, the collection of roles described in Mintzberg's analysis of managerial work emphasizes the considerable variety of behaviours required in these types of jobs. In considering these 10 roles, it is essential to keep in mind that the extent to which any particular role is important will vary considerably from one managerial job to another. Obviously, where a job fits within the organization will have a great deal to do with which particular role or roles are emphasized. The front-line supervisor of branch-office bank tellers obviously has a different mix of roles from that of the bank's executive vice president. Nevertheless, Mintzberg maintains that the 10 roles form a "gestalt," or whole, and that to understand the total nature of *any* managerial job, *all* of them must be taken into account.

Managerial Job Dimensions

Another extremely useful way to try to gain an understanding of managerial work is to analyze the dimensions of managerial jobs. One particular approach was developed by British researcher Rosemary Stewart.[18] Stewart proposed that any managerial job (and, in fact, any job anywhere in an organization) can be characterized along three dimensions:

■ the demands made on it;

■ the constraints placed on it; and

■ the choices permitted in it.

A Week in the Managerial Life of Greg K.

Greg K. is director of finance and accounting in a large division of a financial services firm.

QUESTION: Describe the type and range of activities you were involved in, as a manager, this past week.

In my managerial job, I have a pretty wide variety of activities that I am involved in—ranging from division project meetings to staff meetings to time to work on my own projects. Here is a brief overview of my activities this past week:

Monday—In the morning I participated in a conference call with various management-level employees to discuss activity at one of our broker/dealers. The remainder of the day was filled with interacting with staff, completing my assignments, and reacting to various inquiries from other departments, divisions, and auditors.

Tuesday—This morning I participated in a biweekly status call with our third-party administrator for one of our products. Following the conference call, I met with one of my direct reports (accounting manager) for our weekly staff meeting. We discussed the status of various department projects, staffing issues, upcoming projects, and current events affecting the division. Later that day I met with our accounting coordinator to discuss the status of a pricing project that she was working on.

Wednesday—This was a light day as far as standing meetings; however, I attended a one-hour training class regarding upcoming new product features that we will be offering.

Thursday—Thursdays are typically busy in the mornings due to a biweekly technology meeting that I participate in and a weekly product meeting that I attend. This typically takes up two to three hours of my morning when both of the meetings occur. This Thursday the head of our department held a monthly staff meeting to discuss general events affecting the department, the division, and the company.

Friday—Today began with a weekly investment meeting in the morning. I represent our division in this meeting that includes other representatives from all divisions of the company. The remainder of the day was spent working on various normal tasks.

Aside from the meetings that I attend throughout the week, the remainder of my work week typically includes other interactions with staff and completion of my other assignments (responsibilities as a "working manager"). I typically interact at least daily (more often than not, multiple times throughout the day) with our department head (VP of finance). We discuss new requests/projects, staffing, status of current projects, etc. I also interact regularly throughout the day with my direct reports (five direct reports) to discuss projects and questions, and provide feedback. I also am responsible for approving all of our sales-force travel and expense reports and approving sales support requests that come from our sales force.

QUESTION: What do you like best about your job as a manager?

I think I need to answer this from two angles, one from the perspective of my direct assignments and one from a managerial perspective:

Regarding my direct assignments, the most rewarding part of my job is contributing to a division project that directly impacts the division with findings and recommendations that are communicated to senior management. Feeling part of the division team is very rewarding.

As a manager, I enjoy problem solving and coaching my direct reports regarding issues that they face. My company offers several management development programs, and one that I found especially useful concerned leadership. I try to apply facets of the class to situations that arise in everyday work.

QUESTION: In the past year or so, what is the biggest change you have had to respond to?

From a management perspective, the most challenging change over the past year was terminating two employees (not my direct reports, but I was very involved in the process) and adjusting accordingly on all fronts of the job. I had not previously been involved in a termination, so it was very challenging. The process included performance concerns, HR concerns, reallocating resources within the department to ensure completion of all assignments, and communication to other employees (a very delicate matter).

Looking at managerial jobs in this way not only provides further understanding of what managers do, but also permits direct comparisons of different jobs; for example, how the position of "manager of information systems" might compare with that of "financial analyst," or the job of "marketing vice president" versus "plant manager."

Demands. This dimension of managerial jobs refers to what the holder of a particular position *must* do. Demands are of two types: activities or duties that must be carried out and the standards or levels of minimum performance that must be met. Demands can come from several sources, such as the organization at large, the immediate boss, or the way in which work activities are organized. Typical types of demands would include such behaviour as attending required meetings, adhering to schedule deadlines, following certain procedures, and the like. No doubt, for example, Annette Verschuren has sales and performance targets to meet in her position at The Home Depot Canada.

Constraints. Constraints are factors that limit the response of the manager to various demands. One obvious constraint for any manager is the amount of time available for an activity. Other typical constraints include budgets, technology, attitudes of subordinates, and legal regulations. The important point is that any managerial job has a set of constraints, and therefore a key to performing that job effectively is to recognize them and develop a good understanding of how they can be minimized, overcome, or effectively confronted. Someone like Annette Verschuren has had to work within the constraints of deadlines, supplier schedules, customer preferences, and forces in the larger economy she could not control.

Choices. This dimension underscores the fact that despite demands and despite constraints, there is always room for some amount of discretionary behaviour in any managerial job. Thus, there are a number of activities that a manager *may* carry out but does not have to. Choices can involve how work is to be done, what work beyond that absolutely required will be done, who will do particular tasks, and what initiatives not otherwise prohibited will be undertaken from almost infinite possibilities. In her present and past managerial positions, Verschuren would have faced a multitude of choices about how to make staffing decisions, how to demonstrate leadership, how to respond to changing market conditions affecting home improvements, and the like.

Exhibit 2.4	Two Managerial Jobs with Different Demands, Constraints, and Choices	
	Job A: **Project Team** **Manager**	**Job B:** **Fast-Food Restaurant** **Manager**
Demands	■ Develop new product with strong market appeal ■ Hold formal weekly progress meeting with boss ■ Frequent travel to other company sites	■ Maintain attractive appearance of restaurant ■ Keep employee costs as low as possible ■ Meet standards for speed of service
Constraints	■ 12-month deadline for product development ■ Project budget limit of $1 million ■ No choice in selecting team members	■ Most employees have limited formal education ■ Few monetary incentives to reward outstanding performance ■ Federal and provincial health and safety regulations
Choices	■ The organizational structure of the project team ■ Sequencing of project tasks ■ Budget allocations	■ Selection of employee to promote to supervisor ■ Scheduling of shifts and assignments ■ Local advertising promotions

Exhibit 2.4 illustrates these three job dimensions for two different managerial jobs, that of a project team manager in a manufacturing company and a manager of a medium-sized fast-food restaurant. In these examples, though both jobs are definitely managerial in their nature and how their organizations view them, their demands and constraints are quite different. Some of the types of choices permitted, however, are fairly similar. It's the combination of the specifics of these three dimensions that determines what it would be like to be a manager in these or any other positions.

What Skills Do Managers Need?

Like any other human activity, managing involves the exercise of skills; that is, highly developed abilities and competencies. Skills emerge through a combination of aptitude, education, training, and experience. Three types have been identified as critical for managerial tasks, particularly for the leadership component of management: technical, interpersonal, and conceptual (see Exhibit 2.5).

Technical Skills. Technical skills involve specialized knowledge about procedures, processes, equipment, and the like and include the related abilities of knowing how and when to use that knowledge. Research shows that these skills are especially important early in managerial careers (see Exhibit 2.6) when the leadership of lower-level employees is often part of the role and one of the challenges is to gain the respect of those being led. In addition, technical skills seem to be a particularly critical factor in many successful entrepreneurial start-ups, like that involving Mike Lazaridis and Douglas Fregin, two engineers who founded Research In Motion. Technical skills, whether in an entrepreneurial situation or in a larger organizational setting, are frequently necessary for managing effectively, but usually they are not sufficient in and of themselves. In fact, an

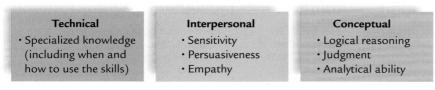

Technical	Interpersonal	Conceptual
• Specialized knowledge (including when and how to use the skills)	• Sensitivity • Persuasiveness • Empathy	• Logical reasoning • Judgment • Analytical ability

Exhibit 2.5 Managers' Skills.

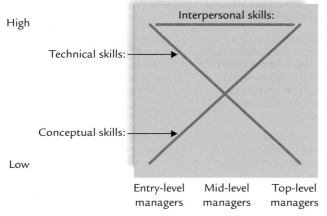

Exhibit 2.6 Relative Importance of Managerial Skills at Different Organizational Levels.

over-reliance on technical skills may actually lower overall managerial effectiveness. The first products engineered and designed by Lazaridis and Fregin were generating sales of $500 000, but they realized that they were engineers first and needed someone who understood the business end of an innovation. In 1992, Jim Balsillie, a business school graduate of the University of Toronto and Harvard, joined Research In Motion as co-CEO. Balsillie became the driver behind the organization's corporate strategy and business development, while Lazaridis (president and co-CEO) and Fregin (vice-president of operations) both preside over the technical side of product strategy and research and development.[19]

Interpersonal Skills. Interpersonal skills like sensitivity, persuasiveness, and empathy have been shown to be important at all levels of management, although particularly so at lower and middle levels. Exhibit 2.7 summarizes the findings of one study that investigated reasons why some fast-rising executives eventually "derailed" or plateaued in their managerial careers, even when they appeared to start out with acceptable levels of interpersonal skills. As put compellingly by a pair of management researchers, referring to those who have these skills but who lack other capabilities, "The charming but not brilliant find that the job gets too big and the problems too complex to get by on interpersonal skills [alone]."[20]

Conceptual Skills. Often called cognitive ability or cognitive complexity, conceptual skills such as logical reasoning, judgment, and analytical abilities are a relatively strong predictor of managerial effectiveness. These skills are often the major factor that determines who reaches the highest levels of the

Exhibit 2.7 Who Succeeds? Who Doesn't?		
Potential Managerial Leaders Share Traits Early on:	**Those Who Don't Quite Make it:**	**Those Who Succeed:**
Bright, with outstanding track records	Have been successful, but generally only in one area or type of job.	Have diverse track records, demonstrated ability in many different situations, and a breadth of knowledge of the business or industry.
Have survived stressful situations	Frequently described as moody or volatile. May be able to keep their temper with superiors during crises but are hostile toward peers and subordinates.	Maintain composure in stressful situations, are predictable during crises, are regarded as calm and confident.
Have a few flaws	Cover up problems while trying to fix them. If the problem can't be hidden, they tend to go on the defensive and even blame someone else for it.	Make a few mistakes, but when they do, they admit to them and handle them with poise and grace.
Ambitious and oriented toward problem solving	May attempt to micromanage a position, ignoring future prospects; may staff with the incorrect people or neglect the talents they have; may depend too much on a single mentor, calling their own decision-making ability into question.	While focusing on problem solutions, keep their minds focused on the next position, help develop competent successors, seek advice from many sources.
Good people skills	May be viewed as charming but political or direct but tactless, cold, and arrogant. People don't like to work with them.	Can get along well with different types of people, are outspoken without being offensive, are viewed as direct and diplomatic.

Source: Adapted from M. W. McCall, Jr. and M. M. Lombardo, "Off the Track: Why and How Successful Executives Get Derailed," *Technical Report #21* (Greensboro, NC: Center for Creative Leadership, 1983), pp. 9–11.

organization. A clear example of someone who was selected for a CEO job precisely because of his conceptual skills is Jack Welch, the well-known former CEO of General Electric. He was appointed to the top position at GE in 1981 and immediately set out to restructure the organization with the objective of making it more globally competitive. His concept of the company included wiping out its bureaucracy to develop a more flexible organization. At the same time, however, he also championed a new corporate culture, one based on greater empowerment of the employee.

Plan of the Book

Now that we have proposed some initial ways to answer the three basic questions of "What is management?" "What do managers do?" and "What skills do managers need?" here in Chapter 2, we want to share with you the overall structure and plan of select chapters in the book. We do this to give you a better understanding of what follows in later chapters. It might even give you some additional insight in answering examination questions that will almost surely come later in the course.

Most books on management, after starting with a set of introductory chapters, group the remaining chapters in clusters around the generally accepted four major functions of management: planning, organizing, directing, and controlling. Our sequence of parts in this book is basically in that order. However, we title the parts in what we consider a more user-friendly and user-useful manner.

This chapter is under the heading "You as a Manager." This chapter is intended to provide you with an introduction to the subject of the book (Chapter 2).

Chapters 4 and 6 focus on the context for managing in organizations: the outside, or external, environment of management, and the ethical issues that are facing every manager at the start of a new century. Chapter 10 presents the cultural environment. Particularly emphasized in these chapters are the various forces outside and inside the organization that affect how, and how well, a person can carry out managerial responsibilities.

Chapter 7 discusses decision making, and Chapter 8 discusses planning for an organization.

In Chapter 13, the topic of communication is explored for its implications in implementing effective leadership in organizations, and Chapter 15 examines the overall issue of managing human resources in the organizational context.

Chapter 14 reviews some of the basic evaluation and control challenges facing managers.

Concluding Comments

As we conclude this chapter, we again want to emphasize the recurring themes you will be encountering throughout the remainder of this book: Management involves constant attention to, and an embracement of, change; it cannot be carried out without an understanding of the impacts of technology on managerial functions and processes, and it requires a global as well as a local, or "own country," focus. When you combine technology, globalization, and frequent change you create a highly complex and challenging environment in which to manage. Managers throughout any organization must manage strategically to confront these challenges effectively. An organization's strategy should focus on resources that exploit opportunities for competitive advantage and sustain it.

Also, here at the end of Chapter 2, we want to remind you of the four perspectives we stressed earlier: (1) The Organizational Context: Management occurs in organizations; (2) The Human Factor: Management means getting things done through people; (3) Managing Paradoxes: Management involves mastering multiple and potentially conflicting situations simultaneously; and (4) Entrepreneurial Mindset: Managers must continuously search for and exploit new opportunities. The challenge for you as a student is to learn more about the implications of these perspectives; that is, to learn more about the subtleties and complexities of the managerial process. This, of course, requires thought and analysis, but that, really, is only the beginning. Understanding management also requires an ability to synthesize and integrate a diverse array of facts, theories, viewpoints, and examples—in a phrase, as we emphasized earlier, to be able to "put it all together" so that the whole is indeed more than the sum of its parts.

Above all else, however, beyond analysis and synthesis, management requires skill in implementation. This is perhaps one of the most difficult skills to develop—how to put into practice the results of analysis and synthesis and how to make decisions. If there is one skill that senior managers seem most concerned about among new managers, it is that of implementation.[21] Most senior managers believe that the typical business graduate is much better at analysis than at implementation. Obviously, acquiring managerial experience helps considerably in developing the skill to be able to implement effectively, as Annette Verschuren has demonstrated. But experience by itself will not guarantee results. What is also needed is a heightened sensitivity to the importance of developing the skill of implementation. The lack of this skill is analogous to an athletic team formulating a good game plan but then fumbling the ball and dropping passes in the game itself—thus being guilty of "not executing." Therefore, as you read through the remainder of this book, keep in mind the message that management is not just about knowing; it is also, and emphatically so, about *doing*.

Key Terms

controlling   (p. 67)
directing   (p. 67)

management   (p. 50)
organizations   (p. 50)

organizing   (p. 66)
planning   (p. 66)

Test Your Comprehension

1. What is management? Explain the different parts of the formal definition.

2. What is an organization?

3. Does management occur outside of organizations? Why or why not?

4. What creates the "personality" of an organization?

5. If you are an effective manager in one organization, will you automatically be as effective in all other organizations? Why or why not?

6. Identify three people skills important for managers.

7. What is meant by managing paradoxes?

8. Explain how a manager's life is both fragmented and integrated.

9. Why is it important for a manager to be both consistent and flexible?

10. What is the trade-off between reflection and action?

11. Why do managers need to be able to think globally but act locally?

12. Explain the types of commitment required of an effective manager.

13. What is an entrepreneurial mindset and how does a manager develop and apply it?

14. What are four traditional components (functions) of the overall management process?

15. What is the importance of each of Mintzberg's 10 managerial roles?

16. Describe Stewart's three managerial job dimensions.

17. What are the three major types of skills managers need to develop? Why is each essential to be an effective manager?

Apply Your Understanding

1. Why is it important to examine management from different perspectives? What do you gain from this type of examination? Think of other possible perspectives or metaphors you could use to describe management (e.g., management is a profession; management means "being in charge"). What does your new perspective tell you about management that adds to your understanding?

2. What do you think is the biggest personal reward of being a manager? What is the biggest potential downside of being a manager?

3. Think about two different managerial-type jobs you have personally observed (within your family, as a worker, as a customer, etc.). Compare them using Stewart's concept of job dimensions. Considering each job's content as analyzed by the three dimensions, which one would you choose? Why?

4. This chapter states that effective managers need technical, interpersonal, and conceptual skills. Do all managers need these in the same mix? In other words, would some managers need more of one than of another? Why? Describe the managerial skills you think you need to develop to be an effective manager, and suggest how this might be done.

Part Three

Options for Organizing a Business

Chapter 3*

Understanding Entrepreneurship, Small Business, and New Venture Creation

*With contributions from Dr. Monica Diochon, St. Francis Xavier University.

Taken from *Business*, Seventh Canadian Edition, by Ricky W. Griffin, Ronald J. Ebert, Frederick A. Starke, and Melanie D. Lang.

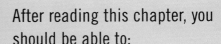

After reading this chapter, you should be able to:

1 Explain the meaning of and interrelationship among the terms *small business*, *new venture creation*, and *entrepreneurship*.

2 Describe the role of small and new businesses in the Canadian economy.

3 Explain the *entrepreneurial process* and describe its three key elements.

4 Describe three alternative strategies for becoming a business owner—*starting a business, buying an existing business*, and *buying a franchise*.

5 Describe four forms of *legal organization* for a business and discuss the advantages and disadvantages of each.

6 Identify four key reasons for success in small businesses and four key reasons for failure.

Family Businesses

Family businesses are a prominent feature in many countries of the world. Most family businesses are small, but some are very large. In addition to the usual challenges facing business firms, family businesses often are threatened by disagreements between family members about how the business should be run. Here are some classic examples.

The Irving Family

The Irving family of New Brunswick is one of the great success stories of Canadian business. The company owns scores of businesses in oil refining, forestry, shipbuilding, food processing, publishing, transportation, and home improvement. The business was started in the nineteenth century by J.D. Irving and was expanded by his son K.C. The empire is now run by K.C.'s three sons, Arthur, J.K., and Jack, who are all in their seventies. In 2007, it became clear that J.K.'s son Jim and Arthur's son Kenneth were competing for a chance to shape the company's fortunes, and they were at odds over the strategic direction the company should take. That disagreement drove a wedge between J.K. and his brothers.

This is a new situation for the Irving family, which has always presented a remarkably united front. The three brothers have a great deal of respect for each other, so when these succession tensions developed, they decided they would try to amicably divide up the businesses. The energy business will go to Arthur's family, and the forestry business to J.K.'s family. Their approach contrasts sharply with what happened to the McCain family, another New Brunswick business dynasty.

The McCain Family

For many years, brothers Wallace and Harrison McCain were the key players at McCain Foods Ltd., the world's largest french fry producer. But in the mid-1990s, the two brothers had a falling out over the question of who would succeed Harrison as the CEO. Wallace wanted his son Michael to get the job, but Harrison wanted someone from outside the family to take over. After a nasty battle, Wallace was removed from the firm. He then took over Maple Leaf Foods and his son Michael eventually became CEO of that company.

The Redstone Family

Shari Redstone is the daughter of Sumner Redstone, the CEO of Viacom Inc., the company that owns MTV, Nickelodeon, Comedy Central, and Paramount Pictures. In 2006, it looked like Shari was being groomed to take over her father's position, but by 2007 their relationship had soured and her father decided that he didn't want her to succeed him when he died. So he negotiated with her to end her involvement in the company. She was not happy.

The dispute came just six months after Mr. Redstone had settled a lawsuit filed by his son Brent that alleged that his father had tried to freeze him out of the business. Sumner eventually bought out his son's interest for $240 million. Mr. Redstone also faced another lawsuit, from a nephew who claimed that he was deprived of his inheritance.

The Mitchell Family

Mitchell's Gourmet Foods Inc. was a Saskatchewan-based family business. A family feud developed when Fred Mitchell claimed that his mother and his brother Charles were trying to wrest control of the business from him. Both sides in the dispute then sued each other. An accommodation of sorts was reached when the disputing parties agreed to divide up the assets of the company. Fred (and his wife, LuAn) kept Mitchell's, and Charles (and his wife, Camille) kept a beef plant the company owned.

Cuddy International

Cuddy International Corp. was founded by Mac Cuddy, who was known as "the turkey king of Canada." Cuddy was a brilliant entrepreneur who created a great company, but then couldn't manage it, partly because he couldn't get along with his five sons and one daughter. All of Mac's sons worked in the family business at one time or another, but Mac was doubtful about their ability to manage the company. Three of his sons—Peter, Bruce, and Brian—made several attempts to take control of the business, but they failed. Eventually, Mac fired Peter and Brian and demoted Bruce (who then quit the business and became a competitor of his father). Squabbles of various sorts were evident, such as the time Peter sued the company, claiming that he had not been given financial information that he was entitled to. He was then sued by the company for making allegedly defamatory remarks at a press conference.

The Antinori Family

Some family businesses manage to avoid feuds. The Antinori family business in Florence, Italy, has been making wine since 1385, and for 26 generations the family has somehow managed to pass on management of the company to the next generation without getting in a big fight. How do they do it? By going against conventional wisdom—which says that you should clearly separate the family's interest from the interest of the business—and instead blurring the two interests as much as possible. For example, the current CEO and his wife live on the top two floors of their fifteenth-century mansion, and the business operates on the bottom two floors. Perhaps more importantly, the company plans far into the future for a company the grandchildren can run.

Maybe there is something about the wine business that makes family feuds less likely. For example, Catherine and Anne Monna and their father, Bernard, run Cassis Monna & Filles near Quebec City. The sisters are the fifth generation of the family to be involved in the wine business.◆

How will this help me?

By understanding the material discussed in this chapter, you'll be better prepared to (1) identify the challenges and opportunities provided in new venture start-ups, (2) assess the risks and benefits of working in a new business, and (3) evaluate the investment potential inherent in a new business.

In this chapter, we begin by looking at the important role that small and new businesses play in the Canadian economy. We then examine entrepreneurship and the process that entrepreneurs use to start a new business from scratch. We also describe two other ways that entrepreneurs can get into business: buying an existing business or buying a franchise. When operating a business, an entrepreneur must also decide which legal form of organization to adopt—sole proprietorship, partnership, corporation, or co-operative—and we discuss the advantages and disadvantages of each form. We conclude the chapter with a discussion of the reasons for success and failure of small businesses.

Small Business, New Venture Creation, and Entrepreneurship

1 Explain the meaning of and interrelationship among the terms *small business*, *new venture creation*, and *entrepreneurship*.

Every day, approximately 380 businesses are started in Canada.[1] New firms create the most jobs, are noted for their entrepreneurship, and are typically small.[2] But does this mean that most small businesses are entrepreneurial? Not necessarily.

The terms *small business*, *new venture*, and *entrepreneurship* are related terms, but each idea is distinct.

Small Business

Defining a "small" business can be tricky. Various measures might be used, including the number of people the business employs, the company's sales revenue, the size of the investment required, or the type of ownership structure the business has. Some of the difficulties in defining a small business are evident when we consider the way the Canadian government collects and reports information on small businesses.

Industry Canada relies on two distinct sources of information, both provided by Statistics Canada: the Business Register (which tracks businesses) and the Labour Force Survey (which tracks individuals). To be included in the Business Register, a business must have at least one paid employee and annual sales revenues of $30 000 or more, or be incorporated. A goods-producing business in the register is considered small if it has fewer than 100 employees, while a service-producing business is considered small if it has fewer than 50 employees.

The Labour Force Survey uses information from *individuals* to make estimates of employment and unemployment levels. Individuals are classified as self-employed if they are working owners of a business that is either incorporated or unincorporated, if they work for themselves but do not have a business (some musicians, for example, would fall into this category), or if they work without pay in a family business.

In its publication *Key Small Business Statistics* (July 2008), Industry Canada reports that there are 2.3 million "business establishments" in Canada and about 2.5 million people who are "self-employed." There is no way of identifying how much overlap there is in these two categories, but we do know that an unincorporated business operated by a self-employed person (with no employees) would *not* be counted among the 2.3 million *businesses* in the Business Register. This is an important point because the majority of businesses in Canada have no employees (just the owner), nor are they incorporated. A study conducted by members of the Entrepreneurship Research Consortium (ERC) tracked a sample of Canadian *nascent entrepreneurs*—people who were trying to start a business—over four years. Only 15 percent of those who reported establishing an operating business had incorporated their firm.[3] These facts need to be kept in mind when considering statistics or research that excludes these firms. When either of these indicators is used to find businesses to study, the number of new firms will be underestimated.

Given all this, we define a **small business** as an owner-managed business with fewer than 100 employees. We do so because it enables us to make better use of existing statistics and because you now are aware of how definitions can influence our understanding of small businesses.

small business An owner-managed business with fewer than 100 employees.

Each year, the Queen's Centre for Business Venturing develops a ranking of the top 50 small- and medium-sized employers to work for. The Top 10 firms in the 2008 study are shown in Table 3.1. Each of these companies exhibited superiority in employee recognition, managing performance, career opportunities, and organizational reputation.[4]

Table 3.1 Top 10 Small- and Medium-Sized Employers in Canada, 2008	
Company	**Location**
1. Protegra Inc.	Winnipeg, Manitoba
2. Miele Canada Limited	Vaughan, Ontario
3. Gibraltar Solutions Inc.	Mississauga, Ontario
4. ISL Engineering and Land Services	Edmonton, Alberta
5. Hood Group	Sherwood Park, Alberta
6. Solutions 2 GO Inc.	Mississauga, Ontario
7. DRN Commerce Inc.	London, Ontario
8. PDL Contact Centres Ltd.	Calgary, Alberta
9. Benefits by Design Inc.	Port Coquitlam, B.C.
10. Heathtech Consultants	Toronto, Ontario

The New Venture/Firm

Various criteria can also be used to determine when a new firm comes into existence. Three of the most common are when it was formed, whether it was incorporated, and if it sold goods and/or services.[5] A business is considered to be new if it has become operational within the previous 12 months, if it adopts any of the main organizational forms (proprietorship, partnership, corporation, or co-operative), and if it sells goods or services. Thus, we define a **new venture (or new firm)** as a recently formed commercial organization that provides goods and/or services for sale.

new venture (or new firm) A recently formed commercial organization that provides goods and/or services for sale.

Entrepreneurship

entrepreneurship The process of identifying an opportunity in the marketplace and accessing the resources needed to capitalize on that opportunity.

entrepreneur A business person who accepts both the risks and the opportunities involved in creating and operating a new business venture.

Entrepreneurship is the process of identifying an opportunity in the marketplace and accessing the resources needed to capitalize on that opportunity.[6] **Entrepreneurs** are people who recognize and seize opportunities. For example, Mark Zuckerberg created the website Facebook, and just a few years later it had close to 40 million active users. By 2008, Zuckerberg was widely thought to be the richest person in the world under the age of 25, with a net worth of over $1.5 billion. It takes more than a good idea to be successful. Zuckerberg worked long hours, and he is constantly tailoring the website to suit its expanding audience.[7]

Another example: Ken Woods and John Gagliardi are two entrepreneurs who recognized an opportunity in the marketplace for higher-quality beer and formed the Ontario-based Black Oak Brewing Company. They've already developed several award-winning beers, such as Black Oak Nut Brown Ale, Pale Ale, and Premium Lager. A website for Toronto beer lovers called The Bar Towel rates these beers very positively.[8]

Each year, the Heritage Foundation publishes an index of economic freedom, which assesses the extent to which entrepreneurs have freedom to pursue new business opportunities. In 2009, the top three countries were Hong Kong, Singapore, and Australia, with freedom scores of 90.0, 87.1, and 82.6, respectively. Canada ranked seventh with a score of 79.6 and North Korea ranked last with a score of 2.0.[9]

Creativity is an important personal attribute that has come to be associated with entrepreneurs, and small businesses provide a great environment to use creativity.[10] But do not assume that only small business owners exhibit entrepreneurial characteristics. Many successful managers in large organizations in both the public and private sectors also exhibit similar characteris-

There are many areas in which small businesses excel. This entrepreneur, for example, has a lucrative business as a dog walker.

tics.[11] Entrepreneurship is evident in a wide range of contexts: in small or new firms, in old firms, in large firms, in firms that grow slowly, in firms that grow rapidly, in non-profit organizations, and in the public sector.[12]

Historically, most innovations have come from individuals in small businesses. As businesses increase in size, however, innovation and creativity tend to become casualties in the battle for higher sales and profits. In some large companies, new ideas are even discouraged, and champions of innovation have been stalled in mid-career. But people who exhibit entrepreneurial characteristics can often create and maintain the innovation and flexibility of a small-business environment within the confines of a large, bureaucratic structure. This is known as **intrapreneuring**, and it is supported by many large firms, including Compaq Computer, Rubbermaid, 3M, and Xerox.

Compaq, which is now part of Hewlett-Packard, is an excellent example of how intrapreneuring works. The firm has one major division called the New Business Group. When a manager or engineer has an idea for a new product or product application, he or she takes it to the New Business Group and "sells" it. The managers in the group are then encouraged to help the innovator develop the idea for field testing. If the product takes off and does well, it is then spun off into its own business group or division. If it doesn't do as well as hoped, it may be maintained as part of the New Business Group or phased out.

Procter & Gamble is also known for encouraging intrapreneurship. It has earned this reputation by having divisions that focus on creating new products for specific markets.[13] The Swiffer product line is one example. Once the basic Swiffer mop was launched successfully, a whole range of products was added, such as the Swiffer WetJet and Swiffer Dusters. A key difference between intrapreneurs and entrepreneurs is that intrapreneurs typically don't have to concern themselves with getting the resources needed to bring the new product to market, since their employer provides the resources.

> **intrapreneuring** Entrepreneurial characteristics that can create and maintain the innovation and flexibility of a small-business environment within the confines of a large, bureaucratic structure.

The Role of Small and New Businesses in the Canadian Economy

Small and new businesses play a key role in the Canadian economy, but recognition of this role is relatively recent. Prior to the 1980s, large businesses were the focus of attention in terms of economic impact within industrialized nations.

> Describe the role of small and new businesses in the Canadian economy.
>
> **2**

Small Businesses

There are 2.3 million business establishments in Canada. Of these, 1.1 million are classified as "employer businesses" (i.e., they have a payroll of at least one person), while the other 1.2 million are classified as "indeterminate" because they have no employees registered with the Canada Revenue Agency.[14]

It may surprise you to learn that 97.8 percent of all employer businesses in Canada are small (they have fewer than 100 employees), and more than half of these have fewer than 5 employees. Medium-sized businesses (100–499 employees) comprise just 1.9 percent of employer businesses, and large businesses (those with 500 or more employees) represent just 0.3 percent of all employer businesses.[15] This pattern is consistent across all provinces in Canada. While one large business has many more employees than one small business, as a group, small businesses provide more jobs than large businesses. Small businesses also lead the way when it comes to innovation and new technology.

Ontario and Quebec together account for the largest proportion of business establishments in Canada (about 56 percent), followed by the western provinces (36 percent) and the Atlantic provinces (7 percent). The Northwest

A common type of small business in Canada is the convenience store. As the name suggests, it emphasizes convenience. It attracts customers from its immediate area through its long hours of operation and the product lines it carries.

Territories, the Yukon, and Nunavut represent just 0.3 percent of Canada's businesses.[16]

The distribution of employment by size of firm varies considerably across industries. Small businesses account for over two-thirds of employment in four industries: non-institutional health care (90 percent), the construction industry (77 percent), other services (73 percent), and accommodation and food (69 percent).[17] In another five industries, at least half of the workforce is employed by small businesses.

The boxed insert entitled "Small Businesses Go Green" provides information on the developing interest in the environment among small business owners.

The Greening of Business

Small Businesses Go Green

Most entrepreneurs and small business owners have plenty of operational problems and crises that demand their attention, so they might not spend much time thinking about how their company could become more eco-friendly. Even if they did find the time, they might think that they couldn't afford to go green. But there are a lot of resources available to help small business owners who are interested in showing more concern for the environment.

John Walker is the CEO of Transition Plus Sustainability Solutions (TPSS), an environmental consulting firm. He says that small business owners are always interested in ways to reduce energy costs, and doing so will make small businesses greener. Making simple changes like choosing energy-efficient lighting and turning off photocopiers and computers overnight is a good place to start. The energy departments in most provinces have websites that provide

information on how companies can save money by using water and energy more efficiently.

For more aggressive or longer-term projects, small business owners can access the federal government's ecoACTION program website, which contains information about programs that help organizations reduce energy costs. The ecoENERGY Retrofit program provides financial incentives of up to 25 percent of project costs to help small- and medium-sized companies implement energy saving projects.

Saving energy is just one possible area for improvement. There are also many other ideas that will appeal to small business owners because implementing the ideas will be inexpensive. Consider the following:

- Use recycled paper.
- Use eco-friendly cleaning supplies.
- Buy pens made of compostable material, not plastic.

▶

▶

- Help staff to organize car pools.
- Encourage staff to bicycle to work by giving them a place to lock their bikes.
- Encourage staff to use public transit.

Various other approaches and resources are also available to small businesses. For example, a Toronto-area initiative called greenTbiz—a project of the Toronto Association of Business Improvement Areas—works free with small businesses to implement environmental programs. The project focusses on recommendations that make financial sense for the small business. Most of the companies that have used the service have fewer than 20 employees.

Another example is Green Enterprise Toronto (GET), which is a group of 385 eco-minded businesses that pay $195 each year to belong to a network where they can trade business, advice, and referrals. All of the businesses in the group are committed to activities like sustainable purchasing, manufacturing, and recycling of products. GET runs regular workshops on topics of importance to small businesses—for example, finance and marketing—but it also offers information on environmental and social responsibility initiatives. Chris Lowry, the director, says that many small business owners have gotten interested in going green after being asked "uncomfortable" questions by their children and staff members about why they aren't doing more for the environment. John Walker, CEO of TPSS, also notes that small business owners are starting to respond to social pressure from customers.

One small business that wants to become more environmentally friendly is the Gladstone Hotel on trendy Queen Street West in Toronto. It occupies a building that is well over 100 years old, so a lot of work is necessary to make the building more energy efficient. The company hired Green Shift consultants to do an environmental audit of the property and to draw up a long-term strategy, which will take several years to implement. A variety of relatively inexpensive actions are being taken, including

- using non-toxic cleaning supplies
- composting waste from the hotel restaurant
- using compostable take-out food containers
- revamping the heating and lighting system

Upgrading an existing business is just one approach; another is to start a business whose whole purpose is to be green. Shannon Boase, for example, founded Earthcycle, a company that makes packaging from palm fibre, a renewable resource that is typically thrown away. She got the idea after working in Malaysia for a company that was developing a new technology that could turn palm husks into biodegradable packaging material for fruits and vegetables. The production activities of Earthcycle are fully integrated, all the way from the plantation to the marketing of the packaging.

Julie Jonas is an environmentalist who thought there would be a market for organic products. So she started an ecommerce business called Zia and Tia Luxury Organics that sells a diverse line of organic products. Customers place orders and Jonas has them shipped directly from the manufacturer to the customer. This reduces the amount of greenhouse gases that are produced because less transportation is required.

Critical Thinking Questions

1. Find a small business in your local area that is committed to being eco-friendly. How did the owner decide to commit to having an eco-friendly business?

2. Interview the owners of several small businesses in your local area. Ask them what they have done to become more environmentally friendly. If they have not done anything, ask them what has prevented them from taking the initiative to be more environmentally friendly.

3. Consider the following statement: *It is unrealistic to expect small business owners to spend much time thinking about or implementing green practices. The failure rate of small businesses is high, so small business owners have to focus all their energies on trying to ensure the survival of their businesses. They simply don't have the time (or money) to "go green."* Do you agree or disagree with the statement? Explain your reasoning.

New Ventures[18]

New ventures are important as a source of job creation and for the introduction of new products and services.[19] In 2007, small business created 100 000 jobs in Canada; this represented 40 percent of all jobs that were created.[20] Between 2002 and 2006, approximately 130 000 new small businesses were started each year in Canada.[21] During that same period, an equal number of small businesses ceased operations each year.[22]

According to Statistics Canada, there were about 877 000 women entrepreneurs in Canada in 2006, and 47 percent of small- and medium-sized enterprises have some degree of female ownership.[23] Between 1996 and 2006, the number of self-employed women increased by 18 percent (compared to 14 percent for men). Women are playing a more prominent role than ever before in starting new ventures. Kyla Eaglesham, the owner of Madeleines, Cherry Pie and Ice Cream, is typical. After doing a lot of research on the ice cream and dessert industry, she left her job as a flight attendant and opened a dessert café in Toronto's trendy Annex neighbourhood. The store attracts customers who want "a little bit of cottage country in the heart of Toronto."[24]

More and more women are starting and successfully operating their own small businesses, and women now account for half of all new businesses that are formed. But women lead only 12 percent of the small- and medium-sized businesses that export goods and services.[25] Women who run businesses from their homes are sometimes called "mompreneurs."[26] One such person is Crystal Dallner, who started a marketing business called Outright Communication soon after her first child was born. The Mompreneur Networking Group organizes seminars and publishes *Mompreneur*, a free magazine that helps women who want to start a business.[27] More information on mompreneurs is provided in Concluding Case 3-1.

Female entrepreneurs are honoured each year at the Canadian Woman Entrepreneur Awards. In 2008, winners included Christina Jennings (Shaftesbury Films, Toronto), Baljit Gill (Kitwanga Lumber Company, Surrey, B.C.), and Nina Gupta (Greenlite Lighting Corp., Pointe Claire, Quebec).[28]

Young entrepreneurs—both men and women—are also involved in creating new ventures in Canada. Consider the following examples:

- Geraldine McManus, who started Ab-Original Wear, buys artwork from Aboriginal artists and then reproduces it on T-shirts, crew-neck shirts, and sweatshirts. The clothing products feature Aboriginal artwork on the front and an inspirational message from a chief or elder on the back. The store also sells crafts made by local Aboriginal artists and miniature log cabins that McManus makes herself from recycled wood.[29]

- The Ben Barry Agency is an Ottawa-based modelling business that promotes models who are considered unorthodox—models of various sizes and ages, different racial backgrounds, and who have physical disabilities. The models have appeared in government advertising campaigns and on fashion runways in shopping malls. Barry works with company management to define their clientele and then chooses models who will best reflect the store's typical shoppers.[30]

- Tell Us About Us (TUAU) is a Winnipeg-based company specializing in market research and customer satisfaction programs. Owners Tyler Gompf and Scott Griffith recently signed a seven-figure deal to provide mystery shopper service to Dunkin' Donuts, Baskin-Robbins, and Togo's in the United States and Canada. The mystery shoppers will note any problems at a retail site and TUAU will then measure how quickly the problems are fixed.[31]

- Sean McCormick is the owner of Blue Moose Clothing Company, the largest manufacturer of mukluks in Canada. McCormick employs 25 people, many of them Aboriginal. He credits Aboriginal Business Canada, which provides money to native entrepreneurs to help them start small businesses.[32]

The Entrepreneurial Process

3 Explain the *entrepreneurial process* and describe its three key elements.

The entrepreneurial process is like a journey. To get to the destination (the start-up of a new venture), the entrepreneur must identify a business opportunity and access the resources needed to capitalize on it. Along the way, social, economic, political, and technological factors in the broader environment will have an influence, but we will focus our attention on understanding the three key process elements—the entrepreneur, the opportunity, and the resources—and how they interact.

As these key elements interact, they may be mismatched or well matched. If elements are mismatched (a "misfit"), the journey may be abandoned before the destination is reached. For example, if an entrepreneur identifies an opportunity for a new health service but does not have the relevant background and skills to deliver the service, the business may never get off the ground. Conversely, if the process elements are well matched (a "fit"), the new business venture will likely become operational. After start-up, the venture's next phase of development will result in one of the following outcomes: growth, stability (staying the same), decline, or demise (ceasing to exist). These ideas are illustrated in Figure 3.1.

The Entrepreneur

Since the entrepreneur is at the heart of the entrepreneurial process, researchers have paid considerable attention to identifying the personal characteristics of entrepreneurs. The profiles provided in Table 3.2 illustrate how wide ranging these characteristics are.[33] Some are behavioural (for example, high energy level), others are personality traits (for example, independence), and still others are skills (for example, problem solving).

While the idea that people are "born" entrepreneurs is still quite popular, nothing could be further from the truth.[34] In fact, entrepreneurial characteristics have been found to be widely distributed in the population.[35] We also know that personal characteristics often have less impact on a person's actions than the situation a person is in.[36] What is really important is not who the person *is* but what the person *does*.[37] The two main things that entrepreneurs need to do are to identify an opportunity and to access resources.

Identifying Opportunities

Identifying opportunities involves generating ideas for new (or improved) products, processes, or services, then screening those ideas so that the one that presents the best opportunity can be developed, and then developing the opportunity.

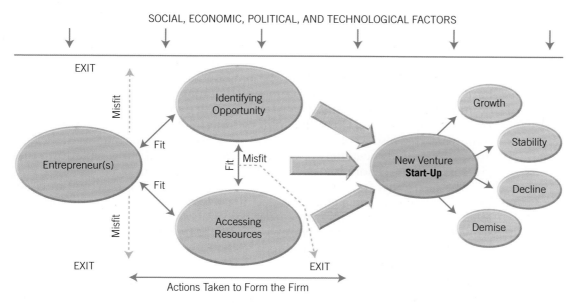

Figure 3.1 The entrepreneurial process in a new venture context.

Table 3.2 Entrepreneurial Characteristics		
Kuratko and Hodgetts (2007)	**Hornday (1982)**	**Timmons and Spinelli (2007)**
Commitment, Determination, and Perseverance	Self-Confidence	Commitment and Determination
Drive to Achieve	Perseverance, Determination	Leadership
Opportunity Orientation	Drive to Achieve	Opportunity Obsession
Initiative and Responsibility	Energy, Diligence	Tolerance of Risk, Ambiguity, and Uncertainty
Persistent Problem Solving	Resourcefulness	Creativity, Self-Reliance, and Adaptability
Seeking Feedback	Calculated Risk Taking	Motivation to Excel
Internal Locus of Control	Need to Achieve	Courage
Tolerance for Ambiguity	Creativity	Creativity and Innovativeness
Calculated Risk Taking	Initiative	Energy, Health, and Emotional Stability
Integrity and Reliability	Flexibility	Values
Tolerance for Failure	Positive Response to Challenges	Capacity to Inspire
High Energy Level	Independence	Intelligence
Creativity and Innovativeness	Perceptiveness	
Vision	Dynamism, Leadership	
Self-Confidence and Optimism	Positive Attitude	
Independence	Ability to Get Along with People	
Team Building	Responsiveness to Suggestions and Criticism	
	Profit Orientation	
	Perceptiveness	

Idea Generation

Typically, generating ideas involves abandoning traditional assumptions about how things work and how they ought to be and involves seeing what others do not. If the prospective new (or improved) product, process, or service can be profitably produced and is attractive relative to other potential venture ideas, it might present an opportunity.

Where do ideas come from? Most new ventures do not emerge from a deliberate search for viable business ideas but from events relating to work or everyday life.[38] Approximately half of all new business ideas come from insights gained or skills learned at a previous job. As employees, prospective entrepreneurs are familiar with the product or service and with the customers, suppliers, and competitors. They can relate those needs to their own personal capabilities and can determine whether they are capable of producing products or services that can fill the void.

Jay Hagan and Scott Gaidano learned how to recover data from damaged hard drives while working for a company that manufactured them. When that company went bankrupt, they started their own business and called it DriveSavers. Likewise, Gina Bianchini met Marc Andreessen while working for a company that also went bankrupt. They discovered a shared interest in the fast-growing world of social networking and together created Ning, a platform that gives users the freedom to design their own online networks.[39]

The next most frequent sources of venture ideas are a personal interest/hobby (16 percent) and a chance happening (11 percent).[40] A chance happening refers to a situation where a venture idea comes about unexpectedly. For example, while on vacation in another country you might try a new snack food that you feel would be in demand if introduced to the Canadian market.

Screening

Entrepreneurs often generate many ideas, and screening them is a key part of the entrepreneurial process. The faster you can weed out the "dead-end" venture ideas, the more time and effort you can devote to the ones that remain. The more of the following characteristics that an idea has, the greater the opportunity it presents.

The Idea Creates or Adds Value for the Customer. A product or service that creates or adds value for the customer is one that solves a significant problem or meets a significant need in new or different ways. Consider Sally Fox's idea for eliminating the dyeing process in textile operations.[41] By cross-breeding long-fibre white cotton and short-fibre coloured cotton, she developed Foxfibre, an environmentally friendly new cotton fibre that is naturally grown in several colours and is long enough to be spun commercially.

The Idea Provides a Competitive Advantage That Can Be Sustained. A competitive advantage exists when potential customers see the product or service as being better than that of competitors. Sustaining a competitive advantage involves maintaining it in the face of competitors' actions or changes in the industry. All other things being equal, the longer markets are in a state of flux, the greater the likelihood of being able to sustain a competitive advantage. Lacking a competitive advantage or developing a competitive advantage that is not sustainable constitute two fatal flaws of many new ventures.[42]

To continue with Sally Fox's story, not too long after she sold her first crop she was running a $10 million business and had well-known companies like Levi's, L.L. Bean, Land's End, and Esprit as customers. But Fox's journey turned out to be bumpy. She had to relocate twice in response to pressure from powerful cotton growers who were afraid that her coloured varieties would contaminate their own crops. Also, once spinning mills began moving to Southeast Asia and South America, Fox's cotton lost the financial advantage it had over traditional cotton. Because the overseas mills were unwilling or unable to process the relatively small quantities of cotton her farmers produced, she lost her big customers. Fox now concentrates on smaller mills and smaller customers, and she is rebuilding her business and her network of growers.

The Idea Is Marketable and Financially Viable. While it is important to determine whether there are enough customers who are willing to buy the product or service, it is also important to determine whether sales will lead to profits.[43] Estimating market demand requires an initial understanding of who the customers are, what their needs are, and how the product or service will satisfy their needs better than competitors' products will. It also requires a thorough understanding of the key competitors who can provide similar products, services, or benefits to the target customer. For example, 10 years ago few people thought that manufacturers of cellphones would be competitors of camera manufacturers in providing real-time photos through digital imaging. Customers define the competition in terms of who can satisfy their needs best.

After learning about the competition and customers, the entrepreneur must prepare a sales forecast. A **sales forecast** is an estimate of how much of a product or service will be purchased by the prospective customers for a specific period of time—typically one year. Total sales revenue is estimated by multiplying the units expected to be sold by the selling price. The sales forecast forms the foundation for determining the financial viability of the venture and the resources needed to start it.

Determining financial viability involves preparing financial forecasts, which are two- to three-year projections of a venture's future financial position and performance. They typically consist of an estimate of *start-up costs*, a *cash budget*, an *income statement*, and a *balance sheet* (see Chapter 11 for more detail about these financial documents). A cash budget forecasts the cash receipts and cash disbursements of the business; the income statement shows the profit

sales forecast An estimate of how much of a product or service will be purchased by the prospective customers for a specific period of time.

or loss; and the balance sheet shows the assets (what the business owns), the liabilities (what it owes), and the owners' equity (owners' investment, including any profits that the business retains). These projections serve as the basis for decisions regarding whether to proceed with the venture, and if so, the amount and type of financing to be used in financing the new business.

exit costs The costs in terms of time, money, and reputation that are incurred when a business shuts down.

The Idea Has Low Exit Costs. The final consideration is the venture's **exit costs**. Exit costs are low if a venture can be shut down without a significant loss of time, money, or reputation.[44] If a venture is not expected to make a profit for a number of years, its exit costs are high, since the project cannot be reasonably abandoned in the short term. On the other hand, if the venture is expected to make a profit quickly, its exit costs will be lower, making the idea more attractive.

Developing the Opportunity

As the "dead-end" venture ideas are weeded out, a clear notion of the business concept and an entry strategy for pursuing it need to be developed. As the process proceeds, the business concept often changes from what was originally envisioned. Some new ventures develop entirely new markets, products, and sources of competitive advantage once the needs of the marketplace and the economies of the business are better understood. So, while a vision of what is to be achieved is important, it is equally important to be responsive to new information and to be on the lookout for opportunities that were not originally anticipated. For example, if customers are not placing orders, as was the case with Sally Fox, it is important to find out why and to make the appropriate adjustments.

franchise An arrangement in which a buyer (franchisee) purchases the right to sell the product or service of the seller (franchiser).

New ventures use one or more of three main entry strategies: They introduce a totally new product or service; they introduce a product or service that will compete directly with existing competitive offerings but add a new twist (such as offering the option of customizing the standard product); or they franchise.[45] A **franchise** is an arrangement in which a buyer (franchisee) purchases the right to sell the product or service of the seller (franchiser). We discuss franchising in more detail later in this chapter.

When capital requirements are high, such as when a manufacturing operation is being proposed, there is a need for considerable research and planning. Similarly, if product development or operations are fairly complex, research and analysis will be needed to ensure that the costs associated with effectively coordinating tasks will be minimized. In these circumstances, or when the aim is to attract potential investors, a comprehensive written business plan will be required. A **business plan** is a document that describes the entrepreneur's proposed business venture, explains why it is an opportunity, and outlines its marketing plan, its operational and financial details, and its managers' skills and abilities.[46] The contents of a business plan are shown in Table 3.3.

business plan A document that describes the entrepreneur's proposed business venture, explains why it is an opportunity, and outlines its marketing plan, its operational and financial details, and its managers' skills and abilities.

If market conditions are changing rapidly, the benefits gained from extensive research and planning diminish quickly. By the time the entrepreneur is ready to start, new competitors may have entered the market, prices may have changed, a location may no longer be available, and so on. Similarly, if the product is highly innovative, market research is of less value because the development of entirely new products involves *creating* needs and wants rather than simply responding to existing needs. Consequently, measuring the capacity of the product or service to fill existing customer needs or wants is less critical.

Contrary to what many people might think, planning does not have to be completed before action is taken. For example, if an electrical contracting business is being proposed in an area where there is a shortage of tradespeople,

Table 3.3   A Business Plan
A well-written business plan is formally structured, easy to read, and avoids confusion. By organizing the information into sections, it makes dealing with the information more manageable. The amount of detail and the order of presentation may vary from one venture to another and according to whom the plan is being prepared for (an investor will require more detail than if the plan is being prepared for internal use by the entrepreneur). An outline for a standard business plan is provided below. While formats vary, with some better suited to the type of venture being proposed than others, most contain the following elements.
I.   **Cover Page**: Name of venture and owners, date prepared, contact person, his/her address, telephone and fax numbers, email address, and the name of the organization the plan is being presented to. The easier it is for the reader to contact the entrepreneur, the more likely the contact will occur.
II.   **Executive Summary**: A one- to three-page overview of the total business plan. Written after the other sections are completed, it highlights their significant points, and aims to create enough excitement to motivate the reader to continue.
III.   **Table of Contents:** This element lists major sections with page numbers for both the body and the appendices of the plan.
IV.   **Company Description**: Explains the type of company and tells whether it is a manufacturing, retail, service, or other type of business. It also describes the proposed form of organization: sole proprietorship, partnership, corporation, or co-operative. A typical organization of this section is as follows: name and location; company objectives; nature and primary product or service of the business; and current status (start-up, buyout, or expansion) and history if applicable.
V.   **Product or Service Description:** Describes the product or service and indicates what is unique about it. This section explains the value that is added for customers—why people will buy the product or service; features of the product or service providing a competitive advantage; legal protection (patents, copyrights, trademarks, if relevant); and dangers of technical or style obsolescence.
VI.   **Marketing:** This section has two key parts, the market analysis and the marketing plan. The market analysis convinces the reader that the entrepreneur understands the market for the product or service and can deal effectively with the competition to achieve sales projections. The marketing plan explains the strategy for achieving sales projections.
VII.   **Operating Plan**: Explains the type of manufacturing or operating system to be used. Describes the facilities, labour, raw materials, and processing requirements.
VIII.   **Management:** Identifies the key players—the management team, active investors, and directors—and cites the experience and competence they possess. This section includes a description of the management team, outside investors and directors and their qualifications, outside resource people, and plans for recruiting and training employees.
IX.   **Financial Plan**: Specifies financial needs and contemplated sources of financing. Presents projected financial statements, including a cash budget, a balance sheet, and an income statement.
1X.   **Supporting Details/Appendix:** Provides supplementary materials to the plan such as résumés and other important supporting data.

it would be important to seek out qualified employees prior to conducting other analyses that are needed to complete the business plan. Such early action also helps to build relationships that can be drawn on later. Obviously, some ventures do not lend themselves to early action, particularly those that are capital intensive. Since most entrepreneurs have limited resources, it is important to concentrate on the issues that can be dealt with *and* that will help determine whether to proceed and how to proceed.[47]

Accessing Resources

Typically, entrepreneurs acquire the various resources needed to make the venture a reality by **bootstrapping**, which means "doing more with less." Usually the term refers to financing techniques whereby entrepreneurs make do with as few resources as possible and use other peoples' resources wherever they can. However, bootstrapping can also refer to the acquisition of other types of resources, such as people, space, equipment, or materials that are loaned or provided free by customers or suppliers.

bootstrapping Financing techniques whereby entrepreneurs make do with as few resources as possible and use other peoples' resources wherever they can. Can also refer to the acquisition of other types of resources, such as people, space, equipment, or materials that are loaned or provided free by customers or suppliers.

Financial Resources

There are two main types of financing—*debt* and *equity*. Briefly, *debt financing* refers to money that is borrowed. The borrower is obliged to repay the full amount of the loan in addition to interest charges on the debt. The most common sources of debt financing are banks (who provide personal loans), trust companies, co-operatives, finance companies, equipment companies, credit unions, government agencies, and suppliers (who provide goods such as inventory to the entrepreneur with an agreement to bill the entrepreneur later).

Equity financing refers to money that the entrepreneur (or others) invests in a business in return for an ownership interest. Equity investors, as owners, are keenly interested in how any profit will be distributed. The most common sources of equity financing are personal savings (new venture founders draw heavily on their own finances to start their businesses), love money (investments from friends, relatives, and business associates), venture capitalists (who loan money to promising new ventures in return for a share of ownership in the business), and private investors (also known as *angels*), who are financially well-off entrepreneurs who wish to recycle their wealth by investing in new businesses. The boxed insert entitled "Looking for Angels" gives more details about angel investing.

Choosing between debt and equity financing involves trade-offs with regard to potential profitability, financial risk, and control. On the one hand, borrowing money increases the potential for higher rates of return to the entrepreneur when the business is performing well. On the other hand, equity makes it possible to reduce risk by giving up some control. Since a business is at its riskiest point during the start-up phase, equity is usually more appropriate and accessible than debt. However, most new venture founders prefer debt because they are reluctant to give up any control to outsiders. To obtain debt financing the entrepreneur must have an adequate equity investment in the business—typically 20 percent of the business's value—and collateral (or security). **Collateral** refers to items (assets) owned by the business (such as a building and equipment) or by the individual (such as a house or car) that the borrower uses to secure a loan or other credit. These items can be seized by the lender if the loan isn't repaid according to the specified terms. To lenders, equity investment demonstrates the commitment of the entrepreneur, because individuals tend to be more committed to a venture if they have a substantial portion of what they own invested in it.

collateral Items (assets) owned by the business (such as a building and equipment) or by the individual (such as a house or car) that the borrower uses to secure a loan or other credit.

Entrepreneurs who want to obtain financing for a start-up business must have collateral like a house or car in order to get a loan. Would you be willing to give your house or car as collateral, knowing that if you couldn't repay the loan the bank would take your house or car?

Business Accountability

Looking for Angels

When small business owners come up with a great idea for a new product, they often find themselves in a Catch-22: They need money to get their product known in the market, but they can't get money because their product is not known in the market. How can they escape from this vicious circle? One answer is angel investors. Consider these stories.

Saxx & Co. makes high-performance men's underwear. The company was started by Trent Kitsch, who developed the idea as part of a project requirement in his MBA program. He put $18 000 of his own money into the company—and he did manage to sell 2000 pairs of Saxx underwear and generate $50 000 in revenue in the process—but he needed a major cash injection to compete with the bigger companies in the industry. Eventually, he received $50 000 from a private investor in return for a 5 percent ownership stake in the business. Kitsch wants to get an additional $500 000, and he is willing to give such an investor 15 percent of the business; he also wants a mentor who has experience in the business.

Kevin Quinn started PowerForward Inc., a company that makes a machine that automatically attaches labels, scratch-and-win cards, or coupons to printed material as it runs through high-speed printing presses. Quinn needed $300 000 to produce the machines so that he could demonstrate that they actually did what he claimed. After several false starts, he approached the ISCM Investment Network in Markham, Ontario. The network does not lend money, but it provides free coaching from mentors who help entrepreneurs like Quinn to better prepare to seek capital. It then introduces the entrepreneurs to angel investors. Quinn was introduced to an angel who invested $250 000. The angel will get a royalty on all machines that Quinn sells.

Chris Beaver, Mark Kerbel, and Roman Kulyk started REGEN Energy Inc., which makes devices to help companies reduce electricity use. The partners needed cash to expand their business, so they approached several venture capital firms. Those firms weren't interested, so they approached angel investors. They found an organization called Maple Leaf Angels, which was in the energy-efficient lighting business. Maple Leaf agreed to sign on as an investor, and one of the individuals at Maple Leaf introduced the partners to the buildings where he was already doing business.

It is important that the angel investor and the small business owner have a clear understanding about issues like who has control over what, the kinds of decisions the angel has to approve, and the amount of regular progress reporting the small business owner will give to the angel.

There are various information sources for small business owners who want to find angels to invest in their business. Angelinvestor.ca, for example, is a Canadian not-for-profit organization that has a directory of angel investors. Another website that contains information about angels is www.angelinvestmentnetwork.ca. Canada has about 25 angel groups. The National Angels Organization is a not-for-profit group that promotes better investment practices and advocates for private investors.

Critical Thinking Questions

1. How are angel investors different from venture capitalists?
2. Are entrepreneurs more accountable to venture capitalists or to angels? Explain your reasoning.
3. Consider the following statement: *Entrepreneurs who have a great new product idea should not try to get money from either venture capitalists or angels. Rather, they should pursue debt or equity capital because they can get larger sums of money that way. They can then use the money to more effectively develop their new product idea.* Do you agree or disagree with the statement? Explain your reasoning.

Besides these conventional sources of financing, the possibilities for creative bootstrap financing are almost endless. For example, an entrepreneur might require an advance payment from customers, in full or in part. Equipment can be leased rather than purchased (which reduces the risk of equipment becoming obsolete). Office furniture can be rented, premises can be shared, and the manufacture of products can be subcontracted, thereby avoiding the expense of procuring material, equipment, and facilities. All of these activities free up cash, which can then be used for other purposes.

Other Resources

Businesses may be owned by one person, but entrepreneurship is not a solo process. There are various stakeholders who provide resources to the venture, including partners, employees, customers, suppliers, professionals, consultants, government agencies, lenders, shareholders, and venture capitalists. Sometimes ownership is shared with one or more of these stakeholders in order to acquire the use of their resources. When ownership is shared, decisions must be made about who to share it with, how much each stakeholder will own, at what cost, and under what conditions. The form of legal organization chosen affects whether ownership can be shared and whether resources can be accessed. We discuss this important point later in the chapter.

Some small businesses are started by friends who decide to team up. For example, Eryn Green and Tamar Wagman teamed up to start Sweetpea, a Toronto-based organic baby food company. Sari Nisker and Casey Soer started Spynga, a Toronto fitness club that focusses on yoga, spinning classes, and holistic health. Candice Versace and Dolly Woo started an upscale clothing shop in Winnipeg. There have been some interpersonal conflicts in all three businesses, but the partners have learned to work together. Stewart Thornhill, who teaches entrepreneurship at the Richard Ivey School of Business, says that friends who operate a business together sometimes have trouble deciding when to quit. He says they should ask themselves this question: "If the person I'm working with wasn't my friend, would I want to be in business with them?"[48]

Deciding whether to share ownership by forming a team involves considering whether having a team is desirable or necessary and whether the aim is to build a company with high growth potential. Whether a team is *necessary* depends upon certain conditions:

- *The size and scope of the venture*: How many people does the venture require? Is it a one-person operation or does it need contributions from others? Can people be hired to fill the key roles as they are required?

- *Personal competencies*: What are the talents, know-how, skills, track record, contacts, and resources that the entrepreneur brings to the venture? How do these match up with what the venture needs to succeed? If gaps are identified, the entrepreneur needs to decide what competencies are needed to complement his or hers and when they are needed.

The nature of the team depends upon the match-up between the lead entrepreneur and the opportunity and how fast and aggressively he or she plans to proceed. Most teams tend to be formed in one of two ways: (a) one person has an idea (or wants to start a business), and then several associates join the team over the first few years of the venture's operation; or (b) an entire team is formed at the outset based on such factors as a shared idea, a friendship, or an experience.

The ideal team consists of people with complementary skills covering the key success areas for the business (for example, marketing, finance, production). Small founding teams tend to work better than big ones. It is quite common for the initial team to consist of just two people—a craftsperson and a salesperson.

If the entrepreneur does not intend to establish a high-growth venture, going solo may be a realistic option. Some new venture founders bring on additional team members only as the business can afford them. Most successful solo businesses are simple types of ventures, such as small retail stores or services.[49] The odds for survival, growth, profitability, and attracting capital are increased by a team approach.[50]

Assessing the "Fit" Between Elements in the Entrepreneurial Process

Assessing the "fit" between the key elements in the entrepreneurial process is an ongoing task, since the shape of the opportunity, and consequently the resources and people needed to capitalize on it, typically changes as the opportunity is developed. It is the entrepreneur who stands to gain the most by attending to these "fits" and any changes they may require, although other stakeholders, such as investors, will be considering them as well.

The Entrepreneur–Opportunity Fit

The entrepreneur needs to decide whether the opportunity, as identified, is something he or she *can do* and *wants to do*. A realistic self-assessment is important. Prospective ventures that are of limited personal interest and that require skills and abilities that do not fit well with those of the entrepreneur should be quickly eliminated. For example, it does little good to identify an opportunity for an ecotourism business in a wilderness area if the entrepreneur is a sedentary urban dweller.

Once the entrepreneur has chosen the opportunity he or she wants to pursue, the success of the venture depends heavily upon the individual or individuals involved. No matter how good the product or service concept is, as the opportunity changes shape, it may demand skills a single entrepreneur lacks. This may prompt a decision to acquire the needed skills either by forming a team or by getting further training.

The Opportunity–Resources Fit

Assessing the opportunity-resources fit involves determining whether the resources needed to capitalize on the opportunity can be acquired. As the opportunity changes shape, so too will the resource requirements. When challenges or risks arise, the aim is to determine whether they can be resolved and, if so, to deal with them as quickly as possible. For example, if the venture requires a greater financial investment than originally anticipated, this does not necessarily mean that the venture should be abandoned. Other options, such as taking on partners or leasing rather than building a facility, may be viable. Of course, some ventures may not be viable regardless of the alternatives considered.

The Entrepreneur–Resources Fit

Once the resource requirements of the venture have been determined, the entrepreneur needs to assess whether he or she has the capacity to meet those requirements. For example, an entrepreneur with a stellar reputation for software development will have an easier time attracting employees for a venture specializing in software development than someone with no track record. If that same entrepreneur is well connected with people in the industry, he or she will be more likely to gain commitments from customers and, in turn, investors.

After the Start-Up

Entrepreneurs must make the right decisions as they work toward the start-up of their new venture, but they must also pay attention to how the business will be run beyond the start-up phase. In this section, we examine three important topics that are relevant to these issues. First, we describe the three main ways that entrepreneurs start up a small business. Next, we look at the four main organizing options that are available to entrepreneurs. We conclude the chapter with a look at the reasons for success and failure in small business.

Starting Up a Small Business

In the previous section, we looked in detail at how entrepreneurs start a business from scratch. But there are two additional ways that entrepreneurs can go into business: buy an already-existing business or buy a franchise.

> Describe three alternative strategies for becoming a business owner— *starting a business*, *buying an existing business*, and *buying a franchise*.
>
> **4**

Buying an Already Existing Business

About one-third of all new businesses that were started in the past decade were bought from someone else. Many experts recommend buying an existing business because the odds of success are better. An existing business has already proven its ability to attract customers. It has also established relationships with lenders, suppliers, and other stakeholders. Moreover, an existing track record gives potential buyers a much clearer picture of what to expect than any estimate of a new business's prospects.

But an entrepreneur who buys someone else's business may not be able to avoid certain problems. For example, the business may have a poor reputation, its location may be poor, it may be difficult to determine an appropriate purchase price, and there may be uncertainty about the exact financial shape the business is in.

Taking Over a Family Business. A special case of buying an existing business involves family businesses. Taking over a family business poses both challenges and opportunities. On the positive side, a family business can provide otherwise unobtainable financial and management resources because of the personal sacrifices of family members. Family businesses often have a strong reputation or goodwill that can result in important community and business relationships. As well, employee loyalty is often high, and an interested, unified family management and shareholders group may emerge. Toronto-based hosiery manufacturer Phantom Industries Inc. is an example of a family-owned business that has been successful through three generations of family members.[51]

On the other hand, major problems can arise in family businesses (see the Opening Case for examples). There may be disagreements over which family members assume control. If the parent sells his or her interest in the business, the price to be paid may be an issue. The expectation of other family members may also be problematic. Some family members may feel that they have a right to a job, promotion, and impressive title simply because they are part of the family.[52] Two other problem areas are choosing an appropriate successor and handling disagreements among family members about the future of the business.

Buying a Franchise

If you drive or walk around any Canadian town, you will notice retail outlets with names like McDonald's, Pizza Pizza, Swiss Chalet, Yogen Früz, 7-Eleven, RE/MAX, Comfort Inn, Blockbuster Video, Sylvan Learning Centre, and Super Lube. What do all these businesses have in common? They are all franchises, operating under licences issued by parent companies to local entrepreneurs who own and manage them.

Franchising became very visible in the 1950s with fast-food franchisers like McDonald's, but it actually started in the early 1800s. In the late 1800s, General Motors began franchising retail dealerships, and similar systems were created by Rexall (pharmacies) in 1902 and by Howard Johnson (restaurants and motels) in 1926. Franchising continues to increase in importance in the twenty-first century. Depending on how it is defined, franchising now accounts for 43 percent of retail sales in Canada. There are thousands of franchise establishments in Canada, and they generate approximately $30 billion in annual sales revenue.[53]

franchising agreement
Outlines the duties and responsibilities of the franchiser and the franchisee.

A franchise is an arrangement that gives franchisees (buyers) the right to sell the product of the franchiser (the seller). A **franchising agreement** outlines the duties and responsibilities of each party. For example, it stipulates the amount and type of payment that franchisees must make to the franchiser. Franchisees usually make an initial payment for the right to operate a local outlet of the franchise; they also make royalty payments to the franchiser ranging from 2 to 30 percent of the franchisee's annual revenues or profits. The franchisee

Franchising is very popular in Canada. It offers individuals who want to run their own business an opportunity to establish themselves quickly in a local market.

also pays an advertising fee so that the franchiser can advertise in the franchisee's local area. Franchise fees vary widely: $30 000 for a Fantastic Sam's hair salon, to $1 million for a Burger King franchise, to hundreds of millions for a professional sports franchise.

The Advantages of Franchising.   Both franchisers and franchisees benefit from the franchising way of doing business (see Table 3.4).

Is Franchising for You?   Do you think you would be happy being a franchisee? The answer depends on a number of factors, including your willingness to work hard, your ability to find a good franchise to buy, and the financial resources you possess. If you are thinking seriously of going into franchising, you should consider several areas of costs that you will incur:

- the franchise sales price
- expenses that will be incurred before the business opens
- training expenses
- operational expenses for the first six months
- personal financial needs for the first six months
- emergency needs

Forms of Business Ownership

Whether they intend to run a small farm, a large factory, an online retail business, a hair salon, or any one of many other types of business, entrepreneurs must decide which form of legal ownership best suits their needs. Four options are available: the sole proprietorship, the partnership, the corporation, and the co-operative.

Describe four forms of *legal organization* for a business and discuss the advantages and disadvantages of each.

5

The Sole Proprietorship

The **sole proprietorship** is a business owned and operated by one person. Legally, if you set up a business as a sole proprietorship, your business is

sole proprietorship A business owned and operated by one person.

Table 3.4 The Benefits of Franchising	
For the Franchiser	**For the Franchisee**
■ The franchiser can attain rapid growth for the chain by signing up many franchisees in many diffeent locations. ■ Franchisees share in the cost of advertising. ■ The franchiser benefits from the investment money provided by franchisees. ■ Advertising money is spent more efficiently (the franchiser teams up with local franchisees to advertise only in the local area). ■ The franchiser benefits because franchisees are motivated to work hard for themselves; the more revenue the franchisee generates, the more money the franchiser makes. ■ The franchiser is freed from all details of a local operation, which are handled by the franchisee.	■ Franchisees own a small business that has access to big business management skills. ■ The franchisee does not have to build up a business from scratch. ■ Franchisee failure rates are lower than are rates for those who start their own business. ■ A well-advertised brand name comes with the franchise and the franchisee's outlet is recognizable because it looks like all other outlets in the chain. ■ The franchiser may send the franchisee to a training program run by the franchiser (e.g., the Canadian Institute of Hamburgerology run by McDonald's). ■ The franchiser may visit the franchisee and provide expert advice on how to run the business. ■ Economies in buying allow franchisees to get lower prices for the raw materials they must purchase. ■ Financial assistance is provided by the franchiser in the form of loans; the franchiser may also help the franchisee obtain loans from local sources. ■ Franchisees are their own bosses and get to keep most of the profit they make.

considered to be an extension of yourself (and not a separate legal entity). Though usually small, a sole proprietorship may be as large as a steel mill or as small as a lemonade stand. While the majority of businesses in Canada are sole proprietorships, this form of ownership accounts for only a small proportion of total business revenues.

Advantages of a Sole Proprietorship

Freedom may be the most important benefit of a sole proprietorship. Sole proprietors answer to no one but themselves since they don't share ownership. A sole proprietorship is also easy to form. If you operate the business under your own name, with no additions, you don't even need to register your business name to start operating as a sole proprietor; you can go into business simply by putting a sign on the door. The simplicity of legal set-up procedures makes this form appealing to self-starters and independent spirits, as do low start-up costs.

Another attractive feature is tax benefits. Most businesses suffer losses in their early stages. Since the business and the proprietor are legally one and the same, these losses can be deducted from income the proprietor earns from personal sources other than the business.

Disadvantages of a Sole Proprietorship

unlimited liability A sole proprietor is personally liable (responsible) for all debts incurred by the business.

A major drawback is **unlimited liability**. A sole proprietor is personally liable (responsible) for all debts incurred by the business. If the business fails to generate enough cash, bills must be paid out of the owner's pocket. Another disadvantage is the lack of continuity; a sole proprietorship legally dissolves when the owner dies. Finally, a sole proprietorship depends on the resources of one person, and that person's managerial and financial limitations may constrain the business. Sole proprietors often find it hard to borrow money to start up or expand. Many bankers fear that they won't be able to recover loans if the owner becomes disabled.

The Partnership

The **partnership**, a form of organization often used by professionals like accountants and lawyers, is established when two or more individuals (partners) agree to combine their financial, managerial, and technical abilities for the purpose of operating a business for profit. Partnerships are often an extension of a business that began as a sole proprietorship. The original owner may want to expand, or the business may have grown too big for a single person to handle.

There are two basic types of partners in a partnership. **General partners** are actively involved in managing the firm and have unlimited liability. **Limited partners** don't participate actively in the business, and their liability is limited to the amount they invested in the partnership. A **general partnership** is the most common type of partnership and is similar in nature to the sole proprietorship in that all the (general) partners are jointly liable for the obligations of the business. The other type of partnership—a **limited partnership**—consists of at least one general partner (who has unlimited liability) and one or more limited partners (who have limited liability). The limited partners cannot participate in the day-to-day management of the business or they risk the loss of their limited liability status.

Advantages of a Partnership

The most striking advantage of a general partnership is the ability to grow by adding talent and money. Partnerships also have a somewhat easier time borrowing funds than do sole proprietorships because banks and other lending institutions prefer to make loans to enterprises that are not dependent on a single individual. Partnerships can also invite new partners to join if they agree to invest money in the firm.

Like a sole proprietorship, a partnership is simple to organize, with few legal requirements. Even so, all partnerships must begin with an agreement of some kind. It may be written, oral, or even unspoken. Wise partners, however, insist on a written agreement to avoid trouble later. This agreement should answer several questions:

- How will disagreements be resolved?

- Who invested what sums of money in the partnership?

- Who will receive what share of the partnership's profits?

- Who does what and who reports to whom?

- How will the partnership be dissolved?

- How will leftover assets be distributed among the partners?

The partnership agreement is strictly a private document. Partners are not required by law to file an agreement with some government agency, and partnerships are not regarded as legal entities. In the eyes of the law, a partnership is nothing more than two or more persons working together. The partnership's lack of legal standing means that the partners are taxed as individuals.

Disadvantages of a Partnership

As with sole proprietorships, unlimited liability is the greatest drawback of a general partnership. By law, each general partner may be held personally liable for all debts incurred in the name of the partnership. And if any partner incurs a debt, even if the other partners know nothing about it, they are all liable if the offending partner cannot pay up. Another problem with partnerships is lack of continuity. When one partner dies or pulls out, the partnership dissolves, even if the other partners agree to stay to continue the business.

partnership A form of organization established when two or more individuals (partners) agree to combine their financial, managerial, and technical abilities for the purpose of operating a business for profit.

general partners Partners who are actively involved in managing the firm and have unlimited liability.

limited partners Partners who generally do not participate actively in the business, and whose liability is limited to the amount they invested in the partnership.

general partnership A type of partnership where all partners are jointly liable for the obligations of the business.

limited partnership A type of partnership with at least one general partner (who has unlimited liability) and one or more limited partners. The limited partners cannot participate in the day-to-day management of the business or they risk the loss of their limited liability status.

A related drawback is the difficulty of transferring ownership. No partner may sell out without the other partners' consent. Thus, the life of a partnership may depend on the ability of retiring partners to find someone compatible with the other partners to buy them out. Finally, a partnership provides little or no guidance in resolving conflict between the partners. For example, suppose one partner wants to expand the business rapidly and the other wants it to grow slowly. If under the partnership agreement the two are equal, it may be difficult for them to decide what to do.

The Corporation

When you think of corporations you probably think of giant businesses such as Air Canada, Imperial Oil, or CN. The very word *corporation* suggests bigness and power. Yet, the tiny corner newsstand has as much right to incorporate as does a giant oil refiner. And the newsstand and oil refiner have the same basic characteristics that all corporations share: legal status as a separate entity, property rights and obligations, and an indefinite lifespan. The Top 10 corporations in Canada are listed in Table 3.5.

corporation A business that is a separate legal entity that is liable for its own debts and whose owners' liability is limited to their investment.

A **corporation** has been defined as "an artificial being, invisible, intangible, and existing only in contemplation of the law."[54] As such, corporations may sue and be sued; buy, hold, and sell property; make and sell products to consumers; and commit crimes and be tried and punished for them. Simply defined, a corporation is a business that is a separate legal entity that is liable for its own debts and whose owners' liability is limited to their investment.

stockholders Investors who buy shares of ownership in the form of stock.

Stockholders—investors who buy shares of ownership in the form of stock—are the real owners of the corporation. Profits may be distributed to stockholders in the form of dividends, although corporations are not required to pay dividends. Instead, they often reinvest any profits in the business.

board of directors The governing body of a corporation whose basic responsibility is to ensure that the corporation is run in a way that is in the best interests of the shareholders.

The **board of directors** is the governing body of a corporation. Its basic responsibility is to ensure that the corporation is run in a way that is in the best interests of the stockholders. The board chooses the president and other officers of the business and delegates the power to run the day-to-day activities of the business to those officers. The board sets policy on paying dividends, on financing major spending, and on executive salaries and benefits. Large corporations tend to have large boards with as many as 20 or 30 directors. Smaller corporations, on the other hand, tend to have no more than 5 directors.

Each year, the *Globe and Mail* analyzes the governance practices of Canadian companies in four areas: board composition, compensation, shareholder rights,

Table 3.5 Top 10 Corporations in Canada, 2008 (ranked by sales revenues)	
Company	**Sales Revenues (in billions of dollars)**
1. Royal Bank of Canada	$37.5
2. Power Corp. of Canada	37.0
3. Manulife Financial Corp.	33.0
4. George Weston Ltd.	32.0
5. EnCana Corp.	32.0
6. Imperial Oil Ltd.	31.2
7. Suncor Energy Inc.	29.0
8. Petro-Canada	27.5
9. Onex Corp.	26.8
10. The Bank of Nova Scotia	26.6

and disclosure. The top-ranked companies in 2008 were Gildan Activewear Inc., Potash Corporation of Saskatchewan, and Manulife Financial Corp. The lowest-ranked companies were TriStar Oil & Gas Ltd., ACE Aviation Holdings Inc., and Galleon Energy Inc.[55]

Inside directors are employees of the company and have primary responsibility for the corporation. That is, they are also top managers, such as the president and executive vice-president. **Outside directors** are not employees of the corporation in the normal course of its business. Attorneys, accountants, university officials, and executives from other firms are commonly used as outside directors.

Corporate officers are the top managers hired by the board to run the corporation on a day-to-day basis. The **chief executive officer (CEO)** is responsible for the firm's overall performance. Other corporate officers typically include the president, who is responsible for internal management, and various vice-presidents, who oversee functional areas such as marketing or operations.

Types of Corporations

There are two types of private sector corporations (corporations can also be found in the municipal, provincial, federal, and nonprofit sectors). The **public corporation** is a business whose shares of stock are widely held and available for sale to the general public. The shares of public corporations like George Weston, Air Canada, and Canadian Pacific are traded on securities exchanges and are widely available to the general public for purchase. By contrast, the shares of stock of a **private corporation** are held by only a few shareholders, are not widely available for purchase, and may have restrictions on their sale. For example, Kroeker Farms, a large agri-business in Manitoba, is owned by nine members of one family. Other private corporations are Para Paints of Canada and Bata Shoes. Most corporations are privately held.

Most new corporations start out as private corporations, because few investors will buy an unknown stock. As the corporation grows and develops a record of success, it may issue shares to the public ("go public") as a way of raising additional money. This is called its **initial public offering (IPO)**. MasterCard went public in 2006 and Visa did the same in 2008. IPOs are not very attractive to investors during stock market declines, but they become more popular when stock markets recover. Globally, there were 1449 IPOs in 2007, and they raised $285 billion.[56]

A public corporation can also "go private," which is the reverse of going public. In 2008, Clearwater Seafoods Income Fund announced that it would be taken private by a consortium led by Clearwater Fine Foods.[57]

During the period from 2000 to 2005, many corporations converted to an **income trust** structure, which allowed them to avoid paying corporate income tax if they distributed all or most of their earnings to investors. For example, Bell Canada Enterprises could have avoided an $800-million tax bill in one year by becoming an income trust. The federal government estimated that it was going to lose billions of dollars of tax revenue because so many corporations were becoming income trusts. In a surprise move in 2006, the Canadian government announced that it would begin taxing income trusts more like corporations by 2011. This announcement caused a significant decline in the market value of income trusts, and it also means that very few corporations will now convert to an income trust structure.[58]

Formation of the Corporation

The two most widely used methods to form a corporation are federal incorporation under the Canada Business Corporations Act and provincial incorporation under any of the provincial corporations acts. The former is used if the company is going to operate in more than one province; the latter is used if

inside directors Members of a corporation's board of directors who are employees of the company and have primary responsibility for the corporation.

outside directors Members of a corporation's board of directors who are not also employees of the corporation on a day-to-day basis.

chief executive officer (CEO) The person responsible for the firm's overall performance.

public corporation A business whose shares of stock are widely held and available for sale to the general public.

private corporation A business whose shares of stock are held by only a few shareholders, are not widely available for purchase, and may have restrictions on their sale.

initial public offering (IPO) The sale of shares of stock in a company for the first time to the general investing public.

income trust Involves corporations distributing all or most of their earnings to investors and thereby reducing the corporation's income tax liability.

the founders intend to carry on business in only one province. Except for banks and certain insurance and loan companies, any company can be federally incorporated under the Canada Business Corporations Act. To do so, it must draw up articles of incorporation. These articles include such information as the name of the corporation, the type and number of shares to be issued, the number of directors the corporation will have, and the location of the company's operations. The specific procedures and information required for provincial incorporation vary from province to province.

All corporations must attach the word *Limited* (Ltd./Ltée), *Incorporated* (Inc.), or *Corporation* (Corp.) to the company name to indicate clearly to customers and suppliers that the owners have limited liability for corporate debts. The same sorts of rules apply in other countries. British firms, for example, use PLC for "public limited company" and German companies use AG for "Aktiengesellschaft" (corporation).

Advantages of Incorporation

limited liability The liability of investors is limited to their personal investment in the corporation.

The biggest advantage of the corporate structure is **limited liability**, which means that the liability of investors is limited to their personal investment in the corporation. In the event of failure, the courts may seize a corporation's assets and sell them to pay debts, but the courts cannot touch the investors' personal possessions. If, for example, you invest $1000 in a corporation that goes bankrupt, you may lose your $1000 but no more. In other words, your liability is limited to $1000.

Another advantage of a corporation is continuity. Because it has a legal life independent of its founders and owners, a corporation can, in theory, continue forever. Shares of stock may be sold or passed on to heirs, and most corporations also benefit from the continuity provided by professional management. Finally, corporations have advantages in raising money. By selling shares of stock, they expand the number of investors and the amount of available funds. The term **stock** refers to a share of ownership in a corporation. Continuity and legal status tend to make lenders more willing to grant loans to corporations.

stock A share of ownership in a corporation.

Disadvantages of Incorporation

One of the disadvantages for a new firm in forming a corporation is the cost (approximately $2500). Corporations also need legal help in meeting government regulations because they are far more heavily regulated than are proprietorships or partnerships. Some people say that **double taxation** is another problem with the corporate form of ownership. By this they mean that a corporation must pay corporate income taxes on its profits, and then shareholders must also pay personal income taxes on the dividends they receive from the corporation. The **dividend** a corporation pays is the amount of money, normally a portion of the profits, which is distributed to the shareholders. Since dividends paid by the corporation are not tax deductible for the corporation, this amounts to double taxation. Others point out that shareholders get a "dividend tax credit," which largely offsets the effect of double taxation.

double taxation A corporation must pay corporate income taxes on its profits, and then shareholders must also pay personal income taxes on the dividends they receive from the corporation.

dividend The amount of money, normally a portion of the profits, which is distributed to the shareholders by the corporation.

The Co-operative

co-operative An incorporated form of business that is organized, owned, and democratically controlled by the people who use its products and services, and whose earnings are distributed on the basis of their use of the co-operative rather than their level of investment.

A **co-operative** is an incorporated form of business that is organized, owned, and democratically controlled by the people who use its products and services, and whose earnings are distributed on the basis of their use of the co-operative rather than their level of investment. As such, it is formed to benefit its owners in the form of reduced prices and/or the distribution of surpluses at year-end. The process works like this: Suppose some farmers believe they can get cheaper fertilizer prices if they form their own company and purchase in large volumes. They might then form a co-operative, which can be either federally or provincially chartered. Prices are generally lower to buyers and, at the end of the fiscal year, any surpluses are distributed to members on the basis of how much they purchased. If Farmer Jones bought 5 percent of all co-op sales, he would receive 5 percent of the surplus.

The co-operative's start-up capital usually comes from shares purchased by the co-operative's members. Sometimes all it takes to qualify for membership in a co-operative is the purchase of one share with a fixed (and often nominal) value. Federal co-operatives, however, can raise capital by issuing investment shares to members or non-members. Co-operatives, like investor-owned corporations, have directors and appointed officers. In a co-operative, each member is entitled to one vote, regardless of how many shares he or she owns.

Types of Co-operatives

There are hundreds of different co-operatives, but they generally function in one of six main areas of business:

- *Consumer co-operatives.* These organizations sell goods to both members and the general public (e.g., co-op gasoline stations, agricultural implement dealers).

- *Financial co-operatives.* These organizations operate much like banks, accepting deposits from members, giving loans, and providing chequing services (e.g., credit unions).

- *Insurance co-operatives.* These organizations provide many types of insurance coverage, such as life, fire, and liability (for example, the Co-operative Hail Insurance Company of Manitoba).

- *Marketing co-operatives.* These organizations sell the produce of their farm members and purchase inputs for the production process (e.g., seed and fertilizer). Some, like Federated Co-operatives, also purchase and market finished products.

- *Service co-operatives.* These organizations provide members with services, such as recreation.

- *Housing co-operatives.* These organizations provide housing for members who purchase a share in the co-operative, which holds the title to the housing complex.

In terms of numbers, co-operatives are the least important form of ownership. However, they are of significance to society and to their members since they may provide services that are not readily available or that cost more than the members would otherwise be willing to pay. Table 3.6 compares the various forms of business ownership using different characteristics.

Advantages of a Co-operative

Co-operatives have many of the same advantages of investor-owned corporations, such as limited liability of owners and continuity. A key benefit of a co-operative relates to its structure. As noted above, each member has only one vote in the affairs of the co-operative, regardless of how many shares he or she holds. This system prevents voting and financial control of the business by a few wealthy individuals. This is particularly attractive to the less-wealthy members of the co-operative.

Unlike corporations, which are not allowed a tax deduction on dividend payments made to shareholders, co-operatives are allowed

Vancouver-based Mountain Equipment Co-op is one of the best-known co-operatives in Canada.

Table 3.6   A Comparison of Four Forms of Business Ownership

Characteristic	Sole Proprietorship	Partnership	Corporation	Co-operative
Protection against liability for bad debts	low	low	high	high
Ease of formation	high	high	medium	medium
Permanence	low	low	high	high
Ease of ownership transfer	low	low	high	high
Ease of raising money	low	medium	high	high
Freedom from regulation	high	high	low	medium
Tax advantages	high	high	low	high

to deduct patronage refunds to members out of before-tax income. Thus, income may only be taxed at the individual member level rather than at both the co-operative and member level.[59]

Disadvantages of a Co-operative

One of the main disadvantages of co-operatives relates to attracting equity investment. Since the benefits from being a member of a co-operative arise through the level of use of the co-operative rather than the level of equity invested, members do not have an incentive to invest in equity capital of the co-operative. Another drawback is that democratic voting arrangements and dividends based purely on patronage turn off some entrepreneurs from forming or joining a co-operative.

Success and Failure in Small Business

6 Identify four key reasons for success in small businesses and four key reasons for failure.

Of every 100 small businesses that begin operation, 96 will still be operating after one year, 85 after three years, and 67 after five years.[60] A study conducted by CIBC World Markets found that small businesses with above-average revenue growth were run by owners who had more education, used professional advisers, adopted the corporate form of ownership, did outsourcing work for other companies, had a high level of internet connectivity, and used the internet to sell outside of Canada.[61]

Reasons for Success

In addition to the specific findings of the CIBC study, four general factors typically explain the success of small business owners:

1. *Hard work, drive, and dedication.* Small business owners must be committed to succeeding and be willing to put in the time and effort to make it happen. Long hours and few vacations generally characterize the first few years of new business ownership.

2. *Market demand for the product or service.* Careful analysis of market conditions can help small business owners assess the probable reception of their products. If the area around a college has only one pizza parlour, a new pizzeria is more likely to succeed than if there are already 10 in operation.

3. *Managerial competence.* Successful small business people have a solid understanding of how to manage a business. They may acquire competence through training (taking courses), experience, or by using the expertise of

others. Few, however, succeed alone or straight out of university or college. Most spend time in successful companies or partner with others to bring expertise to a new business.

4. *Luck*. Luck also plays a role in the success of some firms. For example, after one entrepreneur started an environmental clean-up firm, he struggled to keep his business afloat. Then the government committed a large sum of money for toxic waste clean-up. He was able to get several large contracts, and his business is now thriving.

Reasons for Failure

Small businesses collapse for a number of reasons (see Table 3.7). Entrepreneurs may have no control over some of these factors (for example, weather, fraud, accidents), but they can influence most items on the list. Four general factors are particularly important:

1. *Managerial incompetence or inexperience*. Some entrepreneurs put their faith in common sense, overestimate their own managerial skills, or believe that hard work alone ensures success. If entrepreneurs don't know how to make basic business decisions or don't understand basic management principles, they aren't likely to succeed in the long run.

2. *Neglect*. Some entrepreneurs try to launch ventures in their spare time, and others devote only limited time to their new business. But starting a small business demands an overwhelming time commitment. If you aren't willing to put in the time and effort that a business requires, you aren't likely to survive.

3. *Weak control systems*. Effective control systems keep a business on track and alert owners to potential trouble. If your control systems don't signal impending problems, you may be in serious trouble before you spot more obvious difficulties.

Table 3.7 Causes of Small Business Failure	
Poor management skills	**Personal reasons**
■ poor delegation and organizational ability	■ loss of interest in business
■ lack of depth in management team	■ accident, illness
■ entrepreneurial incompetence, such as a poor understanding of finances and business markets	■ death
■ lack of experience	■ family problems
Inadequate marketing capabilities	**Disasters**
■ difficulty in marketing product	■ fire
■ market too small, non-existent, or declining	■ weather
■ too much competition	■ strikes
■ problems with distribution systems	■ fraud by entrepreneur or others
Inadequate financial capabilities	**Other**
■ weak skills in accounting and finance	■ mishandling of large project
■ lack of budgetary control	■ excessive standard of living
■ inadequate costing systems	■ lack of time to devote to business
■ incorrect valuation of assets	■ difficulties with associates or partners
■ unable to obtain financial backing	■ government policies change
Inadequate production capabilities	
■ poorly designed production systems	
■ old and inefficient production facilities and equipment	
■ inadequate control over quality	
■ problems with inventory control	

4. *Insufficient capital.* Some entrepreneurs are overly optimistic about how soon they'll start earning profits. In most cases, it takes months or even years. Amazon.com didn't earn a profit for 10 years but obviously still required capital to pay employees and to cover other expenses. Experts say you need enough capital to operate at least six months without earning a profit; some recommend enough to last a year.[62]

Test yourself on the material for this chapter at **www.pearsoned.ca/mybusinesslab**.

Summary of Learning Objectives

1. **Explain the meaning of and interrelationship among the terms *small business, new venture creation*, and *entrepreneurship*.** A *small business* has fewer than 100 employees. A *new venture* is one that has become operational within the previous 12 months, has adopted any of four main organizational forms—sole proprietorship, partnership, corporation, or co-operative—and sells goods or services. *Entrepreneurship* is the process of identifying an opportunity in the marketplace and accessing the resources needed to capitalize on it. In relation to small and/or new businesses, entrepreneurship is the process by which a small business or a new business is created.

2. **Describe the role of small and new businesses in the Canadian economy.** New firms create the most jobs, are noted for their entrepreneurship, and are typically small. The small business sector's capacity for entrepreneurship and innovation accounts for much of the job creation this sector contributes to the economy, with start-ups accounting for most of the growth. As the number of businesses has increased, so too has the number of firms led by women. About 98 percent of employer businesses in Canada are small (they have fewer than 100 employees), and the majority of those have fewer than 5 employees. The distribution of employment by size of firm varies considerably across industries. Small businesses account for over two-thirds of employment in four industries: non-institutional health care, construction, other services, and accommodation and food. In another five industries, at least half of the workforce is employed by small businesses.

3. **Explain the *entrepreneurial process* and describe its three key elements.** The *entrepreneurial process* occurs within a social, political, and economic context and consists of three key elements: the entrepreneur, the opportunity, and resources. The *entrepreneur* is the driving force in identifying an opportunity and accessing the resources to capitalize on it. Opportunities don't simply materialize; entrepreneurs create them. *Opportunity* identification involves generating ideas, screening them to determine their potential, and developing the ones that remain. Entrepreneurs typically access the various *resources* needed by *bootstrapping*—doing more with less. These resources are both financial and non-financial. Two types of financing—debt and equity—can be accessed from a range of sources.

4. **Describe three alternative strategies for becoming a business owner—*starting a business, buying an existing business*, and *buying a franchise*.** It is necessary to work through the entrepreneurial process when *starting a business* from scratch. Whether start-up efforts will result in a new business often depends upon how well matched the entrepreneur's skills and abilities are with the opportunity and the resources required, as well as how well matched the opportunity and resources are. Of the ventures that are brought to fruition, some will grow, while others will decline, die, or remain stable.

   Generally, when *buying an existing business*, the odds of success are better. An existing business has already proven its ability to attract customers. It has also established relationships with lenders, suppliers, and other stakeholders. Moreover, an existing track record gives potential buyers a much clearer picture of what to expect than any estimate of a new business's prospects. On the other hand, there may be uncertainty about the exact financial shape the business is in, the business may have a poor reputation, the location may be poor, or it may be difficult to determine an appropriate purchase price. A special case of buying an existing business involves family businesses, which pose both opportunities and challenges.

In *buying a franchise*, the buyer (franchisee) purchases the right to sell the product or service of the seller (franchiser) according to the terms of the franchising agreement. In return the franchiser provides assistance with the business's start-up as well as with ongoing operations once the business opens its doors.

5. Describe four forms of *legal organization* for a business and discuss the advantages and disadvantages of each. A *sole proprietorship* is a business owned and operated by one person. Answering only to themselves, sole proprietors enjoy considerable freedom in running the business. The ease of setting up a sole proprietorship makes it appealing to self-starters, as do the low start-up costs and the tax benefits. A major drawback is unlimited liability. A sole proprietor is personally liable for all debts incurred by the business. Another disadvantage is lack of continuity. A sole proprietorship dissolves when the owner dies. Finally, a sole proprietorship depends on the resources of a single individual.

A *general partnership* is similar to a sole proprietorship in that all partners have unlimited liability for the obligations of the business. The biggest advantage is its ability to grow by adding new talent and money. Because banks prefer to make loans to enterprises that are not dependent on single individuals, it's easier for partnerships to borrow money. They can also invite new partners to join by investing. Although a partnership is easy to form and has few legal requirements, all partnerships should have a partnership agreement. Partners are taxed as individuals, and unlimited liability is a drawback. Each partner may be liable for all partnership debts. Partnerships may lack continuity, and transferring ownership may be hard. No partner may sell out without the consent of the others.

All *corporations* share certain characteristics. They are separate legal entities, they have property rights and obligations, and they have indefinite lifespans. They may sue and be sued; buy, hold, and sell property; make and sell products; and be tried and punished for crimes committed. The biggest advantage of incorporation is limited liability; that is, investor liability is limited to one's personal investments in the corporation. If the business fails, the courts may sell a corporation's assets but cannot touch the personal possessions of investors. Another advantage is continuity—a corporation can continue forever. Shares can be sold or passed on to heirs, and most corporations benefit from the continuity of professional management. Finally, corporations have advantages in raising money. By selling stock, they expand the number of investors and the amount of available funds. Legal protections tend to make lenders more willing to grant loans. Start-up costs and complexity are among the disadvantages of incorporating. Corporations are heavily regulated and must meet complex legal requirements in the provinces in which they're chartered. A potential drawback to incorporation is *double taxation*. A corporation pays income taxes on company profits, and its stockholders pay taxes on income returned by their investments. Thus, corporate profits are taxed twice—at the corporate and at ownership levels (but the dividend tax credit given to owners may offset the effects of double taxation). Of the two types of private sector corporations—public and privately held—the vast majority are privately held. In forming a corporation, a business will incorporate federally if it is going to operate in more than one province and provincially if it is going to operate in only one province.

A *co-operative* is an organization that is formed to benefit its owners in the form of reduced prices and/or the distribution of surpluses at year-end. It is an incorporated business that is organized, owned, and democratically controlled by the people who use its products and services. The distribution of its earnings (or surpluses) is based upon the use of the co-operative rather than the level of investment. In addition to the two main advantages co-operatives share with corporations—limited liability and continuity—they also have two benefits that corporations don't have. Since all members have one vote, this democratic control means that a few people cannot dominate the decision making. Additionally, co-operatives aren't subject to double taxation, since surpluses are distributed to members from pre-tax profits. Co-operatives are not without disadvantages. The main drawback is that co-operatives often have difficulty raising equity, since members gain financial benefit according to their use of the co-operative, not according to the amount they have invested. While there are hundreds of different co-operatives, they usually function in one of six areas of business: consumer co-operatives, financial co-operatives, insurance co-operatives, marketing co-operatives, service co-operatives, or housing co-operatives.

6. Identify four key reasons for success in small businesses and four key reasons for failure. Four basic factors explain most small business success: (1) hard work, drive, and dedication; (2) market demand for the product or service; (3) managerial competence; and (4) luck. Four factors contribute to small business failure: (1) managerial incompetence or inexperience; (2) neglect; (3) weak control systems; and (4) insufficient capital.

Key Terms

board of directors   (p. 102)
bootstrapping   (p. 93)
business plan   (p. 92)
chief executive officer (CEO)
   (p. 103)
collateral   (p. 94)
co-operative   (p. 104)
corporation   (p. 102)
dividend   (p. 104)
double taxation   (p. 104)
entrepreneur   (p. 84)
entrepreneurship   (p. 84)

exit costs (p. 92)
franchise   (p. 92)
franchising agreement   (p. 98)
general partners   (p. 101)
general partnership   (p. 101)
income trust   (p. 103)
initial public offering (IPO)   (p. 103)
inside directors   (p. 103)
intrapreneuring   (p. 85)
limited liability   (p. 104)
limited partners   (p. 101)
limited partnership   (p. 101)

new venture/firm   (p. 84)
outside directors   (p. 103)
partnership   (p. 101)
private corporation   (p. 103)
public corporation   (p. 103)
sales forecast   (p. 91)
small business   (p. 83)
sole proprietorship   (p. 99)
stock   (p. 104)
stockholders   (p. 102)
unlimited liability   (p. 100)

Questions for Analysis

1. What are some of the problems that are encountered when we try to define the term *small business*?

2. Why are new ventures the main source of job creation and new product/service ideas?

3. Do you think that you would be a successful entrepreneur? Why or why not?

4. Consider a new product or service that has recently become available for purchase by consumers. To what extent did this product or service possess the "screening" characteristics that are described in the chapter (adding value, providing competitive advantage, etc.)?

5. Using the product or service you described in Question 4, analyze the extent to which there is a good "fit" between the various elements in the entrepreneurial process.

6. Why might a corporation choose to remain private? Why might it choose to "go public"?

Application Exercises

1. Identify two or three of the fastest-growing businesses in Canada. What role has entrepreneurship played in the growth of these firms?

2. Find a newspaper or magazine article that describes someone who is an entrepreneur. Use the information provided to explain what makes this person an entrepreneur.

3. Spend some time watching what people do and how they do it, and then (1) identify two ways to make what they do easier, and (2) describe two problems you observed and identify strategies for resolving those problems.

4. Interview the owner/manager of a sole proprietorship or general partnership. What characteristics of that business form led the owner to choose it? Does the owner ever contemplate changing the form of ownership of the business? Why or why not?

Building Your Business Skills

Working the Internet

The Purpose of the Assignment

To encourage students to define opportunities and problems for small companies doing business on the internet.

The Situation

Suppose you and two partners own a gift basket store, specializing in special occasion baskets for individual and corporate clients. Your business is doing well in your community, but you believe there may be opportunity for growth through a virtual storefront on the internet.

Assignment

Step 1

Join with two other students and assume the role of business partners. Start by researching internet businesses. Look at books and articles at the library and check the following websites for help:

- Canada Business—Services for Entrepreneurs: www.cbsc.org
- U.S. Small Business Administration: www.sba.gov
- IBM Small Business Center: www.businesscenter.ibm.com
- Apple Small Business Home Page: www.apple.com/business/

These sites may lead you to other sites, so keep an open mind.

Step 2

Based on your research, determine the importance of the following small business issues:

- an analysis of changing company finances as a result of expansion to the internet
- an analysis of your new competitive marketplace (the world) and how it affects your current marketing approach, which focusses on your local community
- identification of sources of management advice as the expansion proceeds
- the role of technology consultants in launching and maintaining the website
- customer service policies in your virtual environment

Questions for Discussion

1. Do you think your business would be successful on the internet? Why or why not?
2. Based on your analysis, how will internet expansion affect your current business practices? What specific changes are you likely to make?
3. Do you think that operating a virtual storefront will be harder or easier than doing business in your local community? Explain your answer.

Exercising Your Ethics: Team Exercise

Public or Private? That Is the Question

The Situation

The Thomas Corporation is a very well-financed private corporation with a solid and growing product line, little debt, and a stable workforce. However, in the past few months, there has been a growing rift among the board of directors that has created considerable differences of opinion as to the future directions of the firm.

The Dilemma

Some board members believe the firm should "go public" with a stock offering. Since each board member owns a large block of corporate stock, each would make a considerable amount of money if the company went public.

Other board members want to maintain the status quo as a private corporation. The biggest advantage of this approach is that the firm maintains its current ability to remain autonomous in its operations.

The third faction of the board also wants to remain private but clearly has a different agenda. Those board members have identified a small public corporation that is currently one of the company's key suppliers. Their idea is to buy the supplying company, shift its assets to the parent firm, sell all of its remaining operations, terminate employees, and then outsource the production of the parts it currently buys from the firm. Their logic is that the firm would gain significant assets and lower its costs.

Team Activity

Assemble a group of four students and assign each group member to one of the following roles:

- an employee at the Thomas Corporation
- a customer of the Thomas Corporation

- an investor in the Thomas Corporation
- a board member who has not yet decided which option is best

Action Steps

1. Before discussing the situation with your group, and from the perspective of your assigned role, which option do you think is best? Write down the reasons for your position.

2. Before discussing the situation with your group, and from the perspective of your assigned role, what are the underlying ethical issues, if any, in this situation? Write down the issues.

3. Gather your group together and reveal, in turn, each member's comments on the situation. Next, reveal the ethical issues listed by each member.

4. Appoint someone to record the main points of agreement and disagreement within the group. How do you explain the results? What accounts for any disagreement?

5. From an ethical standpoint, what does your group conclude is the most appropriate action that should be taken by the Thomas Corporation in this situation?

6. Develop a group response to the following question: What do you think most people would do in this situation?

For additional cases and exercise material, go to **www.pearsoned.ca/mybusinesslab**.

Concluding Case 3-1

Mompreneurs

A Vanier Institute survey revealed that 90 percent of Canadians think that, for two-parent families, the ideal situation is to have one parent stay at home as the primary caregiver. But families often need more income than can be earned by just one parent, so the parent who stays home is often under some pressure to also generate income. How can this be done? One answer is found in the increasing number of Canadian women who have decided to be stay-at-home entrepreneurs (called mompreneurs). They aren't trying to be supermoms who can do everything; rather, they want to use their skills to run a business and at the same time achieve a better work-life balance. Here are some of their interesting success stories.

ABZ for Me

When Tammy Levitt of Thornton, Ontario, learned her son had autism, she stopped working as a graphic artist so she could spend more time with him. Levitt then started an at-home business called ABZ for Me, a children's home decor business. Levitt says running such a business gives her the flexibility to set her own hours. It also allows her to take her son to 20 hours of therapy each week.

Spoon Fed Soup

Carmie Nearing of Calgary had a career as a chef, but when her children came along, the hours she needed to work didn't fit with raising children. She quit and got a 9-to-5 job. But that didn't satisfy her, so she decided to start her own company—called Spoon Fed Soup—to provide gourmet soups to customers. Nearing found that as her business grew, she had to hire employees and spend more and more time dealing with customers. She now realizes that she has a passion for entrepreneurship that goes beyond the simple desire to stay at home with her children.

The Enamoured Heart

When her daughter was born, Lori Bettig of Winnipeg gave up her job in publishing to become a full-time mom. But when a friend showed her a line of personalized "motherhood bracelets," Bettig saw an opportunity to start a home-based business. She set up a website and the business took off. In 2008, Bettig's business—The Enamoured Heart—was nominated for Savvy.com's Mom Entrepreneur of the Year Award. Bettig's daughter has now taken an interest in designing jewellery, and Bettig hopes to someday pass the business on to her daughter.

Zia and Tia Pure Luxury Organics

Julie Jonas of Beaconsfield, Quebec, started an ecommerce company called Zia and Tia Pure Luxury Organics, which sells 450 different organic products, ranging from baby clothes and bedding to adult grooming products, hemp pet beds, and hand-painted furniture. Jonas got the idea for the business after a friend gave her an article about a company that sold organic cotton baby clothes. Jonas likes being a mompreneur because she can be a stay-at-home mother while also building a socially responsible business. She contributes 10 percent of the company's profits to the Half the Sky Foundation, which provides care for orphanages in China.

Outside/In Cosmetics Inc.

Consuelo Clarke of Chilliwack, B.C., started this company, which makes mineral makeup and organic skin care products. However, in just a few months she noticed that work demands were making her family relations deteriorate. She came close to quitting the business, but then decided to let go of some of the business functions, like bookkeeping and sales. That made life simpler for her and freed up time for her to focus on the part of the business that she enjoys.

Robeez

One of the most highly publicized mompreneurs in recent years is Sandra Wilson. After she was downsized out of her airline job, she handcrafted a pair of brightly coloured, soft-soled leather shoes for her 18-month-old son Robert. She thought that other mothers might find them a good product for their children, so she started her own business and called the footwear Robeez after her son. She hand-stitched 20 pairs of her footwear, then went to the Vancouver Gift Show trade exhibition. The orders flooded in and she signed up 15 retailers ready to sell her product.

Wilson's basement became Robeez Footwear's early headquarters, and she quickly learned all there was to know about leather, cutting, sewing, design, sales, and distribution. Wilson hired her first sales representative in March 1995, and by May 1997 Robeez was online. The company moved out of Wilson's basement in May 1999 and into its first commercial space. Since then, the company has relocated and expanded into larger premises to accommodate its rapidly expanding operations. Today, Robeez is recognized as the world's leading manufacturer of soft-soled leather footwear for newborns to four-year-olds. The company has 450 employees and sells more than 90 designs of shoes and booties in over 6500 stores in countries throughout North America, Europe, Australia, and parts of Asia. In 2006, Robeez joined The Stride Rite Corporation's family of well-known footwear brands, including Keds, Sperry Top-Sider, Tommy Hilfiger Footwear, Stride Rite, and Saucony.

Some observers of the mompreneur trend have noted that things are not always as positive as they seem. Barbara Orser, a management professor at the University of Ottawa's School of Management, says that most mompreneurs work long hours, run low-growth businesses, don't make much money, and don't get benefits. She cites a Statistics Canada report showing that only 17 percent of self-employed women earn more than $30 000 per year. In spite of this, increasing numbers of women are becoming mompreneurs (the number of self-employed women increased 18 percent between 1996 and 2006).

It isn't just women who are trying to achieve a better work-life balance. There are also dadpreneurs doing the same thing. For example, Craig Ellis of Calgary (Shift Selling Inc.) and Greg Thorpe (MonkeyRed Designs) are just two examples of men who have started home businesses in order to help raise their children. There do, however, seem to be fewer dadpreneurs than mompreneurs.

Questions for Discussion

1. What is the difference between small business and entrepreneurship? Are mompreneurs entrepreneurs? Explain.

2. Interview a mompreneur and ask the following questions: (a) Why did you start your business? (b) What are the advantages of being a mompreneur? and (c) What are the disadvantages?

3. Why do you think the number of self-employed women is increasing?

4. Why do you think so little attention is been paid to dadpreneurs?

Getting In on the Ground Floor

Larry Gibson, 51, oversees a business empire that employs 80 people full time (plus 110 under contract) and is projected to have sales of $30 million this year. But things didn't start out that way. Gibson got into the flooring business after finding university too slow for his liking. After working as a flooring installer in Halifax, he went west in the late 1970s and worked in Calgary and in the Arctic, honing his commercial estimating skills before returning to Nova Scotia in 1983.

After five years of managing Eaton's flooring business in Halifax, he got word that his division was closing in May 1988. At the time Eaton's still had contracts and warranties outstanding. "So they came to me and said, 'Will you take these contracts on and go out on your own?'" Using personal savings, he and his wife, Patricia, bought a dilapidated Halifax building from which to launch a floor-covering business and took over the chain's local flooring accounts, setting up shop under the Install-a-Flor name.

The weekend before opening the doors in July 1988, Patricia started to cry, wondering if they were doing the right thing. Reassurance was not long in coming. Gibson's phone rang at 8:30 opening day, and on the line—unaware that Gibson's phone was resting on a sawhorse, since his office wasn't furnished yet—was Atlantic property developer Armour Construction. Gibson's earlier bid to install flooring in a 185-unit complex had been accepted. The deal was worth $440 000 over 15 months.

He says that first sale taught him that "if you believe you can do something, then put your mind and heart to it. There's always an element of surprise and the unforeseen, and it can be good or it can be bad. In my case, it was good and lucky." Indeed, Larry Gibson is known for his commitment to hard work, providing the best possible service, and delivering a quality product at a competitive price. He credits the nuns at the convent school in Herring Cove for instilling discipline in him and says the unexpected death of his father when he was 10 helped give him drive.

Mr. Gibson said the first few years of heads-down, all-out work took its toll on his health. "I was gritting my teeth at night and my stomach had a big knot in it, basically, because we started with nothing and always worried about turning that dollar and getting financial institutions and suppliers to believe in me," he recalled. "It was always tight."

Mr. Gibson credits his wife, who handles the business's finances and administration, with helping him through the early days. "I'd go home, we'd sit at the table—most people have salt shakers; we had a calculator. We would do quantity measures on plans and I would bid, bid, bid." That effort resulted in a 633 percent growth over the company's first five years. "When we first started, it was difficult to convince suppliers to sell us their products," recalls Patricia, "because selling to a newcomer is sometimes a bit of a risk. But Larry and I have a policy of 'Never take no for an answer. There's always another way.' We stuck with it and gained people's confidence."

Today, the business includes seven Floors Plus retail stores in Nova Scotia and New Brunswick, as well as specialty and contract divisions that operate internationally and have specialties such as clean room technology—on-site thermal welding and moulding of plastics—that is used in medical operating theatres and food-processing facilities. "Right now we're doing a school in Bermuda," said Mr. Gibson, adding that the business has opened offices in China and Ontario.

Contracting represents 40 percent of the company's business, with retail accounting for another 40 percent and the growing wholesale business, named Dantra (after his two children, Daniel and Tracy, who both work in the family firm), representing 20 percent.

"We have a lack of supply here of specialty products," Mr. Gibson said in explaining the company's diversification. "Nobody's going to come in here and say, 'Listen, I want you to do clean rooms.' You've got to search this stuff out and find a market for it. It's not just about money, it's about service, being a leader and having knowledge about the market."

Market knowledge is market power, and Mr. Gibson has gained that by going all over the world in search of new business opportunities. "We know from travelling the styles that are coming," he said, noting that he is largely in the business of selling fashion. "The (Atlantic) area is a couple of years behind Toronto, New York, and even European or Asian markets. So we know we've got time to react if we react quickly."

Questions for Discussion

1. According to Statistics Canada's Business Register, would Install-a-Flor be considered a small business? Why or why not?

2. Assess the fit between Larry Gibson and the opportunity when Install-a-Flor was started. What personal characteristics contributed most to his success?

3. To what extent did Larry Gibson use bootstrapping in getting his business started? Explain.

4. Assess Larry Gibson's capacity for identifying opportunities according to the characteristics outlined in the opportunity screening section of the chapter.

5. What benefits or drawbacks are evident in this family business?

6. Would you recommend that Install-a-Flor go public?

7. Clearly, Install-a-Flor is no longer a new business. But is it entrepreneurial?

Part
Four

Managing the Organizational Environment

Chapter 4

Assessing External Environments

After reading this chapter, you should be able to:

1 Articulate the role of the external environment in management decisions and effectiveness.

2 Explain the five major dimensions of an organization's general environment.

3 Describe the critical forces in the organization's task environment.

4 Describe the key elements of an organization's global environment.

5 Describe the key considerations in conducting effective environmental scanning.

Taken from *Management*, Canadian Edition, by Michael A. Hitt, J. Stewart Black, Lyman W. Porter, and Andrew J. Gaudes.

Russia's Black Gold

Changing societal values about pollution and renewable energy sources have caused some consumers to rethink their SUV purchases and switch to hybrid vehicles or small cars, like the smart fortwo. SUVs remain enormously popular, however, leaving automakers to grapple with the dilemma about the extent to which they should pursue the hybrid market.

Finding oil and gas reserves hiding beneath thousands of metres of dirt and rock is challenge enough for managers in oil and gas companies. Add to that the challenge of managing operations in locations where political instability, economic turbulence, and social opposition exist—all of which can dramatically affect the organization's performance—and you have a real challenge on your hands. This is the case for oil and gas managers looking at opportunities in the former Soviet Union.

As strange as it might sound, many managers of foreign oil companies long for the old days when permission to explore, drill, extract, transport, or sell oil and gas was tightly controlled by the central oil ministry of the former Soviet Union. But after its fall, if managers wanted to drill in Kazakhstan, for example, and ship crude oil to Italy for refining, they had to negotiate separate agreements with Kazakhstan, Russia, or Georgia, depending on the chosen transportation route. There was no guarantee that the government that signed the agreement one particular day would be the one that was in power the next.

As a result, up until the turn of the century, thousands of wells in Russia lay untapped. The natural pressure pushing the oil to the surface was gone, and the Russians lacked the technology to force the remaining oil out of the ground. Neglect and financial troubles plagued Russia throughout the 1990s and reduced production to an all-time low of 6 million barrels per day in 1996.

But since 1999, a combination of rising world oil prices, the privatization of the market following the Soviet Union's collapse, and increased exports, mostly to Western Europe, have made it more worthwhile than ever to pursue oil and gas production in the former Soviet Union. In 2001, the Russian government proposed changes to the tax code that decreased some of the financing risks that had suppressed investment in oil and gas projects in the past.

Things are so dramatically different, in fact, that today Russia is the world's largest oil and fuel exporter. It has more oil and gas reserves than any other country—nearly 350 billion barrels. That's almost 50 billion more than Saudi Arabia. Russian companies, which are now mostly privatized, have invested billions of dollars and raised production by 40 percent since 1998. They've also watched their stock prices soar as a result. Total revenue for the Russian oil and gas market in 2005 was US$123.5 billion, up 11.7 percent over the previous year. However, the Russian market did not experience the same dramatic growth as Western markets did. This is largely because the Russian market isn't dependent on external suppliers (that is, Russia produces enough oil to satisfy domestic fuel consumption), who have faced wild instability recently because of events like the Iraq war and the crippling effects of Hurricane Katrina in 2005.

In the later part of 2005, the Russian government introduced new restrictions on oil companies that were not majority-owned by Russians. Foreign-owned companies would be prevented from acquiring natural resource rights for Russian oil fields. The move by the Russian government was to ensure that revenues remain in Russia and to reduce the attractiveness of the market to foreign-held companies. As well, the Russian oil and fuel market is not known for ethical practices. Corruption and scandal are rampant, including allegations of bribery and tax evasion and even murder. The richest man in Russia, Mikhail Khodorkovsky, chairman and principal owner of the second-largest oil company, Yukos, was thrown in jail by Russian officials in 2003. The charge laid against Mikhail was tax evasion, and his assets (estimated to be US$15 billion and largely composed of shares in Yukos) were frozen. Many speculate that the Russian government was not pleased with his local influence and ties to the west, so the actions taken were an attempt to silence a potential political rival. Then in 2006, the Yukos Oil Company itself was charged with tax evasion and hit with a tax repayment burden so great (US$27 billion) that it forced the company into bankruptcy and its assets were liquidated.

While the picture in Russia is nonetheless looking brighter than it has in the past, clearly the country's political-legal scenario is still volatile, and other environmental forces continue to pose many risks that managers in the oil and gas industry must confront. Much of the "black gold" available in Russia lies beneath land that is subject to some of the longest and coldest winters in the world. Add to this free-flowing vodka, and workers' living conditions that consist of log cabins and huts without indoor plumbing, and you have an explosive combination. Travellers to the region describe it as similar to the Wild West in the United States back in the 1800s. In Tyumen, things were so wild that many of the elite Black Beret military units were pulled out of Latvia and Estonia and sent to Tyumen to try to keep order.

How does a manager successfully conduct business in such an environment? Most managers of western oil companies don't have much choice but to try. Their efforts to expand production in deep waters offshore have largely failed. Companies such as British Petroleum and ExxonMobil are partnering with Russian players to explore and develop Russian oil fields. Finding the remaining reserves in the rest of the world has become so difficult that many firms are willing to risk the environmental and political turmoil of the former Soviet Union to keep their firms awash in oil. ◆

Sources: BBC News, "Yukos Investor Lawsuit Dismissed," October 26, 2006, news.bbc.co.uk (accessed January 11, 2007); "Oil & Gas in Russia: Industry Profile," *Datamonitor*, May 2006; J. Scott-Joynt, "Khodorkovsky: An Oligarch Undone," May 31, 2005, news.bbc.co.uk (accessed January 11, 2007); *Moscow Times,* "Yukos Told to Work Miracles," January 29, 2004; J. Guyon, "The Game Goes On," *Fortune* (Europe), November 24, 2003, pp. 70–71; B. Powell, "Russia Pumps It Up," *Fortune*, May 13, 2002, pp. 85–91; E. Kreil, "Oil and Gas Joint Ventures in the Former Soviet Union," U.S. Energy Information Agency, www.eia.doe.gov (accessed August 1996); S. Alison, "Russia Sees Second Devaluation as Oil Price Slumps," Reuters Limited, November 23, 1998; A. Konoplyanik, "Special Report—The Russian Oil & Gas Industry: Analysis Raises Questions about Russian Tax Proposal," *Oil & Gas Journal*, August 13, 2001, pp. 54–59; I. Woollen, "Special Report—The Russian Oil & Gas Industry: Central Asian Gas Crucial to Future Russian Gas Supply," *Oil & Gas Journal*, August 13, 2001, pp. 61–65; S. Alexandrovich and R. Morgan, "Special Report—The Russian Oil & Gas Industry: Russian Service Sector Lagging Behind Country's Emerging Oil Boom," *Oil & Gas Journal*, August 13, 2001, pp. 66–71; "Special Report—The Russian Oil & Gas Industry: Russian Oil Firms Mark Dramatic Turnaround in 1999–2000," *Oil & Gas Journal*, August 13, 2001, p. 67; "Special Report—The Russian Oil & Gas Industry: U.S.–Russian JV Entering Second Decade of Operations," *Oil & Gas Journal*, August 13, 2001, pp. 68–69.

Strategic overview

Managers in the oil and gas industry who are thinking about doing business in Russia or other former Soviet Union states should carefully analyze the social, technological, economic, political, and global forces in the external environment. Such an analysis would be a critical first step in strategically deciding whether or not to make an investment in the region. Commonly, a firm that wants to enter high-risk foreign markets like Russia forms a strategic partnership with a local firm so that the partner can help guide them through the local political, business, cultural, and other environmental challenges.[1] As noted later in this chapter, however, the institutional and cultural environments often differ across country borders, affecting the strategic decisions made by firms. For example, the institutional environment in Russia has been chaotic as the country has tried to move central control of the economy to a more market-based system. Because local governments have been given the authority to make many of the policy decisions once made by the central government, the "rules of the game" change frequently. As a result, Russian managers tend to make short-term decisions. Alternatively, China (discussed later in this chapter) has been making a more evolutionary shift from central government control of the economy to a market-oriented system. With a more stable institutional environment, Chinese managers tend to focus more on making long-term strategic decisions than do Russian managers.[2] Managers desiring to do business in Russia or China would do well to understand each of their institutional environments and carefully select strategic partners, making sure the potential partners' short-term or long-term orientation is known since it could affect the amount of commitment they are likely to make. Thus, managers charged with the responsibility of entering these markets should thoroughly scan their environments to help them understand the opportunities and pitfalls.

An analysis of the organization's external environments is critical to developing an effective strategy. Analyzing the general and task environments will provide substantial information, enabling managers to identify the opportunities and threats that exist. Managers must develop strategies that take advantage of the opportunities and avoid or overcome the environmental threats.[3] Without a thorough analysis, they are likely to overlook excellent opportunities, leaving them open for competitors to exploit. Likewise, they may be unprepared to counter or deal with a major threat, and the organization's performance may suffer as a result. For example, senior executives at Polaroid did not perceive the major threat to their business from the development of digital technology. As a result, its senior executives were forced to declare bankruptcy.

What Does the Business Environment Consist of?

The **external environment** is a set of forces and conditions outside the organization that can potentially influence its performance. We divide these forces into two related but distinct categories—the external task environment and the external general environment. The **task environment** consists of forces that have a high potential for affecting the organization on an immediate basis. The **general environment** consists of forces that typically influence the organization's external task environment, thus the organization itself. In addition to an external environment, organizations also have internal environments. The organization's **internal environment** consists of key factors and forces inside the organization that affect how the organization operates. Exhibit 4.1 provides a general illustration of these elements. However, for these concepts to be of much relevance to you as a manager, we need to delve into greater detail. To do this, we will start at the general external environment level and work our way in.

external environment A set of forces and conditions outside the organization that can potentially influence its performance.

task environment Forces that have a high potential for affecting the organization on an immediate basis.

general environment Forces that typically influence the organization's external task environment and thus the organization itself.

internal environment Key factors and forces inside the organization that affect how it operates.

Exhibit 4.1 The Environment of Organizations.

General External Environment

A variety of forces in the general environment can influence an organization's task environment and the organization itself. These forces are typically divided into five major categories: sociocultural, technological, economic, political-legal, and global. Clearly, the impact a given general external environment has varies from industry to industry and firm to firm. As a consequence, it is hard to argue for a particular sequence or order of importance for these general-environment forces. The "STEP Global" (i.e., **S**ociocultural, **T**echnological, **E**conomic, **P**olitical-Legal, and **G**lobal) sequence we use simply makes remembering the categories much easier.

Sociocultural Forces

The sociocultural forces of the general external environment consist primarily of the demographics as well as the cultural characteristics of the societies in which an organization operates.

Demographics are essentially the descriptive elements of the people in a society, such as average age, birth rate, level of education, literacy rate, and

demographics The descriptive elements of the people in a society, such as average age, level of education, financial status, and so on.

so on. For example, in 1920 the average life expectancy in Canada was 59 years for men and 61 years for women, and in 2004 it was 77.8 years for men and 82.6 years for women.[4] As another example of changing demographics, you have no doubt heard about the baby-boom generation. The baby boom was a phenomenon experienced in four industrialized countries: Australia, Canada, New Zealand, and the United States. The term "baby boom" is appropriate given the explosive birth rate, which averaged as high as four babies per woman in Canada. The boom started around 1946–47 and ended in the mid-1960s, with its termination largely being attributed to oral contraception and the migration of women into the workplace. The 20 years or so of high birth rates led to the baby boomers comprising about one-third of the population of North America.

But why should you as a manager care about baby boomers or other demographics? It is because demographics can significantly affect both organizational inputs and outcomes. For example, the average level of education and the birth rate in Canada combined can have a significant impact on the supply of workers with a given level of education and training. Specifically, a low birth rate and a modestly increasing level of education could result in a slow-growing or even declining number of technical workers. Clearly, this could have a significant impact on your ability as a manager in a high-tech firm to find the technicians you need to run your business. This is exactly what happened in the 1990s. Technically knowledgeable workers, such as software programmers, were in short supply in Canada, driving up demand for these types of employees. Or consider that people are living longer and that the largest demographic group in Canadian history is fast approaching the age at which health problems begin to increase. This could create unprecedented demands on the Canadian health care system, creating significant opportunities for some and challenges for others.

As an international example, consider that Japan's population in 2005 declined from the previous year for the first time since World War II, with forecasts expecting the decline to continue. In 2005, the number of people in Japan over 65 years of age comprised 21 percent of the population, more than doubling in size in less than a generation. With one of the world's longest life expectancies (85.5 years for women and 78.5 years for men), fewer workers will be supporting Japan's retirees than at any time in the country's history, and many of Japan's retirees will live so long that they are likely to use up their retirement savings before they die if they retire at age 65.[5] This may present unprecedented opportunities for low-cost senior care centres and may mean that younger workers are faced with higher government taxes to support social security programs for seniors.

Although demographics can give us important statistics about our population, societal values are important translators of those numbers into business implications.[6] **Societal values** are commonly shared desired end states. In practical terms for managers, societal values determine the extent to which an organization's products or services have a market. For example, a switch in values from status to functionality moved firms like Calvin Klein out of the spotlight and L.L.Bean onto centre stage of consumer demand in the early 1990s. This reversed itself in the mid- and late 1990s, as did the fortunes of these two companies. As another example, we can look at the controversy surrounding SUVs (sport utility vehicles) in North America. Throughout the 1990s, SUVs such as the Ford Explorer, Dodge Durango, and Chevy Suburban were the fastest-selling automobiles. However, as concerns about the impact of pollution on global warming increased and fuel prices spiked in 2005 because of the war in Iraq and the devastating hurricane season, people began to create negative sentiment toward SUVs and pressured car companies to make hybrid cars. These hybrids would be powered

societal values Commonly shared desired end states.

by both conventional combustion engines and electric motors—cars that, instead of 5 kilometres to the litre, would get 20 or 30 kilometres to the litre. These changing societal values forced managers at major car companies to weigh the demands for and against SUVs in deciding what vehicles to produce and in what volumes. In 2004, managers at Toyota decided to introduce the first hybrid SUV with other manufacturers following their lead. Time will tell if societal values are sufficiently strong for the decision of these manufacturers to be successful.

Astute managers need the ability to combine demographics and societal values to determine important implications for their organizations.[7] To illustrate this, let's take a look at one demographic fact and one shifting societal value. Demographically, the number of 35 to 45 year olds in North America peaked around 2000. Without significant changes in the number of immigrants, that group will decline in number by 15 percent through the year 2015. Demand for workers in this age group is estimated to grow by 30 percent during this same time period. This creates an anticipated labour shortage. Add to this demographic picture a new generation of 35 to 45 year olds who want a better balance between work and home life and you have an interesting situation.[8]

To help bring out the implications of this combination of demographic and societal value facts, imagine that you are a manager trying to recruit an experienced manager from outside into your firm. There is a labour shortage and the highly qualified person you are trying to recruit does not want to travel as much as the job demands. What do you do? Every day that the job goes unfilled costs you money because the results from that position are not being produced. The labour shortage means that every person you turn down because of their desire to not travel lengthens the time the job remains empty and increases the total cost of the vacancy. Failure to understand these external general-environment forces could lead to a poor recruiting plan costing the company money. In contrast, if you recognize and understand these demographic and sociocultural forces, you might anticipate the hiring challenge and create an appropriate plan. For example, you might borrow from what several consulting firms have done lately. Many consulting firms have instituted policies that require consultants to be at client locations on Tuesdays, Wednesdays, and Thursdays, but not Mondays and Fridays. This saves consultants from having to travel on Sundays to get to client locations on Mondays, or travelling on Saturdays to get home from working at client locations on Fridays. As this example illustrates, a full understanding of both demographics and values can help you as a manager make changes and decisions that can help you increase your effectiveness and your organization's performance.

Technology Forces

Technology is another external environment force that can have brilliant or devastating effects on organizations. A specific technological innovation can spell the birth and growth of one firm and the decline and death of another. For example, the invention of the transistor created firms like Texas Instruments and spelled the death of vacuum-tube manufacturers that did not adapt to this technological environment change. While the technological environment can be quite complicated, managers need to keep in touch with two basic aspects of the technology environment—product and process changes.

Product Technological Changes. **Product technological changes** are those that lead to new features and capabilities of existing products or to

product technological changes Changes that lead to new features and capabilities of existing products or to completely new products.

completely new products. As a manager, you need to know what product technology changes are occurring, especially in your industry. For example, managers at Xerox were caught flat-footed when new, small personal copiers from Canon were able to produce the volume and quality of copies at half the price of larger Xerox machines. Palm created a new product category with the invention and successful launch of the PalmPilot. This had a serious and negative impact on one of the largest makers of paper day planners at the time—FranklinCovey. Because firms increasingly win or lose as a function of their technological advantages and disadvantages, as a manager you need to have a broad view and keep in touch with technological advances at home and abroad. For example, in the multibillion-dollar global disposable diaper industry, absorbency technology shifted from "fluff pulp" (a paper-based product) to absorbent chemicals. This technological change was important because the absorbent chemicals could absorb more than fluff pulp and do so while making the diaper thinner. Procter & Gamble, maker of Pampers, almost lost its dominant position in the US marketplace because it didn't keep up with the new absorbency technology that emerged from Japan.[9]

process technological changes Alterations in how products are made or how enterprises are managed.

Process Technological Changes. **Process technological changes** typically relate to alterations in how products are made or how enterprises are managed. For example, a new computer colouring technology brought back animated feature films from a steep decline in the late 1980s and early 1990s because it substantially lowered production costs compared with the old, individual frame-by-frame, hand-painted technology.[10] As another example, management information system technology (MIS) like that used by retail giant Wal-Mart allows managers to track merchandise on a daily or hourly basis and thereby know which products are selling and which ones are not. This allows them to effectively order merchandise so that they do not run out of hot-selling items (and miss out on the sales revenues) and can avoid overstocking poor-selling items (and tie up valuable cash in inventory). Interestingly, this process technology has helped Wal-Mart go from US$1 billion in annual sales in 1973 to US$1 billion in weekly sales by 1993 and nearly US$1 billion a day now.[11] Cisco is another firm where technological advances in telecommunications and data transmission have significantly affected the way it operates. For example, in 1995 virtually none of Cisco's revenue came from purchase orders over the internet. By 2000, over 70 percent of its nearly US$20 billion in revenue came from internet sales.

Many North American steel manufacturers were driven into bankruptcy because virtually all of the largest firms were slow to adopt an important new process technology—the electric arch furnace. Most large (or what are called integrated) steel companies made steel by starting with raw iron ore and melting and converting it to large steel slabs that were further rolled and refined. Electric arch furnaces allowed so-called "mini-mills" to start with scrap metal, melt it, and make it into steel products. Starting with scrap metal is significantly cheaper than starting with iron ore. While the metal made in mini-mills cannot be made into such things as beams for skyscrapers, it can be made into sheet metal for making car exteriors, washing machines, toasters, and so on. Dofasco, a steel company in Hamilton, Ontario, was the first, and at the time the only, integrated steel company to add this technology to its traditional steel-making processes. However, although the company now enjoys the benefits of the new electric arch furnace technology, it still took it nearly 10 years to adopt the technology after it was first introduced.[12]

A Manager's Challenge   *Technology*

Undoing 230 Years of Success

In 1768, three Scottish printers invented the most famous reference work in the world—the *Encyclopaedia Britannica*. The first was a three-volume edition. It grew from that to a 32-volume edition that children everywhere depended on when it came time to write a report for school. *Encyclopaedia Britannica* became the most authoritative and comprehensive encyclopedia in the business.

In 1920, Sears, Roebuck and Company acquired Britannica. As a consequence, its headquarters moved from Edinburgh to Chicago. It grew under its new owner and became a household name. In 1941, Britannica was sold to William Benton, who continued to build it and then willed it to the Benton Foundation in the early 1970s. Sales continued to grow in the 1970s and 1980s primarily through a direct sales force that called on homes everywhere. The baby-boom generation bought these US$1500 to US$2200 sets for their children in record volume, and by 1990 sales reached a peak of US$650 million and the company had more than 2300 sales representatives.

What happened over the next 10 short years erased over 200 years of success. During this period, Britannica's sales declined by 80 percent. How did this happen? Managers at Britannica dismissed as irrelevant two technological inventions that proved the undoing of the firm's great history.

The first technology they dismissed was the CD-ROM. Managers at Britannica just didn't think that a CD was as attractive or useful as a set of bound (preferably in leather) books. However, their competitors had different ideas. Companies with inferior products such as Encarta, Grolier, and Compton put their encyclopedias on CDs and sold them not for US$1500, but for US$50. Whereas it cost Britannica approximately US$250 to produce an encyclopedia set, it cost only US$1.50 to manufacture a set on a CD. In many cases, however, customers did not even have to pay the US$50 price. Companies like Microsoft found that they could enhance the appeal of their software by bundling these lesser encyclopedias into their main programs free of charge. For a customer, even though the quality of these competitors was not nearly as good as Britannica, the value was better in the minds of many. Why? Customers received lots of information (even if it was less than they would get with Britannica) free. Something for nothing seemed like a better deal to many customers.

As the technological impact of CDs drove Britannica's revenues into a steep dive, executives who at first tried to deny the lasting impact of the technology finally changed

Remember the volumes of encyclopedias that graced the bookcases of homes prior to the internet age? Undeniably, *Encyclopaedia Britannica* was the most authoritative and comprehensive set of volumes in the business. Technology, however, radically changed the business and the company's future prospects. Slow to adapt, *Encyclopaedia Britannica* almost didn't survive.

their minds and gave in. However, in deciding to put *Encyclopaedia Britannica* on CD, managers encountered two significant problems.

First, they faced the problem of how to sell the product. Their direct-sales channel would not work for the CDs because there was no way to price the product high enough for salespeople to receive the US$500 commissions per sale that they were used to getting when they sold bound books. Without a substantial commission, salespeople had little incentive to push the new format. Unfortunately, Britannica did not have other distribution or sales channels for its encyclopedia on CD.

Second, and quite ironically, managers at Britannica discovered that the new technology rendered as a weakness what Britannica's executives had always seen as their greatest strength and differentiator—comprehensiveness. Despite the large storage capacity of CDs, the content of Britannica's encyclopedia could not fit on one CD. However, its "inferior" competitors' encyclopedias fit fine on one CD. Unfortunately for Britannica, customers did not want to hassle with three or four CDs, even if there was better content; they wanted to put one CD into their computer, search, and find the information they desired.

With sales declining and problems increasing, Jacob Safra, a nephew of the banking magnate Edmond Safra, bought Britannica in 1996. Although he put a new management team into place, the nature of competition had changed so dramatically that reviving the business was

▶

nearly an impossible task at that point. The company was dealt a near-fatal blow with the next technological change—the internet.

With the mass-market introduction of the internet, after 1997 it was increasingly easy to access a free encyclopedia or gain needed information from an ever-growing list of websites and information providers at no cost, as long as you were willing to look at the ads on their sites. Reluctantly, Britannica managers set up their own website for reference material and tried to sell their unrivalled volumes of information through a subscription fee of US$20. Unfortunately, this proved unattractive to customers when information from other sources was free.

Britannica spotted a glimmer of hope, though, when the internet ad market collapsed following the burst of the tech bubble in 2001. The company exploited the turmoil by changing its internet model. Not only must a good search engine find all of the relevant documents, it must put the best 20 or 30 at the top. Britannica does this on their website so internet users don't have to weed through a lot of material to find the "good stuff." It also gives anybody access to its entire site, including the beginnings of all articles, the *Merriam-Webster Collegiate Dictionary*, and articles from many popular and professional magazines. However, it charges a membership fee to read full articles.

To solve its sales commission problem, Britannica set up its first direct-marketing team in 2003. The company's sales are now in the US$200 million range—a fraction of what they once were, but the company is surviving. Moreover, all of its products are available on the internet, CD, and DVD. Britannica is also pursuing joint projects with educational product providers, such as the 2006 deals with ToyQuest and The American Education Corporation to provide products with content. Britannica has also pursued deals to supply mobile platforms such as iPods, PDAs, and smart phones with access to content.

While Britannica struggles to find its place in the digital economy, pressure continues to increase from new players. For example, Britannica has hit yet another major wall in regaining market share from the new and powerful Wikipedia, a free internet encyclopedia. Wikipedia is the brainchild of Jimmy Wales and was launched in 2001 as an open-source compendium of world knowledge where content is entered and edited by anyone. Though Wikipedia is deemed less accurate in its entries (but not by much, as *Nature* magazine discovered in random testing of entries), it is 12 times the size of Britannica, easy to use . . . and it's free.

Sources: Book Publishing Report, "Britannica Takes Content to Ever-Growing Mobile Platforms," May 29, 2006, p. 5; M. Naim, "Megaplayers vs. Megapowers," *Foreign Policy*, Jul/Aug 2006, pp. 6–95; P. Gillin, "Why You Should Care about Wikis," *B to B*, January 16, 2006, p. 13; S. Balmond, "Encyclopaedia Britannica Sets Up Direct Team," *Precision Marketing*, May 23, 2003, p. 1; S. Ellerin, "Three Publishers' Site Search Solutions," *EContent*, February 2003, pp. 44–48; P. Evans and T. Wurster, *Blown to Bits* (Cambridge, MA: Harvard Business School Press, 2000).

A Manager's Challenge: "Undoing 230 Years of Success" is a great example of the potential impact of the technological environment and the consequences of failing to adequately recognize or respond to technological changes. It briefly documents the rise and fall of one of the oldest and most revered companies—Encyclopaedia Britannica. As you read this example, ask yourself why you think managers at Encyclopaedia Britannica were unable to anticipate the two major technological changes that nearly did the company in. Why did managers respond so slowly to the change? What do you think managers at Britannica should do going forward? Should they fight, ignore, or embrace the latest technology?

Economic Forces

A wide variety of economic forces in the external environment can also significantly influence organizations. Not all economic forces affect all organizations equally, however. The exact nature of the business and industry determines the specific factors that have the strongest influence on an organization. To better understand these economic forces, we group them into three main categories: current conditions, economic cycles, and structural changes.

Current Economic Conditions. Current economic conditions are those that exist in the short term within a country. It is relatively easy for most students to imagine how current economic conditions can have important effects on an organization. For example, the current level of inflation can directly affect how quickly costs rise, which in turn might squeeze profits. The current level of unemployment can directly influence how easy or difficult it is to find the type of labour an organization needs. Current interest rates can determine how expensive it is to borrow money or even how much money a firm can borrow to finance activities and expansions. For example, Canadian mortgage rates reached a 40-year low in early 2004. Because the cost of borrowing was so low, many people decided that it was time to either buy a house or refinance their existing home loan with a lower rate and lower their mortgage payment. As a result, home builders and mortgage providers have seen a significant increase in business. With the increased demand for housing, the price of existing homes has also increased throughout much of Canada, with the average price of a home surpassing the $200 000 mark in March 2006 for the first time.

Economic Cycles. But economic activity is not static, and current conditions do not necessarily predict future economic conditions. For example, when the Canadian dollar hit a record low of 61.79 cents US on January 21, 2002, few saw this as the onset of a steady increase that would lead to the Canadian dollar reaching parity with the US dollar only 68 months later; a value that had not been seen in over thirty years. Economic activity tends to move in cycles. Although it is difficult to predict exactly when an upturn or downturn in economic conditions will occur, understanding that cycles exist and the key factors that move them is critical for managerial activities like planning. It is also important to understand that specific industry cycles can be more or less pronounced than the general economic cycle of the country. For example, the construction industry tends to have higher peaks and lower valleys than the overall national economy, and the funeral-home business tends to have lower peaks and higher valleys than the overall economy (see Exhibit 4.2). If you were not aware of the impact of economic cycles on your particular industry, you might make poor management decisions. For example, if you were unaware of the exaggerated cycles of the construction industry relative to the peaks and valleys of the general economy, you might not plan for enough labour or materials for the upturn in the cycle and might order more materials than necessary or hire too many people during downturns in the cycle.

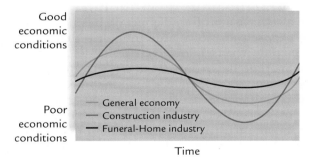

Exhibit 4.2 Overall Economic Cycles and Industry Cycles.

Structural Changes. Perhaps the hardest yet most critical thing to understand about economic conditions is knowing whether changes in the economy are temporary or whether they represent longer-term structural changes. **Structural changes** are changes that significantly affect the dynamics of economic activity now and into the future. For example, the shift from an agrarian (agricultural) to an industrial economy, and then from an industrial to a service economy, were all structural changes that took place in North America. They affected where people worked, what work they did, the education level they needed to do the work, and so on. If structural changes are taking place and you are unaware of them, you can

structural changes Changes that significantly affect the dynamics of economic activity.

easily make poor managerial decisions. For example, the structural shift to a more knowledge-based work environment will likely change not only the nature of workers but also what motivates them. In many service companies, such as engineering firms, consulting firms, and law firms, the company's primary assets (its people) walk out the door every day. This is in contrast to industrial companies like car manufacturers, which have millions of dollars in plant and equipment that stay put even when the workers go home. As a consequence, while a car manufacturer may be able to replace a worker who leaves the assembly line with relative ease and feel only small effects of employee turnover, the same is not true for service companies and for Canada in general, as the structural economic shift from an industrial to an information economy continues.

For example, when a star consultant leaves her firm, she takes with her most of her value to the company—her understanding of client problems and solutions leaves with her. The phone or fax or other hard assets that stay with the company provide comparatively little value. In fact, in some cases the value is so closely tied to the individual that customers leave the company with an individual's departure and redirect their business to wherever the star consultant has gone. Without understanding this structural economic change, you may miss the importance of employee retention and underestimate the role of praising and recognizing the contributions of your star performers so that they stay with your firm. Or you may not see that allowing your employees to travel to client locations on Mondays (instead of Sundays) in the end saves you money because the change in policy helps you retain rather than lose key performers.

Political and Legal Forces

Political and legal forces can also have dramatic impacts on organizations. Laws frame what organizations can and cannot do. As a consequence, they can create both challenges and opportunities. For example, new pollution laws significantly increased the operating costs of coal-burning power plants. At the same time, these laws created new business opportunities for firms like Corning, which developed and sold new filter systems to coal-burning power plants.[13]

Tax laws can also have a profound effect on businesses. In 2005 and 2006, Canadians were exposed to the volatile influence that tax law can have on income trusts. Income trusts allow companies to avoid paying corporate taxes because all income flows directly to the investors, who ultimately pay the income taxes based upon their personal income. Companies were starting to look at becoming income trust organizations rather than corporations to avoid taxes. In November 2005, Minister of Finance Ralph Goodale announced that income trust laws would remain unchanged by the federal government. With the announcement, organizations that had already stated their intent to shift to an income trust organization experienced an increase in value of their shares, and the value of income trust funds that were already in existence also rose. In fall 2006, however, the finance minister of the new government, Jim Flaherty, changed the tax rules governing income trusts to stave off corporations avoiding tax by converting to income trusts: Income trusts will now pay a tax on distributions to shareholders. The results of this new law had an impact on the Toronto Stock Exchange (TSX), where the value of income trust funds dropped by percentages in the double-digits. The value of the Canadian dollar also slipped because of the change in the TSX.[14]

Perhaps one of the most important political aspects of the external general environment is federal government spending. On the one hand, increases or decreases in government spending can have a significant impact on the overall economy. Total government spending at the local, provincial, and federal levels in

2005 and 2006 accounted for between 24.6 percent and 28.6 percent of **gross domestic product**, or GDP (the total dollar value of final goods and services produced by businesses within a nation's borders). The federal government contributed 7.8 percent, the provincial governments 16.8 percent, and the local governments between 6 and 10 percent.[15] It's a significant amount, but it should be noted that for more than 10 years the amount that government contributes in spending has been steadily declining. Regardless, increases or decreases in total government spending can have a significant impact on overall business activity. However, even if total spending remains unchanged, if spending moves from one area to another, such as from education to health care, then government spending can still dramatically affect businesses.

More complicated, but perhaps even more important, is whether government spending pushes the deficit up or down. For example, generally, when federal spending pushes the federal deficit up, interest rates also go up. As interest rates go up, money becomes more expensive for firms to borrow, and as a consequence they typically borrow less. As firms borrow less, they expand their business activities at a slower rate or even contract their overall activity. This can push unemployment up, which in turn pushes consumer spending down. In combination this can create a full-fledged economic downturn. So while the political process governing federal spending and the deficit can be quite complicated, managers cannot afford to ignore the effects.

Global Forces

Although all managers should pay attention to the global environment, its importance depends on the organization's size and scope of business. For small organizations, the other general-environment forces may be more important and have a much stronger impact. However, for medium-sized and large firms, the global environment can be as important as or even more important than any of the other general-environment forces we have discussed. This is especially true as the percentage of international sales increases as part of total sales. For example, 70 percent of Coca-Cola's income comes from international sales in over 200 countries; consequently, the global environment is critical to the company's performance. For global firms that operate in multiple countries and try to integrate those operations into an almost borderless enterprise, the line between the other environmental forces and global environments can blur. As an example, for managers at Nokia, a Finnish company that has only 3 percent of sales from inside Finland, the global economic environment *is* the economic environment. In addition, in order to succeed, managers at Nokia must focus on sociocultural changes around the world. They must also take into consideration technological changes in wireless communication in Europe, North America, Latin America, the Middle East, Africa, and Asia Pacific. As a consequence, while we separate global as a distinct general-environment force, the reality for many companies and managers is that the global environment is intimately intertwined with the other environmental forces.

A Manager's Challenge: "Business in China" helps illustrate the challenge of assessing the global environment and then acting on that assessment. While it may seem thousands of kilometres away, China has the world's largest population—1.3 billion people—with the equivalent of Canada's entire population entering the middle class annually. Consequently, Canadian managers envision great trade opportunities with this growing market, but they must also maintain a high respect for human rights. While reading this managerial challenge box, you might ask yourself what industries may be most sensitive to human rights issues. As a manager in Canada, can you afford to ignore this issue?

gross domestic product The total dollar value of final goods and services produced within a nation's borders.

A Manager's Challenge   *Globalization*

Business in China

"How to deal with China as a big economic power—that is the largest issue . . . in the first half of the 21st century," according to Japan's former foreign minister, Yukihiko Ikeda. Many managers would agree—not just in Japan but also in Taiwan, most of Europe, Canada, Australia, and the United States.

The coming expansion of Chinese industry accompanies monumental changes in its economy and its business infrastructure brought about by its entry into the World Trade Organization in November 2001. The combination of expansion and admission to the world's formal trading system creates an unprecedented opening of what may prove to be the world's largest marketplace for nearly every kind of good and service—from cell phones and tractors to DVDs and blue jeans—and the world's largest source of low-cost manufactured goods. For China, "it is a no-going-back, transforming moment," according to Goldman Sachs's CEO, Henry Paulson. Ironically, that economic opportunity also strikes fear into the hearts of many managers.

It is not just fear of investing billions of dollars into China-based enterprises and failing, though that is a very real concern. Many managers, whether bankers, auto manufacturers, or consumer-goods marketers, already know full well the difficulties of finding and choosing the right Chinese business partners, of coping with a protectionist government bureaucracy, of negotiating myriad cultural differences, and of overcoming China's restrictions on building distribution chains and dealer networks. (These rules often leave foreign managers relying on the same distributors their competitors are using inside China.) Add to these risks those that underlie all international trade—language barriers, currency exchange rate fluctuations, changing consumer preferences—and the picture is already daunting.

Many foreign managers, however, also fear that China's own firms, some of which are still state supported, may reap the largest benefits from its steadily growing consumer demand. Despite a rising standard of living, China is still the world's largest low-wage economy, and it may quickly figure out how to produce many goods more cheaply at home rather than import them from abroad. For example, Taiwan-based computer maker Acer held the number-one position in China for years. However, over the last few years, Legend Holdings, domestic maker of Legend PCs, has substantially increased quality while beating Acer on price. The result is that Legend has replaced Acer in the number-one spot within China. As Legend continued to improve quality, it took its cost

Boasting more than 1.3 billion people, China presents a huge potential market, both in terms of the low-cost labour opportunities it affords and the amount of goods and services that can be sold there. For example, China's construction output in 2006 was valued at US$151 billion and is expected to grow to become the world's largest with an output of US$700 billion by 2015—a boom spawned by the liberalization of free trade, market reforms, and the country's admission into the World Trade Organization in 2001.

advantage and expanded internationally to compete with Acer and other computer manufacturers around the world. In 2004, Legend acquired IBM's PC Division and became the third-largest manufacturer in the world. In 2006, Lenovo Group (Legend's parent company) remained number one in China, with its 2005 revenue in excess of US$13 billion.

Chinese managers in firms less successful than Legend recognize that if inefficient domestic firms are forced to reform, thousands of Chinese workers will lose their jobs over the next several years. In the agricultural industry, where small farms are still the norm, employment losses may be particularly severe. Offsetting these losses, however, has been the injection of foreign investment to the tune of over US$16 billion for the 2008 Olympic Games. An estimated 434 000 new jobs are expected to be created to develop the Olympic sites. However, there is concern for the quick reduction of jobs immediately following the games. Thus, despite the fact that tariffs and distribution barriers are set to drop, Chinese managers may pressure government officials to resist full-scale foreign competition. The rapid changes in China are taking place within a single generation, and adjustments will be very difficult. ▶

Still, the market remains very attractive. China's technology imports alone were well in excess of US$18 billion in 2006, with an annual growth of 57.5 percent. By October 2006, China's trade surplus had already exceeded the 2005 record-setting surplus of US$102 billion, hitting US$133.6 billion. Its economy grew by 11.3 percent in 2005, and a further 10.5 percent in 2006, with the expectation for future growth to be around 10 percent per year. In all of this explosive activity, Canada's participation remains meagre, with exports to China comprising less than 1 percent of all that China imports annually.

For some, like Zhang Xin, who recently earned a computer science degree from one of the country's most prestigious universities and who will go to work for a cellular-phone-network firm in Beijing, it is a land where life is about to change dramatically. The shift in the social structure of China is creating new issues for the country. Canada has been outspoken in promoting human rights in China as the country emerges into an economic powerhouse. For Canadian managers, figuring out how to do business in China by pursuing business opportunities while maintaining Canadian social values has become a delicate balancing act.

Sources: Canada China Business Forum, "Canada Must Balance Values with Interests in China: CCBC President," December 2006, www.ccbc.com (accessed December 23, 2006); *China Daily*, "China's Economy to Grow 10.5 Percent in 2006," October 16, 2006, www.chinadaily.com (accessed December 23, 2006); *China Daily*, "Monthly Trade Surplus Hits New High," November 8, 2006 (accessed December 23, 2006); J. Lee, "A Look Inside both China and North America's Construction Industries," HomebuilderStocks.com, February 2006 (accessed December 23, 2006); B. Powell, "China's Great Step Forward," *Fortune*, September 17, 2001, pp. 128–142; L. P. Norton, "WTO Blows Tradewinds Between Taiwan and China," *Barron's Online*, interactive.wsj.com/pages/barrons.htm (accessed November 19, 2001); J. Brooke, "Tokyo Fears China May Put an End to 'Made in Japan,'" *New York Times*, November 20, 2001, p. A3; Legend Holdings, www.legendholdings.com (accessed December 23, 2006).

The Special Nature of the Global Environment

As we already mentioned, for many companies the global environment is not separate from the other general-environment forces. As we noted, when managers at Nokia think about the sociocultural external environment or the technological external environment, they generally have to think about it in a global context. So while for the sake of simplicity we have separated the sociocultural, technological, economic, and political-legal general-environment forces from global forces, the reality for many managers is that they are not all that separate. The other reality is that while it is possible and even necessary for many managers to analyze the global environment, as a practical matter they often have to break that analysis down into small pieces. Imagine if you were a manager at Nokia trying to do a global economic analysis across the 100-plus countries in which Nokia operates. As a practical matter this is just too unwieldy, which is why many managers focus their more detailed "global environmental analysis" on one country at a time. This is often called country analysis.[16]

As a manager, how do you assess a country and determine which countries are "good" to do business in and which ones are not? Let's take China, for example. Is it a good country in which to do business? During the early 1980s, China looked like a great place for foreign firms to do business. It had announced an economic liberalization plan and was borrowing billions of dollars to build up its economy and infrastructure. It was a nation rich in natural and human resources. However, China had many millions of people employed in state-owned and inefficient enterprises. These firms were naturally reluctant to see efficient, foreign firms come into the country, fearing that they would produce higher-quality goods at lower prices. Government officials were torn because they saw the need to modernize and yet recognized that they could not have thousands of state-owned firms fail and millions upon millions of workers unemployed. As China's government officials alternately tightened and loosened regulations, many managers saw the country as an economic and political yo-yo.

As the situation in China helps illustrate, most countries have both positive and negative aspects in terms of their eligibility for doing business. In the abstract, this means very little. The key to an effective analysis of the country is relating it to a specific industry or organization and its circumstances. Because industries and businesses operate differently and have different needs, specific policies or government actions pose unequal threats. For example, because KFC can source nearly all of its necessary raw materials within China, changes in import duties do not matter. However, Volkswagen must import many components for the cars it builds in China and therefore cares very much about changes in tariffs.

While managers would certainly examine the sociocultural, technological, economic, political, and legal environmental forces when analyzing a foreign country, there are two additional aspects of the external environment that are typically examined in the context of a foreign country, which are not usually part of a "domestic" general external environment analysis. These are the institutional and physical environmental forces. They are often included in analyses of foreign countries primarily because of the vast differences among countries in terms of institutions and physical characteristics.[17]

Institutional Forces. The institutional context involves the key organizations in the country. Although the strength and power of institutions can vary from one country to another, they constitute an important consideration in any environmental analysis.[18] Institutions to assess include the government, labour unions, religious institutions, and business institutions. These organizations are important to analyze in a foreign context because they can be (and often are) dramatically different from those "at home."

Physical Forces. Physical features such as infrastructure (e.g., roads, telecommunications, air links, etc.), arable land, deepwater harbours, mineral resources, forests, and climate can have a dramatic impact on existing and potential operations in a country and can be substantially different from those at home. For example, China has vast coal resources deep in its interior, but they are not an attractive business opportunity because of the poor rail and road infrastructure in those regions.

Pulling Together an Analysis of the General Environment

Even though we have tried to provide a number of examples as we moved through the various elements in the external general environment, it can seem a bit overwhelming. While an analysis of the external general environment is not simple, an integrated example may help to pull all of these concepts together. Let's take Coca-Cola as an example. Exhibit 4.3 provides a brief description of key aspects of the general environment, while Exhibit 4.4 pulls that description into a short summary.

While Exhibits 4.3 and 4.4 are by necessity brief and do not paint a full picture of Coca-Cola's external general environment, you can begin to see how a careful analysis of the general environment can provide useful information to managers in such activities as planning and decision making. For example, the sociocultural information may suggest that managers at Coca-Cola will need to increase their marketing efforts if they are to reach out to ethnic groups who come from countries and cultures in which drinking soft drinks, especially with carbonation, is not common. The information captured in the global dimension of the general external environment may suggest that managers at Coca-Cola should increase their efforts in emerging foreign markets with large populations, like China.

Exhibit 4.3   Description of the General Environment of Coca-Cola

Sociocultural

■ Demographics
Baby boomers drinking less soft drinks as they age.
North American population growth is slowing.

■ Values
Society is increasingly concerned about pollution and recycling.
Increasing focus on health and the negative aspects of caffeine, carbonation, and sugar.

Technological

■ New "canning" technology makes using recycled aluminum easier and cheaper.

■ Internet opens up a new means of running promotion contests and activities.

Economic

■ Slow economy reduces per-person consumption primarily due to fewer social occasions (parties) at which soft drinks might be served.

■ Nearing end of economic downturn and prospects of economic recovery.

■ Stricter liability for illness caused by beverage contamination.

Global

■ Gradual increase in acceptance of carbonated soft drinks in other countries.

■ Widely available electricity and increased ability to afford refrigerators in emerging countries and economies.

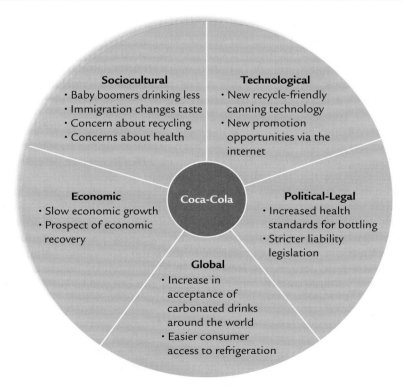

Exhibit 4.4 The General Environment of Coca-Cola.

Task Environment

The task environment is the most immediate external environment within which an organization survives and flourishes. It consists of competitors, customers, suppliers, strategic partners, labour, and regulators. Consequently, it typically has the largest influence on the organization, and the fit between the

Porter's Five Forces by
Michael Hitt

mymanagementlab

organization and its environment is critical for a manager to understand. Forces in the task environment exert a significant influence on the organization. The task environment plays a significant role in the competitive and strategic position of an organization.

Perhaps the most well-known model of analyzing a firm's task environment was developed by Michael Porter, a professor at the Harvard Business School.[19] This framework conceived of the task environment primarily in terms of five environment forces (Porter's Five Forces) that can significantly influence the performance of organizations in the same industry (see Exhibit 4.5). These forces are examined to analyze the industry. The original research was designed to explain why some industries were more profitable as a whole than others and why some companies within industries were more profitable than other firms in the same industry. In general, research has supported the validity of this model.[20] Three of the five forces (nature of rivalry, new entrants, and substitutes) primarily have to do with the "competitor" category of the task environment. While these three aspects of Porter's framework are related to this one category, we examine each of them separately to provide you with a reasonable presentation of the five forces framework. The other two forces in the framework—customers and suppliers—relate directly to the second and third aspects of the task environment that we listed at the beginning of this section. To these five forces of Porter's framework, we add and will discuss the dimensions of strategic partners, labour, and regulators.

The first aspect of the task environment, according to Porter, is competitors and the nature of competition among them. For example, in analyzing this aspect of the task environment you need to know how big and strong your competitors are relative to you. If you are small and weak relative to your competition, you may choose to stay out of their way and go after business that is less interesting to them. In your analysis of competitors, you also need to know their weaknesses. Those weaknesses may represent opportunities that you can exploit.

Apple Inc. took this view; while Apple had been in computers for nearly 30 years, it was a latecomer to the smart phone industry. Competing products such as Palm's Treo and Research In Motion's BlackBerry were dominating the market when Apple stepped in. But despite the convenience of sending and receiving email as well as phone use, Steve Jobs at Apple found the built-in keyboards and command buttons of the Treo and BlackBerry to be cumbersome. To Jobs, this represented a significant weakness in the smart phone industry and a great opportunity for Apple. So Apple developed a smart phone, called the iPhone, that would not have a built-in keyboard. Instead, the iPhone would have a full-body touch screen that would allow for limitless possibilities in arranging touch-sensitive buttons to suit the needs of the user as mobile applications evolve. On the day that Jobs unveiled the iPhone to the public the value of shares in Palm dropped nearly 6 percent, while Research In Motion fell by nearly 8 percent. In contrast, Apple's shares rose by more than 8 percent, buoyed by the optimism that the iPhone would further increase Apple's sales by US$1 billion.

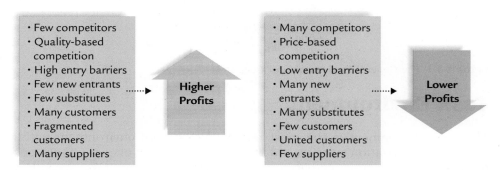

Exhibit 4.5 Profits and Industry Forces.

In addition to understanding your competitors, you also need to consider the nature of competition, or rivalry, in your industry. In general, competition can be based on price or on features of your products or services. Simplified, competitors can try to outdo each other by offering the lowest price to customers or by offering the best product or service. The more competition is based on price, generally the lower the profits. This is primarily because it is easier to lower prices than costs. As prices decline faster than costs, profit margins shrink.

The key for you as a manager is to clearly understand the nature of rivalry in your industry. It is worth noting that in very large industries, like automobile manufacturing, there are quite often different segments. This is important because the nature of rivalry can differ by segment. For example, in the subcompact segment of the auto industry, competition is largely based on price. However, in the luxury automobile segment, competition is primarily based on quality. Issues of safety, engineering, and handling—not price—dominate the ads for Mercedes, Lexus, BMW, and Infiniti. It is only when you have a thorough understanding of this competitive aspect of your industry that you are in a position to combine this information with other data and decide exactly how your company should compete.

New Entrants—Potential New Competitors

The second element of Porter's Five Forces is the extent to which it is easy or difficult for firms to enter the industry. All other elements being equal, new entrants will increase competition. Unless the size of the entire industry pie is expanding, the greater the number of new entrants, the thinner the slice of pie is for each participant. Increased competition (i.e., more entrants) usually leads to lower profit margins because customers have more choices. Unless it is difficult and expensive for customers to switch from one company to another (typically called **switching costs**), companies are forced to pass on greater perceived value to customers when there are more choices. This greater value often presents itself as a reduced price on products to the consumer. For example, if there are five grocery stores within a block of your house, and it costs you very little to go to one store over another, you are likely to go to the store that offers the best deal. As the stores compete for your business, they typically have to lower their profits to offer you a better deal. One grocer may offer shoppers discounts through the use of a loyalty card (the more you purchase at the grocer, the more points you collect, the greater the discount or rewards). This approach attempts to lock in customers by giving them an incentive to shop at one store instead of the others. At the same time, the other grocers may counter this strategy by using their own loyalty cards, or honouring the competitor's loyalty card. One example of this involves gas stations in Fredericton, where select Esso stations will accept Canadian Tire 'Money' at face value for the purchase of gasoline.

switching costs The amount of difficulty and expense involved when customers switch from one company to another.

The factors that keep new entrants out are termed barriers. **Entry barriers** are the obstacles that make it difficult for firms to get into a business. The bigger the barriers, the harder it is to get into the business; the harder it is to get in, the fewer new entrants. For example, the entry barriers in the restaurant business are quite low. Even in major cities, you can be in business for less than $100 000. However, if you wanted to break into the semiconductor business, it would cost you $4 to $6 billion just to build a fabrication plant. This doesn't even take into account the cost of designing or marketing your new chip. Generally, the fewer the new entrants, the fewer the total number of players in the industry. This typically means that each player gets a larger slice of the industry pie. It also means that customers likely have fewer choices, which usually translates into higher profits for the firms already in the industry.

entry barriers Obstacles that make it difficult for firms to get into a business.

standards and practices, primarily to protect the public's interests. Interest groups are nongovernment organizations (often referred to as NGOs) that are organized to serve the interests of their members. While they have no official regulator or enforcement power, they can exert tremendous influence on organizations.[24]

Regulatory agencies are of special note in an organization's external task environment because of the extent to which they can influence and in some cases dictate organization actions. For example, pharmaceutical companies like Merck cannot introduce new drugs for sale without the approval of Health Canada. The federal regulator also prescribes the standards that new drugs have to meet and the processes of testing and development they must go through to meet those standards. In this context, the regulator determines many of the rules of the competitive game among pharmaceutical companies. Regulatory agencies exist at all levels of government, each having an influence on a particular industry and organizations that operate within it. For example, architects and engineers working on new buildings in Winnipeg would have to comply with federal building codes like the National Fire Code of Canada while also adhering to provincial regulations like the Manitoba Building Code and municipal bylaws dictated by the city's long-range policy plan, Plan Winnipeg 2020.

While young managers may not have much experience with regulatory agencies, experienced managers know that municipal agencies regulating land use and property tax assessment, provincial agencies monitoring workplace health and safety and workers' compensation, and federal agencies enforcing the Goods and Services Tax (GST) and the import and export of goods are just a few of the regulators that exert direct and powerful influences on organizations. Managers must understand these regulators and incorporate their policies into their decisions and actions.

Interest groups such as Greenpeace, Amnesty International, the Humane Society, and Mothers Against Drunk Driving (MADD) are often as well recognized by the public as official government agencies. This is primarily because these NGOs have learned that influencing public opinion through the media can have as much influence on organizations as efforts to lobby lawmakers or organizational executives directly. For example, Greenpeace has refined the art of sending small inflatable boats out to try to block shipments they believe are harmful to the environment. They run the boats dangerously close to the cargo ships, creating footage that news stations find hard to resist and that ends up being seen by millions of people.[25]

Task Environment Summary

From this introduction and discussion, it should be fairly clear that these task-environment forces have a powerful influence on organizations and their performance. Task environments are important, but they do not solely determine success or failure. That is, you can position your organization within a task environment and industry so that your organization performs better than your competitors. We mention this because we do not want to create the impression that if you are in an "unattractive" industry (i.e., one in which the task-environment forces are generally aligned to result in lower profits), you are doomed to not do well. Most airlines have lost money because of the nature of the five forces in that industry; however, WestJet has made money. So organizations *can* survive and flourish even in hostile environments.

Exhibits 4.6 and 4.7 provide a summary of the task environment for WestJet, an airline founded in 1996 that is known for its low prices and very buoyant flight crew. To make a profit, it maintains a focus on low cost of operations.

NGOs such as Respect for Animals and the Humane Society apply pressure to governments to ban products that use methods for testing or production that they believe are cruel to animals. Often, NGOs will enlist the services of celebrities to convey the message to government and to sway public opinion. In March 2006, Paul McCartney and his now ex-wife Heather Mills took part in a photo shoot on the ice floes just off the coast of Newfoundland in protest of the annual seal hunt.

Exhibit 4.6 Description of the Task Environment of WestJet

Competitors

■ Rivalry
Primarily based on price, which generally hurts performance.
Many established and big players.

■ New Entrants
With $35 million anyone can start an airline; however, the frequency of past failure makes it less likely for new entrants.

■ Substitutes
As video conferencing gets better with faster connections, it may substitute for some face-to-face business meetings. It is less likely to substitute for leisure, tourist, or personal visit travel.

Customers

■ Business travellers who want convenience.

■ Leisure travellers who want low price.

Suppliers

■ Boeing supplies all of WestJet's planes.

■ Many jet fuel suppliers, such as Imperial Oil.

Strategic Partners

■ Currently not a part of any airline alliance.

■ Initial partner with satellite TV provider (it later bought the company).

Labour

■ Currently not represented by labour unions.

■ Ample supply of pilots and flight attendants due to significant downsizing in other airlines.

Regulators

■ Transport Canada dictates many standards and regulations.

■ Airport authorities determine access and cost of landing slots and gates at airports.

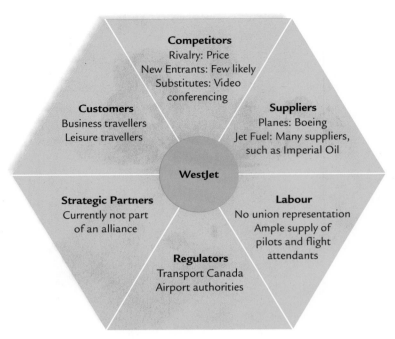

Exhibit 4.7 The Task Environment of WestJet.

The Internal Environment

Much of this text is about the internal organizational environment, and therefore this section should be considered a very brief introduction. Part of the reason that we introduce the internal organizational environment here is that much of the meaning derived from the external environment can only be found when translated into the organizational context. In addition, much of what should be done or can be done in response to the external environment is a function of the nature of the organization's internal environment.

Owners

Owners have legal rights to the assets of a company. The owner of a company could be an individual or a collection of shareholders. As an example of a diversified group of people and institutions owning a public company, consider that in 2006 Research In Motion had nearly 200 million shares outstanding.[26] The structure and nature of ownership is critical when assessing the relationship between the external and internal environment. For example, if a company is privately held, the owner(s) can determine the general objectives of the organization. The owner might determine that maximizing profits is not the ultimate objective and instead place a strong emphasis on giving back to the community. This is the case with Manitoba firm Peak of the Market.[27] Peak of the Market donates more than 1 million pounds of produce to local food banks and also works with charities and not-for-profit organizations. In 2005, Peak of the Market's president and CEO received the Manitoba Lieutenant Governor's Award for outstanding contribution to the community. This would be quite difficult for a public company like Research In Motion, where the owners include a diversified set of shareholders who, for the most part, want a return on their investment. This brings up the issue of what a company's responsibilities are to shareholders, communities, and others, which we will examine in depth in Chapter 6 when we look at managerial ethics and corporate social responsibility.

Board of Directors

Companies often have a board of directors or a set of individuals elected by shareholders of the company who represent the interests of the shareholders. As such the board of directors has the responsibility of overseeing the general management of the company, but it typically does not run the company. The board can consist of individuals from both inside and outside the company. While boards are not there to run the company, they are not there to simply rubber stamp whatever management wants to do. Boards should understand the nature of the business and its operations and review major decisions to ensure that the interests of shareholders are being protected. In the past several years, boards have come under greater scrutiny for not being as active or involved as perhaps they should have been.[28] This has been primarily driven by large corporate bankruptcies reported in the media like Enron, where it seems that the problems that caused the downfall of the firm could have and should have been known to board members far in advance of when they finally came out.

Employees

Employees are an additional force in the internal environment. To some extent we can use the two dimensions of the sociocultural external general-environment force—demographics and values—as a means of examining key aspects of employees. In terms of demographics, factors such as age and distribution of age, gender, and ethnic diversity can all be important to managers. For example, Dofasco executives commissioned a study in 2000 to better understand their workforce. They found that the average age of workers was 47 with 23 years' experience. This information made management realize that over the next several years, many of its skilled workers would retire. The importance of labour in its external task environment took on special significance when managers within Dofasco realized that the external labour pool was shrinking just at the time it would need to replace its aging internal workforce. In response to their findings, Dofasco managers revitalized an apprenticeship program to get young workers into leadership roles within the organization, reducing the development time frame of a good leader in the organization from ten to fifteen years down to five or six.[29]

Employee values are also important for managers to consider when trying to understand internal environmental forces. In Dofasco's case, employees have a strong value for job security and stability in the tasks they perform. In other words, employees want to know they have a secure job, and they want that job to be largely what it has been in the past. This creates some concern among Dofasco managers when they examine aspects of their general and task environments. In the general environment, economic downturn means that they have to lower their costs to remain profitable. This may require shifting workers from one area of the company to another or even laying some workers off. The shifting steel requirements of customers in its task environment means that Dofasco must be more flexible in the mix of existing products it produces and must be innovative in coming up with new products that meet customer needs. Both of these requirements may mean that employees have to be more flexible in what they do, which is in conflict with the values of many employees. As a consequence, this internal-environment force makes responding to external forces much more challenging.

Internal and external environmental forces do not necessarily need to be conflicting. They may be complementary. For example, in the case of WestJet, the fact that there was an increasing supply of airline employees in the external labour environment during its start-up and early operations was

The airline industry in general has been hit hard by profitability problems in recent years. But WestJet, Southwest, JetBlue, Ryanair and other start-up airlines have been successful, in part because of their corporate culture. WestJet employees, who are not unionized, take on different responsibilities when necessary to keep the company's planes in the air and its costs and fares low. Even the CEO of JetBlue, David Neeleman, shown in the photo, would help out where necessary.

significant in part because senior managers wanted to have a non-unionized employee base. Given that unions represent the majority of Canadian airline workers, an excess supply of airline employees (due to the increasingly difficult economic times for air carriers through the 1990s, particularly Canadian Airlines) made it easier for WestJet executives to achieve their internal employee objective.

Culture

Culture is such an important and complex topic that we devote all of Chapter 10 to the subject. As a consequence, we will be brief here about the nature of culture and its role in the internal environment. The culture of an organization is a learned set of assumptions, values, and beliefs that have proven successful enough to be taught to newcomers. The culture of an organization can have a significant impact on how the external environment is perceived and what are easy or difficult responses to it.

We can see an illustration of the interplay between internal and external environments if we return to the case of WestJet. For WestJet, an important element of its task environment is price competition. While it is not the only factor, the price of a plane ticket is significant for customers when they decide which carrier to fly with. If executives at WestJet want to attract customers by offering lower prices and at the same time want to make a profit, the company must have significantly lower costs than its competitors. One of the ways to achieve lower costs is by keeping planes in the air longer rather than having them sit unused. This is greatly facilitated by having shorter turnaround times at the gate. (WestJet targets a 30-minute turnaround, while the industry average is over an hour.) This requires pilots, flight attendants, baggage handlers, and cleaning crews to all pitch in and help. Having a culture in which all employees want to do what is necessary to turn the planes around quickly helps achieve the productivity objective, which in turn lowers costs and ultimately contributes to profits even when WestJet's prices are low.

As you can see from these examples, a practical application of environmental analysis requires keeping the dual elements of the external and internal environments in mind and relating the two. This is not an easy task and there is no magic formula for doing it well. Part of the trick, however, is having a systematic understanding of both external and internal organizational environments.

The first part of this chapter has provided a fairly comprehensive framework for understanding the external general and task environments of organizations as well as the internal environment.

Environmental Scanning and Response

Given all the elements of the environment that we have covered, it should be clear that effective managers need to scan the environment constantly to monitor changes. This chapter helps that process by pointing out the different critical areas to monitor. Trying to monitor everything would simply be overwhelming. Consequently, the first principle of effective environmental scanning is knowing *what* to scan. Again, the environmental forces we have covered constitute a reasonable framework for the "what" when it comes to environmental scanning.

Environmental Scanning by Michael Hitt

However, even if you know what to scan, you will still need a plan for *how* to scan. What do you look for to provide you with information on economic, socio-cultural, legal and political, and technological forces? Where do you look for information on competitors, new entrants, substitutes, customers, and suppliers? Business publications such as *Fortune, Canadian Business, The Economist,* the *Globe and Mail, National Post, Financial Times News,* and *The Wall Street Journal* are probably good starting points. However, for industry-specific information, you will likely need to turn to more specialized trade journals.

An important thing to keep in mind concerning public sources of information is that everyone has equal access to them. Consequently, as a manager you have two basic means of gaining advantage. First, you can work at being superior to others in analyzing publicly available information and anticipating how it relates to your job, company, and industry. Second, you can seek advantage by gaining information from nonpublic sources. This may be as simple as asking people you meet in your business (or even personal) travels about developments in any of the areas mentioned in this chapter. For example, an acquaintance may inform you of rising worker unrest in China that could affect your joint venture there long before word shows up in local or international newspapers. This advance information may help you anticipate and prepare for events rather than just react.

But whether you focus on public or private sources of information, effective scanning has a few basic components (see Exhibit 4.8):

- *Define:* The first step involves determining what type of information you should scan for and where and how you plan to acquire the information.

- *Recognize:* Next you must recognize information as relevant.

- *Analyze:* Once you have recognized information as being relevant, you need to analyze it and determine its implications.

- *Respond:* Finally, the full force of the information lies in its application to your job, company, or industry. Essentially, in this stage you are answering two key questions: What impact will this information have and how can I respond effectively?

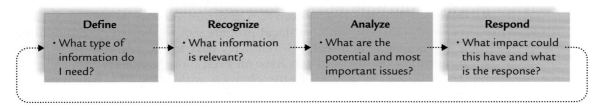

Exhibit 4.8 Environmental Scanning.

Define

Much of this chapter is devoted to addressing this first issue. The categories of the general-environment forces as well as those for the task environment constitute an effective framework for defining what information you need. As we mentioned, both public and private sources should be used in gaining information on all aspects of the external environment.

Recognize

In this digital age, information is not hard to come by. In fact, in many cases you are likely to be overloaded with information even if you use the environmental forces framework from this chapter. As a result, you will need to sift through and determine which information is relevant to your situation. This task is facilitated by asking how specific information you gather might relate to your organization. For example, as we mentioned earlier, even if you know that the economy is currently in a down cycle and is expected to recover within the next 12 months, this information may be more important to a housing construction firm than to a funeral home.

Analyze

Effective analysis has at least two separate but related aspects. First, a good environmental analysis needs to look for and examine the interactive effects of different environmental forces. Second, a good analysis needs to explore the specific implications that environmental forces in isolation and especially in combination likely have for your organization. Interactive effects can be of a complementary or even amplifying nature, or they can be of a mitigating nature. We will examine both through some examples.

To illustrate the importance of examining mitigating interactive effects between or among different environmental forces, let's assume you are a manager in a residential home construction company. During 2000–03, the Canadian economy experienced a slow growth period. Generally, this would cause people to buy fewer homes (new or used) as they worried about their job security and income. However, at the same time interest rates were at 40-year lows. This made owning a home more affordable. Overall, home purchases and mortgage refinancing hit near record highs and continued until the later part of 2006 with much of Canada experiencing unprecedented highs in housing prices. In this case, the low interest rates mitigated and nearly cancelled out what would have normally been a downturn in the economic cycle.

Environmental forces can also serve to reinforce or even amplify each other. For example, the ever-increasing number of retiring university professors in the coming years and the declining number of doctoral students has created a shortfall for nearly every Canadian university. The rise of technology, especially the internet, means that faculty can browse online career search services like chronicle.com and find out the general demand for skills and experience such as theirs and what the market rate is for those skills and experience. In combination, these two forces mean that faculty with valuable and scarce skills have become even harder for universities to hold on to. Add to these two forces the political-legal influence of the North American Free Trade Agreement, which makes it relatively easy for Canadian professors to enter the United States, and you have an even more powerful implication if you are a university administrator charged with attracting and retaining faculty at your school.

Respond

How can organizations respond effectively to changing environmental demands? As we explained at the outset, research as well as experience strongly suggests that responding effectively to changes is key to managerial success over time. As a result, it is impossible and impractical to confine our answer to how organizations can respond effectively to environmental changes to just this section. Still, we can frame many of the general responses in the following four categories: direct influence, strategic response, organizational agility, and information management.

Direct Influence. Managers and organizations are not simply at the mercy of environmental changes; they are not passive receptacles that must take whatever the environment dishes out. Managers do and should try to influence the political-legal process when they believe that existing or proposed legal requirements unjustly restrict their activities. For example, in 2004 McCain Foods filed a complaint with Canadian authorities that US producers of fast-rising pizza were "dumping" product into Canada (selling it below cost), which was hurting Canadian producers of fast-rising pizza. The Canadian Border Services Agency investigated and found that US producers were selling pizzas here nearly 40 percent cheaper than at home. Four Canadian importers and two producers (Kraft Foods and Palermo Villa Inc.) were part of the investigation. The findings resulted in a temporary duty being imposed on pizzas entering Canada from the United States. This example illustrates that pursuing political-legal pressure is a strategy that can be used by managers to alter their competitive environment, regardless of whether their allegations hold merit.

Strategic Response. But suppose it was found that the producers of the pizza were not dumping their product into the Canadian market. How might producers like McCain Foods respond? In this case they might choose among a number of strategic responses. They might use their own foreign operations or form a joint venture with a foreign company to take advantage of lower costs in that locale to produce the pizzas. Alternatively, they may employ a strategy that highlights the quality of the locally produced pizzas in comparison to the imported pizzas. Canadian firms smaller than McCain Foods may opt for a partnership with other Canadian producers to create economies of scale and reduce production costs. For example, the combined purchasing power of two producers might get them lower costs for materials by leveraging their high purchase volumes for pricing discounts. If the firms merged, they might lower costs by eliminating jobs in common support functions like human resources because they only need 50 percent more HR staff to support twice the number of employees.

Organizational Agility. To the extent that environmental change is frequent and unpredictable, managers might respond by creating a more flexible or agile organization. Managers can structure and design organizations for greater (or lesser) flexibility. For example, rules tend to work best when the environment is fairly stable and does not change much. People can follow the rules, and because the environment doesn't change much, following the rules is likely to produce results that fit the environment. On the other hand, in environments that change often, rules tend to not work well. They lead to rigidity and inflexibility. Having people share common values gives them greater flexibility to respond to the changing environment. Because the needs of customers are seen as changing too quickly, managers at WestJet stress the importance of customer service and responding to the needs of customers as they arise. Seventy percent of WestJet's ad budget is used to promote its customer service. And WestJet's corporate culture is deemed the most admired by 107 business executives polled across Canada.[30]

Information Management. If you look back to Exhibit 4.8, you'll notice that the process of environmental scanning is circular, not just linear. In other words, ultimately your response should feed back into your definition. Information management is a specific response that highlights this feedback loop. For example, if you are a manager in a residential-home construction business, you have learned with experience that interest rates are one of the most important forces in the general economic environment. As a consequence, you may develop means of capturing all the indicators and estimators of future interest rates. You may further refine this information management system by determining which indicators or estimators prove to be the most accurate in forecasting future interest rates over time. This information management response actually accelerates and enhances your ability to define, recognize, analyze, and respond to—or perhaps even anticipate—environmental changes.

Summary of Environmental Scanning and Response

By necessity, we have simplified and segmented the discussion of environmental analysis. However, the reality is that one of the greatest challenges you will face as a practising manager is that the environment does not come in nice, segmented pieces. Also, quite often a single event can have an impact across multiple segments of your general and task environment.

One example is the tragic events that took place on September 11, 2001. If you were in any travel-related industry, the potential implications were staggering. Reduction of air travel required cutbacks by airlines, hotels, and resorts. Another example is the 2003 outbreak of severe acute respiratory syndrome (SARS) that killed 800 people around the world, hitting Toronto particularly hard with 44 deaths. The World Health Organization released a travel advisory against nonessential travel to Toronto. The economic impact of the outbreak resulted in an estimated lost revenue of $39 million in April 2003 alone. All gathering places in the Toronto area, such as malls, restaurants, and theatres, had significantly diminished customer traffic. Conferences were cancelled or relocated to other cities and over 800 bus tours were cancelled.[31] Yet another example is the impact of Hurricane Katrina on New Orleans and the Gulf Coast region of the United States in late August 2005. The hurricane is the costliest natural disaster in United States history at an estimated US$150 billion. The cost of oil spiked around the world as available supply diminished because of inaccessible offshore oil rigs in the Gulf, major pipelines being shut down, and damaged refineries. The rising cost of fuel permeated all facets of the Canadian economy, from heating to shipping.

After events like the ones outlined above, managers evaluate and decide upon an appropriate response to the dramatic change in the environment. How will government reaction affect business? How will a manager's customer base be affected? Does this change the customer's propensity to use the products and services offered by the organization? How does a manager respond when her industry is directly affected by the events? How does a manager respond when in a nonrelated industry?

As you can see by just this small set of questions, the analytical task of environmental analysis for managers in situations like this is huge. On the one hand, we presented the task of environmental analysis in an artificially clean and segmented way, but as the three unexpected events above illustrate, actual problems do not present themselves in nice, neat packets. On the other hand, though, imagine trying to analyze the business environment implications without a segmented framework. The task would be overwhelming, to say the least.

Managerial Perspectives Revisited

PERSPECTIVE 1: THE ORGANIZATIONAL CONTEXT While the external environment is not a deterministic force and inevitably dooms an organization to a predetermined level of performance, it does present important demands, constraints, and opportunities. However, these are not absolutes; they have practical application only in the context of a given organization. For example, an increase in older citizens might create an opportunity for a new pharmaceutical company but present a constraint for a hospital with no room or money for expansion. Consequently, effective managers have to analyze the environment from the perspective of their organization. As we discussed, the ultimate practical value of environmental analysis lies in seeing the implications for your organization and determining the appropriate response. In the absence of the organizational context, external general or task environmental analysis is more of an academic exercise than a managerial activity.

PERSPECTIVE 2: THE HUMAN FACTOR Hopefully this chapter has helped illustrate how complex an assessment of the external environment can be while providing a few concepts and tools to make that easier. What we haven't stressed during the chapter but should stress here at the end is that it is rare for a manager to conduct a formal assessment of the external environment on his or her own. In fact, the more complex the company and the environment, the more likely it is that several people will be involved in the assessment based on their particular specialty or area of expertise. For example, as a manager, you may need your sales representatives to give you feedback on what their counterparts are doing out in the field. You may need to rely on people in your technology department to keep up with the technological developments of your competitors. You may need people in financial departments to gauge outside forces like interest rates, stock prices, economic outlook, and so on to provide you with information to make good decisions about where and how to spend money in response to these environmental forces. It is because of this that we want to highlight here that one of the distinguishing capabilities of a manager relative to external environment assessments is the ability to work with and through others to gather, analyze, integrate, and then act on the assessment.

PERSPECTIVE 3: MANAGING PARADOXES One fundamental challenge of environmental assessments is managing to focus on both the near and long terms. Individuals, teams, and companies often have to make changes based on assessments of the current external environment. The present cannot be ignored. But the current economic conditions or state of technology as well as other important aspects of the environment are not likely to remain stable. Consequently, to be effective in assessing the environment and then making strategic, planning, and other decisions, as a manager you will need to be able to manage the paradox of simultaneously considering both the present and the future environmental conditions.

Another potential paradox associated with effective environmental analysis is that of separating and integrating at the same time. On the one hand, you must segment and divide aspects of the environment to analyze and understand the complexities involved. This is precisely why we have divided the external environment into the general and task categories and have further divided each of these into subcategories. However, an environmental analysis of isolated bits and pieces is incomplete. You must also integrate the results of the separate analyses of the various pieces. Effective environmental analysis is not about doing just one or the other, it is about doing both. As stated in this chapter's introduction, the integration of the analyses should help us identify the environmental opportunities and threats that exist. In addition, even though we use the term "environmental analysis," effective management requires both analysis and action. In fact, the practical relevance of the analysis only comes to life with action—organizational response. The actions should be based on the environmental opportunities and threats identified. As a result, as a manager you will need the ability to both think and do; to both conduct an effective environmental analysis and act and react in ways that help you, your subordinates, and the company deal with the external environment.

 PERSPECTIVE 4: ENTREPRENEURIAL MINDSET A critical component of an entrepreneurial mindset is identifying opportunities. Opportunities are most likely to exist in an organization's external environment. Thus, analyzing the external environment is necessary to identify opportunities that the organization can exploit. An organization could identify opportunities afforded by changes in government regulations by analyzing the political-legal environment, for example.

Analyzing changing demographic trends can also provide opportunities. For instance, the aging baby-boomer population in Canada presents many new opportunities for businesses catering to the needs of retiring Canadians. Assessing the environment can broaden managers' knowledge and understanding and allow them to take advantage of entrepreneurial opportunities like this. It also signifies a commitment to acquire new knowledge and skills. Although new knowledge can be tapped from within an organization, the external environment is also an important source. Strategic partnerships can afford access to new knowledge as well.

Concluding Comments

At this point you can see that while some people might think that the task of external environment analysis is the job of specialized analysts, it is not. It is true that in large organizations entire departments may be dedicated to analyzing the economic or political forces in the environment. Although reports from others inside or outside the company can be valuable, you have to be personally aware of and understand these forces. Without such personal awareness and understanding of critical environmental forces, you might not recognize valuable information even if you had it in your hands. As a manager, you must accurately and systematically identify critical factors in the external environment and understand cause-and-effect relationships. Only then will you be able to anticipate, rather than simply react to, external environmental challenges.

Certainly, effective analysis of all the various forces within the industry, domestic, and international environments is a big challenge. However, two even larger challenges remain. The first is to begin to see links among the various forces within an environment. For example, it is one thing to do a good analysis of the substitution and customer forces within the industry environment; it is quite another to see that the lack of substitutes and the fragmented nature of customers combine to offer an unprecedented opportunity for growth. Only in drawing the connections can you plan effectively and exploit opportunities for growth.

The second major challenge is seeing the connections between a particular business and its industry, domestic, and international environments. Seeing relationships among them is a quality of a truly gifted manager. Think of it in terms of the interactions and relationships found in the natural environment. Finding the right conditions to favour growth and survival is as important to businesses as it is to flowers or trees. Organizations thrive or perish according to their fit with their environments.

Meeting the basic challenge of understanding and analyzing individual environmental forces is a significant accomplishment for a manager. Meeting the challenge of seeing relationships among different forces within an environment is exciting. Meeting the challenge of seeing relationships among different environments is a never-ending challenge—one that makes management an exciting and invigorating profession.

Key Terms

demographics   (p. 121)
entry barriers   (p. 135)
external environment   (p. 121)
general environment   (p. 121)
gross domestic product   (p. 129)
internal environment   (p. 121)

process technological
   changes   (p. 124)
product technological
   changes   (p. 123)
societal values   (p. 122)
strategic partners   (p.136)

structural change   (p. 127)
substitutes   (p. 136)
switching costs   (p. 135)
task environment   (p. 121)

Test Your Comprehension

1. Define the external environment.

2. What are key differences between the external, general, and task environments?

3. List four examples of important demographics.

4. Why are societal values important to an assessment of the general external environment?

5. What are the key differences between product and process technological changes?

6. Why is an awareness of both types of change critical to an assessment of the technological environment?

7. Why are economic cycles important to consider in addition to current economic conditions?

8. How are structural economic changes different from economic cycles?

9. Why is government spending important to consider when analyzing the legal and political environment?

10. What are the key features of a country's physical environment?

11. Name three key institutions that should be included in an environmental analysis.

12. What are Porter's Five Forces?

13. If the nature of competition or rivalry in an industry is primarily based on price, do profit margins in that industry tend to increase or decrease?

14. What are entry barriers and why do they matter in an analysis of the industry environment?

15. If there are few new entrants to an industry and if entry barriers are large, do profit margins in that industry tend to increase or decrease?

16. What are switching costs?

17. What is the difference between a substitute and a competing product?

18. What are the four steps to effective environmental scanning?

19. Why is there a feedback loop between Respond and Define in the environmental scanning and response model?

Apply Your Understanding

1. What key environmental changes do you think will increasingly force managers to be proficient at conducting environmental analyses?

2. Are there industries that will be more immune to changes in the global environment and as a consequence will be influenced primarily by their domestic external environment? Name at least two and explain why.

3. What are the most difficult environmental analysis skills to develop? What are some possible means of ensuring that you have these valuable skills?

4. Debate the following statement: Computers and news media have made international environmental analysis simpler.

5. Pick a country and go to the library or the internet to find some information about its resources, government, political and legal systems, and physical infrastructure. What type of business would do well in that country? Why?

Practise Your Capabilities

You are the purchasing manager of a specialty retail company that has just over 20 stores in large shopping malls across Canada. These stores specialize in equipment and clothing targeted at "boarders," that is, guys and girls who surf, skateboard, snowboard, and/or wakeboard. Since the 2006 Winter Olympics increased the number of snowboarding events to six, you have seen a steady increase in the popularity of boarding culture, resulting in an increase in customer traffic to your stores.

The president of the company wants you to come up with an initial analysis and recommendation for the coming year regarding whether the company should anticipate an increase or decrease in sales. Last year sales of equipment declined by 9 percent while sales of clothing dropped by 5 percent. In looking toward the future, you decide to do a quick STEP analysis.

Sociocultural

First, you decide you need some information on the demographics of your target customer (i.e., boys and secondarily girls ages 14–24). Is this group growing or shrinking in Canada? Someone mentioned that www.statcan.ca might be a website that could help you find this information.

Second, you determine that you also need to try to get a sense of the values of the boarding culture and how strongly they are supported in your target customer population. Many of your current customers talk about the freedom that boarding represents. The icon of skateboarding is Tony Hawk, so you decide to check out how well his video game is selling. For wakeboards, it's pros like Sunni-Anne Ball and Chad Sharpe that you need to check out. For snowboarding, it's Jasey-Jay Anderson, Matt Morrison, Mercedes Nicoll, and Maëlle Ricker.

Technology

While you don't feel that technology is affecting your clothing lines that much, you wonder if it might be a factor for equipment. Your top equipment brands are Burton for snowboards, Tony Hawk and Hollywood for skateboards, and Neptune and Connelly for wakeboards. So you go to their websites to see if any new technological changes are on the horizon.

Economic

You also want to get a sense of what is happening with the economy. Unemployment, inflation, exchange rates, and consumer spending seem like important facts to research first.

Political-Legal

While no political or legal issues immediately jump to mind as potentially having a big impact on your business, you wonder about insurance laws affecting skateboarding parks or whether helmets or some sort of headgear might be required in the future for snowboarding or wakeboarding. You've seen a few people get rather nasty cuts on their heads when they crashed and the board they were riding hit them, and they required stitches.

1. After gathering information in each of these four areas, which ones seem to point in a positive direction for your business? Which ones seem to point in a negative direction?

2. Currently, your sales are split about 50/50 between equipment and clothing. Does anything in your analysis indicate that this should be changed in the future?

3. What is your overall recommendation? Should purchases increase?

4. On a broader note, should the company think about increasing or decreasing the number of stores it has?

Part Five

Managing Ethics, Social Responsibility, and Diversity

Chapter 5

Conducting Business Ethically and Responsibly

After reading this chapter, you should be able to:

1 Explain how individuals develop their personal *codes of ethics* and why ethics are important in the workplace.

2 Distinguish *corporate social responsibility* from *ethics*, identify *organizational stakeholders*, and characterize social consciousness today.

3 Show how the concept of social responsibility applies both to environmental issues and to a firm's relationships with customers, employees, and investors.

4 Identify four general *approaches to social responsibility* and describe the four steps a firm must take to implement a *social responsibility program*.

5 Explain how issues of social responsibility and ethics affect small businesses.

Taken from *Business*, Seventh Canadian Edition, by Ricky W. Griffin, Ronald J. Ebert, Frederick A. Starke, and Melanie D. Lang.

What Really Happened at Livent?

Livent Inc. was founded by Garth Drabinsky and Myron Gottlieb. It was a live theatre company with outlets in Toronto, Vancouver, Chicago, and New York. In 1998, questions were raised about Livent's finances by new owners who had bought in to the company. Shortly thereafter, Drabinsky and Gottlieb were fired. They were eventually charged with producing false financial statements to make the company look more profitable than it actually was. The fraud allegedly cost investors and creditors $500 million. Drabinsky and Gottlieb denied any wrongdoing and claimed that the financial manipulations were carried out by subordinates without their knowledge. After a long delay, their trial finally started in 2008.

During the trial, prosecutors called several witnesses who admitted that they had participated in the financial manipulations, but they said that they had done so at the direction of Drabinsky and Gottlieb. Some of their charges were as follows:

- A computer technician said he was asked by the accounting controller to modify accounting software so that changes could be made without auditors detecting them. He said that the vice-president, Gordon Eckstein, told him to carry out the controller's instructions.

- Gordon Eckstein said that he was told by Drabinsky and Gottlieb to carry out the fraud (Eckstein had previously pled guilty).

- John Beer, a private investigator who was hired by KPMG's forensic unit to look into allegations of accounting manipulations, said he found a document in Drabinsky's briefcase that described $21 million of expenses that were omitted from one year's financial statements and "rolled" to the next year.

- Gary Gill, another investigator for KPMG, also testified that he saw an internal company document that contained information about financial manipulations.

- Chris Craib, Livent's accounting controller, testified that he had prepared the document and had given it to Drabinsky and Gottlieb, and that he had attended a meeting where accounting manipulations were openly discussed.

- Another accounting employee said he was amazed to learn of a plan to reclassify $10 million of expenses as fixed assets.

- Chief financial officer Maria Messina (who had formerly worked at KPMG) said she didn't tell her former colleagues about the fraud because she wanted to try to cope with it in-house (she finally exposed the fraud after new investors had taken over managing the company).

- Former controller Grant Malcolm testified that he spent all of his time recording fraudulent manipulations to the company's books. He said he routinely deleted expenses for shows, or moved them to future periods, or transferred them to different shows. He said he prepared a memo for Drabinsky that summarized all the improperly transferred production costs. He also said that two advertising agencies helped with the fraud by moving their billings from an earlier year to a later year. That allowed profit to be higher in the earlier year.

Drabinsky and Gottlieb's defence attorneys repeatedly attacked the credibility of the witnesses and argued that accounting staff had circumvented the accounting controls that Drabinsky had put in place. The defence presented no witnesses, and Drabinsky and Gottlieb did not testify.

In 2009, Drabinsky and Gottlieb were found guilty of fraud and forgery. Drabinsky was sentenced to seven years in jail and Gottlieb to six years. In a related case, the Institute of Chartered Accountants of Ontario found three senior Deloitte & Touche LLP auditors guilty of making errors during an audit of Livent's financial statements. The three were fined $100 000 each.

Drabinsky and Gottlieb are not the only executives who have been charged with wrongdoing in the recent past. In 2005, Bernie Ebbers, the CEO of WorldCom, was found guilty of nine charges of securities fraud and filing false documents. He was sentenced to 25 years in prison. In 2006, Ken Lay, the CEO of Enron, was convicted of conspiracy and securities fraud, but he died before he was sentenced. In 2007, Conrad Black, CEO of Hollinger International, was convicted of fraud and obstruction of justice and was sentenced to six and a half years in prison. In December 2008, Bernie Madoff pleaded guilty to swindling investors in a $50 billion fraud. He is likely to spend the rest of his life in prison. ◆

How will this help me?

There is a growing dilemma in the business world today involving the economic imperatives (real or imagined) facing managers and the pressure to function as good citizens. By understanding the material in this chapter, you'll be better able to assess the ethical and social responsibility issues that you will face as an employee and as a boss or business owner. It will also help you understand the ethical and social responsibility actions of businesses you deal with as a consumer and as an investor.

In this chapter, we'll look at ethics and social responsibility—what they mean and how they apply to a firm's relationships with customers, employees, and investors. Along the way, we look at some general approaches to social responsibility, the steps businesses must take to implement social responsibility programs, and how issues of social responsibility and ethics affect small businesses. But first, we begin this chapter by discussing ethics in the workplace—individual, business, and managerial.

Ethics in the Workplace

1 | Explain how individuals develop their personal *codes of ethics* and why ethics are important in the workplace.

ethics Individual standards or moral values regarding what is right and wrong or good and bad.

ethical behaviour Behaviour that conforms to individual beliefs and social norms about what is right and good.

unethical behaviour Behaviour that individual beliefs and social norms define as wrong and bad.

business ethics Ethical or unethical behaviour by a manager or employee of an organization.

Ethics are beliefs about what is right and wrong or good and bad. An individual's personal values and morals and the social context in which they occur determine whether a particular behaviour is perceived as ethical or unethical. **Ethical behaviour** is behaviour that conforms to individual beliefs and social norms about what is right and good. **Unethical behaviour** is behaviour that individual beliefs and social norms define as wrong and bad. **Business ethics** refers to ethical or unethical behaviour by a manager or employee of an organization.

Individual Ethics

Because ethics are based on both individual beliefs and social concepts, they vary from person to person, from situation to situation, and from culture to culture. Social standards are broad enough to support differences in beliefs. Without violating these general standards, therefore, people may develop personal codes of ethics reflecting a wide range of attitudes and beliefs.

Thus ethical and unethical behaviour is determined partly by the individual and partly by culture. Virtually everyone would agree that if you see someone drop a $20 bill in a store, it would be ethical to return it to the owner. But there will be less agreement if you find $20 and don't know who dropped it. Should you turn it in to the lost-and-found department? Or, since the rightful owner isn't likely to claim it, can you just keep it? The real problem is that each person has a different standard of ethics.

The difference between unethical and illegal behaviour can complicate matters. When CIBC World Markets sued six former employees after they left the company and started a new rival firm, Genuity Capital Markets, CIBC was making a claim of illegal behaviour. But the defendants argued that they had done nothing illegal, or unethical for that matter, because the employees they took with them had already decided to leave CIBC.[1] In another case, damages were awarded to RBC Dominion Securities after one of its branch managers and his subordinates abruptly left as a group to work for a competitor.[2]

Because every situation has some degree of ambiguity, societies may adopt formal laws that reflect prevailing ethical standards or social norms. For example, because most people regard theft as unethical, we have laws against such behaviour and ways of punishing those who steal. We try to make unambiguous laws, but real-world situations can often be interpreted in different ways, and it isn't always easy to apply statutory standards to real-life behaviour. The epidemic of financial scandals in recent years shows how willing people can be to take advantage of potentially ambiguous situations.

In some cultures, ethically ambiguous practices are hallmarks of business activity. Brazilians, for example, apply the philosophy of *jeitinho*—meaning "to find a way"—by using personal connections, bending the rules, or making a "contribution."[3] Suppose you needed to get an official document. You might start out determined to take all the proper bureaucratic steps to get it. However, when you find yourself in a complex maze of rules and regulations and think you'll never get your document, you're likely to resort to *jeitinho* to get the job done.

Individual Values and Codes

How should we deal with business behaviour that we regard as unethical—especially when it's legally ambiguous? We must start with the individuals in a business—its managers, employees, agents, and other legal representatives. Each of these people's personal code of ethics is determined by a combination of factors. We start to form ethical standards as children in response to our perceptions of the behaviour of parents and other adults. Soon we enter school, where peers influence us, and as we grow into adulthood, experience shapes our lives and contributes to our ethical beliefs and our behaviour. We also develop values and morals that contribute to ethical standards. If you put financial gain at the top of your priority list, you may develop a code of ethics that supports the pursuit of material comfort. If you set family and friends as a priority, you'll no doubt adopt different standards.

Because ethics are both personally and culturally defined, differences of opinion can arise as to what is ethical or unethical. For example, many people who would never think of taking a candy bar from a grocery store routinely take home pens and pads of paper from their offices. Other people who view themselves as law-abiding citizens have no qualms about using radar detectors to avoid speeding tickets. In each of the situations, people will choose different sides of the issue and argue that their actions are ethical.

Managerial Ethics

Managerial ethics are the standards of behaviour that guide managers in their work.[4] Although ethics can affect managerial work in any number of ways, it's helpful to classify behaviour in terms of three broad categories.

managerial ethics Standards of behaviour that guide individual managers in their work.

Behaviour Toward Employees

This category covers such matters as hiring and firing, wages and working conditions, privacy, and respect. Ethical and legal guidelines suggest that hiring and firing decisions should be based solely on the ability to perform a job. A manager who discriminates against any ethnic minority in hiring exhibits both unethical and illegal behaviour. But what about the manager who hires a friend or relative when someone else might be more qualified? Such decisions may not be illegal, but in Canada they may be objectionable on ethical grounds (but not necessarily in some other countries).

Wages and working conditions, though regulated by law, are also areas for controversy. Consider a manager who pays a worker less than what is deserved because the manager knows that the employee can't afford to quit. While some people will see the behaviour as unethical, others will see it as simply smart business. It is much easier to judge the behaviour of Enron managers, who encouraged employees to invest retirement funds in Enron stock and then, when financial problems began to surface, refused to permit employees to sell the stock (even though top officials of the company were allowed to sell their stock).

Behaviour Toward the Organization

Ethical issues also arise from employee behaviour toward employers, especially in such areas as conflict of interest, confidentiality, and honesty. A **conflict of interest** occurs when an activity benefits an individual at the expense of the employer. Most companies have policies that forbid buyers from accepting gifts from suppliers. Businesses in highly competitive industries—software or fashion apparel, for example—have safeguards against designers selling company secrets to competitors. Relatively common problems in the general area of honesty include such behaviour as stealing supplies, padding expense accounts, and using a business phone to make personal long-distance calls. Most employees are honest, but most organizations are nevertheless vigilant.

Behaviour Toward Other Economic Agents

Ethics also come into play in the relationship between the firm and its so-called primary agents of interest—mainly customers, competitors, stockholders, suppliers, dealers, and unions. In dealing with such agents, there is room for ethical ambiguity in just about every activity—advertising, financial disclosure, ordering and purchasing, bargaining and negotiation, and other business relationships.

For example, businesses in the pharmaceuticals industry are under criticism because of the rising prices of drugs. They argue that high prices cover the costs of research and development programs to develop new drugs. The solution to such problems seems obvious: Find the right balance between reasonable pricing and *price gouging* (responding to increased demand with steep price increases). But like so many questions involving ethics, there are significant differences of opinion about the proper balance.[5]

Another area of concern is competitive espionage. In 2004, Air Canada sued WestJet for $220 million, claiming that a WestJet executive had accessed Air Canada's confidential reservations database, which contained important competitive information that would be beneficial to WestJet.[6] WestJet eventually admitted its actions were unethical and paid Air Canada $5 million to cover expenses Air Canada incurred while investigating the unauthorized accessing of its website. WestJet also agreed to contribute $10 million to children's charities.

Most people would probably see the WestJet incident as a fairly clear case of unethical behaviour. But what if a manager is given confidential information by an unhappy former employee of a competitor who wants to get revenge on his former employer? Is it acceptable in that case for the manager to use the information? Some people would say it's still unethical, but others might feel that since the manager didn't go looking for the information, it's acceptable to use it.[7]

Difficulties also arise because business practices vary globally. In many countries, bribes are a normal part of doing business, but in Canada and the United States, bribes are seen as clearly unethical and illegal. In 2006, the Gemological Institute of America (GIA) fired several employees after they had accepted bribes from diamond dealers. In return for the bribes, the GIA

The intense competition between Air Canada and WestJet motivated a WestJet executive to access Air Canada's confidential reservations database in the hope of gaining a competitive edge for WestJet.

employees rated the dealers' diamonds higher than they should have been, and this allowed the dealers to sell them for a much higher price.[8]

Assessing Ethical Behaviour

Given the difficulties of distinguishing ethical and unethical behaviour, how can we go about deciding whether a particular action or decision is ethical?[9] A three-step model can be used for applying ethical judgments to situations that may arise during the course of business activities:

1. Gather the relevant factual information.

2. Determine the most appropriate moral values.

3. Make an ethical judgment based on the rightness or wrongness of the proposed activity or policy.

Let's see how this process might work for a common dilemma faced by managers involving their expense accounts. Companies routinely provide managers with accounts to cover work-related expenses when they are travelling on company business and/or entertaining clients for business purposes. Common examples of such expenses include hotel bills, meals, rental cars, and so forth. Employees are expected to claim only those expenses that are accurate and work related. If a manager takes a client to dinner while travelling on business and spends $100, submitting a receipt for that dinner and expecting to be reimbursed for $100 is clearly appropriate. Suppose, however, that the manager also has a $100 dinner the next night in that same city with a good friend for purely social purposes. Submitting that receipt for full reimbursement would be seen by most managers as unethical (although a few might rationalize that it is acceptable because they are underpaid and this is a way to increase their pay).

Other principles that come into play in a case like this include various ethical norms. Consider four such norms and the issues that they raise:

Utility: Does the act optimize what is best for those who are affected by it?

Rights: Does it respect the rights of the individuals involved?

Justice: Is it consistent with what we regard as fair?

Caring: Is it consistent with people's responsibilities to each other?

Figure 5.1 incorporates the consideration of these ethical norms.

Now, let's return to the case of the inflated expense account. The utility norm would acknowledge that the manager benefits from padding an expense account, but others (co-workers and owners) do not. Likewise, most experts would agree that this behaviour does not respect the rights of others. Moreover, it is clearly unfair and compromises the manager's responsibilities to others. This particular act, then, appears to be clearly unethical.

Figure 5.1 also provides mechanisms for considering unique circumstances—those that apply only in certain limited situations. Suppose, for example, that the manager loses the receipt for the legitimate dinner but retains the receipt for the social dinner. Some people will argue that it is acceptable to submit the illegitimate receipt because the manager is only doing so to be reimbursed for what he or she is entitled to. Others, however, will argue that submitting the other receipt is wrong under any circumstances. Changes in the situation can obviously make issues more or less clear-cut.

When judging the ethics of a given behaviour, one of the simplest tests to use is the so-called "newspaper test." This means asking yourself this question:

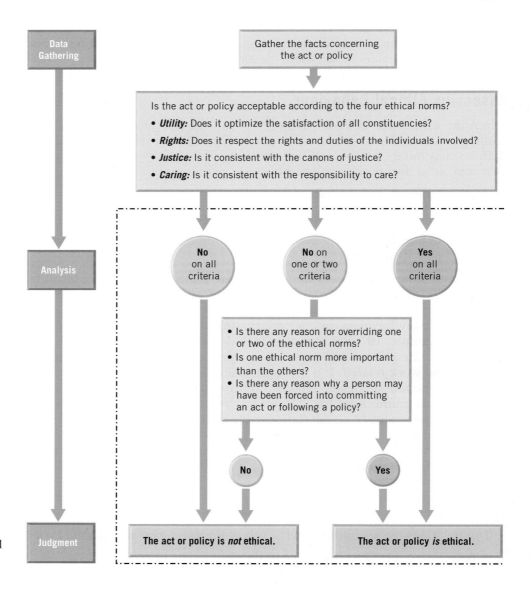

Figure 5.1 Expanded model of ethical judgment making.

If you were to make a decision on an ethical issue and then read about it on the front page of tomorrow's paper, how would you feel? If you would feel embarrassed, you are very likely violating ethical standards and should make a different decision.

Company Practices and Business Ethics

As unethical and even illegal behaviour by both managers and employees plagues more and more companies, many firms have taken steps to encourage ethical behaviour in the workplace. Many, for example, establish codes of conduct and develop clear ethical positions on how the firm and its employees will conduct its business.

Technological developments are creating all sorts of new ethical problems—cloning, satellite reconnaissance, email snooping, and bioengineered foods, to name just a few. For every innovation that promises convenience or safety, there seems to be a related ethical issue. The internet and email, for example, are certainly convenient and efficient, but they present business people with a variety of ethics-related problems. In one sense, electronic communications are merely the modern version of traditional forms of communication, such as regular mail or the telephone. However, they make it possible to run classic swindles, such as Ponzi or pyramid schemes, with greater efficiency than ever before. Federal law-enforcement personnel routinely surf the web looking for illegal or unethical practices, often finding hundreds of questionable sites in a typical sting. Employers are also using email to test employee loyalty, as in the case of the manager who sent false emails to his workers, pretending to be a recruiter from a competing firm. Any employees who responded were skipped for promotion.

If a company truly wishes to promote ethical behaviour on the part of its employees, the single most effective step a company can take is to demonstrate top management commitment to high ethical standards. A now-classic illustration of the power of ethical commitment involved Johnson & Johnson (J&J). In 1982, it was discovered that capsules of the company's Tylenol pain reliever had been laced with cyanide. Managers at J&J quickly recalled all Tylenol bottles still on retailers' shelves and then went public with candid information throughout the crisis. J&J's ethical choices proved to be a crucial factor in its campaign to rescue its product. Both the firm and the brand bounced back much more quickly than anyone had thought possible. When food products made by Maple Leaf Foods were found to be contaminated with listeria, the company took quick action to manage the crisis (see Chapter 1 for more details).[10]

Two of the most common approaches to formalizing commitment are adopting written codes and instituting ethics programs.

Adopting Written Codes

Many companies have adopted written **codes of ethics** that formally acknowledge their intent to do business in an ethical manner. Most codes of ethics are designed to perform one or more of the following functions:

code of ethics Formal, written acknowledgment of a company's intent to do business in an ethical manner.

- They may increase public confidence in a firm or its industry.

- They may help stem the tide of government regulation—that is, aid in self-regulation.

- They may improve internal operations by providing consistent standards of both ethical and legal conduct.

- They can help managers respond to problems that arise as a result of unethical or illegal behaviour.

Our Purpose
To support people in achieving the benefit of wilderness-oriented recreation.

Our **purpose** is what we resolve to do.

Our Vision
Mountain Equipment Co-op is an innovative, thriving co-operative that inspires excellence in products and services, passion for wilderness experiences, leadership for a just world, and action for a healthy planet.

Our **vision** is our picture of the future and outlines where we want to go.

Our Mission
Mountain Equipment Co-op provides quality products and services for self-propelled wilderness-oriented recreation, such as hiking and mountaineering, at the lowest reasonable price in an informative, respectful manner. We are a member-owned co-operative striving for social and environmental leadership.

Our **mission** tells us what business we are in, who we serve, and how. It represents the fundamental reason for MEC's existence.

Our Values
We conduct ourselves ethically and with integrity. We show respect for others in our words and actions. We act in the spirit of community and co-operation. We respect and protect our natural environment. We strive for personal growth, continual learning, and adventure.

Our **values** influence our conduct both collectively as an organization, and individually as employees, directors and members of our community. We strive to have our actions reflect these values, demonstrate personal accountability, and be publicly defensible.

Figure 5.2 Mountain Equipment Co-op's statements of purpose, vision, mission, and values make up their code of ethics.

Figure 5.2 shows the code of ethics adopted by Mountain Equipment Co-op.

Figure 5.3 illustrates the central role that corporate ethics and values should play in corporate policy. Although strategies and practices can change frequently and objectives can change occasionally, an organization's core principles and values should remain steadfast.

Two-thirds of Canada's largest corporations have codes of ethics (90 percent of large U.S. firms do). More and more regulatory and professional associations in Canada are recommending that corporations adopt codes of ethics. The Canada Deposit Insurance Corp., for example, requires that all deposit-taking institutions have a code of conduct that is periodically reviewed and ratified by the board of directors. The Canadian Competition Bureau, the Canadian Institute of Chartered Accountants, and the Ontario Human Rights Commission are all pushing for the adoption of codes of ethics by corporations.[11] Many Canadian and U.S. firms are also adding a position called ethics director or ethics officer.

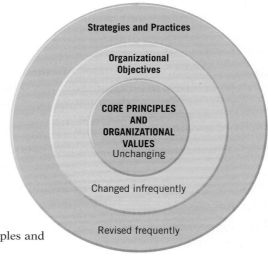

Figure 5.3 Core principles and organizational values.

Instituting Ethics Programs

Can business ethics be "taught," either in the workplace or in schools? While business schools have become important players in the debate about ethics education, most analysts agree that companies must take the chief responsibility for educating employees. In fact, more and more firms are doing so. Imperial Oil, for example, conducts workshops that emphasize ethical concerns for employees. The purpose of these workshops is to help employees put Imperial's ethics statement into practice.

But some firms struggle with ethical dilemmas, particularly in international business situations. A few years ago, a scathing report on Nike's manufacturing partners in Asia called their practices just short of slave labour. Nike responded to the report by acknowledging its mistakes and made a commitment to improve working conditions. Nike plants in Asia, for example, no longer force employees to work on Sundays. Wages have been increased, and supervisors are forbidden to use the extreme punishments that were formerly doled out.[12]

Social Responsibility

Corporate social responsibility (CSR) refers to the way in which a business tries to balance its commitments to **organizational stakeholders**—those groups, individuals, and organizations that are directly affected by the practices of an organization and that therefore have a stake in its performance.[13] Galen Weston, the executive chair of Loblaw Companies Ltd., says that companies that want to be successful need to embrace CSR as part of their core strategy. It can no longer simply be an "add-on." In fact, corporate boards of directors are increasingly considering CSR issues in addition to financial and operational issues.[14]

Everyone seems to accept the idea that attention must be paid to organizational stakeholders. But which ones should be given the most attention? One view, often called *managerial capitalism*, is that a company's only responsibility is to make as much money as possible for its shareholders, as long as it doesn't break any laws. In recent years, this view has been strongly challenged by an opposing view that says that companies must be responsible to a variety of stakeholders, including *customers, employees, investors, suppliers*, and the *local communities* in which they do business.

Most companies that strive to be responsible to their stakeholders concentrate on the five groups shown in Figure 5.4. They may also select other

> **2**
>
> Distinguish *corporate social responsibility* from *ethics*, identify *organizational stakeholders*, and characterize social consciousness today.

corporate social responsibility (CSR) Refers to the way in which a business tries to balance its commitments to organizational stakeholders.

organizational stakeholders that are directly affected by the practices of an organization and that therefore have a stake in its performance.

Starbucks is helping local farmers gain access to credit, working to develop and maintain sustainability of the coffee crop, and building farmer support centres in Costa Rica, Ethiopia, and Rwanda to provide local farmers with agricultural and technical education and support.

stakeholders that are particularly important to the organization and try to address their needs and expectations as well.

Contemporary Social Consciousness

Canadian society and Canadian business have changed dramatically in the last two centuries, and so have views about social responsibility. The late nineteenth century was characterized by the entrepreneurial spirit and the laissez-faire philosophy. During this era of labour strife and predatory business practices, individual citizens and the government both became concerned about unbridled business activity. This concern was translated into laws regulating basic business practices.

During the Great Depression of the 1930s, many people blamed the failure of businesses and banks and the widespread loss of jobs on a general climate of business greed and lack of restraint. Out of the economic turmoil emerged new laws that described an increased expectation that business should protect and enhance the general welfare of society.

During the social unrest of the 1960s and 1970s, business was often characterized as a negative social force. Eventually, increased activism prompted increased government regulation in a variety of areas. Health warnings, for example, were placed on cigarettes, and stricter environmental protection laws were enacted.

Social consciousness and views toward social responsibility continue to evolve in the twenty-first century. The financial excesses that caused the recession that started in 2008 are likely to result in new laws governing business conduct. As well, an increased awareness of the global economy and heightened

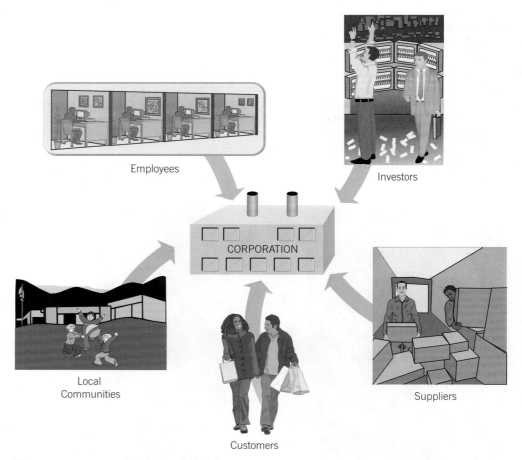

Figure 5.4 Major corporate stakeholders.

campaigning on the part of environmentalists and other activists means that businesses are becoming more sensitive to their social responsibilities.

The production of environmentally safe products has become a potential boom area, as many companies introduce products designed to be "environmentally friendly." Electrolux, a Swedish appliance maker, has developed a line of water-efficient washing machines, a solar-powered lawnmower, and the first refrigerators that are free of ozone-depleting refrigerants. The boxed insert entitled "This Is One Green (and Socially Responsible) Company!" describes the efforts that have been made by retailer Mountain Equipment Co-op to protect the environment and the workers who make the products it sells.

The Greening of Business

This Is One Green (and Socially Responsible) Company!

In 2008, Mountain Equipment Co-op (MEC) opened its twelfth Canadian store in Burlington, Ontario. The retailer was started in 1971 by four students from the University of British Columbia who were committed to protecting the environment. MEC is a co-operative (see Chapter 3), and shares in the company cost $5. The company does not try to maximize shareholder wealth; rather it seeks a balance between financial and social/environmental goals.

MEC directs 1 percent of its sales to charity and to running energy-efficient stores. Jantzi Research Inc. rates MEC as the top company in Canada's retail sector for sustainability practices. MEC also received top marks in North America from the Certified Chartered Accountants for its first sustainability report.

Practising social and environmental responsibility means more than simply giving money to environmental causes and organizations. It also means being conscious of other aspects of social responsibility. For example, products that are sold in MEC stores must be manufactured in safe and healthy workplaces where human and civil rights are respected. The co-op has even stricter standards for MEC-brand products (58 percent of which are manufactured in Canada), which comprise approximately 60 percent of sales. MEC conducts its own Supply Team Evaluation Process, but it also has other organizations do independent audits of its suppliers. These audits ensure that suppliers who produce MEC-brand products:

- Implement and maintain systems to minimize negative impacts of manufacturing and packaging on the environment.
- Implement programs to ensure that waste is disposed of in an environmentally responsible manner.
- Do not use child labour or forced labour.
- Treat their workers with dignity.
- Do not subject their workers to harassment, discrimination, or abuse.

- Allow their workers to join unions and to bargain collectively.
- Pay their workers fairly and directly.
- Provide safe and healthy work environments for workers, which comply with local health and safety laws and regulations.

In its retail outlets, MEC practises what it preaches. The design of its buildings and the material and construction methods used are consistent with care for the environment. MEC's stores are designed to enhance (or at least not detract from) the natural environment, and they are built with resources from the local area. Energy efficiency, pollution control, and recycling potential are all important considerations in MEC buildings. Innovations found in MEC's green buildings include the use of geothermal energy heat pumps in Montreal, a demonstration straw-bale wall in Ottawa, and composting toilets in Winnipeg. When it was built, MEC's Winnipeg store was only the second retail building in Canada that met the national C2000 Green Building Standard (the first one was MEC's Ottawa store). (For information on other green buildings in Canada, see the The Greening of Business box in Chapter 9.)

Critical Thinking Questions

1. Which of the two major views about business— "managerial capitalism" or the "variety of stakeholders" idea—would most likely be held by MEC's shareholders? Why?

2. What are the arguments for and against "managerial capitalism" and the "variety of stakeholders" idea?

3. Consider the following statement: *Businesses should not give money to charity because (1) business executives do not have any training that would help them decide which charities to give money to, (2) businesses are biased in their decisions about which charities to give money to, and (3) business managers don't have any right to give away shareholders' money.* Do you agree or disagree with the statement? Explain your reasoning.

Areas of Social Responsibility

3   Show how the concept of social responsibility applies both to environmental issues and to a firm's relationships with customers, employees, and investors.

In defining their sense of social responsibility, most firms must confront four areas of concern: *responsibilities toward the environment, customers, employees,* and *investors*.

Responsibility Toward the Environment

pollution The injection of harmful substances into the environment.

One critical area of social responsibility involves how the business relates to its physical environment. Controlling **pollution**—the injection of harmful substances into the environment—is a significant challenge for contemporary business. Air, water, and land pollution are the subjects of most anti-pollution efforts by business and governments.[15]

Air Pollution

air pollution When several factors converge to lower air quality.

Air pollution results when several factors converge to lower air quality. Chemicals like the carbon monoxide emitted by automobiles contribute to air pollution. So does smoke and other chemicals emitted by manufacturing plants. Air pollution is particularly bad in China, where 100 coal-fired power plants are being built each year. Each plant uses 1.3 million tonnes of coal and gives off 3.4 million tonnes of carbon dioxide. Only 5 percent of the coal-fired power plants in China are equipped with pollution control equipment.[16] Many industrial companies were forcibly shut down by the Chinese government in advance of the 2008 Olympics in an attempt to improve air quality.

The Kyoto Summit in 1997 was an attempt by various governments to reach an agreement on ways to reduce the threat of pollution. Australia is the world's largest greenhouse gas emitter per capita, contributing 7.3 percent of the world's total. The United States (at 6.5 percent) and Canada (at 6.4 percent) are close behind. Canada is the only one of the three leading emitters that signed the Protocol, but in 2006 the Conservative government said Canada would not be able to meet the targets for reducing pollution and that it would continue with the Protocol only if the targets were renegotiated.[17]

The United Nations is spearheading a move to get rich countries to reduce the impact of their own pollution by paying for cleanups in the developing world. Companies can buy carbon credits, which essentially give them the right to pollute the atmosphere with carbon dioxide. The money collected is then used to help fund clean-air projects in China and other developing countries; these projects would not be affordable otherwise.[18]

Figure 5.5 shows atmospheric carbon dioxide (CO_2) levels for the period 1750 to 2000, and it offers three possible scenarios for future levels under different sets of conditions. The three projections—lowest, middle, highest—were developed by the Intergovernmental Panel on Climate Change, which calculated likely changes in the atmosphere during this century if no efforts were made to reduce so-called greenhouse emissions (waste gases that trap heat in the atmosphere). The criteria for estimating changes are population, economic growth, energy supplies, and technologies; the less pressure exerted by these conditions, the less the increase in CO_2 levels. Energy supplies are measured in exajoules—roughly the annual energy consumption of a large metropolitan area like New York or London.

Under the lowest (or best-case) scenario, by 2100 the population would grow to only 6.4 billion people, economic growth would be no more than 1.2 to 2.0 percent a year, and energy supplies would require only 8000 exajoules of conventional oil. However, under the highest (or worst-case) scenario, the population would increase to 11.3 billion people, annual economic growth would be between 3.0 and 3.5 percent, and energy supplies would require as much as 18 400 exajoules of conventional oil.

There is currently a great deal of discussion and debate about climate change and **global warming**—an increase in the earth's average temperature. Almost everyone agrees that global warming is happening, but there is debate about what is causing it (see Concluding Case 5-1 for more information on this issue). In difficult economic times, like those that developed in 2008–09, the general public is less willing to make personal sacrifices in order to battle climate change. A poll of 12 000 people in 11 different countries showed that less than half of the respondents were willing to make lifestyle changes to reduce carbon emissions, and only 20 percent said they would be willing to spend extra money to fight climate change.[19]

global warming An increase in the earth's average temperature.

Water Pollution

For years, businesses and municipalities dumped their waste into rivers, streams, and lakes with little regard for the effects. Thanks to new legislation and increased awareness on the part of businesses, water quality is improving in many areas. Millar Western Pulp Ltd. built Canada's first zero-discharge pulp mill at Meadow Lake, Saskatchewan. There is no discharge pipe to the river, no dioxin-forming chlorine, and almost no residue. Dow Chemical built a plant at Fort Saskatchewan that will not dump any pollutants into the nearby river.[20]

Land Pollution

Toxic wastes are dangerous chemical and/or radioactive by-products of various manufacturing processes. For example, thousands of hectares of agricultural

toxic wastes Dangerous chemical and/or radioactive by-products of various manufacturing processes.

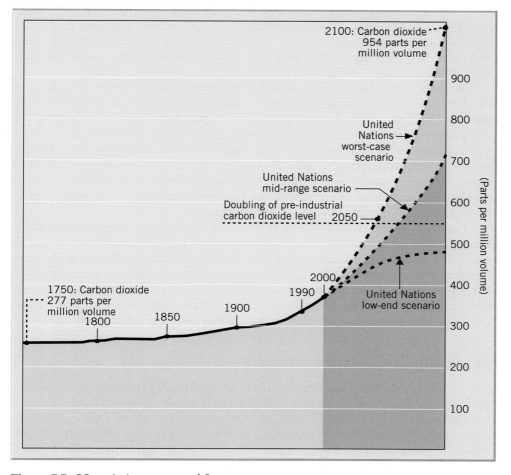

Figure 5.5 CO_2 emissions, past and future.

land were contaminated when five million cubic litres of toxic waste escaped from a holding pond at a zinc mine in Spain that was operated by the Canadian firm Boliden Ltd.[21] Restoring the quality of land is time consuming and costly. Because toxic waste cannot usually be processed into harmless material or destroyed, it must be stored somewhere. The problem is—where? Few people want a toxic waste storage facility in their town.

Recycling.   Changes in forestry practices, limits on certain types of mining, and new forms of solid waste disposal are all attempts to address the issue of land pollution. The conversion of certain waste materials into useful products—**recycling**—has developed as a response to the increased consciousness about land pollution. Some products, such as aluminum beverage cans and glass, can be very efficiently recycled. Others, such as plastics, are more troublesome. Many local communities actively support various recycling programs, including curbside pickup of aluminum, plastics, glass, and pulp paper.

recycling The conversion of certain waste materials into useful products.

An interesting problem that highlights some of the complexities in recycling involves wooden pallets—those splintery wooden platforms used to store and transport consumer goods. Pallets are popular because they provide an efficient method for stacking and moving large quantities of smaller items. Pallets of merchandise can be easily and efficiently moved from factories to trucks to retail stores. Pallets are very recyclable, but since the cost of new ones is so low, many companies just toss used ones aside and get new ones. Many landfills refuse to take pallets, and others assess surcharges for recycling them. Ironically, some environmentalists argue that abandoned pallets actually serve a useful purpose because, in urban areas, they often become refuges for animals such as raccoons and abandoned pets.[22]

biomass Plant and animal waste that can be recycled to produce energy.

Plant and animal waste can also be recycled to produce energy; this is referred to as **biomass**. Waste materials like sawdust, manure, and sludge are increasingly being turned into useful products. Ensyn Corp., for example, converts sawdust into liquid fuel by blasting wood waste with a sand-like substance that is heated. What's left is bio-oil.[23]

Many business firms are now acting to reduce various forms of pollution. Under the Canadian and Ontario environmental protection acts, liability for a business firm can run as high as $2 million per day. To protect themselves, companies must prove that they showed diligence in avoiding an environmental disaster such as an oil or gasoline spill.[24] The Environmental Choice program, sponsored by the federal government, licenses products that meet environmental standards set by the Canadian Standards Association. Firms whose products meet these standards can put the logo—three doves intertwined to form a maple leaf—on their products.[25]

Concern about pollution has influenced the actions of many Canadian firms as they do business abroad. In many cases, there is opposition to a project by the local people because they fear that some sort of pollution will result. For example, in New Caledonia, indigenous people—who were worried about the environmental impact of a proposed nickel mine—stormed the site and stole millions of dollars of equipment.[26] In Peru, indigenous groups threatened violence if Talisman Energy continued drilling for oil on their land.[27]

Responsibility Toward Customers

Social responsibility toward customers generally falls into one of two categories: providing quality products and pricing those products fairly. As with the environment, firms differ in their level of concern about responsibility to customers. Yet unlike environmental problems, customer problems do not require expensive technological solutions. Most such problems can be avoided if companies obey the laws regarding consumer rights, avoid illegal pricing practices, and behave ethically when advertising their products.

Rights of Consumers

Much of the current interest in business responsibility toward customers can be traced to the rise of consumerism. **Consumerism** is a form of social activism dedicated to protecting the rights of consumers in their dealings with businesses. Consumers have the following rights:

1. *The right to safe products.* The right to safe products is not always honoured. In 2008, 20 people died after eating meat made by Maple Leaf Foods that was contaminated with listeria. Company sales dropped by nearly 50 percent once this became public.[28] The government of China has become concerned that negative publicity about faulty toys and contaminated pet food and toothpaste has damaged the "Made in China" label. In a surprising development, Mattel Inc. apologized to China for claiming that a recall of 18 million playsets with dangerous magnets was necessitated by poor quality control at one of its Chinese suppliers. Mattel eventually admitted that its own product design was flawed.[29]

2. *The right to be informed about all relevant aspects of a product.* Food products must list their ingredients. Clothing must be labelled with information about its proper care. And banks must tell you exactly how much interest you are paying on a loan. Cereal companies have come under fire for some of the claims they have made about the oat bran content of their cereals, as well as its likely effects.

3. *The right to be heard.* Many companies today have complaints offices. Retailers like Kmart offer a money-back guarantee if consumers aren't satisfied. Procter & Gamble puts a toll-free number on many of its products; customers can call this number if they have questions or complaints. When companies refuse to respond to consumer complaints, consumer protection agencies such as the Better Business Bureau and consumer interest groups such as the Airline Passengers Association may intervene.

4. *The right to choose what they buy.* Central to this right is free and open competition among companies. In times past, "gentlemen's agreements" were often used to avoid competition or to divide up a market so that firms did not have to truly compete against each other. Such practices are illegal today, and any attempts by business to block competition can result in fines or other penalties.

5. *The right to be educated about purchases.* All prescription drugs now come with detailed information regarding dosage, possible side effects, and potential interactions with other medications.

6. *The right to courteous service.* This right is hard to legislate, but as consumers become increasingly knowledgeable, they are more willing to complain about bad service. Consumer hotlines can also be used to voice service-related issues.

consumerism A social movement that seeks to protect and expand the rights of consumers in their dealings with businesses.

Unfair Pricing

Interfering with competition can also mean illegal pricing practices. **Collusion** among companies—including getting together to "fix" prices—is against the law. Arctic Glacier Inc. of Winnipeg was one of several companies served with subpoenas by the U.S. government as it investigated collusion in the U.S. market for packaged ice. One of Arctic's employees, who claimed he was fired for refusing to take part in a conspiracy to divide up markets, went to the U.S. government and helped them in their investigation. The investigation is underway at the time of this writing.[30] The Canadian Competition Bureau also launched an investigation after hearing allegations from a confidential informant that Mars, Hershey, Nestle, and Cadbury had teamed up in a candy price-fixing

collusion An illegal agreement among companies in an industry to "fix" prices for their products.

scheme.[31] A law firm in Toronto is organizing a class-action lawsuit against the major chocolate companies, alleging a conspiracy to fix prices.[32] Also in 2008, Ultramar, Les Petroles Therrien Inc., and Petro-T pleaded guilty to price-fixing in the retail gasoline market. Ultramar was fined $1.85 million, and the other two companies were both fined $179 000.[33]

Under some circumstances, firms can also come under attack for price gouging. For example, when DaimlerChrysler first launched its PT Cruiser, demand for the vehicles was so strong that some dealers sold them only to customers willing to pay thousands of dollars over sticker prices. Some Ford dealers adopted a similar practice when the new Thunderbird was launched. This illustrates what can happen when there is a shortage of a product.

Ethics in Advertising

In recent years, increased attention has been given to ethics in advertising and product information. Because of controversies surrounding the potential misinterpretation of words and phrases such as *light*, *reduced calories*, *diet*, and *low fat*, food producers are now required to use a standardized format for listing ingredients on product packages. There are several key ethical issues in advertising, including truth-in-advertising claims, the advertising of counterfeit brands, the use of stealth advertising, and advertising that is morally objectionable.

Truth in Advertising. Concerns about truth in advertising are becoming more noticeable on the international scene. In July 2005, for example, Chinese government officials investigated Procter & Gamble's claim that its Pantene shampoo made hair "10 times stronger." A few months earlier, P&G paid a $24 000 fine after one consumer complained that SK-II Skin Cream was not the "miracle water" it claimed to be and that it did not make her skin "look 12 years younger in 28 days."[34]

Advertising of Counterfeit Brands. Another issue concerns the advertising and sale of counterfeit brand names. Canadians tourists who visit New York often go to booths on Canal Street, which is famous for the "bargains" that can be had on supposedly name brand items like Cartier, Panerai, Vacheron, Montblanc, and Louis Vuitton. Many of the items being sold are counterfeit, although it can be very hard to tell the difference between these "knock-offs"

Of all roadway accidents, 25 percent are distraction-related, and the biggest distractions for motorists are handheld gadgets such as cellphones, pagers, and the like. In fulfilling their responsibility to consumers, some companies are conducting tests, which yield important data about roadway accidents. Ford Motor Company, for example, has a Virtual Test Track Experiment simulator that determines how often drivers get distracted. Under normal circumstances, an adult driver will miss about 3 percent of the simulated "events" (like an ice patch or a deer on the road) that Ford contrives for a virtual road trip. If they're on the cellphone, they'll miss about 14 percent. Teenagers miss a scary 54 percent of the events.

and the genuine article. For example, knock-offs of Suzuki motorcycles hit the market just a few weeks after the genuine product became available. These knock-offs were sold to customers as the real thing, but they had not been subjected to rigorous quality control like real Suzuki motorcycles are. Naturally, legitimate manufacturers of these high-end products are trying to stamp out this counterfeit trade in their products.[35] The boxed insert entitled "Counterfeit Products: Who's Accountable?" provides more information about this issue.

Business Accountability

Counterfeit Products: Who's Accountable?

Counterfeit goods are a problem in many different product lines, including perfume, luggage, handbags, pharmaceuticals, designer clothing, shoes, cigarettes, watches, sports memorabilia, and fine wines, to name just a few. An FBI investigation in the United States revealed, for example, that up to 75 percent of sports memorabilia was fake. Wine makers are concerned about the counterfeiting of their products because some of the top names in wine (e.g., Château Mouton Rothschild and Penfolds Grange) cost as much as $3000 a bottle, and this is an incentive for counterfeiters to make a lot of easy money. The counterfeiters buy cheaper wine and then put it in bottles with fake labels. Wineries are fighting counterfeiting by embedding microchips in the label that can be read with an optical scanner, and by laser-etching the wine's name and vintage year into the bottle's glass.

The International Chamber of Commerce estimates that the counterfeit goods trade may be worth as much as $500 billion annually. According to Interpol—the international police organization in Lyon, France—organized crime groups like the Chinese triads and terrorist groups like Hezbollah have gotten into the business of counterfeiting products because of the high rate of return they can make (about as high as the illegal drug trade). Consider an example: One Vietnamese group in New York imported watch components that cost them about 27 cents and then sold them to wholesalers for $12 to $20. The wholesalers then sold them to street vendors for $20 to $30, and the street vendors sold them as Cartier watches for as much as $250. That was still well below the price of a real Cartier watch (about $1800).

While many counterfeit products are sent from China to other countries, shopping for knock-offs in China itself is also very popular with visiting tourists because prices are incredibly low (for example, $10 for a Gucci bag, $15 for a Samsonite suitcase, $7 for a Polo shirt, and $3 for a Rolex watch). While regular tourists are the most frequent purchasers of knock-offs, celebrities are also attracted to counterfeit products. In 2008, for example, Céline Dion was spotted shopping at a knock-off store in Shanghai. But China is not the only country where counterfeit products are made: North Korea turns out two billion packs of cigarettes each year, many of which are fake Marlboros.

The trade in counterfeit goods is harmful to the companies that have spent a lot of time and money developing brand name goods for sale. Every counterfeit product that is sold reduces the sales revenues of the legitimate producers. It also harms governments by denying them tax revenues (most counterfeiters do not pay taxes). Consumers are hurt, too. While it may seem that consumers benefit because they spend very little money for goods that look like the real thing, in fact consumers often pay far too much for counterfeit goods because those goods have very low quality. As well, some counterfeit goods are downright dangerous to use. While a fake handbag simply costs money, fake pharmaceuticals, electrical products, and motorcycles can kill the people who use them.

There is increasing pressure on the Canadian government to do something about counterfeit goods. The Canadian Anti-Counterfeiting Network (CACN) was formed in 2005 to lobby the government for changes in laws. But changes are slow in coming, and other countries (most notably the United States) feel that Canada is not doing enough to discourage the sale of counterfeit goods. Unlike the United States, France, and Italy, Canada doesn't have many famous brand exports, so there aren't very many businesses putting pressure on the government to crack down on counterfeiters. The United States has placed Canada on its official list of countries that don't do enough to control counterfeit products (the list also includes Turkey, Belarus, Vietnam, and Uzbekistan). Canada is moving slowly toward bringing its laws into conformity with the World Intellectual Property Organization (WIPO).

A new approach to reducing counterfeiting is to prosecute anyone who facilitates the sale of counterfeit products, including landlords (who own the buildings where counterfeit goods are being sold), shipping companies, credit-card companies, and others in the supply chain. The argument is that these people are benefitting from the sale of knock-offs, so they should be held accountable. There is also a move in some countries to hold the consumers who buy counterfeit goods accountable. In France and Italy, for example, it is now a crime to buy counterfeit goods.

Individual companies are becoming more aggressive in pursuing counterfeiters. Louis Vuitton, for example, sued

▶

eBay for selling knock-offs of Vuitton products, and in June 2008, a French court levied a fine of $60.8 million against eBay, saying that it should be doing much more to curtail the sale of counterfeit goods. Tiffany & Co., the high-end jeweller, also filed a lawsuit against eBay, charging that it had ignored the sale of fake Tiffany jewellery on eBay's website. But in July 2008, a U.S. federal judge ruled that Tiffany, not eBay, had the responsibility for protecting the Tiffany brand name. A court in Belgium also ruled in favour of eBay after it had been sued by L'Oréal, the cosmetics company.

Critical Thinking Questions

1. How might cultural and individual differences lead to conflicting views about the ethics of selling counterfeit goods?

2. The production and sale of knock-offs obviously benefits some people—for example, the seller of counterfeit goods and perhaps consumers who get products cheap. But it also hurts others—for example, the legitimate manufacturers of products, and consumers who are injured by knock-offs that are faulty. Do you think the benefits of knock-offs exceed the costs, or vice versa? Defend your answer.

3. Consider the following statement: *eBay should not be responsible for monitoring the authenticity of products that are sold through its online business. The responsibility for that lies with the companies who are worried that someone is selling a counterfeit version of their product.* Do you agree or disagree with this statement? Defend your answer.

stealth advertising (undercover or guerrilla advertising) Involves companies paying individuals to extol the virtues of their products to other individuals.

Stealth Advertising. A variation of viral advertising, **stealth advertising** (also called **undercover or guerrilla advertising**) involves companies paying individuals to extol the virtues of their products to other individuals. For example, Student Workforce hires individuals who are 18–30 years old to market products to other people in the same age bracket. One of the people hired is Leanne Plummer, a student at Toronto's Humber College. She says that stealth advertising is more about sharing information than it is about sales.[36]

The ethics of stealth advertising are questionable if the paid individuals do not reveal that they are being paid by a company. In that case, the recipient of the advertising is not aware that it *is* advertising. For example, one advertising agency hired models to pose as "tourists." These models asked real tourists to take their picture with a new Sony Ericsson camera cellphone. The models then talked up the advantages of the new product to the unsuspecting real tourists. Commercial Alert, a U.S.–based consumer protection group, wants a government investigation of these undercover marketing tactics.[37]

Morally Objectionable Advertising. A final ethical issue concerns advertising that is morally objectionable. Benetton, for example, aired a series of commercials featuring inmates on death row. The ads, dubbed "We, on Death Row," prompted such an emotional outcry that Sears dropped the Benetton USA clothing line.[38] Other ads receiving criticism include Victoria's Secret models in skimpy underwear, and campaigns by tobacco and alcohol companies that allegedly target young people.

Responsibility Toward Employees

Organizations also need to employ fair and equitable practices with their employees. Human resource management activities are essential to a smoothly functioning business. These same activities—recruiting, hiring, training, promoting, and compensating—are also the basis for social responsibility toward employees. A company that provides its employees with equal opportunities for rewards and advancement without regard to race, sex, or other irrelevant factors is meeting its social responsibilities. Firms that ignore their responsibility to employees leave themselves open to lawsuits. They also miss the chance to hire better and more highly motivated employees.

Legal and Social Commitments

Some progressive companies go well beyond legal requirements, hiring and training the so-called hard-core unemployed (people with little education or training and a history of unemployment) and those who have disabilities. The Bank of Montreal, for example, sponsors a community college skills upgrading course for individuals with hearing impairments. The Royal Bank provides managers with discrimination awareness training. Rogers Cablesystems Ltd. provides individuals who have mobility restrictions with telephone and customer-service job opportunities.[39] Bell Canada employs more than 1000 people with disabilities (2 percent of its permanent workforce). But, in Canada, over 50 percent of those with physical disabilities are still unemployed.[40]

In addition to their responsibility to employees as resources of the company, firms have a social responsibility to their employees as people. Firms that accept this responsibility ensure that the workplace is safe, both physically and emotionally. They would no more tolerate an abusive manager or one who sexually harasses employees than they would a gas leak.

Business firms also have a responsibility to respect the privacy of their employees. While nearly everyone agrees that companies have the right to exercise some level of control over their employees, there is great controversy about exactly how much is acceptable in areas such as drug testing and computer monitoring. When Canadian National Railways instituted drug testing for train, brake, and yard employees, 12 percent failed. Trucking companies have found that nearly one-third of truckers who have been involved in accidents were on drugs.[41]

Employees are often unaware that they are being monitored by computer software programs like "Spy" and "Peek." This type of monitoring increases employee stress levels because they don't know exactly when the boss is watching them. A lawsuit was brought against Nortel Networks by employees who charged that the firm installed telephone bugs and hidden microphones in one of its plants.[42]

Whistle-Blowers. Respecting employees as people also means respecting their behaviour as ethically responsible individuals. Suppose, for instance, an employee discovers that a business has been engaging in practices that are illegal, unethical, or socially irresponsible. Ideally, this employee should be able to report the problem to management, but management often does not want to hear about such issues. The employee might then decide to inform a regulatory agency or perhaps the media. At this point, he or she becomes a **whistle-blower**—an employee who discovers and tries to put an end to a company's unethical, illegal, or socially irresponsible actions by publicizing them.[43]

Melvin Crothers, who worked in the marketing department at WestJet, paid a price for his whistle-blowing. In 2003, he discovered that a fellow WestJet employee was accessing a restricted Air Canada website in order to obtain data about Air Canada's "load factor" (the proportion of seats filled) on certain flights. He felt that this was unethical, so he tried to talk to WestJet president Clive Beddoe and tell him what was going on. Beddoe was out of town, so Crothers called a former WestJet president who was heading up an Air Canada

whistle-blower An employee who discovers and tries to put an end to a company's unethical, illegal, or socially irresponsible actions by publicizing them.

The safety of workers is an important consideration for all organizations. The required use of hardhats is just one example of precautions that companies can take to protect workers while they are on the job.

discount airline. The conversation led to Air Canada discovering what WestJet was up to, and before long, Air Canada filed a lawsuit against WestJet. Crothers resigned from WestJet four days later.[44]

Whistle-blowers are often demoted—and even fired—when they take their accusations public. Even if they retain their jobs, they may still be treated as outsiders and suffer resentment or hostility from co-workers. Many co-workers see whistle-blowers as people who simply can't be trusted. One recent study suggests that about half of all whistle-blowers eventually get fired, and about half of those who get fired subsequently lose their homes and/or families.[45] New federal legislation to protect whistle-blowers was introduced in Canada in 2003.

Responsibility Toward Investors

It may sound odd to say that a firm can be irresponsible toward investors, since they are the owners of the company. But if managers abuse their firm's financial resources, the ultimate losers are the owners, since they do not receive the earnings, dividends, or capital appreciation due them.

Improper Financial Management

Occasionally, organizations are guilty of financial mismanagement. In the most highly publicized recent case, managers at American International Group became involved in very high-risk insurance that caused the company to be on the hook for billions of dollars. The U.S. government ended up giving hundreds of billions of dollars to the company to keep it afloat. Financial mismanagement can also take many other forms, including executives paying themselves outlandish salaries and bonuses and spending huge amounts of company money for their own personal comfort. In these cases, creditors don't have much leverage and shareholders have few viable options. Trying to force a management changeover is not only difficult, it can also drive down the price of the company's stock, and this is a penalty shareholders are usually unwilling to assign themselves.

Cheque Kiting

cheque kiting Involves writing a cheque from one account, depositing it in a second account, and then immediately spending money from the second account while the money from the first account is still in transit.

Cheque kiting involves writing a cheque from one account, depositing it in a second account, and then immediately spending money from the second account while the money from the first account is still in transit. A cheque from the second account can also be used to replenish the money in the first account, and the process starts all over again. This practice obviously benefits the person doing the cheque kiting, but is irresponsible because it involves using other peoples' money without paying for it.

Insider Trading

insider trading The use of confidential information to gain from the purchase or sale of stock.

Insider trading occurs when someone uses confidential information to gain from the purchase or sale of stock. The most famous case is that of Martha Stewart, but there are many others as well. Barry Landen of Agnico-Eagle Mines was found guilty of insider trading when he sold shares he owned before it became publicly known that the company was going to report poor results. He was sentenced to 45 days in jail and fined $200 000.[46] Andrew Rankin, an investment banking star with RBC Dominion Securities, was originally convicted in 2005 for "tipping" a friend about several big corporate deals that were pending. The friend used this insider information to make over $4 million by buying and selling the stocks of these companies. In 2008, the Ontario Securities Commission agreed to a deal where criminal charges were withdrawn; Rankin was fined $250 000, and he was barred for life from working in the securities industry.[47]

Misrepresentation of Finances

Certain behaviours regarding financial representation are also illegal. In maintaining and reporting its financial status, every corporation must conform to generally accepted accounting principles (see Chapter 11). Sometimes, however, unethical managers project profits far in excess of what they actually expect to earn. As we saw in the opening case, managers at Livent hid losses and/or expenses to boost on-paper profits.

A few years earlier, the same sorts of things happened at Enron, where CFO Andrew Fastow had set up a complex network of partnerships that were often used to hide losses. This allowed Enron to report all the earnings from a partnership as its own while transferring all or most of the costs and losses to the partnership.[48]

"From a purely business viewpoint, taking what doesn't belong to you is usually the cheapest way to go."

Implementing Social Responsibility Programs

Thus far, we have discussed corporate social responsibility (CSR) as if a consensus exists on how firms should behave in most situations. In fact, dramatic differences of opinion exist as to the appropriateness of CSR as a business goal. Some people oppose any business activity that cuts into profits to investors, while others argue that responsibility must take precedence over profits.

Supporters of CSR believe that corporations are citizens just like individuals and therefore need to help improve our lives. Others point to the vast resources controlled by businesses and note that since businesses often create many of the problems social programs are designed to alleviate, they should use their resources to solve the problems. Still others argue that CSR is wise because there is a payoff for the firm.

Opponents of CSR fear that if businesses become too active in social concerns, they will gain too much control over how those concerns are addressed. They point to the influence many businesses have been able to exert on the government agencies that are supposed to regulate them. Other critics of business-sponsored social programs argue that companies lack the expertise needed. For example, they believe that technical experts, not business managers, should decide how best to clean up a polluted river.

The late Max Clarkson, formerly a top-level business executive and director of the Centre for Corporate Social Performance and Ethics at the University of Toronto, said that business firms that had a strong consciousness about ethics and CSR outperform firms that do not. After designing and applying a CSR rating system for companies, he found that companies that had the highest marks on questions of ethics and CSR also had the highest financial performance.[49]

Approaches to Social Responsibility

Given these differences of opinion, it is little wonder that corporations have adopted a variety of approaches to social responsibility. As Figure 5.6 illustrates, the four stances an organization can take concerning its obligations to society fall along a continuum ranging from the lowest to the highest degree of CSR practices.

> Identify four general approaches to social responsibility and describe the four steps a firm must take to implement a social responsibility program.
>
> **4**

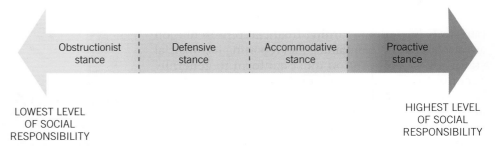

Figure 5.6 Spectrum of approaches to social responsibility.

Obstructionist Stance

obstructionist stance
A business does as little as possible to solve social or environmental problems and denies or covers up their wrongdoings.

Businesses that have an **obstructionist stance** to social responsibility do as little as possible to solve social or environmental problems. When these businesses cross the ethical or legal line that separates acceptable from unacceptable practices, their typical response is to deny or cover up their actions. Firms that adopt this position have little regard for ethical conduct and will generally go to great lengths to hide wrongdoing.

Defensive Stance

defensive stance An organization does only what is legally required and nothing more.

One step removed from the obstructionist stance is the **defensive stance**, where the organization does everything that is required of it legally, but nothing more. For example, a company would install pollution-control equipment dictated by law but would not install higher-quality equipment even though it might further limit pollution. Managers who take a defensive stance insist that their sole job is to generate profits. Tobacco companies generally take this position in their marketing efforts. In Canada and the United States, they are legally required to include warnings to smokers on their products and to limit advertising to prescribed media. Domestically, they follow these rules to the letter of the law, but they use more aggressive marketing methods in countries that have no such rules.

Accommodative Stance

accommodative stance
A company meets all of its legal and ethical requirements, and in some cases even goes beyond what is required.

A firm that adopts an **accommodative stance** meets its legal and ethical requirements but also goes further in certain cases. Such firms voluntarily agree to participate in social programs but only after they are convinced that these programs are worthy of their support. Many organizations respond to requests for donations to community hockey teams, Girl Guides, youth soccer programs, and so forth. The point, however, is that someone has to knock on the firm's door and ask; accommodative organizations are not generally proactively seeking avenues for contributing.

Proactive Stance

proactive stance An organization actively seeks opportunities to be socially responsible.

The highest degree of social responsibility a firm can exhibit is the **proactive stance**. Firms that adopt this approach take to heart the arguments in favour of CSR. They view themselves as citizens in a society and proactively seek opportunities to contribute. The most common—and direct—way to implement this stance is by setting up a foundation to provide direct financial support for various social programs.

Keep in mind that organizations do not always fit neatly into one category or another. The Ronald McDonald House program has been widely applauded, for example, but McDonald's has also come under fire for allegedly misleading consumers about the nutritional value of its food products. The Exercising Your Ethics exercise at the end of the chapter gives you an opportunity to think about the pros and cons of the various stances toward CSR.

Corporate Charitable Donations

Donating money to different causes is one way that business firms try to show that they are socially responsible. In 2008, for example, Great-West Life, London Life, and Canada Life donated $100 000 to the Salvation Army's Christmas campaign.[50] A 2008 survey of 93 large Canadian companies found that 97 percent made a charitable contribution of some sort and that the median value of their contributions was $340 000.[51] Another survey of 2200 companies that was conducted by Imagine Canada found that 91 percent gave to charities or non-profit organizations. Cash donations were provided by 76 percent of the companies, products by 51 percent, and services by 43 percent. More than 80 percent of the companies said that they made contributions because it was a good thing to do, irrespective of any financial benefits they might achieve from giving.[52]

Imagine Canada's "Caring Company" program recommends that corporations give 1 percent of pre-tax profits to charity, but only half of the corporations met that goal in 2008. A survey conducted by the Centre for Philanthropy found that the most of the money given to charities comes from individuals, not corporations. Canadians think that corporations give about 20 percent of the total and that it should be 30 percent.[53]An Environics survey of people in 23 different countries found that two-thirds of them thought that businesses are not doing enough if they simply abide by the law and provide employment.[54]

Businesses have also demonstrated a willingness to give money and products when disasters strike. When seven people died in Walkerton, Ontario, as a result of drinking contaminated water, companies such as Petro-Canada, Shoppers Drug Mart, Sobeys, and Zellers contributed products such as bleach and bottled water. And when tens of thousands of people died in the Asian tsunamis of 2004, companies from around the world rushed aid to the stricken areas. Global Fortune 500 firms donated $580 million in drugs, cellphones, machinery, medical equipment, and water to the relief effort.[55]

Some companies go beyond simply giving money or products. For example, Unilever Canada gives employees four afternoons a year for community activities.[56] Mars Canada sets aside one day each year for employees to volunteer. At Telus Corp.'s annual "day of service" in 2008, employees helped out at a soup kitchen.[57] Many companies take a community-based approach; they try to determine how they can achieve value for the community (and the company) with their donations of time and money.

Managing Social Responsibility Programs

Making a company truly socially responsible takes an organized and managed program (see Figure 5.7).

1. Top management must state strong support for CSR and be considered a factor in strategic planning. Without the support of top management, no program can succeed.

2. A committee of top managers must develop a plan detailing the level of management support. Some companies set aside percentages of profits for social programs. Mountain Equipment Co-op, for example, earmarks 1 percent of its sales revenue for charity. Managers must also set specific priorities. For instance, should the firm train the hard-core unemployed or support the arts?

3. One executive must be put in charge of the firm's agenda. Whether the role is created as a separate job or added to an existing one, the selected individual must monitor the program and ensure that its implementation is consistent with the firm's policy statement and strategic plan.

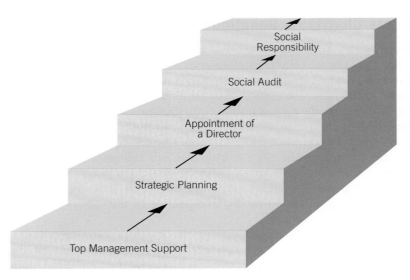

Figure 5.7 Establishing a social responsibility program involves four basic steps.

social audit A systematic analysis of how a firm is using funds earmarked for social-responsibility goals and how effective these expenditures have been.

4. The organization must conduct **social audits**, which are systematic analyses of its success in using funds earmarked for its CSR goals.[58] Suppose a company has a strategic plan calling for spending $100 000 to train 200 hard-core unemployed people and to place 180 of them in jobs. If the firm actually spends $98 000, trains 210 people, and fills 175 jobs, a social audit will confirm the program's success. But if the program costs $150 000, trains only 90 people, and places only 10 of them, the audit will reveal the program's failure. Such failure should prompt a rethinking of the program's implementation and its priorities.

In addition to social audits, Canadian businesses are increasingly publishing sustainability reports. These reports go beyond simple financial reporting and explain how the company is performing on issues such as the environment, employee relations, workplace diversity, and business ethics. The majority of Canadian companies now report at least some sustainability performance information, and about 60 percent of the 100 largest companies in Canada prepare sustainability reports.[59] Social audits and sustainability reports together constitute **triple bottom line reporting**—measuring the social, environmental, and economic performance of a company.[60]

triple bottom line reporting Measuring the social, environmental, and economic performance of a company.

Ronald McDonald House helps the families of children who are in hospital. It is supported by McDonald's and is an example of socially responsible behaviour by a business corporation.

Social Responsibility and the Small Business

Ethics and CSR issues must be faced by managers in all organizations, regardless of size. One key to business success is to decide in advance how to respond to these issues. As the owner of a garden supply store, how would you respond to a building inspector's suggestion that a cash payment would expedite your application for a building permit? As the manager of a nightclub, would you call the police, refuse service, or sell liquor to a customer whose ID card looks forged? As the owner of a small laboratory, would you call the board of health to make sure that it has licensed the company you want to contract to dispose of the lab's medical waste? Who will really be harmed if a small firm pads its income statement to help get a much-needed bank loan?

> Explain how issues of social responsibility and ethics affect small businesses.
>
> **5**

Can a small business afford to set CSR objectives? Should it sponsor hockey teams, make donations to the United Way, and buy light bulbs from the Lions Club? Would you join the Chamber of Commerce and support the Better Business Bureau because it is the responsible thing to do or just because it is good business? The boxed insert entitled "How Green Is That Orange?" describes the social responsibility initiatives of one small business.

Entrepreneurship and New Ventures

How Green Is That Orange?

Ahhh . . . the delicious taste of a fresh wild blueberry juice smoothie! What could be better to quench your thirst? The super juices offered by Arthur's Fresh, an Ontario-based beverage producer, offer much more than just thirst quenching. And it's a good thing because consumers are looking for more than that these days . . . much more. Today's consumers insist on products that are both good for them and good for the environment. Arthur's Fresh is meeting the demands on both fronts. Their fruit smoothies are known for their nutritional benefits. Adding sugar is taboo, and one 325 mL serving is 25 to 50 percent of your required daily intake of fruits and vegetables. The product is sweet; pardon the pun! But what's even sweeter about this product is the way it's produced.

In 2008, Travis Bell, president and founder of Arthur's Fresh, along with his brother Scott (the company CEO), decided to get serious about reducing the environmental footprint of their manufacturing business. Their strategy involved reducing bottle weight (which also reduced transportation costs and emissions), reducing packaging (plastic and cardboard), making responsible raw material sourcing decisions (like "buying local"), changing to bulk hauling transportation providers, and utilizing renewable energy for power generation. They expect to recover their $330 000 investment by 2011, mostly from cost savings associated with transportation and packaging.

The Packaging Association of Canada thought the changes made by the brothers were commendable and recognized them in 2009 with an award for sustainable packaging leadership. Apparently, their customers liked the changes too, since Arthur's Fresh has experienced a 1250 percent increase in sales since 2004. Company sales were $10 million in 2007, and in 2008, *Profit* magazine ranked Arthur's Fresh among Canada's fastest-growing companies.

The company is also involved in social responsibility initiatives that extend beyond concern for the environment. Through its "Seeds of Change" program, Arthur's Fresh gives at least 10 percent of its annual pre-tax profits back to the community for "kid-oriented programs." In 2008, the company was a corporate sponsor for See-Them-Run, a campaign involving two Canadians—Erin van Wiltenburg and Reuben Jentink—who ran 4200 kilometres across the African continent to raise money for youth education programs in Africa. Arthur's Fresh is also a regular donor of juice to food banks throughout the Toronto area. Along with making healthy products and ethical procurement decisions, the company also strongly believes in enriching the lives of children.

For Travis Bell, a fifth-generation fruit farmer from Goderich, Ontario, the decision to develop his part-time business to full-time operations has taken him to greener pastures in more ways than one. So, the next time you pull your chair up to the breakfast table to enjoy a glass of cold O.J., ask yourself, "Exactly how green is that orange?"

Critical Thinking Questions

1. How has Arthur's Fresh addressed the various areas of social responsibility?

2. What further actions might the company take?

Test yourself on the material for this chapter at **www.pearsoned.ca/mybusinesslab**.

Summary of
Learning Objectives

1. Explain how individuals develop their personal *codes of ethics* and why ethics are important in the workplace. Individual codes of ethics are derived from social standards of right and wrong. Ethical behaviour is behaviour that conforms to generally accepted social norms concerning beneficial and harmful actions. Unethical behaviour can result in loss of business, fines, and even imprisonment. Because ethics affect the behaviour of individuals on behalf of the companies that employ them, many firms are adopting formal statements of ethics.

2. Distinguish *corporate social responsibility* from ethics, identify *organizational stakeholders*, and characterize social consciousness today. *Corporate social responsibility* refers to the way a firm attempts to balance its commitments to organizational stakeholders. One way to understand social responsibility is to view it in terms of stakeholders— those groups, individuals, and organizations that are directly affected by the practices of an organization and that therefore have a stake in its performance. Until the second half of the nineteenth century, businesses often paid little attention to stakeholders. Since then, however, both public pressure and government regulation, especially as a result of the Great Depression of the 1930s and the social activism of the 1960s and 1970s, have forced businesses to consider public welfare, at least to some degree. A trend toward increased social consciousness, including a heightened sense of environmental activism, has recently emerged.

3. Show how the concept of corporate social responsibility (CSR) applies to environmental issues and to a firm's relationships with customers, employees, and investors.

With respect to the environment, CSR requires firms to minimize pollution of air, water, and land. With respect to customers, CSR requires firms to provide products of acceptable quality, to price products fairly, and to respect consumers' rights. With respect to employees, CSR requires firms to respect workers both as resources and as people who are more productive when their needs are met. With respect to investors, CSR requires firms to manage their resources and to represent their financial status honestly.

4. Identify four general *approaches to social responsibility* and describe the four steps a firm must take to implement a *social responsibility program*. An *obstructionist stance* on social responsibility is taken by a firm that does as little as possible to address social or environmental problems. The *defensive stance* emphasizes compliance with minimum legal requirements. Companies adopting the *accommodative stance* go beyond minimum activities, if they are asked. The *proactive stance* commits a company to actively contribute to social projects. Implementing a social responsibility program entails four steps: (1) drafting a policy statement with the support of top management, (2) developing a detailed plan, (3) appointing a director to implement the plan, and (4) conducting social audits to monitor results.

5. Explain how issues of social responsibility and ethics affect small businesses. Managers and employees of small businesses face many of the same ethical questions as their counterparts at larger firms. Small businesses also face the same issues of social responsibility and the same need to decide on an approach to social responsibility. The differences are primarily differences of scale.

PEARSON
mybusinesslab™ To improve your grade, visit the MyBusinessLab website at www.pearsoned.ca/mybusinesslab. This online homework and tutorial system allows you to test your understanding and generates a personalized study plan just for you. It provides you with study and practice tools directly related to this chapter's content. MyBusinessLab puts you in control of your own learning!

Key Terms

accommodative stance (p. 176)
air pollution (p. 166)
biomass (p. 168)
business ethics (p. 156)
cheque kiting (p. 174)
code of ethics (p. 161)
collusion (p. 169)
conflict of interest (p. 158)
consumerism (p. 169)
corporate social responsibility (CSR) (p. 163)

defensive stance (p. 176)
ethical behaviour (p. 156)
ethics (p. 156)
global warming (p. 167)
insider trading (p. 174)
managerial ethics (p. 157)
obstructionist stance (p. 176)
organizational stakeholders (p. 163)
pollution (p. 166)
proactive stance (p. 176)

recycling (p. 168)
social audit (p. 178)
stealth (undercover) advertising (p. 172)
toxic wastes (p. 167)
triple bottom line reporting (p. 178)
unethical behaviour (p. 156)
whistle-blower (p. 173)

Questions for Analysis

1. Write a one-paragraph description of an ethical dilemma that you or someone you know faced recently. What was the outcome in the situation? Was it consistent with what you thought should have occurred? Why or why not? Analyze the situation using the ideas presented in the chapter. Make particular reference to the ethical norms of utility, rights, justice, and caring in terms of how they influenced the situation. What would each of these suggest about the correct decision? Does this analysis lead you to a different conclusion about the best outcome? Explain.

2. Develop an example of the way in which your personal code of ethics might clash with the operations of a specific company. How might you try to resolve these differences?

3. What kind of wrongdoing would be most likely to prompt you to be a whistle-blower? What kind of wrongdoing would be least likely? Why?

4. In your opinion, which area of social responsibility is most important? Why? Are there areas other than those noted in the chapter that you consider important?

5. Identify some specific ethical or social responsibility issues that might be faced by small business managers and employees in each of the following areas: environment, customers, employees, and investors.

6. Choose a product or service and explain the social responsibility concerns that are likely to be evident in terms of the environment, customers, employees, and investors.

7. Analyze the forces that are at work from both the company's perspective and the whistle-blower's perspective. Given these forces, what characteristics should a law to protect whistle-blowers have in order to be effective?

8. Pick a product or service that demonstrates the defensive approach to social responsibility. What has been the impact of that stance on the company that is using it? Why did the company adopt a defensive stance?

Application Exercises

1. Develop a list of the major stakeholders of your college or university. As a class, discuss the ways in which you think the school prioritizes these stakeholders. Do you agree or disagree with this prioritization?

2. Using newspapers, magazines, and other business references, identify and describe three companies that take a defensive stance to social responsibility, three that take an accommodative stance, and three that take a proactive stance.

Building Your Business Skills

To Lie or Not to Lie: That Is the Question

The Purpose of This Assignment

To encourage students to apply general concepts of business ethics to specific situations.

Background

Workplace lying, it seems, has become business as usual. According to one survey, one-quarter of working adults said that they had been asked to do something illegal or unethical on the job. Four in 10 did what they were told. Another survey of more than 2000 administrative assistants showed that many employees face ethical dilemmas in their day-to-day work.

Assignment

Step 1

Working with four other students, discuss ways in which you would respond to the following ethical dilemmas. When there is a difference of opinion among group members, try to determine the specific factors that influence different responses.

- Would you lie about your supervisor's whereabouts to someone on the phone?
- Would you lie about who was responsible for a business decision that cost your company thousands of dollars to protect your own or your supervisor's job?
- Would you inflate sales and revenue data on official company accounting statements to increase stock value?
- Would you say that you witnessed a signature when you did not if you were acting in the role of a notary?

- Would you keep silent if you knew that the official minutes of a corporate meeting had been changed?
- Would you destroy or remove information that could hurt your company if it fell into the wrong hands?

Step 2

Research the commitment to business ethics at Johnson & Johnson (www.jnj.com/our_company/our_credo/index. htm) and Texas Instruments (www.ti.com/corp/docs/ company/citizen/ethics/index.shtml) by visiting their respective websites. As a group, discuss ways in which these statements are likely to affect the specific behaviours mentioned in Step 1.

Step 3

Working with group members, draft a corporate code of ethics that would discourage the specific behaviours mentioned in Step 1. Limit your code to a single typewritten page, but make it sufficiently broad to cover different ethical dilemmas.

Questions for Discussion

1. What personal, social, and cultural factors do you think contribute to lying in the workplace?

2. Do you agree or disagree with the following statement? *The term* business ethics *is an oxymoron.* Support your answer with examples from your own work experience or that of a family member.

3. If you were your company's director of human resources, how would you make your code of ethics a "living document"?

4. If you were faced with any of the ethical dilemmas described in Step 1, how would you handle them? How far would you go to maintain your personal ethical standards?

Exercising Your Ethics: Team Exercise

Assessing the Ethics of Trade-Offs

The Situation

Managers must often make choices among options that are presented by environmental circumstances. This exercise will help you better appreciate the nature and complexity of the kinds of trade-offs that often result.

The Dilemma

You are the CEO of a medium-sized, unionized manufacturing corporation that is located in a town of about 15 000 people. The nearest major city is about 200 kilometres away. With about 500 workers, your company is one of the five largest employers in town. A regional recession has caused two of the other largest employers to close down (one went out of business and the other relocated to another area). A new foreign competitor has set up shop in the area, but local unemployment has still risen sharply. All in all, the regional economic climate and the new competitor are hurting your business. Your company's sales have dropped 20 percent this year, and you forecast another drop next year before things begin to turn around.

You face two unpleasant choices:

Choice 1: You can tell your employees that you need them to take cuts in pay and benefits. You know that because of the local unemployment rate, you can easily replace anyone who refuses. Unfortunately, you may need your employees to take another cut next year if your forecasts hold true. At the same time, you have reason to believe that when the economy rebounds (in about two years, according to your forecasts), you can begin reversing pay cuts. Here are the advantages of this choice: You can probably (1) preserve all 500 jobs, (2) maintain your own income, (3) restore pay cuts in the future, and (4) keep the business open indefinitely. And the disadvantages: Pay cuts will (1) pose economic hardships for your employees, and (2) create hard feelings and undercut morale.

Choice 2: You can maintain the status quo as far as your employees are concerned, but in that case, you'll be facing two problems: (1) you'll have to cut your own salary (while you can certainly afford to live on less income, doing so would be a blow to your personal finances); and (2) if economic conditions get worse and/or last longer than forecast, you may have to close down altogether. The firm has a cash surplus, but because you'll have to dip into that fund to maintain stable wages, it will soon run out. The advantages of this option: You can (1) avoid economic hardship for your workers, and (2) maintain good employee relations. The downside: You will reduce your own standard of living and may eventually cost everyone his or her job.

Team Activity

Assemble a group of four students and assign each group member to one of the following roles:

- CEO of the company
- the vice-president of production
- a stockholder
- an employee who is a member of the union

Action Steps

1. Before discussing the situation with your group, and from the perspective of your assigned role, which of the two options do you think is the best choice? Write down the reasons for your position.

2. Before discussing the situation with your group, and from the perspective of your assigned role, what are the underlying ethical issues in this situation? Write down the issues.

3. Gather the group together and reveal, in turn, each member's comments on the best choice of the two options. Next, reveal the ethical issues listed by each member.

4. Appoint someone to record the main points of agreement and disagreement within the group. How do you explain the results? What accounts for any disagreement?

5. From an ethical standpoint, what does your group conclude is the most appropriate action that should be taken by the company? (You may find the concepts of *utility, rights, justice,* and *caring* helpful in making your decision.)

For additional cases and exercise material, go to **www.pearsoned.ca/mybusinesslab**.

Concluding Case 5-1

The Debate over Global Warming

In the 1990s, many scientists came to the conclusion that air pollution and greenhouse gases were causing the temperature of the earth to rise (global warming) and that serious problems were going to be evident in the future unless something was done to reduce carbon dioxide emissions. Recently, a debate has arisen in the scientific community with respect to global warming. The two most extreme positions are held by "Malthusian pessimists" (those who think we are heading toward an inevitable crisis) and the "technological optimists" (those who think that advances in technology will be able to overcome any crisis that might occur). These extreme views make for great party conversation, but what is needed is a careful analysis of the empirical data about climate change. This analysis needs to address two questions: (1) is the global average surface temperature of the earth really increasing, and (2) if it is, what is causing that to happen?

Is Global Warming Occurring?

A strong majority of scientists have concluded that global warming is real, and they point to data generated by the United Nations Intergovernmental Panel on Climate Change (IPCC), which shows that the average global temperature has risen about 0.6 degrees Celsius during the last century. Some scientists who agree that warming is occurring don't think the magnitude is as large as the IPCC claims; their main argument is that the IPCC data are contaminated and therefore exaggerate the amount of warming that has actually occurred. For example, taking temperatures in urban areas—so-called "heat islands"—leads to overestimates of temperature levels.

To the untrained person, it might seem that measuring temperature is a pretty straightforward thing to do, but it is more complex than it appears at first glance. One problem is that the number and location of weather stations is constantly changing, so the comparability of weather data over time is not as good as scientists would like. Another problem is that the methods used to measure temperature change over time. For example, many years ago, the temperature of sea water was measured by lifting a bucket of sea water into a ship and then measuring the temperature of the water. Now, water is pumped into the engine room of a ship and then measured. But doing that might cause the reading to increase because of the warmer temperature in the engine room. Deciding *where* to measure temperature is another problem. Urban heating must be taken into

account, but it is not clear what proportion of urban and rural sites should be included in temperature calculations.

Is Global Warming Caused by Human Activity?

Let us assume for the moment that global warming is a fact. The next obvious question is "What is causing global warming?" Many scientists argue that the rapid increase in carbon dioxide emissions that has occurred during the last 200 years is the cause of global warming. These emissions—which are the result of human industrial activity—trap heat in the atmosphere (the "greenhouse effect") and cause the temperature of the earth to rise. The views of scientists who hold this belief have been widely publicized, and many people accept them as fact. The IPCC has also concluded that greenhouse gases are the cause of global warming.

Other scientists have expressed skepticism about human-caused global warming. Consider some illustrative (and controversial) comments from the skeptics:

■ Reid Bryson, emeritus professor of meteorology and one of the most-cited meteorologists in the world, says the idea that global warming is caused by the release of carbon dioxide into the atmosphere is absurd. He says that warming is occurring simply because we are still coming out of the "little ice age" of the early 1800s.

■ Tad Murty, a professor in the Departments of Civil Engineering and Earth Sciences at the University of Ottawa, says that global warming is the biggest hoax ever perpetrated on humanity. He notes that there have always been cycles of warming and cooling.

■ Tim Patterson, a professor of geology at Carleton University, points out that, 450 million years ago, carbon dioxide levels were ten times higher than they are now and yet the planet was in the depths of an ice age. He also points out that 10 000 years ago, when the earth was coming out of a particularly cold period, temperatures rose as much as 6 degrees Celsius in one decade. That is one hundred times more rapid than the current rise.

Scientists who reject the idea that human activity is the cause of global warming make other, more general arguments. First, they point out that there have been variations in the earth's temperature in the past and that these variations couldn't possibly have been caused by human activity because there weren't any humans. Second, since the thermometer wasn't invented until 1602, we

▶

don't have a very long time period of accurate temperature records to examine as we look for warming trends. Records going back thousands of years are needed before we can say with any confidence that a warming (or cooling) trend is actually occurring. Third, research shows that changes in the earth's climate correlate better with fluctuations in the brightness of the sun than they do with fluctuations in carbon dioxide levels. Analysis of core samples from the sediment in British Columbia fjords shows a consistent 11-year cycle in marine productivity which correlates closely with the known 11-year cycle of sunspots. Scientists predict that by the year 2020 the sun will be entering a phase of weaker output, and they conclude that a period of unusually cool temperatures is likely. Several other research studies of tree rings and freshwater river levels also strongly suggest that the sun drives climate change.

What Does All This Mean?

If the scientists who say that global warming is caused by human activity are right, we had better get moving on initiatives to reduce carbon dioxide emissions. But if the scientists who say that global warming is not caused by human activity are right, there isn't much that we can do about climate change. Regardless of whether global warming is human caused or is a natural occurrence, there are some likely outcomes that will occur because of it. There will be both winners and losers if the average global temperature goes up significantly. In Greenland, for example, rising temperatures mean that more pasture area can be grazed by sheep and cows, and a greater variety of vegetables can be grown than was formerly the case; this will improve Greenland's economic performance. But rising temperatures will also undermine the seal hunting by Greenland's Inuit because of thinning ice and may also cause a decline in polar bear populations.

Questions for Discussion

1. Given the information presented above, as well as other information you have read, do you think the evidence supports the argument that global warming is occurring?

2. Given the information presented above, as well as other information you have read, do you think the evidence supports the argument that global warming is caused by human activity?

3. List some additional winners and losers that are likely as a result of global warming.

4. *While there are some uncertainties about global warming, the problem is significant enough that we need to take immediate action to reduce carbon dioxide emissions. If we don't, in 40 or 50 years it will be too late.* Do you agree or disagree with this statement? Defend your answer.

Pollution on the High Seas

A study by the International Council on Clean Transportation provides some interesting statistics on the global shipping industry.

- Ships transport more than 90 percent of the world's products by volume.

- Ships release more sulfur dioxide than all of the world's cars, trucks, and buses combined.

- Only six countries in the world release more greenhouse gases than ships collectively do.

- Ships produce about one-quarter of the entire world's output of nitrogen-oxide emissions (the ones that cause smog).

- In 1990, land-based sulfur dioxide emissions in Europe were about 10 times higher than sea-based emissions; by 2030, sea-based emissions will exceed land-based emissions.

Pollution from cargo ships is unusually high because they use bunker fuel, which is a tar-like sludge that is left over from the process of refining petroleum. Bunker fuel releases more pollutants than high-grade fuel, but ship owners use it because it is cheap. And refineries are happy to sell it to shippers because it gives them an outlet for a product that would otherwise not have a market.

While increasing concerns are evident about the global shipping industry, regulating ships on the high seas has always been something of a problem. This difficulty is obvious in the work of the International Maritime Organization, which is a United Nations agency that regulates shipping. The 167 nations that comprise its membership have had extreme difficulty agreeing on what to do about the problem of pollution. For example, it took the group 17 years to agree that the sulfur content in marine fuel should not exceed 4.5 percent. But the sulfur content in bunker fuel had already been reduced to half that level by the time the regulation was passed. One frustrated member of the committee said it spent most of one meeting discussing procedural details and the punctuation in its report.

A more effective approach is for ports to set emission rules, since cargo ships obviously have to unload their cargo *somewhere*. Some ports—particularly those in the Baltic Sea region and in the state of California—have already passed laws that prohibit ships from docking unless they use cleaner-burning fuels. California, for example, does not allow ships that use low-grade fuel to sail within 24 miles of its shores. Ports in Germany, Sweden, and Canada have also set targets to reduce air pollution from ships. But this patchwork of regulations has caused ship

owners big problems, because it means that ships need to switch from low- to high-grade fuel as they sail to different locations. Because this process is complicated and dangerous, the International Association of Independent Tanker Owners and the Hong Kong Ship Owners Association both think the UN should simply require ships to stop using bunker fuel.

The problem of pollution is not restricted to ships that carry merchandise; there is also a problem with ships that carry people. More than eight million passengers take an ocean voyage each year, cruising many areas of the world's oceans in search of pristine beaches and clear tropical waters. The tourists and the giant ships that carry them are usually welcomed for the revenues that they bring, but these ships also bring pollution.

A modern cruise ship generates a lot of waste—on a typical day, a ship will produce seven tonnes of solid garbage, 30 000 gallons of sewage, 7000 gallons of bilge water containing oil, and 225 000 gallons of "grey" water from sinks and laundries. Multiply these numbers by more than 167 ships worldwide, cruising 50 weeks per year, and the scope of the environmental damage is staggering.

Environmental groups see the top pollution-related problem as the death of marine life, including extinction. Foreign animals bring parasites and diseases, and in some cases, replace native species entirely. Bacteria that are harmless to human beings can kill corals that provide food and habitat for many species. Oil and toxic chemicals are deadly to wildlife, even in minute quantities. Turtles swallow plastic bags, thinking they are jellyfish, and starve, while seals and birds drown after becoming entangled in the plastic rings that hold beverage cans.

Here again, lack of regulation is the biggest obstacle to solving the problem. Laws and enforcement policies vary considerably from country to country, and even when laws are strict, enforcement may be limited. Cruise lines should be very concerned about clean seas for their own economic well-being, but this is often not the case. Intentional illegal dumping may actually be growing in scope. Over the last decade, for instance, as enforcement has tightened, 10 cruise lines have collectively paid $48.5 million in fines related to illegal dumping. In the largest settlement to date, Royal Caribbean paid $27 million for making illegal alterations to facilities, falsifying records, lying to the U.S. Coast Guard, and deliberately destroying evidence.

Critics are speaking out against the cruise lines' profiteering from an environment that they are destroying, but they note that the companies won't stop as long as the profits continue. Technology exists to make the waste safe, but industry experts estimate that dumping can save a firm millions of dollars annually. From that perspective, the cruise lines are making understandable decisions.

▶

Questions for Discussion

1. What are the major legal issues in this case? What are the major ethical issues?

2. Aside from personal greed, what factors might lead a cruise line to illegally dump waste into the ocean? What factors might cause cargo ships to use low-grade fuel?

3. Are the approaches to social responsibility by the cargo and cruise lines similar or different? Explain.

4. Distinguish between ethical issues and social responsibility issues as they apply to this problem.

Chapter 6

Ethics and Social Responsibility

After reading this chapter, you should be able to:

1 Describe why an understanding of basic approaches to ethical decision making and corporate social responsibility is important.

2 Explain the basic approaches to ethical decision making.

3 Identify the different implications of each approach in real-life situations.

4 Explain the basic approaches to corporate social responsibility.

5 Develop different implications for each approach to corporate social responsibility.

Confidence in the Japanese Construction Sector Collapses

Streamlining of Japan's building-plan review process in 1999 led to systemic corruption within the Japanese construction industry that jeopardized the safety of thousands of building occupants.

Scandal broke in the Japanese construction sector in late 2005 when it was revealed that a respected architect admitted to designing and constructing buildings below the minimum Japanese seismic requirements. The story broke on November 17, 2005, when Japan's Ministry of Land, Infrastructure, and Transport reported that architect Hidetsugu Aneha had knowingly designed 20 condominiums and one hotel that were not fit for occupancy. Of the 21 buildings, which were built in Tokyo, Chiba, and Kanagawa, 13 would not withstand an earthquake with a seismic intensity of 5.0 on the Richter scale—and some would not even withstand a moderate earthquake. This revelation shocked many, since the Japanese city of Kobe had suffered a devastating earthquake only a few years earlier in 1995, where more than 6400 people died from a tremor measuring 7.3 on the Richter scale. The day after the announcement was made, Aneha admitted to the allegations. It was later discovered that he had been falsifying reports since 1998. Through further investigation, the ministry found that Aneha actually falsified data on at least 71 of the 208 buildings he had designed.

Aneha blamed pressure from construction firms to design low-cost structural systems for new buildings and a fear that he would not get work if he didn't comply. In a strange twist, Aneha also blamed the inspection companies he used for their lack of diligence in checking his designs. Following the revelations, hundreds of condominium residents were forced to evacuate their homes, leaving them with the burden of finding new accommodation. The owners of four hotels, which Aneha had assisted in designing, decided to suspend operations while they waited for the buildings to be inspected. Some of the buildings are being retrofitted to increase their earthquake resistance, while others are being demolished. Still others remain vacant as all the stakeholders involved decide what to do.

The architect's deception was made public after eHomes, a privately owned architectural design inspection firm, admitted that it had failed to detect Aneha's fabrication in his structural reports. A representative of eHomes claims that they did not pick up on the faulty data because Aneha had taken measures to conceal it in the volumes of data regularly submitted for inspection and approval. Aneha also admitted that he used eHomes's inspection services because they regularly approved his fraudulent reports. He continued to use the firm's services, anticipating that his false structural calculations would continue to go undetected.

The inspection of building plans was traditionally undertaken by the Japanese government until 1999 when deregulation efforts led to changes in Japan's Building Standards Law. These changes allowed private firms to certify building designs and thereby streamline the building review process. The changes in the system also meant that architects were free to submit their designs to any inspection company for safety certification. Government officials began to realize that some architects were purposely choosing inspection firms with low standards in an effort to have their designs approved quickly, but problems with the new system surfaced only after the Aneha scandal. The changes to the law did incorporate a safeguard, where Japanese authorities were supposed to perform spontaneous, random audits of the operations of design-review firms each year. However, it was discovered after the Aneha scandal that these audits were not conducted with the initially intended frequency.

There is a growing fear that Aneha's case is only the tip of the iceberg for Japanese architecture. Failures in inspection agencies are thought to be the result of declining standards in investigation firms, and now there is concern that the problem is more widespread. Industry experts have suggested that the deterioration of inspection agencies' standards is related to pressure to complete drawing and structural inspections quickly, thus serving more clients and achieving greater profits. Certain inspection firms have acknowledged that the documentation they examine is often lengthy, making it difficult to check all of the information it contains in the short time frames that the industry demands. Since the Aneha scandal went public, the Japanese government visited 105 of 123 building inspection firms, confirming that 18 had failed to carry out proper screening procedures. In the case of eHomes, it was confirmed that they had not detected data fabrications in 37 out of the 99 projects submitted by Aneha. The firm's inspection licence was immediately revoked by the government, which subsequently led to the firm's demise.

Further evidence of poor government monitoring came from the testimony of the president of eHomes, who claimed that public officials did not take action when he informed them that his firm had detected false data. However, eHomes made the discovery only after a re-examination of Aneha's reports, once they had learned that another inspection firm had detected errors in Aneha's work a year earlier. As a result of the Aneha scandal, the Japanese government has recognized the prevalence of falsified structural data and the need to examine and make changes to the building-safety-inspection system to better detect it.

For his part in the scandal, Hidetsugu Aneha was stripped of his licence as an architect and arrested for breaking the Building Standards Law and the Registered Architects Law; the maximum penalty for these violations is 500 000 yen and 300 000 yen, respectively (approximately CDN$5000 and $3000). On the same day, four other individuals that assisted in designing, approving, and building Aneha's flawed designs were arrested. While none of the individuals faced charges directly related to the data fabrication scandal, police hope to build criminal cases against them. A few weeks later, a fifth individual was arrested for allegedly selling a condominium even though he knew that the building's earthquake-resistance data was inaccurate. Through investigation, the Japanese government hopes to determine where its design certification system failed and follow up with a revision of its laws so that scandals like Aneha's become history. ◆

Sources: BBC News, "Japan Construction Scandal Widens," December 14, 2005, news.bbc.co.uk (accessed November 1, 2006); Japan Real Estate, "Architectural Scandal Deepens," November 25, 2005, jrearticles2.blogspot.com (accessed November 1, 2006); *Japan Times Weekly Online,* "Data Scam on Quake Resistance Shakes the Nation," November 26, 2005, www.japantimes.co.jp (accessed November 1, 2006); *Japan Times Weekly Online,* "Rogue Inspection Dragnet Widens," December 3, 2005 (accessed November 1, 2006); *Japan Times Weekly Online,* "The Depths of Data Fabrication," December 10, 2005 (accessed November 1, 2006); *Japan Times Weekly Online,* "Huser Wanted Disclosure Delayed," January 28, 2006 (accessed November 1, 2006); *Japan Times Weekly Online,* "Aneha to Be Arrested Over Quake-Resistance Data," April 22, 2006 (accessed November 1, 2006); *Japan Times Weekly Online,* "Aneha and Seven Associates in Building Fraud Arrested," May 6, 2006 (accessed November 1, 2006); *Japan Times Weekly Online,* "Trail to the Epicenter of Faulty Math," May 13, 2006 (accessed November 1, 2006); *Japan Times Weekly Online,* "Huser Head Arrested in Building Scam," May 27, 2006 (accessed November 1, 2006); *Japan Times Weekly Online,* "Ehomes Head Admits Faking Papers," July 15, 2006 (accessed November 1, 2006).

Strategic overview

Globally, construction is valued at about US$3.2 trillion per year. Corruption in the construction sector is reportedly greater than in any other area in the world economy, and corrupt practices are found in all aspects and stages of the construction process—no area is immune.[1] As the case in Japan illustrates, the design stage plays a dark role in contributing to the scale of corruption in construction. Managers can face pressures that result in ethical and social responsibility issues. Aneha buckled to the pressure of demands for cheaper structural designs with faster completion time frames. As well, once he opened the door to conducting fraudulent practices, he had less reservation in continuing. As Aneha pointed out, the inspectors made it easy for him to continue since their review process was inadequate and didn't catch his false data. What is hard to fathom is the disregard for the safety of thousands by designing and constructing flawed structures, knowing full well that they will collapse when a tremor similar to the Kobe earthquake occurs again.

Should the Japanese government accept partial blame for Aneha's actions and the decay of standards applied in the construction of buildings? How would you feel if you learned that the building you go to school in could collapse under such minimal forces as excessive snow, mild tremors, or heavy rainfall? What if we lost our trust in all that is built, produced, manufactured, or prepared for our consumption? We place a great amount of trust in organizations, assuming that they will conduct themselves in a manner that does not place the public in financial or physical jeopardy, which is why ethics and social responsibility have a powerful role in the discussion of management. Managers in large companies usually act as agents of the owners (as we explain later in this chapter). As such, top executives have an implied obligation to take strategic actions that are in the best interests of the owners or shareholders. If they take actions that help themselves, such as rejecting a takeover bid to keep their jobs, but that may be to the detriment of shareholders, are they acting in an ethical manner? In recent years, numerous executives of top corporations have acted opportunistically, making headlines in the process. Some acted not only unethically but illegally. They harmed both the shareholders and many employees, who lost their jobs when their bosses' misdeeds came to light and the companies went bankrupt.

Both managerial ethics and strategy begin at the top of the organization. For ethical decisions and practices to permeate the firm, top executives must build a culture based on those values. This includes establishing codes of ethics, implementing ethics training for employees, and rewarding ethical behaviour (as discussed later in this chapter). Moreover, it includes behaving in an ethical manner themselves.[2]

An ethical organization is especially important when it comes to implementing the strategies developed by top managers. Managers at the top and throughout the organization along with other employees are likely to face many ethical dilemmas throughout the course of doing business. While the unethical practices that Aneha carried out appear on the grand scale, most organizations face similar pressure situations on a regular basis.

Managers must also grapple with decisions about how to operate their firms efficiently, yet in a socially responsible manner. To do so, top executives may need to establish standards that exceed the requirements of the law. They must also consider the strategic and ethical impact of their decisions on the organization's stakeholders and employees. And their decisions must be perceived to be fair. (We will discuss the various approaches managers can take to organizational "justice" later in this chapter.)

The discussions above coupled with the opening case help to highlight the two key issues of this chapter: managerial ethics and corporate social responsibility. **Managerial ethics** is essentially the study of morality and standards of business conduct. **Corporate social responsibility** is concerned with the obligations that corporations owe to their stakeholders, such as shareholders, employees, customers, and citizens at large.

managerial ethics The study of morality and standards of business conduct.

corporate social responsibility The obligations that corporations owe to their stakeholders, such as shareholders, employees, customers, and citizens at large.

Relevance to You

You may be wondering, "Why should I care about ethics and social responsibility? Aren't these the types of issues philosophers worry about?" To answer this question, you need only pick up recent newspapers or business magazines. Everything from Bay Street insider trading scandals linked to political announcements, to accounting frauds at CIBC and Nortel,[3] to environmental pollution cover-ups seems to be in the press daily. PricewaterhouseCoopers reported that 45 percent of companies around the world have been victim to some form of economic crime over a two-year period. The average cost to those companies was US$2.1 million.[4] For example, in 2004 WestJet was alleged to have repeatedly accessed Air Canada's internal website over a ten-month period. Beginning in May 2003, a former Air Canada employee's password gave WestJet access to confidential corporate information. WestJet executives were reported to have accessed the secure site more than 240 000 times, retrieving flight and scheduling information. Air Canada launched a $220-million lawsuit against the rival airline only to have WestJet launch a countersuit, accusing Air Canada of hiring private investigators to illegally rummage through recycled materials at the home of a WestJet executive. In the end, both parties dropped their suits. WestJet admitted to accessing Air Canada's website and covered the airline's legal fees of $5.5 million and paid $10 million to a children's charity in the two airlines' names. While the worst was avoided by having the two firms settle out of court, the image that they projected to Canadian consumers will be more difficult to drop.[5]

Clearly, poor managerial ethics and corporate social responsibility can generate much negative publicity, hurt a company's stock price and destroy shareholder value, or make it difficult for the firm to recruit high-quality employees. In contrast, well-managed ethical behaviour and corporate social responsibility can have significant, positive consequences for employees, customers, shareholders, and communities. Exhibit 6.1 provides a listing of companies honoured for "Excellence in Ethics" by *Business Ethics* magazine. As you read these examples, ask yourself whether you would be more or less likely to work for one of these firms because of its reputation. As a customer, would you be willing to pay a premium price for the product because of the company's reputation?

South Mountain Company, a US$6 million architecture and construction firm led since 1985 by founder John Abrams, is among the companies honoured for its "Excellence in Ethics" by *Business Ethics* magazine. The company is focused on more than maximum growth and profits. Abrams states that the company is more about workplace democracy and craftsmanship. As a consumer, how important are a company's business ethics to you? Would you be interested in working for a company that did not focus on growth and profit?

The Development of Individual Ethics

At this point in your life, do you think you have a fairly well-established set of ethical beliefs and values? If you do, how did you come by them? What role did family, friends, teachers, religion, job experiences, and life experiences have in the development of your ethical beliefs? To explore this issue, think about a situation in which someone made a different ethical judgment from your own. What if you had been born in a different country, raised by a different family, had attended a different school system, experienced different religious influences, had different friends, or held different jobs? Would you hold the same ethical values you do now? Would you reach the identical ethical judgments that you reach now?

There is little debate that family, friends, teachers, religion, job experiences, and life experiences play a significant role in the development of individual ethical values and judgments. What is debated is which factors play the strongest role, because their influence varies from person to person.[6] This debate is unlikely to be resolved soon. Nor is its resolution necessary for our purposes. The primary reason for raising the issue is to realize that to understand how others make decisions, you need to understand something about their backgrounds.[7]

Simply labelling ethical judgments that are different from your own as wrong is likely to foster feelings of mistrust (in both directions) and hurt working relationships. The greater the diversity in the workforce, or more specifically among your set of colleagues and subordinates, the greater is the need for tolerance and understanding. However, as a manager, tolerance does not mean simply allowing subordinates to come to whatever ethical decisions they individually deem right. Because individual decisions can have consequences for the organization, managers often need to shape and influence the ethical thinking, judgment, and decision making of subordinates.

Consider the following real case that was conveyed to us in a recent conversation (we have disguised the names at the manager's request). Imagine you are the marketing manager in a publishing company. Your assistant manager has just recruited a new sales representative, Martha, from a key competitor. Martha worked for your competitor, Dresden, for 11 months after graduating from college. Dresden pays employees a bonus based on performance after the first year of employment. Martha was expecting a $10 000 bonus from Dresden. In discussions with your assistant manager, Martha

Exhibit 6.1   Excellence in Business Ethics Award Winners

2005 Winners
Intel (CSR Management Award)
For leadership and excellence in corporate social responsibility management.

South Mountain Company (Workplace Democracy Award)
For using employee ownership as the foundation of life-enchancing company.

New Leaf Paper (Environmental Excellence Award)
For mainstreaming ecological principles into the paper industry.

Weaver Street Cooperative (Living Economy Award)
For its sustainable products, community focus, and democratic governance.

2004 Winners
The Gap (Social Reporting Award)
For taking social reporting a quantum step forward by risking unprecedented honesty in reporting factory conditions.

Chroma Technology Corp. (Living Economy Award)
For exemplifying the living economy with practices of employee ownership, fair wages, and environmental stewardship.

Dell, Inc (Environmental Progress Award)
For responding to stakeholders' concerns with industry-leading computer-recycling initiatives.

Clif Bar Inc. (General Excellence Award)
For its ongoing commitment to environmental sustainability, employee well-being, and community involvement.

King Arthur Flour (Social Legacy Award)
For handing down to employee owners a centuries-old tradition of purity, for both the consumer and the environment.

2003 Winners
Organic Valley (Living Economy Award)
For being an exemplar of the living economy: locally rooted, human scale, stakeholder owned, and life serving.

Baxter Healthcare (Environmental Reporting Award)
For rigour, transparency, and leadership in environmental accounting and reporting.

3M (Environmental Excellence Award)
For sustained commitment, innovation, and substantial impact in three decades of environmental stewardship.

Source: www.business-ethics.com, accessed October 24, 2006.

negotiated for a $10 000 signing bonus if Dresden failed to pay her the performance bonus. Part of the reason your assistant manager agreed to do this is because Martha had been exposed to a number of strategic operations and marketing plans in her first year of employment at Dresden. Given her somewhat junior position in the company, she had not been asked to sign, nor had she signed, a "noncompete" clause that would have prevented her from taking a job with a competitor for a specific time period or disclosing or using the knowledge gained during her time at Dresden. Legally, she was free to take the job with you.

Your assistant manager comes to you and asks if it is okay to try to get Martha to disclose as much as she knows about Dresden's marketing plans. What is your response? Do you think Dresden has an ethical obligation to pay Martha the $10 000 bonus even though she plans to leave only a few days short of completing 12 months of employment? If you were Martha, would you have any ethical misgivings about taking the new job and then relating all you knew about your previous employer's strategic plans? Would Dresden's paying you the end-of-year bonus have any bearing on what you would or would not reveal to your new employer?

Understanding Basic Approaches to Ethics

ethical dilemmas Having to
make a choice between two competing
but arguably valid options.

ethical lapses Decisions that are
contrary to an individual's stated beliefs
and the policies of the company.

So how should you make decisions like these? Are there ethical approaches
you can look to for guidance? Yes, there are some basic approaches that have
been around for a long time. This is in part because the challenge of ethical
decision making is not a modern one. **Ethical dilemmas**, or the choice
between two competing but arguably valid options, are not new and have confronted people throughout history.

In the next section we will describe these basic approaches for two reasons. First, they can be helpful in trying to understand how others approach
ethical dilemmas. Second, quite often the lack of a clear approach for making
ethical decisions causes **ethical lapses** or decisions that are contrary to an
individual's stated beliefs and the policies of the company.

In thinking about the first reason, it is important to keep in mind the
increasingly diverse workforce and global business environment. Now more
than ever before you are likely to encounter people who use widely different
approaches and reach very different conclusions about ethical conduct. This
is illustrated in a recent study that examined the extent to which salespeople
from the United States, Japan, and Korea viewed a set of actions as posing an
ethical issue or not. The study found significant difference among these three
nationalities.[8] For example, Korean salespeople did not think that seeking
information from a customer on the price quoted by a competitor in order to
resubmit a more competitive bid was much of an ethical issue. American and
Japanese salespeople saw this as largely unethical behaviour. As a concrete
example of this view, in most places in the United States and Canada a real
estate broker cannot tell you how much someone else offered on a house you
also want to buy. What do you think? Do you think asking a customer for
information on the price submitted by your competitors is ethical or not?

Interestingly, from this same international study, researchers found that
Korean salespeople did not think that giving free gifts was as much of an ethical issue as American salespeople did. Many organizations across Canada
share the American perspective. The issue associated with employees receiving
gifts is twofold: First, a free gift may influence an employee to make a decision
that may not have otherwise been made. Second, a free gift to select employees
within an organization may be perceived by others in the organization as an
unfair benefit. Do you think company policies that prohibit the receipt of gifts
are appropriate or excessive? How do you feel about restaurant serving staff
receiving tips when the cook and cleaning staff do not?

Without understanding how or why others come to different conclusions, it
is easy to label people holding the "wrong" beliefs as inferior. For example, in a
recent study, Chinese and Australian auditors working for the same multinational accounting firm reached different decisions about proper ethical conduct
because of different cultural assumptions. Chinese auditors looked to peers,
while Australian auditors looked to themselves in making ethical decisions. This
reflects the cultural group orientation of the Chinese and the individual orientation of Australians.[9] If either set of auditors has simply judged the other to be
wrong without sensitivity to how culture might influence ethical decisions,
imagine how difficult it might be for them to work together on a global audit
team. In fact, research has shown that ethnocentricity, or the belief that your
perspective is correct and others are inferior, tends to hurt managerial effectiveness, especially in culturally diverse or international contexts.[10] So it is
important for new managers to be able to examine the basic approaches to ethical decision making and recognize that individuals' backgrounds, including
cultural values, influence ethical decisions and behaviour.

As we stated, the second reason for examining basic approaches to ethical
decision making is to avoid ethical lapses. Ethical lapses are more common
than you might think. The pressures coming from both the external and

internal environment can often be overwhelming. This is especially true if managers lack a systematized and explicit framework for thinking through dilemmas. For example, you may believe that Aneha's actions were blatantly wrong. However, if you were in Aneha's situation, where the pressures from the external and internal environment placed you in a position where you must carry out questionable work practices to acquire a contract, you may not find the choice as clear as when you are an observer.

Basic Approaches to Ethical Decision Making

Several frameworks, or approaches, exist to ethical decision making. We will examine four of the most common: the utilitarian, moral rights, universal, and justice approaches. An understanding of basic approaches to ethical decision making will help you as a manager to examine your own personal ethics and work more effectively with employees whose ethical perspectives are different.

Utilitarian Approach

The utilitarian approach focuses on the consequences of an action. Simplified, using a **utilitarian approach** results in "the greatest good." Assume you are trying to sell grain to a developing nation and a customs agent demands an extra fee before he will clear your shipment. From a utilitarian perspective, you would try to determine the consequences of the options available to you. For example, you could (1) pay the money, (2) not pay the money and let the grain sit there, or (3) seek intervention from a third party. Which action would result in the greatest good? If there are starving people waiting for the grain, would you argue that the "good" of saving lives outweighs the "bad" of paying an illegal bribe?

utilitarian approach An approach to ethical decision making that focuses on the consequences of an action.

Keep in mind when talking about whether an outcome is good or bad, people may see the same outcome differently. In other words, the "goodness" or "badness" of an outcome is often subjective. Factors such as culture, economic circumstances, and religion can all affect those subjective judgments. For example, if you were in Aneha's shoes, would you argue that it was the poor reviewing practices of the private firms and inadequate auditing schedule of the Japanese ministry that should be blamed rather than the actions of one architect?

Utilitarian Approach by Stewart Black

mymanagementlab

But many situations are not as clear-cut as to whether they constitute an ethical dilemma or just a business decision. How would you handle a situation in which some members of your staff see an impending decision as strictly business with no ethical implications, while others see it as an ethical dilemma?

For an example of this, take a look at *A Manager's Challenge: "Changing Horses."* In this situation, some members think that a long-term business relationship places certain unwritten obligations on the company to work with a struggling supplier regardless of changes in the business environment. On the other hand, other members of the management team think that the situation is strictly a business-based transaction. They believe that changes in business conditions and performance by the supplier justify changing the relationship. Since the supplier is not meeting its obligations, it's just good business to cut ties with it and move on to a more reliable supplier. If you see this as an ethical dilemma, should you try to influence your co-workers to get them to change their opinions? Or should you change your perspective and simply view it as a business decision like your co-workers do?

Even if you frame the Johannson situation as an ethical dilemma, using the utilitarian approach, what action results in the greatest good and over what time frame? In the short run, continuing to work with Creative

A Manager's Challenge   *Change*

Changing Horses

Caren Wheeler was a young purchasing manager at Johannson Wood Products, a 12-year-old company in the Midwest. As the purchasing manager, she was being asked to make a decision about the continued use of a supplier. This represented a big challenge for Caren. Several other managers in the firm viewed the decision in ethical terms, whereas Caren normally didn't think ethics were relevant unless laws were being broken.

Like many innovative mid-sized firms, Johannson Wood Products had formed strong partnerships with a limited number of suppliers to receive supplies on a just-in-time basis and then ship its finished goods in a timely fashion to retail stores. One of those partner suppliers was Creative Applications.

Creative Applications was a small, family-run company that stored and milled Johannson Wood Products' lumber into finished parts. The partnership, negotiated three years ago, had worked well for Creative Applications. Over 60 percent of its revenues came from Johannson Wood Products. In fact, the agreement had come just when Creative Applications was in financial trouble. Although it was not out of the woods yet, the agreement with Johannson Wood Products was critical to Creative Applications' survival.

Recently, however, the partnership had not worked well for Johannson Wood Products. As its sales increased, Creative Applications was having difficulty meeting deadlines. Caren had mentioned this problem to Steve Jackson, Creative Applications' plant manager (and the son of the owner), but no real improvement occurred.

When Caren met with Tom Masters, the president of Johannson Wood Products, and several other managers to discuss the situation, a variety of opinions emerged. Some saw this as an ethical issue and others did not. First the group focused on Steve Jackson's abrasive personality and management style. Many in the meeting felt that he was "a control freak" and could not delegate authority. Consequently, as demand increased, Steve became a bottleneck in Creative Applications' ability to meet delivery deadlines.

One of Johannson Wood Products' managers, who disliked Steve, stated, "I don't think that continuing a relationship with Creative Applications is going to work for us. It's one of those cases where the management capabilities of a small-time operation can't make the transition to a larger producer. We can't afford to keep nursing along a relationship that's not working."

Another manager felt it was unfair to bring personal feelings for or against Steve into the discussion and replied, "We've always told our vendors that if they were there for us, we'd be there for them. For over two years, Creative Applications really performed for us. Are we going to pull out now that they are facing tough times? Remember 18 months ago, when we pressured them to lease an expensive piece of milling equipment because of our increased volume? The equipment dealer would only do it on a three-year lease. Creative did it even though it elevated their costs. If we pull the rug out from under them now, that's not fair, and will hurt their chances of survival—we're still 60 percent of their business. Is it ethical to just pull the plug now?"

A third individual interjected, "I propose that we make an offer to either purchase Creative Applications or start our own in-house capability for milling the products. Here is a proposal that details the capital that would be required for either option and the potential savings that could be generated over a three-year period."

"Caren, what do you recommend?" asked Tom Masters. Several different issues raced through her mind. First, she had not really thought about the situation from an ethical point of view, yet clearly some of the team members felt there were ethical issues involved. In her gut, she felt just dropping Creative Applications was the *wrong* thing to do, but she didn't have any formal ethical justification for her feelings. However, even those who thought it was an ethical issue did not really have any formal ethical argument for their conclusions. Caren wondered if she should change her normal approach and take a careful look at the situation from both an ethical and business point of view. Should she try to get the others to change their approach and also consider the ethical issues? Johannson Wood Products was always stressing loyal partnership relationships. Was it ethical to just sever the relationship with Creative Applications? On the other hand, the delays being caused by Creative Applications were beginning to hurt Johannson Wood Products' ability to meet store orders faster than its competition. What was the right thing to do and what was the right approach to take?

Source: Adapted from Doug Wallace, "Changing Horses," *Business Ethics*, November–December, 1994, p. 34.

Applications will likely hurt your customers, as your products do not arrive as fast as they would like. If this persists, it may enable your competitors to move past you and take market share away to the point that you have to reduce your size and lay off some employees. On the other hand, demonstrating that you are serious about your promise to work with chosen suppliers could lead to an additional commitment from Creative Applications and other suppliers and result in enhanced performance and product deliveries.

Moral Rights Approach

The **moral rights approach** to ethical decisions focuses on an examination of the moral standing of actions independent of their consequences. According to this approach, some things are just "right" or "wrong," independent of consequences. When two courses of action both have moral standing, then the positive and negative consequences of each should determine which course is more ethical. Using this approach, you should choose the action that is in conformance with moral principles and provides positive consequences. From a moral rights approach, if not honouring unwritten commitments to suppliers is simply wrong (i.e., doesn't have moral standing), then cutting off the supplier to make more money is not justified. The managerial challenge here is that the moral standing of most issues is debatable. For example, you might want to say that it is wrong to lie. But is it wrong to make your competitors think you are about to enter one market when you are really about to enter another so that your company has the element of surprise? Is it just wrong to say you are not working on a particular new technology when you actually are to influence your competitors not to invest in the new technology and thereby have an advantage when you finally perfect it? Again returning to the case of Johannson Wood Products, how would you handle the situation if one employee believes that honouring unwritten, implicit commitments is just right (i.e., has moral standing) and another employee does not? In many companies both explicit policies as well as corporate values often serve a vital role in defining what is right or wrong when there is no universally accepted determination. If the corporate values of Johannson stress honouring not only legal contracts but also implicit promises to suppliers, then should Caren try to get the other managers to change their views and see this as an ethical issue?

moral rights approach An approach to ethical decision making that focuses on examination of the moral standing of actions independent of their consequences.

Moral Rights Approach by Stewart Black
mymanagementlab

Universal Approach

Immanuel Kant, perhaps one of the most famous moral philosophers, articulated the best-known ethical imperative, or **universal approach**. Simplified, Kant's moral imperative was "do unto others as you would have them do unto everyone, including yourself." If you follow this approach, you should choose a course of action that you believe can apply to all people under all situations and that you would want applied to yourself. At the heart of universalism is the issue of rights. For Kant, the basis of all rights stemmed from freedom and autonomy. Actions that limit the freedom and autonomy of individuals generally lacked moral justification. If you were in Hidetsugu Ahena's situation and took a universal approach to the situation he was in, it would be unconscionable to knowingly create structures that will not withstand a moderate earthquake. To justify Ahena's choice under the universal approach, you would have to be willing to accept that your residence is destined to collapse in the next earthquake for the gain of the individuals involved in its construction.

universal approach An approach to ethical decision making where you choose a course of action that you believe can apply to all people under all situations.

Universal Approach by Stewart Black
mymanagementlab

Justice Approach

justice approach An approach to ethical decision making that focuses on how equitably the costs and benefits of actions are distributed.

The **justice approach** focuses on how equitably the costs and benefits of actions are distributed as the principal means of judging ethical behaviour.[11] In general, costs and benefits should be equitably distributed, rules should be impartially applied, and those damaged because of inequity or discrimination should be compensated.

Justice Approach by Stewart Black

mymanagementlab

distributive justice The equitable distribution of rewards and punishment based on performance.

procedural justice Ensuring that those affected by managerial decisions consent to the decision-making process and that the process is administered impartially.

Distributive Justice. Managers ascribing to **distributive justice** distribute rewards and punishments equitably based on performance. This does not mean that everyone gets the same or equal rewards or punishments; rather, they receive equitable rewards and punishments as a function of how much they contribute to or detract from the organization's goals. A manager cannot distribute bonuses, promotions, or benefits based on arbitrary characteristics such as age, gender, religion, or race.

Procedural Justice. Managers ascribing to **procedural justice** make sure that people affected by managerial decisions consent to the decision-making process and that the process is administered impartially.[12] Consent means that people are informed about the process and have the freedom to exit the system if they choose. As with distributive justice, the decision-making process cannot systematically discriminate against people because of arbitrary characteristics such as age, gender, religion, or race. Recent research involving employees across multiple countries consistently suggests that perceived justice is positively related to desired outcomes such as job performance, trust, job satisfaction, and organizational commitment, and is negatively related to outcomes like turnover and other counterproductive work behaviour.[13] Procedural justice is generally studied and interpreted within the context of the organization. However, the findings of a recent study show that factors external to the firm may also have strong effects on counterproductive workplace behaviour. In a study contrasting community violence and an organization's procedural justice, violent crime rates in the community where a plant resided predicted workplace aggression in that plant, whereas the plant's procedural justice climate did not.[14]

compensatory justice If distributive and procedural justice fail, those hurt by the inequitable distribution of rewards are compensated.

Compensatory Justice. The main thesis of **compensatory justice** is that if distributive justice and procedural justice fail or are not followed, then those hurt by the inequitable distribution of rewards should be compensated. This compensation often takes the form of money, but it can also take other forms. For example, compensatory justice is at the heart of affirmative action plans. Typically, affirmative action plans ensure that groups that may have been systematically disadvantaged in the past, such as women or minorities, are given every opportunity in the future. For example, special training programs could be instituted for women who were passed over for promotions in the past because they were denied access to certain experience required for promotion.

Moral Intensity in Ethical Decision Making

moral intensity The degree to which people see an issue as an ethical one.

As we have pointed out thus far in this chapter, one of the challenges of ethical decision making for a manager is that for many issues and consequences, people do not have identical perspectives. They differ in whether they see a situation as involving ethics and in how they would determine their course of action. So the practical question is whether managers can help people come to more common views on the moral intensity of issues.[15] **Moral intensity** is the degree to which people see an issue as an ethical one. This is largely a function of the content of the issue. As a manager you can use this framework both to anticipate the moral intensity of an issue and to diagnose the reasons for differing views about the moral intensity of an issue among people.[16] Moral intensity has six components, as illustrated in Exhibit 6.2: (1) magnitude of the consequences, (2) social consensus, (3) probability of effect, (4) temporal immediacy, (5) proximity, and (6) concentration of effect.[17] In other words, the overall moral intensity of a situation is the result of adding each of these components together.

The **magnitude of the consequences** associated with the outcome of a given action is the level of impact anticipated. This impact is independent of whether the consequences are positive or negative. For example, laying off 100 employees because of a downturn in the economy has less of an impact than if 1000 employees join the ranks of the unemployed. Many people would judge a 20 percent increase in the price of lawn fertilizer to be of a lower magnitude than 500 people killed or seriously injured because of an explosion in the fertilizer plant caused by poor safety procedures.

Social consensus involves the extent to which members of a society agree that an act is either good or bad. For example, in Canada there is strong social consensus regarding the wrongness of driving drunk. However, the extent of the social consensus across provinces differs when it comes to reviewing laws to prevent impaired driving. In a 2006 review of provincial impaired driving legislation, MADD Canada (Mothers Against Drunk Driving) found a wide variation in the measures taken by provincial jurisdictions to reduce impaired driving. MADD Canada's evaluation ranged from a high score of A– (given to Manitoba for their legislative reforms on impaired driving) to an F (given to Nunavut for their poor performance in the same area). This suggests that while there is a general social consensus regarding the wrongness of drunk driving, the consensus breaks down at the point of legislating laws to reduce the occurrence of drunk driving.[18]

The third component of moral intensity is **probability of effect**. Even if a particular action could have severe consequences and people agree about the positive or negative nature of that impact, the intensity of the issue rises and falls depending on how likely people think the consequences are. For example, one of the reasons that the advertising and display of cigarettes in stores is heavily restricted in Canada is because of the strong association between smoking and health problems like lung cancer. However, cigarette smoking itself has not been completely outlawed in part because the probability of effect is not 100 percent. The higher the probability of the consequence, the more intense the sense of ethical obligation is. Because people are highly likely to be injured if they are in a car accident, the intensity regarding the moral obligation of auto manufacturers to make safer cars is increasing. Side-impact air bags are now becoming standard in many of the vehicles available in North America. However, because there is no certainty that you will be in an automobile accident, many of the safety features are not required by law.

Temporal immediacy is the fourth component of moral intensity and is a function of the interval between the time the action occurs and the onset of its consequences. The greater the time interval between the action and its consequences, the less intensity people typically feel toward the issue. For example, even if industrial pollution were certain to lead to global warming and result in catastrophic changes to weather patterns, because the consequences are likely to happen 50 years from now, the moral intensity of industrial pollution is much less than if the effects were to happen next year.

The fifth component is **proximity**. All other factors being equal, the closer the decision maker feels to those affected by the decision the more the decision maker will consider the consequences of the action and feel it has ethical

Social Consequences
+
Probability of Effect
+
Temporal Immediacy
+
Proximity
+
Concentration of Effects
+
Magnitude of the Consequences

Moral Intensity

Exhibit 6.2 Factors of Moral Intensity.

magnitude of the consequences The anticipated level of impact of the outcome of a given action.

social consensus The extent to which members of a society agree that an act is either good or bad.

probability of effect The moral intensity of an issue rises and falls depending on how likely people think the consequences are.

temporal immediacy A function of the interval between the time the action occurs and the onset of its consequences.

proximity The physical, psychological, and emotional closeness the decision maker feels to those affected by the decision.

A Manager's Challenge   *Globalization*

U2-Faced?

Following years of outspoken lobbying on behalf of Africa's poor and sick, the rock group U2 and front man Bono have found themselves recipients of the same criticism that they bestowed upon the wealthy nations of the world. In June 2006, the corporate side of the giant rock group moved operations from their home soil in Ireland to the Netherlands. The decision, as David "Edge" Evans later defended, was based purely on financial grounds: U2 did not want to pay more taxes.

The motivation behind the band's decision to relocate their operations to the Netherlands was that the government of Ireland had decided to change a long-standing leniency on royalty taxes to entertainers in the country. The new tax law requires artists that make more than 500 000 euros (CDN$700 000) to pay tax on half of their creative revenues. U2 was the world's top-grossing band in 2005, bringing in more than 210 million euros (CDN$295 million), with roughly one-third of the band's earnings generated by royalty payments. The Netherlands tax structure for royalties, on the other hand, will result in U2 paying only about 5 percent tax on their royalties. The band members have remained residents of Ireland, as have some of their Irish-based businesses, requiring them to still pay the government of Ireland some taxes based on their income.

Most people wouldn't look twice at such a decision by the typical corporation. However, U2 is not a typical corporation. The tax-saving decision was made by a group that has been active in getting the rich nations of the world to forgive the debt of Africa's poorest nations. Bono, a charismatic figure that has been mentioned as a candidate for the Nobel Peace Prize, has also been a passionate supporter of the Make Poverty History campaign, lobbying nations to increase their financial support to Africa to US$50 billion a year by 2010. Bono has gone so far as to make public pleas while on stage for Ireland's prime minister to increase financial aid from 0.5 percent to 0.7 percent of Ireland's GDP. Bono also pulled no punches when he openly criticized Prime Minister Paul Martin at the outset of the 2005 Canadian federal election campaign for his poor performance in supporting African nations. Bono claimed that he was "crushed" that Canada had not committed to increasing financial aid from 0.3 percent to 0.7 percent of GDP. Bono believed that because Martin was the former finance minister he would be able to "make the numbers work." He also warned Martin that he would feel the impact in the election if he did not increase aid (incidentally, Martin lost the 2005 election).

Many believe that Bono is setting a questionable example by the pursuit of a safe tax haven. To be fair, this is not the first time that super groups have moved operations to pursue tax breaks. For example, the Rolling Stones moved

The rock group U2 decided to relocate their operations to the Netherlands to avoid paying increased taxes in Ireland. The action appeared to many to be in conflict with the band's vocal lobbying of rich nations to increase financial support to Africa.

their operations to the Netherlands in the early 1970s. It is no coincidence that one of U2's directors of U2 Limited is the individual behind the Rolling Stones's Netherlands low-tax strategy. Still, most would agree that the image presented by the Rolling Stones and U2 dramatically differ, with the Stones's sex, drugs, and rock 'n' roll attitude being a stark contrast to U2's active social conscience.

On the other hand, some might argue that U2's move to the Netherlands allows them to not only retain their earnings, but also use their tax savings more effectively toward world debt. Traditionally, U2 has provided anonymous donations as well as the royalties of some of their songs toward debt relief and to reduce the spread of AIDS in Africa. By maintaining complete control of their own finances, U2 can allocate funds where they see the greatest benefit rather than giving their funds to government coffers where it is distributed among numerous public bureaucracies that also rely on tax revenues to function.

There are other implications to the band's decision, as well. Countries cannot increase their spending on aid unless they receive revenue from income taxes. It has been reported that well over US$11 trillion has been stuffed into safe-haven mattresses around the world by wealthy individuals. The net result of the redirection of income is a loss of taxes in the range of US$255 billion to governments, which could go a very long way toward solving Africa's debt problem. How are countries supposed to increase aid if their tax base is eroded by tax havens? By avoiding the increased taxes in their home country, U2 is making it more difficult for Ireland to increase its financial commitment to Africa's needy. And what precedent does this set for other individuals with tremendous wealth?

▶

▶

If the members of U2 were to use the moral intensity framework, how would they assess the positive and negative consequences for relocating to the Netherlands? What is the level of social consensus regarding the rightness or wrongness of moving operations to another nation to reduce taxes? How strongly do people feel about corporations avoiding high taxes by locating in safe havens? How likely is it that U2's relocation will affect Ireland's ability to increase its financial aid to Africa? How close or distant will the public feel toward the argument presented by U2 members, or to the plight of poverty-stricken African nations? When the 2010 goal is to provide US$50 billion in annual financial aid to Africa, how concentrated will the effect of U2's pursuit of tax breaks be perceived by the public?

Sources: F. O'Brien, "Bono Criticized at Home for Irish Tax Manoeuvre," *Globe and Mail*, October 17, 2006; O. Bowcott, "Found What You're Looking For? U2 Inspire Irish Ire by Avoiding Tax," *The Guardian*, August 9, 2006; T. Peterkin, "U2 Move Their Assets Out of Ireland," *The Telegraph*, August 8, 2006; CBC Arts, "Bono 'Crushed' PM Hasn't Reached Foreign Aid Goal," November 25, 2005, www.cbc.ca (accessed October 24, 2006).

implications. Proximity does not just mean physical closeness. Proximity also involves psychological and emotional closeness and identification. Consequently, an affinity between the decision maker and those affected could be a function of many factors, including nationality, cultural background, ethnic similarity, organizational identification, or socioeconomic similarity. For example, if you feel a psychological and emotional affinity for young people in Africa, then decisions by African managers about laying off workers by seniority (meaning younger workers will get laid off first) will have greater moral intensity for you even if you live thousands of kilometres away. Likewise, a decision to close down a poorly performing but slightly profitable factory that could put your parents and neighbours out of work will also likely have greater moral intensity for you than a factory closure in which the affected workers are unknown to you.

The last component is the **concentration of effect**, or the extent to which consequences are focused on a few individuals or dispersed across many. For example, even though laying off 100 people has a lower magnitude of effect than laying off 1000 people, laying off 100 people in a town of 5000 has a greater concentration of effect than laying off 1000 people in a city of 2 million.

concentration of effect The extent to which consequences are focused on a few individuals or dispersed across many.

The importance of these six facets of moral intensity is twofold. First, as a manager, you can use these facets to anticipate issues that are likely to be seen as significant ethical dilemmas in the workplace.[19] If you can better anticipate issues that are likely to become ethical debates, you have more time to prepare and may be more effective at handling ethical dilemmas. Second, if you are working with a group that is using the same basic ethical approach and still can't agree on the ethical course of action, you can use these facets to determine the source of the disagreement.[20] The disagreement may stem from different perceptions of the situation on one or more of the moral intensity components. For example, your group, like Caren Wheeler's, may be arguing over the ethics of terminating a relationship with a long-time supplier. In examining the source of the disagreement, you may discover a difference in perception as to the concentration of effect. For example, once it is clear that you represent 60 percent of the supplier's business, others who were discounting this factor may change their opinions. This alone may make it easier to reach a decision.

The rock group U2 had to deal with significant negative media coverage regarding their decision to relocate their creative operations outside of Ireland and into the tax haven of the Netherlands (see *A Manager's Challenge: "U2-Faced?"*). Members of the band were both caught off guard by the intensity of the global and domestic public scrutiny and somewhat unprepared to respond at first. If U2 members had used the moral intensity framework, could they have predicted public reaction? If they could, would the framework have helped them make some anticipatory changes in how they manage their operations and present their rationale for the decision to relocate?

Making Ethical Decisions

Increasingly, it seems that individuals and organizations are embracing a philosophy of business ethics that was first and perhaps best articulated in 1759 by Adam Smith in his work *The Theory of Moral Sentiments*. Smith's basic thesis was that it is in individuals' and organizations' self-interest to make ethical decisions. Still, a significant challenge remains to you as a manager: How can ethical decisions be fostered and encouraged?

The Manager

As we mentioned at the outset, part of the reason for exploring various approaches to ethical decision making is to help you refine your own approach so that when pressures arise you can make decisions consistent with your ethical framework. To this end, there is perhaps no substitute for taking personal responsibility for ethical decisions. To illustrate this, simply put yourself in Caren Wheeler's position (see *A Manager's Challenge: "Changing Horses"*). If you were Caren, what might the magnitude of consequences be if Creative Applications is dropped as a supplier? How many jobs might be lost? How likely is this? How soon would it happen? If there is some degree of moral intensity to the situation, what approach would you use to come to a decision? Is it right to drop Creative Applications? Caren is expected to provide not only a recommendation but also a rationale for it. What decision would you have made if you were involved in the management of U2's operations? Why?

Even after you have become more comfortable and explicit about how you would resolve ethical dilemmas, the question still remains as to how much you should change your approach to fit in with others or try to change their approach. If you were managing U2's operations, how hard should you work to change the public's perception, persuading them to see the positive benefits of relocating the band's operations to a tax haven? Although it is probably impossible to argue that one of the approaches presented in this chapter is best, applied consistently, each approach does allow a consistent pattern of ethical decision making. This consistency may matter more to those you interact with than whether your decisions are always in agreement with theirs.[21] This is in part because your consistency allows others to better understand your approach and trust you than if they perceive your decision making as random and inconsistent.

The Organization

Just as managers try to foster ethical decisions, organizations have a significant impact on ethical decision making. The overall culture of the company can play a significant role. For example, the emphasis on keeping customers happy and income flowing seemed to contribute to a number of rather lax audits by the accounting firm Arthur Andersen (which subsequently went out of business) for companies like Enron and WorldCom. In contrast, firms can also have a positive impact on ethical decision making and behaviour. In many firms senior managers take explicit and concrete steps to encourage ethical behaviour among their managers. Although there is a variety of ways organizations might accomplish this objective, codes of ethics and whistle-blowing systems are perhaps two of the more visible efforts.

Codes of Ethics. Given the ethical dilemmas that managers face and the different approaches for evaluating ethical behaviour, many firms have adopted codes of ethics to guide their managers' decision making. A **code of ethical conduct** is typically a formal statement of one to three pages that primarily

code of ethical conduct
A formal statement that outlines types of behaviour that are and are not acceptable.

outlines types of behaviour that are and are not acceptable. Exhibit 6.3 reprints the Johnson & Johnson credo, that of one of the most respected organizations in the world. The credo was first adopted in 1945 and has been revised four times to its current version.

An annual study conducted by the *Financial Times* and Pricewaterhouse-Coopers found that more than half of the top 50 most-respected companies in 2005 were US firms; 13 placed in the top 20 (there were no Canadian companies on the list).[22] A separate examination of 84 codes of ethics in US firms found three specific clusters of issues addressed in these statements.[23] The first cluster included items that focused on being a good "organization citizen" and was divided into nine subcategories. The second cluster included items that guided employee behaviour away from unlawful or improper acts that would harm the organization and was divided into twelve subcategories. The third cluster included items that addressed directives to be good to customers and was divided into three subcategories. Exhibit 6.4 provides a list and description of the clusters and specific categories of issues addressed in these written codes. Most firms did have items in each of the three clusters, though not in all 30 subcategories.

A study of codes of ethics for firms in the United Kingdom, France, and Germany found that a higher percentage of German firms had codes of ethics than British or French firms (see Exhibit 6.5).[24] The greater cultural emphasis on explicit communication in Germany may partially explain this finding. Although only about one-third of the European firms in this study had codes of ethics, approximately 85 percent of US firms have formal codes.

In a separate study, researchers found important differences among firms from what are generally considered more similar than different cultures: Canadian, Australian, and US firms.[25] For example, the codes of ethics differed substantially in terms of explicitly commenting on ethical conduct regarding behaviour concerning domestic government officials (59 percent of Canadian, 24 percent of Australian, and 87 percent of US firms).

Exhibit 6.3   Johnson & Johnson Credo

We believe our first responsibility is to the doctors, nurses, and patients, to mothers and all others who use our products and services. In meeting their needs everything we do must be of high quality. We must constantly strive to reduce our costs in order to maintain reasonable prices. Customers' orders must be serviced promptly and accurately. Our suppliers and distributors must have an opportunity to make a fair profit.

We are responsible to our employees: the men and women who work with us throughout the world. Everyone must be considered as an individual. We must respect their dignity and recognize their merit. They must have a sense of security in their jobs. Compensation must be fair and adequate, and working conditions clean, orderly, and safe. Employees must feel free to make suggestions and complaints. There must be equal opportunity for employment, development, and advancement for those qualified. We must provide competent management, and their actions must be just and ethical.

We are responsible to the communities in which we live and work and to the world community as well. We must be good citizens—support good works and charities and bear our fair share of taxes. We must encourage civic improvements and better health and education.

We must maintain in good order the property we are privileged to use, protecting the environment and natural resources.

Our final responsibility is to our stockholders. Business must make a sound profit. We must experiment with new ideas. Research must be carried on, innovative programs developed, and mistakes paid for. New equipment must be purchased, new facilities provided, and new products launched. Reserves must be created to provide for adverse times.

When we operate according to these principles, the stockholders should realize a fair return.

Research on codes of ethics indicates that organizations believe codes of ethics to be the most effective means of encouraging ethical behaviour in their employees.[26] Indeed, if a given firm had a code that covered all 30 categories listed in Exhibit 6.4, employees would have a comprehensive guide for behaviour. Unfortunately, the research does not support a strong link between codes of ethics and actual employee behaviour. Firms without formal codes seem to have no higher or lower incidents of unethical behaviour than those with formal codes.[27]

Successfully Implementing Codes of Ethics. Establishing a formal, written code of ethical conduct is an important first step for organizations to take to encourage ethical behaviour. However, actions speak much louder than words, and employees are unlikely to conform to the formal code unless other actions taken by the organization reinforce the code and communicate that the company is serious about compliance.[28] In some companies, positions of ethics officer or ombudsman are instituted. These individuals are charged with ensuring that the flow of information is rich in both directions. In other

Cluster 1

"Be a dependable organization citizen."

1. Demonstrate courtesy, respect, honesty, and fairness in relationships with customers, suppliers, competitors, and other employees.
2. Comply with safety, health, and security regulations.
3. Do not use abusive language or actions.
4. Dress in businesslike attire.
5. Possession of firearms on company premises is prohibited.
6. Follow directives from supervisors.
7. Be reliable in attendance and punctuality.
8. Manage personal finances in a manner consistent with employment by a fiduciary institution.

Unclustered items

1. Exhibit standards of personal integrity and professional conduct.
2. Racial, ethnic, religious, or sexual harassment is prohibited.
3. Report questionable, unethical, or illegal activities to your manager.
4. Seek opportunities to participate in community services and political activities.
5. Conserve resources and protect the quality of the environment in areas where the company operates.
6. Members of the corporation are not to recommend attorneys, accountants, insurance agents, stockbrokers, real estate agents, or similar individuals to customers.

Cluster 2

"Don't do anything unlawful or improper that will harm the organization."

1. Maintain confidentiality of customer, employee, and corporate records and information.
2. Avoid outside activities that conflict with or impair the performance of duties.
3. Make decisions objectively without regard to friendship or personal gain.
4. The acceptance of any form of bribe is prohibited.
5. Payment to any person, business, political organization, or public official for unlawful or unauthorized purposes is prohibited.
6. Conduct personal and business dealings in compliance with all relevant laws, regulations, and policies.
7. Comply fully with antitrust laws and trade regulations.
8. Comply fully with accepted accounting rules and controls.
9. Do not provide false or misleading information to the corporation, its auditors, or a government agency.
10. Do not use company property or resources for personal benefit or any other improper purpose.
11. Each employee is personally accountable for company funds over which he or she has control.
12. Staff members should not have any interest in any competitor or supplier of the company unless such interest has been fully disclosed to the company.

Cluster 3

"Be good to our customers."

1. Strive to provide products and services of the highest quality.
2. Perform assigned duties to the best of your ability and in the best interest of the corporation, its shareholders, and its customers.
3. Convey true claims for products.

Exhibit 6.4 Categories Found in Corporate Codes of Ethics.

Source: D. Robin, M. Giallourakis, F. R. David, and T. E. Moritz, "A Different Look at Codes of Ethics." Reprinted from *Business Horizons* (January–February 1989), Table 1, and p. 68. Copyright 1989 by Indiana University Kelley School of Business. Used with permission.

words, they have the responsibility of helping information and policies get out to the employees and also to ensure that employees' concerns, observations of misconduct, and the like can flow up and into senior management levels where action to correct things can be taken.

Communication. The first step in effectively implementing a code of ethics is communicating it to all employees. For maximum impact, this communication needs to take a variety of forms and be repeated. It is not enough to simply send out a one-time memo. Rather, the code will need to be communicated in memos, company newsletters, videos, and speeches by senior executives repeatedly over a period of time if people are to take the content of the message seriously.

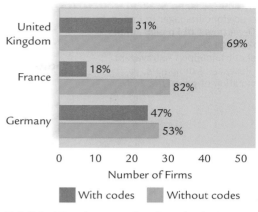

Exhibit 6.5 Adoption of Codes of Ethics.

Training. For the code of ethical conduct to be effective, people will likely need training.[29] For maximum impact, the training needs to be engaging. For example, Motorola developed approximately 80 different short cases. Each case presents a situation requiring a manager to make a decision. Individual participants in the training program were asked to decide what they would do and discuss the ethical aspects of the decision. They then compared their decisions to those of senior executives, including the CEO, and what these executives believe is in keeping with the firm's code of ethics.

Lockheed Martin also takes an engaging approach to ethics training with an interesting, innovative twist. In the late 1990s the company developed a board game based on Scott Adams's *Dilbert* character. The game consisted of 50 ethical dilemmas for which players have to decide among four possible responses. Participants rated this approach much higher in satisfaction than traditional ethics training and seemed to recall the learning points more effectively. Later, when the *Dilbert* craze wore off, Lockheed Martin used real business ethics problems as a basis for discussion. The company also has an ethics hotline employees can call if they are experiencing a business dilemma.[30]

Although officials at organizations often think that ethics training programs are effective, current research is less conclusive. What we can say based on research is that the greater the psychological and emotional involvement of participants in the training, the greater their retention of the learning points. This may explain why Lockheed Martin's experience with ethics training has been so positive.

Reward and Recognition. In addition to communicating the code to employees and training them, it is critical to make sure that those who comply are recognized and rewarded. Otherwise, employees will simply view the written code as the "formal rhetoric, but not the real deal."

The US oil giant ExxonMobil is a company that recognizes the importance of this principle. It regularly celebrates stories of individuals who have honoured the company's code of conduct even when doing so might have cost the company money. For example, one of its drilling teams was setting up to drill for oil in the jungles of a developing country when a government official came by and stated that before they started the drill they needed to pay for an operating permit. However, the official wanted the payment (approximately US$10 000) paid to him personally in cash. This was against the firm's code, so the team manager refused to pay. The drilling team and their expensive equipment sat idle for more than a week at a cost of over US$1 million. Finally, the government official admitted that all the paperwork and permits were in order and the team was allowed to proceed. ExxonMobil celebrated this incident in its newsletter to reinforce to its employees that the company

In 1998, Joanna Gualtieri, a portfolio manager in Canada's Department of Foreign Affairs, reported billions of dollars spent to support extravagant lifestyles of diplomats, in violation of government laws.

takes its code of ethical conduct seriously and rewards people who honour it, even if it costs the company money.

Whistle-Blowing. A **whistle-blower** is an employee who discloses illegal or unethical conduct on the part of others in the organization. While some firms have implemented programs to encourage whistle-blowing, most have not.[31] As a group, whistle-blowers tend *not* to be disgruntled employees but instead are conscientious, high-performing employees who report illegal or unethical incidents. In general, they report these incidents not for notoriety but because they believe the wrongdoings are so grave that they must be exposed.[32] For example, in 2006 four mechanics employed with Air Canada Jazz made public their concerns regarding economic and scheduling pressures taking priority over flight safety. The employees were concerned that the pressure to cut corners on maintenance was going to affect flight safety. The risk taken by the employees in speaking out was great, since there are no protection laws in place for airline workers in Canada. Air Canada Jazz suspended the workers with pay for two weeks, but they also took steps to address the issues raised by the employees.[33] Research suggests that the more employees know about the internal channels through which they can blow the whistle and the stronger the protection of past whistle-blowers, the more likely they are to initially use those internal channels rather than involving external channels like the media.[34]

Following the announcement by the Jazz employees, Canadians in support of whistle-blower protection argued that, similar to the United States, airline workers with life-or-death responsibilities should be free to voice safety concerns without penalty. In a 2005 survey, Canadian CEOs believed almost unanimously that there should be laws in place allowing whistle-blowers to sue employers who penalize them for reporting wrongful practices. Nearly two-thirds in the study also believed that third-party whistle-blower hotlines are more effective in persuading employees to come forward than hotlines

whistle-blower An employee who discloses illegal or unethical conduct on the part of others in the organization.

operated internally.[35] In general, research suggests that the following steps can be effective in encouraging valid whistle-blowing:[36]

- Clearly communicate whistle-blowing procedures to all employees.

- Allow for reporting channels in addition to the chain of command or reporting incidents to one's boss.

- Thoroughly investigate all claims based on a consistent procedure.

- Protect whistle-blowers who make valid claims.

- Provide moderate financial incentives or rewards for valid claims.

- Publicly celebrate employees who make valid claims.

Top Management Example. The impact of setting an example is probably no more evident than in the case of ethical conduct.[37] Top management, both in terms of how they behave personally and how they reward, punish, or ignore the actions of others, can severely damage the best intentions and designs of an implementation plan (e.g., communication, training, whistle-blowing, etc.). When it comes to skirting the law or making decisions that fall short when open to public scrutiny, the example of top management is often correlated with the behaviour of middle managers. Managers are rarely persuaded by top executives to "do as I say, not as I do." Leaders at Enron such as Kenneth Lay and Jeffrey Skilling set an example of reporting growth at any price. Standard accounting rules were ignored so that higher revenues and profits could be recorded immediately. Once one rule, law, or policy is ignored by senior officers, who is to say that others shouldn't be? This pattern of illegal and unethical conduct was not confined to Enron but was complemented by the behaviour of senior partners in the accounting firm that was supposed to monitor and certify Enron's accounting practices—Arthur Andersen. In an effort to retain Enron's auditing business and its more lucrative consulting engagements, leaders at Arthur Andersen ignored Enron's accounting irregularities despite its legal and ethical obligation to report them. In the end, leaders even

"The fish rots from the top of the head." The saying relates to the fact that people in an organization take their cues from the person leading it. Justice John Gomery, who presided over the enquiry on the 1994–2003 federal sponsorship program, stated in his 2005 report that former Prime Minister Jean Chrétien and Chief of Staff Jean Pelletier should be held responsible for mismanaging the flawed $332 million operation that provided lucrative kickbacks to Liberal supporters. While there was no direct evidence linking the two to the wrongdoings, they both failed in taking the most basic of precautions.

instructed subordinates to destroy and shred documents (against company policy and legal statutes) in an effort to hide wrongdoing on both sides.

The net effect of Lay and Skilling's corruption was the complete collapse of Enron and the 2006 conviction of both men for their part in the scandal. Skilling was sentenced to more than 24 years in prison that same fall. Lay's conviction, however, was extinguished in July 2006 when he died of a heart attack before he was sentenced. As for the accounting firm Arthur Andersen, it went from one of the "Big Five" accounting firms with an employee base of 85 000 in 2001 to surrendering its licences and right to practise accounting in 2002. Only 200 employees remain to handle the lawsuits and dissolution of the firm.

But by following the steps outlined earlier, managers can catch problems before they become national media events and seriously damage the firm's reputation. In addition, new laws are being passed by municipal, provincial, and the federal government to protect whistle-blowers. Employers cannot discharge, threaten, or otherwise discriminate against employees because they report a suspected violation of the law.

The Government

The governments of Canada and many other countries have continued to foster ethical behaviour. For example, the Canadian government has enacted a number of laws and regulations designed to reduce the presence of corruption in government and to encourage whistle-blowing when corrupt practices are found. Yet, the conduct of government officials often speaks louder than words.

Canada has traditionally been respected for its business practices, but a series of high-profile scandals within the government had led to a diminished confidence by business people and analysts. Transparency International prepares a Corruption Perceptions Index (CPI) that ranks countries based on the extent that businesspeople and analysts around the world perceive the presence of corruption in public officials and politicians. In 2001, Canada ranked seventh out of 91 countries in the study, with a CPI score of 8.9 out of a possible 10. By comparison, Australia ranked ninth; the United Kingdom thirteenth; the United States sixteenth, and Germany and Japan were twentieth and twenty-first, respectively. In 2005, however, Canada plummeted to fourteenth place with a CPI of 8.4. Australia remained at ninth; the United Kingdom moved up to eleventh; the United States moved down to seventeenth; Germany moved up to sixteenth; and Japan remained twenty-first.[38]

Clearly, making ethical decisions is not easy. It takes an understanding of various frameworks at the individual level and intervention at the organization and government levels if compliance with particular points of view is to be achieved. It's also clear that making the wrong ethical choice can result in serious negative results for individuals, organizations, and even nations.

While this section has focused on making ethical decisions from the individual point of view, the next section examines the general issues of ethics focusing on the organization. Typically, the issues we cover next are discussed under the general banner of corporate social responsibility.

Social Responsibility

Corporate social responsibility is concerned with the constituencies to which corporations are obligated and the nature and extent of those obligations. As media coverage has increased and organizations such as Greenpeace Canada, the David Suzuki Foundation, and Raging Grannies have put more pressure on organizations, they have increasingly come to terms with the amount of resources they should devote to being socially responsible. Consider the following questions that confront managers daily:

- Should a firm implement environmental standards greater than those required by law?

- Should a firm insist on the same high level of safety standards in all its worldwide operations even if the laws of other countries accept lower standards?

- Do all employees, regardless of nationality or employment location, have the same rights?

- Should managerial actions that are illegal or morally unacceptable in one country be allowed in another country in which they are legal or morally acceptable?

- Should managers consider the interests of employees, customers, or general citizens over those of shareholders?

Questions such as these form the substance of social responsibility debates. Both social responsibility and managerial ethics focus on the "oughts" of conducting business. Although several approaches to corporate social responsibility exist, an examination of two fundamental perspectives will help you reflect on how you personally view the issue and how you might effectively interact with others holding differing perspectives.

The Efficiency Perspective

Perhaps no contemporary person presents the **efficiency perspective** of social responsibility more clearly than the Nobel Prize–winning economist Milton Friedman.[39] Quite simply, according to Friedman, the business of business is business. In other words, a manager's responsibility is to maximize profits for the owners of the business. Adam Smith is perhaps the earliest advocate of this approach. Smith concluded over 200 years ago that the best way to advance the well-being of society is to place resources in the hands of individuals and allow market forces to allocate scarce resources to satisfy society's demands.[40]

efficiency perspective The concept that a manager's responsibility is to maximize profits for the owners of the business.

Managers as Owners. When a manager of a business is also the owner, the self-interests of the owner are best achieved by serving the needs of society. If society demands that a product be made within certain environmental and safety standards, then it is in the best interests of the owner to produce the product to meet those standards. Otherwise, customers will likely purchase the product from competitors. Customers are more likely to purchase from firms that comply with widely shared and deeply held social values, so it makes sense for businesses to incorporate those values into their operations and products. To the extent that the cost of incorporating society's values is less than the price customers are willing to pay, the owner makes a profit.

Critics of the efficiency perspective, however, argue that quite often customers and society in general come to demand safety, environmental protection, and so on only after firms have caused significant visible damage. For example, society might hold strong values about not polluting the water and causing health problems. However, if the consequences of polluting a river are not visible and people are not immediately hurt, social pressure might not emerge to cause the owner to align his actions with societal values until years after the fact.

Managers as Agents. In most large organizations today, the manager is not the owner. The corporate form of organization is characterized by the separation of ownership (shareholders) and control (managers). Managers serve as the agents of the organization's owners. Within this context, Friedman argues that managers should "conduct business in accordance with [owners'] desires, which will generally be to make as much money as possible while conforming to the basic rules of society, both those embodied in law and those embodied in ethical custom."[41] From Friedman's perspective, managers have no obligation to act on behalf of society if doing so does not maximize value for the shareholders. For example, packaging products in recycled paper should be undertaken only if doing so maximizes shareholder wealth. Whether such an action satisfies or benefits a small group of activists is irrelevant. Managers have no responsibility to carry out such programs; in fact, they have a responsibility *not* to undertake such action if it is more costly because it does not maximize shareholder wealth. Similarly, charitable donations are not the responsibility of corporations. Instead, managers should maximize the return to shareholders and then shareholders can decide if and to which charities they want to make contributions. Simply put, the profits are not the managers' money, so they have no right to decide how or if it should be distributed to charitable causes.

From the efficiency perspective, it is impossible for managers to maximize shareholders' wealth and simultaneously attempt to fulfill all of society's needs. It is the responsibility of governments to impose taxes and determine expenditures to meet society's needs. If managers pursue actions that benefit society but do not benefit shareholders, then they are exercising political power, not managerial authority.

Concerns with the Efficiency Perspective. The efficiency perspective assumes that markets are competitive and that competitive forces move firms toward fulfilling societal needs as expressed by consumer demand. Firms that do not respond to consumer demands in terms of products, price, delivery, safety, environmental impact, or any other dimension important to consumers will, through competition, be forced to change or be put out of business. Unfortunately, however, corrective action often occurs after people are injured.

Arnold Dworkin, the owner of Kaufman's Bagel and Delicatessen in Illinois, learned to pay attention to public safety the hard way. On a Wednesday, calls trickled in to the restaurant from customers complaining of vomiting, nausea, and stomach pains, and by Friday the restaurant had to be closed. Customers were suffering from salmonella poisoning, which was traced back to the corned beef being cooked at only 90 degrees rather than the 140 degrees required by local health regulations. Although corrective measures were taken, three weeks later another customer was hospitalized with salmonella poisoning. This time the cause was traced to a leaky floorboard above a basement meat-drying table. Kaufman's lost approximately $250 000 in sales and $10 000 in food, and its insurance company paid out more than $750 000 for individual and class-action suits and hospital claims. Interestingly, because Dworkin dealt with the situation in a straightforward manner by disclosing all the information he had to customers and the media, quickly making every repair, and following all the recommended actions suggested by the safety and health board regardless of cost, his business returned to 90 to 95 percent of its original level within two years.[42]

The other major concern with the efficiency perspective is that corporations can impose indirect consequences that may not be completely understood or anticipated. In economic terms, these unintended consequences are called **externalities**. For example, the British government enticed Nissan to build a new automobile plant there with tax and other incentives. However, the trucks going in and out of the plant created traffic congestion and wear on public roads that were not completely accounted for in the government's proposal. The government had to use tax revenue collected from citizens to repair the roads damaged by Nissan, to which it had given tax breaks. These poor road

externalities Indirect or unintended consequences imposed on society that may not be understood or anticipated.

conditions slowed deliveries to the factory and also created inconveniences for the citizens.

However, even when externalities can be anticipated, consumers often cannot correctly factor in or be willing to pay for the costs. For example, the consequences of poor safety controls at a grass fertilizer plant (explosion, fire, toxic fumes, injury, and death) are understood. As a consumer, can you correctly assess the costs of a chemical disaster and the increased price you should pay to cover the needed safety expenditures? If the answer is "No," this may cause the plant manager to skip necessary safety practices to keep costs low and make a profit. It is not until inadequate safety policies and practices result in a chemical disaster and people are killed or injured that the impact of the externality (i.e., the chemical disaster) is fully appreciated by consumers and therefore appropriately priced in the market.

Social Responsibility Perspective

The social responsibility perspective argues that society grants existence to firms; therefore, firms have responsibilities and obligations to society as a whole, not just shareholders. Thus, while the efficiency perspective states that it is *socially responsible* to maximize the return to the shareholder, the social responsibility perspective states that it is *socially irresponsible* to maximize only shareholder wealth because shareholders are not the only ones responsible for the firm's existence. For instance, creditors of a corporation cannot go beyond the assets of the corporation and seek repayment from the assets of the owners. This protection is termed *limited liability*. This privilege is granted to the corporation by society, not by shareholders.[43] Thus, the existence of the firm is not solely a function of shareholders, and therefore, the responsibilities of the firm cannot be restricted just to shareholders.

Stakeholders. In the social responsibility perspective, managers must consider the legitimate concerns of other stakeholders beyond the shareholders. **Stakeholders** are individuals or groups who have an interest in and are affected by the actions of an organization. They include customers, employees, financiers, suppliers, communities, society at large, and shareholders. Customers have a special place within this set of constituencies because they pay the bills with the revenue they provide.[44] Shareholders are also given special status, but in the stakeholder approach, shareholders are viewed as providers of "risk capital" rather than as sole owners. Consequently, shareholders are entitled to *reasonable* return on the capital they put at risk, but they are not entitled to a *maximum* return because they are not solely responsible for the existence of the firm. To maximize the return to shareholders would take away returns owed to the other stakeholders. Thus, managers must make decisions and take actions that provide a reasonable return to shareholders, balanced against the legitimate concerns of customers, employees, financiers, communities, and society at large. While the evidence is not definitive, there is research to suggest that there is a positive relationship between a stakeholder approach and firm performance.[45]

stakeholders Individuals or groups who have an interest in and are affected by the actions of an organization.

Concerns with the Social Responsibility Perspective. One of the key concerns with the social responsibility perspective is that important terms such as "reasonable returns" and "legitimate concerns" cannot be defined adequately. Given that reasonable returns to shareholders and legitimate concerns of other stakeholders could come into conflict, not knowing exactly what is reasonable or legitimate reduces a manager's ability to find the appropriate balance and act in a socially responsible way. This is why from a practical standpoint, even if you believe in the stakeholder framework of corporate social responsibility, making decisions that balance the interests of the different stakeholders is a significant challenge for which there is no magic solution. It is not only possible but also quite likely that customers, employees, financiers, communities, and society at large will have conflicting and competing concerns. Consider the case of a manager in a factory that makes corrugated boxes. His customers want sturdy boxes that can be stacked several levels high. Society increasingly seems to want a higher use of recycled paper. However, boxes made of recycled paper either have higher costs for the same strength or lower strength at the same cost compared to boxes made of nonrecycled paper. In such a case, how would you determine the most socially responsible action? If customers tell you that boxes must meet a certain strength requirement regardless of whether they use recycled paper or not, does this outweigh the desires of the other stakeholders? Should you devote more money to researching and developing stronger recycled boxes even though it takes money away from shareholders by increasing costs and reducing profits?

Comparing the Efficiency and Social Responsibility Perspectives

The efficiency and social responsibility perspectives differ mainly in terms of the constituencies to whom organizations have responsibilities. The two perspectives differ little in their evaluations of actions that either harm or benefit both shareholders and society (see Exhibit 6.6). Their evaluations differ most markedly when actions help one group and harm the other. Actions that benefit shareholders but harm the other legitimate stakeholders would be viewed as managerially responsible from the efficiency perspective, but socially irresponsible from the social responsibility perspective. Actions that harm shareholders but benefit the other legitimate stakeholders would be viewed as managerially irresponsible from the efficiency perspective, but socially responsible from the social responsibility perspective.

Corporate Responses

How corporations react to the various pressures and constituencies connected to the topic of social responsibility varies widely. These reactions can be simplified and laid out on a continuum that ranges from defensive to proactive, as illustrated in Exhibit 6.7. Although we might imagine that firms adopting the efficiency perspective are more likely to be Defenders, Accommodators, and Reactors, and firms adopting the stakeholder perspective are more likely to be Anticipators, we know of no research that

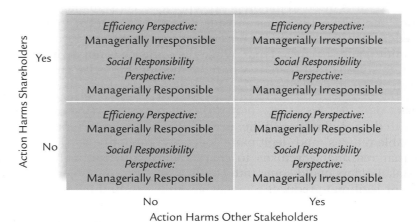

Exhibit 6.6 Comparing Efficiency and Social Responsibility Perspectives.

Exhibit 6.7 Corporate Responses				
	Defenders	**Accommodators**	**Reactors**	**Anticipators**
Belief:	We must fight against efforts to restrict or regulate our activities and profit-making potential.	We will change when legally compelled to do so.	We should respond to significant pressure even if we are not legally required to.	We owe it to society to anticipate and avoid actions with potentially harmful consequences, even if we are not pressured or legally required to do so.
Focus:	Maximize profits.Find legal loopholes. Fight new restrictions and regulations.	Maximize profits. Abide by the letter of the law. Change when legally compelled to do so.	Protect profits. Abide by the law. React to pressure that could affect business results.	Obtain profits. Abide by the law. Anticipate harmful consequences independent of pressures and laws.

has examined this specific association.

Defenders. Companies that might be classified as defenders tend to fight efforts that they see as resulting in greater restriction and regulation of their ability to maximize profits. These firms often operate at the edge of the law and actively seek legal loopholes in conducting their business. Typically, they change only when legally compelled to do so.

Accommodators. These companies are less aggressive in fighting restrictions and regulations than Defenders, but they still change only when legally compelled to do so. This type of firm tends to obey the letter of the law but does not make changes that might restrict profits if it is not required to.

Reactors. Reactor firms make changes when they feel that pressure from constituencies is sufficient such that nonresponsiveness could have a negative economic impact on the firm. For example, the firm might change to recycled paper for boxes only when the pressure from customers becomes strong enough that nonresponsiveness would lead customers to boycott its products or simply to choose a competitor's products that use recycled paper.

Anticipators. Firms in this category tend to believe that they are obligated to a variety of stakeholders—customers, employees, shareholders, general citizens, and so on—not to harm them, independent of laws or pressures that restrict or regulate their actions. Firms in this category not only abide by the law, but they might take action to avoid harming constituencies, even when the constituencies might not be aware of the potential danger. For example, a firm might take steps to protect employees from harmful chemicals within the workplace even before employees suffer negative side effects sufficient for them to demand work environment changes or before safety laws are passed.

A Manager's Challenge: "Not in My Backyard" helps illustrate some of these corporate responses in the face of advancing and accumulating technology. It focuses on how some firms are responding to the need to plan better methods of disposing of old technology. As you read, you might ask yourself what the motivation seems to be for each of the various firms mentioned in exploring new ways to recycle e-waste. For example, the anticipators: Are they motivated primarily to try to help the environment and reduce the accumulation of toxins in landfills, or are they motivated because they believe their competitive position could be enhanced by already meeting future regulations that might be set in place? What would you do if exceeding current environmental requirements potentially hurt your business? For example, what if the cost of safely recycling your products and old technology meant that you had to charge a price higher than your competition? Or what if your market research suggested that while personal users of your equipment support your recycling policy, commercial users were unlikely to pay the premium price for the safety of proper recycling? Or what if commercial sales accounted for half of your company's total sales? What would you do?

A Manager's Challenge   *Technology*

Not in My Backyard: The Safe Disposal of e-Waste

What do you do when your cell phone no longer works? What do you do with the old Sony Discman players that you find when you clean out your closet? What happens to the VHS recorder that has reached the end of its useful life? How do you get rid of these electronic components when they are no longer needed? Do you bury them in your own backyard? Not likely. Most people walk the items to the curb to get picked up by the local garbage collection. For us, the electronic gadget's life is over, but for the environment, it is the beginning of years of decay and leaching of toxins and heavy metals into the soil and water table.

Canada has a voracious appetite for new technology, and as a result we are accumulating a tremendous amount of unwanted, outdated equipment. By 2010, Canada will be throwing away more than 91 000 metric tonnes of electronic equipment such as PCs, cell phones, and printers every year. In Alberta alone, 362 880 kilograms of lead from electronic equipment ends up in landfills annually. Large organizations that have equipment to dispose of end up having it shipped overseas by way of recycling brokers for disassembly. Between 50 and 80 percent of all tossed electronic equipment, or *e-waste*, finds its way to China, India, or other developing countries for dismantling. The reason old technology is sent abroad for recycling is because it's cheap. For about 5 cents a pound a firm can be rid of hundreds of outdated desktops, printers, and fax machines.

The problem with this option is the great global expense associated with the cost-efficient solution. First, it is often children that strip down the old technology into parts by hand, exposing them to an array of toxic chemicals at the most vulnerable stage of their lives. This could have long-term effects for generations to come. Second, while the parts that can be reused are distributed to plants for refurbishing, there is a hazardous contingent of components that cannot be recycled or reused. These items contain toxins such as mercury, cadmium, lead, and polyvinyl chloride and are left in mounds, seeping

It is often children in developing nations that strip old technology shipped from North America into its various components. Exposure to the toxins in the discarded equipment could affect their physical and mental development.

into the soil and groundwater in regions where adequate drinking water is already scarce.

How are we going to properly handle the increasing amount of toxic waste being generated because of our consumption of electronic equipment? One method is by safe handling of the recycling process in our own backyard where it can be properly managed and controlled. Noranda has developed an e-waste recycling facility in Brampton, Ontario, that is designed to safely shred and separate e-waste. Presently they are processing more than a quarter-million kilograms of e-waste each month, breaking it into five centimetre pieces of plastic and metal and separating it through the use of a magnetic screening process. At 45 cents per pound, however, the safer process is not as cost effective as the offshore option. Companies like Hewlett-Packard are buying into the need for a better way to dispose of technology, and they are willing to pay extra to know that their equipment is safely returned to its basic elements. Still, there are many more firms that would rather pay less for the removal of yesterday's equipment, which makes Noranda a niche player with a customer base that is comparatively small. Management at Noranda anticipated this and they have

▶

▶

positioned the firm for the future. They are speculating that it is only a matter of time before legislation is set in place forcing companies to use facilities such as theirs to safely dispose of e-waste.

Another way that the onslaught of e-waste could be managed is by building up financial resources to handle the safe disposal of e-waste. Some governments are starting to implement fees at the point of sale for new technology to cover the cost of its disposal when the item is discarded. Alberta has already set in place an environmental fee that is levied against new equipment when purchased. The fee, which ranges from $5 to $45 for new items including cell phones and large-screen televisions, will be used to safely recycle old equipment. The environmental fee should take the financial edge off the cost of safely collecting and processing e-waste. Ontario's government is also looking into a similar program.

However, the best approach by far is eliminating the presence of toxic materials in products in the first place and having manufacturers take back their own products for recycling. Greenpeace has been lobbying all major producers of technology in the hope that they will voluntarily cut back on their use of hazardous materials and initiate free "take-back" programs wherever their products are sold. In an assessment of various high-tech firms, Greenpeace found that Apple lags behind Dell, Hewlett-Packard, Nokia, and Sony. Greenpeace is focusing their polite campaign on having Apple go green in its production of Macs, iPhones, and iPods, stating "it's not about bruising Apple's image, Apple should be an environmental leader." So while Apple celebrated a momentous achievement in April 2007—the sale of 100 million iPods so far—it causes one to wonder where all of them will end up in a few years.

Sources: K. Benedict and G. Richards, "Eco Fee Boosts TV, PC Prices: Program Aims to Keep Toxins Out of Landfills," *Calgary Herald*, February 1, 2005; G. Semmens and S. Myers, "Green Tax Boosts Price of TVs, PCs: Alberta First with e-Cycle Program," *Calgary Herald*, May 7, 2004; D. McLean, "Dead Computer? Make Sure It Gets a Decent Burial," *Globe and Mail*, June 2, 2005; Greenpeace, www.greenpeace.org/apple (accessed November 6, 2006); Apple Computers, www.apple.com (accessed November 6, 2006).

Managerial Perspectives Revisited

PERSPECTIVE 1: THE ORGANIZATIONAL CONTEXT When it comes to managerial ethics and corporate social responsibility, the context of the organization is extremely important. While no individual manager will likely win a court case by saying "The devil organization made me do it," it is folly to ignore the tremendous impact that the organization has on individual decisions and behaviours. For example, the company may have a code of ethics, but if its culture is contrary to the code, senior managers should not be surprised when individuals act in ways that go against the code. This is perhaps one of the strongest reasons for a well-established whistler-blower system. Even if the "flow" of the company culture is in one direction, a well-established whistle-blower system can allow conscientious employees to swim against the tide. In addition, managers need to understand the general approach the company takes toward social responsibility. Trying to take an efficiency perspective in a stakeholder-orientated company or vice versa will likely lead to frustration. The match between an individual's ethical and social responsibility orientation and the organizational context is critical. For example, applying the tactics of a Defender in an Anticipator organization or vice versa will likely hurt rather than help one's career. While this does not mean that as an individual manager you cannot or should not try to change others around you or the entire organization, it does mean that ignoring the organizational context is naïve.

PERSPECTIVE 2: THE HUMAN FACTOR A manager cannot achieve the desired ethical decisions or approach to social responsibility alone. While personal integrity and ethical decision making is critical for an individual manager, this alone does not satisfy his or her responsibility. Managers are responsible for leading their employees in

ways that limit ethical lapses and increase the odds that they behave responsibly. This means, for example, that if your firm has a code of conduct, you have the responsibility of communicating, supporting, and reinforcing the standard with your subordinates. If the firm has a particular orientation toward social responsibility, as a manager you need to help your employees understand what it means and how it applies to the work they do and the decisions they make. Only if managers inculcate the ethical or social responsibility standards of the company in others can it truly have a pervasive impact.

PERSPECTIVE 3: MANAGING PARADOXES Meeting the challenges required to act ethically and in a socially responsible manner will require managing some important paradoxes. On the one hand, as an individual you may have your own personal standards of integrity, ethics, and social responsibility. On the other hand, as a manager you have a responsibility to uphold the standards of your company. What should you do when there is a conflict between the two? Do you have an obligation to correct inappropriate behaviours or blow the whistle on practices that are not in keeping with company policies or with legal or regulatory standards? The potential paradox between personal and company standards is one of the principal challenges managers face daily regarding ethics and social responsibilities. The other major source of potential paradox is between tolerance and compliance. In diverse cultures encountered by firms that operate globally, differences in ethical values and judgments as well as perspectives on social responsibility are inevitable. Tolerance and understanding of these differences are important. However, at the same time companies are increasingly asking their employees and managers to abide by global standards of conduct and are developing global approaches to social responsibility. As a consequence, managers sometimes face the paradox of balancing tolerance and understanding with integrated standards of conduct.

PERSPECTIVE 4: ENTREPRENEURIAL MINDSET Although managers need to be alert to identify and exploit opportunities, some especially lucrative opportunities may present ethical dilemmas. Therefore, managers will need to remain vigilant in balancing their personal standards and the organizational standards with the opportunities to earn large returns. They will need to understand fully how their actions will affect others, especially the organization's stakeholders, as revealed in U2's decision to relocate their business to the Netherlands. Establishing a values-based culture should help managers remain committed to ethical practices and social responsibilities while simultaneously remaining alert to opportunities and exploiting them. Whatever decisions are ultimately made by the organization shouldn't require a compromise of managers' personal or organizational standards. In fact, emphasizing ethical practices may actually provide the organization with new opportunities because consumers and other stakeholders value such standards. Most people want to work for or do business with ethical and socially responsible organizations.

Concluding Comments

There is no universal opinion concerning managerial ethics or the social responsibility of corporations. Grey areas remain, and important questions go unanswered regardless of which fundamental perspective you adopt concerning ethical behaviour or corporate social responsibility. For example, the efficiency approach argues that managers should seek to maximize shareholders' returns but must do so within the laws and ethical norms of society. In today's increasingly global environment, a given firm may operate in a variety of societies. What if the norms of one society are different than those of another? Which societal norms should be honoured?

A social responsibility approach also operates within equally large grey areas. For example, how can you calculate, let alone incorporate, conflicting needs of constituencies across countries? How can a Korean consumer's needs for low price for paper be balanced against the environmental concerns of Indonesian or Brazilian societies where large forests are being cut down to produce the paper? How can all of these concerns be balanced against the potential worldwide concern for the depletion of critical oxygen-providing trees?

In addition to the difficulty of determining the relative weight of different constituencies, managers face the challenge of trying to determine the weights of different groups within one category of constituencies across national borders. How are such determinations made? For example, firms may have employees in many countries, and the concerns of these employees will most likely differ. Employees in Japan may want the firm to maximize job security, while employees in England may want the firm to maximize current wages and be willing to trade off future job security. Similarly, German consumers may want firms to have high environmental standards, whereas Indonesian consumers may have no such concerns. Which standards should be adopted?

The general debates concerning ethics and social responsibility have raged for generations. The purpose of this chapter has not been to resolve the debate but rather to examine the assumptions and rationales of fundamental perspectives. If there were a magic formula for meeting these challenges, there would likely be little need for bright, capable people (we could just turn the problem over to computer algorithms); nor would there be much excitement in being a manager. We hope this examination enables you to evaluate your own views so that you will be prepared when situations arise concerning ethics or social responsibility. Perhaps then the pressure of the moment will be less likely to cause you to take actions that you might later regret. Understanding the general frameworks also helps you to better appreciate others who have differing perspectives and, thereby, interact more effectively with them.

Key Terms

code of ethical conduct   (p. 202)
compensatory justice   (p. 198)
concentration of effect   (p. 201)
corporate social
   responsibility   (p. 191)
distributive justice   (p. 198)
efficiency perspective   (p. 209)
ethical dilemmas   (p. 194)
ethical lapses   (p. 194)

externalities   (p. 210)
justice approach   (p. 198)
magnitude of the
   consequences   (p. 199)
managerial ethics   (p. 191)
moral intensity   (p. 198)
moral rights approach
   (p. 197)
probability of effect   (p. 199)

procedural justice   (p. 198)
proximity   (p. 199)
social consensus   (p. 199)
stakeholders   (p. 211)
temporal immediacy   (p. 199)
universal approach   (p. 197)
utilitarian approach   (p. 195)
whistle-blower   (p. 206)

Test Your Comprehension

1. Define managerial ethics.

2. What are the key differences between managerial ethics and corporate social responsibility?

3. The utilitarian approach to ethics is often called the "greatest good" approach. What are the key challenges in determining the greatest good?

4. What are the two key elements of the moral rights approach to business ethics?

5. How is the universal approach different from the "golden rule" of do unto others as you would have them do unto you?

6. What are the key elements of distributive, procedural, and compensatory justice and how are the three related to each other?

7. What is moral intensity?

8. What are the six factors that influence moral intensity?

9. How are magnitude of consequences and probability of effect different?

10. Why do temporally immediate consequences usually generate more moral intensity?

11. What are the two types of proximity that can influence moral intensity?

12. According to Adam Smith, it is in the best interests of managers and organizations to make ethical decisions. What is the basis of his argument?

13. What is a code of ethical conduct?

14. What are the most common areas addressed in company codes of conduct?

15. Why do companies without codes of ethical conduct seem to be no worse off than companies with codes of conduct in terms of the number of incidents of ethical wrongdoing?

16. What are five powerful means of enhancing the influence of formal codes of conduct on actual employee behaviour?

17. What is a whistle-blower?

18. What are the key concerns with the efficiency perspective of social responsibility?

19. Who are the major stakeholders to consider from a social responsibility perspective?

Apply Your Understanding

1. How much would you change your ethical values or standards or your view of social responsibility to fit into a company? What if you were sent on assignment to another country where the national standards seemed to differ both from the corporate ones and from your personal standards? How much would you change?

2. Which of the basic approaches to ethical decision making most closely matches your approach for dealing with ethical dilemmas?

3. What is the ethical climate like in your school? What is your school's policy or honour code concerning cheating? What is your ethical responsibility if you see someone cheating?

4. Would you be willing to be a whistle-blower? On what type of issue would you blow the whistle? Inflated overtime submitted on a government contract? Sexual harassment? What organizational and personal factors would you consider?

5. Consider the following scenario: A sales representative from a textbook publisher calls on your professor to try to get him or her to adopt a new textbook. Is it okay for the professor to accept a free lunch from the publisher's sales representative? If it is okay for a professor to accept a free lunch, what about a free game of golf? What about a free set of golf clubs after the game?

Practise Your Capabilities

Your firm has a stated policy that emails constitute company correspondence and therefore are subject to screening. Although the policy explanation is included in the thick orientation document that every new employee receives, most employees aren't aware of the policy. Most of those who are aware of it do not believe that their email or other internet activities are reviewed by the company.

Your boss comes to you with the password to all your subordinates' email accounts and asks you to review them. He has some concern but no hard evidence that one of your subordinates may either be talking with a competitor about coming to work for them or may even be leaking sensitive marketing information to them. He instructs you to not be fooled by what appears in the subject line of the emails because anyone with any smarts would not put the real nature of the email there if they were up to something unethical. Therefore, he wants you to read through all their emails over the last four weeks and monitor them over the next few weeks until the allegation is proven to be true or groundless. He has transferred a small project from you to ensure that you have the time to complete this review over the next week.

1. What would you do? Would you take the assignment?

2. If so, why? If not, why not?

3. If you didn't want to take the assignment, how could you turn it down without hurting your relationship with your boss or potentially damaging your career?

4. Is it ethical to read email that employees may consider private?

5. Is it ethical not to inform employees of what you are about to do?

PEARSON
mymanagementlab To improve your grade, visit the MyManagement Lab website at **www.pearsoned.ca/mymanagementlab**. This online homework and tutorial system allows you to test your understanding and generates a personalized study plan just for you. It provides you with study and practice tools directly related to this chapter's content. MyManagementLab puts you in control of your own learning!

Part Six

The Manager as a Decision Maker

Chapter 7

Individual and Group Decision Making*

After reading this chapter, you should be able to:

1 Explain the traditional model of decision making.

2 Recognize and account for the limits of rationality in the decision-making process.

3 Identify the traps that individuals regularly fall into when making decisions.

4 Describe the role of risk and uncertainty in decision making.

5 List the conditions when decisions are best made individually and when they are best made collectively.

6 Name the steps to facilitate group participation in decision making.

7 Describe the barriers to effective decision making and ways to overcome them.

*Portions of this chapter have been adapted from *Organizational Behavior*, 5th edition, by Richard M. Steers and J. Stewart Black with permission from the authors and the publisher.

Taken from *Management*, Canadian Edition, by Michael A. Hitt, J. Stewart Black, Lyman W. Porter, and Andrew J. Gaudes.

Boeing's Dis-Connexion

Companies sometimes have to make decisions and then later reverse them. In these cases the risk of losing consumer and shareholder confidence must be balanced with the prospect of continuing down the wrong path. Boeing took an innovative leap by pursuing broadband services on commercial flights, but the costly venture proved to be too early for widespread adoption by air carriers and passengers and too uncertain in a post-9/11 world. Connexion by Boeing was terminated in 2006.

After weathering the dot.com collapse and struggling through the fallout of 9/11, Boeing decided to terminate their venture into in-flight WiFi service (called Connexion by Boeing) at the end of 2006.

In spring 2000, Boeing announced that they were developing a high-speed data network for passengers and crew members on Boeing-built planes. A similar service had already been created for installation on private business jets, but this was the first-ever foray into online services for passengers on commercial flights. Phil Condit, then chairman and chief executive officer of Boeing, proclaimed that the service would revolutionize the way people travel. Travellers would be able to send and receive email, browse the internet, or watch movies of live sporting events.

The on-board broadband service was expected to be available in 2001 and generate $100 billion over 10 years. However, with the burst of the dot.com bubble in early 2001, skepticism began forming around the habitually over-optimistic projections being offered by e-business analysts. With the forecast flurry of online commerce now in doubt, further skepticism was generated regarding whether or not passengers would latch on to browsing and shopping on the internet during flights. Moreover, battery technology of the day gave even the most energy-conscious laptop around three hours of power, so the attraction for many on long flights would be limited to executive seating where power outlets are available, or for the occasional travellers who pack two batteries in their briefcases.

In spite of the uncertainty of internet interest by air travellers, Boeing moved forward and was able to secure an agreement in 2001 with Lufthansa for overseas flights and enter into early discussions on a joint venture with three US carriers . . . all prior to the events of September 11. The entire air travel industry took a massive economic hit following 9/11. Air carriers that did not seek bankruptcy protection were recoiling into conservative management practices, reducing flights, laying off staff, cancelling new hardware, and rethinking the addition of extra services on remaining flights. With the installation costs of the wireless equipment running around $795 000 for each plane, the decision to drop wireless in-flight service was simple for air carriers. This further delayed the expected launch of Boeing's WiFi services.

Unfettered, Boeing continued with the development of Connexion, investing more than $1 billion into the venture. Finally, after three years of delays in rolling out the service, the world's first flight with WiFi-based high-speed internet access on a commercial flight left Munich on May 17, 2004, destined for Los Angeles aboard Lufthansa. The cost for unlimited access for the duration of a flight was set at US$29.95, or US$9.95 for the first thirty minutes and 25 cents for each additional minute.

As consumers began warming up to air travel again, more airlines began acquiring the service: China Airlines, Singapore Airlines, All Nippon Airways, Japan Airlines, and SAS Scandinavian Airlines all signed on.

Interestingly, however, no US air carriers installed the service on their planes. By the end of 2004 Connexion had secured 160 corporate accounts where online services would be provided to employees of corporate subscribers. Market watchers started to proclaim Connexion by Boeing as the next big thing in the wireless marketplace. Connexion was being recognized by the mobile network industry and receiving awards for its innovative advances. In 2005 Connexion added even more carriers: Korean Air, Asiana Airlines, and EL AL Israel Airlines. By 2006 more than 170 flights were offering the service every day. On-board broadband was providing all that Boeing had promised in 2000—internet surfing, sending and receiving emails, use of VoIP services like Skype, and even the ability to carry out a video conference—all while travelling at 850 kph 12 000 metres up in the air.

Still, the service was not gaining the interest of enough passengers. The writing was on the wall when Boeing announced a rate change on user fees in early 2006. Connexion was feeling the pressure to make changes to its pricing structure to make the service more attractive and accessible to travellers. Criticism by passengers about the lack of pricing options prompted an announcement by Boeing in January 2006 that they were reducing their rates and offering more pricing options for their in-flight service. Now passengers would be able to get one hour of service for the same price previously charged for thirty minutes. Also, passengers could book two hours for US$14.95, or three hours for US$17.95. As well, passengers could now subscribe to the service for 24 hours, which would cover all connecting flights, for only US$26.95.

The pricing change apparently was not enough to increase passenger use. Just six months after the rate change, with 12 air carriers signed on to the service for a total of 72 long-haul planes, Boeing announced that it was re-evaluating its interest in providing the service. Boeing was going to conduct a market analysis and meet with current clients to determine the future of Connexion. Then, on August 10, 2006, a terrorist plot involving up to 10 transatlantic flights was uncovered in the United Kingdom that led to new restrictions for items allowed on flights. In the UK this included a ban on mobile technology, such as laptops, PDAs, and even MP3 players, for all passengers starting their trip in the UK or transferring from international flights at a UK airport. For the first time, the future use of mobile communications by passengers on flights was in doubt.

One week later Boeing announced that they were exiting the in-flight online market.

Management at Boeing doubted that the market would provide the returns necessary to make the venture viable. The cost of shutting down Connexion was projected to be upwards of $368 million over the remainder of the year. However, management anticipated that by not having to invest further into Connexion, nearly half of that amount would be recovered in 2007 alone. The service was slated for termination at the end of 2006, with passengers enjoying free access to the service for the last two months.

In the meantime, Panasonic announced in September 2006 that it was examining the prospect of picking up the service and providing it to the carriers left by Connexion for a lower price. Panasonic would even use the same hardware already installed on the planes by Boeing. For Panasonic, the critical factor was signing on an initial fleet of 500 planes to the service before they decided to enter into the on-board broadband market. In the end, Panasonic announced in July 2007 that they have devised their own business model, which enables them to launch with as few as 50 planes. Some of the first airline clients are expected to be the initial customers of Connexion and will be commencing operations in early 2008. ◆

Sources: J. Wallace, "Connexion Update: Panasonic Says It Is Close to Starting Internet System," *Seattle Post-Intelligencer*, seattlepi.com (accessed October 18, 2007); Boeing News Release, "Boeing Unveils High-Speed Global Communications Service—Live In-Flight Internet, E-Mail, TV; Available Next Year," April 27, 2000; Boeing News Release, "The New Era of In-flight Connectivity Is Here: Connexion by Boeing and Lufthansa Announce the World Premiere of Airborne Internet," May 11, 2004; Boeing News Release, "Connexion by Boeing Achieves Strong Growth in Availability, Partnerships and Customers Served," December 8, 2004; Boeing News Release, "Connexion by Boeing Continues Evolution of Award-Winning High-Speed In-Flight Internet Service," January 11, 2006; Boeing News Release, "Boeing to Discontinue Connexion by Boeing Service," August 17, 2006; D. Gross, "Wi-Fly: Why Boeing Shouldn't Pull the Plug on Connexion," *Slate*, June 23, 2006; Shephard Group, "Panasonic Reaches for the Connexion Torch," September 19, 2006.

Strategic
overview

In the minds of many, decision making is the most important managerial activity. Management decisions may involve high-profile issues such as acquiring or selling assets, moving into or out of product segments, leaving or entering markets, or launching national or international ad campaigns. Boeing's strategic decision to enter the in-flight broadband market, only to withdraw from it six years later, had a significant impact on the organization. For example, the investment of time and money into nurturing the venture so that it could carry its own takes significant resources away from the core business of Boeing, which is building planes. As well, the decision to abandon the initial investment of more than $1 billion—a decision that will add an additional $368 million of shutdown expenses—is not for the faint of heart.

This illustrates one of the key challenges of managerial decision making at any level—making decisions with uncertainty. Limited information and the presence of inaccurate information and pressure to be responsive can create some of the most powerful challenges in managerial decision making. Consequently, managers need to understand the basic processes of decision making in organizations and the factors that influence them. Several frameworks are available to help explain managerial decision making. Each framework is based on different assumptions about the nature of people at work. So, as an informed manager, you need to understand the models and the assumptions underlying each. The decision by Boeing to terminate Connexion impacts many areas within the organization. Some of the first stakeholders affected by the decision were the employees working at Connexion; Boeing minimized the effect by redeploying staff into other areas within Boeing. The decision also placed Boeing's strategic direction in doubt by investors, since Boeing had already placed significant capital into getting Connexion in the air only to terminate the venture after two years of service. Yet management had to respond to the environment as they saw it. To what extent the terrorist plot in August 2006 played into the decision to pull the plug on Connexion can only be speculated. However, the prospect of having key assumptions (such as passenger use of laptops on flights) thrown out because of increased travel restrictions by a nation with one of the largest air travel hubs in the world would, in all likelihood, not be taken lightly.

Not all managerial decisions are as visible or as important as those described in the Boeing case. Many managerial decisions involve behind-the-scenes issues such as hiring a new employee or changing a production process. In addition, in many situations you must determine the level of involvement of others (e.g., subordinates, peers) in decisions. When are group decisions superior (or inferior) to individual ones? How much participation is realistic in organizations in which managers still assume responsibility for group actions? For example, senior management at Boeing had to decide who to bring into the discussion to terminate

Connexion. As a new manager, you might have to decide how many people to involve in a new-hire decision. In making these choices you need to understand how various factors affect the quality of your decisions. Finally, what approaches can managers use to improve decisions in organizations? A knowledge of effective decision making can help you make the most efficient use of your limited time and resources.

Decision-Making Concepts

A characteristic of effective leaders and effective workgroups is their ability to make decisions that are appropriate, timely, and acceptable. If organizational effectiveness is defined as the ability to secure and use resources in the pursuit of organizational goals, then the decision-making processes that determine how these resources are acquired and used is a key building block. For our purposes here, we define **decision making** as a process of specifying the nature of a particular problem or opportunity and selecting among available alternatives how to solve a problem or capture an opportunity. In this sense decision making has two aspects: the act and the process.

The *act* of decision making involves choosing between alternatives. The *process* of decision making involves several steps that can be divided into two distinct phases. The first, **formulation**, involves identifying a problem or opportunity, acquiring information, developing desired performance expectations, and diagnosing the causes and relationships among factors affecting the problem or opportunity. A **problem** exists when a manager detects a gap between existing and desired performance. This is the situation we commonly associate with decision making, and it is the reason that decision making and problem solving are often talked about interchangeably. For example, you may find that your subordinates just have more work than they can get done. To solve this problem, you may decide to hire an additional worker.

Although as a manager you will confront lots of problems and have to decide how to solve them, you will also encounter opportunities. An **opportunity** exists when a manager detects a chance to achieve a more desirable state than the current one. For example, for managers at Brunswick Corporation this happened when they decided to buy Baja Boats. At the time of the purchase, Brunswick was already the number-one recreational boat builder in North America, with its Sea Ray, Bayliner, PROCRAFT, and other brands. Buying Baja Boats represented an opportunity to expand into a market niche that executives thought would grow in the future and in which they did not have a significant presence at the time.

The **solution** phase of the decision-making process involves generating alternatives, selecting the preferred solution, and implementing the decided course of action. Following the implementation of the solution, the manager monitors the situation to determine the extent to which the decision was successful.

decision making A process of specifying the nature of a particular problem or opportunity and selecting among available alternatives to solve a problem or capture an opportunity.

formulation A process involving identifying a problem or opportunity, acquiring information, developing desired performance expectations, and diagnosing the causes and relationships among factors affecting the problem or opportunity.

problem A gap between existing and desired performance.

opportunity A chance to achieve a more desirable state than the current one.

solution A process involving generating alternatives, selecting the preferred solution, and implementing the decided course of action.

Types of Decisions

Most decisions can be divided into two basic types: programmed or nonprogrammed. A **programmed decision** is a standard response to a simple

programmed decision A routine response to a simple or regularly occurring problem.

or routine problem. The nature of the problem is well defined and clearly understood by the decision maker, as is the array of possible solutions. Examples of programmed decisions can be seen in university admission decisions, reimbursement for managers' travel expenses, and promotion decisions with many unionized personnel. In all these decisions, specific criteria can be identified (e.g., grade-point average and test scores for university admission, per diem allowances for expense account reimbursements, or seniority for union promotions). The programmed decision process is characterized by high levels of certainty for both the problem formulation and the problem solution phases, and rules and procedures typically spell out exactly how to respond.

nonprogrammed decision
A decision about a problem that is either poorly defined or novel.

On the other hand, **nonprogrammed decisions** occur in response to problems that are either poorly defined or novel. Nonprogrammed decisions are unique because they are in response to situations that may never have occurred before, or the situation involves a high level of ambiguity. As a result, decision makers must rely upon their own creativity and intuition in formulating a decision. For example, should a university president with limited funds expand the size of the business school to meet growing student demand, or should she expand the university's science facilities to bring in more federal research contracts? No alternative is clearly correct, and past decisions are of little help; instead, the decision maker must weigh the alternatives and their consequences carefully to make a unique decision—a nonprogrammed decision.

Exhibit 7.1 Decision-Maker Level and Type of Decision.

In most organizations, a significant relationship exists between the programmed and nonprogrammed decisions and organizational hierarchy. As shown in Exhibit 7.1, for example, top managers usually face nonprogrammed decisions, as in the case of the university president. On the other hand, university deans or department heads as well as faculty or students seldom need to make such decisions. Furthermore, lower-level managers (such as first-line supervisors) typically encounter mostly programmed, or routine, decisions. Their options and resources, as well as risks, are usually far less than those of top managers. And, as we might expect, middle managers fall somewhere in between.

standard operating procedure (SOP) Established procedure for action used for programmed decisions that specifies exactly what should be done.

Gresham's law of planning The tendency for managers to let programmed activities overshadow nonprogrammed activities.

One final point should be made here concerning the relationship between programmed and nonprogrammed decisions. Programmed decisions are usually made through structured, bureaucratic techniques. For example, **standard operating procedures (SOP)** are often used for programmed decisions. SOPs specify exactly what should be done—the sequence of steps and exactly how each step should be performed. In contrast, nonprogrammed decisions must be made by managers using available information and their own judgment, often under considerable time pressure. The ambiguity of the problem in part contributes to the uncertainty of the outcome, which in turn leads to interesting and important consequences. Managers tend to let programmed activities overshadow nonprogrammed activities. This tendency is called **Gresham's law of planning**.[1] Thus, if a manager has a series of decisions to make, he or she will tend to make those that are routine and repetitive before focusing on those that are unique and require considerable thought. When asked why they do this, many managers reply that they wish to clear their desks so they can concentrate on the really serious problems. Unfortunately, the reality is that managers often don't actually get to the more difficult and perhaps more important decisions. They may just run out of time or continue to occupy their time with the programmed decisions (and their more certain outcomes) than with the nonprogrammed decisions (and their less certain outcomes).

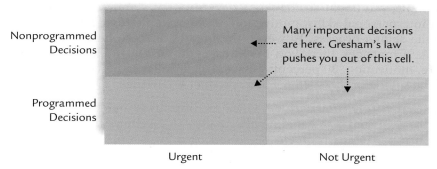

Exhibit 7.2 Gresham's Law and Making Decisions.

The implications of Gresham's law for managerial decision making are clear. As a manager you must make needed decisions in a timely fashion. As a consequence, you may want to check yourself periodically to see where you are spending your "decision-making time" to see if you are falling prey to Gresham's law of planning. The matrix in Exhibit 7.2 may help you with this assessment.

Individual Decision Making

It is no easy task to outline or diagram the details of the decision-making process. Research has been mixed about how individuals and groups make decisions.[2] Even so, at least three attempts to describe the decision-making process are worth noting: (1) the rational/classic model; (2) the administrative, or bounded rationality, model; and (3) the retrospective decision-making model. Each model is useful for understanding the nature of decision processes in organizations. While reading about these models, pay special attention to the assumptions that each makes about the nature of decision makers; also note the differences in focus.

The Rational/Classical Model

The **rational model** (also known as the **classical model**) represents the earliest attempt to model decision processes.[3] It is viewed by some as the classical approach to understanding decision processes. This approach involves seven basic steps (see Exhibit 7.3).

Step 1: Identifying Decision Situations. In the classical model, the decision maker begins by recognizing that a decision-making situation exists, that is, that a problem or an opportunity exists.

Step 2: Developing Objectives and Criteria. Once you have identified the decision-making situation, the next step is to determine the criteria for selecting alternatives. These criteria essentially represent what is important in the outcome. For example, before you can decide which job applicant to hire as an additional salesperson, you need to determine the important characteristics or outcomes needed. When several criteria are involved, it is often necessary to weigh the various criteria.

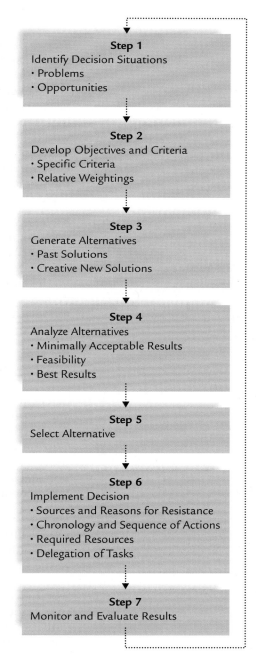

Exhibit 7.3 Classical Decision-Making Model.

rational model (classical model) A seven-step model of decision making that represents the earliest attempt to model decision processes.

For example, you might decide that a new hire's sales ability depends on four things: interpersonal skills, motivation, product knowledge, and understanding of the selling process. However, the impact of these factors may not be equal. As a manager, then, you might assign a weight to each criterion: for example, motivation: 30 percent; interpersonal skills: 25 percent; understanding of the selling process: 25 percent; product knowledge: 20 percent.

Step 3: Generating Alternatives. Once the objectives and criteria are established, the next step is to generate alternatives that achieve the desired result. How can a particular problem be solved or a given opportunity captured? Most of us consider first the alternatives that we have encountered or used in the past. If a current situation is similar to one from the past, past solutions can be effective. However, situations change and to the extent that the current situation is dissimilar to one from the past, or if past solutions have not succeeded, new alternatives must be generated.

Step 4: Analyzing Alternatives. The fourth step in the process involves analyzing the alternatives generated. To begin, you need to determine which alternatives would produce minimally acceptable results. Any alternatives that are unlikely to at least achieve the minimally acceptable outcome can be eliminated. Next, you need to examine the feasibility of the remaining alternatives. Returning to our hiring example, you may have found three candidates for your sales position that would likely produce minimally acceptable sales results. But one candidate's salary requirement exceeds your budget; therefore, that person is not feasible. Once infeasible alternatives are eliminated, the next step is to determine which of the remaining alternatives would produce the most satisfactory outcome. Typically, the criteria and weights produced in step two are applied at this point.

Step 5: Selecting Alternatives. Selecting an alternative flows naturally out of your analysis. The classical model argues that managers will choose the alternative that maximizes the desired outcome. This idea has often been expressed by the term **subjectively expected utility (SEU) model**. This model asserts that managers choose the alternative that they subjectively believe maximizes the desired outcome. The two key components of this model are the expected outcome produced by a given alternative and the probability that the alternative can be implemented.

subjectively expected utility (SEU) model A model of decision making that asserts that managers choose the alternative that they subjectively believe maximizes the desired outcome.

Step 6: Implementing the Decision. In the classical model of decision making, effective decision implementation has four components. First, you assess sources and reasons for potential resistance to the decision. Second, you determine the chronology and sequence of actions designed to overcome resistance to the decision and ensure that the decision is effectively implemented. Setting the chronology and sequence of actions leads naturally into the third step: an assessment of the resources required to implement the decision effectively. Fourth, you need to determine whether you could delegate implementation steps to others and can ensure that those individuals understand and are held accountable for those steps and outcomes.

Step 7: Monitoring and Evaluating Results. The final step in the classical model involves monitoring and evaluating the results. To do this, you must gather information and compare results to the objectives and standards you set at the beginning. This is trickier than it may seem. First, you must gather the right information or the evaluation will be distorted at best and meaningless at worst. In addition, the longer the lead time between actions and results, the more important appropriate performance indicators are, even if they are not easy to gather or evaluate. The key point here is the importance of monitoring and evaluating results to detect problems with the original decision and its implementation so that corrective actions can be taken. If the appropriate information is not gathered, the purpose of this final step is defeated.

A Manager's Challenge   *Technology*

Travel Agencies Find New Technological Paths to Profits

When Delta Air Lines stopped paying commissions to travel agencies for selling tickets on US routes, the decision came as no surprise to Rita Baron and Barbara Hansen. Baron owns Baron Travel in Atlanta, Georgia, and Hansen and her son own Sunflower Travel in Wichita, Kansas. Both owners had to make critical decisions about whether to toss in the towel or use technology to stay in the travel agency game.

A decade ago, travel agents earned at least a 10 percent commission on any airline tickets they sold, and they enjoyed close relationships with airline sales representatives. Starting in 1994, however, many US airlines cut costs by capping commission levels. At the same time, new software technology allowed people to surf the internet in pursuit of airfare bargains and in this way bypass travel agents. By 2001, the airlines were paying travel agencies just US$20 for selling any ticket (regardless of value) on a domestic flight. By 2002, nearly every US airline had entirely eliminated commissions on domestic flights as a way to boost profitability.

Caught in the ongoing financial squeeze of lower revenues from airlines, more than 6000 travel agencies went out of business. Both Baron Travel and Sunflower Travel decided to pass the loss of revenue from disappearing commissions on to customers via service fees in the range of US$40 per ticket. In implementing this decision, Hansen recognized she had to prove her worth to customers. Thus, she uses her extensive industry contacts to search for the lowest possible fares. Now, says Hansen, "we can often beat the fares customers see on the web." She has taken on the technology of the web with old-fashioned person-to-person networking.

To stay in business, Hansen knew she would have to set Sunflower Travel apart from its local and online competitors. Because of her personal interest in the South Pacific, she decided to focus on selling specialized tours to Australia and New Zealand. Once she developed a relationship with an established tour company operating in those countries, she then decided to use the technology that nearly put her out of business to her advantage. She decided to use the internet to promote her tours. For instance, she linked her site with New Zealand's tourism website and offered online wine retailers special Australian food and wine tours.

In this case, the new technology of the internet and a change in commission policy by airlines presented both Hansen and Baron with a problem. Interestingly, each solved essentially the same problem with a different solution.

Sources: T. Pearson, "Why Use a Travel Agent?" *Travel Agent*, September 29, 2003, p. 20; N. Fonti, "Atlanta Travel Agency Experiences Many Industry Changes," *Atlanta Journal-Constitution*, May 17, 2002, www.ajc.com; P. Thomas, "Case Study: Travel Agency Meets Technology's Threat," *Wall Street Journal*, May 21, 2002, p. B4.

A Manager's Challenge: "Travel Agencies Find New Technological Paths to Profits" provides a look at two manager/owners of travel agencies and how they weighed their options and decided not to let new technology put them out of business. In the end they also decided to use the technology to enhance their business. As you read this case, ask yourself if you see the situation as a problem or an opportunity. What do you think of each manager's solution?

To many, the classical model makes considerable sense. However, it is important to understand the assumptions on which it is built:

■ Problems are clear.

■ Objectives are clear.

■ People agree on criteria and weights.

■ All alternatives are known.

■ All consequences can be anticipated.

■ Decision makers are rational:

    ■ They are not biased in recognizing problems.

    ■ They can process all relevant information.

- They appropriately incorporate immediate and future consequences into decision making.
- They search for the alternative that maximizes the desired result.

The potential weaknesses of the classical model are easily exposed if you recall your own decision about what university to attend. How clear was the problem or your objectives? Did everyone (you, your parents, your friends, etc.) agree on the criteria and weights for evaluating alternative schools? Did you know or even consider all the possible alternative universities? Could you fully anticipate the consequences associated with attending each school? Were you completely unbiased in your definition of the problem or the opportunity of which school to attend, and did you objectively review all the relevant information? Did you appropriately emphasize short-term and long-term consequences? Did you search for alternatives until you found the one that maximized your desired outcome? If you answered no to some of these questions, you're not alone. A large body of research has shown that people are not as rational as the classical model assumes.[4] In fact, we can identify a series of factors that inhibit people's ability to accurately identify and analyze problems, as shown in Exhibit 7.4.

Thus, whereas the rational, or classical, model prescribes how decisions *should* be made (i.e., it works as a prescriptive model), it falls short in describing how decisions are *actually* made (i.e., as a descriptive model).

The Bounded Rationality Model

An alternative model, one not constrained by the preceding assumptions, has been presented by Herbert Simon.[5] This model is called the **bounded**

Exhibit 7.4	Factors That Inhibit Accurate Problem Identification and Analysis	
Factor	**Description**	**Illustration**
Information Bias	A reluctance to give or receive negative information.	You are favouring Jane as the candidate and dismiss information about a performance problem she had at her last job.
Uncertainty Absorption	A tendency for information to lose its uncertainty as it is passed along.	It is not clear how well Martha did in her previous job, but by the time the feedback gets to you, she is described as a poor performer.
Selective Perception	A tendency to ignore or avoid certain information, especially ambiguous information.	Jane may have several employment alternatives and may even be considering going back to school, but you ignore all this in making her the offer.
Stereotyping	Deciding about an alternative on the basis of characteristics ascribed by others.	Jane graduated from a private high school and went to a highly rated university on a partial scholarship, so you figure she must be a great hire.
Cognitive Complexity	Limits on the amount of information people can process at one time.	You initially have 200 applicants for the position but decide to eliminate anyone with less than three years' sales experience.
Stress	Reduction of people's ability to cope with informational demands.	Your company's market share is slipping because you don't have enough salespeople in the field, so you feel you just can't look at every bit of information on every candidate.

rationality model (or the **administrative man model**). The theory of bounded rationality is a descriptive model of decision making that was developed as an alternative to the prescriptive theory of subjective expected utility (SEU) mentioned earlier.[6] The reason behind presenting the model is the realization that there are many instances when decision makers arrive at decisions that would not have been predicted by SEU. The key distinguishing characteristic of bounded rationality from SEU is its recognition that human rationality is limited. It assumes that people, although they may seek the best solution, usually settle for less because the decisions they confront typically demand greater information-processing capabilities than they possess. In short, their rationality is limited, or bounded.

As a result of the great complexities surrounding decisions, people will resort to shortcuts and approximations to arrive at decisions that they are comfortable with, even if they are not fully rational. Limits in rationality come about as a result of complex environments, incomplete and insufficient knowledge, inconsistencies in individual preferences and beliefs, conflicting values between people, and errors in calculation.[7]

The concept of bounded rationality has two key implications for decision making. First, Simon and other scholars have argued that people do not actually identify all possible solutions, assess the costs and benefits, and then select the best alternative. Instead, people will examine solutions that are accessible to them with minimal effort until a satisfactory, but not necessarily optimal, solution is found. As Simon described it, **satisficing** occurs when the first solution that meets their needs, whether or not it maximizes utility, will stop the search for alternatives.

In addition, the more alternatives that are available to an individual, the higher the aspirations in a satisfactory solution.[8] For example, if you are intent on going to a movie theatre on a Friday night, but there is only one theatre in your area, you may resolve to see the movie regardless of what it is, simply because the movie will satisfy your desire to go to a theatre. However, if you are in an area where there are multiple theatres your aspirations will rise, which may lead you to quickly pass over the movie in the first scenario for another that you find more appealing.

Second, rather than using explicit criteria and weights to evaluate alternatives, the bounded rationality model argues that people use heuristics. A **heuristic** is a decision-making shortcut that can be based upon preset rules, memory, or past experiences. Thus, instead of looking everywhere for possible solutions, you might use a heuristic to arrive at a solution to a problem or for selecting one opportunity over another. The obvious benefit here is the reduction of time and mental energy expended in arriving at a decision. On the other hand, the obvious cost is that the best solution may not be found because of the shortcut that is taken.

Based on the above, we can imagine that the decision process will be quite different from the rational model. The process does not involve individuals searching for the best solution; rather, they will look for a solution that is *acceptable*. Also, in contrast to the prescriptive rational model, the bounded rationality model is descriptive; that is, it describes how decision makers actually identify solutions to organizational problems.

A Manager's Challenge: "Gaining a New Perspective on Decisions at UPS" illustrates how United Parcel Service (UPS) tries to give managers experiences that will broaden and diversify their knowledge base. The example illustrates how changes in experience base and emphasis on diversity affect not only managers' perceptions, but also the decisions they make. Do you think having similar experiences would influence your perception of future problems? As a consequence, do you think you might change the way you make decisions?

bounded rationality model (administrative man model) A descriptive model of decision making recognizing that people are limited in their capacity to fully assess a problem and usually rely on shortcuts and approximations to arrive at a decision they are comfortable with.

satisficing The tendency for decision makers to accept the first alternative that meets their minimally acceptable requirements rather than pushing them further for an alternative that produces the best results.

Maximizing Satisficing by Stewart Black
mymanagementlab

heuristic A decision-making shortcut that can be based upon pre-set rules, memory, or past experiences.

A Manager's Challenge   *Diversity*

Gaining a New Perspective on Decisions at UPS

Managing diverse perspectives for enhanced decision making is a tough balancing act for managers at United Parcel Service (UPS). On the one hand, UPS has built a successful global delivery business by developing standard procedures for nearly all routine decisions, including how drivers should carry their keys when making deliveries. Yet every year, senior managers send 50 middle managers on a program that is designed to add diversity to the "brown" perspective (that is, the typical UPS perspective) so that these middle managers can make better decisions. The program involves managers spending 30 days in communities far from home that have significant poverty and other problems. UPS founder James Casey initiated the Community Internship Program in 1968. Since then, UPS has invested more than $14 million to send 1100 middle managers through the program, at a cost of $10 000 per participant (plus the manager's regular salary).

Whether managers spend the month cleaning up dilapidated apartments or working with migrant workers, participants say the experience drives home new lessons about diversity. For example, during a month of working with addicts in New York City, division manager Patti Hobbs was impressed by the thoughtful suggestions they offered for keeping teenagers off drugs. Back on the job, she broadened her use of group decision making to involve all staff members in problem-solving discussions rather than only the highest-level managers. "You start to think there's no one person, regardless of position, who has all the answers," she explains. "The answers come from us all."

The program sharpens participants' decision-making skills by taking them out of their comfortable daily work routine. According to Al Demick, UPS's learning and development manager, it "puts people in situations that call on them to use new skills or to use their skills in new ways. Sometimes those are life-and-death situations. People are never quite the same when they come back." Annette Law, a UPS manager from Utah, worked with tenement dwellers in New York City. "I thought I knew all about diversity," she observes. "But what I saw were people just like me, only their opportunities and choices were different." Michael Lockard, a finance and accounting manager, helped inmates in a Chicago prison prepare for release by sharpening their interviewing and job-search skills. The experience shattered Lockard's

Since 1968, UPS has invested more than $14 million to send 1100 middle managers like Flynn Bowen to communities that suffer from poverty and other problems. Initiated by UPS founder James Casey, the Community Internship Program is designed to add diversity to the "brown" perspective.

preconceived notions about inmates and changed the way he approaches decisions at UPS: "I'm much more sensitive to the fact that we must make decisions on a case-by-case basis," he says. "Things are no longer black and white for me."

Because half of all new UPS employees are visible minorities, senior managers believe that the program is an important training ground for the management team. Although executives cannot point to a financial return on this investment, feedback from participants indicates that they not only bring a new perspective to work decisions, but also are inspired to volunteer in their home communities. "We will never really know how many lives we have touched," sums up a recent participant.

Sources: K. Pelkey, "Resident Participates in Company's Community Internship Program," *Farmington Valley Post*, July 24, 2003; J. J. Salopek, "Just Like Me: UPS's Unique Intern Program Transforms the Perspectives of Leaders," *T&D*, October 2002, pp. 52+; L. Lavelle, "For UPS Managers, a School of Hard Knocks," *BusinessWeek*, July 22, 2002, pp. 58–59.

The Retrospective Decision Model

A third model focuses on how decision makers attempt to rationalize their choices after they are made. It has been variously referred to as the **retrospective decision model**[9] or the **implicit favourite model**.[10]

One of the most noted contributors to this perspective was MIT professor Peter Soelberg. As Soelberg observed the job-choice processes of graduating business students, he noticed that in many cases the students identified implicit favourites (that is, the alternative they wanted) very early in the recruiting and choice process. For example, one student might identify a manufacturer in Calgary as a favourite. However, students continued their search for additional alternatives and quickly selected the best alternate (or second) candidate, known as the "confirmation candidate." For example, the student might select a high-tech firm in Ottawa as his alternate firm. Next, the students would attempt to develop decision rules that demonstrated unequivocally that the implicit favourite was superior to the confirmation candidate. They did so by **perceptual distortion** of information—that is, highlighting the positive features of the implicit favourite over the alternative. For example, the student might leave out vacation time as a criterion because his favourite firm in Calgary has a very poor vacation policy compared with the alternative firm in Ottawa. However, the student might heavily weight a criterion of the availability of downhill skiing because it is more abundant in the Calgary region, the student's favoured choice. Finally, after deriving a decision rule that clearly favoured the implicit favourite, the student announced the decision and accepted the job in Calgary.

Ironically, Soelberg noted, the implicit favourite was typically superior to the confirmation candidate on only one or two dimensions. Even so, decision makers generally characterized their decision rules as being multidimensional. For example, in the case of the two firms in Calgary and Ottawa, the jobs offered were quite similar, and the salary, travel, benefits, and promotion prospects were also nearly identical. Yet the student would claim that the Calgary firm was superior on several counts.

The entire process is designed to justify, through the guise of scientific rigor, a decision that has already been made intuitively. By this means, the individual becomes convinced that he or she is acting rationally and making a logical, reasoned decision on an important topic. Consider how many times you have made a decision in a similar way when looking for clothes, cars, stereo systems, and so on. You start with an item that catches your eye and then spend considerable time convincing yourself and your friends that this is the "best" choice. If your implicit favourite is the cheapest among the competition, you emphasize price; if it is not, you emphasize quality or styling. Ultimately, you end up buying the item you favoured, feeling comfortable that you made the right choice. Here, however, we do not want to create the impression that **intuitive decision making**, or the primarily subconscious process of identifying a decision and selecting a preferred alternative, is bad or wrong. Although some firms often base their decision-making practices on rational analyses,[11] some research has found that not only are intuitive decisions often faster in many situations, but the outcome is also as good as or better than a methodical, rational approach.[12]

Influences on Effective Decision Making

From a practical perspective, perhaps the most important question for managers to ask is "What influences effective decision making?" Quite simply, practising managers want to make good decisions. Consequently, it is helpful to briefly examine the major factors that hurt decision quality and then examine what we can do to enhance individual decision quality. At least three general factors influence decision quality (see Exhibit 7.5).[13]

retrospective decision model (implicit favourite model) A decision-making model that focuses on how decision makers attempt to rationalize their choices after they are made.

perceptual distortion Highlighting the positive features of the implicit favourite over the alternative.

intuitive decision making The primarily subconscious process of identifying a decision and selecting a preferred alternative.

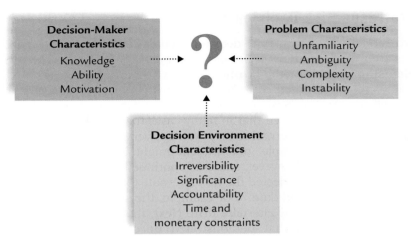

Exhibit 7.5 Influences on the Decision Process.

First, there are the characteristics of the decision maker. Earlier in the chapter we discussed that we may not be as rational as we would like to believe. We can have implicit preferences for alternatives and simply construct rationales for those biases to make it seem as though we are being rational and objective. We can have limitations to our information-processing capabilities and, as a consequence, limit the alternatives we examine. If our motivation is not sufficient, we can easily satisfice and simply accept the first workable solution rather than push to find the best of several workable solutions. If we lack familiarity with the problem or have insufficient knowledge, we can make less than ideal decisions. If we have too much familiarity with the problem, we can be too quick to select solutions that have worked in the past. In the process we might not sufficiently consider what might be different about the past and current situations that might make past solutions inappropriate for the present problem.

Second, the nature of the problem or opportunity itself can influence decision quality. The greater the ambiguity of the problem, the harder it is to be certain of the "right" decision. Also, as we have already discussed, we may shy away from ambiguous problems and, as a consequence, end up with less than ideal outcomes because the needed decisions weren't made soon enough, if at all. The complexity of the problem can also affect the outcome. The more complex the problem is, the more challenging both the decision and its effective implementation are likely to be. The extent to which the problem is stable or volatile can also influence decision effectiveness. Clearly, the more volatile the problem is, the greater the chance that the problem will change and the selected solution won't match the problem.

Third, the environment in which the decision is made influences the decision. Time constraints or any relevant resource constraints (people, money, equipment, etc.) can influence the decision's effectiveness. For example, the more time pressure you are under, the greater the chance that you might "miss" something or become vulnerable to any or all of the bounded rationality limitations we already discussed. If the decision is irreversible and you make the "wrong" decision, you obviously lack the opportunity to modify the decision and correct the results. The importance of the decision can create its own pressures, which in turn can influence the effectiveness of the decision.

Decision-Making Traps

While we all try to make good decisions, we can all fall victim to decision-making traps that lead us away from the optimal solution. Decision-making traps are the result of us searching for shortcuts or using approximations to arrive at a quick conclusion to the tension that goes along with a pending decision. Many of these traps can also be characterized as heuristics that people rely on to make decisions. Four main types of decision-making traps are availability heuristics, the representativeness heuristic, anchoring, and escalation of commitment.[14]

Availability Heuristics. We often rely on our memory of past situations to make decisions for current events. The information that remains intact and is best available to our recollection will be most relied upon when drawing from our memory banks. Considering this, it should be apparent that events that are most recent or had a significant impact on us are the events that we will be able to remember most readily, so these are the events we will most likely use in formulating a judgment. The trap here is that the most recent or the most sensational events in our memory are not necessarily an accurate portrayal of the frequency of such events. Nor does it provide all the information necessary to make a decision.

There are three decision-making biases that emanate from the availability heuristic. The first is **ease of recall**; that is, making a judgment based upon the most recent events or the most vivid in our memory. For example, a manager that is conducting an annual evaluation may give an employee a low performance rating because she saw him arrive at work late the previous week, even though the employee's attendance prior to then was unblemished. The second bias is **retrievability**, which refers to the fact that judgments rely on the memory structures of an individual. Our ability to assemble information may be hampered by how we store and later retrieve that information. For example, you would have an easier time assembling a list of all the people you know that have a first name starting with the letter "S" than searching for people that have the letter "A" as the third letter in their first name. The third decision-making bias is **presumed associations**—the assumption that two events are likely to co-occur based on the recollection of similar associations. For example, the number of media reports that link juveniles dressed in black (Goths) to violent outbursts in academic settings creates an environment where individuals presume that all Goths should be watched closely to ensure they do not harm others in schools.

Representativeness Heuristic. The tendency to judge an event by assessing how closely it relates to a previous similar event is the representativeness heuristic. Individuals will evaluate similarities of current and previous situations using significant or even insignificant features as the basis for a decision. For example, you may see someone that reminds you of another person, possibly because of the way they speak or their facial features, and because of these similarities you may treat the unknown person in the same manner as the person you know.

There are five biases associated with the representativeness heuristic. The first is **insensitivity to base rates**, or the tendency to disregard information that suggests the likelihood of a particular outcome in the presence of other information. For example, if you bought a product that was known to have a 35 percent failure rate, you would likely demand a good warranty or return policy, or simply avoid the product altogether. Yet when you ask most couples engaged to be married if they are preparing a prenuptial agreement they will answer no, even though the rate of failed marriages in Canada is around 38 percent.[15] Individuals will also demonstrate **insensitivity to sample size**, which refers to the tendency to not consider sample size when using information taken from a sample within a given population. People tend to ignore the fact that larger sample sizes are more likely to represent the full population than small samples. A third bias is the **misconception of chance**—people expect small sets of randomly assembled objects or sequences to appear random. For example, if someone rolled a die three

ease of recall Making a judgment based upon the most recent events or the most vivid in our memory.

retrievability A decision-making bias where judgments rely on the memory structures of an individual.

presumed associations The assumption that two events are likely to co-occur based on the recollection of similar associations.

insensitivity to base rates The tendency to disregard information that suggests the likelihood of a particular outcome in the presence of other information.

insensitivity to sample size The tendency to not consider sample size when using information taken from a sample within a given population.

misconception of chance The expectation that small sets of randomly assembled objects or sequences should appear random.

regression to the mean
Overlooking the fact that extreme events or characteristics are exceptional cases that will likely revert back to historic averages over time.

conjunction fallacy The tendency for people to assume that co-occurring events are more likely to occur than if they were independent of each other or grouped with other events.

anchoring Using an initial value received from prior experience or any external information source and giving it disproportionate weight in setting a final value.

escalation of commitment The tendency to exhibit greater levels of commitment to a decision as time passes and investments are made in the decision, even after significant evidence emerges indicating that the original decision was incorrect.

times and each roll was a five, people may anticipate that the fourth roll would not be a five, even though a five has exactly the same odds as any other number appearing—one in six. A fourth tendency that people will fall into is overlooking that extreme events or characteristics will often follow with a **regression to the mean**. If, for example, this year's class of grade four students in a school is on average three inches taller than the previous year's class, the grade four teacher might surmise that, on average, children of the same age are developing earlier. In fact, the next year's class may very well regress to the mean, with the student average height hovering closer to the historic average for students in grade four. A final representativeness bias is the **conjunction fallacy**, or the tendency for people to assume that co-occurring events are more likely to occur than if they were independent of each other or grouped with other events. An example of the conjunction fallacy is the ritual of actions that a hockey goalie will go through in preparation for a game. The goalie believes that if the series of actions are not repeated prior to every game the team will suffer a loss.

Anchoring. Have you ever bought or sold an item, basing its value on a price you saw listed elsewhere? Of course you have. We regularly determine the value of something based upon someone else's set price for similar items. Where we can falter in this approach, however, is if we regard the first bit of information we receive, regardless of its relevancy, as sufficient for the basis of a final value. **Anchoring** is using an initial value received from prior experience or any external information source and giving it disproportionate weight in setting a final value. For example, you have a friend that works as a waiter on weekends at a local restaurant. He reports to you and another friend that he regularly receives over $100 in tips on Saturday evenings. The other friend is enticed by this, and she decides to take a job as a waitress at another restaurant. In the first few weeks of working at this restaurant your friend has been receiving around $80 in tips each shift, but she is disappointed. Her expectation was that she would receive over $100 in tips each shift. Yet she failed to take into account additional information that would help her determine the expected value of tips, such as the average value of a dinner (which can have a significant effect on tipping), the time of her shift, the number of tables she has to tend to in a shift, the usual value of tips received by other servers in the same restaurant, and so on. Your friend may discover that, compared to other serving staff in the same establishment, her tips are on average greater than others.

Escalation of Commitment. The concept of **escalation of commitment** offers an explanation as to why decision makers adhere to a course of action even after they know it is incorrect (that is, why managers "throw good money after bad"). To understand the problem of escalating commitment, consider the following true examples:

- A company overestimated its capability to build an airplane brake that met certain technical specifications at a given cost. Because it won the government contract, the company was forced to invest greater and greater efforts to meet the contract terms. As a result of increasing pressure to meet specifications and deadlines, records and tests of the brake were misrepresented to government officials. Corporate careers and company credibility were increasingly put at stake on the airbrake contract, although many in the firm knew the brake would not work effectively. At the conclusion of the construction period, the government test pilot flew the plane; it skidded off the runway and narrowly missed injuring the pilot.

- An individual purchased a stock at $50 a share, but the price dropped to $20 soon after. Still convinced about the merit of the stock, he bought more shares at the lower price. Soon the price declined further, and the individual was again faced with the decision to buy more, hold what he already had, or sell out entirely.[16]

How do we account for such commitment by individuals and groups to obvious mistakes? At least three explanations are possible. First, we can point to individual limitations in information processing, as first identified by Herbert Simon. People may be limited in both their desire and ability to handle all the information for complex decisions. As a result, errors in judgment may occur. For example, the company in which the stock investor purchased shares may have significant operations in countries where negative changes in exchange rates are occurring or where government regulations have changed. The investor simply may not be able to completely comprehend these issues and how they are hurting the company's performance and subsequent stock price. A second approach is to explain decision errors as a breakdown in rationality because of group dynamics. For example, the stock investor may have received the tip from a trusted friend, or he could be the friend of the company's CEO and therefore has a strong emotional commitment. Although both explanations may help us understand the error, Barry Staw, who has done significant research into escalation of commitment, suggests that they do not go far enough: "A salient feature . . . is that a series of decisions is associated with a course of action rather than an isolated choice."[17]

To help explain such behaviour, Staw turned to the social psychological literature on forced compliance. In studies of forced compliance, individuals are typically made to perform an unpleasant or dissatisfying act (e.g., eating grasshoppers) with no external rewards. In general, after they comply, individuals bias their own attitudes to justify their previous behaviour (e.g., eating grasshoppers is not a bad thing because they are high in protein). This biasing of attitudes is most likely to occur when the individuals feel personally responsible for the negative consequences and when the consequences are difficult to undo.

On the basis of these findings, Staw and his colleagues carried out a series of experiments to find out how willing people would be to continue to commit valued resources to a course of action after it was clear that the original decision had been wrong. They found that decision makers actually allocated more money to company divisions that were showing poor results than to those that were showing good results. Also, decision makers allocated more money to a division when they had been responsible for the original decision to back the division. In short, decision makers were most likely to spend money on projects that had negative consequences when they were responsible.

To find out why, Staw suggested a model of escalating commitment (Exhibit 7.6). This abbreviated model shows that four basic elements determine commitment to an action. First, people are likely to remain committed to a course of action (even when it is clearly incorrect) because of a need to justify previous decisions. When people feel responsible for negative consequences and have a need to demonstrate their own competence, they will often stick to a decision to turn it around or "pull a victory out of defeat." This is a form of retrospective rationality; the individual or members of the group seek explanations so that their previous decisions appear rational. For example, banks that loaned billions of dollars to Asian countries in the late 1980s and early 1990s continued to loan more

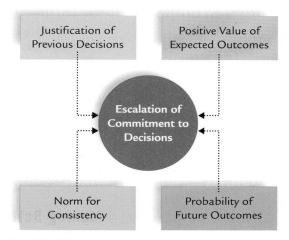

Exhibit 7.6 Contributing Factors to Escalation of Commitment to Decisions.

money even after it was clear that the governments would have great difficulty repaying the loans. They continued these loans in part to support their original decision. If they didn't continue the loans, they might be forced to recognize that their original decision was a mistake. This dynamic is not limited to headline decisions, either.[18] It can affect our continued commitment to personal decisions as well. There is a range of examples, from keeping a car that is a lemon, to sticking with a boyfriend or girlfriend long after it is clear that it is not a good match. In each case we try to avoid admitting openly that the original decision was a mistake.

In addition, commitment to a previous decision is influenced by a norm for consistency. That is, managers who are consistent in their actions are often considered better leaders than those who flip-flop from one course of action to another.

Finally, two additional factors—the perceived probability and value of future outcomes—jointly influence what is called prospective rationality. **Prospective rationality** is simply a belief that future courses of action are rational and correct. When people think they can turn a situation around or that "prosperity is just around the corner," and when the goal is highly prized, they exhibit strong commitment to a continued course of action, influenced in part by the feeling that it is the proper thing to do.

prospective rationality
A belief that future courses of action are rational and correct.

Overcoming Escalation of Commitment. Because escalation of commitment can lead to serious and negative consequences for organizations, we must consider how to minimize its effects.

1. First, as a manager, you should stress in your own mind and to others (superiors, peers, and subordinates) that investments made in the past are sunk costs—that is, they cannot be recovered. All finance theory argues that sunk costs should be ignored in making future decisions, and only future costs and future anticipated benefits should be considered. So when you find yourself in a hole, the first thing to do is stop digging.

2. Second, you must create an atmosphere in which consistency does not dominate. This requires stressing the changing aspects of the competitive, social, cultural, and commercial environment surrounding a business and focusing on the importance of matching current decisions to current and expected future environments rather than to past decisions.

3. Third, you can encourage each member to evaluate the prospects of future outcomes and their expected positive value critically. You can invite experts from outside the group to challenge members' future expectations, if need be.

4. Finally, as a manager, you can reward processes rather than outcomes. This encourages proper evaluation of projects at key stages where the project can be judged at face value and discourages individuals from undertaking risky heroics to pull a project out of the fire. This would mean celebrating failure if processes were followed and providing unambiguous negative feedback if processes were not followed, even if it led to a successful outcome.

In summary, when we consider effective decision-making processes in organizations, we must remain vigilant in knowing where our weaknesses lie. We need to be aware of our limitations in processing information, what shortcuts and approximations we rely on to make decisions, and our tendency to back a losing venture to avoid criticism and embarrassment.

Making Better Decisions

If all of the factors presented above can influence the effectiveness of decisions, what can you do as a manager to avoid these traps and enhance the probability of making a "good" decision?

Analyze the Situation. First, recognizing the decision-making traps is a key factor to success. For example, if you are unaware of Gresham's law or the representativeness heuristic, you have little opportunity to assess whether or not you are falling victim to it. Without this awareness it is almost impossible to deliberately get yourself out of this particular pit if you've fallen into it. As simple as this first step may seem, it is vital. Consequently, one of the first steps to better individual decision making is better decision situation assessment. Exhibit 7.7 provides a simple set of questions related to the three categories of factors diagrammed in Exhibit 7.5 that you can ask yourself to have a clearer picture of the situation and the potential pitfalls.

Scan the Environment. As we discussed, nonprogrammed decisions typically are more ambiguous than routine decisions. As a consequence, there is a greater risk that your decision could be wrong and carry important negative consequences for yourself and others. Going back to our example of the university president who has to choose between expanding the business school or the science facilities, making the wrong decision could be costly, both financially and politically. In fact, her job may depend on making the right decision. If she expands the science facility, there is no guarantee that the added faculty will bring in more contracts and grants. And by doing so, she may be denying admission to a large number of qualified business students. She may also alienate the business faculty and companies that recruit those graduates. In contrast, building the business programs could alienate the science students and faculty, allowing a rival university to get ahead, and possibly prompting many of the university's best scientists to go elsewhere. Clearly, the more complex, ambiguous, and volatile the problem, the more environmental scanning you may want to do prior to making the decision. For example, the university president would want to get as much useful information as she could from outside the organization. In doing so she may discover that a rival school is about to expand its own science complex and wants to hire away the best scientists. On one hand, she may wish to defend what she has, especially if the business school is viewed as less important to the

---

Exhibit 7.7 Questions Related to the Factors That Influence Decision Quality (see Exhibit 7.5)

Decision-Maker Characteristics

1. Do you have an implicit favourite solution?
2. Do you have a tendency to satisfice and go with the first workable solution?
3. Do you feel overwhelmed by the amount of information you are having to process?
4. Do you feel a lack of knowledge about the problem?
5. Are you particularly unfamiliar or familiar with the problem?

Problem Characteristics

1. Does the problem seem quite ambiguous?
2. Is the problem substantially complex?
3. Does the problem seem stable or volatile?

Decision Environment Characteristics

1. Are you under significant time pressures to make the decision?
2. Do you face substantial resource limitations (e.g., people, money, equipment, etc.) relative to the problem and its solution?
3. Is the decision irreversible?
4. Are the problem and your decision of substantial importance?

institution's goals. On the other hand, if the provincial legislature has made it clear that they want more business education, she may have to factor this into her decision as well. Overall, environmental scanning may help you gain useful information that can lead to a higher-quality decision.

Think Through the Process. As we stated earlier in this chapter, even though the rational approach may not always be descriptive of many decision-making processes, you can and most often should use it to guide your own decision making.

Be Creative. Being creative can be an important key to making effective decisions, especially if you discover in doing an analysis of the decision-making situation that you have an "implicit favourite" solution or if you have past experience with a similar but not exactly the same situation. This is also true if the problem is complex or unfamiliar. For example, your problem is how to make a raw egg stand up on the surface of your desk for 10 seconds without assistance and without losing any of the substance inside the egg. In other words, you can't prop it up against something, or use glue, extract the yolk and egg white, and so on. Get creative. Try spinning it. Try balancing it. What works? There is a way to do it.

Know the Right Timing. Clearly, you have to be aware of the timeliness of your decisions. Many decisions involve problems or opportunities that have time constraints. For example, deciding to enter a race after it's half over will not generally work out well. At the same time, deciding to run the race before any of the other competitors or spectators show up may not work out well either. Decisions can be made too early or too late. Making a decision sooner than needed can prevent you from creating a full set of alternatives or from examining them thoroughly. Making a decision too late can leave you with a great set of alternatives and a comprehensive analysis but no beneficial results. In popular management literature, this last tendency is often referred to as "analysis paralysis," or the failure to move and make a decision because you are stuck in the process of analyzing the situation, objectives, alternatives, and so on. To avoid poor timing, ask yourself and others when a decision is needed and why. Make sure the timing of the decision is clear and makes sense.

Increase Your Knowledge. If you are clear about the timing of the decision, you can help yourself avoid the pitfall of analysis paralysis and still increase your knowledge to make a better decision. The old standby foundation questions that you may have been taught in past creative writing exercises are perhaps the best guide for adding relevant knowledge for better decisions: who, what, where, when, why, and how.

Be Flexible. Thankfully, most decisions are not irreversible. As we will explore more fully later in this chapter, much of the sense of irreversibility of decisions comes from the decision maker's desire to seem consistent rather than from the nature of the decision itself. For example, once you jump out of an airplane and start falling, the nature of the decision is irreversible, so you better have a parachute. Consequently, as the rational model of decision making argues, it is important to monitor the outcomes closely and be prepared to modify or even completely change your decision if it seems that the desired outcomes will not materialize.

A Manager's Challenge: "Putting Radio into Orbit" provides an example where managers need to make good decisions in the face of considerable uncertainty. In deciding to launch satellite radio, they must first scan the environment carefully to learn from the actions of others (their successes and mistakes) as well as the nature of the market. In addition, they will need to be creative in coming up with solutions to the problems they face relative to their overall decision to embark on the plan. In reading this case, what is your impression of the industry? Do you think the Canadian market will be as slow to start as the US market was? Do you think the decision to partner with US service providers is the right approach, or should the Canadian providers remain independent?

Group Decision Making

The three models described at the beginning of the chapter (the rational/classical, bounded rationality, and retrospective decision models) attempt to explain certain aspects of individual decision making. However, those models can also illuminate aspects of group decision making. Many of the basic processes remain the same. For instance, using the rational model we can observe that both individuals and groups identify objectives. Both individuals and groups may also attempt to identify all possible outcomes before selecting one and, more than likely, both will fail in that attempt. Both individuals and groups are often observed engaging in satisficing behaviour or using heuristics in the decision process. And both individuals and groups develop implicit favourites and attempt to justify those favourites by procedures that appear to others to be rationalization.

Impact of Groups on Decision Making

What makes group decision making different from individual decision making is the social interaction in the process, which complicates the dynamics. In some situations, group decision making can be an asset, but at other times it can be a liability. The trick for you as a manager is to discover when and how to invite group participation in making decisions. Some assets and liabilities of group decision making are shown in Exhibit 7.8. Going one step further, let's look at what we know about the impact of groups on the decision process itself, especially relative to nonprogrammed decisions:

- In *establishing objectives*, groups are typically superior to individuals in that they bring greater cumulative knowledge to problems.

- In *identifying alternatives*, individual efforts ensure that different and perhaps unique solutions are identified from various functional areas that later can be considered by the group.

- In *evaluating alternatives*, group judgment is often superior to individual judgment because it involves a wider range of viewpoints.

Exhibit 7.8   Assets and Liabilities of Group Decision Making

Assets +	Liabilities −
■ Groups can accumulate more knowledge and facts.	■ Groups often work more slowly than individuals.
■ Groups have a broader perspective and consider more alternatives.	■ Group decisions involve considerable compromise that may lead to less than optimal decisions.
■ Individuals who participate in group decisions are more satisfied with the decision and are more likely to support it.	■ Groups are often dominated by one individual or a small clique, thereby negating many of the virtues of group processes.
■ Group decision processes serve an important communication function, as well as a useful political function.	■ Overreliance on group decision making can inhibit management's ability to act quickly and decisively when necessary.

A Manager's Challenge   *Technology*

Putting Radio into Orbit

Will Canadian listeners on the go tune in to CD-quality satellite radio? Managers at three Canadian satellite radio providers are planning for a resounding "yes" as they introduce satellite broadcasting, or more specifically, subscription radio (since not all of the digital broadcasting is delivered via satellite) to the Canadian market. Along the way, the managers must make a number of key decisions, despite considerable uncertainty about the level of demand, programming content, competition, and financial backing.

Three prospective Canadian satellite providers (Sirius Satellite Radio Canada, XM Canada, and CHUM Subscription Radio Canada) submitted proposals to the CRTC in 2003 and 2004. Following hearings, all three proposals received approval in June 2005, and by December of that same year Sirius and XM were broadcasting in Canada.

The Canadian managers are learning from the experiences of their American counterparts, XM Satellite Radio Holdings and Sirius Satellite Radio, which are partnering with the Canadian affiliates of the same name. Only CHUM will be 100 percent Canadian. The two US services currently use satellites to beam 100 mostly-commercial-free channels of sports, music, news, children's shows, and entertainment programs to subscribers, who pay between $50 and $500 to buy special receivers and an additional monthly fee ranging from $10 to $15. Managers at XM and Sirius have committed billions of dollars in the expectation that truck drivers, commuters, and others who drive for long periods will pay for clear, continuous reception of specialized radio programming anywhere in the United States.

The US companies had an initial bumpy ride because of slow growth in the number of subscribers and new competition from digital radio technology (which makes ordinary radio signals sound much better without any monthly fee). However, growth has dramatically increased: in spring 2005 Sirius was reporting 1.1 million subscribers while XM reported 3.2 million. By July 2006 Sirius had 4.7 million subscribers and XM boasted 6.9 million.

Watching how US companies cope has helped Canadian managers become more knowledgeable about the nature and complexity of the decisions they face. For example, managers at Sirius and XM had little success selling add-on gadgets that equip existing car radios to receive satellite radio signals, so they finally struck deals with major car manufacturers such as Ford, Chrysler, and Honda to install satellite-ready receivers as an option in new cars. In addition, Canadian satellite radio managers realize that although the Canadian market has many similarities to the US market, there are many critical differences as well. The total number of new cars sold in Canada is less than in the United States, accounting for fewer vehicles equipped with satellite radio receivers. As well, managers will have to adhere to specific CRTC requirements for providing Canadian content within the programming packages offered by their service. There are also significant differences in preferences across Canadian regions for radio programming based on language, sports activities, popular music, and news. So far, though, it seems that satellite radio in Canada is here to stay.

Sources: CBC News "Satellite Radio: FAQs," February 10, 2006, www.cbc.ca/news (accessed October 13, 2006); CNET, "CNET's Quick Guide to Satellite Radio," March 1, 2005, reviews.cnet.com (accessed October 14, 2006); Dow Jones Newswires, "FCC Approves Digital Radio," October 10, 2002, www.wsj.com (accessed October 16, 2006); B. Werth, "Companies Push Satellite Radio While Public Interest Lags," *Herald-Times* (Bloomington, IN), September 10, 2002, www.hoosiertimes.com (accessed October 16, 2006).

- In *choosing alternatives,* involving group members often leads to greater acceptance of the final outcome.

- In *implementing the choice,* individual responsibility is generally superior to group responsibility. Whether decisions are made individually or collectively, individuals perform better in carrying out the decision than groups do.[19]

From the list in Exhibit 7.8, you can see that you cannot conclude that either individual or group decision making is superior. Rather, the situation and the individuals involved should guide the choice of decision technique.

One question about the effects of group participation remains to be asked: Why does it seem to work in many instances? A partial answer to this question has been offered by Ronald Ebert and Terence Mitchell.[20] First, they suggest that participation clarifies more fully what is expected. Second, participation increases the likelihood that employees will work for rewards and outcomes they value. Third, it heightens the effects of social influence on behaviour; that is, peers will monitor and exert pressure on each other to conform to expected performance levels. Finally, it enlarges the amount of control employees have over their work activities. In many cases, participation in decision making can be useful in both organizational goal attainment and personal need satisfaction.[21]

Because participation helps involve employees and increases satisfaction and interaction, it has been an important part of quality improvement efforts. For example, team-based efforts to improve products and processes have always worked best when they included significant participation in decision making.

Contingency Model of Participative Decision Making

A central issue facing managers is the extent to which they should allow employees to participate in decisions affecting their jobs. For example, as work situations, time pressures, and even subordinate capabilities change, does the level of participation in decisions need to change? The short answer is "yes." Although many advocates of participation emphasize both case examples and even scientific research showing how participation led to improved decision quality, increased commitment of members to decision outcomes, and increased employee satisfaction, participative decision making is not a panacea. A careful review of the research suggests that it is not appropriate for every situation.[22] If participative decision making is not appropriate for all situations, how can you as a manager determine when it will and won't be effective and, therefore, when you should change your decision-making style or approach from one of making the decision on your own to one of involving others in a participative process?

Participative Decision Makers. To determine some of the variables that make up good participative decisions, researchers have explored the characteristics of the decision makers. Essentially, researchers have asked the question, "When participative decision making is effective, what do the people involved look like?" First and foremost, research suggests that those participating in the decision-making process must have sufficient knowledge about the content of the decision. Companies such as Ford, Federal Express, Procter & Gamble, and Boeing have put together **cross-functional teams** (consisting of members from marketing, finance, operations, human resources, etc.) for new product launches because each member has unique knowledge that adds value to the overall product launch. In contrast, asking people to become involved in decisions that are completely outside their area of expertise does not lead to either better-quality decisions or more commitment to the decisions and their implementation.

cross-functional teams
Employees from different departments, such as finance, marketing, operations, and human resources, who work together in problem solving.

In addition to content knowledge, members also need to have a general desire to participate. Not everyone wants to become involved in decisions. The desire to participate results from the individuals believing that (1) they have relevant content knowledge, (2) their participation will help bring about change, (3) the resulting change will produce outcomes they value or prefer, and (4) participation is valued by the organization and fits with its goals and objectives. When General Motors first started encouraging more employee involvement in decisions, workers resisted the effort because they did not believe it was "for real." This belief was based on the fact that involvement had not been a part of the company's history; in the past, decisions were made by managers and implemented by employees. As a consequence, it took sustained support from top management before workers believed participation was legitimate.

Participative Decision-Making Process. Like individual decision making, participative decision making involves related yet separate processes. Using the classical model of decision making, a participative group moves through the same seven steps, but involvement of group members can vary in each of those steps. Low involvement allows members to communicate their opinions about the problem, alternatives, and solution, but not to influence the final determination. High involvement allows members not only to communicate their opinions, but also to make final determinations. Thus, the degree of involvement could range from high to low on each of the seven elements in the classical decision model. Exhibit 7.9 provides a sample in which a particular group has high involvement in the front end of classical decision making but low involvement on the back end.

Because involvement can vary for each step of the classical decision-making model, a question naturally arises whether any one configuration is better. One study directly examined this question.[23] This study found that high involvement in generating alternatives, planning implementation, and evaluating results was significantly related to higher levels of satisfaction and work-group performance. Involvement in generating alternatives was important because solutions almost always came from the alternatives generated. Involvement in planning the implementation was important because the outcome was affected more by the way a solution was implemented than by the solution itself. And finally, involvement in evaluating results was important because feedback is critical to beginning the decision cycle again.

One of the interesting implications from this line of study is that group members also need to understand group processes for participative decision making to be effective. That is, skills in analysis, communication, and handling conflicts can be as important as knowledge and the desire to participate. For example, one of the critical capabilities in identifying problems is environmental scanning. Not everyone is skilled at scanning the environment and recognizing problems or opportunities, yet it is hard to begin participative decision making without members who can do this. For generating alternatives, a critical capability is creativity. For selecting a solution, a critical capability is managing conflict. It is unlikely that a group can agree on a preferred solution without some conflict, so managing that disagreement effectively is a critical skill.

Exhibit 7.10 provides a summary of the questions a manager should ask in determining whether participative decision making is likely to be effective.

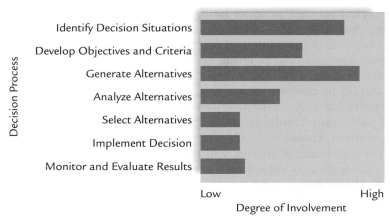

Exhibit 7.9 Sample Configuration of Degree of Involvement and Decision Process.

Exhibit 7.10   Contingency Factors for Effective Participative Decision Making

1. Do potential group members have sufficient content knowledge?

2. Do potential members have sufficient process knowledge?

3. Do members have a desire to participate?

4. Do members believe that their participation will result in changes?

5. Do members positively value the expected outcomes?

6. Do members see participation as legitimate and congruent with other aspects of the organization?

7. If the answer to any of the above questions is no, is it possible to change the conditions?

Source: N. Margulies and J. Stewart Black, "Perspectives on the Implementation of Participative Approaches," *Human Resource Management 26*, no. 3 (1987), pp. 385–412.

On the basis of a long-term research project, Victor Vroom and his colleagues Philip Yetton and Arthur Jago also developed a theory of participation in decision making that has clear managerial implications.[24] It is possible to categorize this model as either a model of leadership or a model of decision making. The model not only considers how managers should behave in decision-making situations, but also prescribes correct leader behaviour regarding the degree of participation. Given its orientation toward leadership behaviour, we cover this theory in depth in Chapter 8.

A Manager's Challenge: "Law Firms Change Decision-Making Style" illustrates one situation in which the move from more involvement in decision making to less involvement seems to have been effective. Clearly, when too many people are involved in decisions and when those decisions involve areas of specialization in which the participating members lack expertise, lower levels of participation are more appropriate than higher levels. This is exactly the situation in many law firms that have experienced significant growth. What is your assessment of the situation and the response? Does the changing situation seem to justify less participation in decisions?

Decision Speed and Quality

Have you ever heard of Gavilan Computer? If you own a laptop you should have, but odds are you haven't. In the early 1980s, Gavilan Computer was at the forefront of computer technology and had a virtual monopoly on the developing—and lucrative—laptop computer market. By 1984, however, Gavilan had filed for bankruptcy. Despite a US$31 million stake from venture capitalists, the company experienced long delays and indecision that cost the company its early technological and market advantage. Competitors entered the market and Gavilan failed to exploit its advantage. As one executive observed, "We missed the window."[25] What happened to Gavilan has occurred with alarming frequency in many corporations—especially those involved in high-tech industries—as the indecisive fall by the wayside.

In a series of studies of decision making in industries characterized by frequent change and turbulence—so-called high-velocity environments—researchers Kathleen Eisenhardt and L. J. Bourgeois attempted to determine what separates successful decision makers and managers from unsuccessful ones.[26] In high-velocity industries (e.g., microelectronics, medical technology, genetic engineering), high-quality, rapid decision making by executives and their companies is closely related to good corporate performance. In these industries, mistakes are costly; information is often ambiguous, obsolete,

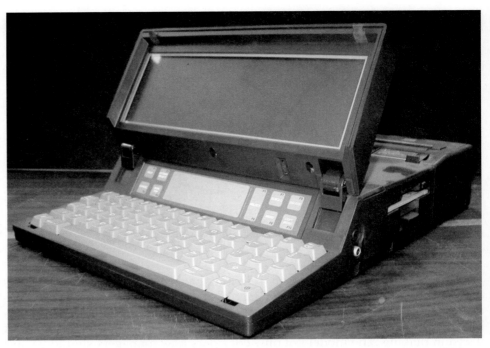

In the early 1980s Gavilan Computer was at the forefront of computer technology. By 1984, Gavilan had filed for bankruptcy.

or simply incorrect; and recovery from missed opportunities is extremely difficult. In view of the importance of speed for organizational innovation, performance, and survival, how do successful decision makers make high-quality, rapid decisions? And how are those decisions implemented quickly?

Eisenhardt and Bourgeois found that five factors influenced a manager's ability to make fast decisions in high-velocity environments (see Exhibit 7.11). These five characteristics are moderated by three mediating processes that determine the manager's and group's ability to deal with the quantity and quality of information:

1. *Accelerated cognitive processing.* The decision maker must be able to process and analyze great amounts of information quickly and efficiently. Some people—and some groups—can simply process information faster and better than others. Obviously, the faster a manager can process what is presented, the quicker the decision can be made.

2. *Smooth group processes.* To be effective, the manager must work with a group that has smooth, harmonious relations. This is not to say that everyone always agrees. Quite the contrary—members of effective groups often disagree. However, it is the way they disagree and resolve their disagreements that counts. Fast decisions are aided by group members who share a common vision and who are mutually supportive and cohesive.

3. *Confidence to act.* Finally, fast decision-making groups must not be afraid to act. As we already noted, some people are reluctant to make decisions in the face of uncertainty, and they tend to wait until they can reduce the uncertainty. They may fall victim to analysis paralysis. Unfortunately, in high-velocity environments, this uncertainty is never eliminated. Thus, to be effective, fast decision makers must be willing to choose when the appropriate time comes even in the face of uncertainty.

Remember that this research is focused on high-velocity environments, not all organizational environments. That is, in businesses that are characterized

A Manager's Challenge *Change*

Law Firms Change Decision-Making Style

Traditionally, all the partners in a law firm participated as a group in making decisions. This system built consensus and commitment and brought diverse backgrounds and opinions to the deliberations. Over time, however, as law firms have merged or added partners, the custom of participative decision making has led to bottlenecks and complications when questions about finance, technology, or other specialized topics appear on the agenda. Not only do the partners need more time to come to an agreement on such issues, but their decisions are also not necessarily better as a result of group participation.

Today law firms face more competition than ever before and feel more pressure to retain and serve corporate clients by keeping up with the faster pace of business. To operate more efficiently and more effectively in such an environment, some large law firms are changing the way they make internal decisions.

For example, Piper Marbury Rudnick & Wolfe is a law firm with 950 attorneys located in offices across the United States. The 300 lawyers at its largest office, located in Chicago, recently changed to a more centralized method of decision making. Instead of bringing all the partners together to vote and then manage the outcome of each decision, the chairperson relies on professional managers who specialize in particular areas of expertise, including marketing, information technology, human resources, and finance. "We realized that because of our size, we had to adopt a corporate model," states the chairperson,

Lee I. Miller. "It streamlines our decision making. We are able to react quickly, decisively."

However, partners accustomed to participative decision making may not easily accept the idea of delegating decisions to professional managers without group input. "At times it's a bitter pill," says a partner at the law firm Stellato & Schwartz. "When you ascend to the position of partner, it's based upon your ability to show loyalty, longevity, and business acumen. Inherent in those qualities is a desire to lead. But sometimes that desire has to be set aside for the good of the team." For their part, the managers who make decisions on behalf of law firms must constantly and carefully evaluate how the outcome of each major decision is likely to affect the firm and its partners, even when dealing with support functions such as human resources and finance.

Consider the situation at Wildman, Harrold, Allen & Dixon, an Illinois law firm where John Holthaus is executive director. As an accountant who holds an MBA degree, Holthaus has the technical and managerial background to make the myriad day-to-day decisions that keep the law firm operating smoothly. One way Holthaus proved his worth was by renegotiating the firm's lease to save on rental expenses. "I view my job as that of a hospital administrator who takes care of all the details so the doctors can take care of their patients," he explains. "I'm trying to make it easier for the attorneys to focus on serving their clients." Knowing that Holthaus understands the law firm's objectives and takes care of the tiniest details, the partners have come to rely on him rather than getting bogged down in endless group meetings to make decisions.

Source: Adapted from John T. Slania, "More Firms Mind Their Business: Corporate Model Helps Streamline Decision Making," *Crain's Chicago Business*, January 28, 2002, p. SR10.

Exhibit 7.11 Factors of Fast Decision Making

1. *Real-time information.* Fast decision makers must have access to and be able to process real-time information—that is, information that describes what is happening right now, not yesterday.

2. *Multiple simultaneous alternatives.* Decision makers examine several possible alternative courses of action simultaneously, not sequentially (e.g., "Let's look at alternatives X, Y, and Z together and see how each looks."). This adds complexity and richness to the analysis and reduces the time involved in information processing.

3. *Two-tiered advice process.* Fast decision makers make use of a two-tiered advisory system, whereby all team members are allowed input but greater weight is given to the more experienced co-workers.

4. *Consensus with qualification.* Fast decision makers attempt to gain widespread consensus on the decision as it is being made, not after it is made.

5. *Decision integration.* Fast decision makers integrate tactical planning and issues of implementation within the decision process itself (e.g., "If we are going to do X, how might we do it?").

by relative stability (e.g., the funeral home industry), rapid decisions may prove disastrous. Because stability allows time for more complete data collection and processing, managers in stable environments have less need for immediate action. Thus, as a manager of a team, you need to assess the time factors that characterize your industry. Then you will be able to make decisions appropriate for your industry.

Problems in Group Decision Making

groupthink A mode of thinking in which the pursuit of agreement among members becomes so dominant that it overrides a realistic appraisal of alternative courses of action.

One of the main problems with group decision making has received a lot of attention in recent years—a phenomenon known as **groupthink**. This phenomenon, first discussed by Irving Janis, refers to a mode of thinking in which the pursuit of agreement among members becomes so dominant that it overrides a realistic appraisal of alternative courses of action.[27] The concept emerged from Janis's studies of high-level policy decisions by government leaders. These included decisions by the US government about Vietnam, the Bay of Pigs invasion, and the Korean War. In analyzing the decision process leading up to each action, Janis found indications pointing to the development of group norms that improved morale at the expense of critical thinking. A model of this process is shown in Exhibit 7.12.

Groupthink by Stewart Black

mymanagementlab

Symptoms of Groupthink.   In studies of both government and business leaders, Janis identified eight primary symptoms of groupthink. The first is the *illusion of invulnerability*. Group members often reassure themselves about obvious dangers, becoming overly optimistic and thus willing to take extraordinary risks. Members fail to respond to clear warning signals. For instance, in the disastrous Bay of Pigs invasion of Cuba in the 1960s, the United States operated on the false assumption that it could keep its invasion of Cuba a secret. Even after news of the plan had leaked out, government leaders remained convinced of their ability to keep it a secret.

Victims of groupthink also tend to collectively *rationalize* and discount warning signs and other negative feedback that could lead to reconsidering the course of action. For example, Motorola discounted the new competitive potential of Nokia in the early 1990s. After all

- Nokia had a 100-year history in the forest products industry, making products like rubber boots for fishermen, not high-tech mobile phones.

- Europe would not likely adopt a unified digital standard because the various countries had never demonstrated any real ability to coordinate and cooperate.

- Even if they did, the markets of these countries (Germany, France, or Italy) paled in comparison to the size of the US mobile phone market.

- Finland (the home of Nokia) had fewer people than Chicago at the time.

We all know what happened. In 1990 Nokia was not even listed in the top 100 recognized brands, but by 2002 Nokia was number six—ahead of Intel and right behind GE. Motorola's 35 percent global market share of mobile phones was cut in half while Nokia's global share went from virtually nothing to 40 percent at its peak. Today Nokia is the number-one cell phone maker in the world.

Next, group members often believe in the inherent morality of the group. Because of this *illusion of morality*, they ignore the ethical or moral consequences of their decisions. While advertising for tobacco products is illegal in Canada, leading tobacco companies in the United States continue to run advertisements about smoking, ignoring the medical evidence of the hazards involved.

Stereotyping the enemy is another symptom of groupthink. In-group members often stereotype leaders of opposition groups in harsh terms that rule out negotiation on differences of opinion. Often they also place tremendous *pressure to conform* on members who temporarily express doubts about the group's shared illusions or who raise questions about the validity of the arguments supporting the group decisions.

Moreover, group members often use *self-censorship* to avoid deviations from group consensus. They often minimize to themselves the seriousness of their doubts. Partly because of self-censorship, the *illusion of unanimity* forms. Members assume that individuals who remain silent agree with the spoken opinions of others and falsely conclude that everyone holds the same opinion.

Finally, victims of groupthink often appoint themselves as *mindguards* to protect the leader and other members of the group from adverse information that could cause conflict over the correctness of a course of action.

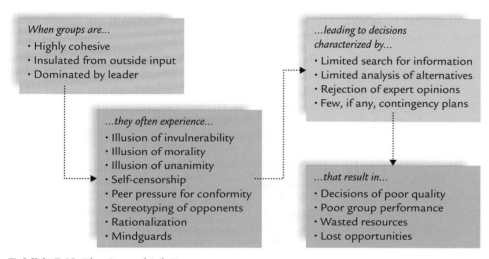

When groups are...
- Highly cohesive
- Insulated from outside input
- Dominated by leader

...they often experience...
- Illusion of invulnerability
- Illusion of morality
- Illusion of unanimity
- Self-censorship
- Peer pressure for conformity
- Stereotyping of opponents
- Rationalization
- Mindguards

...leading to decisions characterized by...
- Limited search for information
- Limited analysis of alternatives
- Rejection of expert opinions
- Few, if any, contingency plans

...that result in...
- Decisions of poor quality
- Poor group performance
- Wasted resources
- Lost opportunities

Exhibit 7.12 The Groupthink Process.

Source: Adapted from Gregory Moorhead, "Groupthink: Hypothesis in Need of Testing," *Group and Organization Studies 7*, no. 4, December 1982, pp. 429–444. Copyright © 1982 by Sage Publications, Inc. Reprinted by permission of Sage Publications, Inc.

Organizational dynamics like groupthink can lead companies to discount competitive threats. When the Finnish company Nokia—which had traditionally manufactured forest industry products, including rubber boots—entered the US mobile phone market in the 1990s, competitors like Motorola didn't take it seriously.

The mindguard may tell the dissident that he or she is being disruptive or nonsupportive or may simply isolate the dissident from other group members.

Consequences of Groupthink. Groupthink can have several adverse consequences for the quality of decision making. First, groups plagued by groupthink often limit their search for possible solutions to one or two alternatives rather than all possible alternatives. Second, such groups frequently fail to re-examine their chosen action after new information or events suggest a change in course. Third, group members spend little time considering nonobvious advantages to alternative courses of action. Fourth, such groups often make little or no attempt to seek expert advice either inside or outside their organization. Fifth, members show interest in facts that support their preferred alternative and either ignore or disregard facts that fail to support it. Finally, groups often ignore possible roadblocks to their choice and, as a result, fail to develop contingency plans. This last consequence is similar to retrospective decision making—the decision is made and then data are selected that support the decision. Because peers reinforce the decision, unwillingness to re-examine and change directions is even more powerful in group decisions than individual decisions.

Overcoming Groupthink. Because a groupthink mentality poses such serious consequences for organizations, we must consider how to minimize its effects. Janis suggests several strategies. To begin, group leaders can reduce groupthink by encouraging each member to evaluate proposals critically. Leaders can also ensure that the group considers a range of alternatives by not stating their own positions and instead promoting open inquiry.

Other strategies for preventing groupthink involve getting more suggestions for viable solutions. Assigning the same problem to two independent groups can achieve this. Or before the group reaches a decision, members can seek advice from other groups in the organization. Another technique is to invite experts outside of the group to challenge group members' views at meetings.

Exhibit 7.13   Guidelines for Overcoming Groupthink

For the Company

- Establish several independent groups to examine the same problem.
- Train managers in groupthink prevention techniques.

For the Leader

- Assign everyone the role of critical evaluator.
- Use outside experts to challenge the group.
- Assign a devil's advocate role to one member of the group.
- Try to be impartial and refrain from stating your own views.

For Group Members

- Try to retain your objectivity and be a critical thinker.
- Discuss group deliberations with a trusted outsider and report back to the group.

For the Deliberation Process

- At times, break the group into subgroups to discuss the problem.
- Take time to study what other companies or groups have done in similar situations.
- Schedule second-chance meetings to provide an opportunity to rethink the issues before making a final decision.

Groupthink may also be prevented with strategies directed at the group members themselves. For example, for each group meeting a member can be appointed to serve as a **devil's advocate**, a person whose role is to challenge the majority position.[28] Also, after reaching preliminary consensus, the group can schedule a second-chance meeting. This allows group members an opportunity to express doubts and rethink the issue.

If groups are aware of groupthink, they can use the steps discussed to minimize the likelihood of falling victim to this problem. These steps, which are summarized in Exhibit 7.13, offer advice for leaders, organizations, individuals, and the process itself.

devil's advocate A group member whose role is to challenge the majority position.

Cultural Dimensions of Decision Making

To this point we have talked about decision making as though it applied the same way the world over. Although we still have much to learn about decision making in different countries and cultures, we can identify several factors that affect how decisions are made. Many stem from the cultural differences we examined in Chapter 10.

One of the factors affecting decision making is the extent to which a culture adopts an individualist or collectivist orientation. For example, in exploring a contingency framework for participative decision making, we cited research suggesting that participation was not effective in all situations and that it should be used when it matches specific elements of a situation. However, it is worth noting that most researchers of participative decision making have come from individualistic cultures such as the United States, Canada, and the United Kingdom. In countries such as Japan, Indonesia, and Korea, managers and employees have a much stronger collectivist orientation. As a consequence, involving others in decision making may not simply be a function of contingency factors, but simply viewed as the "right" thing to do. In collectivist cultures, even when an individual decision maker believes he or she has all the relevant knowledge, a strong collectivist value often leads to the inclusion of others in the decision-making process.

These cultural clashes can often be seen when individuals from opposite cultural orientations must work together. For example, when managers from more individualistic cultures are assigned to work in more collectivist cultures, they quite frequently experience difficulties because they tend to make too many individual decisions and not include others enough.[29]

Basic values concerning hierarchy can also influence decision making across countries.[30] Managers in countries such as Malaysia, India, and Thailand have a higher acceptance of hierarchical differences between people (high power distance, in Hofstede's terms), whereas managers in countries such as Israel, Australia, and Denmark do not. Power distance can significantly affect the problem-analysis stage of decision making, especially when it involves group decisions. In low-power-distance cultures, group members tend to openly and directly disagree with each other in discussing the merits or risks of a given alternative. In high-power-distance cultures, such open discussions are less acceptable when individuals of differing ranks are involved. For example, if a lower-ranked individual in Thailand had a significant difference of opinion with his superior, directly raising this during a group meeting would not be acceptable. Rather, the individual would try to find a time, perhaps after work, when he could present his opinion privately to his superior.

On the surface, one might expect organizations in cultures that have high levels of power distance to suffer from problems of groupthink because employees are less willing to voice their concerns or make critical comments, especially when superiors are present. Interestingly, many of these cultures have developed business practices to counterbalance this potential problem. For example, managers in Japan use a technique called *nemawashi*. This term is borrowed from gardening and refers to the process of gradually snipping the roots of a tree or bush that is to be transplanted to reduce the shock to the plant. In business, *nemawashi* translates into many private or semiprivate meetings in which true opinions are shared before a major decision-making meeting. This allows differences of opinion to be stated while still protecting respected hierarchical status. In addition, meeting after work at a bar or restaurant also allows for more direct discussions and disagreements. Both of these practices serve to counteract groupthink fostered by high power distance.

Another factor that can affect decision making is the extent to which cultures differ in their tolerance of risk. In countries with a relatively low tolerance of uncertainty and risk, such as Japan and Germany, nonprogrammed decisions are avoided as much as possible by using standard operating procedures. For example, the operating manual at BMW for how to work through an engineering problem is thick and detailed. Even though the specific engineering problems may vary, BMW executives have tried to make the decisions as programmed as possible. In contrast, managers in countries with a relatively high tolerance of uncertainty and risk, such as Australia, Canada, and the United States, tend to seek out nonprogrammed decisions and to give senior management more responsibility for nonprogrammed decisions. For example, the employee manual at Nordstrom, an upscale department store in the United States, simply states, "Nordstrom Rules: Rule #1: Use your good judgment in all situations. There will be no additional rules. Please feel free to ask your department manager, store manager, or division general manager any question at any time."

In addition to cultural values and the way they can affect the decision-making process, social and even corporate cultural values can affect nearly every aspect of decision making. For example, what is seen as a problem, what is viewed as an acceptable or desirable outcome, what criteria are used in assessing various alternatives, how an alternative is chosen (by the highest-ranking member, majority votes, consensus, etc.), or who is involved in planning the implementation of a decision can all be influenced by the underlying organizational or national culture. However, knowing the basic building blocks of decision making helps you ask the right questions and discover important differences in decision making when you work with people from other cultures.

Australian, U.S., and Canadian companies like Holt Renfrew are likely to turn to nonprogrammed decision making and give their employees more decision-making latitude.

Strategies for Improving Decision Making

Now that we have focused on the problems and processes involved in decision making, and examined several decision-making models, the differences between individual and group decisions, participation in decision making, constraints on effective decision making, and cultural influences, we can consider additional ways of improving the decision-making process. At the beginning of the chapter we mentioned that decisions could be divided into two phases: problem formulation and problem solution. Strategies to improve decision making can also be divided into the same two categories.[31]

Improving Problem Formulation

Problem formulation focuses on identifying the causes for unsatisfactory behaviour and finding new opportunities and challenges. This process is often inhibited by the failure of group members to look beyond the familiar. Groupthink and escalating commitment often limit critical analysis or comprehensive searches for information and solutions. As a result, improvement in problem formulation may require the use of structured debate. **Structured debate** is a process to improve problem formulation through the use of a devil's advocate, multiple advocacy, and dialectical inquiry (see Exhibit 7.14).

Devil's Advocate. As discussed earlier, a devil's advocate is a group member whose role is to disagree with the group. For example, if you asked a group of North American automobile company executives why their sales are down, they might blame Japanese imports. In this case, a devil's advocate would argue that the problem is not with the Japanese, but with the North Americans themselves and their poor product quality. Through this process, the group is forced to justify its position and, as a consequence, develop a more precise and accurate picture of the problem and its underlying causes.

Multiple Advocacy. **Multiple advocacy** is like the devil's advocate approach except that more than one opposing view is presented. Each group involved in a decision is assigned the responsibility of representing the opinions of its constituents. Thus, if a university is concerned with enhancing racial and cultural diversity on campus, it might establish a commission including Blacks, Hispanics, Asians, women's groups, and so forth. The resulting dialogue should lead to the identification of a useful agenda for discussion.

Dialectical Inquiry. **Dialectical inquiry** occurs when a group or individual is assigned the role of questioning the underlying assumptions of problem formulation. It begins by identifying the prevailing view of the problem and its associated assumptions. Next, an individual is asked to develop an alternative problem that is credible but has different assumptions. By doing so, the accuracy of the original assumptions is examined and possibly altered. As a result, group members are forced to "think outside the box" and look at new ways to analyze a problem. These efforts are particularly helpful in overcoming groupthink and escalating commitment because they question the underlying assumptions of group behaviour.

structured debate A process to improve problem formulation that includes using a devil's advocate, multiple advocacy, and dialectical inquiry.

multiple advocacy A process to improve decision making by assigning several group members to represent the opinions of various constituencies that might have an interest in the decision.

dialectical inquiry A process to improve decision making by assigning a group member (or members) the role of questioning the underlying assumptions associated with the formulation of a problem.

Exhibit 7.14 Techniques for Improving Decision Making	
Structured Debate (Problem Formulation)	**Creativity Stimulants (Problem Solution)**
Devil's advocate	Brainstorming
Multiple advocacy	Nominal group technique
Dialectical inquiry	Delphi technique

Improving Problem Solution

Problem solution involves developing and evaluating alternative courses of action and then selecting and implementing the preferred alternatives. To improve this process, group members must be as thorough and creative as possible. Stimulation of creativity expands the search for and analysis of possible alternatives. Three such mechanisms are useful: brainstorming, the nominal group technique, and the delphi technique.

brainstorming A process of generating many creative solutions without evaluating their merit.

Brainstorming. The process of **brainstorming** generates many creative solutions without evaluating their merit. It is a frequently used mechanism to provide the maximum number of ideas in a short period of time. A group comes together, is given a specific problem, and is told to propose any ideas that come to mind to solve the problem. In such sessions—at least in the early stages—criticism is minimized so as not to inhibit expression. Once all the ideas are on the table, the group considers the positive and negative aspects of each proposal. Through a process of continual refinement, the best possible solution under the circumstances should emerge.

nominal group technique A process of having group members record their proposed solutions, summarize all proposed solutions, and independently rank solutions until a clearly favoured solution emerges.

Nominal Group Technique. The **nominal group technique**, typically referred to as NGT, consists of four phases in group decision making.[32] First, individual members meet as a group, but they begin by sitting silently and independently generating their ideas on a problem in writing. This silent period is followed by a round-robin discussion in which each group member presents an idea to the group. No discussion of the idea is allowed at this time. The ideas are summarized and recorded (perhaps on a whiteboard). After all individuals have presented their ideas, each idea is discussed to clarify and evaluate it. Finally, group members conclude the meeting by silently and independently ranking the various ideas or solutions. The final decision is determined by the pooled outcome of the members' votes.

The NGT allows the group to meet formally, but it does not allow members much discussion; hence the term *nominal* group technique. A chief advantage of this procedure is that everyone independently considers the problem without influence from other group members. As mentioned earlier, this influence represents one of the chief obstacles to open-minded discussions and decision making.

delphi technique A decision-making technique that never allows decision participants to meet face to face but identifies a problem and asks for solutions using a questionnaire.

Delphi Technique. In contrast to NGT, the **delphi technique** never allows decision participants to meet face to face. Instead, a problem is identified and members are asked through a series of carefully designed questionnaires to provide potential solutions. These questionnaires are completed independently. Results of the first questionnaire are then circulated to all group members (who are still physically separated). After viewing the feedback, members are again asked their opinions (to see if the opinions of others on the first questionnaire caused them to change their own minds). This process may continue through several iterations until group members' opinions begin to show consensus.

The decision-making process includes a variety of problems. Individuals and groups have various biases and personal goals that may lead to suboptimal decisions. Moreover, groups often censor themselves. Even so, techniques such as those discussed here aim to minimize many of these problems by insulating individual participants from the undue influence of others. This allows individuals greater freedom of expression, and the group receives far less filtered or slanted information with which to make its decision. Thus, although not perfect, these techniques can give managers mechanisms to improve both the quality and the timeliness of decisions made in organizations.

The Role of Technology

Much has been said in recent years about the role of technology in decision making at the individual and group level.[33] For routine but complex tasks such as scheduling aircraft, raw materials, and material- and component-flow through a factory, computers and software vastly increase decision-making capabilities. These tools can process amounts of information that would be overwhelming for an individual and at a speed that would be impossible for a human being. For example, despite all the problems and huge losses for commercial airlines in the United States during the 1990s, JetBlue, a US discount airline, became a successful start-up in 1998 and made money when other airlines were losing billions. Part of its success was due to the liberal use of new technology. By putting laptops and software in the hands of pilots, the company did away with the dozens and dozens of people typically required to make decisions about flight paths, scheduling, fuel intake, and so on.[34]

There is also a wide variety of technologies available for helping groups communicate and make decisions without having to get together face to face. Technology that allows group members in different locations to view a common document at the same time and make real-time changes is increasingly being used by design teams in industries like automobile manufacturing. The "virtual" aspects can save considerable travel costs and some have argued that the real-time aspects increase group decision effectiveness. Certainly companies are using technology to conduct virtual meetings and bring teams together from all over the world, but whether the benefits of computer-mediated communication are as great as they were hyped up to be is arguable. One review of recent studies comparing decision making in face-to-face versus computer-mediated communication groups found that computer-mediated communication leads to decreased group effectiveness, increased time required to complete tasks, and decreased member satisfaction compared to face-to-face groups.[35] The study concluded by cautioning about the unbridled rush by organizations to adopt computer-mediated communication as a medium for group decision making.

Managerial Perspectives Revisited

PERSPECTIVE 1: THE ORGANIZATIONAL CONTEXT No doubt by this point you see the importance of the organizational context in both individual and group decision making. However, it is worthwhile making the links explicit. For example, time pressures in an organization can significantly affect decision making. On the one hand, the nature of your business may be high velocity and require quick decisions. On the other hand, the culture of your company or just your immediate boss can put pressure on you to make a quick decision when one is not actually needed. Failure to recognize the organizational context could cause you to be late in making a decision in the first situation and unduly early in the second. The cultural diversity of your organization also presents challenges and opportunities. Clearly, when the group and decision-making processes are managed well, cultural diversity can be leveraged for more diverse perspectives regarding the problem or opportunity as well as greater creativity in solving the problem. At the same time, cultural diversity could present challenges in terms of different levels of comfort with ambiguous problems, desire to participate, or how to confront differences of opinion in a group setting with superiors present. The nature of the organization can also influence the degree to which you face programmed and nonprogrammed decisions. In general, managers working in a railroad company likely face more programmed decisions than those working in the fashion industry. However, even within a given industry the culture of the specific company can influence the degree to which you face programmed or nonprogrammed decisions.

PERSPECTIVE 2: THE HUMAN FACTOR Even as a manager, you may encounter decisions that you can and should make individually. However, as a manager it is less likely that these individually made decisions can be implemented completely on your own without the involvement of others. Even when facing situations in which you believe the benefits of involving others in decision making outweigh any disadvantages, you will have to decide the extent to which you involve others in the formulation and solution phases. For example, as the complexity and ambiguity of the problems you face and the decisions you have to make increase, so does the likelihood that you will need to involve others in decisions. Will you work through people with higher involvement primarily in the formulation phase, the solution phase, or both? Clearly, to the extent that you involve others in decision making, the decision formulation and implementation success becomes a function of working effectively with and through others.

PERSPECTIVE 3: MANAGING PARADOXES Managers are likely to encounter paradoxes in decision making. On the one hand, aspiring to follow the rational approach to make and implement decisions can help you avoid common pitfalls of bounded rationality or retrospective decision making. On the other hand, we are limited in our ability to be rational and all too often fall victim to decision-making traps. You will also have to master the potential paradox that is at the heart of Gresham's law. You cannot ignore or simply delegate away all programmed decisions whether they are urgent or not. At the same time, if you allow them to dominate your time and energy, you will be less likely to address nonprogrammed decisions, which often have a bigger impact on your job performance and overall results for the organization. Diversity presents another element of duality. As a manager you get paid in part for your judgment and ability to make decisions. Yet never checking with others as to how they see a situation or never taking into account the diverse perspectives, experience, and capabilities of those around you can lead you to less creative and less effective decisions.

PERSPECTIVE 4: ENTREPRENEURIAL MINDSET Managers' entrepreneurial mindset is reflected in the decisions that they make and by the degree of their commitment to those decisions and the processes by which they are made. Overall, an entrepreneurial mindset in decision making is reflected by applying one's intuition and being creative along with a willingness to take some risks. A manager can enrich entrepreneurial activities in the organization by searching for new information and encouraging others to express diverse viewpoints. Although escalation of commitment to a prior decision and groupthink (if a group participates in the decision) do not reflect an entrepreneurial mindset, the devil's advocate approach, brainstorming, delphi technique, and the nominal group technique can be used by managers to facilitate a more entrepreneurial approach to decision making. Using such approaches displays managers' commitment to be innovative in continuously searching for new opportunities when they make important decisions.

Concluding Comments

Decision making is a critical part of any manager's life. You could construe much of what a manager does as decision making. Motivation could be viewed as a decision regarding how to motivate a subordinate. Strategic management could be viewed as deciding what strategy to pursue. Communication could be viewed as a decision about what to say and how to say it. However central decision making may be to managing, to say that it is everything seems a bit much to us.

Still, as a manager you will make many decisions—large and small. As a consequence, you need a reasonably comprehensive but usable framework for guiding your decisions. We have suggested that thinking about decision making in terms of formation and implementation can fit this need. In formulation, it is important to remember that we often select solutions that meet our minimum objectives rather than spending extra time and energy trying to find the solution that maximizes the objectives. However, to appear rational, we often construct objectives and criteria after the fact to justify the decision we have already made. Groups can add a social dynamic to this tendency and make group members feel even more comfortable that they have been rational than individuals might feel alone. After all, if everyone else feels like it's a good decision, it must be. Managed properly, groups can also be an antidote to many of the limitations we described. Consequently, depending on how well the group dynamics are managed, group decision making can render decisions and results that are significantly better or worse than individuals might achieve on their own.

Thus, making a group decision or involving others in decision making is not a panacea to the common pitfalls. The decision of how much to involve others is a function of several factors including the knowledge and motivation of potential participants in the decision, the nature of the problem and decision, the environment in which the problem exists, and the speed with which the decision needs to be made.

Understanding these basics provides a foundation for awareness of how cultural values can influence decision making. This in turn better enables you as a manager to make effective decisions in an increasingly global and culturally diverse environment.

Key Terms

anchoring   (p. 236)
bounded rationality (administrative man) model   (p. 231)
brainstorming   (p. 254)
conjunction fallacy   (p. 236)
cross-functional teams   (p. 243)
decision making   (p. 225)
delphi technique   (p. 254)
devil's advocate   (p. 251)
dialectical inquiry   (p. 253)
ease of recall   (p. 235)
escalation of commitment   (p. 236)
formulation   (p. 225)
Gresham's law of planning   (p. 226)

groupthink   (p. 248)
heuristic   (p. 231)
insensitivity to base rates   (p. 235)
insensitivity to sample size   (p. 235)
intuitive decision making   (p. 233)
misconception of chance   (p. 235)
multiple advocacy   (p. 253)
nominal group technique   (p. 254)
nonprogrammed decision   (p. 226)
opportunity   (p. 225)
perceptual distortion   (p. 233)
presumed associations   (p. 235)
problem   (p. 225)

programmed decision   (p. 225)
prospective rationality   (p. 238)
rational (classical) model   (p. 228)
regression to the mean   (p. 236)
retrievability   (p. 235)
retrospective decision (implicit favourite) model   (p. 233)
satisficing   (p. 231)
solution   (p. 225)
standard operating procedure (SOP)   (p. 226)
structured debate   (p. 253)
subjectively expected utility (SEU) model   (p. 228)

Test Your Comprehension

1. What are the two fundamental stages in decision making?

2. Describe programmed and nonprogrammed decisions.

3. When are SOPs (standard operating procedures) most often used?

4. Describe Gresham's law of planning.

5. How can selective perception influence decision formulation?

6. What is the basic premise of the rational (classical) model of decision making?

7. How does the rational (classical) model of decision making differ from the bounded rationality model?

8. How can biases negatively affect decision quality?

9. How can managers work to overcome the effects of escalation of commitment to past decisions?

10. What are the key advantages to understanding the bounded rationality model of decision making?

11. What is satisficing? How does it differ from satisfying?

12. What is an implicit favourite?

13. How does the retrospective decision model work?

14. Why is analyzing the decision situation a key step in making better decisions?

15. What are the key assets of group decision making?

16. What are the key liabilities of group decision making?

17. When is it appropriate for a manager to be more participative in decision making?

18. Describe the phenomenon of groupthink. What are its symptoms?

19. How can we overcome groupthink?

20. Compare and contrast the nominal group technique and the delphi technique of decision making.

21. How can cultural values affect decision making?

Apply Your Understanding

1. If your subordinates expect you to be consistent in your decision-making style, but you believe that different decision-making styles (e.g., high involvement of others versus low involvement) are appropriate for specific situations, how can you *change* your decision-making approach but not seem inconsistent to your employees?

2. Think of someone you know personally who is an effective decision maker. What key characteristics would you use to describe this person?

3. What are the strengths and weaknesses of a manager with "good instincts" who seems to make effective decisions but whose approach is more like the retrospective than the rational model?

4. Japanese and Korean managers tend to spend considerably more time on and involve more people in the problem formulation stage of decision making than North American managers do. What are the pros and cons you see with this?

Practise Your Capabilities

While sitting in your office, you get a call from the plant supervisor that a request has come in from a major customer that would require you to adjust your product line for a custom run of this client's rush order. The plant supervisor has delegated the decision of whether you should stop your current run and meet the customer's request to you. He needs the decision by tomorrow morning.

Your line is in the middle of an extended standard run that will produce product for five of your mid-sized customers. Your company competes in part by offering both low cost and quality service. The vast majority of your mid-size customers chose you because of your lower prices. You maintain your profitability with these customers through keeping your costs low. Your principal means of achieving this is through running a high volume of standard products through your product line. Many of your large customers appreciate your low price but are willing to pay a premium for customized service and alterations to the products that come off your line.

If you stop the line to make the changes in equipment needed to run the custom order, you will incur both costs and delays to your current standard run. You are about two-thirds of the way through your standard run. It will take approximately three hours to change over to the custom run and two days to run it.

You have made this particular changeover before, but not in the last six months. You know the basics of the changeover but the person most knowledgeable about the details is off sick today. She left you a voice mail saying that she expects to be back to work tomorrow.

In general your team of nine product-line operators is fairly experienced and does not require close supervision, with the exception of two new members to your team. Your team is generally willing to be involved in decisions, but they are also happy to just "do their jobs."

1. Should you make this decision on your own or should you involve the group?

2. Would you stop the current run and change over for the custom run? Why or why not?

3. If you insist that it's impossible to decide based on the information you have, what additional information must you have to make the decision?

PEARSON

mymanagementlab

To improve your grade, visit the MyManagementLab website at **www.pearsoned.ca/mymanagementlab**. This online homework and tutorial system allows you to test your understanding and generates a personalized study plan just for you. It provides you with study and practice tools directly related to this chapter's content. MyManagementLab puts you in control of your own learning!

Part Seven

The Manager as a Planner and Strategist

Chapter 8

Planning

After reading this chapter, you should be able to:

1 Define planning and explain its purpose.

2 Differentiate between strategic, operational, and tactical plans.

3 Explain the planning process.

4 Identify key contingency factors in planning.

5 Explain budgeting as a planning tool.

6 Describe an MBO planning system.

7 Describe effective goals.

Taken from *Management*, Canadian Edition, by Michael A. Hitt, J. Stewart Black, Lyman W. Porter, and Andrew J. Gaudes.

Procter & Gamble in Eastern Europe

When the Berlin Wall fell in 1989, it opened up Eastern European markets to Western firms for the first time in decades. Procter & Gamble entered the Eastern European market with a careful, elaborate plan. For example, rather than import Tide to the Czech Republic, which would have been too costly, P&G engineers worked with a Czech plant to produce and manufacture Tide there.

Procter & Gamble (P&G), the maker of Tide, Crest, Swiffer, Vidal Sassoon, and hundreds of other well-known consumer brands, relies heavily on its international markets to sustain long-term growth. Currently P&G markets more than 300 products to more than 5 billion consumers in over 180 countries, and the company has over 100 manufacturing plants in 42 countries. P&G's annual revenue in 2006 was in excess of US$68 billion.

Nearly one-quarter of P&G's total revenues are in Western Europe. So it was only natural that P&G corporate and regional executives had a significant interest in the opening of Eastern Europe in 1989 when the Berlin Wall fell. P&G subsequently entered specific Eastern European countries that had been deprived of quality Western material goods. However, rather than enter rapidly and make mistakes, the regional executives formulated a specific plan for doing so. The steps to this plan included: (1) analyzing the environment, (2) setting objectives and strategies, (3) determining resources, and (4) monitoring outcomes.

Analyzing the Environment

Given the instability of the Eastern European countries, P&G executives in Europe took their time to analyze the environment before expanding. In February 1990, company executives from both corporate headquarters and regional operations took a tour of major markets to assess strengths and weaknesses among the countries, including Hungary, the Czech Republic, and Russia. Executives returned with notes and impressions on both the risks and benefits involved in those markets:

RISKS

- Poor infrastructure.
- Unstable governments and tense political atmosphere.

BENEFITS

- 400 million consumers.
- Highly educated and inexpensive work-force.
- Movement to a free market system.

Based on the environmental assessment, the company decided to focus first on Poland, the Czech Republic, and Hungary, and to enter Russia later very cautiously.

Setting Objectives and Strategies

P&G executives' next step was to set objectives for its expansion into Eastern Europe. In addition to long- and short-term financial objectives, they had several strategic objectives. Two important objectives were (1) to achieve the lowest cost and best quality sourcing and (2) to achieve superior distribution.

To provide low-cost, high-quality products, executives determined that they would eventually need regional production capacity, because the high cost of importing goods into the region would make them less affordable to consumers. However, the executives wanted to begin operations quickly without too much risk. So the option of building plants was rejected.

The next option was to acquire local manufacturers, although this carried some risk. For example, how could an Eastern European plant manufacture with the same efficiency and quality as a Western plant? Nonetheless, the strategy was less risky than building the plants from scratch. One such acquisition occurred in the Czech Republic where P&G found a company called Rakona. P&G engineers worked with Czech employees at the Rakona plant to conduct test runs of Ariel detergent—the equivalent of Tide detergent in Western Europe. After only a few weeks, the detergent produced in the Czech plant was identical to that produced in Western Europe.

To achieve the highest market share, P&G executives decided that they had to expand rapidly. But they found that distribution channels in Eastern Europe were very poorly developed. Even under favourable circumstances in Russia, it could take three weeks for a case of detergent to be transferred from the Moscow area across Siberia to Vladivostok on the eastern shore.

Determining Resources

Once objectives and strategies were set, P&G executives determined what resources were needed. The executives figured that the most critical resource was human—the employees who would build the business in Eastern Europe. Both experienced P&G managers from other parts of the world and local men and women would be needed. And these employees would need both technical and managerial skills to succeed.

Monitoring Outcomes

During the implementation of its plan, P&G executives carefully monitored the outcomes, both financial and strategic, in each of the countries they entered. The results have reflected an overall success story in Eastern Europe. After four years of operation, annual sales rose to US$500 million, making the company the largest consumer goods firm in the entire region. Twenty-five brands served the markets, and most were among the top two or three in their product categories. The business also became profitable within the first four years, although it had taken eight years to turn a profit in Western Europe. For Procter & Gamble, the region has now become their most important developing market, surpassing China.

The exclusive distribution arrangements that P&G set in place soon after the opening of Eastern Europe secured for them key markets in Russia and Poland, which made it much more difficult for competitors to get a foothold when they entered later. In Russia, for example, P&G controls around half the laundry detergent sales, shutting out key rival Unilever. The annual revenue for P&G in Russia alone surpassed the

US$1 billion mark in 2004 and has continued to increase.

Today, the company's executives remain optimistic about their long-term business in Eastern Europe. In 2005 P&G acquired Gillette and built the largest production facility for Gillette razor blades in the world in Poland. Because of its careful, thorough planning, the company expects to enjoy high returns over the long term. ◆

Sources: "The Procter & Gamble Company: Company Profile," *Datamonitor*, November, 2006; "From Volatility to Stability," *Soap, Perfumery & Cosmetics*, November 2006; J. Neff, "Entrenched P&G Faces Foes' Inroads," *Advertising Age*, August 28, 2006; "P&G Overhauls Euro Data Strategy," *Precision Marketing*, October 31, 2003, p. 1; Personal communication with John Pepper, 2001; P&G 2001 Annual Report; J. Pepper, "Leading the Change in Eastern Europe," Business Quarterly, Autumn 1995, pp. 26–33.

Strategic overview

The opening case clearly illustrates the importance of a manager's ability to formulate and implement effective plans. Although planning has been an important managerial activity for some time, it is perhaps more important and perplexing now than ever before. On the one hand, the increase in competition means that if an organization, business unit, or individual manager fails to plan and as a consequence drifts off course or loses momentum, competitors are likely to overtake it. On the other hand, the speed of change and rapid flow of information increasingly require plans that are flexible and dynamic. In today's world, a rigid plan can be as fatal as no plan at all. As important as competition and the rate of change are, both must be viewed within the context of globalization for a manager to be successful today and in the future. Increasingly, as a manager you must not only be aware of local competitors, but also those in other parts of the world. In addition, you must recognize that because information flows throughout the world nearly instantaneously, it can create the need for rapid and dramatic changes in your plans.

Effective planning at all organizational levels can have a significant impact on the firm's performance. Without effective planning, P&G might have failed in its efforts to enter and compete successfully in the Eastern European markets. But the company's activities in these markets turned out to be highly effective, in part because managers had a plan and regularly re-evaluated and changed it. Managers need to continuously analyze and understand their external markets and adjust their plans accordingly. Today, the instantaneous availability of information, rapid changes in economies, markets, and the political environments of countries that firms do business in impact planning continuously. Managers need to be prepared to adapt to changes that occur rapidly, no matter what their plans are—or were.

This requires managers to accurately analyze their internal resources. Managers at P&G, for example, determined that people were the most important component of the plan to enter and succeed in the Eastern European markets. Their conclusion is borne out by current research. In fact, some current research suggests that an organization's human capital is absolutely critical to the successful implementation of a firm's strategic plans.[1]

An analysis of the organization's internal resources and external environment helps a manager determine the company's strengths, like the organization's core competencies, along with its weaknesses and how they might affect its future plans.[2] This analysis can also identify the other resources managers will need to implement their plans and ultimately achieve their goals.

An Overview of Planning

objectives The end states or targets that company managers aim for.

plans The means by which managers hope to hit the desired targets.

Few activities are more basic to management than deciding where the company is going and how it is going to get there. Organizational **objectives** are the end states or targets that managers aim for, while **plans** are the means by which

which managers hope to hit the desired targets. **Planning**, then, is essentially a decision-making process that focuses on the future of the organization and how it will achieve its goals. From this perspective, setting organizational objectives has to precede the development of organizational plans. Without objectives or targets, plans make very little sense. Objectives help set direction, focus effort, guide behaviours, and evaluate progress.[3] Interestingly, managers sometimes spend so much time formulating objectives that they neglect to develop detailed plans that will enable them to achieve their goals. This is akin to making a commitment to graduate from university without any idea of what classes to take or when certain classes need to be taken. It is easy to see why organizational results are significantly influenced not just by objectives but also by the plans for hitting the targets. We will now explore the types of plans that exist, the basic planning process, and the methods for implementing plans effectively.

planning A decision-making process that focuses on the future of an organization and how it will achieve its goals.

Types of Plans

Few organizations today of any size offer just one product or service. As a consequence, they cannot develop a single plan to cover all organizational activities. To understand the planning process for complex organizations, we need to differentiate among three types of plans[4] (see Exhibit 8.1).

Strategic/Tactical/ Operational Plans by Michael Hitt

mymanagementlab

Strategic Plans.   **Strategic plans** focus on the broad future of the organization and incorporate both external environmental demands and internal resources into the actions managers need to take to achieve long-term goals. There is some evidence that the rigorous use of strategic plans is associated with superior financial performance.[5] Strategic plans cover the major aspects of the organization including its products, services, finances, technology, and human resources. Although the concept of "long term" has no precise definition, most strategic plans focus on how to achieve goals one to five years into the future. For example, after the passage of NAFTA (North American Free Trade Agreement), the Mexican state of Sonora, which borders Arizona, had a strategic plan to revitalize its economy. In evaluating the state's strengths and weaknesses, government officials decided that the most effective way to

strategic plans Focus on the broad future of the organization and incorporate both external environmental demands and internal resources into managers' actions.

Exhibit 8.1 Types of Plans: Key Differences			
	Strategic plans	**Tactical Plans**	**Operational Plans**
Time Horizon	Typically 3–5 years	Often focused on 1–2 years in the future	Usually focused on the next 12 months or less
Scope	Broadest; originating with a focus on the entire organization	Rarely broader than a strategic business unit	Narrowest; usually centred on departments or smaller units of the organization
Complexity	The most complex and general, because of the different industries and business potentially covered	Somewhat complex but more specific, because of the more limited domain of application	The least complex, because they usually focus on small, homogenous units
Impact	Have the potential to dramatically impact, both positively and negatively, the fortunes and survival of the organization	Can affect specific businesses but generally not the fortunes or survivability of the entire organization	Impact is usually restricted to specific department or organization unit
Interdependence	High interdependence; must take into account the resources and capabilities of the entire organization and its external environments	Moderate interdependence; must take into account the resources and capabilities of several units within a business	Low interdependence; the plan may be linked to higher-level tactical and strategic plans but is less interdependent with them

revitalize its economy was to take advantage of its beautiful beaches and to encourage tourism.

tactical plans Plans that translate strategic plans into specific goals for specific parts of the organization.

Tactical Plans. **Tactical plans** translate strategic plans into specific goals for specific parts of the organization. Consequently, they tend to have somewhat shorter time frames and to be narrower in scope. Instead of focusing on the entire corporation, tactical plans typically affect a single business within an organization. While tactical plans should complement the overall strategic plan, they are often somewhat independent of other tactical plans. For example, the tactical plans of the transportation department for Sonora called for improving the roads leading from the US border to the beach resorts. The tactical plans of the commerce department called for making special low-interest loans available to companies that would build western-style quality hotels in the targeted region. While the tactical plans of the transportation and commerce departments were different, both served to support the overall strategic plan of Sonora. *A Manager's Challenge: "The Bellagio: Using Technology for Effective Tactical Plan Execution"* provides an interesting example of how one company used technology to enhance the execution of an important tactical plan—the hiring of nearly 10 000 workers in five instead of the normal nine to twelve months for a new hotel. As you read this, imagine yourself facing the planning challenge of hiring 10 000 workers in less than half the normal time and still having to ensure that the right people with the right capabilities and characteristics are selected.

operational plans Plans that translate tactical plans into specific goals and actions for small units of the organization and focus on the near term.

Operational Plans. **Operational plans** translate tactical plans into specific goals and actions for small units of the organization and focus on the near term. The near term is typically 12 months or less. These plans are the least complex of the three and rarely have a direct impact beyond the department or unit for which the plan was developed. For example, in the case of the Mexican state of Sonora, the purchasing section within the department of transportation created an operational plan that called for the purchase of several new road graders and a new steamroller to facilitate the expansion of the main highway from a two-lane to a four-lane highway.

As summarized in Exhibit 8.1, strategic, tactical, and operational plans differ from each other on five important dimensions: time horizon, scope, complexity, impact, and interdependence.[6] While these differences matter, the three types of plans should be aligned and integrated with each other. Unfortunately, this type of alignment and integration occurs in only one-third of companies.[7] In addition to types of plans, for a more complete understanding, we need to examine planning at different levels in the organization.

Organizational Levels

In addition to plans that address strategic, tactical, and operational issues of the organization, managers at different levels of the company face different planning challenges. Exhibit 8.2 provides a graphical representation of the three primary levels of a corporation. Managers at each level attempt to address somewhat different questions.

Corporate Level. Most corporations of even moderate size have a corporate headquarters. However, complex and large organizations like Bombardier, a world leader in the manufacture of air and rail transportation solutions with more than US$14 billion in annual revenue, often divide the various businesses of the company into large groups. For Bombardier, these groups include aerospace and transportation. The heads of these groups are typically part of the group of senior executives at the corporate headquarters. Executives at the corporate level in large firms would include both those in the headquarters and those heading up the large corporate groups such as

A Manager's Challenge   *Technology*

The Bellagio: Using Technology for Effective Tactical Plan Execution

When Mirage Resorts decided to build the Bellagio, one of Las Vegas's most luxurious hotels, it was no small feat. The blueprints called for 3000 rooms, a large gallery to hold a fine-art collection, a glass-domed conservatory, a theatre equipped to hold a new water show by the Montreal entertainment group Cirque du Soleil, an eight-acre replica of Italy's Lake Como—along with the most upscale designer shops and gourmet restaurants. The cost of this, before Bellagio's doors even opened, would run about US$1.6 billion. In addition, Mirage had to find a way to recruit nearly 10 000 workers to staff the hotel. Clearly, the company needed a tactical plan to accomplish this.

As construction got underway, Mirage Resorts's human resource executives began the hiring process. Because of the number of jobs that needed to be filled—by the right people—HR executives at the Mirage had to come up with a plan for receiving and sorting through the anticipated tens of thousands of applications. Even after extracting the best candidates from the applications, managers still had to interview thousands of candidates and to make employment offers.

As part of their plan, executives budgeted US$1 million for a computer software system that would screen as many as 75 000 job candidates. The plan was to complete this screening in three months and to eliminate those who were not suitable and extract those who might be. To recruit the initial applicants, executives planned to run large ads in newspapers announcing that they were hiring employees for the new hotel. The plan called for a toll-free number that applicants would call to make an appointment to fill out an application (not for an interview).

Once the applicants were on file in the computer system and the software program had culled out the inappropriate applicants, the plan called for interviews of an estimated 25 000 to 30 000 candidates at a rate of 700 interviews per day! To do this, executives estimated that they would need to hire and specially train 180 interviewers. In other words, the plan called for hiring people to hire people. The results of the interviews would be entered into a database for later reference.

The plan also called for some low-tech screening mechanisms as well. For example, if a candidate showed up to the interview late without notifying someone, he or she would be dropped from the process. Then–vice-president Arte Nathan explained it this way: "If people didn't show up

Opening the Bellagio hotel-casino required its owner, Mirage Resorts, Inc., to hire a whopping 10 000 employees in only five months. The task included screening 75 000 applicants and conducting as many as 700 interviews a day to find the best candidates. Similar to building the hotel, it was no small undertaking. Careful and systematic planning, however, made the hiring process a success.

for their appointments, we figured they'd be no-shows at work, too."

The hiring plan also anticipated the need to conduct as many as 20 000 background checks on candidates that successfully made it through the interviews. This would need to be done in short order—within just a month or two—so the plan was to contract with a professional firm to conduct these background checks on behalf of Mirage Resorts.

This was the plan. So how well did things go? Overall, the plan was well constructed and executed. Instead of the normal nine months it had taken the company to staff a new hotel in the past, this plan resulted in the attracting, screening, and hiring of 10 000 employees in only five months. Arte Nathan also claimed that the process saved the company not only time but direct costs on items such as paper, temporary help, and file space to the tune of US$600 000. Bellagio opened on time and with the right employees trained and in place, in part because of the effective tactical plan for hiring. Since

▶

▶

its opening, the Bellagio has become a major attraction for visitors to Las Vegas. Its popularity prompted a further US$375 million expansion to the facility that opened in December 2004.

Sources: MGM Mirage 2005 Annual Report, www.mgmmirage.com, accessed December 17, 2006; "Bellagio," *Meetings & Conventions*, November 2003, p. 4; E. P. Gunn, "How Mirage Resorts Sifted 75,000 Applications to Hire 9,600 in 24 Weeks," *Fortune*, October 12, 1998, p. 195; J. Gurzinksi, "A Raft of Preparation at Bellagio," *Las Vegas Review Journal*, September 30, 1998.

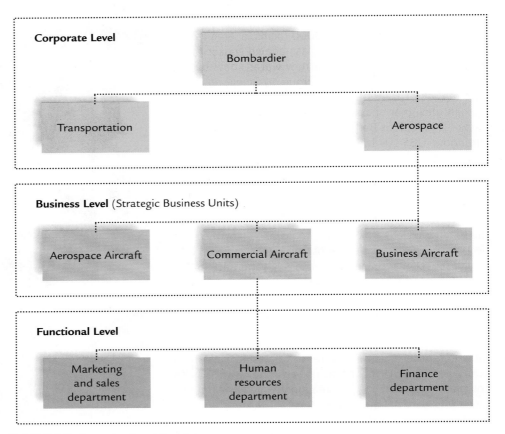

Exhibit 8.2 Organizational Levels.

finance, human resources, legal, and so on. These corporate-level executives would primarily focus on questions such as the following:

- What industries should we get into or out of?

- What markets should the firm be in? For example, is it time to move aggressively into China? If so, what businesses should move first?

- In which businesses should the corporation invest money?

In the case of Bombardier, if coordination across the aerospace and transportation groups or across businesses within the groups is beneficial, it is the responsibility of corporate-level managers to recognize and capture those opportunities.

Business Level. The next level is sometimes referred to as the SBU, or strategic business unit level. At this level managers focus on determining how they are going to compete effectively in the market. For example, within the aerospace area that includes businesses such as amphibious aircraft and commercial aircraft, managers attempt to address questions such as the following:

- Who are our direct competitors?

- What are their strengths and weaknesses?

- What are our strengths and weaknesses?
- What do customers value in the products or services we offer?
- What advantages do we have over competitors?

The planning questions that SBU-level managers face are more focused on how to compete effectively in the business of today than on what businesses to be in tomorrow. If coordination across different departments (finance, marketing, product development, etc.) or units within the SBU is needed, SBU-level managers are responsible for recognizing and capturing those opportunities.

Functional Level. At the functional level, managers focus on how they can facilitate the achievement of the competitive plan of the business. These managers are often heads of departments such as finance, marketing, human resources, or product development. Depending on the SBU's structure, functional managers may include managers responsible for the business within a specific geographic region or managers who are responsible for a specific product like commercial aircraft. Generally, these functional managers attempt to address questions such as the following:

- What activities does my unit need to perform well to meet customer expectations?
- What information about competitors does my unit need to help the business compete effectively?
- What are my unit's strengths and weaknesses?

The main focus of functional managers' planning activities is on how they can support the SBU plan. Functional-level managers are responsible for recognizing and capturing the opportunity, if coordination between individuals within a unit is needed or beneficial.

Interaction between Plan Types and Levels

Strategic plans typically get developed at the corporate level. In fact, strategic planning is arguably the key planning responsibility of corporate managers. Corporate managers, however, tend not to get involved in developing tactical or operational plans. SBU-level managers may be involved in developing strategic plans for their business units and are usually involved in developing tactical plans for their business. However, SBU-level managers typically do not get involved in developing operational plans. In contrast, functional-level managers are not often involved in developing either strategic or tactical plans. Instead, their planning responsibilities tend to focus on the development of operational plans. Exhibit 8.3 illustrates the general pattern of planning responsibility by organizational level. Keep in mind, however, that the specific pattern in any given organization could be different. For example, the size of the organization could affect the pattern. In small organizations, corporate managers might be involved in developing strategic, tactical, *and* operational plans.

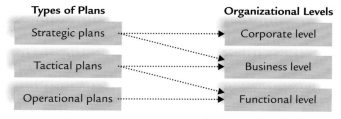

Exhibit 8.3 Interaction between Plans and Levels.

The Planning Process

The planning process has seven key elements: environmental analysis, objectives, requirements, resources, actions, implementation, and outcomes (see Exhibit 8.4). In this section, we will examine each of these elements and their role in the overall planning process.

Analyzing the Environment

The first element of the planning process is an assessment of the environment. Managers who formulate or implement plans in the absence of any assessment of the environment may very well fall short of producing the desired results. In contrast, managers who carefully scan the environment and incorporate the information gathered into the planning process can enjoy greater success in the outcomes of the plans they formulate and implement.[8]

Forecasts. One of the principal tools managers use in assessing the environment is a forecast. Forecasts are or can be made about virtually every critical element in the environment that managers believe could affect the organization or their area of responsibility.[9] For example, if you were in the residential construction business, interest rate forecasts would be important to you. Generally, as interest rates go up and borrowing money becomes more expensive, fewer people purchase new homes. Those that still purchase new homes necessarily have to purchase less expensive homes than they could if interest rates were lower. Planning for the number of houses to build in the coming year would, as a consequence, be influenced by the interest rate forecast.

Interestingly, there is a cascading effect of forecasts. For example, if you forecast that you will build only 1000 homes instead of 1500 homes over the next year because interest rates are expected to rise from 4.5 percent to 5.5 percent, then you might also forecast a decline in revenues. This may lead the purchasing manager to plan for smaller purchases of lumber and may lead the human resource manager to plan for a smaller number of construction workers. The key point for managers is that it's vital to know what the key forecasts are in the company and to keep track of any changes so that any cascading effects can be recognized earlier rather than later.

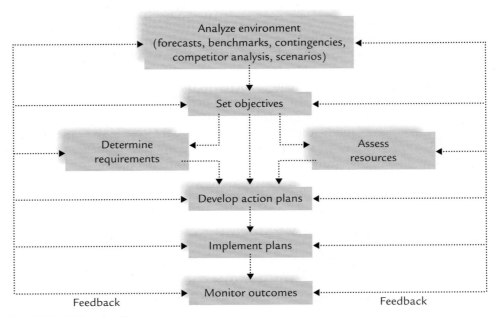

Exhibit 8.4 Planning Process.

Environmental Uncertainty. Obviously, forecasting accurately is a tough business. Things frequently change and don't work out the way we anticipate.[10] In Chapter 4, we talked about the key external general and task environmental forces that can change things. In 1988, no one was predicting the fall of the Berlin Wall in 1989. In early 2000, no one was predicting the worst two years of stock market performance that followed in 2002. The key issue for managers and their planning activities is that the greater the environmental uncertainty, the more flexible their plans need to be. In some cases, managers may even develop contingency plans. **Contingency plans** typically identify key factors that could affect the desired results and specify what different actions will be taken if changes in key events occur.[11]

For example, suppose you were a manager at Boychuk Homes, a home builder in Saskatoon that has built more than 7000 homes over the past 50 years. Clearly, forecasts of future interest rates would be important to you. The forecast might call for interest rates to remain unchanged for the next year. But can you trust the forecast? Rather than just rely on the forecast, you might be better off to develop contingency plans. For instance, what if interest rates go up one point? It is likely that people will buy fewer houses or less expensive houses. Your contingency plan might be to offer reduced financing charges if customers include certain upgrades in their homes like granite countertops. You could perhaps afford to offer buyers this incentive because your profits from the upgrades might be greater than the costs of the finance subsidies. By having this contingency plan in place in advance of the change in interest rates, you can be more prepared to respond.

A Manager's Challenge: "Changing Well-Laid Plans at EMC" provides a great illustration of how dramatically plans may have to change when reality turns out to be different from forecasts. In this case, the forecast of the future was based on such a successful past that few people anticipated how dramatically and quickly things could change. This past success made the future seem deceptively certain, and so EMC did not have contingency plans to fall back on when it became clear that reality would not match forecasts. Why do you think EMC didn't have any contingency plans? Do you think it would have fared better if it had had some contingency plans?

contingency plans Plans that identify key factors that could affect the desired results and specify what actions will be taken if key events change.

Minnesota Mining & Manufacturing (3M) was founded in 1902 by a lawyer, a doctor, two railroad executives, and a meat-market owner hoping to get rich by mining a superhard material called corundum, used to make grinding wheels. But the soft rock 3M was mining turned out to be an inferior abrasive for wheel grinding, so the company began producing sandpaper instead. Unfortunately, it wasn't a very good product because the humidity in Minnesota kept the paper from drying properly. The company's first breakthrough product, Wetordry sandpaper—developed in response to the humidity problem—didn't come out until 1921.

A Manager's Challenge   *Change*

Changing Well-Laid Plans at EMC

If you were a shareholder of the telecommunications corporation EMC during the 1990s, and you sold your shares near the end of that decade, you would likely be retired (and not reading this text). During that period, EMC returned a staggering 84 000 percent to shareholders! By the end of 2000, the company controlled 71 percent of the upper-end data storage market. Seventy percent of its US$8.9 billion in revenues and 92 percent of its US$2.3 billion in operating profits were derived from sales of its storage hardware.

But then the bubble burst. Telecom companies and dot.coms that had spent nearly US$2 billion on EMC products in 2000 spent virtually nothing in 2001 as they struggled for survival. In addition, other key customers froze their IT budgets. As a consequence, EMC saw its revenues plunge. If that weren't enough, IBM and Hitachi launched products and a price war aimed at EMC's most lucrative segment of products. In 2001, EMC tried to maintain prices but could not. It saw its market share drop from 71 percent to 57 percent and watched in horror as gross margins dropped by 25 percentage points to 32 percent as they lowered product prices faster than production costs to compete with IBM and Hitachi.

HR managers had staffing plans and compensation plans, sales managers had sales plans, and R&D managers had research plans for 2001 that were based on a growth trajectory and forecast mirroring results in 2000 and years prior. Suddenly, all of those plans had to change—and not just for one year. The troubles of 2001 did not just mark a bad year, but revealed a turning point for EMC.

Prior to 2001, data storage was a mission-critical function of virtually all firms of moderate or larger sizes. Customer information, financial data, inventory, sales, purchasing, and personnel data all needed to be stored, duplicated, and protected. In addition, IBM, Hitachi, and EMC had their own proprietary systems. In other words, an IBM system could not talk to or work with a Hitachi or EMC system or vice versa. In fact, once a customer selected a storage system, it was, in a sense, held hostage by it because it was just too expensive to switch to another system.

Joe Tucci, EMC's new CEO in 2001, announced a bold change in strategy that would change EMC's future. Tucci was going to split EMC into two companies. The first would continue to make "the best storage hardware in the world." The second would focus on software and services with the ultimate objective of creating software that could manage storage requirements regardless of the hardware (IBM, Hitachi, or EMC). In fact, Tucci wanted 50 percent of revenues to come from software and services by 2004.

This had a profound impact on managers throughout the company. For example, HR managers not only had to scrap their hiring and recruiting plans, but they had to develop plans to downsize (terminate) 19 000 people. In addition, they had to revise future recruiting plans to focus on software engineers and others who could help develop the new integrative software that would be needed to achieve Tucci's revenue target of 50 percent.

Sales managers of the new software group had to implement new motivation and incentive plans. EMC hardware products had traditionally cost its customers millions of dollars. Consequently, commissions were very significant to its sales force. In addition, because the products of its three main rivals were incompatible, motivating salespeople to "kill" the competition was the norm. In the new software sales unit, EMC's products would cost only thousands of dollars—not millions. Furthermore, the salespeople found themselves in the awkward position of telling their customers that whatever storage hardware they now chose (IBM, Hitachi, or EMC) didn't matter—even though these same salespeople had spent years telling them that no hardware could match EMC's.

Some of EMC's R&D managers had to completely shift their plans, as well. Whereas in the past they had simply been concerned with developing technologies to enhance the speed, reliability, and performance of EMC's proprietary products, now they would need to focus on competing products and develop technologies and software language that would not only work with those products but enhance their features, too.

And what does Tucci say about all of EMC's prior plans to which it ultimately laid waste? "Companies that are afraid to disrupt themselves almost 100 percent of the time end up being disrupted [by competitors]. I'm doing what our competitors never thought we had the intestinal fortitude to do." The bold shift by Tucci has resulted in positive results for EMC. Gartner Group identified EMC as the 2005 leader in revenue growth among the nine content management software providers and second in market share of total revenue among all the providers. Tucci was also identified by more than 1700 industry analysts and portfolio managers as the top CEO in the IT hardware industry for 2005, and again in 2006, beating out Steve Jobs of Apple (#2) and Mike Hurd of HP (#3).

Sources: EMC website, www.emc.com, accessed December 18, 2006; T. Eid, "Market Share: Enterprise Content Management Software, Worldwide, 2003–2005," *Gartner Dataquest*, May 18, 2006; A. Asaravala, "EMC Is Resolute," *Intelligent Enterprise*, December 10, 2003, p. 8; EMC Annual Report, 2001; D. Roth, "Can EMC Restore Its Glory?" *Fortune*, July 22, 2002, pp. 107–110.

Benchmarking. A more recent and popular means of assessing the environment is benchmarking. **Benchmarking** is the investigation of the best results among competitors and noncompetitors and the practices that lead to those results.[12] In terms of results, managers might assess competitors that have the highest revenue-to-employee ratio as a means of assessing productivity. Managers would then compare their own revenue-to-employee ratio to get an idea of where they stand relative to the competition. As part of this assessment, they would also investigate the practices that appear to contribute to high revenue-to-employee ratios. For example, they might find that the firms with the highest ratio tend to have fewer levels of managers because they push decision-making authority down in the organization and have a strong focus on participative management and employee involvement.

These same types of assessments might also be made of noncompetitors. The inclusion of noncompetitors has potential pitfalls and benefits that are different from benchmarking competitors. Clearly, noncompetitors can have underlying business factors that make appropriate comparisons difficult. For example, a telemarketing company that sells relatively inexpensive items over the phone will have a much lower revenue-to-employee ratio than a maker of supercomputers. The telemarketing firm has a relatively labour-intensive business, while the maker of supercomputers has a technology-intensive business. These same problems of comparison and relevance can be present when examining the best practices of noncompetitors. The inventory practices of a service firm may be difficult to apply directly to a manufacturing firm. However, by looking outside one's set of competitors, totally new and significantly better ways of doing things can be found.

Consider the case of Outback Steakhouse. Even though the steel industry was totally different from the franchise restaurant industry, Outback found a motivational practice used by several "mini-mills" in the steel industry that it incorporated with great success. Like any franchise restaurant, Outback makes money as its restaurants make money. The person who makes or breaks a restaurant is the local restaurant manager. In particular, the manager must hire the right people and motivate them effectively to ensure good food and service for the customers. The key for Outback is how to motivate its restaurant managers. The "best practice" that Outback adopted was giving the restaurant managers some ownership in the restaurants they managed. That way if a restaurant made money, so did the manager. The manager felt more like an owner and less like an employee. The adoption of this best practice has had a positive effect on

benchmarking The investigation of the best results among competitors and noncompetitors and the practices that lead to those results.

Benchmarking—examining the best practices of one's competitors—can work across industries, too. Outback Steakhouse, an international chain with 13 restaurants in Canada, borrowed an idea used by steel mills to motivate its managers that includes a profit-sharing plan. Outback Steakhouses are managed by a three-person team: a managing partner, manager, and kitchen manager. Because the restaurants are open only for dinner, managers and employees are also able to enjoy a better work–life balance, making Outback an attractive employer.

the success of Outback Steakhouse. Thus, even though benchmarking noncompetitors requires some judgment as to what is relevant or appropriate, it can also lead to ideas and practices that put you ahead of the competition.

Benchmarking can be a useful activity even for young managers. For example, suppose you were a sales manager with five salespeople reporting to you. You might want to benchmark outcomes like revenue-per-salesperson as well as processes like goal setting. How were other sales managers setting goals with their subordinates? The key principle in benchmarking is constant curiosity about what others are accomplishing and how they are doing it.

Setting Objectives

The second element in the planning process is the setting of objectives or desired outcomes. As we mentioned at the beginning of this chapter, it is difficult to establish or implement specific actions without an idea of where those steps are intended to go or what they are expected to achieve.

Priorities and Multiple Objectives. One of the first challenges for managers as they set objectives is to determine priorities.[13] Not all objectives are of equal importance or value. Furthermore, some objectives might be important now and less important later. Without a clear understanding of which objectives are most important and temporal priorities, employees may be working at odds with each other or creating unnecessary conflicts.[14]

Consider your own university. Most universities have multiple and sometimes conflicting objectives. For example, on the one hand students feel they pay tuition to learn leading-edge content from the best professors the school has to offer. Universities cannot ignore the expectations of this important set of its constituents. At the same time, though, to generate leading-edge knowledge universities must hire top researchers and fund their research. Without a clear idea of the university's priorities, department heads may find it difficult to determine how best to plan the allocation of the department budget. How much of the budget should go toward activities that help develop the teaching skills of the faculty? How much should go toward funding research?

Similar potential conflicts might exist for a sales manager weighing the objectives of increasing market share and profitability. In many instances, market share can be gained by lowering prices, but this usually hurts profits. The salespeople who work for the manager would have a difficult time knowing exactly where and how to focus their efforts unless she makes her priorities clear. Are they to sacrifice a sale to protect profit margins? Should they offer a small discount to get the sale? At what point would the discount be considered too big to be acceptable? These are the kinds of practical questions that have to be addressed in setting multiple objectives.

There can also be temporal priorities among objectives.[15] For example, suppose you are launching a new product in an established market with well-positioned competitors. You might decide that your current objective is to gain market share and thereby establish a presence in the market. You tell your salespeople to go after 10 percent market share and to offer discounts of up to 20 percent when needed to get the sale. However, once your product is established at, say, a 10 percent market share, you want your salespeople to focus on profitability objectives over increased market share. Without a clear understanding of this sequence in priorities, your salespeople would not be as able to help you achieve your overall objectives. If there are sequences to objectives, spelling them out in advance can help subordinates better understand what is expected of them.

Measuring Objectives. Once you've made your organization's objectives clear, how are you going to measure them? For example, you might determine that financial performance is the number-one objective. However, financial performance can be measured in a variety of ways.[16] It can be measured in terms of profits relative to sales or profits relative to assets. For example, a retail shoe store could measure a sales clerk's performance based on sales per hour. This would be in contrast to many other retailers that simply measure net sales. How would this small adjustment make a difference? If your sales-people are measured on net sales, they will likely be motivated to work the greatest number of hours they can. In contrast, your sales-per-hour objective might cause clerks to focus on "sales efficiency," or selling the most in every hour they work, rather than working more hours. The best way to improve sales-per-hour is to sell to repeat customers, because as soon as they walk in the door you know the types of things they like, what their budget is, and so on. Specific measures matter. Even slight differences such as net sales versus sales per hour can have important influences on behaviour.[17]

Determining Requirements

The third element in the planning process is the determination of requirements. Managers essentially address the question, "What will it take to get from here to there?" The "there" is essentially the objectives discussed in the previous section. The "here" requires an assessment or knowledge of where things are today.

To begin the process of determining what is required to get from here to there, you first need to understand the key drivers for the journey. For example, let's suppose you are in the athletic shoe manufacturing business, and your objective is to increase your market share from 10 percent to 15 percent. What

A Manager's Challenge   *Globalization*

Ginch Gonch: Thinking outside the Boxer

Jason Sutherland didn't start in the apparel industry. Initially, he was a young award-winning production designer for the film and television industry in Vancouver. Then one day Jason envisioned a new way for men and women to express themselves through their wardrobe, even before they don any outer garments. Jason raised $2 million by selling his home and acquiring investors, and in 2004 he launched Ginch Gonch undergarments. Jason's idea for undergarments was in whimsical protest to the staid line of white, black, and grey underwear offered by companies such as Calvin Klein and The Gap.

Ginch Gonch produces cotton his and hers underwear (briefs, thongs, tanks, and t-shirts) that uses vibrant colours with cartoon-like designs emblazoned on them. The designs hearken back to underwear one may have worn as a kid (i.e., Underoos). The company's mission statement is "Live like a kid," and even the company's name, Ginch Gonch, comes from the Canadian schoolyard slang term for underwear. Ginch Gonch undergarments, however, are not for children. They use premium construction and materials and prints that often have cheeky double meanings. The designer garments are priced in the $25 to $35 range and are marketed primarily to the United States—where consumers spend US$12 billion annually on adult underwear.

Ginch Gonch releases only four design collections a year of finite quantities. When the run is sold out, it is not repeated. Jason likens the limited edition idea to hockey

In stark contrast to undergarment leader Calvin Klein, Vancouver's Ginch Gonch produces cotton his and hers underwear that uses vibrant colours with cartoon-like designs emblazoned on them, which are reminiscent of underwear that one may have worn as a kid.

cards, which become collectibles. Jason's vision of adult self-expression through undergarments was a great success. Positive reviews were coming in from influential news and apparel media such as Fashion File, GQ, and Vogue. In less than a year, Ginch Gonch was shipping $150 000 worth of underwear every month. However, a combination of Jason's lack of understanding of supply chain management and the resounding success of the products was about to threaten the long-term viability of the new-found company.

▶

▶

Ginch Gonch was finding it difficult to complete orders, satisfying only 33 percent of the requests coming in. The fear that unreliable order fulfillment would result in retailers dropping the line, which would put the firm into a tailspin, was very real. The initial source of the problem was their choice in garment factory. Jason and the rest of the Ginch Gonch management team were committed to avoiding sweatshops in the production of their garments, but they also knew that they could not afford the costs of production in Canada. After initially working with a factory in Thailand without satisfactory results, Ginch Gonch searched for a manufacturer in China through an agent. Ginch Gonch went with the fifth factory they toured, but the manufacturer turned out to be a bad relationship characterized by delays and flaws that cost Ginch Gonch time and money since they couldn't fulfill orders.

To add to their order-fulfillment problems, Ginch Gonch failed to consider in their plans the growing resentment in the United States toward outsourcing work to China. They were subsequently caught by surprise when the United States government imposed quotas on Chinese-produced textiles. The policy, which was created to safeguard US garment manufacturers, left Ginch Gonch holding onto thousands of units in Vancouver that were initially destined for the US market. Ginch Gonch was in the unenviable position of possessing inventory they could not distribute without cash to fix their production problems.

Sutherland continued to look for an alternate supplier and found a garment factory in El Salvador that had very good working conditions and a solid financial rating, which alleviated any concerns regarding hardship on workers. The El Salvador government had also increased their appeal to North American firms by providing tax breaks and other financial incentives. Still, the transition did not come without more learning. The factory required new equipment and updated technologies to produce the undergarments to Ginch Gonch's specifications, which created more delays in production. Sutherland and the Ginch Gonch management team continued to look for other suppliers, with the likelihood of ending up with multiple sources around the world.

From their early mistakes, Ginch Gonch learned that planning on one supplier for production could lead to a dangerous dependence where they have little or no control on the timeliness or quality of the product, particularly when the operation is as small as theirs. The optimal arrangement, from their experience, is to have multiple sources for different stages of production and distribution. They also learned that when dealing across nations and cultures, it is necessary to have people skilled in formulating deals with the region to assist with everything from language barriers to local laws. So, while Ginch Gonch's mission is to live like a kid, working in a global market requires the experience and wisdom that comes with time.

Sources: "Ginch Gonch," *Venture*, aired October 18, 2006; L. George, "Manties—They're Panties for Men," *Maclean's*, May 8, 2006; G. Babineau, "Unmentionables: An Adventure in Outsourcing Underwear—Globally," *Canadian Apparel*, March/April 2006; K. Nolan, "Intimates Grow Up—for the Young at Heart," *DSN Retailing Today*, January 9, 2006; "Ginch Gonch Flare Wear," *Body*, March 2005.

is it that drives market share? To drive market share you determine that you need to do two things. First, you need a new line of top-end products since you currently have none. Second, you determine that superior shoe cushion is a key driver of market share for mid-priced running shoes. You discover that running shoe customers make their purchases based on how well a shoe absorbs ground impact. Currently, your cushion technology is not superior. Consequently, it will take new materials to improve the shock absorbency of your shoes.

Assessing Resources

The fourth element in the planning process is an assessment of the required resources and the resources available to you. While this element is closely tied to the identification of requirements, the two are not the same. The easiest way to differentiate the two may be to think of requirements as what is needed to achieve the objectives, and resources as how much is available.

Resources Required. Let's return to our athletic shoe example and the key requirement of a new line of products at the top end of the market. Relative to this key requirement, the first critical question is, "What resources are needed to produce a new high-end product?" Let's suppose you determine that it will take three top product-design engineers two months and a budget of $100 000 to produce a prototype. Further, you determine that it will take new equipment at a cost of $500 000 to manufacture the new high-end shoes. Finally, you determine that it will take an advertising and promotion budget of $2 million to effectively launch the new line. These, of course, do not address all the resources required to design, produce, and sell the new high-end product line, but they do illustrate the financial, human, equipment, and technology resources that might be required.

A Manager's Challenge: "Ginch Gonch: Thinking outside the Boxer" helps illustrate the difficulty of assessing required resources when the task is new to the planners. While planning is often presented as a logical and straightforward managerial function, that presentation can be deceptive. When facing new situations, you often "don't know what you don't know" and therefore have difficulty determining what is required, even if you know what you want to do.

Resources Available. Knowing what resources are required leads naturally to the next question: "What resources are available?" Clearly, for a plan to be effective it must not only be well formulated but it must be feasible to implement.[18] If the resources required significantly exceed those available, either new resources need to be acquired or the plan must be changed. Changing the plan may require going back and changing the objective. In assessing resources available, managers must ask themselves questions such as the following:

- Do we have the needed human talent to meet the requirements?

- Even if we have the needed talent, is it available? Can we take people off what they are currently working on to put them on the new project?

- If we don't have the necessary talent, can we develop or acquire it within the needed time frame?

- Do we have the financial resources available? Can we get additional funding from the debt or equity markets?

- Do we have the required technology or can we gain access to it at a cost-effective price?

While these are certainly not the only questions managers would need to ask, they provide a reflection of the types of questions that would need to be addressed to determine if there is a gap between the resources required and those available. If there is a gap, managers must determine if it can be bridged or if the objectives and key requirements need to be changed to fit the available resources. For example, when a division of business and technology solutions giant EDS changed its strategy to focus on selling solutions to product development problems and not just computer-aided-design (CAD) products, it found that it needed new salespeople with different skills. Before, when they sold CAD products, salespeople from EDS usually talked to middle-level executives in the engineering and product design areas. In trying to sell more integrated solutions, EDS salespeople needed to talk with more senior executives. In the end, EDS managers trained some of their best existing salespeople and recruited new salespeople as well.

Developing Action Plans

The fifth element in the planning process is the development of specific action plans. The action plans are essentially the marching orders that everyone uses to accomplish the established objectives.

Sequence and Timing. A key element of an effective action plan is the sequence and timing of the specific steps or actions that must be taken.[19] One of the common tools used to graphically display the sequence and timing of the specific actions is a Gantt chart (see Exhibit 8.5). Time is typically on the horizontal axis and the tasks to be done are on the vertical axis. The chart shows when actions are to be started and how long they are expected to take for completion. It shows which actions are first, second, or last in the process and whether a preceding action must be completed before a subsequent one can be started or whether there is expected overlap in the timing of specific actions.

In addition to the planned sequence and timing, the actual progress can be charted as well. This allows managers to better assess their progress against the

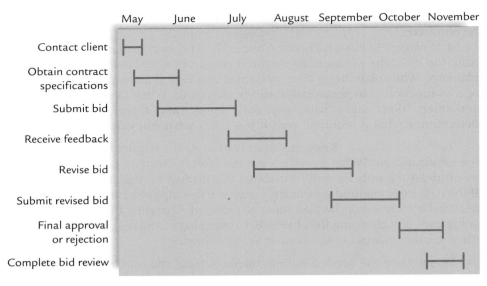

Exhibit 8.5 Gantt Chart.

plan and potentially make adjustments. Today, sophisticated computer programs can assist managers in formulating and implementing plans involving literally hundreds of raw materials and components that must be brought together in the right amounts and sequences for the cost-effective production of finished goods.[20]

Accountability. The second key aspect of effective action plans is a specification of who is accountable for which specific actions. Knowing who is responsible for what can facilitate coordination when more than one person will be executing various actions in the overall plan.[21] Accountability also increases the likelihood that the steps are taken when they should be and done as well as they need to be. Let's go back to our athletic shoe example. You personally take responsibility for hiring the three product-design engineers. You assign one of your subordinates the task of securing space for the designers within the next month. You decide to outsource the manufacturing and assign another subordinate the task of finding reliable contract manufacturers within the next 10 weeks. Finally, you assign another of your subordinates to work with the marketing group to begin generating possible ideas for the promotion and advertising of the launch.

Implementing Plans

Once the action plan has been created, it then needs to be implemented. The quality of the plan implementation can determine the actual results as much as the quality of the plan itself. However, much of the success of the implementation can be assured by doing the previous steps in the planning process well. Plans often fail in the implementation stage because of inadequate assessment of resources required and available. Again let's return to our shoe example. Your subordinate is successful in finding a contract manufacturer with a great reputation. In fact, the company has made shoes for Nike in the past—it even got a good endorsement from Nike when your subordinate checked up on the company. You discover, however, that for your shoes the company will need new sewing machines, and the workers will need training to properly operate the new machines. However, because of the company's poor communication with its workers, the workers mistakenly think the new machines will require fewer workers. As a consequence, they resist the new training for fear they will eventually lose their jobs. Their resistance delays the production of the new shoes, and a critical window of opportunity in the marketplace is lost.

This illustrates in a simple way why plan implementation can be as critical and sometimes more critical than the overall plan objectives. However, no matter how carefully you work out the implementation plan, you will still need to monitor and adjust your implementation efforts because unanticipated events almost always happen.

Monitoring the Implementation. Even if the previous steps in the planning process are done well, there is no guarantee that the plan will be successfully implemented. This is why it is essential for you to monitor the implementation of the plan. In particular, you need to monitor three critical factors.

First, you need to monitor the progress of the plan and its implementation. Are those responsible for taking specific actions well aware of their responsibilities and the timing of their expected actions? Are they adequately motivated and prepared to implement their portion of the plan? Are the necessary actions being taken at the right time? Are they being done at the desired or necessary level of quality? These are the types of questions that you as a manager need to ask to monitor the progress of the implementation. This is why plans often have "milestones" or specific objectives that mark progress along the total journey. For example, you might have a milestone of producing a prototype of your high-end shoe by week nine of your schedule. As week nine approaches, you have a specific means of determining if things are going according to plan or not.

Second, as a manager you need to monitor the level of support that the plan receives as it is being implemented.[22] You cannot assume that just because a plan is in place people will support it. You have to constantly assess whether you are providing the required support for the plan's effective implementation. This support might take the form of encouragement, money, or coaching. Few plans of any complexity or duration can be effectively implemented without continuous support. Are the other key supporters providing the encouragement needed? One of your key responsibilities as a manager is to monitor and ensure that the required support is there. For example, in putting your high-end shoe launch plan into effect, you may want to monitor the level of support from those in the marketing department. The marketing department may need to do a number of things in advance of the launch of the new shoe. They may need to talk with reporters working for magazines like *Runner's World* to start creating some "buzz" about the new shoe; they might need to talk with large retailers like Foot Locker to get them excited about not only ordering the shoe but placing it near the front of their stores in a special display. You cannot afford to have this great shoe coming off the factory line with nowhere to go because of poor support from marketing.

Third, as a manager you need to monitor the level of resistance. Many plans and their implementation involve change. To the extent that they do, you should anticipate and monitor resistance to the plan's implementation. Still, it deserves a bit of space here because resistance has been the cause of death for many plans. One of the general reasons why people resist change is because they have to do new things and anticipate doing them poorly at first. You can use this principle to help you identify possible sources of resistance.

For example, you might expect the marketing department to be thrilled to have a high-end shoe to promote. However, there are several new activities that will be required of the marketing people that they may not be good at initially. Specifically, the launch of your new shoe requires the marketing people to try to get some endorsements or at least use of the shoe by famous runners. Unfortunately, they have never dealt with celebrities. They don't know how to make contact with celebrity runners or how to pitch them on using your shoe. Because people in the department aren't familiar with the process, they may shy away from it—they may even say they are making progress even though they are not really putting much effort into it. Why are they resisting contacting celebrity runners? Even if they see that it is the right thing to do, they resist because they fear failure at first. You may need to provide extra encouragement or even hire a special consultant to help you make the connections and contacts with the celebrity runners.

Real-Time Adjustment. Because we live in a dynamic environment, any plan whose formulation and implementation lasts more than a few days or weeks is likely to need to be adjusted. As the environment changes, what was originally a perfectly acceptable objective may become unrealistic or too easily achieved, and therefore may need to be changed. Likewise, what were perfectly reasonable time frames and required resources at one point may become unreasonable because of sociocultural, technological, economic, or political-legal changes.

This realization has at least two implications. First, it may suggest that as a manager working in a dynamic and changing environment, you need to plan the way a fire department does. A fire department cannot anticipate exactly where or even when fires are likely to break out. Its plans are built upon certain principles of fighting fires and around general categories of fires. If you are a manager in a phone company, one of the key principles is redundancy. If a catastrophic event happens and knocks out your equipment, you have to have a backup system because you won't be able to get new equipment in place fast enough if your original equipment is somehow damaged or destroyed. This lesson is continually reinforced by extreme weather events like Hurricane Juan's devastation in Nova Scotia in September 2003 and the repeated pounding that British Columbia's Vancouver Island and Lower Mainland received from a series of storms in the late fall of 2006. These events prompt managers to ensure that backup equipment and critical replacements are available and ready to roll at a moment's notice. Second, as a manager you need to help your employees recognize and accept the need to adapt plans in real time. You may also need to foster capabilities that enable them to adapt effectively. These capabilities might include skills like good environmental scanning and quick requirement and resource assessment abilities. The key point to remember is that in today's dynamic environment, a fixed and rigid plan may be as dangerous as no plan at all.

Monitoring Outcomes

The final element in the planning process involves monitoring outcomes. If the objectives have been well defined from the outset of the planning process, there should be little question as to what outcomes are to be monitored or how they are to be measured. If the plan was expected to result in increased financial performance and it was to be measured in terms of increased sales, then the outcome should be easy to gauge.

However, most plans also produce unanticipated consequences.[23] The plan and its implementation may produce either negative or positive unanticipated outcomes. Both can be valuable sources of learning. To help illustrate this, let's return once again to our athletic shoe case. Let's suppose that through implementing the plan you discover it takes more advertising money than anticipated to launch your new high-end line of shoes. You find that customers have an image of your firm as a middle-range shoe maker and have difficulty at first believing that you could produce a line of athletic shoes with the technology, quality, and "sizzle" of other makers that are already in the high end of the market. On the unexpected positive side, you also discover that a stitching machine that you bought for your high-end shoes produced a straighter and stronger stitch at a lower price than the machines you were using for your low-end shoes. Using the new machines on both your low-end and high-end shoes will lower your costs, and yet allow you to promote higher quality. This may help you compete with other makers at the lower end of the market who produce lower-quality shoes.

The example above illustrates that managers should capture as much knowledge as they possibly can when monitoring outcomes. There also needs to be a feedback loop so that what they've learned can be used to modify and improve other aspects of the planning process.

Planning Tools

Managers use a variety of planning tools. For example, earlier in this chapter we referred to Gantt charts as one of the tools managers can use to facilitate the timing and sequencing of actions. In this section we discuss a tool that is also widely used: budgets.

Budgets

Budgets are used to quantify and allocate resources to specific activities. In most organizations, budgets are proposed and set on an annual basis. Budgets might address a variety of issues. For example a **capital expenditure budget** specifies the amount of money that is planned for spending on specific items that have long-term use and require significant amounts of money to acquire. These items might include things such as equipment, land, or buildings.

Another common budget is an expense budget. An **expense budget** typically includes all the primary activities on which the unit or organization plans to spend money and the amount that is allocated for each item for the upcoming year. Virtually all profit and not-for-profit organizations of a moderate or larger size have expense budgets, both for planning and for control purposes.

Most organizations have a two-phased process relative to budgets. The first consists of managers looking ahead and planning their needs. They then put together a budget specifying things like expected capital expenditures or expenses. This **proposed budget** provides a plan of how much money is needed and is submitted to a superior or budget review committee. Once the proposed budget is submitted, it gets reviewed, often in the context of other proposed budgets. An **approved budget** specifies what the manager is actually authorized to spend money on and how much.

Regardless of the type of budget, two main approaches to the budgeting process can be taken. The first approach is typically called the **incremental budgeting approach**.[24] In this approach, managers use the approved budget of the previous year and then present arguments for why the upcoming budget should be more or less. This may include particular increases or decreases. Incremental budgeting is efficient because managers do not need to spend significant time justifying the allocation of money toward the same sorts of purchases each year. The principal negative consequence of incremental budgeting is that it can result in "budget momentum." In other words, items that have been given money in the past may be allocated money in the future merely because they have been allocated money in the past. A common frustration with this approach to budgeting is the rampant spending that can occur as a fiscal year approaches its end. In Manitoba, as in many provinces, suppliers of printed material and office equipment saw the provincial government approaching fiscal year end as a boom time for business. Provincial departments would place many orders for supplies and services to be delivered before year end to fully exhaust the current year's budget. If the allocated budget was not fully spent, there was a good chance that departments would receive less money in the subsequent fiscal year. As this example illustrates, incremental budgeting can create a "use it or lose it" mindset, which can in turn lead to the inefficient use of valuable resources and waste, as unnecessary products or services are ordered just to deplete funds.

The **zero-based budgeting approach** assumes that all allocations of funds must be justified from zero each year.[25] In other words, the fact that your department was given $100 000 for computer equipment purchases last year does not provide any justification per se for it receiving money for computers this year. Zero-based budgeting requires starting from a base of zero funds and then justifying the resources being requested for each activity. The benefit of this approach to budgeting is that items that cannot be justified on their own

budgets Used to quantify and allocate resources to specific activities.

capital expenditure budget Specifies the amount of money to be spent on specific items that have long-term use and require significant amounts of money to acquire.

expense budget Includes all primary activities on which a unit or organization plans to spend money and the amount allocated to each for the upcoming year.

proposed budget Provides a plan for how much money is needed and is submitted to a superior or budget review committee.

approved budget Specifies what the manager is actually authorized to spend money on and how much.

incremental budgeting approach Where managers use the approved budget of the previous year and then present arguments for why the upcoming budget should be more or less.

zero-based budgeting approach Assumes that all allocations of funds must be justified from zero each year.

current merits (regardless of their past merits and allocated budgets) will not get money. This then leaves the money available for items or activities that can be justified. In general, this can lead to an overall more effective allocation of the organization's financial resources. However, zero-based budgeting takes time because each item must be justified each year. Some items that need money allocated to them may cost more in time and energy trying to justify their proposed funding than they are worth.

In either approach, budgets are typically used as planning tools by managers to determine priorities, required resources, and keys to implementation. In particular, because money is usually a scarce resource in most organizations—there is almost never as much money available as there are requests for it—allocating money among various activities almost forces a discussion of the relative priority among activities. This is true at all three organization levels. For example, department managers are likely to find they have more demand for money than they have money to allocate. Similarly, corporate officers are likely to find departments and business units requesting more money than the organization has. This leads to a determination of which units and their related activities are of highest priority and should receive budget approval.

In this sense, budgets can be an effective means of integrating and quantifying many aspects of the corporate-, business-, and functional-level plans. While the budgeting process per se does not guarantee that managers will make good decisions about the integration and coordination process, nor that they will make good decisions about priorities, it does raise the likelihood of these key items being discussed and determined.

Goal Setting

Goal setting is a specific planning process for managing performance. Normally we think of it at the individual level, though all of the principles are applicable to setting goals for teams, units, and overall organizations. It is important to examine goals. The research suggests that effective goals can have a significant and positive impact on performance. Much of the research about effective goal setting can be captured in an easy-to-remember and practical acronym—SMART. "Smart" goals have five key characteristics: they are specific, measurable, agreed upon, realistic, and time bound.

Specific. As we mentioned relative to organizational objectives in the planning process, goals for firms, units, subordinates, or for oneself should be specific. For example, you may have received feedback from different people or just sensed that "you need to improve your communication skills." Improvement in this area may in fact yield significant benefits; however, as stated it is too vague. To be effective it must be much more specific. Suppose you decide that "communication skills" is too broad and you narrow the scope and make your goal specifically to improve your listening skills. Is this now a good goal? Is it specific enough? The answer is "no." You need to assess what it is you do or don't do that makes you a less-than-effective listener. Perhaps you often interrupt people when they're speaking because you think you know what they are going to say. You determine that your goal is to not interrupt people and wait for them to finish before saying what you have to say. Is this a good goal? Is it specific? While this alone may not make you a great listener, it is a good goal in terms of being specific, and the research strongly suggests that you are more likely to make progress toward a specific goal than a vague goal.

Measured. One way to determine whether a goal you have set is specific enough is by whether you think you could measure progress and improvement as well as the ultimate result. Could you measure the number of times you interrupted versus the times you listened and waited for others to finish what they had to say? Clearly you could. Could you measure others' perception of whether you were interrupting or listening and waiting for them to say what they had to say? Clearly you could. But having a goal that is measurable is only part of the battle. In addition, you need to actually measure progress toward the goal. Goal setting is most effective when progress toward the goal is measured and measured often. So how often is often? The research does not provide an absolute answer. What we do know is that once a year is not often enough. In fact, twice a year does not seem to be often enough. Beyond that, it seems that the frequency of measurement needs to be related to the nature of the activities associated with the goal. For example, if you talk with people dozens of times per day and therefore have the opportunity to hit (or miss) your goal of not interrupting many times per day, then assessing your progress once a month is too infrequent. Daily self-measurement may be appropriate. However, from a practical perspective, you would be unwise to ask others every day how you are doing on listening and not interrupting. This you may want to do weekly or monthly.

Agreed.   Even if a goal is specific and measurable, if those involved in its achievement do not agree to it, it is unlikely to be met. For organizational goals, this means that a substantial portion of employees must agree to the goal. For unit goals, those in the unit must agree and accept the goal. For subordinate goals, the individual subordinate must accept the goal. Personal goals must be accepted and committed to. Returning to our original example, suppose you lay out the specific goal of not interrupting people and measure progress but do not really accept the goal. (Maybe you don't think interrupting is a bad thing and in fact you believe it saves time in conversations.) In this case, the goal is unlikely to be effective. Obviously, the reverse is true if you accept or are committed to the goal.

Here there is a very practical implication for managers. Because managers are in a position of power, subordinates often say what they believe the manager wants to hear—even when it is not what the subordinates really think. For example, if you say, "Tom, I think this is a challenging but doable goal for you. Don't you?" how is Tom going to reply? A verbal agreement from a subordinate without any real commitment behind the words will likely not result in the goal being achieved. As a consequence, when it comes to the "agreed" part of **SMART** goals, it is important to listen carefully and invite subordinates to candidly express their commitment to or resistance

The Judy Project, named for the late Toronto businesswoman Judy Elder, is a forum for senior executive women offered at the Rotman School of Management. The goal of the Judy Project is to build stronger business organizations through the advancement of more women into senior leadership positions. The week-long seminar provides participants with skills in networking, career planning, goal setting, and leadership styles. While the seminar is only a week in duration, smaller groups of six to eight participants each will continue meeting regularly as an ongoing personal support group for each other.[26]

regarding specific goals. Again, the fundamental objective of this part of SMART goal setting is not superficial agreement but deep commitment.

Realistic.   Now you have a specific, measured, and agreed upon goal. Will it be effective? Not if it is unrealistic—or if it is too easy. Goals that are too easy are not effective and goals that are too difficult are also not effective. To understand why, let's look at each case in turn. First, goals that are too easy are not effective for two reasons. On the one hand, they are not effective because they do not inspire motivation. In general, people are not motivated to try to achieve things that they perceive as being too easy. Often, they wait until the last minute to put any effort into achieving the goal, believing that a little effort at the last minute will enable them to hit the target. On the other hand, easy goals are not effective because they do not deliver substantial results. First, even if they are achieved, easy goals by their nature do not have a big impact on results—organizational, unit, subordinate, or personal. Ironically, because easy goals are seen as easy, the low motivation they inspire often results in the goals being missed. Goals that are too difficult, though, are also not effective. If a goal is seen as impossible or just highly unlikely to be achieved, people are not motivated to try to hit the target. After all, why waste precious time and energy trying to hit an unachievable target? Thus, effective goals must be challenging but achievable or realistic.

To make this concrete, let's return again to a personal goal of not interrupting others and listening to what they have to say. Assuming you have dozens of opportunities each day to hit or miss this target, is it realistic to set a goal of not interrupting 100 percent of the time, especially at first? If it is a challenging but realistic goal, that is fine. But if you see it as unrealistic, it will not be effective. Perhaps the realistic goal is to not interrupt more than 50 percent of the time during the first week.

Time Bound.   Even specific, measured, agreed upon, and realistic goals need to be time bound to be effective. In other words, goals need a specific time span within which they are to be achieved. For goals that will take a long period of time to achieve, say a year or more, shorter time intervals are needed. For example, suppose you think that the right level of listening and

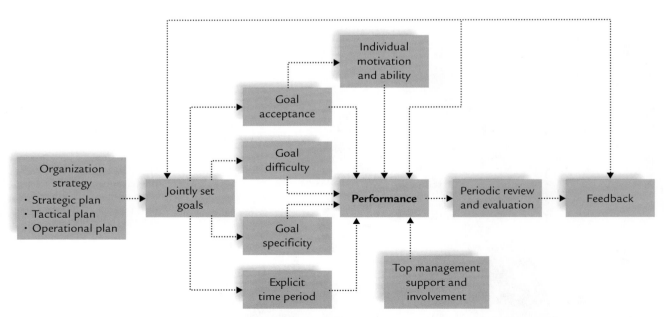

Exhibit 8.6 The Process of MBO.

not interrupting is 80 percent. In other words, you think that in eight out of ten conversations you should not interrupt but should instead listen and wait until the person has said what he or she has to say. Furthermore, you think that it will take you three months to achieve this goal. The three months becomes the general time boundary within which you plan to achieve the goal. However, as we suggested at the end of the section on making the goal realistic, you may have other time frames that become intermediate milestones for your ultimate goal. You may set a time frame of one week for going from 10 percent listening (90 percent interrupting) to 50 percent listening and not interrupting. You may then set a time frame of one month to get to a level of 70 percent listening and not interrupting.

MBO

Management by Objectives (MBO) is a specific type of goal-setting process, similar to SMART. (Exhibit 8.6 provides a graphic illustration of how MBO works.) Research suggests that MBO systems are most effective if top management demonstrates clear support for and involvement in the system.[27] Most of the general characteristics just described are critical to a successful MBO process. First, specific goals are set. The achievement of these goals should translate into results that support the organization's strategic, tactical, and operational plans and objectives. Goals need to be difficult but achievable.

Managerial Perspectives Revisited

As you would expect, when difficult but achievable goals are accomplished, it has a positive impact on performance.[28] Participation by subordinates in setting their goals tends to lead to difficult but achievable goals. In addition, the goals need to be accepted by subordinates. Goal acceptance has a positive impact on both motivation to perform and actual performance,[29] and participation by subordinates in the goal-setting process increases goal acceptance.[30] MBO goals need specific time frames, and periodic review and evaluation are necessary. Based on these reviews, subordinate performance improves according to the quality of feedback given to subordinates.[31] Individuals need to know if what they are doing is on or off target so that they can retain or adjust their behaviours. Also, feedback can affect the goalsetting process. Specific feedback may indicate that the original goals were too easy, too difficult, or just not directed at appropriate targets.

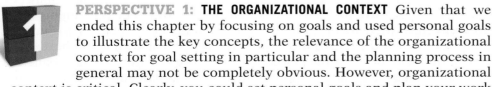

PERSPECTIVE 1: THE ORGANIZATIONAL CONTEXT Given that we ended this chapter by focusing on goals and used personal goals to illustrate the key concepts, the relevance of the organizational context for goal setting in particular and the planning process in general may not be completely obvious. However, organizational context is critical. Clearly, you could set personal goals and plan your work and projects independent of the organizational context. However, this would likely result in suboptimal personal career and organizational results. At a personal level, we are likely to make greater contributions and gain greater recognition for future advancement if our personal goals are aligned with the strategy and direction of the organization. For example, suppose your company had a low-cost strategy and productivity gains were

central to lowering costs in your area of responsibility. How bright would your career prospects be if you were weak at productivity analysis but failed to ever set any improvement goals in that area? The same general principle applies to goals for subordinates, units, and the overall organization. One of the important organizational contexts that we should always consider when setting goals is the strategy of the organization. In addition, the plans that we put in place should consider not only the direction of the company but its culture as well. The details of a plan for change would be different in an organization with a culture that resists change compared to one that embraces it. Thus, many of the details of effective plans have to account for both the direction of the organization and its nature.

PERSPECTIVE 2: THE HUMAN FACTOR Goals and plans for organizations, whether the plans are strategic, tactical, or operational, require input from others and their coordinated efforts to accomplish. In fact, a common mistake of those charged with formulating plans for projects or new-product launches is that they do not think carefully enough about the role that others play in the implementation of the plan. The more complex the plan, the more likely it is that its successful implementation and achievement will depend on multiple people. Managers need to not only develop plans but manage others in the implementation of the plans. This fact is highlighted in the opening case, where P&G determined that the most important resources for successful entry into Eastern European markets were the people—employees and managers—who would ultimately implement its strategy abroad.

PERSPECTIVE 3: MANAGING PARADOXES It should be clear by this point that planning has inherent potential paradoxes. On the one hand, failure to achieve desired results is often a function of not having a thoughtful and detailed plan. As the saying goes, "those who fail to plan, plan to fail." On the other hand, in a dynamic world of change where new competitors appear frequently, innovative technology is developed and used unexpectedly, and customer preferences evolve rapidly, managers cannot afford to rigidly maintain even the most well-developed plans; they must be prepared to modify, adapt, or even discard plans as they go. The need to develop thorough plans and be completely committed to their implementation, yet simultaneously flexible if they need to be changed later, presents something of a paradox to managers. Sometimes the challenge of dealing with change tempts managers to not develop thorough plans in the first place. They might reason that some of their efforts will be wasted if the situation were to change. This is faulty reasoning. The environment will always be undergoing changes. The key to responding to these changes is first detecting them. A thorough plan may be one of the best ways to detect signs that the environment is changing and different from what was expected. A thorough plan can serve as an "image projector." When the environment does not reflect back what you have projected, the more detailed the projection, the more specific the discrepancies that can be detected, and the more refined your adjustments and changes to the plan can be.

PERSPECTIVE 4: ENTREPRENEURIAL MINDSET As discussed in the introduction to this chapter, the strategic planning process helps to identify opportunities. If managers have an entrepreneurial mindset they will be better able to identify those opportunities when analyzing the environment their companies are attempting to do business in, and they will be more likely to formulate a strategy to exploit those opportunities. The required commitment comes primarily in a disciplined approach to plan formulation and an energetic implementation. Sometimes when you have put so much effort into formulating the plan, you can feel as though the implementation will go well with little further effort. But while poor planning quite often guarantees poor implementation, thorough planning does not guarantee effective implementation. To be effective, managers have to be committed to implement it and even to possibly change it as needed. For example, looking back at the discussion on EMC, even though managers spent considerable time formulating their plan to focus on software, because of the history of the company, even its existing customers could have resisted the new plan. It took considerable commitment to overcome the natural obstacles, implementing the planned actions, and then successfully achieving the goals desired. Yet it is important to emphasize that too much commitment to a particular plan without regard for changes in the environment can be detrimental. An entrepreneurial mindset is needed to make plans and implement them, and yet remain flexible and open to new environmental opportunities as things change. The planning process itself provides the overall needed discipline for an organization to excel, while an entrepreneurial mindset helps maintain the necessary flexibility.

Concluding Comments

Planning requires a determination of where the organization wants to go and how it is going to get there. This process includes an assessment of the organization's external and internal environment. Early in their careers, managers typically are more involved in operational plans. Consequently, some organizations or individuals might be tempted to ask why young managers should understand all aspects of the planning process.

The basic answer to this question is twofold. First, lower-level managers are more motivated to implement their specific responsibilities if they know the larger plan. Second, lower-level managers face thousands of specific decisions daily. They cannot make these specific decisions in a way that works toward the organization's overall objectives if they do not understand those objectives. This process would be like facing a series of choices of turning left or right and of slowing down or speeding up without knowing your ultimate destination.

In an ever-globalizing environment, managers are simultaneously faced with three critical planning challenges. First, they must try to learn from the past. Many things that went right or wrong in the past may be helpful in guiding action and shaping plans for the future. Second, managers must keep their ears and eyes closely focused on signals in the current environment— signals from competitors, customers, governments, and so on. The rate of change in the current environment is so fast that too little attention to the present could forfeit the future. Finally, managers must think about and plan for the future. It is the incorporation of three different time perspectives (past, present, and future) that makes planning one of the most challenging managerial activities.

Key Terms

approved budget (p. 281)
benchmarking (p. 273)
budgets (p. 281)
capital expenditure budget
    (p. 281)
contingency plans (p. 271)

expense budget (p. 281)
incremental budgeting
    approach (p. 281)
objectives (p. 264)
operational plans (p. 266)
planning (p. 265)

plans (p. 264)
proposed budget (p. 281)
strategic plans (p. 265)
tactical plans (p. 266)
zero-based budgeting
    approach (p. 281)

Test Your Comprehension

1. What are the key functions of setting objectives?

2. Define strategic plans.

3. Provide an example of a tactical plan.

4. What are the key elements of operational plans?

5. What are the key differences between strategic, tactical, and operational plans?

6. What impact does organizational level have on managerial planning activities?

7. What are the key issues that managers at the corporate level focus on relative to planning?

8. What type of plans do people at the business level primarily undertake?

9. What are the seven elements in the planning process?

10. Why is forecasting critical to the planning process?

11. Under what conditions are contingency plans most beneficial?

12. What is benchmarking and what role does it play in planning?

13. Why is determining the priority of objectives important?

14. In what ways does measuring objectives influence plan implementation and plan changes?

15. What is the difference between defining requirements and assessing resources in the planning process?

16. How can a Gantt chart facilitate the sequence and timing issues in planning?

17. How can budgeting be used as a planning tool?

18. Describe the two basic approaches to budgeting.

19. What are the strengths and weaknesses of incremental and zero-based budgeting?

20. What is the role of MBO in strategy formulation and implementation?

21. What are the five key elements in effective goal setting?

Apply Your Understanding

1. In your university, professors likely have objectives regarding teaching, research, and service to the university. From your perspective what are the relative priorities of these three objectives? If you could, how would you *change* the priorities and why?

2. Think of an action plan in which you were recently involved. Which elements of the planning process were done well? Which ones were done poorly? What was the impact of these strengths and weaknesses on the outcome?

3. As you look at your own experience and capabilities, where are your strengths and weaknesses relative to the seven elements of the planning process? What is your plan of action for strengthening your planning capabilities?

4. Think about the last goal you set for yourself. How SMART was it?

Practise Your Capabilities

Two months ago you were made manager of a group of six gate agents for Provincial Airlines, Newfoundland's regional airline based in St. John's. One of your subordinates comes to you for advice. The previous manager gave him some rather low marks on his performance evaluation. He wants to make some improvements but feels that he cannot do everything at once. Below are the previous manager's comments about the employee.

Punctuality: Joe is usually on time and rarely misses work without prior notification. However, he never shows up early or stays late to help out during busy times.

Customer Service: In general, Joe does not seem to be a happy person. He is never rude to customers but he does not seem to make them happy either. When problems arise, such as delayed flights, Joe gives customers information and answers their questions in a very matter-of-fact manner. He rarely shows any empathy, and a customer has never complimented him for his service when I have been around.

Check-in Knowledge: Joe has a good understanding of check-in processes. He knows who can get upgrades and what is required. He understands seat assignment policies and executes them with great consistency. However, he fails to notice in advance those customers who have too many bags or whose bags are too large, which simply creates delays and customer frustration when they have to check bags as they are about to board the plane.

Security Procedures: While this is an area that is new to everyone and something that seems to change monthly, Joe is relatively up to date. Soon, airport security personnel will conduct all the "at gate screenings," so this aspect will diminish in importance in the future.

Provincial Airlines has introduced a new strategy that emphasizes customer service. In addition, it is trying to reduce delays and improve its on-time performance.

1. What area(s) would you recommend that Joe try to improve? Why?

2. Create one to three SMART goals and have Joe (a classmate) do the same. Compare the goals. How similar are they? Which goals need to be re-evaluated or changed? Assuming that your assessment of Joe is similar to that of his previous boss and that Joe is typical of the other five subordinates you have, what objectives would you set for your team and what plan would you lay out for achieving them? Even if you don't have all the information you need from the brief description above, what questions would you ask and what information would you need to develop a thorough plan?

Part Eight

Organizing

Chapter 9

Organizing the Business Enterprise

After reading this chapter, you should be able to:

1 Discuss the elements that influence a firm's *organizational structure*.

2 Explain how *specialization* and *departmentalization* are the building blocks of organizational structure.

3 Distinguish between *responsibility* and *authority* and explain the differences in decision making in *centralized* and *decentralized* organizations.

4 Explain the differences between *functional*, *divisional*, *project*, and *international organizational structures* and describe the most popular new forms of organizational design.

5 Explain the idea of the *informal organization*.

Taken from *Business*, Seventh Canadian Edition, by Ricky W. Griffin, Ronald J. Ebert, Frederick A. Starke, and Melanie D. Lang.

Reorganizing the Irving Empire

The Irving family of New Brunswick is a legendary success story in Canadian business. The company owns nearly 300 businesses in areas as diverse as oil refining, forestry, shipbuilding, food processing, publishing, transportation, and home improvement, and it has dominated corporate life in New Brunswick for decades. The company represents Canada's third largest fortune and is valued at about $6 billion. The company was founded by J.D. Irving in 1882 when he opened a sawmill in Bouctouche, New Brunswick. The business expanded dramatically under his son K.C. Irving, who then passed it on to his sons J.K., Arthur, and Jack. These three brothers—who are now in their seventies—have five sons working in the business. Two of the most active sons are Ken (Arthur's son), who heads the oil and gas operation, and Jim (J.K.'s son), who oversees the forestry operations. Over time, tensions developed between Ken and Jim regarding the strategic direction of the company because they each wanted more control over the business. These tensions made relations between J.K. and his brothers more difficult and threatened the company's tradition of passing on control of the company to the next generation.

Originally, K.C. Irving set up a structure that saw J.K. (and later his son Jim) running the forestry empire, trucking, food processing, and newspapers. Arthur (and later his son Ken) was in charge of oil refineries and service stations. Jack's responsibilities were in construction, steel, and real estate. The grand plan began to fall apart when Jim began to feel restricted by the structure because it tied his strategy to Ken's. As well, the third brother—Jack—began to feel like an also-ran in the company. As a result, a coalition—composed of Arthur and Jack and their families—developed and began to oppose Jim and his family.

These tensions were surprising because the Irving family had always presented a united front. But once the conflict became public, the key players in the business decided to avoid the problems that many other family businesses have faced when family members disagree. To their credit, the brothers wanted to avoid a bitter family feud like the one that engulfed the McCain brothers in the 1990s. So they started talking about how to achieve an amicable parting. They basically decided to restructure the company and let the two main parts go their separate ways. Jim and his relatives took control of the forestry end of the business, and Ken and his relatives took over the oil and gas business.

The restructuring is a bit complicated because the various businesses in the family empire are controlled by trusts that were set up by K.C. Irving many years ago. In order to divide up the company, the dozens of family members who have an interest will have to agree on what the restructuring will look like. Irving descendants will likely be offered cash or business interests in return for the original trusts being phased out.

The complexity involved in dividing up the trusts is only one problem. The other is the shifting fortunes of the two main businesses (energy and forestry). In 2007, the energy business was in good shape (because of high oil prices) while forestry was suffering (the high Canadian dollar had a negative effect on exports of lumber). This was just the reverse of the situation that existed in the 1990s, when forestry was booming and the energy business was suffering (partly because of cost overruns on a new refinery that was being built in Saint John). At that time, the energy business needed a bailout, and the forestry side of the business provided it. By 2009, however, oil prices had dropped dramatically and so had the Canadian dollar, so the fortunes of the two main parts of the Irving empire were converging once again. ◆

How will this help me?

Companies frequently introduce changes that are designed to improve their organization structures. When this happens, people have to understand their "place" in the organization. By understanding the material in this chapter, you will also be prepared to understand your "place" in the organization that employs you. Similarly, as a boss or owner, you'll be better equipped to create the optimal structure for your own organization.

This chapter examines factors that influence a firm's formal organizational structure. We discuss the building blocks of organizational structure—specialization, departmentalization, and decision-making hierarchy. We also describe a variety of organizational structures and the most popular new forms of organizational design. The chapter concludes with an explanation of the important elements of the informal organization.

What Is Organizational Structure?

> **1** Discuss the elements that influence a firm's *organizational structure*.

In many ways, a business is like an automobile. All automobiles have an engine, four wheels, fenders and other structural components, an interior compartment for passengers, and various operating systems including those for fuel, brakes, and climate control. Each component has a distinct purpose but must also work in harmony with the others. Automobiles made by competing firms all have the same basic components, although the way they look and fit together may vary.

Similarly, all businesses have common structural and operating components, each of which has a specific purpose. Each component must fulfill its own purpose while simultaneously fitting in with the others. And, just like automobiles made by different companies, how these components look and fit together varies from company to company. Thus, **organizational structure** is the specification of the jobs to be done within a business and how those jobs relate to one another.

> **organizational structure** The specification of the jobs to be done within a business and how those jobs relate to one another.

Every institution—be it a for-profit company like Frantic Films, a not-for-profit organization like the University of Saskatchewan, or a government agency like the Canadian Wheat Board—must develop a structure that is appropriate for its own unique situation. What works for Air Canada will not work for Canada Revenue. Likewise, the structure of the Red Cross will not work for the University of Toronto.

Determinants of Organizational Structure

How is an organization's structure determined? Does it happen by chance or is there some logic that managers use to create structure? Does it develop by some combination of circumstance and strategy? Ideally, managers should carefully assess a variety of important factors as they plan for and then create a structure that will allow their organization to function efficiently. But with the busyness that is evident in most organizations, structure may also develop without much planning.

Many elements work together to determine an organization's structure. Chief among these are the organization's purpose, mission, and strategy. A dynamic and rapidly growing enterprise, for example, achieved that position because of its purpose and successful strategies for achieving it. Such a firm will need a structure that contributes to flexibility and growth. A stable organization with only modest growth will function best with a different structure.

Size, technology, and changes in environmental circumstances also affect structure. A large manufacturer operating in a strongly competitive environment requires a different structure than a local barbershop or video store. Moreover, even after a structure has been created, it is rarely free from tinkering—or even outright re-creation. Indeed, most organizations change their structures almost continually.

Since it was first incorporated in 1903, for example, Ford Motor Co. has undergone literally dozens of major structural changes, hundreds of moderate changes, and thousands of minor changes. In just the last 15 years, Ford has initiated several major structural changes. In 1994, the firm announced a major restructuring plan called Ford 2000, which was intended to integrate all of Ford's vast international operations into a single, unified structure by 2000. By 1998, however, midway through implementation of the plan, top Ford executives announced major modifications, indicating that (1) additional changes would be made, (2) some previously planned changes would not be made, and (3) some recently realigned operations would be changed again. In 1999, managers announced another sweeping set of changes intended to eliminate corporate bureaucracy, speed up decision making, and improve communication and working relationships among people at different levels of the organization.[1] In 2001, still more changes were announced that were intended to boost the firm's flagging bottom line and stem a decline in product quality.[2] The problems that developed in the automobile industry in 2007 and 2008 have resulted in further significant structural changes.

The Chain of Command

Most businesses prepare **organization charts** that illustrate the company's structure and show employees where they fit into the firm's operations. Figure 9.1 shows the organization chart for a hypothetical company. Each box represents a job within the company. The solid lines that connect the boxes define the

organization chart Illustrates the company's structure and show employees where they fit into the firm's operations.

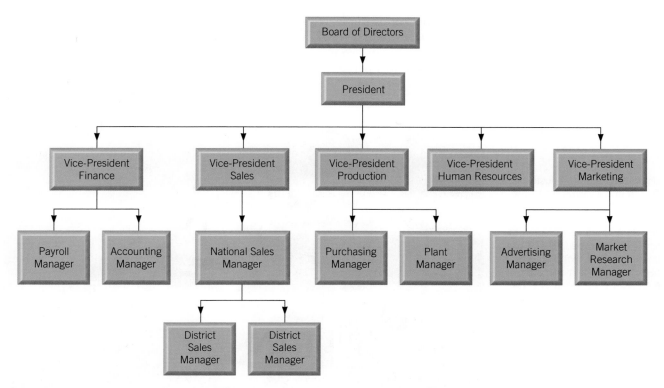

Figure 9.1 An organization chart shows key positions in the organization and interrelationships among them.

chain of command The reporting relationships within the company.

chain of command, or the reporting relationships within the company. For example, the plant manager reports directly to the vice-president of production, who, in turn, reports to the president. When the chain of command is not clear, many different kinds of problems can result.

An actual organization chart would, of course, be far more complex and include individuals at many more levels. Large firms cannot easily draw an organization chart with everyone on it.

The Building Blocks of Organizational Structure

2 Explain how *specialization* and *departmentalization* are the building blocks of organizational structure.

The first step in developing the structure of any business, large or small, is twofold:

- Specialization: determining who will do what
- Departmentalization: determining how people performing certain tasks can best be grouped together

These two tasks are the basic building blocks of all business organization.

Specialization

job specialization The process of identifying the specific jobs that need to be done and designating the people who will perform them.

Job specialization is the process of identifying the specific jobs that need to be done and designating the people who will perform them. In a sense, all organizations have only one major "job"—for example, making a profit by manufacturing and selling something. But this overall job needs to be broken down into smaller components. In turn, each component is assigned to an individual. Consider the manufacture of men's shirts. Because several steps are required to produce a shirt, each job is broken down into its component parts— that is, into a set of tasks to be completed by a series of individuals or machines. One person, for example, cuts material for the shirt body, another cuts material for the sleeves, and a third cuts material for the collar. Components are then shipped to a sewing room, where a fourth person assembles the shirt. In the final stage, a fifth person sews on the buttons.[3]

Organizational and industry-wide growth don't always result in greater job specialization. Animated feature films like *Toy Story 2* are now created by small teams of people who use point-and-click techniques to perform just about every job required by a project. The *Toy Story* movies, as well as *Finding Nemo* and *The Incredibles*, were made by Pixar Animation Studios, which works solely with computer-created animation. According to many experts, Pixar may soon take over industry leadership from Disney.

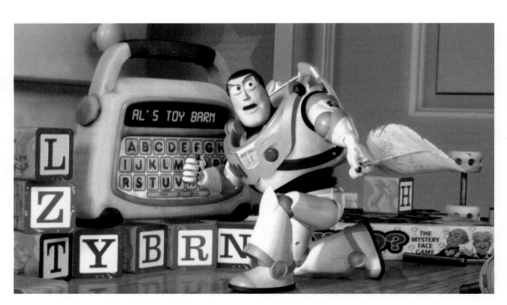

Specialization and Growth

In a very small organization, the owner may perform every job. As the firm grows, however, so does the need to specialize jobs so that others can perform them. To see how specialization can evolve in an organization, consider the case of Mrs. Fields Cookies. When Debbi Fields opened her first store, she did everything herself: bought the equipment, negotiated the lease, baked the cookies, operated the store, and kept the records. As the business grew, however, Fields found that her job was becoming too much for one person. She first hired a bookkeeper to handle her financial records. She then hired an in-store manager and a cookie baker. She herself concentrated on advertising and promotions. Her second store required another set of employees—another manager, another baker, and some salespeople. While Fields focussed her attention on other expansion opportunities, she turned promotions over to a professional advertising director. Thus the job that she once did all by herself was increasingly broken down into components and assigned to different individuals.

Job specialization is a natural part of organizational growth. It is neither a new idea nor limited to factory work. In the ancient art of winemaking, for example, a high degree of specialization has existed for centuries. The activities necessary to make wine—picking and crushing grapes, fermenting the juice, aging and clarifying the wine, and selling it through specialized intermediaries—are performed by individuals who can draw on the knowledge and experience of their predecessors.

Job specialization has certain advantages—individual jobs can be performed more efficiently, the jobs are easier to learn, and it is easier to replace people who leave the organization. On the other hand, if job specialization is carried too far and jobs become too narrowly defined, people get bored, derive less satisfaction from their jobs, and often lose sight of how their contributions fit into the overall organization.

Departmentalization

After jobs are specialized, they must be grouped into logical units. This process is called **departmentalization**. Departmentalized companies benefit from the division of activities. Control and coordination are narrowed and made easier, and top managers can see more easily how various units are performing. Departmentalization allows the firm to treat a department as a **profit centre**—a separate unit responsible for its own costs and profits. Thus, by assessing profits from sales in a particular area—for example, men's clothing—Sears can decide whether to expand or curtail promotions in that area.

departmentalization The process of grouping jobs into logical units.

profit centre A separate company unit responsible for its own costs and profits.

Managers do not group jobs randomly. They group them logically, according to some common thread or purpose. In general, departmentalization may occur along functional, customer, product, geographic, or process lines (or any combination of these).

Functional Departmentalization

Many service and manufacturing companies develop departments according to a group's functions or activities—a form of organization known as **functional departmentalization**. Such firms typically have production, marketing and sales, human resource, and accounting and finance departments. Departments may be further subdivided. For example, the marketing department might be divided geographically or into separate staffs for market research and advertising.

functional departmentalization Departmentalization according to functions or activities.

Customer Departmentalization

Some retail stores actually derive their generic name—department stores— from the manner in which they are structured. Stores like HMV are divided

Many department stores are departmentalized by product. Concentrating different products in different areas of the store makes shopping easier for customers.

customer departmentalization Departmentalization according to the types of customers likely to buy a given product.

into departments—a classical music department, an R&B department, a pop department, and so on. Each department targets a specific customer category (people who want to buy different genres of music). **Customer departmentalization** makes shopping easier by providing identifiable store segments. Thus, a customer shopping for Shania Twain's latest CD can bypass World Music and head straight for Country. Stores can also group products in locations designated for deliveries, special sales, and other service-oriented purposes. In general, when it is departmentalized the store is more efficient and customers get better service—in part because salespeople tend to specialize and gain expertise in their departments.[4]

Product Departmentalization

product departmentalization Dividing an organization according to the specific product or service being created.

Both manufacturers and service providers often opt for **product departmentalization**—dividing an organization according to the specific product or service being created. 3M Corp., which makes both consumer and industrial products, operates different divisions for Post-it brand tape flags, Scotch-Brite scrub sponges, and the Sarns 9000 perfusion system for open-heart surgery.

Geographic Departmentalization

geographic departmentalization Departmentalization according to the area of the country or world supplied.

Some firms may be divided according to the area of the country—or even the world—they serve. This is known as **geographic departmentalization**. In 2009, Nike introduced a new structure that was organized around six geographic regions: North America, Western Europe, Eastern/Central Europe, Greater China, Japan, and emerging markets.[5] Levi Strauss has one division for the United States, one for Europe, and one for the Asia-Pacific region.

The boxed insert entitled "Product vs. Geographical Departmentalization" describes some dilemmas that companies face when they try to choose between product and geographic departmentalization.

Process Departmentalization

process departmentalization Departmentalization according to the production process used to create a good or service.

Other manufacturers favour **process departmentalization**, in which the organization is divided according to the production processes that are used to

Business Accountability

Product vs. Geographical Departmentalization: What's the Right Choice?

Geographic departmentalization ensures quick, responsive reaction to the needs of the company's customers in certain geographic areas. On the other hand, it may also lead to duplicate production and other facilities and compartmentalization of knowledge in those same geographic areas. So it's not easy to decide whether to organize geographically or around products.

Organizing geographically grew in popularity as globalization occurred and firms expanded across national borders. Years ago, when relatively limited communications made it difficult to take the pulse of consumer needs or monitor operations abroad, it made sense to let local managers in foreign countries run their regional or country businesses as more or less autonomous companies. However, two trends are making this structure less popular today. First, information technology is reducing the impediments to cross-border communication. Second, global competition is so intense that firms can't afford to miss an opportunity to quickly transfer product improvements from one region to another.

Many firms are therefore switching from geographic to product departmentalization. For example, food company H.J. Heinz abandoned geographical departmentalization and is now organized by products. Managers in the United States work with those in Europe, Asia, and other regions to apply the best ideas from one region to all the others.

The Canadian Imperial Bank of Commerce (CIBC) also reorganized to break down the walls between the conservative and traditional retail/commercial banking side and the more volatile investment banking side. The company is now organized around product lines.

Exide Corp., the world's largest producer of automotive and industrial batteries, has also shifted from geographical to product departmentalization. Previously, Exide's structure consisted of about 10 "country organizations." The head of each country organization had considerable latitude to make decisions that were best for that country. It also meant that each country manager focussed on products that were marketable in that country. Under the new product system, global business units have been formed to oversee the company's various product lines, such as car and industrial batteries. But the change has not been without problems. For example, when Exide made an

acquisition, some top executives got upset when their unit was made subordinate to the newly acquired unit. It wasn't long before Exide was tinkering with its organization chart again.

PepsiCo was formerly organized around geographic areas. The company had two major divisions: North America and International. When Indra Nooyi became CEO, she reorganized the company into three divisions: Americas Foods, Americas Beverages, and International. The new structure—which is something of a compromise between product and geographic departmentalization—better reflects PepsiCo's focus on snack foods (which accounted for 45 percent of total revenue in 2007).

Either approach—products or geography—can cause problems if taken to an extreme. If a company organizes by products, it can standardize manufacturing, introduce new products around the world faster, and eliminate overlapping activities. But if too much emphasis is placed on product and not enough on geography, a company is likely to find that local decision making is slowed, pricing flexibility is reduced, and products are not tailored to meet the needs of a specific country's customers. Ford Motor Co. experienced exactly these problems when it decided to move toward product departmentalization. The reorganization saved the company $5 billion in its first few years of operation, but Ford's market share declined during the same period. This is what we would expect to happen when too much emphasis is placed on product departmentalization. Ford responded to this drop in market share by giving executives in various regions more authority to decide what types of vehicles were best for their local market. In other words, it moved back a bit toward the geographical model.

Procter & Gamble also encountered problems after it replaced country organizations with global business units in an attempt to globalize P&G brands like Tide, Pampers, and Crest. The reorganization caused great upheaval within the company as thousands of employees shifted into new jobs. As many as half of all company executives took on new roles. The CEO who ordered the change left the company just 17 months into his job.

Questions for Discussion

1. In your own words, explain the dilemma that managers face when they are trying to decide between product and geographic departmentalization.

2. How does the notion of managerial accountability enter into the product vs. geographic departmentalization decision?

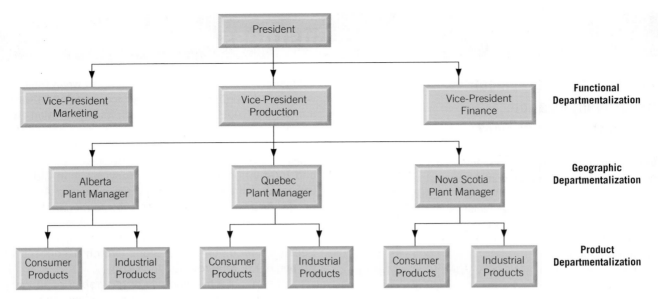

Figure 9.2 Most organizations use multiple bases of departmentalization. This organization, for example, is using functional, geographic, and product departmentalization.

make the product. This principle, for example, is logical for a pickle maker like Vlasic, which has separate departments to transform cucumbers into fresh-packed pickles, pickles cured in brine, and relishes. Cucumbers destined to become fresh-packed pickles must be packed into jars immediately, covered with a solution of water and vinegar, and prepared for sale. Those slated for brined pickles must be aged in brine solution before packing. Relish cucumbers must be minced and combined with a host of other ingredients. Each process requires different equipment and worker skills.

Because different bases of departmentalization have different advantages, larger companies tend to adopt different types of departmentalization for various levels. For example, the company illustrated in Figure 9.2 uses functional departmentalization at the top level. At the middle level, production is divided along geographic lines. At a lower level, departmentalization is based on product groups.

Establishing the Decision-Making Hierarchy

After jobs have been appropriately specialized and grouped into manageable departments, the next step is to answer the question "Who makes which decisions?" This requires the establishment of a decision-making hierarchy, that is, managers must explicitly define reporting relationships among positions so that everyone will know who has responsibility for various decisions and operations. The development of this hierarchy generally involves a three-step process:

1. Assigning tasks: determining who can make decisions and specifying how they should be made

2. Performing tasks: implementing decisions that have been made

3. Distributing authority: determining whether the organization is to be centralized or decentralized

Assigning Tasks

The question of who is supposed to do what and who is entitled to do what in an organization is complex. In any company with more than one person, individuals must work out agreements about responsibilities and authority. **Responsibility** is the duty to perform an assigned task. **Authority** is the power to make the decisions necessary to complete the task.

For example, imagine a mid-level buyer for a department store who encounters an unexpected opportunity to make a large purchase at an extremely good price. Let's assume that an immediate decision is absolutely necessary—but that this decision is one that this buyer has no authority to make without confirmation from above. The company's policies on delegation and authority are inconsistent, since the buyer is responsible for purchasing the clothes that will be sold in the upcoming season but lacks the authority to make the needed purchases.

> Distinguish between *responsibility* and *authority* and explain the differences in decision making in *centralized* and *decentralized* organizations.
>
> **3**

responsibility The duty to perform an assigned task.

authority The power to make the decisions necessary to complete the task.

Performing Tasks

Trouble occurs when appropriate levels of responsibility and authority are not clearly spelled out in the working relationships between managers and subordinates. Here, the issues become delegation and accountability. **Delegation** begins when a manager assigns a task to a subordinate. **Accountability** falls to the subordinate, who must then complete the task. If the subordinate does not perform the assigned task properly and promptly, he or she may be reprimanded or punished, possibly even dismissed.

delegation Assignment of a task, a responsibility, or authority by a manager to a subordinate.

accountability Liability of subordinates for accomplishing tasks assigned by managers.

Fear of Delegating

Unfortunately, many managers have trouble delegating tasks to others. Managers who have trouble delegating typically exhibit several characteristics: they assume that employees can never do anything as well as they can; they fear that their subordinates will "show the manager up" in front of others by doing a superb job; they want to control everything; they fail to do long-range planning because they are bogged down in day-to-day operations; and they are in the dark about industry trends and competitive products because they are too involved in day-to-day operations.

There are remedies for these problems. First, managers should recognize that they cannot do everything themselves. Second, if subordinates cannot do a job, they should be trained so that they can assume more responsibility. Third, managers should recognize that if a subordinate performs well, it reflects favourably on that employee's manager. Effective managers surround themselves with a team of strong subordinates and then delegate sufficient authority to those subordinates so they can get the job done. There are four things to keep in mind when delegating:

- Decide on the nature of the work to be done.

- Match the job with the skills of subordinates.

- Make sure the person chosen understands the objectives he or she is supposed to achieve.

- Make sure subordinates have the time and training necessary to do the task.

Distributing Authority

Delegation involves a specific relationship between managers and subordinates. Most businesses must also make decisions about general patterns of authority throughout the company. This pattern may be largely centralized or decentralized.

Centralized Organizations

centralized organization
Top managers retain most decision-making rights for themselves.

In a **centralized organization**, top management retains the right to make most decisions, and top management must approve most lower-level decisions before they can be implemented.[6] McDonald's practises centralization as a way to maintain standardization. All restaurants must follow precise steps in buying products and making and packaging burgers and other menu items. Most advertising is handled at the corporate level, and a regional manager must approve any local advertising. Restaurants even have to follow prescribed schedules for maintenance and upgrades like floor polishing and parking lot cleaning.[7]

Decentralized Organizations

decentralized organization
Lower- and middle-level managers are allowed to make significant decisions.

In a **decentralized organization**, much of the decision-making authority is delegated to levels of management at various points below the top level. The purpose of decentralization is to make a company more responsive to its environment by breaking the company into more manageable units and giving those units more autonomy. Reducing top-heavy bureaucracies is also a common goal of decentralization.

At FedEx, the commitment to decentralization promotes innovation. Managers are encouraged and rewarded for questioning, challenging, and developing new ideas, which are always given serious consideration. Developments have included teaming up with Motorola and Microsoft to create a proprietary pocket-size PC, sending package information to cellphones, and creating software products for small business logistics.[8]

Jack Welch, the former CEO of General Electric and a long-time proponent of decentralized management, says, "If you don't let managers make their own decisions, you're never going to be anything more than a one-person business."

McDonald's emphasis on centralization ensures standardization in its product offerings. Customers will have a consistent dining experience whenever and wherever they eat at a McDonald's restaurant.

The idea of autonomy for managers sounds pretty reasonable, but decentralization can also cause difficulties for companies. Consider what happened at General Motors. For many years, GM had a decentralized structure that allowed each car division to produce cars that would attract whatever market segment the division was pursuing. This decentralized structure worked so well that GM became the largest automobile manufacturer in the world. But the autonomy given to managers resulted in widely differing car designs that were very expensive to produce. As GM's costs soared, and as competition from foreign car makers became ferocious, GM's sales and overall profitability plummeted. To cope, GM recentralized and head office took away much of the autonomy that managers in various international divisions had.

Now, GM requires its worldwide units to work much more closely together to design cars that can be sold (with modest variations) worldwide. The new, more centralized structure means that engineers in various regions have less authority than they used to have when they are designing cars. A "Global Council" in Detroit now makes key decisions about how much will be spent on new car development. And the council can say "no" to proposed new car designs. For example, when GM engineers at its Daewoo joint venture with South Korea wanted to develop a sport utility vehicle especially suited for the South Korean market, the request was denied.[9] Even with all of these changes, GM's future is in doubt.

Tall and Flat Organizations

Related to the concept of centralized or decentralized authority is the concept of tall or flat organizational structures. With relatively fewer layers of management, decentralized firms tend to have a **flat organizational structure** such as the one shown in Figure 9.3. In contrast, companies with centralized authority systems typically require multiple layers of management and thus have a **tall organizational structure**. The Canadian Forces is an example of such an organization. Because information, whether upward or downward bound, must pass through so many organizational layers, tall structures are prone to delays in information flow.

flat organizational structure An organization with relatively few layers of management.

tall organizational structure An organization with many layers of management.

As organizations grow in size, they typically become at least somewhat taller. For instance, a small firm with only an owner-manager and a few employees is likely to have two layers—the owner-manager and the employees who report to that person. But as the firm grows, more layers will be needed.

Span of Control

As you can see in Figure 9.3, the distribution of authority in an organization also affects the number of people who work for any individual manager. In a flat organizational structure, the number of people managed by one supervisor— the manager's **span of control**—is usually wide. In tall organizations, span of control tends to be relatively narrow. Span of control, however, depends on many factors. Employees' abilities and the supervisor's managerial skills help determine whether span of control is wide or narrow, as do the similarity and simplicity of those tasks performed under the manager's supervision and the extent to which they are interrelated.[10]

span of control The number of people managed by one manager.

If lower-level managers are given more decision-making authority, their supervisor's workload will be lightened because some of the decisions the supervisor previously made are now made by subordinates. The supervisor may then be able to oversee and coordinate the work of more subordinates, resulting in an increased span of control. Similarly, when several employees perform either the same simple task or a group of interrelated tasks, a wider span of control is possible (for example, one supervisor may control an entire assembly line). Because each task is interdependent, if one work station stops, they all

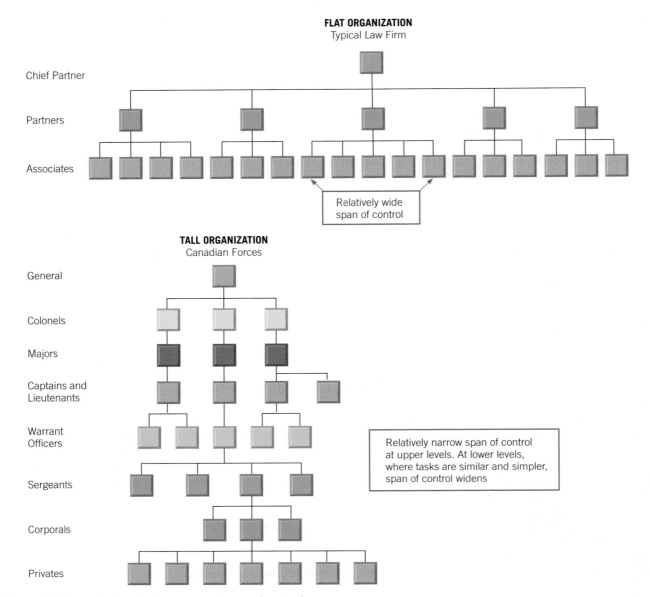

Figure 9.3 Organizational structure and span of control.

downsizing The planned reduction in the scope of an organization's activity.

stop. Having one supervisor ensures that all stations receive equal attention and are well coordinated. **Downsizing**—the planned reduction in the scope of an organization's activity—also affects the span of control. It usually means cutting substantial numbers of managers and workers and reducing the number and variety of products the company produces. Downsizing may eliminate entire layers of management (creating a flatter corporate structure), and the remaining managers end up with larger spans of control.

When jobs are more diversified or prone to change, a narrow span of control is preferable. At Case Corp., farm tractors are made to order in five to six weeks. Farmers can select from among a wide array of options, including engines, tires, power trains, and CD players. A wide assortment of machines and processes is used to construct each tractor. Although workers are highly skilled operators of their assigned machines, each machine is different. In this kind of set-up, the complexities of each machine and the advanced skills needed by each operator mean that one supervisor can oversee only a relatively small number of employees.[11]

Three Forms of Authority

In an organization, it must be clear who will have authority over whom. As individuals are delegated responsibility and authority in a company, a complex web of interactions develops. These interactions may result in one of three forms of authority: line, staff, or committee and team. In reality, like departmentalization, all three forms may be found in a given company, especially a large one.

Line Authority.   **Line authority** is authority that flows up and down the chain of command (refer back to Figure 9.1). Most companies rely heavily on **line departments**—departments directly linked to the production and sales of specific products. For example, Clark Equipment Corp. has a division that produces forklifts and small earth movers (see Figure 9.4). In this division, line departments include purchasing, materials handling, fabrication, painting, and assembly (all of which are directly linked to production) along with sales and distribution (both of which are directly linked to sales).

Each line department is essential to an organization's success. Line employees are the "doers" and producers in a company. If any line department fails to complete its task, the company cannot sell and deliver finished goods. Thus, the authority delegated to line departments is important. A bad decision by the manager in one department can hold up production for an entire plant. For example, say that the painting department manager at Clark Equipment changes a paint application on a batch of forklifts, which then show signs of peeling paint. The batch will have to be repainted (and perhaps partially reassembled) before the machines can be shipped.

Staff Authority.   Most companies also rely on **staff authority**, which is based on technical expertise and involves advising line managers about decisions. Common staff positions include specialists in areas such as law, engineering, accounting, marketing research, and human resource management. Staff members help line departments in making decisions but do not generally have the authority to make final decisions.

Suppose that the fabrication department at Clark Equipment has an employee with a drinking problem. The manager of the department could consult a human resource staff expert for advice on handling the situation. The staff expert might suggest that the worker stay on the job but enter a counselling program. But if the line manager decides that the job is too dangerous to be handled by a person whose judgment is impaired by alcohol, the line manager's decision will most likely prevail.

Typically, the separation between line authority and staff responsibility is clearly delineated. As Figure 9.4 shows, this separation is usually shown in organization charts by solid lines (line authority) and dotted lines (staff responsibility). It may help to understand this separation by remembering that while staff members generally provide expert advice and services to management, line managers are the ones who are directly involved in producing and selling the firm's products.

Committee and Team Authority.   Recently, more and more organizations have started to use **committee and team authority**—authority granted to committees or work teams that play central roles in the firm's daily operations. A committee, for example, may consist of top managers from several major areas. If the work of the committee is especially important, and if the committee will be working together for an extended time, the organization may even grant it special authority as a decision-making body that goes beyond the individual authority possessed by each of its members.

line authority Authority that flows up and down the chain of command.

line departments Departments directly linked to the production and sales of specific products.

staff authority Based on technical expertise and involves advising line managers about decisions.

committee and team authority Authority granted to committees or work teams that play central roles in the firm's daily operations.

CLARK EQUIPMENT CORP.

Staff Managers

Human Resources Department

Engineering Department

Line Managers

Trucks Division

Forks and Small Earth Movers Division

Tools Division

Purchasing

Materials Handling

Fabrication

Painting

Assembly

Sales

Distribution

Figure 9.4 Line and staff organization: Clark Equipment Corp.

At the operating level, many firms today are also using work teams—groups of operating employees empowered to plan and organize their own work and to perform that work with a minimum of supervision. As with permanent committees, the organization will usually find it beneficial to grant special authority to work teams so that they will function more effectively.[12]

Basic Organizational Structures

4 Explain the differences between *functional, divisional, project,* and *international organizational structures* and describe the most popular new forms of organizational design.

A glance at the organization charts of many organizations reveals what appears to be an almost infinite variety of structures. However, closer examination shows that it is possible to identify four basic forms: functional, divisional, project, and international.

The Functional Structure

functional structure The various units in the organization are formed based on the functions that must be carried out to reach organizational goals.

In the **functional structure**, the various units in the organization are formed based on the functions that must be carried out to reach organizational goals. The functional structure makes use of departmentalization by function. Refer back to Figure 9.1 for an example of a functional structure. The advantages and disadvantages of the functional structure are summarized in Table 9.1.

divisional structure Divides the organization into several divisions, each of which operates as a semi-autonomous unit and profit centre.

The Divisional Structure

The **divisional structure** divides the organization into several divisions, each of which operates as a semi-autonomous unit and profit centre (see Figure 9.5). Divisions in organizations can be based on products, customers, or geography. In 2008, Teck Resources Ltd. (formerly Teck Cominco Ltd.)

Business firms are increasingly using work teams and allowing groups of employees to plan and organize their own work with a minimum of supervision. This contributes to employee empowerment.

Table 9.1   Advantages and Disadvantages of a Functional Structure

Advantages	Disadvantages
1. It focusses attention on the key activities that must be performed.	1. Conflicts may arise among the functional areas.
2. Expertise develops within each function.	2. No single function is responsible for overall organizational performance.
3. Employees have clearly defined career paths.	3. Employees in each functional area have a narrow view of the organization.
4. The structure is simple and easy to understand.	4. Decision making is slowed because functional areas must get approval from top management for a variety of decisions.
5. It eliminates duplication of activities.	5. Coordinating highly specialized functions may be difficult.

reorganized its business into separate product divisions for gold, copper, zinc, metallurgical coal, and energy. The company felt that the new structure would increase its competitiveness and allow it to act on opportunities in the five different commodity segments.[13]

H.J. Heinz, one of the world's largest food-processing companies, is divisionalized along seven product lines: food service, infant foods, condiments, Star-Kist tuna, pet foods, frozen foods, and miscellaneous products. Because of its divisional structure, Heinz can evaluate the performance of each division independently. Because divisions are relatively autonomous, a firm can take actions (like selling unprofitable divisions) with minimal disruption to its remaining business operations. The advantages and disadvantages of the divisional structure are summarized in Table 9.2.

Project Organization

Most organizations are characterized by unchanging vertical authority relationships because such a set-up facilitates the production of a product in a routine and repetitive way. Procter & Gamble, for example, produces millions of tubes of Crest toothpaste each year using standardized production methods. The company has done this for years and intends to do so indefinitely.

But some organizations find themselves faced with projects that have a definite starting and ending point. These organizations often use a project structure to deal with the uncertainty encountered in new situations. **Project organization** involves forming a team of specialists from different functional areas of the organization to work on a specific project.[14] A project structure

project organization Involves forming a team of specialists from different functional areas of the organization to work on a specific project.

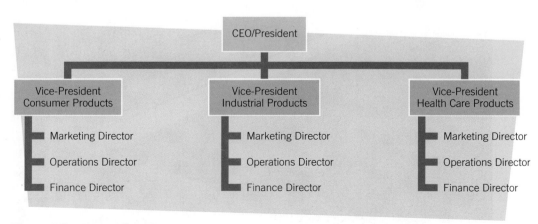

Figure 9.5 Divisional structure.

Table 9.2   Advantages and Disadvantages of a Divisional Structure

Advantages	Disadvantages
1. It accommodates change and expansion.	1. Activities may be duplicated across divisions.
2. It increases accountability.	2. A lack of communication among divisions may occur.
3. It develops expertise in the various divisions.	3. Adding diverse divisions may blur the focus of the organization.
4. It encourages training for top management.	4. Company politics may affect the allocation of resources.

may be temporary or permanent; if it is temporary, the project team disbands once the project is completed and team members return to their regular functional area or are assigned to a new project.

Project organization is used extensively by Canadian firms, for example, in the construction of hydroelectric generating stations like those developed by Hydro-Quebec on La Grande River and by Manitoba Hydro on the Nelson River. Once the generating station is complete, it becomes part of the traditional structure of the utility. Project organization is also used at shipyards. Each ship that is built is treated as a project and supervised by a project manager. The project manager for a given ship is responsible for ensuring that the ship is completed on time and within budget.[15] Project organization has proven useful for coordinating the many elements needed to extract oil from the tar sands. Project management is also used in other kinds of tasks, including construction, military weapons, aerospace, and health-care delivery.[16]

matrix organization A variation of project structure in which the project manager and the regular line managers share authority.

A **matrix organization** is a variation of project structure in which the project manager and the regular line managers share authority. Ford, for example, used a matrix organization to redesign the Ford Thunderbird. A design team composed of people from engineering, marketing, operations, and finance was created to design the new car. During the time the team was working on the Thunderbird project, the engineering, marketing, operations, and finance experts reported primarily to the project manager, but the line managers of the departments they came from also had some say about what work they did. After the team's work was done, team members moved back to their permanent functional jobs.

The project organization structure is very useful for construction projects like this hydroelectric generating station on the La Grande River in Quebec. Installations like this have a specific beginning and ending point. Once the construction is completed, the generating station becomes part of the traditional organizational structure of the provincial utility.

In other companies, the matrix organization is a semi-permanent fixture. Martha Stewart Living Omnimedia Inc. has created a permanent matrix organization for its burgeoning lifestyle business. The company is organized broadly into media and merchandising groups, each of which has specific product and product groups. Layered on top of this structure are teams of lifestyle experts organized into groups such as cooking, crafts, weddings, and so forth. Although each group targets specific customer needs, they all work across all product groups. A wedding expert, for example, might contribute to an article on wedding planning for a Martha Stewart magazine, contribute a story idea for a Martha Stewart cable television program, and supply content for a Martha Stewart website. This same individual might also help select fabrics suitable for wedding gowns that are to be retailed.[17]

The matrix structure does not always work well. In 2009, Carol Bartz—the new CEO at Yahoo—announced a restructuring that was designed to make managers more accountable and to speed up decision making. The new structure essentially did away with the matrix structure and workers no longer report to multiple bosses.[18]

International Organization

Many businesses today manufacture, purchase, and sell in the global market. As a result, several different **international organizational structures** have emerged. Moreover, as competition on a global scale becomes more complex, companies often find that they must experiment with the ways in which they respond.

For example, when Wal-Mart opened its first store outside the United States in 1992, it set up a special projects team to handle the logistics. As more stores were opened abroad in the mid-1990s, the firm created a small international department to handle overseas expansion. By 1999, however, international sales and expansion had become such a major part of Wal-Mart's operations that the firm created a separate international division headed up by a senior vice-president. And by 2002, international operations had become so important to Wal-Mart that the international division was further divided into geographic areas where the firm does business, such as Mexico and Europe. Wal-Mart typifies the form of organization outlined in Figure 9.6.

Other firms have also developed a wide range of approaches to international organization structure. The French food giant Danone Group, for instance,

international organizational structures Organizational structures that are designed to help a company succeed in international markets. International departments, international divisions, or an integrated global organization are all variations of the international organizational structure.

All the signs at this 85 000-square-foot store in Numazu identify it as a Seiyu outlet run by Japan's fifth largest supermarket chain. However, Wal-Mart owns 38 percent of Seiyu, and this giant store is part of Wal-Mart's effort to enter the world's second largest retail market.

Figure 9.6 International division structure.

has three major product groups: dairy products (Danone yogourt), bottled water (Evian), and cookies (Pim's). Danone's structure does not differentiate internationally, but rather integrates global operations within each product group.[19] In contrast, U.S. entertainment companies are finding it advantageous to create a more local identity when they enter foreign markets. For instance, Columbia TriStar, known for such U.S. television programs as *Seinfeld* and *Mad About You*, launched *Chinese Restaurant*, a sitcom filmed and shown only in China. Universal and HBO have also got in on the act by setting up new television production businesses in Germany and Japan.[20]

Finally, some companies adopt a truly global structure in which they acquire resources (including capital), produce goods and services, engage in research and development, and sell products in whatever local market is appropriate, without any consideration of national boundaries. Until a few years ago, for example, General Electric kept its international business operations as separate divisions. Now, however, the company functions as one integrated global organization. GE businesses around the world connect and interact with each other constantly, and managers freely move back and forth among them. This integration is also reflected in the top management team: The head of its audit team is French, the head of quality control is Dutch, and a German runs one of GE's core business groups.[21]

Another kind of "structure" is described in the boxed insert entitled "Green Structures."

Organizational Design for the Twenty-first Century

As the world grows increasingly complex and fast paced, companies continue to seek new forms of organization that permit them to compete effectively. Among the most popular of these new forms are the boundaryless organization, the team organization, the virtual organization, and the learning organization.

Boundaryless Organization

boundaryless organization
Traditional boundaries and structures are minimized or eliminated altogether.

The **boundaryless organization** is one in which traditional boundaries and structures are minimized or eliminated altogether. For example, General Electric's fluid organization structure, in which people, ideas, and information flow freely between businesses and business groups, approximates this concept. Similarly, as firms partner with their suppliers in more efficient ways, external boundaries disappear. Some of Wal-Mart's key suppliers are tied directly into the retailer's vaunted information system. As a result, when Wal-Mart distribution centres start running low on, say, Wrangler blue jeans, the

The Greening of Business

Green Structures

The term *organizational structure* is commonly used to explain theoretical concepts like departmentalization, authority, responsibility, and the hierarchical patterns within organizations. But businesses (and cities) also need physical structures like offices and factories to do their work, and managers in both the public and private sector are beginning to realize that their physical structures present significant opportunities to be eco-friendly. In Charlottetown, P.E.I., for example, a federal government office building is being constructed with photovoltaic panels that will produce 8 to 10 percent of the building's power needs. At the University of Toronto, over 90 percent of the heating requirements for the engineering and computer science building are being recovered from a nearby boiler plant. And Masdar City, Abu Dhabi—which is scheduled for completion in 2016—will be the world's first zero-carbon, zero-waste city that is fully powered by renewable energy.

Some architects think that over the next decade, it may be possible to have buildings that require no energy at all from public utilities. Birgit Siber, an architect at Toronto-based Diamond and Schmitt Architects, says that big box stores are good candidates because they already have relatively low energy requirements. Wal-Mart, for example, has started to open high-efficiency supercentres, which consume 20 percent less energy than their regular supercentres. Gerrit de Boer, president of Toronto-based Idomo Furniture Co., says that his firm will be "off the grid" within 10 years as a result of the geothermal heating system and the photovoltaic solar array that are being installed in the company's 200 000-square-foot building.

Many other organizations are also introducing eco-friendly technologies. When a hybrid heating system was installed at Delta Whistler Village Suites, greenhouse gases were reduced by 45 percent, and the hotel saved $70 000 in energy costs. The hybrid heating system alternates between electricity and fossil fuels, depending on whichever is cheaper at the moment. Manitoba Hydro's new building in Winnipeg contains a geothermal heating and air-conditioning system that provides 100 percent of the energy needed to air condition the building in the summer and 60 percent of the energy needed to heat the building in winter. The building is so energy efficient that it uses just 91 kilowatt hours of energy per square metre of floor space (the Model National Energy Code standards say that a building should not use more than 295 kilowatt hours).

Sunova Credit Union's branch in Oak Bank, Manitoba, became the greenest building in the province when it was completed in the summer of 2009. The building meets the platinum (highest) rating of the Leadership in Energy and Environmental Design (LEED) organization. Very few buildings in Canada have this designation. The building uses recycled building materials and has energy-efficient windows, a solar energy panel, a geothermal heating and cooling system, and a water retention and treatment system. Some automobile dealers are also seeking certification from LEED for buildings at their dealerships. LEED standards are also important in the planning of the facilities and venues for the 2010 Winter Olympics in British Columbia.

Even more innovative ideas are likely to emerge in the future. In Britain, for example, engineers are experimenting with a "heel-strike" technology that harnesses pedestrian footsteps. When people walk around in a building, power is generated each time their heels hit the floor. Pretty clever, but at the moment it appears that not enough energy is generated by heel strikes. Future research will no doubt improve this technology.

The movement toward greener buildings is not limited to commercial buildings. A survey by realtor Royal LePage found that 72 percent of Canadians would look for a greener home when they make their next purchase. Green realtors are now emerging that specialize in finding green homes for clients who are environmentally conscious, and there is even a Green Realty Association in British Columbia. Home buyers have two basic options: they can purchase a home that has been built to be eco-friendly; or they can renovate an older home by improving insulation, replacing windows, installing solar panels, and installing energy efficient appliances and showers.

Critical Thinking Questions

1. What are the advantages of "green" buildings? Are there any disadvantages? Explain.

2. Consider the following statement: *It's a very good idea for companies to build eco-friendly buildings, but it is very expensive to do so, and expenditures like these should not be made. Rather, the focus should be on upgrading their production facilities so that companies can make higher-quality products for consumers and more profits for their shareholders.* Do you agree or disagree with the statement? Explain your reasoning.

manufacturer receives the information as soon as the retailer does. Wrangler proceeds to manufacture new inventory and restock the distribution centre without Wal-Mart having to place a new order.

Team Organization

team organization Relies almost exclusively on project-type teams, with little or no underlying functional hierarchy.

Team organization relies almost exclusively on project-type teams, with little or no underlying functional hierarchy. People "float" from project to project as dictated by their skills and the demands of those projects. At Cypress Semiconductor, units or groups that become large are simply split into smaller units. Not surprisingly, the organization is composed entirely of small units. This strategy allows each unit to change direction, explore new ideas, and try new methods without having to deal with a rigid bureaucratic superstructure. Although few large organizations have actually reached this level of adaptability, Apple Computer and Xerox are among those moving toward it.

Virtual Organization

virtual organization A company with little or no formal structure, which exists only in response to its own needs.

A **virtual organization** has little or no formal structure. Typically, it has only a handful of permanent employees, a very small staff, and a modest administrative facility. As the needs of the organization change, managers bring in temporary workers, lease facilities, and outsource basic support services to meet the demands of each unique situation. As the situation changes, the temporary workforce changes in parallel, with some people leaving the organization and others entering it. Facilities and subcontracted services also change. In other words, the virtual organization exists only in response to its own needs.

Global Research Consortium (GRC) is a virtual organization that offers research and consulting services to firms doing business in Asia. As clients request various services, GRC's staff of three permanent employees subcontracts the work to an appropriate set of several dozen independent consultants and/or researchers with whom it has relationships. At any given time, therefore, GRC may have several projects underway and 20 or 30 people working on various projects. As the projects change, so too does the composition of the organization. Figure 9.7 illustrates a hypothetical virtual organization.

Learning Organization

learning organization Works to integrate continuous improvement with continuous employee learning and development.

The so-called **learning organization** works to integrate continuous improvement with continuous employee learning and development. Specifically, a learning organization works to facilitate the lifelong learning and personal development of all of its employees while continually transforming itself to respond to changing demands and needs.

Figure 9.7 A virtual organization.

The most frequent goals of a learning organization are improved quality, continuous improvement, and performance measurement. The idea is that the most consistent and logical strategy for achieving continuous improvement is constantly upgrading employee talent, skill, and knowledge. For example, if each employee in an organization learns one new thing each day and can translate that knowledge into work-related practice, continuous improvement will logically follow. Indeed, organizations that wholeheartedly embrace this approach believe that only through constant employee learning can continuous improvement really occur.

In recent years, many different organizations have implemented this approach on various levels. Shell Oil Co., for example, recently purchased an executive conference centre called the Shell Learning Center. The facility boasts state-of-the-art classrooms and instructional technology, lodging facilities, a restaurant, and recreational amenities such as a golf course, swimming pool, and tennis courts. Line managers at the firm rotate through the centre and serve as teaching faculty. Teaching assignments last anywhere from a few days to several months. At the same time, all Shell employees routinely attend training programs, seminars, and related activities, all the while gathering the latest information they need to contribute more effectively to the firm. Seminar topics have included time management, balancing work and family demands, and international trade theory.

The Informal Organization

The formal organization of a business is the part that can be seen and represented on the organization chart. The structure of a company, however, is by no means limited to the organization chart and the formal assignment of authority. Frequently, the **informal organization**—the everyday social interactions among employees that transcend formal jobs and job interrelationships—effectively alters a company's formal structure. Indeed, this level of organization is sometimes more powerful than the formal structure. The Exercising Your Ethics boxed insert at the end of the chapter presents an interesting situation that illustrates the informal organization.

Is the informal organization good or bad? On the positive side, the informal organization can help employees feel that they "belong," and it gives them an outlet for "letting off steam" in a safe environment. It also provides information that employees are interested in hearing. On the negative side, the informal organization can reinforce office politics that put the interests of individuals ahead of those of the firm. Likewise, a great deal of harm can be caused by distorted or inaccurate information communicated without management input or review. For example, if the informal organization is generating false information about impending layoffs, valuable employees may act quickly (and unnecessarily) to seek other employment. Among the more important elements of the informal organization are informal groups and the organizational grapevine.

Explain the idea of the *informal organization*.

5

informal organization The everyday social interactions among employees that transcend formal jobs and job interrelationships.

Informal Groups

Informal groups are simply groups of people who decide to interact among themselves even though they may not be required to do so by the formal organization. They may be people who work together or who simply get together for lunch, during breaks, or after work. They may talk about business, the boss, or non-work-related topics such as families, movies, or sports. For example, at the New York Metropolitan Opera, musicians and singers play poker during the intermissions. Most pots are in the $30 to $40 range. Luciano Pavarotti, the famed tenor, once played and lost big.

The impact of informal groups on the organization may be positive (if they work together to support the organization), negative (if they work together in ways that run counter to the organization's interests), or neutral (if what they do is unrelated to the organization).

Organizational Grapevine

The **grapevine** is the informal communication network that runs through the entire organization.[22] The grapevine is found in all organizations except the very smallest, but it does not always follow the same patterns as formal channels of authority and communication, nor does it necessarily coincide with them. Because the grapevine typically passes information orally, messages often become distorted in the process, but most office gossip has at least some kernel of truth to it. Those passing on news may deliberately alter it, either to advance their own goals or to submarine someone else's chances. Listening to and passing on information damaging to someone's reputation can backfire, harming your credibility and making you a target for similar gossip.

In general, the more detailed the information, the less likely it is to be true. Likewise, beware the hush-hush "don't quote me on this" rumour. (Cynics claim that the better the news, the less likely it is to be true.) The higher the source, the greater the likelihood that the grapevine has the real story. Don't reject information from "lower" sources, however. Many an executive assistant can provide valuable insights into a corporation's plans.

Attempts to eliminate the grapevine are fruitless, but managers do have some control over it. By maintaining open channels of communication and responding vigorously to inaccurate information, they can minimize the damage the grapevine can do. In fact, the grapevine can actually be an asset. By getting to know the key people in the grapevine, for example, the manager can partially control the information received and use the grapevine to determine employee reactions to new ideas (e.g., a change in human resource policies or benefit packages). The manager can also receive valuable information from the grapevine and use it to improve decision making.

Wise managers will tune in to the grapevine's message because it is often a corporate early warning system. Ignoring this valuable source of information

The grapevine is a powerful communications network in most organizations. These workers may be talking about any number of things—an upcoming deadline on an important project, tonight's football game, the stock market, rumours about an impending takeover, gossip about forthcoming promotions, or the weather.

can cause managers to be the last to know that they are about to get a new boss or that they have a potentially fatal image problem. The grapevine is not infallible, however. In addition to miscommunication and attempts by some people to manipulate it for their own ends, it may carry rumours with absolutely no basis in fact. Such rumours are most common when there is a complete lack of information (apparently, human nature abhors a vacuum and seeks to fill it with something, even if it is made-up information).

Test yourself on the material for this chapter at **www.pearsoned.ca/mybusinesslab**.

Summary of
Learning Objectives

1. **Discuss the elements that influence a firm's** *organizational structure.* Every business needs structure to operate. *Organizational structure* varies according to a firm's mission, purpose, and strategy. Size, technology, and changes in environmental circumstances also influence structure. In general, while all organizations have the same basic elements, each develops the structure that contributes to the most efficient operations.

2. Explain how *specialization* and *departmentalization* are the building blocks of organizational structure. The building blocks of organizational structure are job specialization and *departmentalization.* As a firm grows, it usually has a greater need for people to perform specialized tasks (specialization). It also has a greater need to group types of work into logical units (departmentalization). Common forms of departmentalization are *customer, product, process, geographic,* and *functional.* Large businesses often use more than one form of departmentalization.

3. Distinguish between *responsibility* and *authority* and explain the differences in decision making in *centralized* and *decentralized* organizations. *Responsibility* is the duty to perform a task; *authority* is the power to make the decisions necessary to complete tasks. *Delegation* begins when a manager assigns a task to a subordinate; *accountability* means that the subordinate must complete the task. *Span of control* refers to the number of people who work for any individual manager. The more people supervised by a manager, the wider his or her span of control. Wide spans are usually desirable when employees perform simple or unrelated tasks. When jobs are diversified or prone to change, a narrower span is generally preferable.

   In a *centralized organization*, only a few individuals in top management have real decision-making authority. In a *decentralized organization*, much authority is delegated to lower-level management. Where both line and line-and-staff systems are involved, *line departments* generally

have authority to make decisions while staff departments have a responsibility to advise. A relatively new concept, *committee and team authority*, empowers committees or work teams involved in a firm's daily operations.

4. Explain the differences between *functional, divisional, project,* and *international organizational structures* and describe the most popular new forms of organizational design. In a *functional organization*, authority is usually distributed among such basic functions as marketing and finance. In a *divisional organization*, the various divisions of a larger company, which may be related or unrelated, operate in a relatively autonomous fashion. In *project organization*, in which individuals report to more than one manager, a company creates teams to address specific problems or to conduct specific projects. A company that has divisions in many countries may require an additional level of *international organization* to coordinate those operations. Four of the most popular new forms of organizational design are (1) *boundaryless organizations* (traditional boundaries and structures are minimized or eliminated), (2) *team organizations* (rely on project-type teams, with little or no functional hierarchy), (3) *virtual organizations* (have little formal structure and only a handful of permanent employees, a small staff, and a modest administrative facility), and (4) *learning organizations* (work to facilitate employees' lifelong learning and personal development while transforming the organization to meet changing demands and needs).

5. Explain the idea of the *informal organization.* The *informal organization* consists of the everyday social interactions among employees that transcend formal jobs and job interrelationships. The informal organization exists within the formal structure of every organization and cannot be suppressed. Effective managers work with the informal organization and try to harness it for the good of the formal organization.

Key Terms

accountability   (p. 301)

authority   (p. 301)

boundaryless organization
   (p. 310)

centralized organization   (p. 302)

chain of command   (p. 296)

committee and team authority
   (p. 305)

customer departmentalization
   (p. 298)

decentralized organization
   (p. 302)

delegation   (p. 301)

departmentalization   (p. 297)

divisional structure   (p. 306)

downsizing   (p. 304)

flat organizational structure
   (p. 303)

functional departmentalization
   (p. 297)

functional structure   (p. 306)

geographic departmentalization
   (p. 298)

grapevine   (p. 314)

informal organization   (p. 313)

international organizational
   structure   (p. 309)

job specialization   (p. 296)

learning organization   (p. 312)

line authority   (p. 305)

line departments   (p. 305)

matrix organization   (p. 308)

organization chart   (p. 295)

organizational structure   (p. 294)

process departmentalization
   (p. 298)

product departmentalization
   (p. 298)

profit centre   (p. 297)

project organization   (p. 307)

responsibility   (p. 301)

span of control   (p. 303)

staff authority   (p. 305)

tall organizational structure
   (p. 303)

team organization   (p. 312)

virtual organization   (p. 312)

Questions for Analysis

1. Explain the significance of size as it relates to organizational structure. Describe the changes that are likely to occur as an organization grows.

2. Why do some managers have difficulties in delegating authority? Why does this problem tend to plague smaller businesses?

3. Draw up an organization chart for your college or university.

4. Describe a hypothetical organizational structure for a small printing firm. Describe changes that might be necessary as the business grows.

5. Compare and contrast the matrix and divisional approaches to organizational structure. How would you feel personally about working in a matrix organization in which you were assigned simultaneously to multiple units and multiple bosses?

6. If a company has a formal organizational structure, why should managers pay attention to the informal organization?

7. Consider the organization where you currently work (or one where you have previously worked). Which of the four basic structural types was it most consistent with? What was the basis of departmentalization in the company? Why was that particular basis of departmentalization used?

8. What kinds of problems might develop in a matrix organization? Why would these problems develop?

Application Exercises

1. Interview the manager of a local service business—a fast-food restaurant. What types of tasks does this manager typically delegate? Is the appropriate authority also delegated in each case?

2. Interview a manager and ask about the informal organization in his or her place of business. What advantages and disadvantages does the manager see with respect to the informal organization? What is the manager's strategy in dealing with the informal organization?

Building Your Business Skills

Getting with the Program

The Purpose of This Assignment

To encourage students to understand the relationship between organizational structure and a company's ability to attract and keep valued employees.

The Situation

You are the founder of a small but growing high-technology company that develops new computer software. With your current workload and new contracts in the pipeline, your business is thriving except for one problem: You cannot find computer programmers for product development. Worse yet, current staff members are being lured away by other high-tech firms. After suffering a particularly discouraging personnel raid in which competitors captured three of your most valued employees, you schedule a meeting with your director of human resources to plan organizational changes designed to encourage worker loyalty. You already pay top dollar, but the continuing exodus tells you that programmers are looking for something more.

Method

Working with three or four classmates, identify some ways in which specific organizational changes might improve the working environment and encourage employee loyalty. As you analyze the following factors, ask yourself the obvious question: If I were a programmer, what organizational changes would encourage me to stay?

Level of job specialization. With many programmers describing their jobs as tedious because of the focus on detail in a narrow work area, what changes, if any, would you make in job specialization? Right now, for instance, few of your programmers have any say in product design.

Decision-making hierarchy. What decision-making authority would encourage people to stay? Is expanding employee authority likely to work better in a centralized or decentralized organization?

Team authority. Can team empowerment make a difference? Taking the point of view of the worker, describe the ideal team.

Intrapreneuring. What can your company do to encourage and reward innovation? (Review the material in Chapter 3 on intrapreneuring before analyzing this factor.)

Questions for Discussion

1. With the average computer programmer earning nearly $70 000 per year and with all competitive firms paying top dollar, why might organizational issues be critical in determining employee loyalty?

2. If you were a programmer, what organizational factors would make a difference to you? Why?

3. As the company founder, how willing would you be to make major organizational changes in light of the shortage of qualified programmers?

Exercising Your Ethics: Team Exercise

To Poach or Not to Poach

The Situation

The Hails Corporation, a manufacturing plant, has recently moved toward an all team-based organization structure. That is, all workers are divided into teams. Each team has the autonomy to divide up the work assigned to it among its individual members. In addition, each team handles its own scheduling for members to take vacations and other time off. The teams also handle the interviews and hiring of new team members when the need arises. Team A has just lost one of its members who moved to another city to be closer to his ailing parents.

The Dilemma

Since moving to the team structure, every time a team has needed new members, it has advertised in the local newspaper and hired someone from outside the company. However, Team A is considering a different approach to fill its opening. Specifically, a key member of another team (Team B) has made it known that she would like to join Team A. She likes the team members, sees the team's work as being enjoyable, and is somewhat bored with her team's current assignment.

The concern is that if Team A chooses this individual to join the team, several problems may occur. For one thing, her current team will clearly be angry with the

▶

members of Team A. Further, "poaching" new team members from other teams inside the plant is likely to become a common occurrence. On the other hand, it seems reasonable that she should have the same opportunity to join Team A as an outsider would. Team A needs to decide how to proceed.

Team Activity

Assemble a group of four students and assign each group member to one of the following roles:

- member of Team A
- member of Team B
- manager of both teams
- investor in Hails Corporation

Action Steps

1. Before discussing the situation with your group, and from the perspective of your assigned role, do you think that the member of Team B should be allowed to join Team A? Write down the reasons for your position.

2. Before discussing the situation with your group, and from the perspective of your assigned role, what are the underlying ethical issues, if any, in this situation? Write down the issues.

3. Gather your group together and reveal, in turn, each member's comments on the situation. Next, reveal the ethical issues listed by each member.

4. Appoint someone to record the main points of agreement and disagreement within the group. How do you explain the results? What accounts for any disagreement?

5. From an ethical standpoint, what does your group conclude is the most appropriate action that should be taken by Hails in this situation? Should Team B's member be allowed to join Team A?

6. Develop a group response to the following questions: Assuming Team A asks the Team B member to join its team, how might it go about minimizing repercussions? Assuming Team A does not ask the Team B member to join its team, how might it go about minimizing repercussions?

For additional cases and exercise material, go to **www.pearsoned.ca/mybusinesslab**.

Concluding Case 9-1

Structure Evolves at Frantic Films

Frantic Films is a Winnipeg-based film and TV production company. Shortly after its founding in 1997, the company was named one of Canada's Hottest 50 Start-Ups by Profit Magazine. By 2004, it ranked #23 on the list of Canada's fastest-growing companies, and in 2005 it ranked #5 on the list of Manitoba's fastest-growing companies. Frantic has also received numerous awards, including the following:

- National Research Council recognition as a Canadian innovation leader
- Lions Gate Innovative Producers Award
- nomination for New Media Visionary Award
- Blizzard Award (for the documentary series *Quest for the Bay*)
- finalist in the Ernst & Young Entrepreneur of the Year award competition (multiple years)

Frantic Films started as a private corporation that was owned and managed by three principal shareholders—Jamie Brown (chief executive officer), Chris Bond (president), and Ken Zorniak (chief operating officer). It originally had three divisions—visual effects, live action, and TV commercials (see Figure 9.8)—but the visual effects division was sold in 2007.

The TV commercial division (Frantic Films Commercial Projects Inc.) produces television commercials for local Winnipeg companies, as well as for national and international clients. It also provides visual effects for commercials produced by other companies. The writers, producers, designers, compositors, animators, and editors create award-winning spots for local, national, and international companies as diverse as the Royal Winnipeg Ballet, the Disney Channel, and Procter & Gamble Canada.

The live action division (Frantic Films Live Action Productions Inc.) produces and owns programs that are broadcast around the world in over 40 countries. The division first develops the ideas for a program, then promotes the idea to broadcasters and financiers. If there is a strong interest, a budget is provided and the division produces the program. Frantic has produced documentary programs such as *Pioneer Quest* (one of the highest-rated documentary series ever broadcast on a Canadian specialty channel), lifestyle series (*'Til Debt Do Us Part*), television movies (*Zeyda and the Hitman*), and feature films (*Lucid*). Once a program is completed, rights are transferred to the releasing company and the individual, single-purpose production companies created for each show are wound up.

Until 2007, the visual effects division (Frantic Films VFX Services Inc.) produced visual effects for TV and movies. Using visual effects software packages such as Maya, Houdini, Digital Fusion, and 3Dstudio Max, the division established a reputation as one of the top visual effects

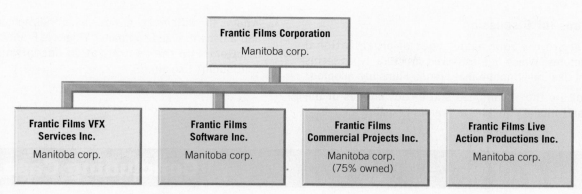

Figure 9.8 Organization chart for Frantic Films.

providers in North America. The majority of the employees at Frantic were in this division. Its output included visual effects for films like *Superman Returns, Stay, X-Men 3, The Italian Job, Catwoman, The Core, Swordfish, Mr. Magorium's Wonder Emporium*, and *Across the Universe*. The division used a matrix structure to complete film projects. This meant that a project team, made up of specialists in areas like 3D animation, 2D animation, compositing, and hardware/software support, was put together. When the project was completed, the team disbanded and its members were assigned to other projects. These teams were typically given specific goals to achieve, and then the team members used their technical expertise to decide how they could best achieve the goal.

Recently, a software division has been created (Frantic Films Software Inc.). It employs seven individuals with specialized expertise, some of whom are computer science grads. When software division employees discovered that off-the-shelf software did not meet their needs, they began creating their own new, stand-alone software to enhance certain visual effects like virtual water and smoke. This software was used to create the fluid-based character Tar Monster in the movie *Scooby-Doo II*.

Each of the divisions at Frantic Films operates fairly independently, but the company is still small enough that individuals from one division sometimes get involved in decisions in other divisions. For example, since the company does not have a marketing vice-president, marketing decisions are often made jointly by Brown, Bond, and Zorniak for each of the divisions.

In 2007, the visual effects division was sold to Prime Focus Ltd., a leader in India's post-production and visual effects services. Office space and a receptionist are now shared with Prime Focus. Jamie Brown says the change will allow the company to get a larger slice of the visual effects pie by pooling its resources with those of Prime Focus. At about the same time as the visual effects division was sold, it was announced that COO Ken Zorniak and President Chris Bond would remain with the company as employees, not owners.

When the company was first formed, the authority structure of the company was quite centralized because the principal shareholders had both the expertise to make decisions and the motivation to do so. But Brown thinks it is important to increase the involvement of lower-level workers in decisions, so he is trying to delegate more authority to them. Some progress has been made in this area. For example, managers in some of the divisions were given the authority to spend up to $5000 without having to get the approval of top management. This change was made because the top managers found that they were spending too much time discussing whether to approve requests for relatively small amounts of money, so they essentially delegated more authority to division managers by giving them the discretion. Brown also encourages employees to make recommendations on various issues to top management. He recognizes that giving employees more discretion can sometimes lead to less-than-optimal decisions, but he also wants to give people more experience in making decisions that affect the company.

Like all rapidly growing companies, Frantic Films has experienced certain "growing pains" with regard to its organizational structure. For example, offices were set up in California and British Columbia to get more visual effects business in those local areas, but until recently, there have not been dedicated salespeople responsible for generating work there. While employees in those offices have been fully employed, they are more costly. The original idea was to have them obtain work that could be sent to the lower-cost Winnipeg office, but more work is being done by a growing workforce in the satellite offices. Top management is now in the process of determining the changes that are needed to make the organization's structure more effective.

Another structural issue is the division of duties between Brown, Bond, and Zorniak. When the company first formed, all three principals were involved in decision making for all the divisions. But as the company grew, each individual gradually became more focussed. For example, Brown had primary responsibility for the live action division, while Zorniak and Bond had primary responsibility for the visual effects division.

Questions for Discussion

1. What are the four basic types of organizational structures? Which of these basic structural types seems most like the structure that Frantic Films has adopted?

2. What are the advantages and disadvantages of the organizational structure at Frantic Films?

3. What is the difference between a centralized company and a decentralized company? Where is Frantic Films positioned on the centralization-decentralization continuum? Explain.

Concluding Case 9-2

Cooking Up a New Structure

A few years ago, Sara Lee CEO John H. Bryan realized that he had a problem. During the 25 years of his tenure, the firm had grown beyond its foundation in food products to encompass dozens of lines of business—everything from cake mixes to insecticide to lingerie. The new businesses were acquisitions, and the original managers controlled each one as if it were a separate company. Calculating the cost of all this duplication, Bryan reached the conclusion that the company could not afford high costs at a time when price competition was heating up.

In an effort to fix things, starting in 1997 Bryan sold or eliminated about one-quarter of the firm's 200 products. He cut redundant factories and the workforce, reduced the number of products, and standardized company-wide processes. He called his extensive restructuring program "deverticalization," and his goal was to remove Sara Lee from manufacturing while strengthening its focus and effectiveness as a marketer. In the meantime, however, he continued to acquire rival firms to sustain the company's growth. Despite Bryan's efforts, Sara Lee continued to suffer from high costs and remained unfocussed and inefficient. Said one industry analyst about Bryan's strategy: "Sometimes, the more chairs you move around, the more dust you see behind the chairs."

In 2000, C. Steven McMillan took over from Bryan at Sara Lee, and in the immortal words of Yogi Berra, "It was déjà vu all over again." McMillan quickly realized that Bryan's moves had had little impact on the firm's performance and that he himself would need to start making some big changes. Borrowing a page from rival Kraft Foods, he began by merging the sales forces that specialized in various brands to create smaller, customer-focussed teams. In meats alone, for instance, Sara Lee had 10 different brands, including Ball Park, Hillshire Farms, Bryan, and Jimmy Dean. "So if you're a Safeway," explained McMillan, "you've got to deal with 10 different organizations and multiple invoices." Teams reduced duplication and were more convenient for buyers—a win-win situation. National retailers like Wal-Mart responded by increasing their orders for Sara Lee products.

McMillan centralized decision making at the firm by shutting down 50 weaker regional brands and reorganizing the firm into three broad product categories: Food and Beverage, Intimates and Underwear, and Household Products. He abolished several layers of corporate hierarchy, including many of the middle managers the firm had inherited from its acquisitions. He created category managers to oversee related lines of business, and the flattened organizational structure led to improved accountability and more centralized control over Sara Lee's far-flung operations.

McMillan also borrowed some tactics from his predecessor, divesting 15 businesses, including Coach leather goods, and laying off 10 percent of his workers. In another move that was widely questioned by industry observers, he paid $2.8 billion for breadmaker Earthgrains. The move increased Sara Lee's market share in baked goods, but many observers felt that McMillan paid too much for a small potential return.

McMillan still had a few tricks up his sleeves. One bold move was developing a chain of retail stores named Inner Self. Each store features a spa-like atmosphere in which to sell Sara Lee's Hanes, Playtex, Bali, and Wonderbra products. Susan Nedved, head of development for Inner Self, thinks that the company-owned stores provide a more realistic and comforting environment for making underwear purchases than do some specialty outlets. "There seems to be an open void for another specialty concept that complements Victoria's Secret," says Nedved. "There was a need for shopping alternatives that really cater to the aging population."

McMillan remains confident that his strategy—more centralization, coordination, and focus—will do the trick at Sara Lee. "I do believe the things we're doing will enhance the growth rate of our company," he says. But many observers are less optimistic. As for Inner Self and underwear, one analyst points out that "even if you fix that business, it's still apparel, and it's not really viewed as a high-value-added business."

Even if McMillan's strategy does manage to cut costs and increase market share, skeptics point out that there is no logic behind the idea of housing baked goods, meats, coffee, underwear, shoe polish, and household cleaners under one corporate roof. Unless McMillan can find some as-yet-undiscovered synergy among such disparate units, Sara Lee is probably headed for a breakup into several smaller, more focussed, more profitable companies.

Questions for Discussion

1. Describe the basic structural components at Sara Lee.
2. What role does specialization play at Sara Lee?
3. What kinds of authority are reflected in this case?
4. What kind of organizational structure does Sara Lee seem to have?
5. What role has the informal organization played in Sara Lee's various acquisitions and divestitures?

Part
Nine

Organizational Culture and Change

Chapter 10

Managing within Cultural Contexts*

After reading this chapter, you should be able to:

1 Explain why a thorough understanding of culture is important for all managers.

2 Explain how culture affects managerial behaviour and practices.

3 Describe the role of fundamental assumptions in corporate, regional, or national cultures.

4 Map aspects of culture in terms of the extent to which they are deeply held and widely shared.

5 Describe the key strategies managers can use to create and change culture.

6 Explain the differences between and describe the implications of high- and low-context cultures.

*Parts of this chapter have been adapted with permission from a chapter written by J. Stewart Black, appearing in J. S. Black, H. Gregersen, M. Mendenhall, and L. Stroh (Eds.), *Globalizing People through International Assignments* (Reading, MA: Addison-Wesley, 1999).

Taken from *Management*, Canadian Edition, by Michael A. Hitt, J. Stewart Black, Lyman W. Porter, and Andrew J. Gaudes.

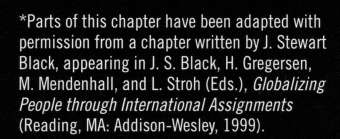

GE Medical's Sick Patient in France

Senior executives at General Electric (GE), in an effort to increase its global strategic position in medical technology, bought France-based Companie Generale de Radiologie (CGR). CGR was owned by the state and manufactured medical equipment with a specific emphasis on X-ray machines and CAT scanners. When GE acquired CGR, it received US$800 million in cash from state-controlled Thomson S.A. in return for GE's RCA consumer electronics business. At the time, the acquisition of CGR was viewed as a brilliant strategic move. Combined with GE's strong position in medical imaging technology in the United States, the acquisition of CGR gave GE an immediate and significant position in Europe. GE executives projected a US$25 million profit for the first full year of operations. However, things did not turn out as the strategic planners projected.

One of the first things managers responsible for the integration did was to organize a training seminar for the French managers. They left T-shirts with the slogan "Go for Number One" for each of the participants. Although the French managers wore them, many were not happy about it. One manager stated, "It was like Hitler was back forcing us to wear uniforms. It was humiliating."

Soon after the takeover, GE executives from Medical Systems headquarters in the United States sent specialists to France to fix CGR's financial control system. Unfortunately, these specialists knew very little about French accounting or financial reporting requirements.

When General Electric (GE) purchased France-based Companie Generale de Radiologie (CGR) to bolster its position in Europe, culture clashes between the two companies were legion. Some GE managers believe that the culture clash sounded a wake-up call to GE not only about its employees abroad, but also about foreign consumers and how they differ from their North American counterparts.

Consequently, they tried to impose a system that was inappropriate for French financial reporting requirements and for the way CGR had traditionally kept records. For example, the two systems differed on what was defined as a cost versus an expense. This cultural conflict (and the working out of an agreeable compromise) took several months and resulted in substantial direct and indirect costs.

GE managers then tried to coordinate and integrate CGR into its Milwaukee-based medical equipment unit in several other ways. For example, because CGR racked up a US$25 million loss instead of the projected US$25 million profit, an executive from Milwaukee was sent to France to turn the operations around. Several cost-cutting measures, including massive layoffs and the closing of roughly half of the 12 CGR plants, shocked the French workforce. Additionally, the profit-hungry culture of GE continued to clash with the state-run, noncompetitive history and culture of CGR.

As a consequence, many valuable managers and engineers left the French subsidiary.

GE managers' efforts to integrate CGR into the GE culture through English-language motivational posters, flying GE flags, and other morale boosters were met with considerable resistance by the French employees. One union leader commented, "They came in here bragging, 'We are GE, we're the best and we've got the methods.'" Although GE officials estimated that GE-CGR would produce a profit in the second year, it lost another US$25 million.

Despite these initial cultural blunders, today GE Medical Systems is one of the strongest global competitors in its field. In fact, some managers believe that the culture clashes experienced in France made everyone aware of the important role that national and organizational cultures play in how people see and react to different events. As a consequence, senior GE Medical Systems managers changed their mental maps to recognize that people do not view the world or management the same everywhere. To facilitate this awareness in others, general cross-cultural training, as well as training specifically in the French business environment and culture, was provided for all employees transferred to France. With this greater awareness of organizational and national culture, GE Medical Systems executives were able to leverage the knowledge and alternative perspectives of managers in the French acquisition into a powerful and globally competitive enterprise. ◆

Sources: Personal communication, 2002; J. S. Black, H. Gregersen, M. Mendenhall and L. Stroh (Eds.), *Globalizing People through International Assignments* (Boston: Addison-Wesley, 1999).

Strategic overview

As the GE Medical Systems example illustrates, even companies that have strong reputations and many years of experience can run aground on unseen cultural reefs as they navigate in today's complex business waters. Culture is important because it is a significant driver of how people see and interpret events and what actions they take. This is true whether the source of the culture is at the national, organizational, or subgroup level. So understanding what constitutes culture and what makes it so powerful in influencing organizations and their performance is important for all managers.

Many people think culture is something an organization, region, or country has—something you can see, hear, touch, smell, or taste. People who take this view often point to clothing, customs, ceremonies, music, historical landmarks, art, and food as examples of culture. For example, you might notice designated parking spots at a company and infer that the culture of the company places high value on status. You might notice that when you exchange business cards with business associates of a given culture they pay very close attention to the title on your card or education qualifications (such as CA or Ph.D.). Based on this observation, you might infer that people from that country place a high value on hierarchy. However, these cultural markers are only the most visible, and in many ways the least powerful, aspects of culture.

Culture can play a major role in organizations, with direct effects on strategic actions chosen by managers and the performance of the strategies selected. For example, most large and many small organizations now sell their goods and services in markets outside their home countries. They also frequently invest in and manage operations in other countries. To sell products in foreign markets and to establish and operate facilities in other countries requires managers to understand the cultures in those countries. Research has shown that most managers who use a strategy of selling their products in foreign markets first market their goods in countries where the cultures are most similar to their domestic environment. It is easier for managers to enter a market where the culture is similar than one which is quite different.[1] They can better understand the similar culture, requiring less adaptation to the customers and employees in that culture. For example, Canadian organizations entering into international markets may first market their products in the United States or England. If the organization is from Quebec and has a strong French influence, it might also market their products in France. As managers gain experience operating in different cultures, they are likely to expand operations to countries where the culture is less similar and thus may operate in many countries. For example, Siemens sells products in 190 different countries and has established 31 separate websites using 38 different languages.[2] To facilitate movement into new international markets, foreign organizations often develop strategic relationships with local organizations. The local business organizations know the culture in those markets, which helps the managers from the foreign company adapt to that culture.[3] Local organizations have contacts with suppliers and government units, but they also can help the managers of their foreign partner learn about and understand the new culture. Developing a better understanding of the culture will help the foreign managers to sell their products in the new market and will also help them to hire and manage the people that they employ in that new market. Thus, as organizations enter more international markets, managers must learn to manage an increasing amount of cultural diversity. That is, they must understand the different cultural values of their customers and employees, respect those differences, and adapt their products and managerial styles to fit the different cultures. An inability to understand and adapt to the local cultures will ultimately produce failure of the international operations. Therefore, success of an international operation hinges on managers understanding cultural differences before they enter foreign markets and adapting their managerial practices thereafter. It also requires that they integrate and use the cultural diversity to their advantage.

Definition of Culture

To appreciate the full importance and impact of culture, we need to take a somewhat complex and broad view of it.[4] Although a team of anthropologists identified over 160 different definitions of culture,[5] we define it as follows: **Culture** is a learned set of assumptions, values, and behaviours that have been accepted as successful enough to be passed on to newcomers. As we mentioned earlier, it is a significant driver of how people see and interpret events and what actions they take.

As the definition suggests, a culture begins when a group of people face a set of challenges. In an organization, the culture might begin to form when the early members face the initial challenges of starting the organization— securing funding, creating products, distributing products to customers, and so on. Early leaders typically have a set of beliefs that guide their behaviours and choices. For example, a leader might believe that tight supervision of employees is best. To the extent that these early decisions and practices work, they typically are retained. This is why early leaders have a significant impact on the exact nature of the company culture.[6] The assumptions, values, and behaviours that are successful are taught to newcomers. In an organization, these newcomers are new hires. In a national culture, newcomers are essentially children born to the group or immigrants who come into the country. So for the newcomers, the culture is learned, not inherited. Culture is taught primarily through symbols and communication, such as stories, speeches, discussions, manuals, novels, poems, art, and so on. Over time, specific assumptions, values, and behaviours come to be shared among the members of the group. However, because circumstances change, what are considered successful responses at one point in time can also evolve and change. As a consequence, culture is adaptive.

With this definition of culture, you can see that the concept potentially can be applied to a group of any size. For example, a large group of people sharing a geographic boundary, such as a country, can have a culture. In fact, many of the studies of culture have used countries as the unit to compare cultural similarities and differences. Within a country, members of the same organization can share an organizational culture. As you might expect, where a smaller group resides within a larger one, such as a company within a country or a work team within a company, research has found that the culture of the smaller group is often influenced by and reflects the culture of the larger group. For example, Japanese companies tend to make decisions by consensus as a reflection of the larger societal cultural value on groups. However, throughout this chapter, whenever we talk about a particular cultural characteristic for a country, region, or company, it is important to keep in mind that there is a distribution of individuals around that characteristic. For example, while Japan as a country tends to have stronger group versus individual orientations, some individuals in Japan are more or less group oriented than the average. Likewise, some Japanese companies may have more or less of a consensus decision-making culture compared to the national culture.

culture A learned set of assumptions, values, and behaviours that have been accepted as successful enough to be passed on to newcomers.

Managerial Relevance of Culture

Before we dive into a deeper understanding of the nature of culture, it may be helpful to first highlight the relevance of culture to you as a manager. Fundamentally, culture is important because it is a strong driver of behaviour. As a consequence, an understanding of culture can be helpful to you in understanding why people behave the way they do and in leveraging culture to help accomplish goals as well as achieve the strategic aims of your organization.

Impact of Culture on Behaviour

As we mentioned, an understanding of culture is critical because culture can dramatically influence important behaviours. For example, culture can influence how people observe and interpret the business world around them.[7] Even when viewing identical situations, culture can influence whether individuals see those situations as opportunities or threats.[8] Culture can lead to different beliefs about the "right" managerial behaviour regarding very specific aspects of management. For example, Swedish managers seldom believe they should have precise answers to most questions subordinates ask, while the vast majority of Japanese managers think they should. Culture can contribute to pre-existing ways of interpreting events, evaluating them, and determining a course of action.[9]

Because culture is not an individual trait but a set of assumptions, values, and beliefs shared by a group, people can and do identify themselves with the culture and the group. To some extent the culture and the group are synonymous in their minds. Research has found that identification with the culture can cause individuals to exert extra effort and make sacrifices to support the culture and the people in it.[10] This means that the greater the extent to which your subordinates identify with the culture of your unit or the company, the harder they are likely to work to make it successful. If culture can significantly influence behaviours, which in turn can influence individual, group, or organizational performance, then it is critical to understand what culture is, how it is formed, and how it can be changed or leveraged.

Cultural Diversity in the Workplace

The impact of culture on perception and behaviour is perhaps more important now than ever before because of the significant increase in cultural diversity you are likely to encounter as a manager. Globalization is a critical factor in this cultural diversity. Even though cultural diversity has always existed among different national, ethnic, regional, and other groups, the globalization of business has increasingly brought that diversity together. As companies globalize and expand operations around the world, they create an increased opportunity and demand for people from different cultures to effectively interact together. One of the key consequences of globalization is that you are much more likely to work with others from a variety of cultural backgrounds. As a result, a thorough understanding of culture—its nature and influence—is a critical component of effective management in these cross-cultural settings.

However, the value of understanding culture is not confined to managers who work in multinational organizations; you do not have to move abroad to encounter cultural diversity. Even if you plan to work in a largely domestic-oriented organization, you will increasingly encounter a culturally diverse workforce and need the ability to understand people with different perspectives and behaviours. To get an idea of the greater cultural diversity you will face, simply consider the following statistics about Canada:[11]

- By 2017, one in five Canadians will be a visible minority (persons other than Aboriginal people that are non-Caucasian in race or non-white in colour), a percentage not seen since the period between 1911 and 1931.

- The highest growth rate for visible minorities will be West Asian, Korean, and Arab, each more than doubling during the period leading up to 2017.

- Nearly half of all visible minorities will be of Chinese and South Asian origin by 2017.

- By the year 2017, young Aboriginal people aged 20 to 29 will increase by 40 percent, which is more than four times the growth rate of the general population of the same age.

These and other statistics point out that as a manager you will encounter an increasingly culturally diverse Canadian workforce. These cultural differences present both challenges and opportunities for managers—challenges that if ignored will have negative consequences for individuals and their organizations, and opportunities that if captured can lead to superior outcomes and organizational competitiveness.

Culture as a Management Tool

Clearly, being an effective manager is not just about understanding others. As we stressed in Chapter 1, managers get paid to accomplish goals with and through other people. Ultimately, as a manager you need to thoroughly understand culture because it can help accomplish your managerial responsibilities. How does culture do this? Since culture is rooted in assumptions and values, once established it guides people's behaviours without overt or constant supervision. For example, as a newcomer to an organization, once you have learned through the words and actions of others that consensus decision making is the "right" way to make decisions in that company, you make decisions that way even if your supervisor is not watching. As we will discuss later in this chapter, while establishing a specific cultural value is not easy, once it is established it serves as a fairly constant guide to and influence on behaviour. An organization's culture can guide what people do and how they do it without you having to monitor and direct your subordinates constantly. This is particularly important with the increasingly complex and geographically dispersed organizations we see today. In many cases, managers may not be present to watch over and direct their people every minute. To the extent that culture can guide behaviour, it can be a powerful management tool.

Culture can also be a powerful means of directing behaviour and accomplishing organizational objectives like outperforming competitors. A recent study conducted by the Massachusetts Institute of Technology found that firms with strong culture had better and more reliable financial performance than firms with weaker cultures. Another study of 160 companies over a 10-year period found companies that outperformed their industry peers excelled in what are called the four primary management practices: (1) strategy, (2) execution, (3) culture, and (4) structure.[12] However, as a manager, you have

Canada and its workforce are becoming more diverse, presenting managers with both challenges and opportunities. By the year 2017, for example, more than one in five Canadians will be a visible minority.

to be careful what you instill as the cultural values. Culture is such a strong force in shaping behaviour that the wrong culture can "lead otherwise good people to do bad things." *A Manager's Challenge: "Overly Aggressive Culture Derails Enron"* helps illustrate this problem. In this example, the culture at Enron stressed the value of achieving growth by any means and at almost any cost. As a consequence, many individuals undertook illegal and unethical actions to keep the company growing or at least make it appear to be growing. As you read this case, you might ask yourself if you have ever been part of an organization whose culture pressured you to make decisions and behave in ways that you thought were wrong. Also, you might put yourself in the shoes of an employee at Enron and ask yourself, "Would Enron's culture have influenced my decisions and ethics?"

Levels of Culture

So far we have talked about culture as though it were a single entity. This is not quite accurate. Culture consists of three distinct but related levels.[13] The structure of these elements is like a tree (see Exhibit 10.1). Some elements are visible. These are often termed **artifacts**, or visible manifestations of a culture such as its art, clothing, food, architecture, and customs. At the beginning of this chapter, we gave the example of designated parking spots as a visible manifestation of an organization's emphasis on status. The base of the culture, like the trunk of a tree, is its values. **Values** are essentially the enduring beliefs that specific conduct or end states are personally or socially preferred to others. However, what holds the tree up is invisible. Most of the components of culture lie below the surface and are hard to see unless you make an effort to uncover them. These are the **assumptions** of the culture, or the beliefs about fundamental aspects of life.

artifacts Visible manifestations of a culture such as its art, clothing, food, architecture, and customs.

values The enduring beliefs that specific conduct or end states are personally or socially preferred to others.

assumptions Beliefs about fundamental aspects of life.

Cultural Assumptions

Understanding cultural assumptions is very relevant and practical for managers. Think of cultural assumptions as the soil in which the overall cultural tree grows. The nature of the soil determines many characteristics of the tree. For example, palm trees need sandy, not clay soil. In contrast, an aspen tree won't grow in the sand. Likewise, certain cultural values and behaviours are only possible with certain underlying cultural assumptions. One of the key implications for managers is that if they understand the fundamental cultural assumptions of a group, they can then begin to understand and even anticipate the values and behaviours of the group. For example, if you know that in the company you just joined hierarchy, or status levels between organization levels, is important, you can anticipate and not be surprised to find that in meetings junior managers (such as yourself) wait for senior managers to speak before sharing their own opinions.

However, we don't want to create the impression that cultural assumptions are deterministic. Even in the natural world different varieties of trees can grow in the same soil. So it is possible for two groups to share the same assumption about hierarchy and exhibit different behaviours. In one group, junior managers only speak after senior managers. In the other group, junior managers never speak in front of senior managers.

Hopefully you can begin to see that although assumptions may seem to be the most abstract level of culture, they are in fact one of the most practical because values and behaviours grow out of assumptions. If you can understand the underlying assumptions, you can begin to understand the types of values

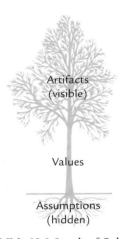

Artifacts
(visible)

Values

Assumptions
(hidden)

Exhibit 10.1 Levels of Culture.

A Manager's Challenge   *Ethics*

Overly Aggressive Culture Derails Enron

While growth is the engine that drives shareholder value, pushing the engine too hard can cause things to overheat and then melt down. Enron's leadership did just that—it fostered a hard-charging culture in which some managers cut ethical and legal corners in the unending quest to report ever-higher earnings. Ultimately, the resulting scandal sent Enron into bankruptcy, put thousands of employees out of work, and drove a major accounting firm out of business.

Under CEO Kenneth Lay, the Houston-based company shifted from its beginnings in oil and natural gas production to a fast-growth strategy aimed at making Enron the "world's greatest energy company." Lay publicly announced extremely ambitious financial targets and promised the workforce stock options that would become increasingly valuable as the company's stock price went up. The message and value were clear: Results matter more than means—what you accomplish matters more than how you do it. "You've got someone at the top saying that the stock price is the most important thing, which is driven by earnings," one insider said. "Whoever could provide earnings quickly would be promoted." Managers' goals, performance measures, compensation, and career advancement were all geared to reinforcing a culture of growth at any price.

This culture was reinforced by selecting people from the outside who fit the company's core values. Jeffrey Skilling was one of the more visible examples of this. He joined Enron as a rising star with a strong entrepreneurial spirit. Knowing that utility customers wanted stable gas costs while gas producers wanted to charge higher prices over time, the Enron division he headed arranged long-term contracts to sell gas to utilities from a pool of suppliers. Instead of using the traditional accounting method to record revenues when received, however, Skilling insisted that Enron record all the expected revenue at the start of each contract. Thanks to this controversial approach, the company's earnings looked significantly better than they actually were, and soon Skilling was promoted to president.

Ironically, higher earnings led management to push for more and more deals so Enron could continue to report improved earnings each quarter. Despite some doubts raised by Arthur Andersen, which audited the company's financial statements, senior managers developed elaborate schemes for making earnings look better while making debt look smaller.

Can a corporation's culture be too strong? Many believe this was the case at Enron. Enron employees were pushed by top managers like CEO Ken Lay (shown in the photo at a senate hearing) and rewarded for delivering bottom-line results—even if it meant crossing ethical and legal boundaries.

Managers also fostered a culture that discouraged any internal objections to questionable activities. In fact, says a former Enron executive, "The whole culture at the vice-president level and above just became a yes-man culture." Personnel practices reinforced this. For example, risk-management employees who had to sign off on potential Enron deals were, in turn, rated by the managers whose deals they were examining. Thus, risk-management employees had a built-in incentive to endorse the deals because performance ratings had a big impact on compensation and job security. Twice a year, management rated each employee as an "A," "B," or "C." The "A" employees received much higher bonuses than the "B" employees; the "C" employees got no bonuses at all—and sometimes were forced to leave the company. Small wonder that few were willing to rock the boat. As one employee put it: "Do you stand up and lose your job?"

But losses began to mount within the special corporate entities, and concerns about Enron's accounting pushed the share price lower and lower. Unable to arrange a merger, the company finally filed for bankruptcy in December 2001. And, as mentioned in Chapter 6, Enron collapsed, Arthur Andersen lost its licence to practise accounting, and Skilling and Lay were convicted of fraud, conspiracy, insider trading, and lying to auditors.

Looking back, experts point to Enron's culture as a major factor in the debacle. Even employees and

▶

managers who felt uneasy about the company's activities went along to avoid conflict. "It was easy to get into, 'Well, everybody else is doing it, so maybe it isn't so bad,'" remembers one ex-Enron employee. Another says: "You do it once, it works, and you do it again. It doesn't take long for the lines to blur between what's legal and what's not."

Sources: "Egg on Enron Faces," *BusinessWeek*, January 12, 2004, p. 80; M. Langbert, "The Enron Mob," *Fortune*, December 22, 2003, p. 9; "The Talent Myth," *New Yorker*, July 22, 2002; J. E. Barnes, M. Barnett, C. H. Schmitt, and M. Lavelle, "How a Titan Came Undone," *U.S. News & World Report*, March 18, 2002, pp. 26+; J. A. Byrne and M. France, "The Environment Was Ripe for Abuse," *BusinessWeek*, February 25, 2002, pp. 118+; K. P. O'Meara, "Enron Board Accused by U.S. Senate Panel," *Insight*, August 19, 2002, pp. 15–17.

and behaviours they support. Without an understanding of assumptions, you might make a number of mistakes in trying to comprehend, change, or even create a new culture. You might mistakenly try to change the existing culture in ways that are not possible because they conflict with the underlying assumptions. For example, if an Australian manager went to Vietnam, she might attempt to reward individual performance, believing it would improve results. However, while Australia has underlying assumptions about the importance of the individual, Vietnam does not. Its cultural assumptions focus on the importance of the group. In fact, in Vietnam, focusing rewards too much on individual performance might actually deliver worse results because people want to fit into the group and not stand out. Without understanding cultural assumptions, you might not recognize that "to change the fruits, you need to change the roots." But we will save a more in-depth discussion of changing culture for later in this chapter.

Most scholars agree that there is a universal category of assumptions represented in all groups.[14] Exhibit 10.2 summarizes these assumptions and provides examples of the specific forms they might take, as well as their management implications.

Humanity's Relationship to the Environment. The first set of assumptions concerns those made about the relationship of humanity to nature. For example, in some groups the cultural assumption is that humans should dominate nature and use it for the wealth and benefit of mankind. In other groups the cultural assumption is that humans and nature should coexist harmoniously. The implications of these differing assumptions can be quite significant. The cultural assumption that people should dominate nature is prevalent in North America and can be seen in structures and industry: damming rivers for electricity, mining iron to make steel for automobiles, or logging trees to make homes. However, the implications of this belief may reach beyond these basic activities to strategic planning or management practices in business as well. Groups that assume humans must subjugate themselves to nature often are characterized by strong notions of fate. As a consequence, the idea of having a strategic planning department may run counter to their belief that it is not possible for humans to dominate something as powerful as the environment.

Human Nature. Different groups also make different assumptions about the nature of people. Some cultures assume people are fundamentally good, while others assume they are inherently evil. You can see the direct influence of this category of assumptions in different organizations. Douglas McGregor captured this notion well in his classic book *The Human Side of Enterprise.*[15] McGregor argued that every manager acted on a theory, or set of assumptions, about people. **Theory X managers** assume that the average human being has an inherent dislike for work and will avoid it if possible. Managers accepting this view of people believe that employees must be

Theory X managers Assume the average human being has an inherent dislike for work and will avoid it if possible.

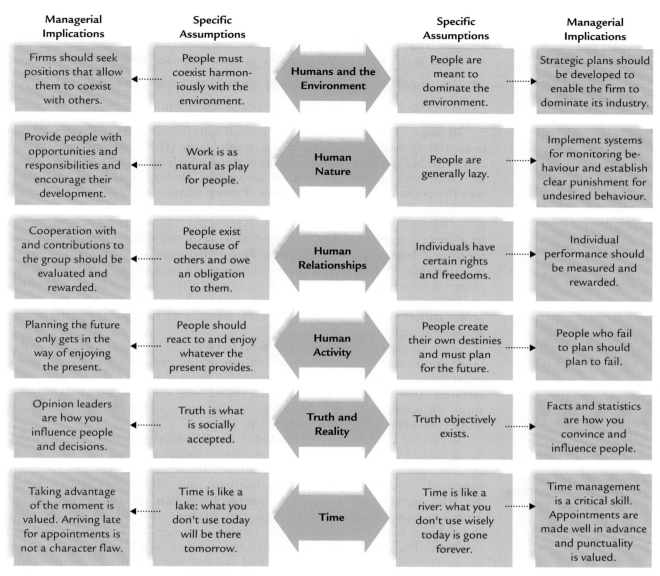

Managerial Implications	Specific Assumptions		Specific Assumptions	Managerial Implications
Firms should seek positions that allow them to coexist with others.	People must coexist harmoniously with the environment.	**Humans and the Environment**	People are meant to dominate the environment.	Strategic plans should be developed to enable the firm to dominate its industry.
Provide people with opportunities and responsibilities and encourage their development.	Work is as natural as play for people.	**Human Nature**	People are generally lazy.	Implement systems for monitoring behaviour and establish clear punishment for undesired behaviour.
Cooperation with and contributions to the group should be evaluated and rewarded.	People exist because of others and owe an obligation to them.	**Human Relationships**	Individuals have certain rights and freedoms.	Individual performance should be measured and rewarded.
Planning the future only gets in the way of enjoying the present.	People should react to and enjoy whatever the present provides.	**Human Activity**	People create their own destinies and must plan for the future.	People who fail to plan should plan to fail.
Opinion leaders are how you influence people and decisions.	Truth is what is socially accepted.	**Truth and Reality**	Truth objectively exists.	Facts and statistics are how you convince and influence people.
Taking advantage of the moment is valued. Arriving late for appointments is not a character flaw.	Time is like a lake: what you don't use today will be there tomorrow.	**Time**	Time is like a river: what you don't use wisely today is gone forever.	Time management is a critical skill. Appointments are made well in advance and punctuality is valued.

Exhibit 10.2 Basic Assumptions and Their Management Implications.

coerced, controlled, directed, and threatened with punishment to get them to strive toward the achievement of organizational objectives. If enough managers in an organization collectively share these assumptions, the organization will have monitoring systems and detailed manuals on exactly what workers' jobs are and exactly how they are to do them. On the other hand, **Theory Y managers** assume that work is as natural as play or rest. Managers accepting this view of people believe that employees exercise self-direction and self-control to accomplish objectives to which they are committed. Commitment to objectives is a function of the rewards associated with their achievement. Organizations in which Theory Y is the dominant assumption would be more likely to involve workers in decision making or even allow them some autonomy and self-direction in their jobs. Research by the GLOBE project has confirmed this cultural dimension and demonstrated that it affects how leaders manage organizations.[16] For example, Hewlett-Packard (HP) is known as an organization with a culture based on more Theory Y assumptions about human nature.[17]

Theory Y managers Assume that work is as natural as play or rest.

Human Relationships. Assumptions about human relationships really deal with a variety of questions:

- What is the right way for people to deal with each other?

- How much power and authority should one person have over another?

- How much should someone be concerned with him- or herself versus others?

power distance The extent to which people accept power and authority differences among people.

In addressing these and other related questions, Geert Hofstede studied over 100 000 employees within a single firm (IBM) across 40 different countries.[18] He found four dimensions along which individuals in these countries differed in terms of human relationships. One of those four dimensions was the construct of power distance. **Power distance** is the extent to which people accept power and authority differences among people. Power distance is not a measure of the extent to which there are power and status differences in a group—most organizations and most societies have richer and poorer, more and less powerful members. Power distance is not the existence or nonexistence of status and power differentials in a society, but rather the extent to which any differences are *accepted*. In Hofstede's study, people from the Philippines, Venezuela, and Mexico had the highest levels of acceptance of power differences. In contrast, Austria, Israel, and Denmark had the lowest levels of acceptance.

Even though North Americans tend to be at the low end of the power distance continuum, the extent to which this assumption exists can vary across organizations. For example, WestJet would be at the lower end of the power distance continuum while Air Canada would be at the higher end. At WestJet, status differentials are minimized while this and other symbols of status are more common and accepted within Air Canada.

individualism The extent to which people base their identities on themselves and are expected to take care of themselves and their immediate families.

A second dimension in Hofstede's study was the extent to which cultures valued individualism or collectivism. **Individualism** can be thought of as the extent to which people base their identities on themselves and are expected to take care of themselves and their immediate families. Hofstede's study found that people from Canada, the United States, Australia, and Great Britain had the highest individual orientations. Individuals from these countries tended to have "I" consciousness and exhibited higher emotional independence from organizations or institutions. They tended to emphasize and reward individual achievement and value individual decisions. **Collectivism** can be thought of as the extent to which identity is a function of the group to which an individual belongs (for example, families, firm members, community members, etc.) and the extent to which group members are expected to look after each other. People from Venezuela, Colombia, and Pakistan had the highest collective orientations. People from these countries tended to have "We" consciousness and exhibited emotional dependence on organizations or institutions to which they belonged. They tended to emphasize group membership and value collective, group decisions.

collectivism The extent to which identity is a function of the group to which an individual belongs.

Once again, even within a society, the extent to which people within organizations share the assumption that individuals matter more than the group or that the group matters more than the individual can vary.

masculine societies Value activities focused on success, money, and possessions.

feminine societies Value activities focused on caring for others and enhancing the quality of life.

Human Activity. Assumptions about human activity concern issues of what is right for people to do and whether they should be active, passive, or fatalistic in these activities. Hofstede's work also addressed this issue. He argued that there were masculine and feminine societies. **Masculine societies** value activities focused on success, money, and possessions. **Feminine societies** value activities focused on caring for others and enhancing the quality of life.

Canada is rated high on the masculine dimension, much like Japan, the United States, and some parts of northern Europe. Workers in these regions believe in phrases such as "people who fail to plan should plan to fail," and "plan the work and work the plan." In other cultures that rated higher on the feminine side, such as Norway and Sweden, emphasis on work is not as great as quality of life and a good work/life balance. Other groups hold the cultural assumption that such preoccupation with planning only gets in the way of enjoying the present.

Truth and Reality. Different groups also form differing assumptions about the nature of reality and truth and how they are verified or established. In many societies, truth is assumed to exist and can be discovered through rigorous examination. In other groups, reality is much more subjective and dependent on what people believe it to be. Consequently, opinion leaders or persuasive stories rather than unshakable facts are used to influence people and business decisions in these cultures.

The famous analogy of the three baseball umpires may serve to illustrate the basic assumptions that people can make about reality and truth. The first umpire stated, "There are balls and there are strikes, and I call them as they are." The second umpire stated, "There are balls and there are strikes, and I call them as I see them." The third umpire stated, "There ain't nothing 'till I call it." Clearly, the nature of the game can change dramatically depending on which umpire is calling the pitch. Have you been in an organization in which the assumption of the first umpire dominated the group? Even if you haven't, you can probably imagine what such an organization would be like.

Hofstede found that cultures differ in the extent to which they need things to be clear or ambiguous. He labelled this **uncertainty avoidance**. Groups high in uncertainty avoidance can be thought of as most comfortable with a first umpire type of culture and least comfortable with a third umpire type of culture. Groups high in uncertainty avoidance create structures and institutions to reduce uncertainty. Groups low in uncertainty avoidance can be thought of as most comfortable with a second or third umpire type of culture and as disliking a first umpire type culture.

uncertainty avoidance The need for things to be clear rather than ambiguous.

Uncertainty Avoidance by Stewart Black
mymanagementlab

Time. Different groups also form differing assumptions about the nature of time. Is time viewed as a river or a lake? Those who view time as a river generally hold linear assumptions about time. Like a river, time moves on in a linear fashion: What you do not take advantage of today will be gone tomorrow. This assumption creates a great emphasis on time management, being punctual for appointments, keeping appointment books, and so on. The phenomenal success of Franklin Quest (now FranklinCovey) through the 1990s, a producer of relatively expensive day planners, is testimony to this orientation in North America. Until the advent of electronic day planners, such as the PalmPilot, Franklin grew at a rate several times that of the general economy. It also enjoyed great success when it expanded into Japan and Korea, two other cultures with linear assumptions about time. In contrast, those who view time as a lake generally hold nonlinear assumptions about time: What you do not dip from the lake today will still be there for you to use tomorrow. This has nearly the opposite effect on management behaviours: being late for an appointment is not seen as a character flaw and setting specific day, hour, and minute schedules is seen as unnecessary.

Hofstede's work also addressed this fundamental assumption. Hofstede found that societies could be segmented based on whether they had a **short-term or long-term orientation**. Short-term–oriented societies tend to view time as a river and focus on immediate results and maximizing time management. Long-term–oriented societies tend to view time as a lake and focus on developing relationships, not expecting immediate results or returns on current efforts.

short-term or long-term orientation Societies that focus on immediate results and those that focus on developing relationships without expecting immediate results.

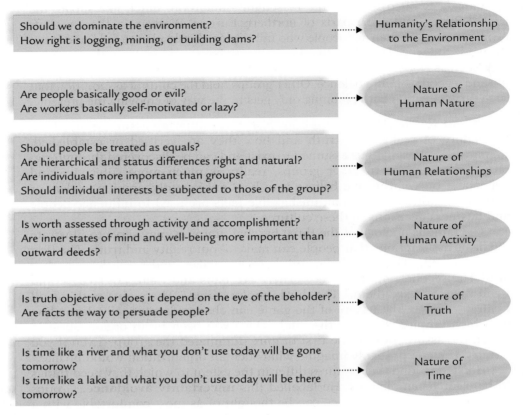

Exhibit 10.3 Questions to Get at Cultural Assumptions.

In spite of its wide acceptance, Hofstede's national culture research has stirred controversy ever since its introduction. Most recently,[19] the underlying assumptions Hofstede made about "culture" as well as the methodology used to collect data and make generalizations have come under scrutiny. Its critics also claim that Hofstede's study erroneously ignores the effects of organizational and occupational culture. Regardless of the criticism and controversy, Hofstede's dimensions of national culture remain widely used and cited in organizational studies.

All groups confront issues represented by these six categories of cultural assumptions. Different organizations can hold differing assumptions; different societies can hold different assumptions. Whether you are trying to understand an organization or a country, you must look at the fundamental assumptions first. In general, this involves asking a general set of questions. Exhibit 10.3 provides illustrative questions for each of the six categories of cultural assumptions. Given that all groups have formed assumptions relative to these six categories, you could use the questions to begin to understand an organization or national culture that is new to you.

Cultural Values

Remember that values are typically defined as enduring beliefs that specific conduct or end states of existence are personally and socially preferred by others.[20] Values are like the trunk of a tree, harder to see than the outline of the branches and leaves from far away but critical to the nourishment and stature of the tree. Fundamentally, values guide behaviour because they define what is good or ought to be and what is bad and ought not to be.

Exhibit 10.4 Classification of Values	
Theoretical people	value the discovery of truth. They are empirical, critical, and rational, aiming to order and systematize their knowledge.
Economic people	value what is useful. They are interested in practical affairs, especially those of business, judging things by their usefulness.
Aesthetic people	value beauty and harmony. They are concerned with grace and symmetry, finding fulfillment in artistic experiences.
Social people	value altruistic and philanthropic love. They are kind, sympathetic, and unselfish, valuing other people as ends in themselves.
Religious people	value unity. They seek communication with the cosmos, mystically relating to its wholeness.

Source: G. W. Allport, P. E. Vernon, and Q. Lindzey, *A Study of Values* (Boston: Houghton Mifflin, 1966).

We can view managerial values as enduring beliefs about specific ways of managing and conducting business that have been deemed successful enough to be passed on. Although some comprehensive frameworks have been proposed for values in general (see Exhibit 10.4 for an early classic), no widely accepted framework for organizing managerial beliefs and values exists. It should also be noted that managers can possess more than one classification at the same time.

Because values address what ought or ought not to be, differences in values often lead to clashes and negative judgments about others. For example, programmers at the 245-employee video game developer Radical Entertainment in Vancouver may play a host of different table games available in their 9000-square-foot employee lounge while trying to solve difficult problems. In contrast, game playing is not likely a common sight in the programming offices of the Canada Revenue Agency's (CRA) Tax Centre in St. John's. Despite their similar jobs (i.e., writing software code), their differing values lead to not only different behaviours, but also assumed attributions about those who are not like them. Radical Entertainment programmers might look on CRA programmers as being boring, dull, and uncreative, and CRA programmers might look on Radical Entertainment programmers as childish or unprofessional.

This tendency to judge different values negatively can be problematic for an organization with operations in multiple countries. For example, Radical Entertainment is one of four integrated studios within Vivendi Games. Massive Entertainment in Sweden is also part of Vivendi's integrated studios, but programmers in Sweden may not play table-top games to help solve problems. What happens when programmers from Massive Entertainment in Malmö, Sweden, have to work on a project with Radical Entertainment's Vancouver programmers? It could be a barrier to productivity if the two sets of programmers do not understand each other and consequently do not trust each other.

Because values define what is good or bad, right or wrong, they not only guide behaviour but are the source of actions that you can see. In part, this is why archeologists and anthropologists seek out artifacts; they hope to find ones that will help them deduce the values of people who are no longer around to observe. In organizations, this is also why artifacts like stories can provide valuable insights into an organization's culture.

Because values guide behaviour, they are critical for any manager to understand. Not recognizing that values could be different even among employees in the same organization can often lead to unproductive clashes among employees.

A company's culture can be the source of strengths, weaknesses, and challenges. What passes for the status quo at Radical Entertainment, such as taking time off to play a table-top game or relax in the log cabin located in the 9000-square-foot employee lounge, is likely taboo in the programming offices of the Canada Revenue Agency. The tendency to judge specific values negatively can be especially problematic within a single organization operating in different countries. Cultural differences from country to country can also pose problems for companies seeking to do business internationally.

Cultural Artifacts and Behaviours

The visible portions of culture are referred to as artifacts and behaviours. In general, the term *"artifact"* is most often associated with physical discoveries that represent an ancient culture and its values, such as buildings, pottery, clothing, tools, food, and art. Archeologists find artifacts when they dig in the jungles and deserts of the world looking for lost civilizations. In modern organizations, important artifacts include such things as office arrangements (individual offices for all versus open offices with no walls), parking arrangements (reserved spaces for some versus open spaces for all), or clothing. Artifacts and behaviours are closely linked. For example, while the clothing worn in an organization or even in a country might be a cultural artifact, wearing a certain style of clothing is a behaviour. But culture can influence behaviours well beyond what to wear. Culture can influence key managerial behaviours, as Exhibit 10.5 illustrates.

Culture A	Managerial Activity	Culture B
Plan for every possible contingency. Develop a plan jointly with boss.	Planning	Accept unexpected surprises. Develop a plan and then seek boss's approval.
Structure department strictly by hierarchy. Communicate frequently face to face and rarely use email.	Organizing	Organize department into free-flowing teams. Communicate infrequently face to face and frequently by email.
Inform subordinates of decisions. Intervene when there are disputes.	Leading	Involve subordinates in decision process. Allow subordinates to solve their own problems.
Closely monitor activities and directly guide behaviour. Emphasize financial results in evaluating performance.	Controlling	Evaluate and then reward based on results. Focus on customer satisfaction in evaluations.

Exhibit 10.5 Culture and Managerial Behaviours.

Cultural Diversity

As a manager, you will encounter greater diversity in organizations in the future. As we mentioned in the beginning of this chapter, diversity comes from two primary sources: (1) increased international activity of organizations and (2) greater diversity in the cultures of employees.

For example, the Organisation for Economic Co-operation and Development (OECD) estimates that there were 1.17 million Canadian-born expatriates residing in other OECD member countries in 2001. The Asia Pacific Foundation of Canada includes both Canadian-born and foreign-born Canadian citizens in their estimate of more than 2.7 million Canadians residing in other countries that same year, or nearly 9 percent of the population.[21] As a consequence, managers in any type of organization need to understand culture in general, and specifically the culture of the countries in which they work and operate. With the globalization of business, there is a greater chance that you will have the opportunity to live and work in a foreign country and experience cultural diversity. However, companies are not just sending people out to their foreign operations; they are also bringing employees into their home-country operations from their foreign subsidiaries. This aspect of globalization also increases the need for an understanding of culture and how it affects people's perspectives and behaviours.

Yet the impact of globalization on cultural diversity is not restricted to employees of a company. Globalization means that as a manager you are increasingly likely to encounter and work with suppliers and customers with different cultural backgrounds. If that weren't enough, new technology has added an interesting twist to the impact of globalization on cultural diversity. New technology now allows people of different cultures to be brought together without ever leaving home. For example, teleconferencing and video conferencing capabilities allow people (employees, suppliers, customers, joint-venture partners, etc.) from all around the world to interact. A lack of understanding of culture can make these interactions less effective because when cultural differences manifest themselves, managers can misinterpret, misunderstand, and as a consequence mistrust each other.[22]

Even if you manage in an organization whose primary focus is domestic, supervisors, peers, and subordinates will not be exactly like you. Differences in age, race, ethnicity, gender, physical abilities, and sexual orientation, as well as work background, income, marital status, military experience, religious beliefs, geographic location, parental status, and education, can all influence the assumptions, values, and behaviours of people.[23] Within an organization, such diversity can enhance competitiveness or, if ignored or unmanaged, lower productivity. As illustrated in Exhibit 10.6, culturally homogeneous groups in

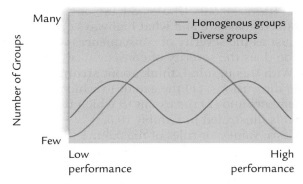

Exhibit 10.6 Effects of Cultural Diversity on Productivity.

Exhibit 10.7   Managing Cultural Diversity for Competitive Advantage

1. Cost	As organizations become more diverse, the cost of a poor job in integrating workers will increase.
2. Resource Acquisition	Companies with the best reputations for managing diversity will win the competition for the best personnel. As the labour pool shrinks and becomes more diverse, this edge will become increasingly important.
3. Marketing	For multinational organizations, the insight and cultural sensitivity that members with roots in other cultures bring should improve marketing efforts.
4. Creativity	Diversity of perspectives and less emphasis on conformity to norms of the past should improve creativity.
5. Problem Solving	Cultural diversity in decision-making and problem-solving groups potentially produces better decisions through consideration of a wider range of and more thorough critical analysis of issues.
6. System Flexibility	Cultural diversity enables the system to be less determinant, less standardized, and therefore more fluid, which will create more flexibility to react to environmental changes.

Source: T. H. Cox and S. Blake, "Managing Cultural Diversity: Implications for Organizational Competitiveness," *Academy of Management Executive* 5, no. 3 (1991), p. 23.

general produce a normal distribution; that is, most groups with culturally similar members produce average results, with a few groups doing quite well and a small minority doing quite poorly. In contrast, most culturally diverse groups either produce significantly worse or superior results with fewer culturally diverse groups producing results in the middle.[24] The culturally diverse teams that did better than culturally similar teams leveraged diverse perspectives, ideas, and innovations into superior performance. The culturally diverse teams that did worse than culturally similar teams were unable to manage the differences among members effectively. This was in part because members of these groups viewed the differences as liabilities rather than assets. Exhibit 10.7 provides a summary of the general arguments for viewing cultural diversity as an asset rather than a liability.

Strong and Weak Cultures

Strong/Weak Culture by Stewart Black

mymanagementlab

strong versus weak cultural values The degree to which the cultural values are shared by organization members.

Culture is not simply the total collection of a group of people's assumptions, values, or artifacts. This is because not all of the assumptions, values, or behaviours are equally influential, nor are they equally shared among members of a group. In other words, their strength varies.

To help in understanding this aspect of culture, think of it in terms of mental road maps and traffic signals. The road map, or culture, tells you what the important and valued goals are and what highways or back roads can get you there. However, just as the severity of consequences for assorted traffic violations varies, so too does the severity of consequences for breaching accepted cultural beliefs. With this in mind, think about **strong versus weak cultural values** along two dimensions: (1) the extent to which they are widely shared among group members and (2) the extent to which they are deeply held. This conceptualization is illustrated in Exhibit 10.8.

The assumptions, values, or rules of the culture that are widely shared and deeply held are generally those that are accompanied by substantial rewards or punishments. For example, an organization that deeply values customer service may provide significant rewards or recognition to employees who take steps to

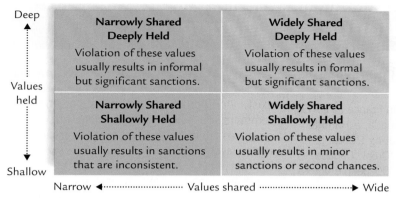

	Deep	
	Narrowly Shared Deeply Held	**Widely Shared Deeply Held**
	Violation of these values usually results in informal but significant sanctions.	Violation of these values usually results in formal but significant sanctions.
Values held	**Narrowly Shared Shallowly Held**	**Widely Shared Shallowly Held**
	Violation of these values usually results in sanctions that are inconsistent.	Violation of these values usually results in minor sanctions or second chances.
	Shallow	

Narrow ◀·················· Values shared ··················▶ Wide

Exhibit 10.8 Matrix of Cultural Strength.

satisfy customers even though their actions are not specifically prescribed in a company manual. Such rewards and recognition would demonstrate the strength of customer satisfaction as a value in the organization's culture and further strengthen that value. *A Manager's Challenge: "The Beauty of L'Oréal Is in Its Employees"* illustrates this even further. As you will read, the value placed upon the employees at L'Oréal Canada creates an environment of support and reward for employees that aspire for upward mobility in the organization.

What about cases in which the value is deeply held but not widely shared? This is perhaps the best definition of a **subculture**. Organization-wide cultures may not develop because the needed conditions, such as consistent reinforcement or time, are not present. Consequently, subcultures can be as common, or in some cases more common, than an overall corporate culture, and in a study conducted in Brazilian companies, subcultural groups have been shown to have a stronger impact on performance than overall corporate culture.[25] For example, while managers in many departments within the Swedish company Ericsson might be comfortable with uncertainty, those in the accounting department are not and operate with a much higher expectation of precision. Subcultures can develop within national cultures as well. For example, in the United Kingdom, belching after a meal is considered by some to be a serious violation of proper behaviour, but this view is not held strongly by all. Consequently, you are unlikely to be put in jail for belching, but you might be cut out of particular social circles if you violate that rule. In other cultures, you may offend a host by *not* belching after a meal because it indicates that you were not satisfied with the meal.

subculture Where values are deeply held but not widely shared.

In the case of widely shared but not deeply held rules, violations of the rules often carry uniform but rather mild punishments. In many cases, infrequent violation of these rules may carry no punishment at all. We might label this a superficial rule because, while it is widely shared, it does not have deep roots. For example, not interrupting people when they are talking to you is a generally accepted rule of conduct in Canada. However, if one occasionally interrupts it is unlikely that this behaviour will be accompanied by any serious punishment.

The importance of conceptualizing cultural values in terms of their strengths is that you then recognize that not all aspects of a culture are created equal. As we will explore shortly, even when we boil culture down to its most fundamental elements, the number of specific assumptions, values, beliefs, rules, behaviours, and customs is nearly infinite. Consequently, trying to learn about all aspects of a new corporate or country culture can be overwhelming. The simplified matrix presented in Exhibit 10.8 provides some mental economy in trying to understand a new culture. This is likely to be of particular relevance to you as you enter a new organization after graduation.

A Manager's Challenge   *Change*

The Beauty of L'Oréal Is in Its Employees

L'Oréal, a company originally established in France in 1909, has a long history in Canada. Cosmair Canada, a Hamilton-based subsidiary of L'Oréal, began distributing L'Oréal products to Canadians in 1958. Today, L'Oréal Canada is headquartered in Montreal, employing 1200 people across the country, including 850 in Montreal. Now the leader in the Canadian cosmetics industry, L'Oréal Canada manufactures and distributes a wide range of products including cosmetics, skin care, sun protection, hair care, and hair colour products.

L'Oréal Canada reports that their success is due to the passionate, enthusiastic, and dedicated people they employ. The company's culture is centred on employee development and professional growth. In order to mould employees to fit the company culture, L'Oréal regularly hires young university graduates who have not yet adopted a corporate culture radically different from their own. Not only does this facilitate learning, it also allows L'Oréal to invest in developing its employees to advance their careers, thereby creating upward mobility and a sense of loyalty to the company. Movement within the company is strongly encouraged as a means of facilitating professional development, whether it is through a change in divisions, professions, or an international transfer.

New recruits undertake a training process that begins with an integration stage that introduces them to L'Oréal's structure, history, strategy, and activities. This stage also functions as a catalyst for new relationships within the company. On-the-job training, which lasts for approximately six months, begins after the integration stage, and is then followed by technical and sales training. The final stage in the training process is the personal and management development stages, which hone management skills and maximize an employee's potential.

Although training ends, the learning never stops at L'Oréal; the company believes in providing its employees with many opportunities to develop professionally and accelerate their careers. Employees are regularly assessed to pinpoint areas where improvement may be needed and where opportunities for career advancement exist. Additionally, communication and management seminars are held in conjunction with various training programs, tailored to the career aspirations and educational levels of the employees. Training is provided via intranet sites, on-site training, and at various management development centres located around the world. For those interested in pursuing post-secondary education, L'Oréal also offers a tuition reimbursement program, further emphasizing the company's commitment to continuous learning.

L'Oréal is also a strong example of well-integrated diversity in the workforce. Employees come from a wide variety of cultures, age groups, and backgrounds, each bringing a different and valuable perspective to the company. Collaboration is encouraged by enabling diverse team structures, which in turn generates creative ideas. In addition to various employee surveys, L'Oréal publishes two in-house newsletters designed to keep employees current on issues and events. Employees are also kept informed by the company's intranet and electronic news screens located throughout the workplace. The Montreal office also provides employees with a coffee bar where they can relax and exchange ideas before work.

L'Oréal offers its employees a flexible benefits package, allowing them to select a plan that best suits their individual needs. Top-up payments for parents taking parental leave, on-site daycare, and Fridays off through the summer are just some of the options that are offered to cater to the needs of young families. Profit sharing, a foosball table in the corporate headquarters lounge, and a wellness program that includes flu shot clinics and skin protection seminars are just a few of the other perquisites of working for L'Oréal Canada. As the leading cosmetics company in Canada, L'Oréal attracts employees who are motivated by competition and have a desire to remain the market leader. In return, L'Oréal can boast a turnover rate of just 2 percent and sales of $747 million in 2007, up 6 percent from the previous year.

Sources: "At a Glance," L'Oréal Canada, www.en.loreal.ca, accessed June 29, 2007; "Our Culture," L'Oréal Canada, www.en.loreal.ca, accessed June 29, 2007; "Ethics and Values," L'Oréal Canada, www.en.loreal.ca, accessed June 29, 2007; "Training and Development," L'Oréal Canada, www.en.loreal.ca, accessed June 29, 2007; "Career Management," L'Oréal Canada, www.en.loreal.ca, accessed June 29, 2007; "Benefits Package," L'Oréal Canada, www.en.loreal.ca, accessed June 29, 2007; Eluta Inc., "Canada's Top 100 Employers 2007: L'Oréal Canada Inc.," www.eluta.ca, accessed June 29, 2007; S. Dougherty, "L'Oréal Canada Invests Serious Time in Each Employee's Potential: Cosmetics Giant Claims Turnover Rate of Just 2% after 3 Years," *Edmonton Journal*, October 14, 2006, p. 15; S. Whittaker, "Good Morale Is More Than a Cosmetic Exercise," working.canada.com, accessed June 29, 2007; A. Pangarkar and T. Kirkwood, "L'Oréal: Selling Learning Internally," www.clomedia.com, accessed June 29, 2007.

Imagine your first day on the job. There are a million things to learn about the culture of the company and therefore how others might expect you to act. Where should you start? First and foremost, because rewards and punishments are greatest for those aspects of culture that are widely shared and deeply held, these values and rules are worth learning early. While true mastery of a culture may require understanding all aspects of the culture, focusing first on the widely shared and deeply held values can facilitate early learning and adjustment. In a practical sense, learning these values first can keep you from making costly mistakes and damaging your job performance and reputation. As a simple example, in some companies coming late to work or leaving early is no big deal. What you accomplish rather than the hours you work is what is valued. In other companies, the fastest way to get your career derailed is to come in late or be seen rushing out the door at 5:00 p.m.

What if you want to be a force for change and improvement in the company? Where should you start (or not start)? To the extent that a specific behaviour is widely shared, deeply held, and directly related to one or more of the six fundamental assumptions, the behaviour will be difficult to change. It might be called a **core value**. If you fail to recognize that you are trying to change a core value, you are likely to make the common mistake of directing too few resources and too little effort at the target of change and as a consequence fail. The point here is not that core values should never change but that if they need to change, the resources directed at the change need to match the requirements.[26]

core value A value that is widely shared and deeply held.

Understanding the core values of a company can also be important when you are looking for a job. As a newcomer to the organization, you should place a premium on making sure that the organization's core values match your own. You are unlikely to be able to change a company's core values and will not be very happy in an organization with core values that clash with yours.

The simple matrix in Exhibit 10.8 can also be of practical value in international business. A business operating in several countries may have to modify its management approach if it conflicts with core values of a foreign country. For example, in North America, most people strongly believe that rewards should be tied to individual behaviour and that they should not be distributed equally among members of a group regardless of individual performance. This belief is supported by deep-rooted assumptions concerning individualism. The success of a company like Wardrop Engineering in Winnipeg can be attributed in part to the cash bonuses paid, which are based upon individual performance and can sometimes increase an employee's salary by more than 50 percent.[27] Imagine the difficulty a firm from a more collectivist country like Japan might have in expanding operations to an individualist country like Canada. In Japan, bonuses are based almost entirely on company performance—everyone at a given rank receives essentially the same bonus, regardless of individual performance. What if Japanese managers tried to implement this type of group or collectivist reward system in Canada? How successful would it be?

Creating and Changing Organization Culture

Since organization culture can be a mechanism for guiding employee behaviour, it is as important as the company's compensation or performance evaluation systems. In fact, to create and reinforce a particular set of values or corporate culture, alignment between the desired values and other systems in the organization, like the compensation system, needs to exist. *A Manager's Challenge: "One Call; That's All"* illustrates how a manager at FedEx managed the demands for cultural change when new technology was introduced in its

A Manager's Challenge   *Technology*

One Call; That's All

In 1998, FedEx saw the internet as an important new technology that could change its business. Management felt that if customers could check on the status of their packages any time of day or night, without having to be put on hold when call centres were busy, they would be even more satisfied. By 1999 the company had created a website where customers could log in and determine the status of their packages.

As customers used the internet and the website to answer basic questions, they increasingly phoned the call centres with more sophisticated questions, along with questions specifically about the website. Unfortunately, call centre reps had no access to the website and were trained in very narrow specialties. Consequently, call centre reps would often pass customers along in a series of call transfers to someone they hoped could answer the customer's question. These transfer calls were often dropped, which frustrated customers. Even when calls were not dropped, customers were still frustrated by what seemed like an endless series of handoffs.

The challenge of changing the technology and its use fell to Laurie Tucker, the manager of all customer service centres. To help senior managers see the basic need for change, she created a short video demonstration for the board. It showed a customer calling in while looking at the website, posing a number of questions while the call centre rep apologized because he could not see the site. Senior management subsequently gave approval for what became known as "OneCall." The vision of OneCall was that a customer should be able, in one call, to get the desired information and not be passed on to someone else.

Call centre reps were initially uneasy about the OneCall vision because they had specialized knowledge and wondered how they could possibly answer all questions a customer might ask. Furthermore, most had little or no experience with the company's website. Not only would reps need web access; they would also need training on how to use the company's website and how to walk people through the site. In addition, call reps had to be cross-trained in various tasks so customers did not get passed along in a frustrating series of handoffs.

Once call reps were given the technology and the training, Tucker and her team also had to change how performance was measured to change the culture from one of specialization to one of full service. Previously, call reps were measured and rewarded on call-time objectives. In other words, the more calls you handled in a day, and therefore, the shorter you made each call, the better. This contradicted the vision of OneCall. As a consequence, the old call-time measures and rewards had to be dropped. Reps were rewarded with bonuses based on customer satisfaction, which included a variety of dimensions such as efficiency, accuracy, and friendliness.

The results of achieving this level of belief were significant. In fact, within a few short months one of the early centres to undergo the transformation generated US$10 million in additional sales from delighted customers. Today, of course, the internet is used by so many businesses, it may sound strange that a company like FedEx once struggled to integrate it effectively. The fact is, however, that new technologies are evolving at an ever-quickening pace, so the same sort of learning and adapting process is constantly ongoing.

Source: A. G. Keane, "Relax, It's a FedEx Ad," *Traffic World*, September 15, 2003, p. 33; personal communication, 2002.

call centres. It also helps illustrate how both performance management and rewards had to be changed to change the culture. As you read this case example, what do you see as the role of technology in changing the culture?

Today's organizations face business environments that are more complicated and more dynamic than perhaps at any other point in history. If an organization tried to create specific policies for all possible situations in such a dynamic environment, the resulting manual would be several phone books thick, and consequently of little practical use. Furthermore, by the time it was printed and distributed, the environment probably would have changed enough to make it obsolete. If, on the other hand, employees could be given a set of assumptions and values to use in assessing situations and determining appropriate actions, then the organization could distribute a simple and short booklet on the company's values and let that guide behaviour. Because of this, organizational culture, which many managers originally thought was a "fluffy" topic, is now being seen as a strategic issue that can have a significant impact on the firm's bottom line.

For example, research has found that the similarity or difference between two organizations forming a joint venture (JV) has a significant impact on the success and performance of the joint venture. The greater the organizational cultural differences between the organizations, the more difficulty the JV has. Also, the more different the managers try to make the JV corporate culture from each of the original partners' culture, the more difficulty the JV has. Successful ventures, however, need not necessarily create an "even" blend of corporate cultures. A study of 17 Hungarian–Western cooperative ventures shows that most have successfully adopted the values, practices, and systems of the Western partner.[28]

But what can managers do to create effective cultures or to change cultures that are ineffective to match the environment? There are at least five critical strategies for effectively managing organizational culture (see Exhibit 10.9). In fact, you can think of them as spokes on a wheel. When all five are in place, the wheel of an organization's culture is much easier to push to where you want it to go.

Selection

One way to create or change a culture is to select individuals whose assumptions, values, and behaviours already match those that you desire. Disney uses this mechanism with great success in creating a culture of "guest" service in its theme parks. In fact, former president of Euro Disney (now called Disneyland Paris) Steve Burke attributes some of that park's early problems to poor selection practices and hiring individuals whose attitudes toward friendly customer service were not compatible with Disney's culture. This was also one of the first things Burke changed upon his arrival in France, which he felt contributed to the dramatic turnaround of the park.[29]

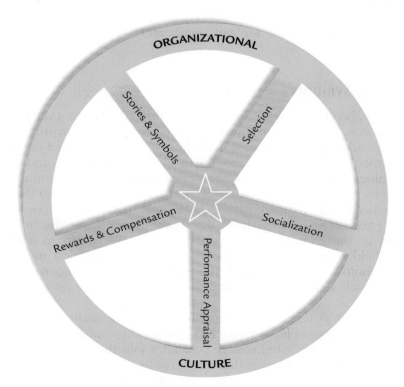

Exhibit 10.9 Strategies to Manage Organizational Culture.

Socialization

Even if selection is not perfect, congruent cultural values can be introduced and reinforced in new hires through socialization. These efforts might include early orientation, training, and arranged interactions with experienced organizational members on a group or individual level. But managers should keep in mind that individuals are not just blank sheets upon which the organization can write whatever cultural scripts it desires. Individuals actively seek out information and try to learn the organization's culture.[30] Consequently, managers should try to facilitate these efforts and monitor them to ensure that individuals are truly coming to a correct understanding of the organization's culture.

Performance Appraisal

Few things signal what the organization values more clearly to newcomers in an organization than what it measures and evaluates. For example, it would do L'Oréal Canada little good to claim that the organization values customer service but then evaluate employees primarily on punctuality.

Rewards and Compensation

Rewards and compensation may be among the most powerful means of signalling what the organization values and reinforcing desired behaviours in newcomers. If we return to the L'Oréal Canada example, it would do the company little good to talk about customer service as a cultural value and then base bonuses on stockroom inventory control. As we explained earlier in this chapter, the best way to get repeat customers who will purchase most of their cosmetics from you is to serve them better than anyone else. As a manager, it is important to remember that although you may not be able to change the formal reward and compensation system of the organization, you directly control many informal rewards that can significantly affect subordinates. For example, what you praise and recognize people for can significantly influence their values and behaviours.

Stories and Symbols

Organizational culture is also created and reinforced through a variety of symbols and stories, which can be a powerful means of communicating company values. Basically, organizational stories tell employees what to do or what not to do. Symbols like physical layout can also communicate and reinforce specific values of the corporate culture. For example, suppose you were hired by Company X and on your first day at work, as you pulled into the parking lot, you noticed that the first two rows of parking spaces were all reserved and that the spaces closest to the front door were reserved for the most senior executives in the company. What values would you begin to suspect the company held relative to hierarchy or participative decision making? You obviously would want more information before drawing final conclusions, but seemingly small symbols can communicate and reinforce an organization's culture.

rituals Symbolic communication of an organization's culture.

Rituals also play a key role in the symbolic communication of an organization's culture. For example, in Japan most major corporations hold a common ritual when their newly hired college graduates join the company. Along with their parents, these new hires gather at a large assembly hall. A representative of the new hires pledges loyalty to the company on their behalf. A representative of all the parents then gives a speech in which he or she commends their children into the company's hands. A senior executive of the company then gives a speech in which he vows on behalf of the company to take care of and continue to nurture these new hires. More effectively than any memo or policy statement, this ritual reinforces the core values of belonging and loyalty.

International Contexts and Cultures

All of the basics of culture that we have covered thus far apply to cultures at a national or local level. However, just as it is sometimes difficult to generalize about an organization-wide corporate culture, so too is it difficult to generalize about national cultures. Important subcultures often exist within the boundaries of a nation. Interestingly, Hofstede's study, which has been criticized because it consisted of subjects from within one company, adds important insights precisely *because* all the subjects are members of the same organization. The organization was IBM, which in general is thought to have a rather strong corporate culture. This strong corporate culture might have dampened the differences across national cultures. Yet, in general, Hofstede found greater differences in cultural values between nationalities than within nationalities.

Perhaps one of the most useful concepts for examining and understanding different cultures is cultural context.[31] **Cultural context** is the degree to which a situation influences behaviour or perception of appropriateness. In high-context cultures, people pay close attention to the situation and its various elements. Key contextual variables are used to determine appropriate and inappropriate behaviour. In low-context cultures, contextual variables have much less impact on the determination of appropriate behaviours. In other words, in low-context cultures the situation may or may not make a difference in what is considered appropriate behaviour, but in high-context cultures the context makes all the difference. For example, in Japan there are five different words for the pronoun "you." The context determines what form of the pronoun "you" would be appropriate in addressing different people. If you are talking to a customer from a large company like Matsushita who holds a significantly higher title than yours and is several years older, you would be expected to use the term *otaku* when addressing the customer. If you were talking to a subordinate who is several years younger than yourself, *kimi* would be the appropriate pronoun. Exhibit 10.10 provides a list of some low- and high-context cultures.

With this in mind, consider some of the issues in managing people who come together from high- and low-context cultures. For example, imagine a team composed of one person each from Canada, Australia, Korea, and Japan. The team meets to discuss a global production problem and report to a senior executive from a client company. For the two individuals from low-context cultures (Canada and Australia), the phrase "Say what you mean and mean what you say" would not only be familiar but would seem right. Consequently, if the senior executive asked if something could be done and the team had already discussed the impossibility of the task, the two team members from the low-context culture would most likely say "no." To say "yes" when you mean "no" would not be right regardless of the fact that a senior executive from a client is in the room. They would likely view someone who would say "yes" when they meant "no" at best with suspicion and at worst as a liar. Yet for the two team members from high-context cultures, the fact that a senior executive from a client is in the room asking the questions makes all the difference in the appropriate response. For them, in this situation saying "yes" when you mean "no" would be entirely appropriate. To say "no" without consideration of the context would be evidence of someone who is

cultural context The degree to which a situation influences behaviour or perception of appropriateness.

High/Low Context Culture by Stewart Black

mymanagementlab

Exhibit 10.10 Low- and High-Context Cultures	
Low-Context Cultures	**High-Context Cultures**
American	Vietnamese
Canadian	Chinese
German	Japanese
Swiss	Korean
Scandinavian	Arab
English	Greek

Source: Adapted from E. Hall, *Beyond Culture* (Garden City, N.Y.: Doubleday, 1976); S. Rosen and O. Shenkar, "Clustering Countries on Attitudinal Dimensions: A Review and Synthesis," *Academy of Management Review* 10, no. 3 (1985), p. 449.

unsophisticated, self-centred, or simply immature. Imagine the consequences if the Canadian replies that what the client is asking for is not possible while the Korean member of the team says it is. Not only would the client be confused, but imagine the attributions that the Canadian and Australian would make about their Japanese and Korean team members and vice versa. Without understanding the influence of cultural context, the trust and effectiveness of the team could break down almost instantly.

From a practical perspective, the key issue is to recognize that neither high-context nor low-context cultures are right or wrong; they are just quite different. These differences can influence a number of important managerial behaviours, including communication, negotiation, decision making, and leadership. While we will examine many of these implications in greater detail in subsequent chapters, *A Manager's Challenge: "When In Rome, How Far Should You Go?"* helps illustrate the concept and some of its implications, by specifically looking at gender stereotypes. It points out that a lack of awareness of this fundamental dimension of cultural differences can lead to misinterpretations, mistaken attributions, mistrust, and ineffectiveness. In contrast, changing yourself and adopting certain behaviours can create goodwill and more effective working relationships. In reading this case, do you think that trying to change oneself and adapt to a new culture can be taken too far? If you were working in a foreign country, which values would be the hardest for you to change?

A Manager's Challenge   *Globalization*

When In Rome, How Far Should You Go?

Women in business face several challenges stemming from gender stereotypes, particularly when conducting business in foreign cultures. The business world remains predominantly male in many countries around the globe, and the idea that women participate in executive positions within a corporation is rarely accepted elsewhere as it is in North America. For example, 57 percent of Canadian women who export their goods or services report having come up against challenges related to their gender. Cultural differences and a lack of respect as business owners are the two most frequently cited reasons for these difficulties when exporting.

To be successful in conducting business abroad, it is essential to learn about and to adapt to cultural differences. Businesswomen should take steps to learn the customs and business etiquette of the country they will be dealing with; this is particularly important when visiting a culture where women do not usually climb to higher corporate positions. Businesswomen should prepare by reading about the culture of the country they will be travelling to. Other travellers can also serve as an excellent source of advice on international business trips.

Respect for local traditions and customs is second only to competence as a necessary ingredient for success abroad. Although there are far fewer women in managerial positions in countries outside North America,

▶

▶

in many countries businesspeople will assume that North American women are competent if they have been sent abroad. Other cultures' opinions of women may sometimes be hard to understand, and might even be offensive, but cultural sensitivity and tolerance should be maintained at all times in an effort to ensure that the business trip is successful.

With careful preparation before departing for a foreign country, there are many ways to break down cultural barriers when conducting business. Greeting a business host in their language is a thoughtful and effective way to show respect during the first meeting. Similarly, distributing business cards with English printed on one side and the host's language printed on the other shows consideration for the other culture while simultaneously communicating rank and position within the company. It should be noted, however, that the appropriate way for handing out and receiving business cards varies significantly between cultures, and should therefore be learned before departure. For example, in China and Japan one should use both hands when accepting a card, whereas in certain parts of the Middle East only the right hand should be used, as the left hand is considered unclean.

As is expected in any business setting, clothing attire should be appropriate and modest; in some cultures the colour of clothing has specific significance. In Japan, for example, red is considered too provocative. Food etiquette is also a necessity and varies significantly between cultures. Specifically, one must learn how to decline food in a polite manner to avoid offending the host.

Of particular concern to businesswomen is how to interact with businessmen in other cultures. Women should be aware that in certain countries businessmen may attempt to flirt with or proposition visiting businesswomen. Instead of becoming offended, it is better to answer with an assertive "no." Another safety measure that women should abide by is to never give out her room

To be successful, managers doing business in another country need not only be competent but also informed about the culture in which they are operating. For example, exchanging business cards is a formal ritual in Asia whereas in North America it's treated more casually.

number, but to plan to meet business contacts in the lobby of the hotel.

All of these recommendations for global businesswomen can be refined down to a few guidelines about working overseas:

1. Learn as much as possible about local and business cultures.
2. Dress conservatively.
3. Be patient.
4. Take cues from those around you.
5. Take advantage of opportunities to socialize.

While all of this advice sounds fine, some women who are faced with conducting business internationally wonder how much they should change and adapt when the local culture is fundamentally different from their own sense of self and from their firm's corporate culture.

Sources: "The Complexities of Women Doing Business Abroad," www.divine.ca, accessed May 17, 2007; Foreign Affairs and International Trade Canada, "Consular Services: Her Own Way: A Woman's Guide to Safe and Successful Travel," August 2006, www.voyage.gc.ca, accessed May 17, 2007, pp. 26–27; R. Bajpai, A. Fung, J. Guyon, P. Hjelt, C. Kano, and R. Tomlinson, "Family Ties," *Fortune*, October 13, 2003, pp. 113–115; S. Taylor, N. Napier Knox, and W. Mayrhofer, "Women in Global Business: Introduction," *International Journal of Human Resource Management*, August 2002, pp. 739–742; K. Melymuka, "Global Woman," *Computerworld*, August 6, 2001, pp. 34–35; Foreign Affairs and International Trade Canada, "Businesswomen in Trade: Research & Stats: Facts and Figures on All Women Exporters," 2002, www.dfait-maeci.gc.ca, accessed May 17, 2007.

Managerial Perspectives Revisited

PERSPECTIVE 1: THE ORGANIZATIONAL CONTEXT The context of the organization plays a central role in the management of culture. As we've pointed out, a strong culture can be an effective influence on daily behaviour even when no one is looking. What the content of that culture should be is largely a function of the organization— what its objectives are, what its history has been, and so on. It is

virtually impossible to say that certain cultural values should be the core ones for every organization. At one organization customer service may be a core value. At another innovation may be a core value. The context of the organization is especially important when cultural change is needed. How entrenched the old culture is constitutes one of the most important factors to understand when contemplating a cultural change. A cultural value that has existed for a long time and has had a history of success can be one of the most difficult elements of an organization to change. This is also true not just for organizations, but for individuals. For example, if you believe in creativity and innovation for the successful management of programmers, and have achieved this through informal "jam sessions" late at night with pizza and rock music, you may have a hard time changing to the more structured approach of programmers in Germany when you are sent there on a special assignment. In this sense, even in the same company, the context of the organizational unit can make all the difference in how even common objectives like innovation are achieved.

PERSPECTIVE 2: THE HUMAN FACTOR Unlike a computer or telephone system, culture only makes a difference with and through people. As a manager, whether you are changing or strengthening a corporate culture, you can only accomplish this by working through people. Part of the challenge is first understanding the different values and beliefs that your employees may have as a function of different family, religious, ethnic, educational, international, or other experiences. If strong organizational cultures are already established then you have to understand where people are today, not just where you want things to be tomorrow. For example, you may want performance to improve, but using individual rewards and recognition may not be the best approach if your subordinates have a strong cultural value regarding groups. In the context of working with peers, subordinates, and even bosses who have different cultural backgrounds from your own, the ability and desire to understand their values and beliefs is critical to determining where common ground might be or what changes might be required of them or you to work effectively together.

PERSPECTIVE 3: MANAGING PARADOXES Respecting cultural differences while trying to foster cooperation for collective achievement is just one of the many paradoxical challenges related to culture. Clearly, insisting on a common culture without understanding or respecting individual or group differences is unlikely to be effective. At the same time, tolerating differences without ensuring some degree of cooperation when needed is also unlikely to produce desired results. This challenge becomes even more acute when individuals from different nationalities and cultures have to work together within an organization. A common culture can provide unifying direction for cross-cultural teams within a company. However, failure to leverage the cultural diversity of the team members could potentially lead to ineffective team decisions and poor performance. How can you balance the dual objectives of integration while simultaneously tolerating cultural differences? Managers who are uncomfortable with this paradox and don't enjoy working through challenges like this are unlikely to be successful in a business world that is increasingly integrated and diverse.

PERSPECTIVE 4: ENTREPRENEURIAL MINDSET An important part of an entrepreneurial mindset is being open to new ideas, opportunities, and perspectives. While this openness is almost always beneficial, it is particularly beneficial in the context of culture. Managers with an entrepreneurial mindset are more likely to be open to and

perceive value in cultural diversity. Diversity in a team setting, for example, should facilitate the development of multiple alternatives and additional opportunities because of the different viewpoints provided by the team's members. An entrepreneurial mindset is also likely to help managers be more open to entering new international markets. This in turn has been shown to provide managers with new technological expertise, which aids them in developing and introducing new products.[32]

Similarly, individuals from different cultures have different behavioural patterns and accomplish tasks differently. This creates other learning opportunities for managers. These learning opportunities can transform managers into innovators and entrepreneurs who will lead their organizations to success. However, absorbing this information and putting it to use requires personal reflection and self-examination. Why? Because understanding people who are different from ourselves, culturally or otherwise, can be challenging.[33] Without a good understanding of your own values and beliefs and why you hold them, the likelihood that you'll realize what others have to offer isn't great.

Concluding Comments

We hope this chapter has demonstrated that what we wear, how we talk, and when we speak are all heavily influenced by cultural assumptions, values, and beliefs. Groups, whether a department, a company, or a country, typically develop a shared set of mental road maps and traffic signals to effectively interact with each other. The managerial challenge relating to culture is three-fold: understanding, changing, and leveraging culture.

In understanding cultures, you should keep in mind that culture consists of assumptions, values, and behaviours and that these elements of a given culture exist because they have been successful in the past. The six basic areas of assumptions that have been presented can facilitate your ability to understand a new culture. This is not to say that every behaviour, custom, or tradition you observe can be traced directly to one of these six categories of assumptions. But many of the fundamental aspects of a culture can be linked to beliefs about humanity's relationship to the environment, human nature, human relationships, human activity, truth and morality, or time. The more widely and deeply the assumptions and values are shared, the stronger the cultural value. The stronger a particular cultural value, the greater the rewards or punishments associated with compliance or non-compliance and the more difficult it is to change.

Changing a culture is always a challenge. Behavioural change and compliance can be achieved with enough monitoring and reinforcement. But doing so will extract a heavy cost of time, energy, and money if the new behaviours are not consistent or compatible with widely shared and strongly held values and assumptions. For example, Japanese executives discontinued wearing traditional kimonos and instead changed to wearing Western clothes in the early 1900s. However, Japanese executives did not adopt Western individualistic values and start wearing all sorts of different styles of business attire. You only need to spend a few moments in any business district in Japan to see that the modern business attire (dark suit, white shirt, modest tie) is as pervasive as traditional kimonos were. Why? Because in Japan people value the group and conforming to it more than individuality. This is a core value, and it has not changed. With this in mind, the challenge in effecting change is to link new desired behaviours to existing values and assumptions. Where this is not possible, old cultural trees—soil, roots, trunk, leaves, and all—must be extracted and replaced with new ones. For most people, this is traumatic, and they usually resist the effort. So to be successful, you must correctly determine not only the behaviour, values, and assumptions that fit with the environmental conditions, but also the change strategy and the amount of *effort needed* to implement it effectively. In addition, the behaviours of those espousing the new culture must be congruent, or in other words, managers must "walk the talk." Employees are quick to pick up on inconsistencies between espoused and actual values and will ignore the "talk" and follow the "walk."[34]

The third challenge lies in using cultural diversity effectively. In today's environment, you will encounter individuals—whether customers, competitors, suppliers, subordinates, bosses, or peers—who have a different cultural background from your own. They will have assumptions, values, beliefs, communication styles, management philosophies, and decision-making processes different from yours. Research suggests that if you simply label those differences as good or bad based on your own assumptions and values, you are not likely to be effective in culturally diverse management situations.[35] If, however, you stop and say, "That's interesting; I wonder why it's that way?" you are more likely to be effective in a diverse environment.

Key Terms

artifacts   (p. 330)
assumptions   (p. 330)
collectivism   (p. 334)
core value   (p. 343)
cultural context   (p. 347)
culture   (p. 327)
feminine societies   (p. 334)

individualism   (p. 334)
masculine societies   (p. 334)
power distance   (p. 334)
rituals   (p. 346)
short-term or long-term orientation   (p. 335)

strong versus weak cultural values   (p. 340)
subculture   (p. 341)
Theory X managers   (p. 332)
Theory Y managers   (p. 333)
uncertainty avoidance   (p. 335)
values   (p. 330)

Test Your Comprehension

1. List three reasons why it is important for you as a manager to have a solid understanding of culture.

2. Define culture.

3. Describe the three levels of culture.

4. What are the key differences between artifacts and assumptions?

5. Describe the six basic assumptions.

6. Do most companies in Canada hold a dominance or harmony assumption regarding humanity's relationship to the environment?

7. What are the key differences between Theory X and Theory Y managers?

8. Define power distance and provide an example of how it affects managerial behaviour.

9. Define individualism and collectivism and provide an example of how they affect managerial behaviour.

10. Would someone from a high-uncertainty-avoidance culture be more likely to believe managers should or

should not have precise answers to questions raised by subordinates?

11. Are individuals who believe "time is a river" more or less likely to be late for appointments?

12. Culturally diverse groups often do significantly better or worse than culturally homogeneous groups. What is the key explanation for this?

13. How does the extent to which cultural values are widely shared and/or deeply held affect the strength or weakness of a culture?

14. What is a subculture?

15. What are two practical reasons for identifying the core values in an organization's or country's culture?

16. What strategies can managers use to create or change culture?

17. What are the key differences between high-context and low-context cultures? How do they affect managerial behaviour?

Apply Your Understanding

1. The stronger an organizational culture, the greater the impact it can have on behaviour; however, the stronger the culture, the more difficult it is to *change*. Unfortunately, the environment changes, and values that fit the environment today may be

inappropriate tomorrow. What can an organization do to keep the positive aspects of a strong culture and still reduce the risk of becoming extinct by not changing its culture fast enough to accommodate environmental shifts?

2. All organizations have cultures. What are the key cultural aspects of your school? What links are there between key assumptions and values and visible artifacts such as clothing, behaviour, or rituals? Compare your school's culture with that of other schools: How do they differ? How are they the same?

3. If you look forward to working with individuals from a variety of cultural backgrounds, or perhaps even working in foreign countries, what can you do to better prepare yourself for those opportunities?

4. What are the key work values you want in an organization you work for? List at least five. How can you assess the extent to which potential employers have these desired values?

Practise Your Capabilities

John Smith accepted a one-year internship to work in a Japanese company in Tokyo. John had studied some Japanese in university but was not yet proficient in the language. Soon after he arrived in Japan, he received a very thorough orientation to the company, including introductions to all the staff in the department to which he was assigned. His job was primarily to edit and proof English correspondence sent to overseas customers and suppliers.

John quickly settled into his job and felt that he was doing well. Still, he felt that despite his efforts to get to know and be friendly with his colleagues, they always seemed a bit cool and standoffish. Then one night one of the younger workers invited him to a group dinner. The group consisted of several younger staff, the assistant manager, and the department manager.

Dinner was a light affair at a local restaurant. Everyone seemed very relaxed and joked with each other and with John. While people spoke mostly in Japanese, everyone, including the assistant and department managers, was careful to chat with John. After dinner the group went to a nearby karaoke bar where they had drinks and sang songs in English. They loved it when John sang "My Way." By the end of the evening, everyone was laughing and joking nonstop. As John left the group to board his train home, he felt that he had finally broken through and become one of the gang.

The next morning he couldn't wait to get to work and enjoy this new level of friendship and personal relationships. He smiled and tried to joke with several colleagues soon after arriving at work, but was stunned when they acted as if the previous evening had not even happened. They were all back to their "business" selves, especially the two managers. Was last night just a chance for them to poke fun at him? Was it all a sham? Were they embarrassed to be seen as friendly with John (a foreigner) in front of people from other departments? Were they all just two-faced hypocrites who could not be trusted?

1. What explains the change in behaviour toward John?

2. What should John do? Should John confront one of his colleagues at work and ask him or her what is going on? Should he just forget it? Should he try to talk with one of the guys after work? Should he give up on trying to become friends?

Part Ten

Accounting and Financial Statements

Chapter 11

Understanding Accounting Issues

After reading this chapter, you should be able to:

1. Explain the role of *accountants* and distinguish among the three types of professional accountants in Canada.

2. Describe how the *accounting equation* is used.

3. Describe three basic *financial statements* and show how they reflect the activity and financial condition of a business.

4. Explain the key standards and principles for reporting financial statements.

5. Explain how computing *financial ratios* can help in analyzing the financial strengths of a business.

6. Explain some of the special issues that arise in *international accounting*.

Taken from *Business*, Seventh Canadian Edition, by Ricky W. Griffin, Ronald J. Ebert, Frederick A. Starke, and Melanie D. Lang.

Accounting for Pensions

Traditional pension plans have historically been defined benefit plans, that is, the company promises to pay a certain defined amount of money to employees when they retire. But the dramatic decline of the stock market in 2008 created large pension short-falls because the market value of the assets that pension plans held declined sharply. The Ontario Teachers' Pension Plan, for example, posted an 18 percent loss in 2008 (the fund's value declined by $21 billion). As of 2008, GM Canada's pension plan was underfunded by more than $6 billion, which means that workers would receive only 50 percent of what they thought they were going to get. The Canada Pension Plan has also been hard hit; during the second quarter of fiscal 2009, the CPP fund declined in value by 6.7 percent ($7.9 billion).

Watson Wyatt Worldwide reported that in 2007 the typical pension plan was 96 percent funded (that is, the market value of a pension plan's assets nearly equalled its liabilities), but in 2008 the typical pension plan was only 69 percent funded. There were predictions that 2009 would be better and that pension fund returns would be about 7.5 percent, but even if that rate of return could be sustained, it would take 15 years for pension funds to return to fully funded status.

There are also problems in funding retiree *benefits* (not pensions). A study of 71 of Canada's largest companies showed that their liabilities for retiree benefits amounted to $16 billion. In one recent year at Suncor Energy Inc., for example, the company's benefits liability was $98 million (almost as much as its pension liability of $99 million). With baby boomers living longer and with large numbers of them heading into retirement, the situation

for both retiree pensions and retiree benefits is likely to get worse before it gets better.

The problems in pension plans have been caused by a variety of factors, but two stand out. First, recent returns on investments held by pension plans have been much lower than anticipated. In the 1990s, returns on pension plan investments averaged 11 percent (higher than the 7.5 percent that had been predicted). But during the economic downturn of 2001–03, the average rate of return for pension plan investments was just 3.1 percent, well below the 7 percent that had been assumed. And during 2008, pension funds *lost* 15 to 30 percent of their value. This situation was made even worse because companies began to invest more heavily in equities as a result of their positive experience in the stock market boom of the 1990s. In 1990, 64 percent of pension assets were invested in fixed-income securities and only 36 percent in the riskier equities. By 2004, however, 56 percent of pension assets were invested in equities and only 37 percent in fixed-income securities.

Second, because pension plan investments had achieved such high returns in the 1990s, many companies took pension plan contribution "holidays" and did not contribute anything to the plans they were sponsoring. When the lower investment returns of the twenty-first century started showing up, pension surpluses quickly became pension

deficits. In retrospect, companies realize they should not have taken contribution holidays.

The crisis in defined benefit pension plans has caused employers to examine alternative ways to deal with pensions. The simplest solution is to drop defined *benefit* pension plans and instead offer employees defined *contribution pension* plans. When the latter is used, the company's liability is known, but the value of the pension plan when a person retires is unknown (its value is determined solely by the rate of return that the investments in the plan have achieved). Defined contribution plans reduce uncertainty for the company, but they create more uncertainty for retirees.

Companies are increasingly shifting to defined contribution pension plans. In the United States, for example, there were 112 000 defined benefit plans in 1985, but now there are only about 29 000. The move away from defined benefit plans is also occurring in Canada, although at a slower rate. But that is likely to change, since Canadian legislation requires companies to bear the full financial burden of pension deficits. The current crisis in defined benefit plans means that, over the next five years, billions of extra dollars will have to be put in to those plans to make up for past investment losses. Companies therefore have an incentive to move away from defined benefit plans and toward defined contribution plans, because with the latter they at least know what their contribution requirements are.

Canadian accounting rules may also need to be re-examined. Under current rules, companies can delay recognizing changes in the value of their pension plans. Using a practice called "smoothing," companies can

▶

spread the reporting of changes over several years. When stock markets were booming, no one scrutinized pension plans much because their value was going up. But when stock markets started dropping, large liabilities began building up (but companies kept that information off their balance sheets). National Bank Financial studied 79 Canadian companies—representing 80 percent of the capitalization of the S&P/TSX—and found that their off-balance sheet pension deficits totalled $21 billion.

Canadian and international accounting regulators are working on changes to accounting rules that will bring more realism to pension reporting. The most obvious change involves ending the practice of smoothing and reporting pension fund returns as they actually take place. This means that income from the pension fund would be reported as investment income and the costs of running the pension fund would be reported as expenses. Regulators recognize that a change like this will increase the volatility in the earnings that corporations report, but they point out that investors will be able to more clearly see what is happening (good or bad) in a company's pension fund. Unfortunately, the economic problems that developed in 2008 made it very difficult to end the practice of smoothing. In fact, companies were given even more time (10 years) to make up for pension shortfalls.

For long-term investors such as the Canada Pension Plan (CPP) Investment Board, understanding how changing regulatory regimes and disruptive technologies could affect a business is critical to the assessment of long-term risk and return. Companies and boards that have yet to examine the quality of their disclosures should undertake this analysis. In a risk-constrained world, their ability to attract stable, long-term capital could depend on it. ◆

How will this
help me?

By understanding the material presented in this chapter, you'll benefit in three ways: (1) If you're an *entrepreneur* thinking about starting your own business, you'll discover your obligations for reporting your firm's financial status; (2) as an *employee*, you'll learn how to evaluate your company's financial condition and its prospects for the future; and (3) as an interested *citizen*, you'll learn about accounting ethics and the regulatory require-ments for maintaining the public's trust in the Canadian business system.

In this chapter, we focus on the development and use of accounting information. We begin by looking at the role of accountants in providing information. We examine how the accounting equation is used in accounting and describe the three basic financial statements. We conclude the chapter with an explanation of the key standards and principles for reporting financial information.

What Is Accounting?

accounting A comprehensive system for collecting, analyzing, and communicating financial information.

bookkeeping Recording accounting transactions.

Accounting is a comprehensive information system for collecting, analyzing, and communicating financial information. As such, it is a system for measuring business performance and translating those measures into information for management decisions. **Bookkeeping** is just one phase of accounting—the recording of accounting transactions. Clearly, accounting is much more comprehensive than bookkeeping because accounting involves more than just the recording of information.

Accounting also uses performance measures to prepare performance reports for owners, the public, and regulatory agencies. To meet these objectives, accountants keep records of such transactions as taxes paid, income received, and expenses incurred, and they analyze the effects of these transactions on particular business activities. By sorting, analyzing, and recording thousands of transactions, accountants can determine how well a business is being managed and how financially strong it is. As the opening case shows, the accounting system can produce distorted results that, in turn, can create huge problems for both owners and managers.

Because businesses engage in many thousands of transactions, ensuring consistent, dependable financial information is mandatory. This is the job of the **accounting information system (AIS)**—an organized procedure for identifying, measuring, recording, and retaining financial information so that it can be used in accounting statements and management reports. The system includes all the people, reports, computers, procedures, and resources for compiling financial transactions.[1]

accounting information system (AIS) An organized procedure for identifying, measuring, recording, and retaining financial information so that it can be used in accounting statements and management reports.

There are numerous users of accounting information:

- *Business managers* use accounting information to set goals, develop plans, set budgets, and evaluate future prospects.

- *Employees and unions* use accounting information to get paid and to plan for and receive such benefits as health care, insurance, vacation time, and retirement pay.

- *Investors and creditors* use accounting information to estimate returns to stockholders, to determine a company's growth prospects, and to decide if the company is a good credit risk before investing or lending.

- *Tax authorities* use accounting information to plan for tax inflows, to determine the tax liabilities of individuals and businesses, and to ensure that correct amounts are paid in a timely fashion.

- *Government regulatory agencies* rely on accounting information to fulfill their duties; the provincial securities commissions, for example, require firms to file financial disclosures so that potential investors have valid information about a company's financial status.

Who Are Accountants and What Do They Do?

At the head of the AIS is the **controller**, who manages all the firm's accounting activities. As chief accounting officer, the controller ensures that the accounting system provides the reports and statements needed for planning, controlling, and decision-making activities. This broad range of activities requires different types of accounting specialists. In this section, we will begin by distinguishing between the two main fields of accounting, *financial* and *managerial*. Then we will discuss the different functions and activities of the three professional accounting groups in Canada.

controller The individual who manages all the firm's accounting activities.

Financial and Managerial Accounting

In any company, two fields of accounting—financial and managerial—can be distinguished by the different users they serve. As we have just seen, it is both convenient and accurate to classify users of accounting information as users outside the company and users inside the company. This same distinction allows us to categorize accounting systems as either *financial* or *managerial*.

Explain the role of *accountants* and distinguish among the three types of professional accountants in Canada.

1

Financial Accounting

A firm's **financial accounting system** is concerned with external users of information—consumer groups, unions, shareholders, and government agencies. It prepares and publishes income statements and balance sheets at regular intervals. All of these documents focus on the activities of *the company as a whole*, rather than on individual departments or divisions.

In reporting data, financial accountants must conform to standard reporting formats and procedures imposed by both the accounting profession and government regulatory agencies. This requirement helps ensure that users can

financial accounting system The process whereby interested groups are kept informed about the financial condition of a firm.

clearly compare information, whether from many different companies or from the same company at different times. The information in such reports is mostly *historical*, that is, it summarizes financial transactions that have occurred during past accounting periods.

Managerial Accounting

managerial (or management) accounting Internal procedures that alert managers to problems and aid them in planning and decision making.

In contrast, **managerial (or management) accounting** serves internal users. Managers at all levels need information to make decisions for their departments, to monitor current projects, and to plan for future activities. Other employees, too, need accounting information. Engineers, for instance, want to know costs for materials and production so they can make product or operations improvements. To set performance goals, salespeople need data on past sales by geographic region. Purchasing agents use information on materials costs to negotiate terms with suppliers.

Reports to these users serve *the company's individual units*, whether departments, projects, plants, or divisions. Internal reports may be designed in any form that will assist internal users in planning, decision making, and controlling. Furthermore, as *projections* and *forecasts* of both financial data and business activities, internal reports are an extremely important part of the management accounting system: They are forward-looking rather than historical in nature.

Professional Accountants

Users of financial statements want to be confident that the accountants who have prepared them have a high level of expertise and credibility. Three professional accounting organizations have developed in Canada to certify accounting expertise.

Chartered Accountants

chartered accountant (CA) An individual who has met certain experience and education requirements and has passed a licensing examination; acts as an outside accountant for other firms.

The Canadian Institute of Chartered Accountants (CICA) grants the **chartered accountant (CA)** designation. To achieve this designation, a person must earn a university degree, then complete an educational program and pass a national exam. About half of all CAs work in CA firms that offer accounting services to the public; the other half work in government or industry. CA firms typically provide audit, tax, and management services (see Table 11.1 for a list of the top 10 CA firms in Canada). CAs focus on external financial reporting, that is, certifying for various interested parties (shareholders, lenders, Canada Customs and Revenue Agency, and so on) that the financial records of a company accurately reflect the true financial condition of the firm. In 2008, there were about 74 000 CAs in Canada.[2]

Certified General Accountants

certified general accountant (CGA) An individual who has completed an education program and passed a national exam; works in private industry or a CGA firm.

The Certified General Accountants Association of Canada grants the **certified general accountant (CGA)** designation. To become a CGA, a person must complete an education program and pass a national exam; to be eligible, a person must have an accounting job with a company. Formerly, CGAs were not allowed to audit the financial statements of publicly held companies, but this is rapidly changing, and now CGAs can audit corporate financial statements in most provinces. Most CGAs work in private companies, but there are a few CGA firms. Some CGAs also work in CA firms. CGAs also focus on external financial reporting and emphasize the use of the computer as a management accounting tool. From time to time, CGA Canada commissions reports on important issues such as pensions (see the opening case). In 2008, there were about 71 000 CGAs in Canada, the Caribbean, and China.[3]

Table 11.1 Top 10 Chartered Accountant Firms in Canada, 2008	
Company	**Annual Revenues (in millions of $)**
1. Deloitte & Touche LLP	$1419
2. KPMG LLP	1122
3. PricewaterhouseCoopers LLP	1062
4. Ernst & Young LLP	856
5. Grant Thornton Canada	442
6. BDO Dunwoody LLP	343
7. Meyers Norris Penhy LLP	260
8. Collins Barrow National Cooperative Inc.	126
9. RSM Richter LLP	117
10. HLB/Schwartz Levitsky Feldman	48

Certified Management Accountants

The Society of Management Accountants of Canada grants the **certified management accountant (CMA)** designation. To achieve the designation, a person must a have university degree, pass a two-part national entrance examination, and complete a strategic leadership program while gaining practical experience in a management accounting environment. CMAs work in organizations of all sizes and focus on applying best management practices in all the operations of a business. CMAs bring a strong market-focus to strategic management and resource deployment, synthesizing and analyzing financial and non-financial information to help organizations maintain a competitive advantage. CMAs emphasize the role of accountants in the planning and overall strategy of the firm in which they work. In 2008, there were about 40 000 CMAs in Canada, with an additional 10 000 students in the program.[4]

certified management accountant (CMA) An individual who has completed a university degree, passed a national examination, and completed a strategic leadership program; works in industry and focuses on internal management accounting.

Accounting Services

CAs and CGAs usually perform several accounting services for their clients. The most common of these are auditing, tax services, and management services.

Auditing

In an **audit**, the accountant examines a company's AIS to determine whether the company's financial reports fairly present its financial operations. Companies normally must provide audited financial reports when applying for loans or when selling stock. The audit will determine whether the firm has controls to prevent errors or fraud from going undetected. Auditors also examine receipts such as shipping documents, cancelled cheques, payroll records, and cash receipts records. In some cases, an auditor may physically check inventories, equipment, or other assets, even if it means descending 200 metres underground in a lead mine.

Detecting fraud is not the primary purpose of audits, but in recent years there has been much publicity about the alleged failure of auditors to detect fraud. Therefore, when audits are being conducted, sometimes **forensic accountants** are used to track down hidden funds in business firms. Because white-collar crime is on the increase, the number of forensic accountants has increased in recent years. Forensic accountants were used to examine Swiss bank accounts for assets deposited by victims of Nazi persecution during the

audit An accountant's examination of a company's financial records to determine whether it used proper procedures to prepare its financial reports.

forensic accountant An accountant who tracks down hidden funds in business firms, usually as part of a criminal investigation.

Business Accountability

Who's Accountable for Offshore Oversight?

Planning on an accounting career for job security? If so, you may want to take a second look at what's happening with business process outsourcing (BPO), which is the use of third parties to perform services that a company would otherwise do internally. Outsourcing is an increasingly popular option for businesses. Universities and hospitals outsource cafeteria operations to food service firms, retailers outsource human resources activities to HR firms, and manufacturing companies outsource shipping and delivery activities to companies like UPS and FedEx. Offshoring is also popular for professional services that have low customer contact and require little customization, such as radiology analysis (e.g., x-rays, CT scans, MRIs), computer software development, and engineering (e.g., product design, testing, and analysis). Worldwide, the outsourcing of finance and accounting services exceeds $40 billion.

The basic philosophy of outsourcing is that businesses do best when they focus on their core activities rather than getting sidetracked into non-core activities. John Gillespie, a partner at Accenture, says that outsourcing of accounting services makes sense because there are a lot of people involved in accounting activities, and there is much routine work that doesn't need to be done by highly paid executives. Accounting's basic number-crunching activities—payroll, accounts receivable, accounts payable, cash accounting, and inventory valuation—are easily outsourced because once the overseas outsourcing provider learns Canadian or U.S. accounting rules, they apply equally to all customers. Data for these activities are transmitted for offshore processing, and results are then transmitted back to the outsourcer.

In addition to cost savings, clients also expect more accurate and faster reporting from outsourcing. On the downside, however, outsourcing increases the risk to data security. Placing private information in faraway hands, especially in the absence of clear-cut legislation on data privacy and security (as in India), increases the chance of violating the client's trust in accounting integrity. In determining what practices to employ for protecting clients, some advocates suggest that, at the very least,

accountants seek clients' permission for using offshore outsourcing. While the accounting profession searches for answers to these outsourcing-related issues, one principle remains clear: The use of third parties in no way diminishes the accountants' accountability for privacy, confidentiality, and security to their clients.

India, with its abundance of well-educated and highly skilled employees, has become the back office of the world. Accounting skills are plentiful, and salaries average just one-fifth of those in Western countries. With over one-third of its university graduates speaking more than two languages fluently, and many speaking as many as six, India is well positioned as an international outsourcing provider. Its Chartered Accountant designation for ensuring professionalism is similar in rigour and esteem to the CPA certification in the United States. The accounting firm Deloitte Touche Tohmatsu forecasts that by 2008 India's financial and accounting services will be boosted by some one million new back-office jobs and technology-related positions, moved there by the world's top 100 financial companies.

While India holds the premier position today in offshore work, other countries—Australia, Ireland, Malaysia, the Philippines, and South Africa—are gearing up with low-cost, high-technology expertise in the battle of accounting outsourcing destinations. Among the brightest contenders, if it can overcome a non-English-speaking tradition, is China, with its population of one billion, rapid economic growth, low-cost labour, and heavy investment in technical education. Its stated goal is to become the world's top outsourcing destination for accounting.

Critical Thinking Questions

1. What factors do you think are most important to consider in deciding which parts of a firm's accounting system, if any, are appropriate for outsourcing?

2. Suppose the accounting firm that prepares your income tax return outsources the work to a third-party tax-service provider overseas. Do you think the accounting firm should get your permission before outsourcing the work? Explain why or why not.

3. What ethical issues, if any, are involved in a decision about outsourcing a firm's accounting activities? Explain.

---

generally accepted accounting principles (GAAP) Standard rules and methods used by accountants in preparing financial reports.

Second World War.[5] Al Rosen, who writes articles about accounting practices, is a well-known Canadian forensic accountant.

One of the auditor's responsibilities is to ensure that the client's accounting system adheres to **generally accepted accounting principles (GAAP)**, a body of theory and procedure developed and monitored by the CICA. At the end of an audit, the auditor will certify whether the client's financial reports

A financial report is an integral component of the financial accounting system.

comply with GAAP. By 2011, Canadian companies will adopt the International Financial Reporting Standards.[6] This will make it easier for investors in other countries to understand the financial statements of Canadian companies, thus making for improved access to global capital markets.

Tax Services

Tax services include helping clients not only with preparing their tax returns but also with their tax planning. Tax laws are complex. A CA's advice can help a business structure (or restructure) its operations and investments and save millions of dollars in taxes. To serve their clients best, of course, accountants must stay abreast of changes in tax laws—no simple matter.

Management Consulting Services

Management consulting services range from personal financial planning to the planning of corporate mergers. Other services include plant layout and design, marketing studies, production scheduling, computer feasibility studies, and design and implementation of accounting systems. Some accounting firms even assist in executive recruitment. Small wonder that the staffs of accounting firms may include engineers, architects, mathematicians, and even psychologists.

management consulting services Specialized accounting services to help managers resolve a variety of problems in finance, production scheduling, and other areas.

Private Accountants

To ensure the fairness of their reports, CAs and CGAs must be independent of the firms they audit. They are employees of accounting firms and provide services for many clients. But businesses also hire their own **private accountants** as salaried employees to deal with the company's day-to-day accounting needs.

Private accountants perform a variety of accounting jobs. An internal auditor at Petro-Canada, for example, might fly to the Hibernia site to confirm the accuracy of oil-flow meters on the offshore drilling platform. But a supervisor responsible for $200 million in monthly accounts payable to vendors and employees may travel no further than the executive suite. The nature of the accounting job thus depends on the specific business and the activities needed to make that business a success. Large businesses employ specialized

private accountant An accountant hired as a salaried employee to deal with a company's day-to-day accounting needs.

Entrepreneurship and New Ventures

New Opportunities in Forensic Accounting

Anyone who watches television knows about the forensic investigations that police officers conduct as they try to catch the bad guys (think *CSI: Miami*). It's pretty interesting stuff. But did you know that forensics is also very relevant to the field of accounting? The numerous corporate financial scandals of the past few years have caused an increase in demand for forensic accountants—individuals who investigate the financial transactions of companies in order to determine whether something fishy is going on. Forensic accountants are also proactive in helping to develop strategies that prevent fraudulent activity from occurring in the first place. In fact, prevention has taken on much greater significance since the Sarbanes-Oxley Act was passed in the United States in 2002. This act requires U.S.-listed companies to analyze their reporting controls and to make any improvements that are necessary. There is also wide speculation that these regulations will soon become mandated in Canada, an effort widely viewed as having major implications for institutions with accounting specializations. This new act will undoubtedly contribute to an increase in demand for specific areas of emphasis within the accounting field.

The CA-designated specialist in investigative and forensic accounting (CA IFA) combines the well-recognized and respected attributes of the CA with an in-depth knowledge and experience in investigative and forensic accounting. This is accomplished through a profession-endorsed certification process that has ongoing experience and education requirements. Individuals who pursue a career in IFA are well positioned to practise in areas such as fraud and economic loss quantification. Some of the responsibilities include testifying as an expert witness, investigating and analyzing financial evidence, and becoming involved in criminal investigations, as well as the rapidly evolving area of computer and internet fraud. If you think that accounting is a less-than-exciting field of study, you may have to rethink your position, given recent developments in forensic accounting. While the work of some accountants is repetitive and routine, the work of forensic accountants is quite varied and compelling.

It is estimated that the number of chartered accountants in Canada who specialize in forensic accounting is rising by as much as 10 percent per year. Exposure to white-collar crime, corporate fraud, and accounting inquiries has escalated for corporations worldwide. In this high-risk business climate, the need for experienced and objective financial and business investigations is critical. According to the latest Kroll Global Fraud Report, companies lost an average of $8.2 million to fraud in the past three years, largely because of the credit crunch and tough economic climate. Blake Coppotelli, senior managing director in Kroll's Business Intelligence & Investigations division, said, "The findings show that fraud is not only widespread but also growing, and we expect to see this increase further as conditions become tougher for business and the full impact of the credit crunch unfolds."

Most of the publicity about financial scandals focuses on large companies, but forensic investigation is needed in businesses of all shapes and sizes. The Atlantic Lottery Corp., for example, hired a forensic accounting firm to review the operations of its small, individually owned lottery retail outlets when reported winnings were higher than statistically possible. That led to widespread concerns that some retailers were cheating by pocketing prizes won by other players, who weren't properly notified of their winnings.

At the other end of the size scale, a major multinational consumer-goods producer became concerned when one of its best-known products began to lose market share in Europe because a competitor was selling its brand at a substantially lower price. Kroll was asked to determine whether the competitor's actions were legitimately supported by lower production costs or whether they reflected unfair market practices. After considerable research, Kroll discovered that the competitor had found a novel means of production that sharply reduced its costs without reducing the quality of its product. Kroll recommended that the company license the technology so that it could also achieve lower costs.

Critical Thinking Questions

1. Visit the Canadian Institute of Chartered Accountants website (www.cica.ca). How much emphasis is placed on forensic accounting? How does a person become a forensic accountant?

2. Interview a forensic accountant and ask the following questions: (a) What general approach do forensic accountants take when investigating the financial statements of companies? (b) What specific techniques are used to determine whether accounting fraud has occurred?

accountants in such areas as budgets, financial planning, internal auditing, payroll, and taxation. Each accounting area has its own challenges and excitement. In small businesses, a single individual may handle all accounting tasks.

The Accounting Equation

All accountants, whether public or private, rely on record keeping. Underlying all record-keeping procedures is the most basic tool of accounting: the **accounting equation**. At various points in the year, accountants use the following equation to balance the data pertaining to financial transactions:

$$\text{Assets} = \text{Liabilities} + \text{Owners' equity}$$

After each transaction (e.g., payments to suppliers, sales to customers, wages to employees, and so on), the accounting equation must be in balance. To understand the importance of this equation, we must first understand the terms *assets*, *liabilities*, and *owners' equity*.[7]

Assets and Liabilities

An **asset** is any economic resource that is expected to benefit a firm or an individual who owns it. Assets include land, buildings, equipment, inventory, and payments due the company (accounts receivable). A **liability** is a debt that the firm owes to an outside party.

Owners' Equity

You may have heard of the equity that a homeowner has in a house—that is, the amount of money that could be made by selling the house and paying off the mortgage. Similarly, **owners' equity** is the amount of money that owners would receive if they sold all of a company's assets and paid all of its liabilities. We can rewrite the accounting equation to highlight this definition:

$$\text{Assets} - \text{Liabilities} = \text{Owners' equity}$$

If a company's assets exceed its liabilities, owners' equity is *positive*; if the company goes out of business, the owners will receive some cash (a gain) after selling assets and paying off liabilities. If liabilities outweigh assets, owners' equity is *negative*; assets are insufficient to pay off all debts. If the company goes out of business, the owners will get no cash and some creditors won't be paid. Owners' equity is meaningful for both investors and lenders. Before lending money to owners, for example, lenders want to know the amount of owners' equity in a business. Owners' equity consists of two sources of capital:

1. The amount that the owners originally invested
2. Profits earned by and reinvested in the company

When a company operates profitably, its assets increase faster than its liabilities. Owners' equity, therefore, will increase if profits are retained in the business instead of paid out as dividends to stockholders. Owners' equity also increases if owners invest more of their own money to increase assets. However, owners' equity can shrink if the company operates at a loss or if owners withdraw assets.

Financial Statements

If your business purchases inventory with cash, you do two things: (1) decrease your cash, and (2) increase your inventory. Similarly, if you purchase supplies on credit, you (1) increase your supplies, and (2) increase your accounts payable. If you invest more money in your business, you (1) increase the company's cash, and (2) increase your owners' equity. In other words, *every transaction affects two accounts*. Accountants thus use a **double-entry accounting system** to record the *dual effects* of financial transactions.

accounting equation The most basic tool of accounting, used to balance the data pertaining to financial transactions: assets = liabilities + owners' equity.

2 Describe how the *accounting equation* is used.

asset Any economic resource that is expected to benefit a firm or an individual who owns it.

liability A debt that the firm owes to an outside party.

owners' equity The amount of money that owners would receive if they sold all of a company's assets and paid all of its liabilities.

3 Describe three basic *financial statements* and show how they reflect the activity and financial condition of a business.

double-entry accounting system A bookkeeping system, developed in the fifteenth century and still in use, that requires every transaction to be entered in two ways—how it affects assets and how it affects liabilities and owners' equity—so that the accounting equation is always in balance.

As we noted earlier, the job of accounting is to summarize the results of a firm's transactions and to issue reports to help managers make informed decisions. Among the most important reports are **financial statements**, which fall into three broad categories—*balance sheets, income statements,* and *statements of cash flows.*[8]

financial statement Any of several types of broad reports regarding a company's financial status; most often used in reference to balance sheets, income statements, and/or statements of cash flows.

Balance Sheets

Balance sheets supply detailed information about the accounting equation factors: assets, liabilities, and owners' equity. Because they also show a firm's financial condition at one point in time, balance sheets are sometimes called *statements of financial position.* Figure 11.1 shows the balance sheet for Perfect Posters.

balance sheets Supply detailed information about the accounting equation factors: assets, liabilities, and owners' equity.

Assets

As we have seen, an asset is any economic resource that a company owns and from which it can expect to derive some future benefit. From an accounting standpoint, most companies have three types of assets: *current, fixed,* and *intangible.*

current assets Cash and other assets that can be converted into cash within a year.

Current Assets. **Current assets** include cash and assets that can be converted into cash within a year. They are normally listed in order of **liquidity**—the ease with which they can be converted into cash. Business debts, for example,

liquidity The ease with which assets can be converted into cash.

o o o o o o o o o	**Perfect Posters, Inc.**
	555 Riverview, Toronto, Ontario

Perfect Posters, Inc.
Balance Sheet
As of December 31, 2009

Assets

Current Assets:		
Cash		$7,050
Marketable securities. . . .		2,300
Accounts receivable.	$26,210	
Less: Allowance of.		
doubtful accounts.	(650)	25,560
Merchandise inventory.		21,250
Prepaid expenses		1,050
Total current assets		**$57,210**
Fixed Assets:		
Land		18,000
Building	65,000	
Less: Accumulated		
depreciation	(22,500)	42,500
Equipment	72,195	
Less: Accumulated		
depreciation	(24,815)	47,380
Total fixed assets. . .		**107,880**
Intangible Assets:		
Patents	7,100	
Trademarks	900	
Total intangible		
assets		**8,000**
Total assets		**$173,090**

Liabilities and Owners' Equity

Current liabilities:		
Accounts payable.	$16,315	
Wages payable.	3,700	
Taxes payable.	1,920	
Total current liabilities		**$21,935**
Long-term liabilities:		
Notes payable, 8%		
due 2010	10,000	
Bonds payable, 9%		
due 2012	30,000	
Total long-term		
liabilities		**40,000**
Total liabilities		**$61,935**
Owners' Equity		
Common stock, $5 par	40,000	
Additional paid-in capital	15,000	
Retained earnings	56,155	
Total owners' equity		**111,155**
Total liabilities and owners' equity . . .		**$173,090**

Figure 11.1 Perfect Posters' balance sheet shows clearly that the firm's total assets equal its total liabilities and owners' equity.

can usually be satisfied only through payments of cash. A company that needs but cannot generate cash (in other words, a company that is not liquid) may thus be forced to sell assets at sacrifice prices or even go out of business.

By definition, cash is completely liquid. *Marketable securities* purchased as short-term investments are slightly less liquid but can be sold quickly if necessary. Marketable securities include stocks or bonds of other companies, government securities, and money market certificates. There are three other important non-liquid assets held by many companies: *accounts receivable*, *merchandise inventory*, and *prepaid expenses*.

Accounts receivable are amounts due from customers who have purchased goods on credit. Most businesses expect to receive payment within 30 days of a sale. In our hypothetical example, the entry labelled *Less: Allowance of doubtful accounts* in Figure 11.1 indicates $650 in receivables that Perfect Posters does not expect to collect. Total accounts receivable assets are decreased accordingly.

Following accounts receivable on the Perfect Posters balance sheet is **merchandise inventory**—the cost of merchandise that has been acquired for sale to customers and is still on hand. Accounting for the value of inventories on the balance sheet is difficult because inventories are flowing in and out throughout the year. Therefore, assumptions must be made about which ones were sold and which ones remain in storage.

Prepaid expenses include supplies on hand and rent paid for the period to come. They are assets because they have been paid for and are available to the company. In all, Perfect Posters' current assets as of December 31, 2009, totalled $57 210.

Fixed Assets. **Fixed assets** (for example, land, buildings, and equipment) have long-term use or value. But as buildings and equipment wear out or become obsolete, their value decreases. To reflect decreasing value, accountants use **depreciation** to spread the cost of an asset over the years of its useful life. Depreciation means calculating an asset's useful life in years, dividing its worth by that many years, and subtracting the resulting amount each year. Each year, therefore, the asset's remaining value decreases on the books. In Figure 11.1, Perfect Posters shows fixed assets of $107 880 after depreciation.

Intangible Assets. Although their worth is hard to set, intangible assets have monetary value. **Intangible assets** usually include the cost of obtaining rights or privileges such as patents, trademarks, copyrights, and franchise fees. **Goodwill** is the amount paid for an existing business beyond the value of its

accounts receivable Amounts due from customers who have purchased goods on credit.

merchandise inventory The cost of merchandise that has been acquired for sale to customers and is still on hand.

prepaid expenses include supplies on hand and rent paid for the period to come.

fixed assets Assets that have long-term use or value to the firm, such as land, buildings, and machinery.

depreciation Distributing the cost of a major asset over the years in which it produces revenues; calculated by each year subtracting the asset's original value divided by the number of years in its productive life.

intangible assets Non-physical assets, such as patents, trademarks, copyrights, and franchise fees, that have economic value but the precise value of which is difficult to calculate.

goodwill The amount paid for an existing business beyond the value of its other assets.

The inventory at this car dealership is part of the company's assets. The cars constitute an economic resource because the firm will benefit financially as it sells them. When they are sold, at the end of the company's accounting period, the dealership will convert the cost of the cars as expenses and show them as costs of goods sold.

other assets. Perfect Posters has no goodwill assets; however, it does own trademarks and patents for specialized storage equipment. These are intangible assets worth $8000. Larger companies, of course, have intangible assets that are worth much more.

Liabilities

current liabilities Debts that must be paid within one year.

Like assets, liabilities are often separated into different categories. **Current liabilities** are debts that must be paid within one year. These include **accounts payable**—unpaid bills to suppliers for materials, as well as wages and taxes that must be paid in the coming year. Perfect Posters has current liabilities of $21 935.

accounts payable Unpaid bills to suppliers for materials, as well as wages and taxes that must be paid in the coming year.

Long-term liabilities are debts that are not due for at least one year. These normally represent borrowed funds on which the company must pay interest. Perfect Posters' long-term liabilities are $40 000.

long-term liabilities Debts that are not due for at least one year.

Owners' Equity

The final section of the balance sheet in Figure 11.1 shows owners' equity broken down into *common stock*, *paid-in capital*, and *retained earnings*. When Perfect Posters was formed, the declared legal value of its common stock was $5 per share. By law, this $40 000 ($5 × 8000 shares) cannot be distributed as dividends. **Paid-in capital** is additional money invested in the firm by its owners. Perfect Posters has $15 000 in paid-in capital.

paid-in capital Additional money invested in the firm by its owners.

retained earnings Net profits minus dividend payments to stockholders.

Retained earnings are net profits minus dividend payments to stockholders. Retained earnings accumulate when profits, which could have been distributed to stockholders, are kept instead for use by the company. At the close of 2009, Perfect Posters had retained earnings of $56 155.

Income Statements

income (profit-and-loss) statement A description of revenues and expenses in a figure showing the firm's annual profit or loss.

The **income statement** is sometimes called a **profit-and-loss statement** because its description of revenues and expenses results in a figure showing the firm's annual profit or loss. In other words,

$$\text{Revenues} - \text{Expenses} = \text{Profit (or loss)}$$

Popularly known as "the bottom line," profit or loss is probably the most important figure in any business enterprise. Figure 11.2 shows the 2009 income statement for Perfect Posters, whose bottom line that year was $12 585. The income statement is divided into three major categories: *revenues, cost of goods sold*, and *operating expenses*.

Revenues

revenues The funds that flow into a business from the sale of goods or services.

When a law firm receives $250 for preparing a will or when a supermarket collects $65 from a customer buying groceries, both are receiving **revenues**—the funds that flow in to a business from the sale of goods or services. In 2009, Perfect Posters reported revenues of $256 425 from the sale of art prints and other posters.

Cost of Goods Sold

cost of goods sold Any expenses directly involved in producing or selling a good or service during a given time period.

In Perfect Posters' income statement, the **cost of goods sold** category shows the costs of obtaining materials to make the products sold during the year. Perfect Posters began 2009 with posters valued at $22 380. Over the year, it spent $103 635 to purchase posters. During 2009, then, the company had $126 015 worth of merchandise available to sell. By the end of the year, it had sold all but $21 250 of those posters, which remained as merchandise inventory. The cost of obtaining the goods sold by the firm was thus $104 765.

```
○○○○○○○○○○○○○○        Perfect Posters, Inc.
                       555 Riverview, Toronto, Ontario
```

Perfect Posters, Inc.
Income Statement
Year ended December 31, 2009

Revenues (gross sales)............			$256,425
Costs of goods sold:			
Merchandise inventory,			
January 1, 2009..............	$22,380		
Merchandise purchases			
during year................	103,635		
Goods available for sale........		$126,015	
Less: Merchandise inventory,			
December 31, 2009.........		21,250	
Cost of goods sold			104,765
Gross profit			**151,660**
Operating expenses:			
Selling and repackaging expenses:			
Salaries and wages........	49,750		
Advertising...............	6,380		
Depreciation—warehouse and ..			
repackaging equipment......	3,350		
Total selling and repackaging			
expenses.................		59,480	
Administrative expenses:			
Salaries and wages..........	55,100		
Supplies...................	4,150		
Utilities...................	3,800		
Depreciation—office equipment .	3,420		
Interest expense................	2,900		
Miscellaneous expenses..........	1,835		
Total administration expenses......		71,205	
Total operating expenses......			**130,685**
Operating income (income before taxes)...			20,975
Income taxes..................			8,390
Net income....................			**$12,585**

Figure 11.2 Perfect Posters' income statement. The final entry on the income statement, the bottom line, reports the firm's profit or loss.

Gross Profit (or Gross Margin). To calculate **gross profit (or gross margin)**, subtract the cost of goods sold from the revenues obtained from goods sold. Perfect Posters' gross profit in 2009 was $151 660 ($256 425 − $104 765). Expressed as a percentage of sales, gross profit is 59.1 percent ($151 660 = $256 425).

Gross profit percentages vary widely across industries. In retailing, Home Depot reports 30 percent; in manufacturing, Harley-Davidson reports 34 percent; and in pharmaceuticals, Wyeth reports 75 percent. For companies with low gross margins, product costs are a big expense. If a company has a high gross margin, it probably has low cost-of-goods-sold but high selling and administrative expenses.

gross profit (or gross margin) A firm's revenues (gross sales) less its cost of goods sold.

Operating Expenses

In addition to costs directly related to acquiring goods, every company has general expenses ranging from erasers to the president's salary. Like cost of goods sold, **operating expenses** are resources that must flow out of a company for it to earn revenues. As you can see in Figure 11.2, Perfect Posters had operating expenses of $130 685 in 2009. This figure consists of $59 480 in selling and repackaging expenses and $71 205 in administrative expenses.

Selling expenses result from activities related to selling the firm's goods or services. These may include salaries for the sales force, delivery costs, and

operating expenses Resources that must flow out of a company for it to earn revenues.

advertising expenses. General and administrative expenses, such as management salaries, insurance expenses, and maintenance costs, are expenses related to the general management of the company.

Operating Income and Net Income. Sometimes managers must determine **operating income**, which compares the gross profit from business operations against operating expenses. This calculation for Perfect Posters ($151 660 – $130 685) reveals an operating income, or income before taxes, of $20 975. Subtracting income taxes from operating income ($20 975 – $8390) reveals **net income** (also called **net profit** or **net earnings**). In 2009, Perfect Posters' net income was $12 585.

operating income Compares the gross profit from business operations against operating expenses.

net income (or net profit or net earnings) A firm's gross profit less its operating expenses and income taxes.

Statement of Cash Flows

Some companies prepare only balance sheets and income statements. However, many firms also report a **statement of cash flows**. This statement describes a company's yearly cash receipts and cash payments. It shows the effects on cash of three business activities:

statement of cash flows A financial statement that describes a firm's generation and use of cash during a given period.

- *Cash flows from operations.* This part of the statement is concerned with the firm's main operating activities: the cash transactions involved in buying and selling goods and services. It reveals how much of the year's profits result from the firm's main line of business (for example, Jaguar's sales of automobiles) rather than from secondary activities (for example, licensing fees a clothing firm paid to Jaguar for using the Jaguar logo on shirts).

- *Cash flows from investing.* This section reports net cash used in or provided by investing. It includes cash receipts and payments from buying and selling stocks, bonds, property, equipment, and other productive assets.

- *Cash flows from financing.* The final section reports net cash from all financing activities. It includes cash inflows from borrowing or issuing stock as well as outflows for payment of dividends and repayment of borrowed money.

The overall change in cash from these three sources provides information to lenders and investors. When creditors and stockholders know how firms

At the end of its accounting period, this pharmaceuticals company will subtract the cost of making the goods that it sold from the revenues received from sales. The difference will be its gross profit (or gross margin). Cost of goods sold does not include the firm's operating expenses, including such selling expenses as advertising and sales commissions. In part, gross margins in the pharmaceuticals industry are high because they do not account for high selling expenses.

obtained and used their funds during the course of a year, it is easier for them to interpret the year-to-year changes in the firm's balance sheet and income statement.

The Budget: An Internal Financial Statement

For planning, controlling, and decision making, the most important internal financial statement is the **budget**—a detailed statement of estimated receipts and expenditures for a period of time in the future. Although that period is usually one year, some companies also prepare budgets for three- or five-year periods, especially when considering major capital expenditures.

budget A detailed financial plan for estimated receipts and expenditures for a period of time in the future, usually one year.

Budgets are also useful for keeping track of weekly or monthly performance. Procter & Gamble, for example, evaluates all of its business units monthly by comparing actual financial results with monthly budgeted amounts. Discrepancies in "actual vs. budget" totals signal potential problems and initiate action to get financial performance back on track.

Although the accounting staff coordinates the budget process, it requires input from many people in the company regarding proposed activities, needed resources, and input sources.[9] Figure 11.3 shows a sample sales budget. In preparing such a budget, the accounting department must obtain from the sales group its projections for units to be sold and expected expenses for each quarter of the coming year. Accountants then draw up the final budget, and throughout the year, the accounting department compares the budget with actual expenditures and revenues.

Reporting Standards and Practices

Accountants follow numerous standard reporting practices and principles when they prepare external reports, including financial statements. The common language dictated by standard practices is designed to give external users confidence in the accuracy and meaning of the information in any financial

Perfect Posters, Inc.
555 Riverview, Toronto, Ontario

Perfect Posters, Inc.
Sales Budget
First Quarter, 2010

	January	February	March	Quarter
Budgeted sales (units)	7,500	6,000	6,500	20,000
Budgeted selling price per unit	$3.50	$3.50	$3.50	$3.50
Budgeted sales revenue	**$26,250**	**$21,000**	**$22,750**	**$70,000**
Expected cash receipts:				
From December sales	$26,210[a]			$26,210
From January sales	17,500[b]	$8,750		26,250
From February sales		14,000	$7,000	21,000
From March sales			15,200	15,200
Total cash receipts:	**$43,710**	**$22,750**	**$22,200**	**$88,660**

[a] This cash from December sales represents a collection of the Account Receivable appearing on the December 31, 2009 Balance Sheet.

[b] The company estimates that two-thirds of each month's sales revenues will result in cash receipts during the same month. The remaining one-third is collected during the following month.

Figure 11.3 Perfect Posters, Inc. sales budget, First Quarter, 2010.

statement. Spelled out in great detail in GAAP, these principles cover a wide range of issues, such as when to recognize revenues from operations, the so-called "matching" of revenues and expenses, and full public disclosure of financial information to the public. Without agreed-upon practices in these and many other accounting categories, users of financial statements would be unable to compare financial information from different companies and thus misunderstand—or be led to misconstrue—a given company's true financial status.

Revenue Recognition

4　Explain the key standards and principles for reporting financial statements.

As we noted earlier, revenues are funds that flow in to a business as a result of its operating activities during the accounting period. *Revenue recognition* is the formal recording and reporting of revenues in the financial statements. Although any firm earns revenues continuously as it makes sales, earnings are not reported until the earnings cycle is completed. This cycle is complete under two conditions:

1. The sale is complete and the product has been delivered.

2. The sale price to the customer has been collected or is collectible (accounts receivable).

The completion of the earning cycle, then, determines the timing for revenue recognition in the firm's financial statements. Revenues are recorded for the accounting period in which sales are completed and collectible (or collected). This practice assures the reader that the statement gives a fair comparison of what was gained for the resources that were given up.

Matching

Net income is calculated by subtracting expenses from revenues. The *matching principle* states that expenses will be matched with revenues to determine net income for an accounting period.[10] Why is this principle important? It permits the user of the statement to see how much net gain resulted from the assets that had to be given up to generate revenues during the period covered in the statement. Consequently, when we match revenue recognition with expense recognition, we get net income for the period.

Consider the hypothetical case of Little Red Wagon Co. Let's see what happens when the books are kept in two different ways:

1. Correct Method: Revenue recognition is matched with expense recognition to determine net income when the earnings cycle is *completed*.

2. Incorrect Method: Revenue recognition occurs *before* the earnings cycle is completed.

Suppose that 500 red wagons are produced and delivered to customers at a sales price of $20 each during 2007. In 2008, 600 red wagons are produced and delivered. In part (A) of Table 11.2, the correct matching method has been used: Revenues are recorded for the accounting period in which sales are completed and collectible from customers, as are the expenses of producing and delivering them. The revenues from sales are matched against the expenses of completing them. By using the matching principle, we see clearly how much better off the company is at the end of each accounting period as a result of that period's operations: It earned $2000 net income for 2007 and $3000 for 2008.

In part (B) of Table 11.2, revenue recognition and the matching principle have been violated. Certain activities of the two accounting periods are disguised and mixed together rather than separated for each period. The result is

Table 11.2   Revenue Recognition and the Matching Principle

(A) The correct method reveals each accounting period's activities and results

	Year ended December 31, 2007	Year ended December 31, 2008
Revenues	$10,000	$12,000
Expenses	8,000	9,000
Net income	2,000	3,000

(B) The incorrect method disguises each accounting period's activities and results

	Year ended December 31, 2007	Year ended December 31, 2008
Revenues	$14,000	$8,000
Expenses	8,000	9,000
Net income	6,000	(1,000)

a distorted performance report that incorrectly shows that 2007 was a better year than 2008. Here's what Little Red Wagon's accountants did wrong: The sales department sold 200 red wagons (with revenues of $4000) to a customer late in 2007. Those *revenues* are included in the $14 000 for 2007. But because the 200 wagons were produced and delivered to the customer in 2008, the *expenses* are recorded, as in (A), for 2008. The result is a distorted picture of operations. It looks as if expenses for 2008 are out of line for such a low sales level, and it looks as if expenses (as compared with revenues) were kept under better control during 2007.

The firm's accountants violated the matching principle by ignoring *the period during which the earnings cycle was completed*. Although $4000 in sales of wagons occurred in 2007, the earnings cycle for those wagons was not completed until they were produced and delivered, which occurred in 2008. Accordingly, both the revenues and expenses for those 200 wagons should have been reported in the same period—namely, in 2008, as was reported in part (A). There, we can see clearly what was gained and what was lost on activities that were completed *in an accounting period*. By requiring this practice, the matching principle provides consistency in reporting and avoids financial distortions.

Full Disclosure

Full disclosure means that financial statements should include not just numbers but also interpretations and explanations by management so that external users can better understand information contained in the statements. Because management knows more about inside events than outsiders, management prepares additional useful information that explains certain events or transactions or discloses the circumstances underlying certain financial results.

Analyzing Financial Statements

Financial statements present a great deal of information, but what does it all mean? How, for example, can statements help investors decide what stock to buy or help managers decide whether to extend credit? Statements provide data, which in turn can be applied to various ratios (comparative numbers). These ratios can then be used to analyze the financial health of one or more companies. They can also be used to check a firm's progress by comparing current and past statements.

> Explain how computing *financial ratios* can help in analyzing the financial strengths of a business.
>
> **5**

Ratios are normally grouped into three major classifications:

- **Solvency ratios**, both short-term and long-term, estimate risk.
- **Profitability ratios** measure potential earnings.
- **Activity ratios** reflect management's use of assets.

Depending on the decisions to be made, a user may apply none, some, or all the ratios in a particular classification.

Solvency Ratios

What are the chances that a borrower will be able to repay a loan and the interest due? This question is first and foremost in the minds of bank lending officers, managers of pension funds and other investors, suppliers, and the borrowing company's own financial managers. Solvency ratios provide measures of the firm's ability to meet its debt obligations.

Short-Term Solvency Ratios

Short-term solvency ratios measure a company's liquidity and its ability to pay immediate debts. The most commonly used ratio is the **current ratio**, which reflects a firm's ability to generate cash to meet obligations through the normal, orderly process of selling inventories and collecting revenues from customers. It is calculated by dividing current assets by current liabilities. The higher a firm's current ratio, the lower the risk to investors. For many years, the guideline was a current ratio of 2:1 or higher—which meant that current assets were at least double current liabilities. More recently, many firms that are financially strong operate with current ratios of less than 2:1.

How does Perfect Posters measure up? Look again at the balance sheet in Figure 11.1. Judging from its current assets and current liabilities at the end of 2009, we see that the company looks like a good credit risk:

$$\frac{\text{Current assets}}{\text{Current liabilities}} = \frac{\$57\ 210}{\$21\ 935} = 2.61$$

Long-Term Solvency

Stakeholders are also concerned about long-term solvency. Has a company been overextended by borrowing so much that it will be unable to repay debts in future years? A firm that can't meet its long-term debt obligations is in danger of collapse or takeover—a risk that makes creditors and investors quite cautious. To evaluate a company's risk of running into this problem, creditors turn to the balance sheet to see the extent to which a firm is financed through borrowed money. Long-term solvency is calculated by dividing **debt**—total liabilities—by owners' equity. The lower a firm's debt, the lower the risk to investors and creditors. Companies with **debt-to-owners'-equity ratios** above 1.0 may be relying too much on debt. In the case of Perfect Posters, we can see from the balance sheet in Figure 11.1 that the debt-to-equity ratio calculates as follows:

$$\frac{\text{Debt}}{\text{Owners' equity}} = \frac{\$61\ 935}{\$111\ 155} = \$0.56$$

Sometimes, high debt can be not only acceptable but also desirable. Borrowing funds gives a firm **leverage**—the ability to make otherwise unaffordable investments. In *leveraged buyouts*, firms have sometimes taken on huge debt in order to get the money to buy out other companies. If owning the purchased company generates profits above the cost of borrowing the

---

solvency ratios Ratios that estimate the financial risk that is evident in a company.

profitability ratios Measures of a firm's overall financial performance in terms of its likely profits; used by investors to assess their probable returns.

activity ratios Measures of how efficiently a firm uses its resources; used by investors to assess their probable returns.

short-term solvency ratios Measure a company's liquidity and its ability to pay immediate debts.

current ratio A form of liquidity ratio calculated as current assets divided by current liabilities.

debt A company's total liabilities.

debt-to-owners'-equity ratio A form of debt ratio calculated as total liabilities divided by owner's equity.

leverage Using borrowed funds to make purchases, thus increasing the user's purchasing power, potential rate of return, and risk of loss.

purchase price, leveraging makes sense. Unfortunately, many buyouts have caused problems because profits fell short of expected levels or because rising interest rates increased payments on the buyer's debt.

Profitability Ratios

Although it is important to know that a company is solvent in both the long term and the short term, safety or risk alone is not an adequate basis for investment decisions. Investors also want some measure of the returns they can expect. Return on equity and earnings per share are two commonly used profitability ratios. (Sometimes these are called *shareholder return ratios* or *performance ratios*.)

Return on Equity

Owners are interested in the net income earned by a business for each dollar invested. **Return on equity** measures this performance by dividing net income (recorded in the income statement, Figure 11.2) by total owners' equity (recorded in the balance sheet, Figure 11.1).[11] For Perfect Posters, the return-on-equity ratio in 2009 can be calculated as follows:

return on equity A form of profitability ratio calculated as net income divided by total owners' equity.

$$\frac{\text{Net income}}{\text{Total owners' equity}} = \frac{\$12\ 585}{\$111\ 155} = 11.3\%$$

Is this figure good or bad? There is no set answer. If Perfect Posters' ratio for 2009 is higher than in previous years, owners and investors should be encouraged. But if 11.3 percent is lower than the ratios of other companies in the same industry, they should be concerned.

Return on Sales

Companies want to generate as much profit as they can from each dollar of sales revenue they receive. The **return on sales** ratio is calculated by dividing net income by sales revenue (see Figure 11.2). For Perfect Posters, the return on sales ratio for 2009 is as follows:

return on sales Calculated by dividing net income by sales revenue.

$$\frac{\text{Net income}}{\text{Sales revenue}} = \frac{\$12\ 585}{\$256\ 425} \times 100 = 4.9\%$$

Is this figure good or bad? Once again, there is no set answer. If Perfect Posters' ratio for 2009 is higher than in previous years, owners and investors should be encouraged, but if 4.9 percent is lower than the ratios of other companies in the same industry, they will likely be concerned.

Earnings per Share

Defined as net income divided by the number of shares of common stock outstanding, **earnings per share** determines the size of the dividend a company can pay to its shareholders. Investors use this ratio to decide whether to buy or sell a company's stock. As the ratio gets higher, the stock value increases, because investors know that the firm can better afford to pay dividends. Naturally, stock will lose market value if the latest financial statements report a decline in earnings per share. For Perfect Posters, we can use the net income total from the income statement in Figure 11.2 to calculate earnings per share as follows:

earnings per share A form of profitability ratio calculated as net income divided by the number of common shares outstanding.

$$\frac{\text{Net income}}{\text{Number of common shares outstanding}} = \frac{\$12\ 585}{\$8\ 000} = \$1.57 \text{ per share}$$

Activity Ratios

The efficiency with which a firm uses resources is linked to profitability. As a potential investor, then, you want to know which company gets more mileage from its resources. Activity ratios measure this efficiency. For example, suppose that two firms use the same amount of resources or assets. If Firm A generates greater profits or sales, it is more efficient and thus has a better activity ratio.

Inventory Turnover Ratio

inventory turnover ratio An activity ratio that measures the average number of times inventory is sold and restocked during the year.

Certain specific measures can be used to explain how one firm earns greater profits than another. One of the most important measures is the **inventory turnover ratio**, which calculates the average number of times that inventory is sold and restocked during the year—that is, how quickly inventory is produced and sold.[12] First, a company needs to know its average inventory—the typical amount of inventory on hand during the year. Average inventory can be calculated by adding end-of-year inventory to beginning-of-year inventory and dividing by two. The company can then calculate the inventory turnover ratio, which is expressed as the cost of goods sold divided by average inventory:

$$\frac{\text{Cost of goods sold}}{\text{Average inventory}} = \frac{\text{Cost of goods sold}}{\text{Beginning inventory} + \text{Ending inventory} \div 2}$$

High inventory turnover ratio means efficient operations. Because a smaller amount of investment is tied up in inventory, the company's funds can be put to work elsewhere to earn greater returns. However, inventory turnover must be compared with both prior years and industry averages. An inventory turnover rate of 5, for example, might be excellent for an auto supply store, but it would be disastrous for a supermarket, where a rate of about 15 is common. Rates can also vary within a company that markets a variety of products. To calculate Perfect Posters' inventory turnover ratio for 2009, we take the merchandise inventory figures for the income statement in Figure 11.2. The ratio can be expressed as follows:

$$\frac{\$104\ 765}{(\$22\ 380 + \$21\ 250) \div 2} = 4.8 \text{ times}$$

The inventory turnover ratio measures the average number of times that a store sells and restocks its inventory in one year. The higher the ratio, the more products that get sold and the more revenue that comes in. Supermarkets must have a higher turnover ratio than, say, auto supply or toy stores. In almost all retail stores, products with the highest ratios get the shelf spaces that generate the most customer traffic and sales.

In other words, new merchandise replaces old merchandise every 76 days (365 days divided by 4.8). The 4.8 ratio is below the average of 7.0 for comparable wholesaling operations, indicating that the business is slightly inefficient.

International Accounting

Many companies, such as McCain Foods, Sabian Cymbals, and Electrovert Ltd., receive large portions of their operating revenues from foreign sales. As well, Canadian companies purchase components from foreign countries. Retailers such as Sears buy merchandise from other countries for sale in Canada. In addition, more and more companies own subsidiaries in foreign countries. With all this international activity, there is obviously a need to keep track of foreign transactions. One of the most basic accounting needs is translating the values of the currencies of different countries.

> Explain some of the special issues that arise in *international accounting.*   **6**

Foreign Currency Exchange

A unique consideration in international accounting is the value of currencies and their exchange rates. The value of any country's currency is subject to occasional change. Political and economic conditions, for instance, affect the stability of a nation's currency and its value relative to the currencies of other countries.

As the currency is traded around the world, market forces determine the currency's value—what buyers are willing to pay for it. The resulting values are called **foreign currency exchange rates**. When a currency becomes unstable—that is, when its value changes frequently—it is regarded as a *weak currency*. The value of the Brazilian real, for example, fluctuated between 0.416 and 0.957—a variation of 130 percent in U.S. dollars—during the period from 1997 to 2002. On the other hand, a *strong currency* historically rises or holds steady in comparison to other currencies.

foreign currency exchange rates What buyers are willing to pay for a given currency.

As changes in exchange rates occur, they must be considered by accountants when recording international transactions. They will affect, perhaps profoundly, the amount that a firm pays for foreign purchases and the amount it gains from sales to foreign buyers.

International Transactions

International purchases, credit sales, and accounting for foreign subsidiaries all involve transactions affected by exchange rates. When a Canadian company imports Bordeaux wine from the French company Pierre Bourgeois, the Canadian company's accountant must be sure that the company's books reflect its true costs. The amount owed to Pierre Bourgeois changes daily along with the exchange rate between euros and Canadian dollars. Thus, the accountant must identify the actual rate *on the day that payment in euros is made* so that the correct Canadian-dollar cost of the purchase is recorded.

"It's up to you now, Miller. The only thing that can save us is an accounting breakthrough."

International Accounting Standards

Professional accounting groups from about 80 countries are members of the International Accounting Standards Board (IASB), which is trying to eliminate national differences in financial reporting procedures.[13] Bankers, investors, and managers want procedures that are comparable from country to country and applicable to all firms regardless of home nation. Standardization is occurring in some areas but is far from universal. IASB financial statements include an income statement, balance sheet, and statement of cash flows similar to those issued by Canadian and U.S. accountants. International standards, however, do not require a uniform format, and variety abounds.

The Greening of Business

The Green Revolution Hits Accounting

If you are asked to think about ways that business firms can reduce the negative impact of their activities on the environment, you're probably most likely to think about changes that companies could make to their production processes that would reduce water or air pollution. But changes can be made in all areas of a business, including the accounting area. In accounting, for example, there is at least one important activity that affects the environment, and that is the use of paper for all those financial statements. The electronic revolution has provided the opportunity to substantially reduce the use of paper, while at the same time making it easier for clients and managers to deal with accounting information. A paperless system not only reduces waste and allows accountants to quickly respond to clients, but it also reduces the overhead of storage, tracking, and accessing documents. With the flexibility of an electronic system, accountants can work virtually anywhere in the world, as long as there is an internet connection available.

For example, traditional accounting firms are spending increasing amounts of valuable time on handling paperwork, such as invoices. The paperless system solution eliminates the need to store paper invoices, by storing their digital images and retrieving the images as needed. Now the firm has easier access to more data, facilitating analyses that save it thousands of dollars.

There are real incentives for companies to embrace environmentally friendly business practices like saving paper. But careful thought has to be given to how this will be done because of the well-known tendency of human beings to resist change. To resolve any resistance that is based on *technical* concerns, management must ensure that the IT infrastructure is working properly and that there is an adequate storage and security system. To deal with resistance that is based on *emotional* concerns, management needs to provide incentives to motivate

people to change to the new system. In the accounting area, one incentive is the potential flexibility that the electronic revolution brings. Having digital images of files reduces the need to travel in order to share documents with clients and other associates. This also enables a company to reduce its dependency on a traditional work environment; now, more employees can choose to work flexible hours and have a more balanced work and family life. Being technically and digitally connected allows for enhanced productivity.

Another incentive is the increased efficiency that will be evident with the use of electronic technology. Increased efficiency means that a given amount of work can be done with fewer people than were previously needed, and this will increase competitiveness. A large number of accountants are expected to retire within the next few years, and increased efficiency means that companies will not have to look for as many people as they would have otherwise. This will save money and simplify recruiting efforts.

It is anticipated that accounting firms increasingly will train their clients to perform more of the initial data entry to allow for the electronic exchange of information. Firms will not be limited by geographic boundaries. They can also bill for higher-level accounting tasks, and the firm can be much more selective about which clients they accept. These new methods will help eliminate the bottom 10 to 20 percent of unproductive clients and allow more time to cultivate the profitable files.

Critical Thinking Questions

1. What other methods can firms use to have a greener accounting system?

2. There are clearly benefits for firms that embrace green accounting practices, but are there also benefits to clients? If so, describe them.

3. Why might there be reluctance on the part of accounting firms or their clients to embrace green initiatives like paperless systems?

Test yourself on the material for this chapter at **www.pearsoned.ca/mybusinesslab**.

Summary of
Learning Objectives

1. Explain the role of *accountants* and distinguish among the three types of professional accountants in Canada. By collecting, analyzing, and communicating financial information, accountants provide business managers and investors with an accurate picture of a firm's financial health. *Chartered Accountants (CAs)* and *Certified General Accountants (CGAs)* provide accounting expertise for client organizations who must report their financial condition to external stakeholders. *Certified Management Accountants (CMAs)* provide accounting expertise for the firms that employ them.

2. Describe how the *accounting equation* is used. Accountants use the following equation to balance the data pertaining to financial transactions:

Assets − Liabilities = Owners' equity

After each financial transaction (e.g., payments to suppliers, sales to customers, wage payments to employees), the accounting equation must be in balance. If it isn't, then an accounting error has occurred. The equation also provides an indication of the firm's financial health. If *assets* exceed *liabilities, owners' equity* is positive; if the firm goes out of business, owners will receive some cash (a gain) after selling assets and paying off liabilities. If liabilities outweigh assets, owners' equity is negative; assets aren't enough to pay off debts. If the company goes under, owners will get no cash and some creditors won't be paid, thus losing their remaining investments in the company.

3. Describe three basic *financial statements* and show how they reflect the activity and financial condition of a business. The *balance sheet* summarizes a company's assets, liabilities, and owners' equity at a given point in time. The *income statement* details revenues and expenses for a given period of time and identifies any profit or loss. The *statement of cash flows* reports cash receipts and payment from operating, investing, and financial activities.

4. Explain the key standards and principles for reporting financial statements. Accountants follow standard reporting practices and principles when they prepare financial statements. Otherwise, users wouldn't be able to compare information from different companies, and they

might misunderstand—or be led to misconstrue—a company's true financial status. Revenue recognition is the formal recording and reporting of revenues in financial statements. All firms earn revenues continuously as they make sales, but earnings are not reported until the earnings cycle is completed. This cycle is complete under two conditions: (a) The sale is complete and the product delivered, and (b) the sale price has been collected or is collectible. This practice assures interested parties that the statement gives a fair comparison of what was gained for the resources that were given up.

5. Explain how computing *financial ratios* can help in analyzing the financial strengths of a business. Drawing upon data from financial statements, ratios can help creditors, investors, and managers assess a firm's finances. The *current, liquidity,* and *debt-to-owners'-equity ratios* all measure solvency, a firm's ability to pay its debt in both the short and long runs. *Return on sales, return on equity,* and *earnings per share* are all ratios that measure profitability. The *inventory turnover ratio* shows how efficiently a firm is using its funds.

6. Explain some of the special issues that arise in *international accounting.* Accounting for foreign transactions involves special procedures, such as translating the values of different countries' currencies and accounting for the effects of exchange rates. Moreover, currencies are subject to change; as they're traded each day around the world, their values are determined by market forces—what buyers are willing to pay for them. The resulting values are *foreign currency exchange rates*, which can be fairly volatile. When a currency becomes unstable—when its value changes frequently—it is called a weak currency. The value of a strong currency historically rises or holds steady in comparison with the U.S. dollar.

International purchases, sales on credit, and accounting for foreign subsidiaries all involve transactions affected by exchange rates. When a Canadian company imports a French product, its accountant must be sure that its books reflect its true costs. The amount owed to the French seller changes daily along with the exchange rate between euros and dollars. The Canadian accountant

▶

must therefore identify the actual rate on the day that payment in euros is made so that the correct Canadian-dollar cost of the product is recorded.

With accounting groups from about 80 countries, the International Accounting Standards Board (IASB) is trying to eliminate national differences in financial reporting. Bankers, investors, and managers want financial reporting that is comparable from country to country and across all firms regardless of home nation. Standardization governs some areas but is far from universal.

PEARSON
mybusinesslab To improve your grade, visit the MyBusinessLab website at www.pearsoned.ca/mybusinesslab. This online homework and tutorial system allows you to test your understanding and generates a personalized study plan just for you. It provides you with study and practice tools directly related to this chapter's content. MyBusinessLab puts you in control of your own learning!

Key Terms

accounting   (p. 358)
accounting equation   (p. 365)
accounting information system (AIS)   (p. 359)
accounts payable   (p. 368)
accounts receivable   (p. 367)
activity ratios   (p. 374)
asset   (p. 365)
audit   (p. 361)
balance sheets   (p. 366)
bookkeeping   (p. 358)
budget   (p. 371)
certified general accountant (CGA)   (p. 360)
certified management accountant (CMA)   (p. 361)
chartered accountant (CA)   (p. 360)
controller   (p. 359)
cost of goods sold   (p. 368)
current assets   (p. 366)
current liabilities   (p. 368)
current ratio   (p. 374)
debt   (p. 374)

debt-to-owners'-equity ratio   (p. 374)
depreciation   (p. 367)
double-entry accounting system   (p. 365)
earnings per share   (p. 375)
financial accounting system   (p. 359)
financial statement   (p. 366)
fixed assets   (p. 367)
foreign currency exchange rates   (p. 377)
forensic accountant   (p. 361)
generally accepted accounting principles (GAAP)   (p. 362)
goodwill   (p. 367)
gross profit (gross margin)   (p. 369)
income (profit-and-loss) statement   (p. 368)
intangible assets   (p. 367)
inventory turnover ratio   (p. 376)
leverage   (p. 374)
liability   (p. 365)

liquidity   (p. 366)
long-term liabilities   (p. 368)
management consulting services   (p. 363)
managerial (management) accounting   (p. 360)
merchandise inventory   (p. 367)
net income (net profit or net earnings)   (p. 370)
operating expenses   (p. 369)
operating income   (p. 370)
owners' equity   (p. 365)
paid-in capital   (p. 368)
prepaid expenses   (p. 367)
private accountant   (p. 363)
profitability ratios   (p. 374)
retained earnings   (p. 368)
return on equity   (p. 375)
return on sales   (p. 368)
revenues   (p. 368)
short-term solvency ratios   (p. 374)
solvency ratios   (p. 374)
statement of cash flows   (p. 370)

Questions for Analysis

1. Balance sheets and income statements are supposed to be objective assessments of the financial condition of a company. But the accounting scandals of the last few years show that certain pressures may be put on accountants as they audit a company's financial statements. Describe these pressures. To what extent do these pressures make the audit more subjective?

2. If you were planning to invest in a company, which of the three types of financial statements would you want most to see? Why?

3. A business hires a professional accountant like a CA or CGA to assess the financial condition of the company. Why would the business also employ a private accountant?

4. How does the double-entry system reduce the chances of mistakes or fraud in accounting?

5. Explain how financial ratios allow managers to monitor their own efficiency and effectiveness.

6. The "credit crunch" of 2008 was highlighted by the inability of banks to convert customers' investments

back to cash when requested, as the investments lacked liquidity. Explain what liquidity is, how it is measured, and why it is important to any company.

7. Suppose that Inflatables Inc., makers of air mattresses for swimming pools, has the following transactions in one week:

   - sold three deluxe mattresses to Al Wett (paid cash $50, remaining $25 on credit) on 7/16
   - received cheque from Ima Flote in payment for mattresses bought on credit ($120) on 7/13
   - received new shipment of 200 mattresses from Airheads Mfg. (total cost $3000, paying 50 percent cash on delivery) on 7/17

   Construct a journal for Inflatables Inc.

8. Dasar Company reports the following data in its September 30, 2009, financial statements:

   Gross sales $225 000

   Current assets $50 000

   Long-term assets $130 000

   Current liabilities $33 000

   Long-term liabilities $52 000

   Net income $11 250

   a. Compute the owners' equity.
   b. Compute the current ratio.
   c. Compute the debt-to-equity ratio.
   d. Compute the return on sales.
   e. Compute the return on owners' equity.

Application Exercises

1. Interview an accountant at a local manufacturing firm. Trace the process by which budgets are developed in that company. How does the firm use budgets? How does budgeting help its managers plan business activities? How does budgeting help them control business activities? Give examples.

2. Interview the manager of a local retail or wholesale business about taking inventory. What is the firm's primary purpose in taking inventory? How often is it done?

3. Interview the manager of a local business and ask about the role of ethics in the company's accounting practices. Is ethics in accounting an important issue to the manager? What steps are taken to ensure ethical practices internally?

Building Your Business Skills

Putting the Buzz in Billing

The Purpose of the Assignment

To encourage students to think about the advantages and disadvantages of using an electronic system for handling accounts receivable and accounts payable.

Assignment

Step 1

Study Figure 11.4. The outside cycle depicts the seven steps involved in issuing paper bills to customers, payment of these bills by customers, and handling by banks of debits and credits for the two accounts. The inside cycle shows the same bill issuance and payment process handled electronically.

Step 2

As the chief financial officer of a provincial hydroelectric utility, you are analyzing the feasibility of switching from a paper to an electronic system of billing and bill payment. You decide to discuss the ramifications of the choice with three business associates (choose three classmates to take on these roles). Your discussion requires that you research electronic payment systems now being developed. Specifically, using online and library research, you

must find out as much as you can about the electronic bill-paying systems being developed by Visa International, Intuit, IBM, and the Checkfree Corp. After you have researched this information, brainstorm the advantages and disadvantages of using an electronic bill-paying system in your company.

Questions for Discussion

1. What cost savings are inherent in the electronic system for both your company and its customers? In your answer, consider such costs as handling, postage, and paper.

2. What consequences would your decision to adopt an electronic system have on others with whom you do business, including manufacturers of cheque-sorting equipment, Canada Post, and banks?

3. Switching to an electronic bill-paying system would require a large capital expenditure for new computers and computer software. How could analyzing the company's income statement help you justify this expenditure?

4. How are consumers likely to respond to paying bills electronically? Are you likely to get a different response from individuals than you get from business customers?

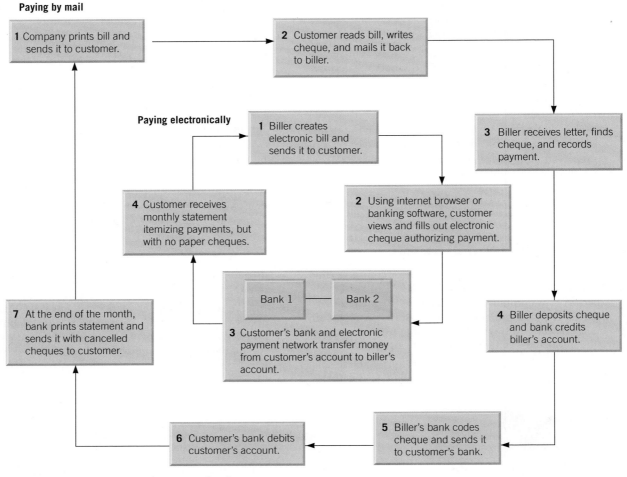

Paying by mail

1 Company prints bill and sends it to customer.

2 Customer reads bill, writes cheque, and mails it back to biller.

3 Biller receives letter, finds cheque, and records payment.

Paying electronically

1 Biller creates electronic bill and sends it to customer.

4 Customer receives monthly statement itemizing payments, but with no paper cheques.

2 Using internet browser or banking software, customer views and fills out electronic cheque authorizing payment.

Bank 1 — Bank 2

3 Customer's bank and electronic payment network transfer money from customer's account to biller's account.

4 Biller deposits cheque and bank credits biller's account.

7 At the end of the month, bank prints statement and sends it with cancelled cheques to customer.

6 Customer's bank debits customer's account.

5 Biller's bank codes cheque and sends it to customer's bank.

Figure 11.4 Managing operations and information.

Exercising Your Ethics: Team Exercise

Confidentially Yours

The Situation

Accountants are often entrusted with private, sensitive information that should be used confidentially. In this exercise, you're encouraged to think about ethical considerations that might arise when an accountant's career choices come up against a professional obligation to maintain confidentiality.

The Dilemma

Assume that you're the head accountant in Turbatron, a large electronics firm that makes components for other manufacturing firms. Your responsibilities include preparing Turbatron's financial statements that are then audited for financial reporting to shareholders. In addition, you regularly prepare confidential budgets for internal use by managers responsible for planning departmental activities, including future investments in new assets. You've also worked with auditors and CA consultants who assess financial problems and suggest solutions.

Now let's suppose that you're approached by another company, Electrolast, one of the electronics industry's most successful firms, and offered a higher-level position. If you accept, your new job will include developing Electrolast's financial plans and serving on the strategic planning committee. Thus, you'd be involved not only in developing strategy but also in evaluating the competition, perhaps even using your knowledge of Turbatron's competitive strengths and weaknesses.

Your contractual commitments with Turbatron do not bar you from employment with other electronics firms.

Team Activity

Assemble a group of four to five students and assign each group member to one of the following roles:

- head accountant (leaving Turbatron)
- general manager of Turbatron

- shareholder of Turbatron
- customer of Turbatron
- general manager of Electrolast (if your team has five members)

Questions for Discussion

1. Before discussing the situation with your group, and from the perspective of your assigned role, are any ethical issues confronting the head accountant in this situation? If so, write them down.

2. Return to your group and reveal the ethical issues identified by each member. Were the issues the same among all roles or did differences in roles result in different issues?

3. Among the ethical issues that were identified, decide as a group which one is most important for the head accountant. Which is most important for Turbatron?

4. What does your group finally recommend be done to resolve the most important ethical issue(s)?

5. What steps do you think Turbatron might take in advance of such a situation to avoid any difficulties it now faces?

For additional cases and exercise material, go to **www.pearsoned.ca/mybusinesslab**.

Concluding Case 11-1

Do We Need to Audit the Auditors?

The large amount of negative publicity that has been given to firms like Enron and WorldCom during the last few years makes for very interesting reading, but it is also making accountants very nervous. More and more investors are asking questions like "How much confidence can I really have when I read in an auditor's statement that a company's practices adhere to generally accepted accounting principles?" or "How can a company go bankrupt shortly after having their books audited by an independent auditor?" In 2002, NFO WorldGroup, a market research firm, gave outside auditors a D grade for their overall performance.

The case of Livent Inc., a live theatre company that formerly had theatres in Vancouver, Toronto, and New York, illustrates the problems that the auditing profession is facing. Livent went bankrupt in the late 1990s amid charges of questionable accounting practices, and in 2009, two of its executives—Garth Drabinsky and Myron Gottlieb—were found guilty of defrauding investors and creditors out of $500 million. Investors lost 95 percent of their investment after Livent first disclosed accounting irregularities in 1998.

In 2000, the Institute of Chartered Accountants of Ontario (ICAO) took disciplinary action against Livent's senior vice-president of finance, who was a chartered accountant. He was fined $25 000 and expelled from the ICAO after admitting that he had filed false financial statements and fraudulently manipulated Livent's books. After that, the ICAO began investigating the role of Deloitte & Touche, the accounting firm that was Livent's auditors, and in 2004, the ICAO laid charges of professional misconduct against four partners at Deloitte & Touche. (A few years earlier, in a U.S. court, a judge concluded that Deloitte had not participated in the fraud.)

Deloitte is also facing several other lawsuits, including one resulting from the collapse of the Italian dairy firm Parmalat. In that case, investors are suing Parmalat executives and two partners in Deloitte's Italian branch for allegedly conspiring to hide nearly $17 billion of debt.

At a disciplinary hearing in April 2004, Deloitte's lawyer argued that the ICAO charges were "rubbish" and that the allegations were simply differences of opinion regarding the application of generally accepted accounting principles. He pointed out that Livent managers had admitted lying to Deloitte auditors to prevent them from finding out about Livent's real financial condition. The lawyer indicated that his clients were angry that they had been charged and criticized the long delay in bringing the ICAO charges forward. He also filed an application with the Ontario Superior Court to drop the charges and prevent the ICAO from pursuing the case further.

William Parrett, the CEO of Deloitte, says that there is an "expectation gap" between what the investing public expects and what external auditors can possibly deliver. While auditors simply certify the accuracy of a company's financial statements (based on information provided by the company), investors want auditors to certify that a company is actually financially healthy. Parrett also says that it is not reasonable to hold auditing firms accountable for the illegal and secretive behaviour of corporate executives. Parrett does agree that auditing firms will have to improve the rigour of their audits, and he said that Deloitte has been working hard to overcome any existing deficiencies. The company has appointed an ethics officer in each of its national companies, has added more resources to audit teams, and rechecks initial audit results.

Parrett's explanation sounds pretty reasonable, but people still want to know how cases like Livent, Parmalat, and Enron happen even after the companies' financial

▶

statements have been audited by an independent accounting firm. One answer is that auditors are sometimes tempted to "look the other way" when they encounter questionable practices. But *why* would accounting firms not point out questionable accounting practices when they find them? One reason is that many accounting firms have historically also done management consulting for the firms they are auditing. The fees generated from this management consulting can be very lucrative, and often exceed the auditing fees the accounting firm receives. Accountants are human beings, so we should not be surprised if they worry that their clients will be upset if auditors question certain accounting practices. And if clients get upset enough, they may not give the accounting firm any more management consulting contracts. The obvious solution to this problem is to prohibit accounting firms from doing both auditing and management consulting for a given client. The Canadian Imperial Bank of Commerce no longer allows its auditors to do any management consulting for CIBC.

One very specific Canadian response so far is the establishment of a new Canadian Public Accountability Board (CPAB), which will oversee supervision, inspection, and discipline of Canada's largest accounting firms. The accounting firms will have to get CPAB clearance before their clients' financial statements are accepted. In short, the auditors are going to be audited.

We should not conclude from all of this that doom and gloom reigns in the auditing business. In fact, things are looking up, partly because the Sarbanes-Oxley Act was passed in 2002 by the U.S. Congress. Section 404 of the act requires U.S.-listed companies to analyze their reporting controls and to make any improvements that are necessary. At each year-end, auditors must certify these controls. Many people in the accounting field believe that Canadian legislators will soon introduce similar legislation. And guess what? That will affect over 4000 Canadian corporations, which in turn will create a substantial increase in demand for the services of auditors. Canadian public accounting firms have already begun recruiting more staff. The increased demand for accountants who are knowledgeable about Sarbanes-Oxley is particularly evident in places like Calgary, the home of many Canadian companies that are listed on U.S. stock exchanges.

Questions for Discussion

1. What role does the Institute of Chartered Accountants of Ontario (ICAO) play in ensuring full disclosure on the part of accountants and auditors? How does the ICAO monitor auditor activity and maintain integrity within the accounting profession? What is the ICAO's relationship to the CPAB?

2. What are some ways to ensure that an auditing firm does not find itself in the position that Deloitte & Touche did in the Livent case?

3. Do you think business practices like disclosure and auditing proceedings are changing as a result of the Sarbanes-Oxley Act? Do you think the number of fraud allegations will decline? Explain your answers.

4. There has been much publicity during the last few years about white-collar fraud. Give some examples of fraud that you are familiar with. What role, if any, did accounting fraud play in these cases?

Concluding Case 11-2

Continuing Concerns in the Accounting Profession

The corporate accounting and insider trading scandals of a few years ago have caused users of financial data to be increasingly concerned that the balance sheets and income statements of corporations may not be exactly what they seem. Those concerns prompted the Canadian Senate Banking Committee to analyze ways to restore investor confidence in financial data. The committee made several recommendations, including forcing CEOs to vouch for the truthfulness of their financial statements, passing new legislation governing the conflicts of interest faced by investment analysts, and requiring companies to have only independent directors on their audit committees.

Most of the really dramatic cases of corporate fraud have occurred in the United States, but Canada has the dubious distinction of having one of its own in the limelight. Canadian-born Bernard Ebbers had risen from Alberta milkman and nightclub bouncer to become CEO of WorldCom Inc., one of the largest companies in the United States. It was alleged that Ebbers conspired with subordinates to "cook the books" when a business downturn occurred. These actions wiped out $100 billion of the company's market value, cost 17 000 people their jobs, and wiped out the life savings of investors. Scott Sullivan, one of Ebbers's subordinates, pled guilty and testified that Ebbers had ordered him to cook the books to hit earnings targets. In 2005, Ebbers was found guilty on nine charges of securities fraud and filing false documents. He was sentenced to 25 years in prison for his role in the collapse of WorldCom.

In addition to outright accounting fraud, concerns have been expressed about the difficulty investors have in understanding what accounting statements really mean. In recent years, two issues in this area have received attention: overstating sales revenue and understating

▶

pension liabilities. The problem of overstating sales revenue is discussed below.

Overstating Sales Revenue

Sometimes companies are tempted to use "creative accounting" to inflate sales revenue, and this yields a distorted picture of how much product or service a company is actually selling. This is done so that the company will not disappoint the expectations of the stock market and then see its stock price drop. There are different ways that sales revenue can be overstated. For example, some software makers sell a lot of product at the end of a quarter and then count all those sales as revenue without taking into account the future costs the firm will incur to support the software or to provide the free upgrades they promised. Or a company that acts as a sales agent for an airline might include the ticket price, plus the commission it earns, as revenue. When the airline firm is paid, the cost goes on the expense line. This approach vastly overstates revenue (but not profit). The company should have included only its sales commissions as revenue.

High-tech firms in particular are seen as too liberal in recording revenues on their financial statements. Because of this, the Ontario Securities Commission is shifting its emphasis from examining prospectuses to analyzing the way companies report income. It has set up a continuous disclosure team to review the financial reports of corporations in a systematic manner. To get a better understanding of the revenue problem, the OSC is also asking companies how they account for revenue from things like service contracts and whether they benchmark their accounting practices against those used by other firms in their industry.

Other Concerns

A variety of other concerns have also been raised during recent years, including the following:

■ There is sometimes a "chummy" relationship between auditors and their clients; this makes it more difficult for auditors to be completely objective.

■ There is considerable "elasticity" in the application of generally accepted accounting principles; thus, companies have a lot of leeway in their accounting practices.

■ If a person from an accounting firm takes a management position with a firm that is a client, future audits may be too "cozy" and fail to be objective.

■ Self-regulation by the accounting industry doesn't work.

■ There has been much fruitless debate in accounting firms about how to deal with stock options that are given to executives (if these are shown as expenses, they depress corporation earnings and lower the stock price).

■ The accounting profession has moved away from establishing broad accounting principles and instead spent much of its time drafting detailed rules; even if these detailed rules are followed, the financial statements that are produced can present a distorted picture of a company's financial condition.

What should be done to resolve these problems? A few of the more commonly heard solutions are as follows:

■ Auditors should clarify their language so that readers of financial statements will have a better idea of how a company is doing before they invest in it.

■ Auditors should give more consideration to the users of financial statements, perhaps emphasizing different data for different user groups.

■ Auditors should be charged with detecting fraud and reporting it when they find it.

■ Firms should be required to change their auditors on a regular basis (for example, once every five years) to prevent "chummy" relationships from developing.

■ Auditors should not be allowed to take jobs with former clients until after a specified time period has passed (say, three to five years).

■ A truly independent monitoring group should be formed that would assess the extent to which companies are meeting standards in their financial reporting.

■ Stock options should be shown as expenses.

■ When earnings forecasts are made, there must be a clear statement of how the forecasted numbers were arrived at.

■ Companies should be required to show how much they paid for auditing services and how much they paid for management consulting from the same auditor.

■ Auditors should be required to rank a company's accounting practices in terms of how "aggressive" they are, rather than just saying the books are okay or not okay.

Questions for Discussion

1. Who are the various users of accounting information? How will each of these users be influenced if sales revenues are overstated and pension liabilities are understated?

2. What are the three basic financial statements that accountants generate for business firms? What does each one show? How will overstating sales revenue and understating pension liabilities affect each of these statements?

3. Read the sections in this chapter on revenue recognition and matching. How is the material in those sections helpful in dealing with the "overstating of sales revenue" problem noted in the case?

4. Consider the following statement: *Since sales revenues and pension returns are measured in dollars, and since dollars are easy to quantify, it should be very clear what sales revenues and investment income a firm had in a given period. It is therefore unnecessary to have policies about how sales revenues and pension returns should be reported.* Do you agree or disagree? Explain.

Tree Planters

At Touchwood Lake, Alberta, 36 rookie tree planters (as well as a group of veteran planters) meet Cal Dyck, who has contracts to plant seven million white and black spruce seedlings in Alberta and Saskatchewan. The trees won't be ready to harvest for 90 years. The tree planting industry was born in the 1970s when the idea of sustainable forestry caught on. Originally, convicts were used, but then forestry companies found out that hippies were cheaper.

During a two-day orientation session, Cal gives the workers a lot of information about tree planting. He knows most of them want to make a lot of money in a short period of time, and he tells them they can do that if they are highly motivated and committed to working hard (planters can burn up to 7000 calories per day). Workers are paid between 10 and 25 cents per tree, depending on the terrain. For a $30 per day charge, Cal will feed the tree planters and move them around to various planting sites. He also provides hot showers.

Among the rookies at the orientation are three friends: Misha (who is studying journalism at Concordia), Megan (a student at the Emily Carr Institute in Vancouver), and Lianne (also a student at the Emily Carr Institute). They will soon learn about the frailty of the human body in the business of tree planting (blisters, tendonitis, twisted ankles, and so on). The orientation also includes all-important demonstrations about how to properly plant a seedling. Spacing the seedlings, planting them at the right depth, choosing the right type of soil, and having the seedlings at the right temperature are all important considerations. The rookies train as a group, but then they're on their own and can work at their own pace. Their work is constantly checked for quality. If planting is not done right, it must be redone.

The rookies plant for just four hours during their first day on the job. While rookies are learning how to plant, they may plant fewer than 100 trees a day, but an experienced veteran can plant 3000 trees in a day. These high-volume planters—called "pounders" because of their intense work ethic—can earn $15 000 during the summer season. They set their own high production goals to motivate themselves to work hard.

For the rookies, the first week is already starting to blur. They eat, sleep, and plant. The work cycle is four days on and one day off. Within just a few weeks, some rookies are already starting to wonder why they are in the bush, especially on days when the rain is pouring down and they are soaked through and through. At Kananaskis, Alberta, work slows down because the terrain is rough and steep. It's only halfway through the season, but some planters already have bad cases of tendonitis from the repeated motions of jamming their shovel into the ground as they plant seedlings. Already eight of the 36 rookies have quit.

Lianne has made $2500 so far, and she is one of the top rookie planters. By season's end, Lianne will have planted more than 98 000 trees. Megan (Lianne's school buddy) is starting to waver. She is fighting a sinus infection and is not even making minimum wage. Misha has decided to quit. A friend of hers is getting married back east and she will not return after the wedding. A week later, Megan quits as well.

At Candle Lake, Saskatchewan, the planting crews are behind schedule as the season nears its end. They still have 1.2 million trees to plant, and the ranks of rookie planters are thinning fast. Only 14 of 36 rookies are still on the job. Smaller work crews mean more work for those who are left, and the opportunity to make more money. After more than three months in the bush, each rookie who is still on the job has planted thousands of trees. Lianne has learned to stop calculating her daily earnings. Brad, a veteran planter, says that he admires the rookies who have pulled through. He says that it's amazing that people can be brought into the bush from the city to do this kind of work.

Questions for Discussion

(Note: Consider the information here when answering the questions below.)

1. Explain what the terms *productivity* and *quality* mean. How are they related in the actual practice of tree planting?

2. Consider the following statement: *The productivity and quality of rookie tree planters is very low, and the turnover rate is very high. Tree planting companies should therefore hire only experienced tree planters.* Do you agree or disagree with the statement? Defend your answer.

3. Why do you think tree planters are paid on a piece-rate basis? What are the advantages and disadvantages of paying tree planters this way?

4. Explain the various forms of employee behaviour. How does each one of these forms of behaviour influence the productivity and quality of tree planters? (Review the relevant material in Chapter 12 before answering this question.)

Video Resource: "Tree Planters," *The National* (May 25, 2007).

African Accountants

In Canada's business jungle, all tracks lead to Bay Street, where lions of modern industry reign. Accountants keep Bay Street's books, but the heat is on for individual business owners to keep better books. Accountants don't like people who bring in shoeboxes full of receipts and then ask the accountant to organize them. Instead, accountants want the material organized before they try to do any calculations. But all this organizing costs money, and small- and mid-sized businesses don't usually have the money to pay for it.

For George Wall, of Wall & Associates, finding enough casual workers to do data organization and entry was a big challenge. He had to pay them up to $20 an hour, and that service was way too pricey for many of his clients. But what if Wall could find workers who would do this work for one-tenth the hourly wage that he had to pay people in Toronto? He found the solution by adopting global outsourcing. It works like this: When that shoebox arrives, each piece of paper is first fed into a high-speed scanner and then stored on a server. While Bay Street sleeps, the material is sent to Kampala, Uganda, over the internet, where the data are keyed in by African accountants who are paid only about $1 a day.

In a freshly painted office in Kampala, a dozen computers have just been taken out of their boxes and a dozen workers have just been hired. Their boss is "20-something" Abu Luaga, a Ugandan with a commerce degree who has the contract to do accounting work for Wall & Associates. He teaches the new hires what to do. His start-up funds came from his family, and he got involved with Wall & Associates through his connections with a Canadian business consultant.

There is much competition from other developing countries to get this kind of business, but Luaga's workers are keen and already trained as bookkeepers. They're eager to see what the developed world has to offer, but many have never had a computer before and need training so that they can recognize various financial documents and learn Canadian accounting jargon. They're also being trained to think the way Canadian businesses do. As well, Luaga reminds them about deadlines and privacy. Because these workers are dealing with sensitive information, no cellphones are allowed in the office and the copying or saving of files or images is prohibited.

What are the implications of all this information flowing from the First World to the Third World and back again? It may be just the kind of miracle Uganda needs. The telecommunications industry has been a bright spot in the Ugandan economy, but Ugandans still make only about $1 a day. The country still relies on money earned by exporting coffee, and the government is dependent on foreign donors for part of its budget. Officials admit that the technical skills of workers aren't as good as those of people in some Asian countries, but this system allows educated Ugandans to work in their home country.

Luaga's workers say the work has already changed their career prospects. But not all Canadian clients have jumped at the chance to zip their documents to Africa. George Wall is convinced they will eventually be comfortable with the idea, and Luaga is banking on it. He's leasing bigger and better office space because he thinks that a new office and clients in Canada will impress other potential clients in Africa.

Questions for Discussion

1. What is the difference between *financial* and *managerial* accounting? Is the work that the African accountants are doing financial or managerial accounting? Explain.

2. Why might Canadian clients be reluctant to have Wall & Associates send their data to Africa for organizing? What can George Wall do to respond to their concerns?

3. Suppose that you read a newspaper editorial condemning the practice of sending documents to Africa on the grounds that this was yet another example of exporting Canadian jobs overseas to low-wage countries. How would you respond?

Video Resource: "African Accountants," *Venture* (February 16, 2003).

Part Eleven

Motivation

Chapter 12

Motivating and Leading Employees

After reading this chapter, you should be able to:

1 Identify and discuss the basic *forms of behaviour* that employees exhibit in organizations.

2 Describe the nature and importance of *individual differences* among employees.

3 Explain the meaning and importance of *psychological contracts* and the *person-job fit* in the workplace.

4 Identify and summarize the most important *models of employee motivation*.

5 Describe the *strategies* used by organizations to improve job satisfaction and employee motivation.

6 Define *leadership* and distinguish it from *management*.

7 Summarize the *approaches to leadership* that developed in the twentieth century.

8 Describe the most recent ideas about effective leadership.

Taken from *Business*, Seventh Canadian Edition, by Ricky W. Griffin, Ronald J. Ebert, Frederick A. Starke, and Melanie D. Lang.

What Do Employees Want?

Every manager wants to have employees who are satisfied and highly motivated; such employees exhibit positive behaviours like persisting even in the face of difficulties, being involved in continuous learning and improvement, and constantly finding ways to improve quality and productivity. These behaviours, in turn, lead to several positive outcomes for the organi-zation: higher customer satisfaction, greater profits, higher quality, and lower employee turnover. But how do managers achieve the goal of having highly motivated and satisfied workers? The most general answer is this: Give employees what they want (within reason, of course).

But what do employees want? Managers often assume that they know the answer to this question, but consider the results of two surveys. The Canadian Payroll Association analyzed the frequency with which 39 specific benefits were provided by companies to their employees. The top five items were term life insurance, car allowances, tuition fees, disability-related employment benefits, and professional membership dues. But another survey of worker opinions found that they rated flexible working hours, casual dress, unlimited internet access, opportunities to telecommute, and nap time as the most desirable. There are obviously major differences in these two lists, so managers are having some difficulty assessing what employees want.

Several other studies are consistent with this conclusion. For example, a Sirota Survey Intelligence study assessed employee satisfaction levels at 237 different companies during the period 1994–2003 and found that only 14 percent of these companies had workforces that could be classified as "enthusiastic." When the stock prices of 28 companies with enthusiastic workforces were compared to the average for publicly traded companies, it was found that they outperformed the average prices by more than two and a half times, while companies with unenthusiastic workforces lagged far behind the average stock prices. Companies with enthusiastic workforces also had fewer customer complaints, lower employee turnover, and higher quality in their products.

Another study of more than 3000 Canadian employees that was conducted by Watson Wyatt Canada revealed the following:

- Forty-six percent would consider changing jobs if a comparable job became available.

- Only 40 percent of employees believe they have real opportunities for advancement with their current employer.

- Only 27 percent of employees see any connection between their job performance and their pay.

In yet another study, the Gallup Organization focussed on the attitudes of 7200 workers in Canada, the United States, and Great Britain. The survey revealed that on most measures of job satisfaction, Canadian workplaces ranked behind those of the United States. For example, only 47 percent of Canadian workers were completely satisfied with their boss, while 60 percent of American workers were. Only 29 percent of Canadian workers were completely satisfied with their opportunities for promotion, while 40 percent of Americans were. And 37 percent of Canadian workers were completely satisfied with the recognition they received, while 48 percent of Americans were. Canadian workers were also less satisfied than American workers on several other issues, including the flexibility of their work hours, workplace safety, relationships with co-workers, and the amount of vacation time they received (even though they usually received more than Americans).

Most employees start work with considerable enthusiasm, but they often lose it. Much of the blame is laid at the feet of managers whose attitudes and behaviours depress employee enthusiasm. These include failing to express appreciation to employees for a job well done, assuming that they are lazy and irresponsible, treating them as disposable objects, failing to build trust with them, and quickly laying them off when the business gets in trouble. Managerial assumptions about employee satisfaction with pay can be particularly problematic. For example, many managers assume that workers will never be satisfied with their pay. But only a minority of workers rate their pay as poor or very poor, and many rate it as good or very good. A Kelly Workforce Index study showed that 58 percent of Canadian workers would be willing to accept a lower wage if they felt their work contributed something important to their organization. A poll by the staffing firm Randstad USA found that 57 percent of workers would be willing to work overtime without pay to impress their boss so that they would be less likely to be laid off as a result of an economic downturn.

One of the simplest ways for managers to motivate workers is to praise them. Yet this occurs far less often than it should. A *Globe and Mail* web poll showed that 27 percent of the 2331 respondents had never received a compliment from their boss. Another 10 percent had not received a compliment in the last year, and 18 percent had not received a compliment in the last month. This result is disturbing, since another survey showed that 89 percent of employees rate recognition of their work as "very important" or "extremely important."

When there is a disconnect between what companies provide for workers and what they really want, we should not be surprised if motivation and satisfaction levels of workers are not high. The real question is this: In the most general sense, what can be done to make worker and company needs more consistent? Part of the answer is provided in yet another survey, this one based on responses by 8000 Canadians. That survey found that the three most important things (for employees of all ages) were to be treated with respect, to be dealt with fairly, and to feel a sense of "connection" with the organization they worked for. Managers can have a very positive influence on all of these things. And that is what this chapter is all about. ◆

How will this help me?

Some people love their jobs, while others hate them. Most people, however, fall somewhere in between. Some of these feelings are caused by the type of leadership employees are experiencing, and some are caused by the type of work that the employees do. After studying the information in this chapter, you'll be better able to understand (1) your own feelings toward your work from the perspective of an employee, (2) the feelings of others toward their work from the perspective of a boss or owner, (3) how you can more effectively function as a leader, and (4) how your manager or boss strives to motivate you through his or her leadership style.

In this chapter, we describe the different forms of behaviour that employees can exhibit at work and how employee attitudes and personality influence their work. Then we look at some important ideas about employee motivation, some strategies and techniques used by organizations to improve employee motivation, and how leadership facilitates employee motivation and performance.

Forms of Employee Behaviour

1 Identify and discuss the basic *forms of behaviour* that employees exhibit in organizations.

employee behaviour The pattern of actions by the members of an organization that directly or indirectly influence the organization's effectiveness.

performance behaviours The behaviours directly targeted at performing a job.

organizational citizenship Behaviours that provide positive benefits to the organization in indirect ways.

counterproductive behaviours Behaviours that detract from organizational performance.

absenteeism Occurs when an employee does not show up for work.

turnover The percentage of an organization's workforce that leaves and must be replaced.

Employee behaviour is the pattern of actions by the members of an organization that directly or indirectly influences the organization's effectiveness. **Performance behaviours** are the behaviours directly targeted at performing a job. An assembly line worker who sits by a moving conveyor and attaches parts to a product as it passes by has relatively simple performance behaviours. By contrast, a research-and-development scientist who works in a lab trying to find new scientific breakthroughs that have commercial potential has much more complex performance behaviours.

Other behaviours—called **organizational citizenship**—provide positive benefits to the organization but in more indirect ways. An employee who does satisfactory work in terms of quantity and quality but refuses to work overtime, won't help newcomers learn the ropes, and is generally unwilling to make any contribution beyond the strict performance requirements of the job is not a good organizational citizen. By contrast, an employee with a satisfactory level of performance who works late when the boss asks and takes time to help newcomers learn their way around is a good organizational citizen.

Counterproductive behaviours are those that detract from organizational performance. **Absenteeism** occurs when an employee does not show up for work. When an employee is absent, legitimately or not, that person's work does not get done and a substitute must be hired to do it, or others in the organization must pick up the slack.

Turnover refers to the percentage of an organization's workforce that leaves and must be replaced. Some turnover is natural and healthy, but high turnover has many negative consequences, including numerous vacancies, disruption in production, decreased productivity, and increased retraining costs. Turnover results from a number of factors, including aspects of the job, the organization, the individual, a poor person-job fit, the labour market, and family influences. One survey of 660 workers showed that 84 percent who worked for a "kind" manager planned to stay with their company a long time, while only 47 percent of those who worked for a "bully" said they planned to stay.[1]

Other forms of counterproductive behaviour may be even more costly for an organization. *Theft and sabotage*, for example, result in direct financial costs for an organization. *Sexual and racial harassment* also cost an organization, both directly (through financial liability if the organization responds inappropriately) and indirectly (by lowering morale, producing fear, and driving off valuable employees). *Workplace aggression and violence* are also counter-productive.

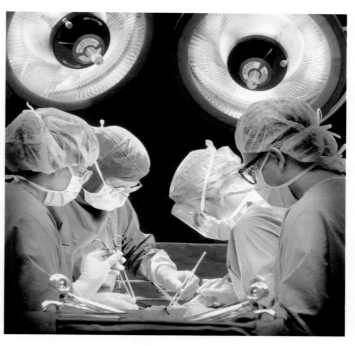

For some jobs, performance behaviours can be narrowly defined and easily measured. But for many other jobs, such as those held by scientists or doctors, performance behaviours are less objective, more diverse, and more difficult to assess.

Individual Differences Among Employees

Individual differences are physical, psychological, and emotional attributes that vary from one person to another. The individual differences that characterize a specific person make that person unique. *Personality* and *attitudes* are two main categories of individual differences.

> Describe the nature and importance of *individual differences* among employees.
>
> **2**

individual differences
Physical, psychological, and emotional attributes that vary from one person to another and that make each person unique.

personality The relatively stable set of psychological attributes that distinguishes one person from another.

Personality

Personality is the relatively stable set of psychological attributes that distinguishes one person from another. Researchers have identified five fundamental traits (the "big five") that are especially relevant to organizations (see Figure 12.1).

- *Agreeableness* is a person's ability to get along with others. A person with a *high* level of agreeableness is gentle, co-operative, forgiving, understanding, and good-natured in their dealings with others. A person with a *low* level of agreeableness is often irritable, short-tempered, uncooperative, and generally antagonistic toward other people. Highly agreeable people are better at developing good working relationships with co-workers, whereas less agreeable people are not likely to have particularly good working relationships.

- *Conscientiousness* refers to the number of things a person tries to accomplish. *Highly conscientious* people tend to focus on relatively few tasks at one time; as a result, they are likely to be organized, systematic, careful, thorough, responsible, and self-disciplined. *Less conscientious* people tend to pursue a wider array of tasks; as a result, they are often more disorganized and irresponsible, as well as less thorough and self-disciplined. Highly conscientious people tend to be relatively higher performers in a variety of different jobs.

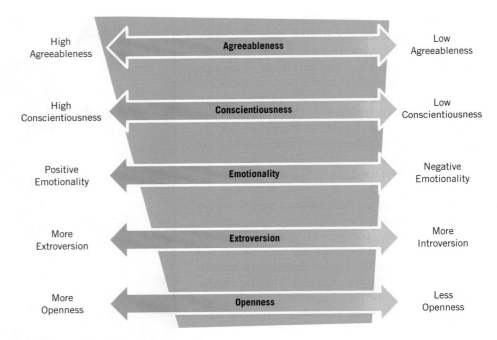

Figure 12.1 The "big five" personality traits.

- *Emotionality* refers to the degree to which people tend to be positive or negative in their outlook and behaviours toward others. People with *positive* emotionality are relatively poised, calm, resilient, and secure; people with *negative* emotionality are more excitable, insecure, reactive, and subject to mood swings. People with positive emotionality are better able to handle job stress, pressure, and tension. Their stability might also cause them to be seen as more reliable than their less-stable counterparts.

- *Extroversion* refers to a person's comfort level with relationships. *Extroverts* are sociable, talkative, assertive, and open to establishing new relationships, while *introverts* are much less sociable, less talkative, less assertive, and more reluctant to begin new relationships. Extroverts tend to be higher overall job performers than introverts and are more likely to be attracted to jobs based on personal relationships, such as sales and marketing positions.

- *Openness* reflects how open or rigid a person is in terms of his or her beliefs. People with *high* levels of openness are curious and willing to listen to new ideas and to change their own ideas, beliefs, and attitudes in response to new information. People with *low* levels of openness tend to be less receptive to new ideas and less willing to change their minds. People with more openness are often better performers due to their flexibility and the likelihood that they will be better accepted by others in the organization.

Emotional Intelligence

emotional intelligence (or emotional quotient [EQ])
The extent to which people possess social skills, are self-aware, can manage their emotions, can motivate themselves, and can express empathy for others.

Emotional intelligence, or emotional quotient (EQ), refers to the extent to which people possess social skills, are self-aware, can manage their emotions, can motivate themselves, and can express empathy for others.[2] Research suggests that people with high EQs may perform better than others, especially in jobs that require a high degree of interpersonal interaction and that involve influencing or directing the work of others. EQ appears to be something that isn't biologically based but that can be developed.[3]

Attitudes

Attitudes reflect our beliefs and feelings about specific ideas, situations, or other people. People in organizations have attitudes about many different things: their salary, their promotion possibilities, their boss, their employee benefits, and so on. People's attitudes also affect their behaviour in organizations. Especially important attitudes are *job satisfaction* and *organizational commitment*.

attitude A reflection of our beliefs and feelings about specific ideas, situations, or other people.

- **Job satisfaction** is the degree of enjoyment that people derive from performing their jobs. (A related concept—*morale*—refers to the overall attitude people have toward their workplace.) A satisfied employee tends to be absent less often, to be a good organizational citizen, and to stay with the organization. Dissatisfied employees tend to be absent more often, may experience stress that disrupts co-workers, and may be continually looking for another job. But a word of caution: Contrary to what a lot of managers believe, high levels of job satisfaction do not *automatically* lead to higher levels of productivity.

job satisfaction The degree of enjoyment that people derive from performing their jobs.

- **Organizational commitment** (sometimes called *job commitment*) reflects an individual's identification with the organization and its mission. Highly committed employees see themselves as true members of the firm, overlook minor sources of dissatisfaction, and see themselves remaining as members of the organization. Less committed employees are more likely to see themselves as outsiders, to express more dissatisfaction about the work situation, and to not see themselves as long-term members of the organization.

organizational commitment (or job commitment) An individual's identification with the organization and its mission.

One way to increase employee commitment is to give employees a voice. BBVA, Spain's second-largest bank, accomplishes this by including employees in the performance evaluation process. Not only is one's own self-evaluation considered, but co-workers also answer questions about each employee's performance. Infosys Technologies in Bangalore, India, started a Voice of Youth program, which gives top-performing young employees a seat on its management council.[4]

Matching People and Jobs

Given the array of individual differences that exist in people and the many different forms of employee behaviour that can occur in organizations, it is important to have a good match between people and the jobs they are performing. Two key concepts for facilitating this match are *psychological contracts* and the *person-job fit*.

Explain the meaning and importance of *psychological contracts* and the *person-job fit* in the workplace.

3

Psychological Contracts

A **psychological contract** is the set of expectations held by an employee concerning what he or she will contribute to an organization (referred to as *contributions*) and what the organization will provide the employee in return (referred to as *inducements*). If either party perceives an inequity in the contract, that party may seek a change. The employee, for example, might ask for a pay raise, promotion, or bigger office, or might put forth less effort or look for a better job elsewhere. The organization can also initiate change by training workers to improve their skills, transferring them to new jobs, or terminating them. Unlike a business contract, a psychological contract is not written on paper, nor are all of its terms explicitly negotiated. Figure 12.2 illustrates the essential features of a psychological contract.

psychological contract The set of expectations held by an employee concerning what he or she will contribute to an organization (referred to as contributions) and what the organization will provide the employee in return (referred to as inducements).

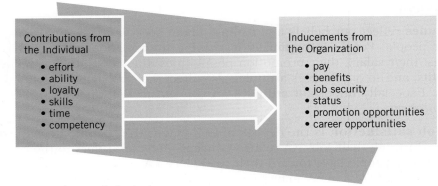

Figure 12.2 The psychological contract.

The downsizing and cutbacks that have occurred in Canadian businesses in recent years have complicated the process of managing psychological contracts. Many organizations, for example, used to offer at least reasonable assurances of job security as a fundamental inducement to employees. Now, however, because job security is less likely, alternative inducements—such as improved benefits packages or more flexible working hours—may be needed instead.

The Person-Job Fit

person-job fit The extent to which a person's contributions and the organization's inducements match one another.

The **person-job fit** refers to the extent to which a person's contributions and the organization's inducements match one another. Each employee has a specific set of needs that he or she wants fulfilled and a set of job-related behaviours and abilities to contribute. If the organization can take perfect advantage of those behaviours and abilities and exactly fulfill those needs, it will have achieved a perfect person-job fit. A good person-job fit, in turn, can result in higher performance and more positive attitudes. A poor person-job fit can have just the opposite effect.

Motivation in the Workplace

4 Identify and summarize the most important *models of employee motivation.*

motivation The set of forces that cause, focus, and sustain workers' behaviour.

Motivation is the set of forces that cause, focus, and sustain workers' behaviour. One worker may be motivated to work hard to produce as much as possible, while another may be motivated to do just enough to get by. As we saw in the opening case, effective managers recognize that because today's workers have diverse and complex needs, they must be motivated in increasingly complex ways. As well, the varying lifestyles of a diverse workforce mean that managers must pay close attention to what their employees expect to receive for their efforts and then try to link rewards with job performance.

Over the years, many theories have been proposed to address the issues of motivation. Three major approaches to motivation in the workplace have been evident—these approaches reflect a chronology of thinking about motivation: *classical theory and scientific management, behaviour theory,* and *contemporary motivation theories*.

Classical Theory and Scientific Management

classical theory of motivation Workers are motivated solely by money.

According to the so-called **classical theory of motivation**, workers are motivated solely by money. In his book *The Principles of Scientific Management* (1911), industrial engineer Frederick Taylor proposed a way for both companies and workers to benefit from this widely accepted view of life in the workplace.[5] If workers are motivated by money, Taylor reasoned, then paying them more would prompt them to produce more. Meanwhile, the firm that analyzed jobs and found better ways to perform them would be able to produce goods more cheaply, make higher profits, and thus pay—and motivate—workers better than its competitors.

Taylor's approach—known as **scientific management**—captured the imagination of many managers in the early twentieth century. Companies across Canada and the United States hired experts to perform *time-and-motion studies*—pioneered by Frank and Lillian Gilbreth—in order to discover the "one best way" of doing a job. Industrial-engineering techniques were applied to each facet of a job to determine how to perform it most efficiently. These studies were the first "scientific" attempts to break down jobs into easily repeated components and to devise more efficient tools and machines for performing them.[6] The results were impressive. For example, studies of workers loading iron on rail cars showed that productivity tripled.

The ideas of Frederick Taylor, the founder of scientific management, had a profound impact on the way manufacturing activities were carried out in the early twentieth century. His basic ideas are still used today.

Early Behavioural Theory

In 1925, a group of Harvard researchers began a study at the Hawthorne Works of the Western Electric Company. Their intent was to examine the relationship between changes in the physical environment and worker output, with an eye to increasing productivity. The results of the experiment at first confused, then amazed, the scientists. Increasing lighting levels improved productivity, but so did lowering lighting levels. And against all expectations, raising the pay of workers failed to increase their productivity. Gradually they pieced together the puzzle. The explanation for the lighting phenomenon lay in workers' response to the attention they were receiving. In essence, they determined that almost any action on the part of management that made workers believe they were receiving special attention caused worker productivity to rise. This result, known as the **Hawthorne effect**, convinced many managers that paying attention to employees is indeed good for business.

Following the Hawthorne studies, managers and researchers alike focussed more attention on how good **human relations**—the interactions

scientific management
Analyzing jobs in order to find better, more efficient ways to perform them.

Hawthorne effect   The tendency for workers' productivity to increase when they feel they are receiving special attention from management.

human relations   The interactions between employers and employees and their attitudes toward one another.

The Hawthorne studies were an important step in developing an appreciation for the human factor at work. These women worked under different lighting conditions as researchers monitored their productivity. The researchers were amazed to find that productivity increased regardless of whether lighting levels increased or decreased.

between employers and employees and their attitudes toward one another—help in motivating employees. As they focussed on the ways in which management thinks about and treats employees, these researchers developed several now-classic motivation theories, including the *human resources model*, the *hierarchy of needs model*, and *two-factor theory*.

The Human-Resources Model: Theories X and Y

Behavioural scientist Douglas McGregor concluded that managers had radically different beliefs about how best to use the human resources at a firm's disposal. He classified these beliefs into sets of assumptions that he labelled "Theory X" and "Theory Y."[7] Managers who subscribe to **Theory X** tend to believe that people are naturally lazy and uncooperative and must therefore be either punished or rewarded to be made productive. By contrast, managers who subscribe to **Theory Y** tend to believe that people are naturally energetic, growth oriented, self-motivated, and interested in being productive.

McGregor generally favoured Theory Y beliefs, and he argued that Theory Y managers are more likely to have satisfied, motivated employees. Of course, the Theory X and Theory Y distinctions are somewhat simplistic and offer little concrete basis for action. Their value lies primarily in their ability to highlight and analyze the behaviour of managers in light of their attitudes toward employees.

Theory X A management approach based on the belief that people must be forced to be productive because they are naturally lazy, irresponsible, and uncooperative.

Theory Y A management approach based on the belief that people want to be productive because they are naturally energetic, responsible, and co-operative.

Maslow's Hierarchy of Needs Model

Psychologist Abraham Maslow's **hierarchy of human needs model** proposed that people have five basic needs, which are arranged in a hierarchy of importance (see Figure 12.3). According to Maslow, lower-level needs must be largely satisfied before a person will be motivated to satisfy higher-level needs.[8]

hierarchy of human needs model Theory of motivation describing five levels of human needs and arguing that basic needs must be fulfilled before people will work to satisfy higher-level needs.

■ *Physiological needs* are survival oriented; they include food, water, shelter, and sleep. Businesses address these needs by providing both comfortable working environments and salaries sufficient to buy food and shelter.

■ *Security needs* include the needs for stability and protection from the unknown. These needs are satisfied when employers offer pension plans and job security.

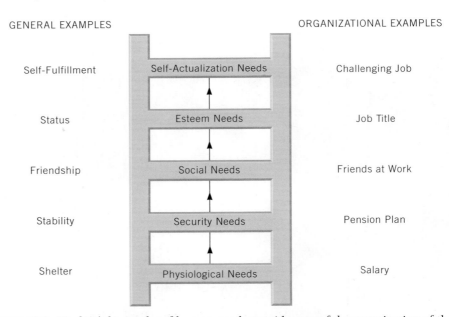

Figure 12.3 Maslow's hierarchy of human needs provides a useful categorization of the different needs people have.

- *Social needs* include the needs for friendship and companionship. Making friends at work can help to satisfy social needs, as can the feeling that you "belong" in a company.

- *Esteem needs* include the need for status and recognition as well as the need for self-respect. Job titles and large offices are among the things that businesses can provide to address these needs.

- Finally, *self-actualization needs* are needs for self-fulfillment. They include the needs to grow and develop one's capabilities and to achieve new and meaningful goals. Challenging job assignments can help satisfy these needs.

According to Maslow, once one set of needs has been satisfied, it ceases to motivate behaviour. For example, if you feel secure in your job, a new pension plan will probably be less important to you than the chance to make new friends and join an informal network among your co-workers. If, however, a lower-level need suddenly becomes unfulfilled, most people immediately refocus on that lower level. Suppose, for example, that you are seeking to meet your esteem needs by working as a divisional manager at a major company. If you learn that your division—and consequently your job—may be eliminated, you might very well find the promise of job security at a new firm as motivating as a promotion once would have been in your old company.

Two-Factor (Motivation-Hygiene) Theory

After studying a group of accountants and engineers, psychologist Frederick Herzberg proposed the **two-factor theory**, which says that job satisfaction and dissatisfaction depend on two factors: *hygiene factors* (such as working conditions, quality of supervision, interpersonal relations, pay, and job security) and *motivating factors* (such as recognition, responsibility, advancement, and achievement).[9] Motivation factors cause movement along a continuum from *no satisfaction* to *satisfaction*. For example, if workers receive no recognition for successful work, they may not be satisfied, but neither will they be dissatisfied. If recognition is provided, they will likely become more satisfied. Hygiene factors cause movement along a different continuum, one from *no dissatisfaction* to *dissatisfaction*. For example, workers will be dissatisfied if they feel that working conditions are poor, but if working conditions are improved, workers will not become *satisfied*; rather, they will no longer be *dissatisfied*. Overall, motivation factors are directly related to the *work* that employees actually perform, while hygiene factors refer to the *environment* in which they perform it (see Figure 12.4).

two-factor theory A theory of human relations developed by Frederick Herzberg that identifies factors that must be present for employees to be satisfied with their jobs and factors that, if increased, lead employees to work harder.

This theory thus suggests that managers follow a two-step approach to enhancing motivation. First, they must ensure that hygiene factors are acceptable. This practice will result in an absence of dissatisfaction. Then they must offer motivating factors as means of improving satisfaction and motivation.

Contemporary Motivation Theory

Recently, more complex models of employee behaviour and motivation have been developed. Two of the most interesting and useful ones are *expectancy theory* and *equity theory*.

Expectancy Theory

Expectancy theory suggests that people are motivated to work toward rewards that they want *and* that they believe they have a reasonable chance of obtaining.[10] A reward that seems out of reach, for example, is not likely to be motivating

expectancy theory The theory that people are motivated to work toward rewards that they want and that they believe they have a reasonable chance of obtaining.

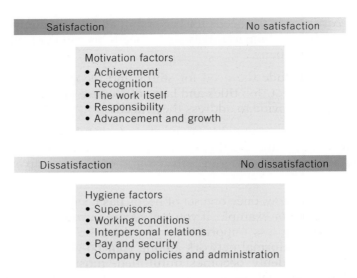

Figure 12.4 According to two-factor theory, job satisfaction depends on two factors.

even if it is very desirable. Figure 12.5 illustrates expectancy theory in terms of issues that are likely to be considered by an individual employee. Consider the case of an assistant department manager who learns that her firm needs to replace a retiring division manager two levels above her in the organization. Even though she wants that job, she does not apply because she doubts that she will be selected. In this case, she is being influenced by the *performance-reward link*. For whatever reason, she believes that her performance will not get her the position. Note that she may think that her performance merits the new job but that performance alone will not be enough. Perhaps she assumes that the reward will go to someone with more seniority.

Now assume that our employee learns that the firm is looking for a production manager on a later shift. She thinks that she could get this job but does not apply because she does not want to change shifts. In this instance, she is being influenced by the *rewards–personal goals link*. Finally, she learns of an opening one level higher—department manager—in her own division. She may well apply for this job because she wants it and because she thinks she has a good chance of getting it. In this case, her consideration of all the links has led to an expectancy that she can reach a desirable outcome.

Expectancy theory helps explain why some people do not work as hard as they can when their salaries are based purely on seniority. Paying employees the same whether they work very hard or just hard enough to get by removes the financial incentive for them to work harder. In other words, they ask themselves, "If I work harder, will I get a pay raise?" and conclude that the answer is no. Similarly, if hard work will result in one or more *undesirable* outcomes—say, a transfer to another location or a promotion to a job that requires unpleasant travel—employees will not be motivated to work hard.

Equity Theory

equity theory The theory that people compare (1) what they contribute to their job with what they get in return, and (2) their input/output ratio with that of other employees.

Equity theory focuses on social comparisons and assumes that people evaluate their treatment in an organization relative to the treatment that others receive. This approach says that people begin by analyzing *inputs* (what they contribute to their jobs in terms of time, effort, education, experience, and so on) relative to *outputs* (what they receive in return in terms of salary, benefits, recognition, security, and so on). The result is a ratio of contribution to return. Then they compare their own ratios with those of other employees and ask whether their ratios are *equal to, greater than,* or *less than* those of the people with whom they

Figure 12.5 Expectancy theory model.

are comparing themselves. Depending on the outcome of their assessments, they experience feelings of equity or inequity.[11]

Suppose that a new graduate gets a starting job at a large manufacturing firm. His starting salary is $30 000 per year, he gets a compact company car, and he shares an office with another employee. If he later learns that another new employee has received the same salary, car, and office arrangement, he will feel equitably treated. If the other newcomer, however, has received $35 000, a full-size company car, and a private office, he is likely to experience feelings of inequity.

Note, however, that the two ratios do not have to be equal—they only need to be *equitable*. Let's assume, for instance, that our new employee has a bachelor's degree and two years of work experience. Perhaps he learns subsequently that the other new employee has an advanced degree and 10 years of work experience. After first feeling inequity, our new employee may now conclude that his comparison person is actually contributing more to the organization. The other employee is therefore entitled to receive more.

When people feel that they are being inequitably treated, they are motivated to do something to restore equity. For example, they may ask for raises, reduce their effort, work shorter hours, or just complain to their bosses. They may also rationalize their situation, find different people with whom to compare themselves, or leave their jobs altogether.

Strategies for Enhancing Motivation

Deciding what motivates workers and provides job satisfaction is only part of the manager's challenge. The other part is to apply that knowledge. Experts have suggested—and many companies have instituted—a wide range of programs designed to make jobs more interesting and rewarding and the work environment more pleasant. Six of the most popular types of programs are *reinforcement/ behaviour modification theory, goal setting theory, participative management, team management, job enrichment and job redesign,* and *modified work schedules*.

> Describe the *strategies* used by organizations to improve job satisfaction and employee motivation.
>
> **5**

Reinforcement/Behaviour Modification Theory

Many managers try to control or modify workers' behaviour through systematic rewards. The first step is to define the specific behaviours that managers want their employees to exhibit (working hard, being courteous to customers, stressing quality) and the specific behaviours they want to eliminate (wasting time, being rude to customers, ignoring quality). The next step is to "shape" employee behaviour by using reinforcement.

Reinforcement means applying (or withholding) positive (or negative) consequences in an attempt to motivate employees to exhibit behaviour the manager wants. A manager has four basic reinforcement options: (1) *positive reinforcement* (apply positive consequences when employees exhibit desired behaviours), (2) *punishment* (apply negative consequences when employees exhibit undesirable behaviours), (3) *omission* (withhold positive consequences

> **reinforcement** Controlling and modifying employee behaviour through the use of systematic rewards and punishments for specific behaviours.

when employees exhibit undesirable behaviours), and (4) *negative reinforcement* (withhold negative consequences when employees exhibit desired behaviours).

Positive reinforcement is the strategy most frequently used. For example, workers at Maple Leaf Sports & Entertainment receive "good job" cards when they do outstanding work. These cards can be redeemed for prizes.[12] WestJet rewarded its employees with a $500 travel credit when they helped deal with major flight disruptions caused by bad weather during December 2008.[13] Positive reinforcement need not be monetary to be effective. Calgary-based Pacesetter Directional and Performance Drilling rewards top employees with time off from work, and Markham, Ontario–based Nobis, a manufacturer of hats and apparel, rewards employees by allowing them to name hats after family and friends.[14] The boxed insert entitled "Employee Engagement" provides further information about rewards.

Rewards work best when people are learning new behaviours, new skills, or new jobs. As workers become more adept, rewards can be used less frequently.

Entrepreneurship and New Ventures

Employee Engagement: The Ultimate Win-Win

"The best way to engage and align employees is to promote transparency, accountability and recognition across all levels of a company," according to I Love Rewards CEO Razor Suleman. I Love Rewards sells solutions for businesses wishing to improve corporate culture, employee engagement, and motivation, and they do this primarily through the development of web-based employee rewards- or incentive-based systems that are customized to suit their clients' needs. Client employees are awarded points for performance, and these points can be redeemed for rewards, including brand name merchandise and travel, which have been carefully selected with the employee demographic in mind.

If companies can motivate their customers with rewards-based systems, why can't it work for employees? Well, companies like Microsoft, Rogers Communications, and Marriott have bought in to the concept and have contracted I Love Rewards to develop incentive-based packages for their employees. News of the successes of this high-growth company is travelling quickly. In the first quarter of 2009, the company reported a 187 percent increase in gross billings year over year. But the future didn't always look so bright for Suleman's agency.

In 2005, Suleman found himself wrestling with his own employee morale and motivation issues. In a span of six months, his company experienced almost 50 percent employee turnover. The solution? Suleman decided to incorporate his marketing expertise into his HR practices. One technique was to introduce group interviews. Suleman decided to directly involve as many as 10 to 12 current employees of his company to interview prospective employees. Employees "sell" the company to the applicant, and by doing so, the company brand is reinforced internally.

Further, having so many staff members directly involved in hiring helps ensure the candidate will be a fit with the company culture. Other newly introduced incentives include flextime and at least four weeks vacation for new hires. Employee involvement extends as well to participation in objective setting, reinforced by an employee share-ownership program. Employees are also privy to the company's financial statements and can query management on any budget line expense. Amidst the hard times, Suleman had been somewhat disenchanted with his business, but his new strategy has paid off. In addition to reduced turnover and increased morale, his fresh approach has earned some other kinds of rewards.

For two years, Suleman's Toronto-based company has been named on Canada's Top 100 Employers list produced by *Maclean's* magazine. *Profit* magazine has included the business on their list of Fastest Growing Companies, and, more recently, WorldBlu, a U.S.-based social enterprise, has included the company on their list of the Most Democratic Workplaces. According to WorldBlu, the current economic crisis has dictated the need for a new business model that promotes transparency and accountability. I Love Rewards' new business model is built on these principles. These characteristics, combined with I Love Rewards' authentic democratic practices, emphasis on culture, and focus on people and recognition, have created a winning combination.

Suleman is now excited about the future of his business. His new strategies for employee engagement may have been just the competitive advantage and vehicle for growth his company was looking for.

Critical Thinking Question

1. Which of the strategies for enhancing job satisfaction and morale has Razor Suleman employed?

Because such actions contribute to positive employer-employee relationships, managers generally prefer giving rewards. They generally dislike punishing employees, partly because workers may respond with anger, resentment, hostility, or even retaliation.

Goal Setting Theory

Goal setting theory focuses on setting goals in order to motivate employees. Research has shown that **SMART goals** (*Specific*, *Measurable*, *Agreed-upon*, *Realistic*, and *Time-framed*) are most likely to result in increased employee performance. On occasion, goal setting may lead to bad behaviour on the part of managers. For example, if managers are told they will receive a bonus if they achieve a certain level of sales revenue, they may focus all their attention on generating sales *revenue*, and not pay any attention to *profits*. At Enron, managers received large bonuses for achieving revenue goals even though the company was failing.[15]

One of the most popular methods for setting performance goals is called **management by objectives (MBO),** which involves managers and subordinates in setting goals and evaluating progress (see Figure 12.6). It is an effort to apply goal setting theory throughout the organization. The motivational impact is perhaps the biggest advantage of MBO. When employees sit down with managers to set goals, they learn more about company-wide objectives, feel that they are an important part of a team, and see how they can improve company-wide performance by achieving their own goals.

Investors Group Financial Services has used MBO for many years to motivate its sales force in selling financial services. The MBO process begins when the vice-president of sales develops general goals for the entire sales force. This sets the stage for Planning Week, which is held annually in various regional centres across Canada. Sales reps review their financial accomplishments and think through their personal and financial goals for the coming year. During Planning Week, they meet with their division managers and reach a consensus about the specific goals the sales reps will pursue during the next year. Each division manager then forwards the proposed objectives for his or her division to the appropriate regional manager. This process continues all the way up to the vice-president of sales, who gives final approval to the overall sales objectives of the company for the coming year.[16]

goal setting theory The theory that people perform better when they set specific, quantified, time-framed goals.

SMART goals Goals that are specific, measurable, agreed upon, realistic, and time framed and which are most likely to result in increased employee performance.

management by objectives (MBO) A system of collaborative goal setting that extends from the top of an organization to its bottom.

Research has shown that goals that are specific, measurable, agreed upon, realistic, and time framed generate high performance in employees.

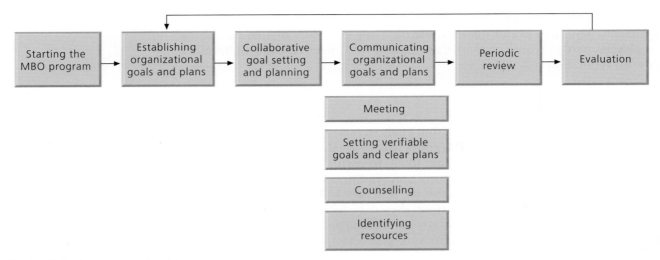

Figure 12.6 Management by objectives.

Participative Management and Empowerment

participative management
and empowerment A method of
increasing employees' job satisfaction
by giving them a voice in how they do
their jobs and how the company is
managed.

Participative management and empowerment involves tapping in to workers' knowledge about the job, encouraging them to be self-motivated and to make suggestions for improvements, and giving them more authority and responsibility so that they feel they are a real part of the company's success. The South Bend, Indiana, manufacturing plant of the Eaton Corporation illustrates empowerment in practice. The traditional factory hierarchy is avoided, and everyone wears the same blue uniforms. There are no time clocks, and workers report their hours on an honour system. Production statistics for each work team are posted where everyone can see them. Each work team is responsible for keeping its own members productive and motivated. Empowerment has meant more authority and more responsibility for workers.

There are many other examples of empowerment:

- At WestJet, front-line staff have the right to issue travel credits to customers they feel have not been treated properly. WestJet thinks that the goodwill generated by the practice will increase repeat business.[17]

- At Toronto's Delta Chelsea Hotel, employees noticed that in the summer months there were fewer business guests and more vacationers' children in the hotel. As a result of employee suggestions, the hotel installed a waterslide, appointed a "kids' concierge," and set up a game room for teens to better serve this market segment.[18]

- AES Corporation is a large energy company where multifunctional teams manage themselves without the assistance of any legal, human resources, or other functional department or any written policies or procedures. No one person is in charge of the teams. As a result of this structure (some call it "empowerment gone mad"), employees exhibit flexibility and continuous learning.[19]

wikis Websites that allow employees
to add content whenever they want on
issues that are of interest to the
business.

quality circle A technique used
to encourage participative management,
whereby a group of employees meet
regularly to consider solutions for
problems in their work area.

To enhance employee productivity, some companies are now using **wikis**—websites that allow employees to add content whenever they want on issues that are of interest to the business. This is part of a move to "mass collaboration" that is going on in business.[20] Another technique to encourage participative management is the **quality circle**, a group of employees who meet regularly to consider solutions for problems in their work area. The Great-West Life Assurance Company, for example, has reported success with its quality circle program.

Empowerment is not desired by all employees. Some will be frustrated by responsibilities they are not equipped to handle, and others will be dissatisfied if they see the invitation to participate as more symbolic than real. A good approach is to invite participation only if employees want to have input, and only if participation will have real value for an organization. The boxed insert entitled "Encouraging Employees to Share Ideas" describes some of the problems that can arise with empowerment.

Business Accountability

Encouraging Employees to Share Ideas

Empowerment can be a tricky process, particularly in an era when layoffs are common and employees may not trust management. The empowerment process typically requires workers to share their job knowledge with other workers or with management. But some workers fear that such sharing will allow others to take credit for their hard-earned knowledge or that sharing their knowledge will weaken their position in the company. So managers who assume that all workers want to be empowered may be in for a rude shock. The following examples demonstrate this difficulty:

- One employee who cut metal shafts for industrial pumps at Blackmer/Dover Resources Inc. in Grand Rapids, Michigan, had a reputation for being both fast and accurate in his work. He refused to share his knowledge with management (or his fellow workers), because he feared that management would use the knowledge to speed up the workflow and that he would then have to work faster. He is not alone. Many workers have developed extra-fast ways of doing their work, but are reluctant to share those ideas with management. Since managers are always under pressure to improve productivity, the refusal of these workers to share information is frustrating.

- A long-time employee at a small Canadian manufacturing plant taught a younger replacement worker how to run a complicated machine. Shortly thereafter, the older worker became ill and was off work for several weeks. When he returned, he found that the younger worker had essentially taken over his job. The older worker had this to say: "To pass on your experience or your knowledge to others, or to pass on to your fellow workers your secrets, how you assemble it faster, better, or more efficiently for the company, be careful; tomorrow you might have lost your job."

- Robin Miller, the executive director of the Winnipeg-based Centre for Education and Work, says that there is a lot of "informal learning" that goes on in companies, but it is not generally recognized or rewarded in Canadian workplaces. If informal learning is not rewarded, we should not be surprised if employees do not share with management the efficient shortcuts they have discovered that allow them to work faster.

The main reason workers conceal knowledge seems to be related to job security. Workers fear that if they share their knowledge, management will use that knowledge to increase output. The increased output will mean that management can get by with fewer workers, so some people will lose their jobs.

In some companies, workers don't share their knowledge because they have become convinced that management doesn't think they have anything to contribute. At the Blackmer/Dover plant, for example, a new plant manager was trying to resolve some production problems that had developed under his predecessor. He asked for worker participation so that he could understand what was wrong in the plant and how things might be improved. Workers were surprised they were being asked for their ideas, because previous management had not solicited worker input. But in this case the workers agreed to help, and the story eventually had a happy ending.

The culture of a country may also moderate the positive effects of empowerment initiatives. One study of a company with operations in the United States, Mexico, Poland, and India found that empowerment was negatively related to job satisfaction in India, but positively related to job satisfaction in the United States, Poland, and Mexico.

Critical Thinking Questions

1. Consider the following statement: *Companies provide jobs for people, so they have every right to expect that employees will do things like sharing their job knowledge with their co-workers because this will make the company more successful and allow it to continue to provide jobs.* Do you agree or disagree with the statement? Explain your reasoning.

2. Why do some workers refuse to share their job knowledge with either their co-workers or with management? What can management do to encourage workers to share their job knowledge?

Team Management

Individual employees are usually given decision-making responsibility for certain narrow activities, such as when to take lunch breaks or how to divide assignments with co-workers. But teams of employees are also being consulted on such decisions as production scheduling, work procedures and schedules, and the hiring of new employees.

Like participation and empowerment, teams are not for everyone. Levi Strauss, for example, encountered major problems when it tried to use teams. Individual workers previously performed repetitive, highly specialized tasks, such as sewing zippers into jeans, and were paid according to the number of parts they completed each day. In an attempt to boost productivity, company management reorganized everyone into teams of 10 to 35 workers and assigned tasks to the entire group. Each team member's pay was determined by the team's level of productivity. In practice, however, faster workers became resentful of slower workers because they reduced the group's total output. Slower workers, meanwhile, resented the pressure put on them by faster-working co-workers. As a result, motivation, satisfaction, and morale all dropped, and Levi's eventually abandoned the teamwork plan altogether.[21]

Team management is widely used to enhance employee motivation and company performance. Although teams are often less effective in traditional and rigidly structured bureaucratic organizations, they do help smaller, more flexible organizations make decisions more quickly and effectively, enhance company-wide communication, and encourage organizational members to feel more like a part of an organization.[22]

Job Enrichment and Job Redesign

Job enrichment and job redesign programs are generally used to increase satisfaction in jobs that are significantly lacking in motivating factors.[23]

Job Enrichment Programs

job enrichment A method of increasing employees' job satisfaction by extending or adding motivating factors such as responsibility or growth.

Job enrichment means adding one or more motivating factors to a job. At one company, a group of eight typists worked in separate cubicles. Their job involved taking calls from dozens of field sales representatives and typing up service orders. They had no client contact; if they had a question about the order, they had to call the sales representative. They also received little performance feedback. Interviews with these workers suggested that they were bored with their

This team of workers at Germany's Apollo car production plant work together to design and manufacture the Apollo sports car. Such teams often help firms make decisions more effectively, enhance communication, and lead to increased employee motivation and satisfaction.

jobs and did not feel valued. As part of a job enrichment program, each typist was paired with a small group of designated sales representatives and became a part of their team. Typists were also given permission to call clients directly if they had questions about the order. Finally, a new feedback system was installed to give the typists more information about their performance. As a result, their performance improved and absenteeism decreased markedly.[24]

Job Redesign Programs

Job redesign acknowledges that different people want different things from their jobs. By restructuring work to achieve a more satisfactory fit between workers and their jobs, **job redesign** can motivate individuals with strong needs for career growth or achievement. Job redesign is usually implemented in one of three ways: through *combining tasks, forming natural work groups,* or *establishing client relationships*.

job redesign A method of increasing employees' job satisfaction by improving the worker-job fit through combining tasks, creating natural work groups, and/or establishing client relationships.

Combining Tasks.   The job of combining tasks involves enlarging jobs and increasing their variety to make employees feel that their work is more meaningful. In turn, employees become more motivated. For example, the job done by a programmer who maintains computer systems might be redesigned to include some system design and system development work. While developing additional skills, the programmer also becomes involved in the overall system package.

Forming Natural Work Groups.   People who do different jobs on the same projects are candidates for natural work groups. These groups are formed to help employees see the place and importance of their jobs in the total structure of the firm. Such groups are valuable to management because the people working on a project are usually the most knowledgeable about it and thus the most capable problem solvers. To see how natural workgroups affect motivation, consider a group where each employee does a small part of the job of assembling radios. One person attaches red wires, while another attaches control knobs. The jobs could be redesigned to allow the group to decide who does what and in what order. The workers can exchange jobs and plan their work schedules. Now they all see themselves as part of a team that assembles radios.

Establishing Client Relationships.   A third way of redesigning a job is to establish client relationships by letting employees interact with customers. This approach increases the variety of a job. It also gives workers greater feelings of control over their jobs and more feedback about their performance. Lotus Software uses this approach as a means of giving necessary independence to creative employees. Instead of responding to instructions from marketing managers on how to develop new products, software writers are encouraged to work directly with customers. Similarly, software writers at Microsoft observe how test users work with programs and discuss problems with them directly rather than receiving feedback from third-party researchers.

Modified Work Schedules

As another way of increasing job satisfaction, many companies are trying out different approaches to working hours and the workweek. Several types of modified work schedules have been tried, including *flextime*, the *compressed workweek, telecommuting,* and *workshare programs*.

Flextime

Flextime allows people to pick their working hours. Figure 12.7 illustrates how a flextime system might be arranged and how different people might use it.

flextime A method of increasing employees' job satisfaction by allowing them some choice in the hours they work.

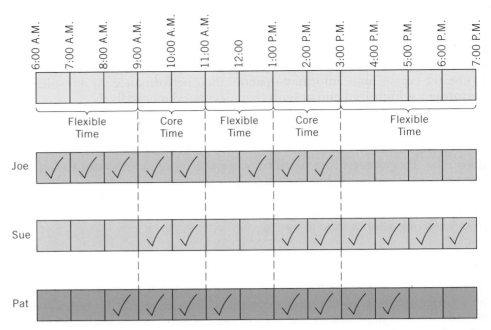

Figure 12.7 Flextime schedules include core time, when everyone must be at work, and flexible time, during which employees can set their own working hours.

The office is open from 6 a.m. until 7 p.m. Each employee works for eight hours each day. Core time is 9 a.m. until 11 a.m. and 1 p.m. until 3 p.m. Joe, being an early riser, comes in at 6 a.m., takes an hour lunch between 11 a.m. and noon, and finishes his day by 3 p.m. Sue, on the other hand, prefers a later day. She comes in at 9 a.m., takes a long lunch from 11 a.m. to 1 p.m., and then works until 7 p.m. Pat works a more traditional day, from 8 a.m. until 5 p.m.

About 70 percent of North American firms offer some variation of flextime.[25] Flextime programs give employees more freedom in their professional and personal lives and allow workers to plan around the work schedules of spouses and the school schedules of young children. The increased feeling of freedom and control over their work life also reduces individuals' levels of stress. Flextime also offers advantages to the company. For example, a Toronto company doing business in Vancouver will benefit if some employees come in at 10 a.m. and work until 7 p.m. to account for the time difference between the two cities. Companies can also benefit from the higher levels of commitment and job satisfaction among flextime workers. In large urban areas, flextime programs reduce traffic congestion that contributes to lost work time.

The Compressed Workweek

compressed workweek Employees work fewer days per week, but more hours on the days they do work.

In the **compressed workweek**, employees work fewer days per week but more hours on the days they do work. The most popular compressed workweek is four days, 10 hours per day, which is used in many companies and municipalities. In 2008, Chrysler began talking with the Canadian Auto Workers Union about instituting the practice because it would cut energy costs and give employees an additional day off each week. Workers at Babcock & Wilcox Canada also negotiated a four-day, 10-hour-day contract.[26]

Telecommuting

telecommuting Allowing employees to do all or some of their work away from the office.

A third variation in work design is **telecommuting**, which allows people to do some or all of their work away from their office. The availability of networked computers, fax machines, cellphones, email, and overnight delivery services makes it possible for many independent professionals to work at home or while travelling. A 2008 survey conducted by WorldatWork found that 40 percent of Canadian businesses offer some form of telecommuting for their employees.[27] In some business functions like customer service and telemarketing, most employees are telecommuters.[28]

When telecommuting was introduced, some managers were concerned that employees would not work as hard at home as they would in the office, but that fear has gradually diminished. When Ikon Office Solutions Inc. implemented a telecommuting program for 250 of its sales staff, the president of the company said there were some initial concerns that telecommuters might not work as hard when they were at home, but they are actually very productive.[29]

Employees like telecommuting because it saves them time and money, and companies like it because it boosts productivity and saves them money as well. A survey by the Computing Technology Industry Association found that two-thirds of employers felt that telecommuting boosted employee productivity and saved the company money.[30] Bell Canada, for example, has reduced its real estate expenses by having 2000 of its workers work at home.[31] Some workers do report feeling isolated and "out of the loop," when they do not see co-workers very often. To avoid this problem, B.C. Tel and Bentall Development Inc. jointly developed a satellite telecommuting office in Langley, British Columbia. It allows workers who used to commute to Burnaby or Vancouver to reduce their travel time considerably and still be able to interact with other workers.[32]

Best Buy is taking modified schedules and alternative work-places to new extremes with its corporate "results-only-work environment" or ROWE. Under ROWE, Best Buy employees can work anytime, anywhere, as long as they achieve results. The program has been so successful that Best Buy has begun introducing the program into its retail stores.

Would-be telecommuters must ask themselves several important questions: Can I meet deadlines even when I'm not being closely supervised? What will it be like to be away from the social context of the office five days a week? Can I renegotiate family rules so my spouse doesn't come home expecting to see dinner on the table just because I've been home all day?

Additional information on telecommuting is provided in Concluding Case 12-1. The boxed insert entitled "The Four-Day Workweek and Telecommuting: Are They Really Green?" raises some interesting issues.

Workshare Programs

A fourth type of modified work schedule, **worksharing** (also called **job sharing**), benefits both employee and employer. This approach allows two people to share one full-time job. For example, two people might share a position advising the human resources department. One person works Mondays through Wednesdays, and the other works Wednesdays through Fridays. A Statistics Canada survey showed that 8 percent of all part-time workers in Canada share a job with someone. People who share jobs are more likely to be women, to be university educated, and to have professional occupations such as teaching and nursing. In addition, job sharers earned more than regular part-time workers.[33]

Short-run worksharing programs can help ease experienced workers into retirement while training their replacements. Worksharing can also allow students in university co-op programs to combine academic learning with practical experience.

Long-run worksharing programs have proven a good solution for people who want only part-time work. For example, five people might decide to share one reservationist's job at Air Canada with each working one day a week. Each person earns some money, remains in the job market, and enjoys some travel benefits.

worksharing (or job sharing)
A method of increasing employee job satisfaction by allowing two people to share one job.

The Greening of Business

The Four-Day Workweek and Telecommuting: Are They Really Green?

For most people, the four-day workweek is attractive because it means they have to work only four days each week instead of five. Most people have lots of leisure-time activities they want to pursue, and the four-day workweek gives them more time to do that.

Recently, the four-day workweek has been touted as good not only for employee morale and satisfaction, but also for the environment. There are two main points that are usually made in support of the argument. First, since workers will be driving to work only four days each week instead of five, they will be using less gas and therefore reducing the amount of greenhouse gases that they put into the atmosphere. Whether the four-day workweek really saves gas obviously depends on what workers do on the fifth day. If they drive their SUV 400 kilometres to go visit relatives, they will burn more gas than they would have by simply driving to and from work. On the other hand, maybe they would have taken such a trip on the weekend if they had to work a traditional five-day workweek.

Second, a four-day workweek should mean that less electricity will be used by businesses because machines, computers, and heating systems will be running at very low levels on the fifth day. While it is true that factory machines will not be running on the fifth day, there may be no actual savings because those machines have already run for 40 hours as a result of the four previous days at 10 hours. Other electricity savings may also be elusive unless the company is committed to turning down the heat and turning off the lights on the fifth day. But that may be impossible, because there always seems to be office

staff that needs to be at work on the fifth day. Even if workers do stay at home on the fifth day, they may do other tasks that require the equivalent amount of electricity or gas that they would have consumed at work (e.g., renovating their home).

These observations show that it may be difficult to determine if the four-day workweek is better for the environment than the five-day workweek is. But telecommuting may be a more effective strategy because workers who telecommute don't come in to the office very much. If they are at home working, they will not be driving their car, so that should save gas. As well, companies that encourage telecommuting may save considerable money on real estate and other operating costs. But even here, we need to analyze what individual workers do as alternate activities before we can conclude that telecommuting is good for the environment.

Critical Thinking Questions

1. Using material contained in this insert as well as other material that you find, develop a list of arguments that the four-day workweek is better for the environment than the five-day workweek. Then develop a list of arguments that the four-day workweek is no better for the environment than the five-day workweek. Which list is most persuasive?

2. Using material contained in this insert as well as other material you can find, develop a list of arguments that telecommuting is better for the environment than the four-day workweek. Then develop a list of arguments that telecommuting is not better than the four-day workweek. Which list is most persuasive?

Leadership and Motivation

6 Define *leadership* and distinguish it from *management*.

leadership The processes and behaviours used by managers to motivate, inspire, and influence subordinates to work toward certain goals.

Leadership refers to the processes and behaviours used by managers to motivate, inspire, and influence subordinates to work toward certain goals. People often assume that "leadership" and "management" mean the same thing, but they are really different concepts. A person can be a manager, a leader, or both.[34] Consider a hospital setting. The chief of staff (chief physician) of a large hospital is clearly a manager by virtue of the position the person occupies. But this individual may or may not be respected or trusted by others and may have to rely solely on the authority vested in the position to get people to do things. Thus, being a manager does not ensure that a person is also a leader. By contrast, an emergency-room nurse with no formal authority may be quite effective at taking charge of a chaotic situation and directing others in how to deal with specific patient problems. Others in the emergency room may respond because they trust the nurse's judgment and have confidence in the nurse's decision-making skills. In this case, the emergency-room nurse is a leader but not a manager.

Finally, the head of pediatrics, supervising a staff of 20 other doctors, nurses, and attendants, may also enjoy the staff's complete respect, confidence, and trust. The staff readily take the head's advice, follow directives without question, and often go far beyond what is necessary to help carry out the unit's mission. Thus, the head of pediatrics is both a manager and a leader. The key distinctions between leadership and management are summarized in Table 12.1.

Organizations need both management *and* leadership if they are to be effective. Leadership is necessary to create and direct change and to help the organization get through tough times, and management is necessary to achieve coordination and to complete administrative activities during times of stability and predictability.[35] Management—in conjunction with leadership—can help achieve planned orderly change. Leadership—in conjunction with management— can keep the organization properly aligned with its environment. In addition, managers and leaders also play a major role in establishing the moral climate of the organization and in determining the role of ethics in its culture.[36]

Approaches to Leadership

Political, religious, and business leaders have profoundly influenced the course of human events throughout history, but careful scientific study of leadership began only about a century ago. In the following paragraphs, we briefly summarize the development of this research.

Summarize the *approaches to leadership* that developed in the twentieth century.

7

The Trait Approach

In the first two decades of the twentieth century, researchers believed that leaders had unique traits that distinguished them from non-leaders. The **trait approach** therefore focussed on identifying the traits that would differentiate leaders from non-leaders. Many traits were proposed as important, including intelligence, dominance, self-confidence, energy, height, and knowledge about the job. As time passed, the list became so long that it lost any practical value. The trait approach was all but abandoned by the middle of the twentieth century, but in recent years it has resurfaced once again. Some researchers now argue that certain traits (for example, intelligence, drive, motivation, honesty, integrity,

trait approach An approach that focuses on identifying the traits that would differentiate leaders from non-leaders.

Table 12.1   Kotter's Distinctions Between Management and Leadership

Activity	Management	Leadership
Creating an Agenda	Planning and budgeting. Establishing detailed steps and timetables for achieving needed results; allocating the resources necessary to make those needed results happen.	Establishing direction. Developing a vision of the future, often the distant future, and strategies for producing the changes needed to achieve that vision.
Developing a Human Network for Achieving the Agenda	Organizing and staffing. Establishing some structure for accomplishing plan requirements, staffing that structure with individuals, delegating responsibility and authority for carrying out the plan, providing policies and procedures to help guide people, and creating methods or systems to monitor implementation.	Aligning people. Communicating the direction by words and deeds to all those whose co-operation may be needed to influence the creation of teams and coalitions that understand the vision and strategies and accept their validity.
Executing Plans	Controlling and problem solving. Monitoring results vs. plan in some detail, identifying deviations, and then planning and organizing to solve these problems.	Motivating and inspiring. Energizing people to overcome major political, bureaucratic, and resource barriers to change, by satisfying very basic, but often unfulfilled, human needs.
Outcomes	Produces a degree of predictability and order and has the potential to consistently produce major results expected by various shareholders (e.g., for customers, always being on time; for stockholders, being on budget).	Produces change, often to a dramatic degree, and has the potential to produce extremely useful change (e.g., new products that customers want, new approaches to labour relations that help make a firm more competitive).

and self-confidence) provide the *potential* for effective leadership, but only if the person is really motivated to be a leader. The implication is that people without these traits are not likely to be successful leaders even if they try.

The *emotional intelligence* idea that was mentioned earlier in this chapter suggests that successful leaders possess five basic traits: *self-awareness* (the ability to understand your mood), *self-regulation* (the ability to control disruptive impulses), *motivation* (a passion for work), *empathy* (the ability to understand the emotional makeup of others), and *social skill* (proficiency in managing relationships). Managers who do not have these traits, it is argued, will not be successful regardless of how intelligent or highly trained they are.[37]

The Behavioural Approach

Because the trait approach was a poor predictor of leadership success, attention shifted from managers' *traits* to their *behaviours*. The goal of the **behavioural approach** was to determine how the behaviours of effective leaders differed from the behaviours of less effective leaders. This research led to the identification of two basic forms of leader behaviour: **task-oriented** (the manager focuses on how tasks should be performed in order to achieve important goals) and **employee-oriented** (the manager focuses on the satisfaction, motivation, and well-being of employees). Task-oriented managers tend to have higher-performing subordinates, but employee-oriented managers have more satisfied subordinates. Researchers have also identified three main leadership styles: the **autocratic style** (the manager issues orders and expects them to be obeyed without question), the **democratic style** (the manager requests input from subordinates before making decisions but retains final decision-making power), and the **free-rein style** (the manager serves as an adviser to subordinates who are given a lot of discretion when making decisions).

Most leaders tend to regularly use one style and may in fact find it difficult to change from one style to another. But some leaders do manage to change their style. For example, Andrall (Andy) Pearson was abrasive, numbers-oriented, and hard to please when he was president and COO of PepsiCo. But now, as director of Yum Brands, he has softened and transformed and seems to truly care about employees.[38]

The Situational (Contingency) Approach

As time passed, researchers began to realize that different situations might demand different leader behaviours. For instance, suppose a new manager takes over a work site where workers are satisfied but not very motivated to work hard. The leader should most likely exhibit task-oriented behaviours in

behavioural approach Determines how the behaviours of effective leaders differ from the behaviours of less effective leaders.

task-oriented A form of leader behaviour in which the manager focuses on how tasks should be performed in order to achieve important goals.

employee-oriented A form of leader behaviour in which the manager focuses on the satisfaction, motivation, and well-being of employees.

autocratic style A form of leader behaviour in which the manager issues orders and expects them to be obeyed without question.

democratic style A form of leader behaviour in which the manager requests input from subordinates before making decisions but retains final decision-making power.

free-rein style A form of leader behaviour in which the manager serves as an adviser to subordinates who are given a lot of discretion when making decisions.

"I like to think of myself as a nice guy. Naturally, sometimes you have to step on a few faces."

order to improve productivity. But suppose a new manager faces a situation where productivity is high but workers are stressed out about their jobs and therefore have low levels of job satisfaction. In this instance, the manager should most likely exhibit employee-oriented behaviours to help improve job satisfaction. This line of thinking led to the development of the *situational approach to leadership*.

The **situational (or contingency) approach** emerged during the 1960s and assumed that appropriate leader behaviour varied from one situation to another. This approach was first proposed as a continuum of leadership behaviour (see Figure 12.8). At one extreme, the leader makes decisions alone; at the other extreme, the leader has employees make decisions with only minimal guidance from the leader. Each point on the continuum is influenced by *characteristics of* the leader (including the leader's value system, confidence in subordinates, personal inclinations, and feelings of security), *characteristics of the subordinates* (including the subordinates' need for independence, readiness to assume responsibility, tolerance for ambiguity, interest in the problem, understanding of goals, knowledge, experience, and expectations), and the *characteristics of the situation* (including the type of organization, group effectiveness, the problem itself, and time pressures).

The leadership continuum focussed attention on leader behaviours as a continuum instead of being two simple alternatives and pointed out that various elements of any given situation affect the success of any given leadership style. Although this framework proposed the importance of certain situational factors, it was only speculative. Later models have developed more detailed and specific predictions of how different forms of leader behaviour influence subordinate satisfaction and productivity.

> **situational (contingency) approach** An approach that emerged during the 1960s and assumed that appropriate leader behaviour varied from one situation to another.

Recent Trends in Leadership

During the last couple of decades, many new ideas about leadership have been developed. We conclude this chapter with a brief discussion of several of these ideas.

> Describe the most recent ideas about effective leadership.   **8**

Transformational Leadership

Transformational leadership refers to the set of abilities that allows a leader to recognize the need for change, to create a vision to guide that change, and to

> **transformational leadership** The set of abilities that allows a leader to recognize the need for change, to create a vision to guide that change, and to execute the change effectively.

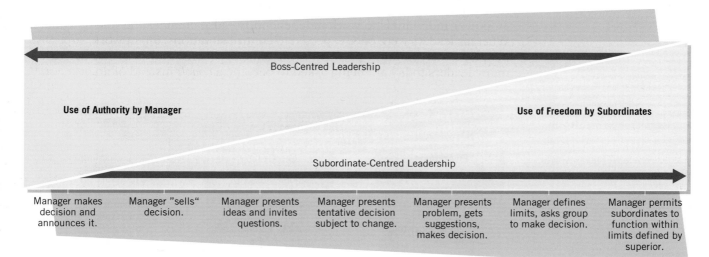

Figure 12.8 The leadership continuum.

transactional leadership
Routine, regimented activities that focus on maintaining stability of operations.

execute the change effectively. By contrast, **transactional leadership** involves routine, regimented activities that focus on maintaining stability of operations.

Many leaders may find it difficult to exercise both types of leadership. For example, when Michael Eisner took over the Walt Disney organization, the company was stagnant and was heading into decline. Relying on his transformational skills, Eisner turned things around in dramatic fashion. He expanded the company's theme parks, built new hotels, improved Disney's movie business, created a successful Disney cruise line, launched several other major initiatives, and changed the company into a global media powerhouse. But when the firm began to plateau and needed some time to let the changes all settle in, Eisner was unsuccessful at changing his own approach from transformational leadership to transactional leadership and was pressured into retiring.

Charismatic Leadership

charismatic leadership A type of influence based on the leader's personal charisma.

Charismatic leadership is a type of influence based on the leader's personal charisma. Figure 12.9 portrays the three key elements of charismatic leadership that most experts acknowledge today.[39]

A highly charismatic supervisor will generally be more successful in influencing a subordinate's behaviour than a supervisor who lacks charisma. Charismatic leaders have a high level of self-confidence and a strong need to influence others. They also communicate high expectations about follower performance and express confidence in their followers. Steve Jobs, the legendary CEO of Apple Inc., commands a cult-like following from both employees and consumers. He exhibits charisma, confidence, originality, brilliance, and vision. He is clearly a leader who can deliver success in businesses that are evolving, highly technical, and demanding. Yet he has also been portrayed as an intimidating, power-hungry, aggressive egotist.[40]

Charismatic leadership ideas are popular among managers today and are the subject of numerous books and articles.[41] One concern is that some charismatic leaders will inspire such blind faith in their followers that the followers may engage in inappropriate, unethical, or even illegal behaviours simply because the leader instructs them to do so. This tendency likely played a role in the collapse of both Enron and Arthur Andersen, as people followed orders from their charismatic bosses to hide information, shred documents, and mislead investigators.

Leaders as Coaches

Many organizations are now attempting to become less hierarchical and to eliminate the old-fashioned command-and-control mentality that is often inherent in bureaucratic organizations. This change—which will motivate and empower individuals to work independently—also changes the role of leaders. Whereas leaders were once expected to control situations, direct work, supervise people, closely monitor performance, make decisions, and structure activities, many leaders today are being asked to become a *coach* instead of an *overseer*.[42]

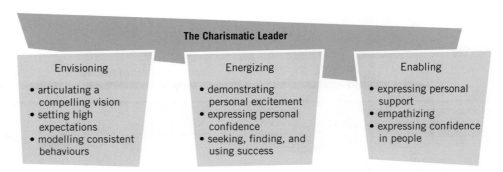

Figure 12.9 Charismatic leadership.

Consider the parallel with an athletic team. The coach selects the players for the team and decides on the general direction to take (such as emphasizing offence versus defence). The coach also helps develop player talent and teaches team members how to execute specific plays. But at game time, it's up to the players to execute plays and get the job done. While the coach may get some of the credit for the victory, he or she didn't actually score any of the points.

For business leaders, a coaching perspective calls for the leader to help select team members and other new employees, to provide some general direction, to help train and develop the team and the skills of its members, and to help the team get the information and other resources it needs. The leader may also have to help resolve conflict among team members and mediate other disputes that arise. And coaches from different teams need to link the activities and functions of their respective teams. Beyond these activities, the leader is expected to keep a low profile and let the group get its work done, with little or no direct oversight from the leader.

Gender and Leadership

Another factor that is altering the face of leadership is the growing number of women advancing to the highest levels in organizations. Given that most leadership theories and research studies have focussed on male leaders, developing a better understanding of how women lead is clearly an important next step. The key question is this: Do women and men lead differently? Some early observers predicted that (consistent with prevailing stereotypes) female leaders would be relatively warm, supportive, and nurturing compared to their male counterparts. But in reality, research suggests that female leaders are not necessarily more nurturing or supportive than male leaders. Likewise, male leaders are not systematically more harsh, controlling, or task focussed than female leaders. Women do seem to have a tendency to be more democratic when making decisions, whereas men have a tendency to be somewhat more autocratic.[43]

Cross-Cultural Leadership

Culture is a broad concept that encompasses both international differences and diversity-based differences within one culture. For instance, when a Japanese firm sends an executive to head up the firm's operation in Canada, that person will need to be sensitive to the cultural differences that exist between the two countries and consider changing his or her leadership style accordingly. Japan is generally characterized by *collectivism* (group before individual), whereas Canada is based more on *individualism* (individual before group). The Japanese

Andrea Jung (left), CEO of Avon Products, and Angela Merkel (right), chancellor of Germany, are exceptional leaders. Jung has transformed Avon and made it a powerhouse in its industry, and Merkel was recently named to *TIME* magazine's list of "people who shape our world."

executive, then, will find it necessary to recognize the importance of individual contributions and rewards and the differences in individual and group roles that exist in Japanese and Canadian businesses.

Cross-cultural factors also play a growing role in organizations as their workforces become more diverse. Most leadership research has analyzed white male leaders, because those individuals have historically dominated leadership positions in North America. But as Asians, blacks, Aboriginals, and Hispanics achieve leadership positions, it will be necessary to reassess how applicable current models of leadership are when applied to the increasingly diverse pool of leaders.

Canadian Versus American Management Styles.   The management style of Canadian managers might look a lot like that of Americans, but there are several notable differences. Most fundamentally, Canadian managers are more subtle and subdued than American managers. Canadian managers also seem more committed to their companies, less willing to mindlessly follow the latest management fad, and more open to different cultures because of the multicultural nature of Canada. All of these characteristics are advantageous for Canadian companies that will increasingly be competing in global markets.[44]

Many Canadian-born managers have achieved significant success in companies that operate outside of Canada. For example, Bob Kelly was appointed CEO of the Bank of New York Mellon Corp., the eleventh largest financial services firm in the United States.[45] Other Canadians who have achieved high positions are Henry McKinnell (CEO of Pfizer, the world's largest pharmaceutical company), Steven McArthur (president of online travel company Expedia), Patricia Arnold (vice-president of Credit Suisse First Boston), Clara Furse (CEO of the London Stock Exchange), Simon Cooper (CEO of The Ritz-Carlton Hotel Company), and Dominic Barton (chair of McKinsey & Company's Asia Region), to name just a few.[46]

Strategic Leadership

strategic leadership A leader's ability to understand the complexities of both the organization and its environment in order to lead change in the organization, which will enhance its competitiveness.

Strategic leadership—which focuses on leadership in top management—is a leader's ability to understand the complexities of both the organization and its environment in order to lead change in the organization, which will enhance its competitiveness. Steve Jobs, CEO of Apple Inc., is an effective strategic leader who recognized the potential growth of MP3 players and the fact that those devices used technology that is similar to that found in computers. He therefore directed the development of the Apple iPod, which has become an enormously successful and profitable product. When he temporarily stepped down as CEO in 2009 because of concerns about his health, observers worried that Apple would lose its competitive advantage.

Ethical Leadership

ethical leadership Leader behaviours that reflect high ethical standards.

In the wake of recent corporate scandals at firms like AIG, Enron, and WorldCom, faith in business leaders has been shaken. High standards of ethical conduct are therefore being held up as a prerequisite for effective leadership. More specifically, business leaders are being called on to maintain high ethical standards for their own conduct, to unfailingly exhibit ethical behaviour, and to hold others in their organizations to the same standards—in short, to practise **ethical leadership**.

Virtual Leadership

virtual leadership The carrying out of leadership activities when the leader does not have regular personal contact with followers.

Virtual leadership involves carrying out leadership activities when the leader does not have regular personal contact with followers. In earlier times, leaders and their employees worked together in the same physical location and engaged in personal (i.e., face-to-face) interactions on a regular basis. But in today's world, leaders and their employees may work in locations that are far from one another. Such arrangements might include people telecommuting from a home office one or two days a week or people actually living and working far from company headquarters and seeing one another in person only very infrequently.

Under virtual leadership, communication between leaders and their subordinates will still occur, but it may be largely by telephone and email. In the future, leaders will have to work harder at creating and maintaining relationships with their employees that go beyond words on a computer screen. Nonverbal communication is not possible with email, so managers will have to work harder to convey appreciation, reinforcement, or constructive feedback to subordinates. Managers should also take advantage of every opportunity whenever they are in face-to-face situations to go further than they might have under different circumstances to develop a strong relationship.

Test yourself on the material for this chapter at **www.pearsoned.ca/mybusinesslab**.

Summary of
Learning Objectives

1. **Identify and discuss the basic *forms of behaviour* that employees exhibit in organizations.** *Employee behaviour* is the pattern of actions by the members of an organization that directly or indirectly influences the organization's effectiveness. *Performance behaviours* are the total set of work-related behaviours that the organization expects employees to display. *Organizational citizenship* refers to the behaviour of individuals who make a positive overall contribution to the organization. *Counterproductive behaviours* are those that detract from, rather than contribute to, organizational performance.

2. **Describe the nature and importance of *individual differences* among employees.** Individual differences are personal attributes that vary from one person to another. *Personality* is the relatively stable set of psychological attributes that distinguish one person from another. The "big five" personality traits are agreeableness, conscientiousness, emotionality, extraversion, and openness. *Emotional intelligence, or emotional quotient (EQ)*, refers to the extent to which people are self-aware, can manage their emotions, can motivate themselves, express empathy for others, and possess social skills. Attitudes reflect our beliefs and feelings about specific ideas, situations, or other people. Especially important attitudes are *job satisfaction* and *organizational commitment*.

3. **Explain the meaning and importance of *psychological contracts* and the *person-job fit* in the workplace.** A *psychological contract* is the overall set of expectations held by employees and the organization regarding what employees will contribute to the organization and what the organization will provide in return. A good *person-job fit* is achieved when the employee's contributions match the inducements the organization offers. Having a good match between people and their jobs can help enhance performance, job satisfaction, and motivation.

4. **Identify and summarize the most important *models of employee motivation*.** *Motivation* is the set of forces that cause people to behave in certain ways. Early approaches to motivation were based first on the assumption that people work only for money and then on the assumption that social needs are the primary way to motivate people. The *hierarchy of human needs model* holds that people at work try to satisfy one or more of five different needs. The *two-factor theory* argues that satisfaction and dissatisfaction depend on hygiene factors, such as working conditions, and motivation factors, such as recognition for a job well done. *Expectancy theory* suggests that people are motivated to work toward rewards that they have a reasonable expectancy of obtaining. *Equity theory* focuses on social comparisons—people evaluating their treatment by the organization relative to the treatment of others.

5. **Describe the *strategies* used by organizations to improve employee motivation.** There are several major strategies and techniques often used to make jobs more interesting and rewarding. When using *reinforcement* theory, a manager has four basic strategies: (1) positive

reinforcement (apply desirable consequences when employees exhibit positive behaviour), (2) punishment (apply undesirable consequences when employees exhibit negative behaviour), (3) omission (withhold desirable consequences when employees exhibit undesirable behaviour), and (4) negative reinforcement (withhold undesirable consequences when employees exhibit positive behaviour).

Management by objectives (MBO) is a system of collaborative goal setting that extends from the top of an organization to the bottom. In *participative management and empowerment*, employees are given a voice in how they do their jobs and in how the company is managed. Using teams can also enhance motivation. *Job enrichment* adds motivating factors to job activities. *Job redesign* is a method of increasing job satisfaction by designing a more satisfactory fit between workers and their jobs. Some companies also use modified work schedules—different approaches to working hours. Common options include *worksharing (job sharing), flextime programs*, and *telecommuting*.

6. Define *leadership* and distinguish it from *management*. *Leadership* refers to the processes and behaviours used by someone to motivate, inspire, and influence the behaviours of others. While leadership and management are related concepts, they are not the same thing. Leadership involves such things as developing a vision, communicating that vision, and directing change. Management, meanwhile, focuses more on outlining procedures, monitoring results, and working toward outcomes.

7. Summarize the *approaches to leadership* that developed in the twentieth century. The *trait approach* to leadership focussed on identifying the traits of successful leaders. The earliest researchers believed that important leadership traits included intelligence, dominance, self-confidence, energy, activity (versus passivity), and knowledge about the job. More recent researchers have started to focus on traits such as emotional intelligence, drive, honesty and integrity, self-confidence, and charisma. The *behavioural approach* identified two basic and common leader behaviours: *task-focussed* and *employee-focussed*

behaviours. The *situational approach* to leadership proposes that there is no single best approach to leadership. Instead, situational factors influence the approach to leadership that is most effective. This approach was proposed as a continuum of leadership behaviour, ranging from having the leader make decisions alone to having employees make decisions with minimal guidance from the leader. Each point on the continuum is influenced by characteristics of the leader, his or her subordinates, and the situation.

8. Describe the most recent ideas about effective leadership. *Transformational leadership* (as distinguished from *transactional leadership*) focuses on the set of abilities that allows a leader to recognize the need for change, to create a vision to guide that change, and to execute the change effectively. *Charismatic leadership* is influence based on the leader's personal charisma. The basic concept of charisma suggests that charismatic leaders are likely to have self-confidence, confidence in their beliefs and ideals, and a need to influence people. They also tend to communicate high expectations about follower performance and to express confidence in their followers.

Many organizations expect their leaders to play the role of coach—to select team members, to provide direction, and to train and develop, but otherwise allow the group to function autonomously. Another factor that is altering the face of leadership is the number of women advancing to higher levels. While there appear to be few differences between men and women leaders, the growing number of women leaders suggests a need for more study. Another changing perspective on leadership relates to cross-cultural issues. In this context, culture encompasses international differences and diversity-based differences within one culture.

Strategic leadership is the leader's ability to lead change in the organization so as to enhance its competitiveness. Business leaders are also being called on to practice *ethical leadership*—that is, to maintain high ethical standards for their own conduct and to hold others in their organizations to the same standards. As more leaders and employees work in different settings, a better understanding of *virtual leadership* is also becoming more important.

Key Terms

absenteeism   (p. 392)

attitude   (p. 395)

autocratic style   (p. 412)

behavioural approach   (p. 412)

charismatic leadership   (p. 414)

classical theory of motivation
    (p. 396)

compressed workweek   (p. 408)

counterproductive behaviours
    (p. 392)

democratic style   (p. 412)

emotional intelligence (emotional
    quotient [EQ])   (p. 394)

employee behaviour   (p. 392)

employee-oriented   (p. 412)

equity theory   (p. 400)

ethical leadership   (p. 416)

expectancy theory   (p. 399)

flextime   (p. 407)

free-rein style   (p. 412)

goal setting theory   (p. 403)

Hawthorne effect   (p. 397)

hierarchy of human needs model
    (p. 398)

human relations   (p. 397)

individual differences   (p. 393)

job enrichment   (p. 406)

job redesign   (p. 407)

job satisfaction   (p. 395)

leadership   (p. 410)

management by objectives (MBO)
    (p. 403)

motivation   (p. 396)

organizational citizenship   (p. 392)

organizational commitment
    (p. 395)

participative management and
    empowerment   (p. 404)

performance behaviours   (p. 392)

personality   (p. 393)

person-job fit   (p. 396)

psychological contract   (p. 395)

quality circle   (p. 404)

reinforcement   (p. 401)

scientific management   (p. 397)

situational (contingency) approach
    (p. 413)

SMART goals   (p. 403)

strategic leadership   (p. 416)

task-oriented   (p. 412)

telecommuting   (p. 408)

Theory X   (p. 398)

Theory Y   (p. 398)

trait approach   (p. 411)

transactional leadership   (p. 414)

transformational leadership
    (p. 413)

turnover   (p. 392)

two-factor theory   (p. 399)

virtual leadership   (p. 416)

wikis   (p. 404)

worksharing (job sharing)   (p. 409)

Questions for Analysis

1. Describe the psychological contract you currently have or have had in the past with an employer. If you have never worked, describe the psychological contract that you have with the instructor in this class.

2. Explain how each of the "big five" personality traits influence leadership effectiveness.

3. Compare and contrast the needs-based theories of Maslow and Herzberg with expectancy theory and equity theory.

4. How can participative management programs enhance employee satisfaction and motivation? Why do some employees not want to get involved in participative management?

5. What is the relationship between performance behaviours and organizational citizenship behaviours? Which are more important to an organization?

6. As a manager, under what sort of circumstances might you apply each of the theories of motivation discussed in this chapter? Which would be easiest to use? Which would be hardest? Why?

7. Suppose you realize one day that you are dissatisfied with your job. Short of quitting, what might you do to improve your situation?

8. List two Canadian and two U.S. managers who you think would also qualify as great leaders. Explain your choices.

Application Exercises

1. Ask a manager what traits the manager thinks are necessary for success. How does the manager's list compare with the "big five" list in this chapter? How many differences are there? Why would these differences exist?

2. Interview the manager of a local company and ask what strategies the company uses to enhance employee job satisfaction. Also ask the manager whether he or she believes that leadership can be taught. What are the implications of the manager's answer?

Building Your Business Skills

Too Much of a Good Thing

The Purpose of the Assignment

To encourage students to apply different motivational theories to a workplace problem involving poor productivity.

The Situation

Consider a small company that makes its employees feel as if they are members of a large family. Unfortunately, this company is going broke because too few members are working hard enough to make money for it. They are happy, comfortable, complacent—and lazy. With sales dropping, the company brings in management consultants to analyze the situation and make recommendations. The outsiders quickly identify a motivational problem affecting the sales force: Sales reps are paid a handsome salary and receive automatic year-end bonuses regardless of performance. They are also treated to bagels every Friday and regular group birthday lunches that cost as much as $200 each. Employees feel satisfied but have little incentive to work very hard. Eager to return to profitability, the company's owners wait to hear your recommendations.

Assignment

Step 1

In groups of four, step into the role of management consultants. Start by analyzing your client's workforce motivation problems from the following perspectives (the questions focus on key motivational issues):

Job satisfaction and morale. As part of a long-standing family-owned business, employees are happy and loyal, in part because they are treated so well. Can high morale have a downside? How can it breed stagnation, and what can managers do to prevent stagnation from taking hold?

Theory X versus Theory Y. Although the behaviour of these workers seems to make a case for Theory X, why is it difficult to draw this conclusion about a company that focuses more on satisfaction than on sales and profits?

Two-factor theory. Analyze the various ways in which improving such motivational factors as recognition, added responsibility, advancement, and growth might reduce the importance of hygiene factors, including pay and security.

Expectancy theory. Analyze the effect on productivity of redesigning the company's sales force compensation structure, namely, by paying lower base salaries while offering greater earnings potential through a sales-based incentive system. How would linking performance with increased pay that is achievable through hard work motivate employees? How would the threat of job loss motivate greater effort?

Step 2

Write a short report based on your analysis and make recommendations to the company's owners. The goal of your report is to change the working environment in ways that will motivate greater effort and generate greater productivity.

Questions for Discussion

1. What is your group's most important recommendation? Why do you think it is likely to succeed?

2. Changing the corporate culture to make it less paternalistic may reduce employees' sense of belonging to a family. If you were an employee, would you consider a greater focus on profits to be an improvement or a problem? How would it affect your motivation and productivity?

3. What steps would you take to improve the attitude and productivity of long-time employees who resist change?

Exercising Your Ethics: Team Exercise

Taking One for the Team

The Situation

You are a skilled technician who has worked for a major electronics firm for the past 10 years. You love your job—it is interesting, stimulating, and enjoyable, and you are well-paid for what you do. The plant where you work is one of five manufacturing centres your firm operates in a major metropolitan area. The firm is currently developing a new prototype for one of its next-generation products. To ensure that all perspectives are reflected, the company

has identified a set of technicians from each plant who will work together as a team for the next two months.

The Dilemma

You have just met with your new teammates and are quite confused about what you might do next. As it turns out, the technicians from two of the manufacturing centres have heard rumours that your company is planning to close at least three of the centres and move production to a lower-cost factory in another country. These individuals are very upset. Moreover, they have made it clear that

►

▶

they (1) do not intend to put forth much extra effort on this project, and (2) are all looking for new jobs. You and the other technicians, though, have heard none of these rumours. Moreover, these individuals seem as excited as you are about their jobs.

Team Activity

First, working alone, write a brief summary of how you would handle this situation. For instance, would you seek more information or just go about your work? Would you start looking for another job, would you try to form a sub-group with just those technicians who share your views, or would you try to work with everyone?

Second, form a small group with some of your class-mates. Share with each other the various ideas you each identified. Then, formulate a group description of what you think most people in your situation would do and share your description with the rest of the class.

For additional cases and exercise material, go to **www.pearsoned.ca/mybusinesslab**.

Concluding Case 12-1

What About Telecommuting?

On any given day, many business offices are vacant because employees are either at off-site meetings, travelling, on vacation, out sick, or attending training sessions. Many companies now recognize that there are advantages for both employees and for the company if they allow employees to work from home and "telecommute." About 1.5 million Canadians work at home at least one or two days a week, and some work from home almost all the time. Consider three fairly typical stories.

Edward Moffat works for Sun Microsystems of Canada. He signed up for the company's "open work" program, which allowed him to work largely from home (or anywhere for that matter). He wasn't in the office much anyway, because he travelled a lot. Now Ed works out of his Brampton, Ontario home 9 days out of 10. He doesn't have to pay $300 per month in highway tolls, his gas costs and car maintenance costs have gone way down, and he spends less on lunch. He thinks all those things combined save him about $50 per day. He also gets to see his wife and children more frequently. The company estimates that telecommuting saved it $71 million in real estate costs alone (because fewer employee offices are needed), and the turnover rate is half what it is for non-telecommuters.

Sylvie Bolduc decided to take advantage of Bell Canada's telework option, partly because she was sick of the 90-minute drive to work every day. She says she is a disciplined person and doesn't feel the need to constantly interact with co-workers. She has online meetings with staff on a regular basis and makes trips to the office every two weeks to catch up on other developments. She says she wants to work like this the rest of her life. Bell's program means that 11 000 tonnes of greenhouse gases are not being put into the atmosphere, because fewer employees are driving to and from work.

Deborah Corber started telecommuting at her job when her family relocated to her hometown of Montreal. Later, she worked out of her home after she started her own consulting firm. She says the biggest challenge was isolation, because she likes bouncing ideas off colleagues. She also had trouble separating her personal and professional life and felt that she was spending way too much time in her office in her home. In 2007, she decided to stop working at home, and she now shares space with several colleagues in an office close to her home.

These three stories show how varied employee experiences are with the idea of telecommuting. They also show that there are advantages and disadvantages associated with telecommuting.

Advantages for employees

- health benefits (for example, lower stress levels)
- lower costs (reduced car expenses)
- better use of time (no commuting long distances, no interruptions)

Disadvantages for employees

- feeling "out of the loop" (not being knowledgeable about important business issues or interesting personal gossip)
- having difficulty separating personal and professional life (work intrudes at home)
- feeling ill-suited for telework (lack of discipline and feeling lonely)
- finding it difficult to work closely with colleagues when necessary
- fear of career derailment

Advantages for the Employer

- increased productivity (two-thirds of employers surveyed said that employee productivity went up)
- cost savings (fewer offices and office supplies are needed; lower vehicle expenses)
- lower electric bills (fewer lights and computers are turned on in offices)
- access to qualified staff (who otherwise wouldn't be available because they don't live in the area or don't want to drive so far to work)
- lower travel expenses (teleconferencing, email, networking systems take the place of travel)
- lower employee turnover

Disadvantages for the Employer

- requires a change in management thinking (forces managers to adopt an attitude of trust regarding employees)
- bosses have to spend more time with subordinates on the phone or other media (they may prefer face-to-face communication)
- bosses don't know when employees are actually working (may threaten the control of bosses who are used to having employees in sight)
- telecommuting may not work well for companies where customers are frequently in the office
- telecommuting may not work well if colleagues frequently need intense face-to-face collaboration to complete rush jobs on time

These advantages and disadvantages mean that telecommuting must be carefully thought through so that it is beneficial to both employees and to the company. It does not mean simply telling workers that they can now work at home. Rather, there must be a clear understanding between the bosses and workers about things like the nature of the arrangement, the type of tasks that can be completed away from the office, maintaining safety and confidentiality in the employee's home office, what telecommuting might mean for the employee's career path, and so on.

Questions for Discussion

1. How is telecommuting different from other forms of modified work schedules? How is it similar?

2. Do you think that telecommuting will become more prominent in the future? Explain the reasons for your position.

3. Interview a friend or relative who telecommutes in their job. What advantages and disadvantages do they see in such an arrangement? Compare their responses with the advantages and disadvantages listed above. If there are major differences, try to explain them.

Concluding Case 12-2

Leadership and Management

We generally think of leadership and management as being important mainly in business firms, but leadership and management are relevant in many different contexts. Consider the activity of polar exploration. In the nineteenth century, much time, money, and effort was spent by English, Norwegian, and American explorers as they tried to reach the North and South Poles. To achieve their goals, explorers first had to secure financial support to pay for their expeditions. But that was only the beginning. Ships and personnel had to be acquired, and tonnes of supplies and animals had to be taken across the ocean to the starting point for the expedition. All of this required a great deal of planning and organizing, both of which are key functions of management. But leadership was also crucial because these expeditions were attempting to achieve goals that were at the very edge of human capability. They were also very dangerous, and many men died on these expeditions. Leaders who could generate high motivation and commitment among their followers were therefore critical to the success of their expeditions. John Franklin, Ernest Shackleton, Roald Amundsen, and Robert Scott were particularly notable.

John Franklin (1786–1847)

John Franklin was an English explorer who hungered for fame and promotion through the ranks of the English navy. Franklin has been described as recklessly ambitious, humourless, sensitive, unimaginative, dogged, brave, indecisive, calm when danger threatened, courageous, charming, humble, and easygoing. In 1845, he led a group of 129 men in an attempt to discover the Northwest Passage. Critics of Franklin noted that he ignored the harsh environment he was entering and simply tried to transport the "civilized" English environment with him rather than adapting to the Arctic environment as the Inuit did. His expedition was last seen by a whaling ship in Baffin Bay in June 1845. His group was never seen again by white people, but his expedition may have encountered Inuit hunters somewhere in their travels. His ships were crushed by the ice and eventually all 129 members of the expedition died as they tried to find their way home.

Ernest Shackleton (1874–1922)

Ernest Shackleton was an Anglo-Irish explorer who became famous for his dramatic expeditions to the Antarctic as he tried to reach the South Pole. Shackleton has been described as quick tempered, impatient, self-confident, ruthless, egotistical, moody, optimistic, persuasive, restless, and ambitious. He was a strong leader who made things happen. His followers did whatever he ordered because they had complete faith in him. They affectionately called him "The Boss." Shackleton showed great concern for the men under his command, and he put his followers' welfare ahead of his own. His inspirational leadership motivated his men to give that extra ounce of effort in life-and-death situations.

In 1914, Shackleton decided to trek across the Antarctic, but his ship, the *Endurance*, became locked in the ice and he never even reached the continent. After the ship was crushed by the ice and sank, his party camped out for some weeks until the ice broke up. They then took to small boats and made their way to nearby Elephant Island, a desolate, isolated, and windswept speck of land in the South Atlantic Ocean. Knowing that rescue would never come there, Shackleton and a small group of men then sailed a tiny open boat across almost 1300 kilometres of ocean to South Georgia, where they organized a relief party for the men back on Elephant Island. In the end, not a man was lost and Shackleton's leadership reputation became legendary.

Robert Scott (1868–1912) and Roald Amundsen (1872–1928)

In 1911–12, the Englishman Robert Scott and the Norwegian Roald Amundsen became involved in a race to see who would be the first human being to reach the South Pole. The trip to the Pole was made in conditions that are hard to imagine. On foot or on skis, the explorers made their way across 1200 kilometres of ice and snow, through –40°C temperatures and over mountains nearly 3000 metres high. Once at the Pole, they had to turn around and fight their way back to the coast through the same conditions.

Roald Amundsen was very successful because he learned to adapt his behaviour to the environment in which he was working. He avoided almost all of the mistakes that other explorers made. For example, he learned that most expeditions actually had two leaders: the expedition commander (who typically had no navigation experience) and the ship's captain. This could lead to dissension. He also learned that there was typically conflict between the scientific staff and the sailors on the expedition. Amundsen therefore studied science and navigation and became an expert at both, so there was no divided command on his expeditions. He also took only small numbers of men so there were fewer people to feed. In sharp contrast to most other explorers, he adopted the successful strategies of the Inuit to survive in polar climates.

Amundsen was a meticulous planner because he realized that planning was absolutely essential for a successful expedition to the Pole. In the crucial areas of food and fuel, Amundsen developed a system for laying out supply depots so that they could be found even in a raging blizzard. This ensured that the Norwegians had enough supplies to make it safely back to their base camp after they had reached the Pole. By studying polar conditions, he knew that sled dogs were the best animals to haul supplies. He also knew that going to the Pole on skis

was far superior to walking. Amundsen carefully selected the four men who would accompany him and who would live in very close quarters during the three-month trip to the Pole and back. Amundsen's men had complete confidence in his abilities, and he, in turn, allowed them to participate in many of the important decisions that had to be made during the expedition.

Robert Scott was a sharp contrast to Amundsen. Because he left the planning of important details of the expedition to the last minute, major mistakes were made in decisions about animals and equipment. For example, Scott decided to rely on ponies for hauling supplies, but this decision ignored the obvious fact that ponies were inferior to huskies for hauling supplies in bitterly cold weather. Scott did take skis along, but few people in his party knew how to use them properly. They therefore wasted precious energy and covered fewer kilometres each day than they might have. Scott's planning of supply depots was also haphazard, and insufficient care was taken in the storage of fuel. In the extreme cold of the Antarctic, much of the fuel that Scott had stored in supply depots evaporated. On his return trip, therefore, he consistently ran short of fuel. (Amundsen had no such problems because he had designed an airtight seal for his fuel containers.) Scott's leadership ability was also questionable. There was dissension in the ranks because of poor communication, conflicting orders, and interpersonal disagreements. Scott did not inspire confidence in his men, and he did not allow them to participate in important decisions.

Who won the race? Although both men managed to reach the South Pole, Amundsen beat Scott to the prize by a full month. In the end, Scott's men paid dearly for their leader's shortcomings: They all died of starvation and exposure as they attempted to get back to their base camp on the coast.

Questions for Discussion

1. What is the difference between leaders and managers? Were the explorers described above leaders? Were they managers?

2. Compare the leadership ability of each of the polar explorers in terms of the five traits that are thought to predict effective leadership.

3. What is emotional intelligence? To what extent did the polar explorers exhibit emotional intelligence?

4. Use any one of the contingency leadership theories discussed in the chapter to analyze the appropriateness of the leadership styles used by Scott and Amundsen. Were they using the right style? Explain.

5. What makes a leader charismatic? Which of the polar explorers do you think was the most charismatic? Explain.

Flair Bartending

Remember the movie in which Tom Cruise played a flashy bartender? That style of bartending actually has a name. It's called "flair bartending." Gavin MacMillan is the top-ranked Canadian flair bartender and second-ranked in the world. He's also an author and the owner of a bartender-for-hire business called Movers and Shakers. Now he's developing a brand-new idea for a bartender school called Bartender 1. Eventually, he wants to franchise the idea across Canada, the United States, and the world.

Potential franchisees will like his idea to use an actual bar to teach students flair bartending. Gavin doesn't rent space; rather, he borrows a bar for an evening to hold his classes. On one Monday evening, he is at a Toronto bar that is closed, but he has talked the owner into letting him run his class there for free. In return, the bar gets first pick of the graduates of Gavin's bartending school. In his first class of 12 students, Gavin has incurred $11 000 of expenses but receives only $6000 in revenues. He hopes to reduce the cost of running future classes by reusing demonstration equipment. He needs to prove this concept will really work before trying to franchise it.

Later, a Mississauga bar owner lets Gavin hold a class at his establishment. Gavin doesn't have a problem finding students who want to be bartenders, but he does have a problem finding people who can be instructors. There are only about 10 flair bartenders in Toronto and 40 in all of Canada. Finding teachers is not Gavin's only problem. He is a perfectionist who is always fussing over the little things. Sometimes he focuses so much on the details that he doesn't see the big picture. A third problem is his lack of time to do all the things he wants to do.

He has designed, built, and financed a portable bar that he hopes to sell to golf courses and hotels. He brings his idea to an entrepreneurial self-help session run by a business group that he joined. He says that he wants to make 10 of the portable bars in order to be more cost-effective, and he wants the other participants in the group to help him with ideas to market the bar. But one of the group members questions whether Gavin should even pursue the idea, because he already has too many balls in the air. He needs to prioritize.

Two months later, Gavin is conducting a two-day bartending course at the University of Guelph. His school is now making money, and everything is going well because he listened to the advice to focus on just a few projects. He has stopped putting energy into his portable bar for the moment and has begun delegating duties to others.

Gavin says he wants to make his business a great success. He is thinking big. He wants to earn enough money to buy a yacht with a helicopter pad on it.

Questions for Discussion

1. What are the big-five personality traits? How do you think Gavin MacMillan would score on each of these five traits? What might this imply for his success as an entrepreneur?

2. Do a little research and find out what the difference is between *extrinsic motivation* and *intrinsic motivation*. Do you think Gavin is extrinsically or intrinsically motivated?

3. Gavin says that he wants to eventually have a yacht with a helicopter pad on it. How does setting a goal like this motivate a person?

4. What recommendations would you have for Gavin in the area of being more focussed in his goal setting?

Video Resource: "Flair Bartending," *Dreamers and Schemers* (November 8, 2006).

Clash of the Co-workers

Venture conducted a survey to determine workers' perceptions of the main causes of conflict in the workplace. Respondents were presented with a list of 10 common worker complaints and asked to list their top three. The top three vote-getters were (1) people who talk too loudly on the phone, (2) office gossip, and (3) co-workers who waste your time. *Venture* further examined the impact of office gossip. It also looked at the issues of co-workers who don't pull their weight and clashes between older and younger workers.

Office Gossip

Office gossip can poison a workplace. A tanning salon owner who had worked hard to build her company encountered big problems when employees started spreading rumours about one another. After one salon manager disciplined a worker, other workers began spreading rumours that the salon manager was incompetent. When the owner became aware of the excessive gossip that was evident at the company, she called all employees into the head office and asked them to sign a contract that prohibited gossip. One behaviour that is prohibited is talking about a co-worker when that co-worker isn't present. A year after introducing the contract idea, the salon owner is getting calls from other companies asking about the policy.

Bob Summerhurst, a human resources specialist, says that gossip occurs when bosses play favourites or when they don't communicate properly. Any information void will be filled with gossip, and that gossip is often negative. His solution is not a ban on gossip but rather regular meetings of managers and employees.

Co-workers Who Don't Pull Their Weight

Jerry Steinberg, a Vancouver teacher, says that workers with children are often treated as "special" and he thinks it's unfair. He says an extra burden is being borne by people like himself when they are asked to work a few extra hours a week to cover for parents who are tending to their children. The problem is worst during the holiday season because people with no children are asked to work holidays so that workers with children can spend time with their kids.

Steinberg is speaking up about his concerns. He has started a website called No Kidding where child-free members can vent their frustrations about the unfair treatment they are receiving at their workplace. But Steinberg says it is hard to stand up for yourself because you don't want to rock the boat or be a whiner. He recognizes that it sounds heartless to be unsympathetic to parents' wishes to spend time with their children. But he also observes that these people made a choice to have children, and they shouldn't expect to have an advantage because they made that choice. He is also unhappy about the extra benefits that parents get. He has a simple solution for that problem: Give each employee a certain dollar amount that they can spend on whatever benefits they want.

The Generation Gap

Young people in their 20s have generally grown up in an environment where their baby-boomer parents gave them lots of things. Now those young people are entering the workforce, and they want more things—benefits, money, authority, and free time. And they want them right now.

Consider John and Ryan, who are recent college grads. They are part of a generation that is a problem for business. They feel that they work very hard, but they don't necessarily want to do what their predecessors did (like wearing a suit and tie to work, or working from 9 to 5). Mike Farrell, who researches attitudes of young people, notes that most young people are plugged in and well-informed, and these are qualities that employers crave. Theresa Williams, who hires workers for the Halifax *Chronicle-Herald*, recognizes that young people today are different from their predecessors. For example, they don't seem grateful to be offered a job like people in her generation were. She tries to overcome the difficulties in recruiting young people by emphasizing the good working conditions at the *Chronicle-Herald*.

The way students look for jobs is also changing. The job fair approach is still used, but some companies find it doesn't attract the kind of employees they want. One company therefore came up with a gimmick: They posted a job competition on the internet, with the prize being a job for a year, a free apartment, and a trip home for the holidays. The two winners—John and Ryan—moved to Halifax. A year later, they moved out of their free apartment but stayed on with the company. Now they are helping to design this year's job competition, and they're on board with "the old guys."

Questions for Discussion

1. What are the various forms of employee behaviour that can be observed in organizations, and what is the impact of the various forms on organizations? Identify the forms of employee behaviour that are evident in each of the three situations described above and how they affected the organization in which they occurred.

2. What is the difference between *management* and *leadership*? What is the relevance of management and leadership in each of the situations described above?

3. What is the difference between the *formal organization* and the *informal organization*? How is the distinction relevant for each of the three situations described above?

4. Consider the following statement with respect to the first incident described above (office gossip): *The grapevine carries a lot of inaccurate information that prevents employees from doing their jobs well. To overcome this problem, managers should provide accurate information through formal communication channels, and that will negate the need for the grapevine.* Do you agree or disagree with the statement? Explain your reasoning.

Video Resource: "Clash of the Co-workers," *Venture* (March 26, 2006).

Part 1: The Contemporary Business Environment

Goal of the Exercise

In Chapter 3 we discussed how the starting point for virtually every new business is a *business plan*. Business plans describe the business strategy for any new business and demonstrate how that strategy will be implemented. One benefit of a business plan is that, in preparing it, would-be entrepreneurs must develop their idea on paper and firm up their thinking about how to launch their business before investing time and money in it. In this exercise, you'll get started on creating your own business plan.

Exercise Background: Part 1 of the Business Plan

The starting point for any business plan is coming up with a "great idea." This might be a business that you've already considered setting up. If you don't have ideas for a business already, look around. What are some businesses that you come into contact with on a regular basis? Restaurants, childcare services, and specialty stores are a few examples you might consider. You may also wish to create a business that is connected with a talent or interest you have, such as crafts, cooking, or car repair. It's important that you create a company "from scratch" rather than use a company that already exists. You'll learn more if you use your own ideas.

Once you have your business idea, your next step is to create an "identity" for your business. This includes determining a name for your business and an idea of what your business will do. It also includes identifying the type of ownership your business will take, topics we discussed in Chapter 3. The first part of the plan also briefly looks at who your ideal customers are and at how your business will stand out from the crowd. It also looks at how the business will interact with the community and demonstrate social responsibility, topics we discussed in Chapter 5. Finally, almost all business plans today include a perspective on the impact of global business.

Your Assignment

Step 1

To complete this assignment, you first need to download the *Business Plan Student Template* file from this book's Companion Website at www.prenhall.com/ebert. This is a Microsoft Word file you can use to complete your business plan. For this assignment, you will fill in Part 1 of the plan.

Step 2

Once you have the *Business Plan Student Template* file, you can begin to answer the following questions in Part 1: The Contemporary Business Environment.

1. What is the name of your business?

Hint: When you think of the name of your business, make sure that it captures the spirit of the business you're creating.

2. What will your business do?

Hint: Imagine that you are explaining your idea to a family member or a friend. Keep your description to 30 words or less.

3. What form of business ownership (sole proprietorship, partnership, or corporation) will your business take? Why did you choose this form?

Hint: For more information on types of business ownership, refer to the discussion in Chapter 3.

4. Briefly describe your ideal customers. What are they like in terms of age, income level, and so on?

Hint: You don't have to give too much detail in this part of the plan; you'll provide more details about customers and marketing in later parts of the plan.

5. Why will customers choose to buy from your business instead of your competition?

Hint: In this section, describe what will be unique about your business. For example, is the product special or will you offer the product at a lower price?

6. All businesses have to deal with ethical issues. One way to address these issues is to create a code of ethics. List three core principles your business will follow.

Hint: To help you consider the ethical issues that your business might face, refer to the discussion in Chapter 5.

7. A business shows social responsibility by respecting all of its stakeholders. What steps will you take to create a socially responsible business?

Hint: Refer to the discussion of social responsibility in Chapter 5. What steps can you take to be a "good citizen" in the community? Consider also how you may need to be socially responsible toward your customers and, if applicable, investors, employees, and suppliers.

8. Will you sell your product in another country? If so, what countries and why? What challenges will you face?

Hint: Consider how you will expand internationally (i.e., independent agent, licensing, etc.). Do you expect global competition for your product? What advantages will foreign competitors have?

Note: Once you have answered the questions, save your Word document. You'll be answering additional questions in later chapters.

Part 2(a): The Business of Managing

Goal of the Exercise

In Part 1 of the business plan project, you formulated a basic identity for your business. Part 2(a) of the business plan project asks you to think about the goals of your business, some internal and external factors affecting the business, and the organizational structure of the business.

Exercise Background: Part 2(a) of the Business Plan

As you learned in Chapter 1, every business sets goals. In this part of the plan, you'll define some of the goals for your business. Part 2(a) of the business plan also asks you to perform a basic SWOT analysis for your business. As you'll recall from Chapter 1, a SWOT analysis looks at the business's *strengths*, *weaknesses*, *opportunities*, and *threats*. The strengths and weaknesses are internal factors—things that the business can control. The opportunities and threats are generally external factors that affect the business, such as the following:

Socio-cultural forces—Will changes in population or culture help your business or hurt it?

Economic forces—Will changes in the economy help your business or hurt it?

Technological forces—Will changes in technology help your business or hurt it?

Competitive forces—Does your business face much competition or very little?

Political-legal forces—Will changes in laws help your business or hurt it?

Each of these forces will affect different businesses in different ways, and some of these may not apply to your business at all.

Part 2(a) of the business plan also asks you to determine how the business is to be run. One thing you'll need to do is create an organizational chart to get you thinking about the different tasks needed for a successful business.

Your Assignment

Step 1

Open the saved *Business Plan* file you began working on in Part 1. You will continue to work from the same file you started working on in Part 1.

Step 2

For the purposes of this assignment, you will answer the questions in "Part 2(a): The Business of Managing."

1. Provide a brief mission statement for your business.

Hint: Refer to the discussion of mission statements in Chapter 1. Be sure to include the name of your business, how you will stand out from your competition, and why a customer will buy from you.

2. Consider the goals for your business. What are three of your business goals for the first year? What are two intermediate-to-long-term goals?

Hint: Refer to the discussion of goal setting in Chapter 1. Be as specific and realistic as possible with the goals you set. For example, if you plan on selling a service, how many customers do you want by the end of the first year, and how much do you want each customer to spend?

3. Perform a basic SWOT analysis for your business, listing its main strengths, weaknesses, opportunities, and threats.

Hint: We explained previously what factors you should consider in your basic SWOT analysis. Look around at your world, talk to classmates, or talk to your instructor for other ideas in performing your SWOT analysis.

4. Who will manage the business?

Hint: Refer to the discussion of managers in Chapter 1. Think about how many levels of management as well as what kinds of managers your business needs.

5. Show how the "team" fits together by creating a simple organizational chart for your business. Your chart should indicate who will work for each manager as well as each person's job title.

Hint: As you create your organizational chart, consider the different tasks involved in the business. Whom will each person report to? Refer to the discussion of organizational structure in Chapter 9 for information to get you started.

Note: Once you have answered the questions, save your Word document. You'll be answering additional questions in later chapters.

Part 2(b): The Business of Managing

Goal of the Exercise

At this point, your business has an identity and you've described the factors that will affect your business and how you will operate it. Part 2(b) of the business plan project asks you to think about your employees, the jobs they will be performing, and the ways in which you can lead and motivate them.

Exercise Background: Part 2(b) of the Business Plan

To complete this part of the plan, you need to refer back to the organizational chart that you created in Part 2(a). In this part of the business plan exercise, you'll take the different job titles you created in the organizational chart and give thought to the *skills* that employees will need to bring to the job *before* they begin. You'll also consider the *training* you'll need to provide *after* they are hired, as well as how you'll compensate your employees. Part 2(b) of the business plan also asks you to consider how you'll lead your employees and keep them happy and motivated.

Your Assignment

Step 1

Open the *Business Plan* file you have been working on.

Step 2

For the purposes of this assignment, you will answer the questions in "Part 2(b): The Business of Managing."

1. What do you see as the "corporate culture" of your business? What types of employee behaviours, such as organizational citizenship, will you expect?

Hint: Will your business demand a casual environment or a more professional environment? Refer to the discussion on

employee behaviour in Chapter 12 for information on organizational citizenship and other employee behaviours.

2. What is your philosophy on leadership? How will you manage your employees day-to-day?

Hint: Refer to the discussion on leadership in Chapter 12 to help you formulate your thoughts.

3. Looking back at your organizational chart in Part 2(a), briefly create a job description for each team member.

Hint: A job description lists the duties and responsibilities of a job; its working conditions; and the tools, materials, equipment, and information used to perform it. Imagine your business on a typical day. Who is working and what are each person's responsibilities?

4. Next, create a job specification for each job, listing the skills and other credentials and qualifications needed to perform the job effectively.

Hint: As you write your job specifications, consider what you would write if you were making an ad for the position. What would the new employee need to bring to the job in order to qualify for the position?

5. What sort of training, if any, will your employees need once they are hired? How will you provide this training?

Hint: Will you offer your employees on-the-job training? Off-the-job training? Vestibule training?

6. A major factor in retaining skilled workers is a company's compensation system—the total package of rewards that it offers employees in return for their labour. Part of this compensation system includes wages/salaries. What wages or salaries will you offer for each job? Why did you decide on that pay rate?

7. Incentive programs are special programs designed to motivate high performance. What incentives will you use to motivate your workforce?

Hint: Be creative and look beyond a simple answer, such as giving pay increases. Ask yourself, who are my employees and what is important to them?

Note: Once you have answered the questions, save your Word document. You'll be answering additional questions in later chapters.

Crafting a Business Plan

Part 3: Managing Operations and Information

Goal of the Exercise

This part of the business plan project asks you to think about your business in terms of operations, accounting concepts, and information technology (IT) needs and costs.

Exercise Background: Part 3 of the Business Plan

An increasingly important part of a business plan is a consideration of how IT—computers, the internet, software, and so on—influences businesses. This part of the business plan asks you to assess how you will use technology to improve your business. Will you, for example, use a database to keep track of your customers? How will you protect your business from hackers and other IT security risks?

This part of the business plan also asks you to consider the costs of doing business, such as salaries, rent, and utilities. You'll also be asked to complete the following financial statements:

- *Balance Sheet.* The balance sheet is a foundation for financial reporting. This report identifies the valued items of the business (its *assets*) as well as the debts that it owes (its *liabilities*). This information gives the owner and potential investors a "snapshot" view of the health of the business.

- *Income Statement (or Profit-and-Loss Statement).* This is the focus of the financial plan. This document will show you what it takes to be profitable and successful as a business owner for your first year. You'll also be asked to consider various factors relating to operating your business.

Your Assignment

Step 1

Open the saved *Business Plan* file you have been working on.

Step 2

For the purposes of this assignment, you will answer the following questions in "Part 3: Managing Operations and Information":

1. What kinds of IT resources will your business require?

Hint: Think about the employees in your business and what they will need in order to do their jobs. What computer hardware and software will they need? Will your business need a network and an internet connection? What type of network?

2. How will you use IT to keep track of your customers and potential customers?

Hint: Many businesses—even small businesses—use databases to keep track of their customers. Will your business require a database? What about other information systems?

3. What are the *costs* of doing business? Equipment, supplies, salaries, rent, utilities, and insurance are just some of these expenses. Estimate what it will cost to do business for one year.

Hint: The Business Plan Student Template provides a table for you to insert the costs associated with doing business. Note that these are just estimates—just try your best to include accurate costs for the expenses you think will be a part of doing business.

4. How much will you charge for your product? How many products do you believe you can sell in one year (or how many customers do you think your business can attract)? Multiply the price that you will charge by the number of products that you hope to sell or the amount you hope each customer will spend. This will give you an estimate of your *revenues* for one year.

Hint: You will use the amounts you calculate in the costs and revenues questions in this part of the plan in the accounting statements, so be as realistic as you can.

5. Create a balance sheet and an income statement (profit-and-loss statement) for your business.

Hint: You will have two options for creating these reports. The first option is to use the Microsoft Word versions that are found within the Business Plan Student Template itself. The second option is to use the specific Microsoft Excel templates created for each statement, which are found on the book's MyBusinessLab. These Excel files are handy to use because they already have the worksheet calculations preset—all you have to do is "plug in" the numbers and the calculations will be performed automatically for you. If you make adjustments to the different values in the Excel worksheets, you'll automatically see how changes to expenses, for example, can improve the "bottom line."

6. Create a floor plan of the business. What does it look like when you walk through the door?

Hint: When sketching your floor plan, consider where equipment, supplies, and furniture will be located.

7. Explain what types of raw materials and supplies you will need to run your business. How will you produce your good or service? What equipment do you need? What hours will you operate?

8. What steps will you take to ensure that the quality of the product or service stays at a high level? Who will be responsible for maintaining quality standards?

Note: Once you have answered the questions, save your Word document. You'll be answering additional questions in later chapters.

Part Twelve

Communication

Chapter 13

Communication and Negotiation

After reading this chapter, you should be able to:

1 Explain why communication is vital for effective management.

2 Describe the basic process of communication.

3 Explain how culture can influence communication.

4 Identify key barriers to effective communication.

5 Describe approaches to overcoming communication barriers.

6 Describe the basic process of negotiation.

Taken from *Management*, Canadian Edition, by Michael A. Hitt, J. Stewart Black, Lyman W. Porter, and Andrew J. Gaudes.

A Communication Collision

It was a car lover's dream. Two brothers, Jack and John Goudy, left their desk jobs to open their own auto repair shop. At first, just the two brothers did brake jobs and replaced exhaust systems. Then, as business grew, they hired a few workers and moved to a larger shop. Within a decade, Two J's Auto Repair was cranking in sales of half a million dollars per year, but then those sales reached a plateau and gradually began to decline. So John, who was in charge of sales and accounting, searched for a new way to improve business. He found it by using technology. John began integrating cutting-edge technology into the shop operations. But he had to convince his workers, including Jack (who spent more time in the shop than in the office), that his strategy for rebuilding Two J's would be successful.

John convened a staff meeting to communicate his new strategy to the employees. Armed with graphs and charts, he talked about profit sharing, employee involvement, and state-of-the-art technology. "From today on, we're a completely different business," he predicted. He did not know how prophetic that statement would prove to be. John's audience did not share his enthusiasm; in fact, they did not understand his message at all because they had received no previous training in the areas of finance, human resources, or the use of technology. They didn't understand the vocabulary he used or the ideas he was presenting. "It was a sea of blank faces with an occasional mutter here and there," John recalls. Thus, the flow of miscommunication at Two J's began.

John purchased a new computer, which reduced the amount of paper communication generated by the office. But employees

When Jack and John Goudy left their desk jobs to open their auto repair shop, it seemed like a car lover's dream. But poor communication between the two and their staff members turned the one-time dream into a nightmare. Fortunately, they realized their "failure to communicate" and were able to improve the situation.

eventually discovered that the original estimates and the final invoices did not match each other, which caused them to believe that he was withholding work hours—and pay. He installed a closed-circuit TV in the shop so that, when customers phoned to inquire about the status of their repairs, he could glance quickly at the monitor and answer them. Unfortunately, shop workers believed that John had installed the TV as a surveillance tool to monitor them, and they resented what they perceived to be a lack of trust.

Although John had provided his employees with an elaborate explanation of the profit-sharing plan (which they did not understand), they were skeptical of it because of mixed messages he sent: John often groaned about poor profits but would suddenly arrive at work driving a new sports car. Sensing declining morale, John started to hold daily "release meetings," designed to let employees voice their

frustrations and concerns. But even these backfired. "John talked about working together like a football team," says one employee. But the meetings quickly dissolved into lectures. "John talked, we listened." Another employee observes, "It was clear John didn't care much about what we thought. He was too excited about his big ideas."

Jack, meanwhile, tried to serve as a go-between for John and the workers. "John wasn't working in the shop anymore," he explains. "Unfortunately, he dismissed their ideas when they offered suggestions." Eventually, even Jack and John could be heard fighting in the office. "They routinely got into yelling matches, one threatening to walk out on the other," says one veteran Two J's worker.

Finally, despite John's efforts to attract new customers and provide better, faster repairs through technology, workers began to leave the shop for jobs with other companies. At first, he did not understand what had gone so wrong; he had not realized how gruelling running his own business could be. He also knew that he was not a strong communicator. "Every day there were questions," he comments. "After a while, they just ground me down." When the company hit rock bottom, John started to get the message. He began to recognize the importance of communication—not only with customers, but also with his own workers—and proceeded to make small changes. "Now [when I attend staff meetings], I bring a yellow pad, scribble, and listen."

This chapter is about the importance of communication—whether it takes place via yellow pad or computer—throughout an organization. ◆

Source: Elizabeth Conlin, "Company Profile: Collision Course," *Inc.* 14, no. 13 (December 1992), pp. 132–142.

Strategic
overview

Effective communication is crucial for managers in formulating a successful strategy and implementing it. Strategy formulation requires a substantial amount of communication. To identify a potentially successful strategy, managers must analyze their external environment, such as their competitors, their markets, industry forces, and government regulations. This first requires them to absorb and evaluate a large amount of information communicated to them before taking action based on it. Taking action to support the strategy then means communicating the relevant information to others in the organization, convincing them of your strategy, and explaining what they have to do to implement it.

In the opening case example, John's strategy for Two J's Auto Repair was to use technology to give customers better service by making faster repairs and providing them with more information about the repairs in progress. However, his strategy failed

because of poor communication. First, he developed the strategy alone, which means he may not have gathered and evaluated enough information from his employees. Second, the implementation of the strategy was unsuccessful because he communicated it poorly, to them and his brother.

For example, Two J's employees did not understand the reason why the new technology was being implemented, and John didn't listen effectively to them. Besides needing better listening and receiving skills, it appeared there were interpersonal barriers between him and his employees that he needed to overcome before any new strategy could be successfully implemented. Without doing these three things—gathering adequate amounts of information, including information from his employees; properly listening and communicating his goals to them; and using good communication skills to foster better interpersonal relations, the strategy John designed for Two J's predictably failed.

communication The process of transferring information, meaning, and understanding from sender to receiver.

Most of us take communication for granted because we do it every day. Communicating effectively, however, is not easy.[1] Accurate and persuasive communication within and between organizations, person to person, person to group, or group to group, is frequently, and sometimes unexpectedly, difficult, as the opening case example demonstrates. Receivers often do not have a complete understanding of what senders mean. But the heart of **communication** is exactly that: the process of transferring information, meaning, and understanding from sender to receiver. And carrying out that process convincingly and proficiently is absolutely essential for a manager to exercise leadership. In fact, leadership is unlikely to be successful in the absence of excellent communication skills. The first step for a manager to become an outstanding leader, therefore, is to become an outstanding communicator.

In this chapter, we start with an overview of the basic communication process, followed by an examination of the modes and media of communication. These topics provide a background for the next section on the organizational context of the communication process as it affects managers. Although the organization can facilitate managerial communication, it also can be one of the key barriers to communication—interpersonal, organizational, and cultural—which are discussed in the following section. This section in turn is followed by one that, appropriately, highlights some of the steps that managers can take to reduce or overcome these barriers.

The final parts of this chapter focus on one particular area of communication that is especially critical for managers—negotiation. In those sections, we discuss the impact of cultural influences on negotiation strategies and on the negotiation process itself. Throughout this chapter we need to keep in mind a basic perspective: Although communication is a universal human activity, successful communication is not habitual. It requires motivation, skill, and knowledge.

Basic Model of Communication

How do people communicate? How do they send and receive messages? What factors can disrupt communication? Let's look first at the basic model of the communication process (Exhibit 13.1).[2]

Exhibit 13.1 Basic Communication Model.

All communication involves four actions and five components. The four actions are encoding, sending, receiving, and decoding. The five components are sender, message, medium, noise, and receiver. The actions and components combine to transfer meaning from the sender to the receiver. The sender originates the message by **encoding** it, that is, by constructing the message. The message is the content of the communication. The sender then transmits the message through a **medium**. A medium is the method or means of transmission, not the message itself. Examples of media are spoken words, video, written memos, faxes, and emails. The receiver acquires, or receives, the message by hearing it, reading it, or having it appear on a fax or computer. The receiver then begins **decoding** the message, that is, interpreting it. Sometimes distractions interfere with the message; these interferences are called **noise**. Noise contributes to misinterpretations of the original message, and it is only through feedback, or verification of the original message, that communication problems may be located and corrected.

encoding The act of constructing a message.

medium The mode or form of transmission of a message.

decoding The act of interpreting a message.

noise Potential interference with the transmission or decoding of a message.

The basic model of communication is fundamental and universal; that is, it occurs whenever communication takes place, regardless of the culture or organization. However, while the basic acts and components of the communication process are the same everywhere, how the acts are carried out and the nature of the components are deeply influenced by cultural, organizational, and even personal contexts.[3] Who can send messages to whom, what kinds and what volumes of messages are sent, what medium is used to transmit messages, what sort of interference or noise is likely to occur, and what cues are available for decoding messages are just some of the many examples of the types of communication issues that can vary from manager to manager, from organization to organization, and from country to country.

Modes of Communication

Communication can occur in either a verbal mode or a nonverbal mode, as shown in Exhibit 13.2. Each mode has particular characteristics and issues that an effective manager must understand.

Verbal Communication

Most of us think of spoken words when we think of verbal communication. The key, however, is not that the words are spoken but that words—language—are

Exhibit 13.2   Modes of Communication

	Verbal mode (Language Used to Convey Meaning)		Nonverbal Mode
	Oral	**Written**	
Examples	■ Conversation ■ Speeches ■ Telephone calls ■ Video conferences	■ Letters ■ Memos ■ Reports ■ Email ■ Fax	■ Dress ■ Speech intonation ■ Gestures ■ Facial expressions
Advantages	■ Vivid ■ Stimulating ■ Commands attention ■ Difficult to ignore ■ Flexible ■ Adaptive	■ Decreased misinterpretation ■ Precise	■ Effectiveness of communication increases with congruence to oral presentation ■ Can emphasize meaning
Disadvantages	■ Transitory ■ Subject to misinterpretation	■ Precision loss in translation ■ Inflexible ■ Easier to ignore	■ Meanings of nonverbal communication not universal

used to convey meaning. Consequently, when we talk about verbal communication, we mean *both* oral and written communication.

Oral Communication. The spoken word has the potential advantages of being vivid, stimulating, and of commanding attention. In most organizational situations, it is difficult for receivers—the listeners—to ignore either the speaker or the words spoken. Just think about the last time someone spoke to you directly. Even if you weren't interested in what the person had to say, wouldn't it have been difficult to simply ignore the person, turn, and walk away?

Also, oral communication is exceptionally flexible for both the sender and receiver. While you are speaking, you may try to make a point a certain way, but along the way change your words for the listener to understand you. Because oral communication is generally interactive, it can be quite responsive and adaptive to circumstances. However, this mode of communication has the major disadvantages of being transitory (unless recorded) and subject to considerable misinterpretation. Even when individuals use the same language, the subtle nuances of the spoken word may be missed or incorrect meaning may be attached to them. Oral communication between those whose first languages differ, as in many management situations today, simply multiplies the chances of intended meaning going awry.

Written Communication. When messages are put in writing, as in letters, memos, email, and the like, the opportunity for misunderstanding the words of the sender are decreased. The receiver may still misinterpret the intended message, of course, but there is no uncertainty about exactly what words the sender has used. In that sense, written communication has precision. However, not everyone writes well, and so greater precision does not necessarily lead to greater understanding. This is further complicated when the words need translation from one language to another. For example, North Americans often write "at your earliest convenience" when requesting action, meaning that the request is somewhat urgent, but Europeans frequently interpret it to mean they can respond whenever they want. Because the writer/sender does not know immediately how well or poorly the message is getting across, written communication has the disadvantage of not being very flexible. In addition, it is often not as vivid or compelling as oral communication. Although you might find it difficult to ignore someone speaking to you, it would probably be much easier to ignore an email you received.

Nonverbal Communication

In direct interpersonal communication, nonverbal actions and behaviours often constitute significant messages. A whole range of actions, or lack of them, has the potential for communicating. Body language, posture, the way you dress, speak words, use gestures, handle utensils, exhibit facial expressions, and set the physical distance to the receiver are just some of the many forms of nonverbal communication.

As a manager, keep in mind that when verbal and nonverbal messages are contradictory, receivers often give more weight to the nonverbal signals than to the words used. For example, you may say to employees, "I have an open-door policy. Come and talk to me whenever you need to." However, if you never seem to be able to find the time to see them or rarely look up from your work when employees enter, they will soon come to believe the nonverbal message, "I'm busy," rather than the verbal message, "I encourage you to talk with me."

Of course, when nonverbal messages are consistent with the spoken message, the odds of effective communication taking place are increased. For example, suppose that in addition to saying you had an open-door policy you looked up when employees entered, made eye contact with them, smiled, and turned away from your computer and the report on which you were working. In combination, what sort of message do you think you would be sending?

The problem for managers in many of today's organizations where they work with employees from different cultural backgrounds and often work across international borders is that there are no universal meanings to the various nonverbal actions. For example, the traditional "OK" sign in North America is a gesture for money in Japan and is a rather rude gesture in Brazil. You might think that just toning down your nonverbal gestures would be a good way to avoid inadvertent wrong messages. Such an effort would be fine in Finland, but someone in Italy or Greece might infer from your subdued nonverbal cues that you are uninterested in the discussion. Because there is no simple answer, you should learn about the nonverbal cues and gestures of countries and cultures you deal with the most.

Media of Communication

The means of communication, or, in other words, *how* or by what methods information is transmitted from sender to receiver, are typically referred to as communication media (or, in the singular, medium). In organizations, there are basically a limited number of types of media that can be used. These range from the very personal and direct face-to-face interaction to the very impersonal and indirect posted notice or bulletin board that is frequently used in organizational settings. In between are telephone conversations, electronic messages, letters, memos, and reports.

It is obvious that these different media have different sets of characteristics, such as the following:

- Personal–impersonal nature
- Speed in sending and receiving

- Availability of multiple cues to assist receivers in acquiring accurate meaning from the messages

- Opportunity to receive immediate and continuing feedback from the receiver

media richness Different media are classified as rich or lean based on their capacity to facilitate shared meaning.

The term that has been used to summarize the nature of these characteristics of different media is called "**media richness**."[4] Different media are classified as rich or lean based on their "capacity to facilitate shared meaning."[5] (See Exhibit 13.3.) Thus, interpersonal, face-to-face interactions, for example, would be regarded as rich because they provide several types of information and multiple ways to obtain mutual understanding between sender and receiver, whereas a general email message sent to a number of receivers would be regarded as leaner because it lacks some of the features listed above. The general principle here is that the more ambiguous the message to be communicated and the more complex the issue, the richer the medium of communication should be.

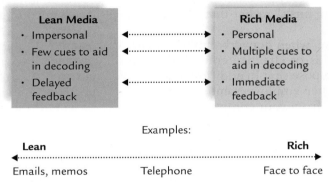

Exhibit 13.3 Factors Contributing to Media Richness.

The concept of media richness has important implications for managers when they communicate. It serves to emphasize that different media have different capabilities for conveying meaning, and that managers therefore should be sensitive to matching message with medium. Using face-to-face meetings to convey simple, straightforward information, such as the time of a meeting next week, would be an unnecessary waste of a rich medium. That is, it would involve too much time and effort of both sender and receivers to obtain shared meaning of a relatively unambiguous message. On the other hand, using a memo, for example, rather than a face-to-face meeting, would probably be a poor choice for settling a serious disagreement with subordinates. The medium would be too lean to enable the manager to resolve a complicated, highly ambiguous matter.

Often, of course, time pressures and distance may make it relatively costly for a manager to use a richer rather than a leaner medium. That is why, in recent years, technological advances in such communication media as instant messaging (see *A Manager's Challenge: "Staying Connected through Instant Messaging and VoIP"*) or video conferencing often provide acceptable trade-offs between an ideally rich, face-to-face medium for resolving complex issues, on the one hand, and an ideally low-cost written memo (whether sent via email or otherwise), on the other hand.[6] The key point, if you are a manager, is to choose a medium that best suits the degree of potential ambiguity in the message, consistent with the constraints of circumstances and the resources of you and your organization. The choice of an appropriate medium should not be left to chance.

A Manager's Challenge   *Technology*

Staying Connected through Instant Messaging and VoIP

A growing number of managers are using instant messaging (IM) and voice over internet protocol (VoIP) technology to stay in touch with colleagues and subordinates located in the same office or even thousands of miles away. With instant messaging, sales representatives who need immediate answers to clinch a deal simply bring up the IM software and send the boss a brief, to-the-point question that automatically appears in a box on his screen. In turn, the manager can type a quick response to suggest a particular strategy or approve a special discount. If personal discussion is required, the sales rep can go to the VoIP software to engage in a conversation from her computer—with or without a video image. No waiting for answers to email messages, no small talk—just instant communication to keep the business running smoothly and productively.

With IM and VoIP applications users can tell at a glance whether a particular person is online and available to receive a message. If necessary, they can type messages and exchange files or engage in a conference call with several people at one time, essentially convening online meetings. Clearly, IM and VoIP, with their live interaction and support for mobile employees, are helping companies keep their workforces connected at a fraction of the cost (in terms of both time and money) of conventional phone calls and letters.

Despite the benefits, not everyone is a fan of IM and VoIP communication. Why? Because, by and large, IM and VoIP initially came into the corporate world through the back door. Many employees downloaded free IM and VoIP software from sites such as Skype, Yahoo! and AOL onto company computers without permission from top managers, who tend to view it as a new tool for goofing off and chatting with one's friends. However, the new methods of communicating are becoming legitimized by firms such as Telus and Bell, who are offering VoIP business solutions across sectors such as finance, government, and education. Doctors and nurses at Toronto's Mount Sinai Hospital are now using a VoIP network to better serve their patients.

Even when IM and VoIP are used for legitimate managerial business purposes, some managers say they

Toronto's Mount Sinai Hospital has deployed 550 wireless VoIP handsets throughout the hospital. The shift to VoIP is better able to support a mobile workplace, making it easier for doctors and nurses to provide more effective health care.

have difficulty staying focused on tasks like writing reports when messages suddenly appear on the computer screen. Others feel pressure to stay close to their computers, even late into the evening, in case colleagues in other time zones have questions or need decisions made. Moreover, free downloadable software creates security holes because the messages and files being shared never pass through a server. That means they can't be scanned for viruses, nor can they be monitored by management or archived.

Nonetheless, these new communications technologies are coming into their own in the business workplace as software developers devise industrial-strength versions with security and auditing features.

Sources: V. Ho, "VoIP Faces Challenges in Healthcare," *itworldcanada.com*, accessed May 28, 2007; "VoIP Right for Businesses of All Shapes and Sizes," *Globe and Mail*, April 13, 2005, p. B11; D. Robb, "Instant Messaging: A Portal to Online Threats?" *Government Procurement*, December 2003, pp. 10–13; M. Sarrell, "Corporate IM," *PC Magazine,* November 11, 2003, p. 132; Y. Bhattacharjee, "A Swarm of Little Notes," *Time*, September 16, 2002, pp. A4+; A. Stuart, "IM Is Here. RU Ready 2 Try It?" *Inc.*, July 1, 2002, pp. 76–81.

Air traffic controllers communicate with pilots of aircraft, providing instruction, information, and clearances during their flight. Controllers will also hand off aircraft from one area control centre (ACC) to another. Clear communication is imperative between the controllers and pilots to prevent accidents.

The Organizational Context of Communication

Managers do not deal with communication in the abstract, but rather within an organizational context. The structure and processes of organizations powerfully shape the nature and effectiveness of communication that takes place within and between them.[7] Organizations, whether businesses, hospitals, or government agencies, have a set of defining characteristics, all of which affect communication in one way or another.[8] Thus, organizations

- are composed of individuals and groups;
- are oriented toward goals;
- have differentiated functions;
- have intended coordination; and
- have continuity through time.

Organizations of any size, regardless of country, are not simply a random set of individuals who by chance come together for a brief period with no purpose. The fact that they have goal orientations, structures, and coordination greatly influences the nature and amount of communication that takes place. This influence can be analyzed in terms of directions, channels, and patterns of communication.

Directions of Communication within Organizations

Because organizations of any degree of complexity have both differentiated functions and more than one level of positions with more or less responsibility, the directions of communication within them can be classified according to the level for which they are intended:

downward communication
Messages sent from higher organizational levels to lower levels.

- **Downward communication** is sent from higher organizational levels to lower levels; for example, from the organization's top executives to its employees, or from supervisors to subordinates.

■ **Upward communication** is sent from lower organizational levels to higher levels; for example, from nonmanagement employees to their supervisors, or from a manager to her boss.

■ **Lateral communication** is sent across essentially equivalent levels of an organization; for example, from one clerical assistant to another, from the manager of Product A to the manager of Product B, or from the marketing department to the engineering design department.

upward communication
Messages sent from lower organizational levels to higher levels.

lateral communication
Messages sent across essentially equivalent levels of an organization.

The contents of communications within organizations usually vary according to the direction of the communication activity. As shown in Exhibit 13.4, downward communication typically involves such matters as goals, objectives, directions, decisions, and feedback. Upward communication commonly focuses on information, suggestions, questions, problems, and requests for clarification. Lateral communication is oriented toward exchanges of information—both formal and informal—that assist or affect coordination and joint problem solving.

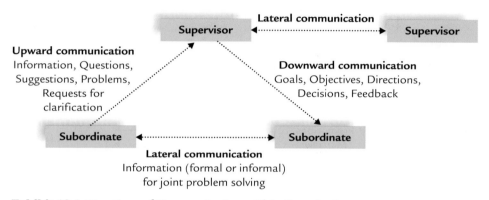

Exhibit 13.4 Directions of Communication within Organizations.

While the subject matter of communication in a particular direction tends to be fairly similar in most medium-sized to large organizations, the culture of the organization (or the culture of the country in which the organization operates) can affect the process. For example, in an organization in which authority and hierarchy are stressed, upward communication might be more formal than in an organization with a more egalitarian culture. As a simple illustration, in a strongly hierarchical organization, a conversation might start with the subordinate addressing a superior several levels above as Mr. or Ms. Jones. In many countries, such as Korea, the conversation might start by addressing the superior by his or her title, such as Director Park. In organizations with less emphasis on hierarchy, the conversation might start by addressing the superior by his or her first name. Likewise, organizational or country culture can influence the frequency and flavour of upward communications. For example, in organizations with strong hierarchical values, upward communication tends to be less frequent.

In summary, organizational communications flow upward, downward, and laterally. The direction of the communication has a significant impact on the type of communication that is likely to take place. In addition, the culture of the organization and the region or country in which the organization is located can further determine the exact form that communication will have and even the frequency of each direction of communication.

Channels of Communication within Organizations

Organizational channels, or routes of communication, consist of two fundamental types: formal and informal. Both types are essential for organizational functioning, and neither type can easily substitute for the other.

formal communication channels Routes that are authorized, planned, and regulated by the organization and that are directly connected to its official structure.

Formal communication channels are those that are authorized, planned, and regulated by the organization and that are directly connected to its official structure. Thus, the organization's designated structure indicates the normal paths for downward, upward, and lateral formal communication. Formal communication channels (shown in Exhibit 13.5) are like highlighted roads on a road map. They specify organizational members who are responsible for tasks and communicating information to levels above and below them and back and forth to adjacent units. Also, formal channels indicate the persons or positions to whom work-related messages should be sent. Formal channels can be modified, and thus they have some flexibility, but they can seldom be disregarded.

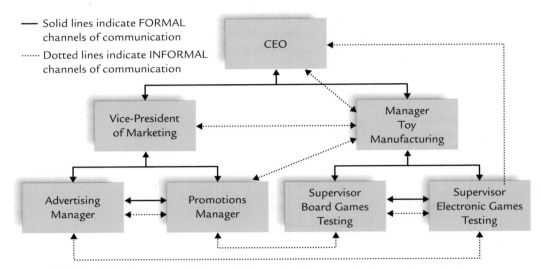

Exhibit 13.5 Formal and Informal Channels of Communication in Organizations.

informal communication channels Routes that are not pre-specified by the organization but that develop through typical and customary activities of people at work.

Informal communication channels are communication routes that are not pre-specified by the organization but that develop through typical interpersonal activities of people at work. Channels can come into existence and change or disappear rapidly, depending on circumstances. However, they may also endure in many work situations, especially where individuals have been working together over a period of time. If a specific pattern becomes well-established, it would ordinarily be called a "network" (to be discussed later).

Several important features of informal communication channels should be noted:

- They tend to operate more often in the lateral than in the vertical direction compared to formal channels (see Exhibit 13.6) because they are not designated by the organization and its top officials.

- Information flowing through informal channels often moves extremely fast, mainly because senders are highly motivated to pass on information. The so-called "grapevine," a term applied to an informal network that supports the exchange of rumours or gossip between people, is a classic example of entrenched methods supporting rapid transmission of messages through informal channels.[9] In recent years, the communication capabilities of the internet have facilitated the emergence of large-scale, word-of-mouth networks. Some researchers propose that these mechanisms are poised to have a significant impact on informal information flow in organizations.[10]

- Informal channels carry work-related as well as nonwork information. The fact that channels are informal does not mean that only gossip and other messages unrelated to jobs and tasks are carried by them. In fact, crucial work-related information is frequently communicated in this way. Of course, some of the messages passed through informal channels may contain inaccuracies or be negative, and thus are seen by some managers as a source of problems. However—and this is important to emphasize— few organizations could exist for very long if they had to rely only on formal communication channels!

Exhibit 13.6 Characteristics of Formal and Informal Communication Channels	
Formal Communication Channels	**Informal Communication Channels**
■ Authorized, planned, and regulated by the organization ■ Reflect the organization's formal structure ■ Define who has responsibility for information dissemination and indicate the proper recipients of work-related information ■ May be modified by the organization ■ Minor to severe consequences for ignoring them	■ Develop through interpersonal activities of organization members ■ Not specified by the organization ■ May be short lived or long lasting ■ Are more often lateral than vertical ■ Information flow can be very fast ■ Used for both work-related and nonwork information

Patterns of Organizational Communication

Identifiable patterns of communication that occur with some regularity within and between organizations, whether using formal or informal channels, are typically called **communication networks**. Put another way, communication networks are stable systems of interconnections. Thus, networks involve consistent linkages between particular sets of senders and receivers. For example, as shown in Exhibit 13.7, a middle-level divisional marketing manager in Calgary might have a particular network that involves her boss in Montreal, three key managers in other departments in the Montreal headquarters, her seven subordinates located in major western cities, and two outside vendors of market research data. Another network for the same manager might involve two lower-level managers in other units in the Calgary office and her former colleague and old friend who is now a sales supervisor in Winnipeg and who has access to inside information on how well new marketing approaches are working in that region.

An example of a larger, more organization-wide network would be McCain Foods's worldwide pattern of communication relationships between its headquarters in Florenceville, New Brunswick, and its production plants. Of course, networks can also be formed across organizations as well as within. This is what often happens when sets of managers from two companies, such as BASF South East Asia and Shell Eastern Petroleum Ltd., for example, have to work together on issues that arise in an international joint venture, in this case the Ellba Eastern plant on Jurong Island, Singapore.[11] A particular challenge in building an effective network for a project that was to last for a number of months and which involved a number of participants from different organizations is illustrated in *A Manager's Challenge, "Communication Is Secret Weapon for Change."* The challenge here was to change the way communication had been carried out in the past—and thus to develop more effective networking processes—on this type of large, complex project that has many sources of senders and receivers.

The importance of communication networks to managers is that they can provide significant and regular sources of information, both of the

communication networks
Identifiable patterns of communication within and between organizations, whether using formal or informal channels.

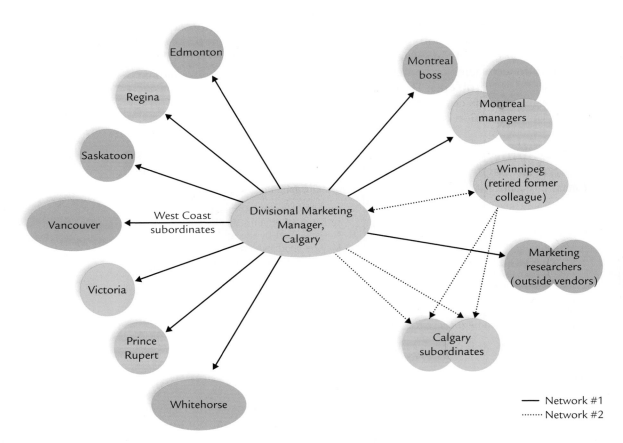

Exhibit 13.7 Examples of Two Organizational Communication Networks.

— Network #1
······· Network #2

formal and informal type, that might otherwise take a much longer time to obtain if the various links had to be set up from scratch each time some new topic or problem came up. Also, when managers are members of established networks, it can make it easier for them to influence the other people or groups involved in the networks. Consequently, for both of these reasons, managers need to pay particular attention to what networks they can and want to be a part of, and to the composition of those networks. It is no accident that the term **networking** has come to signify a process that has the potential for gaining advantages for a manager (or anyone for that matter) by having one or more sets of individuals or groups with which one can interact easily and regularly, and with whom one can communicate a sense of confidence and trust.

In traditional Western organizations, it has always been relatively easy for males in management positions to establish various networks with other males (thus providing the basis for the phrase "old boys' network"). However, at least until very recently, it has been much harder for women and members of underrepresented ethnic groups to establish similar helpful networks in their organizations. Research suggests, in fact, that organizational networks involving individuals from these groups are different in terms of both composition and relationships from the old Western networks that were composed primarily of Caucasian males.[12] It does not make such networks any less important or useful to managers from these groups, but it does serve to emphasize that network patterns of communication in organizations can vary based on a number of different situational circumstances, including the age, gender, and ethnicity of the individuals involved.

A Manager's Challenge   *Change*

Communication Is Secret Weapon for Change

Imagine the complications of managing communication among the workforces of several competitors who must work on the same government project. Increasingly, after intensive bidding battles to win contracts for complex systems of equipment, managers at major manufacturing firms must face this situation when they have to collaborate with the very competitors they have just outbid.

Consider what happened when BAE Systems, one of Europe's largest aerospace and defence companies, won a multimillion-dollar contract. As a condition of being designated the prime contractor by the UK Ministry of Defence to design a very large and sophisticated new product, BAE was required to work with a number of companies to finish on schedule and within budget. "With products as complex as [this one], the days of single-source suppliers are over," and "we had to become more collaborative," said Ian Haddleton, BAE's integrated systems solutions manager. As many as 1000 people from BAE and other firms were going to participate in the months-long redesign project. Therefore, in preparation, management decided to foster closer collaboration by making major changes in the company's approach to communication in carrying out such a complicated endeavour.

To start, BAE managers "agreed on a set of values with our customer that is now the guideline and principle for anyone working on the project," Haddleton explained.

Based on these values, all project participants would be able to determine what information was important and with whom it should be shared. As an example, employees of BAE and other collaborating companies agreed to air concerns early in the project so they could be adequately analyzed and addressed before key design decisions were locked in place.

Next, BAE managers set up a web-based data exchange system to support collaborative communication among the hundreds of project participants. "With a project of this size and the number of companies involved, it's always difficult to know who is responsible for what, and whom to ask when needing advice or information," Haddleton noted. The data exchange system stored the latest information about each participant's role and responsibility. It also allowed participants to upload project-related data (such as proposed design specifications) so that others could post comments, questions, and suggested changes for all to review. And because the system was web-based, BAE could control access and not have to ask other companies to replace their proprietary communications systems.

Changing their approach to communication helped BAE's managers become more effective in keeping the product's design on course month after month. "Now, more than ever before, it's much easier for us to function as an extended team," summarized Haddleton. "The way we work today is certainly an improvement over the way things used to be done."

Sources: S. Windsor-Lewis, "Communicating to Avert Industrial Action at BAE Systems," *Strategic Communication Management*, December 2003–January 2004, pp. 18–22; "Product Development's Secret Weapon: Communication," *Design News*, June 17, 2002, pp. S1+; "BAE Systems Strengthens AMS after MBDA Missile Merger," *Defense Daily*, May 1, 2001; F. Tusa, "The Rise of European EW," *Journal of Electronic Defense*, June 2001, pp. 54+.

Barriers to Communication

Although the organizational context provides numerous opportunities for effective and productive communication, it likewise can present many barriers that interfere with the communication process. Such barriers can arise from several different sources, including interpersonal, organizational, and cultural (see Exhibit 13.8).

Interpersonal Barriers

Obstacles to interpersonal communication can occur with either the sender or the receiver. The burden is simultaneously on both the sender and the receiver to ensure accurate communication. It is, however, the sender's obligation to choose the language and words—that is, to encode the message—carefully to carry the greatest precision of meaning. Precision is especially

Exhibit 13.8 Barriers to Communication

Level	Origin of Barrier	Affects Communication Between:
Interpersonal	■ Selective perception ■ Frame of reference ■ Individual differences ■ Emotion ■ Language ■ Nonverbal cues	■ Individuals or groups
Organizational	■ Hierarchical (barriers resulting from formal structure) ■ Functional (barriers resulting from differences between functional departments)	■ Individuals and/or groups within an organization ■ Individuals and/or groups in different organizations
Cultural	■ Language ■ High/low-context culture ■ Stereotyping ■ Ethnocentrism ■ Cultural distance	■ Individuals or groups in different organizations with different national cultures ■ Individuals or groups from different organizational cultures ■ Individuals or groups from diverse cultural backgrounds within an organization

selective perception The process of screening out some parts of an intended message because they contradict our beliefs or desires.

frames of reference Existing sets of attitudes that provide quick ways of interpreting complex messages.

Selective Perception by Lyman Porter

mymanagementlab

important if the sender is trying to persuade the receiver to do something in a language or communication style different from what the receiver prefers. For example, if you are trying to convince your boss to authorize a new project and you use an informal style and choice of words, your boss may not be receptive if she prefers a more formal approach. You will probably need to adjust your style for the communication to be effective.

The receiver, of course, is often the source of communication breakdowns. For example, the receiver might have a **selective perception** problem.[13] That is, the receiver may unintentionally screen out some parts of the intended message because they contradict his beliefs or desires. For example, you might stress the increased productivity that would result from a proposed project, but your boss is focusing on the estimated cost of the project. Although selective perception is a natural human tendency, it hinders accurate communication, especially when sensitive or highly important topics are being discussed. Another way to state this point is that individuals tend to adopt **frames of reference**, or simplified ways of interpreting messages, that help them make sense of complex communications. These shortcuts, however, may prevent the intended message from being received.[14]

Individual differences between senders and receivers in terms of such basic characteristics as their age, gender, ethnicity, or level of education sometimes can be the source of communication barriers. In general, it would be reasonable to assume that the fewer the differences between the two parties on these kinds of attributes, the lower the communication barriers. Even where these kinds of differences exist, however, such as a difference in gender between sender and receiver, the research evidence tends not to find consistently serious impediments to effective communication related to that characteristic.[15] It is more a matter of a manager being very alert to the *possibility* that individual differences in sender and receiver characteristics could impose a significant obstacle to good communication in a specific instance, rather than assuming it will never be a barrier or, conversely, will always be a barrier.

Emotions can be another barrier.[16] How the receiver feels at the time can influence what gets heard or how it gets interpreted. You certainly have had the experience of feeling that someone was "touchy" or overly sensitive when responding to your message. As a consequence, comments that normally would be taken as mere statements get interpreted as criticisms.

Language can also be a barrier. Even for people who speak the same language, a given word or set of words can mean different things to different people.[17] For example, the word "cool" has been applied not only to denote something that is cold, but for large sums of money, someone who is calm, or something that is fashionable.

Nonverbal cues can also be barriers to effective communication in two basic ways. First, people can send nonverbal signals without being aware of them, and therefore create unintentional consequences.[18] For example, you might make minimal eye contact with your boss while trying to convince her to approve your proposed project, and yet be unaware that you are doing so. Your boss might think the project has merit but interprets your low level of eye contact as an indication that you are hiding something. Your boss could then reject a project that she might otherwise have authorized. Second, as we have already touched on, nonverbal cues can mean different things to different people.[19] A weak handshake might indicate politeness in Indonesia but communicate lack of confidence in Alberta.

Organizational Barriers

Just as interpersonal barriers can limit communication, so can organizational barriers. Such barriers can interfere with communication between individuals or groups within the same organization, between individuals or groups from two different organizations, or between entire organizations. The basis of these barriers lies within the hierarchical structure of organizations. All organizations of any complexity have specialized functions and more than one level of authority. This specialization creates a situation that is ripe for communication difficulties. For example, one person might come from marketing and the other from research and development. The person in marketing might think nothing of exaggerating while the person from research and development always understates her points. Consequently, the marketer might see the R&D scientist as unimaginative and boring, while the scientist might view the marketer as superficial and careless. In addition, the two parties might come from different levels in the organization. The differences between responsibility and level of authority could cause a senior executive to expect an explanation of the broad impacts of a proposed project on the entire organization, and a junior technical expert to focus on the detailed schedule of the project.

Cultural Barriers

Communication and culture are tightly intertwined. Culture cannot exist without communication, and human communication only occurs within a cultural context. Since the act of communicating is so closely connected to the surrounding environment, culture can ease or hinder it. Thus, similarity in cultures between senders and receivers facilitates successful communication—the intended meaning has a higher probability of getting transferred. Differences in culture hinder the process. The greater the cultural differences between sender and receiver, the greater the expected difficulty in communicating. Therefore, other things being equal, it should be easier, for example, for a Canadian manager to communicate with an Australian subordinate than with a Greek subordinate.

Organizational cultures can also differ. The industry of an organization, for example, can influence its internal culture, as we pointed out in Chapter 10. Therefore, it is more likely that an executive at CanWest Global could communicate successfully with an executive at CBC than with an executive at Imperial Oil. It is not that extreme cultural differences prevent good communication; rather, the possibilities for breakdowns in communication increase in proportion to the degree of differences in the background and customs of the two parties.

The extent to which a sender and receiver differ in a high-context or low-context communication style also significantly influences the effectiveness of the communication. As we discussed in Chapter 10, individuals in high-context cultures tend to pay great attention to the situational factors surrounding the communication process and as a consequence substantially alter what they say and how they say it based on the context.[20] (See Exhibit 13.9.) Individuals in low-context cultures tend to pay less attention to the context and so make fewer and smaller adjustments from situation to situation.[21] Although the greatest differences in high- and low-context cultures occur across countries, there are also such differences across organizations. For example, Japan is a high-context culture that has three distinct levels of language that a speaker uses, depending on his or her status compared with that of the listener. Thus, there are actually five different words for "you" that are used, depending on relative rank and status. However, even within Japan, communication is much more high context at Mitsubishi Heavy Industries than at Nintendo.

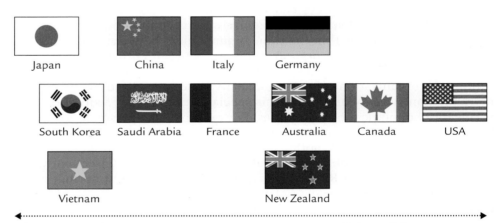

High-Context Cultures
- More and greater adjustments in messages
- Rank of receiver will probably affect message and medium
- Nonverbal communication cues may be very important
- Medium may be as important as message

Low-Context Cultures
- Fewer and smaller adjustments in messages
- Rank of receiver may or may not affect message or medium
- Nonverbal communication cues not as important
- Message is more important than medium

Exhibit 13.9 Communication Differences in High-and Low-Context Cultures.

Source: www.crwflags.com/fotw/flags

What is most problematic when individuals from high- and low-context cultures communicate is that each often forms negative interpretations about the other's communication approach. Individuals from low-context cultures tend to interpret the wide swings in words and style indicative of people from high-context cultures as evidence of insincerity, hypocrisy, and even instability. These interpretations make trust difficult and at the extreme can make effective communication impossible. On the other hand, individuals from high-context cultures view the lack of change in communication style of individuals from low-context cultures as evidence of immaturity, selfishness, or lack of sophistication.

In Japanese culture, managers are taught that to communicate effectively, you should "say what you mean, and mean what you say."[22] Vague directives and instructions are seen as a sign of poor communication skills. The assumption, therefore, is that the burden of proof for effective communication is on the speaker. In contrast, in cultures such as those in Arabic countries and in Latin America, the assumption is that both the speaker and the listener share the burden for communicating effectively. In cultures like these, chances of unpleasant encounters and direct confrontations and disagreements tend to decrease.

Probably the greatest single cultural barrier that can affect communication across different departmental, organizational, regional, or national cultures is ethnocentrism.[23] **Ethnocentrism** is the belief in the superiority of one's own group and the related tendency to view others in terms of the values of one's own group. Ethnocentrism leads individuals to divide their interpersonal worlds into in-groups and out-groups. In-groups are groups of people with whom you identify and about whom you care.[24] Members of the in-group tend to be trusted, listened to, and have information shared with them. Members of out-groups tend to be viewed with skepticism, if not suspicion, and are not given full information. This type of behaviour exists in organizations as well as in interpersonal interactions. When British European Airways merged with British Overseas Airways Corporation some years ago to form British Airways, the ethnocentric orientation of each side almost led to the bankruptcy of the merged unit, which lost nearly US$1 billion before the communication barriers were overcome.

ethnocentrism The belief in the superiority and importance of one's own group.

Ethnocentrism by Lyman Porter

mymanagementlab

Another cross-cultural barrier to communication closely related to ethnocentrism is **stereotyping**, the tendency to oversimplify and generalize about groups of people. The more firmly held the stereotype by a communicator, the harder it is to overcome preconceived expectations and focus on the specifics of the message that is being sent or received. Stereotyping occurs both within and between cultures and thus it affects communication in virtually all organizational settings. For example, suppose you are a technical service manager in a software company and the president has a definite stereotype of people in your position. Generally, the president sees technical service managers as focused on details and unable to see the big picture. With a strong stereotype of this sort, the president may not recognize that you understand and are considering the competitive implications (not just the technical ones) of a new software tool.

stereotyping The tendency to oversimplify and generalize about groups of people.

Another major cultural barrier to communication can be labelled **cultural distance**.[25] This concept refers to the overall difference between two cultures' basic characteristics such as language, level of economic development, and entrenched traditions and customs. Cultural distance was illustrated by a study that gathered 21 senior executives from major corporations in Japan, the United States, Brazil, the United Kingdom, and India for a five-week period of cultural explorations. The executives attended lectures and seminars, built rafts and climbed cliffs together, and even travelled in fact-finding teams to the countries represented. Nevertheless, observers reported that communication remained a problem the entire five weeks.[26] Although much of the difficulty came from obvious language differences, a more subtle difficulty came from cultural differences. Many of the Japanese managers, attempting to fit in, adopted American nicknames, but they actually hated being called by them. The Americans couldn't understand why the Japanese were so quiet, not realizing that they felt that it was unwise to speak first at a meeting. The more senior the

cultural distance The overall difference between two cultures' basic characteristics such as language, level of economic development, and traditions and customs.

Cross-cultural communication problems can stem from language differences, but more subtle problems occur because of cultural differences and biases such as *stereotyping* (the tendency to oversimplify and generalize about groups of people) and *ethnocentrism* (the belief that one's own culture or group is superior).

Japanese executive, the more he listens, and the executives on this trip were quite senior. Similarly, a development project undertaken by Alcan Aluminum of Canada and the National Nonferrous Corporation of China brought together managers from both firms to learn more about each other's culture. Even though a set of managers from China spent a whole year in Canada studying North American business methods, effective communication remained an elusive goal throughout the period for both sides.[27] Such examples emphasize that the degree of cultural distance between organizational employees from different nationalities represents a potentially very difficult communication barrier to overcome. The severity of the problem should not be underestimated.

Improving Communication

The various barriers discussed in the preceding section can interfere with effective communication, but there are ways to deal with—or overcome—them and improve your communication capabilities. How important is it for you to have a commitment to developing good communication skills? Consider this: "In the *Wall Street Journal*/Harris Interactive survey, recruiters rated [business] school graduates on a variety of attributes—and then rated the attributes in terms of how important they are in a job candidate. Topping the list of 24 attributes are communication and interpersonal skills."[28] As the *Wall Street Journal* article went on to say: "Interpersonal communication . . . skills are what corporate recruiters crave most but find most elusive in MBA graduates."

Given the obvious importance of this topic, in the remainder of this section we discuss some of the most essential approaches that are necessary for you to consider in improving your communication abilities as a manager in organizations.

Improving Listening Skills

When the subject is improving communication skills, most people first think of improving their speaking or writing skills. However, contrary to popular belief, probably the single best thing you can do to enhance your communication skills is to focus on improving your receiving rather than sending skills.

Be More Open-Minded. Stereotyping, ethnocentricity, rigid frames of reference, and selective listening can all become barriers to comprehending the intended message of a sender, so one of the first things to do to enhance listening skills is to spend time developing a greater awareness of your personal tendencies in the direction of any of these problems. Once you have a better awareness of these tendencies, you can monitor and control them during conversations. Part of the reason for direct and conscious attention to this area is that most people speak at about 120 words per minute and yet can listen at a rate of about 1000 words per minute.[29] This creates the opportunity for our minds to wander or make judgments about what we are hearing. These tendencies can distort what is heard and how it is interpreted.

Develop Empathy. Once personal tendencies have been examined, the next step is to develop empathy. **Empathy** is identifying with and understanding the other person's feelings, situation, and motives. To some extent, this requires thinking about the situation of other people. What are their feelings relative to the topic at hand? What are their motivations? Why are they talking about this particular subject? These and other questions can help you enhance your understanding of the personal context of the message being sent.

empathy The ability to put yourself in someone else's place and to understand his or her feelings, situation, and motives.

Listen Actively. The next step to improving communication is to take actions to ensure that you—the receiver—hear and understand what the sender is trying to communicate. In conversations, making eye contact is a good way to help speakers feel comfortable and convinced that you are sincerely interested in understanding what they have to say. It is important to focus on the content of the message being sent regardless of the style of its delivery. Even if people are not choosing the best words or are making grammatical errors, they may have something quite valuable to communicate. Focusing on style over substance can cause the value of the message to be missed. To make sure you understand what is being said, ask clarifying questions. Also, even when you think you have understood the message, it is a good idea to paraphrase, that is, restate what you think the message is. This can be put in the form of a question or statement. For example, you could ask, "So are you saying that . . . ?" Or you could say something like, "What I understand you to be saying is. . . ."

Observe Nonverbal Cues. As we discussed earlier in this chapter, nonverbal cues are critical to effective communication.[30] Listening more open-mindedly and actively to the words is only part of the task. You also need to concentrate on observing nonverbal cues. In cross-cultural settings, this means that you need to remember that a nonverbal cue or gesture can have different meanings in different cultures. There is little substitute for learning about the nonverbal cues and gestures of the culture of those with whom you will be interacting.

Improving Sending Skills

There are many situations in which you will be the sender of a message. Effective communication can be enhanced by developing better sending skills.

Simplify Your Language. One of the first things a sender can do to enhance communication is to simplify the language in the message. Clearly, what is simple will vary, depending on the audience. Simplifying may involve eliminating jargon that might not be familiar to all members of the audience. It may also involve choosing more succinct and active words and shorter sentences. Perhaps the best clue for spotting complicated and passive language is excessive use of prepositions. The more prepositions in a sentence, the higher the likelihood that the language could be simplified and the message could be stated more directly.

Organize Your Writing. Executives consistently complain about the poor writing skills of new managers.[31] Their complaints lie not in spelling or grammar mistakes, though clearly these should be eliminated, but in the lack of logical thought processes. As a manager, you are likely to write more reports and memos than you may want, and the effectiveness of those written communications will have an important impact on your career. Consequently, developing good writing skills is vital to being an effective manager. Nothing substitutes for practice.

Understand Your Audience. Perhaps the single best thing a sender can do to enhance the effectiveness of communications is to understand the audience.[32] For example, consider the following questions, which come from the material we have covered thus far in this chapter:

- What is the direction of the communication (up, lateral, or down), and does the receiver have any expectations concerning this type of communication?

- Is the communication formal or informal, and how should it be structured to have the intended impact on the receiver?

- Are there expectations from the receiver about the explicitness or implicitness of the message you want to send?

- Does the receiver have any biases for or against certain modes of communication (e.g., for or against email, face-to-face conversations, and so on)?

If you do not understand the person or persons to whom you are sending a message, it is almost impossible to answer these questions. Knowing your audience (i.e., the receiver or receivers) is critical to improving your sending skills. Knowledge of the audience is particularly important in cross-cultural settings. Exhibit 13.10 lists some ways to improve cross-cultural communication.

Organization-Level Improvements in Communication

Organizations can take steps to change their policies and methods for how and when managers should communicate. Unfortunately, guidelines for this more structural approach are not as well developed as those for individual

Exhibit 13.10   Tips on Being a More Effective Cross-Cultural Communicator

1. Study general principles that apply to all types of intercultural communication.

2. Learn about the fundamental characteristics of the other cultures with which you will be working.

3. For high-context cultures, learn as many details in advance about the target organization(s) and their specific individual representatives.

4. For high-context cultures, use at least a few words or phrases in the listener's language.

5. For high-context cultures, be especially careful about body language and tone of voice.

6. For low-context cultures, organize written communications so that the major points are immediately and directly stated.

7. Study and respect communicators' preferences for greater degrees of formality, especially compared with the typical North American approach of casual informality.

managers. A study of research and development laboratories within 14 large multinational firms, however, provides some suggestions.[33] The study produced strong evidence for the importance of **gatekeepers**, or so-called "boundary-spanning" individuals who are at the communication interface between separate organizations or between units within an organization. Large companies especially need to be able to structure the activities of gatekeepers to maximize their usefulness to the communication process and to make sure that the most critical information is both sent and received. Findings from the study indicated that communication could be improved by implementing rules and procedures that increased formal communication, replacing some face-to-face communication with electronic communication, developing particular communication networks, and even creating a centralized office to manage communication activities.

gatekeepers Individuals who are at the communication interface between separate organizations or between different units within an organization.

Communication and Negotiation

In the last sections of this chapter, we focus on one particular type of communication that is especially crucial for a manager—negotiation. **Negotiation** can be thought of as the process of conferring to arrive at an agreement between two or more parties, each with their own interests and preferences. The purpose of negotiation is to see whether the parties can arrive at an agreement that serves their mutual interests. Since reaching an agreement inherently involves communication, negotiation and communication are inseparably linked. Thus, the negotiation process can be considered a special part of the general communication process.

negotiation The process of conferring to arrive at an agreement between different parties, each with their own interests and preferences.

The Importance of Negotiation to Managers

Today's managers often find themselves in the role of negotiator. This can occur in different types of situations. One type is during the ongoing, day-to-day activities of the manager's organizational unit, where there is a need to negotiate a settlement or resolution of some kind of disagreement. This could be a disagreement between the manager and his own boss, between the manager and another manager from a different unit, or between the manager and one or more of his subordinates. Disagreements could also occur between subordinates or between entire departments. Typically, in these kinds of circumstances, the manager would function as an individual negotiator.

The other basic type of negotiation situation in which managers could find themselves would be where they are part of a formally appointed negotiating team representing their unit or organization in discussions with representatives from another unit or organization. In either kind of negotiating situation, managers are taking on the role of facilitator—attempting to ensure that all parties can agree on a common course of action. Also, regardless of the specific features of the situation, the principles of effective approaches to negotiation can help settle any kind of disagreement a manager might encounter—inside or outside an organization.

Achieving More Effective Negotiations

Managers have available several potentially helpful approaches to increasing their chances of achieving successful negotiation outcomes (see Exhibit 13.11). One especially useful principle to keep in mind when serving as a negotiator is to focus on the parties' *interests*, not their positions.[34] Each side to a dispute has interests, whether or not they enter into negotiations with fixed positions. **Interests** are a party's concerns and desires—what they want, in other words.

interests In negotiation, a party's concerns and desires—in other words, what they want.

positions In negotiation, a party's stance regarding their interests.

Positions, on the other hand, are a party's stance regarding those interests. An example of an interest would be the desire by a subordinate to receive a specific challenging new assignment. A position in this example would be a statement by the subordinate that "I am the one who should receive this new sales territory because. . . ." It is easier to get agreement on interests than on positions because (1) for a given interest there are probably several possible positions that could satisfy it, and (2) behind two opposed positions there are likely to be at least some interests that are shared rather than in direct conflict.[35] Thus, if such mutually compatible interests can be identified, the chances of reaching an acceptable conclusion to the negotiations are increased. In the example above, even though the boss is not able to give the desired new sales territory to this particular subordinate, a common interest may be identified—such as the desire of both parties to see that the subordinate's good performance in the past is rewarded with some other kind of challenging new assignment in the future—even though it can't be this particular assignment now.

Less effective	More effective
◄ ·· ►	
• Positions	• Interests
• People Involved	• Problem/Issue
• Maintaining/Increasing	• Decreasing/Lessening
Competition	Competition
(Win/Lose Focus)	(Collaborative Focus)

Exhibit 13.11 Improving Effectiveness of Negotiations.

A second sound principle for negotiations (again, see Exhibit 13.11) is to focus on the problem or issue rather than on the people involved. The key point here is that a negotiator should endeavour to concentrate on the substance of the disagreement rather than on who is doing the disagreeing or what they are like as people. This principle is well summarized in the advice to negotiators to "be hard on the problem, soft on the people."[36]

Another helpful principle for managers who are involved in negotiations is to try to lessen the competition between the two parties (an "I win, you lose" situation) by establishing an atmosphere of collaboration (a "we all win" situation). **Collaboration** is an attempt to get both parties to attack a problem and solve it together, rather than have one party defeat the other, as in a win–lose athletic contest. Thus, both parties should be encouraged to develop creative solutions that increase the total amount of resources available to be shared or divided by the two parties.

collaboration A part of negotiation in which parties work together to attack and solve a problem.

Finally, if managers find that negotiations are extremely complex and the parties seem emotionally invested in the outcome, they can often request intervention by a neutral third party. Sometimes disinterested managers within the organization may be asked to serve in this role. The third-party negotiator can serve the role of judge, mediator, or devil's advocate. In the role of a judge, the manager handles negotiations and decides on the best possible course of action, which the parties then agree to follow. In mediation, the manager controls the negotiation process, but someone else makes the final decision based on the arguments presented—possibly a senior executive in the organization. As we have discussed in other chapters, a devil's advocate asks questions that may oppose the positions of both parties. The attempt here is for all parties to think about positions that they may not originally have considered.

Key Factors in Cross-National Negotiations

As noted earlier, as a manager you may find yourself a member of negotiating teams. With the greater frequency of international assignments, this may particularly be the case when working in situations that require negotiations across national borders. Because of the advances in transportation and communication technologies, along with expanding capital flows worldwide, organizations are engaging in ever-larger amounts of foreign trade and international business partnerships. Together, all of this activity increases the importance of your being able to negotiate successfully in cross-national circumstances as well as in your own organization or country.

Analysis has shown that there are three principal variables that determine the outcome of negotiations in general, and especially in these kinds of cross-national situations: (1) the people involved, (2) the situation, and (3) the process itself.[37] Research from an array of internationally oriented studies also indicates that each of these variables is strongly influenced by cultural differences.[38]

People. Although there are some cultural differences in preferred negotiator characteristics, there seem to be some traits and abilities that are fairly universal for the task of negotiation. They include good listening skills, strong orientation toward people, and high self-esteem, among others.[39] In addition, an ability to be influential in the home organization appears to be a commonly preferred personal attribute.

Research has also found that negotiators will modify or adapt their behaviour when working in cross-cultural negotiations. However, there were differences found in the extent that negotiators will adjust their approach to accommodate individuals from another country. American negotiators were found to be the most tenacious in their behaviour across cultures, making minimal adjustments, while Japanese negotiators were found to be more accommodating, tending to make more adjustments. The same study also compared intracultural negotiations (negotiations with differing cultural groups within a country) between anglophone and francophone Canadians. The study found that francophone Canadians were much more accommodating with anglophone Canadians than with cross-cultural negotiators (negotiations with differing cultural groups outside of Canada), and anglophone negotiators enjoyed more joint profits across teams when negotiating with francophones than with cross-cultural negotiators.[40]

Situations of Negotiations. The second major variable affecting negotiation outcomes is the set of situational circumstances. Probably the most important are the location of the negotiations, the physical arrangements, the emphasis on speed and time, and the composition of the negotiating teams.

Location. Typically, there is a strong tendency to want to negotiate on your own turf or at neutral sites, especially for critical negotiations. The so-called "home court advantage" seems to be universal; everyone feels more comfortable and confident and has greater access to information and resources when negotiating at home. For international negotiations, negotiations conducted in a manager's own offices or even in his or her home country can be a psychological advantage.

Characteristics of locations, however, can vary by culture. For example, in North America negotiations regularly occur in a formal setting, such as an office or conference room. In contrast, in Japan and Mexico, where relationship building is crucial, major parts of the process are likely to occur in an informal or nonwork setting, such as a restaurant or golf course. In Korea, the final contract produced from the negotiations is likely to be signed in a formal and public setting rather than in someone's office.

Physical Arrangements. The usual North American approach to setting up a room for negotiations is to place the parties on opposite sides of a table facing each other, which has the obvious effect of emphasizing competing interests. Other arrangements are possible, including seating the parties at right angles or along the same side "facing the problem," or at a round table where all are part of the total problem-solving effort.[41]

Emphasis on Speed and Time. North Americans typically avoid wasting time. They want to "get right to the point" or "get down to business." Other cultures differ from that viewpoint. In Mexico or China, for example, the norm is to invest considerable time in relationship building and other activities not directly related to the central negotiation process. Consequently, in such cultures speed is sacrificed and the effectiveness and efficiency of subsequent negotiations often hinge on how well relationships have been developed.

Composition of the Negotiating Teams. The composition and size of teams representing the parties can also influence negotiations. For example, the more people involved at the negotiation table, the more preparation that needs to be done to ensure that the team presents a united front. The composition of the team in terms of decision-making authority is also important. If individuals at the table have authority to make binding decisions, the negotiations are generally more efficient than if they do not.

Team composition can vary significantly by culture. In countries that are sensitive to status differences and ranks (for example, Singapore, India, Venezuela, Japan), having similar status, position, age, and authority between the negotiating teams is much more important than in other countries (like New Zealand, Canada, United States). The size of negotiating teams also can differ markedly by culture. In the North American individualistic-oriented culture, team size is ordinarily much smaller than in more collectivist-oriented cultures such as those of Taiwan, China, and Japan. The resulting mismatch in size can communicate unintended messages. Taiwanese, for example, might interpret a single negotiator or a small team as a sign that the other party does not consider the negotiations to be important. Similarly, someone from North America might interpret the presence of a large team from a Taiwanese firm as an attempt to intimidate them with numbers.

The Negotiation Process. The third—and probably most crucial—variable determining the outcome of negotiations is the negotiating process itself. The five common stages in this process, which are basically the same across all cultures,[42] are described below and shown in Exhibit 13.12.

Stage 1: Planning and Preparation. This stage involves laying the foundations through advance planning and analysis prior to any face-to-face interactions. At this stage, individuals or teams conduct background research, gather relevant information, and plan their strategy and tactics. In addition, preliminary decisions are made about what the objectives will be and what can and cannot be conceded during the course of the negotiations.

Stage 2: Relationship Building between Negotiating Parties. This stage is commonly referred to as "nontask time," in which each side attempts to establish comfortable working relationships with the other side. North Americans are generally inclined to make this stage briefer and believe such activities are relatively unimportant. On the other hand, negotiators from some other cultures such as Latin America, the Middle East, and Asia believe exactly the opposite. Research suggests three behavioural elements emerge during this stage: developing trust, developing personal rapport, and establishing long-term association.[43]

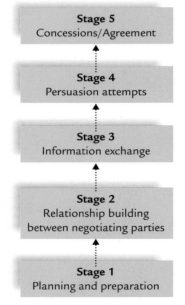

Exhibit 13.12
The Five Stages in the Negotiating Process.

Stage 5
Concessions/Agreement

Stage 4
Persuasion attempts

Stage 3
Information exchange

Stage 2
Relationship building between negotiating parties

Stage 1
Planning and preparation

Stage 3: Information Exchange. In this stage, each party attempts to learn about the needs and demands of its counterparts. North American managers often attempt to hurry through these activities with an attitude of "you tell me what you want, and I will tell you what I want."[44] In contrast, managers from Asian cultures take a much more indirect, more drawn out, and more thorough approach to acquiring and exchanging information. Arabic and Latin American managers appear to follow a similar approach, except that the latter are even more leisurely in their use of time at this stage.[45]

Stage 4: Persuasion Attempts. This stage focuses on attempts to modify the position of the other party and to influence that side to accept the negotiator's desired set of exchanges (for example, an exchange of a certain price for a certain quantity or quality of goods or services). North American managers usually treat this as the most important stage, with assertive and straightforward efforts to obtain a desired conclusion. Such persuasion can sometimes involve the use of warnings or threats to try to force the other party to agree.[46] Managers from Arabic countries tend to show tactics similar to those of North Americans at the persuasion stage, but they are less inclined to hurry. Negotiators from Asian cultures take a slow, careful approach but do not tend to use direct assertiveness in persuasion until later in the negotiations. As reported in one research study, "when not sure of the offer, they frequently resort to the tactics of 'pretending to lack authority' or 'deliberately delaying [a] counter offer'."[47] Managers from Latin American cultures tend to use a mixture of approaches during this stage by showing a moderate degree of assertiveness but also a willingness to use the tactic of "calculated delay" when this seems advisable.[48]

Stage 5: Concessions/Agreement. At this final point, if reasonable progress has been made, compromises and concessions are made that permit each party to take away something of value. Since North American managers tend to begin the negotiation process with positions fairly close to what they will finally accept, they do not have much leeway for concessions.[49] Managers from Arabic and Latin American countries seem to open negotiations from more extreme positions, which permit them to offer concessions late in the process. Managers from Asian countries often employ "normative appeals" (such as "it's your obligation") to try to get the other party to offer concessions.[50]

Managerial Perspectives Revisited

PERSPECTIVE 1: THE ORGANIZATIONAL CONTEXT Almost all types and forms of managerial communication are affected by the organizational context. The structure and characteristics of organizations can facilitate or impede effective communication. The policies and procedures of the organization likewise can help or hinder a manager's attempts to send and receive information and meaning to and from different sources. Particularly affected by the organizational context is the direction of communication. The meaning of transmitted information varies considerably depending on whether it is being sent or received upward, downward, or laterally. The organizational context also presents major challenges and opportunities to build powerful communication networks.

PERSPECTIVE 2: THE HUMAN FACTOR The very phrase "interpersonal communication" suggests the centrality of the people aspects of communication. As we discussed earlier in this chapter, among the chief barriers to successful communication are the interpersonal ones. Managers who can gain insight into this kind of potential barrier and how such processes as selective perception and frames of reference can affect communication will increase their chances of becoming more effective communicators. We also observed in the latter part of the chapter how certain characteristics of people help determine the likelihood of constructive outcomes of negotiations in cross-cultural circumstances.

PERSPECTIVE 3: MANAGING PARADOXES Communication can be a source of paradoxes to be managed. For example, a manager has to be alert to how both verbal and nonverbal modes of communicating affect potential receivers. A verbal message may convey one meaning, but a nonverbal message may convey another. Oral and written communication can also present paradoxes. Managers often attempt to reinforce their intended messages by sending them by both modes of communication, but this does not guarantee successful communication. In other words, being effective at communicating in one mode is not the same thing as being effective in the other. If they are ineffective at one or both, their messages can be misunderstood, causing more confusion rather than more collaboration among their employees. Therefore, it is critical for most managers to hone both forms. In the area of negotiations, another paradox to be managed is the necessity to pay attention to the differences between "interests" and "positions."

PERSPECTIVE 4: ENTREPRENEURIAL MINDSET As we have said, a key component of being entrepreneurial is identifying opportunities. To identify opportunities, managers have to gather substantial amounts of information and analyze them. They must remain alert to unique trends and changes in markets and customer needs. Gathering this information requires managers to communicate with many people and engage in active listening. Furthermore, exploiting opportunities requires them to communicate their ideas and strategies effectively to others in the organization.

The other relevant observation that can be made here is that communication is an area (as with leadership in general) where people can develop and definitely improve their skills if they have sufficient desire to do so. Those with an entrepreneurial mindset are more likely to try. The same is true for becoming a more skilled negotiator: A commitment to improving can result in positive benefits.

Concluding Comments

As emphasized at the beginning of this chapter, being a good communicator and knowing how the communication process works is essential for becoming an effective manager and leader. In fact, most experienced managers will tell you that communication skills are vital to career success, and a variety of studies emphatically support this claim. Of course, the first step is to understand the nuances of the basic communication process. But that is only a starting point. Although the process seems simple enough, the major challenge is to be able to implement that process successfully on a regular and consistent basis.

That, in turn, requires applying your knowledge about the nature of organizations and some of the other key functions of managing (such as planning, organizing, and leading) that have already been discussed in previous chapters.

If good communication were easy, then everyone would be able to do it well most of the time. However, in any organizational context, there are always barriers and obstacles that interfere with effective communication. It is critically important, therefore, to be very aware of these potential obstructions so you can take steps to overcome and deal with them. Communication is an excellent example of a management activity where there is a great cost to naïveté and inexperience and a great benefit to be gained by awareness and analytical insight. Very few people are naturally superb communicators, but there is ample opportunity to become a much better communicator if you focus on developing that awareness and insight.

It also will be especially helpful in your management career if you can add some understanding of the process of negotiation to your repertoire of communication skills. As we noted in this chapter, negotiation is a particular type or form of communication because of the up-front recognition and acknowledgment of different interests and preferences as the starting point for the process. Various factors, like cultural differences, can increase the difficulty and complexity of the process. Again, however, like communication in general, being able to become a better negotiator is a capability that can be honed. Gaining negotiation experience is especially helpful, particularly if that experience is followed by careful analysis and attention to what was learned from the process.

Key Terms

collaboration (p. 454)
communication (p. 434)
communication networks (p. 443)
cultural distance (p. 449)
decoding (p. 435)
downward communication (p. 440)
empathy (p. 451)
encoding (p. 435)
ethnocentrism (p. 449)

formal communication
 channels (p. 442)
frames of reference (p. 446)
gatekeepers (p. 453)
informal communication
 channels (p. 442)
interests (p. 453)
lateral communication (p. 441)
media richness (p. 438)

medium (p. 435)
negotiation (p. 453)
networking (p. 444)
noise (p. 435)
positions (p. 454)
selective perception (p. 446)
stereotyping (p. 449)
upward communication (p. 441)

Test Your Comprehension

1. What is communication?

2. What are the parts of the communication model?

3. What is noise? How does it affect the communication process?

4. Why is oral communication usually more compelling than written communication?

5. Which mode of communication is the most flexible? The least flexible? Why?

6. Why is it important for nonverbal cues to be consistent with verbal cues? What happens if they are not?

7. What is meant by "media richness"?

8. What are some of the characteristics of media that you should consider when deciding which one to use for a given message?

9. What are the typical differences in content of upward, downward, and lateral communication within organizations?

10. What are the differences between formal and informal communication channels? When would you use each?

11. What is a communication network?

12. Why is networking important?

13. What are the three types of barriers to effective communication?

14. How are selective perception and frames of reference related?

15. In what way can emotions become a barrier to effective communication?

16. What are the principal differences between high-context and low-context cultures relative to communication?

17. What is ethnocentrism, and how does it impair effective communication?

18. What is cultural distance?

19. What are the two basic methods for improving your communication ability?

20. Discuss the four ways to improve your listening skills.

21. What are some of the methods used to improve your sending skills?

22. What can organizations do to improve communication within them?

23. In negotiation, what is the difference between an "interest" and a "position"?

24. What are four helpful principles for effective negotiation?

25. What are the key factors in cross-national negotiations?

26. Describe each of the five stages of negotiations and how they can contribute to the overall outcome.

Apply Your Understanding

1. Despite the considerable emphasis that most companies and other types of organizations put on communication, why do you think that many employees feel there is inadequate communication with and from their managers?

2. Assume that you are now working in the first, truly management position in your career. What is likely to be the most important communication issue/problem you will face in the first few months in that position?

3. Will the continued increase in electronic communication within and between organizations be likely to increase or decrease the communication issues/problems faced by the typical manager? Explain the reasoning behind your answer.

4. How can knowledge of the basics of negotiation assist managers in doing their day-to-day activities, especially in regard to exercising leadership and influence? Can you provide examples?

Practise Your Capabilities

When Chris Barnes was promoted to manager in the production department at Telmark Plastics, sales had been increasing for three years and productivity and morale in the department were high. Lately, however, orders have been slowing down. Some days there haven't been enough orders to keep all of the workers busy. And it isn't just in Chris's department. An economic downturn has sent the entire company into a tailspin. The CEO has instructed all managers to find ways to cut costs by 22 percent immediately.

Feeling very pressured and too busy to talk to any of the workers right away to get their opinions, on Tuesday Chris sent the following short memo to the production department employees:

> TO: Production Workers:
> I have been instructed to cut costs by 22 percent. This means we will need to make some tough decisions. We will have a meeting to discuss alternatives on Friday afternoon at 5:00 p.m.

Through the rest of the week, Chris noticed clusters of workers having intense conversations that stopped whenever he approached. Productivity was slipping. There was more absenteeism than normal. Every member of the department appeared angry, depressed, and worried.

On Friday afternoon, as soon as Chris entered the meeting room the yelling started. The entire evening shift seemed to think they would probably all be laid off. The day shift had somehow come to the conclusion that they were going to have to take significant pay cuts or maybe be replaced by less expensive workers. Chris finally managed to calm everybody down and told them that the meeting wasn't to announce layoffs or pay cuts, but to discuss any other ways they could think of to cut costs. Didn't they read the memo?

Chris had expected everyone to show up with creative ideas on how to cut costs, not expectations of being laid off! What had gone wrong?

1. Comment on Chris's choice of media for (a) the announcement and (b) the meeting. Would you have made the same choices?

2. Identify any barriers to communication in this situation. How could they have been reduced?

3. If you were Chris, what would you do following the meeting to improve the communication between yourself and your workers?

PEARSON

mymanagementlab™

To improve your grade, visit the MyManagementLab website at **www.pearsoned.ca/mymanagementlab.** This online homework and tutorial system allows you to test your understanding and generates a personalized study plan just for you. It provides you with study and practice tools directly related to this chapter's content. MyManagementLab puts you in control of your own learning!

Part Thirteen

Organizational Control

Chapter 14

Control

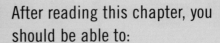

After reading this chapter, you should be able to:

1 Discuss the effects of too much or too little control in an organization.

2 Describe the four basic elements of the control process and the issues involved in each.

3 Differentiate between the different levels of control and compare their implications for managers.

4 Explain the concept of standards and why they are so important in organizations.

5 Compare bureaucratic and clan controls.

6 Identify the important qualities required for information to be useful in the control process.

Taken from *Management*, Canadian Edition, by Michael A. Hitt, J. Stewart Black, Lyman W. Porter, and Andrew J. Gaudes.

How Much Control Is Enough?

Workers are shown exiting the Barings Bank building in London, after it was purchased by Dutch financial group ING for only 1£. Some parts of Barings were integrated into ING while other parts were sold or shut down. Barings had been one of the oldest and most prestigious banks in Great Britain before employee Nick Leeson bankrupted it by speculating in the Nikkei 225 (Japan's version of the Dow Jones index).

Can a single individual topple an entire multinational corporation? The answer is, surprisingly, yes. The lack of control at Barings Bank sank the 233-year-old British bank and rocked the financial world. In early 1995, a 28-year-old trader caused one of the most spectacular collapses in modern financial history. When the dust finally settled, Barings had suffered trading losses in excess of US$1 billion. Ironically, just two years earlier, Peter Baring, the company's CEO, had stated in a speech, "[Financial] derivatives need to be well controlled and understood, but we believe we do that well here."

Baring Brothers was one of the oldest and most prestigious banks in Great Britain, and was even a bank to the House of Windsor. Barings's money helped to keep British armies in the field during the Napoleonic Wars. The Baring family had run the firm for 233 years, and Peter Baring was carrying on the tradition.

In 1992, Barings sent Nick Leeson to assume a post as the chief trader of Baring Futures in Singapore. Leeson traded futures contracts on the Nikkei 225, Japan's version of the Dow Jones index. His job was to exploit the small differences in the buying and selling of these contracts, otherwise known as arbitrage. The trading of futures was considered a relatively safe bet because they generally only resulted in small profits or losses at one time. But Leeson became more sophisticated in his trading knowledge, and he became more "bullish" (that is, he took greater risks).

On January 17, 1995, a massive earthquake devastated Kobe, Japan, and the Nikkei responded with uncertainty. Later that month, the Nikkei plunged more than 1000 points. For Barings and for Leeson, this natural disaster turned into a financial disaster. The traders in the Far East panicked, Leeson in particular.

Leeson made huge investments, betting on the rebound of the Nikkei. While traders at other investment banks cut their losses, Leeson proceeded to put Barings's money into billions of dollars worth of futures contracts that would only make money if the Nikkei rose. Traders in Tokyo and Singapore watched, but they figured that the bets that Barings was making were offset by hedges in other areas.

However, this turned out not to be the case. For every percentage point that the Nikkei slipped, Barings lost tens of millions of dollars. Eventually, the losses exceeded Barings's net worth.

Whether senior management really knew what was going on in Singapore is not clear. Someone at the London headquarters knew—because Leeson had made the investments with borrowed funds, a common practice. As Leeson's bets lost, Barings in London funnelled US$900 million to Singapore to offset the losses. By late February, the Nikkei had not bounced back, and Leeson and his wife skipped town.

Barings went bankrupt on February 26, 1995. As British regulators took control of the bank, Interpol, the international intelligence agency, sent out an alert to all governments in neighbouring countries to find Leeson. A few days after the bank's collapse, the "rogue trader" walked into the arms of police at Germany's Frankfurt airport. Leeson was convicted of fraud and sentenced to six and a half years in a Singapore prison, but served only four years, being released in 1999. While in prison he wrote a book entitled *Rogue Trader*, which is an account of his fraudulent acts. A *New York Times* review of the book was not very complimentary, but it did state that the book should be read by "banking managers and auditors everywhere," suggesting that there are lessons to be learned in the lack of control employed by Barings at the time of Leeson's reckless endeavours. ◆

Sources: P. Dwyer, "Descent into the Abyss," *BusinessWeek*, July 1, 1996, pp. 28–29; F. Norris, "Upper-Class Twits Made Me Do It," *New York Times*, March 31, 1996; S. D. Kaye, "Ripples from a Fallen Bank," *U.S. News & World Report*, March 13, 1995, pp. 68–72; B. Powell, D. Pedersen, and M. Elliott, "Busted!" *Newsweek*, March 13, 1995, pp. 36–43.

Strategic overview

As shown in the opening case on Barings, control is a critically important component of management activities in organizations, and it can play an important role in how an organization's strategy is developed and implemented and in the evaluation of its success. Oftentimes, control is exercised based on the financial outcomes of a strategy, like an organization's profits. However, control is sometimes focused on the type of strategy selected and the manner in which it is implemented. While controls focused on strategy (as opposed to financial outcomes) are difficult to develop and apply, they are crucial to ensuring that the organization remains innovative. Financial controls often focus on achieving short-term results like meeting the firm's profit goals for a quarter or a year. But when the focus is on strategy, managers must look toward longer-term results, like investing in the development of innovative new products. In fact, the types of controls implemented can affect the formulation of future strategies. Research has shown that when managers use controls focused on strategy, they are better able to focus on the long term and develop more effective organizational strategies.[1]

The type of control can also affect both the formulation and implementation of strategies by managers. Bureaucratic controls tend to focus on controlling behaviour in organizations with rules and regulations. Universities often employ bureaucratic controls because of the large number of students, faculty, and employees whose behaviour they must oversee. However, these controls are frequently tight and may constrain the types of strategies that can be pursued. For this reason, universities often make major changes only very slowly. Alternatively, controls based on the organization's culture (called "clan controls," and explained later in this chapter) better ensure that the strategies chosen fit well with the values of the organization. For example, WestJet has a unique culture and uses it to select new employees who share the organization's values. This same culture, or clan control, governs the behaviour of both managers and employees, who then have the same vision for the organization. Because all of the employees understand WestJet's culture and "buy into it," managers are better able to develop effective strategies that match the firm's values and implement them.

Regardless of the types of controls used, managers shouldn't feel so controlled or constrained that they can't respond to environmental changes such as challenges from competitors and the prospect of innovative products being introduced to the market. Many organizations now employ the balanced scorecard approach (explained later in this chapter) to ensure that managers are able to balance controls and needed flexibility to continue to learn, innovate, and change.

Probably the most critical part of that challenge, for individual managers as well as for organizations, is where to draw the line between too much control and too little control. Most of us can think of examples from our own work or other group experiences where we have encountered the downside of excessive control by individuals or supervisors or the organization itself through its rules and regulations. At the extreme, overcontrol conjures up images of "Big Brother," where you cannot make a move without first obtaining permission from someone higher up in the organizational structure.[2] More typically, too much control can result in resentment and limited motivation.

At the other extreme, too little control, as illustrated in the opening example, can expose an organization and its managers to very costly risks. Take, for example, the opening case in Chapter 6 where Japanese architect Hidetsugu Aneha was able to falsify structural documents because of the infrequent auditing undertaken by the Japanese government on privatized plan inspectors. In milder forms, undercontrol contributes to sloppy operations and failure to use resources efficiently and effectively. Errors or mistakes can increase, and the organization may not know where or when problems are occurring and, most importantly, how to fix them. In severe cases, the potential consequences can be catastrophic for the organization, as they were for Barings, or for the public, as they could have been for the occupants of the under-designed buildings in Japan.

Exercising control, then, presents not only major challenges for managers but also difficult dilemmas. The issue gets further complicated by the fact that, as we will discuss later, there are different types of control. A certain type of control may be quite effective in one situation but very ineffective or even damaging in different circumstances. The bottom line is that managers, no matter where they are in an organization or at what level, will have to deal with fundamental questions of control.

Managerial control problems occur in sophisticated organizations and in all countries. The example in the opening paragraphs makes this abundantly clear. If a major multinational corporation like Barings can have difficulties with control, so can smaller organizations with fewer resources and less sophisticated systems. Likewise, if these kinds of problems can develop within a firm headquartered in the United Kingdom and doing business across the globe, they can occur in any location or culture where managerial activity takes place. Exercising effective control is a universal and exceedingly important managerial challenge.

To explore the issue of control, we first look at the role that control plays in organizations and the way it relates to other managerial functions such as strategy and planning. Next, the four basic elements of the control process—establishing standards, measuring performance, comparing performance against standards, and evaluating results (and, if necessary, taking action)—are reviewed. Following this is a discussion of the different levels of control (strategic, tactical, and operational) and the various forms of control. This chapter concludes with an examination of factors that can influence the effectiveness of controls, such as their focus, amount, and the cost of implementing them. How consideration of these factors leads to crucial managerial choices is also explored.

The Control Function in Management

On the face of it, the word "control" sounds negative. It can mean restraints, constraints, or checks. This clearly connotes restricted freedom of action—an idea that many people, especially in some cultures, may find troublesome. Certainly, within the context of organizations, **control** involves regulation of activities and behaviours (see Exhibit 14.1). To control in an organizational setting means to adjust or bring conformity to specifications or objectives. In this sense, then, the control responsibilities of managers are bound to restrict someone's freedom. A manager cannot control without restricting. However, whether this is good or bad for the individual or group that is being controlled, for the manager who determines the amount and type of control, or for the organization at large depends on the consequences of the control and whose perspectives are being considered.

control The regulation of activities and behaviours within organizations; adjustment or conformity to specifications or objectives.

Some amount of control in organizations is unavoidable. The very essence of organizations is that individuals give up total independence so that common goals and objectives can be accomplished. As one organizational scholar put it, "The coordination and order created out of the diverse interests and potentially diverse behaviours of members is largely a function of control."[3] Thus, control is a fundamental characteristic of organized activity. Managers should always keep in mind, however, that control is a means for achieving a goal and is not the goal itself (as is well demonstrated in *A Manager's Challenge: "The Keg"*).

The managerial function of control comes at the end of a chain of the other major functions of planning, organizing, and leading. (Indeed, that is why a chapter on control is almost always found toward the end of most management textbooks.) If those prior functions are carried out well, generating positive responses to controls will be much easier. Conversely, if major problems exist in planning, organizing, or leading, almost no amount of attention to control is likely to work very well. In this sense, effective control is a managerial function that depends heavily on the other functions that precede it. When these preceding functions work well, control tends to work well. When they don't, control can become a major headache for a manager.

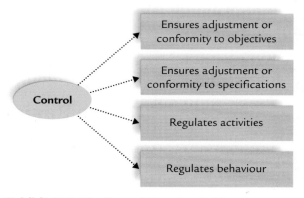

Exhibit 14.1 The Control Function in Management.

A Manager's Challenge   *Change*

The Keg

For fine restaurants, cooking is an art, not a science. The reputation of the food at these restaurants is usually a function of the chef's creativity. So the ideas of standardization and tight control are generally alien to upscale restaurants.

This is not the case with The Keg Steakhouse & Bar, a company that operates over 90 steakhouses across North America. Since the first Keg restaurant opened in North Vancouver in 1971, the company has continued to expand, making it the largest casual-restaurant brand and one of the most popular steakhouses in Canada. The Keg was originally created as a private company and later became public, trading on the Vancouver and Toronto Stock Exchanges.

As a result of a few changes in ownership since its establishment in 1971, The Keg has operated a number of nonsteak restaurant concepts including The Old Spaghetti Factory, Brandy's Cocktail Lounges, Crock & Block, and others. After it was purchased by Canadian entrepreneur David Aisenstat in 1997, The Keg began to focus once again on its "core steakhouse and bar concept." With this change in focus, The Keg became increasingly dedicated to providing its consumers with steaks of the highest quality. To accomplish this goal, steaks are aged to ensure tenderness, and are then seasoned with a "special blend of seasonings" to give the steaks a distinct flavour. Steaks are not the only

menu items for which preparation is carefully controlled to ensure consistent quality across all Keg locations; all desserts are made by its dessert supplier in Toronto.

Over the years, The Keg has experienced several challenges because of changes in the external environment. A particularly difficult year for the restaurant industry was 2003, with the SARS scare, continued terrorism threats, hurricanes, the increasing value of the Canadian dollar, and the mad cow disease scare. Despite these pressures in its operating environment, The Keg managed to increase its sales to $292 million from $277 million the previous year. In 2004, while the amount of money spent at Canadian steakhouses declined 13 percent from the previous year, The Keg's sales continued to climb. According to the company's 2006 annual report, The Keg reached a sales record of more than $372 million, which was an increase of $46 million, or 14.4 percent, from 2005.

The Keg has managed to survive periods of difficulty and has continued to grow and prosper by continually enforcing specific controls. The entrees are consistent between locations, as cooks are instructed to follow head office's precise preparation instructions, which are sent to each restaurant on DVD. The Keg has very few suppliers, which are "monitored almost fanatically" in an effort to ensure that all food meets the company's "detailed and so-specific" quality requirements. The result of these controls is a consistent atmosphere and a dependable menu that creates loyal customers.

Sources: The Keg Steakhouse & Bar, "The Keg History," www.kegincomefund.com (accessed April 25, 2007); Annual Report 2006, www.kegincomefund.com (accessed April 25, 2007); The Keg Steakhouse & Bar, "News 2005: Keg Chews Up the Competition Even As Industry Sales Drop," www.kegincomefund.com (accessed April 25, 2007); K. Wells, "The Keg: A Rare Treat," *The Telegram*, May 3, 2005, p. B1; R. Harris, "Consistency Pays Off," *Marketing*, September 6, 2004, p. 4; W. Hanley, "Keg Boss Gives Street Steak, Sizzle," *National Post*, October 25, 2003, p. IN1; W. Chow, "Well Done! The Keg at 30: Steakhouse Mogul David Aisenstat Celebrates with Ambitious Expansion," *Vancouver Sun*, September 21, 2001, p. F10.

Control can also be thought of as a "causal" variable because the results of control efforts can inform and improve the planning process of the organization. Control is thus part of a feedback loop into planning and organizing (see Exhibit 14.2) that can help managers adapt to changing circumstances and conditions. When either the internal or external organizational environment changes, good control systems let managers know if the current ways of operating are still meeting the organization's objectives.

The Basic Control Process

The basic elements of the control process in an organizational setting are simple and straightforward (see Exhibit 14.3):

1. Establish standards

2. Measure performance

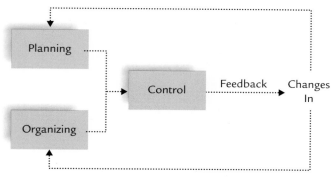

Exhibit 14.2 Control's Feedback Loop.

3. Compare performance against standards

4. Evaluate results (of the comparison) and, if necessary, take action

Each of these basic components involves important managerial attention and decisions.

Establish Standards

Specifying what management expects is absolutely critical at each step of the control process. This starts at the top of the organization and, ideally, should eventually involve every level of employee. First and foremost, those at the highest levels should be able to articulate a vision and formulate broad strategic goals for the organization. For instance, part of the vision of the Royal Canadian Mint is to be "a world-class brand that exceeds expectations with outstanding products and services."[4] From this example, it is easy to see how particular **standards**, or targets of performance, might be developed. Without a strategic vision and goals for the overall organization, managers in various parts of the organization find it difficult to develop meaningful and agreed-upon performance yardsticks.

The establishment of standards—wherever they exist throughout the organization—requires as much specificity as possible. The reason for this is that measuring performance against standards cannot readily be accomplished if the standards are vague. A standard of "efficiently respond to customer complaints," for example, does not provide usable guidelines for determining whether the standard has been met. A standard of "responds, on average, to three customer complaints per hour" would permit an objective measurement of performance.

However, for some aspects of performance, especially in higher-level and more complex jobs like those in research laboratories, it is often not possible nor even desirable to set up easily quantified standards (like number of discoveries per year). In these kinds of positions, the most important elements of performance may be the most difficult to measure, like the probable long-term impact of a given discovery. Moreover, as in the example in the preceding paragraph, the *quality* of response to customer complaints may be more important than the *rate* of response. However, quality is often more difficult to measure. As shown in Exhibit 14.4, the more abstract the standard, the greater the possibility of confusion in measuring performance, and the greater the problem of gaining the acceptance of those measurements by members whose performance is being assessed.

Other issues also can arise in the establishment of standards (see Exhibit 14.5). One revolves around the decision regarding who should set the standards. In general, research has shown that in setting standards, participation by those who will be affected is beneficial in two respects.[5] First, because they have had

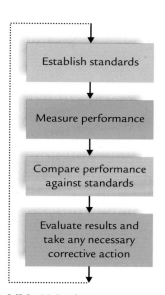

Exhibit 14.3 The Basic Elements in the Control Process.

standards Targets of performance.

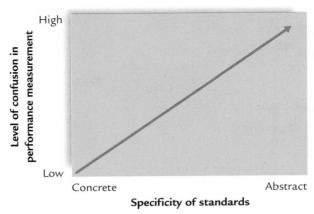

Exhibit 14.4 The Effect of Specificity of Standards on Performance Measurement.

some opportunity to influence the standards being set, those affected are more likely to be committed to meeting them. Second, involving those who have to meet the standards often results in a useful exchange of information and expertise that, in turn, results in more appropriate standards. At Siemens AG's top-notch medical solutions plant in Forchheim, Germany, for example, managers are striving to achieve a cost-savings goal of 10 percent per year while at the same time improving quality manufacturing performance. To do so, they have involved all of the workgroups in the control process, and each group meets weekly with their manager to examine the past week's performance and set goals for the following week. The initiative led to a shortening of delivery time by 90 percent (from 22 weeks to 2 weeks) and substantial improvements in reliability.[6]

Another issue is the degree of difficulty of the standards themselves. As we saw in the chapter on motivation, the research on goal setting points to the conclusion that difficult but achievable goals seem to result in the highest levels of performance.[7] Similar views have been expressed regarding goals in the budgetary process. Thus, "the ideal budget is one that is challenging but

If anyone knows how to put on the "ritz," it's the Ritz-Carlton's 32 000 employees located at its 63 hotels worldwide in 21 countries. Each Ritz employee gets over 100 hours of customer service training annually. A daily "SQI" (service quality indicator) in every hotel is displayed on TV screens for hotel personnel to see. The SQI monitors production and guest service processes up to the minute so service problems are apparent and can be immediately remedied.

attainable."[8] Achievable budget standards are regarded as desirable because they reduce the motivation to manipulate data or to focus only on short-term actions at the expense of long-term objectives. Achievable budgets also have the potential for increasing morale and generating a "winning atmosphere."[9] This assumes, as noted, that the budgetary targets are not only attainable, but also reasonably difficult. Here, again, where to draw the line between goals that are too challenging and those that are not challenging enough is itself another managerial challenge.

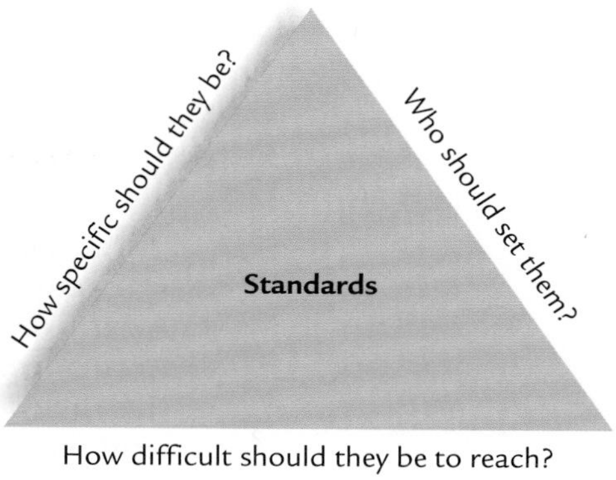

An interesting side note on the topic of budgets is that some companies have rejected the use of budgets and the wrangling over what the data indicate. In the absence of budgets, they use alternative financial and nonfinancial goals and measures. Companies that have rejected budgets require employees to measure themselves against the performance of competitors and against internal peer groups. Since employees do not know whether they have succeeded until they can look back on the results of a given period, they must make sure that they beat the competition. A key feature of many companies that have rejected budgets is the use of rolling forecasts, which are created every few months and typically cover five to eight quarters.[10]

Exhibit 14.5 Issues in Establishing Standards.

Measure Performance

The second step in the basic control process is the measurement of performance—the actions of people and equipment that the organization wants to monitor (see Exhibit 14.6). When readily quantifiable criteria do not exist, however, it becomes especially important to obtain as much consensus as possible about the way in which performance is to be assessed. To use an analogy, when true/false or multiple-choice tests are used in a class, the score a student receives is seldom contested (even though the quality of the questions often is). On the other hand, the score given to the answers on a test composed of essay questions is frequently disputed between student and teacher. The more the instructor and the class members can agree in advance about the qualities of good answers and on how the essay questions will be graded,

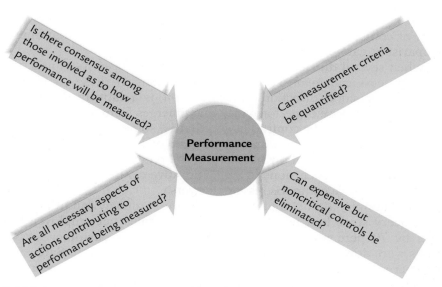

Exhibit 14.6 Issues in the Measurement of Performance.

the more likely the measurement process will be accepted. This occurs even though that process is clearly subjective. Similarly, in work situations, gaining up-front commitment to the performance measurement methods will reduce later complaints about what those measurements show and what they mean to individuals and to the organization.

Since performance in many jobs involves multiple activities, it is important for measurement to be comprehensive. If only some aspects of performance are measured, results can be misleading; they can skew the data that are used for the next two steps in the control process, especially taking action to change performance. The Royal Bank of Canada, Kodak, Motorola, and Hydro-Québec are just a few of the more than 73 percent of North American companies that use a comprehensive control technology called the "Stage-Gate" process throughout the life of a project. The Stage-Gate was developed by Dr. Robert G. Cooper, a marketing professor at McMaster University's DeGroote School of Business. Each project is divided into several stages with "gates" between them. Collectively, the gates act as comprehensive quality control checks that have to be passed before the gate will open, allowing the project to move on to the next stage. This allows management to review the progress of the project at each gate and decide whether it merits continued funding.[11] A potential danger, of course, is that promising new products might be killed too soon by overeager, stage-gate keepers.

Finally, even though measurement should be comprehensive, not everything that possibly could be measured should be measured. Measurement has a cost, and the usefulness of the information obtained may not justify the costs. The issue here is one of criticality, that is, what is measured should be highly relevant to the goals of the organization. Activities that are necessary but do not provide relevant indicators of progress toward goals do not justify the expense to measure them. What is easy to measure may not be what is most important to control. Furthermore, from the perspective of many managers in operations, what gets measured in an organization is often what gets done.

Compare Performance against Standards

Comparing performance results against previously set standards is the third step in the control process. Just as performance measurement is strongly influenced by the standards, so are comparisons affected by the kinds of measurements available. If key measurements have not already been built into the system, it is usually not possible to go back and reconstruct them for purposes of comparison. Sometimes managers realize too late that appropriate comparisons cannot be made.

When several dimensions of performance have been measured, this step in the process can involve multiple comparisons. If those comparisons all point in the same direction, interpretation is relatively straightforward. However, the picture of performance that emerges from a set of comparisons may be inconsistent or contradictory. That is, some comparisons may show good adherence to standards and targets, and others may reveal problems. So managers need to know how to interpret the patterns of comparisons and to draw appropriate conclusions. A single negative comparison may outweigh a number of positive comparisons, or vice versa.

For example, after a major restructuring, Safeway found that its sales per grocery store had nearly tripled and its sales per employee had also risen by 70 percent. Overall profits were up, but customer satisfaction scores were down. What were managers to make of this? In Safeway's case, sales per store and per employee as well as overall profits were up because it had sold off or closed its least profitable stores (many of which were operating at a loss). All of this might paint a very positive picture. However, the fact that customer satisfaction was down was potentially a bad sign.

Grocery stores make money through volume. Therefore, if dissatisfied customers were to start spending less at Safeway and more at competitors, the positive results could deteriorate rapidly. Consequently, placing too much emphasis on per-store sales compared with customer satisfaction would be a control mistake.

In this third control step, managers need to compare expected performance with actual performance. These comparisons often involve both subjective estimates as well as objective ones. However, even if the comparison involves only objective, quantitative numbers, judgment is still needed. For example, suppose Safeway's customer satisfaction numbers were down from 5.5 to 5.2. Anyone can calculate that customer satisfaction had declined by 0.3 points. However, the key question is whether this drop is significant. The answer to this question requires managerial judgment.

Evaluate Results and Take Action

The fourth step, evaluating results and taking action, is arguably the most difficult managerial task in the entire control process. The results that emerge from the performance comparisons may or may not require action. Managers need to consider whether any single comparison or a pattern of comparisons requires action to be taken. If actual performance deviates from expected performance, how much of a difference is required before something is done about that difference? That question has no single answer. It requires evaluation of the importance and magnitude of the deviation.

An analogy illustrates what is involved in this type of judgment. In industrialized countries, the directors of the national banking system—in Canada, the board of directors and governor of the Bank of Canada—periodically receive the most current data about the national economy; for example, the unemployment rate, the consumer price index, the index of consumer confidence, the rate of new starts in home building, and the like. These data are compared against predetermined benchmarks to make a decision about whether to take action (for example, to increase interest rates). The problem for the board, as for any manager in an organization, is to determine which data are most important and how much of a change is significant. However, the issue is even more complicated than that. Managers must determine whether a slight change in the same direction for all of the indicators is more or less important than a major change in just one indicator. As any macroeconomist would testify regarding the national economy, this type of judgment is not easy.

The other basic judgment that must be made in this fourth step is what action to take if the pattern and size of deviations from expected performance are determined to be significant. Managers need knowledge about the causes of the deviation as well as about the potential actions that are possible.

Clearly, the evaluation and action step of control requires managers to have strong diagnostic skills as well as a certain level of expertise. Sometimes, the causes of a problem may be easily recognized, but the decisions about which actions to take to correct them may be extremely difficult. Conversely, the most effective actions may be well known, if only the causes could be clearly identified.

If a manager discovers major negative differences between performance and standards, some type of action is clearly needed because failure to act can lead to more severe problems in the future. However, if the deviations are major but positive, the necessity for action is usually much less (see Exhibit 14.7). Such positive differences, though, may in fact provide valuable insights about unexpected opportunities that should be pursued. For example, a major maker of baby food discovered stronger-than-expected sales of its new line of toddler foods in Florida, which has a higher-than-average

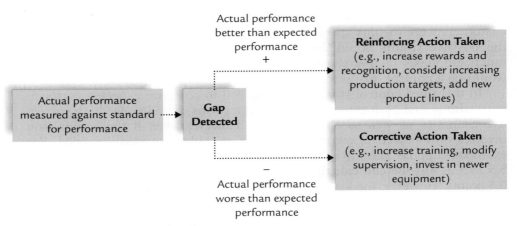

Exhibit 14.7 Outcomes of Performance Measurement.

percentage of elderly residents. Further investigation revealed that the increased sales were not because of a higher-than-expected number of toddlers; rather, they were due to older customers with teeth problems who bought the product because it was easier to chew. This led to a whole new line of packaged foods targeted at this particular consumer segment.

To help maintain positive performance, employees who are doing better than expected can be given increased recognition and rewards to reinforce their excellent performance. Likewise, sales that exceed their forecast may mean that production should be increased or the product line should be extended. Costs that are below target may suggest an efficient practice that could be duplicated for other employees to follow, to reduce the costs even further. In short, it is as important to evaluate surprises on the upside as it is on the downside.

One other issue is involved in determining what action managers should take in the case of significant deviations from standards (whether in the positive or negative direction). This is the judgment about whether the standards are correct and the performance is the problem, or whether the performance is appropriate but the standards are too difficult or too easy. That is why a broken-line feedback arrow is shown from "Evaluate Results" to "Establish Standards" in Exhibit 14.3, indicating that the standards may need to be adjusted. Over time, standards are sometimes modified as experience is gained and the feasibility of existing standards is better understood. If a great deal of effort and care has been used in setting the standards and participation in setting them was broad, then the issue is probably likely to be one of performance. If, however, the standards have been set hastily or without appropriate input from the relevant parties, then performance may not be the problem. This kind of issue points out once again the tight interconnection of the four basic steps of the control process.

Scope of Control in the Organization

Even though the four steps of the control process are similar wherever they occur in organizations, the scope of what is being controlled can vary widely. This, in turn, affects how the steps are actually put into use. A bank provides a simple illustration. The bank manager may need to assess whether she has an adequate level of deposits relative to outstanding loans. The scope is quite broad because the outcome of this assessment could affect the entire organization. If the ratio is too low, the bank may need to reduce its level of lending or try to get more deposits. On the other hand, the manager may also need to evaluate the ratio of human bank tellers to automatic teller machines at each branch. In this case, the scope is much narrower because the issue only involves a small part of the bank's total set of activities. In the former instance we would label the scope as "strategic," and in the latter instance it would be regarded as an "operational" control issue. These represent two of the three major categories of control scope. The third and intermediate level, between strategic and operational, is a category typically called "tactical." (Refer back to Chapter 8, "Planning," for a discussion of the three categories of "strategic," "tactical," and "operational.")

In the remainder of this section, we look at the issues involved in each of these three types of control classified by the breadth of their scope. However, it is useful to remember that no hard-and-fast boundaries separate the three types (see Exhibit 14.8). The differences between strategic and tactical control issues are often blurred, and likewise, it is not always clear whether a control issue should be considered tactical or operational. Nevertheless, the three categories help remind managers where they should focus their attention.

Strategic, Tactical, and Operational Control Systems by Michael Hitt

mymanagementlab

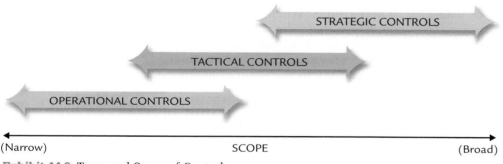

Exhibit 14.8 Types and Scope of Control.

Strategic Control

Strategy refers to the direction for the organization as a whole. It is linked to the mission of the organization and to the basic plans for achieving that mission. Thus, **strategic control** is focused on how the organization as a whole fits its external environment and meets its long-range objectives and goals. Strategic control systems, where they exist, are designed to determine how well those types of objectives and goals are being met.

A particular challenge in formulating strategic controls is the fact that strategic goals are broad and, especially, long term. This means that such goals typically are more abstract than goals for particular units. Consequently, setting strategic standards and measuring strategic performance can be especially challenging. For this reason, research has shown that only a relatively small number of firms in both Europe and North America have set what could be termed strategic control systems.[12] The numbers will undoubtedly increase in the future, but important obstacles interfere with establishing such systems.

A significant factor that affects whether strategic control systems can be set up and whether they will be effective is the unpredictability of the external environments in which many organizations operate and from which they obtain resources. This also makes it difficult to develop standards and measures that are relevant for more than short periods of time. In fact, it is particularly difficult for firms to develop useful criteria for assessing the long-term performance of individual managers.[13]

Environmental conditions for large companies affect how much leeway each division or unit is given in determining its own competitive strategies for

strategic control Assessment and regulation of how the organization as a whole fits its external environment and meets its long-range objectives and goals.

dealing with its particular markets.[14] The issue is essentially one of how much strategic control systems should be centralized versus decentralized, and how much variation should be allowed by unit. Such a decision involves not only matters of strategy but also of organizational structure. Sometimes, in fact, because of changes in the external environment, companies find they have to reverse course on their overall strategic approach to controls. Thus, McDonald's has restructured its US operations to reinstate controls it had abandoned in the mid-1990s. Why? Because it was experiencing a decreased earnings trend. To deal with this, it is controlling not only its ingredients but also the experience customers have in its restaurants. It has gone back to more inspections of every store and the use of mystery shoppers. It is also making more use of extensive customer surveys.[15]

Research indicates, however, that "the efficiencies of managing through centralized control may be greater . . . when the operating environments of divisions in multidivisional organizations are relatively stable and predictable" (see Exhibit 14.9).[16] When there is more uncertainty in the environment, centralized control becomes less efficient. In other words, in relatively turbulent environments, it is difficult for centralized strategic control systems to keep up with events, and consequently, more responsibility for control must be delegated to major units. When the environment is changing rapidly, as it is for many companies these days, too much reliance on organization-wide strategic goals and standards of performance that are set too far in advance can interfere with the needed speed and flexibility of the various operating units to respond effectively to the environment, especially in complex organizations with many types of units.[17]

As shown in Exhibit 14.10, both the degree to which it is possible to precisely measure how well performance conforms with strategic goals and the degree of turbulence or uncertainty in the environment can affect the value of having strategic control systems.[18] They are most likely to be useful when measurement is easy and operating environments are relatively calm, as in the case of the cement industry, for example. Although this industry basically follows the ups and downs of the construction industry, the factors that significantly affect these movements are relatively well-known. For instance, changes in interest rates have a significant impact on building booms and busts. As rates go down and money is cheaper to borrow, construction increases. As rates go up and money becomes more expensive to borrow, construction decreases. Thus, for a cement firm, strategic controls like being number one in sales in a region can be relatively useful. Conversely, strategic controls are probably least useful when exact measurement is difficult and the environment is fluctuating rapidly.

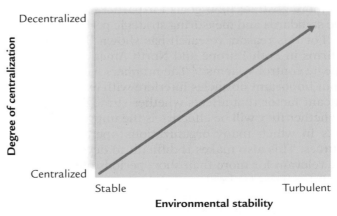

Exhibit 14.9 Degree of Centralization of Control in Relation to Environmental Stability.

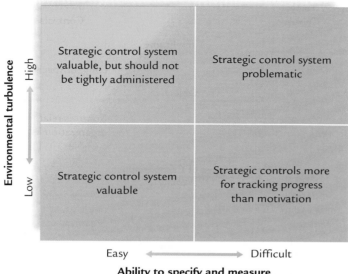

Exhibit 14.10 Approaches to Strategic Control.

Source: M. Goold and J. J. Quinn, "The Paradox of Strategic Controls," *Strategic Management Journal* 11, no. 1 (1990), pp. 43–57 (p. 55).

Tactical Control

Tactical control focuses on the implementation of strategy. Thus, this level covers the fundamental control arrangements of the organization, those with which its members have to live day to day. Tactical control forms the heart and, one might say, the soul of an organization's total set of controls. Four of the most important types of tactical control systems are financial controls, budgets, the supervisory structure, and human resource policies and procedures.

The first two types of control, financial and budgetary, contain elements of both strategic and tactical control systems. To the extent that they focus on the entire organization, they tend to be more toward the strategic end of the continuum (see Exhibit 14.11), and the more they focus on specific units within an overall organization, they tend to be toward the tactical end. We have chosen to discuss them in this section since they most often focus on organizational units, but keep in mind that they, especially financial controls, can also be used for some strategic control considerations.

Financial Controls. Financial controls include several important quantitative ratios involving key financial statistics. Although such financial data are always generated at the overall organizational level as well as at the organizational-unit level, they are especially useful at the unit level as a form of tactical control.

The data used for the most important financial controls involve a basic cost-benefit analysis. For example, ratios relevant to the **profitability** of a given unit are constructed from revenue data (benefit) in relation to given amounts of investment (cost). The ratio is called **ROI** (**return on investment**, or alternatively, **ROE**, **return on equity**) and compares the amount of net profit before taxes (the numerator of the ratio) to the total amount of assets invested (the denominator). Thus, a unit that has a profit of $500 000 for a given year from invested assets of $10 million would have an ROI of 0.05 for

Tactical control The assessment and regulation of the day-to-day functions of the organization and its major units in the implementation of its strategy.

profitability The ratio of cost to benefit.

ROI (return on investment) A measure of profitability obtained by dividing net income by the total amount of assets invested.

ROE (return on equity) An alternative term for ROI.

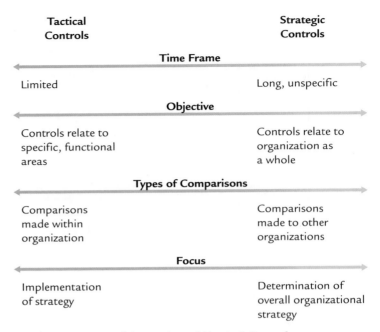

	Tactical Controls		Strategic Controls
Time Frame			
	Limited		Long, unspecific
Objective			
	Controls relate to specific, functional areas		Controls relate to organization as a whole
Types of Comparisons			
	Comparisons made within organization		Comparisons made to other organizations
Focus			
	Implementation of strategy		Determination of overall organizational strategy

Exhibit 14.11 Characteristics of Strategic and Tactical Controls.

that year. If another unit generated that same amount of profit on invested assets of only $5 million, its ROI would be 0.10 and would thus be considered to have had superior financial performance since it generated equal benefit for less cost.

liquidity A measure of how well a unit can meet its short-term cash requirements.

leverage The ratio of total debt to total assets.

efficiency (activity) The ratio of amount of sales to total cost of inventory.

Other financial ratios that are commonly used to assess unit performance include those related to **liquidity** (current assets in relation to current liabilities), which provides an indication of how well the unit can meet its short-term cash requirements; **leverage** (total debt to total assets), which provides an indication of ability to meet long-term financial obligations; and **efficiency** or **activity** (for example, the amount of sales in a given period relative to the cost of inventory used to generate those sales), measuring how efficiently assets are used.

Examples of these four types of ratios for two organizations in the retail industry for the year 2006 are shown in Exhibit 14.12. It can be seen from the exhibit that West 49 had a lower ROI than Le Château that year, somewhat less liquidity, a slightly less favourable leverage ratio, and a less efficient use of inventory. Thus, if these had been two units within the same organization, one would say that for this year Le Château as a unit was doing better overall insofar as financial performance was concerned.

The important point here is not the detailed steps that need to be taken to calculate the ratios. Rather, it is that when the ratios are calculated, they can be used to compare one organization, or one unit, to another. Thus, it is the comparative nature of the ratios that provides managers with information needed to take action during control. The numbers used to calculate a ratio, such as inventory turnover, for example, will show whether the ratio is relatively unfavourable, and if so, an examination of the two components used in the ratio will also indicate whether the problem seems to be in the amount of sales (too low) or in the amount of inventory (too high) or both. In other words, financial ratios can provide a very useful diagnostic tool for managers to determine where to take control action to improve situations.

break-even point (B-E P) The amount of a product that must be sold to cover a firm's fixed and variable costs.

Another financial measure, the **break-even point (B-E P)**, is sometimes used for control purposes in business organizations. Essentially, a B-E P analysis is a quantitative formula used to determine what volume of some product

Exhibit 14.12 Examples of Company Financial Ratios

Ratio	Formula	Company			
		Le Château, 2006 In $ millions		West 49, 2006 In $ millions	
PROFIT Return on Investment	$\dfrac{\text{Net Profit before Taxes}}{\text{Total Assets}}$	$\dfrac{38.4}{185.7}$	0.207	$\dfrac{6.9}{102.1}$	0.067
LIQUIDITY Current Ratio	$\dfrac{\text{Current Assets}}{\text{Current Liabilities}}$	$\dfrac{107.1}{61.6}$	1.74	$\dfrac{33.2}{26.9}$	1.23
LEVERAGE Debt to Assets	$\dfrac{\text{Total Debt}}{\text{Total Assets}}$	$\dfrac{77.5}{185.7}$	0.417	$\dfrac{43.3}{102.1}$	0.424
ACTIVITY Inventory Turnover	$\dfrac{\text{Sales}}{\text{Inventory}}$	$\dfrac{303.9}{41.0}$	7.41	$\dfrac{195.3}{24.0}$	8.14

or service must be sold before a firm's fixed and variable costs are covered by the next sale. That is, the break-even point is where the selling price of a unit of a product (or service) minus its variable costs exceeds the fixed costs for that unit. Clearly, the lower the fixed costs are, the fewer the units of goods or services that need to be sold for a break-even point to be reached. Likewise, the lower the variable costs, the higher the profit per unit and therefore the fewer the units that need to be sold to reach that point. Break-even analysis, then, provides a way for managers to gauge whether new products or services have a potential to turn a profit. Managers can therefore exercise control *before* new ventures are undertaken. Even more important for ongoing operations, a break-even analysis focuses managers' attention on reducing or controlling the two categories of costs—fixed and variable—to take the pressure off the need to sell larger volumes.

An example of where a break-even analysis can illustrate comparisons between two organizations or business units is provided by the airline industry. Many of the larger airlines have set up separate subsidiary airlines to handle short-haul commuter routes, for example, Jazz, which is a part of Air Canada. These commuter airlines can operate on relatively small volumes of passenger traffic because their costs—like lower wage bases for their pilots—produce lower break-even points. Similarly, certain independent airlines—if they are especially efficient—can charge very low fares on many of their routes and still make a profit. Canadian air carrier WestJet replicated the model applied by US discount air carrier Southwest Airlines, which uses a flexible point-to-point route system instead of the hub-and-spoke system of most other airlines and avoided the cost of meals by serving only snacks long before other airlines did.[19]

Although a B-E P analysis can provide extremely useful information for managers for control purposes, such an analysis also has limitations. Looking strictly at the numbers of a B-E P analysis may discourage certain decisions that could ultimately result in very profitable activities that do not initially appear to be profitable. Also, it is not always easy to allocate costs between fixed and variable categories, and it is sometimes difficult to project costs accurately, especially variable costs. Like other financial controls, a B-E P analysis can be an aid to exercising effective control, but it is not by itself a guarantee of wise decisions. What it does do, however, is highlight the potential advantages to be gained by controlling specific types of costs.

Budgetary control A type of tactical control based on responsibility for meeting financial targets and evaluating how well those targets have been met.

Budgetary Controls. Budgets are used in almost every organization (as we discussed in Chapter 8 on planning), and like financial controls can sometimes be considered elements of a strategic system. **Budgetary controls**, however, are more usefully viewed as a significant tactical control because they focus on how well strategies are being implemented. In contrast to purely strategic control, budgetary controls.

■ typically cover a relatively limited time frame (usually twelve-month or three-month periods)

■ focus exclusively on one type of objective (financial)

■ usually cannot be used to compare a total organization's progress relative to its competitors[20]

Anyone occupying a managerial position is controlled by budgets and uses budgets to control others. A budget is a commitment to a forecast to make an agreed-upon outcome happen.[21] Thus, it is more than a forecast, which is simply a prediction. A budget is designed to influence behaviour so that forecasts or plans for expenditures and (where relevant) revenues can be achieved. It "controls" by assigning responsibility for meeting financial targets and for evaluating how well those targets have been met. It would be difficult indeed to maintain an organization if none of its members were held accountable for limits on expenditures.

When using budgets as a form of control, managers face several important issues, as shown in Exhibit 14.13. One is the question of whether to use a fixed budget for a specific period, usually 12 months, and stick with those numbers, or to revise it midway during the period based on changes in operating conditions. Ace Hardware, for example, now uses a rolling planning and budgetary process. With the old annual type of process, the conditions on which Ace's budget were based were frequently out of date by the time the budget was finalized. In the middle of a recent year, however, the company's sale1s were within 5 percent of the expected amount and closely tracked the budget. "We haven't had sales so close to budget at this point in the year in

Exhibit 14.13 Issues in Budgetary Control	
Issue	**Questions**
Rolling budgets and revision	Should the budget period be for 12 months followed by another 12-month budget a year later, or should a calendar quarter be added each time a new calendar quarter begins? Should the budget remain fixed for the budget period or should it be revised periodically during the period?
Fixed or flexible budgets	Should performance be evaluated against the original budget or against a budget that incorporates the actual activity level of the business?
Bonuses based on budgets	Should incentive compensation, if any, be based on actual versus budgeted performance, or on actual performance against some other standard?
Evaluation criteria	Should the budget used to evaluate performance include only those items over which the evaluated manager has control, or should it include all unit costs and revenues appropriate to the managerial unit?
Tightness of the budget	What degree of "stretch" should there be in the budget?

Source: Adapted from N. C. Churchill, "Budget Choices: Planning vs. Control," *Harvard Business Review* 62, no. 4 (1984), pp. 150–64 (p. 151).

five years," said the company's manager of financial planning and analysis.[22] A rolling budgetary process with relatively frequent revisions has the advantage of being more current and therefore more accurate; however, it also can take more managerial time and effort.

Another budget issue is whether compensation bonuses should be based on the achievement of budgetary targets. This sounds good, but it has the great disadvantage of encouraging budget game-playing, because the person being evaluated has an incentive to provide high-cost and low-revenue estimates. This way, by creating "budgetary slack" with relatively easy targets, the person has a higher probability of hitting the targets and earning a bonus. Thus, managers who supervise the preparation of budgets need to be alert to how a bonus system of this type can distort estimates and undermine control. Managers also need to make sure that they don't inadvertently create a short-term focus on the part of subordinates attempting to meet budgetary targets at the expense of achievement of more important, longer-term organizational goals.[23]

A third budgetary control issue involves the question of whether those responsible for meeting specified targets should be evaluated only on expenditures and revenues over which they have direct control, or whether they should be evaluated on a final "net" figure based on all costs and revenues for a given unit. The former results in a more direct link between managerial behaviour and budgetary responsibility, but the latter is the ultimate "bottom line," especially for publicly held corporations. For example, as a manager of a sales unit, you might have strong control over the revenues that your unit generates and the money spent on travel expenses. When these travel expenses are subtracted from sales, your unit might look very good. However, if your unit also uses marketing and promotion materials to get these sales, they may need to be factored into the overall assessment. Otherwise, you may overspend on marketing and promotion activities.

The final and perhaps most important managerial control issue regarding budgets is how tight or loose to make them. Should a budget require those charged with meeting it to make an extra "stretch"? As we have said before, research indicates that the best performance results come from goals that are challenging but achievable. Since budgets represent goals, this conclusion seems highly relevant to the issue of budgetary control.

Supervisory Structure Controls. The basic **supervisory structure** of an organization is probably the most widespread tactical control system that a typical organizational member encounters. The amount and form of such control varies considerably from organization to organization, but almost always exists in some form. In organizations of any size, there is always someone or some group to which an employee or manager reports. Even the most collegial and least bureaucratic types of work organizations, such as research laboratories and not-for-profit enterprises, have some sort of reporting structure that regulates the activities of each member.

supervisory structure A type of tactical control based on reporting levels in an organization.

Human Resource Controls. **Human resource policies and procedures** are a fourth major type of tactical control that affects everyone working in an organization. They provide a number of different opportunities for control (see Exhibit 14.14):

Human resource policies and procedures A type of tactical control based on the organization's overall approach to using its human resources.

- Selection procedures can specify the range of abilities that will be brought into the organization.

- Training can improve skills and elevate performance to meet standards.

- Appraisal and evaluation methods can reinforce desired behaviour and discourage undesirable levels of performance.

- Compensation can be used to motivate employees and increase their efforts in particular directions.

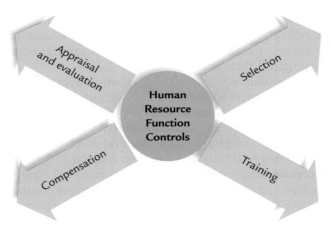

Exhibit 14.14 Opportunities for Control in the Human Resource Function.

An example of using human resource procedures to reinforce desired behaviour occurred when Standard Life of Scotland, one of the largest insurance companies in Europe, changed its performance evaluation and reward systems to a "contribution management system." The new system focused on the importance (not just the number) of an employee's accomplishments, the effort to develop the competencies to accomplish critical tasks, and the employee's contribution to customer satisfaction and the overall performance of the business. The change in approach required employees to be highly involved in goal setting, training plans, and reward determinations. As a result of these changes in HR procedures, the company has gone from being one of the lowest-ranked on performance and customer satisfaction to one of the highest within the United Kingdom. It was also voted "Company of the Year" five years running in its industry.[24]

Because the effects of human resource policies and procedures are so extensive, they are very powerful means of control. When used with skill and deftness, they are a significant aid to the achievement of organizational objectives, as in the above Standard Life example. When used ineptly and with heavy-handedness, however, they can hinder organizational progress.

Contrasting Approaches to Using Tactical Controls. The ways in which tactical control systems are implemented say a great deal about an organization (what it is like to work there and how effective the control is). These control systems characterize an organization and are a critical part of its identity. For these reasons, it is important to specify and discuss the two fundamental approaches to tactical control: (1) imposed, or bureaucratic, control and (2) elicited, or commitment or clan, control (see Exhibit 14.15).[25] Most organizations use a combination of these two approaches, but also tend to emphasize one over the other.

Bureaucratic control stresses adherence to rules and regulations and a formal, impersonal administration of control systems. Thus, for instance, Imperial Oil Limited has a thick operating manual for refinery managers. It specifies everything from which types of capital budget requests need which type of approval to equipment maintenance schedules. This approach highlights rational planning and orderliness. It heavily emphasizes detecting deviance from standards. But its foremost feature, in a control sense, is that control is *imposed* on the person, group, or activity. From an employee's perspective, "others" do the controlling.

Commitment, **or clan**, **control** stresses obtaining consensus on what goals should be pursued and then developing a shared sense of responsibility for achieving those goals. It is called a "clan" approach to control because of the emphasis on generating shared values, as in a set of close relatives, and on

Bureaucratic control An approach to tactical control that stresses adherence to rules and regulations and is imposed by others.

Commitment (clan) control An approach to tactical control that emphasizes consensus and shared responsibility for meeting goals.

Exhibit 14.15   Control in Bureaucracy and Clan Structures

Type of Control	Social Requirements[a]	Control Approach	Informational Requirements
Bureaucracy	■ Norm of reciprocity ■ Legitimate authority	■ Adherence to rules and regulations ■ Formal and impersonal ■ Emphasis on detecting deviance ■ Imposed on the individual	■ Rules
Clan	■ Norm of reciprocity ■ Legitimate authority ■ Shared values, beliefs	■ Stresses group consensus on goals and their measurement ■ Mutual assistance in meeting performance standards ■ Uses deviations as guidelines in diagnosing problems ■ Control comes from the individuals or groups	■ Traditions

[a]Social requirements are the basic agreements between people that, at a minimum, are necessary for a form of control to be employed.
Source: Adapted from William G. Ouchi, "A Conceptual Framework for the Design of Organizational Control Mechanisms," *Management Science* 25, no. 9 (1980), pp. 833–87 (p. 838).

mutual assistance in meeting performance standards. Clan control is consistent with strong cultures where values are widely shared and deeply held (see Chapter 10). A firm using a clan approach may, for example, emphasize care in the employee selection process to make sure that those coming into the organization have values similar to those that are prominent in its culture. The firm may have no real policy manual, and employees may be given general goals and basic budgets within which they need to work rather than specific constraints. A clan-based firm would rely on the employees' understanding of and commitment to the organizational objectives as the primary means of control. Unlike the bureaucratic approach, the clan approach tends to treat deviations from standards more as a basis for diagnosis than for corrective action. Its foremost feature, in a control sense, is that control is viewed as being *elicited from* rather than imposed on the person, group, or activity. From an employee's perspective, the employee or his or her group, rather than others, does the controlling.

You might wonder why every organization doesn't use a commitment approach. It sounds as if it would function better for both the organization and those who work in it. However, things are not that simple. Creating a genuine clan-like atmosphere among employees, especially in large organizations, is extremely difficult. It takes time and also considerable managerial effort. It may not succeed, or more likely, will succeed only partially. If a true clan-like, high-commitment culture is not created, an organization cannot rely on self-control by individuals or groups to exercise sufficient control. However distasteful it may sound, some amount of bureaucratic managerial control seems necessary for most complex organizations.

Even from the perspective of the organization's members or employees, self-imposed clan control may not be as satisfying as it would seem at first glance. A detailed study of a small manufacturing company illustrates the point.[26] This company converted its traditional hierarchical structure, which emphasized a high degree of supervisory control, to a structure that was built around self-managed work teams. In the first phase of the transition, the teams spent a good deal of time developing consensus on what constituted, both collectively and individually, good work and good patterns of behaviour. In the second phase, the teams developed strong norms regarding expected behaviour. Experienced team members expected new workers to buy into the teams' values and act according to their norms.

Under the old system, supervisors tolerated some slackness among the workers. But in the team system, the members exercised their newfound authority with much less patience. In converting to a clan approach to control, the teams' norms tended to become formalized—that is, they became self-imposed rules. As one team member said, "If we can just get our code of conduct in writing, then everyone will know what to do. We won't have so many problems . . . if we can just get it written down." The researcher studying this company stated, "The teams had now created, in effect, a nearly perfect form of control . . . an essentially total system of control almost impossible to resist. . . . The team members had become their own masters and their own slaves." Such clan control had developed into (in the researcher's term) an "iron cage."

The previous example serves to emphasize the point that no single approach to managerial control will work well in all situations. It also shows that whatever approach is chosen will have its own unique problems as well as advantages.

Operational Control

Operational control The assessment and regulation of the specific activities and methods an organization uses to produce goods and services.

pre-control A type of operational control that focuses on the quality, quantity, and characteristics of the inputs into the production process.

concurrent control A type of operational control that evaluates the conversion of inputs to outputs while it is happening.

post-control A type of operational control that checks quality after production of goods or services outputs.

Operational control, as the name implies, regulates the activities or methods an organization uses to produce the goods and services it supplies to customers and clients. It is control applied in the core and support processes toward the transformation of inputs into outputs, such as the actions that produce a car, administer therapy to an ill patient, cook and serve a restaurant meal, send a satellite into the sky, or write computer software. In short, operational control "is where the rubber meets the road."

The overall management of operations involves a number of critical and often technical issues. Here we focus specifically on an overview of the control process relating to operations. Operational control can be analyzed by relating it to the three basic elements involved in any type of service or goods production: inputs, transformation, and outputs (Exhibit 14.16).[27] These three elements can be related to the location of control in the production process: before transformation occurs, or **pre-control** (also known as feedforward); during transformation, or **concurrent control**; and after transformation takes place, or **post-control** (also known as feedback).

Pre-control of Operations. This form of operational control focuses on the quality, quantity, and characteristics of the inputs into the production process—for example, the purity of steel, the grade of beef, the number of passengers, the age of patients, the test scores of entering students, the aptitudes of job applicants.

The more stringent the control over the quality of inputs, the less need for control at the later two stages. The higher the quality of recruits to the Royal Canadian Mounted Police, for example, the easier it is to train them to be competent police officers. However, there is a cost involved in exacting pre-control standards. Higher-quality inputs typically cost more, and the effort to ensure that the quality is high also increases costs. Nevertheless, in many cases those costs will be well justified by what is saved in the later control steps and by the positive evaluation of the eventual goods and services. In other words, customers may be willing to pay more for better products and services.

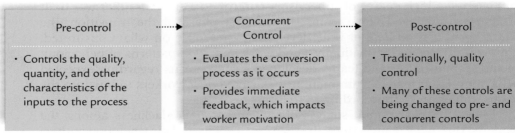

Exhibit 14.16 Operational Controls.

Because of the potentially disastrous effects a lethal virus could have if it began to spread in a city, the design, construction, and management of a high-containment laboratory require a great deal of pre-, concurrent, and post-control. The Canadian Science Centre for Human and Animal Health in Winnipeg is Canada's only Level-4 lab—one of approximately 15 in the world—and is capable of housing the world's deadliest pathogens, such as Ebola and Junin. The lab took 10 years and $172 million to design and build. Part of the pre-control process in the opening of the lab was allowing poured concrete, initially for the foundation and later for walls in high-containment areas, to cure for 12 full months, as well as covering such walls with an epoxy coating. In June 1999 the lab opened and in 2000 it received its first cargo of six of the world's most deadly viruses. Since opening, the lab has been pivotal in Canada's battle against diseases such as SARS, bird flu, and Mad Cow.

Concurrent Control of Operations. Concurrent control involves real-time assessment of the quality of the transformation process; that is, evaluating the conversion of inputs to outputs while it is happening. For example, eVineyard, a US internet wine retailer, created its business plan based on having a virtual, concurrent control of inventory. Because of the regulatory complexities of distributing liquor products for interstate sales, wine has to be passed through a local wholesaler and retailer before it gets shipped to the consumer. eVineyard set up local retail "shops" next door to local wholesalers and paid cash for daily shipments. "We don't buy wine until we have an order, so we don't have inventory cost," explained one of the company's marketing managers. In fact, eVineyard takes possession of bottles just long enough to package and ship them to buyers. This type of concurrent control enabled the company to hold down its costs and prices and survive the dot.com crash as well as to take over competitors wine.com and wineshopper.com. eVineyard has since adopted the name wine.com for its internet presence.[28]

Other typical examples of concurrent control are the monitoring of a customer service representative's performance while handling a telephone inquiry or the inspection of fruit while a batch is proceeding along a conveyer belt to the canning machinery. This type of control is designed to provide immediate feedback so that operations can be changed rapidly to decrease errors or increase quality. To have effective concurrent control procedures, however, managers must give considerable attention in advance to how such systems are designed and implemented. Also, managers need to be aware that this kind of control can have strong impacts on the motivation of those carrying out the operations, since the feedback is so immediate and often very direct.

Post-control of Operations. Post-control was the traditional form of control in manufacturing—checking quality *after* a product (TV sets, shoes, furniture, etc.) was produced. Thus, companies typically have had quality control inspectors or whole departments that checked the rate of defective products and then decided what to do if those rates were too high. For example, Toyota inspects each car coming off the assembly line against a basic list of criteria. It also randomly inspects cars based on a significantly longer and more detailed list of quality criteria. In recent years, quality control at many companies has been greatly diminished in favour of pre- and concurrent controls. The adage has been "*Build* quality into the product, rather than inspect quality into the product."[29] Also, the more contemporary approach to operational control has been to shift control responsibilities to operations personnel and away from separate evaluators at the end of the process.

Factors in Control Effectiveness

Regardless of good intentions, control systems in organizations may break down completely, as illustrated in the opening case of this chapter, or they may not work very well. There can be many reasons for this, but alert managers can take the initiative to reduce these possibilities. The effectiveness of control is very much under the control of managers. Again, there are no automatic prescriptions or heuristics for managing the control process well. Instead, managers can use certain potential sources of influence to increase the probabilities of success. In this section, we look at some of the key factors that determine the effectiveness of controls (see Exhibit 14.17).

Exhibit 14.17	Key Factors in Determining the Effectiveness of Controls
Key Factor	**Concerns**
Focus of control	■ What will be controlled? ■ Where should controls be located in the organizational structure? ■ Who is responsible for which controls?
Amount of control	■ Is there a balance between over- and undercontrol?
Quality of information collected by the controls	■ Is the information useful? ■ Is the information accurate? ■ Is the information timely? ■ Is the information objective?
Flexibility of controls	■ Are the controls able to respond to varying conditions?
Favourable cost–benefit ratio	■ Is the information being gathered worth the cost of gathering it?
Source of control	■ Is control imposed by others? ■ Is control decided by those who are affected?

Focus of Control

The decision of where to focus control in an organization involves critical choices based on what actions and outcomes should receive the greatest attention. The guiding principle for focusing control is that it should be closely linked to the strategic goals and, particularly, the planning process of the organization. For example, the Royal Bank of Canada placed a strategic focus on customer service. As a consequence, while the company would probably not be wise to ignore other controls, the focus would need to be on how to address the needs of customers and maintain a high level of customer satisfaction.

To be most effective, planning should be part of the control process, and control should be part of the planning process. Priorities should be set to select what is to be intensely monitored and controlled and what is to be given less attention. As software firms have found out, for example, little is to be gained from requiring star programmers to come to work on a precise schedule, given that the real objective is to produce innovative software. It is worth considerable control effort in that kind of organization, however, to make sure that the software that is written is as absolutely error-free as possible. Conversely, it is extremely important for restaurants to have their serving personnel be on time so that service is given promptly, whereas an occasional small mistake in taking a customer's order could be tolerated.

One approach to determining the focus of control that has become popular in the last decade or so is the "**balanced scorecard.**" Essentially, the advocates of this approach argue that historically—since the early years of the twentieth century—there has been an overfocus on financial measurements such as ratios and budgetary control procedures and a corresponding neglect of other important areas of measurement of a company's performance.[30] To remedy this, the developers of the balanced scorecard approach proposed an integrated and "balanced" set of measures for four critical areas ("perspectives," as they called them):[31]

balanced scorecard An integrated and "balanced" set of measures for four critical areas or perspectives: financial, customers, internal business, and innovation and learning.

- The (traditional) financial perspective: How do shareholders perceive the company?

- The customer perspective: How do customers perceive the company?

- The internal business perspective: How well is the company doing in excelling in internal business operations and procedures?

- The innovation and learning perspective: How well is the company doing at innovating, improving, and creating value?

Balanced Scorecard by Michael Hitt

mymanagementlab

It is also argued by the originators of this approach that the financial perspective primarily pays attention to the past, while the other three categories are much more future oriented. In effect, a presumed advantage of the balanced scorecard is that it requires managers to link measures of organizational success more closely to strategic objectives and to assess whether success in one area may be coming at the expense of poor performance in another area. It is intended, therefore, to bring greater focus and concentration on a total set of the most important areas of evaluation and control.

Many organizations are adopting some form of a balanced scorecard approach. Carleton University, Nova Scotia Power, and St. Michael's Hospital in Toronto, for example, use the balanced scorecard to help improve organizational performance. However, only 17.3 percent of Canadian organizations are using the management tool.[32]

As might be expected, however, some issues have been raised about the details of the balanced scorecard approach. One is whether these are the "correct" areas to measure and whether there are only four. A missing area, for example, is how employees perceive the organization and whether it is doing a good job of attracting and retaining talent. Another issue is whether each and every organization needs balance across all four areas or whether companies should concentrate on only one or two of the areas or some other sort of mix.[33] Still another issue—which is common to any system or overall approach to control measurement—concerns the degree of difficulty in designing and implementing the types of measures called for in this comprehensive approach.[34] Regardless of these issues, however, it is clear that the balanced scorecard has introduced a fresh and needed approach to focusing control on more than just financial numbers.

Focus of control refers not only to what should be controlled, but also to where control should be located in the organizational structure. This means paying careful attention to which people or positions in the structure have responsibility for different types and areas of control and how broad or

A Manager's Challenge   *Technology*

Control: Too Much or Too Little?

Controls that are too tight can keep an organization from functioning at its best; however, controls that appear too restrictive for one organization may be just right for another. Consider the fast-food giant McDonald's, which began as a "mom and pop" shop in San Bernardino, California, in 1954 and has since grown into a successful multinational corporation. McDonald's position as a leader in fast food can be attributed in part by the systemization of its operations. Every element of the supply chain is standardized and streamlined, from employee job descriptions to equipment and materials. The replication of predetermined policies and procedures across all restaurants facilitates training and results in consistent performance.

The strict controls that McDonald's imposes on all aspects of its operations are in place to achieve its goal of consistency in product and meeting or exceeding industry and government standards. Whether you are in Tokyo, Cairo, Stockholm, or Yellowknife, a Big Mac should look and taste the same. Quality and safety inspections are critical in maintaining these high standards, which is why McDonald's and its suppliers follow strict safety protocols and test products thousands of times before they are sold to consumers.

McDonald's imposes strict requirements from its suppliers to maintain consistency across stores. To provide burgers with consistent tastes and textures, all of McDonald's burger suppliers are required to test cook patties using the same grills as McDonald's before they are shipped. Once food products reach the various locations, McDonald's uses specialized equipment, such as rapid bun toasters, video display systems, and heated preparation tables, to ensure consistent food preparation. Employees are trained on how to prepare the different menu items and how to handle food safely, while supervisors and "mystery shoppers" monitor their compliance with these procedures.

In contrast to McDonald's, The Cabin Restaurant is a fast-food restaurant with far less stringent controls. The small, one-room restaurant in Fredericton, New Brunswick, has remained the only location since its establishment, also in 1954. A 1950s-style diner with burgundy booths, chrome-plated stools at a soda counter, and a miniature jukebox at every booth, The Cabin's atmosphere has remained relatively unchanged.

The Cabin offers its clientele simple, homemade recipes that are prepared without following specific cooking instructions or measuring the ingredients. Unlike McDonald's, meals at the Cabin are not mass produced by suppliers; they are traditional recipes that are made from base ingredients on site. Many of The Cabin's recipes simply could not be mass produced without losing the homemade taste that has kept some customers coming back for more than 40 years. Current owners David Halfyard and Linda Beardall point out that many customers enjoy old-fashioned recipes that remind them of the meals they ate growing up. Every Thursday, many regular patrons make sure they stop by the restaurant, knowing that this is the day that employee Jude Sampson makes her famous bread pudding from a secret family recipe.

Despite several changes in ownership and fewer controls than gigantic competitors like McDonald's, The Cabin Restaurant remains a successful business, with many regular customers who would prefer the cozy, one-of-a-kind atmosphere to a multinational franchise any day.

Sources: L. Stewart, "Aaah . . . The Comfort of Comfort Food; They're Our Favourite Foods—the Ones That Soothe Us When We Need It the Most," *The Daily Gleaner*, January 19, 2007, p. C1; P. Nelson, "A Step Back in Time: The Cabin in Fredericton Has Been Serving Homecooked Meals to Its Loyal Patrons for at Least 50 Years," *New Brunswick Telegraph-Journal*, April 12, 2003; S. Biggs, "'McDonald-ize' Your Shop," *Bodyshop* 32, no. 3 (2002), p. 30; McDonald's Canada, "FAQs," "Commitment to Quality," "Food Safety," "Our Beef Story," "Our Potato Story," "Food Freshness," 2006, www.mcdonalds.ca (accessed June 14, 2007); McDonald's Corporation, "Fact Sheet: Food Safety at McDonald's," "Fact Sheet: Food Quality at McDonald's," 2006, www.mcdonalds.com (accessed June 14, 2007).

narrow their scope of responsibility is. Control responsibility that is too diffuse can lead to omissions, and responsibility that is too concentrated can result in bottlenecks and decision delays. For example, if too many different people are assigned responsibility for quality control of a complex set of equipment, each may assume that one of the others has taken care of a particular problem, and as a consequence, some aspect of control gets left undone. On the other hand, if only one person is charged with inspecting all the pieces of equipment, that person may get overloaded, with the result that some critical detail gets inadvertently overlooked. Either way, effective control could be compromised.

Amount of Control

As we discussed at the beginning of this chapter, one of the greatest control challenges for any organization or manager is to determine the appropriate amount of control. To complicate the matter further, not all organizations need to employ the same level of control, as illustrated in *A Manager's Challenge: "Control: Too Much or Too Little?"*

Effective control involves finding a balance between overcontrol and undercontrol. Often, less-experienced managers tend to apply more control than is necessary in their eagerness to demonstrate that they are "in charge." This in turn can produce unintended resentment and resistance. Thus, new managers need to be aware of this tendency and moderate it.

If this were not a big enough challenge in itself, it is compounded in multinational corporations. In those organizations, perceptions of what is too much control can vary considerably from one country and culture to another. For example, tight monitoring of a manager's time and movements is more accepted in countries like Thailand; however, managers in Australia are likely to react quite strongly and negatively to tight monitoring.

When managers have more experience, they have a better basis for gauging the minimum levels of control that will get the job done without incurring unjustified risks. Even seasoned managers often find it difficult to correctly judge the degree of control required, and problems of undercontrol can crop up where least expected. No predetermined "right" amounts of control apply to all work situations. The best guideline for a manager to follow is to view the amount of control as something that, within limits, can be adjusted. Additionally, the undesirable consequences of excessive control and the dangers of too little control need to be made part of careful assessments of performance requirements and not inadvertently or casually overlooked. As we have already mentioned, involving those who will be directly influenced by the control measures in setting the amount of control increases the chances that an appropriate level of control is set from the outset. Furthermore, if adjustments need to be made, this initial involvement will likely reduce the resistance to these changes.

Quality of Information

Effective control requires knowledge based on data—that is, it requires good information. Four characteristics that determine the quality of information are usefulness, accuracy, timeliness, and objectivity.

Usefulness. Not all data collected for control purposes are equally useful in managerial operations and decisions. Sometimes data that were once useful continue to be collected, even though the original purposes for obtaining that information have disappeared. Such a situation was discovered several years ago in a division of BorgWarner Incorporated. BorgWarner is a US$4.6 billion company that develops engine and powertrain products for the automotive industry. It has plants and offices located around the world, including Simcoe, Ontario. Because of major changes in the operating environment at an automotive transmission unit, the company decided to find out which accounting reports, if any, were actually helpful to managers. Did the information contained in the reports actually assist managers to do their jobs better? The answer was a resounding "no." Investigation indicated that the accounting department thought it was gathering data that two separate groups could use: corporate managers and plant managers. Yet it turned out that the information being disseminated was of assistance only to the first group. As a result, the accounting department worked with operations managers in the plants to develop control reports that would help them do their particular jobs more effectively.[35]

Accuracy. Data or numbers that are inaccurate or misleading not only fail to provide a good basis for control steps, but also breed cynicism among those whose performance is being measured. Since control actions, especially those designed to change behaviour that does not meet agreed-upon standards, can have such powerful effects, it is vital that substantial effort be put into obtaining data that are absolutely valid; no information is better than inaccurate information.

Timeliness. Even accurate data, if they arrive too late, are not useful. This is true for any organizational actions, but especially so for purposes of control. In the fast-paced world of global business, data that are out of date are of virtually no use. For effective control, information must arrive on time to those who can take action and make any required changes. In everyday life, for example, information that reaches truck drivers 10 minutes after the wrong route has been taken is not very useful. Effective control systems require speed.

Objectivity. Objectivity, especially as it relates to control, can be a double-edged sword. Almost everyone would agree that objective facts are better than subjective, and possibly biased, opinions. However, for some kinds of performances, objective data may not be possible to obtain or may even be misleading. In diving competitions, for example, objective measurement of the exact height that a diver jumps off a springboard may be much less important than the subjective opinion of an experienced judge on the form of the dive. Similarly, in organizations, some of the most easily measured activities, and therefore the most easily controlled, may be relatively insignificant for the achievement of major, strategic goals. All other factors being equal, objective information would be preferred, but in many situations those other factors may not be equal and thoughtful judgments rather than unimportant "facts" may provide the best basis for action decisions.

For example, in a customer service call centre, it is relatively easy to gather objective data on the length of time a customer service agent spends on the phone with each caller. However, comparing the number of callers served by each agent may not tell you the most important thing—how well each customer was served. In fact, if the number of calls answered becomes the key performance measure, customer service agents may begin to provide poor service to get customers off the phone quickly and move on to the next customer, thereby maximizing the number of calls they take in a day. In this case, it is clear that the objective data (the number of calls taken) may not be the most important data (that is, how well the customer is served). Measuring customer service effectively may require having a supervisor randomly listen in on service calls or going to the cost and effort of trying to measure customer satisfaction by polling customers who have called in to the service centre.

Flexibility

For control to be effective, its procedures must respond to changing conditions. Organizations and managers become accustomed to control procedures that are already in place; it is a human tendency to stay the course when things appear to be going well. But that tendency can defeat effective control. Well-designed control systems should be able to account for changing circumstances and adjust accordingly. Rigidity of control systems is not usually a feature to be prized—flexibility is.[36]

Favourable Cost–Benefit Ratio

The designs of some control systems look good on paper, but they prove to be impractical or costly to use. To be effective, the benefits of controls must outweigh both the direct financial costs and the indirect costs of inconvenience and awkwardness in implementation. Elaborate, complicated control systems immediately raise the issue of whether they will be worth the expense involved. Sometimes, the simplest systems are nearly as effective. Consider again our customer service call centre example. While objective customer satisfaction data may be preferable to subjective supervisor evaluations, obtaining satisfaction ratings directly from customers may cost significantly more and not provide much better information than well-trained supervisors.

Of course, some situations may call for intricate controls because of the extremely high costs that would occur from unacceptable performance. Organizations that must carry out certain activities associated with high levels of hazard—such as hospitals, virology laboratories, nuclear power plants, and air traffic control agencies—need to invest heavily in control systems that ensure an exceedingly high degree of reliability. Consequently, they have to make costly investments—for example, in continual training, backup staffing, and very expensive equipment—to control operations and reduce the possibility of a catastrophic accident to absolute minimum levels.[37] In such cases, high control costs are obviously justified.

Sources

The source of control often affects the willingness of organization members to work cooperatively with the system. As we discussed earlier, in recent years many organizations have changed from bureaucratic control to control that relies more on members' monitoring their own or their team's performance. Thus, the source of control has shifted, and the change may increase positive reactions because employees have more trust in a process over which they have some influence.

Similarly, controls that provide information from equipment or instruments often seem less resented and more fair than controls involving what can be viewed as the sometimes arbitrary actions of supervisors. This principle was illustrated at Unum Insurance Company, a leading provider of income protection that started in the United Kingdom in 1970 and now has offices in North America. Several years ago it installed an elaborate information system (involving a more-than-US\$30 000 investment in hardware and software per employee) to help improve the performance of the company's information-systems professionals by measuring the amount of work to be done, identifying errors as they occur, and assisting in correcting those errors. The affected employees accepted the errors identified by the new system more readily than they had from supervisors because the system had no personal "axe to grind."[38] For any type of control, the source has a great deal to do with the acceptability of the system. Acceptability, in turn, affects how well control systems work in practice and not just in theory.

Managerial Perspectives Revisited

1

PERSPECTIVE 1: THE ORGANIZATIONAL CONTEXT Organizations could not function as organizations without control. It's as simple as that. It is not a question of whether to have control or not have control. Instead, the basic issues involve how much and what type. Early in the chapter we emphasized that control as an organizational and managerial process is closely connected to other major organizational processes, such as planning, organizing, and leading. Control is affected by these processes, but in turn control also affects them. Thus, control is integral to an organization's entire set of activities.

2

PERSPECTIVE 2: THE HUMAN FACTOR Within any organizational setting, for the process of control to work effectively it needs the cooperation of the people who are affected by it. Many aspects of control, as we pointed out, are impersonal in nature, as when instruments provide information on whether some product or process is within quality boundaries. However, it ultimately is up to people at some level, or several levels, to take action based on that information. If the people affected by managerial control activities are working to defeat and impede control, eventually the quality and quantity of organizational performance are affected. On the other hand, if they are supportive, performance can be enhanced. Often the reactions of the people affected by control are a good barometer of whether the organization is heading in the right direction in its other activities.

3

PERSPECTIVE 3: MANAGING PARADOXES There are two major potential paradoxes for managers to consider with respect to the topic of control. First, managers need to make sure that they and their associates view control as a "means" and not as an "end." Sometimes managers get so obsessed with the necessity and importance of control that they send the unintended message that it is in fact *the* objective, rather than simply being a way to assist in meeting organizational goals. Second, managers need to determine where the most appropriate balance is between overcontrol and undercontrol. Either condition, if not detected and modified, can lead to unfortunate consequences.

4

PERSPECTIVE 4: ENTREPRENEURIAL MINDSET If managers adopt an entrepreneurial mindset they are more likely to develop balanced controls—controls that meet both the firm's financial and strategic objectives. These managers understand the importance of adhering to financial budgets and constraints, but they aren't blinded to entrepreneurial opportunities that may exist and require money to develop. Moreover, the *types* of control used depend on a manager's entrepreneurial mindset. On the one hand, a strong managerial emphasis on financial control has been found to produce less innovation, while a managerial emphasis on strategic control tends to facilitate innovation within an organization.[39] Why? Financial controls tend to cause managers to focus on short-term gains rather than long-term opportunities.

In addition, the use of clan control versus bureaucratic control by a manager is likely to help him or her take a long-term perspective and be more innovative—especially when these values are inculcated within the organization's culture. When this occurs, members of the organization are highly committed and share a strong set of mutually agreed-upon values. Such a commitment may be easier to obtain in a smaller organization, but many larger organizations can nonetheless benefit from clan control because they have more committed members whose efforts they can mobilize than do their competitors of similar size and complexity.

Concluding Comments

Control is a crucial, albeit many times difficult and sometimes even unpleasant, managerial function. As we have emphasized repeatedly throughout this chapter, the challenge for managers is to make wise decisions about how much and where control needs to be used, and then how to apply that control. Control is essential, but many a manager and even many an organization have run into severe difficulties because the control process has not been well handled.

Knowing the basic elements of the control process is a helpful start in gaining perspective about how to exercise appropriate control. Understanding some of the pitfalls and obstacles that can interfere at each of these steps provides a basis for avoiding unnecessary "rookie" mistakes. Not many managers would have the aspiration to be a great "controller," but likewise, most would not like to be known as excessively naïve about the need for control. Keeping in mind the factors that influence control effectiveness—such as the focus, amount, and degree of flexibility—is a way to reduce the chances of unintended control blunders and improve the probabilities of success.

Clearly, control is a matter of both science and art. On the one hand, there are a variety of quantitative measures available to assess individual, group, and organizational performance. Particular areas, such as finance and operations, tend to use many quantitative control measures because they deal with things that are easy to count (money, products, defects, etc.). However, the fact that something can be easily measured doesn't mean it should be. Likewise, the fact that something is hard to measure doesn't mean it shouldn't be. The key to managerial success relative to control is making good judgments and *then* good measurements. Without good judgment concerning what, how, and when to measure something, the measurements are of little value. Control can add real value to an organization, but that outcome is not guaranteed unless managers with judgment make it happen.

Key Terms

balanced scorecard   (p. 487)
break-even point (B-E P)   (p. 478)
budgetary control   (p. 480)
bureaucratic control   (p. 482)
commitment (clan)
   control   (p. 482)
concurrent control   (p. 484)
control   (p. 467)

efficiency (activity)   (p. 478)
human resource policies and
   procedures   (p. 481)
leverage   (p. 478)
liquidity   (p. 478)
operational control   (p. 484)
post-control   (p. 484)
pre-control   (p. 484)

profitability   (p. 477)
ROE (return on equity)   (p. 477)
ROI (return on
   investment)   (p. 477)
standards   (p. 469)
strategic control   (p. 475)
supervisory structure   (p. 481)
tactical control   (p. 477)

Test Your Comprehension

1. What is meant by "control" in organizations?
2. How is the control function linked to other managerial functions?
3. What is meant when control is described as a causal variable, as well as being a dependent variable?
4. What are the four elements of the control process?
5. Who is responsible for setting standards?
6. What are standards and how are they used in organizations?
7. What are the key issues managers must consider when establishing standards?
8. When measuring performance, can nonquantifiable data be helpful? How?
9. What is the limiting factor in comparing performance against standards?
10. Which is the most difficult managerial task in the control process? Why?
11. What happens when a gap is detected between expected performance and actual performance?
12. What is the difference between "reinforcing action" and "corrective action"? When would you use each?
13. Compare strategic, tactical, and operational control. Why are the boundaries between each not always clear?
14. When are strategic controls more useful? Less useful?
15. What is the relationship of the external organizational environment to the development of strategic controls?
16. Contrast budgetary control with strategic control.
17. What is the main focus of tactical control?
18. List and discuss four types of tactical controls.
19. Describe four managerial control issues involving budgets.
20. What is the fundamental difference between bureaucratic control and commitment (clan) control?
21. Define operational control.
22. What is the relationship between pre-, concurrent, and post-controls of operations? Which type is best?
23. What are the seven factors of control effectiveness?
24. What are the advantages and the problems involved in using a balanced scorecard approach?
25. What factors determine the usefulness of information to the control process?

Apply Your Understanding

1. Do you think it is possible for an international firm to have a common control system even for a single activity, like manufacturing, when it has plants in countries such as India, Australia, Japan, Canada, and Germany? Explain your answer.
2. If you were the manager of your university's control system for exams, would you tighten or loosen the amount of control? What signals would you look for to determine whether your adjustments were appropriate?
3. In general, do you think that people respond to control systems or that control systems respond to people? In other words, will people generally conform to the tightness or looseness of a control system, or should the tightness or looseness of the control system depend on the nature of the people involved?
4. If you were a worker and management wanted to tighten controls over your job, what would they need to do to get you to go along with the tighter controls?

Practise Your Capabilities

Charlie had begun her career at one of Le Château's retail stores as a sales clerk during high school. She loved it there. Le Château stocked cutting-edge fashions with stock changing as rapidly as the customers' styles. It was a high-energy, fast-changing environment in which to work. An internship during college helped her gain her first entry-level management job in the chain after graduation. Promotions had been steady, and two months ago Charlie began her new job as assistant store manager. If she performed well in this position, the next step would be to manage her own store. She had decided that she would impress upper management by controlling costs and improving the efficiency of the store. Her predecessor in the assistant manager position—who had received a promotion—had been, in her opinion, far too easygoing. He had allowed the sales and stock personnel to perform their jobs more or less as they saw fit, within broad limits. When Charlie took over as the new assistant manager, however, she decided to "tighten things up."

Charlie's first action was to make a thorough review of the company rules and procedures for stock and sales personnel. For three weeks, she made daily inspections of the stock rooms to make sure all of the boxes were stacked properly and neatly, and that all boxes that were opened were immediately unpacked and the merchandise put away. She noted every example of incorrect storage. On the sales floor, she inspected every garment display, sometimes even rearranging them. She watched each move the sales clerks made, and once or twice noted the specific amount of time spent in conversation between employees and compared it to the time they spent with customers. She timed lunches and rest breaks and reviewed everyone's time cards. After three weeks of review and inspections, she called a meeting for Monday morning, before customers arrived, to announce the changes she would be making.

"I really want our store to shine! We need to impress top management with our efficiency and level of sales. Remember, there are bonuses available for increases in sales above the company average, for cost containment in the stock rooms, and even for low absenteeism and tardiness. So, from now on, this store is going to run like clockwork. There will be no more skirting the rules. We will be working according to the letter of the law. I am issuing a copy of the company policy manual to each of you along with the rules you will be following in implementing these policies. I have several ideas on how we can improve the operation of this store and help us all qualify for those bonuses." Charlie then went on to tell the store personnel about all of the new forms she was having printed that would detail each task with signature lines where each employee would sign off whenever he or she finished a specific task. Arrival, departure, and break times would be much more closely monitored than before. Additionally, sales personnel would constantly be walking the sales floor looking for customers to increase sales. There should be very little time for idle conversation. There were so many new rules to explain that the meeting took over two hours. Charlie ended the meeting by saying: "Let's have the best, most efficient, store in the chain! I know you can do it."

1. How do you think the store personnel are going to respond to Charlie's new rules and regulations, in light of the fact that they should have increased opportunities to earn bonuses? Why?

2. Using the concepts in this chapter, analyze the types of control that Charlie is using.

To improve your grade, visit the MyManagementLab website at **www.pearsoned.ca/mymanagementlab**. This online homework and tutorial system allows you to test your understanding and generates a personalized study plan just for you. It provides you with study and practice tools directly related to this chapter's content. MyManagementLab puts you in control of your own learning!

Part
Fourteen

Managing
Human
Resources

Chapter 15

Human Resources

After reading this chapter, you should be able to:

1 Explain how the management of human resources is a role both for the human resource management department and for all managers.

2 Describe the key means by which companies find job candidates.

3 Explain how companies select job candidates.

4 Highlight the keys to effective socialization and training.

5 Describe the common methods of managing performance.

6 Discuss the various compensation and reward systems commonly used.

7 Explain how various laws affect core HR activities.

Taken from *Management*, Canadian Edition, by Michael A. Hitt, J. Stewart Black, Lyman W. Porter, and Andrew J. Gaudes.

HRM at HOK Toronto

The boom/bust cycle is common to the building industry and architecture profession, since construction activity and demand for design professionals has traditionally fluctuated with the economy. HOK in Toronto is an architectural firm that is applying a multifaceted strategy to address the challenge of acquiring and keeping good people.

The Canadian building industry has enjoyed a significant period of growth over the last decade or so. For the past 11 years, the value of building permits issued in Canada has steadily increased, reaching a value of more than $66 billion in 2006. Architectural design firms have also benefited from this dramatic growth. However, growth has come with the burden of searching for the right design personnel that can both emulate the character of the firm and cover the demand for work that is arriving at the design firm's door.

A growing market was not always the case for the building industry in Canada. During the declining economy of the late 1980s and early 1990s the building industry experienced a flat period, with few large projects and not enough work to go around. Architecture firms were forced to cut back on the number of employees, letting go architects, technologists, and office support that, at the time, were only contributing to the overhead of the firm and putting the company further into the red with every passing month. It was a period of low morale; job stability was foremost in an employee's mind, stifling creativity and affecting innovation and production.

This cycle is common to the building industry and architecture profession, since construction activity and demand for design professionals has traditionally fluctuated with the economy—periods of dramatic growth offset by periods of stagnation and decline. What is particularly difficult for the architectural design sector of the building industry is that when design professionals are let go, all too often they leave the industry altogether, which results in a declining number of professionals available to reinsert into positions when the economy is in an upswing.

While the current extended growth in the building sector has been long enough to have people enter architecture schools and graduate into entry positions in firms, the recent bust-to-boom cycle has created a new challenge for human resources specific to the current generation: Managers must contend with a gap that exists between older senior designers and younger entry-level designers, which is a joint result of economic cycles and the baby-boom generation. Many designers who would have comprised the middle set of professionals in architecture firms today were laid off in the 1990s, as they were the junior designers at that time. The length of the downturn led to many designers deciding to leave the profession.

The personnel that remained in design firms eventually moved into senior roles in their organizations, and as the economy strengthened a new younger cohort entered the field. The net effect of the lost middle cohort is that design firms are largely composed of two groups: a cohort of experienced senior designers that are poised to retire, and a junior cohort that is, by and large, too inexperienced to assume the role of senior designers. Given the current conditions, the next 10 years could prove to be the most challenging as key people leave the industry and create a void of experience and networks.

Some design firms are initiating human resource management strategies with the hope of increasing recruiting and strengthening retention, as well as preparing for future economic cycles. HOK is a multidisciplinary architecture and design firm with 26 global offices that is applying a multifaceted strategy to address the challenges of acquiring and keeping good people. HOK's Toronto office has 290 employees. The objective of management is to ensure that HOK Toronto can maintain a medley of creative employees across all ages and levels of experience who can pour their innovation into new projects for the firm.

Given the nature of the industry, personnel have a particular sensitivity to their surroundings. HOK in Toronto has designed an innovative workplace environment with great consideration for comfort. The office has been designed to be bright and airy, including abundant natural light and fresh air with ergonomically designed workspaces and windows that employees can open.

HOK also accommodates employees' personal lives with customizable work hours that may involve alternative arrangements such as a four-day workweek, unpaid leave that protects the employee's position, or even sabbatical arrangements where an employee can work four years with a fifth year off. Guaranteed access to daycare in downtown Toronto has proven to be a high-value benefit, given the scarcity of spaces available to professionals with young children in the Toronto area. A similar benefit is provided for employees that have infirm parents, where elder care is available on a back-up basis when care requirements and work demands conflict.

Another facet to HOK's strategy is providing internal development to move staff up through the ranks via mentorship and coaching, as well as offering lateral moves to different projects, which is particularly appealing for design professionals searching for variety. Forty hours of paid time for study and exam writing toward professional designations in architecture and interior design is also offered to employees.

Although the above programs are already in place, the management at HOK continues to look for new ways to further enhance the appeal of their firm to new and existing employees at all levels. ◆

Sources: "Dealing with the Labour Shortage," *Canadian HR Reporter* 20, no. 15 (September 10, 2007), p. 11; HOK Toronto website, www.hok.com (accessed October 7, 2007); "Country Profile, Canada: Construction," *Economist Intelligence Unit*, 2007, p. 50.

Strategic
overview

Historically, many organizations have promoted the idea that people are their most important asset. Unfortunately, their actions didn't support their claims. For example, when the economy enters a recession and organizations encounter reduced demand for their goods and services, they cut costs by laying off employees. Recently, organizations have begun to reassess the importance of their employees. One of the reasons for this change is the realization that employees generally possess the knowledge that enables the firm to compete effectively in the marketplace. In fact, much of the knowledge in a firm is held by its employees, making employees critical assets. The firm's employees are also its most unique resource and cannot be easily imitated by competitors. Firms that have greater knowledge about technology, customers, manufacturing processes, and the products and services consumers want can win competitive battles. But it is predicated on the ability of the organization to learn, innovate, and change its processes.[1] To do these things effectively requires human talent.[2]

As a result, human resource management has evolved in recent years, particularly the strategic aspects of it.[3] In this chapter, we underscore the importance of this link. As the opening case on HOK Toronto suggests, organizations must have adequate amounts of human capital to implement a strategy of any value. However, the company must also have quality human capital, especially among its managers. As such, the company's human resource efforts should be aimed at identifying and selecting employees who have the knowledge, skills, and capabilities the organization needs to compete, and fostering and retaining those employees with good compensation and reward systems.

In general, human resource management (HRM) encompasses the activities of acquiring, maintaining, and developing the organization's people—its human resources. The traditional view of these activities focuses on planning for staffing needs, recruiting and selecting employees, orienting and training staff, appraising their performance, providing compensation and benefits, and managing their career movement and development. From this perspective, HRM involves both the activities of the human resource department and its specialized staff as well as all managers. While the HR department likely sets policies and practices for hiring people, for example, managers are quite often involved in selecting employees because once hired, the new employees are going to go to work for them. Similarly, while the HR department may set up the exact performance appraisal forms and processes, managers are the ones who actually assess employee performance. Thus, while it is important for you to understand the role of a company's human resource department, it is even more important for you as a future manager to understand your role in managing human resources. How can you manage your human resources effectively? In general, you need the following capabilities:

- The ability to recruit and select the right people.

- The ability to effectively socialize and train people in your unit.

- The ability to effectively evaluate their performance.

- The ability to determine reward systems that will motivate high performance.

- To know what additional experience or education your subordinates need to develop to advance in their careers.

One of the most enlightening studies on the importance of effective human resource management and career success looked at cases of career derailment. The study found that the number-one reason for managerial career derailment (in other words, the number-one reason why managers who got on were subsequently bumped off the upwardly mobile career track) was their inability to successfully carry out the activities associated with effective human resource management.[4] Consequently, managers who gain a competitive advantage at human resource management activities place themselves squarely in a superior position for upward movement and greater opportunities and responsibilities. While the bulk of this chapter focuses on the key elements of effective human resource management, the actual practices in HR are heavily influenced by laws and regulations. Managers need to be familiar with these laws and regulations and how they affect different HR activities. Consequently, a summary of them appears at the end of the chapter.

The employment challenges at HOK Toronto illustrate two key issues: (1) a firm's ability to survive and prosper in the future is increasingly a function of the human resources they have, and (2) as a manager, your own career success or failure may depend on how well you manage human resources during both good economic times and bad. We can all think of firms whose success seems tied to products, technology, or strategy, but not people. Where would Apple be without the Macintosh, iMac, or iPod? Would Research In Motion (RIM) be an important competitor in mobile communications without the BlackBerry? Clearly, these and other "golden eggs" seem to lie at the heart of certain firms' fortunes. But the real key to any golden egg is the goose that laid it. Such valuable resources do not just materialize. Without bright, capable, and motivated people, Apple would not have developed the Macintosh or iMac. Without people who recognized the growing need for data transmission and email communication, RIM would not have seized the advantage in this arena. In short, people invent and use technology; people gather, analyze, and disseminate information; people formulate and implement strategy. Thus, HOK Toronto's dependence on people for its future success is not unique or even uncommon. Both the quality of a firm's strategy and the success of its implementation depend on getting the right people and maximizing their performance and potential.

The Strategic Role of Human Resource Management

As we discussed in the chapter on strategic management, competitive advantage comes through creating and leveraging products that provide value to customers but are hard for competitors to imitate. Since people are behind every product or idea that a company generates, having a human resource strategy in place is essential. For example, WestJet has moved its way up to the second-largest air carrier in Canada, becoming one of the most admired corporate cultures in the country. In an industry that is more known for losses and bankruptcies than success stories, what has WestJet accomplished that so many before failed to do? Senior management at WestJet believe that it is the people that work for them and the company's commitment to putting people first. This type of human resource strategy creates happy employees, who in turn treat customers better, which ultimately leads to a better bottom line.

HR and Strategy Formulation

While the traditional view of HR as a function has not involved strategy formulation, it is a perspective that is changing.[5] Increasingly, executives are looking at their people and their present and future capabilities to determine what the company's competitive strategy ought to be.[6] As one executive put it, "In football, if you have a quarterback with a great arm, does it make sense to design an offense built upon the run?" Recall from our discussion of competitive advantage in the strategic management chapter that competitive advantage comes largely from creating value for customers through resources that are hard for competitors to copy. The capabilities employees possess are often hard for competitors to copy. To the extent that these capabilities also create value for customers, they become a source of competitive advantage and can therefore play a role in what the company's competitive strategy ought to be.

HR and Strategy Implementation

Exhibit 15.1 General Framework of HRM.

Clearly, not every strategy is or should be driven by a firm's human resources. However, it is hard to think of a strategy that can be effectively implemented without the proper management of its human resources. Consequently, both executives in charge of the HR function and managers throughout an organization need to manage their human resources in a way that supports and helps implement the strategy.[7]

Exhibit 15.1 incorporates these various perspectives into a strategic framework of human resource management (HRM). As the figure illustrates, specific human resource activities (planning, job analysis, recruiting, selecting, socializing and training, job design, performance appraisal, compensation, and development) exist within the context of the firm's strategy and environment. The fit of these human resource activities with the strategy and environment leads to competitive advantage for the organization and for the individual manager.[8]

Human Resource Management Activities That Get the Right People

To this point, we have explored the link between competitive advantage and human resource management and have also briefly examined the importance of the fit between HRM practices and the firm's strategy. We now outline the key HRM activities listed in Exhibit 15.1.

Simplified, there are two main HRM goals: (1) getting the right people and (2) maximizing their performance and potential. Although there are a number of activities related to these two general categories, all managers need to get the right people into the right place at the right time and then help them maximize their performance and future potential. For example, a brilliantly creative person might be right for a firm that competes through product innovation, like Research In Motion, but might be wrong for an organization that competes via cost leadership and low fares, like WestJet.

Getting the right people cannot be accomplished without understanding and aligning HRM activities with the corporate strategy. Although it is necessary to discuss each of these activities separately, you should not forget that they are related and that success or failure in one activity can significantly influence the success or failure of another.

Planning

Human resource planning is concerned with assessing the future human resource needs (demand), determining the availability of the type of people needed (supply), and creating plans for how to meet the need (fulfillment). At the organizational level, HR planning is sometimes a shared responsibility among HR specialists and executives in other functional areas like accounting, finance, marketing, and operations.

Forecasting Demand. The key objective is to determine how many and what type of employees the firm needs at a point in the future, say, one or five years hence, considering the firm's strategy and the general business and economic environment. For example, many Japanese electronics firms estimated in the mid-1990s that the product segments of music and games would increase at double-digit rates for 20 years. Much of the assembly work of putting together the various components of the music- and game-playing machines would require relative low-skilled and low-cost labour.

Assessing Supply. At the time, much of what these firms produced for export to other countries was assembled in Japan. As they looked at the future labour supply in Japan, however, two key facts emerged. First, based on demographic trends, it was clear that the population of Japan in the age range of 19 to 35 (the most common age of assembly workers) was going to shrink. Second, based on economic growth expectations, many of these companies forecast that labour costs were going to increase significantly. Thus, many of the managers in electronics firms in Japan determined that the demand for low-cost and low-skilled labour for product assembly would outstrip the supply of these types of workers in Japan.

Formulating Fulfillment Plans. The firms determined that demand would outstrip supply by approximately 2 to 3 million people by the turn of the century. To address this shortfall, many of these senior executives and government officials examined the possibility of allowing immigrants into Japan to fill the labour shortage and lower the labour costs. However, this approach generally lacked political and popular support. As a consequence, many executives of these electronics firms decided to automate some aspects of component manufacturing and also examined the automation of final assembly. However, while some components could be manufactured cost-effectively through automation, automating final assembly looked to be too costly. As a consequence, most of the executives in these firms decided to aggressively move final assembly operations offshore to countries with a good supply of semi-skilled and low-cost labour, such as China, Vietnam, and Indonesia.

Even though the human resource management department might be specially charged with looking at HR planning, individual managers must also be skilled planners as well. As a manager you will want to be able to determine the number and types of employees you will need in your units, assess the supply in the marketplace, and develop a plan to get the right people. Just as with the organization, as a manager you cannot distinguish between a "right" and "wrong" employee without thoughtful consideration of your firm's strategy. For example, after his first departure from Apple, Steve Jobs started a company called NeXT to compete in the high-end computer and work station market. Within just a few years, Jobs decided to shift the firm's strategic orientation from hardware to software. For managers in product development, this meant that they needed more programmers than engineers and that they initially needed fewer employees overall. Because the market for software programmers was tight, NeXT managers focused their efforts on attracting dissatisfied programmers at other companies and highlighted the exciting things that they were doing at NeXT.

To fulfill your employment needs, you may need to consider the use of *part-time* or *temporary* employees. This can give you the flexibility to meet significant but temporary increased demand for employees. It allows you to reduce your workforce more easily if demand falls, as well as to try out employees before hiring them permanently if demand remains strong.

You may decide to *outsource* specific workforce demands.[9] For example, many companies now outsource their call centre jobs involving customer service or telemarketing to other companies like Blue Ocean Contact Centers. In a sense, this offloads the fluctuations in demand for call centre representatives to another company that specializes in these tasks and has concentrated capabilities in hiring and training people for these jobs.

Job Analysis

job analysis Determination of the scope and depth of jobs and the requisite skills, abilities, and knowledge that people need to perform their jobs successfully.

Job analysis is a critical but often overlooked human resource activity. **Job analysis** is concerned primarily with determining the scope and depth of jobs and the requisite skills, abilities, and knowledge that people need to perform their jobs successfully.

The data and insights that come from a job analysis are typically used to create a *job description*, or a list of duties and capabilities required for the job. Typically, this leads to a *job specification*, or a statement that describes the skills, experience, and education that a candidate should have to perform the job.

Recruiting

Recruiting is primarily concerned with determining what the desired candidate pool consists of and attracting those candidates to specific positions within the organization. As with the other activities we have already discussed, the desired pool of candidates cannot be determined without considering the firm's strategy. Whom you want is a function of whom you need—whether you can get the type of person you want is a different story. Can you offer them what they want? Can your competitor offer them more?

Let's consider the first question. The key to knowing whether you can offer people what they want is to actually find out what they do want. Consider the case of UPS in Germany. When UPS expanded into Germany, managers had a difficult time selecting good drivers because they simply were not attracting high-quality applicants. Several factors contributed to this, most notably the fact that the brown UPS uniforms were the same colour as those of the Nazi youth group during World War II. UPS was not offering what high-quality prospective drivers wanted and was, in fact, offering something (brown uniforms) they did not want.

The second question is not simply a matter of whether you can offer candidates more money than your competitors. People are not motivated only by money. Rather, it is important to consider the work environment, the nature of the work, the flexibility of the benefits, and the opportunity for advancement as factors that could attract candidates to your organization.

Once you have assessed these two questions, a variety of approaches can be used to generate job candidates. Each one has its strengths and weaknesses and, as a consequence, should be used as the situation dictates. Some companies try to persuade firms and their managers to go "high-tech" to select their candidates. These companies use tools like skills tests, psychological tests, and even artificial intelligence to make candidate selection faster, cheaper, and better. After reading *A Manager's Challenge: "Guru's Gamble on a High-Tech Selection System,"* what do you think? Would you be inclined to use such a service?

job posting An internal recruiting method whereby a job, its pay, level, description, and qualifications are posted or announced to all current employees.

Job Posting. **Job posting** is a popular internal recruiting method whereby a job, its pay, level, description, and qualifications are posted or announced to all current employees. Increasingly, posting is done electronically through email. Job postings help ensure that all qualified employees have an opportunity to apply for a particular job. Job posting can also help current employees have a better idea of the types of jobs available and the qualifications needed to be successful in

A Manager's Challenge *Technology*

Guru's Gamble on a High-Tech Selection System

How can managers seeking to fill an open position determine which candidate represents the best match with their company's needs and work style? Former Guru.com founder and one of the most influential people in the recruiting industry, Ray Marcy, thought he had a high-tech answer to this perennial challenge. Marcy realized that managers who post job openings often receive hundreds of responses. Then they have to spend hours (perhaps even days) wading through each applicant's credentials to narrow the field and select the most qualified candidates.

Marcy proposed a radically different approach to the selection process. He believed that Guru could use artificial intelligence (AI) software to sift through candidates for open positions and identify a handful of highly qualified finalists from which client companies could select. As a result, managers seeking to hire a new employee would invest far less time in the selection process, but wind up with a far better match between the candidate, the job, and the company.

To implement this approach at Guru, Marcy hired an industrial psychologist to develop psychological tests that would show what companies were actually seeking in job candidates. In addition, he hired an AI expert to create the technology that would electronically evaluate candidates for posted jobs. Despite this high-tech emphasis, Marcy also recognized the importance of maintaining human contact during the selection process.

If you were a manager posting an open job on the website, a Guru "talent agent" would immediately call to learn more about the position's requirements and the company's work style. The agent would ask you if you are seeking to hire someone who is independent, accommodating, risk-taking, creative, or has other work-style traits. Next, the talent agent uses the AI system to identify qualified candidates from among those in Guru's database and other job-search databases. Using Guru's online system, these candidates complete a work-style assessment test so the talent agent can compare their styles with the styles desired by the hiring manager. Finally, the talent agent sends the hiring manager information on the three candidates whose background and work styles most closely match what you are seeking. The entire process,

As a manager, would you be inclined to use skills tests, psychological tests, and even artificial intelligence to ferret out the best job applicant? If so, how much would you be willing to pay to screen each candidate? What is the value of this approach for selecting the best employees?

from the time you submit an open position to the time you receive a listing of matching candidates, takes 48 hours or less.

Guru's fee for screening and recommending candidates was US$7500, about one-third of the cost of using a traditional search firm to fill an open position. However, some techno-savvy companies have built their own internal systems to help their managers select candidates for open positions, and other online job sites have similar tools.

Moreover, before Guru could fully capitalize on the artificial intelligence screening system, the marketplace changed dramatically. Tech firms laid off thousands of workers following a crash in the economy's tech sector, and employers found themselves less willing to pay high fees to hire them. As the firm took shape, assessment did not become the core activity of Guru.com's business—hiring freelancers did. Today, Guru.com is the world's largest online market for freelance talent with more than 600 000 active professionals in over 160 categories listed. Over time, many placement firms applied similar elaborate automated screening methods to minimize time in reviewing candidates.

Source: Guru.com Facts, www.guru.com (accessed October 4, 2007); S. Fister Gale, "Putting Job Candidates to the Test," Workforce Management, 2003 Vender Directory 82, no. 11, p. 90; S. Clifford, "Guru's Gamble," Business 2.0, July 2002, pp. 92–93.

those jobs. This can allow them to plan their careers. On the negative side, job postings can generate unqualified applicants who need to receive explanations about why they were unqualified and did not get the job. Without adequate explanation, they are likely to wonder whether the job was really "open" when it was posted. If employees begin to doubt the process of posting jobs, it can generate skepticism and limit candidates and therefore also the posting's effectiveness.

Advertisements. Advertisements in general or specialized publications can also be an effective means of generating job candidates. National business newspapers such as the *Globe and Mail* and the *National Post* cast a wide net. Professional magazines such as *Canadian HR Reporter* cast a very specialized net. Regional or local publications, such as your city newspaper, focus on the local labour pool. Increasingly, the internet is being used as a source of advertising job openings. As use of the internet matures, it is likely to develop regional and industrial segments that will facilitate a more targeted advertising of jobs.[10] The major downside of advertisements is the time and expense of screening out and rejecting unqualified candidates.

Employment Agencies. Employment agencies can also be effective in generating job candidates in some fields. The agency's effectiveness is largely a function of how well it understands your organization and the requirements of the specific job. Agencies tend to be expensive and usually not cost effective for low-level and low-paying jobs. In contrast, most openings at the senior management level use executive search firms as part of their recruiting efforts. As their fee for finding an acceptable candidate, these firms typically charge at least one-third of the successful candidate's first-year compensation.

Employee Referrals. Managers may find current employees a great source for job candidates. Current employees with tenure in the organization understand the organization, its culture, and often the particular job that needs to be filled. They usually know something about an applicant as well: work history, educational background, skills and abilities, personal characteristics, and so on. Given that their recommendation puts their own reputation on the line to some degree, current employees tend to recommend individuals whom they believe will do well. Their personal relationship with the recommended candidate allows employees not to just sell the company on the individual but to sell the individual on the company. In general, research suggests that current employee referrals are one of the most effective recruiting methods. Employee referrals are less effective when the firm is looking for a different type of employee than it currently has. Current employees tend to recommend people like themselves. So a company pushing into international activities or new technology may find that its employees don't know people in these new areas to refer.

School Placement Centres. School placement centres are also a popular source of job candidates. Placement centre offices can range from those found in high schools, technical schools, and colleges to universities and advanced degree programs. If given adequate time and clear job specifications and requirements, school placement centres can do much of the pre-screening, filtering out unqualified candidates. This can save the firm significant time and money in the recruiting process. Schools are increasingly using video conferencing capabilities to set up "virtual" interviews and online job fairs. Technology helps firms broaden the field, allowing them to reach places to which they may not be able to travel physically. The weakness of school placement centres is that they often deal with so many companies and students that they might not know enough about either to conduct ideal screening.

The Internet. Companies are discovering that the internet is a powerful recruiting tool. Most major companies use their corporate websites to list jobs and attract candidates. In addition to using their own sites, companies are increasingly using sites like Monster.ca. Monster.ca now has over 2 million resumés and 25 000 posted positions in its database and is part of the even larger Monster Worldwide network. Workopolis.com and Canjobs.com are two other sites where companies frequently post ads for Canadian positions.

Selecting

Successful selection is a function of effective planning, analyzing, and recruiting, as well as applying appropriate selection techniques.[11] Even if you get the right set of candidates before you, you need to be able to determine which one is best for the job. For example, international banks have no trouble attracting people to overseas positions, because international experience is important in the increasingly global banking industry. However, managers selected for overseas assignments sometimes fail and have to return home early at a significant cost to the employer. The early returns not only cost the company but also hurt employees' careers. These failures are partly a function of poor specification of the characteristics that predicted success in an overseas assignment and limited use of effective selection techniques.[12]

One of the key points to keep in mind relative to any selection technique is that if legally challenged, the organization must be able to demonstrate that the selection technique is valid. A **valid selection technique** is one that can differentiate between those who would be more successful in the job and those who would be less successful. For example, educational background is often used in selecting new hires because knowledge typically has a proven relationship with job performance. That is, it is hard to perform well in a job for which you do not have the requisite education and knowledge. There are a variety of selection techniques; each has its own strengths and weaknesses.

valid selection technique
A screening process that differentiates those who would be successful in a job from those who would not.

Valid Selection Techniques by Stewart Black

PEARSON
mymanagementlab

Interviews. The most widely used selection technique is the interview. In most cases, the interview is unstructured. An **unstructured interview** is one in which interviewers have a general idea of the types of questions they might ask but do not have a standard set. As a consequence, interviewers might ask different candidates different questions. With different questions and responses, comparing candidates can be like comparing apples and oranges. Not surprisingly, a major weakness of unstructured interviews is that they tend to have low levels of validity.[13] In contrast, **structured interviews**, in which interviewers ask a standard set of questions of all candidates about qualifications and capabilities related to job performance, can be quite valid. Validity can be further enhanced by carefully recording interviewee responses on a standardized form and taking approximately the same time in each interview. Exhibit 15.2 provides tips for interviewers and Exhibit 15.3 provides tips for interviewees.[14]

unstructured interview
An interview in which interviewers have a general idea of the questions they might ask but do not have a standard set.

structured interview An interview in which interviewers ask a standard set of questions of all candidates about qualifications and capabilities related to job performance.

Work Sampling. There are a variety of techniques that could be classified as work sampling. Essentially, all these techniques attempt to simulate or exactly duplicate the job the person would be doing if hired. The underlying rationale is straightforward: If you perform poorly or well in the work sample, you would likely perform similarly in the real job. In general, the main strength of work sampling techniques is that they make a reasonably accurate prediction of how an individual will do in a job. The main drawback is that they tend to be time and cost intensive. Research supports the validity of work sampling techniques.

Assessment Centres. **Assessment centres** use work sampling techniques. Typically, candidates are required to go through a number of exercises, and each exercise is designed to capture one or more key aspects of the job. For example, a supervisor's job might require good prioritization skills. The assessment centre might have an "in-basket" exercise to assess this skill.

assessment centres A work sampling technique in which candidates perform a number of exercises, each one designed to capture one or more key aspects of the job.

Exhibit 15.2 Tips for Interviewers

1. Plan the interview by reviewing the candidate and the job specifications.
2. Establish rapport with a friendly greeting and start the interview with a nonjob question.
3. Follow a structured set of questions.
4. Avoid questions that require or solicit a simple *yes* or *no* response.
5. Try not to telegraph, or give cues for, the desired answer.
6. Make sure the candidate has plenty of time to answer—do not monopolize the conversation.
7. Listen carefully and paraphrase key candidate answers to be sure you understand what they meant to say.
8. Ask for specific, not general, examples of the candidate's experience and accomplishments.
9. Leave time at the end of the interview to answer questions from the candidate.
10. At the close make sure the candidate knows what the next steps are and approximate timing.
11. After the candidate leaves, review your notes and highlight important points while they are fresh in your mind.

Exhibit 15.3 Tips for Interviewees

- Prepare for the interview by researching the company through articles and its own website.
- Smile and provide a warm greeting and firm handshake if the interviewer extends his or her hand.
- Make sure that your overall appearance (hair style, clothing, makeup, and so on) match the nature of the business and culture of the company.
- Watch your nonverbal behaviour to ensure that you maintain good eye contact and convey enthusiasm without being overly expressive with your hands or other body movements.
- Try to solicit the interviewer's needs early in the interview.
- Early in the interview be sure to get a complete picture of the job through questions like "Can you tell me about what has led people to succeed in this job in the past?"
- Explicitly relate yourself and your capabilities to the interviewer's needs through statements like "You mentioned that one of the keys to this position is the ability to motivate others. In my experience at XYZ. . . ."
- Take your time before answering; you do not need to begin talking the instant the interviewer asks a question.
- Conclude the interview by thanking the person for the opportunity and expressing your interest in the company and the position.

The exercise consists of an in-basket filled with letters, memos, and reports that the candidate must read and then prioritize. The individual's ability to recognize and respond to high-priority items comes out during the exercise. In general, research supports assessment centres as an effective selection method for new hires as well as for individuals moving up in a firm.[15]

work simulation Situations in which job candidates perform work they would do if hired or work that closely simulates the tasks they would perform.

Work Simulation. **Work simulation** techniques typically involve situations in which job candidates perform work that they would do if hired, or work that closely simulates the tasks they would perform. Work simulation can also be an effective training technique. An example of this can be found at Atomic Energy of Canada Limited (AECL). AECL is in the business of designing, building, and maintaining nuclear reactors in Canada and around the world. They use simulation technology to train employees in areas where they would otherwise be exposed to hazardous materials. This approach allows the employees to gain the experience without being unnecessarily exposed to environmental hazards.

Written Tests. Written tests are also widely used to select job candidates. This is due in part to the fact that the tests can be administered cost effectively to a large number of job candidates. Cognitive ability and intelligence tests measure an individual's general cognitive complexity and intellectual ability. Although the validity of these tests has been mixed, they do seem to be acceptable predictors for supervisory and management jobs. Personality tests are more controversial. While they can be reasonably good predictors of people's ability to work well with other particular personalities, they have not been good overall predictors of job performance.[16] Integrity tests are a more recent development. These tests try to assess the general level of a person's honesty. In general, they seem to be of debatable validity.[17] Written tests have the advantage of being inexpensive to administer, but the results are more valid regarding general performance and success than for success in a specific job.

Background and Reference Checks. Background checks attempt to verify factual information that applicants provide. Service Canada has found that up to 60 percent of applicants use misleading information. As a consequence, checking to make sure applicants graduated with the degrees they claim, from the schools they cite, and held the jobs with the responsibilities they describe can be quite valuable. The objective of reference checks is to get candid evaluations from those who have worked with the job candidate. It is important that managers not only ask applicants for three references, but that they also check the references to confirm that what the applicant has stated in his or her resumé or during an interview is true.

Physical Examinations. Companies that require physical examinations as part of the selecting process typically do so because the job has high physical demands. In addition to helping them select physically qualified candidates, physical exams also protect firms. First, the physical exam information may help firms reduce insurance claims. Second, it may help protect the firm from lawsuits by identifying high-risk applicants, like someone who might experience a heart attack from the physical strains of the job. However, managers must be careful to ensure that the physical requirements being screened in the examination are in fact related to job performance and are not sources for discrimination.[18] Physical examinations can also be used for screening out people who are inappropriate for the physical demands of the job. Drug testing is another screening mechanism companies use to ensure that employees' judgment and capabilities are not impaired while on the job.

Human Resource Management Activities that Maximize Performance

Once the right people are in the right positions, the organization needs to ensure that they are performing well. What constitutes maximum performance and potential is largely a function of the organization's strategy. For example, 3M Canada chooses to compete on new-product innovation and strives to have the majority of its revenue come from products that are less than five years old, such as FireStrap. FireStrap is a product designed to contain a fire by not permitting it to pass through walls. For this level of innovation, 3M needs employees like Larry Whitty, the developer of FireStrap, who can think of and test new ideas. For 3M, maximum performance and potential are largely defined in terms of employee innovations. Based on this, 3M undertakes a variety of activities to maximize employee creativity. Five specific categories of activities can significantly influence employee performance and potential.

Socialization and Training

Just as early life experiences can shape the general character, personality, and behaviour of people, so too can early training and socialization experiences shape important aspects of employees' performance.[19] For example, early training and socialization affects (1) the probability that new hires will stay with the firm, (2) the extent to which they will perform well, and (3) the degree to which they will develop to their full potential.[20]

Managers can use a variety of training methods to enhance the performance and potential of employees. We cover several here. Although early career training is important, in today's changing environment, training and learning are likely to become career-long endeavours.

Orientation. One of the first opportunities for an organization to shape the expectations and behaviour of new employees is during orientation programs.[21] Typically, these programs provide a broad overview of the industry, the company and its business activities, its key competitors, and general information about working in the company (such as key policies, pay procedures, and fringe benefits). Work-unit orientation sessions are typically more narrow and are generally designed to help the new employee get up to speed on the new job, co-workers, work-unit policies and procedures, and expectations. To maximize the effectiveness of orientation programs, managers should consider the following recommendations:[22]

- Keep paperwork to a minimum to avoid information overload. Do include paperwork that must be completed immediately.

- Include an informal meeting with the individual's immediate supervisor.

- Alternate heavy information, such as that related to benefits and insurance, with lighter live or video presentations from corporate officers.

- Provide a glossary of terms unique to the organization.

- Match each new employee with a "buddy" (that is, an experienced worker) based more on personality compatibility than similarity of jobs.

On-the-Job Training Techniques. On-the-job training (OJT) is the most widely used training technique in organizations. As Exhibit 15.4 illustrates, there are a wide variety of techniques that a manager can use to train employees. Over your career, you will likely be exposed to most, if not all, of these approaches.

Off-the-Job Training Techniques. Off-the-job training can also be used with positive effect. The most common off-the-job training approach is the classroom-based program. The program may be only an hour, or it may be several weeks in length. It may be conducted by in-house experts (employees of the company) or by outside experts from the industry or the education field, such as university professors. The program may involve lectures, case studies, discussions, videos, or simulations. Individual-based programs are also increasingly popular. Formal correspondence courses are sometimes used when employees have different learning speeds and motivations but the learning objectives are clear. Computer-assisted programs are also used when employees have different learning speeds and motivations. Current technology now allows for text, graphics, and a variety of visual displays as well as interaction. Many programs now adjust content and difficulty level in real time based on how well the individual is doing.

Training Objectives. Orientation and training programs can have a variety of objectives. However, at a fundamental level, these programs are intended to

Exhibit 15.4   On-the-Job Training Techniques

1. *Expanded Responsibilities.* This training technique expands the job duties, assignments, and responsibilities of an individual.

2. *Job Rotation.* Also called *cross-training*, this practice moves individuals to various types of jobs within the organization at the same level or next-immediate-higher level for periods of time from an hour or two to as long as a year.

3. *Staff Development Meetings.* Meetings are usually held offsite to discuss facts of each individual's job and to develop ideas for improving job performance.

4. *"Assistant to" Positions.* Promising employees serve as staff assistants to higher-skill-level jobs for a specified period of time (often one to three months) to become more familiar with the higher-skilled positions in the organization.

5. *Problem-Solving Conferences.* Conferences are held to solve a specific problem being experienced by a group or the organization as a whole. It involves brainstorming and other creative means to come up with solutions to the basic problems.

6. *Mentoring.* A guide or knowledgeable person higher up in the organization helps a new employee "learn the ropes" of the organization and provides other advice.

7. *Special Assignments.* Special tasks or responsibilities are given to an individual for a specified period of time. The assignment may be writing up a report, investigating the feasibility for a new project, process, service, or product, preparing a newsletter, or evaluating a company policy or procedure.

8. *Company Trainers.* Special programs can cover such topics as safety, new personnel procedures, new products or services, affirmative action, and technical programs.

9. *Outside Consultants.* Recognized experts are brought to the company to conduct training on such topics as goal setting, communications, assessment techniques, safety, and other current topics of importance. They often supplement training done by company trainers.

10. *Consultant Advisory Reviews.* Experts in specialized fields meet with various managers and employee groups to investigate and help solve particular problems. The emphasis is on problem solving rather than training.

11. *Reading Matter.* A formal program is created to circulate books, journals, selected articles, new business material, and so on to selected employees. An effective program also includes periodic scheduled meetings to discuss the material.

12. *Apprenticeship.* Training is provided through working under a journeyman or master in a craft. The apprentice works alongside a person skilled in the craft and is taught by that person. Apprenticeship programs also often include some classroom work.

Source: Adapted from W. P. Anthony, D. L. Perrewé, and K. M. Kacmar, *Strategic Human Resource Management* (Fort Worth, TX: Harcourt Brace Jovanovich, 1993).

address employee technical, interpersonal, or conceptual abilities. Technical skills can range from being able to read and perform simple math to being able to program a supercomputer.

Because very few employees work in isolation, improved interpersonal abilities are the target of a wide variety of training programs. Programs might address skills such as effective listening, conflict resolution, negotiation, and coaching. In a recent study, executives cited poor interpersonal skills as one of the biggest problems in new university or MBA graduates.[23]

The final category is conceptual abilities. This category includes a variety of skills and abilities, such as problem solving, decision making, planning, and organizing. A given training program might be designed to address just one of these categories, two, or all four.

Regardless of the category the program is designed to target, most successful programs provide participants with several things:

- An understanding of what is and is not the correct behaviour.

- A clear knowledge of why certain behaviours are correct or incorrect.

■ Sufficient opportunities to practise the desired behaviours.

■ Feedback on performance with further opportunities to practise and improve.

An important part of well-designed training is an evaluation of its effectiveness.[24] Perhaps the simplest means of assessing training is what is often called the "smile index," or the satisfaction of participants with the training. This is quite often gathered just after the training is finished via a questionnaire. Clearly, it is unlikely that any aspect of the training that participants do not like will be retained by them and have a positive impact on their knowledge or behaviours. However, the fact that participants enjoyed the training or thought it was useful does not guarantee that it will have the intended impact. A more rigorous assessment of training would involve a pre-training and post-training assessment. For example, if the training were primarily intended to convey knowledge, then a "pre and post" assessment design would involve assessing the knowledge level of participants before the training and at some point afterward. These basics would also apply to an assessment of the skills they learned. In addition, if the training is intended to improve job performance, like quality, you might assess the impact of the training by comparing important metrics, such as defects per 1000 before and after the training.

While a reduction in defects might tell you if the training had the intended effect, it does not tell you if the training was cost effective. Determining this is much more complicated. In general you have to assess both the direct (the cost of trainers) and indirect costs (the productivity lost while workers were in training instead of on the job). You then have to compare these costs to the benefits, such as the savings from fewer returns because of higher quality. However, one key challenge is determining the period over which to add up the benefits. For example, if higher quality is saving you $100 per day in returns, should you estimate the total value of these savings over a week, a month, a year, or several years? Your answer dramatically influences the total benefit quantification and therefore the final determination of whether the training costs are exceeded by the benefits, and if so by how much.

Job Design

job design The structuring or restructuring of key job components.

Job design is focused on the structuring or restructuring of key job components. A job design typically includes the responsibilities. Thus, while job analysis focuses on what the components of a job are, job design is the process of determining which components ought to be put together and how they should be arranged to enhance performance.[25] For example, does an assembly-line worker work in isolation and repetitively attach a given part to a product, or does he work in a team with others building an entire unit?

In some texts, job design would be much earlier in the sequence than we have placed it. In general, for a brand new job that has never been filled before, job design does take place early in the sequence. Also, jobs were traditionally designed and then appropriate people were selected to fit into the jobs. The reality of today's dynamic environment has changed that approach. In some cases, it is possible and appropriate to design jobs and then try to match people to them, but in other cases jobs might need to be designed or redesigned to fit the available people. There are also situations that require a combination of both fitting the person to the job and fitting the job to the person. For example, **job sharing** involves two people working part time in the same job. Effective job sharing requires two individuals who can coordinate well and have similar capabilities. It has become popular with working

job sharing A situation in which two people share the same job by each working part time.

mothers who are faced with balancing family and economic and professional demands. Increasingly, technology is allowing managers to design and redesign jobs in ways not possible before.

During the early and mid-1990s, re-engineering became a popular concept regarding the design or redesign of work. **Re-engineering** is the fundamental rethinking and radical redesign of business processes to achieve dramatic improvements in critical, contemporary measures of performance, such as cost, quality, service, or speed.[26] Computer and information technology advancements have allowed organizations to design more enriched, satisfying, and productive jobs. Increasingly, organizations are looking at ways to give employees more flexibility in the way their work is accomplished. Technology is one way to provide that flexibility. Maximizing subordinates' performance and your unit's performance is your goal as a manager regarding effective job design.

> **re-engineering** The fundamental rethinking and radical redesign of business processes to achieve dramatic improvements in critical, contemporary measures of performance.

Performance Appraisal

Before organizations or managers can encourage or correct the actions of employees, they must know how the employees are doing. Performance appraisal is concerned with (1) establishing performance objectives and standards, (2) measuring performance against those standards, and (3) providing feedback to employees concerning that measurement and evaluation.[27] As we stated before, the objectives of the job and the standards against which performance is measured must be driven by the strategy of the firm.

For most managers, performance appraisal is perhaps the most important, yet most difficult, human resource activity. This difficulty is not only because of the complexity of evaluating past performance and setting future performance targets, but because performance appraisals involve communicating to employees how they are doing relative to established targets. Often employees are not quite measuring up to established standards and require feedback for corrective action; however, few people like to give or receive negative feedback. Still, without this feedback, neither individuals nor organizations can maximize performance. As a consequence, all managers need to understand the key factors that drive effective performance appraisal systems and be skilled at implementing them.

Graphic Rating Scales. Perhaps the most popular method of providing performance feedback is through graphic rating scales (see Exhibit 15.5 for an example). A graphic rating scale typically lists a set of qualities on which the

Employee name: _____	Dept. _____				
	Excellent	Good	Average	Fair	Poor
1. Quality of work	☐	☐	☐	☐	☐
2. Quantity of work	☐	☐	☐	☐	☐
3. Cooperation	☐	☐	☐	☐	☐
4. Dependability	☐	☐	☐	☐	☐
5. Initiative	☐	☐	☐	☐	☐
6. Job knowledge	☐	☐	☐	☐	☐
7. Attitude	☐	☐	☐	☐	☐

Exhibit 15.5 Graphic Rating Scale.

employee is evaluated. The level of performance on each of these items is then rated in terms of a graduated scale. The scale typically ranges from 1 to 5. The degree of specificity concerning the definition of each point on the scale can range from one-word descriptors (e.g., 1 = poor) to complete sentences (e.g., 1 = Does not meet the minimum standards).

The popularity of graphic ratings is due to two main factors. First, they are relatively quick and easy for managers to complete. Given that most managers have many employees whom they must evaluate and that managers typically are not rewarded for writing up high-quality evaluations, they have a natural incentive to complete the evaluations as quickly as possible. Second, because the evaluation items and the rating scale are common across all employees, it is easy to quantify the results and compare employees' performance ratings.

However, there are two key limitations that as a manager you should keep in mind relative to graphic rating scales. First, the characteristics being evaluated may not be clearly defined; thus they are left to individual interpretation. Consequently, one manager might focus her interpretation of "interpersonal skills" on conflict resolution abilities, while another manager might focus his interpretation on listening skills. Given the two different interpretations, it is difficult to compare the employees evaluated by the two different managers. Furthermore, the two different managers might have different interpretations of the rating scale. One manager might only allow the top 5 percent of employees to receive a high rating of "5 = excellent." Another manager might interpret a "5" as applicable to the top 20 percent of employees. Once again, the different interpretations would make comparing employees rated by different managers difficult.[28] This incomparability is important because over 85 percent of firms use performance appraisals to determine merit increases, bonuses, and promotions.

Behaviourally Anchored Rating Scales. **Behaviourally anchored rating scales (BARS)** are designed to keep many of the advantages of the graphic rating scales and reduce the disadvantages. The general design of BARS is similar to graphic rating scales in that managers rate employee characteristics using a quantitative scale. However, the characteristics are specified in greater detail and described in terms of behaviours rather than abstract qualities. Likewise, the scales are much more tied to descriptions of specific behaviours rather than ambiguous terms (see Exhibit 15.6 for an example). The greater specificity and link to behaviours reduces, but does not eliminate, the potential for noncomparability of ratings across different evaluators.[29] However, some potential for manager bias remains.[30]

360-Degree Feedback. The primary rationale behind 360-degree feedback appraisal systems is that an individual's performance should be viewed from multiple perspectives.[31] Most **360-degree feedback** systems involve collecting appraisal evaluations from an individual's boss, peers, and subordinates. In some companies, evaluations are also collected from suppliers and customers, depending on the nature of interaction the employee has with these constituencies. The positive aspect of 360-degree feedback is that because data are gathered from multiple sources, employees are encouraged to focus on all key constituencies. This reduces the tendency, for example, to simply cozy up to the boss and work poorly with peers or subordinates. The major drawback is the time and energy it takes to collect, process, and effectively feed the data back to the individual. In addition, a recent study shows that 360-degree feedback might not have the validity attributed to it. Lowest-performing employees sometimes give themselves the highest ratings. These individuals were relatively easy to spot because their supervisor ratings were significantly lower. However, a problem occurs for "modest" employees, or employees who underrate themselves. This research suggests that more modest feedback recipients might be underrated by their supervisors.

Position: _____

Job dimensions: _____

Plans work and organizes time carefully so as to maximize resources and meet commitments.	9	
	8	Even though this associate has a report due on another project, he or she would be well prepared for the assigned discussion on your project.
	7	This associate would keep a calendar or schedule on which deadlines and activities are carefully noted, and which would be consulted before making new commitments.
	6	As program chief, this associate would manage arrangements for enlisting resources for a special project reasonably well, but would probably omit one or two details that would have to be handled by improvisation.
Plans and organizes time and effort primarily for large segments of a task. Usually meets commitments, but may overlook what are considered secondary details.	5	This associate would meet a deadline in handing in a report, but the report might be below usual standard if other deadlines occur on the same day the report is due.
	4	This associate's evaluations are likely not to reflect abilities because of overcommitments in other activities.
	3	This associate would plan more by enthusiasm than by timetable and frequently have to work late the night before an assignment is due, although it would be completed on time.
	2	This associate would often be late for meetings, although others in similar circumstances do not seem to find it difficult to be on time.
Appears to do little planning. May perform effectively, despite what seems to be a disorganized approach, by concerted effort, although deadlines may be missed.	1	This associate never makes a deadline, even with sufficient notice.

Exhibit 15.6 Behaviourally Anchored Rating Scale.

Source: Table from *Strategic Human Resource Management* by William P. Anthony, Pamela L. Perrewé, and K. Michele Kacmar, p. 456. Copyright © 1993 by Harcourt Brace & Company, reproduced by permission of the publisher.

The study also found that peers often overestimated the performance of poor performers.[32]

Effective Performance Feedback. Regardless of the system of evaluating employee performance, the results of the evaluation need to be fed back effectively to employees to make a positive difference in their performance. There are two important points to keep in mind. First, if expectations concerning unacceptable, acceptable, or superior performance were not clear to the employee prior to the appraisal, negative assessments will not likely influence motivation or performance. Consequently, performance expectations must be clear and acceptable to the employee from the beginning. Second, if the employee believes that, as the manager, you are biased in your observations, your assessment will not have the effect you desire. This is why recording both positive and negative **critical incidents** is important. This simply involves the recording of important, specific incidents in which the employee's behaviour and performance were above or below expectations. This record then allows you to avoid remembering only the most recent events and also facilitates your ability to talk about specifics in the appraisal interview.[33] This brings us to a brief list of recommendations for an effective performance appraisal interview:

1. Review key work objectives, goals, or standards against which the employee's performance is measured.
2. Summarize the employee's overall performance by reviewing specific positive and negative incidents.
3. Discuss causes of weak performance and listen carefully to the employee's explanation.
4. Discuss alternative means of improving future performance and encourage employee input.
5. Establish an agreed approach, timetable, and review process for future improvement.
6. Establish key objectives, timetables, and standards for the upcoming performance period.
7. Leave the meeting on an encouraging and positive note.

These may seem like simple steps, but they can go a long way to improving the effectiveness of one of the most difficult yet important human resource challenges you face as a manager.

Compensation

Although rewards and compensation can be instrumental in getting the right people, their primary function is retaining and maximizing the performance of employees once they have entered the organization. Rewards by their nature are designed to encourage desired behaviours. As already discussed, desired behaviours must be linked to the firm's strategy. Thus, reward systems must also be linked to the firm's strategy.

Unfortunately, employees are often rewarded for doing one thing and yet expected to do another. For example, most stockbrokers at retail brokerage firms are rewarded with bonuses based on the volume of transactions they complete. This leads many brokers to "churn" individual investors' accounts. That is, brokers buy and sell shares to generate commissions even though the investment objectives of the investors did not justify such frequent transactions. As a consequence of this churning and the associated fees charged to customers, investors often take their accounts to competing brokerage firms. In the end, the reward structures encourage churning, but churning ultimately hurts firm revenue and broker commissions because customers leave.

pay structure A range of pay for a particular position or classification of positions.

broadband systems Pay structures in which the range of pay is large and covers a wide variety of jobs.

Pay. Most firms establish a pay structure based on level in the company and type of position. A **pay structure** establishes a range of pay for a particular position or classification of positions. Traditionally, pay structures have been hierarchical and segmented. Most companies are now moving to **broadband systems** in which the range of pay is large and covers a wide variety of jobs.[34] Exhibit 15.7 provides a graphic illustration of a traditional pay structure and a more modern broadband system. The major advantage to a broadband system is the greater flexibility it gives organizations to match pay to individual value and changing labour market conditions.

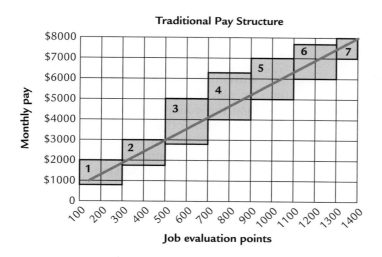

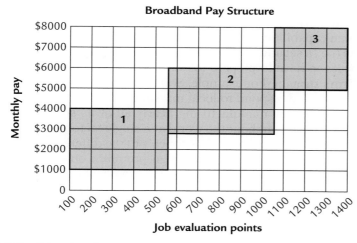

Exhibit 15.7 Traditional and Contemporary Pay Structures.

Another important pay trend is the movement away from an individual's total compensation package being primarily composed of salary and toward a greater portion of compensation being at risk.[35] **At-risk compensation** is simply pay that varies depending on specified conditions. These conditions might include the general profitability of the company; hitting particular budget, revenue, or cost savings targets for a unit; or meeting specific individual performance targets. Increasingly, companies are placing a higher portion of total compensation "at risk." This is primarily because if total compensation is made up of salary and if salaries are raised at a level comparable to inflation, inflation and subsequent salary increases can add significantly to company costs. On the other hand, if a higher percentage of compensation is tied to performance, higher compensation costs only occur with higher performance. Consequently, **incentive plans**, or approaches that tie some compensation to performance, are increasingly being spread throughout the organization, whereas traditionally they were reserved for only the most senior managers.

at-risk compensation Pay that varies depending on specified conditions, including the profitability of the company; hitting particular budget, revenue, or cost savings targets for a unit; or meeting specified individual performance targets.

incentive plans Systems that tie some compensation to performance.

Benefits. Traditional benefit plans include items such as medical, dental, and life insurance. In the past, companies used to compete for employees and retain them in part through offering attractive benefit plans. However, as companies added more and more features to the plans to make them attractive to a broader base of employees with differing needs, companies found themselves paying 20 to 40 percent of salary in benefits. To reduce the soaring benefit costs and still meet differing employee needs, companies began to offer

cafeteria-style plans Benefit plans in which employees have a set number of "benefit dollars" that they can use to purchase benefits that fit their particular needs.

cafeteria-style plans, in which employees had a set number of "benefit dollars" that they could use to purchase the specific benefits that fit their particular needs.

Rewards and Motivation. Although much of the responsibility for reward and compensation systems is placed on the human resource department, effective rewards are more than the dollars paid out in salaries and bonuses or the dollars tied up in health care and other benefits. And though individual managers can influence pay increases and the like, they also have the greatest control over equally powerful rewards such as recognition and praise. Consequently, it is important for you to understand the broad range of rewards and how they influence the performance of your employees.

Career Systems and Development

career paths Sets and sequences of positions and experiences.

One of the most powerful motivators for people to join organizations and to perform is the opportunity to grow and develop.[36] Career and employee development systems are designed to respond to that particular motivation and to ensure that the human capabilities needed in the organization are being developed. The **career paths** (i.e., a set and sequence of positions and experiences) organizations want employees to have to prepare for certain responsibilities is largely a function of the firm's strategy. For example, Sony is simultaneously trying to capture global efficiencies and respond to local market conditions. Sony tries to capture economic efficiencies by manufacturing nearly all of its small, handheld video cameras for markets throughout the world at a single factory in Japan. Yet it also tries to sell these cameras in a way that appeals to the different local tastes across the globe. Consequently, Sony places a high premium on international experience for career paths that lead to the top of the organization. Sony also competes on integrated team design. That is, individuals from various functional areas such as market research, engineering, sales, and finance work together at the outset of a new product development. Therefore, Sony places a premium on employees' working in several functional areas over the course of their careers, or what is referred to as **cross-functional job rotation**.[37]

cross-functional job rotation Opportunities for employees to work in different functional areas and gain additional expertise.

While responsibility for organizational career and development systems is often that of the human resource function, individual managers are those most knowledgeable about the development needs of specific employees and are often those to whom individual employees go in search of career guidance. In addition, managers develop reputations as being effective or ineffective at employee development, and these reputations influence the quality of subordinates managers attract, which in turn affects the performance of their units. Thus, while some may view employee career pathing and development as an activity for which the HR department is responsible, it is actually a critical activity at which all managers must be skilled.

dual-career couples Couples in which both partners work full time in professional, managerial, or administrative jobs.

Promotion. Employees can and should expand and improve their capabilities in their jobs, and development need not involve promotion. However, for a large percentage of an organization's employees, job development is the means to gain promotion to positions of greater responsibility and pay. In large companies promotions often involve relocations as well. With the increasing percentage of couples who both work, these relocations, especially international relocations, can be challenging.[38] **Dual-career couples**, or couples in which both partners work full time in professional, managerial, or administrative jobs, frequently do not want to be separated, and yet finding a job for the other partner, especially in a foreign country, can be a serious obstacle to an individual's accepting a promotion and transfer. Furthermore, work visa restrictions may prevent employment of the spouse in a foreign country even if a transfer or interim job can be located. To cope with this challenge, companies are expanding their spouse relocation assistance programs and are also forming informal associations so employees interested in relocating can exchange information about transfers and job opportunities to help each other out.[39]

Termination. Despite your best efforts to recruit, hire, train, compensate, and manage the performance of your employees, you may find that you have to terminate or fire an employee. Firing for cause usually involves the termination of an employee for criminal behaviour like theft of company property, or violation of company policies like sharing confidential information with competitors. Most companies have detailed and written policies about the criteria for "cause terminations" and the steps that a manager must follow to fire an employee who meets these conditions. An employee can also be fired for *failure to perform*. Again, most companies have detailed policies about what must be done first before an employee can be fired for poor performance. Often these policies involve the following:

1. Informing the employee of the performance standards.

2. Formally and specifically documenting incidents of poor performance.

3. Informing the employee of these performance failures, reiterating the standards, and setting time frames and actions for performance improvement.

4. Formally informing the employee of the consequences of failure to meet the standards and time frame established for performance improvement.

If the employee's performance does not improve sufficiently subsequent to taking these measures, many companies require his or her manager to work with a specialist in the HR department to actually fire the employee.

Layoffs. Layoffs involve the termination of groups of employees because of economic or business reasons and are not a function of the employees' performance per se. Research has demonstrated that companies suffer in their ability to attract and retain good employees in the future if they do not conduct layoffs in a *reasonable* manner. Clearly, "reasonable" is open to interpretation, but practices that seem to be perceived as reasonable include outplacement aids such as resumé-writing assistance, career counselling, office space access, secretarial help, and job-hunting assistance. Often these activities are outsourced to companies that specialize in helping laid-off workers find employment.

Labour Relations

Labour relations come into play when employees are represented by formal unions who negotiate on their behalf regarding wages, benefits, and other terms of their employment. Some industries, like the airlines, have a large proportion of employees represented by unions. For example, in the airline industry not only are some of the lower-paid employees, like baggage handlers, represented by unions, but highly paid employees, like pilots, are also represented by unions. Managers must find a balance between meeting the needs of the unionized employees on such core issues as compensation, benefits, and job security, and meeting the needs of the business including controlling costs, remaining flexible to respond to a changing environment, and sustaining a reputation that allows the company to attract and retain needed employees now and in the future.

Laws and Regulations Affecting HRM

Perhaps more than any other area of management, laws and regulations affect human resource management. Exhibit 15.8 provides a summary of areas where major developments in labour legislation in employee standards occurred in Canadian jurisdictions over a one-year period (September 2005 to August 2006). The basic intent of such legislation has been to ensure that equal opportunity is provided for both job applicants and current employees. Because the laws were intended to correct past inequalities, many organizations have voluntarily implemented or been pressured by employees and other constituencies to implement **affirmative action programs** to ensure that organizational changes are made. These programs may involve such things as taking extra effort to inform minority candidates about job opportunities, providing special training programs for disadvantaged candidates, or paying special attention to the racial or gender mix of employees who are promoted.

As businesses globalize, laws within Canada can have an impact on how Canadian businesses operate in other countries. Countries to which managers might be sent for development opportunities only complicate the situation. For example, Japan is Canada's second-largest export market and the fifth greatest source of investment in Canada. Therefore, Canadian firms are likely to send **expatriate employees**—employees sent overseas on lengthy, but temporary assignments—to operations in Japan. However, in Japan, less than 3 percent of senior management are women. This may suggest that in a traditionally male-dominated society, female expatriate managers from Canada

affirmative action programs
Hiring and training programs intended to correct past inequalities for certain categories of people based on gender, race and ethnicity, age, or religion.

expatriate employees
Employees sent overseas on lengthy, but temporary, assignments.

Exhibit 15.8	Major Developments in Canadian Labour Legislation on Employment Standards in 2005–2006
Type of Legislation	**Jurisdiction**
Compassionate Care Leave and Benefits	Canada, British Columbia
Parental Insurance	Quebec
Emergency Leave and Related Matters	Ontario
Minimum Wages	Manitoba, New Brunswick, Prince Edward Island, Quebec, Yukon
Prohibited Wage Deductions	Prince Edward Island
Banking Industry and Commission-Paid salespeople Hours of Work	Canada
Construction Industry Workers	Manitoba, Yukon, Nova Scotia
Garment Industry Minimum Wages	Quebec
Recorded Visual and Audio Visual Entertainment Production Industry	Ontario
Apprentices of Defined Trades	Manitoba
Retail Establishments and Hours of Operation	Nova Scotia
Administration and Enforcement of *Employment Standards Act*	British Columbia, Ontario, Saskatchewan, Yukon
Wage Earner Protection Program	Canada
Human Rights in the Workplace	Ontario, Newfoundland and Labrador
Mandatory Retirement	Ontario, Newfoundland and Labrador
Pay Equity	Quebec
Whistle-Blower Protection	Canada, Manitoba

Source: Human Resources and Social Development Canada website www.hrsdc.gc.ca (accessed September 30, 2007).

may face a severe **glass ceiling**—an invisible barrier that prevents women from being promoted to the highest executive ranks. Yet Canada's *Employment Equity Act* of 1995 states that the gender of Canadian employees cannot be a barrier to employment opportunities.[40]

Keep in mind that the intent of most of the legislation and regulation in Canada and the United States is designed to provide equal opportunity. This, however, does not prevent organizations from using certain criteria that you might think of as discriminatory, if it can be demonstrated that the criteria are **bona fide occupational qualifications (BFOQ)**, or qualifications that have a direct and material impact on job performance and outcomes.[41] For example, you might think that not hiring male employees who have a mustache or beard (or requiring them to shave them before being hired) would constitute discrimination. However, Disney has such a policy for its theme park workers and has prevailed when taken to court. Disney was able to retain the policy despite legal challenges because the company was able to demonstrate statistically that customers reacted better to and were more satisfied with clean-shaven park employees than those with beards and mustaches. In Disney's case, being clean shaven is a BFOQ.

Sexual Harassment

Sexual harassment is a major workplace issue, given the devastating impact it can have on people who are victims of harassment, the negative impact it has on an organization's workplace and reputation, and the significant financial penalties that can be assessed against organizations that allow it to occur. Sexual harassment takes two basic forms. The first is sometimes called *quid pro quo* and involves requests or implied suggestions that sexual relations are required in exchange for continued employment or benefits like promotion. The second form involves actions that create a "hostile environment." A hostile environment can be created through jokes, touching, comments, pictures, and other means of communicating unwanted sexual innuendo. Sexual harassment suits have increased dramatically over the last several years. As a consequence of the judgments (which are often several hundred thousand dollars), companies are increasingly offering training programs to try to help managers understand the law and avoid such incidents.

Workforce Diversity

Effective management of workforce diversity is a growing managerial challenge. Historically, diversity was defined in terms of differences along traditional racial categories. Today, most organizations think of workforce diversity in terms of a wide range of factors, including age, gender, race, religion, cultural background, education, and mental and physical disabilities. Eight percent of the Canadian workforce are visible minorities, 1 percent are Aboriginal Peoples, 60 percent are women, and 5 percent are persons with disabilities.[42] The diversity of backgrounds raises a variety of human resource management questions. For example, with the need to reach out to such a diverse group of potential employees, what types of recruiting efforts will be effective and avoid unintended discrimination? How can the diverse backgrounds, perspectives, and talents of employees be effectively managed?

Managing Workforce Diversity. While there are ethical arguments for why organizations should embrace diversity, efforts to effectively manage workforce diversity typically are justified in terms of business reasons:

- Need to attract enough capable workers to meet turnover and growth demands of the business

- Enhanced creativity and innovation when solving problems

- Knowledge and understanding of the diverse marketplace and customers

glass ceiling An invisible barrier that prevents women from promotion to the highest executive ranks.

bona fide occupational qualifications (BFOQ) Qualifications that have a direct and material impact on job performance and outcomes.

Canada Council for the Arts is an arm's length federal agency providing services and grants to Canadian artists and arts organizations and is a leader in recruiting traditionally underrepresented groups. The agency currently meets or exceeds average Canadian levels of diversity in the workforce, with 11% of their workforce composed of visible minorities, 6% Aboriginal Peoples, 73% women, and 5% persons with disabilities.[43]

The experience of most organizations, however, is that these advantages are hard to obtain. Just as multiple perspectives, values, and ways of thinking can bring new insights and creativity to a problem, they can also create a significant management challenge. Diverse workgroups often encounter the following problems:

- Communication problems and misunderstandings

- Mistrust

- Conflict and incompatible approaches to resolving the conflict

- Lower group cohesiveness and greater subgroup formation based on elements of diversity such as language, race, or gender

Given the potential benefits and the significant challenges of effectively managing workforce diversity, we review some general guidelines for you as a manager to follow:

- *Know yourself.* How much exposure have you had to people with ethnic, racial, religious, educational, or cultural backgrounds different from your own? How tolerant and understanding of the differences have you been? How comfortable were you? How curious were you?

- *Prepare yourself and your employees.* How skilled are you and your employees at listening, conflict resolution, negotiation, and communication?

- *Provide support.* To what extent are there support groups for employees with minority backgrounds to keep them from feeling unappreciated and wanting to leave the organization? To what extent do minority employees have mentors who can help them understand and become an effective part of the organization?

- *Guide behaviour.* To what extent do you monitor the behaviour of your subordinates and peers? How consistent are you in providing positive reinforcement of behaviours that foster tolerance of and effective use of diversity? To what extent do you privately provide negative feedback to individuals who display intolerance or other problem behaviours?

From both a domestic and international perspective, workforce diversity is only going to increase. One of the ways you can distinguish yourself from others and add value to your organization is through your ability to work effectively with subordinates, peers, customers, and suppliers with diverse backgrounds. *A Manager's Challenge: "Marriott Provides a Step Up"* profiles one company in which senior managers have changed how they help middle managers successfully meet the diversity challenge. As you read the box, you might ask yourself which HR practices you would find most helpful to you if you were a manager in the Marriott company.

Globalization

Globalization also poses a significant challenge to human resource management. Many argue that the world is getting smaller. However, from a human resource perspective, the world is getting larger! If you look at the history of almost any multinational corporation (MNC), at its beginning the firm operated in one or a very limited number of countries. As it grew, it expanded into

A Manager's Challenge   *Change*

Marriott Provides a Step Up

For managers at Marriott International, maintaining a core of workers to handle entry-level jobs and provide excellent service is critical to supporting its competitive position and continued growth. Moreover, nearly one-third of Marriott's managers started in hourly wage positions, another reason why this group is vital to the company's success. However, given the changing composition and nature of the entry-level workforce, Marriott managers have come to recognize that compensation alone will not attract, motivate, or help retain the workers they need. Managing a diverse workforce who speak some 50 languages can be a real human resource challenge.

To learn more about the changes in its workforce, Marriott managers conducted a study and learned that about one-quarter of the workers had literacy problems. In response, Marriott initiated an on-site English as a second language (ESL) program during work hours. The business reason? Workers who speak English can better serve English-speaking hotel guests.

However, managers were still busy offering advice about family conflicts and childcare solutions and sometimes lending money to employees for urgent bills. Instead of dealing with customers, some managers were spending too much time doing social work. As a result, Marriott managers changed their approach to human resource management. They added programs such as the Associate Resource Line, a confidential service that counsels employees across a broad spectrum of personal matters. They also started up social services referrals and childcare referrals to attract and motivate hourly workers—and keep turnover lower than that of competitors.

More than 50 languages are spoken among Marriott's 151 000 employees in 67 countries around the world. The hotel chain has been honoured for its work–life practices by many organizations, including *Diversity*, Inc., *Working Mother*, and *Latina Style* magazines. In an industry where the hourly employee turnover rate is 80 to 90 percent, Marriott's 35 percent turnover rate is exceptionally low.

By responding to the changing composition and needs of the entry-level workforce, managers help sustain Marriott's competitive position and its reputation for exceptional service. The company's continued growth has delivered even more opportunities for employee personal and professional growth, which managers highlight to attract and retain employees.

Sources: Marriott International, Inc 2006 Annual Report, www.marriott.com (accessed October 8, 2007); Adapted from A. Wheat, "The Anatomy of a Great Workplace," Fortune, February 4, 2002, pp. 75+; J. Hickman, "America's 50 Best Companies for Minorities," Fortune, July 8, 2002, pp. 110+; "America's 50 Best Companies for Minorities," Fortune, July 9, 2001, pp. 122+; J. Gordon, "The New Paternalism," Forbes, November 2, 1998; "Best Companies for Asians, Blacks, and Hispanics," Fortune, August 2, 1998.

more and more countries. Telecommunication and transportation technologies in particular have facilitated this expansion. Now companies like McCain Foods operate in more than 110 countries around the world. For McCain, that translates into employees speaking a multitude of languages and practising a variety of religions, dealing with 110 different governments, and coping with hundreds of different customs, holidays, and traditions. As companies expand into new countries and cultures, the world for them gets larger and more complicated.

As firms expand outside their home countries, they will confront a variety of HRM challenges. For example, do the selection techniques that work in one country also work in another? Can one performance appraisal form be applied in all operations around the globe? Must reward systems be adapted and changed from one country to the next? If they must be adapted, how can a firm avoid the risk of employees perceiving these differences as inequitable? What must a firm do to ensure that it provides development opportunities for employees in all its operations? How does any global firm ensure that it finds and develops the best possible talent wherever in its worldwide operations that talent might be located? When a firm needs to send employees outside their native countries as a means of developing their international skills and abilities, how does it effectively select these individuals? How should these employees be trained prior to their international assignments? How can these individuals be effectively evaluated when factors such as real changes in exchange rates, government price controls, and other external factors significantly influence bottom-line results of overseas operations? These are just a sampling of the questions and human resource management challenges raised by today's increasingly global environment.

Managerial Perspectives Revisited

PERSPECTIVE 1: THE ORGANIZATIONAL CONTEXT The organizational context is extremely important when it comes to human resource management. In many ways the appropriate HR practices are a function of the organization. Change the context of the organization—its strategy, culture, or industry—and you are likely to need to change the characteristics or capabilities needed in the employees you want to recruit, how you orient them, what training they need, and how you manage their performance or structure their compensation.

PERSPECTIVE 2: THE HUMAN FACTOR From one perspective, human resource management is all about working through others; it is about achieving results by attracting, selecting, training, appraising, compensating, and developing others. Because human resource management also typically involves the policies and practices of the company through the human resource department, as a manager, effective HRM will likely also involve working with and through people in your HR department.

PERSPECTIVE 3: MANAGING PARADOXES Meeting the HRM challenge creates some important potential paradoxes. On the one hand, individual managers have their own personal views on the effective management of human resources. On the other hand, as managers in an organization, they have to work with, support, and uphold the policies and practices of the company. At times there may be a conflict between the two. In such cases, do managers have an obligation to try to correct company practices that are not in keeping with what their values are or what they believe—or that may be inappropriate or even illegal? This dynamic tension between personal and company standards is one of the principal paradoxes managers face when it comes to managing and motivating the firm's people.

4   PERSPECTIVE 4: **ENTREPRENEURIAL MINDSET** The entrepreneurial mindset is reflected in the behaviour and actions of a firm's employees. WestJet employees are a good example of workers who hold and display an entrepreneurial mindset. Employees at WestJet are given more latitude in making on-the-spot decisions and exercise a greater interest in the well-being of the customer and, at the same time, the company. Part of this may be attributed to the fact that more than 87 percent of WestJet employees are shareholders, taking part in an employee share purchase plan that the company matches with equal contributions. It may also be the culture of WestJet, where the emphasis is on putting people first. Either way, the approach to managing employees at WestJet is attracting and retaining quality employees that are in turn rewarded for their commitment.

To maintain a company's competitive edge, managers should be committed to constantly improving their human resource management capabilities. While the HR department is designed to support and facilitate the effective management of human resources in the company, it's no substitute for individual managers taking the initiative to engage in key HR activities.

Concluding Comments

In this chapter, we presented human resource management as a set of activities performed by all managers rather than a set of functions locked within a human resource department. A company's human resources are its most fundamental source of competitive advantage. In addition, individual managers can create competitive advantages for themselves in their careers through superior management of human resources. In particular, managers who can match their management of human resources with the strategy of the organization may find themselves in a superior position relative to their peers.

As a manager, it is unlikely that you will want to leave activities such as recruitment, selection, training, or development of your employees entirely to the human resource department. While human resource departments in most companies play a formal role in all the activities we have covered in this chapter, if you want to get the right people and maximize their performance, you will need to be involved in and skilled at these activities as well.

Relegating HR activities to a specific department is an old school of thought and not reflective of today's environment. As business continues to push toward being knowledge based, the effective management of intelligent employees becomes increasingly important. As an executive of an engineering service firm said to us, "I watch the company's assets walk out the door at the close of business each day." From that perspective, effective human resource management becomes a central component of every manager's job.

Key Terms

affirmative action
    programs   (p. 520)
assessment centres   (p. 507)
at-risk compensation   (p. 517)
behaviourally anchored rating
    scales (BARS)   (p. 514)
bona fide occupational
    qualifications (BFOQ)   (p. 521)
broadband systems   (p. 516)
cafeteria-style plans   (p. 518)

career paths   (p. 518)
critical incidents   (p. 516)
cross-functional job
    rotation   (p. 518)
dual-career couples   (p. 518)
expatriate employees   (p. 520)
glass ceiling   (p. 521)
incentive plans   (p. 517)
job analysis   (p. 504)
job design   (p. 512)

job posting   (p. 504)
job sharing   (p. 512)
pay structure   (p. 516)
re-engineering   (p. 513)
structured interview   (p. 507)
360-degree feedback   (p. 514)
unstructured interview   (p. 507)
valid selection technique
    (p. 507)
work simulation   (p. 508)

Test Your Comprehension

1. What are the key human resource activities at which a manager must be skilled?

2. Why is it important to keep the firm's strategy in mind when engaged in HR activities like selection?

3. What are two advantages of part-time or temporary employees in meeting a firm's workforce needs?

4. What are the principal aspects of job analysis?

5. How can job posting help a firm with its internal management of human resources?

6. Describe five effective means of recruiting new employees.

7. What does it mean for a selection technique to be valid?

8. What is the primary difference between structured and unstructured interviews and what effect does this difference have?

9. What is the basic rationale for work sampling as a selection method?

10. Identify three written tests used in selection and describe their validity.

11. Why are reference checks of little use in selection?

12. List the five things that can be done to make orientation programs more effective.

13. Define *re-engineering* and explain its use in organizations.

14. What are the key differences between graphic rating scales and behaviourally anchored rating scales?

15. List seven steps that can be taken to make performance appraisal sessions more effective.

16. Why are organizations moving away from traditional pay structures to more broadband pay structures?

17. What is a cafeteria-style benefit plan?

18. What does it mean to fire someone for cause?

19. What is the purpose of affirmative action programs?

20. What is a BFOQ?

21. What is the difference between quid pro quo and a hostile environment in cases of sexual harassment?

22. Describe three things you can do to improve your capability to manage greater diversity in the workforce.

Apply Your Understanding

1. What do you think will change most dramatically in the future in terms of what it will take to attract young people to companies?

2. Think about the best and worst bosses you've ever had. To what extent did human resource management skills differentiate the two? In particular, which skills?

3. As you look forward to a future management position, what HRM strengths and weaknesses do you feel you have?

4. If you look at your university, what HR activities does it perform well? What are needed improvements?

5. What do you think will be the most challenging HR activities in the future?

Practise Your Capabilities

You are the captain of a firefighting squad consisting of two trucks and 12 firefighters. You have two females in your squad. As firefighters your squad is on duty for 24 hours and then off duty for 24 hours at a time. When on duty you all live together in the firehouse where you eat, sleep, train, relax, and hang out together. Some days are so intense with calls that you do not have time for anything else. Other days by comparison are quite slow.

The effectiveness of your team is a function of skill and trust. The techniques of suppressing a fire or evacuating people from a burning building may be lost on the average person, but the depth of these required skills are vital. A significant amount of trust is also required to be effective. For example, if you were injured in a burning building, you would want to know that your team members would be able to get you out.

In most firehouses, including yours, the addition of women has happened only recently. All women firefighters have to pass the same physical and skill tests given to the men. However, firehouses have traditionally had a strong flavour of male-oriented conversation, humour, and activities such as lifting weights as a means of helping the team bond.

One of your newest female recruits has come to you complaining of a sexually hostile work environment. She complained that the jokes she overhears are full of offensive humour and that several of the guys have offensive pictures inside their lockers. Because the firehouse is an older one, there are not separate locker rooms or showers. Although separate shower times have been scheduled, the recruit also complained that some of the guys had "accidentally" walked in when she was showering because they "forgot" the schedule.

The other female member of the squad, who has been in the unit for nearly a year, disagrees with the description of the environment as sexually hostile, but would not really go into any details or specifics.

1. What actions would you take?

2. Suppose, in talking individually with the guys in the squad, some say that they can see that a couple of the younger, single guys might be a bit "macho" in their conversations among themselves. What would you do if these younger guys report that they feel the new female recruit is simply eavesdropping on private conversations?

3. How would the fact that the new female recruit seems to be as physically strong and more skilled than two of the younger "macho" guys in the squad affect your actions? What would you do differently if she were not a good performer?

Part
Fifteen

Marketing

Chapter 16

Understanding Marketing Processes and Consumer Behaviour

After reading this chapter, you should be able to:

1 Explain the concept of *marketing* and describe the five forces that constitute the *external marketing environment*.

2 Explain the purpose of a *marketing plan* and identify the four components of the *marketing mix*.

3 Explain *market segmentation* and show how it is used in *target marketing*.

4 Explain the purpose and value of *market research*.

5 Describe the key factors that influence the *consumer buying process*.

6 Discuss the three categories of *organizational markets* and explain how *organizational buying behaviour* differs from consumer buying behaviour.

7 Describe the *international* and *small business marketing mixes*.

Taken from *Business*, Seventh Canadian Edition, by Ricky W. Griffin, Ronald J. Ebert, Frederick A. Starke, and Melanie D. Lang.

Why So Serious?

The five Batman movies released between 1989 and 2008 grossed more than $1.6 billion worldwide. It would be understandable, then, if the producers decided to skimp on the marketing budget for film #6. If ever a movie could be expected to market itself, it would be *The Dark Knight*. Instead, the producers teamed with 42 Entertainment, a California-based creator of alternate reality games, to immerse fans in one of the most elaborate viral marketing campaigns ever conceived. The fun began over a year before the movie opened, with the appearance of posters and a website "supporting" one of the film's characters, Harvey Dent, in his campaign for district attorney of Gotham City. Visitors to the website quickly discovered a link to a similar site— www.whysoserious.com—that appeared to have been vandalized by the movie's main villain, the Joker.

The emergence of the Joker set in motion a series of games in which fans vied with one another to solve puzzles. The fastest fans received cellphones that let them access information that led them deeper into the puzzle. Meanwhile, the websites multiplied: fake newspapers with articles like "Batman Stops Mob Melee"; safety tips from the Gotham Police Department; even a link to Betty's House of Pies, a restaurant that plays a small but crucial role in the movie's plot.

The appeal of viral marketing, according to Jonathan Waite, owner of the Alternate Reality Gaming Network, is that "you're not a passive onlooker; you're taking an active role. And any time you take an active role, you're emotionally connecting." Or, as one blogger put it, "I've never been a fan of the Batman series, but this sort of thing makes me want to go see it."

The Dark Knight's innovative marketing campaign helped catapult the movie to a record-breaking box office debut, earning over $158 million in its opening weekend. Domestically and internationally, the film was a great success, earning more than $873 million worldwide. That was more than half the money earned by the previous five Batman movies combined. Was it the innovative marketing tactics or the captivating line-up of stars that contributed to the film's success? We may never know. ◆

How will this help me?

Marketing is a business activity that focuses on providing value to customers so they will want to purchase goods and services that companies offer for sale. If you understand the marketing methods and ideas that are presented in this chapter, you will benefit in two ways: (1) You'll be better prepared to enhance your career by using effective marketing ideas, both as an employee and as a manager; and (2) you'll be a more informed consumer, with greater awareness of how businesses use marketing to influence your purchases.

We start this chapter by looking at how marketing provides value, satisfaction, and utility to customers in order to motivate them to purchase goods and services. We then look at the marketing plan and the components of the marketing mix and discuss market segmentation and how it is used in target marketing. Next, we look at the idea of market research and how this activity helps companies develop and sell goods and services. The chapter concludes with a discussion of the key factors that influence the buying processes of consumers and organizational buyers.

What Is Marketing?

1 Explain the concept of *marketing* and describe the five forces that constitute the *external marketing environment.*

marketing Planning and executing the development, pricing, promotion, and distribution of ideas, goods, and services to create exchanges that satisfy both buyers' and sellers' objectives.

marketing concept The idea that the whole firm is directed toward serving present and potential customers at a profit.

What do you think of when you hear the word **marketing**? If you are like most people, you probably think of advertising for something like detergent or soft drinks. But marketing is more than just advertising. Marketing is "the process of planning and executing the conception, pricing, promotion, and distribution of ideas, goods, and services to create exchanges that satisfy individual and organizational goals."[1]

Because we are all consumers and because we all buy goods and services, we are influenced by the marketing activities of companies that want us to buy their products. But as consumers, we are in fact the essential ingredients in the marketing process. Every day, we express needs for such essentials as food, clothing, and shelter and wants for such non-essentials as entertainment and leisure activities. Our needs and wants are the forces that drive marketing.

The **marketing concept** means that the whole firm is coordinated to achieve one goal—to serve its present and potential customers and to do so at a profit. This concept means that a firm must get to know what customers really want and follow closely the changes in tastes that occur. The various departments of the firm—marketing, production, finance, and human resources—must operate as a system, well coordinated and unified in the pursuit of a common goal—customer satisfaction.

We begin our study of marketing by looking at how marketing focuses on providing value and utility for consumers. We then explore the marketing environment and the development of marketing strategy. Finally, we focus on the four activities that compose the marketing mix: *developing, pricing, promoting,* and *placing products.*

Providing Value and Satisfaction

What attracts buyers to one product instead of another? While our desires for the many goods and services available to us may be unbounded, limited financial resources force most of us to be selective. Accordingly, consumers buy products that offer the best value when it comes to meeting their needs and wants.

Value and Benefits

Value compares a product's benefits with its costs. The benefits of a high-value product are much greater than its costs. Benefits include not only the functions of the product but also the emotional satisfactions associated with owning, experiencing, or possessing it. Every product has costs, including sales price, the expenditure of the buyer's time, and the emotional costs of making a purchase decision. The satisfied buyer perceives the benefits derived from the purchase to be greater than its costs.

value Relative comparison of a product's benefits vs. its costs.

Thus the simple but important ratio for value:

$$\text{Value} = \frac{\text{Benefits}}{\text{Costs}}$$

Marketing strategies focus on increasing value for customers. Marketing resources are deployed to add value to products to satisfy customers' needs and wants. Satisfying customers may mean developing an entirely new product that performs better (provides greater benefits) than existing products. Or it may mean keeping a store open extra hours during a busy season (adding the benefit of greater shopping convenience). Some companies simply offer price reductions (the benefit of lower cost). Customers may also gain benefits from an informational promotion that explains how a product can be used in new ways.

Value and Utility

To understand how marketing creates value for customers, we need to know the kind of benefits that buyers get from a firm's goods or services. Products provide consumers with **utility**—the ability of a product to satisfy a human want or need. Marketing strives to provide four kinds of utility.

utility Ability of a product to satisfy a human want or need.

■ When a company turns out ornaments in time for Christmas, it creates time utility: It makes products available when consumers want them.

■ When a department store opens its annual Christmas department, it creates place utility: It makes products available where customers can conveniently purchase them.

■ When the store sells ornaments, it provides ownership utility by conveniently transferring ownership from store to customer.

■ By making products available in the first place—by turning raw materials into finished ornaments—the ornament maker creates form utility.

Marketing plays a role in all four areas—determining the timing, place, terms of sale, and product features that provide utility and add value for customers. Marketers, therefore, must begin with an understanding of customers' wants and needs. Their methods for creating utility are described in this and the following two chapters.

Goods, Services, and Ideas

The marketing of tangible goods is obvious in everyday life. You walk into a department store and are given a free scented paper strip as an initial product sample of a new perfume. A pharmaceutical company proclaims the virtues of its new cold medicine. Your local auto dealer offers to sell you an automobile with no interest charges for four years. These products—the perfume, the cold medicine, and the car—are all **consumer goods**: products that you, the consumer, buy for personal use. Firms that sell products to consumers for personal consumption are engaged in consumer marketing.

consumer goods Products purchased by individuals for their personal use.

Business Accountability

When Smoke Gets in Your Eyes

In Canada, government restriction on the advertising of cigarettes has a long history. Television advertising of cigarettes has been prohibited since 1971, and various other restrictions (including some rather dramatic label requirements) have come into force since then. Recent legislation discourages tobacco companies from sponsoring sports and cultural events so that they can get their brands prominently displayed to consumers. At a charity dinner in Toronto in 2004, for example, the Rothmans, Benson & Hedges table simply said "anonymous" in spite of the fact that the company had paid thousands of dollars to sponsor the table. Tobacco companies are still allowed to advertise in magazines and newspapers, but the rules are so restrictive they generally don't try anymore. Yves-Thomas Dorval, a spokesman for Imperial Tobacco Canada Ltd., says that since "promotion" is essentially prohibited by law, tobacco companies are focussing on the three other *P*s of marketing (price, place, and product).

Clashes between stop-smoking groups and tobacco companies are common, particularly when tobacco companies appear to be ignoring the spirit of the restrictions that have been placed on them. For example, as part of the TD Canada Trust Toronto Jazz Festival, Imperial Tobacco set up an outdoor smoking lounge in Nathan Phillips Square. The lounge was criticized by the Ontario Tobacco-Free Network, which called on the mayor of Toronto to stop Imperial from using "scantily clad girls" to promote cigarettes on city property.

All of these situations are interesting, but an important question remains: Who is accountable for the negative effects of tobacco use? Government agencies in both Canada and the United States (Health Canada and the American Public Health Association, respectively) seem to take the position that it is the companies who sell cigarettes that bear most of the responsibility. Not surprisingly, cigarette companies argue that because tobacco use is an individual behaviour choice for which potential health risks are well-known, accountability falls to the consumer instead of the producer of the product.

Coalitions of health advocacy groups—including the World Health Organization and other grassroots public health organizations—are insisting that corporate accountability be formally acknowledged. In the United States, the $39 billion in settlement revenues that was given to states during a recent five-year period is cited as tangible recognition of the industry's accountability, but only for after-effects. Not far enough, insist the health advocates, arguing that the more than 400 000 tobacco-related deaths each year in North America are preventable: Companies should also be accountable for effective pre-ventive measures that are absent now and are likely to remain so until more regulation is imposed on them. Tobacco firms, in response, point to several recent court rulings in the United States that denied more than $50 billion in claims brought by health maintenance organizations (HMOs) and insurance companies for reimbursement of tobacco-related health expenses. They point to these cases as supportive of the industry's argument that it is not accountable.

While the issue of accountability simmers, marketing finds itself on both sides of the controversy. Advertising expenditures by Canadian and U.S. tobacco companies have soared to more than $11 billion each year. Health advocates cite "predatory marketing practices" as the industry advertises in youth magazines and develops advertising campaigns targeted at Hispanic, Asian, and other population groups that as yet may not be fully aware of health risks from smoking. Young adults with low incomes and lower education levels are representative of the target-market demographics of smoking. Consider the following statistics:

- The rate of smoking among people who did not complete high school is three times the rate for those with an undergraduate university degree.
- Smoking among pregnant women is 15 times greater for those who did not graduate from high school than it is for those with a university education.
- About one-third of people living below the poverty line are smokers, compared with only one-quarter of those above the poverty line.
- Low-wage workers smoke more than those with high wages.

Health advocates say that tobacco companies have increasingly paid retailers to display tobacco advertising, have used "buy one, get one free" promotions, and have set up promotional racks and giveaways that make cigarettes easier to buy among these targeted smokers.

Marketing by health advocacy groups has embraced "idea-and-information" messages to promote the stop-smoking idea and to appeal for more corporate accountability. The American Legacy Foundation's award-winning TV "truth" campaign debunks the idea that smoking is glamorous and features information about the social costs and health consequences of tobacco. A report by the U.S. National Cancer Institute publicized the idea that "light" cigarettes don't reduce health risks and often simply lead to brand switching rather than quitting. Community-based and grassroots efforts include counter-marketing campaigns to educate higher risk groups—targeted by the tobacco industry—about tobacco's harmful effects. Media ads and promotional materials targeted at ▶

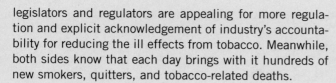

legislators and regulators are appealing for more regulation and explicit acknowledgement of industry's accountability for reducing the ill effects from tobacco. Meanwhile, both sides know that each day brings with it hundreds of new smokers, quitters, and tobacco-related deaths.

Critical Thinking Questions

1. Who is more accountable for the health risks associated with smoking, the tobacco companies or the people who decide to smoke cigarettes? Explain your reasoning.

2. Should tobacco companies be held more accountable for the health problems of low-income, low-education smokers than for the health problems of high-income, high-education smokers?

3. Consider the following statement: *There is overwhelming evidence that cigarettes cause a variety of serious health problems. The Canadian government, in its role of protecting consumers, should therefore ban the sale of cigarettes.* Do you agree or disagree with this statement? Explain your reasoning.

Marketing is also important for **industrial goods**, which are products used by companies to produce other products. Surgical instruments and earth movers are industrial goods, as are such components and raw materials as integrated circuits, steel, and unformed plastic. Firms that sell products to other manufacturers are engaged in industrial marketing.

industrial goods Products purchased by companies to use directly or indirectly to produce other products.

Marketing is also relevant for **services**—intangible products such as time, expertise, or some activity that you can purchase. Service marketing has become a major growth area in Canada. Insurance companies, airlines, investment counsellors, health clinics, and accountants all engage in service marketing, both to individuals and to other companies.

services Intangible products, such as time, expertise, or an activity that can be purchased.

Finally, marketers also promote ideas. Television ads, for example, can remind us that teaching is an honourable profession and that teachers are "heroes." Other ads stress the importance of driving only when sober and the advantages of not smoking.

Relationship Marketing

Although marketing often focuses on single transactions for products, services, or ideas, marketers also take a longer-term perspective. Thus, **relationship marketing** emphasizes lasting relationships with customers and suppliers. Stronger relationships—including stronger economic and social ties—can result in greater long-term satisfaction and customer loyalty.[2]

relationship marketing A type of marketing that emphasizes lasting relationships with customers and suppliers.

Each of these advertisements provides information about a specific product, service, or idea. The soy milk, for example, is a tangible consumer product. The advertisement for the fitness club promotes a service that can be enjoyed. The public service ad promotes the idea of healthy behaviour.

Banks, for example, offer economic incentives to encourage longer-lasting relationships. Customers who purchase more of the bank's products (for example, chequing accounts, savings accounts, and loans) accumulate credits toward free or reduced-price services, such as unlimited monthly transactions. Motorcycle manufacturer Harley-Davidson offers social incentives through the Harley Owners Group (H.O.G.), which gives motorcyclists the opportunity to bond with other riders and to develop long-term friendships. For companies needing assistance and ideas, Loyalty Works designs and manages incentive and loyalty marketing programs. Their programs focus not only on building loyal customers but also on aligning channel partners and employees for an integrated approach to improving relationship marketing.

The Marketing Environment

external environment Outside factors that influence marketing programs by posing opportunities or threats.

Marketing plans, decisions, and strategies are not determined unilaterally by any business—not even by marketers as experienced and influential as Coca-Cola and Procter & Gamble. Rather, they are strongly influenced by powerful outside forces. As you can see in Figure 16.1, any marketing program must recognize the outside factors that compose a company's **external environment**. In this section, we will describe five of these environmental factors: the political/legal, social/cultural, technological, economic, and competitive environments.

Political and Legal Environment

Political activities, both foreign and domestic, have profound effects on business. Legislation on the use of cellphones in cars and legislation on pollution can determine the destinies of entire industries. Marketing managers therefore try to maintain favourable political/legal environments in several ways. For example, to gain public support for their products and activities, marketing uses advertising campaigns for public awareness on issues of local, regional, or national importance. They also lobby and contribute to political candidates (although there are legal restrictions on how much they can contribute). Such activities sometimes result in favourable laws and regulations and may even open new international business opportunities.

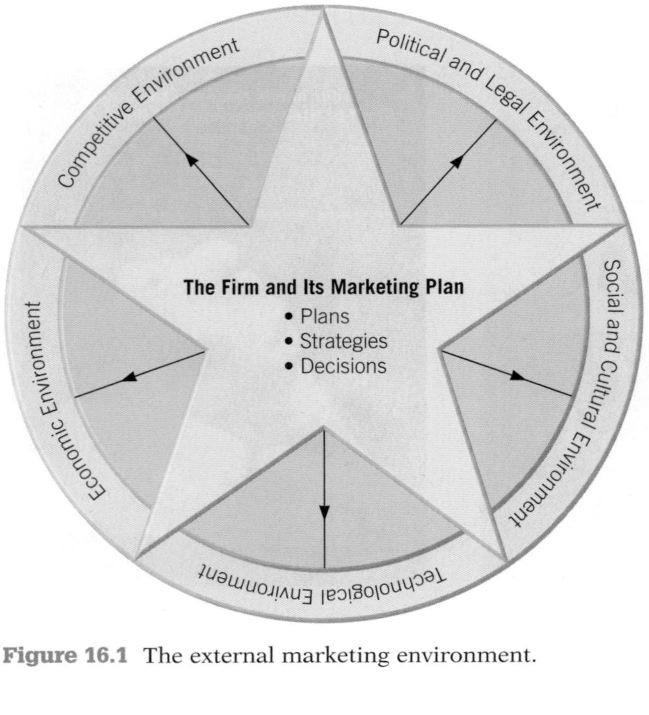

Social and Cultural Environment

More people are working at home, more women are entering the workforce, the number of single-parent families is increasing, food preferences and physical activities reflect the growing concern for healthy lifestyles, and the growing recognition of cultural diversity continues. These and other issues reflect the values, beliefs, and ideas that form the fabric of Canadian society today. These broad attitudes toward issues have direct effects on business. Today, for example, as we continue to insist on a "greener" Canada, we have seen the demise of Freon in air conditioners and increased reliance on recycling materials in the goods that we consume.

Changing social values force companies to develop and promote new products for both indi-

Figure 16.1 The external marketing environment.

vidual consumers and industrial customers. For example, although most of us value privacy, web surfers are discovering that a loss of privacy is often a price for the convenience of internet shopping. Dot-com sites regularly collect personal information that they use for marketing purposes and which they often sell to other firms. Responding to the growing demand for better privacy protection, firms like iNetPrivacy offer such products as Anonymity 4 Proxy software, which allows you to surf the internet anonymously.

Technological Environment

New technologies affect marketing in several ways. Obviously, they create new goods (say, the satellite dish) and services (home television shopping). New products make some existing products obsolete (for example, music downloads are replacing compact discs), and many of them change our values and lifestyles. In turn, they often stimulate new goods and services not directly related to the new technology itself. Cellphones, for example, not only facilitate business communication but also free up time for recreation and leisure.

Consider the phenomenon of DNA "fingerprinting": The O.J. Simpson trial (United States), the Guy Paul Morin case (Canada), and the television show *CSI: Crime Scene Investigation* have made just about everyone aware of its availability to law-enforcement officials. Bear in mind, however, that it is also the focal point of a new industry—one that involves biological science and laboratory analysis and instrumentation as well as criminology. DNA fingerprinting, then, is a product. Along with its technical developments, therefore, it involves marketing decisions—such as pricing and promotion. This has been the case with literally thousands of technological breakthroughs in such fields as genetics, electronics, aeronautics, medicine, information sciences, communications systems, transportation, the internet, and emarketing.

Economic Environment

Economic conditions determine spending patterns by consumers, businesses, and governments. Thus they influence every marketer's plans for product offerings, pricing, and promotional strategies. Among the more significant economic variables, marketers are concerned with inflation, interest rates, recession, and recovery. In other words, they must monitor the general business cycle, which typically features a pattern of transition from periods of prosperity to recession to recovery (return to prosperity). Not surprisingly, consumer spending increases as consumer confidence in economic conditions grows during periods of prosperity. Conversely, spending decreases during low-growth periods, when unemployment rises and purchasing power declines.

Traditionally, analysis of economic conditions focussed on the national economy and the government's policies for controlling or moderating it. Increasingly, however, as nations form more and more economic connections, the global economy is becoming more prominent in the thinking of marketers everywhere.[3]

Marketing strategies are strongly influenced by powerful outside forces. For example, new technologies create new products, such as the Chinese cellphone "filling station" kiosk shown here. Called *shouji jiayouzhan* in Chinese, these kiosks enable customers to recharge their cellphones as they would refuel their cars. The screens on the kiosks also provide marketers with a new way to display ads to waiting customers.

At U.S.-based Wal-Mart, for example, more than 18 percent of all sales revenue comes from the retailer's international division. International sales were up 9.9 percent for 2009, which suggests that some U.S. companies can remain profitable from strong international sales despite a U.S. economic slowdown.

Competitive Environment

In a competitive environment, marketers must convince buyers that they should purchase their products rather than those of some other seller. In a broad sense, because both consumers and commercial buyers have limited

The Greening of Business

Guelph Thinks Green

The first important plastic, celluloid, was discovered in 1869 by the American inventor John W. Hyatt and manufactured by him in 1872. However, plastics did not come into modern industrial use until 1909, after the production of bakelite by the American chemist L.H. Baekeland. The majority of plastics that have been manufactured since then are still in existence. As little as 4 percent of plastics produced have been recycled, and only 2 percent have been incinerated. The remaining masses are either buried, blowing around, sitting in a landfill, or floating in our oceans. Larger populations, continuous consumption, and increased demand for products have taken a terrible toll on our environment. Today's consumers are becoming more aware of their impact on the environment and are starting to look for ways to reduce waste.

A group of University of Guelph students decided to look more closely at a niche market to try to address waste issues. Green World Solutions (GWS) was created by Kwasi Danso, Jonathan Wolff, and Ashley van Herten. This ambitious group recognized that, in order to make a difference to the environment, consumers must become collectively accountable for their actions. Their research brought GWS in contact with the patent holder of a revolutionary additive that makes plastic biodegradable. GWS has aligned itself with the Canadian exclusive holder of this additive and has begun discussions and developing pricing strategies for manufacturing a variety of household items.

One product idea was a pet waste bag but, before the idea could be launched, GWS needed to conduct significant market research to determine competitiveness and product feasibility. What they found was surprising: Most of the biodegradable bags for pet waste were currently on the market were not biodegradable in a landfill. The ideal environment for the breakdown of the materials could only be found in commercial composts. This new revelation did not make sense to GWS, as consumers were led to believe the products currently on the market would compost when left in a garbage can. This new informa-tion—showing that current product offerings needed to be improved—gave GWS the basis for demonstrating to consumers that their product was superior to others already on the market.

GWS is constantly testing this biodegradable additive with additional products in order to help all industries make an easy environmental choice. As this is a new market and environmental interest is at an all-time high, GWS is also spending considerable time and effort in creating a strong, recognizable brand image as an environmentally conscious company. Their name is descriptive and appealing to the targeted audience, and the logo shows imagery of a clean blue and green earth.

Green World Solutions has now incorporated and will shortly be commencing production on biodegradable waste bags. The next steps for GWS are to actively promote environmental consumerism and to spread awareness of the importance of taking action for one's own footprint. Green World Solutions foresees tremendous opportunity in the biodegradable retail plastic industry and has future goals for the consumer household market.

Neil Seldman is a waste recycling expert and president of the Institute for Local Self-Reliance, an organization with a long track record of promoting sustainable communities. He explains that saving money by altering plastic consumption is not limited to supermarkets and retailers through the elimination of plastic bags. According to Seldman, "There is a lot of money to be made in alternative plastics and in managing refillable reusables."

Critical Thinking Questions

1. Research some other plastics products that might benefit from having a biodegradability additive. What do you think would be the biggest barrier to getting the new product in the mainstream market?

2. What are some of the concerns that businesses would have when undertaking new initiatives like those at GWS? What concerns might consumers have?

3. Research the waste management industry. What can you learn from their websites about the benefits of new biodegradable plastics?

resources to spend, every dollar spent to buy one product is no longer available for other purchases. Each marketing program, therefore, seeks to make its product the most attractive; theoretically, a failed program loses the buyer's dollar forever (or at least until it is time for the next purchase decision).

By studying the competition, marketers determine how best to position their own products for three specific types of competition:

- **Substitute products** are dissimilar from those of competitors but can fulfill the same need. For example, your cholesterol level may be controlled with either a physical-fitness program or a drug regimen; the fitness program and the drugs compete as substitute products.

- **Brand competition** occurs between similar products, such as the auditing services provided by large accounting firms like Ernst & Young and KPMG. The competition is based on buyers' perceptions of the benefits of products offered by particular companies.

- **International competition** matches the products of domestic marketers against those of foreign competitors—say, a flight on Swiss International Air Lines vs. Air Canada. The intensity of international competition has been heightened by the formation of alliances such as the European Union and NAFTA.

substitute product A product that is dissimilar from those of competitors but that can fulfill the same need.

brand competition Competitive marketing that appeals to consumer perceptions of similar products.

international competition Competitive marketing of domestic against foreign products.

Strategy: The Marketing Mix

As a business activity, marketing requires management. Although many individuals also contribute to the marketing of a product, a company's **marketing managers** are typically responsible for planning and implementing all the marketing-mix activities that result in the transfer of goods or services to its customers. These activities culminate in the **marketing plan**—a detailed and focussed strategy for gearing marketing activities to meet consumer needs and wants. Marketing, therefore, begins when a company identifies a consumer need and develops a product to meet it.

In planning and implementing strategies, marketing managers develop the four basic components (often called the "four Ps") of the **marketing mix** (see Figure 16.2). In this section, we briefly describe each of those components: *product*, *price*, *place*, and *promotion*.

The importance of these four elements varies, depending on the product that is being sold. Price might play a large role in selling fresh meat but a very small role in selling newspapers. Distribution might be crucial in marketing gasoline but not so important for lumber. Promotion is vital in toy marketing but of little consequence in marketing nails. The product is important in every case, but probably less so for toothpaste than for cars.

> Explain the purpose of a *marketing plan* and identify the four components of the *marketing mix*.
>
> **2**

marketing managers Managers responsible for planning and implementing all the marketing-mix activities that result in the transfer of goods or services to customers.

marketing plan A detailed strategy for gearing the marketing mix to meet consumer needs and wants.

marketing mix The combination of product, pricing, promotion, and distribution strategies used in marketing a product.

Product

Marketing begins with a **product**—a good, a service, or an idea designed to fill a consumer need or want. Conceiving and developing new products is a constant

product A good, service, or idea that satisfies buyers' needs and demands.

Figure 16.2 Choosing the marketing mix for a business.

challenge for marketers, who must always consider the factor of change—changing technology, changing consumer wants and needs, and changing economic conditions. Meeting consumer needs, then, often means changing existing products to keep pace with emerging markets and competitors. Mass-customization allows marketers to provide products that satisfy very specific needs of consumers.

product differentiation The creation of a product or product image that differs enough from existing products to attract consumers.

Producers often promote particular features of products to distinguish them in the marketplace. **Product differentiation** is the creation of a feature or image that makes a product differ enough from existing products to attract consumers. For example, Crest toothpaste has nine different products for different consumer needs. People looking for alternatives in a car might consider an electric vehicle (EV); GM's EV1 used the slogan "A different driving experience," which appealed to early users looking for a unique driving technology that also helps the environment.

Price

price That part of the marketing mix concerned with choosing the appropriate price for a product to meet the firm's profit objectives and buyers' purchasing objectives.

Price refers not only to the actual amount of money that consumers must pay for a product or service but also to the total value of things that consumers are willing to give up in return for being able to have the benefits of the product or service. For example, if a person wants to own a Chrysler 300, that person may have to take money out of a savings account to pay for the car. The value of the interest that would have been earned on the savings account is part of the value that the customer gives up to own the car. From the seller's perspective, determining the best price at which to sell a product is often a balancing act. On the one hand, prices must support a variety of costs—operating, administrative, research, and marketing costs. On the other hand, prices can't be so high that consumers turn to competitors' products. Successful pricing means finding a profitable middle ground between these two requirements.

Both low- and high-price strategies can be effective in different situations. Low prices, for example, generally lead to larger sales volumes. High prices usually limit market size but increase profits per unit. High prices may also

Jann Wenner started *Rolling Stone* magazine in 1967, and it's been the cash cow of Wenner Media ever since. In 1985, Wenner bought *Us* magazine and set out to compete with *People*, perhaps the most successful magazine ever published. Wenner's latest strategy calls for greater differentiation between the two products. *People* is news driven, reporting on ordinary people as well as celebrities, and Wenner intends to punch up *Us* with more coverage of celebrity sex and glitter. So far, he hasn't been successful. *People* reaches 3.7 million readers, *Us* about 900 000.

attract customers by implying that a product is of high quality. We discuss pricing in more detail in Chapter 18.

Place (Distribution)

In the marketing mix, place refers to **distribution**. Placing a product in the proper outlet—say, a retail store—requires decisions about several activities, all of which are concerned with getting the product from the producer to the consumer. Decisions about warehousing and inventory control are distribution decisions, as are decisions about transportation options.

Firms must also make decisions about the channels through which they distribute products. Many manufacturers, for instance, sell goods to other companies that, in turn, distribute them to retailers. Others sell directly to major retailers such as Sears, Wal-Mart, or Safeway. Still others sell directly to final consumers. We explain distribution decisions further in Chapter 18.

Promotion

The most highly visible component of the marketing mix is **promotion**, which refers to techniques for communicating information about products. The most important promotional tools include advertising, personal selling, sales promotions, and public relations. One example of a promotional tactic used to entice consumers is the loyalty program. Rupert Duchesne, CEO of Group Aeroplan Inc., is convinced that loyalty marketing is boundaryless, and he has identified four components of loyalty: travel loyalty, financial services loyalty, retail loyalty, and data analytics (getting information on where consumers travel, how much they spend, and which stores they frequent).[4] We describe promotional activities more fully in Chapter 17.

Product, price, place, and promotion focus on the seller's perspective. From the buyer's perspective, each of the four Ps provides a certain benefit. In effect, the seller's four Ps are a mirror image of the buyer's four Cs: customer solution (product), customer cost (price), customer convenience (place), and customer communication (promotion).[5]

Apple's latest iPhone features an application that allows travellers to wirelessly map an entire city layout.

distribution That part of the marketing mix concerned with getting products from the producer to the buyer, including physical transportation and choice of sales outlets.

promotion Techniques for communicating information about products.

Target Marketing and Market Segmentation

Marketing managers long ago recognized that they cannot be "all things to all people." People have different tastes, different interests, different goals, different lifestyles, and so on. The marketing concept's recognition of consumers' various needs and wants has led marketing managers to think in terms of target marketing. **Target markets** are groups of people with similar wants and needs.

Target marketing clearly requires **market segmentation**, dividing a market into categories of customer types or "segments." For example, Mr. Big & Tall sells to men who are taller and heavier than average. Certain special interest magazines are oriented toward people with specific interests (see Table 16.1). Once they have identified market segments, companies may adopt a variety of product strategies. Some firms decide to provide a range of products to the market in an attempt to market their products to more than one segment. For example, General Motors of Canada offers compact cars, vans, trucks, luxury cars, and sports cars with various features and prices. Its strategy is to provide an automobile for nearly every segment of the market.

In contrast, some businesses restrict production to one market segment. Rolls-Royce understands that only a relatively small number of people are

Explain *market segmentation* and show how it is used in *target marketing*.	**3**

target market Any group of people who have similar wants and needs and may be expected to show interest in the same product(s).

market segmentation Dividing a market into categories according to traits customers have in common.

Table 16.1 Magazines with Specific Target Audiences

Accounting	Fishing/Hunting
CAmagazine	*Canadian Fly Fisher*
CGA Magazine	*Outdoor Canada*
CMA Management	*B.C. Outdoors Sport Fishing*
Agriculture	**Automotive**
Agro-Nouvelles	*Aftermarket Canada*
Meat & Poultry Magazine	*Bodyshop*
Country Life in B.C.	*World of Wheels*
Sports	**Boating**
Cycle Canada	*Boating Business*
Chalk and Cue	*Canadian Boating*
Athletics Canada	*Porthole Magazine*
Gardening	**Music**
Canadian Gardening	*CHART Magazine*
The Gardener for the Prairies	*CODA Magazine*
Gardening Life	*Opus*

willing to pay $310 000 for exclusive touring limousines. Rolls, therefore, makes no attempt to cover the entire range of possible products; instead, it markets to only a very small segment of the total automobile buyers market. In contrast, U.S. retailer Target has deals with Mossimo Giannulli and Isaac Mizrahi. Through these partnerships, says Target vice-president Trish Adams, "our guests have learned, and come to expect, that high fashion doesn't have to mean high prices." The key to luxury today lies in creating an emotional rapport between the consumer and the product.[6]

Table 16.2 shows how a marketer of home electronics equipment might segment the radio market. Note that segmentation is a strategy for analyzing consumers, not products. The analysis in Table 16.2, for example, identifies consumer users—joggers, commuters, and travellers. Only indirectly, then, does it focus on the uses of the product itself. In marketing, the process of fixing, adapting, and communicating the nature of the product itself is called positioning.

Table 16.2 Possible Segmentation of the Radio Market

Segmentation	Product/Target Market
Age	Inexpensive, unbreakable, portable models for young children
	Inexpensive equipment—possibly portable—for teens
	Moderate-to-expensive equipment for adults
Consumer attitude	Sophisticated components for audio buffs
	All-in-one units in furniture cabinets for those concerned with room appearance
Product use	Miniature models for joggers and commuters
	"Boom box" portables for taking outdoors
	Car stereo systems for travelling
	Components and all-in-one units for home use
Location	Battery-powered models for use where electricity is unavailable
	AC current for North American users
	DC current for other users

Identifying Market Segments

By definition, the members of a market segment must share some common traits or behaviours that will affect their purchasing decisions. In identifying market segments, researchers look at geographic, demographic, psychographic, and product-use variables.

Geographic Variables

In some cases, where people live affects their buying decisions. The heavy rainfall in British Columbia prompts its inhabitants to purchase more umbrellas than does the climate in Arizona's desert. Urban residents have less demand for pickup trucks than do their rural counterparts. Sailboats sell better along both coasts than they do in the prairie provinces. **Geographic variables** are the geographical units, from countries to neighbourhoods, that may be considered in a segmentation strategy.

geographic variables
Geographical units that may be considered in a segmentation strategy.

These patterns affect marketing decisions about what products to offer, at what price to sell them, how to promote them, and how to distribute them. For example, consider the marketing of down parkas in rural Saskatchewan. Demand will be high, price competition may be limited, local newspaper advertising may be very effective, and the best location may be one easily reached from several small towns.

Although the marketability of some products is geographically sensitive, others enjoy nearly universal acceptance. Coca-Cola, for example, gets more than 70 percent of its sales from markets outside the United States. It is the market leader in Great Britain, China, Germany, Japan, Brazil, and Spain. By contrast, Pepsi earns 78 percent of its income from the United States. Coke's chief competitor in most countries is not Pepsi but a local soft drink.

Demographic Variables

Demographic variables describe populations by identifying characteristics such as age, income, gender, ethnic background, marital status, race, religion, and social class. These are objective criteria that cannot be altered. Marketers must work with or around them. Table 16.3 lists some demographic market

demographic variables
Characteristics of populations that may be considered in developing a segmentation strategy.

Table 16.3 Demographic Market Segmentation	
Age	Under 5; 5–11; 12–19; 20–34; 35–49; 50–64; 65+
Education	Grade school or less; some high school; graduated high school; some college or university; college diploma or university degree; advanced degree
Family life cycle	Young single; young married without children; young married with children; older married with children under 18; older married without children under 18; older single; other
Family size	1, 2–3, 4–5, 6+
Income	Under $9000; $9000–$14 999; $15 000–$25 000; over $25 000
Nationality	Including but not limited to African, Asian, British, Eastern European, French, German, Irish, Italian, Latin American, Middle Eastern, and Scandinavian
Race	Including but not limited to Inuit, Asian, black, and white
Religion	Including but not limited to Buddhist, Catholic, Hindu, Jewish, Muslim, and Protestant
Sex	Male, female
Language	Including but not limited to English, French, Inuktitut, Italian, Ukrainian, and German

"I'd get out of children and into older people."

segments. Depending on the marketer's purpose, a segment can be a single classification (aged 20–34) or a combination of categories (aged 20–34, married with children, earning $25 000–$34 999). Foreign competitors, for example, are gaining market share in auto sales by appealing to young buyers (under age 30) with limited incomes (under $30 000). While companies such as Hyundai, Kia, and Daewoo are winning entry-level customers with high-quality vehicles and generous warranties, Volkswagen targets under-35 buyers with its entertainment-styled VW Jetta.[7]

Another important demographic variable is ethnicity. Canada's great ethnic diversity requires companies to pay close attention to ethnicity as a segmentation variable. For example, Rogers Communication Inc.'s television advertising campaign for its Bollywood Oye! video-on-demand service is designed to promote its business to South Asian communities in Canada. Rogers currently has 78 multicultural channels in more than 20 languages and wants to be a leader in customizing services to suit specific ethnic groups. Visible minorities in Canada control $76 billion in annual buying power, and to be effective in multicultural marketing, companies must really understand the underlying values that ethnic minority customers hold.[8]

Psychographic Variables

psychographic variables Psychological traits that a group has in common, including motives, attitudes, activities, interests, and opinions.

Members of a market can also be segmented according to such **psychographic variables** as lifestyle, opinions, interests, and attitudes. One company that is using psychographic variables to revive its brand is Burberry, whose plaid-lined gabardine raincoats have been a symbol of British tradition since 1856. After a recent downturn in sales, Burberry is repositioning itself as a global luxury brand, like Gucci and Louis Vuitton. The strategy calls for luring top-of-the-line, fashion-conscious customers. Burberry pictures today's luxury-product shopper as a world traveller who identifies with prestige fashion brands and monitors social and fashion trends in *Harper's Bazaar*.[9] Robert Polet, chief executive of the Gucci Group, agrees with this strategy. "We're not in the business of selling handbags. We are in the business of selling dreams."[10]

Psychographics are particularly important to marketers because, unlike demographics and geographics, they can sometimes be changed by marketing efforts. Many companies have succeeded in changing at least some consumers' opinions by running ads highlighting products that have been improved directly in response to consumer desires. For example, Las Vegas began courting the gay community a few years ago as part of a broader effort to target a range of minority audiences. Studies showed that the gay and lesbian travel market was among the most lucrative. According to research from Community Marketing Inc., a gay and lesbian market research company, gay and lesbian travel accounts for $55 billion of the overall U.S. travel market.[11]

Product-Use Variables

product-use variables The ways in which consumers use a product, the benefits they expect from it, their reasons for purchasing it, and their loyalty to it.

The term **product-use variables** refers to the ways in which consumers use a product, the benefits they expect from it, their reasons for purchasing it, and

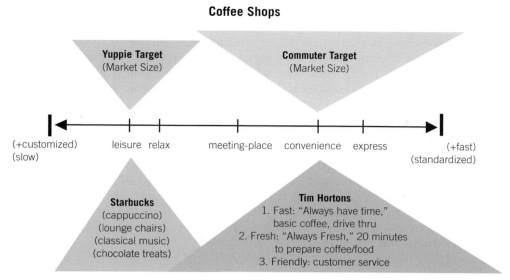

Figure 16.3 Product positioning.

their loyalty to it.[12] A women's shoemaker might identify three segments—wearers of athletic, casual, and dress shoes. Each segment is looking for different benefits in a shoe. A woman buying an athletic shoe may not care about its appearance but may care a great deal about arch support and traction in the sole. A woman buying a casual shoe will want it to look good and feel comfortable. A woman buying a dress shoe may require a specific colour or style and may even accept some discomfort. Speaking of shoes, when Nike—the leader in the $15.5 billion athletic footwear industry—found that women's footwear accounted for about one-third of industry sales but generated only about one-fifth of Nike's business, they changed their strategy and introduced a marketing campaign that focussed on differences between the way men and women think about sports and the way they shop for clothing. According to Nike marketers, women are more interested in image trends and active lifestyles than in athletic competition and sports celebrities.

Whatever basis is used for segmenting a market, care must be taken to position the product correctly. A product's position refers to the important attributes that consumers use to assess the product. For example, a low-priced car like the Ford Focus tends to be positioned on the basis of economy, while a Porsche is positioned in terms of high performance. In Figure 16.3, the product positioning chart shows that Tim Hortons emphasizes a standardized product and provides fast service to people in a hurry, while Starbucks provides more customized products in more leisurely surroundings.

Market Segmentation: A Caution

Segmentation must be done carefully. A group of people may share an age category, income level, or some other segmentation variable, but their spending habits may be quite different. Look at your friends in school. You may all be approximately the same age, but you have different needs and wants. Some of you may wear cashmere sweaters, while others wear sweatshirts. The same holds true for income. University professors and truck drivers frequently have about the same level of income. However, their spending patterns, values, tastes, and wants are generally quite different.

In Canada, the two dominant cultures—English and French—have historically shown significant differences in consumer attitudes and behaviour.

Researchers have found, for example, that compared with English Canadians, French Canadians are more involved with home and family, attend ballet more often, travel less, eat more chocolate, and are less interested in convenience food. But this does not necessarily mean that companies must have different product offerings for Quebec. The adoption process for new products varies from one individual to another according to socio-economic and demographic characteristics.

Marketers are very interested in a person's system of values because values can have a big influence on an individual's tendency to adopt a new product. One study using business school students from France, Quebec, and the rest of North America identified three types of consumers: the conservatives, the dynamics, and the hedonists. The conservatives are typically those consumers who are least likely to adopt new products, while the hedonists (pleasure seekers) are categorized as innovators and are the most likely to adopt a new product. Those individuals in the dynamics category are somewhat likely to adopt new products, but are often seen as imitators.[13]

Market Research

4 Explain the purpose and value of *market research*.

market research The systematic study of what buyers need and how best to meet those needs.

Market research—the study of what buyers need and how best to meet those needs—can address any element in the marketing mix. Business firms spend millions of dollars each year as they try to figure out their customers' habits and preferences. Market research can greatly improve the accuracy and effectiveness of market segmentation.[14] For example, comic books have historically not been of much interest to girls, but DC Comics and Marvel Entertainment are convinced they can change that after observing the success of upstart companies like Tokyopop and Viz Media, who produce translated Japanese comics called *manga*. These companies have succeeded in attracting female readers by having "girl-friendly" content and by distributing their products in both comic book shops and mainstream bookstores. The total comics and graphic novel market was $640 million in 2007, and manga comics accounted for $200 million of that total.[15]

The place of market research in the overall marketing process is shown in Figure 16.4. Ultimately, its role is to increase the firm's competitiveness by understanding the relationship among the firm's customers, its marketing variables, and its marketing decisions. Market researchers use a variety of methods to obtain, interpret, and use information about customers. They determine the kinds of information that are needed for decisions on marketing strategy, goal setting, and target-market selection. In doing so, they may conduct studies on how customers will respond to proposed changes in the current marketing mix. One researcher, for example, might study consumer response to an experimental paint formula (new product). Another might explore the response to a price reduction (new price) on calculators. A third might check response to a proposed advertising campaign (new promotion). Marketers can also try to learn whether customers are more likely to purchase a given product in a specialty shop or on the internet (new place).

Most companies will benefit from market research, but they need not do the research themselves. Using a new tool and a virtual store developed by Kimberly-Clark Corp., Safeway stores asked participants to walk through the "store" and shop for items. The shoppers were actually in a virtual store and were surrounded by three screens showing a typical store aisle. A retina-tracking device recorded their every glance. When Safeway tested the display inside its stores, sales of items in that section increased.[16]

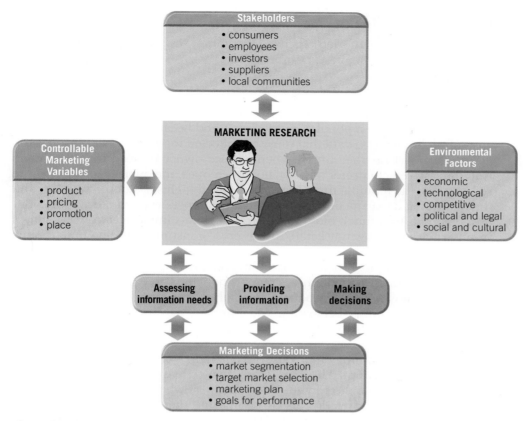

Figure 16.4 Market research and the marketing process.

The Research Process

Market research can occur at almost any point in a product's existence. Most commonly, however, it is used when a new or altered product is being considered. These are the five steps in performing market research:[17]

1. Study the current situation. What is the need and what is being done to meet it at this point?

2. Select a research method. In choosing a method, marketers must bear in mind the effectiveness and costs of different methods.

3. Collect data. **Secondary data** is information already available as a result of previous research by the firm or other agencies. For example, Statistics Canada publishes a great deal of data that is useful for business firms. Using secondary data can save time, effort, and money. But in some cases secondary data are unavailable or inadequate, so **primary data**—new research by the firm or its agents—must be obtained. Hostess Frito-Lay, the maker of Doritos, spent a year studying how to best reach its target market—teenagers. The researchers hung around shopping malls, schools, and fast-food outlets to watch teens.[18]

4. Analyze the data. Data are not useful until they have been organized into information.

5. Prepare a report. This report should include a summary of the study's methodology and findings. It should also identify alternative solutions (where appropriate) and make recommendations for the appropriate course of action.

secondary data Information already available to market researchers as a result of previous research by the firm or other agencies.

primary data Information developed through new research by the firm or its agents.

Research Methods

The four basic types of methods used by market researchers are observation, surveys, focus groups, and experimentation.

Observation

observation A market research technique involving viewing or otherwise monitoring consumer buying patterns.

Probably the oldest form of market research is simple **observation** of what is happening. It is also a popular research method because it is relatively low in cost, often drawing on data that must be collected for some other reason, such as reordering. In earlier times, when a store owner noticed that customers were buying red children's wagons, not green ones, the owner reordered more red wagons, the manufacturer's records showed high sales of red wagons, and the marketing department concluded that customers wanted red wagons. But observation is now much more sophisticated. For example, electronic scanners in supermarkets allow marketers to "observe" consumers' preferences rapidly and with tremendous accuracy.

Another example: Procter & Gamble sent video crews into about 80 households in the United Kingdom, Germany, and China to capture people's daily routines and how they use products. By analyzing the tapes, P&G hoped to get insights into consumer behaviour. The company can use this information to develop new products to satisfy needs that consumers didn't even know they had.[19]

Using video equipment to observe consumer behaviour is called video mining. It is being adopted by many stores in North America, which use hidden cameras to determine the percentage of shoppers who buy and the percentage who only browse. Stores do this by comparing the number of people taped with the number of transactions the store records. Some consumer organizations are raising privacy concerns, since shoppers are unaware that they are being taped.[20]

Surveys

survey A market research technique based on questioning a representative sample of consumers about purchasing attitudes and practices.

Sometimes marketers need to ask questions about new marketing ideas or about how well the firm is doing its marketing tasks. One way to get answers is by conducting a **survey**. When Sara Lee Corp. acquired Kiwi shoe polish, they surveyed 3500 people in eight countries about shoe care needs. They learned that people do not care as much about the shine on their shoes as they do about how fresh and comfortable they are on the inside. The firm has since unveiled several new products under the Kiwi name and is doing quite well.[21]

Because no firm can afford to survey everyone, marketers must be careful to get a representative group of respondents when they do surveys. They must also construct the survey questions so that they get honest answers that address the specific issue being researched. Surveys can be expensive to carry out and may vary widely in their accuracy.

In the past, surveys have been mailed to individuals for their completion, but online surveys are now gaining in popularity because the company gets immediate results and because the process is a less intrusive way of gathering data. At Hudson's Bay Co., customers can use online surveys to tell the company how happy or unhappy they are about the service they received at any of the Bay's department stores. The company can then make any changes that are needed to keep customers happy. The Bay used to hire mystery shoppers to find out how well it was serving the public, but that program ended when the online survey system was adopted.[22]

Focus Groups

focus group A market research technique involving a small group of people brought together and allowed to discuss selected issues in depth.

Many firms also use **focus groups**, where six to 15 people are brought together to talk about a product or service. A moderator leads the group's discussion, and employees from the sponsoring company may observe the proceedings from behind a one-way mirror. The people in the focus group are not usually told which company is sponsoring the research. The comments of people in the focus group are taped, and then researchers go through the data looking for common themes.

When Procter & Gamble was developing a new air freshener, it asked people in focus groups to describe their "desired scent experience." They discovered that people get used to a scent after about half an hour and no longer notice it. P&G used this information to develop a "scent player," called Febreze Scentstories, which gives off one of five different scents every 30 minutes.[23] Focus groups at farm implement manufacturer John Deere have suggested many improvements in farm tractors, including different ways to change the oil filter and making the steps to the tractor cab wider.[24]

Consumers don't necessarily express their real feelings when participating in focus groups or when filling out surveys. They may say one thing and think something else. This has led marketers to look at other ways of gathering information. Sensory Logic Inc., for example, studies facial expressions and eye movements to determine what consumers really think of a product.[25]

Experimentation

The last major form of market research, **experimentation**, also tries to get answers to questions that surveys cannot address. As in science, experimentation in market research attempts to compare the responses of the same or similar individuals under different circumstances. For example, a firm trying to decide whether to include walnuts in a new candy bar probably would not learn much by asking people what they thought of the idea. But if it made some bars with nuts and some without and then asked people to try both, the responses could be very helpful.[26]

experimentation A market research technique in which the reactions of similar people are compared under different circumstances.

Data Warehousing and Data Mining

Almost everything you do leaves a trail of information about you. Your preferences in movie rentals, television viewing, internet sites, and groceries; the destinations of your phone calls, your credit-card charges, your financial status; personal information about age, gender, marital status, and even health—these are just some of the items in a huge cache of data that are stored about

As they watch a sitcom with six commercial breaks, these women are participating in a marketing research experiment. The researchers think that their results will be more accurate than questionnaire and focus group responses because they're getting them straight from the subjects' brains. A spike in a subject's left prefrontal cortex means that she probably likes a product or an ad. A spike in the right prefrontal cortex is bad news for the advertiser. Using machines designed to detect brain tumours, researchers can even tell which part of an ad makes a dent in the subject's long-term memory.

Retailers such as Wal-Mart rely on data warehousing and mining to keep shelves stocked with in-demand merchandise.

each of us. The collection, storage, and retrieval of such data in electronic files is called **data warehousing**. For marketing researchers, the data warehouse is a gold mine of clues about consumer behaviour.[27]

The Uses of Data Mining

After collecting information, marketers use **data mining**—the application of electronic technologies for searching, sifting, and reorganizing pools of data—to uncover useful marketing information and to plan for new products that will appeal to target segments in the marketplace.[28] Using data mining, for example, the insurance company Farmers Group discovered that a sports car is not an exceptionally high insurance risk if it's not the only family car. The company thus issued more liberal policies on Corvettes and Porsches and so generated more revenue without significantly increasing payout claims. Among retailers, Wal-Mart has long been a data-mining pioneer, maintaining perhaps the world's largest privately held data warehouse. Data include demographics, markdowns, returns, inventory, and other data for forecasting sales and the effects of marketing promotions.[29]

data warehousing Process of collecting, storing, and retrieving data in electronic form.

data mining Application of electronic technologies for searching, sifting, and reorganizing data to collect marketing information and target products in the marketplace.

Understanding Consumer Behaviour

Market research in its many forms can be of great help to marketing managers in understanding how the common traits of a market segment affect consumers' purchasing decisions. Why do people buy DVDs? What desire are they fulfilling? Is there a psychological or sociological explanation for why consumers purchase one product and not another? These questions and many others are addressed in the area of marketing known as **consumer behaviour**, which focuses on the decision process by which customers come to purchase and consume a product or service.

consumer behaviour The study of the process by which customers come to purchase and consume a product or service.

Influences on Consumer Behaviour

To understand consumer behaviour, marketers draw heavily on the fields of psychology and sociology. The result is a focus on four major influences on consumer behaviour: psychological, personal, social, and cultural. By identifying the four influences that are most active, marketers try to explain consumer choices and predict future purchasing behaviour.

- Psychological influences include an individual's motivations, perceptions, ability to learn, and attitudes.

- Personal influences include lifestyle, personality, economic status, and life-cycle stage.

- Social influences include family; opinion leaders (people whose opinions are sought by others); and reference groups such as friends, co-workers, and professional associates.

- Cultural influences include culture (the "way of living" that distinguishes one large group from another), subculture (smaller groups, such as ethnic groups, with shared values), and social class (the cultural ranking of groups according to criteria such as background, occupation, and income).

Although these factors can have a strong impact on a consumer's choices, their effect on actual purchases is sometimes weak or negligible. Some consumers, for example, regularly purchase certain products because they are satisfied with their performance. Such people (for example, users of Craftsman tools) are less subject to influence and stick with preferred brand names. On the other hand, the clothes you wear and the food you eat often reflect social and psychological influences on your consuming behaviour.

The Consumer Buying Process

Researchers who have studied consumer behaviour have constructed models that help marketing managers understand how consumers come to purchase products. Figure 16.5 presents one such model. At the heart of this and similar models is an awareness of the psychosocial influences that lead to consumption. Ultimately, marketing managers use this information to develop marketing plans.

> Describe the key factors that influence the *consumer buying process.*
>
> **5**

Problem/Need Recognition

The buying process begins when a consumer becomes aware of a problem or need. After strenuous exercise, you may recognize that you are thirsty and need refreshment. After the birth of twins, you may find your one-bedroom

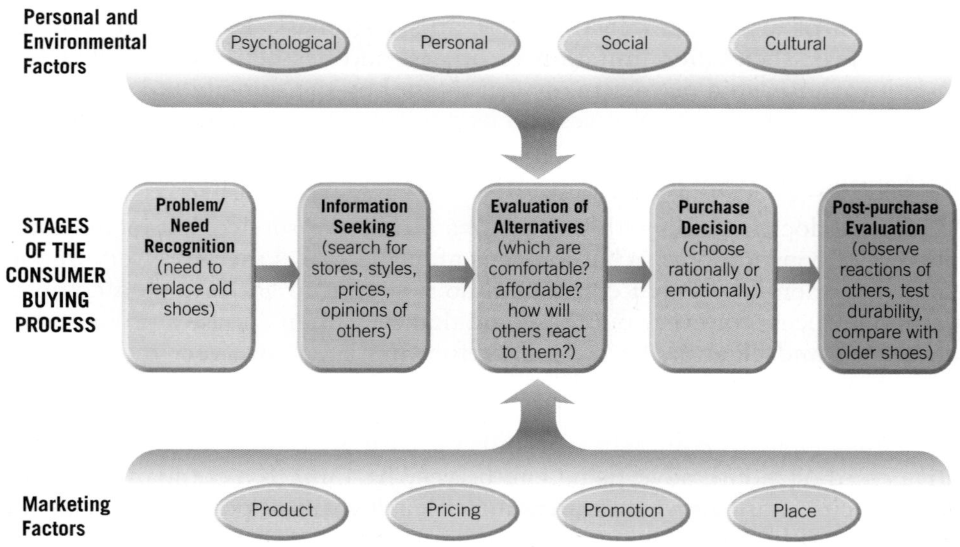

Figure 16.5 Consumer buying process.

apartment too small for comfort. After standing in the rain to buy movie tickets, you may decide to buy an umbrella. Need recognition also occurs when you have a chance to change your purchasing habits. For example, the income from your first job after graduation will allow you to purchase items that were too expensive when you were a student. You may also discover a need for professional clothing, apartment furnishings, and a car. Credit cards and credit issuing companies recognize this shift and market their credit cards to graduates.

Information Seeking

Having recognized a need, consumers seek information. This search is not always extensive. If you are thirsty, you may ask where the pop machine is, but that may be the extent of your information search. Other times you simply rely on your memory for information. Before making major purchases, most people seek information from personal sources, marketing sources, public sources, and experience. For example, if you move to a new town, you will want to find out who is the best local dentist, physician, hair stylist, butcher, or pizza maker. To get this information, you may check with personal sources such as acquaintances, co-workers, and relatives. Before buying an exercise bike, you may read the latest issue of *Consumer Reports*—a public source of consumer ratings—on such equipment. You may also ask market sources such as the sales clerk or rely on direct experience. For example, you might test ride the bike to learn more before you buy. The internet has become an important source of information; almost three quarters (73 percent) of Canadians aged 16 and older rely on the internet to gather information.[30]

Evaluation of Alternatives

If you are in the market for a set of golf clubs, you probably have some idea of who produces clubs and how they differ. You may have accumulated some of this knowledge during the information-seeking stage and combined it with what you knew before. Based on product attributes such as colour, taste, price, prestige, quality, and service record, you will decide which product best meets your needs.

Purchase Decisions

rational motives Those reasons for purchasing a product that involve a logical evaluation of product attributes such as cost, quality, and usefulness.

emotional motives Those reasons for purchasing a product that involve non-objective factors.

Ultimately, you make a purchase decision. You may decide to defer the purchase until a later time or you may decide to buy now. "Buy" decisions are based on rational and emotional motives. **Rational motives** involve a logical evaluation of a product's cost, quality, and usefulness. **Emotional motives** include fear, sociability, imitation of others, and aesthetics. You might buy mouthwash to avoid ostracism, or you might buy the same brand of jeans as your friends. Emotional motives can lead to irrational purchase decisions.

Post-purchase Evaluations

Marketing does not stop with the sale of a product or service, but includes the process of consumption. What happens after the sale is therefore very important. Marketers know that consumers do not want to go through a complex decision process for every purchase and that they often choose a product they have used and liked in the past. Therefore marketers are very motivated to keep consumers happy so they will make repeat purchases of the product. Unfortunately for marketers, when consumers are not satisfied with a purchase they typically complain to friends rather than to the company. This negative word-of-mouth advertising can be very harmful to a company. In more extreme cases, unhappy consumers may file a lawsuit or publicly criticize the product and the company.

People can complain about products or services at www.complaints.com. Dissatisfied customers can have a very negative impact on a company's marketing effort. **Word-of-mouth marketing (also known as buzz marketing)** is therefore a very powerful marketing tool. It can, however, be the most devastating, since businesses cannot control it.[31]

word-of-mouth marketing (also buzz marketing) Opinions about the value of products, passed among consumers in informal discussions.

Organizational Marketing and Buying Behaviour

Buying behaviour is observable daily in the consumer market, where marketing activities, including buying-selling transactions, are visible to the public. Equally important, however, but far less visible, are organizational (or commercial) markets—organizations that buy goods and services to be used in creating and delivering consumer products. Marketing to these buyers involves different kinds of organizational markets, and buying behaviours that are quite different from those found in consumer markets.

Discuss the three categories of *organizational markets* and explain how *organizational buying behaviour* differs from consumer buying behaviour.

6

Organizational Markets

Organizational or commercial markets fall into three categories: *industrial, reseller,* and *government/institutional markets*.

Industrial Market

The **industrial market** includes businesses that buy goods falling into one of two categories—goods to be converted into other products and goods that are used up during production. This market includes farmers, manufacturers, and some retailers. For example, Seth Thomas purchases electronics, metal components, and glass to make clocks for the consumer market. The company also buys office supplies, tools, and factory equipment—items never seen by clock buyers—to be used during production.

industrial market Businesses that buy goods to be converted into other products that will be sold to ultimate consumers.

Reseller Market

Before products reach consumers, they pass through a **reseller market** consisting of intermediaries, including wholesalers and retailers, who buy the finished goods and resell them (wholesalers and retailers are discussed in Chapter 18). Retailers like department stores, drugstores, and supermarkets buy clothing, appliances, foods, medicines, and other merchandise for resale to the consumer market. Retailers also buy such services as maintenance, housekeeping, and communications.

reseller market Intermediaries like wholesalers and retailers who buy finished products and resell them.

Government and Institutional Market

Federal, provincial, and municipal governments purchase millions of dollars worth of computer equipment, buildings, paper clips, and other items. The **institutional market** consists of non-governmental organizations, such as hospitals, churches, museums, and charitable organizations, which also compose a substantial market for goods and services. Like organizations in other commercial markets, these institutions use supplies and equipment, as well as legal, accounting, and transportation services.

institutional market Non-government organizations such as hospitals, churches, and schools.

Organizational Buying Behaviour

In some respects, industrial buying behaviour bears little resemblance to consumer buying practices. Differences include the buyers' purchasing skills and an emphasis on buyer-seller relationships.

Differences in Buyers

Unlike most consumers, organizational buyers are professional, specialized, and expert (or at least well-informed).

- As professionals, organizational buyers are trained in methods for negotiating purchase terms. Once buyer-seller agreements have been reached, buyers also arrange for formal contracts.

- As a rule, industrial buyers are company specialists in a line of items. As one of several buyers for a large bakery, for example, you may specialize in food ingredients. Another buyer may specialize in baking equipment (industrial ovens and mixers), while a third may buy office equipment and supplies.

- Industrial buyers are often experts about the products they buy. On a regular basis, organizational buyers study competing products and alternative suppliers by attending trade shows, by reading trade magazines, and by conducting technical discussions with sellers' representatives.

Differences in the Buyer-Seller Relationship

Consumer-seller relationships are often impersonal, short-lived, one-time interactions. In contrast, industrial situations often involve frequent and enduring buyer-seller relationships. The development of a long-term relationship provides each party with access to the technical strengths of the other as well as the security of knowing what future business to expect. Thus, a buyer and a supplier may form a design team to create products of benefit to both. Accordingly, industrial sellers emphasize personal selling by trained representatives who understand the needs of each customer.

The International Marketing Mix

7 Describe the *international* and *small business marketing mixes.*

Marketing products internationally means mounting a strategy to support global business operations. This is no easy task, since foreign customers may differ from domestic buyers in language, customs, business practices, and consumer behaviour. When companies decide to go global, marketers must consider how each element of the marketing mix might be affected.

International Products

Some products (for example, Budweiser, Coca-Cola, and Marlboro) can be sold in many different countries with virtually no changes, but often only a redesigned (or completely different) product will meet the needs of foreign buyers. To sell its computers in Japan, for example, Apple had to develop a Japanese-language operating system.

Mattel, the maker of Barbie dolls, is just one company that has learned some interesting lessons about the international market. When it conducted focus groups with kids in dozens of countries, it found that worldwide demand existed for many of the same products. Mattel discovered, in essence, that children have similar tastes no matter where they live. Mattel's experience with its famous Barbie doll is illustrative. The dolls sold in Japan, for example, had always had black hair and Asian features, not the blonde, blue-eyed appearance of Barbie dolls sold in North America. This seemed to make intuitive sense, but now Mattel is finding that the original Barbie doll is selling just as well in Asia as in North America.

Mattel's experience is not unique. Various other companies that sell products to international consumers have found the same phenomenon:

- The Harry Potter book series already had a global following when the first Harry Potter movie was released.

- Harlequin Enterprises, which sells millions of romance novels in many different countries, uses the same book covers around the world. The pictures of Caucasians on the book covers do not seem to deter customers in other countries from buying Harlequin romance novels.

- Sports is another universal language. Basketball stars like Michael Jordan and Shaquille O'Neal have high name recognition overseas. In a poll of Chinese students in rural Shaanxi province, Michael Jordan tied with former Chinese premier Zhou En-lai for the title "World's Greatest Man."

But there are still important differences between countries, and these cannot be ignored. For example, German children aren't attracted to action toys the way Canadian and American children are. There are also differences even within basic product lines. American kids, for example, want NASCAR toy cars, while European children want Formula One models.

International Pricing

When pricing for international markets, marketers must handle all the considerations of domestic pricing while also considering the higher costs of transporting and selling products abroad. Some products cost more overseas than in Canada because of the added costs of delivery. Due to the higher costs of buildings, rent, equipment, and imported meat, a McDonald's Big Mac that sells for C$2.99 in Canada has a price tag of over C$10 in Japan. In contrast, products like jet airplanes are priced the same worldwide because delivery costs are incidental; the huge development and production costs are the major considerations regardless of customer location.

International Promotion

Some standard Canadian promotional techniques do not always succeed in other countries. In fact, many Europeans believe that a product must be inherently shoddy if a company does any hard-sell advertising. International marketers must also be aware that cultural differences can cause negative reactions to products that are advertised improperly. Some Europeans, for example, are offended by television commercials that show weapons or violence. Advertising practices are regulated accordingly. Quebec is the only province, and in fact the only jurisdiction in North America, in which commercial advertising to persons under 13 is generally prohibited. Meanwhile, liquor and cigarette commercials that are banned from Canadian and U.S. television are thriving in many Asian and European markets.

Symbolism, too, is a sometimes-surprising consideration. In France, for instance, yellow flowers suggest infidelity. In Mexico, they are signs of death—an association made in Brazil with the colour purple. Clearly, product promotions must be carefully matched to the customs and cultural values of each country.

International Distribution

In some industries, delays in starting new distribution networks can be costly. Therefore, companies with existing distribution systems often enjoy an advantage over new businesses. Several companies have gained advantages in

Feathercraft is a small British Columbia manufacturer that has been successful selling kayaks in the Japanese market.

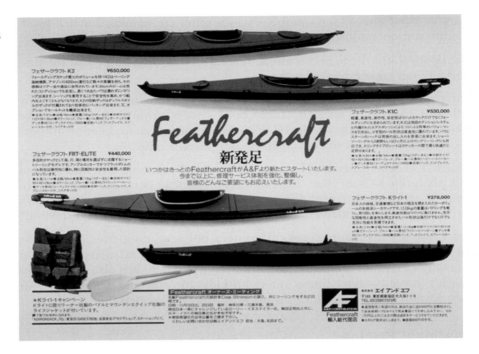

time-based competition by buying existing businesses. Procter & Gamble, for example, saved three years of start-up time by buying Revlon's Max Factor and Betrix cosmetics, both of which are well-established in foreign markets. P&G can thus immediately use these companies' distribution and marketing networks for selling its own brands in the United Kingdom, Germany, and Japan.

Other companies contract with foreign firms or individuals to distribute and sell their products abroad. Foreign agents may perform personal selling and advertising, provide information about local markets, or serve as exporters' representatives. But having to manage interactions with foreign personnel complicates a marketing manager's responsibilities. In addition, packaging practices in Canada must sometimes be adapted to withstand the rigours of transport to foreign ports and storage under conditions that differ radically from domestic conditions.

Small Business and the Marketing Mix

As we noted in Chapter 3, far more small businesses fail than succeed, yet many of today's largest firms were yesterday's small businesses. McDonald's began with one restaurant, a concept, and one individual (Ray Kroc) who had tremendous foresight. Behind the success of many small firms lies a skilful application of the marketing concept and careful consideration of each element in the marketing mix.

Small Business Products

Some new products—and firms—are doomed at the start simply because few consumers want or need what they have to offer. Too often, enthusiastic entrepreneurs introduce products that they and their friends like, but they fail to estimate realistic market potential. Other small businesses offer new products before they have clear pictures of their target segments and how to reach them. They try to be everything to everyone, and they end up serving no one well. In contrast, sound product planning has paid off for many small firms.

"Keep it simple" is a familiar key to success—that is, fulfill a specific need and do it efficiently.

Small Business Pricing

Haphazard pricing that is often little more than guesswork can sink even a firm with a good product. Most often, small business pricing errors result from a failure to project operating expenses accurately. Owners of failing businesses have often been heard to utter statements like "I didn't realize how much it costs to run the business!" and "If I price the product high enough to cover my expenses, no one will buy it!" But when small businesses set prices by carefully assessing costs, many earn very satisfactory profits—sometimes enough to expand or diversify.

Small Business Promotion

Successful small businesses plan for promotional expenses as part of start-up costs. Some hold down costs by taking advantage of less expensive promotional methods. Local newspapers, for example, are sources of publicity when they publish articles about new or unique businesses. Other small businesses have succeeded by identifying themselves and their products with associated groups, organizations, and events. Thus a custom-crafts gallery might join with a local art league and local artists to organize public showings of their combined products.

Small Business Distribution

Problems in arranging distribution can make or break small businesses. Perhaps the most critical aspect of distribution is facility location, especially for new service businesses. The ability of many small businesses—retailers, veterinary clinics, and gourmet coffee shops—to attract and retain customers depends partly on the choice of location.

In distribution, as in other aspects of the marketing mix, however, smaller companies may have advantages over larger competitors, even in highly complex industries. They may be quicker, for example, in applying service technologies. Everex Systems Inc. sells personal computers to wholesalers and dealers through a system the company calls "Zero Response Time." Phone orders are reviewed every two hours so that the factory can adjust assembly to match demand.

Test yourself on the material for this chapter at **www.pearsoned.ca/mybusinesslab**.

Summary of
Learning Objectives

1. **Explain the concept of *marketing* and describe the five forces that constitute the *external marketing environment*.** *Marketing* is the process of planning and executing the conception, pricing, promotion, and distribution of ideas, goods, and services to create exchanges that satisfy individual and organizational goals. Products provide consumers with *utility*—the ability of a product to satisfy a human want or need. Marketing can be used to promote consumer and industrial goods and services, as well as ideas. The *external environment* consists of the outside

▶

forces that influence marketing strategy and decision making. The *political/legal environment* includes laws and regulations, both domestic and foreign, that may define or constrain business activities. The *social and cultural environment* is the context within which people's values, beliefs, and ideas affect marketing decisions. The *technological environment* includes the technological developments that affect existing and new products. The *economic environment* consists of the conditions—such as inflation, recession, and interest rates—that influence both consumer and organizational spending patterns. Finally, the *competitive environment* is the environment in which marketers must persuade buyers to purchase their product rather than that of their competitors.

2. **Explain the purpose of a** *marketing plan* **and identify the four components of the** *marketing mix.* Marketing managers plan and implement all the marketing activities that result in the transfer of products to customers. These activities culminate in the *marketing plan*—a detailed strategy for focussing the effort to meet consumer needs and wants. Marketing managers rely on the four Ps of marketing, or the *marketing mix:* (1) *Product:* Marketing begins with a product, a good, a service, or an idea designed to fill a consumer need or want. Product differentiation is the creation of a feature or image that makes a product differ from competitors. (2) *Pricing:* Pricing is the strategy of selecting the most appropriate price at which to sell a product. (3) *Place* (Distribution): All distribution activities are concerned with getting a product from the producer to the consumer. (4) *Promotion:* Promotion refers to techniques for communicating information about products and includes advertising.

3. **Explain** *market segmentation* **and show how it is used in** *target marketing.* Marketers think in terms of *target markets*—groups of people who have similar wants and needs and who can be expected to show interest in the same products. Target marketing requires *market segmentation*—dividing a market into customer types or "segments." Four of the most important influences are (1) *geographic variables* (the geographical units that may be considered in developing a segmentation strategy); (2) *demographic variables* (population traits such as age, income, gender, ethnic background, marital status, race, religion, and social class); (3) *psychographic variables* (such as lifestyles, interests, and attitudes); and (4) *product-use variables* (the ways in which consumers use a product, the benefits they expect from it, their reasons for purchasing it, and their loyalty to it).

4. **Explain the purpose and value of** *market research. Market research* is the study of what buyers need and of the best ways to meet those needs. This process involves a study of the current situation, the selection of a research method, the collection of data, the analysis of data, and the preparation of a report that may include recommendations for action. The four most common research methods are *observation, surveys, focus groups,* and *experimentation.*

5. **Describe the key factors that influence the** *consumer buying process. Consumer behaviour* is the study of the process by which customers decide to purchase products. The result is a focus on four major influences on consumer behaviour: (1) *Psychological influences* include motivations, perceptions, ability to learn, and attitudes; (2) *Personal influences* include lifestyle, personality, and economic status; (3) *Social influences* include family, opinion leaders, and such reference groups as friends, co-workers, and professional associates; (4) *Cultural influences* include culture, subculture, and social class. By identifying which influences are most active in certain circumstances, marketers try to explain consumer choices and predict future purchasing behaviour.

6. **Discuss the three categories of** *organizational markets* **and explain how** *organizational buying behaviour* **differs from** *consumer buying behaviour. Organizational (or commercial)* markets, in which organizations buy goods and services to be used in creating and delivering consumer products, fall into three categories: (1) *The industrial market* consists of businesses that buy goods to be converted into other products or goods that are used during production. (2) Before products reach consumers, they pass through a *reseller market* consisting of intermediaries that buy finished goods and resell them. (3) The third category is *government and institutional markets.* Federal, provincial, and local governments buy durable and nondurable products. The institutional market consists of non-governmental buyers such as hospitals, churches, museums, and charities. Organizational buying behaviour differs from consumer buyer behaviour in two major ways: (1) *Differences in buyers:* Organizational buyers are professionals trained in arranging buyer-seller relationships and negotiating purchase terms. They are usually specialists in a line of items and are often experts about the products they are buying. (2) *Differences in the buyer-seller relationship:* Whereas consumer-seller relationships are often fleeting, one-time interactions, industrial situations often involve frequent, enduring buyer-seller relationships.

7. **Describe the** *international* **and** *small business marketing mixes.* When they decide to go global, marketers must reconsider each element of the marketing mix. (1) *International products:* Whereas some products can be sold abroad with virtually no changes, sometimes only a

redesigned product will meet the needs of foreign buyers. (2) *International pricing:* When pricing for international markets, marketers must consider the higher costs of transporting and selling products abroad. (3) *International distribution:* In some industries, companies have gained advantages by buying businesses already established in foreign markets. (4) *International promotion:* Occasionally, a good ad campaign can be transported to another country virtually intact. Quite often, however, standard Canadian promotional tactics do not succeed in other countries.

Behind the success of many small firms lies an understanding of each element in the marketing mix. (1) *Small business products:* Understanding of what customers need and want has paid off for many small firms. (2) *Small business pricing:* Haphazard pricing can sink even a firm with a good product. Small business pricing errors usually result from failure to project operating expenses accurately. But when small businesses set prices by carefully assessing costs, many earn satisfactory profits. (3) *Small business distribution:* Perhaps the most critical aspect of distribution is facility location. The ability of many small businesses to attract and retain customers depends partly on the choice of location. (4) *Small business promotion:* Successful small businesses plan for promotional expenses as part of start-up costs. Some take advantage of less expensive promotional methods.

PEARSON
mybusinesslab
To improve your grade, visit the MyBusinessLab website at www.pearsoned.ca/mybusinesslab. This online homework and tutorial system allows you to test your understanding and generates a personalized study plan just for you. It provides you with study and practice tools directly related to this chapter's content. MyBusinessLab puts you in control of your own learning!

Key Terms

brand competition   (p. 539)
consumer behaviour   (p. 550)
consumer goods   (p. 533)
data mining   (p. 550)
data warehousing   (p. 550)
demographic variables   (p. 543)
distribution   (p. 541)
emotional motives   (p. 552)
experimentation   (p. 549)
external environment   (p. 536)
focus group   (p. 548)
geographic variables   (p. 543)
industrial goods   (p. 535)
industrial market   (p. 553)
institutional market   (p. 553)

international competition   (p. 539)
market research   (p. 546)
market segmentation   (p. 541)
marketing   (p. 532)
marketing concept   (p. 532)
marketing managers   (p. 539)
marketing mix   (p. 539)
marketing plan   (p. 539)
observation   (p. 548)
price   (p. 540)
primary data   (p. 547)
product   (p. 539)
product differentiation   (p. 540)
product-use variables   (p. 544)
promotion   (p. 541)

psychographic variables   (p. 544)
rational motives   (p. 552)
relationship marketing   (p. 535)
reseller market   (p. 553)
secondary data   (p. 547)
services   (p. 535)
substitute product   (p. 539)
survey   (p. 548)
target market   (p. 541)
utility   (p. 533)
value   (p. 533)
word-of-mouth (buzz) marketing
   (p. 553)

Questions for Analysis

1. Why and how is market segmentation used in target marketing?

2. Select an everyday product (books, CDs, skateboards, dog food, or shoes, for example). Show how different versions of your product are aimed toward different market segments. Explain how the marketing mix differs for each segment.

3. Select another product and describe the consumer buying process that likely occurs before it is purchased.

4. Explain the key differences between consumer buying behaviour and organizational buying behaviour.

5. What is the value to consumers of things like loyalty cards and discount cards? Why would companies offer consumers such cards?

6. Why has the in-store use of hidden cameras become so popular? Is this "video mining" ethical? If not, how could it be made more acceptable?

7. If you were starting your own small business, what are the key marketing pitfalls you would try to avoid?

8. Select a product or service that you regularly use. Explain the relative importance of each of the four elements in the marketing mix (product, price, promotion, and place). Then select another product and determine the extent to which the relative emphasis changes. If it changed, why did it change?

Application Exercises

1. Interview the marketing manager of a local business. Identify the degree to which this person's job is focussed on each element in the marketing mix.

2. Select a product made by a foreign company and sold in Canada. What is the product's target market? What is the basis on which the target market is segmented? Do you think that this basis is appropriate? How might another approach, if any, be beneficial? Why?

Building Your Business Skills

Dealing in Segments and Variables

The Purpose of the Assignment

To encourage students to analyze the ways in which various market segmentation variables affect business success.

The Situation

You and four partners are thinking of purchasing a heating and air conditioning (H/AC) dealership that specializes in residential applications priced between $2000 and $40 000. You are now in the process of deciding where that dealership should be. You are considering four locations: Miami, Florida; Toronto, Ontario; Vancouver, British Columbia; and Dallas, Texas.

Assignment

Step 1

Working with four classmates (your partnership group), do library research to learn how H/AC makers market their residential products. Check for articles in *The Globe and Mail*, *Canadian Business*, *The Wall Street Journal*, and other business publications.

Step 2

Continue your research. This time, focus on the specific marketing variables that define each prospective location. Check Statistics Canada data at your library and on the internet and contact local chambers of commerce (by phone and via the internet) to learn about the following factors for each location:

- geography
- demography (especially age, income, gender, family status, and social class)
- psychographic variables (lifestyles, interests, and attitudes)

Step 3

Meet with group members to analyze which location holds the greatest promise as a dealership site. Base your decision on your analysis of market segment variables and their effects on H/AC sales.

Questions for Discussion

1. Which location did you choose? Describe the market segmentation factors that influenced your decision.

2. Identify the two most important variables you believe will have the greatest impact on the dealership's success. Why are these factors so important?

3. Which factors were least important in your decision? Why?

4. When equipment manufacturers advertise residential H/AC products, they often show them in different climate situations (in winter, summer, or high-humidity conditions). Which market segments are these ads targeting? Describe these segments in terms of demographic and psychographic characteristics.

Exercising Your Ethics: Team Exercise

A Big Push for Publicity

The Situation

Marsden Corp. is known as a "good citizen" and prides itself on the publicity it receives from sponsoring civic programs and other community projects. The company's executive vice-president, Jane Martin, has just been named chairperson of annual fundraising for the Coalition for Community Services (CCS), which is a group of community services organizations that depend on voluntary donations. In the highly visible chairperson's role, Martin has organized the support of officials at other firms to ensure that the fundraising target is met or surpassed.

The Dilemma

Martin began a meeting of 30 department managers to appeal for 100 percent employee participation in CCS giving in the fundraising drive. As follow-up the week before the drive officially started, she met with each manager, saying "I expect you to give your fair share and for you to ensure that all your employees do likewise. I don't care what it takes, just do it. Make it clear that employees will at least donate cash. Even better, get them to sign up for weekly payroll deductions to the CCS fund because it nets more money than one-time cash donations."

An hour after meeting with Martin, Nathan Smith was both surprised and confused. As a newly appointed department manager, he was unsure how to go about soliciting donations from his 25 subordinates. Remembering Martin's comment, "I don't care what it takes, just do it," Nathan wondered what to do if someone did not give. Personally, too, he was feeling uneasy. How much should he give? With his family's pressing financial needs, he would rather not give money to CCS. He began to wonder if his donation to CCS would affect his career at Marsden.

Team Activity

Assemble a group of four to five students and assign each group member to one of the following roles:

- Nathan Smith (employee)
- Jane Martin (employer)
- director of CCS (customer)
- Marsden stockholder (investor)
- Marsden CEO (use this role only if your group has five members)

Questions for Discussion

1. Before discussing the situation with your group, and from the perspective of your assigned role, do you think there are any ethical issues with Marsden's fundraising program? If so, write them down.

2. Before discussing the situation with your group, and from the perspective of your assigned role, are any problems likely to arise from Marsden's fundraising program? If so, write them down.

3. Together with your group, share the ethical issues you identified. Then share the potential problems you listed. Did the different roles you were assigned result in different ethical issues and problems?

4. For the various ethical issues that were identified, decide as a group which one is the most important for Marsden to resolve. Likewise, for potential problems that were identified, which is the most important one for Marsden?

5. From an ethical standpoint, what does your group recommend be done to resolve the most important ethical issue? How should the most important problem be resolved? Identify the advantages and drawbacks of your recommendations.

For additional cases and exercise material, go to **www.pearsoned.ca/mybusinesslab**.

Concluding Case 16-1

Dell-ivering on Consumer Electronics

There's a good reason why competitors don't match Dell's success in selling computers. From the outset, Michael Dell's vision recognized a market with different kinds of potential users—the business sector, non-business organizations such as schools and other institutions, as well as the growing segment of PC users in homes—each with different needs and resources. Choosing to focus more on the business and institutional segments, Dell envisioned an unheard-of combination of service features for PC customers: high-quality products, lowest cost, ease in ordering and receiving products, live interaction with expert technical assistance for building a PC "the way you like it," super-fast deliveries, and after-the-sale communications to ensure product performance and keep users informed about upgrades to enhance their PCs.

The market response has been overwhelming, resulting in Dell's dominant position as industry leader. Dell's unique vision for integrating all stages of marketing—developing the product and related services, pricing it, selling to consumers directly via telephone or the internet, delivering directly to customers from efficient manufacturing plants, and using promotional messages for product awareness and use—are unmatched by competitors that are struggling to copy Dell's way of doing business.

As if that were not enough to cause headaches in the PC industry, Dell recently launched itself into the broader consumer electronics market for even greater revenue growth. Giant electronics retailers like Best Buy may soon be looking over their shoulders if Dell's customer-friendly business model is successfully carried over into flat-panel TVs, DVD recorders, MP3 players, and digital cameras. Plans even call for opening an online music-downloading store on the same popular website where PC users buy other Dell products. The potential range of products is enormous because music, movies, photos, and other entertainment are increasingly digital and, thus, are becoming compatible extensions of PCs. Commenting on the company's new thrust, chairman Michael Dell states, "The whole new ballgame is these worlds [computing and consumer electronics] converging, and that's a world we're comfortable in."

But will they necessarily succeed? Some experts think the crossover into consumer products could be a problem because, unlike Gateway's and Hewlett-Packard's focus on the consumer segment, Dell's primary PC focus has been on business and institutional markets. A classic example of a failed crossover is IBM's ill-fated attempt in the 1980s to woo consumers with its downsized PC Jr.

With hugely successful sales and technical support for business customers, IBM never understood the consumer market, and Big Blue's efforts proved a mismatch that ended with the withdrawal of the PC Jr. from the marketplace in the late 1990s. But Dell CEO Kevin Rollins says such risks are largely offset by Dell's brand familiarity in both business and consumer markets.

Price is equally important to consumers, says industry analyst Peter Kastner. "Dell's no-middleman model almost guarantees a value-based price," and that means more intense price-for-performance competition than exists now in consumer electronics. The bottom line for consumers will be lower prices while other firms in the industry try to imitate Dell's low-price, high-value business model.

For masses of electronics lovers, Dell's entry comes as welcome news. Consumers will see prices fall as competition drives down profit margins and prices. Retailers and etailers, in contrast, will experience what might be called "reverse sticker shock." Sellers currently enjoying net profit margins of 25 to 40 percent on consumer electronics may have to survive on the modest 10 percent margin to which PC sellers are accustomed. That leaves lots of room for Dell to push electronics prices down, gain large volume sales, and reap high total profits while competing firms in the industry try to imitate its low-price, high-value business model.

Dell's promotional efforts first are aimed at building brand familiarity by dramatically increasing daily interaction with consumers. Electronics lovers from Canada, Japan, the United States, and Brazil who are accustomed to such brands as Sony and Samsung may be surprised to see the Dell name on TVs, pocket PCs, MP3 players, and the Digital Jukebox, among its upcoming line of products. Winning this massive customer base is essential for high-volume sales, and Dell plans to attract consumers to its new Dell.com website with Music Store, an online music-downloading service that will include the major labels and performers. Unlike Apple's iTunes service, which is available only to users of Apple products, Dell's downloading version is open to the public, not just to Dell PC users. It has the additional advantage of working with Microsoft Windows and, promises CEO Kevin Rollins, at prices below those of competitors.

The new Dell.com is reportedly designed to appeal to consumers and to set it apart from Dell's business products. Its main screen will provide easy ways to find not only electronics equipment but also music, radio stations, photos, and other media, all of which capitalize on the logical linkages between home computers and consumer electronics. More and more consumers in the "digital

▶

▶

home" are viewing DVDs, video clips, games, and photos through their computers. So Dell plans to sell related media products the same way it sells other PC peripherals such as printers.

Because consumer buying habits don't change overnight, no one at Dell expects to dominate the electronics market the way it does in PCs, where it leads with a 31.4 percent market share and 21.8 percent growth rate in sales worldwide (while Hewlett-Packard's market share decreased to 25 percent). Before buying an expensive flat-screen TV, for example, most consumers want to see the quality of its picture first-hand rather than buying through catalogues or a website. As Forrester Research analyst Jed Kolko notes, "With video products it's harder to demonstrate value online." Consumers hold similar reservations about the sound quality of audio products. Only with the passage of time can Dell establish relationships with consumers by informing them, by convincing them to switch over from an already-crowded list of competing sellers—including newcomers such as Apex Digital, which is already underpricing more established brands—and by demonstrating superior product value in the Dell brand. Both industry experts and electronics consumers will soon witness Dell's bottom-line results in this new venture.

Questions for Discussion

1. What social and technological factors have influenced the growth of the consumer electronics market?

2. What demographics would you use to define the flat-screen TV target market? How about the target market for home PCs?

3. Identify the main factors favouring success for Dell's crossover into consumer electronics. What prominent factors suggest major problems or even failure for this crossover attempt?

4. Applying the textbook's definition for product value to Dell's plans, what are the "benefits" in Dell's consumer electronics offerings? What are the "costs"?

5. Applying the textbook's definition for product value to electronics retailers such as Best Buy, what are the "benefits" and "costs"? How well or poorly does Dell's product value ratio stack up against its competitors' ratios?

An Old Company with New Potential

Bell Canada is Canada's largest communications company and offers consumers solutions to all of their communication needs. Bell has responded to the ever-changing needs of consumers by providing telephone services, wireless communications, high-speed internet, digital television, and VOIP. It is no surprise, then, that with the changing scale of entertainment technologies Bell would open an online video store.

The idea behind this is not new, but the new service offering at Bell Canada certainly is. Currently, iTunes offers the same service, but at present the service rights do not extend into Canada. Bell believes that an online video store is another way to offer affordable convenience to consumers looking for entertainment options, and the corporation is looking at ways to expand their entertainment categories. At this time, the Bell Video Store offers approximately 1500 movies, TV shows, documentaries, and music videos available for download at any time on any day of the week. Part of the success can be attributed to partnership agreements with Paramount Digital Entertainment for first-time release of its digital content in Canada and with Canadian broadcaster Corus Entertainment for its animated content. Collectively, this team of entertainment and communication experts may change the way consumers enjoy video entertainment.

Not everyone is overjoyed with Bell's announcement to launch an online video store, and most of the skepticism surrounds the untimely launch of the store in the midst of a legal battle that involves one of Bell's competitors in the United States. While Bell has been working on the development of the new service offering for quite some time, the choice to open the online store now poses unavoidable comparisons to the FCC investigation of Comcast in the United States, where a company called Vuze accused Comcast of inhibiting its legal P2P (peer-to-peer) video sales, while at the same time offering their own video-on-demand through its cable system. To counteract such a comparison, Bell claims that 5 percent of its users generate 60 percent of its total traffic and that 60 percent of this total traffic is P2P that is negatively affecting 95 percent of all customers. The Canadian Radio-television and Telecommunications Commission (CRTC) wants to see the calculations, and it has requested that Bell Canada provide full disclosure. "Provide full rationale and evidence in support of Bell Canada's view that 95 percent of its customers were being negatively affected," says the first of the CRTC interrogatories. Bell believes that this is simply procedural and that soon everyone, including the critics, will see the full benefit this new service has to offer.

Bell is the first online service in Canada to offer download-to-own movies the same day they become available in retail stores and download-to-rent shortly thereafter. Kevin Crull, president of Bell Residential Services, explains that "the Video Store is another first for Bell, offering 24/7 access to the most hit videos in Canada without ever having to leave the comfort and convenience of home." The actual benefit will be experienced by the consumer, who will have the opportunity to enjoy a wide selection of entertainment options. Bell currently provides a download-to-own service starting at $4.99 and a download-to-rent service starting at $1.99. With download-to-rent, customers have access to their movie for 30 days after they have downloaded it, but once they hit play, they have just 24 hours to view the film (as many times as they like). This service also offers consumers the opportunity to use the Bell Video Store media player on a PC or laptop and to be able to begin viewing their video only a few moments after purchasing it. Also, consumers with a Media Center PC will be able to use their remote to watch Bell Video Store content right on their TV.

While this feature sounds advantageous for consumers, what are the implications for those who use a Mac? Similar to all new offerings, this new launch has certain product limitations that will inhibit full market integration. Bell Video Store does not work with Macs or Linux machines because the site uses Windows Media DRM, and, surprisingly, not even the creators of the store are happy with this situation.

One interesting and amusing comment made on the FAQ page of the Bell Video Store explicitly states that while the two systems are not compatible, "We're hoping that one day Microsoft, Apple, the content owners, and video sites like ours will have a big group hug and we can all share content... Please share any ideas on how we can get MAC and PC to play nice together." While these limitations seem large, the software does work with all XP or Vista software, and the content can also be used with Xbox 360 or be downloaded to other portable devices. Because iTunes is not currently being offered in Canada, consumers will have more options when choosing online video content. There is tremendous added value to consumers because "the Bell Video Store will also bring additional value to Bell digital TV subscribers," explains Crull. New experiences will be created through heightened product delivery options of online viewing.

When any company updates its product offerings, there are bound to be comments and criticisms, but what Bell has demonstrated is a keen desire to offer its consumers a vast array of entertainment options in a highly competitive atmosphere. Some critics argue that Bell is using its significant size to gain a foothold in this new

▶

market. Only time will tell whether this new launch is a smart move for Bell, or if the old saying holds any truth—the bigger they are, the harder they fall.

Questions for Discussion

1. Assess the relative importance of the four Ps in Bell's new venture.

2. What are market strengths and weaknesses of Bell's new venture? Create a SWOT analysis and explain your findings. (Review the SWOT material in Chapter 1 before answering this question.)

3. Are there any product limitations that might affect consumer willingness to adopt the new technology?

4. How important is timing and PR with this type of new product launch?

Chapter 17

Developing and Promoting Goods and Services

After reading this chapter, you should be able to:

1 Explain the definition of a product as a *value package*.

2 Describe the new product development process and trace the stages of the *product life cycle*.

3 Explain the importance of *branding*, *packaging*, and *labelling*.

4 Identify the important objectives of *promotion* and discuss the considerations in selecting a *promotional mix*.

5 Discuss the most important *advertising* strategies and describe the key *advertising media*.

6 Outline the tasks involved in *personal selling* and list the steps in the personal selling process.

7 Describe the various types of *sales promotions*, and distinguish between *publicity* and *public relations*.

8 Describe the development of international and small business *promotion* strategies.

Taken from *Business*, Seventh Canadian Edition, by Ricky W. Griffin, Ronald J. Ebert, Frederick A. Starke, and Melanie D. Lang.

Psst! Did You Hear the Latest?

Word-of-mouth advertising is probably the oldest form of advertising. Ever since the first brand names developed hundreds of years ago, consumers have been exchanging information with each other about the positive and negative features of the products they buy. In the eighteenth and nineteenth centuries, marketing was very fragmented and most products were promoted only in local areas at retailers like the general store. Word-of-mouth advertising was therefore mostly confined to local or regional markets because existing technology did not allow consumers to be well connected.

By the 1930s, the development of radio, and later television, allowed businesses to market their products nationwide. Word of mouth did not disappear, but it was overshadowed by mass marketing. More recently, word-of-mouth advertising has again gained prominence, partly because of the internet. PQ Media predicts that spending in the United States on word-of-mouth advertising will reach $3.7 billion by 2011 because companies recognize the emerging importance of social networking sites like YouTube and Facebook and of personal blogs.

Word-of-mouth advertising is relatively cheap, and the messages that it carries are trusted by those who hear them. A Nielsen study showed that 78 percent of consumers trust word-of-mouth messages. Newspapers were trusted by 63 percent of consumers, television by 56 percent, and text ads on cellphones by only 18 percent.

Word of mouth is a double-edged sword. If consumers are spreading positive messages about a product, sales will likely soar. For example, Nike spent very little money advertising its Presto line of stretchy sneakers, but kids and teens spread the word to each other about the shoes and the fashion statement they could make by having them. If, however, consumers are spreading negative messages, sales will suffer. The movie *Snakes on a Plane*, which starred Samuel L. Jackson, bombed at the box office because most of the word of mouth focussed on how bad the film was. And when Pontiac gave away one of its new G6 models on the Oprah Winfrey show, the company hoped that the publicity would generate significant word of mouth among potential customers. But sales did not materialize.

Procter & Gamble—which is famous for its television commercials—is very active in word-of-mouth advertising. When the company introduced a new cleaning product called Dawn Direct Foam, it provided information about the product to Vocalpoint, a group of 450 000 brand "evangelists" who talk up P&G products. The new product launch was a success. P&G has another word-of-mouth unit called Tremors, which includes over 200 000 teenagers who are active on social networks. These individuals are often early adopters of new products. P&G is planning to use Canada as a testing ground for online advertising spending, especially in light of the fact that an Ipsos Reid survey showed that Canadian consumers spend 39 percent of their media consumption time on the internet, 26 percent on TV, and 11 percent on print media. This large percentage of media consumption time spent on the internet means great opportunities for word of mouth.

Many other companies also recognize the importance of word-of-mouth advertising:

■ The Sprinkles Cupcake chain is expanding even during a recession by choosing locations in affluent areas and then relying on word of mouth to bring customers in.

■ Lee Jeans recruited 1000 "agents" who each received a pair of One True Fit jeans and a promotional kit that included a list of people to target with information about the Lee brand.

■ Algordonza is a Swiss-based company that makes artificial diamonds from the carbon found in the ashes of people who have been cremated. It sells about 700 diamonds each year to friends and relatives of the deceased. The company does not advertise but relies on word of mouth to make people aware of its product.

■ Volkswagen Canada cancelled a scheduled advertising campaign for its new Eos automobile because the cars were rapidly being sold due to positive word of mouth about the car among consumers.

■ Google did no marketing of its Gmail; instead they gave out Gmail accounts to only certain "power users" and the resulting word of mouth increased demand for the service.

A group called The Influencers is Canada's first word-of-mouth community. It has created its own word-of-mouth campaign for promoting word-of-mouth advertising and cites various interesting statistics:

- The average person has 56 word-of-mouth conversations each week.

- Ninety-three percent of customers say word of mouth is the most trustworthy source of product information.

- Word of mouth is rated as the most reliable of 15 different marketing influences.

- Seventy-seven percent of word-of-mouth advertising is face to face.

- Forty-four percent of Canadians avoid buying products that overwhelm them with advertising. ◆

How will this help me?

By understanding the material in this chapter, you can benefit in three ways: (1) As an employee and as a manager, you'll be better able to use the concepts of developing and promoting products in your career; (2) as a consumer, you'll have a clearer picture of how the complex process of new product development and promotion leads to more consumer choice; and (3) as an investor, you'll be better prepared to evaluate a company's marketing program and its competitive potential before buying the company's stock.

In Chapter 16, we introduced the four basic elements in the marketing mix: product, promotion, price, and place (distribution). In this chapter, we focus on two of these components—products and how they are promoted. We begin by looking at the different classifications of products, the new product development process, the product life-cycle idea, and the branding of products. We then discuss the various aspects of promotion—advertising, personal selling, sales promotion, and publicity. As you read this chapter and the one that follows, keep in mind that it is virtually impossible to focus on just one element of the marketing mix (for example, the product) without having to also deal with the others (price, promotion, and distribution).

What Is a Product?

1 Explain the definition of a product as a *value package*.

In developing the marketing mix for any product—whether ideas, goods, or services—marketers must consider what consumers really buy when they purchase products. Only then can they plan their strategies effectively. In this section we look first at product features and benefits, then explain the major classifications of products, then discuss the product mix.

Product Features and Benefits

features Qualities—tangible and intangible—that a company builds in to its products.

Product **features** are the qualities—tangible and intangible—that a company builds in to its products, such as a 12-horsepower motor on a lawn mower. Products are therefore much more than just visible features. In buying a product, consumers are also buying an image and a reputation. The marketers of Swatch Chrono watches, for example, are well aware that the brand name, packaging, labelling, and after-the-purchase service are also indispensable parts of their product. Advertisements remind consumers that they don't just get "real" features like shock and water resistance, quartz precision, and Swiss manufacture. They also get Swatch's commitment that its products will be young and trendy, active and sporty, and stylistically cool and clean.

To attract buyers, product features must also provide benefits. The lawn mower, for example, must produce an important intangible benefit—an attractive lawn. Today's consumers regard a product as a bundle of attributes, which, taken together, marketers call the **value package**. Increasingly, buyers expect to receive products with greater value—with more benefits at reasonable costs. For example, the possible attributes in a personal computer value package are

value package Product marketed as a bundle of value-adding attributes, including reasonable cost.

things like easy access to understandable pre-purchase information, choices of colour, attractive software packages, fast ordering via the internet, speedy delivery, and internet chat room capability. Although the computer includes physical features—like processing devices and other hardware—most items in the value package are services or intangibles that, collectively, add value by providing benefits that increase the customer's satisfaction.

Look carefully at the ad in Figure 17.1 for SAS Institute (www.sas.com), a designer of statistical software. In this ad, SAS does not emphasize the technical features of its products, nor even the criteria that companies use in selecting software—efficiency, compatibility, support. Rather, the ad focuses on the customer-oriented benefits that a buyer of SAS software can expect from using the firm's products. These benefits are being marketed as part of a complete value package.

Figure 17.1 SAS ad.

Classifying Goods and Services

Buyers fall into two basic groups, consumer and industrial. Marketing products and services to consumers is vastly different from marketing them to companies.

Classifying Consumer Products

Consumer products are commonly divided into three categories that reflect buyers' behaviour: convenience, shopping, and specialty products.

- **Convenience goods** (such as milk and newspapers) and **convenience services** (such as those offered by fast-food restaurants) are consumed rapidly and regularly. They are relatively inexpensive and are purchased frequently and with little expenditure of time and effort.

- **Shopping goods** (such as stereos and tires) and **shopping services** (such as insurance) are more expensive and are purchased less frequently than convenience goods and services. Consumers often compare brands, sometimes in different stores. They may also evaluate alternatives in terms of style, performance, colour, price, and other criteria.

- **Specialty goods** (such as wedding gowns) and **specialty services** (such as catering for wedding receptions) are extremely important and expensive purchases. Consumers usually have strong preferences, will accept no substitutes, and will often spend a great deal of time and money to get a specific product or service.

Classifying Industrial Products

Industrial products are usually divided into two categories, based on how much they cost and how they will be used.

- **Expense items** are materials and services that are consumed within a year by firms producing other goods or services. The most obvious expense items are industrial goods used directly in the production process, for example, bulk loads of tea processed into tea bags.

- **Capital items** are permanent—that is, expensive and long-lasting—goods and services. All these items have expected lives of more than a year. Buildings (offices, factories), fixed equipment (water towers, baking ovens), and accessory equipment (computers, airplanes) are capital goods. **Capital services** are those for which long-term commitments are made. These may include

convenience goods/services Relatively inexpensive consumer goods or services that are bought and used rapidly and regularly, causing consumers to spend little time looking for them or comparing their prices.

shopping goods/services Moderately expensive consumer goods or services that are purchased infrequently, causing consumers to spend some time comparing their prices.

specialty goods/services Very expensive consumer goods or services that are purchased rarely, causing consumers to spend a great deal of time locating the exact item desired.

expense items Relatively inexpensive industrial goods that are consumed rapidly and regularly.

capital items Expensive, long-lasting industrial goods that are used in producing other goods or services and have a long life.

capital services Services for which long-term commitments are made.

purchases for employee food services, building and equipment maintenance, or legal services.

The Product Mix

The group of consumer or industrial products a company has available for sale is known as the firm's **product mix**. Black & Decker, for example, makes toasters, vacuum cleaners, electric drills, and a variety of other appliances and tools. 3M makes everything from Post-it Notes to laser optics.

Product Lines

A **product line** is a group of products that are closely related because they function in a similar manner or are sold to the same customer group, who will use them in similar ways. Many companies that begin with a single product find that, over time, the initial product fails to suit every consumer shopping for the product type. To meet market demand, they introduce similar products designed to reach more customers. For example, ServiceMaster originally offered mothproofing and carpet cleaning, then subsequently expanded into other closely related services for homeowners—lawn care (TruGreen, ChemLawn), pest control (Terminix), and cleaning (Merry Maids).

Companies may also introduce multiple product lines that go well beyond their existing product line. After years of serving residential customers, ServiceMaster added business and industry services (landscaping and janitorial), education services (management of schools and institutions, including physical facilities and financial and personnel resources), and health-care services (management of support services like plant operations, asset management, and laundry/linen supply for long-term care facilities).

Developing New Products

All products and services—including once-popular TV shows like *Seinfeld, Everybody Loves Raymond, Friends,* and *Frasier*—eventually fall out of favour with consumers. Firms must therefore develop and introduce new products. Levi's jeans, for example, was once one of Canada's most popular brands, but the company failed to keep pace with changing tastes and lost market share. The company got back on track when it introduced the new Signature brand of casual clothing. The brand has become very popular, and Levi's has opened Signature stores in several countries.

While new product development is critical, it is also very risky. Consider the battle between Toshiba (HD DVD) and Sony (Blu-ray) for global dominance in the format of high-definition DVDs. Both companies invested millions of dollars in their respective products, and experts predicted that there would be a prolonged fight between the two companies. But in less than two years, Toshiba gave up the fight and stopped producing its product. Why? Because Sony was successful in convincing movie studios like Warner to release movies only in the Blu-ray format. Major retail outlets like Wal-Mart and Netflix also announced they would sell only the Blu-ray format. Sony's success with Blu-ray is in marked contrast to its failure in the 1980s to get its Betamax format adopted for VCRs. In that earlier fight, Sony lost out when consumers preferred the VHS format.[1]

The Time Frame of New Product Development

Companies often face multi-year time horizons, high risks, and lots of uncertainty when developing new products. In 2004, Montreal-based Bombardier announced that it would build a new C-series line of regional passenger jets. In 2006, it shelved the project, but it restarted it in 2007. In 2008, Bombardier announced that it had received the first orders for the new plane, which will not enter service until 2013.[2] Two other commercial airplane manufacturers have also had delays with their new planes. Boeing's 787 Dreamliner was originally supposed to be available to buyers in 2008, but a strike by machinists and incomplete work by suppliers will delay the introduction of the new plane until 2010. Boeing's main competitor, Airbus, has experienced its own problems. It had to redesign its A350, which pushed back the planned start of production by nearly three years.[3] Other products that have experienced delays are high-definition television and the hydrogen fuel cell.

Pharmaceutical companies spend large amounts of money on research and development, yet bring relatively few new products to market each year.

Product Mortality Rates

It takes about 50 new product ideas to generate one product that finally reaches the market, and then only 10 percent of these products become successful. Creating a successful new product has become increasingly difficult, even for the most experienced marketers, because the number of new products hitting the market each year has increased dramatically.

Speed to Market

The more rapidly a product moves from the laboratory to the marketplace, the more likely it is to survive. By introducing new products ahead of competitors, companies establish market leadership and become entrenched in the market before being challenged by newer competitors. The importance of **speed to market**—a firm's success in responding to customer demand or market changes—can be seen in this statistic: A product that is only three months late to market (three months behind the leader) loses 12 percent of its lifetime profit potential. A product that is six months late will lose 33 percent.[4]

speed to market Strategy of introducing new products to respond quickly to customer and/or market changes.

The Seven-Step Development Process

To increase their chances of developing successful new products or services, many firms use a basic seven-step process (see Figure 17.2). Steps 2, 3, 4, 6, and 7 are the same for both products and services, but there are some differences in Steps 1 and 5.

1. *Product ideas.* Product development begins with a search for ideas for new products. Product ideas can come from consumers, the sales force, research and development, or engineering. Developing services ideas includes a task called defining the **service package**, which involves identification of the tangible and intangible features that define the service and state service specifications.

service package Identification of the tangible and intangible features that define the service.

2. *Screening.* This stage is an attempt to eliminate all product ideas that do not mesh with the firm's abilities, expertise, or objectives. Representatives from marketing, engineering, and production must have input at this stage.

3. *Concept testing.* Once ideas have been culled, companies use market research to solicit consumers' input. Firms can identify benefits that the product must provide as well as an appropriate price level for the product.

4. *Business analysis.* This involves developing a comparison of costs and benefits for the proposed product. Preliminary sales projections are compared with cost projections from finance and production to determine whether the product can meet minimum profitability goals.

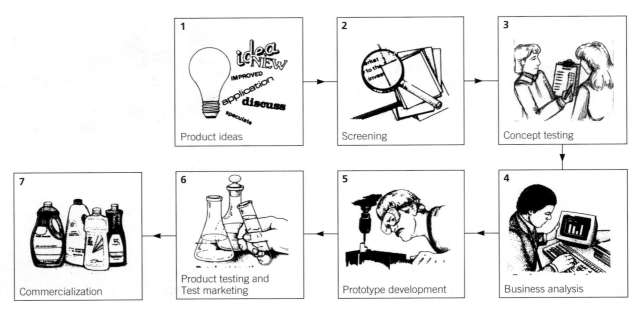

Figure 17.2 The new product development process.

5. *Prototype development.* Using input from the concept-testing phase, engineering and/or research and development produce a preliminary version of the product. Prototypes can be extremely expensive, often requiring extensive hand crafting, tooling, and development of components, but this phase can help identify potential production problems. **Service process design** involves selecting the process (identifying each step in the service, including the sequence and the timing), identifying worker requirements (specifying employee behaviours, skills, capabilities, and interactions with customers), and determining facilities requirements (designating all of the equipment that supports delivery of the service).

6. *Product testing and test marketing.* The company begins limited production of the item. If the product meets performance requirements, it is made available for sale in limited areas (test markets). This stage is very costly, since promotional campaigns and distribution channels must be established. Test marketing gives a company its first information on how consumers will respond to a product under real market conditions.

7. *Commercialization.* If test-marketing results are positive, the company will begin full-scale production and marketing of the product. Gradual commercialization, with the firm providing the product to more and more areas over time, prevents undue strain on the firm's initial production capabilities, but delays in commercialization may give competitors a chance to bring out their own version.

The Product Life Cycle

The concept of the **product life cycle (PLC)** is based on the idea that products have a limited profit-producing life. This life may be a matter of months, years, or decades, depending on the ability of the product to attract customers over time. Products such as Kellogg's Corn Flakes, Coca-Cola, Ivory soap, Argo cornstarch, and Caramilk candy bars have had extremely long product life cycles.

service process design
Selecting the process, identifying worker requirements, and determining facilities requirements so that the service can be effectively provided.

product life cycle (PLC) The concept that the profit-producing life of any product goes through a cycle of introduction, growth, maturity (levelling off), and decline.

Stages in the Product Life Cycle (PLC)

The life cycle for both goods and services is a natural process in which products are born, grow in stature, mature, and finally decline and die.[5] In Figure 17.3(a), the four phases of the PLC are applied to several products with which you are familiar.

1. *Introduction.* The introduction stage begins when the product reaches the marketplace. During this stage, marketers focus on making potential consumers aware of the product and its benefits. Because of extensive promotional and development costs, profits are non-existent.

2. *Growth.* If the new product attracts and satisfies enough consumers, sales begin to climb rapidly. During this stage, the product begins to show a profit. Other firms in the industry move speedily to introduce their own versions.

3. *Maturity.* Sales growth begins to slow. Although the product earns its highest profit level early in this stage, increased competition eventually leads to price cutting and lower profits. Toward the end of the stage, sales start to fall.

4. *Decline.* During this final stage, sales and profits continue to fall. New products in the introduction stage take away sales. Companies remove or reduce promotional support (ads and salespeople) but may let the product linger to provide some profits.

Figure 17.3(b) plots the relationship of the PLC to a product's typical sales, costs, and profits. Although the early stages of the PLC often show negative cash flows, successful products usually recover those losses and, in fact, continue

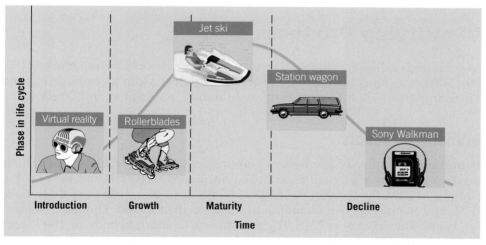

(a)

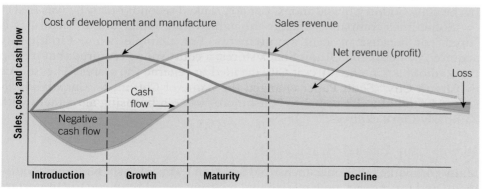

(b)

Figure 17.3 The product life cycle: stages, sales, cost, and profit.

to generate profits until the decline stage. For most products, profitable life spans are short—thus, the importance placed by so many firms on the constant replenishment of product lines. In the pension industry, for example, "defined benefit" programs are approaching the end of their life cycle, while "defined contribution" plans are in the growth stage.

Extending Product Life: An Alternative to New Products

Companies try to keep products in the maturity stage as long as they can. Sales of TV sets, for example, have been revitalized by such feature changes as colour, portability, miniaturization, stereo capability, and high definition. Companies can extend product life through a number of creative means. Foreign markets, for example, offer three possibilities for lengthening product life cycles:

product extension The process of marketing an existing, unmodified product globally.

1. In **product extension**, an existing product is marketed globally instead of just domestically. Coca-Cola and Levi's 501 jeans are prime examples of international product extensions.

product adaptation The process of modifying a product to have greater appeal in foreign markets.

2. With **product adaptation**, the product is modified for greater appeal in different countries. In Germany, a McDonald's meal includes beer, and in Japan, Ford puts the steering wheel on the right side. After Kraft Foods changed the shape of the traditional round Oreo Cookie to be long and thin (and coated the cookie in chocolate), it became the best-selling cookie in China. The new shape is also sold in Canada.[6]

reintroduction The process of reviving for new markets products that are obsolete in older ones.

3. **Reintroduction** means reviving, for new markets, products that are becoming obsolete in older ones. NCR, for instance, has reintroduced manually operated cash registers in Latin America.

Identifying Products

As we noted earlier, developing a product's features is only part of a marketer's job. Marketers must also identify products so that consumers recognize them. Three important tools for this task are branding, packaging, and labelling.

Branding Products

3 Explain the importance of *branding, packaging,* and *labelling*.

Branding is the use of symbols to communicate the qualities of a particular product made by a particular producer. According to Interbrand Best Global Brands, in 2008 the three most successful brands in the world were Coca-Cola, IBM, and Microsoft. Two Canadian firms made the top 100: Thomson Reuters (#44) and BlackBerry (#73).[7] The top three Canadian brands in 2009 were Shoppers Drug Mart, Canadian Tire, and Rona.[8] Countries can also be branded. In the 2008 Country Brand Index, Canada ranked second (Australia was first).[9]

branding The use of symbols to communicate the qualities of a particular product made by a particular producer.

Sometimes companies change the name of a popular brand because it is "tired," or because of legal requirements. For example, when Circuit City acquired 874 Canadian RadioShack stores, a court ruling required that it drop the RadioShack name. Circuit City decided to rename the stores "The Source by Circuit City." Scott Paper changed the name of Cottonelle, Canada's best-selling brand of toilet paper, to "Cashmere" when a licensing agreement with Kimberly-Clark expired.[10]

Adding Value Through Brand Equity

Many companies that once measured assets in terms of cash, buildings, equipment, and inventories now realize that a strong brand is an equally important asset. Widely known and admired brands are valuable because of their power to attract customers. Those with higher **brand equity** generate greater brand awareness and loyalty on the part of consumers, have larger market shares than competing brands, and are perceived to have greater quality. In the 2009 survey of Canadian brand equity, the top three companies were the Royal Bank of Canada (whose brand equity was valued at $5.3 billion), BlackBerry ($4.6 billion), and TD Canada Trust ($4.0 billion).[11]

brand equity Degree of consumers' loyalty to and awareness of a brand and its resultant market share.

Ebusiness and International Branding

The expensive and fierce struggle for brand recognition is very evident in the branding battles among dot-com firms. Collectively, the top internet brands—Google, America Online, Yahoo!, and Amazon.com—spend billions each year. Cisco Systems Inc., the network-equipment manufacturer, developed a successful promotional campaign that increased its brand awareness by 80 percent. The campaign also lifted Cisco's reputation as an internet expert above that of Microsoft, IBM, and Lucent.[12]

Firms that sell products internationally must consider how product names will translate in various languages. In Spanish, for example, the name of Chevrolet's now-defunct Nova simply became no va—"it does not go." Not surprisingly, sales were poor in South America. Similarly, Rolls-Royce was once going to name a new touring car Silver Mist, but changed the name to Silver Shadow when it discovered that *mist* is German for *manure*.[13]

Differences in approaches to brand names are evident even within countries. When Headspace Marketing Inc. asked 1000 Quebecers to rate how well 12 different brands had adapted to the needs and expectations of Quebecers, they found that the top three brands were Tim Hortons, Canadian Tire, and Bureau en gros (in that order). Tim Hortons ranked much higher than Starbucks (which ranked last) even though Tim Hortons did very little to adapt its product line to the Quebec market and Starbucks did a lot. However, Tim Hortons got involved with community charities and activities and used Quebec actors in their ad campaigns. This apparently made the Tim Hortons brand "resonate" better with Quebecers.[14]

The experience of Tim Hortons is not unusual. Consider the "brand wars" between Coke and Pepsi in Quebec. Coke sells better than Pepsi in most places in the world, but not in Quebec. Why is that? Perhaps it's because Pepsi customizes its advertisements to meet distinct Quebecois tastes. One now-famous ad shows what happens when a European tourist orders a Coke in Quebec: a hush comes over the restaurant, wildlife stops in the forest, and traffic comes to a halt. The waiter finally opens a Pepsi for the tourist, who then says, "Ah! Ici, c'est Pepsi."[15] Bombardier's national ad campaign uses the slogan "Planes. Trains. Canadian Spirit" except in Quebec, where the slogan is "Planes. Trains. A Source of Pride."[16]

Types of Brand Names

Virtually every product has a brand name of some form. However, different types of brand names tell consumers something about the product's origin.

National Brands. Brand name products that are produced and distributed by the manufacturer are called **national brands**. These brands, such as Scotch tape, are often widely recognized by consumers because of large national advertising campaigns. The costs of developing a positive image for a national brand are high, so some companies use their national brand on several related products. Procter & Gamble markets Ivory shampoo, capitalizing on the widely recognized name of its soaps.

national brands Products distributed by and carrying a name associated with the manufacturer.

Licensed Brands. More and more nationally recognized companies and personalities have sold other companies the right to place their names on

SpongeBob macaroni and cheese is Kraft Foods' top-selling licensed pasta product, and SpongeBob Band-Aids now outsell Scooby Doo bandages. There are SpongeBob dolls and bowling balls, and the brand also appears on toothpaste and underwear. SpongeBob belongs to Nickelodeon Enterprises, a children's TV programmer that's been the highest-rated basic cable network since 1995. Product licensing is worth about $2.5 billion to Nickelodeon each year.

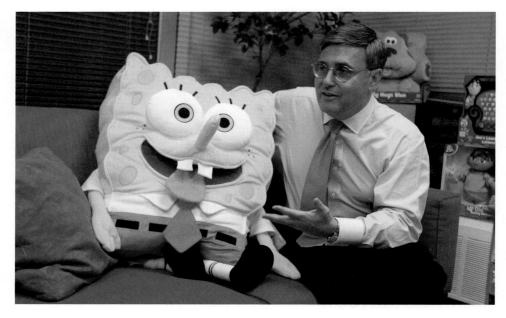

licensed brands Products for which the right to use a brand name, a celebrity's name, or some other well-known identification mark was sold to another company to use on a product.

products, which are **licensed brands**. The Olympic logo generates millions in revenues for the International Olympic Committee, which licenses its name on clothing, tableware, coins, licence plates, and countless other merchandise items. Harley-Davidson's famous logo—emblazoned on boots, eyewear, gloves, purses, lighters, and watches—brings the motorcycle maker more than $210 million annually. Licensing for character-based brands—Punisher, Spider-Man, and Pokémon—is equally lucrative. Nelvana and U.S.-based Sears signed a licensing agreement allowing Sears to set up Franklin the Turtle boutiques at its stores. These boutiques market Franklin clothing and accessories that are available exclusively at Sears.[17]

Private Brands. When a wholesaler or retailer develops a brand and has the manufacturer place that brand name on the product, the resulting product name is a **private brand**. Sears has two well-known private brands—Craftsman tools and Kenmore appliances. J. Sainsbury PLC, the largest supermarket chain in Britain, introduced its own private brand of cola in a can that looks strikingly like the one used by Coke. The product is made by Cott Corp. of Toronto, which also makes the "American Choice" label for Wal-Mart. Loblaw Companies Ltd. created a line of upscale products under the private brand President's Choice. Shoppers Drug Mart produces a line of products under the Life label.[18] E.D. Smith, a maker of jams and pie fillings, makes private label items for retailers like Wal-Mart and Pizza Pizza Ltd.[19]

private brands Products promoted by and carrying a name associated with the retailer or wholesaler, not the manufacturer.

Brand Loyalty

Brand loyalty means that when customers need a particular item, they will go back to the same brand and buy the company's products. Brand loyalty exists at three levels: *brand awareness* (customers recognize the brand name), *brand preference* (consumers have a favourable attitude toward the product), and *brand insistence* (consumers demand the product and are willing to go out of their way to get it). Brand insistence implies a lot of consumer trust in a brand. Canadians have less trust in brands than they did 20 years ago, but some well-known brands like Becel margarine, Robin Hood flour, Wal-Mart, and Black & Decker are still viewed positively.[20]

Brand loyalty is strong in several sports, including baseball, basketball, and soccer, and fans respond to marketing efforts by companies like Nike and

brand loyalty Customers' recognition of, preference for, and insistence on buying a product with a certain brand name.

Adidas. But in some other sports (for example, skateboarding) brand loyalty is difficult to develop. Because skateboarders go through a lot of boards each year, they are reluctant to buy brand name boards, which cost three to five times what "blank" boards cost. The International Association of Skateboard Companies estimates that 50 to 70 percent of all boards sold are blank, not branded.[21]

Brand loyalty can have a major impact on a company's profits. In the beer industry, for example, each market share point is worth about $25 million in profit. This is why companies like Labatt and Molson have such fierce competitive battles for market share.[22]

Trademarks, Patents, and Copyrights

Because brand development is very expensive, a company does not want another company using its name and confusing consumers. Companies can apply to the Canadian government and receive a **trademark**, the exclusive legal right to use a brand name. Trademarks are granted for 15 years and may be renewed for further periods of 15 years, but only if the company continues to protect its brand name. In 2008, a European court ruled that the construction toys made by Lego AS can no longer be protected by trademark law. Montreal-based Mega Brands Inc., which makes a competitive product called Mega Bloks, had challenged Lego's trademark.[23]

> **trademark** The exclusive legal right to use a brand name.

Exactly what can be trademarked is not always clear. If the company allows the name to lapse into common usage, the courts may take away protection. Common usage occurs when the company fails to use the ® symbol for its brand. It also occurs if the company fails to correct those who do not acknowledge the brand as a trademark. Windsurfer (a popular brand of sailboards by WSI Inc.) lost its trademark. Like the trampoline, yo-yo, and thermos, the brand name has become the common term for the product and can now be used by any sailboard company. But companies owning brands like Xerox, Coke, Jell-O, and Scotch tape have successfully defended their brand names.

Companies want to be sure that both product brands and new product ideas are protected. A **patent** protects an invention or idea for a period of 20 years. The cost is $1000 to $1500; it takes from nine months to three years to secure a patent from the Canadian Patent Office.[24] Patents can be very valuable. In 2006, Research In Motion (RIM), maker of the immensely popular BlackBerry device, agreed to pay $612.5 million to NTP Inc., a U.S. firm that claimed RIM was infringing on some patents it held.[25] Two months later, RIM was sued by another U.S. company claiming that RIM had also infringed on its patents.[26] In yet another patent dispute, Pfizer Inc. reached an agreement in 2008 with an Indian generic drug maker that will keep a cheaper version of the cholesterol-lowering drug Lipitor out of the U.S. market until 2011. Sales revenues of Lipitor are about US$13 billion annually, so this is a very important deal for Pfizer.[27]

> **patent** Exclusive legal right to use and license a manufactured item or substance, manufacturing process, or object design.

Copyrights give exclusive ownership rights to the creators of books, articles, designs, illustrations, photos, films, and music. Computer programs and even semiconductor chips are also protected. In Canada, the copyright process is relatively simple, requiring only the use of the copyright symbol © and the date. Copyrights extend to creators for their entire lives and to their estates for 50 years thereafter in Canada (70 years in the United States). Copyrights apply to the tangible expressions of an idea, not to the idea itself. For example, the idea of cloning dinosaurs from fossil DNA cannot be copyrighted, but Michael Crichton, the author of *Jurassic Park*, had a copyright for his novel (which is now held by his estate) because it is the tangible result of the basic idea.

> **copyright** Exclusive ownership rights belonging to the creators of books, articles, designs, illustrations, photos, films, and music.

There is much debate about how copyrights apply to material that appears on the internet. In 2005, the Author's Guild and several publishers sued Google, claiming that its book-scanning project was infringing on their copyrights.

In 2008, Google agreed to pay US$125 million to settle the lawsuits. Google can now make available millions of books online.[28]

Packaging Products

packaging Physical container in which a product is sold, advertised, or protected.

Except for products like fresh fruits and vegetables and structural steel, almost all products need some form of **packaging** so they can be transported to the market. Packaging also serves several other functions: It is an in-store advertisement that makes the product attractive; it clearly displays the brand; it identifies product features and benefits; and it reduces the risk of damage, breakage, or spoilage. The package is the marketer's last chance to say "buy me" to the consumer.

Companies are paying close attention to consumer concerns about packaging. Beyond concerns about product tampering, packaging must be tight enough to withstand shipping but not so tight that it frustrates consumers when they try to open the package. Nestlé—which spends more than $6 billion annually on packaging—spent nine months coming up with a new, easier-to-open lid and an easier-to-grip container for its Country Creamery ice cream. In general, companies have found that packaging costs can be as high as 15 percent of the total cost to make a product, and features like zip-lock tops can add 20 percent to the price that is charged.[29]

Labelling Products

label That part of a product's packaging that identifies the product's name and contents and sometimes its benefits.

Every product has a **label** on its package. Like packaging, labelling can help market the product. First, it identifies the product or the brand, such as the name Campbell on a can of soup or Chiquita on a banana. Labels also promote products by getting consumers' attention. Attractive colours and graphics provide visual cues to products that otherwise might be overlooked on the shelf. Finally, the label describes the product by providing information about nutritional content, directions for use, proper disposal, and safety.

Consumer Packaging and Labelling Act A federal law that provides comprehensive rules for packaging and labelling of consumer products.

The federal government regulates the information on package labels. The **Consumer Packaging and Labelling Act** has two main purposes: The first is to provide a comprehensive set of rules for packaging and labelling of consumer products, and the second is to ensure that manufacturers provide full and factual information on labels. All pre-packaged products must state in French and English the quantity enclosed in metric units, as well as the name and description of the product.

Sellers are very sensitive to what is on the label of the products they sell. For example, the Maple Leaf is on all beer that Labatt Brewing Co. Ltd. sells in Canada—except in Quebec. There, the label has a stylized sheaf of wheat instead of the Maple Leaf. Interestingly, the Maple Leaf is much more prominent on Labatt's beer sold in the United States.[30] Many companies use different labels for their products in Quebec than they do for products sold elsewhere in Canada.

Promoting Products and Services

4 Identify the important objectives of *promotion* and discuss the considerations in selecting a *promotional mix.*

promotion Any technique designed to sell a product.

As we noted in Chapter 16, **promotion** is any technique designed to sell a product. It is part of the *communication mix*: the total message a company sends to consumers about its product. Promotional techniques, especially advertising, must communicate the uses, features, and benefits of products. Sales promotions also include various programs that add value beyond the benefits inherent in the product. For example, it is nice to get a high-quality product at a reasonable price, but it is even better when the seller offers a rebate or a bonus pack with "20 percent more *free*."

Information and Exchange Values

In free market systems, businesses use promotional methods to accomplish four objectives with potential customers:

- make them aware of products
- make them knowledgeable about products
- persuade them to like products
- persuade them to purchase products

Successful promotions provide communication about the product and create exchanges that satisfy the objectives of customers (who get a desired product) and sellers (who get sales and profits). The promotion program can determine the success or failure of any business or product, whether it is in the introduction stage (promoting for new product awareness) or the maturity stage (promoting brand benefits and customer loyalty).

Promotional Objectives

The ultimate objective of any promotion is to increase sales. However, marketers also use promotion to *communicate information, position products, add value,* and *control sales volume*.[31]

Communicating Information

Consumers cannot buy a product unless they have been informed about it. Information can advise customers about the availability of a product, educate them on the latest technological advances, or announce the candidacy of someone running for a government office. Information may be communicated in writing (newspapers and magazines), verbally (radio, in person, or over the telephone), or visually (television, the internet, a matchbook cover, or a billboard). Today, the communication of information regarding a company's products or services is so important that marketers try to place it wherever consumers may be. The average Canadian sees about 3000 marketing messages every day, much more than the average consumer saw 30 years ago.[32] The boxed insert entitled "Promoting a Green Business Image" describes how companies communicate information about their green initiatives to consumers.

Positioning Products

As we saw in Chapter 16, **product positioning** establishes an easily identifiable image of a product in the minds of consumers. For example, by selling only in department stores, Estée Lauder products are positioned as more upscale than cosmetics sold in drugstores. With product positioning, the company is trying to appeal to a specific segment of the market rather than to the market as a whole.

product positioning The establishment of an easily identifiable image of a product in the minds of consumers.

Adding Value

Today's value-conscious customers gain benefits when the promotional mix is shifted so that it communicates value-added benefits in its products. Burger King, for instance, shifted its promotional mix by cutting back on advertising dollars and using those funds for customer discounts. Receiving the same food at a lower price is added value for Burger King's customers.

The Greening of Business

Promoting a Green Business Image

In addition to their traditional role of promoting their products and services, Canadian businesses are also promoting themselves as "green" enterprises. They are doing this because the market for green products has increased rapidly during the last few years as consumers have become more concerned about the environment. For example, the image of Canada's oil sands producers is that of environmental "bad boys," so the companies have banded together to get out the word that they are investing in new technology that will reduce the impact of oil sands activity on the air, land, and water. The campaign includes a new website and a national advertising campaign that is designed to provide information and correct misperceptions that consumers may have about oil sands development.

Even companies that have a good reputation for being green are stepping up their efforts. The Body Shop unveiled a major advertising campaign in 2008 that aggressively touted its long-standing commitment to having a corporate culture of concern for the environment. The company is advertising because its competitors are touting their own commitment to the environment, and The Body Shop wants to stand out from the crowd.

Convincing customers that a business is green is becoming increasingly difficult because consumers have become quite cynical and because watchdog groups carefully scrutinize green claims. A Gandalf Group survey of 1500 Canadians found that the majority of consumers think that (a) environmental claims by businesses are just a marketing ploy, and (b) labelling regulations are needed so buyers can understand what terms like *eco-friendly* mean. These consumer attitudes have developed partly because some companies have tried to claim that their products are more eco-friendly than they really are. The term *greenwashing* has been coined to describe the practice of exaggerating or making false claims about the environmental impact of a product or service (it is a modern variation of the older term *whitewashing*, which means making things look better than they actually are). EnviroMedia publishes a Greenwashing Index that ranks the eco-friendly advertising claims of various companies.

Charges of greenwashing can create very negative publicity for a company. A case in point—World Wildlife Fund (WWF) accused Shell Oil of greenwashing after Shell advertised that its Alberta oil sands operations were "sustainable." WWF filed a complaint with the U.K. Advertising Standards Authority, and in 2008 the authority ruled that the advertisement was misleading and confusing to consumers. WWF publicized the ruling—and made critical comments about Shell—on a large digital billboard in central London.

Another oil company that has had difficulties is BP. Its slogan "Beyond Petroleum" promotes its green image, and the company has been praised by the Natural Resource Defense Council in the United States as a leader in the industry's move toward renewable energy. But BP is involved in extracting oil from the Alberta oil sands, which Greenpeace has called "the greatest climate crime in history." BP has also been cited for environmental offences several times during the last decade.

Some green advertising campaigns may strike consumers as downright audacious. Much to the dismay of animal rights activists, the Fur Council of Canada—which emphasizes its ties with Aboriginal Canadians and its made-in-Canada attributes—is now promoting itself as a green industry. Its billboard and print advertisements stress the sustainability of the fur industry and point out that trappers are the first to sound the alarm when wildlife habitats are threatened. The trapping industry has endured much negative publicity during the last couple of decades, so this advertising campaign will likely make consumers sit up and take notice.

In response to concerns about greenwashing, the Canadian Competition Bureau, in co-operation with the Canadian Standards Association, has drafted industry guidelines that will require companies to back up their environmental claims with scientific evidence. Laws prohibiting misleading advertising already exist, but environmental claims are difficult to assess since there are no consistent definitions and standards that can be used to judge whether a product is really eco-friendly. The new guidelines will create national definitions for terms like *recyclable* and will also prohibit vague claims about products (for example, "our product is non-toxic"). In 2008, Lululemon Athletics Inc. was required to remove its unsubstantiated claims about the health benefits of seaweed from one of its clothing lines.

Critical Thinking Questions

1. What is your reaction to the Fur Council of Canada's green advertising campaign? What would you say to an animal rights activist who is outraged at the claims the Fur Council is making?

2. Consider the following statement: *The Competition Bureau's plan to create national guidelines to define terms like "recyclable" is well intentioned, but it will not work in practice, because companies will figure out ways to get around the rules and still make unwarranted claims about how "green" they are.* Do you agree or disagree with the statement? Explain your reasoning.

Controlling Sales Volume

Many companies, such as Hallmark Cards, experience seasonal sales patterns. By increasing promotional activities in slow periods, these firms can achieve more stable sales volume throughout the year. They can thus keep production and distribution systems running evenly. Promotions can even turn slow seasons into peak sales periods. For example, greeting card companies and florists together have done much to create Grandparents Day. The result has been increased consumer demand for cards and flowers in the middle of what was once a slow season for both industries.

Promotional Strategies

Once a firm's promotional objectives are clear, it must develop a promotional strategy to achieve these objectives. A company using a **push strategy** will aggressively "push" its product through wholesalers and retailers, who in turn persuade customers to buy the product. In contrast, a company using a **pull strategy** appeals directly to customers, who then demand the product from retailers, who in turn demand the product from wholesalers. Generally speaking, makers of industrial products use a push strategy, and makers of consumer products use a pull strategy, but many large firms use a combination of the two. For example, General Foods uses advertising to create consumer demand (pull) for its cereals, but it also pushes wholesalers and retailers to stock these products (push).

In rare cases, a company may purposely avoid both strategies. For example, Langlitz Leathers makes leather jackets that cost as much as $800. They are worn by rebels like Hells Angels, musicians like Bruce Springsteen, and actors like Sylvester Stallone. Even though the company does virtually no advertising, customers who want a Langlitz have to wait several months to get one after they place their order.[33]

push strategy A promotional strategy whereby a company aggressively pushes its product through wholesalers and retailers, who persuade customers to buy it.

pull strategy A promotional strategy in which a company appeals directly to customers, who demand the product from retailers, who demand the product from wholesalers.

The Promotional Mix

As we noted in Chapter 16, there are four types of promotional tools: advertising, personal selling, sales promotions, and publicity/public relations. The best combination of these tools—the **promotional mix**—depends on many factors, with the most important being the target audience. In establishing a promotional mix, marketers match promotional tools with the five stages in the buyer decision process we described in Chapter 16:

promotional mix That portion of marketing concerned with choosing the best combination of advertising, personal selling, sales promotions, and publicity to sell a product.

1. *Buyers recognize the need to make a purchase.* At this stage, marketers must make sure that buyers are aware of their products. Advertising and publicity, which can reach many people quickly, are important.

2. *Buyers seek information about available products.* Advertising and personal selling are important because both can be used to educate consumers.

3. *Buyers compare competing products.* Personal selling can be vital. Sales representatives can demonstrate product quality and performance in comparison with competitors' products.

4. *Buyers purchase products.* Sales promotion is effective because it can give consumers an incentive to buy. Personal selling can help by bringing products to convenient purchase locations.

5. *Buyers evaluate products after purchase.* Advertising, or even personal selling, is sometimes used to remind consumers that they made wise purchases.[34] Figure 17.4 summarizes the effective promotional tools for each stage of the consumer buying process, and Figure 17.5 shows different combinations of products, promotional tools, and target consumers.

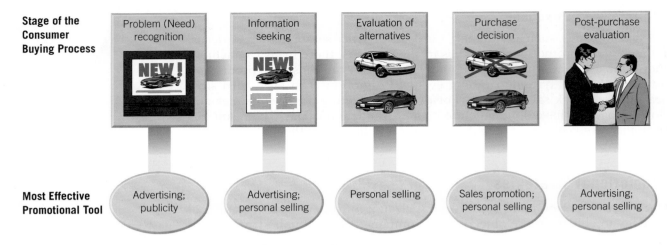

Stage of the Consumer Buying Process	Problem (Need) recognition	Information seeking	Evaluation of alternatives	Purchase decision	Post-purchase evaluation
Most Effective Promotional Tool	Advertising; publicity	Advertising; personal selling	Personal selling	Sales promotion; personal selling	Advertising; personal selling

Figure 17.4 The consumer buying process and promotional mix.

Goods Promotion: House (real estate)
Tool: Personal selling
Consumer: House buyer

Service Promotion:
Weight-loss program
Tool: Sales promotion (coupon)
Consumer: Overweight person

You loved it as a girl...
Come back as a leader

Girl greatness starts here.

Girl Guides of Canada
Guides du Canada
Join today!
1-800-565-8111
girlguides.ca

Organizational Promotion: Scouts Canada
Tool: Publicity
Consumer: Young men and women

Event Promotion: Rock concert
Tool: Advertising
Consumer: Cheering fan

Person or Idea Promotion:
Candidate for prime minister
Tool: Publicity/advertising/personal sales
Consumer: Voter

Figure 17.5 Each promotional tool should be properly matched with the product being promoted and the target consumer.

Advertising Promotions

What candy bar is "one of life's sweet mysteries"? What soap is "99 and 44/100% pure"? What is the store where "the lowest price is the law"? What product is "only available in Canada—pity"? If you are like most Canadians, you can answer these questions because of **advertising**, which is a promotional tool consisting of paid, non-personal communication used by an identified sponsor to inform an audience about a product. (The answers are Caramilk, Ivory soap, Zellers, and Red Rose tea, respectively.) Consumers remember brand names more easily if the company has a catchy advertising slogan. Buckley's Mixture, a well-known product in Canada, is also sold in the United States. In one television advertisement, the announcer intones, "Buckley's Mixture, the famous Canadian cough remedy, is now available here. It tastes awful, and it works."[35]

advertising A promotional tool consisting of paid, non-personal communication used by an identified sponsor to inform an audience about a product.

Advertising Strategies

Advertising strategies depend on which stage of the product life cycle the product is in. During the introduction stage, **informative advertising** can help develop an awareness of the company and its product among buyers and can establish a primary demand for the product. For example, before a new textbook is published, instructors receive direct-mail advertisements notifying them of the book's contents and availability. During the growth stage, **persuasive advertising** can influence a larger number of consumers to buy the company's products. During the maturity stage, **comparative advertising**—which involves comparing the company's brand name with a competitor's brand name in such a way that the competitor's brand looks inferior—is often used. When Procter & Gamble aired advertisements claiming that its Bounty brand had more absorbency than Scott Paper's competing product, Scott retaliated by producing an advertisement that said that Scott Clean Ultra was 60 percent more absorbent than P&G's Bounty.[36] During the latter part of the maturity stage and all of the decline stage, **reminder advertising** keeps the product's name in front of the consumer.

informative advertising An advertising strategy, appropriate to the introduction stage of the product life cycle, in which the goal is to make potential customers aware that a product exists.

persuasive advertising An advertising strategy, appropriate to the growth stage of the product life cycle, in which the goal is to influence the customer to buy the firm's product rather than the similar product of a competitor.

comparative advertising An advertising strategy, appropriate to the maturity stage of the product life cycle, in which the goal is to influence the customer to switch from a competitor's similar product to the firm's product by directly comparing the two products.

Advertising Media

Consumers tend to ignore the bulk of advertising messages that bombard them. Marketers must therefore find out who their customers are, which media they pay attention to, what messages appeal to them, and how to get their attention. Thus, marketers use several different **advertising media**—specific communication outlets for carrying a seller's message to potential customers. For example, IBM uses television ads to keep its name fresh in the minds of consumers, newspaper and magazine ads to educate them about product features, and trade publications to introduce new software. Often marketers turn to a multimedia company so that the seller's message is the same across the different advertising media. The combination of media through which a company chooses to advertise its products is called its **media mix**. Although different industries use different mixes, most depend on multiple media to advertise their products and services. The top 10 multimedia companies in Canada are listed in Table 17.1.

An advertiser selects media with a number of factors in mind. The marketer must first ask: Which medium will reach the people I want to reach? If a firm is selling hog breeding equipment, it might choose a business magazine read mostly by hog farmers. If it is selling silverware, it might choose a magazine for brides. If it is selling toothpaste, the choice might be a general audience television program or a general audience magazine such as Reader's Digest (or Sélection du Reader's Digest, for exposure to a similar audience of francophones).

reminder advertising An advertising strategy, appropriate to the latter part of the maturity stage of the product life cycle, in which the goal is to keep the product's name in the minds of customers.

advertising media The specific communication devices—television, radio, newspapers, direct mail, magazines, billboards, the internet—used to carry a firm's advertising message to potential customers.

media mix The combination of media through which a company chooses to advertise its products.

Table 17.1   Top 10 Multimedia Companies in Canada, 2008

Company	Annual Revenues (in billions of $)
1. Rogers Cable Inc.	$3.8
2. CanWest Global Communications Corp.	3.1
3. Shaw Communications Inc.	3.1
4. Vidéotron Ltée	1.8
5. Rogers Media Inc.	1.4
6. Bell ExpressVu LP	1.3
7. Cogeco Inc.	1.1
8. Astral Media Inc.	0.8
9. Corus Entertainment Inc.	0.7
10. Canadian Broadcasting Corp.	0.5

Newspapers

Newspapers offer excellent coverage. Most local markets have at least one daily newspaper, and many people read the paper every day. This medium offers flexible, rapid coverage since ads can change from day to day. It also offers believable coverage since ads are presented side by side with news. However, newspapers are generally thrown out after one day, they often are not printed in colour, they have poor reproduction quality, and they do not usually allow advertisers to target their audience. Advertisers spent $1.7 billion on newspaper advertising in Canada in 2007.[37]

In recent years the volume of classified ads placed in newspapers has declined as advertisers have shifted their emphasis to the internet. The *Toronto Star* has tried to counter this trend by giving a free internet posting to anyone who buys a classified ad in the newspaper.[38]

Television

Television allows advertisers to combine sight, sound, and motion, thus appealing to almost all of the viewer's senses. Information on viewer demographics for a particular program allows advertisers to promote to their target audiences. One disadvantage of television is that too many commercials cause viewers to confuse products. In addition, viewers who record programs on DVRs (digital video recorders) often fast-forward through the ads appearing on the TV shows they have recorded. The brevity of TV ads also makes television a poor medium in which to educate viewers about complex products.

Television is the most expensive medium in which to advertise. Worldwide, advertisers spent US$146.8 billion on television advertising in 2005.[39] Spending on television advertising in Canada totalled $3.3 billion in 2007.[40] A 30-second commercial during the NFL Super Bowl costs about US$2.4 million.[41]

Direct Mail

direct mail Printed advertisements, such as flyers, mailed or faxed directly to consumers' homes or places of business.

Direct mail involves flyers or other types of printed advertisements that are mailed directly to consumers' homes or places of business. Direct mail allows the company to select its audience and personalize its message. Although many people discard "junk mail," targeted recipients with stronger-than-average interest are more likely to buy. Direct mail involves the largest advance costs of any advertising technique, but it appears to have the highest cost-effectiveness. Particularly effective have been "fax attacks," in which advertisers send their "mail" messages electronically via fax machines and get higher response rates than they would if they used Canada Post. Advertisers spent $1.7 billion on direct mail promotion in 2007.[42]

Radio

A tremendous number of people listen to the radio each day, and radio ads are inexpensive. In addition, since most radio is programmed locally, this medium gives advertisers a high degree of customer selectivity. For example, radio stations are segmented into listening categories such as rock and roll, country and western, jazz, talk shows, news, and religious programming. Like television, however, radio ads are very short, and radio permits only an audio presentation. People tend to use the radio as "background" while they are doing other things, and this means they may pay little attention to advertisements. Spending on radio advertisements totalled $1.4 billion in Canada in 2007.[43]

Magazines

The many different magazines on the market provide a high level of consumer selectivity. The person who reads *Popular Photography* is more likely to be interested in the latest specialized lenses from Canon than is a *Gourmet* magazine subscriber. Magazine advertising allows for excellent reproduction of photographs and artwork that not only grab buyers' attention but also may convince them of the product's value. And magazines allow advertisers plenty of space for detailed product information. Magazines have a long life and tend to be passed from person to person, thus doubling and tripling the number of exposures. The Canadian magazine with the largest readership is *Reader's Digest*, followed by *Canadian Living* (*Chatelaine* and *Canadian Geographic* are tied for third).[44] Spending on magazine advertisements totalled $718 million in Canada in 2007.[45]

Outdoor Advertising

Outdoor advertising—billboards; signs; and advertisements on buses, taxis, and subways—is relatively inexpensive, faces little competition for customers' attention, and is subject to high repeat exposure. Like many other areas of advertising, outdoor advertising has gone high-tech. Winnipeg-based Side-track Technologies Inc., for example, has developed a system of 360 digital strips that are placed at intervals along subway walls. When a train passes by, the strips blend together, creating the impression of an artificial video. The strips can be changed remotely, thus allowing a company like McDonald's to

Speed and creativity have given billboards like these a new prominence in the world of advertising media. Instead of relying on highly skilled human artists, outdoor ad sellers can now commission digital creations that not only turn heads but cost less than most other media. Whereas it used to take a month to launch a billboard-based campaign, it now takes just days.

advertise Egg McMuffins during the morning commute and Big Macs during the afternoon commute.[46]

Titan Worldwide has developed an LED display that shows commercials on New York City buses. The display contains GPS technology, so it can target audiences based on the time of day and postal code where the bus is located. The technology will also be introduced to Canada and Ireland.[47] Many billboards now feature animation and changing images, and today's billboard messages are cheaper because they can be digitally printed in colour in large quantities. On the downside, outdoor ads can present only limited information, and sellers have little control over who sees their advertisements. Worldwide spending on outdoor advertising in 2005 totalled $23.2 billion, while in Canada the total was $422 million in 2007.[48]

Word-of-Mouth Advertising

word-of-mouth advertising
Opinions about the value of products passed among consumers in informal discussions.

As noted in the opening case, **word-of-mouth advertising** occurs when consumers talk to each other about products they are using. According to the Word of Mouth Marketing Association, there are several varieties of word-of-mouth advertising. These include buzz marketing (using high-profile news to get consumers talking about a product), viral marketing (consumers passing product information around on the internet), product seeding (providing free product samples to influential consumers), and cause marketing (involving consumers who feel strongly about a cause such as reducing poverty).[49]

Consumers form very strong opinions about products as a result of conversations with friends and acquaintances, so when consumers start talking about a new product or idea, the information can build momentum and spread like wildfire. This "spreading the word" can happen without any expenditure of money by the company selling the product in question. But companies do spend money developing formal word-of-mouth advertising campaigns because they recognize how powerful they are. The now-famous "Evolution" ad for Dove soap (which showed an "ordinary" girl being transformed into a goddess) was posted on YouTube instead of the traditional places. It was eventually viewed by 300 million people and generated huge publicity for the brand. The only cost to the company was that incurred in making the video.[50]

The Internet

ecommerce Buying and selling processes that make use of electronic technology.

internet marketing The promotional efforts of companies to sell their products and services to consumers over the internet.

Ecommerce refers to buying and selling processes that make use of electronic technology, while **internet marketing** refers to the promotional efforts of companies to sell their products and services to consumers over the internet.[51] The internet is the most recent advertising medium to arise, and thousands of well-known and lesser-known firms have placed ads there. Online ad sales were valued at $1.2 billion in 2007, more than double the amount for 2006.[52] Craigslist.org offers free local classified advertising on over 200 websites around the world. More information about internet marketing is provided in Chapter 18.

MySpace is using a "hypertargeting" system to categorize its users into different categories like "rodeo watcher" or "scrapbook enthusiast." Live Nation, a concert promoter, saw increased traffic on its Coldplay page after it placed ads on MySpace that were directed at fans of Coldplay and other similar bands. This sounds very positive for marketers, but privacy concerns have arisen about technologies that track consumers as they surf the web. For example, a company called NebuAd has developed ad-tracking software that has gotten the attention of critics who claim that it violates wiretap laws.[53]

Online marketing can be profitable for companies, but what happens when consumers turn against them? With so many individuals participating in social networking sites like Facebook or MySpace and keeping personal blogs, it's increasingly common for a single unhappy customer to wage war against a company for selling faulty products or providing poor service. Individuals may post negative reviews of products on blogs, upload angry videos outlining complaints on YouTube, or join public discussion forums where they can voice their opinion. While companies benefit from the viral spread of good news, they must also be on guard for an online backlash that can damage their reputation.[54]

YouTube—the most popular online video site—began selling ads within videos in 2007. The ads appear on the bottom 20 percent of the screen; if the consumer doesn't click on the ad within 10 seconds, it disappears. YouTube found that 75 percent of viewers clicked on the ad and watched it in its entirety. The ads also had higher click-through rates than standard display ads that appear on websites.[55] Changes are occurring in the way consumers navigate the web, and more online searches now take place on YouTube than on Yahoo. Companies are therefore changing their advertising strategies. Pizza Hut, for example, started buying mobile search ads and buying ads through Facebook.[56]

Internet advertising offers advantages for both buyers and sellers. For buyers, advantages include convenience (websites can be accessed 24 hours a day, and there is no need to fight traffic at shopping malls), privacy (no face-to-face high-pressure sales tactics are possible), selection (the products and services that are available are almost unlimited), useful information (about competing products and services), and control (consumers can "build" custom products for themselves).

For sellers, advantages include reach (access to consumers around the world), direct distribution (eliminating intermediaries), reduced expenses (which would normally be incurred when owning "bricks-and-mortar" outlets), relationship building (with customers on interactive websites), flexibility (sellers can quickly change prices or the terms of sale based on market developments), and feedback (sellers can measure the success of messages by counting how many people see each ad and tracking the number of click-throughs to their own website).[57]

While internet marketing has some obvious advantages for both buyers and sellers, it also has weaknesses, including profitability problems (many internet marketers are unprofitable and the failure rate is high), information overload (consumers may not know what to do with all the information available to them), and limited markets (consumers who use the web are typically more highly educated).

In addition to these weaknesses, internet marketers must also cope with consumer concerns about two security-related issues. An Angus Reid/Globe and Mail poll of 1500 Canadians found that their main concern about internet marketing was security. People who had made at least one purchase on the internet were more likely to list security as their top concern than were those who had never purchased anything on the internet. In particular, people were concerned that their credit-card number might end up in the wrong hands, and that their privacy would be invaded if they purchased on the internet.[58]

Consumers also object to "spyware" software, which monitors websites they visit and observes their shopping habits. This software is often implanted on their personal computers as they wander the web. It then generates "pop-up" advertisements that are targeted to that particular consumer. Because people are often unaware that such spyware is on their computer, the technique has generated a lot of anger among consumers. Consumers can, however, get free anti-spyware software that removes spyware from their computer. Spyware is also a concern for companies that sell from their own websites because the pop-ups are designed to divert web surfers from the products offered by the website.[59] If it going to reach its full potential, internet marketing is going to have to improve its image.

Virtual Advertising

virtual advertising A technique that uses digital implants of brands or products onto live or taped programming, giving the illusion that the product is part of the show.

Virtual advertising uses digital implants of brands or products onto live or taped programming, giving the illusion that the product is part of the show. With this technique, an advertiser's product can appear as part of the television show—when viewers are paying more attention—instead of during commercial breaks. In a televised basketball game, for example, the digital image of a brand—for example, the round face of a Rolex watch or an Acura hubcap—can be electronically enlarged and superimposed on centre court without physically changing the playing floor. For videotaped movies, digital images can be inserted easily. A Kmart shopping bag can be digitally added to the table in a kitchen scene, or a Philips Flat TV can be superimposed on the wall for display during a dramatic scene.[60]

A variation of virtual advertising is described in the boxed insert entitled "Fuelling the World of Branded Entertainment."

Other Advertising Media

A combination of many additional media, including catalogues, sidewalk handouts, Yellow Pages, skywriting, telephone calls, special events, and door-to-

Entrepreneurship and New Ventures

Fuelling the World of Branded Entertainment

The casual gaming industry develops non-violent, easy-to-play video games that appeal to a wide variety of users. Industry sales are $2.3 billion worldwide, expected annual growth is 20 percent, and the market is about 200 million people.

Fuel Industries of Ottawa, Ontario, founded in 1999, has positioned itself as an up-and-comer in this industry by winning contracts that typically would be awarded to big-name companies like DreamWorks Animation and Pixar Animation Studios. The company's success has not gone unnoticed. In 2008, *Canadian Business* magazine recognized Fuel as one of the country's fastest growing businesses in Canada.

Fuel doesn't just develop online video games. Rather, it is pioneering a new model of branded online entertainment (referred to as "advergames"). Essentially, an advergame is an online video game and advertising rolled into one. The theory behind the concept is simple: If consumers are having fun while interacting with the entertainment, they are more likely to remember and feel positive toward the brand. Instead of trying to make an impression during a traditional 60-second commercial, advergames keep consumers engaged for as long as 600 seconds! Many companies are beginning to see the benefits of this market-ing strategy.

Fuel was launched into the branded digital promotion business when it created an advergame called Fairies and Dragons that helped McDonald's promote its Happy Meal in 40 European countries. With every Happy Meal, kids received a fairy or dragon toy along with a CD-ROM that contained three games and 10 hours of game play. That approach differed noticeably from the usual tactic of licensing characters from established entertainment companies like Disney. Plans are underway to launch the same concept for McDonald's in other regions, including Australia, Japan, and North America.

Since their success with McDonald's, Fuel has done similar work for U.S. toy company JAKKS Pacific's branded game Girl Gourmet Cupcake Maker. The company is also behind the development of Spark City, an online game targeted to tween girl gamers. This virtual world is part of the All Girl Arcade website. The branded element appears through the integration with television and retail. As an example, Fuel is adding a movie theatre to Spark City and the "agency is in talks with broadcasters and film companies looking to run trailers in the theatre."

So, what's the cost to get your brand into Spark City? It could be anywhere between $25 000 and $200 000. But is there a risk of virtual world burnout among customers as branded sites flourish? According to Virtual Worlds Management, a Texas-based company, the future looks good, but "the cream will definitely rise to the top." Therefore, if a company chooses this strategy, as with any product, branded sites need to be developed to address the needs and wants of the selected target market.

Critical Thinking Questions

1. Discuss how marketers can build relationships with customers through newer methods of virtual advertising like advergames.

2. What are the advantages and disadvantages of internet advertising?

Once the master of mass-marketing (especially the 30-second TV spot), Coca-Cola has bowed to audience fragmentation and the advent of devices like TiVo, which allow people to skip TV ads altogether. Coke has begun experimenting with alternative approaches to promotion, focussing on events and activities that can be integrated into the daily routines of targeted consumers. In Europe, the company posts interactive websites built around music, and in the United States it has installed Coke Red Lounges in a few select malls, offering teenagers exclusive piped-in music, movies, and videos.

door communications, make up the remaining advertisements to which Canadians are exposed.

Types of Advertising

Regardless of the media used, advertisements fall into one of several categories. **Brand advertising** promotes a specific brand, such as the Canon Rebel digital camera, Air Canada, or Nike Air Jordan basketball shoes. A variation on brand advertising, **product advertising,** promotes a general type of product or service such as dental services and milk. The "Got Milk?" advertisements are an example of product advertising. **Advocacy advertising** promotes a particular candidate or viewpoint, as in ads for political candidates at election time and anti-drug commercials. **Institutional advertising** promotes a firm's long-term image rather than a specific product.

In consumer markets, local stores usually sponsor **retail advertising** to encourage consumers to visit the store and buy its products and services. Larger retailers, such as Kmart and The Bay, use retail advertising both locally and nationally. Often retail advertising is actually **co-operative advertising**, with the cost of the advertising shared by the retailer and the manufacturer.

In industrial markets, to communicate with companies that distribute its products, some firms use **trade advertising** publications. For example, a firm that makes plumbing fixtures might advertise in Hardware Retailer to persuade large hardware stores to carry its products. And to reach the professional purchasing agent and managers at firms buying raw materials or components, companies use **industrial advertising**.

Preparing an Advertising Campaign

An **advertising campaign** is the arrangement of ads in selected media to reach target audiences. It includes several activities that, taken together, constitute a program for meeting a marketing objective, such as introducing a new product or changing a company's image in the public mind. A campaign typically includes six steps:

1. Identifying the target audience
2. Defining the objectives of the advertising messages
3. Establishing the advertising budget

brand advertising Advertising that promotes a specific brand-name product.

product advertising A variation on brand advertising that promotes a general type of product or service.

advocacy advertising Advertising that promotes a particular viewpoint or candidate.

institutional advertising Advertising that promotes a firm's long-term image, not a specific product.

retail advertising Advertising by retailers designed to reach end-users of a consumer product.

co-operative advertising Advertising in which a manufacturer together with a retailer or a wholesaler advertise to reach customers.

trade advertising Advertising by manufacturers designed to reach potential wholesalers and retailers.

industrial advertising Advertising by manufacturers designed to reach other manufacturers' professional purchasing agents and managers of firms buying raw materials or components.

advertising campaign The arrangement of ads in selected media to reach target audiences.

4. Creating the advertising messages

5. Selecting the appropriate media

6. Evaluating advertising effectiveness

advertising agencies Firms that specialize in creating and placing advertisements in the media for clients.

Advertising agencies—independent companies that provide some or all of their clients' advertising needs—help in the development of advertising campaigns by providing specialized services. The agency works together with the client company to determine the campaign's central message, create detailed message content, identify advertising media, and negotiate media purchases.[61] The advantage offered by agencies is expertise in developing advertising themes, message content, and artwork, as well as in coordinating advertising production and advising on relevant legal matters. As payment for its services, the agency usually receives a percentage, traditionally 15 percent of the media purchase cost. For example, if an agency purchases a $1-million television commitment for a client's campaign, it would receive $150 000 for its services.

The globalization of business has affected advertising agencies, both in Canada and elsewhere. Increasingly, large U.S. companies are using one single agency (often headquartered somewhere other than Canada). The Association of Quebec Advertising Agencies says that big U.S. companies often bypass Montreal-based advertising agencies when they are developing advertising campaigns for Quebec. The group says that it is pointless to try to simply translate into French a campaign that is developed by a New York or Toronto agency for the rest of Canada.[62]

Personal Selling

6 Outline the tasks involved in *personal selling* and list the steps in the personal selling process.

Virtually everyone has done some personal selling. Perhaps as a child you had a lemonade stand or sold candy for the drama club. Or you may have gone on a job interview, selling your abilities as an employee to the interviewer's company. In personal selling, a salesperson communicates one-on-one with a potential customer to identify the customer's need and match that need with the seller's product.

personal selling Promotional tool in which a salesperson communicates one-on-one with potential customers.

Personal selling—the oldest form of selling—provides the personal link between seller and buyer. It adds to a firm's credibility because it provides buyers with someone to interact with and to answer their questions. Because it involves personal interaction, personal selling requires a level of trust between the buyer and the seller. When a buyer feels cheated by the seller, that trust has been broken and a negative attitude toward salespeople in general can develop.

Personal selling is the most expensive form of promotion per contact because presentations are generally made to one or two individuals at a time. Personal selling expenses include salespeople's compensation and their overhead, usually travel, food, and lodging. The average cost of each industrial sales call has been estimated at nearly $300.[63]

Costs have prompted many companies to turn to telemarketing—using telephone solicitations to conduct the personal selling process. Telemarketing is useful in handling any stage of this process and in arranging appointments for salespeople. It cuts the cost of personal sales visits to industrial customers, each of whom requires about four visits to complete a sale. Such savings are stimulating the growth of telemarketing, which provides 150 000 jobs in Canada and generates $25 billion in annual sales. Telemarketing returns $6.25 for every dollar that is spent.[64]

Because many consumers are annoyed by telemarketing pitches, a do-not-call registry was set up in Canada in 2008, and six million people quickly registered. Heavy fines can be levied on companies that ignore the new rules.

A survey by VoxPop showed that 80 percent of Canadians who registered now receive fewer tele-marketing calls than they used to,[65] but in 2009, it was discovered that some unscrupulous marketers were actually using the registry to call people. Michael Geist, a Canada Research Chair in Internet and E-commerce Law at the University of Ottawa, says the government's registry is flawed.[66]

Sales Force Management

Sales force management means setting goals at top levels of the organization, setting specific objectives for individual salespeople, organizing the sales force to meet those objectives, and implementing and evaluating the success of the overall sales plan.

Personal Selling Situations

Managers of both telemarketers and traditional salespeople must consider the ways in which personal sales activities are affected by the differences between consumer and industrial products:

In personal selling, the salesperson has the opportunity to explain in detail the benefits of the product or service, and can also respond to concerns that the customer may express regarding the product or service.

- **Retail selling** is selling a consumer product for the buyer's personal or household use.

- **Industrial selling** is selling products to other businesses, either for the purpose of manufacturing other products or or resale.

Levi's, for instance, sells jeans to the retail clothing chain Gap Inc. (industrial selling). In turn, consumers purchase Levi's jeans at one of Gap's stores (retail selling). Each of these situations has distinct characteristics. In retail selling, the buyer usually comes to the seller, but in industrial selling, the salesperson comes to the buyer.

Personal Selling Tasks

Improving sales efficiency requires marketers to consider salespeople's tasks. Three basic tasks are generally associated with selling: order processing, creative selling, and missionary selling. Sales jobs usually require salespeople to perform all three tasks to some degree, depending on the product and the company.

Order Processing. In **order processing**, a salesperson receives an order and oversees the handling and delivery of that order. Route salespeople are often order processors. They call on regular customers to check the customer's supply of bread, milk, snack foods, or soft drinks. Then, with the customer's consent, they determine the size of the reorder, fill the order from their trucks, and stack the customer's shelves.

Creative Selling. When the benefits of a product are not clear, **creative selling** may persuade buyers that they have a need for it. Most industrial products involve creative selling because the buyer has not used the product before or may not be familiar with its features and uses. Creative selling is also crucial for high-priced consumer products, such as homes, where buyers comparison shop. Any new product can benefit from creative selling that differentiates it from other products.

sales force management Setting goals at top levels of an organization; setting practical objectives for salespeople; organizing a sales force to meet those objectives; implementing and evaluating the success of a sales plan.

retail selling Selling a consumer product for the buyer's own personal or household use.

industrial selling Selling products to other businesses, either for manufacturing other products or for resale.

order processing In personal sales, the receiving and follow-through on handling and delivery of an order by a salesperson.

creative selling In personal sales, the use of techniques designed to persuade a customer to buy a product when the benefits of the product are not readily apparent or the item is very expensive.

missionary selling In personal sales, the indirect promotion of a product by offering technical assistance and/or promoting the company's image.

Missionary Selling. The goal of **missionary selling** is to promote the company and its products over the long term, rather than to make a quick sale. Drug company representatives promote their companies' drugs to doctors who, in turn, may eventually prescribe them to their patients. The sale is actually made at the drugstore.

The Personal Selling Process

Although all three sales tasks are important to an organization using personal selling, perhaps the most complicated is creative selling. It is the creative salesperson who is responsible for most of the steps in the personal selling process described below.

prospecting In personal sales, the process of identifying potential customers.

qualifying In personal sales, the process of determining whether potential customers have the authority to buy and the ability to pay for a product.

Prospecting and Qualifying. **Prospecting** is the process of identifying potential customers. Salespeople find prospects through past company records, existing customers, friends, relatives, company personnel, and business associates. **Qualifying** means determining whether prospects have the authority to buy and the ability to pay.

Approaching. The *approach* refers to the first few minutes that a salesperson has contact with a qualified prospect. The success of later stages depends on the prospect's first impression of the salesperson, since this impression affects the salesperson's credibility. Salespeople need to present a neat, professional appearance and to greet prospects in a strong, confident manner.

Presenting and Demonstrating. Presenting involves a full explanation of the product, its features, and its uses. It links the product's benefits to the prospect's needs. A presentation may or may not include a demonstration of the product, but it is wise to demonstrate a product whenever possible, since most people have trouble visualizing what they have been told.

Handling Objections. Prospects may have objections to various aspects of the product, including its price. Objections show the salesperson that the buyer is interested in the presentation and which parts of the presentation the buyer is unsure of or has a problem with. They tell the salesperson what customers feel is important and, essentially, how to sell to them.

closing In personal sales, the process of asking the customer to buy the product.

Closing. The most critical part of the selling process is the **closing**, in which the salesperson asks the prospective customer to buy the product. Successful salespeople recognize the signs that a customer is ready to buy. For example, prospects who start to figure out monthly payments for the product are clearly indicating that they are ready to buy. Salespeople can ask directly for the sale or they can indirectly imply a close.

Following Up. The sales process does not end with the close of the sale. Sales follow-up activities include fast processing of the customer's order and on-time delivery. Training in the proper care and use of the product and speedy service if repairs are needed may also be part of the follow-up.

Sales Promotions

sales promotions Short-term promotional activities designed to stimulate consumer buying or co-operation from distributors and other members of the trade.

Sales promotions are short-term promotional activities designed to stimulate consumer buying or co-operation from distributors, sales agents, or other members of the trade. For example, soap may be bound into packages of four with the promotion. "Buy three and get one free." Sales promotions are important because they enhance product recognition and increase the likelihood that buyers will try products. To be successful, sales promotions must be convenient and accessible when the decision to purchase occurs. If Harley-Davidson has a one-week motorcycle promotion and there is no dealer in your area, the promotion is neither convenient nor accessible to you, and you will not buy. But if the Bay offers a 20 percent off coupon that you can save for later use, the promotion is convenient and accessible.

Describe the various types of *sales promotions*, and distinguish between *publicity* and *public relations*. **7**

Types of Sales Promotions

The best-known sales promotions are coupons, point-of-purchase displays, purchasing incentives (such as free samples, trading stamps, and premiums), trade shows, and contests and sweepstakes.

- Certificates entitling the bearer to stated savings off a product's regular price are **coupons**. Coupons may be used to encourage customers to try new products, to attract customers away from competitors, or to induce current customers to buy more of a product. They appear in newspapers and magazines and are often sent through direct mail.

- To grab customers' attention as they walk through a store, some companies use **point-of-purchase (POP) displays**, which often coincide with a sale on the item(s) being displayed. Displays are located at the end of an aisle or near the checkout in supermarkets to make it easier for customers to find a product and easier for manufacturers to eliminate competitors from consideration.

- Free samples and premiums are purchasing incentives. **Free samples** allow customers to try a product for a few days at no cost. They may be given out at local retail outlets or sent by manufacturers to consumers via direct mail. **Premiums** are free or reduced-price items, such as pens, pencils, calendars, and coffee mugs, given to consumers in return for buying a specified product. For example, in one sales promotion, Molson Canadian included a free T-shirt with certain packages of its beer.[67] Premiums may not work as well as originally hoped, since customers may switch to a new brand just to get the premiums that company is offering and then return to their customary brand.

coupon A method of sales promotion featuring a certificate that entitles the bearer to stated savings off a product's regular price.

point-of-purchase (POP) displays A method of sales promotion in which a product display is so located in a retail store as to encourage consumers to buy the product.

free samples A method of sales promotion in which a small sample of product is offered free, allowing customers to try a product for a few days at no cost.

premium A method of sales promotion in which some item is offered free or at a bargain price to customers in return for buying a specified product.

Best Buy, a chain once known for consumer electronics and appliances, is now the biggest retailer of CDs and DVDs. To promote its entertainment products, Best Buy uses promotional tie-ins, such as a deal to become the exclusive retailer of a U2 DVD. Meanwhile, CEO Brian Dunn has continued to pursue a strategy of putting electronics and entertainment under one roof.

trade shows A method of sales promotion in which members of a particular industry gather for displays and product demonstrations designed to sell products to customers.

- **Trade shows** allow companies to rent booths to display and demonstrate their products to customers who have a special interest or who are ready to buy. Trade shows are relatively inexpensive and are very effective, since the buyer comes to the seller already interested in a given type of product.

- Customers, distributors, and sales representatives may all be persuaded to increase sales of a product through the use of contests and sweepstakes. For example, distributors and sales agents may win a trip to Hawaii for selling the most pillows in the month of February, or customers may win $1 million in a magazine sweepstake.

Publicity and Public Relations

publicity Information about a company that is made available to consumers by the news media; it is not controlled by the company, but it does not cost the company any money.

Much to the delight of marketing managers with tight budgets, **publicity** is free. Moreover, because it is presented in a news format, consumers see publicity as objective and highly believable. However, marketers often have little control over publicity, and that can have a very negative effect on the company. For example, a YouTube video showing what appeared to be a Guinness beer commercial portrayed several people in a suggestive sexual arrangement with the title "Share One with a Friend." Guinness was quick to distance itself from the fake advertisement, saying that was not how they wanted their product portrayed. In another case, the restaurant chain Olive Garden was placed in a difficult position when it received favourable publicity from Playboy Playmate Kendra Wilkinson, who at that time was one of Hugh Hefner's three live-in girlfriends and who was featured in the E! series *The Girls Next Door*. She gave several on-air plugs for the restaurant chain, but the restaurant is concerned because Wilkinson's reputation is not consistent with the company's wholesome, family-friendly image.[68]

public relations A company-influenced activity that attempts to establish a sense of goodwill between the company and its customers through public-service announcements that enhance the company's image.

Public relations is company-influenced activity that attempts to establish a sense of goodwill between the company and its customers through public-service announcements that enhance the company's image. For example, a bank may announce that senior citizens' groups can have free use of one of the bank's meeting rooms for their social activities. Corporate sponsorships of athletic events also help promote a company's image. Organizers of the 2012 Olympic Games announced in 2008 that Cadbury PLC had paid approximately $40 million to be a sponsor of the Games. It will be the sole supplier of confectionery sold in the Olympic Park.[69]

International Promotion Strategies

8 Describe the development of international and small business *promotion* strategies.

Recent decades have witnessed a profound shift from "home-country" marketing to "multi-country" marketing and now to "global" marketing. Nowhere is this rapidly growing global orientation more evident than in marketing promotions, especially advertising.

Emergence of the Global Perspective

global perspective A company's approach to directing its marketing toward worldwide rather than local or regional markets.

Every company that markets products in several countries faces a basic choice—use a decentralized approach (maintaining separate marketing for each country) or adopt a global perspective (directing a coordinated marketing program at one worldwide audience). The **global perspective** is a philosophy that directs marketing toward worldwide rather than toward local or regional markets.

Before creating an international advertisement like this Chinese ad for Coca-Cola, it is crucial to research what differences—such as meaning of words, traditions, and taboos—exist between different societies. For example, German manufacturers of backpacks label them as "body bags," which is not terribly enticing to the Canadian consumer. Gerber baby food is not sold in France because the French translation of gerber is "to vomit."

The Movement Toward Global Advertising

A truly global perspective means designing products for multinational appeal— that is, genuinely global products.[70] A few brands, such as Coca-Cola, McDonald's, Mercedes-Benz, Rolex, and Xerox, enjoy global recognition and have become truly global brands. One universal advertising program would obviously be more efficient and cost-effective than developing different programs for each of many countries. For several reasons, however, global advertising is not feasible for many companies. Four factors make global advertising a challenging proposition:

- *Product variations.* Even if a product has universal appeal, some variations (slightly different products) are usually preferred in different cultures. In the magazine business, Hearst Corp. has expanded to 33 editions of *Cosmopolitan* magazine, including one for Central America; English and Spanish editions for the United States; and local editions for Italy, Turkey, Russia, Hong Kong, and Japan. *Reader's Digest* has 48 editions in 19 languages. Many companies have found that without a local or national identity, universal ads don't cause consumers to buy. Coca-Cola's "think global, act local" strategy and Nestlé's approach to small-scale local advertising call for ads tailored to different areas. Such ads are designed to produce variations on a universal theme while appealing to local emotions, ideas, and values. Advertising agencies have set up worldwide agency networks that can coordinate a campaign's central theme while allowing regional variations.

- *Language differences.* Compared with those in other languages, ads in English require less print space and airtime because English is a more efficient and precise language than most others. But translations can be inexact and confusing. When Coke first went to China many years ago, the direct translation of *Coca-Cola* came out "Bite the wax tadpole" in Chinese.

- *Cultural receptiveness.* There are differences across nations regarding the mass advertising of sensitive products (such as birth control or personal hygiene products), not to mention those for which advertising may be legally restricted (alcohol, cigarettes). A Canadian in Paris may be surprised to see nudity in billboard ads and even more surprised to find that France is the only country in the European Union (EU) that bans advertising or selling wine on the internet. In the EU and through much of Asia, comparative advertising is considered distasteful or even illegal.

■ *Image differences.* Any company's image can vary from nation to nation, regardless of advertising appeals for universal recognition. American Express, IBM, and Nestlé have better images in the United States than in the United Kingdom, where Heinz, Coca-Cola, and Ford have better images.

Promotional Practices in Small Business

Although small businesses generally have fewer resources, cost-effective promotions can improve sales and enable small firms to compete with much larger firms.

Small Business Advertising

Few developments in history have provided more advertising opportunities than the internet. Cheaper access to computing equipment, to online services, and to website expertise puts cyberspace within the grasp of nearly every firm. Still, owners must decide which audiences to target and what messages to send. And even though the web can instantaneously reach distant customers, other methods depend on the market that the small business is trying to reach—local, national, or international.

Non-primetime ads on local or cable TV have good impact at costs within the reach of many small firms. More often, however, small firms use newspaper, radio, and, increasingly, direct mail to reach local markets. For year-round advertising, the Yellow Pages is popular for both industrial and consumer products. However, many small businesses, especially those selling to consumer markets, rely more on seasonal advertising.

Many small businesses have grown by using direct mail, particularly catalogues. By purchasing mailing lists from other companies, small firms can cut costs with targeted mailings. The ability to target an audience also makes specialized magazines attractive to small businesses. When it comes to international markets, television, radio, and newspapers are too expensive for small businesses. Most small firms find direct mail and carefully targeted magazine ads the most effective tools.

The Role of Personal Selling in Small Business

As with advertising, small business personal selling strategies depend on intended markets. Some small firms maintain sales forces, especially in local markets, where clients can be quickly visited. But most small companies cannot afford to establish international offices, although some entrepreneurs do visit prospective customers in other countries. For most small businesses, even sending sales representatives abroad is too expensive. Some contract with sales agencies—companies that act on behalf of several clients. Because the costs of a national sales force are high, small companies prefer sales agencies and such methods as telemarketing. By combining telemarketing with catalogues or other print media, small businesses can sometimes compete with larger companies on a national scale. Syncsort Inc. combined a telemarketing staff with eight national sales reps to become the number-one developer of computer software for sorting data into convenient formats (IBM is number two).

Small Business Promotions

Small companies also use sales promotions to market their products. Large firms tend to rely on coupons, POP displays, and sales contests, but small firms prefer premiums and special sales because they are less expensive.[71] An automobile dealership, for example, might offer you a fishing reel if you come in to road test a new car. Service companies ranging from martial arts centres to dry cleaners frequently feature special sale prices.

Test yourself on the material for this chapter at **www.pearsoned.ca/mybusinesslab.**

Summary of
Learning Objectives

1. **Explain the definition of a product as a** *value package*. A *product* is a good, service, or idea that is marketed to satisfy consumer needs and wants. Consumers regard a product as a bundle of attributes that, taken together, constitute the *value package*. Consumers expect to receive products with greater value, that is, products with more benefits at a reasonable price. A successful product is a value package that provides the right *features* and offers the right benefits. Features are the qualities, tangible and intangible, that a company builds into its products.

2. **Describe the new** *product development process* **and trace the stages of the** *product life cycle*. Many firms adopt some version of a basic seven-step new product development process: (1) *Product ideas:* searching for ideas for new products; (2) *Screening:* eliminating all product ideas that do not mesh with the firm's abilities or objectives; (3) *Concept testing:* using market research to get consumers' input about product benefits and prices; (4) *Business analysis:* comparing manufacturing costs and benefits to see whether a product meets minimum profitability goals; (5) *Prototype development:* producing a preliminary version of a product; (6) *Product testing* and *test marketing:* going into limited production, testing the product to see if it meets performance requirements, and, if so, selling it on a limited basis; and (7) *Commercialization:* beginning full-scale production and marketing.

The *product life cycle (PLC)* is a series of four stages or phases characterizing a product's profit-producing life: (1) I*ntroduction:* Marketers focus on making potential consumers aware of the product and its benefits; (2) *Growth:* Sales begin to climb and the product begins to show a profit; (3) *Maturity:* Although the product earns its highest profit level, increased competition eventually leads to price cutting and lower profits, and sales start to fall; (4) *Decline:* Sales and profits are further lost to new products in the introduction stage.

3. **Explain the importance of** *branding, packaging,* **and** *labelling. Branding* is a process of using symbols to communicate the qualities of a particular product made by a particular producer. Brands are designed to signal uniform quality. *Packaging* refers to the physical container in which a product is sold, advertised, or protected. A package makes the product attractive, displays the brand name, and identifies features and benefits. It also reduces the risk of damage, breakage, or spoilage, and it lessens the likelihood of theft. Every product has a *label* on its package that identifies its name, manufacturer, and contents. Like packaging, labelling can help market a product.

4. Identify the important objectives of *promotion* and discuss the considerations in selecting a *promotional mix. Promotion* is any technique designed to sell a product. Besides the ultimate objective of increasing sales, marketers may use promotion to accomplish any of the following four goals: (1) c*ommunicating information*, (2) *positioning products*, (3) *adding value*, and (4) *controlling sales volume.*

There are four types of promotional tools: *advertising, personal selling, sales promotions,* and *publicity* and *public relations.* The best combination of these tools—the best

▶

promotional mix—depends on several factors, the most important of which is the target audience and buyer decision process. Marketers try to match promotional tools with stages in the buyer decision process.

5. Discuss the most important *advertising* strategies and describe the key *advertising media*. The advertising strategies used for a product most often depend on the stage of the product life cycle the product is in. As products become established and competition increases, advertisers may choose one of three strategies: (1) *persuasive advertising*, (2) *comparative advertising*, and (3) *reminder advertising*.

Marketers use several different advertising media-specific communication devices for conveying a seller's message to potential customers: (1) *television*, (2) *newspapers*, (3) *direct mail*, (4) *radio*, (5) *magazines*, (6) *outdoor advertising*, (7) *internet advertising*, and (8) *virtual advertising*.

6. Outline the tasks involved in *personal selling* and list the steps in the personal selling process. There are three basic tasks in personal selling: (1) *order processing*, (2) *creative selling*, and (3) *missionary selling*. The creative salesperson goes through most of the following six steps in the personal selling process: (1) *Prospecting* and *qualifying*: Prospecting identifies potential customers, who are then qualified to determine whether they have the authority to buy and ability to pay. (2) *Approaching*: The first few minutes of contact with a qualified prospect make up the approach. (3) *Presenting* and *demonstrating*: After the approach, the salesperson makes a presentation. (4) *Handling objections*: Objections pinpoint the parts of the presentation with which the buyer has a problem and which the salesperson must overcome. (5) *Closing*: In the closing, the salesperson asks the prospective customer to buy the product. (6) *Following up*: To cement lasting relationships with buyers, sellers supply additional after-sale services.

7. Describe the various types of *sales promotions*, and distinguish between *publicity* and *public relations*. Sales promotions are short-term promotional activities designed to stimulate consumer buying or co-operation from members of the trade. The following are the best-known forms of promotions: (1) *Coupons* are certificates entitling bearers to savings off regular prices. (2) *Point-of-purchase (POP) displays* are used by companies to grab customers' attention as they move through stores. (3) *Free samples* are purchasing incentives that allow customers to try products without risk. (4) *Premiums* are gifts to consumers in return for buying certain products. (5) Industries sponsor *trade shows*, at which companies rent booths to display and demonstrate products to customers with a special interest in them. (6) *Contests* are a means to persuade customers, distributors, and sales reps to increase sales.

Publicity is a promotional tool in which information about a company or product is created and transmitted by general mass media. It is free, and because it is presented in a news format, consumers often see it as objective and credible. However, marketers often have little control over it, and it can be as easily detrimental as beneficial. *Public relations* is company-influenced publicity that seeks to build good relations with the public and to deal with unfavourable events.

8. Describe the development of *international and small business promotion* strategies. Recent decades have witnessed a profound shift from home-country marketing to global marketing. Every company that markets its products in several countries faces a basic choice: Use a *decentralized approach*, with separate marketing management for each country, or adopt a *global perspective*, directing marketing toward a worldwide rather than a local or regional market. There are four factors that determine whether global advertising is feasible: (1) *product variations*, (2) *language differences*, (3) *cultural receptiveness*, and (4) *image differences*. In recognizing national differences, many global marketers try to build on a universal advertising theme that nevertheless allows for variations. In doing so, they rely on help from different advertising agencies in various geographic regions.

Key Terms

advertising   (p. 583)
advertising agencies   (p. 590)
advertising campaign   (p. 589)
advertising media   (p. 583)
advocacy advertising   (p. 589)
brand advertising   (p. 589)
brand equity   (p. 575)
brand loyalty   (p. 576)
branding   (p. 574)
capital items   (p. 569)
capital services   (p. 569)
closing   (p. 592)
comparative advertising   (p. 583)
Consumer Packaging and
   Labelling Act   (p. 578)
convenience goods/services   (p. 569)
co-operative advertising   (p. 589)
copyright   (p. 577)
coupon   (p. 593)
creative selling   (p. 591)
direct mail   (p. 584)
ecommerce   (p. 586)
expense items   (p. 569)
features   (p. 568)
free samples   (p. 593)
global perspective   (p. 594)

industrial advertising   (p. 589)
industrial selling   (p. 591)
informative advertising   (p. 583)
institutional advertising   (p. 589)
internet marketing   (p. 586)
label   (p. 578)
licensed brands   (p. 576)
media mix   (p. 583)
missionary selling   (p. 592)
national brands   (p. 575)
order processing   (p. 591)
packaging   (p. 578)
patent   (p. 577)
personal selling   (p. 590)
persuasive advertising   (p. 583)
point-of-purchase (POP) displays
   (p. 593)
premium   (p. 593)
private brands   (p. 576)
product adaptation   (p. 574)
product advertising   (p. 589)
product extension   (p. 574)
product life cycle (PLC)   (p. 572)
product line   (p. 570)
product mix   (p. 570)
product positioning   (p. 579)

promotion   (p. 578)
promotional mix   (p. 581)
prospecting   (p. 592)
public relations   (p. 594)
publicity   (p. 594)
pull strategy   (p. 581)
push strategy   (p. 581)
qualifying   (p. 592)
reintroduction   (p. 574)
reminder advertising   (p. 583)
retail advertising   (p. 589)
retail selling   (p. 591)
sales force management   (p. 591)
sales promotions   (p. 592)
service package   (p. 571)
service process design   (p. 572)
shopping goods/services   (p. 569)
specialty goods/services   (p. 569)
speed to market   (p. 571)
trade advertising   (p. 589)
trade shows   (p. 594)
trademark   (p. 577)
value package   (p. 568)
virtual advertising   (p. 588)
word-of-mouth advertising
   (p. 586)

Questions for Analysis

1. What impact do the different levels of brand loyalty (recognition, preference, insistence) have on the consumer buying process that was described in Chapter 16?

2. Why would a business use a push strategy rather than a pull strategy?

3. Analyze several advertisements that use comparative advertising. Do these advertisements leave you with a positive or negative image of the company? Also, analyze differences in the comparative advertisements that are shown on U.S. and Canadian television networks. Do these differences affect your opinion of the advertiser?

4. How would you expect the branding, packaging, and labelling of convenience, shopping, and specialty goods to differ? Why? Give examples to illustrate your answers.

5. Choose two advertising campaigns that have recently been conducted by business firms in your area. Choose one that you think is effective and one that you think is ineffective. What differences in the campaigns make one better than the other?

6. Select a good or service that you have purchased recently. Try to retrace the relevant steps in the buyer decision process as you experienced it. Which steps were most important to you? Which steps were least important?

7. Find examples of publicity about some business, either a local firm or a national firm. Did the publicity have, or is it likely to have, positive or negative consequences for the business? Why?

Application Exercises

1. Interview the manager of a local manufacturing firm. Identify the company's different products according to their positions in the product life cycle.

2. Select a product that is sold nationally. Identify as many media used in its promotion as you can. Which medium is used most often? On the whole, do you think the campaign is effective? What criteria did you use to make your judgment about effectiveness?

3. Interview the owner of a local small business. Identify the company's promotional objectives and strategies, and the elements in its promotional mix. What, if any, changes would you suggest? Why?

4. Check out your college's or university's website and determine how effective it is as a tool for promoting your school.

Building Your Business Skills

Greeting Start-up Decisions

The Purpose of the Assignment

To encourage students to analyze the potential usefulness of two promotional methods—personal selling and direct mail—for a start-up greeting card company.

Assignment

You are the marketing adviser for a local start-up company that makes and sells specialty greeting cards in a city of 400 000. Last year's sales totalled 14 000 cards, including personalized holiday cards, birthday cards, and special-events cards for individuals. Although revenues increased last year, you see a way of further boosting sales by expanding into card shops, grocery stores, and gift shops. You see two alternatives for entering these outlets:

1. Use direct mail to reach more individual customers for specialty cards

2. Use personal selling to gain display space in retail stores

   Your challenge is to convince the owner of the start-up company which alternative is the more financially sound decision.

Step 1

Get together with four or five classmates to research the two kinds of product segments, personalized cards and retail store cards. Find out which of the two kinds of marketing promotions will be more effective for each of the two segments. What will be the reaction to each method from customers, retailers, and card company owners?

Step 2

Draft a proposal to the company owner. Leaving budget and production details to other staffers, list as many reasons as possible for adopting direct mail. Then list as many reasons as possible for adopting personal selling. Defend each reason. Consider the following reasons in your argument:

- Competitive environment: Analyze the impact of other card suppliers that offer personalized cards and cards for sale in retail stores.

- Expectations of target markets: Who buys personalized cards, and who buys ready-made cards from retail stores?

- Overall cost of the promotional effort: Which method—direct mail or personal selling—will be more costly?

- Marketing effectiveness: Which promotional method will result in greater consumer response?

Now respond to the following items:

1. Why do you think some buyers want personalized cards? Why do some consumers want ready-made cards from retail stores?

2. Today's computer operating systems provide easy access to software for designing and making cards on home PCs. How does the availability of this product affect your recommendation?

3. What was your most convincing argument for using direct mail? And for using personal selling?

4. Can a start-up company compete in retail stores against industry giants such as Hallmark?

Exercising Your Ethics: Team Exercise

Cleaning Up in Sales

The Situation

Selling a product—whether a good or a service—requires the salesperson to believe in it, to be confident of his or her sales skills, and to keep commitments made to clients. Because so many people and resources are involved in delivering a product, numerous uncertainties and problems can give rise to ethical issues. This exercise encourages you to examine some of the ethical issues that can surface in the selling process for industrial products.

The Dilemma

Cleaning Technologies Corporation (CTC) is a U.S.-based company that manufactures equipment for industrial cleaners. The Canadian division of CTC has just hired Denise Skilsel and six other new graduates, and these seven individuals have just completed the sales training program for a new line of high-tech machinery that CTC has developed. As a new salesperson, Skilsel is eager to meet potential clients, all of whom are professional buyers for companies—such as laundries and dry cleaners, carpet cleaners, and military cleaners—that use CTC products or those of competitors. Skilsel is especially enthusiastic about several facts that she learned during training: CTC's equipment is the most technically advanced in the industry, carries a 10-year performance guarantee, and is safe—both functionally and environmentally.

The first month was difficult but successful. In visits to seven firms, Skilsel successfully closed three sales, earning large commissions (pay is based on sales results) as well as praise from the sales manager. Moreover, after listening to her presentations, two more potential buyers had given verbal commitments and were about to sign for much bigger orders than any Skilsel had closed to date. As she was catching her flight to close those sales, Skilsel received two calls—one from a client and one from a competitor.

The client, just getting started with CTC equipment, was having some trouble: Employees stationed nearby were getting sick when the equipment was running. The competitor told Skilsel that the U.S. Environmental Protection Agency (EPA) had received complaints from some of CTC's U.S. customers that the new technology was environmentally unsafe because of noxious emissions.

Team Activity

Assemble a group of four students and assign each group member to one of the following roles:

- Denise Skilsel: CTC salesperson (employee)
- CTC sales manager (employer)
- CTC customer
- CTC investor

Action Steps

1. Before discussing the situation with your group, and from the perspective of your assigned role, what do you recommend that Skilsel say to the two client firms she is scheduled to visit? Write down your recommendation.

2. Gather your group together and reveal, in turn, each member's recommendation.

3. Appoint someone to record the main points of agreement and disagreement within the group. How do you explain the results? What accounts for any disagreement?

4. Identify any ethical issues involved in group members' recommendations. Which issues, if any, are more critical than others?

5. From an ethical standpoint, what does your group finally recommend that Skilsel say to the two client firms she is scheduled to visit? Explain your result.

6. Identify the advantages and drawbacks resulting from your recommendations.

Measuring the Effectiveness of Advertising

Business firms spend a lot of money each year on advertising, so it is not surprising that they want to know what effect their advertising is having. For example, marketers are asking advertising agencies more probing questions about advertising campaigns and media buys: How are the media plans developed, who buys the current mix of media, and how well have they performed? Faced with growing accountability to perform, ad agencies are, in turn, imposing more accountability on media outlets where they place advertisements. Local and national TV may no longer rely solely on Nielsen ratings as evidence for ad effectiveness; more convincing proof of performance would show how much they contribute to advertiser's sales. Newsprint, magazines, radio, and other media will also be asked for more convincing evidence of effectiveness. New ways to test the effects of media on consumer attention, persuasion and consumer thinking, and responsiveness in buying behaviour are in the development stage. Reliable measurements will allow media planners in advertising agencies to compare bottom-line results from alternative media expenditures—newsprint, radio, magazines, local TV, national TV—and to pinpoint the best combination of media buys for the agency's client.

In general, advertisers want to know what television programs consumers are watching, or what websites they are visiting, so they can effectively direct their advertisements. If it can be demonstrated that some TV shows or internet websites are more popular than others, advertisers are willing to pay more to have their ads appear in those places.

Measuring Television Viewership

Nielsen Media Research is the most well-known company providing information on television viewing habits of the general public. It gets its revenues by selling its viewer data to advertising agencies, television networks, and cable companies. In the past, the system involved having selected viewers write down the channel number they were watching and who was watching TV each quarter-hour of the day. But this system was cumbersome, and consumers often made errors when they were filling out the forms. The system gradually began to break down as technology changed. For example, when remote controls became popular, so did channel surfing, but channel surfing is virtually impossible to reflect in a diary. The introduction of digital video recorders (DVRs) and the delivery of shows via cellphone, computer, and iPod has made Nielsen's old system obsolete.

Nielsen initially responded to criticisms by attaching electronic meters to household TVs. The meter determined what channel was being watched and who was watching, but viewers still had to punch in a pre-assigned number on their remote control whenever they started to watch. These meters likely improved the accuracy of in-home viewing data, but they did not address the growing problem of measuring viewing habits of people who were not at home but who were still watching TV. For example, measuring the viewing habits of students who live away from home at university is not easy. Nielsen also doesn't monitor viewing in offices, bars, hotels, prisons, and many other out-of-home venues.

Cable companies argue that Nielsen's system doesn't accurately capture the large number of people who watch cable TV. Differences can be substantial with different measuring systems. For example, in a side-by-side analysis in New York City, an episode of *The Simpsons* on the Fox network showed a 27 percent decline when the new electronic meters were used, but shows on Comedy Central cable saw gains of 225 percent using the same electronic measurement.

In Montreal and Quebec City, consumers are being paid to carry a pager-sized device that records each advertisement they see or hear and every store or restaurant they go into. BBM Canada is using something called the Personal Portable Meter (PPM) to determine television ratings. These devices, which listen for cues that broadcasters have embedded in their broadcasts, enable BBM to assess television viewing outside peoples' homes. (The system has also been introduced for radio listeners in Montreal.) The new system will eventually allow advertisers to correlate the advertisements people hear with the products they buy. They can therefore determine how effective their advertisements are.

In 2006, Nielsen announced that it would introduce new technology that would allow it to capture DVR viewing on a daily basis. It will also begin measuring video-on-demand and testing ways of measuring viewing on the internet and on hand-held devices such as iPods and cellphones. If these new measuring systems show significantly different viewing patterns than historical data, it will likely result in advertisers shifting their money around. Nielsen also has invested in a company called NeuroFocus, which is developing a system for scanning the human brain to determine if people are paying attention to (and remembering) ads they see.

But even if these improvements are made, some critics will not be happy. The vice-president at one advertising space–buying company, for example, says that the only thing that is important to measure is "live" viewing.

▶

The use of DVRs has led to a sharp drop in "live" television viewing, and people who are watching a DVR program may not even be watching the ads. Not surprisingly, TV companies disagree with that assessment. They argue that ad rates should be determined by the total viewership an ad gets.

Measuring Internet Viewership

Two web measurement services—comScore and Nielsen Online—gather data on internet use by getting people to agree to let their online surfing and purchasing patterns be monitored. The behaviour of these individuals is then extrapolated to the larger population. Since this method is similar to the traditional assessment method that Nielsen used to measure television viewing habits, there are also concerns about its accuracy. To overcome these concerns, Google Inc. introduced a new service designed to more accurately measure internet use. Because it shows which websites various target audiences visit, the new system should help advertisers figure out which are the best places to buy online ads. Google's system uses data from web servers, and this should allow for a better understanding of how the internet is used by consumers. Both comScore and Nielsen Online charge advertisers for the data they provide, but Google will provide the information free of charge. Google also introduced a new system to help advertisers determine how web surfers respond to the ads they see on the various sites they visit. The system works by comparing people who have seen the ads with people who haven't.

No system is perfect, and it is clear that using web servers to gather data has some problems of its own. For example, measurement is based on "cookies" (tracking data), but some users delete cookies and then another cookie is attached when they later revisit a website. This can lead to overstatement of the number of website visits. As well, the system has trouble telling whether a website visit is from an actual consumer or from a technology that visits different websites.

One of the potentially serious problems with gathering data about consumer behaviour is "click fraud." It can occur in several ways, such as when a web developer repeatedly clicks on a website in order to make it seem like there is a great deal of interest in it. Or computers can be programmed to repeatedly click on ads to simulate a real consumer clicking on ads on a webpage. When this happens, advertisers get a bigger bill but no extra sales revenue. When click fraud occurs, the money spent on advertising is obviously wasted. Click Forensics Inc., a click fraud reporting service, reports that the click fraud rate is about 16 percent. But Google claims that only 2 out of 10 000 clicks are fraudulent.

Questions for Discussion

1. The viewership data that Nielsen develops is important in determining how much advertisers pay to place their ads on TV. What are the advantages and disadvantages of the system? Are there alternative systems that might work better? Explain.

2. The argument has been made that counting DVR viewing isn't useful, because people don't watch program advertisements when using a DVR and because advertisements simply don't have the same urgency as they do when the program actually airs. Do you agree or disagree with this argument? Give reasons. Whatever your position, how do you think uncertainty over issues like this influences the value of the data that are produced? What could be done to improve the data?

3. Suppose that you are buying advertising space on TV. Would you be more likely to accept Nielsen data for, say, sports programs than you would for dramas? Explain. What kind of biases might you have and why?

4. What are the strong and weak points of measuring viewership for internet advertisements?

Concluding Case 17 -2

The Changing Face of Advertising

A long time ago (in the 1960s and 1970s), advertising was simple. Sellers of products paid for radio, TV, and newspaper advertisements to get the attention of prospective customers. Consumers basically put up with advertisements because they knew that advertisers were providing radio, TV, or newspaper content in return for their advertisements being shown. But consumers have never liked most advertisements, and when they are given an opportunity to avoid them, they take it. And that opportunity has increasingly been provided as consumers are given the tools to help them avoid advertisements.

In TV, the problem (from the advertisers' perspective) is caused by VCRs and digital video recorders like TiVo. Although these devices were primarily designed to allow consumers to record TV shows when they had other commitments, consumers quickly discovered that they could fast-forward through those annoying advertisements.

This obviously defeated the purpose for which TV advertisements were produced. It is estimated that by 2010 almost half of all television programming will be watched this way and that consumers will fast-forward through 80 percent of the advertisements they might otherwise have seen.

In radio, the development of satellite radio poses another threat to advertisers. Earth-based radio stations beam their signal to orbiting satellites, which in turn beam the signal to a satellite radio company such as Sirius Satellite. These companies then make the signal available to consumers who pay a monthly fee for the service. In 2005, the Canadian Radio-television and Telecommunications Commission approved licences for Canadian companies to start providing ad-free satellite radio service. In addition to allowing listeners to avoid advertisements, satellite radio may threaten the competitive position of existing AM radio stations because the satellite radio companies are required to have only 10 percent Canadian content, while existing AM radio stations are required to have 35 percent Canadian content. However, consumer interest in satellite radio has to date been much higher in the United States than in Canada.

Advertisers are not sitting idly by as these trends unfold. Instead, they are using several new tactics to reach consumers. These include stealth advertising, product placement, cellphone advertising, and interactive television advertising.

Stealth Advertising

As the name implies, stealth advertising is designed to advertise a company's product without consumers knowing that they are the target of an actual advertisement. (For more information on stealth advertising, see Chapter 5.)

Product Placement

Product placement (also called embedded advertising) involves using brand name products as part of the actual storyline of TV shows. For example, Home Depot has been able to embed its brand name into shows like *Trading Spaces*, *Survivor*, and *The Apprentice*. In one installment of *Canadian Idol*, the Subway logo was clearly displayed on water bottles in front of the judges. Other products either mentioned or displayed during the program were sponsored by Disney World, Coca-Cola, and Nokia. Many companies are using product placement, including Bell Canada (on CBC's *Making the Cut*) and Buick (on *Desperate Housewives*).

Product placement is not limited to TV advertising; it can also be found in movies, novels, video games, pop songs, music videos, and Broadway plays. It is also rapidly increasing in importance. PQ Media estimated that spending in the United States on product placements in all media was $2.9 billion in 2007, with television accounting for $2 billion. In Canada, $32 million was spent on product placement in 2007, with television accounting for $26 million. More and more time is being devoted to product placement on prime-time television shows. On the big U.S. networks, nine minutes of each hour is devoted to showing products as part of the program's storyline. There are also nearly 14 minutes of traditional commercials each hour, so nearly 23 minutes (37 percent of each hour) is taken up with advertisements of one sort or another.

Product placement must be done carefully because it is a complex type of advertising. Pat Wilkinson, director of marketing for Home Depot Canada, says that for every dollar the company spends on branded entertainment, it must spend an additional $3–$5 to make it deliver further results. And Michael Beckerman, the chief marketing officer for the Bank of Montreal, says that product placements must be "natural." He says that if a person is watching, say, *Desperate Housewives* and the characters started talking about BMO mutual funds, viewers would see it as a blatant advertisement, and it would not likely be effective.

Cellphone Advertising

Capitalizing on new technology and the popularity of cellphones, Maiden Group PLC and Filter UK Ltd. have developed a system where transmitters detect cellphones that are equipped with Bluetooth, a short-range wireless technology, and then the transmitters beam out text messages to these cellphones. For example, passengers in the first-class lounge who were waiting to board a Virgin Atlantic Airways flight at London's Heathrow airport were asked if they would like to watch a video-clip about a new SUV on their phone. The transmitters are also installed in billboards in train stations in the United Kingdom. In one test, the transmitters discovered 87 000 Bluetooth-equipped phones at the railway station; 13 000 of the cellphone users agreed to view the advertisement when asked. Cellphone advertising is important to advertisers because people are spending less time watching TV or reading newspapers.

Interactive Television Advertising

Interactive television advertising allows viewers of advertisements to opt for more information about products if they are interested. Consider this example: Sony Corp. produced a TV advertisement for the action movie *XXX: State of the Union* that included an icon that appeared on TV screens. The icon invited viewers to press a button on their remote to learn more about the movie. If they pushed the button, they got access to a 30-minute program that included 10 minutes of the actual movie as well as interviews with the stars. A unit of Chrysler also developed an interactive ad that lets viewers go to a special screen where they can customize a car.

▶

One new variation of interactive advertising is nanogaming, which is a blend of trivia games and social networking that allows television viewers to use their knowledge to predict what will happen next on a program. For example, viewers might guess who will score on the next play in a football game, or predict who will be the next person to be kicked off a show like *Big Brother*. Viewers who make correct predictions earn points that can be redeemed for merchandise. Advertisers like nanogaming because it can only be done if the viewer is actually tuned in to the live broadcast of the program (not just watching it on a DVR). This prevents viewers from fast-forwarding through advertisements.

The idea of giving consumers an opportunity to interact with advertisers is also evident on the internet. Procter & Gamble developed an online contest for its Crest Whitening Expressions brand where internet users voted for their favourite potential new flavour. Crest promised to make a product based on the winning flavour. Over 785 000 votes were recorded over a three-month period. To promote its Malibu Maxx vehicle, GM Canada ran an online search for the Canadian couple with the greatest height difference.

Contestants logged on to www.LongandShort.gmcanada.com and completed a survey.

Questions for Discussion

1. Consumers are taking advantage of ways to avoid seeing advertisements, but companies are also developing new techniques to increase the visibility of their products. What do you think will be the eventual outcome in this "contest"? Give examples to demonstrate your reasoning.

2. Will the emphasis on each of the four Ps of marketing (product, price, promotion, and place) change in importance as consumers get more opportunities to avoid viewing advertisements? Why or why not?

3. To what extent will the changes that are occurring in advertising affect the new product development process in companies?

4. Does the value of brand names increase or decrease when consumers are able to take advantage of ways to avoid seeing advertisements?

Chapter 18

Pricing and Distributing Goods and Services

After reading this chapter, you should be able to:

1 Identify the various *pricing objectives* that govern pricing decisions and describe the price-setting tools used in making these decisions.

2 Discuss *pricing strategies* and tactics for existing and new products.

3 Explain the distribution mix, the different *channels of distribution,* and different *distribution strategies.*

4 Explain the differences between *merchant wholesalers* and *agents/ brokers,* and describe the activities of e-intermediaries.

5 Identify the different types of *retailing* and *retail stores.*

6 Define *physical distribution* and describe the major activities in *warehousing* operations.

7 Compare the five basic forms of *transportation* and explain how distribution can be used as a marketing strategy.

Taken from *Business*, Seventh Canadian Edition, by Ricky W. Griffin, Ronald J. Ebert, Frederick A. Starke, and Melanie D. Lang.

Buyers and Sellers Jockey for Position

Retail shoppers want to get the lowest price possible, and retailer sellers want to get the highest price possible to protect their profit margins. As a result, there is always a certain level of tension between sellers of goods and the customers who buy them. As a result of the recession that started in 2008, this tension has reached a new level.

Stores continue to trumpet low prices as they always have, but they don't want to attract just the "cherry-picking" customers (those who go from store to store buying only on-sale items). Rather, retailers want customers who buy a variety of products, because this allows the retailer to keep profit margins higher. When you go into a Zellers store, for example, you might see boxes of canned Coca-Cola near the entrance with a bargain price of three for $9.99. But you'll have to look harder to find the discount price of $58.97 on Sesame Street's Elmo. As you are looking for Elmo, the store hopes you will find some other item that you need that is not on sale.

Wal-Mart tries to cope with cherry-picking consumers by placing products that customers might overlook close to high-demand items (e.g., placing reduced-priced slippers next to higher-priced boots). Canadian Tire and Loblaw Companies Ltd. have also noted the cherry-picking trend. In addition to strategically placing sale items, retailers can cope with cherry-pickers by limiting quantities (e.g., "one per customer"), advertising higher-margin items, and developing promotional programs that encourage shoppers to buy a broad range of products.

Retailers aren't the only ones struggling with low margins. Manufacturers are also faced with pricing dilemmas. For example, when Unilever Canada Ltd. was faced with big cost increases in the price of soybean oil used

in Hellmann's mayonnaise, it debated about whether it should increase the price or simply absorb the cost increase. It finally decided to do neither. Instead, it kept the price the same but decreased the size of the mayonnaise jar from 950 mL to 890 mL and changed the container from glass to plastic (which cut manufacturing costs).

This practice has become very common because marketers believe that people don't notice the change in quantity like they do the change in price. Other examples of this strategy are as follows:

- General Motors started charging extra for antilock brakes instead of including them at no charge as it used to (this also constituted a price increase).

- Juicy Fruit gum reduced the number of pieces in a pack from 17 to 15 while keeping the price the same.

- Tropicana orange juice reduced its container size from 2.84 litres to 2.63 litres.

- General Mills introduced smaller boxes for Cheerios and Wheaties, and Kellogg Co. did the same with many of its cereals.

Here is an interesting statistic that is relevant for the issue of prices: In November 2008, only two of the 30 companies that make up the Dow Jones Industrial Average had higher stock prices than they did in November 2007 before the recession hit. Those two companies—McDonald's and Wal-Mart—are legendary for their low prices, and both of them benefited as consumers "traded down" to cheaper meals and consumer products as a result of the recession. There are many other examples as well. Consider the recent success of so-called dollar stores—retailers that offer ultra-cheap prices on a limited selection of goods. These include stores like The Silver Dollar, Dollarama, and Buck or Two. Sales revenues for this type of retail outlet have doubled in the last five years, and the number of stores has tripled. While dollar stores originally targeted low-income shoppers, they now are appealing to buyers at all income levels, and they are gaining the attention of companies that once ignored them. Procter & Gamble, for example, created a special version of Dawn dish soap that sells for $1, and Kraft Foods sells boxes of macaroni and cheese in dollar stores.

Pricing issues are very significant in the cigarette industry. For many years, the North American cigarette market has been an oligopoly that is dominated by a few very large tobacco companies like Imperial Tobacco, R.J. Reynolds, Philip Morris, Brown & Williamson, and Lorillard Tobacco. The pricing strategy that has historically been used by these companies is to increase prices to maintain (or increase) profits. This strategy worked for decades because customers were very loyal to their favourite brand. But now, some new cigarette manufacturing companies have started up and are pricing their cigarettes as much as 50 percent lower than the "majors." The majors are likely to have less control over the market than they used to, and they are going to have much more difficulty simply raising prices in the future. ◆

How will this help me?

By understanding the material presented in this chapter, you will benefit in three ways: (1) As a consumer, you will have a better understanding of how a product's development, promotion, and distribution affect its selling price; (2) as an investor, you'll be better prepared to evaluate a company's marketing program and its competitive potential before buying the company's stock; and (3) as an employee and/or manager, you'll be able to use your knowledge about product pricing and distribution to further your career.

In this chapter, we continue with our analysis of the four Ps of marketing by looking first at price and then at place (channels of distribution). As the opening case shows, the price element of the marketing mix has become intensely competitive during the last few years. But price is not the only important element. We analyze the distribution function of marketing as well, because consumers also want products and services to be available in the right place at the right time.

Pricing Objectives and Tools

1 Identify the various *pricing objectives* that govern pricing decisions and describe the price-setting tools used in making these decisions.

pricing Deciding what the company will receive in exchange for its product.

pricing objectives Goals that producers hope to attain in pricing products for sale.

In **pricing**, managers decide what the company will receive in exchange for its products. In this section, we first discuss the objectives that influence a firm's pricing decisions. Then we describe the major tools that companies use to achieve those objectives.

Pricing to Meet Business Objectives

Different companies have different **pricing objectives**. Some firms want to maximize profit, while others try to achieve a high market share. Pricing decisions are also influenced by the need to survive in the marketplace, by social and ethical concerns, and even by corporate image.

Profit-Maximizing Objectives

Pricing to maximize profits is tricky. If prices are set too low, the company will probably sell many units of its product, but it may miss the opportunity to make additional profit on each unit—and may in fact lose money on each exchange. Conversely, if prices are set too high, the company will make a large profit on each item but will sell fewer units, resulting in excess inventory and a need to reduce production operations. Again, the firm loses money. To avoid these problems, companies try to set prices to sell the number of units that will generate the highest possible total profits.

The strategy of charging prices based on market conditions is increasingly evident. For example, Coca-Cola tested a vending machine that automatically raised the price of a Coke as the temperature climbed. It also tried setting prices at different vending machines at different levels, depending on how many customers used the machine.[1] The Ottawa Senators increased prices 20 percent for games against the Toronto Maple Leafs and the Detroit Red Wings.[2]

In the public sector, governments are also using prices, not to maximize profit, but to manage traffic patterns. An experimental dynamic-pricing system of toll-road fees has been introduced in Stockholm, Sweden, in an attempt to reduce traffic congestion. In the busiest time of the day, road users must pay fees that are double those charged during lighter traffic times. During the trial period, declines were evident in the number of vehicles using the roads, the number of personal injuries, and the amount of emissions from motor vehicles.[3] In the United Kingdom, one auto insurer has introduced a system where car insurance premiums vary depending on how much, where, and when a person drives. For example, a 40-year-old driver who is driving on a divided highway at 2 p.m. might pay only one pence per mile to drive, but a teenager driving at 1 a.m. would pay dramatically more (about one *pound* per mile).[4] In Canada, Skymeter Corp. is developing a technology that tracks how far a car travels and where it parks. It does away with the need for highway toll booths and parking attendants. A GPS unit on the car's dashboard makes the measurements and calculations.[5]

"O.K., who *can* put a price on love? Jim?"

Managers in business firms calculate profits by comparing revenues against costs for materials and labour to create the product. But they also consider the capital resources (plant and equipment) that the company must tie up to generate that level of profit. The costs of marketing (such as maintaining a large sales staff) can also be substantial. Concern over the efficient use of these resources has led many firms to set prices so as to achieve a targeted level of return on sales or capital investment.[6]

Market Share Objectives

In the long run, a business must make a profit to survive. Nevertheless, many companies initially set low prices for new products. They are willing to accept minimal profits—even losses—to get buyers to try products. In other words, they use pricing to establish **market share**—a company's percentage of the total market sales for a specific product. Even with established products, market share may outweigh profits as a pricing objective. For a product like Philadelphia brand cream cheese, dominating a market means that consumers are more likely to buy it because they are familiar with a well-known, highly visible product.

market share A company's percentage of the total market sales for a specific product.

Other Pricing Objectives

In some instances, neither profit maximizing nor market share is the best objective. During difficult economic times, for instance, loss containment and survival may become a company's main objectives. Not long after the recession began in 2008, for example, retailers began cutting prices in an attempt to attract customers. A few years earlier, Universal cut the price it charged for CDs by one-third as a response to consumer complaints about high CD prices.[7]

Price-Setting Tools

Whatever a company's objectives, managers must measure the potential impact before deciding on final prices. Two basic tools are often used for this purpose: *cost-oriented pricing* and *break-even analysis*. These tools are often combined to identify prices that will allow the company to reach its objectives.

Cost-Oriented Pricing

Cost-oriented pricing considers the firm's desire to make a profit and takes into account the need to cover production costs. A music store manager, for instance, would price CDs by calculating the cost of making them available to shoppers. Included in this figure would be store rent, employee wages, utilities, product displays, insurance, and, of course, the cost of buying CDs from the manufacturer.

Let's assume that the cost from the manufacturer is $8 per CD. If the store sells CDs for this price, it will not make any profit. Nor will it make a profit if it sells CDs for $8.50 each or even for $10 or $11. The manager must account for product and other costs and set a figure for profit. Together, these figures constitute markup. In this case, a reasonable markup of $7 over costs would result in a $15 selling price. Markup is usually stated as a percentage of selling price. Markup percentage is thus calculated as follows:

$$\text{Markup percentage} = \frac{\text{Markup}}{\text{Sales price}}$$

In the case of our CD retailer, the markup percentage is 46.7:

$$\text{Markup percentage} = \frac{\$7}{\$15} = 46.7\%$$

In other words, out of every dollar taken in, 46.7 cents will be gross profit for the store. From this profit the store must still pay rent, utilities, insurance, and all other costs. Markup can also be expressed as a percentage of cost: The $7 markup is 87.5 percent of the $8 cost of a CD ($7 ÷ $8).

In some industries, cost-oriented pricing doesn't seem to be used. When you go to a first-run movie theatre, for example, you pay the same price for each film you see. But it may cost as little as $2 million or as much as $200 million to make a film. Shouldn't the admission price be based on how much the film cost to make? After all, you pay a lot more for a Lincoln Continental than you do for a Ford because the Lincoln costs more to make. Shouldn't the same pricing system apply to Hollywood? Apparently not. Consumers are simply not willing to pay more than a certain amount to see a movie. The boxed insert entitled "Men and Cars: Unrequited Love" describes a situation where, unlike the movie example, the price of a service may not be a big concern for customers.

Break-Even Analysis: Cost-Volume-Profit Relationships

variable costs Those costs that change with the number of goods or services produced or sold.

fixed costs Those costs unaffected by the number of goods or services produced or sold.

break-even analysis An assessment of how many units must be sold at a given price before the company begins to make a profit.

break-even point The number of units that must be sold at a given price before the company covers all of its variable and fixed costs.

Using cost-oriented pricing, a firm will cover its **variable costs**—costs that change with the number of goods or services produced or sold. It will also make some money toward paying its **fixed costs**—costs that are unaffected by the number of goods or services produced or sold. But how many units must the company sell before all of its fixed costs are covered and it begins to make a profit? To determine this figure, it needs a **break-even analysis**.[8]

To continue our music store example, suppose again that the variable cost for each CD (in this case, the cost of buying the CD from the producer) is $8. This means that the store's annual variable costs depend on how many CDs are sold—the number of CDs sold multiplied by $8 cost per CD. Say that fixed costs for keeping the store open for one year are $100 000. These costs are unaffected by the number of CDs sold; costs for lighting, rent, insurance, and salaries are steady however many CDs the store sells. Therefore, how many CDs must be sold to cover both fixed and variable costs and to start to generate some profit? The answer is the **break-even point**, which is 14 286 CDs. We arrive at this number through the following equation:

$$\text{Break-even point (in units)} = \frac{\text{Total fixed costs}}{\text{Price} - \text{Variable cost}}$$

$$= \frac{\$100\ 000}{\$15 - \$8} = 14\ 286 \text{ CDs}$$

Entrepreneurship and New Ventures

Men and Cars: Unrequited Love

Men have always had a bit of a love affair with their cars, but the customers of Auto Vault are downright obsessive. You would be too if you had $500 000 invested in a Lamborghini, or some other exotic coupe. Auto Vault, a Toronto-based secure car-storage facility for luxury automobiles and motorcycles, is owned and operated by Gary Shapiro. Shapiro got the idea for Auto Vault when working in sales at a high-end auto dealership. Potential customers complained that money wasn't the issue when it came to making a purchase; rather, the problem was where they would store the vehicle. Shapiro's company was launched in 2004, and it has been experiencing steady growth since inception, expanding from 80 customers at the end of its first year of operations to 400 in 2008.

For a $229 monthly fee, customers can purchase Auto Vault's Gold Package, which includes an exterior dust cover, interior mats and steering wheel cover, access to dedicated staff, secure parking, security monitoring, valet delivery, and detailing. But if you think your "baby" deserves more than that, then sign up for the Platinum Package. For $299 per month, you can get all the features of the Gold Package, plus tire pressure monitoring, battery and fluid checks, scheduled vehicle start-ups, and visual inspections.

Aside from the storage and services, Auto Vault's customers are purchasing peace of mind. They trust Shapiro and they like him. "I was once called 'likeable' in a newspaper article.... I hope I am, it would make it easier to convince someone to hand over the keys to a

$500 000 car and their American Express card," said Shapiro. Shapiro is also known for his discretion; people are not told who owns which car and some of his customers even have cars that are unknown to their families. Finally, the location is secret and disclosed to customers only after Shapiro meets with them.

As part of his service offering, Shapiro also likes to maintain personal contact with his clients, and this is done through his handling of all incoming calls. "Word spread that I take good care of people," he said. This has helped him to get referrals, and according to Shapiro, he doesn't have to push his product; customers come to him. Gary Shapiro thinks he can extend his business to another level, however.

His next venture is a $15-million storage facility to be converted into parking condos. For $40 000, plus monthly maintenance fees, prestige car owners can purchase their own customized unit (average size is 400 square feet) and Shapiro's imagination for what his car condo can offer has no boundaries. He's talking about such features as decor to match your car's colour, 24-hour concierge service, a detailing service, and common areas with large-screen TVs, among other things. This romance between men and cars . . . it must be true love! And price is no object.

Critical Thinking Question

1. Review the various types of pricing strategies and distribution options and identify the choices made by Auto Vault. Do you think Shapiro's pricing reflected the market he was targeting? Why or why not?

Figure 18.1 shows the break-even point graphically. If the store sells fewer than 14 286 CDs, it loses money for the year. If sales exceed 14 286 CDs, profits grow by $7 for each CD sold. If the store sells exactly 14 286 CDs, it

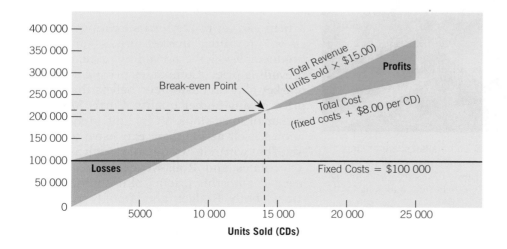

Figure 18.1 Break-even analysis.

will cover all of its costs but will earn zero profit. Zero profitability at the break-even point can also be seen by using the following profit equation:

$$\text{Profit} = \text{total revenue} - (\text{total fixed costs} + \text{total variable costs})$$
$$= (14\,286\ \text{CDs} \times \$15) - (\$100\,000\ \text{fixed costs} + [14\,286\ \text{CDs} \times \$8\ \text{variable costs}])$$

The music store owner would certainly like to hit the break-even quantity as early as possible so that profits will start rolling in. Why not charge $20 per CD and reach the break-even point earlier?. At a price of $20 per CD, sales at the store would drop. In setting a price, the manager must consider how much CD buyers will pay and what the store's local competitors charge.

Pricing Strategies and Tactics

2 Discuss *pricing strategies* and tactics for existing and new products.

The pricing tools discussed in the previous section provide guidance for managers trying to set prices on specific goods. But they do not provide general direction for managers trying to decide on a pricing philosophy for their company. In this section, we discuss *pricing strategy*—that is, pricing as a planning activity that affects the marketing mix. We then describe some basic *pricing tactics*—ways in which managers implement a firm's pricing strategies.

Pricing Strategies

Let's begin this section by asking two questions. First, can a manager really identify a single "best" price for a product? Probably not. One study of prices for popular non-aspirin pain relievers (such as Tylenol and Advil) found variations of 100 percent.[9] Such large price differences may reflect some differences in product costs, but the bigger issue is likely differing brand images that attract different types of customers. In turn, these images reflect vastly different pricing philosophies and strategies. Second, just how important is pricing as an element in the marketing mix? As we have already seen, it is a mistake to try to isolate any element in the marketing mix from the others. Nevertheless, pricing is a critical variable because it has a major impact on company revenues, and it is extremely important to consumers.

Pricing Existing Products

A firm can set prices for its existing products *above* prevailing market prices for similar products, *below* the prevailing price, or *at* the prevailing price. Companies pricing above the market play on customers' beliefs that higher price means higher quality. Curtis Mathes, a maker of televisions, VCRs, and stereos, promotes itself as the most expensive television set, "but worth it." Companies such as Godiva chocolates and Rolls-Royce have also succeeded with this pricing philosophy. In contrast, both Budget and Dollar car rental companies promote themselves as low-priced alternatives to Hertz and Avis. Pricing below

Using low-cost direct-to-consumer selling and market share pricing, Dell profitably dominated the personal computer market, while its competitors—Apple IBM, Compaq, and Hewlett-Packard—sold through retailers, adding extra costs that prevented them from matching Dell's low prices. Competitors have switched to direct-to-consumer sales, but Dell is strongly anchored as the industry's number-two PC maker after Hewlett-Packard.

the prevailing market price can succeed if the firm can offer a product of acceptable quality while keeping costs below those of higher-priced options.

In some industries, a dominant firm establishes product prices and other companies follow along. This is called **price leadership**. (Don't confuse this approach with *price fixing*, the illegal process of producers agreeing among themselves what prices will be charged.) Price leadership is often evident in products such as structural steel, gasoline, and many processed foods because these products differ little in quality from one firm to another. Companies compete through advertising campaigns, personal selling, and service, not price.

price leadership The dominant firm in the industry establishes product prices and other companies follow suit.

Pricing New Products

Companies introducing new products into the market have to consider two contrasting pricing policy options—coming in with either a very high price or a very low one. **Price skimming**—setting an initially high price to cover costs and generate a profit—may generate a large profit on each item sold. The revenue is often needed to cover development and introduction costs. Skimming works only if marketers can convince consumers that a product is truly different from those already on the market. High-definition TVs, microwave ovens, electronic calculators, video games, and video cameras were all introduced at high skimming prices. In contrast, **penetration pricing**—setting an initially low price to establish a new product in the market—seeks to create consumer interest and stimulate trial purchases.

price skimming The decision to price a new product as high as possible to earn the maximum profit on each unit sold.

penetration pricing The decision to price a new product very low to sell the most units possible and to build customer loyalty.

Whatever price strategy a company is using, it must be communicated to buyers. Wal-Mart consistently communicates a low-price strategy to consumers, but some other retailers do not. Zellers, for example, tried to compete with Wal-Mart by adopting an "everyday low prices" (EDLP) policy a few years ago but abandoned it and returned to its former practice of promotional markdowns on some products to attract customers to its stores.[10]

Fixed vs. Dynamic Pricing for Ebusiness

The electronic marketplace has introduced a highly variable pricing system as an alternative to more conventional—and more stable—pricing structures for both consumer and business-to-business (B2B) products. *Dynamic pricing* works because information flows on the web notify millions of buyers of instantaneous changes in product availability. To attract sales that might be lost under traditional fixed-price structures, sellers can alter prices privately, on a one-to-one, customer-to-customer basis.[11]

Roy Cooper scours the markets of Quito, Ecuador, for tapestries, baskets, and religious relics. He pays $10 to $15 for selected items and then posts them on eBay, where they usually sell at substantial markups. His online enterprise nets Cooper about $1300 a month ($2500 in November and December). His Ecuadorian suppliers, whose average income is $1460 per year, seem happy with their share. In a country where only 2.7 percent of the population has ever been online, very few people have heard of dynamic pricing.

Pricing Tactics

Regardless of its general pricing strategy, a company may adopt one or more specific pricing tactics, such as *price lining* or *psychological pricing*. Managers must also decide whether to use *discounting* tactics.

Price Lining

price lining The practice of offering all items in certain categories at a limited number of predetermined price points.

Companies selling multiple items in a product category often use **price lining**—offering all items in certain categories at a limited number of prices. Three or four *price points* are set at which a particular product will be sold. For example, all men's suits might be priced at $175, $250, or $400. The store's buyers select suits that can be purchased and sold profitably at one of these three prices.

Psychological Pricing

psychological pricing The practice of setting prices to take advantage of the nonlogical reactions of consumers to certain types of prices.

odd-even pricing A form of psychological pricing in which prices are not stated in even dollar amounts.

discount Any price reduction offered by the seller to persuade customers to purchase a product.

Psychological pricing is based on the idea that customers are not completely rational when making buying decisions. One type of psychological pricing, **odd-even pricing**, assumes that customers prefer prices that are not stated in even dollar amounts. Thus, customers may regard a price of $99.95 as significantly lower than a price of $100.00. But Wal-Mart is going against this trend. In an attempt to make it easier for money-conscious customers to calculate their bill before they get to the cash register, Wal-Mart is rounding prices to the nearest dollar on many products.[12]

Discounting

cash discount A form of discount in which customers paying cash, rather than buying on credit, pay lower prices.

seasonal discount A form of discount in which lower prices are offered to customers making a purchase at a time of year when sales are traditionally slow.

trade discount A discount given to firms involved in a product's distribution.

The price that is set for a product is not always the price at which all items are actually sold. Many times a company offers a price reduction—a **discount**—to stimulate sales. In recent years, **cash discounts** have become popular. Stores may also offer **seasonal discounts** to stimulate the sales of products during times of the year when most customers do not normally buy the product. **Trade discounts** are available to companies or individuals in a product's distribution channel (for example, wholesalers, retailers, and interior designers

If the manufacturer says a product should retail for $349, why does every retailer sell it for, say, $229? Such discrepancies between a manufacturer's suggested retail price and the actual retail price are the norm in the electronics industry, and consumers have come to expect discounted prices. "You can't have a discount until there's a price to discount it from," explains an editor at Consumer Reports, but the practice raises an interesting question: If no one charges suggested retail prices, is anyone really getting a discount?

pay less for fabric than the typical consumer does). **Quantity discounts** involve lower prices for purchases in large quantities. Discounts for cases of motor oil or soft drinks at retail stores are examples of quantity discounts.

quantity discount A form of discount in which customers buying large amounts of a product pay lower prices.

International Pricing

When Procter & Gamble reviewed its prospects for marketing products in new overseas markets, it encountered an unsettling fact: Because it typically priced products to cover hefty R&D costs, profitably priced items were out of reach for too many foreign consumers. The solution was, in effect, to reverse the process. Now P&G conducts research to find out what foreign buyers can afford and then develops products that they can buy. P&G penetrates markets with lower-priced items and encourages customers to trade up as they become able to afford higher-quality products.

As P&G's experience shows, pricing products for other countries is complicated because additional factors are involved. Income and spending trends must be analyzed. In addition, the number of intermediaries varies from country to country, as does their effect on a product's cost. Exchange rates change daily, there may be shipping costs, import tariffs must be considered, and different types of pricing agreements may be permitted.

The Distribution Mix

The success of any product depends in part on its **distribution mix**—the combination of distribution channels a firm uses to get a product to end-users. In this section, we explain the need for *intermediaries*, then discuss the basic *distribution strategies*, and then consider some special issues in channel relationships.

> Explain the distribution mix, the different *channels of distribution*, and different *distribution strategies*.
>
> **3**

distribution mix The combination of distribution channels a firm selects to get a product to end-users.

Intermediaries and Distribution Channels

Once called *middlemen*, **intermediaries** are the individuals and firms who help distribute a producer's goods. **Wholesalers** sell products to other businesses, which resell them to final consumers. **Retailers** sell products directly to consumers. While some firms rely on independent intermediaries, others employ their own distribution networks and sales forces. Intermediaries are appearing in places where most people might think they aren't needed. A Canadian company called Imagine This Sold Ltd. began operating in 2004. For a percentage of the selling price, it provides expertise to people who are trying to sell items on eBay. This company exists because trading has become so competitive on eBay that more expertise is needed to succeed than a lot of people thought.[13]

intermediary Any individual or firm other than the producer who participates in a product's distribution.

wholesalers Intermediaries who sell products to other businesses, which in turn resell them to the end-users.

retailers Intermediaries who sell products to end-users.

Distribution of Consumer Products

A **distribution channel** is the path that a product follows from producer to end-user. Figure 18.2 shows how eight primary distribution channels can be identified according to the kinds of channel members involved in getting products to buyers. Note that all channels must begin with a producer and end with a consumer or an industrial user. Channels 1 through 4 are most often used for the distribution of consumer goods and services.

distribution channel The path a product follows from the producer to the end-user.

Channel 1: Direct Distribution of Consumer Products. In a **direct channel**, the product travels from the producer to the consumer without intermediaries. Using their own sales forces, companies such as Avon, Fuller Brush, and

direct channel A distribution channel in which the product travels from the producer to the consumer without passing through any intermediary.

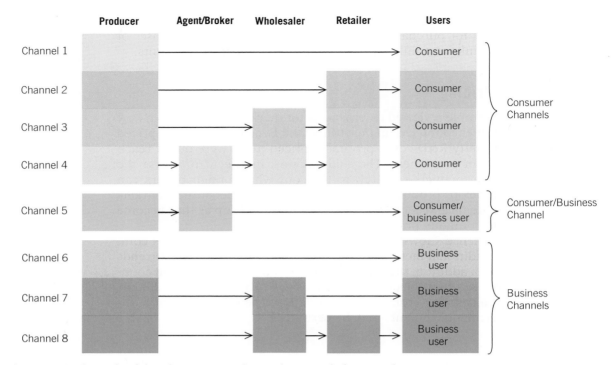

Figure 18.2 Channels of distribution: How the product travels from producer to consumer or user.

Tupperware use this channel. The direct channel is also prominent on the internet, where consumers can purchase airline reservations (and thousands of other products and services) directly from internet sites.

Channel 2: Retail Distribution of Consumer Products. In Channel 2, producers distribute products through retailers. Goodyear, for example, maintains its own system of retail outlets. Levi's has its own outlets but also produces jeans for other retailers such as Gap Inc.

Channel 3: Wholesale Distribution of Consumer Products. Faced with the rising cost of store space, many retailers found that they could not afford both retail and storage space. Thus, wholesalers entered the distribution network to perform the storage function. The combination convenience store/gas station is an example of Channel 3. With approximately 90 percent of the space used to display merchandise, only 10 percent is left for storage and office facilities. Wholesalers store merchandise and restock it frequently. Wholesalers are prominent in ecommerce because internet stores give customers access to information and product displays 24 hours a day. Buyers can also place orders electronically and confirm delivery almost instantaneously. In the diamond industry, retail companies can access wholesalers such as Diasqua Group, visually examine diamonds, place orders, and receive delivery dates, all over the internet.

sales agents (or brokers)
Independent business people who represent a business and receive a commission in return, but never take legal possession of the product.

Channel 4: Distribution Through Sales Agents or Brokers. **Sales agents (or brokers)** represent producers and sell to wholesalers, retailers, or both. They receive commissions based on the prices of the goods they sell. Lafferty and Co. Food Brokers Inc. represents several prominent food manufacturers—Pillsbury, Old El Paso, and Sunkist. To relieve manufacturers of sales activities, Lafferty arranges sales of their products to other companies, allowing manufacturers to do what they do best—produce food products—rather than divert resources to sales and distribution. Agents generally deal in the related product lines of a few producers and work on a long-term basis. Travel agents,

MANKOFF

*"On the one hand, eliminating the middleman would result in lower costs, increased
sales, and greater consumer satisfaction; on the other hand, we're the middleman."*

for example, represent airlines, car-rental companies, and hotels. In contrast,
brokers match sellers and buyers as needed. The real estate industry relies on
brokers to match buyers and sellers of property.

The Pros and Cons of Non-direct Distribution

Each link in the distribution chain makes a profit by charging a markup or
commission. Thus, non-direct distribution means higher prices. The more
intermediaries in the channel, the higher the final price will be. Calculated as
a percentage of cost, *markups* are applied each time a product is sold. They
may range from 10 to 40 percent for manufacturers, from 2 to 25 percent for
wholesalers, and from 5 to 100 percent for retailers. *E-intermediaries*—wholesalers and agents who use internet channels—also charge markups. In general,
markup levels depend on competitive conditions and practices in a particular
industry.

Intermediaries provide *added value* by saving consumers both time and
money. Moreover, the value accumulates with each link in the supply chain.
Intermediaries provide time-saving information and make the right quantities
of products available where and when consumers need them. Figure 18.3 illustrates the problem of making chili without benefit of a common intermediary—the supermarket. As a consumer/buyer, you would obviously spend a lot
more time, money, and energy if you tried to gather all the ingredients from
one retailer at a time.

Even if intermediaries are eliminated, the costs associated with their
functions are not. Intermediaries exist because they do necessary jobs in cost-
efficient ways. For example, in this do-it-yourself era, more and more people
are trying to save money by opting to sell their homes without using the
services of a real estate agent. Since the agent's fee is normally between 5 and
6 percent of the purchase price of the house, the savings can be substantial.
But the seller has to do all the work that brokers would normally do to earn
their fee.

Remember this: Although intermediaries like real estate agents provide an
essential service, this does not mean that they necessarily provide a *low-cost*
service. Ebrokers have emerged who charge a flat rate for selling a home, and
that rate is far below what traditional real estate brokers charge. It is not surprising that this development has been viewed with some alarm by traditional

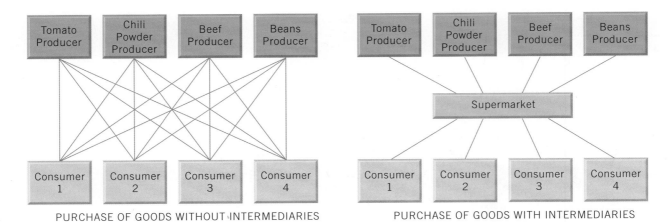

Figure 18.3 Advantages of intermediaries.

real estate agents. What's worse, in 2007 the Canadian Competition Bureau launched an inquiry into changes the Canadian Real Estate Association (CREA) made to its operating procedures. Ebrokers claimed these changes were designed to maintain high fees for traditional real estate brokers by cutting ebrokers out of the CREAs Multiple Listing Service.[14]

Channel 5: Distribution by Agents to Consumers and Businesses. Channel 5 differs from previous channels in two ways: (1) An agent functions as the sole intermediary, and (2) the agent distributes to both consumers and business customers. Consider Vancouver-based Uniglobe Travel International, a travel agent representing airlines, car-rental companies, and hotels. Uniglobe books flight reservations and arranges complete recreational-travel services for consumers. The firm also services companies whose employees need lodging and transportation for business travel.

Ecommerce works well in this channel because it directly informs more people about products. At Uniglobe, for instance, an online subsidiary combines a high-tech website with an old-fashioned human touch in a specialty market—booking cruises. Customers can scan for destinations, cruise lines, restaurants, and cabin locations for many different ships. Using Uniglobe's online chat function, travellers can simply open a window to speak in real time with one of 75 cruise specialists. The strategy has paid off: Uniglobe.com leads the market in online cruise bookings.[15]

Distribution of Business Products

Industrial channels are important because every company is also a customer that buys other companies' products. The Kellogg Co., for example, buys grain to make breakfast cereals, and Imperial Tobacco buys tobacco to make cigarettes. **Industrial (business) distribution** is the network of channel members involved in the flow of manufactured goods to business customers. Business products are traditionally distributed through Channels 6, 7, and 8 (refer back to Figure 18.2).

industrial (business) distribution The network of channel members involved in the flow of manufactured goods to business customers.

Channel 6: Direct Distribution of Business Products. Most business goods are sold directly by the manufacturer to the industrial buyer. Lawless Container Corp., for instance, produces packaging containers for direct sale to Fisher-Price (toys), Dirt Devil (vacuum cleaners), and Mr. Coffee (coffee makers). Many manufacturers maintain **sales offices** as contact points with customers and headquarters for salespeople. Ecommerce technologies have popularized channel 6. Dell Computer Corp., a pioneer in direct internet sales, now gets about two-thirds of its sales from other businesses, governments, and schools.[16]

sales offices Offices maintained by sellers of industrial goods to provide points of contact with their customers.

Channel 7: Wholesale Distribution of Industrial Products. Channel 7 mostly handles accessory equipment (computers, fax machines, and other office equipment) and supplies (USB memory sticks, pencils, and copier paper). Manufacturers produce these items in large quantities, but companies buy them in small quantities. For example, few companies order truckloads of paper clips, so intermediaries help end-users by breaking down large quantities into smaller sales units.

Channel 8: Wholesale Distribution to Business Retailers. In the office-products industry, channel 7 is being displaced by a channel that looks very much like channel 3 for consumer products. Instead of buying office supplies from wholesalers (channel 7), many businesses are now shopping at office discount stores such as Staples, Office Depot, and Office Max. Before selling to large companies, these warehouse-like superstores originally targeted retail consumers and small businesses that bought supplies at retail stores (and at retail prices). Today, however, small business buyers shop at discount stores designed for industrial users, selecting from 7000 items at prices 20 to 75 percent lower than retail.

Distribution Strategies

Three strategies—*intensive, exclusive,* and *selective distribution*—provide different degrees of market coverage for products. **Intensive distribution** means distributing a product through as many channels and channel members (using both wholesalers and retailers) as possible. For example, as Figure 18.4 shows, Caramilk bars flood the market through all suitable outlets. Intensive distribution is normally used for low-cost consumer goods such as candy and magazines.

In contrast, **exclusive distribution** occurs when a manufacturer grants the exclusive right to distribute or sell a product to one wholesaler or retailer in a given geographic area. Exclusive distribution agreements are most common for high-cost prestige products. For example, Jaguar or Rolls-Royce automobiles are typically sold by only one dealer in a large metropolitan area.

Selective distribution falls between intensive and exclusive distribution. A company that uses this strategy selects only wholesalers and retailers who will give special attention to the product in terms of sales efforts, display position,

intensive distribution A distribution strategy in which a product is distributed in nearly every possible outlet, using many channels and channel members.

exclusive distribution A distribution strategy in which a product's distribution is limited to only one wholesaler or retailer in a given geographic area.

selective distribution A distribution strategy that falls between intensive and exclusive distribution, calling for the use of a limited number of outlets for a product.

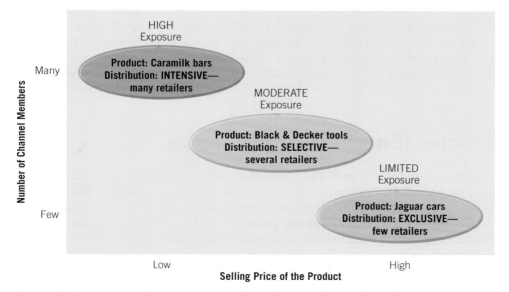

Figure 18.4 Amounts of market exposure from the three kinds of distribution.

and so on. Selective distribution policies have been applied to virtually every type of consumer product. They are often used by companies like Black & Decker, whose product lines do not require intense market exposure to increase sales. Para Paints uses a selective distribution policy because it keeps its high-end paint products out of the "big-box" stores such as Canadian Tire and Home Depot. Doing so has increased Para's margins (because big-box stores demand steep discounts), and has also increased sales by 15 to 20 percent because the independent stores that sell Para paint have remained loyal to Para.[17]

Channel Conflict and Channel Leadership

channel conflict Conflict arising when the members of a distribution channel disagree over the roles they should play or the rewards they should receive.

Channel conflict occurs when members of the distribution channel disagree over the roles they should play or the rewards they should receive. John Deere, for example, would object if its dealers began distributing Russian and Japanese tractors. Similarly, when a manufacturer-owned factory outlet store discounts the company's apparel or housewares, it runs the risk of alienating the independent retailers who also sell the manufacturer's products. Channel conflict may also arise if one member has more power than others or is viewed as receiving preferential treatment. Such conflicts defeat the purpose of the system by disrupting the flow of goods to their destinations.

Conflicts are resolved when members' efforts are better coordinated. A key factor in coordinating the activities of independent organizations is channel leadership. Usually, one channel member—the **channel captain**—can determine the roles and rewards of other members. Often, the channel captain is a manufacturer, particularly if the manufacturer's product is in high demand. In some industries, an influential wholesaler or a large retailer such as Wal-Mart may emerge as the channel captain because of its large sales volumes.

channel captain The channel member that is the most powerful in determining the roles and rewards of organizations involved in a given channel of distribution.

vertical marketing system (VMS) A system in which there is a high degree of coordination among all the units in the distribution channel so that a product moves efficiently from manufacturer to consumer.

To overcome problems posed by channel conflict and issues of channel leadership, the **vertical marketing system (VMS)** has emerged. In a VMS, separate businesses join to form a unified distribution channel, with one member coordinating the activities of the whole channel. There are three main types of VMS arrangements. In a *corporate* VMS, all stages in the channel are under single ownership. The Limited, for example, owns both the production facilities that manufacture its apparel and the retail stores that sell it. In a *contractual* VMS, channel members sign contracts agreeing to specific duties and rewards. The Independent Grocers' Alliance (IGA), for example, consists of independent retail grocers joined with a wholesaler who contractually leads—but does not own—the VMS. Most franchises are contractual VMSs. In an *administered* VMS, channel members are less formally coordinated than in a corporate or contractual VMS. Instead, one or more of the members emerge as leader(s) and maintain control as a result of power and influence. Although the administered VMS is more fragile than the corporate and contractual forms, it is more unified than channels relying on independent members.

Wholesaling

4 | Explain the differences between *merchant wholesalers* and *agents/brokers*, and describe the activities of e-intermediaries.

Now that you know something about distribution channels, we can consider the role played by intermediaries. Wholesalers provide a variety of functions for their customers, who are buying products for resale to consumers or to businesses. In addition to storing products and providing an assortment of products for their customers, wholesalers offer delivery, credit, and information about products. The specific services that wholesalers offer depend on the type of intermediary involved: *merchant wholesaler, agent/broker,* or *e-intermediary*.

Merchant Wholesalers

Most wholesalers are independent operators who derive their income from sales of goods produced by a variety of manufacturers. All **merchant wholesalers** take title to merchandise, that is, they buy and own the goods they resell to other businesses. They usually provide storage and a means of delivery.

A **full-service merchant wholesaler** provides credit, marketing, and merchandising services. Approximately 80 percent of all merchant wholesalers are full-service wholesalers. **Limited-function merchant wholesalers** provide only a few services, sometimes merely storage. Their customers are normally small operations that pay cash and pick up their own goods. One such wholesaler, the **drop shipper**, receives orders from customers, negotiates with producers to supply goods, takes title to them, and arranges for shipment to customers.

Other limited-function wholesalers, known as **rack jobbers**, market consumer goods—mostly non-food items—directly to retail stores.[18] Procter & Gamble, for example, uses rack jobbers to distribute products like Pampers diapers. After marking prices, setting up display racks, and displaying diapers in one store, the rack jobber moves on to another outlet to check inventories and shelve products.

merchant wholesaler An independent wholesaler that buys and takes legal possession of goods before selling them to customers.

full-service merchant wholesaler A merchant wholesaler that provides storage and delivery in addition to wholesaling services.

limited-function merchant wholesaler An independent wholesaler that provides only wholesaling—not warehousing or transportation—services.

drop shipper A type of wholesaler that does not carry inventory or handle the product.

rack jobber A limited-function merchant wholesaler specializing in non-food merchandise that sets up and maintains display racks of some products in retail stores.

Agents and Brokers

Agents and brokers, including internet e-agents, serve as the sales and merchandising arms of manufacturers that do not have their own sales forces. They work on commissions, usually about 4 to 5 percent of net sales. Unlike merchant wholesalers, they do not take title to the merchandise they sell. The value of agents and brokers lies primarily in their knowledge of markets and their merchandising expertise. They also provide a wide range of services, including shelf and display merchandising and advertising layout. Finally, they maintain product saleability by removing open, torn, or dirty packages; arranging products neatly; and generally keeping them attractively displayed. Many supermarket products are handled through brokers.

Retailing

If you are like most Canadians, you buy nearly all the goods and services you consume from retailers. Most retailers are small operations, often consisting of just the owners and part-time help. But there are a few very large retailers, and these account for billions of dollars of sales each year in Canada (see Table 18.1).

Identify the different types of *retailing* and *retail stores*.

5

Types of Retail Outlets

Retail operations in Canada vary as widely by type as they do by size. They can be classified in various ways—by pricing strategies, location, range of services, or range of product lines. Choosing the right types of retail outlets is a crucial aspect of every seller's distribution strategy. There are two basic categories of retail stores: *product line retailers* and *bargain retailers*.

Product Line Retailers

Retailers that feature broad product lines include **department stores**, which are organized into specialized departments such as shoes, furniture, women's clothing, and so forth. Stores are usually large and handle a wide range of

department stores Large retail stores that offer a wide variety of high-quality items divided into specialized departments.

Table 18.1 Top 10 Retailers in Canada, 2008

Company	Annual Revenues (in billions of $)
1. Wal-Mart Canada Corp.	$16.6
2. Costco Wholesale Canada Ltd.	10.1
3. Canadian Tire Corp. Ltd.	9.1
4. Home Depot Canada	6.1
5. Sears Canada Inc.	5.7
6. Best Buy Canada Ltd.	5.5
7. Rona Inc.	4.8
8. Home Hardware Stores Ltd.	4.8
9. Liquor Control Board of Ontario	4.1
10. B.C. Liquor Distribution Branch	2.6

supermarkets Large retail stores that offer a variety of food and food-related items divided into specialized departments.

specialty stores Small retail stores that carry one line of related products.

category killers Retailers who carry a deep selection of goods in a narrow product line.

bargain retailers Retail outlets that emphasize low prices as a means of attracting consumers.

discount houses Bargain retail stores that offer major items such as televisions and large appliances at discount prices.

catalogue showroom A bargain retail store in which customers place orders for items described in a catalogue and pick up those items from an on-premises warehouse.

factory outlets Bargain retail stores that are owned by the manufacturers whose products they sell.

warehouse club (or wholesale club) Huge, membership-only, combined retail–wholesale operations that sell brand-name merchandise.

convenience stores Retail stores that offer high accessibility, extended hours, and fast service on selected items.

goods. In addition, they usually offer a variety of services, such as generous return policies, credit plans, and delivery. Similarly, **supermarkets** are divided into departments of related products—food products, household products, and so on. The emphasis is on wide selection and self-service.

In contrast, **specialty stores** are small stores that carry one line of related products. They serve specific market segments with full product lines in narrow product fields and often feature knowledgeable sales personnel. Sunglass Hut International, for instance, has 1600 outlets in Canada, the United States, Europe, and Australia that carry a deep selection of competitively priced sunglasses. Retailers who carry an extremely deep selection of goods in a relatively narrow product line and who hire technical experts to give customers advice are called **category killers**. Home Depot and Staples are examples of category killers.

Bargain Retailers

Bargain retailers carry wide ranges of products and come in many forms. The first **discount houses** sold large numbers of items (such as televisions and other appliances) at substantial price reductions to certain customers. As name-brand items became more common, they offered better product assortments while still transacting cash-only sales in low-rent facilities. As they became firmly entrenched, they began moving to better locations, improving decor, and selling better-quality merchandise at higher prices. They also began offering a few department store services, such as credit plans and non-cash sales. Wal-Mart and Zellers are bargain retailers.

Catalogue showrooms use mail catalogues to attract customers into showrooms to view display samples, place orders, and wait briefly while clerks retrieve orders from attached warehouses. **Factory outlets** are manufacturer-owned stores that avoid wholesalers and retailers by selling merchandise directly from factory to consumer. The **warehouse club (or wholesale club)** offers large discounts on a wide range of brand name merchandise to customers who pay annual membership fees. **Convenience stores** such as 7-Eleven and Circle K offer ease of purchase, easily accessible locations, extended store hours, and speedy service. They differ from most bargain retailers in that they do not feature low prices. Like bargain retailers, they control prices by keeping in-store service to a minimum.

The boxed insert entitled "Green Retailing" describes how retailers are joining the green movement.

The Greening of Business

Green Retailing

When people think about green practices in business, the first thing they typically think about is factories doing something to reduce air and water pollution. But the green movement has become active in both manufacturing and service companies, including the retailing sector. Here are some examples of the green movement in retailing:

- Nature's Path Foods reduced packaging sizes by 10 percent, and this meant a 20 percent reduction in transportation emissions.
- Cities as different as San Francisco, California, and Leaf Rapids, Manitoba, have banned the use of plastic bags; several grocers in Nova Scotia are also considering the move.
- Wal-Mart and other retailers are training their cashiers to ask customers if they even need a bag of any kind.
- In 2007, Loblaw opened four Superstores where customers have to use reusable bags; more than 14 million reusable bags have been sold by Loblaw, and the number of plastic bags given to customers has been reduced by 20 percent.
- Many stores, including IKEA and No Frills, charge customers for plastic bags and try to encourage consumers to stop using the bags.

Canadians use 55 million plastic bags each week. While they are convenient, they also cause problems. Because they are derived from oil, they can take up to 1000 years to degrade. Even when they do degrade, the toxins they contain get into the soil. They are also an eyesore when they blow around landfills and elsewhere.

Mountain Equipment Co-op (MEC) wants to convince customers to stop using disposable bags altogether, so it makes a five-cent donation to environmental groups each time a customer declines to take a plastic bag. Between 2006 and 2008, MEC contributed $207 000 to environmental groups as a result of the program. MEC also offers compostable bags to its customers. These bags, which are eaten by micro-organisms and become compost, are even more environmentally friendly than biodegradable bags (which are still out there in the environment even after they degrade).

Reusable cloth bags and collapsible plastic crates are increasing in popularity as substitutes for plastic bags. Most major retailers sell them. One really green alternative is reusable bags that are themselves made from recycled plastic bottles.

It is not just retailers who are trying to change consumer behaviour. Consumers are also starting to demand that retailers provide more eco-friendly packaging that is biodegradable, recycled, or reusable. One alternative to traditional plastic bottles is corn-derived PLA polymer. Another is polyethylene terephthalate plastic bottles, which can be produced from recycled material. And remember that old-fashioned glass is 100 percent recyclable. Consumers want less packaging overall, whatever type it is.

Critical Thinking Questions

1. All things considered, which type of shopping bag is best: plastic, paper, or reusable cloth?

Non-store Retailing

Not all goods and services are sold in stores. In fact, some retailers sell all or most of their products without bricks-and-mortar stores. For example, certain types of consumer goods—soft drinks, candy, and cigarettes—lend themselves to distribution in *vending machines*. Non-store retailing also includes **direct-response retailing**, in which firms contact customers directly to inform them about products and to take sales orders. **Mail order (or catalogue marketing)** is a popular form of direct-response retailing. So is **telemarketing**—the use of the telephone to sell directly.

The oldest form of direct-response retailing is **direct selling**, which is still used by companies that sell door-to-door or through home-selling parties. Avon Products has more than four million sales reps in 100 different countries[19], and Tupperware has more than 60 000 salespeople in Russia alone.[20] The Fuller Brush Company, which was started in 1906 by Arthur Fuller, a self-described

direct-response retailing A type of retailing in which firms make direct contact with customers both to inform them about products and to receive sales orders.

mail order (or catalogue marketing) A form of non-store retailing in which customers place orders for merchandise shown in catalogues and receive their orders via mail.

telemarketing Use of the telephone to sell directly to consumers.

direct selling Form of non-store retailing typified by door-to-door sales.

"country bumpkin" from Nova Scotia, used to be well-known in door-to-door selling. But sweeping changes in North American society—women leaving the home to work, mass retailing, and the globalization of business—caused the company to fall on hard times. Two of its most famous salespeople were the Reverend Billy Graham and disc jockey Dick Clark.

An increasingly important category of non-store retailing includes **e-intermediaries**—internet-based channel members who perform one or both of the following functions: (1) They collect information about sellers and provide it for consumers, or (2) they help deliver internet products to buyers. We will examine three types of e-intermediaries—*syndicated sellers, shopping agents,* and *eretailers.*

e-intermediaries Internet-based distribution-channel members that collect information about sellers and present it in convenient form to consumers and/or help deliver internet products to consumers.

Syndicated Sellers

syndicated selling Occurs when a website offers other websites a commission for referring customers.

Syndicated selling occurs when one website offers another a commission for referring customers. For example, Expedia's webpage shows a list of car rental companies, and when Expedia customers click on, say, the Dollar banner for a car rental, they are transferred from the Expedia site to the Dollar site. Dollar pays Expedia a fee for each booking that comes through this channel. Although the new intermediary increases the cost of Dollar's supply chain, it adds value for customers because they are efficiently guided to a car-rental agency.[21]

Shopping Agents

shopping agent (e-agent) A type of intermediary that helps internet consumers by gathering and sorting information they need to make purchases.

Shopping agents (e-agents) help internet consumers by gathering and sorting information. Although they don't take possession of products, they know which websites and stores to visit, give accurate comparison prices, identify product features, and help consumers complete transactions by presenting information in a usable format—all in a matter of seconds. PriceScan.com is a well-known cyber-shopping agent. Since e-agents have become so plentiful, unsure shoppers are turning to rating sites, such as eSmarts.com, that evaluate and compare e-agents.

Ecommerce intermediaries called *business-to-business (B2B) brokers* have also emerged for business customers. The pricing process between B2B buyers and sellers of commodities can be outsourced, for example, to an internet company like FreeMarkets Inc. (which merged with Ariba). As a pricing broker, FreeMarkets links any large-volume buyer with potential suppliers that bid to become the supplier for the industrial customer. Client companies (the commodity buyers), such as Quaker Oats or Emerson Electric, pay FreeMarkets a fixed annual subscription fee and receive networking into FreeMarkets's auction headquarters, where real-time bids come in from suppliers at remote locations. The website (www.freemarkets.com) provides up-to-date information until the bidding ends with the low-price supplier. In conducting the pricing transactions electronically, FreeMarkets doesn't take possession of any products. Rather, it brings together timely information and links businesses to one another.[22]

Electronic Retailing

electronic retailing (etailing) Allows consumers to shop from home using the internet.

Electronic retailing (also called *etailing*) allows consumers to shop from home using the internet. Sears Canada, one of the most popular etailers in Canada, offers more than 10 000 items for sale on its website.[23] Etailing is made possible by communications networks that let sellers post product information on consumers' PCs. Electronic retailing includes *electronic catalogues, internet-based stores, electronic storefronts and cybermalls,* and *interactive and video marketing.*

Electronic Catalogues. **Ecatalogues** use the internet to display products for both retail and business customers. Using electronic displays (instead of traditional mail catalogues), firms give millions of users instant access to pages of product information. The seller avoids mail-distribution and printing costs, and once an online catalogue is in place, there is little cost in maintaining and accessing it. Popular consumer ecatalogues include JCPenney, L.L.Bean, and Victoria's Secret. Top B2B ecatalogues include Dell Computer and Office Depot.[24]

ecatalogues Non-store retailing that uses the internet to display products and services for both retail shoppers and business customers.

Internet-Based Stores. In 2007, Canadians bought $12.8 billion worth of goods and services over the internet. That was up 61 percent from just two years earlier. As large as these numbers seem, they still represent only about 1.5 percent of the $853 billion that consumers spent on goods and services in 2007.[25] Ice.com, a Montreal-based company, is a typical internet-based store. It sells mid- and low-priced jewellery over the internet to mostly U.S. customers. The company is profitable because it deals in products that are high value, high margin, small size, and easy to ship to customers.[26] Using the internet to do *comparison shopping* is increasing rapidly. Internet sites like Ask Jeeves Inc., Google Inc., and Yahoo! Inc. allow consumers to compare prices and products before making a purchase.

Approximately 32 000 Canadians make a significant portion of their annual income by selling goods and services on eBay alone. These "small retailers" who use sites like eBay, Kijiji, and Craigslist often do not pay income tax or sales tax on their sales, so both the Canada Revenue Agency and the federal government are losing millions of dollars in tax revenues each year. The Federal Court of Appeal has ordered eBay to provide information on people who sell more than $1000 per month on its site.[27] eBay is also planning to retreat from its recently adopted strategy of selling new goods over the internet and will return to its original strategy of being the web's flea market.[28]

Electronic Storefronts and Cybermalls. Today, a seller's website is an **electronic storefront** (or *virtual storefront*) from which consumers collect information about products and buying opportunities, place orders, and pay for purchases. Producers of large product lines, such as Dell Computer, dedicate storefronts to their own product lines. Other sites, such as CDNOW, which offers CDs and audio and videotapes, are category sellers whose storefronts feature products from many manufacturers.

electronic storefront A seller's website in which consumers collect information about products and buying opportunities, place sales orders, and pay for their purchases.

Search engines like Yahoo! serve as **cybermalls**—collections of virtual storefronts representing diverse products. After entering a cybermall, shoppers can navigate by choosing from a list of stores (L.L.Bean or Lands' End), product listings (computers or MP3 players), or departments (apparel or bath/beauty). When your virtual shopping cart is full, you check out and pay your bill. The value-added properties of cybermalls are obvious—speed, convenience, 24-hour access, and efficient searching.

cybermalls Collections of virtual storefronts representing diverse products.

From Door-to-Door to Esales? Not surprisingly, cyberspace is encroaching on door-to-door distribution. Amway is famous for a **multilevel marketing** channel in which self-employed distributors get commissions for recruiting new customers and new Amway reps. Now Amway is expanding this system to the internet with a spinoff called Quixstar. With help from Quixstar, you can start your own at-home internet business. You will be paid for directing new customers to the Quixstar site and for encouraging others to become Quixstar reps. The internet's huge at-home sales potential is also luring other famous door-to-door names—Tupperware, Avon, and Mary Kay. Such firms are racing to board the internet train even though they are courting potential channel conflict. Thousands of loyal door-to-door sales reps stand to lose customers to their own companies' internet outlets.[29]

multilevel marketing A system in which salespeople earn a commission on their own sales and on the sales of any other salespeople they recruit.

Veteran QVC host Bob Bowersox is getting ready to offer bedding made by a company called Northern Lights, which distributes regularly through the TV home-shopping channel. Northern Lights, which sells sheets, pillows, and other bedding products, markets through such electronic retailing outlets as eBay and Shopping.com, as well as QVC.

Interactive and Video Marketing. Both retail and B2B customers interact with multimedia sites using voice, graphics, animation, film clips, and access to live human advice. One good example of **interactive marketing** is LivePerson.com, a leading provider of real-time sales and customer service for over 3000 websites. When customers log on to the sites of Toyota, Earthlink, Hewlett-Packard, Verizon, Microsoft—all of which are LivePerson clients—they can enter a live chat room where a service operator initiates a secure one-on-one text chat. Questions and answers go back and forth to help customers get answers to specific questions before deciding on a product. Another form of interaction is the so-called banner ad that changes as the user's mouse moves about the page, revealing new drop-down, check, and search boxes.[30]

interactive marketing Selling products and services by allowing customers to interact with multimedia websites using voice, graphics, animation, film clips, and access to live human advice.

Video marketing, a long-established form of interactive marketing, lets viewers shop at home from TV screens by phoning in or emailing orders. Most cable systems offer video marketing through home-shopping channels that display and demonstrate products and allow viewers to phone in or email orders. One U.S. network, QVC, also operates in the United Kingdom, Germany, Mexico, and South America.

video marketing Selling to consumers by showing products on television that consumers can buy by telephone or mail.

Physical Distribution

6 Define *physical distribution* and describe the major activities in *warehousing* operations.

Physical distribution refers to the activities needed to move products efficiently from manufacturer to consumer. The goals of physical distribution are to keep customers satisfied, to make goods available when and where consumers want them, and to keep costs low. Physical distribution includes *warehousing* and *transportation operations*, as well as *distribution for ecustomers*.

physical distribution Those activities needed to move a product from the manufacturer to the end-consumer.

Warehousing Operations

Storing, or **warehousing**, is a major part of distribution management. In selecting a strategy, managers must keep in mind both the different characteristics and costs of warehousing operations.

warehousing That part of the distribution process concerned with storing goods.

Types of Warehouses

There are two basic types of warehouses—*private* and *public*. Facilities can be further divided according to use as *storage warehouses* or *distribution centres*.

Public and Private Warehouses.   **Public warehouses** are independently owned and operated. Because companies rent only the space they need, they are popular with firms needing storage only during peak periods. Manufacturers who need multiple storage locations to get products to multiple markets also use public warehouses. **Private warehouses** are owned by a single manufacturer, wholesaler, or retailer. Most are run by large firms that deal in mass quantities and need regular storage.

Storage Warehouses and Distribution Centres.   **Storage warehouses** provide storage for extended periods. Producers of seasonal items, such as agricultural crops, use this type of warehouse. **Distribution centres** provide short-term storage of products whose demand is both constant and high. Retail chains, wholesalers, and manufacturers who need to break down large quantities of merchandise into the smaller quantities that stores or customers demand also use them. Distribution centres are common in the grocery and food industry. Kellogg's, for example, stores virtually no products at its plants. Instead, it ships cereals from factories to regional distribution centres.

public warehouse An independently owned and operated warehouse that stores the goods of many firms.

private warehouse A warehouse owned and used by just one company.

storage warehouse A warehouse used to provide storage of goods for extended periods of time.

distribution centre A warehouse used to provide storage of goods for only short periods before they are shipped to retail stores.

Warehousing Costs

Typical warehouse costs include such obvious expenses as storage-space rental or mortgage payments (usually computed on a square-foot basis), insurance, and wages. They also include the costs of *inventory control and materials handling.*

Inventory Control.   **Inventory control** means ensuring that an adequate supply of a product is in stock at all times, while avoiding an excessive inventory of supplies.

Materials Handling.   Most warehouse personnel are involved in **materials handling**—the transportation, arrangement, and orderly retrieval of inventoried goods. Holding down materials-handling costs requires making decisions about product placement within the warehouse as well as decisions about whether to store products as individual units, in multiple packages, or in sealed containers. A **unitization** strategy calls for standardizing the weight and form of materials. A GE warehouse, for example, receives apartment-size refrigerators from Europe in containers of 56 refrigerators each. Dealing with the huge containers rather than individual boxes not only makes handling easier but also reduces theft and damage. It also optimizes shipping space and makes restocking easier.

inventory control The part of warehouse operations that keeps track of what is on hand and ensures adequate supplies of products are in stock at all times.

materials handling The transportation and arrangement of goods within a warehouse and orderly retrieval of goods from inventory.

unitization Standardizing the weight and form of materials.

Transportation Operations

The major transportation modes are rail, water, truck, air, and pipeline. In the early part of the twentieth century, railroads dominated the Canadian transportation system, but by the 1970s, truck and air transportation had become important as well. Using operating revenue as the criterion, the most important modes of transportation in Canada are now trucks, air, and rail.

Cost is a major factor when a company chooses a transportation method, but it is not the only consideration. A company must also consider the nature of its products, the distance the product must travel, timeliness, and customers' needs. A company shipping orchids or other perishable goods will probably use air transport, while a company shipping sand or coal will use rail or water transport.

Compare the five basic forms of *transportation* and explain how distribution can be used as a marketing strategy.

7

Transportation Modes

Each of the major transportation modes has advantages and disadvantages. Key differences in cost are most directly related to delivery speed.

Trucks. The advantages of trucks include flexibility, fast service, and dependability. All sections of Canada except the Far North can be reached by truck. Trucks are a particularly good choice for short-distance distribution and more expensive products. Large furniture and appliance retailers in major cities, for example, use trucks to shuttle merchandise between their stores and to make deliveries to customers. Trucks can, however, be delayed by bad weather. They also are limited in the volume they can carry in a single load.

Planes. Air is the fastest available transportation mode, and in Canada's Far North, it may be the *only* available transportation. Other advantages include greatly reduced costs in packing, handling, unpacking, and final preparations necessary for sale to the consumer. Also, eliminating the need to store certain commodities can reduce inventory-carrying costs. Fresh fish, for example, can be flown to restaurants each day, avoiding the risk of spoilage that comes with packaging and storing. However, air freight is the most expensive form of transportation.

Railroads. Railroads have been the backbone of the Canadian transportation system since the late 1800s. Until the 1960s, when trucking firms lowered their rates and attracted many customers, railroads carried a wide variety of products. Railroads are now used primarily to transport heavy, bulky items such as cars, steel, and coal.

Water Carriers. Of all the transportation modes, transportation by water is the least expensive. Unfortunately, it is also the slowest. Boats and barges are mainly used for extremely heavy, bulky materials and products (like sand, gravel, oil, and steel) for which transit times are relatively unimportant. The St. Lawrence Seaway is a vital link in Canada's domestic water transportation system. Water transportation is also important in Canada's Far North, where barges deliver commodities such as fuel oil to isolated hamlets along the western edge of Hudson's Bay during the summer months. Northern Transportation Company Ltd. moves freight on the Athabasca River because of demand created by the oil sands projects in Northern Alberta.[31] In international trade, manufacturers often use water carriers for long distance ocean transportation because many ships are now specially constructed to load and store large standardized containers.

Pipelines. Traditionally, pipelines have transported liquids and gases, and they provide a constant flow of these products and are unaffected by weather conditions. Like water transportation, pipelines are slow in terms of overall delivery time. They also have a lack of adaptability to other products, and limited routes make pipelines a relatively unimportant transportation method for most industries.

Changes in Transportation Operations

For many years, transport companies specialized in one mode or another. With deregulation, however, this pattern has changed. New developments in cost-efficiency and competitiveness include *intermodal transportation, containerization,* and *order fulfillment through ecommerce channels.*

intermodal transportation
The combined use of different modes of transportation.

Intermodal Transportation. The combined use of different modes of transportation—**intermodal transportation**—has come into widespread use. For example, shipping by a combination of truck and rail ("piggyback"), water and rail ("fishyback"), or air and rail ("birdyback") has improved flexibility and reduced costs.

A container train crosses the Salmon River bridge in New Brunswick.

Containerization. To make intermodal transport more efficient, **container-ization** uses standardized heavy-duty containers into which many items are sealed at point of shipment; the containers are opened only at their final destination. Containers may be stowed on ships for ocean transit, transferred to trucks, loaded onto railcars, and delivered to final destinations by other trucks. Unloaded containers are then returned for future use.

containerization The use of standardized heavy-duty containers in which many items are sealed at the point of shipment; they are opened only at the final destination.

Order Fulfillment Through Ecommerce Channels. New ecommerce companies often focus on sales, only to discover that delays in after-sale distribution cause customer dissatisfaction. **Order fulfillment** begins when the sale is made and involves getting the product to each customer in good condition and on time. But the volume of a firm's transactions can be huge, and fulfillment performance—in terms of timing, content, and terms of payment—has been disappointing for many ebusinesses.

order fulfillment All activities involved in completing a sales transaction, beginning with making the sale and ending with on-time delivery to the customer.

To improve on-time deliveries, many businesses, such as Amazon.com, maintain distribution centres and ship from their own warehouses. Other etailers, however, entrust order-filling to distribution specialists such as UPS. The clients of Atomic Box, a much smaller company, range from manufacturers to dot-coms that prefer to concentrate on selling while outsourcing logistics and storage activities. The company maintains 325 000 square feet of warehousing through which it annually delivers products worth more than $200 million. It handles the flow of goods and information in both B2B and business-to-consumer transactions.

Companies like Atomic Box and UPS process customer orders, ship goods, provide information about product availability, inform customers about the real-time status of their orders, and handle returns. To perform these tasks, the client's computer system must be integrated with that of the distribution specialist. In deciding whether to build their own distribution centres or to use third-party distributors, clients must consider fixed costs as well as the need for shipping expertise. Because the capital investment required for a 1-million-square-foot distribution centre is $60 to $80 million, only high-volume companies can afford it. The alternative is paying a third-party distributor about 10 percent of each sale to fulfill orders.[32]

Companies Specializing in Transportation

The major modes of transportation are available from one or more of four types of transporting companies: *common carriers*, *freight forwarders*, *contract carriers*, and *private carriers*.

Common carriers transport merchandise for any shipper—manufacturers, wholesalers, retailers, and even individual consumers. They maintain regular schedules and charge competitive prices. The best examples of common carriers are truck lines and railroads.

Not all transportation companies own their own vehicles. A **freight forwarder** is a common carrier that leases bulk space from other carriers, such as railroads or airlines. It then resells parts of that space to smaller shippers. Once it has enough contracts to fill the bulk space, the freight forwarder picks up whatever merchandise is to be shipped. It then transports the goods to the bulk carrier, which makes delivery to an agreed-on destination and handles billing and any inquiries concerning the shipment.

Some transportation companies will transport products for any firm for a contracted amount and time period. These **contract carriers** are usually self-employed operators who own the vehicle that transports the products. When they have delivered a contracted load to its destination, they generally try to locate another contract shipment (often with a different manufacturer) for the return trip.

A few manufacturers and retailers maintain their own transportation systems (usually a fleet of trucks) to carry their own products. The use of such **private carriers** is generally limited to very large manufacturers such as Kraft Foods and Canada Safeway.

Distribution as a Marketing Strategy

Distribution is an increasingly important way of competing for sales. Instead of just offering advantages in product features and quality, price, and promotion, many firms have turned to distribution as a cornerstone of their business strategies. This approach means assessing and improving the entire stream of activities—wholesaling, warehousing, and transportation—involved in getting products to customers.

The Use of Hubs

One approach to streamlining is the use of **hubs**—central distribution outlets that control all or most of a firm's distribution activities. Two contrasting strategies have emerged from this approach: *supply-side and "pre-staging" hubs* on the one hand and *distribution-side hubs* on the other.

Supply-Side and "Pre-staging" Hubs. *Supply-side hubs* are located at the same site where production activities take place. They make sense when large shipments flow regularly to a single industrial user, such as an automobile manufacturer. But these incoming shipments can create a lot of congestion, so some firms use *pre-staging hubs*, which are located near the factory. For example, Saturn maintains a pre-staging hub—managed by Ryder System—where all incoming material is organized to ensure that Saturn's production schedule at the factory is not disrupted. At the hub, long-haul tractors are disconnected from trailers and sent on return trips to any of 339 suppliers in many different geographical areas. Responding to Saturn's up-to-the-minute needs, hub headquarters arranges transport for pre-sorted and pre-inspected materials to the factory by loading them onto specially designed tractors.

The chief job of the hub, then, is to coordinate the customer's materials needs with supply-chain transportation. If the hub is successful, factory inventories are virtually eliminated, storage-space requirements are reduced, and

---

common carriers Transportation companies that transport goods for any firm or individual wishing to make a shipment.

freight forwarders Common carriers that lease bulk space from other carriers and resell that space to firms making small shipments.

contract carriers Independent transporters who contract to serve as transporters for industrial customers only.

private carriers Transportation systems owned by the shipper.

hubs Central distribution outlets that control all or most of a firm's distribution activities.

long-haul trucks are kept moving instead of being queued up at the unloading dock. By outsourcing distribution activities to its hub, Saturn can focus on what it does best—manufacturing. Meanwhile, Ryder is paid for its special skills in handling transportation flows.

Distribution-Side Hubs. Whereas supply-side hubs are located near industrial customers, *distribution-side hubs* may be located much farther away, especially if customers are geographically dispersed. UPS, for example, has a large distribution-side hub at Burlington, Ontario.[33] National Semiconductor, one of the world's largest chip makers, airfreights chips worldwide from a single centre in Singapore.

Test yourself on the material for this chapter at **www.pearsoned.ca/mybusinesslab**.

Summary of
Learning Objectives

1. **Identify the various *pricing objectives* that govern pricing decisions and describe the price-setting tools used in making these decisions.** *Pricing objectives* are the goals that producers hope to achieve as a result of pricing decisions. These objectives may include (1) pricing to maximize profits, and (2) pricing to achieve *market share* objectives. Sometimes, neither profit maximizing nor market share is the best objective. During difficult economic times, loss containment and survival may be the main objectives. Managers use two basic pricing tools, which are often combined: (1) *cost-oriented pricing,* and (2) *break-even analysis.* Break-even analysis assesses total costs versus revenues for various sales volumes. It shows, at any particular sales price, the financial result—the amount of loss or profit—for each possible sales volume.

2. **Discuss *pricing strategies* and tactics for existing and new products.** There are three *strategies* for pricing existing products: (1) pricing above the market, (2) pricing below the market, (3) and pricing at or near the market. Companies pricing new products must often choose between two pricing policy options: (1) *price skimming* (setting an initially high price), or (2) *penetration pricing* (setting an initially low price).

   Regardless of its pricing strategy, a company may adopt various *pricing tactics*, including *price lining* (offering all items in certain categories at a limited number of prices), *psychological pricing* (taking advantage of the fact that customers are not completely rational when making buying decisions), and using *discounts* to stimulate sales.

3. **Explain the distribution mix, the different *channels of distribution*, and different *distribution strategies*.** The *distribution mix* refers to the combination of distribution channels a firm selects to get a product to end-users. In selecting a distribution mix, a firm may use all or any of eight distribution channels. The first four are aimed at getting products to consumers, the fifth is for consumers or business customers, and the last three are aimed at getting products to business customers (see Figure 18.2). There are three basic *distribution strategies:* (1) *intensive* (make products available in as many outlets as possible), (2) *selective* (make products available in a few outlets), and (3) *exclusive* (make products available in only one outlet in a geographic area).

4. **Explain the differences between *merchant wholesalers* and *agents/brokers*, and describe the activities of e-intermediaries.** *Merchant wholesalers* buy products from manufacturers (i.e., they take title to the products) and sell them to other businesses, usually providing storage and delivery. A *full-service merchant wholesaler* also provides credit, marketing, and merchandising. *Limited-function merchant wholesalers* provide only a few services, sometimes merely storage. *Agents and brokers* are independent representatives of many companies and work on commissions. They serve as sales and merchandising arms of producers that don't have sales forces.

   E-intermediaries are internet-based channel members who perform one or both of two functions: (1) They collect information about sellers and present it to consumers; (2) they help deliver internet products. There are three types of e-intermediaries: *syndicated sellers*, *shopping agents*, and *business-to-business brokers*.

5. **Identify the different types of *retailing* and *retail stores*.** Retail operations fall under two classifications. (1) *Product line retailers* feature broad product lines. Types of stores

include *department stores* and *supermarkets*, which are divided into departments of related products. Small *specialty stores* serve clearly defined market segments by offering full product lines in narrow product fields. (2) *Bargain retailers* carry wide ranges of products and come in many forms, such as *discount houses, catalogue showrooms, factory outlets, warehouse clubs* (or *wholesale clubs*), and *convenience stores.*

Important forms of non-store retailing include *direct-response retailing, mail order* (or *catalogue marketing*), *telemarketing,* and *direct selling. Electronic retailing* uses communications networks that allow sellers to connect to consumers' computers. Sellers provide members with internet access to product displays. Buyers can examine detailed descriptions, compare brands, send for free information, or purchase by credit card. *Ecatalogues* use the internet to display products for both retail and business customers. A seller's website is an *electronic storefront* in which consumers collect information about products, place orders, and pay for purchases. Search engines such as Yahoo! serve as *cybermalls.* In a *multilevel marketing channel,* self-employed distributors get commissions for recruiting new customers and reps. Both retail and B2B customers participate in *interactive marketing. Video marketing* lets viewers shop at home from television screens.

6. **Define *physical distribution* and describe the major activities in *warehousing* operations.** *Physical distribution* (which includes *warehousing*) refers to the activities needed to move products from manufacturer to consumer. These activities make goods available when and where consumers want them, keep costs low, and provide customer services. There are two types of warehouses: *private warehouses* are owned and used by a single manufacturer, wholesaler, or retailer; while *public warehouses* are independently owned and operated and permit companies to rent only the space they need. *Storage warehouses* provide storage for extended periods. *Distribution centres* store products whose market demand is constant and high. Retail chains, wholesalers, and manufacturers use them to break down large quantities of merchandise into the smaller quantities that stores or customers demand. In addition to keeping track of what is on hand at any time, *inventory control* involves the balancing act of ensuring that an adequate supply of a product is in stock at all times and avoiding excessive supplies of inventory. *Materials handling* refers to the transportation, arrangement, and orderly retrieval of inventoried goods.

7. **Compare the five basic forms of *transportation* and explain how distribution can be used as a marketing strategy.** The advantages of trucks include flexibility, fast service, and dependability. Railroads are now used primarily to transport heavy, bulky items such as cars and steel. Air transport is the fastest available mode of transportation but also the most expensive. Transportation by water is the least expensive but the slowest. Pipelines are slow and inflexible, but do provide a constant flow of products and are unaffected by weather. Many firms regard distribution as a cornerstone of business strategy. One approach to streamlining distribution is the use of *hubs.* Supply-side hubs make the most sense when large shipments flow regularly to a single industrial user. To clear congestion, some firms operate pre-staging hubs, at which all incoming supplies are managed to meet production schedules. Whereas supply-side hubs are located near industrial customers, distribution-side hubs may be located much farther away, especially if customers are geographically dispersed. From these facilities, finished products, which may be produced in plants throughout the world, can be shipped to customer locations around the globe.

Key Terms

bargain retailers   (p. 622)
break-even analysis   (p. 610)
break-even point   (p. 610)
cash discount   (p. 614)
catalogue showroom   (p. 622)
category killers   (p. 622)
channel captain   (p. 620)
channel conflict   (p. 620)
common carriers   (p. 630)
containerization   (p. 629)
contract carriers   (p. 630)
convenience stores   (p. 622)
cybermalls   (p. 625)
department stores   (p. 621)
direct channel   (p. 615)
direct selling   (p. 623)
direct-response retailing   (p. 623)
discount   (p. 614)
discount houses   (p. 622)
distribution centre   (p. 627)
distribution channel   (p. 615)
distribution mix   (p. 615)
drop shipper   (p. 621)
ecatalogues   (p. 625
e-intermediaries   (p. 624)
electronic retailing (etailing)
    (p. 624)
electronic storefront   (p. 625)
exclusive distribution   (p. 619)

factory outlets   (p. 622)
fixed costs   (p. 610)
freight forwarders   (p. 630)
full-service merchant wholesaler
    (p. 621)
hubs   (p. 630)
industrial (business) distribution
    (p. 618)
intensive distribution   (p. 619)
interactive marketing   (p. 626)
intermediary   (p. 615)
intermodal transportation   (p. 628)
inventory control   (p. 627)
limited-function merchant
    wholesaler   (p. 621)
mail order (catalogue marketing)
    (p. 623)
market share   (p. 609)
materials handling   (p. 627)
merchant wholesaler   (p. 621)
multilevel marketing   (p. 625)
odd-even pricing   (p. 614)
order fulfillment   (p. 629)
penetration pricing   (p. 613)
physical distribution   (p. 626)
price leadership   (p. 613)
price lining   (p. 614)
price skimming   (p. 613)
pricing   (p. 608)

pricing objectives   (p. 608)
private carriers   (p. 630)
private warehouse   (p. 627)
psychological pricing   (p. 614)
public warehouse   (p. 627)
quantity discount   (p. 615)
rack jobber   (p. 621)
retailers   (p. 615)
sales agents (or brokers)   (p. 616)
sales offices   (p. 618)
seasonal discount   (p. 614)
selective distribution   (p. 619)
shopping agent (e-agent)   (p. 624)
specialty stores   (p. 622)
storage warehouse   (p. 627)
supermarkets   (p. 622)
syndicated selling   (p. 624)
telemarketing   (p. 623)
trade discount   (p. 614)
unitization   (p. 627)
variable costs   (p. 610)
vertical marketing system (VMS)
    (p. 620)
video marketing   (p. 626)
warehouse club (wholesale club)
    (p. 622)
warehousing   (p. 626)
wholesalers   (p. 615)

Questions for Analysis

1. How do cost-oriented pricing and break-even analysis help managers measure the potential impact of prices?

2. From the manufacturer's point of view, what are the advantages and disadvantages of using intermediaries to distribute products? From the end-user's point of view?

3. In what key ways do the four channels used only for consumer products differ from the channels used only for industrial products?

4. Explain how the activities of e-agents (internet shopping agents) or brokers differ from those of traditional agents/brokers.

5. Suppose that a small publisher selling to book distributors has fixed operating costs of $600 000 each year and variable costs of $3 per book. How many books must the firm sell to break even if the selling price is $6? If the company expects to sell 50 000 books next year and decides on a 40 percent markup, what will the selling price be?

6. Novelties Ltd. produces miniature Canadian flag decals. The fixed costs for their latest project are $5000. The variable costs are $0.70/flag, and the company should be able to sell them for $2 apiece. How many flags must Novelties Ltd. sell to break even? How many flags must the company sell to make a profit of $2000? If

the maximum number of flags the company can sell is 5000, should it get involved in this project?

7. Consider the various kinds of non-store retailing. Give examples of two products that typify the kinds of products sold to at-home shoppers through each form of non-store retailing. Are different products best suited to each form of non-store retailing? Explain.

8. A retailer buys a product from a manufacturer for $25 and sells it for $45. What is the markup percentage? Explain what the term *markup percentage* means.

9. Suppose that your company produces industrial products for other firms. How would you go about determining the prices of your products? Describe the method you would use to arrive at a pricing decision.

10. Give three examples (other than those provided in the chapter) of products that use intensive distribution. Do the same for products that use exclusive distribution and selective distribution. For which category was it easiest to find examples? Why?

11. If you could own a firm that transports products, would you prefer to operate an intermodal transportation business or one that specializes in a single mode of transportation (say, truck or air)? Explain your choice.

Application Exercises

1. Select a product with which you are familiar and analyze various possible pricing objectives for it. What information would you want to have if you were to adopt a profit-maximizing objective? A market-share objective? An image objective?

2. Interview the manager of a local manufacturing firm. Identify the firm's distribution strategy and the channels of distribution that it uses. Where applicable, describe the types of wholesalers or retail stores used to distribute the firm's products.

3. Choose any consumer item at your local supermarket and trace the chain of physical distribution activities that brought it to the store shelf.

Building Your Business Skills

Are You Sold on the Net?

The Purpose of the Assignment

To encourage students to consider the value of online retailing as an element in a company's distribution system.

The Situation

As the distribution manager of a privately owned clothing manufacturer specializing in camping gear and outdoor clothing, you are convinced that your product line is perfect for online distribution. However, the owner of the company is reluctant to expand distribution from a successful network of retail stores and a catalogue operation. Your challenge is to convince the boss that retailing via the internet can boost sales.

Assignment

Step 1

Join together with four or five classmates to research the advantages and disadvantages of an online distribution system for your company. Among the factors to consider are the following:

- The likelihood that target consumers are internet shoppers. Young, affluent consumers who are comfortable with the web generally purchase camping gear.

- The industry trend to online distribution. Are similar companies doing it? Have they been successful?

- The opportunity to expand inventory without increasing the cost of retail space or catalogue production and mailing charges.

- The opportunity to have a store that never closes.

- The lack of trust many people have about doing business on the web. Many consumers are reluctant to provide credit-card data over the web.

- The difficulty that electronic shoppers have in finding a website when they do not know the store's name.

- The frustration and waiting time involved in web searches.

- The certainty that the site will not reach consumers who do not use computers or who are uncomfortable with the web.

Step 2

Based on your findings, write a persuasive memo to the company's owner stating your position about expanding to an online distribution system. Include information that will counter expected objections.

Questions for Discussion

1. What place does online distribution have in the distribution network of this company?

2. In your view, is online distribution the wave of the future? Is it likely to increase in importance as a distribution system for apparel companies? Why or why not?

Exercising Your Ethics: Team Exercise

The Chain of Responsibility

The Situation

Because several stages are involved when distribution chains move products from supply sources to end-consumers, the process offers ample opportunity for ethical issues to arise. This exercise encourages you to examine some of the ethical issues that can emerge during transactions among suppliers and customers.

The Dilemma

A customer bought an expensive wedding gift at a local store and asked that it be shipped to the bride in another province. Several weeks after the wedding, the customer

▶

▶

contacted the bride, who had not confirmed the arrival of the gift. It hadn't arrived. Charging that the merchandise had not been delivered, the customer requested a refund from the retailer. The store manager uncovered the following facts:

■ All shipments from the store are handled by a well-known national delivery firm.

■ The delivery firm verified that the package had been delivered to the designated address two days after the sale.

■ Normally, the delivery firm does not obtain recipient signatures; deliveries are made to the address of record, regardless of the name on the package.

The gift giver argued that even though the package had been delivered to the right address, it had not been delivered to the named recipient. It turns out that, unbeknownst to the gift giver, the bride had moved. It stood to reason, then, that the gift was in the hands of the new occupant at the bride's former address. The manager informed the gift giver that the store had fulfilled its obligation. The cause of the problem, she explained, was the incorrect address given by the customer. She refused to refund the customer's money and suggested that the customer might want to recover the gift by contacting the stranger who received it at the bride's old address.

Team Activity

Assemble a group of four students and assign each group member to one of the following roles:

■ customer (the person who had originally purchased the gift)

■ employee (of the store where the gift was purchased)

■ bride (the person who was supposed to receive the gift)

■ customer service manager (of the delivery company)

Questions for Discussion

1. Before discussing the situation with your group, and from the perspective of your assigned role, do you think there are any ethical issues in this situation? If so, write them down.

2. Before discussing the situation with your group, and from the perspective of your assigned role, decide how this dispute should be resolved.

3. Together with your group, share the ethical issues that were identified. What responsibilities does each party—the customer, the store, and the delivery company—have in this situation?

4. What does your group recommend be done to resolve this dispute? What are the advantages and disadvantages of your recommendations?

For additional cases and exercise material, go to **www.pearsoned.ca/mybusinesslab**.

Concluding Case 18-1

This Distribution Net's for You

For many years, two Canadian beer brands—Molson Canadian and Labatt's Blue—have been locked in an intense battle for market share dominance in the Canadian market. But now there is a new brand that just may be the top-selling beer in Canada. That beer is Budweiser, which is brewed by Labatt as part of an agreement with Anheuser-Busch (AB) of St. Louis, Missouri. Those familiar with the beer industry estimate that Molson has about 11 percent of the Canadian market, and Labatt has about 20 percent (11 percent from Budweiser and about 9 percent from Blue). The talk in the industry is that Molson Canadian is a brand in crisis because of competition from various sources, including American beers, cheap discount beers, chic micro-breweries, and trendy imports.

This development may come as an unpleasant surprise to Canadians, but if you ask beer connoisseurs to name the world's largest-selling brand, they'll likely say Budweiser. The secret to AB's market leadership is a combination of

factors: good-tasting products, four generations of brand development and recognition, and a superior distribution system that has become a formidable competitive weapon. AB's state-of-the-art distribution system is a cornerstone in Budweiser's marketing strategy.

BudNet, AB's nationwide data network, is a space-age information technology that's integrated into AB's long-established distribution channel. The information technology and the distribution network, working together, are part and parcel of a strategy for moving product to more consumers. While sales reps from AB's 700 beer distributors continue with traditional services—convincing retailers to put more Bud products on the shelf, order taking, rearranging displays, restocking shelves, and installing promotional materials and displays—they also gather real-time data that AB uses for product promotions and sales strategies.

Here's how they do it. First, the several thousand sales reps and drivers for AB wholesalers are the eyes and ears of the system. When reps visit customer stores, they

▶

bring book-size, hand-held PCs and scanners for gathering retail sales data. Commenting on using the PC in a customer's store, sales rep Derek Gurden says, "First I'll scroll through and check accounts receivable, make sure everything's current. Then it'll show me an inventory screen with a four-week history. I get past sales, package placements—facts and numbers on how much of the sales they did when they had a display in a certain location." But information doesn't stop with just AB products: Gurden walks through the store noting what competitors are doing—product displays, shelf space, packaging—inputting what he sees in painstaking detail. "Honestly? I think I know more about these guys' businesses than they do. At least in the beer section," says Gurden.

Connecting their PCs to a cellphone, the reps transmit marketing data along with new sales orders to the warehouse, where the distributor compiles the data, then transmits it daily to AB corporate headquarters, where marketing specialists analyze it to see what beer lovers are buying. They know how much the consumer pays, time of sales, whether it's in bottles or cans, cold or warm, and the kind of store, all correlated with recent sales promotions for each sale. The accumulated data are stored in a digital "data warehouse" for fast retrieval and scientific analysis of consumer behaviour. Using the detailed analysis possible with data mining, computers comb through possible matchups between different sales promotions and consumer buying patterns, along with competitors' marketing actions, so brand managers can design marketing promotions to suit the ethnic makeup of various markets. The resulting new promotional plans are entered into BudNet, where distributors log on daily to get the latest recommendations for store displays and stock rotations. The results—AB's steadily increasing market share—seem to confirm what August Busch IV, president for domestic operations, told a recent gathering of distributors: "Brewers and wholesalers with a clear, data-driven focus will have a distinct competitive advantage."

In 2004, AB reached its highest domestic market share ever in the United States: 50.1 percent—more than two and a half times the volume of Miller Brewing Company, the second largest U.S. brewer. And, as noted earlier, AB is also doing very well in Canada. This lofty market position in both countries stems from BudNet's technology, with up-to-the-minute information on consumer buying patterns and competitors' distribution and sales activities. It replaces slow-moving weekly or monthly written reports that once flowed from retailer to wholesaler to brewer, a practice that still exists at some of AB's competitors. By providing current field intelligence to its marketing specialists, wholesaler reps are essential in AB's "Seamless Selling" program, a strategy for removing barriers between brewer, wholesalers, and retailers.

Seamless Selling energizes the entire supply chain for fast reaction in moving millions of barrels of brew annually in the right varieties of customer-ready packages from brewer to consumer. Using product managers' overnight analysis of what products consumers will buy in different kinds of stores—convenience stores, supermarkets, spirits shops, restaurants—and in various geographic regions and neighbourhoods, AB's distribution network responds with next-day deliveries.

BudNet's evolution is no accident. In 1997, chairman August Busch III announced AB's commitment to industry leadership in mining customers' buying patterns, with a technology investment costing $100 million. Since then, comments Joe Patti, vice-president for retail planning, "Wholesaler and store-level data have become the lifeblood of our organization."

The introduction of hand-held PCs provides greater efficiencies at the distributor level, too, for day-to-day scheduling of deliveries to retail stores. Before PCs, sales orders were accumulated from store to store throughout the day and delivered at day's end from sales reps to the warehouse. Sorting through large batches of orders presented a huge surge in evening workload and warehouse congestion, causing excessive time to pick products from storage, load them into delivery trucks, maintain accurate warehouse records, and have trucks loaded for delivery starting early the next morning. Even worse, when sales reps were late getting back at day's end, the evening's warehousing activities were delayed, causing costly overtime to load trucks for morning deliveries. With hand-held PCs, congestion has all but vanished. Sales reps communicate in real time with the warehouse, so sales orders flow in throughout the day. In addition to savings on costly overtime, it reduces administrative time in the warehouse and, even more importantly, gives sales reps more time with customers. The resulting increase in distributors' sales improves AB's chances for even greater gains in market share.

Questions for Discussion

1. In what ways has BudNet changed the wholesaler rep's job, as compared to pre-BudNet days?

2. Among the eight channels of distribution described in the text, which channel is used for distributing Anheuser-Busch products? Do you think another channel might be better?

3. Considering the roles and activities of each member in the distribution channel, which channel member is the channel captain? Explain your reasoning.

4. What are the warehousing activities performed by AB wholesalers? What are their transportation activities?

5. In what specific ways does BudNet remove barriers between brewer, wholesalers, and retailers so that the supply chain is more effective than before?

Changing Distribution Channels in the Music Business

Physical distribution of music in the form of CDs is rapidly declining, and digital distribution of music is rapidly increasing. A 2008 report by PricewaterhouseCoopers LLP predicts that by 2011 physical music sales in Canada will decline to just $275 million. That's down from $572 million in 2007. The study also predicts that by 2011 digital sales from sites such as iTunes will increase to $366 million. Thus, sometime in 2010 more music will be distributed digitally than physically.

The increase in digital music delivery has been dramatic. In 2007, digital music sales were just $122 million in Canada. That was only one-quarter of the volume of physical music sales. Music piracy is getting worse as consumers share music on the internet, and this is hastening the decline of physical music sales (which declined 11.9 percent in 2006 and 19.8 percent in 2007). In response to these declines, record stores have shifted their emphasis away from CDs and toward DVDs and video games.

The evolution of retail music sales shows how dramatically changes in technology can influence channels of distribution. For decades, consumers visited music stores, looked over the merchandise, and then decided what to buy (originally breakable records, then vinyl records, then eight-track tapes, then cassettes, and finally CDs). Then came internet stores offering thousands of titles among CDs and cassettes. Customers searched the lists, placed orders electronically or over the phone, and then received their music by mail.

Then came an online music service called Napster, where customers downloaded free software onto their computers that allowed them to put their music on Napster's website and trade with anyone else who was live on the internet at the same time. Not surprisingly, recording industry executives were not impressed with this new channel of distribution. They argued that file-sharing denied music artists the royalties they were due. The threat from Napster was seen as so great that the Recording Industry Association of America (RIAA) decided to prosecute. The courts soon shut Napster down for copyright infringement. But the victory was short-lived, and other file-sharing services like Morpheus, Kazaa, and Grokster popped up.

To combat illegal downloading, the recording industry launched two online music services—MusicNet and Pressplay. If customers used MusicNet, they paid $9.95 a month and got 100 downloads (but they couldn't copy them, and the deal expired at the end of the month). If they used Pressplay, they got 100 downloads for $24.95 per month (and the right to burn 20 tracks to a CD). Other similar services are offered by iTunes (the industry leader), Microsoft, Yahoo!, and a rejuvenated Napster.

The recording industry also filed lawsuits against Grokster and StreamCast Networks (the makers of Morpheus), and in 2005 the U.S. Supreme Court ruled that the entertainment industry could sue companies like Grokster and Morpheus. A few months later, Grokster agreed to shut down and pay $50 million to settle piracy complaints by the music industry. Grokster then announced plans to launch a legal service called 3G, which would require customers to pay a fee to get access to songs that could be downloaded.

In 2009, a Swedish court delivered another blow to illegal file-sharing when it found four men guilty of illegally posting online a pirated copy of the film *X-Men Origins: Wolverine*. Their website—called Pirate Bay—indexed songs, movies, and TV shows. It is visited by more than 22 million people each day. The men were sentenced to one year in jail and ordered to pay $3.6 million in damages to various entertainment companies.

But will the Swedish court ruling stop the illegal downloading of music? Grokster and Morpheus software is in the hands of millions of consumers who can still engage in illegal downloading, and more file-sharing software becomes available all the time. Overseas programmers also offer new software to consumers and they are beyond the reach of the law in North America. A survey by Forrester Research found that 80 percent of consumers who were surveyed said they were not going to stop free downloading.

Music companies should never underestimate how clever consumers can be when they are highly motivated to get something for free. Consider what happened with Apple's iTunes software. There is an option on the software called "share my music," which allows users to make their library of songs available to any other computer running iTunes. The software allows people to listen to other peoples' collection of music but not to copy it. Or so Apple thought when it developed the software. Then, some clever programmers figured out a way to get around the restriction and they started using iTunes software to facilitate illegal downloading.

It is hard to predict how this story will end, but for related developments, see Concluding Case 1-2.

Questions for Discussion

1. Consider the traditional channels of distribution for music albums. Which channel elements are most affected by the presence of services like Grokster, Kazaa, and Morpheus? Explain how those elements are affected.

2. Why is the music industry so concerned about internet distribution? Are there any opportunities for the recording industry in internet distribution?

3. Develop arguments opposing the legality of services offered by Grokster and Morpheus. Then take the reverse position and develop an argument in favour of these services.

4. What types of ethical or social responsibility issues does file-sharing raise?

5. What other products, besides music albums, are the most likely candidates for distribution on the internet, now and in the future?

The "Feel-Better" Bracelet

Q-Ray advertisements say that its "Serious Performance Bracelet is designed to help people play, work, and live better." According to the ads, the $200 bracelet—which makes people feel better by balancing natural positive and negative forces—is ionized using a special secret process. Golfers claim that the bracelet reduces their pain, so *Marketplace* went looking for answers at the golf course. Sandra Post, a champion golfer, is a paid spokesperson for the bracelet. When Wendy Mesley of *Marketplace* interviews her, Post emphasizes the jewellery aspect of the Q-Ray, not its pain-relief qualities. Mesley also interviews golfers Frank and Sam. Frank tells her that the bracelet has reduced his arthritis pain, but Sam (who also wears one of the bracelets) thinks the pain relief is mostly in people's heads.

Advertising that a product provides pain relief is a tricky business. Even though a lot of people wear the Q-Ray for pain relief, the company cannot advertise that its product relieves pain unless there are medical studies that clearly show this. And there are no such studies. Until 2006, people in Q-Ray ads said that the bracelet had cured their pain. But now they can't say that, because the U.S. Federal Trade Commission ruled that such advertising is deceptive.

Andrew Park brought the Q-Ray to North America, and now his son Charles is marketing the product in Canada. Park says that 150 000 Q-Rays have been sold in Canada at a price of $200 each. In an interview with Mesley, Park says that the company does not make pain-relief claims for the product in its advertisements. But then Mesley shows a hidden camera film clip to Park in which he is making a pain-relief claim during the shooting of an infomercial. Park says that he believes that the product reduces pain, and that if you believe the bracelet will relieve your pain, it will. Mesley also plays a hidden camera clip showing retail salespeople telling customers that the Q-Ray reduces the pain of arthritis. Park says he can't control what retailers tell their customers.

Marketplace also asks Christopher Yip, an engineer at the University of Toronto, to test a Q-Ray bracelet to determine if it is ionized. Yip finds that the bracelet does not hold an electrical charge and is therefore not ionized. When Park is confronted with this evidence, he says that he never claimed that the bracelet would hold an electrical charge. Rather, he simply says that the bracelet is ionized using an "exclusive ionization process." Hidden camera film of retail salespeople shows them explaining ionization by saying things like "it picks up the iron in your blood and speeds up circulation" and "negative ions are collected in the ends of the bracelet." Retail salespeople say they aren't sure what ionization is.

Mesley also shows Park a hidden camera interview with the Q-Ray sales coordinator. The coordinator mentions several types of pain that Q-Ray bracelets relieve—migraine, carpal tunnel, and arthritis. Park says that he will have to meet with the sales coordinator and inform her that she cannot make these pain-relief claims.

Questions for Discussion

1. Is the Q-Ray bracelet a convenience, shopping, or specialty good? Explain your reasoning. Also analyze the "value package" provided by the Q-Ray bracelet.

2. Briefly describe the variables that are typically used to segment markets and what each involves. Which variable is Q-Ray using?

3. Consider the following statement: *People suffering from chronic pain need hope, and a product like Q-Ray provides hope. Even though it might be scientifically difficult to prove that the bracelet relieves pain, if people believe the product will reduce their pain, that might become a self-fulfilling prophecy and the person's pain will be relieved. So companies like Q-Ray should not be prohibited from advertising that their product has pain-relieving qualities.* Do you agree or disagree with this statement? Defend your answer.

4. Which of the four Ps is most important in the marketing of the Q-Ray bracelet? Explain your reasoning.

Video Resource: "Buyer Belief," *Marketplace* (November 14, 2007).

Shall We Dance?

Baby boomers (those born between 1946 and 1964) now make up one-third of Canada's population, and they control 55 percent of the disposable income in Canada. The needs and wants of this demographic group have created many new business opportunities in the health, leisure, and security industries. Many entrepreneurs are now chasing "boomer bucks."

Consider Beverly and Robert Tang, who are former North American dance champions. They want to capitalize on boomers' love of dancing. Their timing is good, since television has boosted interest in ballroom dancing with immensely popular shows like *Dancing with the Stars*. The Tangs want to cash in on the dance craze by targeting baby boomers (mostly women) because boomers have the money to spend on dancing lessons. And they want their company—Dancescape—to be a world-class dance lifestyle company that is the basis for a global dance brand.

It's Thursday night at a Ukrainian church hall, and baby boomers are dancing under the instruction of the Tangs. The Tangs spend a lot of time giving instruction, but they have also invested $20 000 to make a learn-to-dance video. It's already selling in the United States and they're working on Canadian and British distribution. A key element of their plan is three websites where dancers can shop, socialize, and download dance videos. The Tangs hope their website will be the new "Facebook for dancers." But to build their brand and build their business, they need $1.4 million. They manage to get an audience with Tim Draper, a venture capitalist who has made millions on the internet. He likes karaoke, and he invested in Hotmail, so they know he's open to new ideas. To prepare for their meeting with him, they hire a brand coach to help them prepare their sales pitch. Unfortunately, after working with them, the coach thinks they aren't ready to meet with Draper. The coach thinks they are spending so much time running the business that they don't have time to refine and polish their sales pitch.

On pitch day, Tim Draper gets an impromptu lesson from Beverly and also listens to Robert's sales pitch. The sales pitch gets off to a rocky start when Robert calls Tim "Steve" on two different occasions. That is very embarrassing. Draper listens carefully to Robert's sales pitch but makes no commitment. But he doesn't give them a flat "No" either. They're still hopeful he may come through.

Marketplace talks with two experts about the prospects of success for Dancescape. Lina Ko works for National Public Relations, a company that does surveys with boomers. She also has a blog that provides insights into Canadian consumers' needs and wants. The other expert is Robert Herjavec, who owns a computer company. He says it's good that the Tangs are doing something they love, because "you should love what you do and you'll never work a day in your life." But, he observes, that doesn't automatically mean that you'll have a viable business doing what you love. He notes that the Tangs are promoting dancing to the boomer generation, but they are trying to do it using the technology of the Facebook generation. He is not convinced that boomers are technologically savvy enough for this to work. He also has concerns because he wants to see young people dancing, not boomer-age people. He thinks the Tangs need a viral marketing idea that will have broad appeal. Selling their videos through niche stores limits their market and is inconsistent with their goal of being a global brand.

Ko disagrees with Herjavec and says that the perception that boomers are not technically savvy is incorrect. She also notes that the dancing concept is good because boomers are interested in exercising and dancing is good exercise. Dancing also makes people feel younger than they really are. The targeting of women is also a good idea because women have a big influence on family purchase decisions. But Ko thinks that the Tangs should revamp their language. Boomers don't want to hear the word *retirement*. Rather, they want to reinvent themselves. Ko also says that the Tangs need to further segment the boomer market because boomers in their 40s are quite different than boomers in their 60s.

Questions for Discussion

1. What is the difference between *goods, services*, and *ideas*? Are the Tangs marketing a good, a service, or an idea? Explain your reasoning.

2. Which of the four Ps of marketing do you think is most important in the case of dancing lessons? Explain your reasoning.

3. Which variables do marketers generally use to identify market segments? Which variables are being used by the Tangs? Be specific.

Video Resource: "Boomer Bonanza," *Fortune Hunters* (March 8, 2008).

Part 4: Principles of Marketing

Goal of the Exercise

So far, your business has an identity; you've described the factors that will affect your business; and you've examined your employees, the jobs they'll be performing, and the ways in which you can motivate them. Part 4 of the business plan project asks you to think about marketing's four Ps—product, price, place (distribution), and promotion—and how they apply to your business. You'll also examine how you might target your marketing toward a certain group of consumers.

Exercise Background: Part 4 of the Business Plan

In Part 1, you briefly described what your business will do. The first step in Part 4 of the plan is to more fully describe the product (good or service) you are planning to sell. Once you have a clear picture of the product, you'll need to describe how this product will "stand out" in the marketplace—that is, how will it differentiate itself from other products?

In Part 1, you also briefly described who your customers would be. The first step in Part 4 of the plan is to describe your ideal buyer, or target market, in more detail, listing their income level, educational level, lifestyle, age, and so forth. This part of the business plan project also asks you to discuss the price of your products, as well as where the buyer can find your product.

Finally, you'll examine how your business will get the attention and interest of the buyer through its promotional mix—advertising, personal selling, sales promotions, and publicity and public relations.

This part of the business plan encourages you to be creative. Have fun! Provide as many details as you possibly can, as this reflects an understanding of your product and your buyer. Marketing is all about finding a need and filling it. Does your product fill a need in the marketplace?

Your Assignment

Step 1

Open the saved *Business Plan* file you have been working on.

Step 2

For the purposes of this assignment, you will answer the following questions in "Part 4: Principles of Marketing":

1. Describe your target market in terms of age, education level, income, and other demographic variables.

Hint: Refer to Chapter 16 for more information on the aspects of target marketing and market segmentation that you may want to consider. Be as detailed as possible about who you think your customers will be.

2. Describe the features and benefits of your product or service.

Hint: As you learned in Chapter 17, a product is a bundle of attributes—features and benefits. What features does your product have—what does it look like and what does it do? How will the product benefit the buyer?

3. How will you make your product stand out in the crowd?

Hint: There are many ways to stand out in the crowd, such as a unique product, outstanding service, or a great location. What makes your great idea special? Does it fill an unmet need in the marketplace? How will you differentiate your product to make sure that it succeeds?

4. What pricing strategy will you choose for your product, and what are the reasons for this strategy?

Hint: Refer to this chapter for more information on pricing strategies and tactics. Since your business is new, so is the product. Therefore, you probably want to choose between price skimming and penetration pricing. Which will you choose, and why?

5. Where will customers find your product or service? (That is, what issues of the distribution mix should you consider?)

Hint: If your business does not sell its product directly to consumers, what types of retail stores will sell your product? If your product will be sold to another business, which channel of distribution will you use? Refer to Chapter 18 for more information on aspects of distribution you may want to consider.

6. How will you advertise to your target market? Why have you chosen these forms of advertisement?

Hint: Marketers use several different advertising media—specific communication devices for carrying a seller's message to potential customers—each having its advantages and drawbacks. Refer to Chapter 17 for a discussion of the types of advertising media you may wish to consider here.

7. What other methods of promotion will you use, and why?

Hint: There's more to promotion than simple advertising. Other methods include personal selling, sales promotions, and publicity and public relations. Refer to the discussion of promotion in this chapter for ideas on how to promote your product that go beyond just advertising.

Note: Once you have answered the questions, save your Word document. You'll be answering additional questions in later chapters.

Notes, Sources, and Credits

Reference Notes

Chapter 1

1. Grant Buckler, "Workplace Wheel of Fortune," *The Globe and Mail*, December 18, 2007, B8.

2. Peter Burrows, "The Hottest Property in the Valley?," *Business Week*, August 30, 1999, 69–74.

3. www.paultan.org/archives/2007/08/02volkswagen-experiences-the-power-of-word-of-mouth.

4. Alex Taylor III, "How a Top Boss Manages His Day," *Fortune*, June 19, 1989, 95–100.

5. "On a Roll," *Canadian Business*, October 9–22, 2006, 51.

6. Joann Lublin, "Top Brass Try Life in the Trenches," *The Wall Street Journal*, June 25, 2007, B1, B3.

7. Virginia Galt, "Lousy People Skills Are Biggest Hurdle for Leaders," *The Globe and Mail*, October 15, 2005, B11.

8. *The Leader-Post* (Regina), www.2.canada.com/reginaleaderpost/news/business_agriculture/story.html?id=cd94cd.

9. Jerry Useem, "Boeing vs. Boeing," *Fortune*, October 2, 2000, 148–160; "Airbus Prepares to 'Bet the Company' as It Builds a Huge New Jet," *The Wall Street Journal*, November 3, 1999, A1, A10.

10. Peter Tingling, "Fact or Fantasy?," *National Post*, April 21, 2009, FP12.

11. Charles P. Wallace, "Adidas—Back in the Game," *Fortune*, August 18, 1997, 176–182.

12. Barry M. Staw and Jerry Ross, "Good Money After Bad," *Psychology Today*, February 1988, 30–33.

13. Gerry McNamara and Philip Bromiley, "Risk and Return in Organizational Decision Making," *Academy of Management Journal* 42 (1999): 330–339.

14. Brian O'Reilly, "What it Takes to Start a Startup," *Fortune*, June 7, 1999, 135–140.

15. "Kodak Deems Transformation Complete," *The Globe and Mail*, January 31, 2008, B10.

16. Sinclair Stewart and Derek DeCloet, "It's Mr. Focus v. Mr. Diversification," *The Globe and Mail*, June 3, 2006, B4.

17. Gordon Pitts, "Taking a Stand: How One CEO Gained Respect," *The Globe and Mail*, January 31, 2006, B8.

18. Bertrand Marotte, "Gildan Takes T-shirt Making to the Cutting-Edge of Casual Apparel," *The Globe and Mail*, July 3, 2004, B3.

19. Amy Hoffman, "Potash Strike Leaves Slippery Side Effects," *The Globe and Mail*, November 17, 2008, B1.

20. Steve Ladurantaye, "Maple Leaf Battered by Meat Recall Costs," *The Globe and Mail*, October 30, 2008, B3.

21. Kristine Owram, "Maple Leaf Claims 'Progress' After Recall," *The Globe and Mail*, February 25, 2009, B5.

22. Richard Bloom, "How Parmalat Juggled the Struggle," *The Globe and Mail*, May 23, 2005, B3.

23. Ric Dolphin, "Magna Force," *Canadian Business*, May 1988.

24. Isadore Sharp, "Quality for All Seasons," *Canadian Business Review* (Spring 1990): 21–23.

25. Bruce McDougall, "The Thinking Man's Assembly Line," *Canadian Business*, November 1991, 40–44.

26. Peter Verburg, "Prepare for Takeoff," *Canadian Business*, December 25, 2000, 95–99.

27. Sanam Islam, "Execs See Link to Bottom Line; Gap is Closing; More Firms Keen to be Seen as Best Corporate Culture," *National Post*, November 12, 2008, FP16.

28. Wallace Immen, "Half of Workers Don't Fit In," *The Globe and Mail*, October 22, 2008, C2.

29. Derek Sankey, "Cult-Like Culture is Key," *Financial Post*, July 28, 2008, www.nationalpost.com/story-printer.html?id=684225.

30. Calvin Leung, "Culture Club," *Canadian Business*, October 9–22, 2006, 115, 116, 118, 120; "Golden Rule Is Measure of Success: 10 Most Admired Corporate Cultures," *National Post*, December 3, 2008, FP16.

31. Neal Boudette, "Nardelli Tries to Shift Chrysler's Culture," *The Wall Street Journal*, June 18, 2008, B1.

32. Gordon Pitts, "It Boiled Down to a Culture Clash," *The Globe and Mail*, June 11, 2005, B5.

Chapter 2

1. G. Davenport (trans. 1976). *Herakleitos and Diogenes*. Pt. 1, Fragment 23.

2. M. A. Hitt, R. D. Ireland, and R. E. Hoskisson, *Strategic Management: Competitiveness and Globalization* (Cincinnati, OH: Southwestern Publishing Co., 2003).

3. A. S. DeNisi, M. A. Hitt, and S. E. Jackson, "The Knowledge-Based Approach to Sustainable Competitive Advantage," in S. E. Jackson, M. A. Hitt, and A. S. DeNisi (eds.), *Managing Knowledge for Sustained Competitive Advantage* (San Francisco, CA: Jossey-Bass, 2003).

4. D. A. Sirmon, M. A. Hitt, and R. D. Ireland, "Managing the Firm's Resources in Order to Achieve and Maintain a Competitive Advantage." Paper presented at the Academy of Management Conference, August, 2003.

5. Team Fredericton, www.teamfredericton.com (accessed July 7, 2007); RBC Financial Group, www.rbc.com (accessed July 7, 2007).

6. Radical Entertainment, www.radical.ca (accessed July 8, 2007).

7. R. E. Mueller, "The Inadvertent Entrepreneur: Accepting Change Is a Shortcut to Success," February 15, 1995, *Success* 47, no. 11 (2000), p. 22.

8. S. Martin, "Thoughts on a Long Ride: An Interview with Ray Fowler," *Monitor on Psychology* 33, no. 11 (2002), p. 37.

9. Z. Olijnyk, "Richard Currie," *Canadian Business*, April 11, 2005, pp. 78–79; S. Howland, "Richard Currie Named Chancellor of the University of New Brunswick," www.unb.ca (accessed July 7, 2007).

10. Roots Canada, www.roots.ca (accessed July 8, 2007).

11. McDonald's, www.mcdonalds.com/countries/index.html (accessed July 5, 2007); IAmFood.com, www.iamfood.com (accessed July 5, 2007); A Japanese Exchange Program, japan.lisd.k12.mi.us (accessed July 5, 2007).

12. M. A. Hitt, R. D. Ireland, S. M. Camp, and D. S. Sexton, *Strategic Entrepreneurship: Creating a New Mindset* (Oxford, UK: Blackwell Publishing, 2000).

13. R. McGrath and I. MacMillan, *The Entrepreneurial Mindset* (Boston: Harvard Business School Press, 2000).

14. R. D. Ireland, M. A. Hitt, and D. G. Sirmon, "A Model of Strategic Entrepreneurship: The Construct and Its Dimensions," *Journal of Management* 29: 963–989.

15. Ibid.

16. S. J. Carroll and D. J. Gillen, "Are Classical Management Functions Useful in Describing Managerial Jobs and Behavior?" *Academy of Management Review* 12 (1987), pp. 39–51.

17. H. Mintzberg, "The Manager's Job: Folklore and Fact," *Harvard Business Review* 5, no. 4 (1975), pp. 49–61.

18. R. Stewart, "A Model for Understanding Managerial Jobs and

Behavior," *Academy of Management Review* 7 (1982), pp. 7–13.

19. C. Gagné, "The Other RIM Guy," *Canadian Business*, December 5, 2005, www.canadianbusiness.com (accessed July 7, 2007); Research in Motion, www.rim.net (accessed July 7, 2007).

20. M. W. McCall and M. M. Lombardo, *Off the Track* (Greensboro, NC: Center for Creative Leadership, 1983).

21. L. W. Porter and L. E. McKibbin, *Management Education and Development: Drift or Thrust into the 21st Century?* (New York: McGraw-Hill, 1988).

Chapter 3

1. Statistics Canada, *Business Dynamics in Canada*, Catalogue no. 61-534-XIE (Ottawa: Minister of Industry, 2006).

2. P. D. Reynolds, S. M. Camp, W. D. Bygrave, E. Autio, and M. Hay, *Global Entrepreneurship Monitor: 2001 Executive Report* (Kansas City, MO: Kauffman Center for Entrepreneurial Leadership, 2001); P. D. Reynolds, M. Hay, W. D. Bygrave, S. M. Camp, and E. Autio, *Global Entrepreneurship Monitor: 2000 Executive Report* (Kansas City, MO: Kauffman Center for Entrepreneurial Leadership, 2000).

3. Monica Diochon, Teresa Menzies, and Yvon Gasse, "Exploring the Relationship Between Start-up Activities and New Venture Emergence: A Longitudinal Study of Canadian Nascent Entrepreneurs," *International Journal of Management and Enterprise Development* 2, no. 3/4 (2005): 408–426.

4. Queen's School of Business, "Queen's Centre for Business Venturing Announces Canada's Best Small and Medium Employers," January 14, 2009, www.business.queensu.ca/news/2009/01-14-09-BSME.php.

5. Nancy M. Carter, William B. Gartner, and Paul D. Reynolds, "Firm Founding," in *Handbook of Entrepreneurial Dynamics: The Process of Business Creation*, ed. W. B. Gartner, K. G. Shaver, N. M. Carter, and P. D. Reynolds (Thousand Oaks, CA: Sage, 2004), 311–323.

6. William D. Bygrave and C. W. Hofer, "Theorizing About Entrepreneurship," *Entrepreneurship Theory and Practice* 16, no. 2 (Winter 1991): 14; Donald Sexton and Nancy Bowman-Upton, *Entrepreneurship: Creativity and Growth* (New York, NY: MacMillan Publishing Company, 1991), 7.

7. Fred Vogelstein, "How Mark Zuckerberg Turned Facebook Into the Web's Hottest Platform," *Wired*, September 6, 2007, www.wired.com/techbiz/startups/news/2007/09/ff_facebook?currentPage=3; Ellen McGirt, "Hacker, Dropout, CEO," *Fast Company*, May 2007, www.fastcompany.com/magazine/115/open_features-hacker-dropout-ceo.html.

8. John Cooper, "A Pint of Success," *CMA Management* (December 1999–January 2000): 44–46.

9. www.heritage.org/index/ranking.aspx

10. Angela Dale, "Self-Employment and Entrepreneurship: Notes on Two Problematic Concepts," in *Deciphering the Enterprise Culture*, ed. Roger Burrows (London: Routledge, 1991), 45, 48.

11. Donald Sexton and Nancy Bowman-Upton, *Entrepreneurship: Creativity and Growth* (New York, NY: MacMillan Publishing Company, 1991), 11.

12. Allan A. Gibb, "The Enterprise Culture and Education: Understanding Enterprise Education and Its Links with Small Business, Entrepreneurship and Wider Educational Goals," *International Small Business Journal* 11 no. 3 (1993): 13–34; Donald Sexton and Nancy Bowman-Upton, *Entrepreneurship: Creativity and Growth*, (New York, NY: MacMillan Publishing Company, 1991).

13. Terrence Belford, "Intrapreneurs Combine Big-biz Clout with Entrepreneurial Style," *CanWest News*, March 23, retrieved from CBCA Current Events database. (Document ID: 1009719591).

14. Industry Canada, Small Business Research and Policy, *Key Small Business Statistics*, Table 1 (Ottawa: Public Works and Government Services Canada, July 2008), www.ic.gc.ca/eic/site/sbrp-rppe.nsf/eng/rd02300.html.

15. Industry Canada, Small Business Research and Policy, *Key Small Business Statistics*, Table 3 (Ottawa: Public Works and Government Services Canada, July 2008), www.ic.gc.ca/eic/site/sbrp-rppe.nsf/eng/rd02300.html.

16. Industry Canada, Small Business Research and Policy, *Key Small Business Statistics* (Ottawa: Public Works and Government Services Canada, July 2008), www.ic.gc.ca/eic/site/sbrp-rppe.nsf/eng/rd02371.html.

17. Industry Canada, Small Business Research and Policy, *Key Small Business Statistics* (Ottawa: Public Works and Government Services Canada, 2006), 10.

18. Since government statistics exclude businesses without employees, a business counted as "new" could possibly have been operating for several years before being statistically counted as a new business. This can happen because an unincorporated business operated by a self-employed person (with no employees) would *not* be included in Statistics Canada's business register. If such a business operated for several years prior to hiring employees it would only be classified as a new business when the employees were first acquired.

19. William B. Gartner, Kelly G. Shaver, Nancy M. Carter, and Paul D. Reynolds, *Handbook of Entrepreneurial Dynamics* (Thousand Oaks, CA: Sage Publications, Inc., 2004), ix.

20. Industry Canada, *Key Small Business Statistics* (Ottawa: Public Works and Government Services Canada, January 2009), 3.

21. Ibid.

22. Ibid., 10.

23. Ibid., 4.

24. Richard Bloom, "Building a Future on Sweet Dreams," *The Globe and Mail*, October 21, 2004, B9.

25. Lauren McKeon, "Tied to Home," *Canadian Business*, April 14, 2008, 33.

26. Roma Luciw, "Stay-at-Home Moms Stay the Business Course," *The Globe and Mail*, March 3, 2007, B10.

27. www.rbcroyalbank.com/sme/women/top_news.html.

28. RBC Canadian Woman Entrepreneur Award, www.theawards.ca/cwea/past-winners.cfm.

29. Murray McNeill, "Patience Pays Off for Native Owner," *Winnipeg Free Press*, November 6, 2002, B3.

30. Sarah Kennedy, "Self-Styled Pioneer Aims to Alter Face of Fashion," *The Globe and Mail*, July 1, 2002, B12.

31. Geoff Kirbyson, "Market-Research Firm Lands Major Contract," *Winnipeg Free Press*, July 19, 2004, D7.

32. Dianne Rinehart, "Seed Money Gives Wing to Aboriginal Ventures," *The Globe and Mail*, October 17, 2007, E8.

33. Donald F. Kuratko and Richard M. Hodgetts, *Entrepreneurship: Theory, Process, Practice*, 7th ed. (Mason, OH: Thomson South-Western, 2007), 118–125; John A. Hornday, "Research About Living Entrepreneurs," in *Encyclopedia of Entrepreneurship*, ed. Calvin Kent, Donald Sexton, and Karl Vesper (Englewood Cliffs, NJ: Prentice Hall, 1982), 26–27; Jeffry A. Timmons and Stephen Spinelli, *New Venture Creation: Entrepreneurship for the 21st Century*, 7th ed. (Boston, MA: McGraw-Hill Irwin, 2007), 9.

34. Jeffry A. Timmons and Stephen Spinelli, *New Venture Creation: Entrepreneurship for the 21st Century*, 7th ed. (Boston, MA: McGraw-Hill Irwin, 2007), 19.

35. J. D. Kyle, R. Blais, R. Blatt, and A. J. Szonyi, "The Culture of the Entrepreneur: Fact or Fiction," *Journal of Small Business and Entrepreneurship* (1991): 3–14.

36. R. H. Brockhaus and Pam S. Horwitz, "The Psychology of the Entrepreneur," in *The Art and Science of Entrepreneurship*, ed. D. L Sexton and Raymond W. Smilor (Cambridge, MA: Ballinger Pub. Co., 1986); William B. Gartner, "What Are We Talking About When We Talk About Entrepreneurship?," *Journal of Business Venturing* 5 no. 1 (1990): 15–29; Allan A. Gibb, "The Enterprise Culture and Education: Understanding Enterprise

Education and Its Links with Small Business, Entrepreneurship and Wider Educational Goals," *International Small Business Journal* 11 no. 3 (1993): 13–34; J. C. Mitchell, "Case and Situation Analysis," *Sociological Review* 31 no. 2 (1983): 187–211.

37. Donald Sexton and Nancy Bowman-Upton, *Entrepreneurship: Creativity and Growth* (New York, NY: MacMillan Publishing Company, 1991); Karl H. Vesper, *New Venture Strategies* (Englewood Cliffs, NJ: Prentice Hall, 1990); W. D. Bygrave and C. W. Hofer, "Theorizing About Entrepreneurship," *Entrepreneurship Theory and Practice* 16 no. 2 (Winter 1991): 14.

38. Walter Good, *Building a Dream* (Toronto: McGraw-Hill Ryerson, 1998), 40.

39. Ronald Ebert and Ricky Griffin, *Business Essentials* (Upper Saddle River, NJ: Prentice Hall, 2009), 137.

40. Wayne A. Long and W. Ed McMullan, *Developing New Ventures* (San Diego: Harcourt Brace Jovanovich, 1990), 374–375.

41. "Sally Fox: Innovation in the Field," www.vreseis.com/sally_fox_story.htm.

42. Michael E. Porter, "Know Your Place," *Inc*. 13 no. 9 (September 1992): 90–93.

43. Howard H. Stevenson, H. Irving Grousbeck, Michael J. Roberts, and Amarnath Bhide, *New Business Ventures and the Entrepreneur* (Boston: Irwin McGraw-Hill, 1999), 19.

44. Ibid., 21.

45. Marc J. Dollinger, *Entrepreneurship: Strategies and Resources* (Upper Saddle River, NJ: Prentice Hall, 1999), 94–101.

46. Thomas W. Zimmerer and Norman M. Scarborough, *Essentials of Entrepreneurship and Small Business Management*, 4th ed. (Upper Saddle River, NJ: Pearson Prentice Hall, 2005), 359.

47. Michael E. Porter, "Know Your Place," *Inc*. 13 no. 9 (September 1992): 90–93.

48. Dianne Rinehart, "It's Not Just Business, It's Personal," *The Globe and Mail*, October 10, 2007, B13.

49. Karl H. Vesper, *New Venture Mechanics* (Englewood Cliffs, NJ: Prentice Hall, 1993), 105.

50. Jeffry A. Timmons, *New Venture Creation* (Boston: Irwin McGraw-Hill, 1999), 277.

51. Lisa Stephens, "With Some Shape Shifting, This Company Has Legs," *The Globe and Mail*, October 5, 2005, B10.

52. George Anders, Carol Hymowitz, Joann Lublin, and Don Clark, "All in the Family," *The Wall Street Journal*, August 1, 2005, B1, B4.

53. Mary Agnes Welch, "When Name Is Everything," *Winnipeg Free Press*, May 12, 2002, B1–B2.

54. Quoted in Lowell B. Howard, *Business Law* (Woodbury, NY: Barron's Woodbury Press, 1965), 332.

55. "How They Stack Up," *The Globe and Mail*, November 10, 2008, B7.

56. "NYSE Euronext Takes Top Spot in IPOs," *The Globe and Mail*, December 29, 2007, B7.

57. "Clearwater Foods Going Private," *National Post*, August 15, 2008, www.nationalpost.com/story-printer.html?id=725985.

58. Terry Pedwell, "Income Trusts Face Tough Rules," *Winnipeg Free Press*, November 1, 2006, B7.

59. "An Overview of Available Business Structures," www.umanitoba.ca/afs/agric_economics/MRAC/structures.html#Cooperatives.

60. Industry Canada, *Key Small Business Statistics* (Ottawa: Public Works and Government Services Canada, January 2009), 12.

61. Kevin Marron, "Want to Succeed? Read This," *The Globe and Mail*, October 19, 2005, E1, E5. Several excellent articles on starting and operating a small business are found in Section E, "Report on Small Business" in *The Globe and Mail*, October 19, 2005.

62. See Norman M. Scarborough and Thomas W. Zimmerer, *Effective Small Business Management: An Entrepreneurial Approach*, 7th ed. (Upper Saddle River, NJ: Prentice Hall, 2003).

Chapter 4

1. M. A. Hitt, M. T. Dacin, E. Levitas, J. L. Arregle, and A. Borza, "Partner Selection in Emerging and Developed Market Contexts: Resource-Based and Organizational Learning Perspectives," *Academy of Management Journal* 43 (2000), pp. 449–467.

2. M. A. Hitt, D. Ahlstrom, M. T. Dacin, E. Levitas, and L. Svobodina, "The Institutional Effects on Strategic Alliance Partner Selection in Transition Economies: China Versus Russia," *Organization Science*, in press.

3. M. A. Hitt, R. D. Ireland, and R. E. Hoskisson, *Strategic Management: Competitiveness and Globalization* (Cincinnati, OH: South-Western Publishing Co., 2005).

4. Statistics Canada, www.statcan.ca (accessed January 4, 2007).

5. Statistics Canada, www.statcan.ca (accessed January 4, 2007); S. Moffett, "For Ailing Japan, Longevity Takes Bite Out of Economy," *Wall Street Journal*, February 11, 2003, p. 1.

6. A. Sagie and Z. Aycan, "A Cross-Cultural Analysis of Participative Decision-Making in Organizations," *Human Relations* 56, no. 4 (2003), pp. 453–473.

7. S. P. Seithi and P. Steidlmeier, "The Evolution of Business' Role in Society," *Business and Society Review* 94 (Summer 1995), pp. 9–12; L. L. Martins, K. A. Eddleston, and J. E. Veiga, "Moderators of the Relationship between Work–Family Conflict and Career Satisfaction," *Academy of Management Journal* 45, no. 2 (2002), pp. 399–409.

8. S. Gelsi, "Class for the Masses," *Brandweek* 38, no. 13 (1997), pp. 23–33.

9. J. Lawrence, "P&G Losing Ground in Product Innovation," *Advertising Age* 64, no. 48 (1993), p. 44; J. Lawrence, "It's Diaper D-Day with P&G Rollout," *Advertising Age* 64, no. 39 (1993), pp. 1, 60; J. Lawrence, "Kimberly, P&G Rev Up to Market Latest Twist in Disposable Diapers," *Advertising Age* 63, no. 26 (1992), pp. 3, 51.

10. B. Johnstone, "Rainbow Warriors," *Far Eastern Economic Review* 147, no. 7 (1999), p. 90.

11. Wal-Mart Annual Report, "2006 Annual Report: Building Smiles."

12. Personal communication with Dofasco senior management, 2003.

13. "Glass Fibers Make Smokestacks Cleaner," *Machine Design* 67, no. 18 (1995), p. 123.

14. CBC News, "Flaherty Imposes New Tax on Income Trusts," November 1, 2006, www.cbcnews.ca (accessed January 4, 2007).

15. Government of Canada, "Making Sense Out of Dollars 2005–2006," Government of Canada, www.admfincs.forces.gc.ca (accessed December 21, 2006).

16. A. K. Sundaram and J. S. Black, *The International Business Environment* (Upper Saddle River, NJ: Prentice Hall, 1995).

17. J. E. Oxley and B. Yeung, "E-Commerce Readiness: Institutional Environment and International Competitiveness," *Journal of International Business Studies* 32, no. 4 (2001), pp. 705–723.

18. C. M. Lau, D. K. Tse, and N. Zhou, "Institutional Forces and Organizational Culture in China: Effects on Change Schemas, Firm Commitment and Job Satisfaction," *Journal of International Business Studies* 33, no. 3 (2002), pp. 533–550.

19. M. Porter, *Competitive Strategy: Techniques for Analyzing Industries and Competitors* (New York: Free Press, 1980).

20. S. Slater and E. Olson, "A Fresh Look at Industry and Market Analysis," *Business Horizons* 45, no. 1 (2002), pp. 15–22.

21. N. Stein, "The De Beers Story: A New Cut on an Old Monopoly," *Fortune*, February 19, 2001, pp. 186–206; "Glass

with Attitude," *Economist* 345, no. 8048 (1997), pp. 113–115.

22. R. D. Ireland, M. A. Hitt, and D. Vaidyanath, "Alliance Management as a Source of Competitive Advantage," *Journal of Management* 28, no. 3 (2002), pp. 413–446; B. R. Koka and J. E. Prescott, "Strategic Alliances as Social Capital: A Multidimensional View," *Strategic Management Journal* 23, no. 9 (2002), pp. 795–816; D. Rigby and C. Zook, "Open-Market Innovation," *Harvard Business Review* 80, no. 10 (2002), pp. 80–89.

23. Canadian Auto Workers Union, www.caw.ca (accessed December 24, 2006).

24. D. Martin, "Gilded and Gelded: Hard-Won Lessons from the PR Wars," *Harvard Business Review* 81, no. 10 (2003), pp. 44–54; P. Christmann and G. Taylor, "Globalization and the Environment: Strategies for International Voluntary Environmental Initiatives," *Academy of Management Executive* 16, no. 3 (2002), pp. 121–135.

25. Greenpeace, www.greenpeace.org (accessed March 1, 2003).

26. Research in Motion, www.rim.net.on (accessed January 4, 2007).

27. Peak of the Market, www.peakmarket.com (accessed on January 4, 2007).

28. S. Finkelstein and A. C. Mooney, "Not the Usual Suspects: How to Use Board Process to Make Boards Better," *Academy of Management Executive* 17, no. 2 (2003), pp. 101–113; J. M. Ivancevich, T. N. Duening, J. A. Gilbert, and R. Konopaske, "Deterring White-Collar Crime," *Academy of Management Executive* 17, no. 2 (2003), pp. 114–127.

29. www.swlearning.com (accessed January 4, 2007).

30. Natalie Williams, "Why It's (Still) Good to Be WestJet," *Strategy*, November 2005, www.strategymag.com (accessed January 4, 2007).

31. CBC News, "In Depth Report on SARS," www.cbc.ca (accessed January 4, 2007).

Chapter 5

1. Sinclair Stewart, "CIBC Sues 6 Former Employees, Alleges They Took Confidential Data, Recruited Colleagues to Upstart Genuity," *The Globe and Mail*, January 6, 2005, B1, B4.

2. Howard Levitt, "Managers Have Duty to Remain Loyal to Employer; Court Penalizes Merrill Lynch for Taking RBC Staff," *National Post*, November 12, 2008, FP15.

3. Ronald Ebert and Ricky Griffin, *Business Essentials* (Upper Saddle River, NJ: Prentice Hall, 2009), 21.

4. Thomas Donaldson and Thomas W. Dunfee, "Toward a Unified Conception of Business Ethics: An Integrative Social Contracts Theory," *Academy of Management Review* 19, no. 2 (1994): 252–284.

5. "Drug Companies Face Assault on Prices," *The Wall Street Journal*, May 11, 2000, B1, B4.

6. John Saunders, "Bitter Air Carrier Dogfight Heads to Court," *The Globe and Mail*, July 8, 2004, B3.

7. Andrew Crane, "Spying Doesn't Pay; Intelligence Gathering is Still an Ethical and Legal Minefield," *National Post*, November 11, 2008, FP12.

8. Ann Zimmerman and Anita Raghavan, "Diamond Group Widens Probe of Bribe Charges," *The Wall Street Journal*, March 8, 2006, B1–B2.

9. This section follows the logic of Gerald F. Cavanaugh, *American Business Values with International Perspectives*, 4th ed. (Upper Saddle River, NJ: Prentice Hall, 1998), Chapter 3.

10. Steve Ladurantaye, "Maple Leaf Battered by Meat Recall Costs," *The Globe and Mail*, October 30, 2008, B3; Kristine Owram, "Maple Leaf Claims 'Progress' After Recall," *The Globe and Mail*, February 25, 2009, B5.

11. Mark Schwartz, "Heat's on to Get an Effective Code," *The Globe and Mail*, November 27, 1997, B2.

12. Julie Schmidt, "Nike's Image Problem," *USA Today*, October 4, 1999, 1B, 2B.

13. Jeffrey S. Harrison and R. Edward Freeman, "Stakeholders, Social Responsibility, and Performance: Empirical Evidence and Theoretical Perspectives," *Academy of Management Journal* 42, no. 5 (1999): 479–485. See also David P. Baron, *Business and Its Environment*, 3rd ed. (Upper Saddle River, NJ: Prentice Hall, 2000), Chapter 17.

14. Richard Blackwell, "The Double-Edged Sword of Corporate Altruism," *The Globe and Mail*, November 10, 2008, B5.

15. Jeremy Main, "Here Comes the Big New Cleanup," *Fortune*, November 21, 1988, 102–118.

16. Neil Reynolds, "The Dirty Truth of China's Energy," *The Globe and Mail*, March 28, 2007, B2.

17. Bill Curry, "Ottawa Wants Kyoto Softened," *The Globe and Mail*, May 12, 2006, A1, A7.

18. Jeffrey Ball, "U.N. Effort to Curtail Emissions in Turmoil," *The Wall Street Journal*, April 12–13, 2008, A1, A5.

19. "Going Green Losing Its Shine Among World's Citizens: Poll," *Winnipeg Free Press*, November 28, 2008, A20.

20. Catherine Collins, "The Race for Zero," *Canadian Business*, March 1991, 52–56.

21. Allan Robinson and Allan Freeman, "Mining's Dam Problem," *The Globe and Mail*, May 16, 1998, B1–B2.

22. Daniel Machalaba, "As Old Pallets Pile Up, Critics Hammer Them as New Eco-Menace," *The Wall Street Journal*, April 1, 1998, A1.

23. Egle Procuta, "One Man's Garbage is Another's Gold," *The Globe and Mail*, April 11, 2006, B7.

24. Geoffrey Scotton, "Cleanups Can Hurt, Companies Warned," *Financial Post*, June 25, 1991, 4.

25. Marc Huber, "A Double-Edged Endorsement," *Canadian Business*, January 1990, 69–71.

26. Patrick Barta, "Goro No Tropical Paradise for Inco," *The Globe and Mail*, July 12, 2006, B5.

27. Claudia Cattaneo, "Talisman Braces for Jungle Standoff; Threats of Violence," *National Post*, November 14, 2008, FP1.

28. Steve Ladurantaye, "Maple Leaf Battered by Meat Recall Costs," *The Globe and Mail*, October 30, 2008, B3.

29. Nicholas Casey, Nicholas Zamiska, and Andy Pasztor, "Mattel Seeks to Placate China With Apology on Toys," *The Wall Street Journal*, September 22–23, 2007, A1, A7.

30. John Wilke, "U.S. Probes Ice Makers Collusion Case," *The Wall Street Journal*, August 7, 2008, B1, B10.

31. Paul Waldie, "Chocolate Bar Makers Probe Over Prices," *The Globe and Mail*, November 28, 2007, B1, B10.

32. "Chocolate Makers Face Legal Challenges," *The Globe and Mail*, February 20, 2008, B9.

33. Jason Magder, Jack Branswell, and Ken Meaney, "Gas Firms Guilty of Price-Fixing," *Winnipeg Free Press*, June 13, 2008, A15.

34. Jonathan Cheng, "False Ads: Chinese Consumers Awaken to a Western Problem," *The Wall Street Journal*, July 8, 2005, B9.

35. Shawn McCarthy, "Crackdown on New York's Canal Street," *The Globe and Mail*, August 30, 2004, B1, B11.

36. Holly Shaw, "Buzzing Influencers," *National Post*, March 13, 2008, FP12.

37. Tim Barker, "Word-of-Mouth Advertising Grows in Influence, Concern," *Orlando Sentinel*, March 17, 2006, A1, A19.

38. Michael McCarthy and Lorrie Grant, "Sears Drops Benetton After Controversial Death Row Ads," *USA Today*, February 18, 2000, 2B.

39. Shona McKay, "Willing and Able," *Report on Business Magazine*, October 1991, 58–63.

40. "Why Business Is Hiring the Mentally Abled," *Canadian Business*, May 1991, 19.

41. J. Southerst, "In Pursuit of Drugs," *Canadian Transportation*, November 1989, 58–65.

42. G. Bylinsky, "How Companies Spy on Employees," *Fortune*, November 4, 1991, 131–140.

43. Jerald Greenberg and Robert A. Baron, *Behavior in Organizations: Understanding and Managing the Human Side of Work*, 7th ed. (Upper Saddle River, NJ: Prentice Hall, 2000), 374–375.

44. Brent Jang and Patrick Brethour, "This WestJet Staffer Blew the Whistle on His Employer's Corporate Spying. He's Still Waiting for Someone to Say Thanks," *The Globe and Mail*, October 18, 2006, A1, A12.

45. Cora Daniels, "'It's a Living Hell,'" *Fortune*, April 15, 2002, 367–368.

46. Janet McFarland, "Former Agnico Executive Sentenced to Jail Time," *The Globe and Mail*, January 30, 2009, B3.

47. Janet McFarland and Brent Jang, "Andrew Rankin: Barred From Trading Stocks, but Cleared of Criminal Charges," *The Globe and Mail*, February 22, 2008, B1, B4.

48. Greg Farrell, "Enron Law Firm Called Accounting Practices 'Creative'," *USA Today*, January 16, 2002, 1B.

49. Daniel Stoffman, "Good Behavior and the Bottom Line," *Canadian Business*, May 1991, 28–32.

50. "Great-West Life, London Life and Canada Life Donate $100,000 to the Salvation Army to Help Provide a Brighter Christmas for Many Across Canada," *Canada NewsWire*, December 18, 2008.

51. Diana McLaren, "Spirit of Philanthropy Is Thriving," *The Globe and Mail*, December 10, 2008, B7.

52. "Survey Shows Canadian Businesses Engaged in Meeting Community Need," *Canada NewsWire*, February 7, 2008, 1.

53. Tom Kierans, "Charity Begins at Work," *Report on Business Magazine*, June 1990, 23.

54. Theresa Ebden and Dawn Walton, "Walkerton Recipient of New-Style Corporate Giving," *The Globe and Mail*, June 3, 2000, B1, B6.

55. Alan Muller and Gail Whiteman, "Exploring the Geography of Philanthropic Disaster Response: A Study of Fortune Global 500 Firms," *Journal of Business Ethics* 84 (2009): 589–603.

56. Diane McLaren, "Doing Their Part—With Goals in Mind," *The Globe and Mail*, December 10, 2008, B7.

57. Kira Vermond, "A Great Way to Engage Your Employees," *The Globe and Mail*, July 26, 2008, B16.

58. Sandra Waddock and Neil Smith, "Corporate Responsibility Audits: Doing Well by Doing Good," *Sloan Management Review* (Winter 2000): 75–85.

59. Richard Blackwell, "The Double-Edged Sword of Corporate Altruism," *The Globe and Mail*, November 10, 2008, B5.

60. Alison Arnot, "The Triple Bottom Line," *CGA Magazine* (January–February 2004): 27–32.

Chapter 6

1. "Transparency International Corruption Perceptions Index 2005," Transparency International, 2005, www.transparency.org (accessed November 4, 2006).

2. M. A. Hitt, R. D. Ireland, and R. E. Hoskisson, *Strategic Management: Competitiveness and Globalization* (Cincinnati, OH: South-Western Publishing, 2005).

3. Canadian Imperial Bank of Commerce was charged with and later settled on aiding and abetting the Enron Corporation in accounting fraud. CBC News, "CIBC Agrees to $80 Million US Penalty over Enron Accounting Fraud," December 23, 2003, www.cbcnews.ca (accessed January 13, 2007). Nortel Networks was found to have committed accounting fraud to get out of the slump following the dot.com bubble burst. CBC News, "In Depth: Canada's Tech Giant," December 1, 2006, www.cbcnews.ca (accessed January 13, 2007).

4. PricewaterhouseCoopers, "Global Economics Crime Survey 2005," www.pwc.com (accessed October 24, 2006).

5. CBC News, "WestJet Countersues Air Canada," June 30, 2004, www.cbcnews.ca (accessed October 25, 2006); CBC News "Air Canada Seeking $220 Million in Suit Against WestJet," July 22, 2004, www.cbcnews.ca (accessed October 25, 2006); CBC News, "Air Canada Settles Spying Lawsuit," May 30, 2006, www.cbcnews.ca (accessed October 25, 2006).

6. D. Peterson, A. Rhoads, and B. C. Vaught, "Ethical Beliefs of Business Professionals: A Study of Gender, Age, and External Factors," *Journal of Business Ethics* 31, no. 3 (2001), pp. 225–232; E. Marnburg, "The Questionable Use of Moral Development Theory in Studies of Business Ethics: Discussion and Empirical Findings," *Journal of Business Ethics* 32, no. 4 (2001), pp. 275–283.

7. J. Tsalikis, B. Seaton, and P. Tomaras, "A New Perspective on Cross-Cultural Ethical Evaluations: The Use of Conjoint Analysis," *Journal of Business Ethics* 35, no. 4 (2002), pp. 281–292; L. Thorne and S. B. Saunders, "The Socio-Cultural Embeddedness of Individuals' Ethical Reasoning in Organizations (Cross-Cultural Ethics)," *Journal of Business Ethics* 35, no. 1 (2002), pp. 1–14; J. B. Hamilton III and S. B. Knouse, "Multinational Enterprise Decision Principles for Dealing with Cross-Cultural Ethical Conflicts," *Journal of Business Ethics* 31, no. 1

(2001), pp. 77–94; C. J. Robertson and W. F. Crittenden, "Mapping Moral Philosophies: Strategic Implications for Multinational Firms," *Strategic Management Journal* 24, no. 4 (2003), pp. 385–392.

8. A. J. Dubinsky, M. A. Jolson, M. Kotabe, and C. U. Lim, "A Cross-National Investigation of Industrial Salespeople's Ethical Perceptions," *Journal of International Business Studies*, Fourth Quarter 1991, pp. 651–669; J. K. Giacobbe-Miller, D. J. Miller, W. Zhang, and V. I. Victorov, "Country and Organization-Level Adaptation to Foreign Workplace Ideologies: A Comparative Study of Distributive Justice Values in China, Russia and the United States," *Journal of International Business Studies* 34, no. 4 (2003), pp. 389–406.

9. A. Kolk and R. VanTulder, "Ethics in International Business," *Journal of World Business*, February 2004, pp. 49–61; J. Tsui and C. Windsor, "Some Cross-Cultural Evidence of Ethical Reasoning," *Journal of Business Ethics* 31 (2001), pp. 143–150; C. J. Robertson and W. F. Crittenden, "Mapping Moral Philosophies: Strategic Implications for Multinational Firms," *Strategic Management Journal* 24, no. 4 (2003), pp. 385–392.

10. J. S. Black, H. B. Gregersen, and M. E. Mendenhall, *Global Assignments* (San Francisco, CA:Jossey-Bass, 1992).

11. J. Rawls, *A Theory of Justice* (Cambridge, MA: Harvard University Press, 1971); J. Greenberg, "A Taxonomy of Organizational Justice Theories," *Academy of Management Review* 12 (1987), pp. 9–22; Giacobbe-Miller et al., "Country and Organization-Level Adaptation to Foreign Workplace Ideologies," pp. 389–406.

12. T. Donaldson and T. W. Dunfee, "Toward a Unified Conception of Business Ethics," *Academy of Management Review* 19 (1994), pp. 252–284; J. A. Colquitt, R. A. Noe, and C. L. Jackson, "Justice in Teams: Antecedents and Consequences of Procedural Justice Climate," *Personnel Psychology* 55, no. 1 (2002), pp. 83–109.

13. R. Pillai, E. Williams, and J. J. Tan, "Are the Scales Tipped in Favor of Procedural or Distributive Justice? An Investigation of the U.S., India, Germany, and Hong Kong (China)," *International Journal of Conflict Management* 12, no. 4 (2001), pp. 312–332; D. Fields, M. Pang, and C. Chiu, "Distributive and Procedural Justice as Predictors of Employee Outcomes in Hong Kong," *Journal of Organizational Behavior* 21, no. 5 (2000), pp. 547–562; Y. Cohen-Charash and P. E. Spector, "The Role of Justice in Organizations: A Meta-analysis," *Organizational Behavior and Human Decision Processes* 86, no. 2 (2001), pp. 278–321; J. A. Colquitt, D. E. Conlon, M. J. Wesson, C. Porter, and Y. K. Ng,

"Justice at the Millennium: A Meta-analytic Review of 25 Years of Organizational Justice Research," *Journal of Applied Psychology* 86, no. 3 (2001), pp. 424–445; S. L. Blader, C. C. Chang, and T. R. Tyler," Procedural Justice and Retaliation in Organizations: Comparing Cross-Nationally the Importance of Fair Group Processes," *International Journal of Conflict Management* 12, no. 4 (2001), pp. 295–311; J. Greenberg, "Who Stole the Money, and When? Individual and Situational Determinants of Employee Theft," *Organizational Behavior and Human Decision Processes* 89, no. 1 (2002), pp. 985–1003; B. J. Tepper and E. C. Taylor, "Relationships among Supervisors' and Subordinates' Procedural Justice Perceptions and Organizational Citizenship Behaviors," *Academy of Management Journal* 46, no. 1 (2003), pp. 97–105.

14. J. Dietz, S. L. Robinson, R. Folger, R. A. Baron, and M. Schultz, "The Impact of Community Violence and an Organization's Procedural Justice Climate on Workplace Aggression," *Academy of Management Journal* 46, no. 3 (2003), pp. 317–326.

15. J. M. Jones, "Ethical Decision Making by Individuals in Organizations: An Issue-Contingent Model," *Academy of Management Review* 16 (1991), pp. 366–395.

16. J. Paolillo and S. J. Vitell, "An Empirical Investigation of the Influence of Selected Personal, Organizational and Moral Intensity Factors on Ethical Decision Making," *Journal of Business Ethics* 35, no. 1 (2002), pp. 65–74.

17. Ibid.

18. Mothers Against Drunk Driving, www.madd.ca (accessed October 25, 2006).

19. A. Chia and L. S. Mee, "The Effects of Issue Characteristics on the Recognition of Moral Issues," *Journal of Business Ethics* 27 (2000), pp. 255–269.

20. D. Carlson, K. M. Kacmar, and L. L. Wadsworth, "The Impact of Moral Intensity Dimensions on Ethical Decision Making: Assessing the Relevance of Orientation," *Journal of Managerial Issues* 14, no. 1 (2002), pp. 15–30; J. M. Dukerich, M. J. Waller, E. George, and G. P. Huber, "Moral Intensity and Managerial Problem Solving," *Journal of Business Ethics* 24, no. 1 (2000), pp. 29–38.

21. P. S. Ring and A. Van De Ven, "Developmental Process of Cooperative Interorganizational Relationships," *Academy of Management Review* 19 (1994), pp. 90–118.

22. "World's Most Respected Companies 2005," Finfacts Ireland, www.finfacts.com (accessed October 25, 2006).

23. D. Robin, M. Giallourakis, F. R. David, and T. Moritz, "A Different

Look at Codes of Ethics," *Business Horizons*, January–February 1989, pp. 66–73.

24. C. C. Langlois and B. B. Schlegelmilch, "Do Corporate Codes of Ethics Reflect National Character? Evidence from Europe and the United States," *Journal of International Business Studies*, Fourth Quarter 1991, pp. 519–539.

25. G. Wood, "A Cross-Cultural Comparison of the Content of Codes of Ethics: USA, Canada, and Australia," *Journal of Business Ethics* 25, no. 4 (2000), pp. 281–298.

26. Robin et al., "A Different Look at Codes of Ethics."

27. Ibid.

28. L. P. White and L. W. Lam, "A Proposed Infrastructural Model for the Establishment of Organizational Ethical Systems," *Journal of Business Ethics* 28, no. 1 (2000), pp. 35–42; S. A. DiPiazza, "Ethics in Action," *Executive Excellence* 19, no. 1 (2002), pp. 15–16.

29. C. Verschoor, "To Talk about Ethics, We Must Train on Ethics," *Strategic Finance* 81, no. 10 (2000), pp. 24, 26; T. Donaldson, "Editor's Comments: Taking Ethics Seriously—A Mission Now More Possible," *Academy of Management Review* 28, no. 3 (2003), pp. 363–366.

30. "Stronger Than Ever," *LM Today*, January 2004, p. 8; K. Shelton," "The Dilbert Dilemma," *Executive Excellence*, November 2003, p. 2; R. Carey, "The Ethics Challenge," *Successful Meetings* 47, no. 5 (1998), pp. 57–58.

31. M. McClearn, "A Snitch in Time," *Canadian Business*, June 18, 2004, pp. 60–67; M. P. Miceli and J. P. Near, *Blowing the Whistle* (Lexington, MA: Lexington Books, 1992).

32. Miceli and Near, *Blowing the Whistle*.

33. "Pearson Four Suspended: Whistle-Blowing Jazz Mechanics Cited Safety Concerns," *Hamilton Spectator*, www.hamiltonspectator.com (accessed August 25, 2006).

34. M. P. Miceli and J. P. Near, "The Relationships among Beliefs, Organizational Position, and Whistle-Blowing Status: A Discriminant Analysis," *Academy of Management Journal* 27 (1984), pp. 687–705.

35. BDO Dunwoody/Chamber Weekly CEO/Business Leader Poll by Compas Inc., "Whistleblowing," *Financial Post*, May 30, 2005, www.bdo.ca (accessed October 24, 2006).

36. Miceli and Near, *Blowing the Whistle*.

37. R. Sims and J. Brinkmann, "Leaders as Moral Role Models: The Case of John Gutfreund at Salomon Brothers," *Journal of Business Ethics* 35, no. 4 (2002), pp. 327–339; R. Galford and A. S. Drapeau, "The Enemies of Trust,"

Harvard Business Review 81, no. 2 (2003), pp. 88–95; L. R. Offermann and A. B. Malamut, "When Leaders Harass: The Impact of Target Perceptions of Organizational Leadership and Climate on Harassment Reporting and Outcomes," *Journal of Applied Psychology* 87, no. 5 (2002), pp. 885–893.

38. "Transparency International Corruption Perceptions Index 2001," Transparency International, 2001, www.transparency.org (accessed October 25, 2006); "Transparency International Corruption Perceptions Index 2005," Transparency International, 2005, www.transparency.org (accessed October 25, 2006).

39. M. Friedman, "The Social Responsibility of Business Is to Increase Its Profits," *New York Magazine*, September 13, 1970, pp. 32–33, 122, 126.

40. A. Smith, *An Inquiry into the Nature and Causes of the Wealth of Nations*, ed. R. H. Campbell and A. S. Skinner (Oxford, UK: Clarendon Press, 1976).

41. Friedman, "The Social Responsibility of Business Is to Increase Its Profits," p. 32; C. E. Bagley, "The Ethical Leader's Decision Tree," *Harvard Business Review* 81, no. 2 (2003), pp. 18–19.

42. M. Rothman, "Nightmare at Kaufman's," *Business Ethics*, November–December 1994, pp. 15–16.

43. J. Joha, L. Serbet, and A. Sundaram, "Cross-Border Liability of Multinational Enterprises: Border Taxes and Capital Structure," *Financial Management*, Winter 1991, pp. 54–67; C. Handy, "What's a Business For?" *Harvard Business Review* 80, no. 12 (2002), pp. 49–55.

44. Joha, Serbet, and Sundaram, "Cross-Border Liability of Multinational Enterprises: Border Taxes and Capital Structure."

45. B. Ruf, K. Muralidhar, R. Brown, J. Janney, and K. Paul, "An Empirical Investigation of the Relationship between Change in Corporate Social Performance and Financial Performance: A Stakeholder Theory Perspective," *Journal of Business Ethics* 32, no. 2 (2001), pp. 143–156; C. Sanchez, "Value Shift: Why Companies Must Merge Social and Financial Imperatives to Achieve Superior Performance," *Academy of Management Executive* 17, no. 2 (2003), pp. 142–144.

Chapter 7

1. H. A. Simon, *The New Science of Management Decisions* (Upper Saddle River, NJ: Prentice Hall, 1977).

2. G. R. Ungson and D. N. Braunstein, *Decision Making* (Boston: Kent, 1982).

3. D. Miller and M. Star, *The Structure of Human Decisions* (Upper Saddle River, NJ: Prentice Hall, 1967).

4. Simon, *The New Science of Management Decisions*; J. Parking, "Organizational Decision Making and the Project Manager," *International Journal of Project Management* 14, no. 5 (1996), pp. 257–263.

5. H. A. Simon, *Administrative Behavior* (New York: The Free Press, 1957).

6. H. A. Simon, G. B. Dantzig, R. Hogarth, C. R. Plott, H. Raiffa, T. C. Schelling, K. A. Shepsle, R. Thaler, A. Tversky, and S. Winter, "Decision Making and Problem Solving," *Interfaces* 17, no. 5 (1987), pp. 11–31.

7. H. A. Simon, "Rational Decision Making in Business Organizations," *The American Economic Review* 69, no. 4 (1979), pp. 493–513.

8. J. G. March and H. A. Simon, *Organizations* (New York: Wiley, 1958) pp. 140–141.

9. F. Phillips, "The Distortion of Criteria after Decision Making," *Organizational Behavior and Human Decision Processes* 88, no. 2 (2002), pp. 768–784.

10. P. Soelberg, "Unprogrammed Decision Making," *Industrial Management* (1967), pp. 19–29; D. Cray, G. H. Haines, and G. R. Mallory, "Programmed Strategic Decision Making," *British Journal of Management* 5, no. 3 (1994), pp. 191–204.

11. G. Loveman, "Diamonds in the Data Mine," *Harvard Business Review* 81, no. 5 (2003), pp. 109–113; E. Bonabeau, "Don't Trust Your Gut," *Harvard Business Review* 81, no. 5 (2003), pp. 116–123.

12. J. Johnson, et al. "Vigilant and Hypervigilant Decision Making," *Journal of Applied Psychology* 82, no. 4, pp. 614–622; E. Bonabeau, "Don't Trust Your Gut."

13. T. R. Mitchell and J. R. Larson, *People in Organizations* (New York: McGraw-Hill, 1987).

14. M. Bazerman, *Judgment in Managerial Decision Making*, Sixth Edition (New York: Wiley, 2005).

15. "Divorces," *The Daily*, March 9, 2005, Statistics Canada, www.statcan.ca (accessed January 7, 2007).

16. B. M. Staw, "The Escalation of Commitment to a Course of Action," *Academy of Management Review* 6 (1981), pp. 577–587; G. Whyte, A. M. Saks, and S. Hook, "When Success Breeds Failure," *Journal of Organizational Behavior* 18, no. 5 (1997), pp. 415–432; D. R. Bobocel and J. P. Meyer, "Escalating Commitment to a Failing Course of Action," *Journal of Applied Psychology* 79, no. 3 (1994), pp. 360–363; J. Ross and M. Straw, "Organizational Escalation and Exit: Lessons from the Shoreham Nuclear Power Plant," *Academy of Management Journal* 36, no. 4 (1993), pp. 701–732.

17. Staw, "The Escalation of Commitment to a Course of Action," p. 578.

18. G. McNamara, H. Moon, and P. Bromiley, "Banking on Commitment: Intended and Unintended Consequences of an Organization's Attempt to Attenuate Escalation of Commitment," *Academy of Management Journal* 45, no. 2 (2002), pp. 443–452.

19. E. Harrison, *The Managerial Decision Making Process* (Boston: Houghton Mifflin, 1975); J. R. Hough and M. A. White, "Environmental Dynamism and Strategic Decision-Making Rationality: An Examination at the Decision Level," *Strategic Management Journal* 24, no. 5 (2003), pp. 481–489.

20. R. Ebert and T. Mitchell, *Organizational Decision Processes: Concepts and Analysis* (New York: Crane, Russak, 1975).

21. S. S. K. Lam, X. P. Chen, and J. Schaubroeck, "Participative Decision Making and Employee Performance in Different Cultures: The Moderating Effects of Allocentrism/Idiocentrism and Efficacy," *Academy of Management Journal* 45, no. 5 (2002), pp. 905–914.

22. N. Margulies and J. S. Black, "Perspectives on the Implementation of Participative Approaches," *Human Resource Management* 26, no. 3 (1987), pp. 385–412.

23. J. S. Black and H. B. Gregersen, "Participative Decision Making: An Integration of Multiple Perspectives," *Human Relations* 50 (1997), pp. 859–878.

24. V. Vroom and P. Yetton, *Leadership and Decision Making* (Pittsburgh: University of Pittsburgh Press, 1973); V. Vroom and A. Jago, *The New Leadership: Managing Participation in Organizations* (Upper Saddle River, NJ: Prentice Hall, 1988).

25. R. Hof, "Why Once-Ambitious Computer Firm Quit," *Peninsula Times Tribune*, September 29, 1984, p. B1.

26. K. Eisenhardt and L. J. Bourgeois, "Making Fast Strategic Decisions in High-Velocity Environments," *Academy of Management Journal* 32 (1989), pp. 543–576; Hough and White, "Environmental Dynamism and Strategic Decision-Making Rationality."

27. I. Janis, *Victims of Groupthink* (Boston: Houghton Mifflin, 1972); M. E. Turner and A. R. Pratkamis, "Twenty-Five Years of Groupthink Theory and Research: Lessons from the Evaluation of a Theory," *Organizational Behavior and Human Decision Processes* 73, nos. 2, 3 (1998), pp. 105–115; J. K. Esser, "Alive and Well after 25 Years: A Review of Groupthink Research," *Organizational Behavior and Human Decision Processes* 73, nos. 2, 3 (1998), pp. 116–141.

28. S. Schulz-Hardt, M. Jochims, and D. Frey, "Productive Conflict in Group Decision Making: Genuine and Contrived Dissent as Strategies to Counteract Biased Information Seeking,"

Organizational Behavior and Human Decision Processes 88, no. 2 (2002), pp. 563–586.

29. J. S. Black, H. B. Gregersen, and M. E. Mendenhall, *Global Assignments* (San Francisco: Jossey-Bass, 1992).

30. K. Y. Ng and L. Van Dyne, "Individualism-Collectivism as a Boundary Condition for Effectiveness of Minority Influence in Decision Making," *Organizational Behavior and Human Decision Processes* 84, no. 2 (2001), pp. 198–225.

31. C. Schwenk and H. Thomas, "Formulating the Mess: The Role of Decision Aids in Problem Formulation," *Omega* 11 (1983), pp. 239–252.

32. A. Van De Ven and A. Delbecq, "The Effectiveness of Nominal, Delphi, and Interacting Group Decision-Making Processes," *Academy of Management Journal* 17 (1974), pp. 607–626.

33. B. B. Baltes, M. W. Dickson, M. P. Sherman, C. C. Bauer, and J. S. LaGanke "Computer-Mediated Communication and Group Decision Making: A Meta-Analysis," *Organizational Behavior and Human Decision Processes* 87, no. 1 (2002), pp. 156–179; Bonabeau, "Don't Trust Your Gut."

34. J. Levere, "Low-Fare Airline Aims to Build on Attitude and Hostility," *New York Times*, December 1, 2000.

35. Baltes et al., "Computer-Mediated Communication and Group Decision Making: A Meta-Analysis."

Chapter 8

1. M. A. Hitt, L. Bierman, K. Shimizu, and R. Kochhar, "Direct and Moderating Effects of Human Capital on Strategy and Performance in Human Service Firms: A Resource-Based Perspective," *Academy of Management Journal* 44 (2001), pp. 13–28.

2. M. A. Hitt, R. D. Ireland, and R. E. Hoskisson, *Strategic Management: Competitiveness and Globalization* (Cincinnati, OH: South-Western Publishing Co., 2005).

3. J. A. Pearce, K. Robbins, and R. Robinson, "The Impact of Grand Planning Formality on Financial Performance," *Strategic Management Journal*, March–April 1987, pp. 125–134.

4. R. Van Wingerden, "Managing Change," *International Journal of Technology Management* 21, nos. 5/6 (2001), pp. 487–495.

5. D. Rheault, "Freshening Up Strategic Planning: More than Fill-in the Blanks," *Journal of Business Strategy* 24, no. 6 (2003), pp. 33–38; B. Walters, I. Clarke, S. Henley, and M. Shandiz, "Strategic Decision-Making among Top Executives in Acute-Care Hospitals," *Health Marketing Quarterly* 19, no. 1 (2001), pp. 43–59.

6. J. Camillus, "Reinventing Strategic Planning," *Strategy and Leadership*, May–June 1996, pp. 6–12; L. Olson, "Strategic Lessons," *Association Management* 44, no. 6 (1992), pp. 35–39; J. J. Murphy, "Identifying Strategic Issues," *Long Range Planning* 22, no. 2 (1989), pp. 101–105.

7. "The Times that Try Men's Souls," *Journal of Business Strategy*, January/February 1999, p. 4.

8. C. Ngamkroeckjoti and L. Johri, "Management of Environmental Scanning Processes in Large Companies in Thailand," *Business Process Management Journal* 6, no. 4 (2000), p. 331; M. A. Peteraf and M. E. Bergen, "Scanning Dynamic Competitive Landscapes: A Market-Based and Resource-Based Framework," *Strategic Management Journal* 24, no. 10 (2003), pp. 1027–1041; M. D. Watkins and M. H. Bazerman, "Predictable Surprises: The Disasters You Should Have Seen Coming," *Harvard Business Review* 81, no. 3 (2003), pp. 72–80.

9. C. Jain, "Forecasting Process at Wyeth Ayerst Global Pharmaceuticals," *Journal of Business Forecasting Methods & Systems*, Winter 2001/2002, pp. 3–6; E. A. Boyd and I. O. Bilegan, "Revenue Management and E-commerce," *Management Science* 49, no. 10 (2003), pp. 1363–1386; M. Spann and B. Skiera, "Internet-Based Virtual Stock Markets for Business Forecasting," *Management Science* 49, no. 10 (2003), pp. 1310–1326.

10. G. Vastag, S. Kerekes, and D. Rondinelli, "Evolution of Corporate Environmental Management Approaches: A Framework and Application," *International Journal of Production Economics* 43, nos. 2/3 (1996), pp. 193–211; B. Boyd and J. Faulk, "Executive Scanning and Perceived Uncertainty: A Multidimensional Model," *Journal of Management* 22, no. 1 (1996), pp. 1–21; D. Lane and R. Maxfield, "Strategy under Complexity: Fostering Generative Relationships," *Long Range Planning* 29, no. 2 (1996), pp. 215–231; Watkins and Bazerman, "Predictable Surprises."

11. Michael J. Hileman, "Future Operations Planning Will Measure Plan Achievability," *Oil and Gas Journal*, March 18, 2002, pp. 84–87; L. Rouleau and F. Segui, "Strategy and Organization Theories: Common Forms of Discourse," *Journal of Management Studies* 32, no. 1 (1995), pp. 101–117.

12. "Benchmarking Strategies," *Brand Strategy*, December/January 2004, p. 3; A. Kouzmin, E. Loffler, H. Klages, and N. Korac-Kakabadse, "Benchmarking and Performance Measurement in Public Sectors: Toward Learning for Agency Effectiveness," *International Journal of Public Sector Management* 12, no. 2 (1999), p. 121; R. Bergstrom, "Benchmarking," *Automotive Production* 108, no. 9 (1996), pp. 63–65; J. Vezmar,

"Competitive Intelligence at Xerox," *Competitive Intelligence Review* 1, no. 3 (1996), pp. 15–19; David J. Smith, Y. Hwang, B. K. W. Pei, and J. H. Reneau, "The Performance Effects of Congruence between Product Competitive Strategies and Purchasing Management Design," *Management Science* 48, no. 7 (2002), pp. 866–885.

13. C. Barker, C. Thunhurst, and D. Ross, "An Approach to Setting Priorities in Health Planning," *Journal of Management in Medicine* 12, no. 2 (1998), p. 92; A. Bhid, "The Questions Every Entrepreneur Must Ask," *Harvard Business Review* 74, no. 6, pp. 120–130.

14. E. A. Locke and G. P. Latham, *A Theory of Goal Setting and Task Performance* (Upper Saddle River, NJ: Prentice Hall, 1990); A. Lederer and A. Mendelow, "Information Systems Planning and the Challenge of Shifting Priorities," *Information and Management* 24, no. 6 (1993), pp. 319–328.

15. D. Federa and T. Miller, "Capital Allocation Techniques," *Topics in Health Care Financing* 19, no. 1 (1992), pp. 68–78.

16. F. Sunderland and M. Kane, "Measuring Productivity on a Value Basis," *National Productivity Review* 15, no. 4 (1996), pp. 57–76; S. D. Pugh, J. Dietz, J. W. Wiley, and S. M. Brooks, "Driving Service Effectiveness through Employee–Customer Linkages," *Academy of Management Executive* 16, no. 4 (2002), pp. 73–84.

17. J. P. Morgan, "EVA Measures Competitiveness," *Purchasing*, September 4, 2003, pp. 16–18; K. Lehn and A. Makhiji, "EVA and MVA: As Performance Measures and Signals for Strategic Change," *Strategy and Leadership* 24, no. 3 (1996), pp. 34–38; R. Kaplan and D. Norton, "Strategic Learning and the Balanced Score Card," *Strategy and Leadership* 24, no. 5 (1996), pp. 18–24; I. Morgan and J. Rao, "Aligning Service Strategy through Super-Measure Management," *Academy of Management Executive* 16, no. 4 (2002), pp. 121–131; L. Aiman-Smith and S. G. Green, "Implementing New Manufacturing Technology: The Related Effects of Technology Characteristics and User Learning Activities," *Academy of Management Journal* 45, no. 2 (2002), pp. 421–430; L. G. Love, R. L. Priem, and G. T. Lumpkin, "Explicitly Articulated Strategy and Firm Performance under Alternative Levels of Centralization," *Journal of Management* 28, no. 5 (2002), pp. 611–627.

18. Bhid, "The Questions Every Entrepreneur Must Ask."

19. L. Rivenbark and M. Frost, "Strategic Planning for Success," *HR Magazine*, July 2003, pp. 120–121; L. Kempfer, "Planning for Success," *Computer-Aided Engineering* 13, no. 4 (1994), pp. 18–22; P. Sweet, "A Planner's Best Friend?" *Accountancy* 113, no. 1206

(1994), pp. 56–58; J. Rakos, "The Virtues of the Time-Bar Chart," *Computing Canada* 18, no. 17 (1992), p. 32.

20. S. Mallya, S. Banerjee, and W. G. Bistline, "A Decision Support System for Production/Distribution Planning in Continuous Manufacturing," *Decision Sciences*, Summer 2001, pp. 545–556; P. Cowling and M. Johansson, "Using Real Time Information for Effective Dynamic Scheduling," *European Journal of Operational Research*, June 1, 2002, pp. 230–244; S. G. Taylor, "Finite Capacity Scheduling Alternatives," *Production and Inventory Management Journal*, Third Quarter 2001, pp. 70–74.

21. F. Harrison, "Strategic Control at the CEO Level," *Long Range Planning* 24, no. 6 (1991), pp. 78–87; A. Di Primo, "When Turnaround Management Works," *Journal of Business Strategy* 9, no. 1 (1988), pp. 61–64.

22. W. R. Guffey and B. J. Nienhaus, "Determinants of Employee Support for the Strategic Plan of a Business Unit," *S.A.M. Advanced Management Journal*, Spring 2002, pp. 23–30.

23. M. Ishman, "Commitment-Compliance: Counterforces in Implementing Production and Inventory Control Systems," *Production and Inventory Management Journal* 36, no. 1 (1995), pp. 33–37.

24. J. White, "Almost Nothing New under the Sun: Why the Work of Budgeting Remains Incremental," *Public Budgeting and Finance* 14, no. 1 (1994), pp. 113–134.

25. W. Llewellyn, "A Review of the Budgeting System," *Assessment* 1, no. 5 (1994), pp. 47–50.

26. L. Bogomolny, "Melting the Glass Ceiling," *Canadian Business*, 79, no. 9, pp. 11–12.

27. H. Weihrich, *Management Excellence: Productivity through MBO* (New York: McGraw-Hill, 1985); H. Levinson, "Management by Whose Objectives?" *Harvard Business Review* 81, no. 1 (2003), pp. 107–116.

28. G. P. Latham and L. M. Saari, "The Effects of Holding Goal Difficulty Constant on Assigned and Participatively Set Goals," *Academy of Management Journal*, March 1979, pp. 163–168; A. Drach-Zahavy and M. Erez, "Challenge versus Threat Effects on the Goal-Performance Relationship," *Organizational Behavior and Human Decision Processes* 88, no. 2 (2002), pp. 667–682.

29. M. Erez, P. C. Earley, and C. L. Hulin, "The Impact of Participation on Goal Acceptance and Performance: A Two-Step Model," *Academy of Management Journal*, March 1985, pp. 50–66.

30. Locke and Latham, *A Theory of Goal Setting and Task Performance*.

31. P. Mali, *MBO Update* (New York: Wiley, 1986); J. M. Jackman and M. H. Strober, "Fear of Feedback," *Harvard Business Review* 81, no. 4 (2003), pp. 101–107; R. E. Kaplan, "Know Your Strengths," *Harvard Business Review* 80, no. 3 (2002), pp. 20–21.

Chapter 9

1. Robert L. Simison, "Ford Rolls Out New Model of Corporate Culture," *The Wall Street Journal*, January 13, 1999, B1, B4.

2. Joann Muller, "Ford: Why It's Worse Than You Think," *Business Week*, June 25, 2001, 80–84.

3. John A. Wagner and John R. Hollenbeck, *Management of Organizational Behavior* (Englewood Cliffs, NJ: Prentice Hall, 1992), 563–565.

4. Jay Diamond and Gerald Pintel, *Retailing*, 6th ed. (Upper Saddle River, NJ: Prentice Hall, 1996), 83–84.

5. "Nike Redefines Its Regions Amid Spending Pullback," *The Globe and Mail*, March 21, 2009, B7.

6. Michael E. Raynor and Joseph L. Bower, "Lead from the Center," *Harvard Business Review* (May 2001): 93–102.

7. Bruce Horovitz, "Restoring the Golden-Arch Shine," *USA Today*, June 16, 1999, 3B.

8. *Hoover's Handbook of American Business 2006* (Austin, TX: Hoover's Business Press, 2006); Brian Dumaine, "How I Delivered the Goods," *Fortune Small Business*, October 2002.

9. Lee Hawkins, "Reversing 80 Years of History, GM Is Reining in Global Fiefs," *The Wall Street Journal*, October 6, 2004, A1, A14.

10. Gary Yukl, *Leadership in Organizations*, 5th ed. (Upper Saddle River, NJ: Prentice Hall, 2002), 35–36.

11. "Multi-Tasking: Cost-Reduction Strategy at Case Corp.," *Machinery Systems Inc.*, www.machinerysystems.com/RavingFan/CaseCorp.html, July 20, 2001.

12. Donna Fenn, "The Buyers," *Inc.* (June 1996): 46–48+.

13. "Teck to Drop Cominco, Split Into Five Units," *The Globe and Mail*, October 2, 2008, B7.

14. J. Galbraith, "Matrix Organization Designs: How to Combine Functional and Project Forms," *Business Horizons* (1971): 29–40; H.F. Kolodny, "Evolution to a Matrix Organization," *Academy of Management Review* 4 (1979): 543–553.

15. Interview with Tom Ward, operations manager for Genstar Shipyards.

16. Lawton R. Burns, "Matrix Management in Hospitals: Testing Theories of Matrix Structure and Development," *Administrative Science Quarterly* 34 (1989): 48–50.

17. Diane Brady, "Martha Inc.," *Business Week*, January 17, 2000, 62–66.

18. Miguel Helft, "Yahoo Chief Rearranges Managers Once Again," *The New York Times*, February 27, 2009, B5.

19. Gail Edmondson, "Danone Hits Its Stride," *Business Week*, February 1, 1999, 52–53.

20. Frank Rose, "Think Globally, Script Locally," *Fortune*, November 8, 1999, 156–160.

21. Thomas A. Stewart, "See Jack. See Jack Run," *Fortune*, September 27, 1999, 124–127+.

22. Jerald Greenberg and Robert A. Baron, *Behavior in Organizations: Understanding and Managing the Human Side of Work*, 7th ed. (Upper Saddle River, NJ: Prentice Hall, 2000), 308–309.

Chapter 10

1. A. K. Gupta and V. G. Govindarajan, "Converting Global Presence into Global Competitive Advantage," *Academy of Management Executive* 15, no. 2 (2001), pp. 45–57.

2. M. A. Hitt, R. D. Ireland, and R. E. Hoskisson, *Strategic Management: Competitiveness and Globalization* (Cincinnati, OH: South-Western Publishing, 2005).

3. M. Koza and A. Lewin, "Managing Partnerships and Strategic Alliances: Raising the Odds of Success," *European Management Journal* 18, no. 2 (2000), pp. 146–151; M. Peng, "The Resource-Based View and International Business," *Journal of Management* 27 (2001), pp. 803–829.

4. E. Schein, "Coming to a New Awareness of Organizational Culture," *Sloan Management Review*, Winter (1984), pp. 3–16.

5. A. L. Kroeber and C. Kluckhohn, *Culture: A Critical Review of Concepts and Definitions* (Cambridge, MA: Harvard University Press, 1952).

6. Schein, "Coming to a New Awareness of Organizational Culture."

7. A. L. Wilkins and W. Ouchi, "Efficient Cultures: Exploring the Relationship between Culture and Organizational Effectiveness," *Administrative Science Quarterly* 28 (1983), pp. 468–481; K. A. Wade-Benzoni, T. Okumura, J. M. Brett, and D. A. Moore, "Cognitions and Behavior in Asymmetric Social Dilemmas: A Comparison of Two Cultures," *Journal of Applied Psychology* 87, no. 1 (2002), pp. 87–95; M. J. Gelfand, M. Higgins, L. H. Nishii, and J. L. Raver, "Culture and Egocentric Perceptions of Fairness in Conflict and Negotiation," *Journal of Applied Psychology* 87, no. 5 (2002), pp. 833–845.

8. J. E. Dutton and S. Jackson, "Categorizing Strategic Issues: Links to Organizational Actions," *Academy of Management Review* 12 (1987), pp. 76–90; Gelfand et al., "Culture and Egocentric Perceptions of Fairness in Conflict and Negotiation."

9. R. G. Eord and R. J. Foti, "Schema Theories, Information Processing, and Organizational Behavior," *The Thinking Organization*, ed. H. P. Simes and D. A. Gioia (San Francisco: Jossey-Bass, 1986); Wilkins and Ouchi, "Efficient Cultures"; Gelfand et al., "Culture and Egocentric Perceptions of Fairness in Conflict and Negotiation."

10. D. Druckman, "Nationalism, Patriotism, and Group Loyalty: A Social-Psychological Perspective," *Merson International Studies Review* (1994), pp. 43–68.

11. Statistics Canada, www.statscan.ca (accessed July 2, 2007); A. Belanger and E. C. Malenfant, "Ethnocultural Diversity in Canada: Prospects for 2017," *Canadian Social Trends*, Winter 2005, pp. 18–21.

12. A. Zuckerman, "Strong Corporate Cultures and Firm Performance: Are There Tradeoffs?" *Academy of Management Executive* 16, no. 4 (2002), pp. 158–160; N. Nohria, W. Joyce, and B. Robertson, "What Really Works," *Harvard Business Review* 81, no. 7 (2003), pp. 42–52.

13. Schein, "Coming to a New Awareness of Organizational Culture."

14. Ibid.

15. D. McGregor, *The Human Side of Enterprise* (New York: McGraw-Hill, 1960).

16. R. J. House, "Cultural Influences on Leaders and Organizations," in *Advances in Global Leadership*, vol. 1, pp. 171–233 (JAI Press, 1999); J. C. Kennedy, "Leadership in Malaysia: Traditional Values, International Outlook," *Academy of Management Executive* 16, no. 3 (2002), pp. 15–26.

17. J. Foley, "Hewlett-Packard Reaches a Cultural Crossroads," *Information Week*, July 23, 2001, p. 47.

18. G. Hofstede, *Culture's Consequences* (Beverly Hills, CA: Sage, 1980); G. Hofstede, "Dimensions Do Not Exist: A Reply to Brendan McSweeney," *Human Relations* 55, no. 11 (2002), pp. 1355–1631; A. Sagie and Z. Aycan, "A Cross-Cultural Analysis of Participative Decision-Making in Organizations," *Human Relations* 56, no. 4 (2003), pp. 453–473; D. Williamson, "Foreword from a Critique of Hofstede's Model of National Culture," *Human Relations* 55, no. 11 (2002), pp. 1373–1395.

19. B. McSweeney, "Hofstede's Model of National Cultural Differences and Their Consequences: A Triumph of Faith—A Failure of Analysis," *Human Relations* 55, no. 1 (2002), pp. 89–118.

20. J. Rokeach, *The Nature of Human Values* (New York: Free Press, 1973): T. Lenartowicz and J. P. Johnson,

"A Cross-National Assessment of the Values of Latin American Managers: Contrasting Hues or Shades of Gray?" *Journal of International Business Studies* 34, no. 3 (2003), p. 266.

21. Kenny Zhang, "Recognizing the Canadian Diaspora," *Canada Asia* 41, March 2006.

22. N. Adler, *International Dimensions of Organizational Behavior* (Boston, MA: Kent Publishing, 1994).

23. "Delphi Makes Another Investment in China," *Automotive News*, December 22, 2003, p. 25; M. Loden and J. Rosener, *Workforce America! Managing Employee Diversity as a Vital Resource* (New York: Irwin, 1991).

24. Adler, *International Dimensions of Organizational Behavior*.

25. M. K. Kozan, "Subcultures and Conflict Management Style," *Management International Review* 42, no. 1 (2002), pp. 89–105; C. M. Byles, "Brazil's Distinct Subcultures: Do They Matter to Business Performance?" *Academy of Management Executive* 16, no. 2 (2002), pp. 165–166.

26. S. Black and H. Gregersen, *Leading Strategic Change* (Upper Saddle River, NJ: Prentice Hall, 2002); M. Cortsjens and J. Merrihue, "Optimal Marketing," *Harvard Business Review* 81, no. 10 (2003), pp. 114–122.

27. R. Yerema, "Every Company Likes to Say They Treat Their Staff like Valued Assets. Here Are the Very Best That Are Actually Doing It." *Maclean's*, October 13, 2006, www.mcleans.ca (accessed July 2, 2007).

28. V. Pothukuchi, F. Damanpour, J. Choi, C. Chen, C. Chao, and S. H. Park, "National and Organizational Culture Differences and International Joint Venture Performance," *Journal of International Business Studies* 33, no. 2 (2002), pp. 243–265; C. Fey and P. W. Beamish, "Organizational Climate Similarity and Performance: International Joint Ventures in Russia," *Organization Studies* 22, no. 5 (2001), pp. 853–882; W. M. Danis and A. Parkhe, "Hungarian-Western Partnerships: A Grounded Theoretical Model of Integration Processes and Outcomes," *Journal of International Business Studies* 33, no. 3 (2002), pp. 423–455.

29. Personal communication, 1998.

30. V. D. Miller and F. M. Jablin, "Information Seeking during Organizational Entry: Influences, Tactics, and a Model of the Process," *Academy of Management Review* 16 (1991), pp. 92–120; R. M. Kramer, "When Paranoia Makes Sense," *Harvard Business Review* 80, no. 7 (2002), pp. 62–69; R. Galford and A. S. Drapeau, "The Enemies of Trust," *Harvard Business Review* 81, no. 2 (2003), pp. 88–95.

31. E. Hall, *Beyond Culture* (Garden City, NY: Doubleday, 1976).

32. S. A. Zahra, R. D. Ireland, and M. A. Hitt, "International Expansion by New Venture Firms: International Diversity, Mode of Entry, Technological Learning and Performance," *Academy of Management Journal* 43 (2000), pp. 925–950.

33. S. Black, H. Gregersen, M. Mendenhall, and L. Stroh, *Globalizing People through International Assignments* (Reading, MA: Addison-Wesley, 1999); J. L. Graham and N. M. Lam, "The Chinese Negotiation," *Harvard Business Review* 81, no. 10 (2003), pp. 82–91.

34. M. Murphy and K. M. Davey, "Ambiguity, Ambivalence and Indifference in Organizational Values," *Human Resource Management Journal* 12, no. 1 (2002), pp. 17–32; Galford and Drapeau, "The Enemies of Trust."

35. Black et al., *Globalizing People through International Assignments*; Graham and Lam, "The Chinese Negotiation."

Chapter 11

1. Ronald Hilton, *Managerial Accounting*, 2nd ed. (New York: McGraw-Hill, 1994), 7.

2. "Canada's Chartered Accountants Congratulate 2,701 Candidates Who Passed the 2008 Uniform Evaluation," *CICA*, media release, www.cica.ca/news/media-centre/media-releases-and-backgrounders/2008/item8644.aspx.

3. "CGA-Canada Announces 2008 Fellowship Recipients," *Canada NewsWire*, www.newswire.ca/en/releases/archive/February2009/05/c5463.html.

4. Certified Management Accountants of Canada, www.cma-canada.org.

5. Elizabeth MacDonald, "Accounting Sleuths Ferret Hidden Assets," *The Wall Street Journal*, December 18, 1996, B1–B2.

6. Philip Mathias, "Non-Profits Fight Move to GAAP Accounting," *Financial Post*, March 5, 1994, 15.

7. Bruce Horovitz, "Restoring the "Golden-Arch Shine," *USA Today*, June 16, 1999, 3B.

8. Charles T. Horngren, Walter T. Harrison Jr., and Linda Smith Bamber, *Accounting*, 5th ed. (Upper Saddle River, NJ: Prentice Hall, 2002), 17–20.

9. Ronald Hilton, *Managerial Accounting*, 2nd ed. (New York: McGraw-Hill, 1994), 402–403.

10. Billie Cunningham, Loren Nikolai, and John Bazley, *Accounting: Information for Business Decisions* (Fort Worth, TX: Dryden, 2000), 133–134.

11. Charles T. Horngren, Walter T. Harrison Jr., and Linda Smith Bamber, *Accounting*, 4th ed. (Upper Saddle River, NJ: Prentice Hall, 1999), 562–563; Arthur J. Keown et al., *The Foundations of Finance: The Logic and Practice of Financial Management*, 2nd ed. (Upper Saddle River, NJ: Prentice Hall, 1998), 89–95.

12. Charles T. Horngren, Walter T. Harrison Jr., and Linda Smith Bamber, *Accounting*, 4th ed. (Upper Saddle River, NJ: Prentice Hall, 1999), 201–202.

13. Alvin C. Burns and Ronald F. Bush, *Marketing Research*, 3rd ed. (Upper Saddle River, NJ: Prentice Hall, 2000), 70–84.

Chapter 12

1. "Bosses: Killing Them with Kindness Pays Off," *The Globe and Mail*, October 8, 2008, C3.

2. Daniel Goleman, *Emotional Intelligence: Why It Can Matter More Than IQ* (New York: Bantam Books, 1995); also Kenneth Law, Chi-Sum Wong, and Lynda Song, "The Construct and Criterion Validity of Emotional Intelligence and Its Potential Utility for Management Studies," *Journal of Applied Psychology* 89 no. 3 (2004): 78–90.

3. Daniel Goleman, "Leadership That Gets Results," *Harvard Business Review*, March–April 2000, 78–90.

4. Doris Burke, Corey Hajim, John Elliott, Jenny Mero, and Christopher Tkaczyk, "The Top Ten Companies for Leaders," *Fortune*, October 1, 2007, http://money.cnn.com/galleries/2007/fortune/0709/gallery.leaders_global_topten.fortune/index.html.

5. Frederick W. Taylor, *Principles of Scientific Management* (New York: Harper and Brothers, 1911).

6. See Daniel Wren, *The History of Management Thought* (New York: John Wiley & Sons, 2004).

7. Douglas McGregor, *The Human Side of Enterprise* (New York: McGraw-Hill, 1960).

8. Abraham Maslow, "A Theory of Human Motivation," *Psychological Review* (July 1943): 370–396.

9. Frederick Herzberg, Bernard Mausner, and Barbara Bloch Snydeman, *The Motivation to Work* (New York: Wiley, 1959).

10. Victor Vroom, *Work and Motivation* (New York: Wiley, 1964); Craig Pinder, *Work Motivation* (Glenview, IL: Scott, Foresman, 1984).

11. J. Stacy Adams, "Toward an Understanding of Inequity," *Journal of Abnormal and Social Psychology* 75 no. 5 (1963): 422–436.

12. Andy Holloway, "How the Game Is Played," *Canadian Business*, April 2, 2001, 26–35.

13. Brent Jang, "'WestJetters' Reap Rewards for Wild-Weather Work," *The Globe and Mail*, January 8, 2009, B7.

14. Deena Waisberg, "Tip of the Hat to Excellence; Employers get Creative with Rewards to Keep Top Performers," *National Post*, November 19, 2008, FP15.

15. For more information on some of the potential problems with goal setting, see Drake Bennett, "Do Goals Undermine Good Management?," *National Post*, March 24, 2009, FP10; also Wallace Immen, "The Goal: To Set Goals That Really Can Be Met," *The Globe and Mail*, March 20, 2009, B12.

16. Interviews with Sterling McLeod and Wayne Walker, senior vice-presidents of sales for Investors Group Financial Services.

17. Brent Jang, "High-Flying WestJet Morale Gets Put to the Test," *The Globe and Mail*, November 25, 2005, B3.

18. Virginia Galt, "Change Is a Good Thing When Everyone Is Involved," *The Globe and Mail*, June 25, 2005, B11.

19. Robert Grant, "AES Corporation: Rewriting the Rules of Management," *Contemporary Strategy Analysis* (Hoboken, NJ: John Wiley & Sons, 2007), www.blackwellpublishing.com/grant/docs/17AES.pdf.

20. Patricia Kitchen, "Tap Your Employees," *Orlando Sentinel*, March 14, 2007, F1.

21. Gregory Moorhead and Ricky W. Griffin, *Organizational Behavior*, 6th ed. (Boston: Houghton Mifflin, 2001), Chapter 7.

22. Ibid.

23. Ibid.

24. Ricky Griffin, *Task Design* (Glenview, IL: Scott, Foresman, 1982).

25. Kira Vermond, "Punching In on the Variable Clock," *The Globe and Mail*, March 22, 2008, B14.

26. Tavia Grant, "Lower Costs, Higher Morale Benefits of Four-Day Work Week," *The Globe and Mail*, August 18, 2008, B4.

27. Paul Lima, "With New Advances in Technology, Why Are We Still Jumping in the Car?," *The Globe and Mail*, October 20, 2008, E9.

28. Joyce Rosenberg, "Out of Sight, On Your Mind: Learning to Trust Telecommuters," *The Globe and Mail*, September 20, 2008, B19.

29. Paul Lima, "With New Advances in Technology, Why Are We Still Jumping in the Car?," *The Globe and Mail*, October 20, 2008, E9.

30. "Productivity Rises for Teleworkers: Survey," *The Globe and Mail*, October 15, 2008, C7.

31. Randi Chapnik Myers, "The Back and Forth of Working from Home," *The Globe and Mail*, March 8, 2008, B16.

32. Margot Gibb-Clark, "Satellite Office a Hit with Staff," *The Globe and Mail*, November 18, 1991, B4.

33. Dawn Walton, "Survey Focuses on Job Sharing," *The Globe and Mail*, June 10, 1997, B4.

34. John Kotter, "What Leaders Really Do," *Harvard Business Review*, December 2001, 85–94.

35. Ronald Heifetz and Marty Linsky, "A Survival Guide for Leaders," *Harvard Business Review*, June 2002, 65–74.

36. Frederick Reichheld, "Lead for Loyalty," *Harvard Business Review*, July–August 2001, 76–83.

37. Daniel Goleman, "What Makes a Leader?" *Harvard Business Review*, November–December 1998, 93–99.

38. David Dorsey, "Andy Pearson Finds Love," *Fast Company*, August 2001, 78–86.

39. David A. Waldman and Francis J. Yammarino, "CEO Charismatic Leadership: Levels-of-Management and Levels-of-Analysis Effects," *Academy of Management Review* 24 no. 2 (1999): 266–285.

40. Ronald Ebert and Ricky Griffin, *Business Essentials* (Upper Saddle River, NJ: Prentice Hall, 2009), 129.

41. Jane Howell and Boas Shamir, "The Role of Followers in the Charismatic Leadership Process: Relationships and Their Consequences," *Academy of Management Review* 30 no. 1 (2005): 96–112.

42. J. Richard Hackman and Ruth Wageman, "A Theory of Team Coaching," *Academy of Management Review* 30 no. 2 (2005): 269–287.

43. "How Women Lead," *Newsweek*, October 24, 2005, 46–70.

44. Madelaine Drohan, "What Makes a Canadian Manager?," *The Globe and Mail*, Feburary 25, 1997, B18.

45. Sinclair Stewart, "Passed by at TD, CEO Hits Stride in New York," *The Globe and Mail*, December 5, 2006, B1, B21.

46. Zena Olijnyk, Mark Brown, Andy Holloway, Calvin Leung, Alex Mlynek, Erin Pooley, Jeff Sanford, Andrew Wahl, and Thomas Watson, "Canada's Global Leaders," *Canadian Business*, March 28–April 10, 2005, 37–43.

Chapter 13

1. S. Bing, "Business as a Second Language," *Fortune*, 1998, pp. 57–58.

2. K. Krone, F. M. Jablin, and L. L. Putnam, "Communication Theory and Organizational Communication: Multiple Perspectives," in F. M. Japlin, L. L. Putnam, K. H. Roberts, and L. W. Porter (eds.), *Handbook of Organizational Communication: An Interdisciplinary Perspective* (Newbury Park, CA: Sage Publications, 1987).

3. H. C. Triandis, *Culture and Social Behavior* (New York: McGraw-Hill, 1994); B. A. Bechky, "Sharing Meaning across Occupational Communities: The Transformation of Understanding on a Production Floor," *Organization Science* 14, no. 3 (2003), p. 312; M. Becerra and A. K. Gupta, "Perceived Trustworthiness within the Organization: The Moderating Impact of Communication Frequency on Trustor and Trustee Effects," *Organization Science* 14, no. 1 (2003), pp. 32–44.

4. R. L. Daft and R. H. Lengel, "Information Richness: A New Approach to Managerial Behavior and Organization Design," in L. L. Cummings and B. Staw (eds.), *Research in Organizational Behavior*, vol. 6 (Greenwich, CT: JAI, 1984), pp. 191–223; R. L. Daft and R. H. Lengel, "Organizational Information Requirements, Media Richness and Structural Design," *Management Science* 32 (1986), pp. 554–572; K. Miller, *Organizational Communication: Approaches and Processes*, 2nd ed. (Belmont, CA: Wadsworth, 1999).

5. L. K. Trevino, R. L. Daft, and R. H. Lengel, "Understanding Managers' Media Concerns," in J. Fulk and C. Steinfeile (eds.), *Organizations and Communication Technology* (Newbury Park, CA: Sage Publications, 1990); Anonymous, "How to Create Communications Materials Employees Will Actually Use," *Harvard Business Review* 80, no. 1 (1990), p. 102.

6. B. B. Baltes, M. W. Dickson, M. P. Sherman, C. C. Bauer, and J. S. LaGanke, "Computer-Mediated Communication and Group Decision Making: A Meta-Analysis," *Organizational Behavior and Human Decision Processes* 87, no. 1 (2002), pp. 156–179.

7. J. Yates and W. J. Orlikowski, "Genres of Organizational Communication: A Structurational Approach to Studying Communication and Media," *Academy of Management Review* 17 (1992), pp. 299–326.

8. L. W. Porter, E. E. Lawler, III, and J. R. Hackman, *Behavior in Organizations* (New York: McGraw-Hill, 1975).

9. K. Davis, "The Care and Cultivation of the Corporate Grapevine," *Dun's Review* 102, no. 1 (1973), pp. 44–47.

10. C. Dellarocas, "The Digitization of Word of Mouth: Promise and Challenges of Online Feedback Mechanisms," *Management Science* 49, no. 10 (2003), pp. 1407–1424.

11. "BASF Launches SM/PO Venture," *Chemical Market Reporter* 262, no. 11 (2002), p. 23.

12. "He Said, She Said," *Communications* 46, no. 9 (2003), p. 11; H. Ibarra, "Homophily and Differential Returns: Sex Differences in Network Structure and Access in an Advertising Firm," *Administrative Science Quarterly* 37 (1992), pp. 422–447; H. Ibarra, "Personal Networks of Women and Minorities in Management: A Conceptual Framework,"

NOTES, SOURCES, AND CREDITS **N–12**

Academy of Management Review 18 (1993), pp. 56–87; H. Ibarra, "Race, Opportunity, and Diversity of Social Circles in Managerial Networks," *Academy of Management Journal* 38 (1995), pp. 673–703; K. A. Mollica, B. Gray, and L. K. Trevino, "Racial Homophily and Its Persistence in Newcomers' Social Networks," *Organization Science* 14, no. 2 (2003), pp. 123–136.

13. J. M. Beyer et al., "The Selective Perception of Managers Revisited," *Academy of Management Journal* 40 (1997), pp. 716–737.

14. A. Tversky and D. Kahneman, "Rational Choice and the Framing of Decisions," *Journal of Business* 59 (1986), pp. S251–278; I. Grugulis, "Nothing Serious? Candidates' Use of Humour in Management Training," *Human Relations* 55, no. 4 (2002), pp. 387–406.

15. C. M. Jones, "Shifting Sands: Women, Men, and Communication," *Journal of Communication* 49 (1999), pp. 148–155.

16. C. R. Rogers and F. J. Roethlisberger, "Barriers and Gateways to Communication," *Harvard Business Review* 69, no. 6 (1991), pp. 105–111; L. Perlow and S. Williams, "Is Silence Killing Your Company?" *Harvard Business Review* 81, no. 5 (2003), pp. 52–58.

17. R. Wilkinson, "Do You Speak Obscuranta?" *Supervision* 49, no. 9 (1988), pp. 3–5; C. Argyris, "Four Steps to Chaos," *Harvard Business Review* 81, no. 10 (2003), p. 140.

18. R. Harrison, *Beyond Words: An Introduction to Nonverbal Communication* (Upper Saddle River, NJ: Prentice Hall, 1974); A. Kristof-Brown, M. R. Barrick, and M. Franke, "Applicant Impression Management: Dispositional Influences and Consequences for Recruiter Perceptions of Fit and Similarity," *Journal of Management* 28, no. 1 (2002), pp. 27–46; H. A. Elfenbein and N. Ambady, "Predicting Workplace Outcomes from the Ability to Eavesdrop on Feelings," *Journal of Applied Psychology* 87, no. 5 (2002), pp. 963–971.

19. J. A. Mausehund, S. A. Timm, and A. S. King, "Diversity Training: Effects of an Intervention Treatment on Nonverbal Awareness," *Business Communication Quarterly* 58, no. 1 (1995), pp. 27–30.

20. J. H. Robinson, "Professional Communication in Korea: Playing Things by Eye," *IEEE Transactions on Professional Communication* 39, no. 3 (1996), pp. 129–134; G. E. Kersten, S. T. Koeszegi, and R. Vetschera, "The Effects of Culture in Computer-Mediated Negotiations," *Journal of Information Technology Theory and Application* 5, no. 2 (2003), pp. 1–28.

21. T. E. McNamara and K. Hayashi, "Culture and Management: Japan and the West towards a Transnational Corporate Culture," *Management Japan* 27, no. 2 (1994), pp. 3–13.

22. S. Okazaki and J. Alonso, "Right Messages for the Right Site: On-line Creative Strategies by Japanese Multinational Corporations," *Journal of Marketing Communications* 9, no. 4 (2002), pp. 221–240; M. Rosch and K. G. Segler, "Communication with Japanese," *Management International Review* 27, no. 4 (1987), pp. 56–67.

23. C. Gouttefarde, "Host National Culture Shock: What Management Can Do," *European Business Review* 92, no. 4 (1992), pp. 1–3.

24. H. Triandis, "Cross-Cultural Contributions to Theory in Social Psychology," in W. B. Gudykunst and Y. Y. Kim (eds.), *Reading on Communication with Strangers* (New York: McGraw-Hill, 1992), p. 75; R. S. Marshall and D. M. Boush, "Dynamic Decision-Making: A Cross-Cultural Comparison of U.S. and Peruvian Export Managers," *Journal of International Business Studies* 32, no. 4 (2001), pp. 873–893; T. R. Tyler and S. L. Blader, "Autonomous vs. Comparative Status: Must We Be Better Than Others to Feel Good about Ourselves?" *Organizational Behavior and Human Decision Processes* 89, no. 1 (2002), pp. 813–838; L. Huff and L. Kelley, "Levels of Organizational Trust in Individualist versus Collectivist Societies: A Seven-Nation Study," *Organization Science* 14, no. 1 (2003), pp. 81–90; A. C. Lewis and S. J. Sherman, "Hiring You Makes Me Look Bad: Social-Identity Based Reversal of the Ingroup Favoritism Effect," *Organizational Behavior and Human Decision Processes* 90, no. 2 (2003), pp. 262–276.

25. S. Carlson, "International Transmission of Information and the Business Firm," *Annals of the American Academy of Political and Social Science* 412 (1974), pp. 55–63; Marshall and Boush, "Dynamic Decision-Making"; Y. Luo, "Building Trust in Cross-Cultural Collaborations: Toward a Contingency Perspective," *Journal of Management* 28, no. 5 (2002), pp. 669–694.

26. J. Main, "How 21 Men Got Global in 35 Days," *Fortune*, 1989, pp. 71–79.

27. C. Peter, P. Scott, and J. Calvert, "Chinese Business Face: Communication Behaviors and Teaching Approaches," *Business Communication Quarterly* 66, no. 4 (2003), pp. 19–23; R. S. Burnert, "Ni Zao: Good Morning, China," *Business Horizons* 33, no. 6 (1990), pp. 65–71.

28. R. Alsop, "Playing Well with Others," *Wall Street Journal*, September 9, 2002, p. R1-1; Kristof-Brown, Barrick, and Franke, "Applicant Impression Management."

29. T. D. Lewis and G. H. Graham, "Six Ways to Improve Your Communication Skills," *Internal Auditor* (1988), p. 25.

30. G. M. Barton, "Manage Words Effectively," *Personnel Journal* 69, no. 1 (1990), pp. 32–40.

31. L. W. Porter and L. E. McKibbin, *Management Education and Development: Drift or Thrust into the 21st Century* (New York: McGraw-Hill, 1988).

32. S. L. Silk, "Making Your Speech Memorable," *Association Management* 46, no. 1 (1994), pp. L59–L62.

33. A. DeMeyer, "Tech Talk: How Managers Are Stimulating Global R&D Communication," *Sloan Management Review* 32, no. 3 (1991), pp. 49–58.

34. R. Fisher and W. Ury, *Getting to Yes* (London: Simon & Schuster, 1987); K. A. Wade-Benzoni et al., "Barriers to Resolution in Ideologically Based Negotiations: The Role of Values and Institutions," *Academy of Management Review* 27, no. 1 (2002), pp. 41–57.

35. Ibid.

36. Ibid., p. 54.

37. N. J. Adler, *International Dimensions of Organizational Behavior*, 2nd ed. (Boston: PWS-Kent, 1991), p. 185.

38. G. Fisher, *International Negotiations* (Chicago: Intercultural Press, 1980); J. L. Graham, "Brazilian, Japanese, and American Business Negotiations," *Journal of International Business Studies* 14, no. 1 (1983), pp. 47–61; J. L. Graham and N. M. Lam, "The Chinese Negotiation," *Harvard Business Review* 81, no. 10 (2003), pp. 82–91; J. K. Sebenius, "The Hidden Challenge of Cross-Border Negotiations," *Harvard Business Review* 80, no. 3 (2002), pp. 76–85; L. J. Kray, A. D. Galinsky, and L. Thompson, "Reversing the Gender Gap in Negotiations: An Exploration of Stereotype Regeneration," *Organizational Behavior and Human Decision Processes* 87, no. 2 (2002), pp. 386–409.

39. J. L. Graham and R. A. Herberger Jr., "Negotiators Abroad Don't Shoot from the Hip," *Harvard Business Review* 83, no. 4 (1983), pp. 160–168.

40. N. J. Adler and J. L. Graham, "Cross-Cultural Interaction: The International Comparison Fallacy?" *Journal of International Business Studies* 20, no. 3 (1989), pp. 515–537.

41. Fisher and Ury, *Getting to Yes.*

42. M. Lee, "10 Myths about Multicultural Customers," *Selling*, November 2003, pp. 10–12; K. Kumar, S. Noneth, and C. Yauger, "Cultural Approaches to the Process of Business Negotiation: Understanding Cross-Cultural Differences in Negotiating Behaviors," in C. L. Swanson (ed.), *International Research in the Business Disciplines* (Greenwich, CT: JAI Press, 1993), pp. 79–90; B. M. Hawrysh and

J. L. Zaichkowsky, "Cultural Approaches to Negotiations: Understanding the Japanese," *International Marketing Review* 7, no. 2 (1990), pp. 28–42.

43. Kumar et al., "Cultural Approaches to the Process of Business Negotiations."

44. Graham and Herberger, "Negotiators Abroad Don't Shoot from the Hip."

45. Kumar et al., "Cultural Approaches to the Process of Business Negotiations."

46. N. Woliansky, "We Do (Do Not) Accept Your Offer," *Management Review* 75, no. 12 (1989), pp. 54–55; Kumar et al., "Cultural Approaches to the Process of Business Negotiations."

47. Kumar et al., "Cultural Approaches to the Process of Business Negotiations," p. 86.

48. Graham and Herberger, "Negotiators Abroad Don't Shoot from the Hip."

49. Adler and Graham, "Cross-Cultural Interaction"; C. Barnum and N. Wolniasky, "Why Americans Fail at Overseas Negotiations," *Management Review* 75, no. 10 (1989), pp. 55–57.

50. Kumar et al., "Cultural Approaches to the Process of Business Negotiations."

Chapter 14

1. R. E. Hoskisson and M. A. Hitt, *Downscoping: How to Tame the Diversified Firm* (New York: Oxford University Press, 1994).

2. G. Orwell, *1984: A Novel* (New York: New American Library, 1950); D. E. W. Marginson, "Management Control Systems and Their Effects on Strategy Formation at Middle-Management Levels: Evidence from a U.K. Organization," *Strategic Management Journal* 23, no. 11 (2002), pp. 1019–1031; M. Goold and A. Campbell, "Do You Have a Well-Designed Organization?" *Harvard Business Review* 80, no. 3 (2002), pp. 117–124; W. Nasrallah, R. Levitt, and P. Glynn, "Interaction Value Analysis: When Structured Communication Benefits Organizations," *Organization Science* 14, no. 5 (2003), pp. 541–557.

3. A. S. Tannenbaum (ed.), *Control in Organizations* (New York: McGraw-Hill, 1968); Marginson, "Management Control Systems and Their Effects"; Goold and Campbell, "Do You Have a Well-Designed Organization?"; Nasrallah, Levitt, and Glynn, "Interaction Value Analysis."

4. External Forces, Internal Strength: Royal Canadian Mint Annual Report 2006.

5. V. Govindarajan, "Impact of Participation in the Budgetary Process on Managerial Attitudes and Performance: Universalistic and Contingency Perspectives," *Decision Sciences* 7 (1986), pp. 496–516.

6. D. Drickhamer, "Europe's Best Plants: Medical Marvel," *Industry Week* 257, no. 3 (2002), pp. 47–49.

7. E. A. Locke, "The Ubiquity of the Technique of Goal Setting in Theories of and Approaches to Employee Motivation," *Academy of Management Review* 3 (1978), pp. 594–601; A. Drach-Zachavy and M. Erez, "Challenge versus Threat Effects on the Goal-Performance Relationship," *Organizational Behavior and Human Decision Processes* 88, no. 2 (2002), pp. 667–682.

8. R. N. Anthony and J. S. Reece, *Accounting Principles*, 7th ed. (Chicago: Richard D. Irwin, 1995).

9. Ibid.

10. J. Hope and R. Fraser, "Who Needs Budgets?" *Harvard Business Review* 81, no. 2 (2003), pp. 108–115.

11. F. D. Buggie, "Set the 'Fuzzy Front End' in Concrete," *Research Technology Management* 45, no. 4 (2002), pp. 11–14; Product Development Inc., "Product Innovation Guru Dr. Robert G. Cooper and Nine Leading Companies Address Business Executives at the 1st Annual Stage-Gate® Leadership Summit," press release March 13, 2007, www.prod-dev.com (accessed June 14, 2007).

12. Marginson, "Management Control Systems and Their Effects"; M. Goold and J. J. Quinn, "The Paradox of Strategic Controls," *Strategic Management Journal* 77 (1990), pp. 43–57.

13. J. Hogan and B. Holland, "Using Theory to Evaluate Personality and Job-Performance Relations: A Socioanalytic Perspective," *Journal of Applied Psychology* 88, no. 1 (2003), p. 100; P. Lorange and D. C. Murphy, "Strategy and Human Resources: Concepts and Practice," *Human Resource Management* 22, nos. 1/2 (1983), pp. 111–135.

14. J. A. Alexander, "Adaptive Change in Corporate Control Practices," *Academy of Management Journal* 34 (1991), pp. 162–193; V. Govindarajan and J. Fisher, "Strategy, Control Systems, and Resource Sharing: Effects on Business-Unit Performance," *Academy of Management Journal* 33 (1990), pp. 259–285.

15. A. Zuber, "McD Restructures to Beef Up Performance," *Nation's Restaurant News* 35, no. 44 (2001), pp. 1, 6.

16. Alexander, "Adaptive Change in Corporate Control Practices," p. 181.

17. G. Hamel and L. Valikangas, "The Quest for Resilience," *Harvard Business Review* 81, no. 9 (2003), pp. 52–63; Goold and Quinn, "The Paradox of Strategic Controls."

18. Goold and Quinn, "The Paradox of Strategic Controls," Figure 2, p. 55.

19. L. Strauss, "Come Fly with Me," *Barron's* 52, no. 33 (2002), p. T8.

20. Goold and Quinn, "The Paradox of Strategic Controls."

21. N. C. Churchill, "Budget Choice: Planning vs. Control," *Harvard Business Review* 62, no. 4 (1984), pp. 150–164.

22. R. Whiting, "Crystal-Ball Glance into Fiscal Future," *Information Week*, July 22, 2002, p. 37.

23. W. A. Van der Stede, "The Relationship between Two Consequences of Budgetary Controls: Budgetary Slack Creation and Managerial Short-Term Orientation," *Accounting, Organizations, and Society* 25 (2000), pp. 609–622.

24. D. Brown, "Using Competencies and Rewards to Enhance Business Performance and Customer Service at the Standard Life Assurance Company," *Compensation and Benefits Review* 33, no. 4 (2001), pp. 14–24.

25. J. R. Barker, "Tightening the Iron Cage: Concertive Control in Self-Managing Teams," *Administrative Science Quarterly* 38 (1993), pp. 408–437; Goold and Quinn, "The Paradox of Strategic Controls"; W. G. Ouchi, "A Conceptual Framework for the Design of Organisational Control Mechanisms," *Management Science* 25 (1979), pp. 833–848; W. G. Ouchi, "Markets, Bureaucracies, and Clans," *Administrative Science Quarterly* 25 (1980), pp. 129–141; R. E. Walton, "From Control to Commitment in the Workplace," *Harvard Business Review* 63, no. 2 (1985), pp. 76–84.

26. Barker, "Tightening the Iron Cage."

27. W. H. Newman, *Constructive Control: Design and Use of Control Systems* (Upper Saddle River, NJ: Prentice Hall, 1975).

28. P. Odell, "Wine.com Plans Big October E-Mailing," *Direct* 14, no. 11 (2002), p. 11; E. Gunn, "A Good Year," SmartBusinessMag.com, pp. 40–42.

29. R. N. Anthony, J. Dearden, and V. Govindarajan, *Management Control Systems*, 8th ed. (Burr Ridge, IL: Richard D. Irwin; 1995).

30. R. S. Kaplan and D. P. Norton, "The Balanced Scorecard—Measures That Drive Performance," *Harvard Business Review* 70, no. 1 (1992), pp. 71–80; A. Neely and M. Bourne, "Why Measurement Initiatives Fail," *Quality Focus* 4, no. 4 (2000), pp. 3–6.

31. Kaplan and Norton, "The Balanced Scorecard."

32. Kidwell, Ho, Blake, Wraith, Roubi, and Richardson, "New Management Techniques: An International Comparison," February 2002, www.nysscpa.org/cpajournal (accessed June 14, 2007).

33. E. M. Olson and S. E Slater, "The Balanced Scorecard, Competitive Strategy, and Performance," *Business Horizons* 45, no. 3 (2002), pp. 3–6.

34. Neely and Bourne, "Why Quality Initiatives Fail."

35. G. F. Hanks, M. A. Freid, and J. Huber," Shifting Gears at Borg-Warner

Automotive," *Management Accounting* 75, no. 8 (1994), pp. 25–29.

36. G. A. Bigley and K. H. Roberts, "The Incident Command System: High-Reliability Organizing for Complex and Volatile Task Environments," *Academy of Management Journal* 44 (2001), pp. 1281–1299.

37. K. H. Roberts, "Managing High Reliability Organizations," *California Management Review* 34, no. 4 (1990), pp. 101–113.

38. D. M. Iadipaolo, "Monster or Monitor? Have Tracking Systems Gone Mad?" *Insurance and Technology* 17, no. 6 (1992), pp. 47–54.

39. M. A. Hitt, R. E. Hoskisson, R. A. Johnson, and D. D. Moesel, "The Market for Corporate Control and Firm Innovation," *Academy of Management Journal* 39 (1996), pp. 1084–1119.

Chapter 15

1. S. A. Snell, M. A. Shadur, and P. M. Wright, "Human Resources Strategy: The Era of Our Ways," in M. A. Hitt, R. E. Freeman, and J. S. Harrison (eds.), *Handbook of Strategic Management* (Oxford, UK: Blackwell Publishing, 2001).

2. M. A. Hitt and R. D. Ireland, "The Essence of Strategic Leadership: Managing Human and Social Capital," *Journal of Leadership and Organization Studies* 9 (2002), pp. 3–14.

3. P. M. Wright, B. B. Dunford, and S. A. Snell, "Human Resources and the Resource-Based View of the Firm," *Journal of Management* 27 (2001), pp. 701–721.

4. M. W. McCall and M. M. Lombardo, *Off the Track: Why and How Successful Executives Get Derailed* (Greensboro, NC: Center for Creative Leadership, 1983).

5. D. Ulrich, *Human Resource Champions* (Boston: Harvard Business School Press, 1997).

6. R. W. Rowden, "Potential Roles of the Human Resource Management Professional in the Strategic Planning Process," *S.A.M. Advanced Management Journal* 64, no. 3 (1999), pp. 22–27.

7. M. Huselid, S. Jackson, and R. Schuler, "Technical and Strategic Human Resource Management Effectiveness as Determinants of Firm Performance," *Academy of Management Journal* 40 (1997), pp. 171–188; K. S. Law, D. K. Tse, and N. Zhou, "Does Human Resource Management Matter in a Transitional Economy? China as an Example," *Journal of International Business Studies* 34, no. 3 (2003), pp. 255–265; S. L. Rynes, K. G. Brown, and A. E. Colbert, "Seven Common Misconceptions about Human Resource Practices: Research Findings versus Practitioner Beliefs," *Academy of*

Management Executive 16, no. 3 (2002), pp. 92–102; R. Batt, "Managing Customer Services: Human Resource Practices, Quit Rates, and Sales Growth," *Academy of Management Journal* 45, no. 3 (2002), pp. 587–597.

8. J. Pfeffer, *Competitive Advantage through People: Unleashing the Power of the Workforce* (Boston: Harvard Business School Press, 1994).

9. S. Bates, "Growing Pains Are Cited in Study of HR Outsourcing," *HRMagazine* 47, no. 8 (2002), p. 10; D. P. Lepak and S. A. Snell, "Examining the Human Resource Architecture: The Relationships among Human Capital, Employment, and Human Resource Configurations," *Journal of Management* 28, no. 4 (2002), pp. 517–543.

10. M. O'Daniel, "Online Assistance for Job Seekers," *New Strait Times*, November 11, 2003; L. Goff, "Job Surfing," *Computer-World* 30, no. 36 (1996), p. 81; M. K. McGee, "Job Hunting on the Internet," *InformationWeek* 576 (1996), p. 98.

11. D. Terpstra, "The Search for Effective Methods," *HR Focus* 73, no. 5 (1996), pp. 16–17.

12. J. S. Black, H. B. Gregersen, M. E. Mendenhall, and L. Stroh, *Global People through International Assignments* (Reading, MA: Addison-Wesley, 1999).

13. J. Conway, R. Jako, and D. Goodman, "A Meta-Analysis of Interrater and Internal Consistency Reliability of Selection Interviews," *Journal of Applied Psychology* 80, no. 5 (1995), pp. 565–579; M. McDaniel, D. Whetzel, F. Schmidt, and S. Maurer, "The Validity of Employment Interviews: A Comprehensive Review and Meta-Analysis," *Journal of Applied Psychology* 79, no. 4 (1994), pp. 599–616.

14. G. Dessler, *Human Resource Management*, 8th ed. (Upper Saddle River, NJ: Prentice Hall, 2000), Chapter 6.

15. L. Rudner, "Pre-Employment Testing and Employee Productivity," *Public Management* 21, no. 2 (1992), pp. 133–150; P. Lowry, "The Assessment Center: Effects of Varying Consensus Procedures," *Public Personnel Management* 21, no. 2 (1992), pp. 171–183; T. Payne, N. Anderson, and T. Smith, "Assessment Centres: Selection Systems and Cost-Effectiveness," *Personnel Review* 21, no. 4 (1992), pp. 48–56; D. J. Schleicher, D. V. Day, B. Mayes, and R. E. Riggio, "A New Frame for Frame-of-Reference Training: Enhancing the Construct Validity of Assessment Centers," *Journal of Applied Psychology* 87, no. 4 (2002), pp. 735–746; F. Lievens, "Trying to Understand the Different Pieces of the Construct Validity Puzzle of Assessment Centers: An Examination of Assessor and Assessee Effects," *Journal of Applied Psychology* 87, no. 4 (2002), pp. 675–686; W. Arthur

Jr., E. A. Day, T. L. McNelly, and P. S. Edens, "A Meta-Analysis of the Criterion-Related Validity of Assessment Center Dimensions," *Personnel Psychology* 56, no. 1 (2003), pp. 125–154; D. J. Woehr and W. Arthur Jr., "The Construct-Related Validity of Assessment Center Ratings: A Review and Meta-Analysis of the Role of Methodological Factors," *Journal of Management* 29, no. 2 (2003), p. 231; K. Dayan, R. Kasten, and S. Fox, "Entry-Level Police Candidate Assessment Center: An Efficient Tool for a Hammer to Kill a Fly?" *Personnel Psychology* 55, no. 4 (2002), pp. 827–849.

16. R. Bentley, "Candidates Face Alternative Testing," *Computer Weekly*, November 18, 2003, p. 54; S. Adler, "Personality Tests for Salesforce Selection," *Review of Business* 16, no. 1 (1994), pp. 27–31.

17. M. McCullough, "Can Integrity Testing Improve Market Conduct?" *LIMRA's Marketfacts* 15, no. 2 (1996), pp. 15–16; H. J. Bernardin and D. Cooke, "Validity of an Honesty Test in Predicting Theft among Convenience Store Employees," *Academy of Management Journal* 36, no. 50 (1993), pp. 1097–1108.

18. B. Murphy, W. Barlow, and D. Hatch, "Employer-Mandated Physicals for Over-70 Employees Violate the ADEA," *Personnel Journal* 72, no. 6 (1993): p. 24; R. Ledman and D. Brown, "The Americans with Disabilities Act," *SAM Advanced Management Journal* 58, no. 2 (1993), pp. 17–20.

19. C. Fisher, "Organizational Socialization: An Integrative Review," in K. Rowland and J. Ferris (eds.), *Research in Personnel and Human Resource Management* 4 (1986), pp. 101–145.

20. T. J. Fogarty, "Socialization and Organizational Outcomes in Large Public Accounting Firms," *Journal of Managerial Issues* 12, no. 1 (2000), pp. 13–33; M. K. Ahuja and J. E. Galvin, "Socialization in Virtual Groups," *Journal of Management* 29, no. 2 (2003), p. 161; E. W. Morrison, "Newcomers' Relationships: The Role of Social Network Ties during Socialization," *Academy of Management Journal* 45, no. 6 (2002), pp. 1149–1160.

21. B. Jacobson and B. Kaye, "Service Means Success," *Training and Development* 45, no. 5 (1991), pp. 53–58; J. Brechlin and A. Rossett, "Orienting New Employees," *Training* 28, no. 4 (1991), pp. 45–51.

22. W. P. Anthony, P. L. Perrewé, and K. M. Kacmar, *Strategic Human Resource Management* (Fort Worth, TX: Harcourt Brace Jovanovich, 1993).

23. L. W. Porter and L. E. McKibbin, *Management Education and Development* (New York: McGraw-Hill, 1988); A. Kristof-Brown, M. R. Barrick, and M. Franke, "Applicant Impression Management: Dispositional Influences

and Consequences for Recruiter Perceptions of Fit and Similarity," *Journal of Management* 28, no. 1 (2002), pp. 27–46.

24. J. De Kok, "The Impact of Firm-Provided Training on Production," *International Small Business Journal* 20, no. 3 (2002), pp. 271–295.

25. J. K. Eskildsen and J. J. Dahlgaard, "A Causal Model for Employee Satisfaction," *Total Quality Management* 11, no. 8 (2000), pp. 1081–1094.

26. M. Hammer and J. Champy, *Reengineering the Corporation* (New York: HarperCollins, 1993); D. A. Buchanan, "Demands, Instabilities, Manipulations, Careers: The Lived Experience of Driving Change," *Human Relations* 56, no. 6 (2003), p. 663.

27. T. Redman, E. Snape, and G. McElwee, "Appraising Employee Performance: A Vital Organizational Activity?" *Education and Training* 35, no. 2 (1993), pp. 3–10; R. Bretz, G. Milkovitch, and W. Read, "The Current State of Performance Appraisal Research and Practice," *Journal of Management* 18, no. 2 (1992), pp. 321–352.

28. R. Cardy and G. Dobbins, *Performance Appraisal* (Cincinnati, OH: South-Western Publishing, 1994).

29. L. Gomez-Mejia, "Evaluating Employee Performance: Does the Appraisal Instrument Make a Difference?" *Journal of Organizational Behavior Management* 9, no. 2 (1988), pp. 155–272.

30. C. Rarick and G. Baxter, "Behaviorally Anchored Rating Scales: An Effective Performance Appraisal Approach," *Advanced Management Journal* 51, no. 1 (1986), pp. 36–39; D. Naffziger, "BARS, RJPs, and Recruiting," *Personnel Administrator* 30, no. 8 (1985), pp. 85–96; M. Hosoda, E. F. Stone-Romero, and G. Coats, "The Effects of Physical Attractiveness on Job-Related Outcomes: A Meta-Analysis of Experimental Studies," *Personnel Psychology* 51, no. 2 (2003), p. 431; T. J. Watson, "Ethical Choice in Managerial Work: The Scope for Moral Choices in an Ethically Irrational World," *Human Relations* 56, no. 2 (2003), pp. 167–185.

31. K. Clark, "Judgment Day," *U.S. News & World Report* 134, no. 2 (2003), p. 31; D. Bohl, "Minisurvey: 360 Degree Appraisals Yield Superior Results," *Compensation and Benefits Review* 28, no. 5 (1996), pp. 16–19.

32. P. W. B. Atkins and R. E. Wood, "Self versus Others' Ratings as Predictors of Assessment Center Ratings: Validation Evidence for 360-Degree Feedback Programs," *Personnel Psychology* 55, no. 4 (2002), pp. 871–904.

33. J. Lawrie,"Steps toward an Objective Appraisal," *Supervisory Management* 34, no. 5 (1989), pp. 17–24.

34. "Changing with the Times," *IRS Employment Review*, February 21, 2003, pp. 14–17; J. Kanin-Lovers and M. Cameron, "Broadbanding—A Step Forward or a Step Backward?" *Journal of Compensation and Benefits* 9, no. 5 (1994), pp. 39–42.

35. L. Stroh, J. Brett, J. Baumann, and A. Reilly, "Agency Theory and Variable Pay Compensation Strategies," *Academy of Management Journal* 39, no. 3 (1996), pp. 751–767.

36. J. Herman, "Beating the Midlife Career Crisis," *Fortune*, 1993, pp. 52–62.

37. Personal communication with vice-president of human resources at Sony.

38. A. M. Chaker, "Luring Moms Back to Work," *Wall Street Journal*, December 30, 2003, pp. D1–D2; A. Leibowitz and J. Merman, "Explaining Changes in Married Mothers' Employment over Time," *Demography* 32, no. 3 (1995), pp. 365–378; S. Werner, "Recent Developments in International Management Research: A Review of 20 Top Management Journals," *Journal of Management* 28, no. 3 (2002), pp. 277–305.

39. J. S. Black and H. B. Gregersen, *So You're Going Overseas: A Handbook for Personal and Professional Success* (San Diego, CA: Global Business Publishers, 1999).

40. Foreign Affairs and International Trade Canada, www.infoexpert.gc.ca (accessed October 3, 2007); The Center for the Advancement of Working Women, www.miraikan.go.jp (accessed October 3, 2007); Government of Canada *Employment Equity Act*, 1995, c 44.

41. E. P. Gray, "The National Origin of BFOQ under Title VII," *Employee Relations Law Journal* 11, no. 2 (1985), pp. 311–321.

42. Canada Council for the Arts, "Cultural Diversity—The Cornerstone of Canadian Society," www.canadacouncil.ca (accessed October 3, 2007).

43. Ibid.

Chapter 16

1. American Marketing Association, "Marketing Services Guide," August 23, 2001, www.ama.org/about/ama/markdef.asp. 2; Philip Kotler, *Marketing Management*, 11th ed. (Upper Saddle River, NJ: Prentice Hall, 2003), 76–78.

3. Warren J. Keegan and Mark C. Green, *Global Marketing*, 3rd ed. (Upper Saddle River, NJ: Prentice Hall, 2003), 8–15.

4. Jennifer Wells, "Hoarding, Frustrating, Winning," *The Globe and Mail*, August 23, 2008, B4.

5. Philip Kotler and Peggy Cunningham, *Marketing Management* (Toronto: Prentice Hall, 2004), 18.

6. Peter Gumbel, "Mass vs. Class," *Fortune*, September 17, 2007, 82.

7. Chris Isidore, "Sweet Spot: Luxury SUV's are Hot," *CNNMoney*, January 7,

2004, http://money.cnn.com/2004/01/06/news/companies/detroit_luxury_suv/index.htm.

8. Aparita Bhandari, "Ethnic Marketing—It's More Than Skin Deep," *The Globe and Mail*, September 7, 2005, B3.

9. Lauren Goldstein, "Dressing Up an Old Brand," *Fortune*, November 9, 1998, 154–156.

10. Peter Gumbel, "Mass vs. Class," *Fortune*, September 17, 2007, 82.

11. Tamara Audi, "Las Vegas Goes All Out to Attract Gay Travelers," *The Wall Street Journal*, November 2, 2007, B1.

12. Philip Kotler, *Marketing Management*, 11th ed. (Upper Saddle River, NJ: Prentice Hall, 2003), 292–294.

13. Naoufel Daghfous, John V. Petrof, and Frank Pons, "Values and Innovations: A Cross-cultural Study," *The Journal of Consumer Marketing* 16 no. 4 (2009): 314–331.

14. John Morton, "How to Spot the Really Important Prospects," *Business Marketing* (January 1990): 62–67.

15. Matt Phillips, "Pow! Romance! Comics Court Girls," *The Wall Street Journal*, June 8, 2007, B1.

16. Ellen Byron, "A Virtual View of the Store Aisle," *The Wall Street Journal*, October 3, 2007, B1.

17. Alvin C. Burns and Ronald F. Bush, *Marketing Research*, 3rd ed. (Upper Saddle River, NJ: Prentice Hall, 2000), 70–84.

18. Marina Strauss, "First You Have to Get Their Attention," *The Globe and Mail*, July 12, 1991, B1.

19. Emily Nelson, "P&G Checks Out Real Life," *The Wall Street Journal*, May 17, 2001, B1, B4.

20. Joseph Pereira, "Spying on the Sales Floor," *The Wall Street Journal*, December 21, 2004, B1, B4.

21. Julie Jargon, "Kiwi Goes beyond Shine in Effort to Step Up Sales," *The Wall Street Journal*, December 20, 2007, B1.

22. Marina Strauss, "Mining Customer Feedback, Firms Go Undercover and Online," *The Globe and Mail*, May 13, 2004, B1, B25.

23. Deborah Ball, Sarah Ellison, and Janet Adamy, "Probing Shoppers' Psyche," *The Wall Street Journal*, October 28, 2004, B1, B8.

24. Oliver Bertin, "John Deere Reaps the Fruits of Its Labours," *The Globe and Mail*, September 2, 1991, B1, B3.

25. Peter Morton, "Marketing at Face Value," *National Post*, July 11, 2007, FP3.

26. Alvin C. Burns and Ronald F. Bush, *Marketing Research*, 3rd ed. (Upper Saddle River, NJ: Prentice Hall, 2000), 140–148.

27. Kenneth C. Laudon and Jane P. Laudon, *Management Information*

Systems: Managing the Digital Firm, 7th ed. (Upper Saddle River, NJ: Prentice Hall, 2002), 221–222.

28. Ibid., 222–224.

29. Paul S. Foote and Malini Krishnamurthi, "Forecasting Using Data Warehousing Model: Wal-Mart's Experience," *The Journal of Business Forecasting Methods & Systems*, Fall 2001, 13–17.

30. www.statcan.gc.ca.

31. Thomas Russell, Glenn Verrill, and W. Ronald Lane, *Kleppner's Advertising Procedure*, 11th ed. (Englewood Cliffs, NJ: Prentice Hall, 1990); James Engel, Martin Warshaw, and Thomas Kinnear, *Promotional Strategy*, 6th ed. (Homewood, IL: Richard D. Irwin, 1987).

Chapter 17

1. Barrie McKenna and Matt Hartley, "Stringer Makes His Mark," *The Globe and Mail*, February 20, 2008, B1, B6.

2. Eric Reguly, "Beaudoin's Big, Bold Bet," *The Globe and Mail*, July 14, 2008, B1, B10.

3. Susanna Ray, "Dreamliner a Scheduling Nightmare; Delayed Yet Again; Boeing This Time Cites Strike and Fastener Problem," *National Post*, December 12, 2008, FP12.

4. James C. Anderson and James A. Narus, *Business Market Management: Understanding, Creating, and Delivering Value* (Upper Saddle River, NJ: Prentice Hall, 1999), 203–206.

5. Philip Kotler, *Marketing Management*, 11th ed. (Upper Saddle River, NJ: Prentice Hall, 2003), 328–339.

6. Julie Jargon, "The Iconic Oreo Squares Off in Kraft's Battle for Global Taste Buds," *The Globe and Mail*, May 1, 2008, B13.

7. Jennifer Wells, "Canadian Companies Hop on the Global Brand Wagon," *The Globe and Mail*, September 19, 2008, B7.

8. "30 Second Spot: Dispatches from the World of Media and Advertising," *The Globe and Mail*, January 16, 2009, B5.

9. "Australia Ranks #1 as World's Top Country Brand for Third Consecutive Year, Global Study Reveals," *Country Brand Index: 2008*, www.countrybrandindex.com/press-release.

10. Keith McArthur, "How to Survive an Identity Crisis," *The Globe and Mail*, November 14, 2005, B1, B11.

11. "Canada's Most Valuable Brands 2009," *Brand Finance Canada*, Spring 2009, www.brandfinance.com/Uploads/pdfs/BrandFinanceCanadaMostValuableBrands2009.pdf.

12. John Frook, "Cisco Scores with Its Latest Generation of Empowering Tools," *B to B*, August 20, 2001, 20.

13. Cyndee Miller, "Little Relief Seen for New Product Failure Rate," *Marketing News*, June 21, 1993, 1; Nancy J. Kim, "Back to the Drawing Board," *The Bergen Record* (New Jersey), December 4, 1994, B1, B4.

14. Marina Strauss, "The Secret to Gaining Success in Quebec," *The Globe and Mail*, September 27, 2005, B4.

15. Konrad Yakabuski, "How Pepsi Won Quebec," *The Globe and Mail*, August 28, 2008, B1-B2.

16. Bertrand Marotte, "I Am Canadian—But Not Necessarily in Quebec Marketing," *The Globe and Mail*, December 8, 2007, B8.

17. Brian Milner, "Canada's Franklin the Turtle Heads South," *The Globe and Mail*, February 14, 2000, B1, B10.

18. Marina Strauss, "Shoppers Sees Gold in Private Labels," *The Globe and Mail*, January 3, 2005, B1–B2.

19. Richard Bloom, "Taking on the World, One Jar at a Time," *The Globe and Mail*, July 4, 2005, B3.

20. Marina Strauss, "Consumers Less Trusting of Brands," *The Globe and Mail*, February 13, 2003, B3.

21. Paul Glader, "Avid Boarders Bypass Branded Gear," *The Wall Street Journal*, July 27, 2007, B1–B2.

22. Keith McArthur, "Why Molson Is Crying in Its Beer," *The Globe and Mail*, July 10, 2004, B4.

23. "Mega Brands Wins Case over Lego," *The Globe and Mail*, November 13, 2008, B3.

24. David Square, "Mouse Pad Gets Oodles of Nibbles," *Winnipeg Free Press*, July 26, 1997, B10.

25. Paul Waldie, "How RIM's Big Deal Was Done," *The Globe and Mail*, March 6, 2006, B1, B14.

26. Simon Avery, "RIM Faces New U.S. Fight Over Patents," *The Globe and Mail*, May 2, 2006, B3.

27. Avery Johnson, "Pfizer Buys More Time for Lipitor," *The Wall Street Journal*, June 19, 2008, B1.

28. "Google to Pay US$125 Million to Settle Copyright Lawsuits Over Book Project," *National Post*, October 29, 2008, FP6.

29. Deborah Ball, "The Perils of Packaging: Nestle Aims for Easier Openings," *The Wall Street Journal*, November 17, 2005, B1, B5.

30. Keith McArthur, "Oh? Canada? Ads Beg to Differ," *The Globe and Mail*, July 1, 2004, B1, B18.

31. William Pride and O.C. Ferrell, *Marketing*, 5th ed. (Boston: Houghton Mifflin, 1987).

32. Calvin Leung, "Marketing Ubiquity," *Canadian Business*, February 18, 2008, 28.

33. Robert Berner, "The Rolls-Royce of Leather Jackets Is Hard to Come By," *The Wall Street Journal*, November 22, 1996, A1, A10.

34. Kenneth E. Clow and Donald Baack, *Integrated Advertising, Promotion, and Marketing Communications* (Upper Saddle River, NJ: Prentice Hall, 2002), Chapter 5.

35. John Heinzl, "Buckley Wants U.S. to Swallow Its Bad Taste," *The Globe and Mail*, November 11, 1999, B1, B12.

36. Marina Strauss, "Towel War Turns to Name-Naming," *The Globe and Mail*, December 5, 1995, B1, B10.

37. Canadian Media Directors Council, *Media Digest, 2008-2009*, Components of Net Advertising Revenue by Medium, (Toronto: Marketing, 2008), 14, www.cmdc.ca/pdf/2008_09_Media_Digest.pdf.

38. Andrew Wahl, "Red All Over," *Canadian Business*, February 13–26, 2006, 53–54.

39. Aaron O. Patrick, "Technology Boosts Outdoor Ads as Competition Becomes Fiercer," *The Wall Street Journal*, August 23, 2006, A1, A10.

40. Canadian Media Directors Council, *Media Digest, 2008-2009*, Components of Net Advertising Revenue by Medium, (Toronto: Marketing, 2008), 14, www.cmdc.ca/pdf/2008_09_Media_Digest.pdf.

41. Allan Kreda, "Advertisers Lured by Super Bowl's Glitz, Huge Ratings," *The Globe and Mail*, December 30, 2004, B3.

42. Canadian Media Directors Council, *Media Digest, 2008-2009*, Components of Net Advertising Revenue by Medium, (Toronto: Marketing, 2008), 14, www.cmdc.ca/pdf/2008_09_Media_Digest.pdf.

43. Ibid.

44. James Adams, *Reader's Digest* Still Rules Magazine Roost," *The Globe and Mail*, March 27, 2009, B2.

45. Canadian Media Directors Council, *Media Digest, 2008-2009*, Components of Net Advertising Revenue by Medium, (Toronto: Marketing, 2008), 14, www.cmdc.ca/pdf/2008_09_Media_Digest.pdf.

46. Matt Hartley, "Tunnel Visionaries," *The Globe and Mail*, January 31, 2008, B18.

47. "30 Second Spot: Dispatches from the World of Media and Advertising," *The Globe and Mail*, October 31, 2008, B8.

48. Aaron O. Patrick, "Technology Boosts Outdoor Ads as Competition Becomes Fiercer," *The Wall Street Journal*, August 23, 2006, A1, A10; Grant Robertson, "Growth in Internet Ads Outpaces All Others," *The Globe and Mail*, June 23, 2006, B4; Canadian Media Directors Council, *Media Digest, 2008-2009*, Components of Net Advertising Revenue by Medium, (Toronto: Marketing, 2008), 14, www.cmdc.ca/pdf/2008_09_Media_Digest.pdf.

49. Mike Blaney, "Word of Mouth Advertising," blog, www.themarketingguy.wordpress.com/2007/10/09/word-of-mouth-advertising.

50. Sarah Scott, "Ready for Their Close-Up," *Financial Post Business*, September 2007, 40–45.

51. Philip Kotler, Gary Armstrong, and Peggy H. Cunningham, *Principles of Marketing*, 6th Canadian ed. (Toronto: Pearson, 2005), 88.

52. Canadian Media Directors Council, *Media Digest, 2008-2009*, Components of Net Advertising Revenue by Medium, (Toronto: Marketing, 2008), 14, www.cmdc.ca/pdf/2008_09_Media_Digest.pdf.

53. Amol Sharma and Emily Steel, "Ads Critical to MySpace," *The Wall Street Journal*, August 4, 2008, B5.

54. Ronald Ebert and Ricky Griffin, *Business Essentials* (Upper Saddle River, NJ: Prentice Hall, 2009), 161.

55. Emily Steel, "YouTube Launches Video Ads," *The Wall Street Journal*, August 22, 2007, B9.

56. Emily Steel, "As Search Habits Change, Advertisers Look Past Google, Yahoo," *The Globe and Mail*, January 20, 2009, B10.

57. Philip Kotler, Gary Armstrong, and Peggy H. Cunningham, *Principles of Marketing*, 6th Canadian ed. (Toronto: Pearson, 2005), 89–91.

58. Simon Tuck, "Security Rated Top On-Line Fear," *The Globe and Mail*, July 5, 1999, B5.

59. James Hagerty and Dennis Berman, "New Battleground in Web Privacy War: Ads That Snoop," *The Wall Street Journal*, August 27, 2003, A1, A8.

60. Stuart Elliott, "Real or Virtual? You Call It," *The New York Times*, October 1, 1999, C1, C6.

61. William Wells, John Burnett, and Sandra Moriarty, *Advertising: Principles and Practice*, 5th ed. (Upper Saddle River, NJ: Prentice Hall, 2000), 77–83.

62. Ann Gibbon, "Ad Group Tries to Demystify Quebec," *The Globe and Mail*, November 25, 1993, B6.

63. "Regulators Wary of Ads Rapping Rivals," *The Globe and Mail*, May 23, 1991, B4.

64. Simon Avery, "Do Not Call List Could Give Boost to Direct Mail," *The Globe and Mail*, September 29, 2008, B3.

65. Hollie Shaw, "Do Not Call List a Ringing Success," *National Post*, March 13, 2009, FP12.

66. Oliver Moore, "Clement Blasts Do-Not-Call Scammers," *The Globe and Mail*, January 26, 2009, A4.

67. John Heinzl, "Beer Firms Rethink Giveaways," *The Globe and Mail*, March 3, 2003, B1, B5.

68. Grant Robertson, "Thanks, But No Thanks," *The Globe and Mail*, August 29, 2008, B5; Rebecca Dana, "When You're Here, You're Family—But What About a Playboy Model?," *The Wall Street Journal*, August 13, 2008, A1, A14.

69. "2012 Games Boost Finances with Cadbury Sponsorship," *The Globe and Mail*, October 21, 2008, B15.

70. Warren J. Keegan, *Global Marketing Management*, 7th ed. (Upper Saddle River, NJ: Prentice Hall, 2002), Chapter 14.

71. Norman M. Scarborough and Thomas W. Zimmerer, *Effective Small Business Management: An Entrepreneurial Approach*, 6th ed. (Upper Saddle River, NJ: Prentice Hall, 2000), Chapter 11.

Chapter 18

1. Constance L. Hays, "Coke Tests Weather-Linked Pricing," *The Globe and Mail*, October 29, 1999, B11.

2. Stefan Fatsis, "The Barry Bonds Tax: Teams Raise Prices for Good Games," *The Wall Street Journal*, December 3, 2002, D1, D8.

3. Leila Abboud and Jenny Clevstrom, "Swedes Try Toll Plan to Unsnarl Traffic," *The Globe and Mail*, August 29, 2006, B10; Lawrence Solomon, "Sweden Proves Congestion Tolls Work," *National Post*, August 4, 2007, FP13.

4. Lawrence Solomon, "Revolution on the Road: Pay-Per-Mile Insurance," *National Post*, October 14, 2006, FP15.

5. David George-Cosh, "Cisco Joins Skymeter to Help Unsnarl City Traffic," *National Post*, October 6, 2008, www.nationalpost.com/story-printer.html?id=862402.

6. Stephen Kindel, "Tortoise Gains on Hare," *Financial World*, February 23, 1988, 18–20.

7. Ethan Smith, "Universal Slashes CD Prices in Bid to Revive Music Industry," *The Wall Street Journal*, September 4, 2003, B1, B8.

8. Chester Zelasko, "Acesulfame-K," *Better Life Institute*, May 17, 2001, www.betterlifeunlimited.com/healthnews/health_az/display.aspx?id=69141141052.

9. Stewart A. Washburn, "Establishing Strategy and Determining Cost in the Pricing Decision," *Business Marketing*, July 1985, 64–78.

10. Marina Strauss, "Why Everyday Low Prices Failed Zellers," *The Globe and Mail*, March 22, 2005, B8.

11. Judy Strauss and Raymond Frost, *E-Marketing*, 2nd ed. (Upper Saddle River, NJ: Prentice Hall, 2001), 166–167; Eloise Coupey, *Marketing and the Internet* (Upper Saddle River, NJ: Prentice Hall, 2001), 281–283.

12. "Wal-Mart Rounds Prices to Lure Shoppers," *The Globe and Mail*, April 15, 2009, B12.

13. Marina Strauss, "Taking 'e' Out of E-commerce: Meet the eBay Middleman," *The Globe and Mail*, October 6, 2004, B1, B19.

14. Paul Waldie, "Battle over Real Estate Listings Spurs Probe," *The Globe and Mail*, March 26, 2007, B1–B2.

15. Ahmad Diba, "An Old-Line Agency Finds an Online Niche," *Fortune*, April 3, 2000, 258.

16. *Fiscal 2001 In Review*, Dell Annual Report, April 22, 2002, www.dell.com/downloads/global/corporate/annual/2001_DELL_Annual.pdf; Qiao Song, "Legend Outlines Role in China's Wireless Future," *ebn*, March 25, 2002, 3; Faith Hung, "Legend Looks to Defend Its Turf—WTO Entry Will Force China's Top PC Maker to Fend Off Unrestricted Rivals," *ebn*, December 17, 2001, 44; Neel Chowdhury, "Dell Cracks China," *Fortune*, June 21, 1999, 120–124.

17. Keith McArthur, "Para Paints' Bold Stroke," *The Globe and Mail*, October 18, 1999, M1.

18. Dale M. Lewison, *Retailing*, 5th ed. (New York: Macmillan, 1994), 454; Louis Stern and Adel I. El-Ansary, *Marketing Channels*, 4th ed. (Englewood Cliffs, NJ: Prentice Hall, 1992), 129–130.

19. Direct Selling Association, www.dsa.org.

20. Gordon Pitts, "Tupperware Shows the World How to Party," *The Globe and Mail*, February 9, 2008, B3.

21. Expedia.com, www.expedia.com.

22. Ann Bednarz, "Acquisitions Tighten Supply-Chain Market," *Network World*, February 9, 2004, 21–22.

23. Marina Strauss, "E-tailing in Age of Refinement," *The Globe and Mail*, August 3, 2005, B6.

24. "Did You Know?" *Catalog News.com*, www.catalog-news.com, April 8, 2002; Judy Strauss and Raymond Frost, *E-Marketing* (Upper Saddle River, NJ: Prentice Hall, 2001), 140.

25. "More Than 8.4 Million Canadians Spent $12.8 Billion over the Internet in 2007," *National Post*, November 18, 2008, FP6.

26. Zena Olijnyk, "Dot-Com Wonder Boys," *Canadian Business*, April 14, 2003, 30–36.

27. Vito Pilieci, "Taxman Eyes Internet Sellers," *Winnipeg Free Press*, November 18, 2008, B5.

28. Geoffrey Fowler, "EBay Retreats in Web Retailing," *The Wall Street Journal*, March 12, 2009, A1, A11.

29. Peter Elkind, "Shhhhh! Amway's on the Web," *Fortune*, March 6, 2000, 76.

30. "LivePerson.com™," www.liveperson.com, April 19, 2000.

31. Gordon Jaremko, "River Highway in Canada's North Open for Business," *Winnipeg Free Press*, July 25, 2006, B10.

32. Anne T. Coughlan et al., *Marketing Channels*, 6th ed. (Upper Saddle River, NJ: Prentice Hall, 2001), 458–462.

33. "Just One Word: Logistics," *Financial Post Business*, June 2007, 14–23.

Sources

Chapter 1

Corporate Culture Carrie Tait, "CIBC Shuffles the Deck," *National Post*, January 8, 2008, www.nationalpost.com/ story; Meagan Fitzpatrick, "RCMP 'Horribly Broken,' Need Fix Quickly: Report," *Winnipeg Free Press*, June 16, 2007, A9; Roma Luciw, "No. 1 Employee Not Always Your No. 1 Manager," *The Globe and Mail*, February 17, 2007, B10; Calvin Leung, "Culture Club," *Canadian Business*, October 9–22, 2006, 115–120; Andrew Wahl, "Culture Shock," *Canadian Business*, October 10–23, 2005, 115–116; Gordon Pitts, "It Boiled Down to a Culture Clash," *The Globe and Mail*, June 11, 2005, B5; Sinclair Stewart and Andrew Willis, "Hunkin Is De-Risking the Place," *The Globe and Mail*, December 11, 2004, B4; Doug Nairne, "Mounties Riding the Vision Thing," *Winnipeg Free Press*, September 16, 1996, A5.

Business Accountability Henry Mintzberg, *The Nature of Managerial Work* (New York: Harper and Row, 1973); Harvey Schachter, "Monday Morning Manager," *The Globe and Mail*, November 8, 2005, B2.

The Greening of Business "Rona Wins Kudos on Green Initiative," *The Globe and Mail*, November 22, 2008, B7; Marjo Johne, "Shoppers Get a Brand New Bag," *The Globe and Mail*, October 20, 2008, E5; John Murphy, "Honda CEO Vies for Green Mantle," *The Wall Street Journal*, June 16, 2008, B1–B2; "Deadline Set for Big Polluters," *National Post*, December 13, 2007, www.nationalpost.com/ news/canada/story.html?id=164992; *Agriculture and Agri-Food Canada, Going Green: The Future of the Retail Food Industry, July 2007*, www.ats.agr.gc.ca/us/4351_e.htm; "Google Sets Goal of Making Renewables Cheaper Than Coal," *Clean Edge News*, November 28, 2007, www.cleanedge.com/ story.php?nID=5036; Sharda Prashad, "Good Green Goals," *TheStar.com*, April 22, 2007, www.thestar.com/ printArticle/205855.

Entrepreneurship and New Ventures *Photo-Kicks Martial Arts Photography*, http://photo-kicks.com; Inc.com 5000, www.lnc.com/inc5000/2007/company-profile.html?id+200705920; Joanne Schneider, "Action: Filmmakers Open Studios in Columbia," *Columbia Business Times*, February 20, 2009, www.columbiabusinesstimes.com/3527/2009/ 02/20/action-filmmakers-open-studios-in-columbia.

Concluding Case 1-1 Vanessa O'Connell, "Coach Targets China—and Queens," *The Wall Street Journal*, May 29, 2008, B1; "Coach's Drive Picks Up the Pace," *Business Week*, March 29, 2004, 98–100; Julia Boorstin, "How Coach Got Hot," *Fortune*, October 28, 2003, 131–134; Marilyn Much, "Consumer Research Is His Bag," *Investor's Business Daily*, December 16, 2003; "S&P Stock Picks and Pans: Accumulate Coach," *Business Week*, October 22, 2003.

Concluding Case 1-2 Brian Milner, "The Unmaking of a Dynasty," *Cigar Aficionado*, January 20, 2009, www.cigaraficionado.com/Cigar/CA_Profiles/ People_Profile/0,2540,176,00.html; Mathew Ingram, "Nokia's Deal with Record Firms Could Have Music Fans Hanging Up," *The Globe and Mail*, July 2, 2008, R3; "Warner Music to Sell Tunes on Amazon.com," *The Globe and Mail*, December 28, 2007, B4; Simon Avery, "Music Firms Hope to Leave the Blues Behind," *The Globe and Mail*, April 5, 2007, B14; Shawn McCarthy, "Bronfman Is Eager to Gain Redemption for His Music Gambit," *The Globe and Mail*, January 4, 2005, B4; Shawn McCarthy, "Bronfman Jumps Back into Music with Winning Bid," *The Globe and Mail*, November 25, 2003; Brian Milner, "Broken Spirits," *Report on Business Magazine*, September 2002, 26–38; Brian Milner, "Seagram's Top Gun Shoots for the Stars," *The Globe and Mail*, June 6, 1998, B1, B6; Brian Milner, "Seagram Snares Polygram," *The Globe and Mail*, May 22, 1998, B1, B4; Brian Milner, "The Selling of Edgar Bronfman Jr.," *The Globe and Mail*, February 15, 1999, B15.

Chapter 3

Family Businesses Burke Campbell, "Sisters Toast Family Roots as Business Bears Fruit," *National Post*, September 29, 2008, www.nationalpost.com/ story-printer.html?id=846427; Gabriel Kahn, "A Vintage Strategy Faces Modernity," *The Wall Street Journal*, April 5–6, 2008, A6; Chris Morris, "Rumours of Irving Family Corporate Breakup Swirl," *Winnipeg Free Press*, November 23, 2007, B14; Gordon Pitts and Jacquie McNish, "Shaking the Family Tree," *The Globe and Mail*, November 22, 2007, B1, B9; Gordon Pitts and Jacquie McNish, "Irving Brothers Look to Break Up Empire," *The Globe and Mail*, November 21, 2007, B1, B6; Martin Peers, Matthew Karnitschnig, and Merissa Marr, "Shaken from the Family Tree," *The Globe and Mail*, July 20, 2007, B6; Paul Waldie, "Mitchell's Feud Goes Public," *The Globe and Mail*, November 30, 2002, B3; Gordon Pitts, "The Cuddy Situation is an Extreme Case of Family Company Dysfunctionality," *The Globe and Mail*, April 17, 2000, B9; David Berman, "Carving Up Cuddy," *Canadian Business*, March 27, 1998, 39–44.

Table 3.1 www.business.queensu.ca/ news/2009/01-14-09-BSME.php.

Table 3.5 *Financial Post Magazine*, June 2009, 42.

The Greening of Business Laura Ramsay, "Small Firms Can Go Green Too: There's Lots of Help out There," *The Globe and Mail*, October 14, 2008, E1; Burke Campbell, "Entrepreneur's Green Inspiration from the East," *National Post*, September 22, 2008, www.nationalpost.com/story-printer.html?id= 812446; Stephanie Whittaker, "Mompreneur Finds Online Niche for Organic Stock," *National Post*, March 31, 2008, www.nationalpost.com/ todays_paper/story.html?id=411279.

Business Accountability Rasha Mourtada, "Help Me Get an Angel in My Underwear," *The Globe and Mail*, January 28, 2008, B13; Terrence Belford, "When Money Is the Mother of Invention," *The Globe and Mail*, October 17, 2007, E7; Marjo Johne, "Moolah from Heaven," *The Globe and Mail*, July 24, 2007, B14.

Concluding Case 3-1 Alexandra Lopez-Pacheco, "Home-Preneurs Want it All; She Said," *National Post*, December 22, 2008, FP4; David Hatton, "Home-Preneurs Want it All; He Said," *National Post*, December 22, 2008, FP4; Daryl-Lynn Carlson, "A Beautiful Balance with Help from Outsourcing," *National Post*, September 8, 2008, www.nationalpost. com/story-printer.html?id=776154; Melissa Martin, "Mompreneurial Spirit," *Winnipeg Free Press*, September 2, 2008, D1, D5; Stephanie Whittaker, "Mompreneur Finds Online Niche for Organic Stock," *National Post*, March 31, 2008, www.nationalpost.com/todays_ paper/story.html?id=411279; Robeez Footwear Ltd., www.robeez.com/en-us/ about/sandra.htm?PriceCat=1&Lang= EN-US; Rebecca Gardiner, "It Pays to be Nice," *Profit* 24 no. 6 (2005): 23.

Concluding Case 3-2 Marlene Cartash, "My Best Sale: Asked to Recall the Defining Moment of Their Selling Careers, 10 Celebrated Entrepreneurs Cited Gutsy Moves That Still Fill Them with Pride," *Profit* 13 no. 4 (1995): 34–41; Bruce Erskine, "Gibson Got in on Ground Floor," *The Halifax Herald Limited*, April 26, 2006, www. thechronicleherald.ca/external/bbi/ index11.html. Used with permission.

Chapter 5

What Really Happened at Livent? Jacquie McNish, "Convictions Seen as Much-Needed Regulatory Win," *The Globe and Mail*, March 26, 2009, B4; Janet McFarland, "ICAO Appeal Panel Upholds Deloitte Decision," *The Globe and Mail*, February 19, 2009, B9; Grant McCool and John Poirier, "Madoff Mess Manoeuvres," *National Post*, December 18, 2008, FP3; Shannon Kari, "Livent Defence Calls No Witnesses; Final Arguments," *National Post*, November 4, 2008, FP5; Janet McFarland, "File Listed Livent 'Problems': Investigator," *The Globe and Mail*, October 22, 2008, B9; Janet McFarland, "Livent Brass Pulled 'Numbers out of a Hat'," *The Globe and Mail*, September 9, 2008, B2; Janet McFarland, "Ex-Livent Official Tells of 'Absurd' Plan," *The Globe and Mail*, September 3, 2008, B5; Janet McFarland, "Livent Staff Dodged Drabinsky's Controls, Lawyer Says," *The Globe and Mail*, July 18, 2008, B2; Janet McFarland, "Livent Software Was Altered, Court Hears," *The Globe and Mail*, July 17, 2008, B9; Janet McFarland, "Ad Firms Helped Livent, Ex-Official Says," *The*

Globe and Mail, July 16, 2008, B7; Janet McFarland, "All His Time Spent on Fraud: Ex-Livent Official," *The Globe and Mail*, July 15, 2008, B4; Janet McFarland, "Ex-CFO Testified She Hid Fraud at Livent," *The Globe and Mail*, June 12, 2008, B3.

The Greening of Business Hollie Shaw, "Keeping It Green; Outdoor-Recreation Retailer Finds Ways to Draw Customers," *National Post*, November 28, 2008, FP14; Laura Pratt, "Sustainability Reporting," *CGA Magazine*, September–October 2007, 18–21; Sharda Prashad, "Good Green Goals," *TheStar.com*, April 22, 2007, www.thestar.com/printArticle/205855; Ralph Shaw, "Peak Performance (Mountain Equipment Co-op)," *Alternatives Journal* 31 no. 1 (2005): 19–20.

Business Accountability "EBay Claims Court Victory in Belgium over L'Oreal in Counterfeit Goods Case," *National Post*, August 13, 2008, www.nationalpost.com/story-printer.html?id=718982; "EBay Quashes Tiffany Trademark Suit," *The Globe and Mail*, July 15, 2008, B6; "The End of Louis Vuitton on eBay?," *ETonline.com*, June 30, 2008, www.etonline.com/news/2008/06/63035; Maureen Fan, "China's Olympic Turnabout on Knockoffs," June 13, 2008, A1; Aileen McCabe, "China's Knock-Off Shops Help the Rich Scrape By," *Winnipeg Free Press*, April 19, 2008, C19; Daryl-Lynn Carlson, "The Costly Reality of Fakes," *The National Post*, December 5, 2007; Daryl-Lynn Carlson, "Canada's IP Protection Laws Soft," *The National Post*, December 5, 2007; Paul Waldie, "Court Clobbers Store for Selling Vuitton Fakes," *The Globe and Mail*, November 26, 2007, B3; Jonathan Cheng, "A Small Firm Takes on Chinese Pirates," *The Wall Street Journal*, July 5, 2007, B1–B2; Stacy Meichtry, "Swell or Swill?," *The Wall Street Journal*, August 10, 2006, B1–B2; Alessandra Galloni, "As Luxury Industry Goes Global, Knock-Off Merchants Follow," *The Wall Street Journal*, January 31, 2006, A1, A13; Alessandra Galloni, "Bagging Fakes and Sellers," *The Wall Street Journal*, January 31, 2006, B1–B2; Gordon Fairclough, "Tobacco Firms Trace Fakes to North Korea," *The Wall Street Journal*, January 27, 2006, B1–B2; Jeff Sanford, "Knock-Off Nation," *Canadian Business*, November 8–21, 2004, 67–71; Shawn McCarthy, "Crackdown on New York's Canal Street," *The Globe and Mail*, August 30, 2004, B1, B11.

Entrepreneurship and New Ventures "Frequently Asked Questions," Arthur's Juice," http://arthursjuice.ca/en_faq.asp; The Packaging Association of Canada, "Presentation Highlights and Speaker Profiles," www.pac.ca/ePromos/NA09_Walmart_Sus_Conf_3info.htm#Travis_Bell; Karen Davidson, "New Products Sport Green Nutrition," *The Grower*, May 1, 2009; Randy Ray, "Fresh Ideas for Green Manufacturing," *The Globe and Mail*, April 22, 2009, E10;

Cleve Dheensaw, "100 Marathons Earn Place on Walk of Fame," *Times Colonist*, October 11, 2008; Rick Spence, "Top 100 List Reveals Healthy Economy," *Financial Post*, June 2, 2008, FP5; Ken Ramstead, "The Juices Are Flowing," *Canadian Grocer* 121 no. 3 (2007): 53.

Concluding Case 5-1 Ross McKitrick, "Contaminated Data," *National Post*, December 5, 2007; Lawrence Solomon, "Open Mind Sees Climate Clearly," *National Post*, June 29, 2007, FP15; "List of Scientists Opposing the Mainstream Scientific Assessment of Global Warming," http://en.wikipedia.org/wiki/List_of_Scientists_opposing_global_warming_consensus; Christopher Essex, "There Is No Global Temperature," *National Post*, June 23, 2007, FP15; Timothy Patterson, "Read the Sunspots," *National Post*, June 20, 2007, FP17; David Ebner, "The Greening of the Oil Sands," *The Globe and Mail*, January 6, 2007, B4; Lauren Etter, "For Icy Greenland, Global Warming Has a Bright Side," *The Wall Street Journal*, July 18, 2006, A1, A12; Patrick Brethour, "Canada's Big Emitters Brace for Investment Climate Change," *The Globe and Mail*, February 19, 2005, B4; Jared Diamond, *Collapse: How Societies Choose to Fail or Succeed* (New York: Penguin Books, 2005), 493–494; Robert Park, *Voodoo Science* (Oxford: Oxford University Press, 2000), 31–34, 43–45; James Trefil, *101 Things You Don't Know about Science and No One Else Does Either* (Boston: Houghton Mifflin, 1996), 124–126, 142.

Concluding Case 5-2 Bruce Stanley, "Ships Draw Fire for Rising Role in Air Pollution," *The Wall Street Journal*, November 27, 2007, A1, A16; Bill McAllister, "Alaska Still Out Front on Environmental Monitoring," *The Juneau Empire*, May 29, 2004; Marilyn Adams, "Former Carnival Exec Says He Was Fired for Helping Federal Inquiry," *USA Today*, November 8–10, 2003; Marilyn Adams, "Cruise-Ship Dumping Poisons Seas, Frustrates U.S. Enforcers," *USA Today*, November 8–10, 2003; Michael Connor, "Norwegian Cruise Line Pleads Guilty in Pollution Case," *Reuters*, December 7, 2002; "What Is a Dead Zone?" *Oceana Interactive*, June 10, 2004, www.oceana.org/index.cfm?sectionID511&fuseaction59#25.

Chapter 9

Reorganizing the Irving Empire Chris Morris, "Rumours of Irving Family Corporate Breakup Swirl," *Winnipeg Free Press*, November 23, 2007, B14; Gordon Pitts and Jacquie McNish, "Shaking the Family Tree," *The Globe and Mail*, November 22, 2007, B1, B9; Gordon Pitts and Jacquie McNish, "Irving Brothers Look to Break Up Empire," *The Globe and Mail*, November 21, 2007, B1, B6.

Business Accountability Betsy Morris, "The Pepsi Challenge," *Fortune*,

February 19, 2008, www.money.cnn.com/2008/02/18/news/companies/morris_nooyi.fortune/index.htm; "PepsiCo Unveils New Organizations Structure, Names CEOs of Three Principal Operating Units," May 11, 2007, *FLEXNEWS*, www.flex-news-food.com/pages/12058/pepsi/pepsico-unveils-new-organizational-structure-names-ceos-three-principal-operating-units.html; Joann Lublin, "Place vs. Product: It's Tough to Choose a Management Model," *The Wall Street Journal*, June 27, 2001, A1, A4; Richard Blackwell, "New CIBC Boss Promises Shakeup," *The Globe and Mail*, April 2, 1999, B1, B4; Rekha Bach, "Heinz's Johnson to Divest Operations, Scrap Management of Firm by Region," *The Wall Street Journal*, December 1997, B10–B12; Jana Parker-Pope and Joann Lublin, "P&G Will Make Jager CEO Ahead of Schedule," *The Wall Street Journal*, September 1998, B1, B8.

The Greening of Business Gerald Flood, "At One with the World," *Winnipeg Free Press*, April 19, 2009, B1–B2; Jay Somerset, "A Building with an Energy All Its Own," *The Globe and Mail*, November 11, 2008, B9; Marta Gold, "More Realtors Turning Green," *Winnipeg Free Press*, August 24, 2008, F2; Murray McNeill, "Green Is the New Green at Credit Union Branches," *Winnipeg Free Press*, August 20, 2008, B6, B8; "Delta Hotels Expands Green Initiatives with Hybrid Heating," press release, www.sempapower.com/media/newsarticles/16.06.08%20-%20Delta%20Hotels%20Expands%20Green%20Initiatives%20with%20Hybrid%20Heating.pdf, August 15, 2008; Peter Mitham, "Going for the Gold in Green," *The Globe and Mail*, August 5, 2008, B5; John D. Stoll, "Car Dealers Set 'Green' Blueprints," *The Wall Street Journal*, May 15, 2008, B1; *Agriculture and Agri-Food Canada, Going Green: The Future of the Retail Food Industry*, July 2007, www.ats.agr.gc.ca/us/4351_e.htm.

Concluding Case 9-1 Randall King, "Frantic Films Sells Division," *Winnipeg Free Press*, November 28, 2007, B7; interviews with Jamie Brown, CEO of Frantic Films; documents provided by Frantic Films.

Concluding Case 9-2 "Our Brands," *Sara Lee*, www.saralee.com, July 3, 2002; Deborah Cohen, "Sara Lee Opens Alternative to Victoria's Secret," *The Wall Street Journal*, January 3, 2003, B4; Julie Forster, "Sara Lee: Changing the Recipe—Again," *Business Week*, September 10, 2001, 87–89; "Sara Lee: Looking Shapely," *Business Week*, October 1, 2002, 52.

Chapter 11

Accounting for Pensions Boyd Erman, "Teachers' Books Worst-Ever Year after 18 Percent Plunge," *The Globe and Mail*, April 3, 2009, B4; Janet McFarland, "Who's Responsible?," *The Globe and Mail*, March 6, 2009, B1; Lori McLeod,

"Pension Plans Suffer Historic Losses," *The Globe and Mail*, January 9, 2009, A1; Janet McFarland, "Returns Forecast This Year Will Do Little to Offset 2008 Shortfalls," *The Globe and Mail*, January 14, 2009, B3; Janet McFarland, "Relief Falls Short, Pension Plans Warn," *The Globe and Mail*, November 28, 2008, B1; Elizabeth Church, "Pension Funding Shortfall Increases Dramatically," *The Globe and Mail*, November 8, 2005, B5; Elizabeth Church, "Pension Fund Shortfall Soars in First Half," *The Globe and Mail*, November 23, 2005, B1, B7; Elizabeth Church, "Cost of Retiree Benefit Liabilities 'Sleeping Giant'," *The Globe and Mail*, August 23, 2004, B4; Paul Waldie and Karen Howlett, "Reports Reveal Tight Grip of Ebbers on WorldCom," *The Globe and Mail*, June 11, 2003, B1, B7; Barrie McKenna, Karen Howlett, and Paul Waldie, "Probes Cite Ebbers in 'Fraud'," *The Globe and Mail*, June 10, 2003, B1, B16; Elizabeth Church, "Accounting Overhaul Coming," *The Globe and Mail*, December 23, 2002, B1, B6; Richard Blackwell, "OSC Targets Tech Accounting," *The Globe and Mail*, September 26, 2000, B1, B6.

Table 11.1 *Financial Post Magazine*, June 2009, 98.

Business Accountability Lawrence M. Gill, "Questions Loom as Accountants Outsource Work Abroad," *Chicago Lawyer*, January 26, 2004,; Jim Peterson, "Turf Battle Shows Signs of Truce," *International Herald Tribune*, November 8, 2003, 17; Beth Ellyn Rosenthal, "Deloitte Study Discovers 75 Percent of Global Financial Institutions Plan to Outsource Offshore," *BPO Outsourcing Journal*, June 2003, www.bpo-outsourcing-journal.com/jun2003-deloitte.html; Todd Furniss and Michel Janssen, "Offshore Outsourcing Part 1: The Brand of India," *BPO Outsourcing Journal*, December 2003, www.bpo-outsourcing-journal.com/dec2003-india.html; "How to Evaluate an Outsourcing Provider and Watch the Bottom Line," *The CPA Journal*, June 2002, 19; Liz Loxton, "Offshoring—Offshore Accounting," *Accountancy*, February 2004, 48; Thomas J. Smedinghoff and Creighton R. Meland, Jr., "Financial Institution Outsourcing: Managing the Risks," *Outsourcing Journal*, May 2002, www.outsourcing-journal.com/may2002-legal.html; Todd Furniss, "China: The Next Big Wave in Offshore Outsourcing," *BPO Outsourcing Journal*, June 2003, www.bpo-outsourcing-journal.com/jun2003-everest.html; "Cover Feature—Outsourcing the Finance Function—Out with the Count," *Accountancy*, September 1, 2001, 32.

Entrepreneurship and New Ventures *The Daily Gleaner*, A1, from Canadian Newsstand Core database, (Document ID: 1652944261); Randy Ray, "It Is a Sexy Environment and Ee are the CSIs," *The Globe and Mail*, October 10, 2007, B8; Chartered Accountants of Canada, www.cica.ca; Elisabeth Bumiller, "Bush Signs Bill Aimed at Fraud in Corporations," *The New York Times*, July 31, 2007; Kroll Investigative Services, www.kroll.com; *Stephen Llewellyn*, "Some Lottery Retailers Don't Obey the Rules; Winnings 20% Failed Anti-Cheating Test," *The Daily Gleaner*, February 28, 2009.

The Greening of Business Ken Garen, "Are You Ready to Prosper?," *The Practical Accountant*, June 2008, SR29; Jeff Sanford, "The Next Pension Crisis," *Canadian Business Journal* 80 14 (August 2007): 62–63; Dom Serafini, "Regulations Are the Consumers' Best Friends," *Intermedia*, July 2004, 32, 2, ABI/INFORM Global database, 23.

Concluding Case 11-1 Jeff Buckstein, "SOX Provision Holds Management's Feet to the Fire," *The Globe and Mail*, April 19, 2006, B13; Claire Gagne, "The *Sarbanes-Oxley Act* Restores Shine to Auditors' Reputation—and Fills Their Coffers," *Canadian Business*, September 27–October 10, 2004, 47–49; Karen Howlett, "Livent's Auditors Charged with Misconduct," *The Globe and Mail*, April 6, 2004, B1, B4; Karen Howlett, "Accounting Hearing Is Told Misconduct Charges Against Auditors Are 'Rubbish'," *The Globe and Mail*, April 14, 2004, B3; Shawn McCarthy, "Investors Expect Too Much: Deloitte CEO," *The Globe and Mail*, October 17, 2005, B10; Elizabeth Church, "Accounting Overhaul Coming," *The Globe and Mail*, December 23, 2002, B1, B6; Richard Blackwell, "Auditing Firms Get Tighter Rules," *The Globe and Mail*, July 18, 2002, B1, B4; John Partridge and Karen Howlett, "CIBC Restricts Its Auditors," *The Globe and Mail*, March 1, 2002, B1, B4; Lily Nguyen, "Accountants Primed for Change," *The Globe and Mail*, February 4, 2002, B9; Richard Blackwell, "Accountants to Issue New Rules," *The Globe and Mail*, March 28, 2002, B1, B7; John Gray, "Hide and Seek," *Canadian Business*, April 1, 2002, 28–32; Steve Liesman, Jonathan Weil, and Michael Schroeder, "Accounting Debacles Spark Calls for Change: Here's the Rundown," *The Wall Street Journal*, February 6, 2002, A1, A8; Edward Clifford, "Big Accounting Firms Face Insurance Crunch," *The Globe and Mail*, November 13, 1993, B3; Patricia Lush, "Gap Widens Between Views on Auditor's Role in Canada," *The Globe and Mail*, February 14, 1986, B3; Chris Robinson, "Auditor's Role Raises Tough Questions," *The Financial Post*, June 22, 1985.

Concluding Case 11–2 Elizabeth Church, "Pension Funding Shortfall Increases Dramatically," *The Globe and Mail*, November 8, 2005, B5; Elizabeth Church, "Pension Fund Shortfall Soars in First Half," *The Globe and Mail*, November 23, 2005, B1, B7; Elizabeth Church, "Cost of Retiree Benefit Liabilities 'Sleeping Giant'," *The Globe and Mail*, August 23, 2004, B4; Paul Waldie and Karen Howlett, "Reports Reveal Tight Grip of Ebbers on WorldCom," *The Globe and Mail*, June 11, 2003, B1, B7; Barrie McKenna, Karen Howlett, and Paul Waldie, "Probes Cite Ebbers in 'Fraud'," *The Globe and Mail*, June 10, 2003, B1, B16; Elizabeth Church, "Accounting Overhaul Coming," *The Globe and Mail*, December 23, 2002, B1, B6; Richard Blackwell, "OSC Targets Tech Accounting," *The Globe and Mail*, September 26, 2000, B1, B6.

Chapter 12

What Do Employees Want? Wallace Immen, "Meaning Means More Than Money at Work: Poll," *The Globe and Mail*, February 27, 2009, B14; Wallace Immen, "Hey, Boss, Shine Your Shoes? Keep Me Around," *The Globe and Mail*, October 22, 2008, C3; Tavia Grant, "Favourite Perk? Not a Blackberry," *The Globe and Mail*, September 10, 2008, C1; Wallace Immen, "Boomers, Gen-Yers Agree: It's All about Respect," *The Globe and Mail*, January 24, 2007, C1; Wallace Immen, "The Continuing Divide over Stress Leave," *The Globe and Mail*, June 10, 2005, C1; Jeff Buckstein, "In Praise of Praise in the Workplace," *The Globe and Mail*, June 15, 2005, C1, C5; Virginia Galt, "This Just In: Half Your Employees Ready to Jump Ship," *The Globe and Mail*, January 26, 2005, B1, B9; David Sirota, Louis Mischkind, and Michael Meltzer, "Nothing Beats an Enthusiastic Employee," *The Globe and Mail*, July 29, 2005, C1; Virginia Galt, "Business's Next Challenge: Tackling Mental Health in the Workplace," *The Globe and Mail*, April 12, 2005, B1, B20; Virginia Galt, "Canadians Take Dour View on Jobs, Bosses, Angels," *The Globe and Mail*, October 18, 2004, B1, B7; Virginia Galt, "Worker Stress Costing Economy Billions, Panel Warns," *The Globe and Mail*, July 21, 2000, B9; "A Better Workplace," *Time*, April 17, 2000, 87.

Entrepreneurship and New Ventures Leena Rao, "I Love Rewards Raises $5.9 Million For Employee Rewards Program," *TechCrunch*, www.techcrunch.com/2009/05/07/i-love-rewards-raises-59-million-for-employee-rewards-program/; Chris Atchison, "Masters of One," *Profit* 28 no. 2 (2009): 18; "I Love Rewards Reports Record Results as Demand for Rewards and Recognition Programs Grows," *Canada NewsWire*, April 24, 2009; "I Love Rewards Named One of the World's Most Democratic Workplaces," *Marketwire*, April 14, 2009; Ari Weinzweig, "Ask Inc.: Tough Questions, Smart Answers," *Inc.* 29 no. 12 (2007): 84; Ryan McCarthy, "'Help Wanted' Meets 'Buy it Now': Why More Companies Are Integrating Marketing and Recruiting," *Inc.* 29 no. 11 (2007): 50.

Business Accountability Virginia Galt, "Ideas: Employees' Best-Kept Secrets," *The Globe and Mail*, June 18, 2005, B11; Frederick A. Starke, Bruno Dyck, and Michael Mauws, "Coping with the Sudden Loss of an Indispensable Worker," *Journal of Applied Behavioural Science* 39 no. 2 (2003): 208–229; Timothy Aeppel,

"On Factory Floors, Top Workers Hide Secrets to Success," *The Wall Street Journal*, July 1, 2002, A1, A10; Christopher Robert, Tahira Probst, Joseph Martocchio, Fritz Drasgow, and John Lawler, "Empowerment and Continuous Improvement in the United States, Mexico, Poland, and India: Predicting Fit on the Basis of the Dimensions of Power Distance and Individualism," *Journal of Applied Psychology*, October 2000, 643–658; Timothy Aeppel, "Not All Workers Find Idea of Empowerment as Neat as It Sounds," *The Wall Street Journal*, September 8, 1997, A1, A13.

Concluding Case 12-1 Joyce Rosenberg, "Out of Sight, On Your Mind; Learning to Trust Telecommuters," *The Globe and Mail*, September 20, 2008, B19; "Productivity Rises for Teleworkers: Survey," *The Globe and Mail*, October 15, 2008, C7; Randi Chapnik Myers, "The Back and Forth of Working from Home," *The Globe and Mail*, March 8, 2008, B16; Paul Lima, "With New Advances in Technology, Why Are We Still Jumping in the Car?," *The Globe and Mail*, October 20, 2008, E9; Kira Vermond, "In Support of Ditching the Commute," *The Globe and Mail*, November 17, 2007, B23.

Concluding Case 12-2 Roland Huntford, *The Last Place on Earth* (New York: Atheneum, 1985); Pierre Berton, *The Arctic Grail* (Toronto: McClelland and Stewart, 1988), esp. 125–196, 435–486, and 531–548; Roland Huntford, *Shackleton* (London: Hodder and Stoughton, 1985).

Chapter 16

Why So Serious? "Batman Film Series," May 23, 2008, http://en.wikipedia.org/wiki/Batman_%28film_series%29; Claude Brodesser-Akner, "Hyping Joker-Without Exploiting Heath's Death," *Advertising Age*, May 12, 2008, http://adage.com/article.php?article_id=126981; Chungaiz, "New Batman Dark Knight Marketing Continues, Fantastic!, blog," December 13, 2007, www.altogetherdigital.com/20071213/new-batman-dark-knight-marketing-continues-fantastic; Chris Lee, "The Dark Knight Marketing Blitz," *Los Angeles Times*, March 24, 2008, articles.latimes.com/2008/mar/24/entertainment/et-batmanviral24. See also http://batman.wikibruce.com/Timeline; www.42entertainment.com; http://whysoserious.com.

Business Accountability Keith McArthur, "A Year Later: No Medium for the Message," *The Globe and Mail*, November 1, 2004, B3; Cheryl Healton and Kathleen Nelson, "Reversal of Misfortune: Viewing Tobacco as a Social Justice Issue," *American Journal of Public Health*, February 2004, 186t; *Federal Trade Commission Cigarette Report for 2001*, June 15, 2003, www.ftc.gov/os/2003/06/cigreport.pdf.

The Greening of Business Statistics Canada, "Canadian Economic Accounts," *The Daily*, March 3, 2008, www.statcan.gc.ca/daily-quotidien/080303/dq080303a-eng.htm; "Industry Statistics & Trends," *American Pet Products Manufacturing Association*, www.americanpetproducts.org/press_industrytrends.asp; Blair Coursey, "North America: Plastic Waste—More Dangerous *Than* Global Warming," *Ethical Corporation*, May 8, 2007; Statistics Canada, "*Canadian Economic Accounts*," *The Daily*, March 3, 2008, www.statcan.gc.ca/daily-quotidien/080303/dq080303a-eng.htm.

Concluding Case 16-1 Joel Hruska, "Apple, Dell Big Market Share Winners for the First Quarter," *Ars Technica*, April 17, 2008; Kevin Maney, "Dell to Dive into Consumer Electronics Market," *USA Today*, September 25, 2003, 1B–2B; David Teather, "Michael Dell Quits as Chief of His Own Company," *The Guardian*, March 5, 2004.

Concluding Case 16-2 Nate Anderson, "Bell Canada Opens Online Video Store as P2P Debate Rages On," *Ars Technica*, May 22, 2008; Etan Vlessing, "Bell Canada in Deal with Paramount," *Hollywood Reporter*, May 21, 2008; Jack Kapica, "Bell Launches Video Download Store," *The Globe and Mail*, May 21, 2008; Jason Laszlo, "New Bell Video Store Offers the Most Download-to-own and Rent Movies and TV shows in Canada," *Bell Canada Enterprises*, May 21, 2008.

Chapter 17

Psst! Did You Hear the Latest? Hollie Shaw, "Reaching Out via Web; Marketers Look for Creative Ways to Draw in Consumers," *National Post*, November 7, 2008, FP14; Nick Turner, "Cupcake Business Reaps Sweet Rewards; Location and Word of Mouth Key to Success," *National Post*, October 27, 2008, FP9; Sam Cage, "Word of Mouth Sells 'Remembrance' Gems," *National Post*, September 15, 2008; Sinclair Stewart, "Hey, Did You Hear about That Great New Toothpaste?," *The Globe and Mail*, November 20, 2007, B3; Erin White, "Word of Mouth Makes Nike Slip-On Sneakers Take Off," *The Globe and Mail*, June 7, 2001, B1, B4; Mike Blaney, "*Word of Mouth Advertising*," blog, www.themarketingguy.wordpress.com/2007/10/09/word-of-mouth-advertising; www.theinfluencers.ca/why_wom.php.

Table 17.1 *Financial Post Magazine*, June, 2009, 87.

The Greening of Business Hollie Shaw, "Making the Case That Wearing Fur Can Be Eco-Friendly," *Winnipeg Free Press*, December 5, 2008, B6; Daryl-Lynn Carlson, "Advertising Guidelines Target 'Greenwashing'," *Winnipeg Free Press*, November 21, 2008, B6; Marina Strauss, "Standing Out in a Sea of Green," *The Globe and Mail*, August 16, 2008, B3; Randy Boswell, "Oil Sands Ad 'Greenwash' Environment Group Crows," *The Globe and Mail*, August 14, 2008, C8; Richard Blackwell, "Eco-Friendly? Canadians Want to See the Proof," *The Globe and Mail*, July 28, 2008, B1, B3; Shawn McCarthy, "Oil Sands Tries Image Makeover," *The Globe and Mail*, June 24, 2008, B1, B7; Sharon Epperson, "BP's Fundamental but Obscured Energy Contradiction," *CNBC.com*, May 21, 2008, www.cnbc.com/id/24758394; Carly Weeks, "New Scrutiny for Green Claims," *The Globe and Mail*, March 11, 2008, B1, B6; "Oil Company BP Pleads Guilty to Environmental Crime," *International Herald Tribune*, November 29, 2007, www.iht.com/articles/ap/2007/11/30/business/NA-FIN-US-BP-Settlement-Alaska.php?page=1; Terry Macalister, "Greenpeace Calls BP's Oil Sands Plan an Environmental Crime," *Guardian.co.uk*, December 7, 2007, www.guardian.co.uk/business/2007/dec/07/bp.

Entrepreneurship and New Ventures Jonathan Paul, "RPGs look for Brands to Play With," *Strategy*, April 2009, 33; Frank Armstrong, "Fairytale Ending for Tiny Ottawa Firm," *The Globe and Mail*, November 11, 2008; Lana Castleman, "Virtual Worlds on the Menu at Kids Marketing Agencies," *KidScreen*, October 2008, 79; Lana Castleman, "McDonald's Is Lovin' Customer Content," *KidScreen*, May 2008, 26; Rob Gerlsbeck, "Fuel Industries," *Marketing* 112, 21 (2007): 22.

Concluding Case 17-1 Grant Surridge, "People, Lend Them Your Ears; More Accurate Radio Monitoring," *National Post*, November 26, 2008, FP1; Emily Steel, "Google Set to Roll Out Web-Measurement Tool," *The Wall Street Journal*, June 24, 2008, B14; Jennifer Wells, "The Brain Guy Wants to Get Inside Your Head," *The Globe and Mail*, March 15, 2008, B4–B5; "TV Networks Pay Back Advertisers," *National Post*, December 13, 2007; David George-Cosh, "Fighting Click Fraud: Is It Really Down for the Count?," *The Globe and Mail*, August 23, 2007, B7; Brooks Barnes, "New TV Ratings Will Produce Ad-Price Fight," *The Wall Street Journal*, December 22, 2005, B1, B3; Brooks Barnes, "Where're the Ratings, Dude?," *The Wall Street Journal*, March 7, 2005, B1, B6; Keith McArthur, "New TV Ratings Devices Know What You're Watching," *The Globe and Mail*, November 29, 2004, B1, B12; Keith McArthur, "Advertisers Wary of Plan to Fuse TV Ratings Systems," *The Globe and Mail*, July 13, 2004, B1, B20; Brooks Barnes, "For Nielsen, Fixing Old Ratings System Causes New Static," *The Wall Street Journal*, September 16, 2004, A1, A8; Elizabeth Jensen, "Networks Blast Nielsen, Blame Faulty Ratings for Drop in Viewership," *The Wall Street Journal*, November 22, 1996, A1, A8.

Concluding Case 17-2 Jennifer Wells, "Ad Nauseam," *The Globe and Mail*, July 25, 2008, B5; "30-Second Spot: Dispatches from the World of Media and Advertising," *The Globe and Mail*, December 19, 2008, B6; Scott Valentine, "Interactive TV-Watching Had Advertisers Sitting Up," *The Globe and Mail*, January 24, 2008, B8; Grant Robertson, "Radio Rivals Resort to Merger," *The Globe and Mail*, February 20, 2007, B1, B6; Keith McArthur and Grant Robertson, "CRTC Ponders Impact of Product Placement," *The Globe and Mail*, November 21, 2005, B1, B10; Grant Robertson and Richard Blackwell, "Eased Satellite Radio Rules Could 'Shock' System," *The Globe and Mail*, September 25, 2005, B7; Tessa Wegert, "On-Line Marketing Concept Gives Consumers a Say," *The Globe and Mail*, October 13, 2005, B13; Aaron Patrick, "Commercials by Cellphone," *The Wall Street Journal*, August 22, 2005, B1, B3; Frazier Moore, "You Can't Fast-Forward Past These Commercials," *Winnipeg Free Press*, July 25, 2005, D3; Simon Tuck, "CRTC Turns Radio on Its Head with Landmark Satellite Ruling," *The Globe and Mail*, June 17, 2005, B1, B6; Eric Reguly, "Blame the *Act*, Not the Regulator," *The Globe and Mail*, June 16, 2005, B2; Joe Flint and Brian Steinberg, "Proctor & Gamble Tweaks Its Traditional TV Ad Strategy," *The Wall Street Journal*, June 13, 2005, B6; Peter Grant, "Interactive Ads Start to Click on Cable and Satellite TV," *The Wall Street Journal*, May 26, 2005, B1, B6; Keith McArthur, "Branded Content Generates Buzz," *The Globe and Mail*, April 6, 2005, B4; Keith McArthur, "A Year Later: No Medium for the Message," *The Globe and Mail*, November 1, 2004, B3.

Chapter 18

Buyers and Sellers Jockey for Position
"Consumers Trade Down, McDonald's Sales Go Up," *The Globe and Mail*, December 9, 2008, B12; Marina Strauss, "Stores Aim to Convert 'Cherry Pickers'," *The Globe and Mail*, November 19, 2008, B11; Janet Adamy, "McDonald's Strategy to Take Sales from Pricier Restaurants Working," *National Post*, October 23, 2008, FP2; David Hutton, "Consumers Get Less Bang for Their Buck," *The Globe and Mail*, July 8, 2008, B2; Ann Zimmerman, "Behind the Dollar-Store Boom: A Nation of Bargain Hunters," *The Wall Street Journal*, December 13, 2004, A1, A10; Gordon Fairclough, "Four Biggest Cigarette Makers Can't Raise Prices as They Did," *The Wall Street Journal*, October 25, 2002, A1, A8; Timothy Aeppel, "After Cost Cutting, Companies Turn toward Price Increases," *The Wall Street Journal*, September 18, 2002, A1, A12.

Table 18.1 *Financial Post Magazine*, June, 2009, 86.

Entrepreneurship and New Ventures
Auto Vault, www.autovaultcanada.com; Deirdre Kelly, "Nowhere to Park the Lamborghini?" *The Globe and Mail*, September 20, 2008, M3; Jerry Langton, "Driven by Love of Hot Wheels; Entrepreneur Cashes in on Need for Secure Storage for Owners' Exotic Cars with Auto Vault, Car Condo," *The Toronto Star*, May 12, 2008, B01; Joshua Knelman, "Auto Focus: This 40,000 Square-foot Car Park Protects Your Precious Ride from All the Elements—Criminal and Climactic," *Toronto Life*, May 2005, 27; "Storing Your 'Baby' for Winter," *The Expositor*, www.brantfordexpositor.ca/ArticleDisplay.aspx?archive=true&e=1283051.

The Greening of Business Marjo Johne, "Shoppers Get a Brand New Bag," *The Globe and Mail*, October 20, 2008, E5; *Agriculture and Agri-Food Canada, Going Green: The Future of the Retail Food Industry, July 2007*, www.ats.agr.gc.ca/us/4351_e.htm.

Concluding Case 18-1 Keith McArthur, "Why Molson *Is* Crying in *Its* Beer," *The Globe and Mail*, July 10, 2004, B4; Kevin Kelleher, "66,207,896 Bottles of Beer on the Wall," *Business 2.0*, January/February 2004, 47–49; Tim Davis, "Surfin' the Net, Bud Style," *Beverage World*, August 1995, 28; "This Budnet's for You," *Progressive Grocer*, May 1996, 16; *2003 Annual Report* (St. Louis: Anheuser-Busch Companies Inc., 2004).

Concluding Case 18-2 Matt Hartley, "From Pirate Bay, a Torpedo to Illegal File-Sharing," *The Globe and Mail*, April 18, 2009, B3; Grant Robertson, "Death Knell Sounds for CDs," *The Globe and Mail*, June 19, 2008, B3; Shawn McCarthy, "U.S. Court Shuts Door on Internet File-Sharing," *The Globe and Mail*, June 28, 2005, B3; "File Sharing Firm Will Shut Down," *Winnipeg Free Press*, November 8, 2005, A11; Nick Wingfield, "Online Music's Latest Tune," *The Wall Street Journal*, August 27, 2004, B1, B2; Nick Wingfield, "New File-Swapping Software Limits Sharers to a Select Few," *The Wall Street Journal*, October 4, 2004, B1, B4; Sarah McBride, "Stop the Music!," *The Wall Street Journal*, August 23, 2004, B1; also Vauhini Vara, "On Campus, iTunes Finds an Illicit Groove," *The Wall Street Journal*, August 23, 2004, B1–B2; Nick Wingfield and Sarah McBride, "Green Light for Grokster," *The Wall Street Journal*, August 20, 2004, B1, B3; Nick Wingfield, "The Day the Music Died," *The Wall Street Journal*, May 2, 2003, B8; "The End of File-Shares as We Know Them," *Winnipeg Free Press*, July 4, 2003, A8; Ted Birdis, "Music Industry Escalates Net Fight," *Winnipeg Free Press*, June 26, 2003, A12; Matthew Ingram, "Digital Music Industry Gets New Spin on Napster Judge's Decision," *The Globe and Mail*, February 26, 2002; Nick Wingfield, "Napster Boy, Interrupted," *The Wall Street Journal*, October 1, 2002, B1, B3; Anna Matthews and Charles Goldsmith, "Music Industry Faces New Threats on Web," *The Wall Street Journal*, February 21, 2003, B1, B4.

acquired needs theory a motivation theory that focuses on learned needs that become enduring predispositions for affiliation, power, and achievement

affirmative action programs hiring and training programs intended to correct past inequalities for certain categories of people based on gender, race and ethnicity, age, or religion

anchoring using an initial value received from prior experience or any external information source and giving it disproportionate weight in setting a final value

approved budget specifies what the manager is actually authorized to spend money on and how much

artifacts visible manifestations of a culture such as its art, clothing, food, architecture, and customs

assessment centres a work sampling technique in which candidates perform a number of exercises, each one designed to capture one or more key aspects of the job

assumptions beliefs about fundamental aspects of life

at-risk compensation pay that varies depending on specified conditions, including the profitability of the company; hitting particular budget, revenue, or cost savings targets for a unit; or meeting specified individual performance targets

balanced scorecard an integrated and "balanced" set of measures for four critical areas or perspectives: financial, customers, internal business, and innovation and learning

behavioural process orientation a key distinguishing feature of the OD approach to organizational change that focuses on new forms of behaviour and new relationships

behaviourally anchored rating scales (BARS) a performance appraisal system in which the rater places detailed employee characteristics on a rating scale

benchmarking the investigation of the best results among competitors and noncompetitors and the practices that lead to those results; identification, analysis, and comparison of the best practices of competitors against an organization's own practices

bona fide occupational qualifications (BFOQ) qualifications that have a direct and material impact on job performance and outcomes

boundaryless organization an organization where barriers to effective integration are overcome by people empowered to work across boundaries

bounded rationality model (administrative man model) a descriptive model of decision making recognizing that people are limited in their capacity to fully assess a problem and usually rely on shortcuts and approximations to arrive at a decision they are comfortable with

brainstorming a process of generating many creative solutions without evaluating their merit

break-even point (B-E P) the amount of a product that must be sold to cover a firm's fixed and variable costs

broadband systems pay structures in which the range of pay is large and covers a wide variety of jobs

budgetary control a type of tactical control based on responsibility for meeting financial targets and evaluating how well those targets have been met

budgets used to quantify and allocate resources to specific activities

bureaucratic control an approach to tactical control that stresses adherence to rules and regulations and is imposed by others

cafeteria-style plans benefit plans in which employees have a set number of "benefit dollars" that they can use to purchase benefits that fit their particular needs

capital expenditure budget specifies the amount of money to be spent on specific items that have long-term use and require significant amounts of money to acquire

career paths sets and sequences of positions and experiences

cash cows products or SBUs that have relatively high market share in markets with unattractive futures

centralized organizations organizations that restrict decision making to fewer individuals, usually at the top of the organization

change agents individuals who are responsible for implementing change efforts; they can be either internal or external to the organization

charismatic leader someone who has influence over others based on individual inspirational qualities rather than formal power

code of ethical conduct a formal statement that outlines types of behaviour that are and are not acceptable

coercive power a type of position power based on a person's authority to administer punishments, either by withholding something that is desired or by giving out something that is not desired

cognitive specialization the extent to which people in different units within an organization think about different things or about similar things differently

cohesion the degree to which members are motivated to remain in the group

collaboration a part of negotiation in which parties work together to attack and solve a problem

collectivism the extent to which identity is a function of the group to which an individual belongs

command (supervisory) group a group whose members consist of a supervisor or manager and all those who report to that person

commitment (clan) control an approach to tactical control that emphasizes consensus and shared responsibility for meeting goals

committee a group that is either permanent or temporary (ad hoc) whose members meet only occasionally and otherwise report to different permanent supervisors in an organization's structure

communication the process of transferring information, meaning, and understanding from sender to receiver

communication networks identifiable patterns of communication within and between organizations, whether using formal or informal channels

compensatory justice if distributive and procedural justice fail, those hurt by the inequitable distribution of rewards are compensated

competitive advantage the ability of a firm to win consistently over the long term in a competitive situation

concentration of effect the extent to which consequences are focused on a few individuals or dispersed across many

concurrent control a type of operational control that evaluates the conversion of inputs to outputs while it is happening

conformity close adherence to the group's norms by individual members

confrontation a means of helping people perceive contrasts by providing an inescapable experience

conjunction fallacy the tendency for people to assume that co-occurring events are more likely to occur than if they were independent of each other or grouped with other events

content theories motivation theories that focus on what needs a person is trying to satisfy and what features of the work environment seem to satisfy those needs

context-driven competencies competencies that are specific to both the unique nature of the particular tasks and the particular composition of the team

contingency plans plans that identify key factors that could affect the desired results and specify what actions will be taken if key events change

contrast a means by which people perceive differences

control the regulation of activities and behaviours within organizations; adjustment or conformity to specifications or objectives

controlling regulating the work of those for whom a manager is responsible

core competency focusing on an interrelated set of activities that can deliver competitive advantage in the short term and into the future

core value a value that is widely shared and deeply held

corporate social responsibility the obligations that corporations owe to their stakeholders, such as shareholders, employees, customers, and citizens at large

cost leadership striving to be the lowest-cost producer of a product or provider of a service and yet charge only slightly less than industry average prices

critical incidents recording of specific incidents in which the employee's behaviour and performance were above or below expectations

cross-functional job rotation opportunities for employees to work in different functional areas and gain additional expertise

cross-functional teams employees from different departments, such as finance, marketing, operations, and human resources, who work together in problem solving

cultural context the degree to which a situation influences behaviour or perception of appropriateness

cultural distance the overall difference between two cultures' basic characteristics such as language, level of economic development, and traditions and customs

culture a learned set of assumptions, values, and behaviours that have been accepted as successful enough to be passed on to newcomers

customer segment a group of customers who have similar preferences or place similar value on product features

decentralized organizations organizations that tend to push decision-making authority down to the lowest level possible

decision making a process of specifying the nature of a particular problem or opportunity and selecting among available alternatives to solve a problem or capture an opportunity

decoding the act of interpreting a message

delphi technique a decision-making technique that never allows decision participants to meet face to face but identifies a problem and asks for solutions using a questionnaire

demographics the descriptive elements of the people in a society, such as average age, level of education, financial status, and so on

devil's advocate a group member whose role is to challenge the majority position

dialectical inquiry a process to improve decision making by assigning a group member (or members) the role of questioning the underlying assumptions associated with the formulation of a problem

differentiation a strategy for making a product or service different from those of competitors

directing the process of attempting to influence other people to attain organizational objectives

distributive justice the equitable distribution of rewards and punishment based on performance

dogs products or SBUs that have relatively low market share in unattractive markets

downward communication messages sent from higher organizational levels to lower levels

dual-career couples couples in which both partners work full time in professional, managerial, or administrative jobs

early wins early and consistent positive reinforcement of desired change

ease of recall making a judgment based upon the most recent events or the most vivid in our memory

effective leadership influence that assists a group or an organization to meet its goals and objectives and perform successfully

efficiency (activity) the ratio of amount of sales to total cost of inventory

efficiency perspective the concept that a manager's responsibility is to maximize profits for the owners of the business

80/20 rule a "rule" that suggests that 80 percent of the desired outcome is provided by 20 percent of the contributing factors

emotional intelligence an awareness of others' feelings and a sensitivity to one's own emotions and the ability to control them

empathy the ability to put yourself in someone else's place and to understand his or her feelings, situation, and motives

encoding the act of constructing a message

entry barriers obstacles that make it difficult for firms to get into a business

equity theory a motivation theory that focuses on individuals' comparisons of their circumstances with those of others and how such comparisons may motivate certain kinds of behaviour

escalation of commitment the tendency to exhibit greater levels of commitment to a decision as time passes and investments are made in the decision, even after significant evidence emerges indicating that the original decision was incorrect

ethical dilemmas having to make a choice between two competing but arguably valid options

ethical lapses decisions that are contrary to an individual's stated beliefs and the policies of the company

ethnocentrism the belief in the superiority and importance of one's own group

expatriate employees employees sent overseas on lengthy, but temporary, assignments

expectancy theory a motivation theory that focuses on the thought processes people use when they face particular choices among alternatives, especially alternative courses of action

expense budget includes all primary activities on which a unit or organization plans to spend money and the amount allocated to each for the upcoming year

expert power a type of personal power based on specialized knowledge not readily available to many people

external environment a set of forces and conditions outside the organization that can potentially influence its performance

externalities indirect or unintended consequences imposed on society that may not be understood or anticipated

extinction the absence of positive consequences for behaviour, lessening the likelihood of that behaviour being repeated in the future

feminine societies value activities focused on caring for others and enhancing the quality of life

flat organizational structure a structure that has fewer layers in its hierarchy than a tall organization

focus groups small groups involved in intense discussions of the positive and negative features of products or services

force field analysis uses the concept of equilibrium, a condition that occurs when the forces for change, the "driving forces," are balanced by forces opposing change, the "restraining forces," and results in a relatively steady state

formal communication channels routes that are authorized, planned, and regulated by the organization and that are directly connected to its official structure

formal group a group that is designated, created, and sanctioned by the organization to carry out its basic work and to fulfill its overall mission

formalization the official and defined structures and systems in decision making, communication, and control in an organization

formulation a process involving identifying a problem or opportunity, acquiring information, developing desired performance expectations, and diagnosing the causes and relationships among factors affecting the problem or opportunity

frames of reference existing sets of attitudes that provide quick ways of interpreting complex messages

gatekeepers individuals who are at the communication interface between separate organizations or between different units within an organization

general environment forces that typically influence the organization's external task environment and thus the organization itself

glass ceiling an invisible barrier that prevents women from promotion to the highest executive ranks

globalization the tendency to integrate activities on a coordinated, worldwide basis

goal-setting theory a theory that assumes human action is directed by conscious goals and intentions

Gresham's law of planning the tendency for managers to let programmed activities overshadow nonprogrammed activities

gross domestic product the total dollar value of final goods and services produced within a nation's borders

group a set of people, limited in number (usually from 3 to 20), who have some degree of mutual interaction and shared objectives

groupthink a mode of thinking in which the pursuit of agreement among members becomes so dominant that it overrides a realistic appraisal of alternative courses of action

heuristic a decision-making shortcut that can be based upon pre-set rules, memory, or past experiences

human resource policies and procedures a type of tactical control based on the organization's overall approach to using its human resources

hybrid a structure that combines one or more organizational structures to gain the advantages and reduce the disadvantages of any particular structure

in-group the group to which a person belongs

incentive plans systems that tie some compensation to performance

incremental budgeting approach where managers use the approved budget of the previous year and then present arguments for why the upcoming budget should be more or less

individualism the extent to which people base their identities on themselves and are expected to take care of themselves and their immediate families

informal communication channels routes that are not pre-specified by the organization but that develop through typical and

customary activities of people at work

informal group a group whose members interact voluntarily

informal organization the unofficial but influential means of communication, decision making, and control that are part of the habitual way things get done in an organization

insensitivity to base rates the tendency to disregard information that suggests the likelihood of a particular outcome in the presence of other information

insensitivity to sample size the tendency to not consider sample size when using information taken from a sample within a given population

integration the extent to which various parts of an organization cooperate and interact with each other

interdependence the degree to which one unit or person depends on another to accomplish a task

interests in negotiation, a party's concerns and desires—in other words, what they want

intergroup conflict differences that occur between groups

internal environment key factors and forces inside the organization that affect how it operates

interventions sets of structured activities, or action steps, designed to improve organizations

intragroup conflict differences that occur within groups

intuitive decision making the primarily subconscious process of identifying a decision and selecting a preferred alternative

job analysis determination of the scope and depth of jobs and the requisite skills, abilities, and knowledge that people need to perform their jobs successfully

job characteristics model an approach that focuses on the motivational attributes of jobs through emphasizing three sets of variables: core job characteristics, critical psychological states, and outcomes

job design the structuring or restructuring of key job components

job enrichment increasing the complexity of a job to provide greater responsibility, accomplishment, and achievement

job posting an internal recruiting method whereby a job, its pay, level, description, and qualifications are posted or announced to all current employees

job sharing a situation in which two people share the same job by each working part time

justice approach an approach to ethical decision making that focuses on how equitably the costs and benefits of actions are distributed

lateral communication messages sent across essentially equivalent levels of an organization

legitimate power (formal authority) a type of position power granted to a person by the organization

leverage the ratio of total debt to total assets

liaisons individuals designated to act as a bridge or connection between different areas of a company

line of authority specifies who reports to whom

liquidity a measure of how well a unit can meet its short-term cash requirements

localization the tendency to differentiate activities country by country

LPC (least preferred co-worker) theory a contingency theory of leadership that identifies the types of situations in which task-oriented or person-oriented leaders would be most effective

magnitude of the consequences the anticipated level of impact of the outcome of a given action

management the process of assembling and using sets of resources in a goal-directed manner to accomplish tasks in an organizational setting

managerial ethics the study of morality and standards of business conduct

managerial grid a method for measuring the degree to which managers are task oriented and people oriented

masculine societies value activities focused on success, money, and possessions

Maslow's need hierarchy a theory that states people fulfill basic needs, such as physiological and safety needs, before making efforts to satisfy other needs, such as social and belongingness, esteem, and self-actualization needs

media richness different media are classified as rich or lean based on their capacity to facilitate shared meaning

medium the mode or form of transmission of a message

mental map habitual cognitive patterns

misconception of chance the expectation that small sets of randomly assembled objects or sequences should appear random

mission statement a statement that articulates the fundamental purpose of the organization and often contains several components

moral intensity the degree to which people see an issue as an ethical one

moral rights approach an approach to ethical decision making that focuses on examination of the moral standing of actions independent of their consequences

motivation the set of forces that energize, direct, and sustain behaviour

movement changing perceptions based on the level of certainty or uncertainty associated with the change

multiple advocacy a process to improve decision making by assigning several group members to represent the opinions of various constituencies that might have an interest in the decision

negative reinforcements undesirable consequences that, by being removed or avoided, increase the likelihood of a behaviour being repeated in the future

negotiation the process of conferring to arrive at an agreement between different parties, each with their own interests and preferences

network structures formal or informal relationships among units or organizations (e.g., along the firm's value chain)

networking a process of developing regular patterns of communication with particular individuals or groups to send and receive information

neutralizers of leadership aspects of the organization or work situation that can defeat the best efforts of leaders

niche strategy a limited scope or breadth of focus

noise potential interference with the transmission or decoding of a message

nominal group technique a process of having group members record their proposed solutions, summarize all proposed solutions, and independently rank solutions until a clearly favoured solution emerges

nonprogrammed decision a decision about a problem that is either poorly defined or novel

normative decision model a contingency model that prescribes standards to determine the extent to which subordinates should be allowed to participate in decision making

norms a group's shared standards that guide the behaviour of its individual members

objectives the end states or targets that company managers aim for

operational control the assessment and regulation of the specific activities and methods an organization uses to produce goods and services

operational plans plans that translate tactical plans into specific goals and actions for small units of the organization and focus on the near term

opportunity a chance to achieve a more desirable state than the current one

organizational charts an illustration of the relationships among units and lines of authority among supervisors and subordinates

organizational design the process of assessing the organization's strategy and environmental demands and then determining the appropriate organizational structures

organizational development (OD) an approach to organizational change that has a strong behavioural and people orientation, emphasizing planned, strategic, long-range efforts focusing on people and their interrelationships in organizations

organizational leadership an interpersonal process involving attempts to influence other people in attaining some goal

organizational learning exhibited by an organization that is skilled at creating, acquiring, and transferring knowledge, and at modifying its behaviour to reflect new knowledge and insights

organizational renewal a concept of organizational change that proposes a goal of flexibility and capability for continual change

organizational structure the sum of the ways an organization divides its labour into distinct tasks and then coordinates them

organizations interconnected sets of individuals and groups who attempt to accomplish common goals through differentiated functions and intended coordination

organizing systematically putting resources together

outsourcing the practice of taking a significant activity within the organization and contracting it out to an independent party

paternalism where a leader is regarded as the provider "father" who will take care of the subordinate in return for responsible behaviour and performance

path–goal theory of leadership a contingency theory of leadership that focuses on the leader's role in increasing subordinate satisfaction and effort by increasing personal payoffs for goal attainment and making the path to these payoffs easier

pay structure a range of pay for a particular position or classification of positions

people behaviours behaviours that focus on interaction, such as being friendly and supportive, showing trust and confidence, being concerned about others, and supplying recognition

perceptual distortion highlighting the positive features of the implicit favourite over the alternative

personal power power based on a person's individual characteristics

planning estimating future conditions and circumstances and making decisions about appropriate courses of action; a decision-making process that focuses on the future of an organization and how it will achieve its goals,

plans the means by which managers hope to hit the desired targets

portfolio analysis techniques designed to assist managers in assessing the attractiveness of a market

position power power based on an organizational structure

positions in negotiation, a party's stance regarding their interests

positive reinforcements desirable consequences that, by being given or applied, increase the likelihood of behaviour being repeated in the future

post-control a type of operational control that checks quality after production of goods or services outputs

power the capacity or ability to influence

power distance the extent to which people accept power and authority differences among people

pre-control a type of operational control that focuses on the quality, quantity, and characteristics of the inputs into the production process

presumed associations the assumption that two events are

likely to co-occur based on the recollection of similar associations

primary activities activities that are directly involved in the creation of a product or service, getting it into the hands of the customer, and keeping it there

probability of effect the moral intensity of an issue rises and falls depending on how likely people think the consequences are

problem a gap between existing and desired performance

procedural justice ensuring that those affected by managerial decisions consent to the decision-making process and that the process is administered impartially

process costs the increasing costs of coordination as group size increases

process redesign (re-engineering) involves a fundamental redesign of business processes to achieve dramatic improvements

process technological changes alterations in how products are made or how enterprises are managed

process theories motivation theories that deal with the way different variables combine to influence the amount of effort people put forth

product technological changes changes that lead to new features and capabilities of existing products or to completely new products

profit centre a unit or product line in which the related expenses are deducted from the revenue generated

profitability the ratio of cost to benefit

programmed decision a routine response to a simple or regularly occurring problem

project/task force a temporary group put together by an organization for a particular purpose

proposed budget provides a plan for how much money is needed and is submitted to a superior or budget review committee

prospective rationality a belief that future courses of action are rational and correct

proximity the physical, psychological, and emotional closeness the decision maker feels to those affected by the decision

punishments undesirable consequences that are applied to decrease the likelihood of behaviour being repeated in the future

question marks products or SBUs that have relatively low market share in attractive markets

rational model (classical model) a seven-step model of decision making that represents the earliest attempt to model decision processes

re-engineering the fundamental rethinking and radical redesign of business processes to achieve dramatic improvements in critical, contemporary measures of performance

referent power a type of personal power gained when people are attracted to, or identify with, that person; this power is gained because people "refer" to that person

refreezing the process of reinforcing change so that it becomes established

regression to the mean overlooking the fact that extreme events or characteristics are exceptional cases that will likely revert back to historic averages over time

relationship (affective) conflict interpersonal differences among group members

retrievability a decision-making bias where judgments rely on the memory structures of an individual

retrospective decision model (implicit favourite model) a decision-making model that focuses on how decision makers attempt to rationalize their choices after they are made

reward power a type of position power based on a person's authority to give out rewards

rituals symbolic communication of an organization's culture

ROE (return on equity) an alternative term for ROI

ROI (return on investment) a measure of profitability obtained by dividing net income by the total amount of assets invested

role ambiguity a situation in which the expected behaviours for a group member are not clearly defined

role conflict a situation in which a member of a group faces two or more contrasting sets of expectations

satisficing the tendency for decision makers to accept the first alternative that meets their minimally acceptable requirements rather than pushing them further for an alternative that produces the best results

selective perception the process of screening out some parts of an intended message because they contradict our beliefs or desires

self-efficacy an individual's confidence about his or her abilities to mobilize motivation, cognitive resources, and courses of action needed to successfully execute a specific task within a given context

self-managing (autonomous) work-group a group that has no formally appointed supervisor but is similar to command groups in that the members coordinate their organizational work as if they all reported to the same formally appointed supervisor; members usually appoint their own informal team leader

short-term or long-term orientation societies that focus on immediate results and those that focus on developing relationships without expecting immediate results

situational leadership model a model that states that different types of appropriate leadership are "contingent" on some other variable, in this case "the situation"

social cognitive theory (SCT) a theory that focuses on how individuals think about, or "cognitively process," information obtained from their social environment

social consensus the extent to which members of a society agree that an act is either good or bad

social intelligence the ability to "read" other people and their intentions and adjust one's own behaviour in response

social loafing the phenomenon of reduced effort per person in large groups

societal values commonly shared desired end states

solution a process involving generating alternatives, selecting the preferred solution, and implementing the decided course of action

span of control the number of employees reporting to a given supervisor

specialization the extent to which tasks are divided into subtasks and performed by individuals with specialized skills

stakeholders individuals or groups who have an interest in and are affected by the actions of an organization

standard operating procedure (SOP) established procedure for action used for programmed decisions that specifies exactly what should be done

standards targets of performance

stars products that have relatively high market share in markets with attractive futures

status the standing or prestige that a person has in a group

stereotyping the tendency to oversimplify and generalize about groups of people

strategic control assessment and regulation of how the organization as a whole fits its external environment and meets its long-range objectives and goals

strategic objectives objectives that translate the strategic vision and mission of a firm into concrete and measurable goals

strategic partners organizations that work closely with a firm in the pursuit of mutually beneficial goals

strategic plans focus on the broad future of the organization and incorporate both external environmental demands and internal resources into managers' actions

strategic scope the scope of a firm's strategy or breadth of focus

strategic vision what an organization ultimately wants to be and do

strong versus weak cultural values the degree to which the cultural values are shared by organization members

structural changes changes that significantly affect the dynamics of economic activity

structured debate a process to improve problem formulation that includes the using a devil's advocate, multiple advocacy, and dialectical inquiry

structured interview an interview in which interviewers ask a standard set of questions of all candidates about qualifications and capabilities related to job performance

subculture where values are deeply held but not widely shared

subjectively expected utility (SEU) model a model of decision making that asserts that managers choose the alternative that they subjectively believe maximizes the desired outcome

substitutes alternative products or services that can substitute for existing products or services

substitutes for leadership alternative approaches that can at least partially substitute for the need for leadership or can sometimes overcome poor leadership

substitution whether or not the customer's need that you fulfill can be met by alternative means

supernormal returns the profits that are above the average for a comparable set of firms

supervisory structure a type of tactical control based on reporting levels in an organization

support activities activities that facilitate the creation of a product or service and its transfer to the customer

switching costs the amount of difficulty and expense involved when customers switch from one company to another

SWOT analysis an analysis that requires managers to consider their firm's Strengths, Weaknesses, Opportunities, and Threats for its continued operation

T-groups groups of individuals participating in organizational development sessions away from the workplace; also called basic-skills training groups

tactical control the assessment and regulation of the day-to-day functions of the organization and its major units in the implementation of its strategy

tactical plans plans that translate strategic plans into specific goals for specific parts of the organization

tall organizational structure a structure that has multiple layers or is high in terms of vertical differentiation

task behaviours behaviours that specify and identify the roles and tasks of leaders and their subordinates, such as planning, scheduling, setting standards, and devising procedures

task (substantive) conflict conflict that focuses on differences in ideas and courses of action in addressing the issues facing a group

task-contingent competencies competencies that are needed in teams that perform a specific and recurring set of tasks but have varying sets of members

task environment forces that have a high potential for affecting the organization on an immediate basis

task specialization specialization by what employees do

team a type of group that has additional characteristics: a high degree of interdependent, coordinated interaction and a strong sense of members' personal responsibility for achieving specified outcomes

team-contingent competencies competencies that are specific to the particular team, but applicable across a wide range of tasks

temporal immediacy a function of the interval between the time the action occurs and the onset of its consequences

Theory X managers assume the average human being has an inherent dislike for work and will avoid it if possible

Theory Y managers assume that work is as natural as play or rest

360-degree feedback a performance appraisal system in which information is gathered from supervisors, co-workers, subordinates, and sometimes suppliers and customers

traits relatively enduring characteristics of a person

transactional leadership leadership that focuses on motivating followers' self-interests by exchanging rewards for their compliance; emphasis is on having subordinates implement procedures correctly and make needed, but relatively routine, changes

transformational leadership leadership that motivates followers to ignore self-interests and work for the larger good of the organization

to achieve significant accomplishments; emphasis is on articulating a vision that will convince subordinates to make major changes

transportable competencies competencies that can be used in any situation

two-factor theory a motivation theory that focuses on the presumed different effects of intrinsic job factors (motivation) and extrinsic situational factors (hygiene factors)

uncertainty the extent to which future input, throughput, and output factors cannot be forecast accurately

uncertainty avoidance the need for things to be clear rather than ambiguous

unfreezing undoing old patterns

unity of command the notion that an employee should have one and only one boss

universal approach an approach to ethical decision making where you choose a course of action that you believe can apply to all people under all situations

unstructured interview an interview in which interviewers have a general idea of the questions they might ask but do not have a standard set

upward communication messages sent from lower organizational levels to higher levels

utilitarian approach an approach to ethical decision making that focuses on the consequences of an action

valid selection technique a screening process that differentiates those who would be successful in a job from those who would not

value chain a set of key activities that directly produce or support the production of what a firm ultimately offers to customers

value proposition the ratio of what customers get from a firm to how much they pay relative to alternatives from competitors

values the enduring beliefs that specific conduct or end states are personally or socially preferred to others

virtual team a group composed of individuals who do not work together in close physical proximity

whistle-blower an employee who discloses illegal or unethical conduct on the part of others in the organization

work centrality the degree of general importance that working has in the life of an individual at a point in time

work simulation situations in which job candidates perform work they would do if hired or work that closely simulates the tasks they would perform

zero-based budgeting approach assumes that all allocations of funds must be justified from zero each year